Dear West Customer:

West Academic Publishing has changed the look of its American Casebook Series®.

In keeping with our efforts to promote sustainability, we have replaced our former covers with book covers that are more environmentally friendly. Our casebooks will now be covered in a 100% renewable natural fiber. In addition, we have migrated to an ink supplier that favors vegetable-based materials, such as soy.

Using soy inks and natural fibers to print our textbooks reduces VOC emissions. Moreover, our primary paper supplier is certified by the Forest Stewardship Council, which is testament to our commitment to conservation and responsible business management.

The new cover design has migrated from the long-standing brown cover to a contemporary charcoal fabric cover with silver-stamped lettering and black accents. Please know that inside the cover, our books continue to provide the same trusted content that you've come to expect from West.

We've retained the ample margins that you have told us you appreciate in our texts while moving to a new, larger font, improving readability. We hope that you will find these books a pleasing addition to your bookshelf.

Another visible change is that you will no longer see the brand name Thomson West on our print products. With the recent merger of Thomson and Reuters, I am pleased to announce that books published under the West Academic Publishing imprint will once again display the West brand.

It will likely be several years before all of our casebooks are published with the new cover and interior design. We ask for your patience as the new covers are rolled out on new and revised books knowing that behind both the new and old covers, you will find the finest in legal education materials for teaching and learning.

Thank you for your continued patronage of the West brand, which is both rooted in history and forward looking towards future innovations in legal education. We invite you to be a part of our next evolution.

Best regards,

Heidi M. Hellekson
Publisher, West Academic Publishing

Torts and Compensation

Personal Accountability and Social Responsibility for Injury

Sixth Edition

∎ ∎ ∎

By

Dan B. Dobbs

Regents Professor and
Rosenstiel Distinguished Professor of Law Emeritus
University of Arizona

Paul T. Hayden

Professor of Law and Jacob J. Becker Fellow
Loyola Law School, Los Angeles

Ellen M. Bublick

Dan B. Dobbs Professor of Law
University of Arizona

AMERICAN CASEBOOK SERIES®

WEST®

A Thomson Reuters business

Mat #40657423

American Casebook Series is a trademark registered in the U.S. Patent and Trademark Office.

COPYRIGHT © 1985, 1993 WEST PUBLISHING CO.
© West, a Thomson business, 1997, 2001, 2005
© 2009 Thomson Reuters

    610 Opperman Drive
    St. Paul, MN 55123
    1–800–313–9378

Printed in the United States of America

ISBN: 978–0–314–18490–0

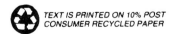
TEXT IS PRINTED ON 10% POST
CONSUMER RECYCLED PAPER

In thanks to and in memory of those lawyers, scholars, and students, living and dead, who have taught me most in tort law: Robert A. Leflar, Tom Pryor, Robert G. Byrd, Page Keeton, Wex Malone, and most of all, my students.—D.B.D.

To Diane, without whom my accomplishments would be fewer and far less meaningful.—P.T.H.

To David, Harrison and Daniel, who have taught me the value of everything.—E.M.B.

*

PREFACE TO THE SIXTH EDITION

This casebook is a teaching tool. We strive to produce a book that presents contemporary cases and issues, but equally one that presents the unchallenged core of lawyering, judging and thoughtful criticism. We also want to engage students without mystifying them.

While the foundation of tort law is timeless, the law is anything but static. This edition, as with our earlier editions, thus reflects new developments in cases, topics and academic commentary that have occurred in the last few years. There are sixteen new main cases, many new case abstracts and hundreds of citations to newer cases. These new materials not only carry a contemporary feel for the issues and outcomes, but often add perceptibly to the clarity and the challenges the issues present.

New cases are not the only occasion for changes. We have all learned from experience in teaching these materials, and have tried to profit from every question raised by students and every suggestion made by teachers. This edition's changes reflect that added experience, even if we have not made every change every person has suggested.

Of course, adding pages upon pages of new material would produce a casebook of unworkable length. We remain committed to providing a book that is as lean as possible, consistent with fully covering core materials and giving professors sufficient leeway to cover some topics but not others. To that end, we have tried to hold each edition to around 1000 pages and we have managed to cut this edition below that mark. We made many cuts simply by tightening materials, or by replacing older with newer. We also cut some materials entirely, either because they seemed redundant or too specialized, or in the belief that few professors had time to reach them.

This book deals centrally with injuries to persons, and reading about and discussing such serious matters can be difficult. But we have always approached torts by trying to present the reality of conflicts in tort law and we continue to do so in this edition. Tort law is about real people and real injuries, and the cases in this book reflect that reality. Of course, much of that tort law reality is leavened more than occasionally by the absurd and unexpected. A torts class using this book will then be more than an exercise in solemn analysis of tragic situations; our experience tells us that smiles and laughter are neither rare nor inappropriate as students and professors discuss the law. We believe a good book will challenge students, yet provide a good time when possible.

Our primary criterion in selecting cases for inclusion in this book is whether they provide opportunities for analysis and for strengthening important lawyering skills such as reading, interpretation, evaluation and synthesis of legal materials. This book has never been merely a collection of illusory "majority rules." We hope students using this book will realize early on that both the cases and the notes aim to sharpen intellectual skills and the understanding of legal process as well as to impart information.

Torts is a varied subject that crosses a wide range of types of conduct and types of injuries. Personal injury torts remain its solid core for most first-year classes, however, and we focus mainly on such torts, including products liability. But most personal injuries are redressed through alternative means, such as workers' compensation, social security, or private insurance. A picture of injury law, therefore, includes those topics and they remain a part of the Sixth Edition. And while we recognize the importance of economic torts to the real world, we continue to limit our coverage of such torts to core rules. This means that these materials cannot substitute for advanced courses that cover defamation, misrepresentation, intellectual property, interference with contract, employment law and the like. Our book does provide an introduction to those topics that should suffice to help students recognize that tort law is not exclusively injury law, and perhaps to help them decide on advanced electives.

A Note on Editing Conventions

The main "cases" reproduced in this (and almost any) casebook are opinions of appellate judges. Such opinions are rarely succinct. They almost always include a good deal of matter on procedural points and discussions of many arguments made by lawyers that are not relevant to the ideas we want to highlight and develop. They also usually include many citations to cases as precedent or example. Editing is therefore necessary.

When we omit text in opinions, we indicate the omission by ellipses. Sometimes we add an editorial summary of some point ourselves; we put that in brackets. We don't usually mark out omissions of citations of precedent and academic commentary at all, because such citations are so prevalent that every page would be cluttered with dots if we did. We likewise omit footnotes in opinions without marking the omission; when we retain footnotes we also retain their original numbering. Finally, in quoted materials, we usually omit any internal quotation marks to make materials more readable.

We repeatedly cite a number of standard works on torts in this book. A major work in six volumes is Fowler V. Harper, Fleming James, Jr., and Oscar S. Gray, The Law of Torts (3d ed. 2007), with some volumes in the second edition (1986) with current supplements. We usually cite this work as Harper, James & Gray, giving the appropriate section and publication date. A second work is Dan B. Dobbs, The Law of Torts (2000), a one volume edition with the same section numbers as the two-volume lawyer's edition of the same work. It is cited as Dobbs on Torts.

This edition contains numerous citations to the Restatements of Torts, and sometimes to the Restatements of Agency or other areas of relevant law. The Restatements of the Law in various editions are the product of the American Law Institute, a private law-reform group. The Restatements are not themselves law, but have proven quite influential with courts, many of which have voluntarily adopted the black-letter rules these Restatements contain. The newest torts Restatements are designated as the Restatement

(Third) of Torts, with subtitles to indicate the particular area covered—for instance, the Restatement of the Law of Torts: Liability for Physical Harm. As we go to press work on the Third Restatement is not complete and citations are necessarily to the most current drafts rather than to a final edition.

DAN B. DOBBS

PAUL T. HAYDEN

ELLEN M. BUBLICK

February 2009

*

ACKNOWLEDGEMENTS

Many people have aided our work on this edition. Thanks to research assistants Victoria Torrilhon and Mark Sorokin of the University of Arizona, James E. Rogers College of Law for their exemplary work and good company over the summer months. Thanks also to Grace Campbell for her thoughtful editorial suggestions. Paul gives special thanks to his colleagues David Leonard and Dan Selmi for their helpful suggestions on this edition; to Loyola Law School, Los Angeles, for generous financial support; and to his family for their patience and understanding. Ellen also thanks Barbara Lopez for critical help with the manuscript; Maureen Garmon for effective design of research structures; Barbara Atwood for assistance with procedure-related issues; Jim Rogers for generous financial support of research at the college; and Toni Massaro for support of this project and her thoughtful guidance. All of us thank our students, past and present, who continue to inspire and invigorate us.

*

Summary of Contents

TABLE OF CONTENTS

TABLE OF CASES

The principal cases are in bold type. Cases cited or discussed in the text are in roman type. References are to pages. Cases cited in principal cases and within other quoted materials are not included.

TORTS AND COMPENSATION

PERSONAL ACCOUNTABILITY AND SOCIAL RESPONSIBILITY FOR INJURY

Sixth Edition

*

PART 1

A FIRST LOOK AT TORTS

■ ■ ■

CHAPTER 1

TORT LAW: AIMS, APPROACHES, AND PROCESSES

■ ■ ■

§ 1. WHAT IS TORT LAW?

Tort as wrongdoing. Torts are wrongs recognized by law as grounds for a lawsuit. These wrongs include an intentional punch in the nose and also a negligent car wreck. They include medical malpractice and some environmental pollution. The list of tortious wrongs is very long. All torts involve conduct that falls below some legal standard. In almost all cases, the defendant is in some sense at fault, either because he intends harm or because he takes unreasonable risks of harm.

Harm required. In all tort cases, the defendant's wrong results in a harm to another person (or entity, such as a corporation), that the law is willing to say constitutes a legal injury. The injured person is said to have a "cause of action," that is, a claim against the person who committed the tort. This claim can be pursued in court. Most of the cases in this book involve some kind of physical injury or threat of physical injury. Some torts, however, involve harm that is purely commercial and others involve intangible harm such as harm to reputation.

Torts, crimes, and contracts. A breach of contract is often grounds for a lawsuit, but a breach of contract is often not considered to be a tort at all. It must ordinarily be redressed under the rules for contracts, not the rules for torts. Some torts are also crimes. A punch in the nose is a tort called battery, but it may also be a crime. Sometimes a defendant who attacked the plaintiff is prosecuted criminally and is also held liable to the plaintiff for the tort. The two fields of law often overlap. However, they are not identical. Some acts that cause no harm at all to individuals might be crimes but not torts. Conversely, some acts cause harm and are torts but are not crimes. That is because criminal law aims at vindicating public interests, while tort law aims at vindicating individual rights and redressing private harms.

Non-tort systems. Physical injuries inflicted by one person upon another are commonly addressed by tort law, but there are alternatives to tort law. Toward the end of this book, several chapters consider alternatives such as workers' compensation systems, which require employers to buy insurance and to pay for all on-the-job injuries even when the employer is not at fault. This is important for tort lawyers and also for those who wish to understand the way society deals with injuries. However, for now we are going to concentrate on the way tort law deals with injuries.

Common questions in tort law. Much of the law of torts is concerned with three questions: (1) what conduct counts as tortious or wrongful? (2) Did the conduct cause the kind of harm the law will recognize? (3) What defenses can be raised against liability if the defendant has committed a tort? The answer to these questions turns in part on why we have tort law and what its aims are. Before we look at those, however, we can get a better idea of what tort law *is* by looking briefly at what it *does* and what it aims to do.

§ 2.   THE AIMS AND APPROACHES IN TORT LAW—JUSTICE AND POLICY, COMPENSATION AND DETERRENCE

A.   SOME BROAD (AND CONFLICTING) AIMS

DAN B. DOBBS, THE LAW OF TORTS §§ 8–11 & § 13

Copyright © 2000 by Westgroup

[Section 8]
Justice, Policy, and Process Aims of Tort Law

... *Morality or corrective justice.* Particular aims of tort law are usually erected under one of two large systems of thought. The first bases tort law on moral responsibility or corrective justice. It attempts to hold defendants liable for harms they wrongfully caused and no others. Good social effects may result when courts act to right the wrongs done by defendants, but in this system of thought that is not the point of imposing liability. Liability is imposed instead when and only when it is "right" to do so. As stated in a recent decision of the House of Lords, "The overall object of tort law is to define cases in which the law may justly hold one party liable to compensate another." *Fairchild v. Glenhaven Funeral Servs.*, [2002] 3 All E.R. 305, 2002 WL 820081 (H.L. 2002).

Social utility or policy. The second large system of thought reverses the emphasis; it bases tort law on social policy or a good-for-all-of-us view. Social policy may coincide with justice in particular cases, but the dominant concern is not justice to the individual; it is to provide a system of rules that, overall, works toward the good of society.

Process. One kind of utility or social policy is inward looking. Rules must be made with the legal process itself in mind. They must be the kind of rules judges and juries can understand and apply in a practical way, and they must not leave too much to the judge's or the jury's discretion. These and a host of similar considerations focus on the litigation process itself as a good to be preserved rather than on the abstract ideal of justice or social utility.

Potential conflicts. The first two ways of looking at tort law are usually regarded as antithetical to each other. Although justice and policy often point to the same result, they do not always do so, and when they do not, one of these views must prevail or both must be compromised. The legal process view might also conflict with the aims of justice or those of policy.

Suppose a city, facing a raging and spreading fire, attempts to create a firebreak by blowing up a row of houses. Because time is critical, the city insists upon doing so before the plaintiff, who owns one of the houses, can remove his furniture. When the whole thing is over, the plaintiff claims damages from the city for the value of the furniture he could have saved. The city has acted for the good of its residents generally, but the plaintiff is the one who pays the costs. If the city's action is to be judged by a standard of social policy, some jurists might say the city should not be liable. On the other hand, if it is judged by corrective justice standards, the city should pay for the damage it did. Otherwise, the city would get the advantage of its action (whatever that advantage might be) but would pay none of the costs. There are more subtle examples, but this one is enough to suggest the potential conflict between a decision based upon (supposed) social policy and one based upon justice to the individual.

[Section 9]
Ideas of Corrective Justice

... *Fault and corrective justice.* Tort law imposes liability upon defendants for conduct the law treats as wrong. In most instances, the conduct adjudged as wrong can be viewed as morally faulty conduct: it is intentional misconduct or at least unreasonably risky conduct likely to cause harm to others. In these cases, tort law seems to be commensurate with corrective justice ideals. The defendant's fault is a wrong that has harmed the plaintiff in some recognizable way; tort liability, by requiring the wrongdoer to compensate the plaintiff, can put the accounts right between the parties.

Conversely, it can be argued that in a corrective justice scheme, it would be wrong to impose liability upon a defendant who is not at fault in causing the plaintiff's harm. Society may wish to compensate injured people by the use of public funds, but it cannot justly force one innocent individual to compensate another.

These views emphasize individual accountability for fault, accompanied by individual freedom to act without fault. They are consistent with an ideal of social responsibility for victims, however; they do not speak against government compensation for victims when the defendant is not at fault, only against compensation by the faultless defendant.

Strict liability and corrective justice. When tort law imposes liability without fault, does it go beyond the principle of corrective justice? At least *some* strict liability seems commensurate with corrective justice. For example, suppose a long-standing custom in our neighborhood permits any neighbor to borrow garden equipment from any other neighbor, but the custom is equally strong that if the equipment is damaged or lost while in the borrower's possession, the borrower must make the loss good. Suppose I borrow your lawnmower and without my fault it is damaged when a truck backs over it in my driveway. A rule that imposes liability upon me would be a strict liability rule because I was not at fault. Even so, liability seems to accord with corrective justice so long as you and I both know of the custom.

Uniting the potential for gains and losses. Some thinkers have advocated a general regime of strict liability on the ground that strict liability is a morally based system and therefore within the principle of corrective justice. One idea behind this view is that when I make choices about my conduct, I am entitled to the gains that may result from that conduct (including my personal pleasure), so I should also take responsibility for the losses. If I choose to hang-glide off the mountainside, either for personal pleasure or as part of a demonstration that brings me profit, then I should pay any damages I do when I cannot control the glider and land on your vegetable garden or your cat. This line of thought works best when an active person causes harm to a person or thing at rest. When two hang-gliders (or car drivers) crash into each other without fault, it is much harder to work out a system of strict liability that is also based on corrective justice.

[Paragraphs on strict liability for nonreciprocal risks and strict liability dictated by community standards are omitted.]

Fault again. Although innovative thinkers have sought to justify strict liability within a corrective justice framework, many of the cases they consider seem to entail special kinds of fault, for example, fault as judged by the fairness of imposing nonreciprocal risks or as judged by deviations from community-accepted norms. Whatever is to be said of strict liability theories of corrective justice, the great majority of tort cases turn on some kind of perception that the defendant is at fault in a significant way. At least for those cases, tort law begins with corrective justice ideals, even if those ideals may be modified by pragmatic, process, or policy considerations in particular cases.

[Section 10]
Compensation, Risk Distribution, Fault

... *Risk distribution or loss spreading....* [S]ome commentators have argued that tort liability should be strict or expansive in order to secure compensation for more injured persons. Some defendants if not all were seen as good "risk distributors" who should be liable for any harms they cause regardless of fault because they can "distribute" the costs of paying compensation. This means that some defendants, such as products manufacturers, could pay compensation for injuries they cause and then recoup some or all of those costs by raising the price of products. In this view, each individual purchaser of the products will pay a tiny fraction of the costs of injuries inflicted by those products and the injured person will not be compelled to bear the entire cost alone. Loss would thus cause less social dislocation. At the same time, an enterprise would be forced to internalize losses typically generated by the business itself.

Limited acceptance of risk distribution arguments. The common law of tort has not in fact generally adopted views that compensation is more important than corrective justice or that liability should be strict. Distribution arguments and strict liability have gone hand in hand, but only in a few kinds of cases. They have not supplanted fault as the most common basis for tort liability.

Moral and policy reasons for limiting compensation to cases of fault. Since compensation *is* indeed important and one of the goals of tort law, why is it that courts do not adopt strict liability across the board and order compensation in every case in which the defendant causes harm? The most obvious possibility is that judges feel heavily committed to a system of corrective justice and turn to social policy only when they feel social policy and corrective justice coincide at least in part. It is also possible, however, that in spite of social policy favoring compensation, other social policies counsel only limited compensation through the tort system.

First, the role of judges in framing schemes of distribution is doubtful. The risk distribution arguments may be sound, but sometimes may better be addressed to legislatures. In fact, some legislation in effect adopts such arguments. Workers' compensation statutes, for example, impose strict liability upon employers when workers are injured on the job. The cost or loss is distributed in part to workers themselves, whose wages might be higher but for the employer's cost of insuring against their injury. Part of it is distributed to customers who buy the employer's products or services. Second, an invariable award of compensation that must be paid by a defendant may eliminate any deterrent effect that the award would have if it were confined to cases of fault. Third, the tort system is an extremely expensive system to operate. If compensation is the most important goal, the tort system is a poor way to accomplish it because other means are cheaper. . . .

[Section 11]
Fostering Freedom, Deterring Unsafe Conduct; Economic Analysis

Deterrence. Courts and writers almost always recognize that another aim of tort law is to deter certain kinds of conduct by imposing liability when that conduct causes harm. The idea of deterrence is not so much that an individual, having been held liable for a tort, would thereafter conduct himself better. It is rather the idea that all persons, recognizing potential tort liability, would tend to avoid conduct that could lead to tort liability. They might sometimes engage in the conduct in question, but only if they would get more out of it than the tort liability would cost. Some critics believe that tort law fails to provide systematic deterrence.

Deterrence in corrective justice and social policy systems. Both corrective justice and social policy goals can agree that deterrence is acceptable, but the two approaches might call for deterring quite different conduct. If you focus on conduct that is wrongful in the sense of being unjust to an individual, you might regard any given act as wrongful even though it is economically useful in society. If you focus on social policy, you might want to forgive defendants who cause harms by their socially useful activities....

Economic analysis. As the example suggests, one particular kind of social policy consideration is the economic one. If economics is defined broadly enough to include a consideration of all human wants and desires, then perhaps all social policies are in a sense economic policies.

For instance, economic analysis of the personal injury part of tort law might attempt to suggest rules for finding the right balance between the number of injuries and the freedom of defendants to act. People in general ought to be free to build buildings, including cheaper ones, if they do so carefully; the law wants to protect their freedom and indeed encourage the enterprise because economically sound decisions are indeed good for the community as a whole. So one line of economic thought suggests that in deciding [liability of a builder whose carefully-constructed building collapses and causes harm] the costs of injury should be weighed, but so should the social (economic) utility of the cheaper building. This line of thought in fact accords with a great many decisions in the courts that do not mention economics at all. Depending on how much the builder saved and how high the injury costs were, this line of thought might lead a court to deny any recovery against the builder....

Note

Considerations of costs and utilities are often identified with the drive for efficiency, meaning the greatest net good for the community. Efficiency in turn is contrasted with fairness or justice.

[Section 13]
Process Values in Tort Law

... Process values are values we attach to the legal process itself, in particular, the process of deciding disputes. Jury trial rights, discussed later, are one part of the dispute resolution process, but there are others. Many process values are represented in procedural codes and in constitutional prescriptions. Due process is a prized right even if it is not precisely formulated: we should hold the trial before the verdict; each party should be entitled to know what the other claims; disputing parties must be able to present their side of the dispute.

Adopting, formulating, and applying tort rules. ... A judge might justly award damages to an injured plaintiff even if there were no rules at all, but the process of adjudication would then itself be suspect and in a sense unjust. So rules adopted must be rules that can be seen, understood, and applied, at least by the professionals involved in litigation. Judges striving to formulate or apply tort rules attempt to meet this modest concern for the litigation process itself.

Process goals. No authoritative list of process values guides judges, so lawyers can argue that any given rule is undesirable because it does not appropriately respect process concerns. Broadly phrased, the legal process should be designed not only to get good results in accord with justice and policy, but also to leave participants with a sense of humane participation in the process. That might include the felt need to tell one's side of the story and relate a sense of injustice. It might also include a sense that justice is not only done but seen to be done. There is also a practical side to process. Rules should be structured to permit efficient decision making—no litigant should be compelled to spend weeks getting a decision that can be made as well in a day.

Loose rule formulation that diminishes judicial accountability. ... If rules are too abstract, they may fail to constrain the judge or the jury. They may instead effectively permit the decision makers to do as they like.... A rule that merely told people "be good" has at least two process defects. First, it fails to point to evidence a lawyer could adduce or arguments she could make. Second, the rule is so undefined that it fails to constrain the judge in appropriate ways. If too many rules were like this, the judge's decision would be a ukase of a judicial czar, not an adjudication of facts and law. The judges' rational explanations of what they do is usually the only effective check on them. If their decisions are not subject to professional scrutiny because the rules are so uncertain that anything goes, judges are likely to become in time more arbitrary and ultimately less just.

Tight rule formulation that eliminates needed flexibility. Conversely, however, precise rules may constrain the decision makers too much, leaving no room for justly deciding the individual's case which is at the heart of our concept of justice. A rule that says "be good" violates the process interest in understandable, reasonably precise rules. At the other extreme, a rule that says "never, ever, drive more than 40 miles per hour in this zone" may leave too little flexibility for the case of the driver rushing his child to the emergency room.

Rules guiding lawyers' investigation and arguments. Although some rules are actually read and understood by the people whose conduct they regulate, many tort rules are not. Rules often attempt to reflect the way people should behave even if they have not read the statutes and the cases. Thus, many tort rules are mainly read and understood by lawyers. Judges formulating tort rules must have in mind that lawyers use rules in very practical ways, to know what arguments and what facts are relevant so that investigation can proceed accordingly....

Rules failing to specify provable facts. Rules also detract from good process when they call for facts that cannot be proved with reasonable confidence or proved within a reasonable length of time. Suppose that it is normally a tort to touch someone who has not consented to a touching, but that it is not a tort to touch someone who has consented to it. If the plaintiff plays in a game of tag or football, consent seems apparent even if it is not expressed. If judges were to say that anyone touching the plaintiff is liable unless the plaintiff actually, subjectively consents to the touching, the rule would not point to evidence that can be reached by the defendant's lawyer, since no one can produce evidence about the plaintiff's state of mind except so far as it is outwardly or objectively expressed. That might or might not lead to unjust results, but it leads to process concerns because we would not be very sure of our basis for judging the question of subjective consent if we are not permitted to consider the outward signs. . . .

NOTE

Many writers have addressed the goals or methods of tort law. Major contributions and differing views about justice vs. deterrence (or moral vs. economic analysis) are discussed in Gary T. Schwartz, *Mixed Theories of Tort Law: Affirming Both Deterrence and Corrective Justice*, 75 TEX. L. REV. 1801 (1997). For a more recent look at the tensions, see Kenneth W. Simons, *Tort Negligence, Cost–Benefit Analysis, and Tradeoffs: A Closer Look at the Controversy*, 41 LOYOLA L.A. L. REV. 1171 (2008). There is also an admirably succinct summary in William E. Nelson, *From Fairness to Efficiency: the Transformation of Tort Law in New York*, 1920–1980, 47 BUFF. L. REV. 117 (1999). David A. Fischer, *Successive Causes and the Enigma of Duplicated Harm*, 66 TENN. L. REV. 1127 (1999), concludes that when courts have been forced to choose between the goals of fairness and efficiency, they have opted for fairness. Louis Kaplow & Steven Shavell argue in *Fairness versus Welfare*, 114 HARV. L. REV. 961 (2001), that courts err whenever they accord independent weight to notions of fairness such as corrective justice, and instead should focus on individual well-being. The materials in this book may help you determine for yourself whether either of these conclusions is well-founded.

B.   APPLYING SOME APPROACHES

A great deal can be said about approaches to tort law or its goals, but for those without experience in reading actual cases and encountering actual tort problems, the goals are so abstract that they almost elude the grasp. The best approach may be to keep the goals or approaches in mind while reading cases. In many instances the different approaches will lead to the same outcome. When they do not, the differences are worth thinking about. To leave this topic with a sense of how some of these approaches might differ, consider the following hypothetical case and the approaches taken by the three judges.

PROSSER v. KEETON

143 Unrep. Case 1113

Allen, J., stated the facts for the court: Prosser was the owner of a valuable watch. It was stolen on or about April 1 by a person then unknown, but later discovered to be one Thurlow. Thurlow, in possession of the stolen watch, represented to Keeton that the watch was Thurlow's and that, because his mother was ill, he needed to sell it to raise funds. Thurlow and Keeton were both members of the same church and knew each other slightly. Keeton, because of this connection, reasonably believed that Thurlow was indeed the owner and he paid Thurlow $500 for the watch, a sum which approximated its real value. Thurlow immediately disappeared. About a month later, however, Prosser saw Keeton wearing the watch and identified it by a secret mark on the back. There is no question about the identification and Prosser demanded its return. Keeton argued that as he had paid for it, he would not return it. The trial judge held that Keeton, though in good faith, was a converter and liable to return the watch or pay its reasonable value. Keeton appeals.

Allen, J. The thief obviously did not obtain title to the watch. (It would be absurd to say that Prosser could not sue the thief if he had discovered the theft immediately.) If the thief did not have title, how could he transfer the title he did not have? Obviously he could not do so. And if the thief could not transfer title, then Keeton did not get title from the thief. It is true that Keeton paid money, but that can hardly go to show that the thief could suddenly convey a title he did not have. Since Keeton obtained no title, he has no right to the watch and he is a converter, liable to Prosser.

Bateman, J. A rule of law should work justice between the parties. Neither Prosser nor Keeton were guilty of wrongdoing, but as the thief has disappeared, one or the other must bear the loss. Purchasers are generally in no position to determine the true ownership of watches and this purchaser in particular had every reason to believe that the thief was honest. Watch owners, though undoubtedly victims of theft, are in better position to guard against theft than purchasers are to discover it. Justice therefore requires us to hold that the purchaser, Keeton, takes good title by operation of law.

Compton, J. The law may give the good faith purchaser title if there is an apt reason of policy for doing so, and this is true even if the thief could not give title. There is no reason of justice to make Prosser bear the loss. It has not been established by evidence that Prosser in particular or watch owners in general can protect themselves from thieves any better than purchasers can. Justice does not help us put the loss on either Prosser or Keeton. However, social policy, which transcends the question of justice between two individuals, does speak to this issue. Social policy in an enterprise society demands that exchange of goods be fostered. If every buyer had to investigate the provenance of the goods he or she purchased, the process of production and the satisfaction of human needs and wants would be made much more costly if it was not stopped altogether. Social policy, therefore, requires us to hold that Keeton should be given title to the watch by operation of the law.

NOTES

1. **Formal styles of legal reasoning.** Judge Allen's reasoning might be described as "formal," or less flatteringly, as "conceptual" or "mechanical." Does Allen appeal either to justice or to policy?

2. **Justice and morality.** If a lawyer today were asked to mount an argument against formalistic reasoning, the answer might well be something like this: "Formalistic reasoning takes the eye off the ball. The real problems for which courts were instituted are justice and social policy." Judge Bateman's decision in *Prosser v. Keeton* emphasized justice, and concluded that it was "just" for the owner to bear the risk of theft rather than the purchaser. Might she have argued instead that it is unjust to deprive an owner of property by force or theft? This would have put her in accord with Judge Allen. Is her opinion more likely to be predictable and "correct" than Judge Allen's?

3. **Policy.** When the demands of justice conflict with demands of policy, which should prevail? If ideas of justice can be manipulated in an argument maybe ideas of policy can be, too. Is there any policy argument in favor of holding Keeton liable?

4. **A question.** Suppose someone says to you: "Why should the courts bother with such a small case? After all, it is just a watch. People shouldn't burden the courts with small claims like this." Do you find any responses in considerations of justice? Of social policy?

FLORIDA 2008 SESSION LAW SERVICE
TWENTIETH LEGISLATURE, SECOND REGULAR SESSION

Chapter 2008–269
C.S.H.B. No. 787

PERSONAL INJURIES—NEGLIGENCE—BRIAN DAIAGI

An act for the relief of Brian Daiagi by the South Florida Water Management District; authorizing and directing the South Florida Water Management District to compensate Brian Daiagi for personal injuries that he suffered due to the negligence of the South Florida Water Management District; providing a limitation on attorney's fees, lobbying fees, costs, and other similar expenses relating to the claim; providing an effective date.

WHEREAS, on the morning of August 10, 1992, Brian Daiagi, a 20-year-old single resident of Broward County, was traveling on a dirt bike westbound on the shoulder of Griffin Road with Richard Truntz, an off-duty police officer with the Hollywood Police Department, who was also on a dirt bike, and

WHEREAS, across the shoulder of the road, hidden in tall grass and unbeknownst to both of them, was a drainage culvert that ran perpendicular to and across the shoulder of the road on which they were traveling, and

WHEREAS, this drainage culvert that was placed on land owned by the South Florida Water Management District had been there for many years and, at one point, Bell South was to have erected a security fence around the drainage culvert, having obtained permission to lay telephone cables on the road shoulder, but Bell South ultimately failed to erect the security fence, and

WHEREAS, despite having notice that the security fence had not been erected, the South Florida Water Management District did not act to protect or warn of the hidden drainage culvert, and

WHEREAS, on August 10, 1992, at approximately 3:00 p.m., when the two riders were returning to Brian Daiagi's home, Richard Truntz was unable to get his dirt bike out of first gear and could ride only very slowly and suggested that Brian ride ahead and meet him later at Mr. Daiagi's house, and

WHEREAS, while wearing a helmet and full protective gear and traveling at approximately 25 m.p.h., Brian Daiagi drove his dirt bike into the hidden drainage culvert, and

WHEREAS, Mr. Daiagi had never ridden his dirt bike in the area where the accident occurred, and had moved to this western area of Broward County approximately 3 weeks prior to the accident, and

WHEREAS, the drainage culvert cannot be seen with the naked eye and was completely obscured by long grass along the road, and

WHEREAS, the South Florida Water Management District is responsible for cutting the grass in this area, and

WHEREAS, testimony at the trial of the case indicated that the grass was at least "knee high" and obscured the culvert from ordinary view, and Richard Truntz testified that he would also have driven into the culvert except for the fact that he was traveling in first gear and was able to stop 2 feet short of the culvert only by breaking hard, and

WHEREAS, the South Florida Water Management District acknowledged during the trial that it had knowledge that "passers-by" used the road shoulder and took the position that Brian Daiagi was "an invitee" on the premises, and

WHEREAS, Brian Daiagi sustained a crush fracture to his spine, was rendered a paraplegic as a result of the incident, was paralyzed from the waist down, and, according to Dr. Barth Green who treated Mr. Daiagi for his injuries, will always be confined to a wheelchair within a reasonable degree of medical probability, and

WHEREAS, the specific injuries include a T10–T11 fracture with complete paraplegia below the navel; comminuted fracture of the vertebrae at T11;

multiple fractures of the spine at L1, L2, L3, and L4; posttraumatic stress disorder; depression; pain secondary to the spinal cord injury; bowel dysfunction; nonfunctioning bladder that requires 24–hour catheterization; and complete sexual impotence, and

WHEREAS, there was no testimony that Brian Daiagi was speeding at the time of the accident and the South Florida Water Management District claimed that Mr. Daiagi was not looking where he was going, and

WHEREAS, the trial court allowed the jury to visit the scene of the accident and the jury agreed by their verdict that the drainage culvert was completely obscured and could not be seen and, at the time the jury visited the site, the grass was above knee level, and

WHEREAS, an engineer and accident reconstructionist who was called by Mr. Daiagi as an expert witness testified that Mr. Daiagi's speed, based upon where he was found on the other side of the culvert, was approximately 25.6 m.p.h., requiring 90 feet in which to stop, at which distance Mr. Daiagi could not have seen the culvert, and

WHEREAS, at the time of the accident, Mr. Daiagi was working in a jewelry store and is now 36 years of age and lives in western Broward County, and

WHEREAS, a verdict was rendered in the case on September 29, 2000, finding that the South Florida Water Management District was 80–percent negligent in causing the injuries sustained by Brian Daiagi, and awarding damages totaling $4,344,000, which took into account a finding of 20–percent comparative negligence by Mr. Daiagi, and

WHEREAS, the verdict was later reduced by the trial court due to collateral source payments pursuant to health insurance, resulting in an amended final judgment entered by the trial court on May 10, 2001, in the amount of $4,008,616.63, and

WHEREAS, the South Florida Water Management District appealed the verdict to the Fourth District Court of Appeals and the verdict was upheld in a unanimous opinion by the appellate court on July 17, 2002, Case Number 4D01–1918, NOW, THEREFORE,

Be It Enacted by the Legislature of the State of Florida:

Section 1. **The facts stated in the preamble to this act are found and declared to be true.**

Section 2. **The South Florida Water Management District is authorized and directed to appropriate from funds of the district not otherwise appropriated and to draw a warrant in the amount of $3,908,616.63, payable to Brian Daiagi, to compensate him for personal injuries and damages suffered as a result of the negligence of the South Florida Water Management District.**

Section 3. **This award is intended to provide the sole compensation for all present and future claims arising out of the factual situation described in this act which resulted in injury to Brian Daiagi.**

The total amount paid for attorney's fees, lobbying fees, costs, and other similar expenses relating to this claim may not exceed 25 percent of the amount awarded under this act.

Section 4. This act shall take effect upon becoming a law.

Approved by the Governor May 19, 2008.

Filed in Office Secretary of State May 19, 2008.

NOTES

1. **The legislature's role.** Normally courts decide tort cases and enforce judgments against defendants. In this case, a jury found for Brian Daiagi and determined that his damages were $4.28 million. That judgment was upheld by a Florida Court of Appeals. See *South Florida Water Management Dist. v. Daiagi*, 824 So.2d 216 (Fla. Dist. Ct. App. 2002). However, under a Florida tort claims statute, the liability of government agencies is limited to $200,000 per incident unless the Florida legislature authorizes a damage payment in excess of this amount. See FLA. STAT. ANN. § 768.28(5) (West 2008). Sixteen years after Daiagi was injured, the Florida legislature passed this law which authorized him to collect the judgment.

2. **Legal remedy for injury.** In the United States there are millions of disabling injuries each year. This Florida legislation concerns just one. Because physical injuries cannot be undone, the tort law focuses on whether a legal remedy for the injury should be available, what kind, and against whom. On the facts stated in this case, should Brian Daiagi be able to recover money from the South Florida Water Management District? Would liability promote accountability, deterrence, compensation?

3. **The importance of specific facts.** The legislature noted the Water Management District's position that Daiagi was an "invitee" on the premises. As we will see in chapter 12, this means that unlike a trespasser, Daiagi was authorized to be on the land. Are there other facts that would make a difference to the question of whether Daiagi should be allowed to recover for his damages? What if there had been a similar accident in the same place six months earlier? What if a Water Management District employee sent an email to a supervisor cautioning that Bell South had not put up the fence and warning that something tragic might happen if the District did not correct the situation? What if Daiagi had not been wearing a helmet? What else?

§ 3.   IMPLEMENTING TORT LAW PURPOSES WITH DAMAGES AWARDS

In a few cases the remedy for a tort is an injunction. That is, the court will order the defendant to cease committing a tort like a nuisance or a continuing contamination of the plaintiff's land. In the overwhelming majority of injury cases, however, the remedy is compensatory damages, an award of money to compensate for the tort committed by the defendant.

HOLDEN v. WAL–MART STORES, INC.

608 N.W.2d 187 (Neb. 2000)

CONNOLLY, J. . . .

The appellant, Debra J. Holden, fell after stepping in a hole in the parking lot of a store owned by the appellee, Wal–Mart Stores, Inc. Holden subsequently underwent knee replacement surgery and sustained medical bills of at least $25,000. . . .

In July 1992, Holden was injured after she fell in the parking lot of a Wal–Mart in Scottsbluff, Nebraska. Prior to the fall, Holden had been issued a handicapped parking permit dated June 2, 1992, because prior problems with her knees and feet made it difficult for her to walk distances. On the day of the fall, Holden parked in a handicapped parking space at Wal–Mart. When she pulled into the stall, she did not notice any holes in the surface of the parking lot. After she got out of her van and was walking toward the rear of it, she fell and experienced immediate pain, the worst of which was in her right knee. After she composed herself, she saw that the cause of the fall was that her foot had twisted in a hole. Following the fall, Holden went to the emergency room. Holden subsequently underwent knee replacement surgery and brought the instant action against Wal–Mart seeking damages. . . .

[Dr. Diane Gilles, an orthopedic surgeon, testified about Holden's earlier knee problems, but also testified] that if Holden had not fallen, she probably could have waited between 5 to 10 years before requiring a total knee replacement. Gilles also testified that prior to the fall, Holden had an 87–percent lower extremity impairment and a 35–percent whole person impairment and that after the fall, this increased to a 97–percent lower extremity impairment and 39–percent whole person impairment. Gilles' charges for treatment related to the fall were $646.75.

The record reflects that Holden first saw Dr. Mark Alan McFerran, another orthopedic surgeon, on January 10, 1994. McFerran subsequently performed a total knee replacement and placed Holden on maximum medical improvement in May 1995. . . . McFerran also testified that he thought the fall at Wal–Mart hastened the need for Holden to have her knee replaced.

The total of McFerran's charges was $24,707.91. McFerran testified that the hardware involved in the knee replacement has a lifespan of 15 to 20 years, after which Holden would require another replacement costing between $40,000 and $50,000, barring complications. Holden presented evidence regarding the pain she experienced after the fall and her need for assistance due to the fall.

The jury returned a verdict finding 40 percent negligence on the part of Holden and 60 percent negligence on the part of Wal–Mart. The jury determined total damages to be $6,000. As a result, Holden recovered $3,600. . . .

[On appeal Holden contended] that the jury erred in its computation of damages, arguing that the jury made a mistake.

"An award of damages may be set aside as excessive or inadequate when, and not unless, it is so excessive or inadequate as to be the result of passion, prejudice, mistake, or some other means not apparent in the record.... If an award of damages shocks the conscience, it necessarily follows that the award was the result of passion, prejudice, mistake, or some other means not apparent in the record."

We conclude that the award in the instant case was not the result of a mistake.... Evidence was presented at trial regarding Holden's previous problems with her right knee, and there was conflicting evidence regarding the effect of the fall on this preexisting condition. Holden testified regarding the additional pain and difficulties the fall caused, and her physicians indicated that the fall sped up the need for her to have knee replacement surgery. However, there was also evidence that Holden had been having similar knee pain causing difficulty in her life prior to the fall. However, she did not report the additional pain in several following appointments with her physicians. The evidence was strong that Holden would, at some point, have undergone knee replacement surgery regardless of the fall. However, when she might have done so was unclear.

[T]he jury could have reached any number of factual conclusions. A jury is entitled to determine what portion of a claimed injury was proximately caused by the incident and what portion of the medical bills was reasonably required. The jury in this case could have determined that the fall was the proximate cause of only a small portion of Holden's damages. The evidence for such a determination is apparent from the record, and we will not disturb that determination on appeal....

Affirmed.

NOTES

1. **Liability.** Most cases in this book will be considering whether the defendant should be liable to the plaintiff at all. In this case, assume that the judge and jury, considering the detailed testimony not available to us, properly imposed liability. That will permit us to focus on the question of appropriate compensation.

2. **The jury damages award.** Did the jury get the award about right or was the award too low because it was less than the plaintiff's actual medical expense? Actually, you might consider whether we have facts sufficient to permit us to judge either way.

3. **Judge and jury.** The appellate judges seem to recognize an important role for the jury, yet also seem to say that the judges will reject the jury's verdict in some cases. Can you say when judges will do that? Is *Holden* more about process values than about, say, appropriate deterrence or exact compensation?

4. **A check on awards that "shock the conscience."** The *Holden* court states the rule that a trial judge may set aside a jury's award of damages

if it "shocks the conscience." This was found to be the case in *Advocat, Inc. v. Sauer*, 111 S.W.3d 346 (Ark. 2003). The jury awarded $15 million in compensatory damages against the operators of a nursing home they found to have been grossly negligent in causing the decedent's death from malnutrition and dehydration. The court used its *remittitur* power to lower the award by two-thirds, to $5 million. An award of punitive damages was similarly reduced by the trial judge.

5. **Compensatory damages elements.** The injured person has the burden of proving damages. Upon an offer of adequate proof, the plaintiff can recover any (1) lost wages or lost earning capacity, (2) medical expenses, and (3) pain and suffering endured, including mental or emotional pain. Upon proper proof, the plaintiff can recover not only for such losses that have already occurred, but also for such losses that will probably arise in the future. A damages award, if any, is subject to some adjustments. For instance, adjustments may be made to account for delay in payment, for inflation and other items. We leave aside those more technical details for now. The gist of the damages rules is that the defendant has wrongfully reduced the plaintiff's net assets, tangible and intangible, and should be required to restore them. Is this consistent with some or all of the broad goals of tort law?

6. **Punitive damages.** In a very few cases, juries are permitted to award punitive damages in addition to compensatory damages. Virtually all states authorize punitive damages only when a tortfeasor has acted maliciously or wilfully or wantonly in causing injury. Punitive damages are intended to provide a measure of added deterrence and perhaps some punishment for the wrongdoer's serious misconduct.

7. **Attorney fees costs to the plaintiff.** One of the most important institutional rules covering most litigation in the United States is that a losing party is not required to pay the winning party's attorney fees. As a result, the almost universal system of litigation finance in this country is that plaintiffs' attorneys are paid by contingent fees. They are paid nothing if they lose, and a percentage of the recovery if they win. The percentage may vary from around 25% to 40%, sometimes higher. The percentage may sound high, but considering the lawyer's investment of time and effort and the fact that the lawyer will be paid nothing in some cases, such fees are usually not a bad deal for the client who could not afford to pay a lawyer otherwise. State rules of professional responsibility prohibit lawyers from charging or collecting fees that are unreasonable, excessive or unconscionable. *See* ABA MODEL RULES OF PROFESSIONAL CONDUCT 1.5(a) (prohibiting unreasonable fees). These rules apply to all kinds of fees, including contingent fees, and a lawyer may be disciplined by the state bar for any violation. Many states also limit the percentage that can be charged in particular kinds of cases, such as medical malpractice.

8. **Criticisms of damages.** You may have heard or read many criticisms of tort law—that it is out of control, that Americans litigate trivial matters, that they are greedy, and that they seek something for nothing. No doubt greed shows up in lawsuits as well as in corporate board rooms and elsewhere. However, it is important to know that the studies available do *not* support the claim that litigation by individuals has increased or that juries

often run amok. One prominent study is Deborah Jones Merritt & Kathryn Ann Barry, *Is the Tort System in Crisis? New Empirical Evidence,* 60 OHIO ST. L. J. 315 (1999). A 2008 report issued by the Bureau of Justice Statistics estimates the median award in tort cases at $24,000, slightly lower than the $35,000 median award in contract cases. In all cases, only 4% of plaintiffs received awards over one million dollars. In addition, from 1992 to 2005 the number of tort cases decreased by 40%. Did plaintiffs fare better with juries rather than judges? Quite to the contrary. *See* LYNN LANGTON & THOMAS H. COHEN, BUREAU OF JUSTICE STATISTICS, U.S. DEP'T. OF JUSTICE, NCJ 223851, CIVIL BENCH AND JURY TRIALS IN STATE COURTS, 2005 (October 2008).

9. **A case example.** You might want to be cautious about forming judgments about all tort law based upon anecdotes or media presentations rather than an understanding of the whole system. One case that grabbed media attention and comes in for vituperative comment involved a large judgment for a woman who was burned by scalding coffee handed her by McDonald's. Sitting in the car, she held the container between her legs to take the top off and the coffee spilled. It was hot enough to inflict third degree burns—which covered her groin and genital area. Third degree burns can burn entirely though the skin and vessels and all the way to the bone. She was hospitalized, underwent skin grafts, had excruciating pain, and was permanently disfigured. She asked McDonald's to pay her $11,000 hospital bills, but McDonald's refused. She hired an attorney who demanded $90,000 in damages, but McDonald's refused that, too. The attorney then filed a suit and discovered that McDonald's intentionally kept its coffee hot enough to inflict third degree burns and in fact had known of at least 700 people who had been burned by its scalding coffee. He now demanded more and punitive damages, to boot. The jury awarded the plaintiff $200,000 in compensatory damages, reduced to $160,000 because it considered that she was partly at fault. The jury then added a whopping sum as punitive damages because McDonald's was reckless or even malicious. The jury's verdict for that was $2.7 million, a large sum meant to deter such misconduct. Even so it only represented about two days' of McDonald's revenues from coffee sales. The judge reduced the punitive award to $480,000, for a total award of $640,000. Media and web commentators present a different picture. They often leave out the fact that most of the award was for deterrence, not compensation, that it was reduced as part of the ordinary mechanisms of tort law (the judge's review) and that the coffee was not merely "hot," but capable of great harm, which it in fact caused quite needlessly. You can read comments on the web in essence saying that "an old woman" spilled coffee on herself and got something for nothing, omitting to note that the jury reduced the compensatory damages by $40,000 for the plaintiff's supposed fault in spilling the coffee, and perhaps betraying a contempt for "old women." You'll want to judge for yourself, but as professionals we should decide on the basis of more facts than appear in the popular media. For these facts and others, and also for the media portrayals, you can find a summary of the McDonald's case in Mark B. Greenlee, *Kramer v. Java World: Images, Issues, and Idols in the Debate over Tort Reform,* 26 CAP. U. L. REV. 701 (1997).

10. **Pain and suffering.** One difficulty in assessing proper compensation is that for many of us, our main assets are not in the form of money or

property but in the form of good health and freedom from pain. Although pain is not quantifiable, freedom from pain has economic value. We can see that in the expenditures people make to gain pleasure and avoid pain. You could also imagine that someone offered you money for the right to break your leg. If you would accept such an awful offer at all, you would almost certainly demand even more money if the break would entail pain. The amount of money you would demand to suffer pain is not the measure of a tortfeasor's liability (he is only liable for reasonable compensation, not what you would demand). Even so, if freedom from pain is an intangible asset, pain inflicted by a defendant represents a real loss and should be compensated somehow.

11. **Estimating damages.** How does the jury know what to award for pain and suffering? Remember that the jury's ultimate decision on this element of damages represents a collective judgment of a group. If jurors are randomly chosen, does that tend to guarantee that awards are likely to represent the community's sense of an appropriate award on the facts of the particular case? Remember, too, that the jury is not merely reading an abbreviated media account but is instead seeing all the witnesses and learning of all the harms actually done.

12. **Calculating plaintiff's losses.** In *Estevez v. United States*, 72 F. Supp. 2d 205 (S.D.N.Y. 1999), the defendant's employee carelessly caused a car accident that injured a two-year-old child. The child was hospitalized for weeks and underwent surgeries to repair his aorta, kidney and bowel as well as some arteries and veins. In addition, the child had to wear a spinal fracture brace and was placed on breathing and feeding tubes for a period of time. Because of the injuries, he faced increased risks for future medical problems, required increased medical monitoring, and could anticipate a shortened work life expectancy. The court awarded $138,000 in past hospital and medical costs, $85,415 for future cardiac procedures, $1,800 for needed x-rays of his leg, $40,000 for orthotic devices he would need over the course of a lifetime, $11,700 for tendon lengthening surgery, $93,600 for physical therapy, $432,887 in lost wages for a 6.67 reduced work-life expectancy, $500,000 for past pain and suffering and $750,000 for future pain and suffering, an award that the court said amounted to "little more than $10,000 per year for a permanent limp and leg shortening, a damaged spine, potential abdominal adhesions, risk of infection of the Gortex patch [on the aorta], and the continued discomfort of medical monitoring and associated procedures." After plaintiff's total award of $1,993,902 was reduced by 25% for attorney fees, his total adjusted award was $1,511,052. Although tort damage amounts may sound quite high, so far as pecuniary damages go, each item must be proved. Actual costs to the victim can be quite high when you calculate future costs of medical treatment and lost wages.

13. **A measurement question.** Consider another case. Mr. Cho, with a medical appointment, asked Buckner to move his truck, which was blocking Cho's car. Buckner refused. Cho then honked at Buckner. This seems to have triggered Buckner's response: he kicked Mr. Cho in the head, knocking him down. When Mrs. Cho came out, Buckner knocked her down, kicked her down a second time, then hit her in the chest, causing a third fall. Mrs. Cho had medical bills of more than $8,600, Mr. Cho of more than $1,300. If we are the jury, what amount do we award the Chos as compensatory damages? *Norfolk Beverage Co., Inc. v. Cho*, 525 S.E.2d 287 (Va. 2000).

Chapter 2

Reading Torts Cases: Trial Procedures

■ ■ ■

§ 1. LOOKING FOR FACTS, RULES, AND REASONS

Reading cases to understand principles and predict law. This course presents real cases that involve individual human beings as plaintiffs, defendants, lawyers and judges. The "cases" in this book are actually the explanations judges give for the legal decisions that they make. By reading these explanations carefully, good lawyers can learn the governing legal principles. They can also envision what other legal rules could develop from these principles. In addition, they can learn to identify recurring issues, distinguish seemingly similar cases, and find similarities in cases that are seemingly different. Why are these skills important? One reason is that these are skills needed to make professional estimates about likely outcomes of a case if a client must sue or defend. Another is that these skills are needed to construct sound and persuasive legal arguments to courts.

Facts. The facts of a case are likely to influence the judge in deciding on appropriate legal rules. If the case is about a four-year-old who causes harm, the judge's observations about "the liability of children" may really be observations only about the liability of very young children. The facts that influence the judge's decision may be an explicit part of the case or an implicit part of the judge's reasoning. The scope of a rule will require interpretation on your part, and it means that you must understand the facts in the case very well indeed. When you identify the important facts of a case be sure to include facts necessary to the judge's decision. You may also include facts that determine the scope of the rule, facts that demonstrate the overall context of the case, and facts that help in remembering the case.

Procedure and procedural issues. Reading cases well requires attention to both the substantive legal issues raised by the parties and the legal procedures through which those issues are raised. The legal procedure that triggered the court's ruling is important to understanding the legal rule of the case—did the lower court dismiss the plaintiff's complaint

20

before any evidence had been gathered, grant summary judgment for the defendant after reviewing all of the material facts, or reverse a judgment against the defendant after a full trial and verdict? The allocation of decision-making power between judge and jury is a major process element in many tort cases. Suppose: (1) The issue is whether the judge should dismiss the plaintiff's claim without letting a jury decide it, and that the judge lets the jury decide. (2) The jury decides for the defendant. (3) The judge upholds the jury's verdict. Process values explain this sequence. In item (1), by refusing to dismiss the case the judge is not saying that the plaintiff should win. The judge is saying instead that the decision on the particular issue in light of the facts stated should be made by the jury, not by the judge. So the jury's verdict either way will be upheld on those particular facts. In other cases, judges will take the case away from the jury, allocating power to themselves instead of the jury. The appropriate sphere of judge and jury is often the basic concern in applying legal rules, so a reader of cases must pay attention to which procedure triggers the appeal. One example of a statement about procedure might be—summary judgment granted by the trial court and upheld by the appellate court.

Substantive issues. The substantive issue raised by the litigants as shaped by the court will also affect the holding. It is helpful to recognize both the procedural issue—"should the trial court's motion for summary judgment be upheld?"—and the substantive question presented to the court—"is intent to harm required to show a battery?"

Holding and rules. The holding of the court is the court's response to the issues raised by the parties. The procedural form of the holding might be as simple as "reversed." However, a fuller statement of the holding might also include the rule of law the court stated in response to the substantive issue raised in the case. For example, a statement of a holding that includes both the procedural holding and the rule of the case might be "Reversed, for the defendant; a battery cannot be proved without proof that the defendant intended harm or offense." Rules of a case are helpful because they may be used to resolve similar cases later on. Sometimes a judge clearly earmarks a rule. More often, you must interpret what you read.

Reasoning. The rules in most judicial decisions are interpreted in part by following the judge's reasoning. Ideally, the judge's reasoning explains why the rule exists (or why the judge is creating the rule) and how it applies to the case. The judge's reasoning may include analogies to other cases or legal doctrines, reference to persuasive authorities, and discussion of fairness or policy concerns. What the judge emphasizes in reasoning about the rule tells you a great deal about what the rule is and what its limits might be.

Application of rules. Although rules found in yesterday's cases will help resolve today's disputes, they usually will not do so simply or directly. You will find you must reason about how the rule is to be applied in your client's situation. You will also find that any given rule must ordinarily be made to work effectively with other rules.

Rules point lawyers to evidence required and arguments available. Frequently, the rules in yesterday's cases do not actually resolve today's disputes at all. Instead, their most important function is to point to evidence that lawyers will need to gather for a trial and to arguments that lawyers will need to construct in presenting or defending a claim.

§ 2. PROCEDURES AT TRIAL

The cases you read are usually the decisions of appeals court judges. Less often they are decisions of trial court judges who occasionally decide to provide a written explanation of their decisions. The judges are usually addressing the facts that are shown by a transcript of the trial. Since all decisions about tort law are made in deciding some procedural point, it is necessary to have a basic idea what the trial procedure is like.

Trial procedure can be complicated, but the basic plan of a trial is very simple. It is designed to resolve two kinds of disputes. The first kind of dispute is about the facts, about what happened. Almost all trials involve at least some factual dispute. The second kind of dispute is about the law. Most trials also involve disputes about what the legal rules are, or how they should apply to the particular case.

Although we've listed trial procedures in the order in which they typically arise in a trial, some of the procedures—the ones marked with an asterisk—are the main procedural devices that raise legal issues which will appear in the tort cases in this book. The procedures that most frequently raise legal issues reflect the fact that the judge is a gatekeeper who screens out evidence that is improper and often screens out whole cases, preventing the evidence or the case from being considered by the jury. When the judge screens out the whole case, the jury decides nothing and lawyers say the case did not "get to the jury," meaning that the judge decided that the plaintiff must lose under some rule of law or that the plaintiff's evidence was insufficient to permit reasonable people to find the facts essential for the plaintiff to win. In fact, the first question lawyers are likely to ask when they evaluate a new case is: Can this case get to the jury?—meaning, will the judge screen the case out or will the jury be permitted to make the ultimate decision in the case?

You may want to look back at these pages as you encounter these procedures in cases. In the appendix following this section, we narrate a hypothetical case so you can see the procedures being applied.

For our discussion here, it may be helpful to imagine a very simple kind of case in which the plaintiff contends that the defendant struck her. Defendant denies this completely. How does this get to court and what happens there?

Complaint. Plaintiff's lawyer, having investigated the facts, writes up a document called a complaint or petition. This document states the facts as claimed by the client. This document is formally filed with the court (in the court clerk's office) and a copy is served on (delivered to) the defendant, often by an officer of the court such as the sheriff or the federal marshal.

The Motion to Dismiss or Demurrer. If the defendant believes that the plaintiff's complaint does not state facts that show a good legal claim, the appropriate response is to file a motion to dismiss the complaint. The effect of this motion is to say to the judge, "Take all the facts stated in the complaint as if they were proved; even so, they do not show a valid legal claim."

Since the facts alleged are temporarily assumed to be true for purpose of considering this motion, there is no factual dispute. The issue raised is one of law, for the judge to decide, not the jury. Suppose plaintiff's lawyer wrote up, filed and served a complaint stating not that the defendant struck the plaintiff, but instead that the defendant frowned at the plaintiff. Frowning is not a tort, so defendant's motion to dismiss would be sustained.

Conceivably the plaintiff's complaint would be rewritten or amended to add important allegations. This would usually be permitted. However, in most cases in this casebook, the issue is on appeal for the very reason that the plaintiff *cannot* add any provable facts that will help.

Notice that the motion to dismiss comes at a very early stage of the case—before the defendant has filed an answer or along with the defendant's answer. In other words, it comes before any time has been invested in developing proof or calling a jury.

If the motion to dismiss or demurrer is denied, the case will proceed and defendant will file an answer.

Answer. The defendant, within the time allowed, must file some sort of paper taking a position on the complaint. Very often it is an "answer." An answer usually disputes the factual claims of the plaintiff. For example, if plaintiff's complaint states "Defendant struck the plaintiff in the face," the defendant might answer saying he denies that he struck the plaintiff. This reveals what facts are in dispute between the parties. Because the dispute is about the facts, the parties will gather evidence for presentation to a jury.

Discovery. Discovery is the portion of the case in which both parties gather information about the underlying claims. For example, the defendant might interview the plaintiff in order to obtain new information or reveal inaccuracies. Did the plaintiff seek medical treatment after the event? What did the plaintiff tell the doctor at the time? Discovery is not limited to gathering information from the parties. The parties may also seek information from others who know about the event. For example, if other people were in the room at the time that the defendant allegedly struck the plaintiff, the parties might interview those witnesses (at times under oath) and ask what they saw. The parties can investigate facts through written requests for documents as well as oral interviews. For example, either party could ask the doctor to produce written records of the plaintiff's visit.

* *The Motion for Summary Judgment.* The motion to dismiss assumes all the facts stated in the complaint are true and argues that, even so, the complaint fails to show a good legal claim. On the other hand, the summary judgment motion, which occurs after the parties have gathered new facts during the process of discovery, is based on a developed set of facts. If the moving party, almost always the defendant, shows that (1) there is no real dispute about important facts and (2) on the undisputed facts, the law compels judgment for the defendant, summary judgment will be granted.

Suppose the parties go through discovery and the plaintiff states, "he hit me," while the defendant states, "I did not." The defendant cannot get summary judgment because the fact asserted is important to the controversy and is directly disputed by the plaintiff. It will be for the jury to decide which party is speaking truthfully.

Pretrial briefs and motions in limine. After a case is set for trial, the parties may want the judge to decide in advance whether to include or exclude certain types of evidence and whether to apply particular legal rules. The parties may file motions or briefs asking the judge to shape the trial in a particular way. For example, in a motion in limine the defendant might ask the trial judge to keep out evidence that the defendant hit another person five years earlier on the ground that evidence of the earlier incident might prejudice the jury against the defendant.

Selection of a jury. When the case comes up for trial, prospective jurors are questioned by the judge and perhaps by the lawyers to determine whether they are biased about issues in the case or about one of the parties. Lawyers may "strike" or eliminate some prospects. Of those who remain, 12 (or sometimes six or eight) are then "put in the box" as jurors for the particular case.

Opening statements. At this point the judge will ask the plaintiff's lawyer to state the case for the plaintiff. This is not an argument but a preliminary view of the testimony the plaintiff will put on. The defendant's lawyer makes a similar opening statement.

Plaintiff's case. The plaintiff's attorney then calls the first witnesses. By asking questions, the lawyer elicits answers that establish what the witness knows about the facts relevant to the case. After each witness is questioned by the plaintiff's lawyer, the defendant's lawyer has an opportunity to cross-examine the witness, by asking questions that may put the matters in a different light, or may give them a different emphasis, or may show that the witness was mistaken, lying, or biased. The two examinations of the witness thus can give the jury a basis for judging how much the witness really knew and how credible the witness might be.

The Motion for Directed Verdict. Defendants usually move for a directed verdict (sometimes referred to in federal courts as a motion for judgment as a matter of law) at the end of the plaintiff's evidence and again when the defendant's evidence is completed. Such motions assert that the proof offered by the plaintiff is legally insufficient to warrant a jury's verdict for the plaintiff. More rarely, a plaintiff might move for directed verdict, but such a motion is seldom granted in view of the plaintiff's burden of proof.

The judge considers the evidence in the light most favorable to the plaintiff. That is, the judge takes into account all the reasonable inferences the jury would be allowed to draw from the testimony. Considering all the evidence in this light, the judge will grant the motion for a directed verdict if a jury of reasonable persons could not differ on the evidence, or if the facts taken in this favorable light do not establish any legal claims. The standard can be stated in other ways, but the basic idea is that the judge is not to take over the jury's role. So a directed verdict should be denied if there is room for reasonable jurors to disagree. This almost always involves some interaction of fact and law—do the facts, taken in a light favorable to the plaintiff, establish the elements required by law?

A motion for directed verdict is somewhat similar to both a motion to dismiss and to a summary judgment motion, but it is based on the *evidence produced in full at the trial*, not on general allegations of the complaint and not on the claim that the facts are undisputed.

Defendant's case. When all of the plaintiff's witnesses have been examined and cross-examined, the defendant puts on witnesses who give the defense side of the story. These witnesses, answering questions on the defense counsel's examination, often give a different factual picture from that given by the plaintiff's witnesses. After each witness is examined, the plaintiff's counsel cross-examines.

Objections to Evidence and Offers of Evidence. Not only before the trial, but also during the trial, the parties can object to evidence that is presented. Evidence that is not relevant to help prove any element involved in the case should be excluded by the judge, especially if the evidence is likely to mislead the jury or to be "prejudicial." A trial judge's admission of evidence over objection, or her refusal to admit evidence because of objection, raises legal issues. Rulings on admission of evidence are often rulings based on a specific principle of law.

Closing arguments. Plaintiff's lawyer, then defendant's lawyer, then plaintiff's lawyer in rebuttal, make closing arguments to the jury. These are arguments, not statements of fact. They are aimed at persuading the jury on the basis of the testimony that one side or the other should be believed.

Proposed Jury Instructions and Objections to Them. Instructions are the trial judge's statements of law to the jury. They tell the jury what it must consider and what facts must be found to exist before the plaintiff can recover, or before a defense applies. Instructions must accurately state the law. Lawyers must actively object to instructions they feel are incorrect statements of law, or propose instructions of their own. Once the judge listens to each party's suggested instructions and decides which are appropriate, the judge instructs or "charges" the jury. Thus, a judge might instruct the jury that if it finds that the defendant intentionally struck the plaintiff with intent to harm, it should bring in a verdict for the plaintiff. Notice that this leaves the fact-finding to the jury and the legal rules to the judge. Since an instruction is supposed to represent a correct statement of the law, and one on which the jury will act, an erroneous statement of the law would be ground for appeal.

Jury Verdict. After receiving instructions from the judge, the jury members talk with each other and consider whether the evidence presented in the trial meets or does not meet the legal rules articulated by the judge. The jury reaches a verdict on the plaintiff's claim, and when applicable decides on an appropriate remedy. For example, if the jury finds that the defendant struck the plaintiff in a way that provides the plaintiff with a recognizable claim against the defendant, the jury might also award the plaintiff a sum of money it deems fair compensation.

* *The Motion J.N.O.V.—A Post-trial Motion for Judgment as a Matter of Law.* The post-trial motion N.O.V. (like a motion for directed verdict, also referred to as a motion for judgment as a matter of law in federal courts) is a virtual renewal of the motion for directed verdict. (N.O.V. is for the Latin *non obstante veredicto,* meaning notwithstanding the verdict.) The motion asserts that the evidence is not legally sufficient to justify a jury verdict for the plaintiff. A judge who is unwilling to grant a directed verdict before the jury reaches its decision may grant a J.N.O.V. after the verdict is reported. There may be several reasons for this. For example, the judge may firmly believe the jury will find for the defendant even without a directed verdict. Or the judge may believe that the jury will come in with a verdict for the plaintiff, but that it will be small and reasonable. Afterwards, when the J. N.O.V. motion is presented, the judge may have some second thoughts.

The legal issue presented by the J.N.O.V. motion is the legal sufficiency of the evidence. It should be granted on proof that would warrant the grant of a directed verdict motion.

* *The Motion for New Trial.* The parties are entitled not only to a trial but to one that is carried out without any serious legal error. If an error was committed in the trial and the judge now recognizes this, there is the possibility that the error influenced the jury. If this seems to be a strong possibility, a new trial should be granted.

A second kind of new trial motion is unique. This asks the judge to grant a new trial, not because of error, but because the verdict is against the weight of the evidence or because the damages award was unconscionably high (or possibly unconscionably low). These motions really ask the judge to use something like discretion. The judge cannot substitute herself for the jury and make the ultimate decision in the case merely because she differs from the jury about what is right. Still, the judge does have considerable power to grant a *new trial*. If a new trial is granted, a new jury will hear the evidence. This may be done in many states because the first jury's verdict is against the weight of the evidence (though not legally wrong), or because the damages award was excessive. Judges do not often grant such motions.

Appeals. When a case has been resolved by a judge or jury, a party may ask a higher court to review the determination. Typically, state court systems have two levels of courts of appeal—intermediate appellate courts and a state supreme court. If an intermediate appellate court affirms the trial court's ruling, the non-prevailing party can accept the appellate court ruling or appeal further to the state supreme court. In rare cases, after a state supreme court has resolved the controversy, the tort issue can be appealed further to the United States Supreme Court. It is unusual for tort cases to be resolved by the Supreme Court because tort law is generally state law for which state courts are generally considered the final arbiter.

When a court of appeals reverses a lower court's decision, the case typically returns to the place it left off in the trial process. For example, if the trial court dismisses the plaintiff's complaint and the court of appeals reverses the dismissal, the plaintiff will not necessarily prevail. Instead, the case will be returned to the lower court and the defendant will have to answer the complaint, after which the discovery process will begin, and so forth.

Appendix: A Narrative Case with Procedural Rulings

A Complaint and Answer

Rosa Light makes an appointment with an attorney, Lawton. Careful questioning by Lawton develops the story summarized here: "Two months ago, when I was about eight months pregnant, I was at a dance with Bill Burton. He got angry with me because I danced with his brother, who is a terrible flirt. Anyway, Bill hit me in the stomach. Two or three weeks after that I had the baby. I had no permanent bad effects from the blow and the baby had no obvious injury, but I want to sue Bill. Can I?"

Lawton writes up a complaint for Rosa, asserting that Bill committed a battery against her. Lawton also writes up a complaint on behalf of the child, Adrian. This complaint alleges the same facts, and in addition says in part: "On information and belief it is alleged that the plaintiff Adrian Light felt the blow and suffered pain from it."

The complaint is then filed in the office of the clerk of the Superior Court and a copy is served on (or handed to) Bill. Bill's lawyer gets a different story. Bill says in substance: "I did try to pull my brother away from Rosa and when I did she came flying at me, trying to scratch me. I held her at arm's length—well, maybe I had to push a little—but didn't hit her in the stomach or anywhere else."

Bill's lawyer, Atwood, files a paper which combines two documents: First, he files an "answer," in which he says Bill denies the facts alleged; Bill did not hit Rosa at all. This is extended to say that to the extent Bill touched Rosa at all, it was in justifiable self defense. This answer raises factual issues to be decided by the trier of fact.

The Defendant Demurs or Moves to Dismiss

Atwood also includes in the papers a motion known as a *demurrer* at common law and as a *motion to dismiss* in federal rule types of procedural systems. The paper asks the court to dismiss the claim of the child, Adrian, on the ground that even if the facts claimed by Rosa and Adrian were true, no law supports any claim by the child.

Judge Yacashin Ponders and Decides

The *Light* file comes to Judge Rebecca Yacashin in the usual course of her work as a Superior Court Judge. Her first reaction is that the motion to dismiss the child's claim should be granted, since the facts alleged in the complaint do not appear to her to show a battery to the child, though undoubtedly the complaint states facts showing a battery to the mother. On second thought, she recognizes that the case is novel and she is loath to dismiss it without study. She therefore has the clerk send a formal note to each lawyer asking that each submit a brief or memorandum within ten days, stating arguments for or against the motion, together with any pertinent cases. The memorandum submitted by Atwood on Bill's behalf argues: "An unborn child is not a person to whom a tort can be committed." Judge Yacashin considers this argument and the cases cited by each party. She then concludes that the argument does not represent the law. Accordingly, she signs a formal order denying the motion to dismiss. The order is mailed to each lawyer.

Defense Planning: Discovery

"Does this mean we'll have to have a trial?" Bill asks. "Maybe," Atwood says, "but not necessarily. We could take depositions of witnesses and of the plaintiff, and maybe we could get some helpful stuff, maybe even an admission that the baby wasn't hurt. If we could get the plaintiff to admit that the baby wasn't hurt, we could file a motion for summary judgment, because I believe that if the baby wasn't hurt or at least offended, there wasn't any battery, even if the baby is a person who can sue for a tort before her birth."

Bill says, "But they won't admit that. They already said in their complaint that the baby felt pain." "You are right, but maybe we can do something even better. Maybe we can file an affidavit of a doctor saying that the baby felt nothing. Affidavits can't be used at trial as proof, but they can be used to show there is no real dispute about the facts. If the plaintiffs can't deny the affidavit by an affidavit of their own, the judge will have to say there is no dispute about the facts for a jury to decide, and that means she'll have to decide on the law."

The Defense Motion for Summary Judgment
and Judge Yacashin's Ruling

Atwood is able to get an affidavit, but it is not quite so good as he had hoped. The doctor gave an affidavit saying that the child might have felt a blow, but could not differentiate it from many other movements or feelings, or attribute it to a human being. Atwood files this affidavit along with his motion for summary judgment.

Judge Yacashin begins working through the summary judgment motion in *Light v. Burton*. "I've already ruled that the baby, though not born at the time, is a person who could be victimized by a tort," she reflects. "But it is true that there is no battery if the plaintiff is not hurt or offended." She reads the affidavit from the defendant's doctor. "So the baby could not tell the blow was from a human source or distinguish it from other discomforts." The plaintiff, however, has filed a counter-affidavit from another doctor saying that, while it was true that before birth the baby could not distinguish one blow from another, it would feel pain as an unpleasant sensation if the blow was hard enough. Judge Yacashin would be glad to get rid of the case, but she concludes that the defendant's affidavit does not really establish a fact helpful to the defendant. She writes a brief statement of her reasons for denying the summary judgment motion as follows:

> "The defendant's affidavit establishes that the baby could not distinguish this harm from other harms, but it does not establish that there is no harm. The plaintiff's complaint alleges, and her affidavit supports, the idea that the baby before birth could and did feel unpleasant sensations as the result of the blow, if there was a blow. The facts shown by the defendant and left undisputed by the plaintiff do not warrant judgment in his favor, since I hold that the child's feelings would constitute 'harm' under the law of battery. The case will have to go to trial, therefore, on the factual issues raised by the complaint and answer."

Pre-trial, Trial, and Admission of Evidence

Months later, after a pre-trial conference in which the judge attempts to get issues clarified and to encourage settlement, the case is scheduled for the actual trial and a jury is impaneled.

Rosa Light's attorney, Lawton, begins putting on his case. After Rosa has testified to the main events stated in her complaint, Lawton asks:

Q.   What happened after Bill Burton hit you?

A.   He pulled his brother by the arm outside.

Q.   What did you do?

A.   I went to the window and watched while Bill beat his brother up. Then I got sick.

At this point Atwood stands up and says, "We object, Your Honor. This testimony should be stricken and the jury cautioned." Judge Yacashin says, "Overruled. Go on Mr. Lawton."

Motions for Directed Verdict

The trial proceeds in normal fashion. The plaintiff's witnesses are examined and cross-examined. When the plaintiff's case is completed, the defendant's attorney approaches the bench. "We move for a directed verdict as to the infant plaintiff, Your Honor," Atwood says in a voice the jury could not hear. "The plaintiff has failed to prove an essential element of her case: harm or offense. There is no offense without consciousness. As to harm, the Restatement Second of Torts requires 'physical impairment of the condition of another's body, or physical pain or illness.' [§ 15]. There is no testimony even remotely supporting the idea that there was physical pain or illness. We do not think the Supreme Court of this state would accept a passing discomfort as 'harm,' and this is the most the testimony would support." Lawton answers: "Doctor Veillicht testified, Your Honor, that the child in the womb could feel a blow like that attributed to the defendant and would feel it as a negative thing, pain in the sense that the baby would try to avoid it." Judge Yacashin: "I'm going to deny the motion and instruct the jury as to the definition of harm."

After Judge Yacashin denies the motion for directed verdict, the defendant proceeds to introduce his evidence, and again witnesses are examined and cross-examined. When the defendant completes his proof, Atwood again moves for directed verdict and it is again denied.

Closing Arguments and Instructions to the Jury

The lawyers then give their closing arguments, summarizing the evidence favorable to each side and discounting evidence against them, each trying to persuade the jury that his client was telling the truth. In addition, Lawton talks considerably about the importance of damages. Atwood urges the jury to keep things in perspective.

After the closing arguments, there is a recess for lunch. Judge Yacashin asks the lawyers to meet with her in chambers before resuming the afternoon session. In chambers, she reminds them that they had previously submitted proposed instructions to the jury, had also previously seen the instructions she expected to give, and had made their "record" of objections and requests about those instructions.

"Now the evidence always takes a few unexpected turns," she adds, "and I think I had better add an instruction. I've been worried about the question of harm to the fetus. There is no evidence of any pathological harm. As you know, Mr. Atwood, I refused to grant your motion for directed verdict, which you made on the ground that there was no harm as a matter of law. The only definition of harm we've seen here is the Restatement's definition and our Supreme Court often follows the Restatement. So I think there may be enough evidence to get to the jury on this, but I do think we need a very careful statement to the jury. Does either of you have a proposed instruction?"

"I do not, Your Honor; whatever you think will suit us," Lawton says.

"I do have one," Atwood says, and he passes copies. His proposed instruction would tell the jury that before the infant plaintiff could recover, it would be necessary to find that harm was done and that harm would require either an identifiable physical symptom or sign, or some identifiable medical condition, and that it could not be a transitory feeling.

"We would object to that, of course," Lawton comments.

"Yes, I think that may be too strong," the judge says, "but maybe something along those lines." She begins writing on the instruction proposed by Atwood and comes up with this:

"You are instructed as to the infant plaintiff there can be a recovery only if there is a battery as the Court has already defined that term to you. As to the infant plaintiff, this will require, in addition to an intentional unpermitted blow by the defendant, that the infant plaintiff has suffered harm. Harm is defined to include any physical impairment of the body, physical pain, or illness. It is not necessary that there be any permanent ill-effects, but on the other hand a trivial and transitory feeling on the part of the fetus would not constitute harm for this purpose."

Lawton objects to the last clause, and his objection is written down as part of the record. Atwood objects to the instruction so far as it fails to require some identifiable medical condition or the pain of a conscious, living being. This objection is also noted. The judge and lawyers then return to the courtroom for the remainder of the trial.

The Jury's Verdict

Judge Yacashin duly instructs the jury, which then adjourns to the privacy of the jury room. For the lawyers it is a waiting time. When the bailiff announces that the jury is coming in, Judge Yacashin takes the bench. The lawyers go to their tables and the jury files in.

"Have you reached a verdict?" Judge Yacashin asks.

"We have, Your Honor," the foreman says.

"Please hand it to the bailiff." The bailiff hands the paper to the judge. The form has been provided by the judge and filled in or crossed out by the jury. "We the jury," Judge Yacashin reads out loud, "find for the plaintiff Rosa Light in the sum of $10,000 and for the plaintiff Adrian Light in the sum of $5,000." "Is this your verdict?"

"It is, Your Honor."

Judge Yacashin thanks the jurors for their services, explains their obligation to return for further jury duty at a later date, discharges them, and adjourns the court.

J.N.O.V. and New Trial Motions and the Final Judgment

One motion, or pair of motions, remains to be asserted by the defendant's lawyer, Atwood. He files a written motion two days later, in two parts. The first part moves for "Judgment N.O.V."—a judgment notwithstanding the verdict. The second part moves in the alternative for a new trial for errors committed in the trial, and especially the error in the instruction on the battery to the child.

Judge Yacashin denies the motions and enters a judgment on the verdict. The judgment is usually the last formal order. It is signed by the judge and reflects the jury's verdict. Here it provides that the plaintiff Rosa should have and recover from the defendant $10,000 and that the plaintiff Adrian should have and recover from the defendant $5,000.

Getting to the Appeal

These are the kinds of events that have occurred before the appeal. At this point the appeal process takes over. Here Atwood files notice of appeal, and in the course of the next few months provides the Appellate Court with excerpts from the trial record and files a brief arguing that the trial judge committed error in a number of respects. You can test yourself by determining what specific rulings or actions by the judge might constitute grounds for appeal. You can check the footnote for an answer.[1]

The Appellate Court Decides

Having seen Atwood's brief for the appellant, Lawton files a brief for the appellee. The Appellate Court schedules oral arguments for some months later and after those are heard, the judges of the appellate court and their law clerks research the law further. They hold conferences about the case and draft an opinion. The various judges comment on the proposed opinion and finally they agree on a final draft. If a judge still disagrees he or she may write a dissent. The opinion is then formally announced and a copy is sent to the lawyers. This "opinion," or formal explanation of the court's decision, is then published in "advance sheets" and by on-line services (such as Westlaw), and finally in an official state volume as well as a "regional reporter." (Which regional reporter a case is reported in depends on which state court decided the case.) Each published opinion is given a citation so it can be found easily by lawyers and others researching the law in the library or on-line. For example, the appeals court's decision in *Light v. Burton* (which is a fictional case, of course) might be reported in volume 665 of the Northwest Reporter, Second Series, beginning on page 87. If the deciding court was the Court of Appeals of Michigan, and if the opinion was filed in 2004, the citation would look like this: 665 N.W.2d 87 (Mich. Ct. App. 2004). A court's published opinion is the "case" with which law study begins, in an effort to isolate principles and rules, and to learn how arguments can be constructed to persuade judges.

REFERENCE: Kenney F. Hegland, Introduction to the Study and Practice of Law (Nutshell Series 4th Ed. 2003).

---

1. Each of the procedural devices listed above is the basis for a potential appeal. The judge, Atwood argues, should have granted the motion to dismiss, the summary judgment, and the directed verdict motion; she should have instructed the jury as Atwood requested, and should not have admitted the evidence to which he objected. Each of these arguments is supported by propositions of law, for which Atwood argues in his appellate brief.

PART 2

FAULT-BASED LIABILITY FOR PHYSICAL HARMS TO PERSONS AND PROPERTY

■ ■ ■

TOPIC A

DIRECT INTENTIONAL WRONGS

■ ■ ■

CHAPTER 3

ESTABLISHING A CLAIM FOR INTENTIONAL TORT TO PERSON OR PROPERTY

■ ■ ■

Every type of tort claim has its own *elements*, or particular things that a plaintiff must prove in order to succeed on that claim. A plaintiff must first allege, in good faith, facts comprising these required elements—in other words, a "prima facie case," or a case good "on the face of it," or at first look. If the plaintiff does not, the judge will dismiss the complaint. But making allegations is not enough to win. The plaintiff must then go on to *prove* the prima facie case of some particular tort. The plaintiff bears the burden of proof on each element, meaning if the plaintiff fails to prove a prima facie case, the defendant will win even without putting on a defense. In this chapter we will explore the required elements of a number of intentional tort claims. In the next chapter we will see a number of defenses that may allow the defendant to escape liability even where a prima facie case has been proved.

§ 1. BATTERY

A. REQUIRING FAULT

VAN CAMP v. McAFOOS
156 N.W.2d 878 (Iowa 1968)

BECKER, JUSTICE.

This case comes to us on appeal from the trial court's action in sustaining defendant's motion to dismiss. We are therefore limited to what can be gleaned from the pleadings.

In Division I of her petition plaintiff sues Mark McAfoos alleging in pertinent part, "That at said time and place defendant Mark McAfoos was operating a tricycle on said public sidewalk, and drove the tricycle into the rear of the plaintiff without warning, striking the right leg of the plaintiff thereby causing an injury to the Achilles" tendon of that leg.

"That as a direct and proximate cause of the defendant's action, plaintiff's tendon was injured and subsequently required surgery. . . ." [In another part of the petition the plaintiff alleged that Mark was three years, one month old.]

The trial court sustained the motion to dismiss as to Division I stating in part, "It is not alleged that the defendant was negligent. It is not alleged that the action of the defendant was willful or wrongful in any manner. Under these circumstances it is difficult to see how the Division as now set out states any basis upon which the plaintiff could recover."

The question presented is, did plaintiff plead a cause of action. . . .

I. Plaintiff's sole assignment of error as to Division I is "The trial court erred in failing to recognize categories of tort liability other than negligence, in evaluating the pleading in plaintiff's first division."

. . . She stands firmly on the proposition that invasion of her person is in itself a wrong and she need plead no more. We do not agree. . . . In essence plaintiff urges a person has a right not to be injuriously touched or struck as she lawfully uses a public sidewalk. She was injuriously struck by Mark. Therefore Mark is liable. She argues that no more need be pleaded. It follows that no more need be proved in order to justify submission of the case. Plaintiff's posture satisfies us she would have us impose liability without fault. We are not prepared to extend this concept to childish acts (by children).

II. Plaintiff's reply brief states "If the absence of a single word or conclusory label remains the *sine qua non* of pleading a valid cause of action, we have restored today's jurisprudence to the specious procedural formalism of the 18th Century common courts."

The trial court's ruling was not a return to legal formalism. Plaintiff makes it abundantly clear she insists on a right to recovery by proof of an accident caused by another, independent of fault or wrong doing. Where an essential element of the cause of action is missing, the question is not what may be shown under the pleading but whether a cause of action has been pled.

. . . Unless and until we are ready to recognize liability without fault for otherwise innocent childish actions, fault must be discernible in the pleading and in proof. . . . Intentionally wrongful or negligently wrongful use of the tricycle is neither pled nor can it be made out from the bare allegation defendant "operated a tricycle on said public sidewalk and drove the tricycle into the rear of the plaintiff without warning." . . .

III. Plaintiff cites many cases from other jurisdictions holding a child of tender years may be liable *in tort*; *Garratt v. Dailey*, 46 Wash. 2d 197, 279 P.2d 1091. All of the foregoing cases involve the fault concept. Many turn on the question of whether the child could be guilty of the fault charged but each case has fault as one of the essential elements of liability. We need not disagree with those authorities. Whatever her motive, plaintiff has chosen to plead in such a way as to avoid bringing herself within the scope of those cases. . . .

Affirmed.

NOTES

1. **Overview.** Casebook editors may select cases and materials with more than one purpose in mind. At any given point, several themes may be in progress. *McAfoos* displays both a substantive and a procedural theme. The substantive or tort law theme has to do with the basis or grounds of liability. The procedural theme has to do with how legal issues are raised in court. Most cases in this book will raise one or more points that bear analysis and further thought. Notes like these should help you develop that analysis or furnish related information.

Substantive Issues

2. **Historical strict liability and the rules today.** From the early days of tort law, about the 13th century until perhaps as late as the 18th century, anyone who acted affirmatively and directly (like Mark McAfoos) might be held liable for harm done, even though he was not at fault. In these cases the plaintiff used a form for suing called *Trespass* and he would win unless the defendant had some special defense, called justification or excuse. An example of a defense would be self-defense. If the harm caused was indirect, on the other hand, the defendant was not responsible unless he was at fault in some way. If Mark McAfoos had left his tricycle on the walk and the plaintiff had bumped into it in the dark, this would have been an indirect harm and even in the early English law Mark would not have been liable without fault. Cases of indirect harm required the plaintiff in that period to select a Form of Action for suing called *Trespass on the Case*, or just *Case*. Does *McAfoos* implicitly or expressly reject the older rule that a defendant can be liable for direct harms even in the absence of fault?

3. **What is fault?** What would it take to show fault in *McAfoos*? Suppose McAfoos said that he ran into Ms. Van Camp on purpose because he wanted to hear her get angry. If McAfoos caused the accident, how could it have happened without his fault? In *McAfoos,* the Iowa Supreme Court upheld the dismissal of plaintiff's claim because no fault at all had been pleaded—neither "intentionally wrongful" nor "negligently wrongful" use of the tricycle. Both intentional misconduct and negligent misconduct can be forms of fault. However, not just any form of fault would have been sufficient to maintain a cause of action for battery—an intentional tort. In later cases we will learn more about the particular type of fault that must be pleaded to state a claim for battery.

4. **Tort law and the states.** With few exceptions, tort law is made by the courts and legislatures of the various states, not by the federal government. When you read McAfoos how can you tell which state court wrote the opinion? If *McAfoos* tells us that fault is required to maintain a battery claim in Iowa, do we know whether fault is required in Illinois?

5. **Evaluation of the legal rule.** How does the rule or principle in *McAfoos* stack up against the aims of tort law? Consider whether it attempts to do justice and whether it reflects appropriate standards of deterring wrongdoing. Evaluation is important to lawyers. It is one process by which lawyers become sure they have grasped the rule and its implications. It is also a process by which lawyers begin to formulate legal arguments.

6. **Grasping a principle.** *McAfoos* involved a child on a tricycle. But the principle or reason behind the case might apply to many other situations. One function of a lawyer is to recognize the possibility of applying the principle of a case to a new set of facts. Try it:

—H becomes angry with his wife, W, and repeatedly hits her with his fist, breaking her jaw and bruising her face. Would the principle or idea in *McAfoos* either establish or exclude liability?

—The defendant's yard has a tree near the sidewalk. The tree appears to be sound and healthy, but in fact it is rotten and it blows over in a wind. It strikes a passerby. Can you predict from *McAfoos* whether a court would impose liability?

Procedural Issues

7. **Facts and rules.** Cases today are begun by a complaint or petition, a document that states the main facts on which the plaintiff relies. If the facts are in dispute, the jury decides what the facts were. In *McAfoos*, the parties seemed to disagree over the legal rules rather than the facts. Did you notice the procedural device used to resolve this difference?

B. ELEMENTS OF BATTERY

There are many types of tort claims. Conceptually, one way to organize these claims is to group them along two dimensions—the interests they protect, and the levels of culpability they require. In terms of interests, tort actions can protect against 1) physical injury to person or property; 2) dignitary and emotional harm; and 3) economic harm. With respect to culpability, tort rules may impose liability for serious wrongdoing (intent or malice), negligence (lack of reasonable care), and even when the defendant is guilty of no fault (strict liability). *See* Thomas C. Grey, *Accidental Torts*, 54 VAND. L. REV. 1225 (2001). Our exploration of tort claims begins with causes of action that protect against intentional physical injuries.

> "[T]he least touching of another in anger is a battery.... If any of them use violence against the other, to force his way in a rude inordinate manner, it is a battery...." *Cole v. Turner*, 6 Mod. Rep. 149, 90 Eng. Rep. 958 (Nisi Prius 1704).

SNYDER v. TURK
627 N.E.2d 1053 (Ohio Ct. App. 1993)

RICHARD K. WILSON, JUDGE....

[Defendant was a surgeon performing a gall-bladder operation. The procedure did not go well. Evidence would permit these findings: The defendant became frustrated with the operation itself and with the plaintiff, a scrub nurse in the operating room. Defendant's perception was that the plaintiff was making mistakes and complicating an already difficult procedure. The defendant finally became so exasperated when the plaintiff handed him an instrument he considered inappropriate that he grabbed her shoulder and pulled her face down toward the surgical opening, saying, "Can't you see where I'm working? I'm working in a hole. I need long instruments."]

The parties agree that a "battery" is defined as an intentional, unconsented-to contact with another. The appellee contends that there is no liability for the commission of a battery absent proof of an intent to inflict personal injury. Dr. Turk further contends that the directed verdict was properly granted on the battery liability issue because of the absence of evidence that he intended to inflict personal injury. . . .

A person is subject to liability for battery when he acts intending to cause a harmful or offensive contact, and when a harmful contact results. Contact which is offensive to a reasonable sense of personal dignity is offensive contact. . . .

A motion for a directed verdict assumes the truth of the evidence supporting the facts essential to the claim after giving the nonmovant the benefit of all reasonable inferences from the evidence and refers the application of a reasonable-minds test to such evidence. It is in the nature of a demurrer to the evidence.

Applying the above test we believe that reasonable minds could conclude that Dr. Turk intended to commit an offensive contact. The first assignment of error is sustained.

COHEN v. SMITH

648 N.E.2d 329 (Ill. App. Ct. 1995)

JUSTICE CHAPMAN delivered the opinion of the court:

Patricia Cohen was admitted to St. Joseph Memorial Hospital ("Hospital") to deliver her baby. After an examination, Cohen was informed that it would be necessary for her to have a cesarean section. Cohen and her husband allegedly informed her physician, who in turn advised the Hospital staff, that the couple's religious beliefs prohibited Cohen from being seen unclothed by a male. Cohen's doctor assured her husband that their religious convictions would be respected.

During Cohen's cesarean section, Roger Smith, a male nurse on staff at the Hospital, allegedly observed and touched Cohen's naked body. Cohen and her husband filed suit against Nurse Smith and the Hospital. The trial court allowed defendants' motions to dismiss. We reverse.

In reviewing a motion to dismiss for failure to state a cause of action, the court must view all well-pleaded facts in the light most favorable to the plaintiff. A trial court may dismiss a cause of action for failing to state a cause of action, based solely on the pleadings, only if it is clearly apparent that no set of alleged facts can be proven which will entitle a plaintiff to recovery....

The Restatement (Second) of Torts provides that an actor commits a battery if: "(a) he acts intending to cause a harmful or offensive contact with the person of the other or a third person, or an imminent apprehension of such a contact, and (b) a harmful [or offensive]¹ contact with the person of the other directly or indirectly results." (Restatement (Second) of Torts, § 13 (1965).) Liability for battery emphasizes the plaintiff's lack of consent to the touching. "Offensive contact" is said to occur when the contact "offends a reasonable sense of personal dignity."

Historically, battery was first and foremost a systematic substitution for private retribution. (W. Prosser & Keeton, Torts § 9, at 41 (5th ed. 1984) (Prosser).) Protecting personal integrity has always been viewed as an important basis for battery. "Consequently, the defendant is liable not only for contacts which do actual physical harm, but also for those relatively trivial ones which are merely offensive and insulting." This application of battery to remedy offensive and insulting conduct is deeply ingrained in our legal history. As early as 1784, a Pennsylvania defendant was prosecuted for striking the cane of a French ambassador. The court furthered the distinction between harmful offensive batteries and non-harmful offensive batteries: "As to the assault, this is, perhaps, one of that kind, in which the insult is more to be considered than the actual damage; for, though no great bodily pain is suffered by a blow on the palm of the hand, or the skirt of the coat, yet these are clearly within the definition of assault and battery, and among gentlemen too often induce duelling and terminate in murder." (Respublica v. De Longchamps (Pa.1784), 1 Dall. 111, 1 L.Ed. 59, in Gregory, Kalven, & Epstein, Cases & Materials on Torts 904–905 (1977).)....

Although most people in modern society have come to accept the necessity of being seen unclothed and being touched by members of the opposite sex during medical treatment, the plaintiffs had not accepted these procedures and, according to their complaint, had informed defendants of their convictions. This case is similar to cases involving Jehovah's Witnesses who were unwilling to accept blood transfusions because of religious convictions. Although most people do not share the Jehovah's Witnesses' beliefs about blood transfusions, our society, and our courts, accept their right to have that belief. Similarly, the courts have consistently recognized individuals' rights to refuse medical treatment even if such a refusal would result in an increased likelihood of the individual's death.

A person's right to refuse or accept medical care is not one to be interfered with lightly. As Justice Cardozo stated, "Every human being of adult years and sound mind has a right to determine what shall be done

---

1. The editors of this casebook inserted the bracketed phrase. It appears in Restatement § 18, not § 13, which the court is quoting.—Eds.

with his own body; and a surgeon who performs an operation without his patient's consent commits an assault, for which he is liable in damages."

Accepting as true the plaintiffs' allegations that they informed defendants of their religious beliefs and that defendants persisted in treating Patricia Cohen as they would have treated a patient without those beliefs, we conclude that the trial court erred in dismissing both the battery and the intentional infliction of emotional distress counts.

MULLINS v. PARKVIEW HOSPITAL, INC.

865 N.E.2d 608 (Ind. 2007)

SULLIVAN, JUSTICE. . . .

[Before undergoing a hysterectomy at a teaching hospital, the plaintiff Ruth Mullins told her gynecologist that she wanted privacy during the surgery. Toward that end, she crossed out the portion of the consent form that consented to "the presence of healthcare learners" during the procedure. On the day of the surgery Mullins received assurance from the attending anesthesiologist that she would personally handle the anesthesia. As soon as Mullins was unconscious, the anesthesiologist permitted an Emergency Medical Technician student, LaRea VanHoey to practice intubation on the plaintiff. It was VanHoey's first day attempting intubation on live patients and she lacerated the plaintiff's esophagus. Mullins required additional surgery and recuperation time as a result of the laceration. She filed suit for battery among other claims. The lower court granted summary judgment for all defendants on all counts, but the Court of Appeals held that Mullins had an actionable battery claim against VanHoey, the gynecologist, the anesthesiologist and both doctors' practices. VanHoey appealed.]

When [the anesthesiologist] granted VanHoey permission to attempt intubation, VanHoey had no reason to suspect that Ruth [Mullins] had insisted on modifying the standard consent form. VanHoey could properly rely on her previous experience attempting to intubate a patient that day, her preceptor's direction, and [the doctor's] authority as the anesthesiologist for the surgery. . . . [G]iven VanHoey's status, she was under no obligation to obtain consent herself or inquire into the consent under which [the anesthesiologist] was acting. . . .

VanHoey may indeed have "touched Mrs. Mullins in a harmful and offensive manner without permission," as the Mullinses claim. However, even if true, this characterization of events does not satisfy all the elements required to show a battery; at most, the Mullinses have asserted that VanHoey "act[ed]" and that "harmful contact with [Mullins] directly resulted." *See* Restatement (Second) of Torts § 13. The Mullinses must also show that VanHoey "act[ed] *intending* to cause a harmful or offensive contact with [Mullins]." . . .

When we accept the facts alleged by the Mullinses and construe the evidence in their favor as the non-moving party, there is still no indication that VanHoey intended to harm Ruth. . . .

Because there is no genuine issue of material fact as to VanHoey's intent to cause a harmful contact with Ruth, VanHoey was entitled to summary judgment on the Mullinses' battery claim.''

NOTES

1. **Elements of battery.** What are the elements of a cause of action for battery? What sources would you look to in order to find these elements?

2. **The role of physical harm.** Under the Restatement rule quoted in *Cohen,* must the plaintiff prove an actual harm such as pain or a bruise? See if you can support a yes or no answer.

3. **Testing the rules.** In the light of the rules stated or applied in the prior cases, how should the following cases be resolved?

   a. Karen Whitley was standing in front of her locker at school when LeGault shoved her. The shove caused no physical harm. LeGault argued that she was not liable because (1) no harm was done by her shove and (2) no intent to harm was proven. *Whitley v. Andersen,* 37 Colo.App. 486, 551 P.2d 1083 (1976), *aff'd,* 570 P.2d 525 (Colo. 1977).

   b. The plaintiff's employer was engaged in teasing and horseplay with an automobile condenser that had been electrically charged, giving employees a mild shock. He shocked the plaintiff, who was trying to avoid it. The plaintiff, quite unexpectedly, developed a serious nerve problem that required surgery. *Caudle v. Betts,* 512 So.2d 389 (La. 1987).

4. **Motive versus intent.** Suppose the defendant has a good motive—administering medical treatment over the plaintiff's objection. Can this still be a battery? *See, e.g., Roberson v. Provident House,* 576 So.2d 992 (La. 1991). Is this what happened in *Mullins?*

5. **Procedure: motion to dismiss.** The plaintiff in *Cohen* prevailed in overturning the trial court's dismissal. Does that mean that the plaintiff won the case? What if, on remand, the plaintiff cannot produce evidence that Nurse Smith knew of Patricia Cohen's wishes? As discussed in chapter 2, it is important to pay attention to the procedure that triggers the appeal.

6. **Procedure: motion for summary judgment.** Remember that summary judgment is granted where there is no genuine issue of material fact and the moving party is entitled to judgment as a matter of law. What would it have taken take for the *Mullins* court to deny Van Hoey's summary judgment motion? Suppose there was evidence that the anesthesiologist expressly told Van Hoey, ''Mrs. Mullins doesn't want students involved in her treatment, but she'll never know. Go ahead and intubate her.'' Would analysis of a summary judgment motion in that situation have been different?

7. **Bodily contact.** Neither harm nor offense would be sufficient for a claim in the absence of bodily contact. Does this require that the defendant's

body directly touch the plaintiff's body? Imagine a defendant who fires a bullet into the plaintiff's body and seeks to escape liability for battery on the ground that there was no touching. Reasoning from the purposes of battery law, would courts treat the bullet as a touching? Now consider a defendant who shakes the limb of a tree on which the plaintiff is sitting, but does not touch the plaintiff. A classic case on this point is *Fisher v. Carrousel Motor Hotel, Inc.*, 424 S.W.2d 627 (Tex. 1967). The plaintiff, Fisher, was a mathematician attending a meeting on telemetry equipment. He and the others at the meeting adjourned for lunch in the defendant's hotel. As the plaintiff was about to be served, he was approached by the manager, who "snatched the plate from Fisher's hand and shouted that he, a Negro, could not be served in the club." The court said: "[T]he intentional grabbing of plaintiff's plate constituted a battery. The intentional snatching of an object from one's hand is as clearly an offensive invasion of his person as would be an actual contact with the body." Would summary judgment have been appropriate on a claim of battery against the anesthesiologist in *Mullins* on the ground that the anesthesiologist was not the one to touch the patient during the intubation?

8. **What counts as a touching?** Would it be a touching if a talk-show host blew cigar smoke in the face of an anti-smoking advocate in order to humiliate him? *See Leichtman v. WLW Jacor Communications Inc.*, 634 N.E.2d 697 (Ohio 1994) (yes—tobacco smoke, as particulate matter, has the physical properties capable of making contact). What about being touched by light waves or sound waves? Your noisy neighbor bombards you with loud music every night. Could this be a battery? Or what if a defendant intentionally exposes the plaintiff to high levels of ozone, resulting in injury—battery? *See Swope v. Columbian Chems. Co.*, 281 F.3d 185 (5th Cir. 2002).

9. **Nominal damages.** Why award damages to a plaintiff who suffered trivial harm or offense, as in the *Leichtman* case in the previous paragraph? That court wrote, "No matter how trivial the incident, a battery is actionable, even if damages are only one dollar. The rationale is explained by Roscoe Pound in his essay 'Liability': '[I]n civilized society men must be able to assume that others will do them no intentional injury—that others will commit no intentioned aggressions upon them.' Pound, An Introduction to the Philosophy of Law (1922) 169."

———————

A.R.B. v. ELKIN, 98 S.W.3d 99 (Mo. Ct. App. 2003). A male and a female, no longer living with their father, brought an action for battery against him. They claimed and he admitted numerous acts of sexual abuse, some involving physical touchings of the plaintiffs. The trial judge rejected a claim for damages for the children's counseling because the invoices had not been produced on discovery. He rejected an award of damages for emotional harm, fear, and the like on the ground that medical evidence was required to show such injury and none had been admitted. He then awarded the male $100 "nominal" damages because he had been physically harmed, but awarded nothing to the female plaintiff. *Held*, reversed and remanded for further proceedings. The trial judge erred in requiring proof of medically diagnosable emotional injury. Upon proof of battery or assault, the plaintiff is entitled to recover nominal damages plus "compensatory damages for bodily pain, humiliation, mental anguish and other injuries that occur as a necessary and natural consequence of the tortious conduct. There is no fixed measure or standard available to the trier of fact in determining the measure of damages for pain and suffering. The measure of damages is simply that which is fair and reasonable." Further, punitive damages should also have been considered.

NOTES

1. **Damages for offensive conduct.** When a battery is proved and the contact is offensive but not physically harmful, courts have traditionally permitted juries to award substantial damages even though the plaintiff has no pecuniary loss. The award is not limited to nominal damages, and the award might reach hundreds and even thousands of dollars. *See* DAN DOBBS, THE LAW OF REMEDIES § 7.3 (2) (1993). Is this a good idea? In addition to compensatory damages, courts may allow punitive damages against an intentional tortfeasor who is guilty of "malice" or wanton misconduct.

2. **Emotional distress damages.** Inflicting emotional distress is not very often a tort in itself. However, when emotional distress results from a trespassory tort like battery, assault, or false imprisonment, damages for the distress are readily recoverable. Sometimes jurists say that emotional distress damages resulting from such torts are "parasitic" to the tort, meaning that emotional distress resulting in such cases is not stand-alone distress, but is attached to or flows from some recognized tort. *See Lyons v. Zale Jewelry Co.,* 150 So.2d 154 (Miss. 1963).

C. DEFINING INTENT

GARRATT v. DAILEY

279 P.2d 1091 (Wash. 1955)

HILL, JUSTICE. . . .

Brian Dailey (age five years, nine months) was visiting with Naomi Garratt, an adult and a sister of the plaintiff, Ruth Garratt, likewise an adult, in the back yard of the plaintiff's home, on July 16, 1951. It is plaintiff's contention that she came out into the back yard to talk with Naomi and that, as she started to sit down in a wood and canvas lawn chair, Brian deliberately pulled it out from under her. The only one of the three persons present so testifying was Naomi Garratt. (Ruth Garratt, the plaintiff, did not testify as to how or why she fell.)

The trial court, unwilling to accept this testimony, adopted instead Brian Dailey's version of what happened, and made the following findings:

"III. . . . that while Naomi Garratt and Brian Dailey were in the back yard the plaintiff, Ruth Garratt, came out of her house into the back yard. Some time subsequent thereto defendant, Brian Dailey, picked up a lightly built wood and canvas lawn chair which was then and there located in the back yard of the above described premises, moved it sideways a few feet and seated himself therein, at which time he discovered the plaintiff, Ruth Garratt, about to sit down at the place where the lawn chair had formerly been, at which time he hurriedly got up from the chair and attempted to move it toward Ruth Garratt to aid her in sitting down in the chair; that due to the defendant's small size and lack of dexterity he was unable to get the lawn chair under the plaintiff in time to prevent her from falling to the ground. That plaintiff fell to the ground and sustained a fracture of her hip, and other injuries and damages as hereinafter set forth.

"IV.   That the preponderance of the evidence in this case establishes that when the defendant, Brian Dailey, moved the chair in question *he did not have any wilful or unlawful purpose* in doing so; that *he did not have any intent to injure the plaintiff, or any intent to bring about any unauthorized or offensive contact with her person* or any object appurtenant thereto; that the circumstances which immediately preceded the fall of the plaintiff established that the defendant, *Brian Dailey, did not have purpose, intent or design to perform a prank or to effect an assault and battery upon the person of the plaintiff.*" (Italics ours, for a purpose hereinafter indicated.)

It is conceded that Ruth Garratt's fall resulted in a fractured hip and other painful and serious injuries. To obviate the necessity of a retrial in the event this court determines that she was entitled to a judgment against Brian Dailey, the amount of her damage was found to be $11,000. Plaintiff appeals from a judgment dismissing the action and asks for the entry of a judgment in that amount or a new trial.

The authorities generally, but with certain notable exceptions, state that when a minor has committed a tort with force he is liable to be proceeded against as any other person would be.

In our analysis of the applicable law, we start with the basic premise that Brian, whether five or fifty-five, must have committed some wrongful act before he could be liable for appellant's injuries....

It is urged that Brian's action in moving the chair constituted a battery. A definition (not all-inclusive but sufficient for our purpose) of a battery is the intentional infliction of a harmful bodily contact upon another. The rule that determines liability for battery is given in 1 RESTATEMENT TORTS, 29, § 13, as:

"An act which, directly or indirectly, is the legal cause of a harmful contact with another's person makes the actor liable to the other, if

"(a) the act is done with the intention of bringing about a harmful or offensive contact...."

... In the comment on clause (a), the Restatement says:

"Character of actor's intentions. In order that an act may be done with the intention of bringing about a harmful or offensive contact ..., the act must be done for the purpose of causing the contact ... or with knowledge on the part of the actor that such contact ... is substantially certain to be produced." See, also, Prosser on Torts 41, § 8.

We have here the conceded volitional act of Brian, i.e., the moving of a chair. Had the plaintiff proved to the satisfaction of the trial court that Brian moved the chair while she was in the act of sitting down, Brian's action would patently have been for the purpose or with the intent of causing the plaintiff's bodily contact with the ground, and she would be entitled to a judgment against him for the resulting damages.

The plaintiff based her case on that theory, and the trial court held that she failed in her proof and accepted Brian's version of the facts rather than that given by the eyewitness who testified for the plaintiff. After the trial court determined that the plaintiff had not established her theory of a battery (i.e., that Brian had pulled the chair out from under the plaintiff while she was in the act of sitting down), it then became concerned with whether a battery was established under the facts as it found them to be.

In this connection, we quote another portion of the comment on the "Character of actor's intention," relating to a clause (a) of the rule of the Restatement heretofore set forth:

> "It is not enough that the act itself is intentionally done and this, even though the actor realizes or should realize that it contains a very grave risk of bringing about the contact or apprehension. Such realization may make the actor's conduct negligent or even reckless but unless he realizes that to a substantial certainty, the contact or apprehension will result, the actor has not that intention which is necessary to make him liable under the rule stated in this section."

A battery would be established if, in addition to plaintiff's fall, it was proved that, when Brian moved the chair, he knew with substantial certainty that the plaintiff would attempt to sit down where the chair had been. If Brian had any of the intents which the trial court found, in the italicized portions of the findings of fact quoted above, that he did not have, he would of course have had the knowledge to which we have referred. The mere absence of any intent to injure the plaintiff or to play a prank on her or to embarrass her, or to commit an assault and battery on her would not absolve him from liability if in fact he had such knowledge.

Without such knowledge, there would be nothing wrongful about Brian's act in moving the chair and, there being no wrongful act, there would be no liability.

While a finding that Brian had no such knowledge can be inferred from the findings made, we believe that before the plaintiff's action in such a case should be dismissed there should be no question but that the trial court had passed upon that issue; hence, the case should be remanded for clarifications of the findings to specifically cover the question of Brian's knowledge, because intent could be inferred therefrom. If the court finds that he had such knowledge the necessary intent will be established and the plaintiff will be entitled to recover, even though there was no purpose to injure or embarrass the plaintiff. If Brian did not have such knowledge, there was no wrongful act by him and the basic premise of liability on the theory of a battery was not established.

It will be noted that the law of battery as we have discussed it is the law applicable to adults, and no significance has been attached to the fact that Brian was a child less than six years of age when the alleged battery occurred. The only circumstance where Brian's age is of any consequence is in determining what he knew, and there his experience, capacity, and understanding are of course material. . . .

The cause is remanded for clarification, with instructions to make definite findings on the issue of whether Brian Dailey knew with substantial certainty that the plaintiff would attempt to sit down where the chair which he moved had been, and to change the judgment if the findings warrant it. . . .

NOTES

1. **Subsequent history of the case.** On remand, the trial court found that the plaintiff was in the act of sitting down when Brian moved the chair, and that Brian knew this. On the basis of the substantial certainty test, the judge found for the plaintiff. This was affirmed on the second appeal, *Garratt v. Dailey*, 304 P.2d 681 (Wash. 1956).

2. **Defining intent.** What is the definition of intent accepted by the *Garratt* court? Imagine that defendant hates the plaintiff, sees him at a distance and hurls a stone, hoping to hit the plaintiff but believing that success is extremely unlikely. The stone does in fact hit the plaintiff, however. Is this a battery? Is the intent involved the same intent on which Brian Dailey was held liable? The Restatement Third of Torts defines intent to produce a consequence as either a purpose to produce that consequence or knowledge that the consequence is substantially certain to result. RESTATEMENT (THIRD) OF TORTS: LIABILITY FOR PHYSICAL HARM § 1 (Proposed Final Draft No.1, 2005).

3. **Distinguishing intent from negligence.** Legal fault usually takes the form of intent or the form of negligence. Negligence is a large subject, to be considered beginning in Chapter 5. In general, negligence is conduct that creates an unreasonable risk of harm. Driving too fast would be an example. Can you distinguish between *Garratt v. Dailey* intent on the one hand and negligence on the other? Test it out: Defendant became highly intoxicated and drove his car on the wrong side of the highway, causing a head-on collision that seriously injured the plaintiff. *Garratt v. Dailey* intent, or negligence? What about fumes from a manufacturing plant, molecules of which are overwhelmingly likely to hit someone, though not necessarily likely to do harm? *See* ID. § 1, cmt. *e* (discussing the limits of ''substantial certainty'' intent).

4. **Reckless, wilful and wanton conduct.** Wilful or wanton conduct is "a course of action which shows actual or deliberate intent to harm or which, if the course of action is not intentional, shows an utter indifference to or conscious disregard for a person's own safety or the safety or property of others. [It is] a hybrid between acts considered negligent and behavior found to be intentionally tortious." *Pfister v. Shusta,* 657 N.E.2d 1013 (Ill. 1995). Recklessness is defined in much the same way. The newest Restatement adds that "When a person's conduct creates a known risk that can be reduced by relatively modest precautions," that conduct should be considered reckless rather than simply negligent. RESTATEMENT (THIRD), *supra,* § 2, cmt. *a. See Boyd v. National R.R. Passenger Corp.,* 845 N.E.2d 356 (Mass. 2006) (placing emphasis on the seriousness of the risk). While line-drawing can be difficult, courts sometimes distinguish recklessness or wanton misconduct from intent or negligence because of certain rules of damages or because of different statutes of limitation. Conduct that falls short of intentional wrongdoing, for example, may still be reckless or wanton so that punitive damages would be justified.

5. **The object of intent.** To establish the intentional tort of battery, what must be the object of the defendant's intent? To contact the plaintiff? To harm her? To offend? All three?

WHITE v. MUNIZ

999 P.2d 814 (Colo. 2000)

JUSTICE KOURLIS delivered the Opinion of the Court. . . .

In October of 1993, Barbara White placed her eighty-three year-old grandmother, Helen Everly, in an assisted living facility, the Beatrice Hover Personal Care Center. Within a few days of admission, Everly started exhibiting erratic behavior. She became agitated easily, and occasionally acted aggressively toward others. [A physician concluded that she had progressive dementia, loss of memory, impulse control and judgment, a degenerative dementia of the Alzheimer type.]

On November 21, 1993, the caregiver in charge of Everly's wing asked Sherry Lynn Muniz, a shift supervisor at Hover, to change Everly's adult diaper. The caregiver informed Muniz that Everly was not cooperating in that effort. This did not surprise Muniz because she knew that Everly sometimes acted obstinately. Indeed, initially Everly refused to allow Muniz to change her diaper, but eventually Muniz thought that Everly relented. However, as Muniz reached toward the diaper, Everly struck Muniz on the jaw and ordered her out of the room.

[Muniz sued Everly and White as her representative for assault and battery. After the evidence was presented, the trial judge instructed the jury in part as follows.]

The fact that a person may suffer from Dementia, Alzheimer type, does not prevent a finding that she acted intentionally. You may find that she acted intentionally if she intended to do what she did, even though her reasons and motives were entirely irrational. However, she must have appreciated the offensiveness of her conduct.

Muniz's counsel objected to the last sentence of the instruction, claiming that it misstated the law. [The jury found for Everly and White. The Court of Appeals held the instruction to be error and reversed.]

The question we here address is whether an intentional tort requires some proof that the tortfeasor not only intended to contact another person, but also intended that the contact be harmful or offensive to the other person.

State courts and legal commentators generally agree that an intentional tort requires some proof that the tortfeasor intended harm or offense. See W. Page Keeton et al., Prosser and Keeton on the Law of Torts § 8 (5th ed.1984); Dan B. Dobbs, The Law of Torts § 30 (2000). According to the Restatement (Second) of Torts [§ 13],

(1) An actor is subject to liability to another for battery if

(a) he acts intending to cause a harmful or offensive contact with the person of the other or a third person, or an imminent apprehension of such a contact, and

(b) an offensive [or harmful] contact with the person of the other directly or indirectly results. . . .

[Historically,] the actor had to understand that his contact would be harmful or offensive. See Keeton, supra, § 8; Dobbs, supra, § 29. The actor need not have intended, however, the harm that actually resulted from his action. Thus, if a slight punch to the victim resulted in traumatic injuries, the actor would be liable for all the damages resulting from the battery even if he only intended to knock the wind out of the victim.

Juries may find it difficult to determine the mental state of an actor, but they may rely on circumstantial evidence in reaching their conclusion. No person can pinpoint the thoughts in the mind of another, but a jury can examine the facts to conclude what another must have been thinking. For example, a person of reasonable intelligence knows with substantial certainty that a stone thrown into a crowd will strike someone and result in an offensive or harmful contact to that person. Hence, if an actor of average intelligence performs such an act, the jury can determine that the actor had the requisite intent to cause a harmful or offensive contact, even though the actor denies having such thoughts.

More recently, some courts around the nation have abandoned this dual intent requirement in an intentional tort setting, that being an intent to contact and an intent that the contact be harmful or offensive, and have required only that the tortfeasor intend a contact with another that results in a harmful or offensive touching. Under this view, a victim need only prove that a voluntary movement by the tortfeasor resulted in a contact which a reasonable person would find offensive or to which the victim did not consent. These courts would find intent in contact to the back of a friend that results in a severe, unexpected injury even though the actor did not intend the contact to be harmful or offensive. The actor thus could be held liable for battery because a reasonable person would find an injury offensive or harmful, irrespective of the intent of the actor to harm or offend. . . .

Because Colorado law requires a dual intent, we apply here the Restatement's definition of the term. As a result, we reject the arguments of Muniz and find that the trial court delivered an adequate instruction to the jury.

Operating in accordance with this instruction, the jury had to find that Everly appreciated the offensiveness of her conduct in order to be liable for the intentional tort of battery. It necessarily had to consider her mental capabilities in making such a finding, including her age, infirmity, education, skill, or any other characteristic as to which the jury had evidence. We presume that the jury "looked into the mind of Everly," and reasoned that Everly did not possess the necessary intent to commit an assault or a battery.

A jury can, of course, find a mentally deficient person liable for an intentional tort, but in order to do so, the jury must find that the actor intended offensive or harmful consequences. As a result, insanity is not a defense to an intentional tort according to the ordinary use of that term, but is a characteristic, like infancy, that may make it more difficult to prove the intent element of battery. Our decision today does not create a special rule for the elderly, but applies Colorado's intent requirement in the context of a woman suffering the effects of Alzheimer's. . . .

[Jury verdict reinstated.]

———————

WAGNER v. STATE, 122 P.3d 599 (Utah 2005). While waiting in a department store customer service line, plaintiff Tracy Wagner was suddenly attacked from behind by Sam Giese, a mentally disabled patient who was brought to the store as a part of a state treatment program. Under a statute, the state would not be liable for the patient's conduct if that conduct "arose out of battery." In her suit against the state, plaintiff asserted that the conduct was not a battery. The trial agreed and dismissed plaintiff's complaint, which dismissal was upheld in the court of appeals. The Wagners argue that Mr. Giese's attack could not legally constitute a battery because battery requires the actor to intend harm or offense through his deliberate contact, an intent Mr. Giese was mentally incompetent to form. The State, on the other hand, argues that the only intent required for battery is simply an intent to make a contact. *Held,* affirmed.

"Utah has adopted the Second Restatement of Torts to define the elements of [battery], including the element of intent. . . . [We] agree with the State that only intent to make contact is necessary. . . . We hold that the actor need not intend that his contact be harmful or offensive in order to commit a battery so long as he deliberately made the contact and so long as that contact satisfies our legal test for what is harmful or offensive.... [The court deemed the practical consequences of a dual intent rule unworkable]. For example, a man who decides to flatter a woman he spots in a crowd with an unpetitioned-for kiss, one of the examples of battery Prosser provides, would find no objection under the Wagners' proposed rule so long as his intentional contact was initiated with no intent to injure or offend. He would be held civilly liable for his conduct only if he intended to harm or offend her through his kiss. A woman in such circumstances would not enjoy the presumption of the law in favor of preserving her bodily integrity; instead, her right to be free from physical contact with strangers would depend upon whether she could prove that the stranger hoped to harm or offend her through his contact. So long as he could show that he meant only flattery and the communication of positive feelings towards her in stroking her, kissing her, or hugging her, she must be subjected to it and will find no protection for her bodily integrity in our civil law."

NOTES

1. **Single versus dual intent.** Think about *White v. Muniz* and *Wagner v. State*. For each case, what would the plaintiff have to prove in order to hold the defendant liable for battery? In a state that follows a "dual intent" requirement, as in *White*, is it more or less difficult to hold a child or mentally disabled person liable for the tort of battery?

2. **Making a choice.** Courts that adopt a single intent rule and courts that adopt a dual intent rule both trace the origins of those rules to the Restatement Second of Torts and to Dean Prosser's treatise, suggesting that those authorities might be somewhat unclear. Which court's construction of the intent rule for battery is more just? Which represents better policy? The issue has provoked strong reactions from judges. *See White v. University of Idaho*, 797 P.2d 108 (Idaho 1990) (Bistlin, J., dissenting) ("the Court's opinion has a chilling effect on any thought of ever again tapping a dancing gent on the shoulder to ask, 'May I?' Today it is learned that so doing is a battery even though no harm or offense is intended. One lives and learns.") Scholars have also disputed the point. For an argument that the single-intent rule reflects sound policy, *see* Kenneth Simons, *A Restatement (Third) of Intentional Torts?*, 48 ARIZ. L. REV. 1061 (2006). For an argument that the dual-intent rule is better advised, *see* DAN B. DOBBS, THE LAW OF TORTS § 30 (Supp. 2008).

3. **Single-intent outside the context of defendant incapacity.** Whether courts adopt a single or dual intent rule may be important to cases involving children and people with diminished mental capacity where intent to harm or offend can be difficult to establish. However, the rule is important to other contexts too. Suppose the defendant hugs her husband in an ordinary way but, surprisingly, this breaks a vertebra. Is this a battery because contact was intended and it turned out to be harmful? Is this what happened in *Mullins v. Parkview Hospital?* Would the defendant's motion for summary

judgment in *Mullins* have come out differently under a single intent rule? Would imposing liability on the defendant for intent to contact which happens to produce harm or offense necessarily reflect wrongdoing on the part of the defendant?

4. **Insanity.** When a defendant intends to harm the plaintiff but does so because of insanity, ordinary rules of battery apply. The usual American view is that insanity is not an excuse from tort liability. In *Polmatier v. Russ*, 537 A.2d 468 (Conn. 1988), defendant Russ shot his father in law, Arthur Polmatier, causing his death. Russ was found not guilty by reason of insanity on a murder charge in criminal court, but in the tort action, a judgment was entered for the plaintiff. The court held that the judgment against defendant was appropriate even though Russ could not make a rational choice, and shot his father in law for "crazy" or schizophrenic reasons (including Russ' belief that Polmatier was a spy for the red Chinese, and that Russ was a supreme being who could make his bed fly out of the window). According to the court "[a]n insane person may have an intent to invade the interests of another, even though his reasons and motives for forming that intention may be entirely irrational." Because Russ intended shoot Polmatier, plaintiff was entitled to prevail.

5. **Insanity in common law and civil law countries**. Canada, like the United States, is a common law country in which most tort law is made by judicial decision in concrete cases. Canadian case law, like American, refuses any blanket immunity for insane persons. The question is whether the defendant had the requisite intent; if so, the fact that the intent arose from insanity is not relevant. Sparse English authority seems to agree. The civil law, as contrasted with the common law, begins with general principles formally stated in codes of law. Civil law courts do decide particular cases, of course, but they begin analysis by considering a Code provision. Civil law, rooted in Roman jurisprudence, is the dominant legal system in Europe, Central and South America, and elsewhere outside the Anglo–American legal communities. It is also an important heritage in Louisiana by way of the French connection and in the Southwest by way of the Spanish connection. The traditional civil law held that a mentally unsound person "cannot commit a fault." This can be seen today in the German Civil Code § 827, excluding civil responsibility for one who is unable to exercise free will, except where he brought on temporary disability by use of alcohol or similar means. But civil law countries today are divided. In Mexico, the Código Civil para el Distrito Federal § 1911 provides that the incompetent person is liable unless some other person such as a guardian is liable.

6. **Options.** Should people with diminished mental capacity be held to the same rules of liability as others? If you were writing a statute to resolve the problem of injury caused by insane persons, would you want to consider any other options besides liability or non-liability? Crime victims' compensation statutes have been enacted in many states. Under these statutes the state may create a fund for the partial compensation of crime victims, at least where the criminal himself is not made to pay. *See* Charlene Smith, *Victim Compensation: Hard Questions and Suggested Remedies*, 17 RUTGERS L. J. 51 (1985). Would this be a good solution for the problem represented by *Wagner* and *Polmatier?*

NOTE: CHILD LIABILITY

1. *General rule.* As recognized in *Garratt v. Dailey*, in most states children may be liable for torts they commit as long as the injured plaintiff can prove the required elements, including intent. That is, in most states a child cannot escape tort liability simply because of young age. Does *Van Camp v. McAfoos* stand in opposition to this general rule?

2. *Young children.* In some states, however, particularly young children are "conclusively presumed to be incapable of harmful intent." Age seven is frequently used as the cut-off point. *See, e.g., DeLuca v. Bowden,* 329 N.E.2d 109 (Ohio 1975); *Carey v. Reeve,* 781 P.2d 904 (Wash. Ct. App. 1989). A few states go even further and hold that children under a particular age (again, often seven) are conclusively presumed to be incapable of committing any tort at all. *See, e.g., Queen Ins. Co. v. Hammond,* 132 N.W.2d 792 (Mich. 1965).

3. *Other solutions.* Will small children always be liable in states that do not grant blanket immunity to children under a particular age? Notice that the child's age would be relevant to show either that he could not or did not form an adequate intent to touch, to offend or to harm. Should we say as a matter of law that a child of four cannot harbor an intent to strike a babysitter in a harmful or offensive way, or is it a matter of assessing the intent in the particular case? *Bailey v. C.S.,* 12 S.W.3d 159 (Tex. App. 2000) (four-year-old hit babysitter in the throat, crushing larynx). What about holding a child liable for intended harms, but not for intended offense? This was approved in *Horton v. Reaves,* 526 P.2d 304 (Colo. 1974).

NOTE: PARENTAL LIABILITY FOR THE TORTS OF THEIR MINOR CHILDREN

Why should a person injured by the tortious action of a child not just sue the child's parents and seek damages from them? The answer is that such a lawsuit is possible only if a statute authorizes such a suit—in which case the statutory requirements for recovery must be met—or if the parents are themselves at fault in some way. That is, the common law rule is that parents are not vicariously liable for the torts of their children simply by virtue of their being parents.

Statutes imposing liability on parents for their children's torts exist in virtually every state, but they are usually limited in two significant ways: First, the child's tort must have been committed willfully or wantonly. Second, the damages that may be obtained are limited. Some states cap damages at a very low amount, while others are less restrictive. *Compare* CT. GEN. STAT. § 52–572 (2008) (capping damages at $5,000 for injury to persons or property); *with* FLA. STAT. ANN. § 741.24 (2008) (providing no cap on damages for theft and destruction of property but limiting recovery to the amount of actual damages incurred) *and* CAL. CIV. CODE § 1714.1 (2008) (capping damages at $25,000 per tort). When parents are sued under a parental liability statute, the court may interpret the statutory terms in a way that differs from the contours of common law "intent." The court's inquiry in a statutory claim will be whether the child's acts fit the statutory definition that gives rise to parental liability. *See, e.g., Walker v. Kelly*, 314 A.2d 785 (Conn. Cir. Ct. 1973) (holding that the statutory term "wilfully or maliciously" means "caused by design"). A child's parents will not be liable under a statute for every common-law intentional tort committed by the child.

Plaintiffs who sue parents for the parents' own fault will often allege that the parents negligently supervised their child, and that this caused the plaintiffs' harm. This negligence theory is explored in greater detail in Chapter 18. We can say now that such claims are very difficult to win. Indeed, such a claim failed in *Van Camp v. McAfoos* because the plaintiffs did not prove that the parents were at fault. On the other hand, what if a parent tells his minor child, "throw a rock at Susie's dad," and the child does so, hitting Susie's dad. Would *that* be actionable? Why?

If parents often are not legally liable for a child's torts, how can the injured plaintiff hope to see any money in a suit against a child? Children do not usually have adequate assets to pay a judgment. Often the parents' insurance policy may well cover minor children living in the household. Such a policy would pay any judgment rendered against the child.

STOSHAK v. EAST BATON ROUGE PARISH SCHOOL, 959 So. 2d 996 (La. Ct. App. 2007). While trying to break up a fight, Baton Rouge High School teacher John Stoshak was struck in the back of the head by a punch thrown by one of two fighting students. Stoshak fell to the ground and lost consciousness. In an affidavit, Stoshak stated that he "did not believe either of the boys had punched him deliberately; rather, he got in the way of the fighting boys who were, in his words, 'tear[ing] each other up.'" Under a Louisiana law referred to as the "assault pay provision," Stoshak was entitled to broader disability benefits if his injury resulted from "an assault and battery by any student or person" while he was acting in his capacity as a member of the teaching staff of a public school. The trial court ruled on undisputed facts that Stoshak was not the victim of an "assault or battery by any student or person" and thus was not entitled to the highest level of sick leave benefits provided for in the state statute. Held, reversed. "Under the tort law, a battery has been defined as a 'harmful or offensive contact with a person, resulting from an act intended to cause the plaintiff to suffer such a contact.' In defining what type of conduct constitutes a battery, our courts have employed the doctrine of transferred intent. Under this theory, if a person intended to inflict serious bodily injury while trying to hit another person, but missed and accidentally hit someone else instead, such intent is transferred to the actual victim. We must presume that in enacting La. R.S. 17:1201(C) [the assault pay provision], the legislature was cognizant of the fact that our courts have interpreted the term 'battery' to encompass an unintentional injury of one person if the person inflicting the injury specifically intended to injure someone else. The legislature authorized the highest level of benefits to a teacher injured as a result of 'assault or battery by any student or person.' There is no language in this provision requiring that the teacher be the intended victim of an assault or battery, and we decline to read such a requirement into the statute.... Applying this construction of the statute, we hold that as a matter of law, Mr. Stoshak is entitled to benefits under the 'assault pay' provision...."

BASKA v. SCHERZER, 156 P.3d 617 (Kan. 2007). Celeste Baska had given her daughter Ashley, a high school senior, permission to organize a scavenger hunt and party. Around midnight, a fight broke out between Harry Scherzer, Jr. and Calvin Madrigal. Baska yelled at the boys to stop fighting. When they did not, Baska placed herself between them and was punched in the face, losing several teeth and receiving injuries to her neck and jaw. Baska sued Madrigal and Scherzer for personal injuries. In depositions, both Madrigal and Scherzer testified that they did not intend to strike or injure Baska. Instead, each testified that it was his intent only to strike and injure the other defendant. Madrigal and Scherzer then filed motions for summary judgment based on the 1–year statute of limitations for assault and battery. [The statute of limitations for negligence actions was longer and would not have barred the plaintiff's claim]. Held, Baska's cause of action was an action for assault and battery, not negligence. The court explained: "[T]he doctrine of transferred intent states that '[t]he tort of battery or of assault and battery may be committed, although the person struck or hit by the defendant is not the one whom he intended to strike or hit.' The comments to the Restatement (Second) of Torts, in describing the intent necessary for battery, explain:

> 'The intention which is necessary to make the actor liable [for civil battery] is not necessarily an intention to cause a harmful or offensive contact or an apprehension of such contact to the plaintiff himself or otherwise to cause him bodily harm. It is enough that the actor intends to produce such an effect upon some other person and that his act so intended is the legal cause of a harmful contact to the other. It is not necessary that the actor know or have reason even to suspect that the other is in the vicinity of the third person whom the actor intends to affect and, therefore, that he should recognize that his act, though directed against the third person, involves a risk of causing bodily harm to the other so that the act would be negligent toward him.' Restatement (Second) of Torts § 16, comment b (1964)....

The undisputed facts in this case show that the defendants intended to strike and cause harm to one another. When Baska intervened and stepped between the two boys, she was 'unintentionally' struck by punches intended for the defendants. Had the defendants struck each other and brought suit, they would be liable to one another for assault and battery. Under the doctrine of transferred intent, which has long been recognized in this state, the fact that the defendants struck the plaintiff does not change the fact that their actions (punching) were intentional. . . . The trial court correctly granted defendant's motion for summary judgment."

NOTES

1. **Forms of transferred intent.** The doctrine of transferred intent has wide acceptance. This case demonstrates one form of transferred intent. How would you state the rule?

2. **The extended liability principle.** The defendant who commits an intentional tort, at least if it involves conscious wrongdoing, is liable for all damages caused, not merely those intended or foreseeable. We will call this the extended liability principle. This principle explains the result in most transferred intent cases, as where the defendant intends a battery to one person and then accidentally causes a battery to another as well. *See* Osborne M. Reynolds, Jr., *Transferred Intent: Should its "Curious Survival" Continue?*, 50 OKLA. L. REV. 529 (1997). No doubt there is a limit somewhere.

3. **Accepting or rejecting the rule in light of policy rationales.** If the purpose of the transferred intent rule is to afford broad recovery to people injured in situations in which harms were at least to some extent intended, might courts choose to employ the transferred intent rule only when the rule would effectuate those policies? In *Baska* the transferred intent rule was employed not to assist the plaintiff in recovering for damages caused by intentional misdeeds but to bar her recovery altogether. For an argument that the transferred intent doctrine often works against plaintiffs and should be abolished or at least limited see Vincent R. Johnson, *Transferred Intent in American Tort Law*, 87 MARQ. L. REV. 903 (2004). Would there be any other way to address the problem in *Baska?*

4. **The effects of classifying a tort as intentional.** The Restatement Third of Torts calls it "somewhat ironic" that "intentional torts are generally deemed considerably more serious than torts of mere negligence," and yet "in certain circumstances the plaintiff is worse off if the tort committed against the plaintiff is classified as intentional rather than negligent." RESTATEMENT THIRD OF TORTS: LIABILITY FOR PHYSICAL HARM § 5 cmt. *a* (Proposed Final Draft No. 1, 2005). How could a plaintiff be worse off with a judgment against the defendant for an intentional tort in contrast to a negligent or reckless tort? One reason is that many insurance policies pay judgments for negligent and reckless acts but do not cover intentional torts, thereby limiting the plaintiff's potential source of recovery. Another reason is that statutes of limitation for intentional torts are often much shorter than are statutes of limitation for negligent torts. Because of this phenomenon plaintiffs sometimes try to "underplead" intentional tort cases and style them as claims for negligence. *See* Ellen Smith Pryor, *The Stories We Tell*, 75 TEX. L. REV. 1721 (1997). At other times, classifying a tort as intentional tort may help the plaintiff. For example, judgments in intentional tort cases may be more difficult for a defendant to discharge in bankruptcy.

REFERENCES: DOBBS ON TORTS §§ 24, 28–31 (2000); HARPER, JAMES AND GRAY ON TORTS § 3.3 (3d ed. 2006).

§ 2. ASSAULT

CULLISON v. MEDLEY

570 N.E.2d 27 (Ind. 1991)

KRAHULIK, JUSTICE.

Dan R. Cullison (Appellant–Plaintiff below) petitions this Court to accept transfer of this cause in order to reverse the trial court's entry of summary judgment against him and in favor of the Appellees–Defendants below (collectively "the Medleys")....

According to Cullison's deposition testimony, on February 2, 1986, he encountered Sandy, the 16-year-old daughter of Ernest, in a Linton, Indiana, grocery store parking lot. They exchanged pleasantries and Cullison invited her to have a Coke with him and to come to his home to talk further. A few hours later, someone knocked on the door of his mobile home. Cullison got out of bed and answered the door. He testified that he saw a person standing in the darkness who said that she wanted to talk to him. Cullison answered that he would have to get dressed because he had been in bed. Cullison went back to his bedroom, dressed, and returned to the darkened living room of his trailer. When he entered the living room and turned the lights on, he was confronted by Sandy Medley, as well as by father Ernest, brother Ron, mother Doris, and brother-in-law Terry Simmons. Ernest was on crutches due to knee surgery and had a revolver in a holster strapped to his thigh. Cullison testified that Sandy called him a "pervert" and told him he was "sick," mother Doris berated him while keeping her hand in her pocket, convincing Cullison that she also was carrying a pistol. Ron and Terry said nothing to Cullison, but their presence in his trailer home further intimidated him. Primarily, however, Cullison's attention was riveted to the gun carried by Ernest. Cullison testified that, while Ernest never withdrew the gun from his holster, he "grabbed for the gun a few times and shook the gun" at plaintiff while threatening to "jump astraddle" of Cullison if he did not leave Sandy alone. Cullison testified that Ernest "kept grabbing at it with his hand, like he was going to take it out," and "took it to mean he was going to shoot me" when Ernest threatened to "jump astraddle" of Cullison. Although no one actually touched Cullison, his testimony was that he feared he was about to be shot throughout the episode because Ernest kept moving his hand toward the gun as if to draw the revolver from the holster while threatening Cullison to leave Sandy alone.

As the Medleys were leaving, Cullison suffered chest pains and feared that he was having a heart attack. Approximately two months later, Cullison testified that Ernest glared at him in a menacing manner while again armed with a handgun at a restaurant in Linton. On one of these occasions, Ernest stood next to the booth where Cullison was seated while wearing a pistol and a holster approximately one foot from Cullison's face. Shortly after the incident at his home, Cullison learned that Ernest had previously shot a man. This added greatly to his fear and apprehension of Ernest on the later occasions when Ernest glared at him and stood next to the booth at which he was seated while armed with a handgun in a holster.

Cullison testified that as a result of the incident, he sought psychological counseling and therapy and continued to see a therapist for approximately 18 months. Additionally, Cullison sought psychiatric help and received prescription medication which prevented him from operating power tools or driving an automobile, thus injuring Cullison in his sole proprietorship construction business. Additionally, Cullison testified that he suffered from nervousness, depression, sleeplessness, inability to concentrate and impotency following his run-in with the Medleys. . . .

[Cullison sued the Meleys for a number of torts, including assault. The defendants moved for summary judgment on all claims. The trial court granted the motion and the appeals court affirmed.]

. . . In count two of his complaint, Cullison alleged an assault. The Court of Appeals decided that, because Ernest never removed his gun from the holster, his threat that he was going to "jump astraddle" of Cullison constituted conditional language which did not express any present intent to harm Cullison and, therefore, was not an assault. Further, the Court of Appeals decided that even if it were to find an assault, summary judgment was still appropriate because Cullison alleged only emotional distress and made no showing that the Medleys' actions were malicious, callous, or willful or that the alleged injuries he suffered were a foreseeable result of the Medleys' conduct. We disagree.

It is axiomatic that assault, unlike battery, is effectuated when one acts intending to cause a harmful or offensive contact with the person of the other or an imminent apprehension of such contact. It is the right to be free from the apprehension of a battery which is protected by the tort action which we call an assault. As this Court held approximately 90 years ago in *Kline v. Kline* (1901), 158 Ind. 602, 64 N.E. 9, an assault constitutes "a touching of the mind, if not of the body." Because it is a touching of the mind, as opposed to the body, the damages which are recoverable for an assault are damages for mental trauma and distress. "Any act of such a nature as to excite an apprehension of a battery may constitute an assault. It is an assault to shake a fist under another's nose, to aim or strike at him with a weapon, or to hold it in a threatening position, to rise or advance to strike another, to surround him with a display of force. . . ." W. PROSSER & J. KEETON, PROSSER AND KEETON ON TORTS § 10 (5th ed. 1984). Additionally, the apprehension must be one which would normally be aroused in the mind of a reasonable person. *Id.* Finally, the tort is complete with the invasion of the plaintiff's mental peace.

The facts alleged and testified to by Cullison could, if believed, entitle him to recover for an assault against the Medleys. A jury could reasonably conclude that the Medleys intended to frighten Cullison by surrounding him in his trailer and threatening him with bodily harm while one of them was armed with a revolver, even if that revolver was not removed from the its holster. Cullison testified that Ernest kept grabbing at the pistol as if he were going to take it out, and that Cullison thought Ernest was going to shoot him. It is for the jury to determine whether Cullison's apprehension of being shot or otherwise injured was one which would normally be aroused in the mind of a reasonable person. It was error for the trial court to enter summary judgment on the count two allegation of assault. . . .

[Reversed in part and remanded.]

NOTES

1. **Applying *Cullison*.** In *Raess v. Doescher*, 883 N.E.2d 790 (Ind. 2008), "defendant [a cardiovascular surgeon], angry at the plaintiff about reports to the hospital administration about the defendant's treatment of other perfusionists [individuals who operate the heart/lung machine during open heart surgeries], aggressively and rapidly advanced on the plaintiff with clenched fists, piercing eyes, beet-red face, popping veins, and screaming and swearing at him. The plaintiff backed up against a wall and put his hands up, believing that the defendant was going to hit him, '[t]hat he was going to smack the s* *t out of me or do something.' Then the defendant suddenly stopped, turned, and stormed past the plaintiff and left the room, momentarily stopping to declare to the plaintiff 'you're finished, you're history.'" Under *Cullison*, would these facts, if proved, entitle the plaintiff to recover on the assault claim?

2. **Assault and battery.** "Assault" has a technical meaning in tort law. Newspapers may use the term as a euphemism for sexual battery. Even judges, particularly in older cases, may use the term assault to mean a battery. But the two torts are different. One can find cases, especially older ones, that say, "Every battery necessarily involves an assault." *McGlone v. Hauger*, 104 N.E. 116 (Ind. Ct. App. 1914). Can this be an accurate formulation? Suppose the defendant struck a sleeping plaintiff with a baseball bat. Would that be an assault? In *Koffman v. Garnett*, 574 S.E.2d 258 (Va. 2003), a 260–pound football coach slammed a 144–pound 13-year-old student to the ground to demonstrate proper tackling technique. Because the student "had no warning of an imminent forceful tackle," the pleadings were insufficient to state a claim for assault.

3. **Apprehension.** What does "apprehension" mean? One common meaning of that word is "fear," and certainly the plaintiff in *Cullison* was probably fearful. But apprehension in the context of assault does not mean fear, but rather an awareness of an imminent touching that would be a battery if completed. *See* DOBBS ON TORTS § 34 (2000).

4. **"Words alone."** Courts have sometimes said that words alone cannot count as an assault. But isn't it almost impossible to imagine words alone, divorced from any act at all? The Restatement says that "Words alone do not make the actor liable for assault unless together with other acts or circumstances they put the other in reasonable apprehension [of imminent contact]." RESTATEMENT (SECOND) OF TORTS § 31. Suppose someone stands perfectly still at the entrance to a dark alley. He is masked and holding a gun. He says: "I am

now going to shoot you dead." Surely this could be reasonably understood as a threat of imminent bodily harm. Maybe "words alone" is another shorthand or inaccurate statement. Perhaps it means that the plaintiff must reasonably apprehend an immediate touching and that in most cases words alone will not suffice to create such an apprehension.

5. **Words negating intent to effect immediate touching.** Sometimes acts seem threatening but the threat is countered by words. The defendant draws back his arm as if to strike, but at the same time he is saying "If the police officer were not here, I'd punch your nose." The words clearly mean he is *not* going to punch your nose. If there are no facts to make it reasonable to believe that the defendant will strike you in spite of the police officer's presence, this does not look like an assault.

6. **Words offering a choice of tortious alternatives.** Suppose the defendant says in a menacing way "I won't beat you to a pulp if you give me your basketball tickets; otherwise you are going to be pretty bloody." Is this an assault, even though the threatened battery can be avoided by complying with the aggressor's demands? In *Gouin v. Gouin*, 249 F. Supp. 2d 62 (D. Mass. 2003), the plaintiff and defendant, an estranged married couple, were engaged in a number of ongoing disputes. As a result of one, the plaintiff sued the defendant for assault, alleging that the defendant said to her during an argument about their son, "You can either do it my way or I can beat you half to death." She further alleged that the defendant knowingly acted as he did "to instill fear in her so that she would comply with his wishes." Are these allegations sufficient to state a claim for assault?

7. **Imminent apprehension.** To state a claim for assault, the plaintiff must have been placed in "imminent" apprehension of a harmful or offensive touching. What does that phrase mean? The Restatement Second explains in a comment that "The apprehension created must be one of imminent contact, as distinguished from any contact in the future. 'Imminent' does not mean immediate, in the sense of instantaneous contact. . . . It means rather that there will be no significant delay." § 29(1), comment *b*. In *Dickens v. Puryear*, 276 S.E.2d 325 (N.C. 1981), the plaintiff, a 31-year-old man, "shared sex, alcohol and marijuana" with defendant's 17-year-old daughter. The defendant and some of his friends lured the plaintiff into a rural area, where they beat him, handcuffed him to a piece of farm machinery, and threatened him with castration while brandishing knives. The court had no problem labeling many of these acts as batteries and assaults. But the defendant also "told plaintiff to go home, pull his telephone off the wall, pack his clothes, and leave the state of North Carolina; otherwise he would be killed." He was then freed, and sued the defendant almost three years later in a North Carolina Court. Was this last threat imminent for the purposes of assault? What do you see as the strongest arguments on each side?

8. **Revisiting transferred intent.** In *Stoshak* and *Baska*, the defendants intended a battery against one another and inadvertently struck the plaintiff, committing a battery based on the doctrine of transferred intent. A second form of transferred intent occurs when a defendant intends to commit one tort and ends up committing another. For example, the defendant intends to commit an assault but instead commits battery. In *Alteiri v. Colasso*, 362

A.2d 798 (Conn. 1975), the defendant threw a stone into a neighbor's backyard with the intent to scare, but not strike, someone other than the plaintiff. The stone struck and permanently injured the plaintiff. *Held*, "[T]he jury could logically and legally return a plaintiff's verdict for willful battery." We now have a second meaning for transferred intent.

NOTE: RELATED STATUTORY CLAIMS

Legislatures have crafted some causes of action that allow plaintiffs to sue for damages on particular facts that might also give rise to common-law actions for assault. For example, the federal Free Access to Clinic Entrances Act (FACE), 18 U.S.C.A. § 248, creates a civil claim against anyone who by threat, force, or physical obstruction intentionally injures, intimidates, or interferes with a person seeking to obtain or provide "reproductive health services." In *Planned Parenthood of the Columbia/Willamette, Inc. v. American Coalition of Life Activists,* 290 F.3d 1058 (9th Cir. 2002), defendants published "wanted" posters, describing plaintiffs as murderers (because they provided abortions) and giving names and addresses. When such posters had been posted about other abortion providers, the providers had been murdered, but not by the defendants. Should the court permit the jury to find a threat in violation of the statute and uphold an award of damages to the abortion providers?

Statutes in a number of states create a claim against stalkers who follow or stalk someone. The stalkers almost always seem to be men and their victims women. The California statute creates a statutory tort called stalking based on a pattern of conduct the "intent of which was to follow, alarm, or harass the plaintiff," with resulting reasonable fear by the plaintiff for herself or an immediate family member. In addition, the defendant must either make a credible threat or violate a restraining order. Cal. Civ. Code § 1708.7.

§ 3.   FALSE IMPRISONMENT

McCANN v. WAL–MART STORES, INC.

210 F.3d 51 (1st Cir. 2000)

This case involves a claim for false imprisonment. On December 11, 1996, Debra McCann and two of her children—Jillian, then 16, and Jonathan, then 12—were shopping at the Wal–Mart store in Bangor, Maine. . . . [T]he McCanns went to a register and paid for their purchases. One of their receipts was time stamped at 10:10 p.m.

As the McCanns were leaving the store, two Wal–Mart employees, Jean Taylor and Karla Hughes, stepped out in front of the McCanns' shopping cart, blocking their path to the exit. Taylor may have actually put her hand on the cart. The employees told Debra McCann that the children were not allowed in the store because they had been caught stealing on a prior occasion. In fact, the employees were mistaken; the son of a different family had been caught shoplifting in the store about two weeks before, and Taylor and Hughes confused the two families.

Despite Debra McCann's protestations, Taylor said that they had the records, that the police were being called, and that the McCanns "had to go with her." Debra McCann testified that she did not resist Taylor's direction because she believed that she had to go with Taylor and that the police were coming. Taylor and Hughes then brought the McCanns past the registers in the store to an area near the store exit. Taylor stood near the McCanns while Hughes purportedly went to call the police. During this time, Debra McCann tried to show Taylor her identification, but Taylor refused to look at it. . . .

Although Wal–Mart's employees had said they were calling the police, they actually called a store security officer who would be able to identify the earlier shoplifter. Eventually, the security officer, Rhonda Bickmore, arrived at the store and informed Hughes that the McCanns were not the family whose son had been caught shoplifting. Hughes then acknowledged her mistake to the McCanns, and the McCanns left the store at approximately 11:15 p.m. . . .

The jury awarded the McCanns $20,000 in compensatory damages on their claim that they were falsely imprisoned in the Wal–Mart store by Wal–Mart employees. Wal–Mart has now appealed. . . .

Although nuances vary from state to state, the gist of the common law tort is conduct by the actor which is intended to, and does in fact, "confine" another "within boundaries fixed by the actor" where, in addition, the victim is either "conscious of the confinement or is harmed by it." . . .

While "confinement" can be imposed by physical barriers or physical force, much less will do—although how much less becomes cloudy at the margins. It is generally settled that mere threats of physical force can suffice, and it is also settled . . . that the threats may be implicit as well as explicit, and that confinement can also be based on a false assertion of legal authority to confine. Indeed, the Restatement provides that confinement may occur by other unspecified means of "duress." . . .

The evidence, taken favorably to the McCanns, showed that Wal–Mart employees . . . told the McCanns that they had to come with the Wal–Mart employees and that Wal–Mart was calling the police, and then stood guard over the McCanns while waiting for a security guard to arrive. The direction to the McCanns, the reference to the police, and the continued presence of the Wal–Mart employees (who at one point told Jonathan McCann that he could not leave to go to the bathroom) were enough to induce reasonable people to believe either that they would be restrained physically if they sought to leave, or that the store was claiming lawful authority to confine them until the police arrived, or both.

Wal–Mart asserts that under Maine law, the jury had to find "actual, physical restraint," a phrase it takes from [Knowlton v. Ross, 114 Me. 18, 95 A. 281 (1915).] While there is no complete definition of false imprisonment by Maine's highest court, this is a good example of taking language out of context. In Knowlton, the wife of a man who owed a hotel for past bills entered the hotel office and was allegedly told that she would go to jail if she did not pay the bill.... The court noted that the defendants did not ask Mrs. Knowlton into the room (another guest had sent for her), did not touch her, and did not tell her she could not leave. The court also said that any threat of jail to Mrs. Knowlton was only "evidence of an intention to imprison at some future time." In context, the reference to the necessity of "actual, physical restraint" is best understood as a reminder that a plaintiff must be actually confined—which Mrs. Knowlton was not.

Taking too literally the phrase "actual, physical restraint" would put Maine law broadly at odds with not only the Restatement but with a practically uniform body of common law in other states that accepts the mere threat of physical force, or a claim of lawful authority to restrain, as enough to satisfy the confinement requirement for false imprisonment (assuming always that the victim submits). It is true that in a diversity case, we are bound by Maine law, as Wal–Mart reminds us; but we are not required to treat a descriptive phrase as a general rule or attribute to elderly Maine cases an entirely improbable breadth....

Affirmed.

NOTES

1. **Elements.** "False imprisonment occurs when a person confines another intentionally without lawful privilege and against his consent within a limited area for any appreciable time, however short." *Bennett v. Ohio Dep't of Rehab. & Correction*, 573 N.E.2d 633 (Ohio 1991). In addition, it is usually said that the plaintiff must have been aware of the confinement at the time or else must have sustained actual harm. Notice that bad motive is not one of the elements, only intent.

2. **Exclusion.** Confinement implies limited range of movement and it is not enough to exclude the plaintiff from some place such as a bar or restaurant. Suppose you are prevented from leaving Taiwan. Is that false imprisonment? *Shen v. Leo A. Daly Co.*, 222 F.3d 472 (8th Cir. 2000).

3. **Confinement by physical barrier or force.** Suppose the plaintiff is locked in a room but knows of a safe and reasonable means of escape. Is she confined? Suppose the defendant refuses to stop a moving car, the doors of which are not locked. Is his passenger confined?

4. **Confinement by threats or duress.** *(a) Threats or demands*. When the claim is confinement by explicit or implicit threat or duress, factual details are critical. Suppose that in *McCann* the store guards had not mentioned police but had said, "You must wait until our supervisor arrives." Suppose instead that they had said "if you leave, we'll see that you are prosecuted." What if a female employee is surrounded by six burly men who accuse her of theft? You can think of many variations. The central issue is whether the facts show confinement. *(b) Assertion of authority*. Submission to an officer's assertion of arrest under colorable legal authority is sufficient to show confinement. *(c) Duress of goods*. The defendant grabs the plaintiff's pants

from a dressing room and refuses to return them. Plaintiff wishes to leave but doesn't want to leave without her pants. Is this an implicit threat that results in confinement? *See Thorsen v. Kaufmann's Department Stores*, 55 Pa. D. & C.4th 565 (Com. Pl. 2000).

5. **Confinement by contractual requirement.** In *Segal v. First Psychiatric Planners, Inc.*, 864 N.E.2d 574 (Mass. App. Ct. 2007), plaintiff alleged that on her arrival at the hospital she signed an admissions document she could not read due to blurry vision. Plaintiff wanted to leave the day after her admission, but the form she signed required her to stay for three days. On these facts, the court said a colorable false imprisonment claim had been raised.

6. **Asking the police to confine.** The defendant requests a police officer to confine the plaintiff and the officer does so without a warrant or other privilege. The officer is liable. *See Fuerschbach v. Southwest Airlines Co.*, 439 F.3d 1197 (10th Cir. 2006) (upholding liability of officers who participated in a practical joke by staging an arrest of an airline employee). The defendant who instigates or induces an officer to unlawfully detain another may also be subject to liability. *See Hunter v. The Buckle, Inc.*, 488 F. Supp. 2d 1157 (D. Kan. 2007).

7. **Damages.** False imprisonment is a trespassory tort, so the plaintiff can recover damages even if she sustains no actual harm. Actual harm is required, however, to support a claim where the plaintiff was not aware of the confinement at the time it took place. The Restatement supposes a case in which defendant locks a baby in a bank vault with a time lock. The baby is not conscious of confinement but has difficulty breathing and suffers actual harm, so recovery is permitted. RESTATEMENT (SECOND) OF TORTS § 42 & *ill.* 3 (1965).

8. **Privileges.** When an officer of the law improperly arrests a person, the tort is usually called false arrest. The rules requiring confinement are the same, but the officer, and sometimes others, may have defenses. A proper arrest based upon warrant or probable cause is of course not a tort. Privileges and affirmative defenses are considered in Chapter 4.

9. **Duration of privilege.** Even when an arrest and detention are originally justified, the legal justification may "dissipate over time." In such cases the defendant may lose its justification to detain the arrestee. In *State of Maryland v. Dett,* 891 A.2d 1113 (Md. 2006) a woman stopped for a traffic violation was arrested for an outstanding warrant. Shortly thereafter, information suggested that she was not the person for whom the warrant had been issued. However, she was detained for almost four days before she was released. In that circumstance, summary judgment for defendant on the plaintiff's suit for false imprisonment was improper.

§ 4. TORTS TO PROPERTY

Many torts may involve intentional invasions of property interests. One might, for example, be defrauded in a way that causes loss of property. Only three torts, however, involve direct application of force and thus furnish substantial analogy to personal injury cases such as those involved in battery or false imprisonment. These torts are trespass to land, conversion of chattels, and trespass to chattels.

A. TRESPASS TO LAND

1. Intentional entry. Trespass to land usually requires an intentional entry upon land of another. This might be accomplished by personal entry or by intentionally causing an object to enter the land. The right of the landowner extends downward beneath the surface and to at least a reasonable height above ground, so that if one were to dig beneath the surface or fly very close to the ground this would also constitute a trespass. In one situation intentional *entry* is not required. This occurs when one unintentionally enters, as where a car goes out of control without fault, and then refuses to leave. The refusal to leave is now considered a trespass.

2. Intent. The object of intent need not be "to trespass." It is enough that defendant intended to enter the land. Once intent to enter is shown, the defendant does not escape liability merely because the defendant did not intend to harm plaintiff's property. Similarly, it is no defense that defendant reasonably believes that this is the defendant's own land or that there is a right to be there. Is there intent to enter if the defendant does not have a purpose to enter the plaintiff's land but is substantially certain of entry? Plaintiffs in *Amaral v. Cuppels,* 831 N.E.2d 915 (Mass. App. Ct. 2005), occupied newly-constructed homes near the ninth tee of a pre-existing golf course. One plaintiff collected over 1800 golf balls that had landed on her property in a five year period. When the golf course did not resolve the problem, plaintiff sued the golf course owner for trespass, seeking monetary and injunctive relief. The court declared that "the projection of golf balls from the defendant's property onto the plaintiffs' properties constitutes a continuing trespass," because the golf balls deprive plaintiffs of the exclusive possession of their land. The court rejected defendants' argument that plaintiffs had to accept the incursions because they had moved in after the golf course was built. The court wrote, "[t]o the extent that the ordinary use of the defendants' golf course requires land beyond the course boundaries to accommodate the travel of errant shots, it is incumbent on the defendants to acquire either the fee in the additional land itself, or the right to use the additional land for that purpose."

3. Trespass and nuisance. Many trespass cases also raise issues of nuisance. According to a passage in Prosser cited by the *Amaral* court, the distinction between the torts of trespass and nuisance is that "trespass is an invasion of the plaintiff's interest in the exclusive possession of his land, while nuisance is an interference with his use and enjoyment of it. The difference is that between walking across his lawn and establishing a bawdy house next door; between felling a tree across his boundary line and keeping him awake at night with the noise of a rolling mill."

4. Injunction and damages. On remand, the defendant golf course owners in *Amaral* were permanently enjoined from operating their golf course so as to cause golf balls to be cast upon the plaintiffs' property. Damages could also be awarded. The *Amaral* plaintiffs suffered physical harm to property from the trespass, including broken windows and window screens. When physical harm is inflicted, the defendant is liable for damages measured either by the cost of repairing damage or by the diminution in the value of the premises resulting from the tort, depending on circumstances. *See* 1 DAN DOBBS, LAW OF REMEDIES § 5.1 (1993). In *Robert v. Scarlata*, 899 A.2d 666 (Conn. App. Ct. 2006), defendants appropriated a portion of plaintiff's land for their own purposes, against the express wishes of the plaintiff. After five years, defendants removed all of their belongings from the 105–square foot plot, leaving it much as it was before they encroached upon it. The court found that the trespass was temporary and resulted in no permanent harm. Plaintiff was awarded $500 in damages, representing the diminution in value of his land during the period of occupation. However, with trespassory torts, the defendant is liable for damages even if no physical or economic harm is done. Parasitic damages may also be recovered as in any other trespassory tort: the trespasser whose bawdy songs upset the placid home life may be liable for mental distress.

5. Punitive damages without harm. Punitive damages may be awarded if the trespass is deliberate or "malicious." In *Jacque v. Steenberg Homes, Inc.*, 563 N.W.2d 154 (Wis. 1997) the defendant wished to deliver a mobile home by hauling it across the plaintiff's fields. The plaintiff refused permission, but the assistant manager instructed his workers to cut a path and drive it across the plaintiff's land. The jury found no actual damages but awarded $100,000 punitive damages. Courts frequently say that punitive damages cannot be awarded unless the plaintiff first shows actual loss or damages. No such loss was shown in *Jacque,* but the court said that "in the case of intentional trespass to land, the nominal damage award represents the recognition that, although immeasurable in mere dollars, actual harm has occurred." It thus held the punitive award proper.

6. Extended liability. The trespasser is liable for damages inflicted even if he never intended harm and could not foresee it. Suppose the defendant knows he is trespassing on a farm, and throws his cigarette into what appears to be a puddle of water. The "water" is really gasoline leaked from a tractor, and it spreads a fire that burns down the farmer's barn. The extended liability rule makes the trespasser liable for loss of the barn.

7. Limiting extended liability. There are almost certainly limits to this rule. It might not apply fairly to trespassers who reasonably believe they are rightfully on the land, for example. Beyond that, it may be that the extended damages for which the trespasser is liable are those that are somehow related to security of possession. Suppose that while trespassing, the defendant sees the landowner commit murder. He reports the murder and the landowner is convicted and subjected to a life sentence. The extended liability rule does not suggest that the trespasser is liable for the murderer's imprisonment merely because the trespass provided the information essential to conviction. *Cf. Food Lion, Inc. v. Capital Cities/ABC, Inc.*, 194 F.3d 505 (4th Cir. 1999) (trespassing journalists not liable for publishing truth they obtained while trespassing).

8. Hypotheticals.

(a) An unidentified cat perches atop a fence that divides the Plunkett property from the Durfee property. The cat sets up an intolerable caterwauling in the middle of the night and Durfee hurls a shoe at the cat from her side of the line. The cat dodges and continues its serenade, but the shoe falls on Plunkett's property. Do these facts make a prima facie case of trespass?

(b) John Dangle took off from a mountain point in a hang-glider. He passed over Pergolesi's land at a height of 250 feet. Shortly thereafter a shotgun blast from an unidentified source ripped holes in the glider's surfaces and Dangle lost control. He landed safely in Burger's back yard. No damage was done to Burger's property. Is Dangle a trespasser as to either Pergolesi or Burger?

B. CONVERSION OF CHATTELS—TROVER

Dubbs steals Pedrick's watch. This is a conversion and Dubbs is a converter. He has, as it is said, "converted the watch to his own use." In other words, Dubbs has exercised substantial "dominion" over the watch and interfered with Pedrick's ability to control it. In such a case Pedrick can sue for the value of the watch at the time and place of the taking. In the earlier common law the form of action used to redress this conversion was known as *Trover*, and this is the word under which conversion cases are usually indexed even today.

NOTES

1. **Intent.** Conversion is an intentional tort. The defendant must intend to exercise substantial dominion over the chattel. But, as in the case of trespass to land, there is no requirement that the defendant be conscious of wrongdoing. One who takes another's watch in the honest belief that it is the person's own is still a converter if the dominion thus exercised is sufficiently substantial and the act interferes with another's right to exercise control. *See Kelley v. LaForce*, 288 F.3d 1 (1st Cir. 2002) (even if police officers believed they were putting Pub into possession of its rightful owner, they still acted with intent to deprive plaintiff, the rightful owner of the Pub, of possession).

2. **How conversion is accomplished.** In each of the following cases, suppose the defendant reasonably but mistakenly believes he has a right to deal with the property.

(a) Defendant decides to burn his copy of a torts casebook and throws it in the fire. By mistake he got the plaintiff's copy instead.

(b) Defendant restaurant holds a coat checked by A and also one checked by B. By mistake defendant gives B's coat to A, who disappears and is never found. B's coat is far more valuable than A's.

(c) Defendant, honestly believing that Turvey has the right to sell a watch, buys it from him. The watch in fact was stolen from plaintiff.

One of the more difficult issues is what constitutes substantial dominion. It is clear that dominion is exercised in all the above cases, including where the property is damaged by the defendant. But in other cases defendant merely takes the property for a short period of time, as in the case of a joyride. If he takes a car for a joyride and it is destroyed in the process, he is no doubt liable. But suppose he takes it and returns it. Is this a conversion? These facts and many variations on them raise questions of degree which cannot be resolved firmly on principle. The American Law Institute concludes that it is all a matter of how serious the interference is. Since a finding of conversion will mean that the defendant pays the full value of the chattel, the ALI concluded that the interference should be serious enough to justify imposing such liability and that a number of factors were important including:

(a) extent and duration of control;

(b) the defendant's intent to assert a right to the property;

(c) the defendant's good faith;

(d) the harm done; and

(e) expense or inconvenience caused.

See RESTATEMENT (SECOND) OF TORTS § 222A (1965).

3. **New forms of property.** What types of property may be converted? The traditional common law rule was that conversion would lie only for tangible personal property. Thus neither land nor intangible property such as paper money or promissory notes could be converted. The rules today seem more liberal. One can convert shares of stock or bonds and other documents which are strongly identified with the right itself. There are also a number of interesting conversion cases surrounding intellectual property and biotechnology. Is theft of a lucrative domain name conversion? *See Kremen v. Cohen*, 337 F.3d 1024 (9th Cir. 2003) (yes, the plaintiff had a property interest in the sex.com domain name).

What if a doctor takes and without authorization sells or uses the plaintiff's egg or pre-embryo? In *Unruh–Haxton v. Regents of University of California*, 76 Cal.Rptr.3d 146 (Ct. App. 2008), plaintiffs underwent fertility treatments at a clinic owned by the Regents of the University of California. They were given a fertility drug that caused them to produce multiple eggs, which were then harvested for fertilization outside of the women's bodies. The women who underwent the procedure planned to implant the pre-embryos or freeze them for their own later use. However, after the eggs were harvested, some women were told that their eggs were not suitable for fertilization while others were told that the eggs had been fertilized and the resulting pre-embryos frozen. Patients allege that in fact, the doctors sold the eggs for research or implanted the pre-embryos in other women. The court held that the conversion claim survives demurrer. "The allegations of stealing and then selling a person's genetic material for financial gain is an intentional act of egregious abuse against a particularly vulnerable and trusting victim" and one that could be conversion.

Is the sale or use of a patient's blood or blood cells different than the sale or use of a patient's egg or pre-embryo? In a California Supreme Court case, a patient went through a course of treatments by a physician, who withdrew blood or blood cells at least ostensibly in the course of treatment and (a) sold one unit of blood to a blood bank and (b) used another unit to develop a unique line of cells that were commercially valuable for making an important drug. Along with others in the venture, but not with the patient or with the patient's knowledge, the doctor patented the products in order to reap the commercial gains. Is the doctor guilty of conversion anywhere along the line? The California Supreme Court held that the use of blood cells to develop a cell-line as a commercial product was NOT a conversion. The court seemed to say that the patient lacked a property interest in his own body tissues once they were removed, but its main concern was not to hinder development of socially useful medical treatments. *Moore v. Regents of the Univ. of Cal.*, 793 P.2d 479 (Cal. 1990). The court did say, however, that the physician was under a fiduciary duty to disclose some of the facts to the patient. Rejection of the conversion claim probably means that the plaintiff's recovery would not equal the commercial value of the product drawn from his body. The *Unruh* decision made no mention of *Moore*.

4. **Aiding and abetting.** Conversion may be accomplished by aiding and abetting another's conversion. In *Montgomery v. Devoid*, 915 A.2d 270 (Vt. 2006), a son stole $80,000 in cash, giving some to his father, who also stored some vehicles the son had stolen. The Court held that the father might be found liable along with the son.

5. **Serial conversions.** Dubbs steals Pedrick's watch, then sells the watch to Byer. Dubbs is a converter and so is Byer, since both have exercised substantial dominion and have intended to do so. Pedrick could sue either or both, though he could collect only once.

6. **Bona fide purchasers.** Byer in the preceding illustration is liable even if she buys in good faith, that is, even if she is a bona fide purchaser for value and without notice of Pedrick's rights. The theory is that Byer cannot purchase from Dubbs any more than Dubbs has. Dubbs has no title and thus cannot transfer title to Byer.

There is one special wrinkle in this rule. If Dubbs does not steal the watch but tricks Pedrick into selling it to him, then Dubbs *does* get title. Since Dubbs got it by a trick or fraud, Pedrick could go to court and have the sale voided; he could get his watch back because of Dubbs' fraud. However, he is not *required* to do this. He may do nothing at all and keep the money Dubbs paid him. At any rate, until Pederick does go to court, Dubbs has title to the watch. This means that Dubbs could transfer title to someone else, including Byer. In this kind of case Byer would obtain good title and would *not* be a converter if she were a bona fide purchaser for value and without notice of Pedrick's rights. On the other hand, if Byer knew of the fraud practiced on Pedrick, and bought the watch anyway, she would also be a converter, along with Dubbs.

7. **The Uniform Commercial Code.** A comprehensive statute enacted in almost all states regulates many commercial dealings. One provision of the code covers this kind of case: Orwell takes his bike to the Merchant Bike Shop

for repair. The bike shop repairs the bike but before Orwell returns, sells it to Dalzell. Under the rules stated above, Dalzell would be liable, since Merchant had no title to pass. The UCC, however, provides that if goods are entrusted to the possession of a merchant who deals in goods of that kind, the merchant has the legal power to transfer all the rights of the "entrustor." Is Dalzell liable or not? Suppose Orwell had stolen the bike, then taken it to Merchant for repair. Would Dalzell be liable?

8. **Remedies.** The usual remedy for conversion is damages, measured by the value of the chattel at the time of conversion. At times, however, the value of the chattel fluctuates in the market, as in the case of shares of stock or commodities. The plaintiff, who has lost her property, may be forced to replace it in a rising market. If so, the time of conversion rule would be unfair. Some courts have accordingly permitted the plaintiff to recover the highest market value of the chattel that occurs within a reasonable time for replacement. The plaintiff might, instead of seeking value of the chattel, seek "replevin" or "claim and delivery," that is, an actual return of the chattel itself. This might also be possible in some instances through an injunction suit brought in equity.

REFERENCES: *See generally* DOBBS ON TORTS §§ 61–67 (2000); HARPER, JAMES & GRAY, LAW OF TORTS, Chapter 2 (3d ed. 2006).

C. TRESPASS TO CHATTELS

SCHOOL OF VISUAL ARTS v. KUPREWICZ, 771 N.Y.S.2d 804 (N.Y. Sup. Ct. 2003). The defendant, a former employee of the School of Visual Arts, allegedly caused large volumes of pornographic email and unsolicited job applications to be sent to the plaintiff, resulting in depleted hard disk space, drained processing power, and other adverse affects on plaintiff's computer system. The school and its director of human resources brought suit against the defendant for trespass to chattels. In the trial court, *held*—motion to dismiss the trespass to chattels claim denied. "To establish a trespass to chattels, [plaintiff] must prove that Kuprewicz intentionally, and without justification or consent, physically interfered with the use and enjoyment of personal property in [plaintiff]'s possession, and that [plaintiff] was harmed thereby. Thus, one who intentionally interferes with another's chattel is liable only if there results in harm to 'the owner's materially valuable interest in the physical condition, quality, or value of the chattel, or if the owner is deprived of the use of the chattel for a substantial time.' RESTATEMENT (SECOND) OF TORTS § 218, cmt. *e*. Furthermore, to sustain this cause of action, the defendant must act with the intention of interfering with the property or with knowledge that such interference is substantially certain to result.... The Court concludes that accepting these factual allegations as true, SVA has sufficiently stated a cause of action for trespass to chattels, and has alleged facts constituting each element of this claim.... It is important to note that by this decision, the Court does not hold that the mere sending of unsolicited e-mail communications will automatically subject the sender to tort liability. The Court merely concludes that.... accepting [plaintiff]'s factual allegations of damage to its computer systems, the complaint states a valid cause of action for trespass to chattels."

―――――――――

Trespass to chattels involves something short of a conversion. Liability is based on actual damage.

Is there a trespass to chattel, a conversion, or no tort at all in the following cases?

(a) Defendant pets the plaintiff's dog although the plaintiff has repeatedly told him not to do so. The dog is not harmed.

(b) Defendant leans against the plaintiff's car.

(c) Defendant takes the car for a joyride against the plaintiff's will, and puts the dog in the front seat with him.

(d) Defendant, angered at the dog's barking, kicks the dog, then pushes the car over a cliff, causing substantial damages.

Trespass to chattels has traditionally involved the plaintiff's tangible chattel. However, as in *School of Visual Arts,* recent cases have held that clogging a company's email or computer systems with large amounts of unwanted email or other electronic interference can count as a trespass to chattels. *See, e.g., Compuserve Inc. v. Cyber Promotions, Inc.,* 962 F.Supp. 1015 (S.D. Ohio 1997) (unsolicited email and advertisements found to have damaged plaintiff's business reputation and goodwill); *Register.com v. Verio, Inc.,* 356 F.3d 393 (2d Cir. 2004) (defendant's use of a "search robot" that could overtax plaintiff's servers). *Cf. Intel Corp. v. Hamidi*, 71 P.3d 296 (Cal. 2003) (sending spam email not a trespass to chattels where it neither interferes with possessor's use or possession of a legally protected right in the plaintiff's computer system itself).

§ 5. FORCIBLE HARMS AS CIVIL RIGHTS VIOLATIONS

A. THE § 1983 CLAIM

42 U.S.C.A. § 1983

Every person who, under color of any statute, ordinance, regulation, custom, or usage, of any State or Territory or the District of Columbia, subjects, or causes to be subjected, any citizen of the United States or other persons within the jurisdiction thereof to the deprivation of any rights, privileges, or immunities secured by the Constitution and laws, shall be liable to the party injured in an action at law, suit in equity, or other proper proceeding for redress.

NOTES

1. This statute, which was passed by the Congress as one of several civil rights statutes which followed the Civil War, is usually known by its section number in the present code—"1983." The statute was designed to prevent states from denying freed persons the rights given to them by the federal government. However, the statute is not limited to use is race discrimination cases. Section 1983 claims of various kinds make up a substantial portion of the federal court docket.

2. Notice that section 1983 creates a federal cause of action—one governed by federal law. Although the plaintiff may sue in either federal or state court, state courts must follow precedent set by federal courts in interpreting the statute and the rights it protects.

3. What elements must the plaintiff prove to establish the § 1983 action? Try to glean these from the statute itself.

———————

YANG v. HARDIN, 37 F.3d 282 (7th Cir. 1994). The defendants, uniformed Chicago police officers, answered a burglary call from a store owner. One officer (Brown) entered the store to investigate as another (Hardin) filled out a police report by the front door. Yang thought he saw Brown stealing some merchandise and asked him to return it. At first Brown denied wrongdoing, but then reached into his jacket and pulled out a pair of "L.A. Raiders" shorts and threw them at Yang. Officers Brown and Hardin then proceeded to enter their police car to drive away. When Yang followed, Officer Brown shoved Yang. Hardin did nothing in response to Yang's pleas to call the police sergeant. Brown then drove the squad car away with Yang holding on to the driver's side door. Brown drove fast and zigzagged in an attempt to throw Yang off, also striking him repeatedly in the ribs with his left elbow. Throughout the drive, Officer Hardin sat in the passenger seat, doing nothing and saying nothing. After two blocks the car stopped and Yang let go. Brown got out of the car and punched Yang in the face, then did the same to Yang's brother who had run after the car. Hardin then got out of the car, pulled his gun and pointed it at the Yang brothers, shouting obscenities. Officers Hardin and Brown got back in the police car and drove away. In Yang's § 1983 suit, the trial court found against Brown but in favor of Hardin. Held, the judgment for Hardin must be reversed. Hardin's failure to intervene deprived Yang of his liberty rights under the Due Process Clause of the Fourteenth Amendment and his rights under the Fourth Amendment to be free from unreasonable seizure. "An officer who is present and fails to intervene to prevent other law enforcement officers from infringing the constitutional rights of citizens is liable under § 1983 if that officer had reason to know: (1) that excessive force was being used, (2) that a citizen has been unjustifiably arrested, or (3) that any constitutional violation has been committed by a law enforcement official; and the officer had a realistic opportunity to intervene to prevent the harm from occurring."

NOTES

1. **Elements.** A § 1983 tort requires the plaintiff to establish that someone, usually a state or municipal official, acted under color of state law and also that the action deprived the plaintiff of a federal right. Although the federal right involved might be based on some other federal statute, most often it has been based on the federal constitution itself.

2. **Color of law.** This phrase in § 1983 means the exercise of power "possessed by virtue of state law and made possible only because [of] the authority of state law," even where that authority is misused. *West v. Atkins*, 487 U.S. 42 (1988) (doctor hired by state to provide medical services at prison acted under color of law in providing allegedly inadequate treatment). This definition is sufficiently broad to include some acts of off-duty officers. *See, e.g., Memphis, Tenn. Area Local, Am. Postal Workers Union, AFL–CIO v. City of Memphis*, 361 F.3d 898 (6th Cir. 2004) (off-duty police officers hired by private company to harass and threaten union picketers through the use of their status as police officers); *Chapman v. Higbee Co.*, 319 F.3d 825 (6th Cir. 2003) (en banc) (off-duty sheriff, in uniform working as a department store security guard, strip-searched the plaintiff who was suspected of shoplifting). It also includes acts of private persons who conspire with state officials and acts of private persons who willingly participate in a state-enforced "custom or usage" that violates federal rights—segregation, for example. *See Adickes v. Kress & Co.*, 398 U.S. 144 (1970).

3. **Liability of public entities.** The officer (or private person held to be acting under color of state law) who violates the plaintiff's federal rights may be held personally liable. If the officer acts on behalf of a local public entity such as a city, the city may be held as well. However, cities are liable under § 1983 only under special conditions that can be considered later. States—as distinguished from cities and individual officers—are simply not liable under § 1983 at all.

NOTE: INTERNATIONAL CIVIL RIGHTS

Some intentional torts find parallels not only in the statutory civil rights claims but also in international law, which may take the form of "customary international law" or of specific international instruments such as treaties. For instance, victims have recovered both for unlawful detention and for torture inflicted in the Bosnia war. A recent example is *Mehinovic v. Vuckovic,* 198 F. Supp. 2d 1322 (N.D. Ga. 2002).

A federal statute called the Alien Tort Statute, 28 U.S.C. § 1350, gives federal district courts jurisdiction over "all causes where an alien sues for a tort only in violation of the law of nations or a treaty of the United States." In *Sosa v. Alvarez–Machain*, 542 U.S. 692 (2004), the Court held that the statute should apply only to a modest number of causes of action recognized under the "law of nations," such as piracy, offenses against ambassadors, and violations of safe conduct. Thus in the case of a Mexican national detained for a day illegally in Mexico before being transferred to U.S. custody, no norm of international law was violated and no federal cause of action was stated under the ATS. For a more detailed analysis of the ATS, *see* JULIE A. DAVIES & PAUL T. HAYDEN, GLOBAL ISSUES IN TORT LAW Ch. 3 (2008).

B. EXEMPLARS OF CONSTITUTIONAL VIOLATIONS

Three constitutional provisions are most frequently invoked in the physical-attack civil rights cases: (a) The Fourteenth Amendment's due process clause, guaranteeing citizens freedom from the deprivation of rights in life, liberty, and property without due process of law; (b) the Fourth Amendment, guaranteeing citizens freedom from unreasonable searches or seizures; and (c) the Eighth Amendment, prohibiting cruel and unusual punishment. In a § 1983 case, the court focuses on whether the constitutional provision itself was violated, not on whether some common-law tort was committed.

MEALS v. CITY OF MEMPHIS, 493 F.3d 720 (6th Cir. 2007). Officer King was running radar when she saw a car pass at a high rate of speed. She was chasing the car in order to make a traffic stop. The car, driven by John Harris, traveled at a high rate of speed, went through a busy intersection without stopping, headed the wrong way against traffic and crossed a grass median before striking head-on James Harvey Meals and William Meals. William Meals suffered a fractured spine and permanent paraplegia. The city had a pursuit policy that required discontinuation of the pursuit "when there is a clear danger to the pursuing officers or the public." In a civil rights suit against the city and Officer King, the court analyzed the case under the Fourteenth Amendment's due process clause. Pursuant to earlier Supreme Court precedent, abuse of governmental power violates due process rights only when it shocks the conscience. In this context the test means that the officer must have had the intent to injure. There was no evidence of intent to injure in this case. The officer's alleged violation of city policy, even if recklessness, is insufficient to show a due process violation.

ALEXANDER v. DEANGELO, 329 F.3d 912 (7th Cir. 2003). The plaintiff sued police officers who had involved her in a sting operation. Allegedly the officers wished her to pose as a prostitute, offering oral sex to the sting target in return for money. To induce her cooperation, the officers threatened her with arrest and a 40–year prison term, knowing that such a term could never be imposed. She did cooperate in obtaining evidence from the sting target, but then refused to testify and filed a § 1983 suit. Posner, J.: "[S]ex procured by threats that the threatener has no legal right to make is a common form of rape," and rape is a battery. "The liberty protected by [the Fourteenth Amendment due process clause] includes bodily integrity, and is infringed by a serious, as distinct from a nominal or trivial, battery.... [M]ost batteries are too trivial to amount to deprivations of liberty. Rape, however, is not only a battery, but a very serious battery, and a rape committed under color of state law is therefore actionable under 42 U.S.C. § 1983 as a deprivation of liberty without due process of law.''

Notes

1. **Common law torts and § 1983.** (a) Many § 1983 claims also constitute common law torts under state law. It is not uncommon to see § 1983 used to redress claims that appear to be batteries, assaults, and false arrests and imprisonments. There are even § 1983 cases that seem to involve something like conversion and trespass to land.

(b) In most cases, the plaintiff can sue under § 1983 even though she could just as well claim under state tort law. *See Zinermon v. Burch*, 494 U.S. 113 (1990). As a practical matter, plaintiffs often support their claims by pointing both to common law theories like battery and to constitutional torts.

(c) The plaintiff can usually claim both federal rights violations and common law torts in the same suit. That suit can be brought in either federal or state court and in either case both federal and common law theories can be pursued.

2. **Practical value of § 1983.** Why sue under § 1983 rather than for simple common law torts? Reasons may include: (1) A § 1983 claim permits suit in federal court; a state tort claim ordinarily would not. A federal forum might be desirable in some cases because the judge seems more favorable or because the juries are drawn from a wider area and have a different demographic composition. (2) A § 1983 claim permits the prevailing plaintiff to recover reasonable attorney's fees, pursuant to another federal statute, 42 U.S.C. § 1988. (Remember that the rule for ordinary tort cases is usually the opposite, and each person pays his or her own attorney. In tort cases the practice is for the plaintiff's attorney to take a contingent fee, ranging from about one-fourth to one-half of the plaintiff's judgment.) (3) A § 1983 claim might sometimes avoid defenses or immunities that would defeat a common law claim.

3. **Qualified immunity.** One significant barrier to plaintiffs' success in § 1983 actions is that an officer may assert a qualified immunity that protects him from being held liable if his conduct did not violate clearly established statutory or constitutional rights of which a reasonable person would have been aware. *Harlow v. Fitzgerald*, 457 U.S. 800 (1982). Indeed, the court in *Alexander* held that despite the fact that a rape could be actionable under § 1983, the officers involved in the case were immune from liability because "[w]e cannot say that it would have been obvious to the average officer that the deceit involved in this case rose to the level of a constitutional violation."

4. **Corporal punishment as a civil rights violation?** A principal calls a 13-year-old student to his office for disciplinary reasons, then beats him repeatedly with a metal cane. Does the student have a civil rights action

on the ground that this shocks the conscience? *See Kirkland v. Greene County Bd. of Educ.*, 347 F.3d 903 (11th Cir. 2003).

BROWN v. MUHLENBERG TOWNSHIP, 269 F.3d 205 (3rd Cir. 2001). The plaintiffs' pet, a Rottweiler named Immi, wandered into an adjacent parking lot. Police Officer Robert Eberly spotted Immi, approached her as she backed away and then shot her five times. Immi had not displayed any aggressive behavior, and at the time of the shooting, the owner screamed to the officer not to shoot. The Browns claim that Officer Eberly violated their right to be free from unreasonable governmental seizures of property under the Fourth Amendment. Held, Officer Eberly's destruction of Immi could be found to be an unreasonable seizure. Under the Fourth Amendment "[t]he right of the people to be secure in their persons, houses, papers, and effects, against unreasonable searches and seizures, shall not be violated.... The people's 'effects' include their personal property. A Fourth Amendment 'seizure' of personal property occurs when 'there is some meaningful interference with an individual's possessory interests in that property.' Destroying property meaningfully interferes with an individual's possessory interest in that property.... Immi was property protected by the Fourth Amendment and Officer Eberly's destruction of her constituted a Fourth Amendment seizure.... To be constitutionally permissible, then, Officer Eberly's seizure must have been 'reasonable.'.... Where the governmental interest justifying a seizure is sufficiently compelling and the nature and extent of the intrusion occasioned by the seizure is not disproportionate to that interest, the seizure may be reasonable even though effected without a warrant...." Although the state has an interest in restraining stray pets so they don't pose a danger to others, the state may not, consistent with the Fourth Amendment, "destroy a pet when it poses no immediate danger and the owner is looking on, obviously desirous of retaining custody."

GRAHAM v. CONNOR, 490 U.S. 386 (1989). The plaintiff was a diabetic who hurried into a convenience store to purchase orange juice to counteract an insulin reaction he felt coming on. Lines at the counter made him fearful that it would take too long, so he left almost immediately to search elsewhere. A police officer saw him enter and quickly come out. The officer became suspicious and after following the plaintiff for a distance pulled him over. The "sugar reaction" was explained to the officer, but he went to his car to call for backup. Graham got out of his car and ran around it twice, then passed out. Backup arrived, Graham was rolled over on the sidewalk, and his hands were cuffed behind him. Graham came to and asked officers to check his wallet for his diabetes card, but they told him to shut up. After inflicting some other indignities they threw him head-first into the police car and refused to let him have orange juice a friend brought. In the Supreme Court, *held:* (1) The specific provisions of the Fourth Amendment rather than the general concept of due process provides the constitutional standard that governs "a free citizen's claim that law enforcement officials used excessive force in the course of making an arrest, investigatory stop, or other seizure of his person." (2) Subjective tests based on malice or good faith have no application. The test is the one specified in the Fourth Amendment, reasonableness. (3) Reasonableness would be judged objectively, through the eyes of a reasonable person at the scene. This would allow for errors made in emergent circumstances, but would not allow an officer to escape the consequences of unreasonable force merely because he did not act maliciously. Conversely, the officer's evil motives do not make the use of force actionable if it is otherwise reasonable.

NOTE

In *Curley v. Klem*, 298 F.3d 271 (3d Cir. 2002), a police officer had been pursuing a killer-carjacker who was driving a Camry. Klem had a description of the suspect as a tall black man. Klem came upon the Camry, which had crashed at a toll booth. Officer Curley, a black man, was responding to a radio call and was approaching the Camry with gun drawn. Klem shot Curley, thinking he was the killer. If this was excessive force, should it matter to the analysis of Curley's civil rights case that Klem thought he was firing at a dangerous criminal suspect?

HUDSON v. McMILLIAN, 503 U.S. 1 (1992). The plaintiff, a prisoner, claimed that guards beat him in violation of the Constitution's prohibition against cruel and unusual punishment. In the Supreme Court, *held*: (1) Application of unreasonable force to a prisoner does not violate the Eighth Amendment. By its terms, that amendment is violated only by application of cruel or unusual punishment. (2) But the test of liability is not whether the injury was minor or major. Although not every push or shove is actionable, prison officials are liable for sadistic or malicious use of force against inmates regardless of the amount of injury. "Otherwise, the Eighth Amendment would permit any physical punishment, no matter how diabolic or inhuman, inflicting less than some arbitrary quantity of injury." Justice Thomas dissented. He argued that a serious injury is always required in Eighth Amendment cases.

CHAPTER 4

DEFENSES TO INTENTIONAL TORTS—PRIVILEGES

■ ■ ■

The defenses encountered in this chapter are for the most part purely affirmative defenses. That is, the defendant must affirmatively raise these defenses, usually by answer to the complaint, and the *proof* must affirmatively convince the jury that the facts supporting the defense are established. The defendant has the burden of proving affirmative defenses.

§ 1. PROTECTING AGAINST THE APPARENT MISCONDUCT OF THE PLAINTIFF

A. SELF–DEFENSE

1. **Rule.** One is privileged to use reasonable force to defend against harmful or offensive bodily contact and against confinement. Some states have specific legislation which defines the standard for both tort and criminal actions. RESTATEMENT (SECOND) OF TORTS § 70 states that an actor is privileged to use that amount bodily harm or confinement in self-defense which "the actor correctly or reasonably believes to be necessary for his protection." The privilege depends on apparent necessity of self-defense, not on actual reality. Thus if the defendant reasonably, but mistakenly believes she is being attacked, she is privileged to use reasonable force to forestall the attack or minimize its effects.

2. **Reasonable deadly force.** What force is reasonable in self-defense will vary with the facts. Is deadly force never reasonable? The general rule is that the defendant's privilege extends only so far as reasonably necessary to prevent death or serious bodily harm. *See First Midwest Bank v. Denson*, 562 N.E.2d 1256 (Ill. App. Ct. 1990) (upholding jury verdict for sixty-seven-year-old landlord who shot and killed evicted tenant who landlord believed was about to push him down the stairs).

3. **Retreat**. The defendant who is attacked is not required to retreat or otherwise avoid the need for self-defense. When the defendant is threatened with sexual attack, or force likely to cause death or serious

bodily harm, the defendant is privileged to respond with reasonable deadly force. However, some states require reasonable retreat before deadly force is used when the defendant is not at home. *See* RESTATEMENT (SECOND) OF TORTS § 65 (1965); HARPER, JAMES & GRAY, LAW OF TORTS § 3.11 (3d ed. 2007). Others have no such requirement. DOBBS ON TORTS § 71 (2000).

4. **Excessive force.** The privilege covers only reasonable force. Any excessive force is unprivileged and the defendant is liable for it. A defendant who retaliates or continues the "defense" after the fight is over is likewise liable. Sometimes, excessive force is characterized as negligence, allowing the plaintiff to reach the defendant's insurance. Defining excessive force is a matter of degree and depends very much on the facts of each case. Suppose Pearson attacks Doolittle by punching him in the nose. Doolittle, reasonably perceiving that other blows may follow, proceeds to knock Pearson down, straddle his chest, and beat him for five minutes. Is this excessive force? What if Doolittle honestly believes such force is required to subdue Pearson, but his belief is unreasonable—is the excess slapping a battery, or merely a negligent tort?

5. **Provocation.** Provocation is generally not sufficient to raise the self-defense privilege. Insults and arguments, for example, do not justify a physical attack by the insulted defendant. Distinguish acts that create the reasonable appearance of an attack from mere provocation.

6. **Assault and imprisonment in self-defense.** The Restatement specifically recognizes that one may be privileged, given appropriate facts, to commit what otherwise would be an assault or a false imprisonment in self-defense. *See* RESTATEMENT (SECOND) OF TORTS § 67 (1965). One point of special interest is the rule in § 70 of the Second Restatement that the defendant may be privileged to put the plaintiff in apprehension of a harmful or offensive bodily contact even though the contact itself would not be privileged. Would this authorize defendant to point a gun at the plaintiff to forestall a punch in the nose, even though the defendant would not be privileged to fire it?

B. DEFENSE OF THIRD PERSONS

At one time, the privilege to defend third persons was limited to permit only defense of family and servants. This seems to have little support today and in general one may defend others on the same basis that he may defend himself or herself. Suppose defendant sees A striking B. Believing that B is attacked, defendant seizes A and delivers a stunning blow. B then runs off. It turns out that A was a police officer attempting to carry out a lawful arrest which B was resisting. Some courts have held that the defendant is liable for battery to the officer on the ground that the mistake destroys the privilege. Others have held that the privilege covers even this case, as long as the defendant's belief was reasonable. The Restatement (Second) of Torts § 76 has followed this latter view.

C. ARREST AND DETENTION

PETERS v. MENARD, INC.

589 N.W.2d 395 (Wis. 1999)

N. PATRICK CROOKS, J. . . .

On May 5, 1994, Chad Wright, an employee of API [a security company], was working as a plain clothes security guard at Menard's La Crosse, Wisconsin, store. He observed a person he later identified as Brian Peters take a box containing a drill off of a shelf. Wright saw Peters place the box into his shopping cart and push the cart through an exit door located in the carpet department. The door led to Menard's lumber yard, where Wright continued to watch Peters. Peters pushed the cart to a parked truck and placed the drill box into the back seat of the truck's extended cab. He then returned the cart to the store, walked back to the truck, and sat down in the back seat. . . .

Wright walked to the truck and asked to speak with the rear seat passenger, Brian Peters. When Peters got out of the truck, Wright identified himself and asked about the drill. Wright could see the drill box, which appeared to be open, in the truck's back seat. According to the driver of the truck, Wright's tone of voice clearly indicated that he was upset. . . .

Peters denied any knowledge of a stolen drill. . . . Wright eventually requested that Peters take the box and accompany him back into the store to speak with the store manager. At that point, Peters took off running. . . .

Wright ran after Peters, closing within ten feet of Peters at times. . . .

According to Wright, Kind [another API employee] took over the pursuit at that point, and Wright lagged behind. Kind followed Peters onto the bike path, where he chased Peters for about 100 yards. Throughout the chase, both guards shouted "stop" repeatedly at Peters, to no avail. . . .

Wright and Kind terminated their pursuit. According to Kind, the chase had gone on for about seven minutes. Peters continued to run into a flooded marsh area toward the swollen La Crosse River. . . . After a few seconds, however, Wright heard splashing. The guards ran to the flooded area and Wright saw Peters enter the flooded La Crosse River. . . .

In their depositions, both security guards elaborated on their reasons for undertaking the chase in the first place. Wright stated that he pursued Peters in order to identify Peters as the person he observed shoplifting the drill. According to Wright, his purpose was to achieve a detention so that he could "present Peters to a law enforcement officer." In addition, although Wright did not actually observe the drill or its box on Peters' person, he thought that the box he observed in the truck had been opened and expressed concern that Peters may try to discard the drill during the chase. . . .

Unfortunately, the fast-moving current swept Peters back to the river's middle, where he went underwater. . . .

[Peters' estate and family brought suit against the defendants for Peters' death.]

We begin by addressing the certified question [from the court of appeals]: whether a merchant or its agents are immune from liability under Wis. Stat. § 943.50(3) for actions taken while attempting to detain a suspected shoplifter by pursuing him or her off of the merchant's premises.

The plain language of Wis. Stat. § 943.50(3) allows "[a] merchant, a merchant's adult employee or a merchant's security agent who has reasonable cause for believing that a person has violated this section in his or her presence" to "detain the person in a reasonable manner for a reasonable length of time to deliver the person to a peace officer. . . ." [and it] provides immunity from civil or criminal liability to "[a]ny merchant, merchant's adult employee or merchant's security agent who acts in good faith in any act authorized under this section." It is clear from this language that immunity from liability for detaining a person exists only when three "reasonableness" requirements are met. These requirements are: (1) there must be reasonable cause to believe that the person violated § 943.50; (2) the manner of the detention and the actions taken in an attempt to detain must be reasonable; and (3) the length of time of the detention and the actions taken in an attempt to detain must be reasonable. . . .

[W]hen the legislature enacts a statute, it is presumed to do so with full knowledge of the existing law. Section 120A of the Restatement (Second) of Torts existed when Wis. Stat. § 943.50 was enacted in 1969. Section 120A provides:

> One who reasonably believes that another has tortiously taken a chattel upon his premises, or has failed to make due cash payment for a chattel purchased or services rendered there, is privileged, without arresting the other, to detain him on the premises for the time necessary for a reasonable investigation of the facts.

Restatement (Second) of Torts § 120A (1964). There is a caveat to § 120A, which reads, "The Institute expresses no opinion as to whether there may be circumstances under which this privilege may extend to the detention of one who has left the premises but is in their immediate vicinity." There is also a comment on the caveat, part of which states, "[T]he Caveat is intended to leave open the question whether the privilege extends to the detention of one who has left the premises but is still in their immediate vicinity, as, for example, where the person suspected has gone out of the door of a shop, and is half-way across the sidewalk on the way to his [or her] car."

Although § 120A of the Restatement contains language expressly restricting merchants to detentions "on the premises," Wis. Stat. § 943.50(3) contains no such phrase.... The legislature's conspicuous omission from § 943.50(3) of the Restatement's "on the premises" language plainly suggests that the legislature intended to allow merchants to follow suspected shoplifters off of the store's premises in order to detain them....

We agree that the common law permitted the pursuit in this case, provided that the three "reasonableness" requirements of the statute were met.

Finally, public policy supports a construction of "detain" which would include pursuit.... A decision by this court denying immunity under Wis. Stat. § 943.50(3) to merchants or their agents who pursue suspected shoplifters while attempting to detain them would have at least two adverse effects on society. First, it would strip merchants of much of their ability to recover shoplifted merchandise and apprehend shoplifters. Shoplifting is a widespread societal problem. A failure to catch shoplifters would likely result in merchants raising their prices to make up for increased losses of stolen goods. Second, shoplifters, knowing that merchants could not pursue them, would be encouraged to dash out of stores with their stolen loot as fast as their legs could carry them. The potential would increase for injuries to innocent shoppers caused by fleeing shoplifters. Indeed, this court has already encountered a case involving a store customer who was injured when a fleeing shoplifter collided with her. In short, a ruling by this court that "detain" does not include pursuit would invite shoplifters to flee and increase the risk of harm to merchants and innocent customers. This court will not adopt a ruling which would create such an undesirable risk.... We hold that Wis. Stat. § 943.50(3) provides immunity to a merchant or its agents for actions taken while attempting to detain a person, including pursuit, as long as the statute's three "reasonableness" requirements are met....

[The court would have left determinations of the three reasonableness requirements for decision at trial, but it concluded that a separate statute barred recovery here because the decedent's own conduct was more unreasonable than the store's.]

NOTES

1. **Statutes and common law privilege.** Many states have statutes similar to the Wisconsin statute. The common law also recognized a privilege to arrest or detain, but the common law privilege was narrower. Police officers were privileged to make an arrest under a warrant that appears to be authorized and also where they had "probable cause" to believe that a felony has been committed by the arrested person. A private person also often had a privilege to make an arrest for felonies that were in fact committed under some circumstances. But the private person had no privilege to arrest for misdemeanors (minor crimes) unless the misdemeanor was committed in his

presence or the misdemeanor was a breach of the peace. These common law rules are summarized in Restatement (Second) of Torts §§ 112–139 (1965). Shoplifting items of minor cost, as in *Peters*, would be a misdemeanor only. These rules left a gap covered by the statutes and also covered, as an extension of the older common law, by Restatement § 120A, quoted in *Peters*.

2. **The policy of a broad privilege to detain.** What type of reasoning did the *Peters* court use to justify its holding that permits pursuit beyond the premises? Is this reasoning persuasive?

3. **Rules v. standards.** Under Wisconsin law, a flexible reasonableness standard is used to determine whether a merchant can detain a person off premises. Is it better to have a flexible reasonableness standard than a fixed rule that says storekeepers can pursue shoplifters "on the premises" or "within 50 feet of the premises?" Under Wisconsin's standard, would it have been reasonable for security to pursue the shoplifter so far? Should the judge or the jury decide this question?

4. **Mistake.** What if a shopkeeper suspects a patron of theft and detains the patron for investigation, but then learns that his suspicions were incorrect? In *Great Atlantic & Pacific Tea Co. v. Paul*, 261 A.2d 731 (Md. 1970), an assistant store manager detained a shopper based on a suspicion that the shopper had concealed a can of tick spray in his coat. An ensuing investigation revealed that the shopper did not have any unpurchased items. Held, the shopkeeper is liable for false imprisonment. Maryland had not adopted the Restatement's right to detain, but had a common law privilege to detain a person believed to have tortiously taken property. However, "[t]his common law right is exercised at the shopkeeper's peril... and if the person detained does not unlawfully have any of the arrester's property in his possession, the arrester is liable for false imprisonment." Would a mistaken shopkeeper have enjoyed better protection under the Restatement? According to the court, even if Maryland had adopted the Restatement's right to a reasonable detention in light of a reasonable belief that property had been taken, the merchant's claim might have fallen short of the Restatement provisions. The shopkeeper might not have been reasonable in the belief that property had been taken, and the shopkeeper's manner and method of the detention might not have been "necessary for a reasonable investigation of the facts."

5. **Reporting crime.** A person who induces another to confine the plaintiff may be held liable for the false imprisonment, but people are privileged to report suspected crime to appropriate authorities so long as they act in good faith and make no knowing, "malicious," or false statements. *See Holcomb v. Walter's Dimmick Petroleum,* Inc., 858 N.E.2d 103 (Ind. 2006); *Highfill v. Hale,* 186 S.W.3d 277 (Mo. 2006).

D. DEFENSE AND REPOSSESSION OF PROPERTY

KATKO v. BRINEY
183 N.W.2d 657 (Iowa 1971)

Moore, Chief Justice.

[Defendant Bertha Briney inherited an unoccupied farm house. For ten years there were a series of housebreaking events, with damage to this property. She and her husband boarded up the windows and posted no trespass signs and eventually they set up a shotgun trap in one of the rooms. The gun was rigged to an old iron bed, barrel pointed at the door. A wire ran from the doorknob to the trigger. It was pointed to hit the legs of an intruder. Mr. Briney admitted he was "mad and tired of being tormented," but said he did not intend to injure anyone. There was no warning of the gun. The plaintiff and one McDonough had been to the house before. They were looking for old bottles and jars. They broke into the house, and plaintiff started to enter the bedroom. The shotgun went off, and much of his right leg, including part of the tibia, was blown away. He spent 40 days in the hospital. The jury found for the plaintiff in the sum of $20,000 actual damages and $10,000 punitive damages.] ...

Plaintiff testified he knew he had no right to break and enter the house with intent to steal bottles and fruit jars therefrom. He further testified he had entered a plea of guilty to larceny in the nighttime of property of less than $20 value from a private building. He stated he had been fined $50 and costs and paroled during good behavior from a 60–day jail sentence. . . .

The main thrust of defendants' defense in the trial court and on this appeal is that "the law permits use of a spring gun in a dwelling or warehouse for the purpose of preventing the unlawful entry of a burglar or thief." . . .

Instruction 6 stated: "An owner of premises is prohibited from willfully or intentionally injuring a trespasser by means of force that either takes life or inflicts great bodily injury; and therefore a person owning a premise is prohibited from setting out 'spring guns' and like dangerous devices which will likely take life or inflict great bodily injury, for the purpose of harming trespassers. The fact that the trespasser may be acting in violation of the law does not change the rule. The only time when such conduct of setting a 'spring gun' or a like dangerous device is justified would be when the trespasser was committing a felony of violence or a felony punishable by death, or where the trespasser was endangering human life by his act."

The overwhelming weight of authority, both textbook and case law, supports the trial court's statement of the applicable principles of law.

Restatement of Torts, section 85, page 180, states: "The value of human life and limb, not only to the individual concerned but also to society, so outweighs the interest of a possessor of land in excluding from it those whom he is not willing to admit thereto that a possessor of land has ... no privilege to use force intended or likely to cause death or serious harm against another whom the possessor sees about to enter his premises or meddle with his chattel, unless the intrusion threatens death or serious bodily harm to the occupiers or users of the premises. . . . A possessor of land cannot do indirectly and by a mechanical device that which, were he present, he could not do immediately and in person." . . .

Affirmed.

NOTES

1. **Home invasion.** Would the case have been different if the trespasser had been entering the defendants' dwelling while the defendant was at home? *See Graves v. Trudell*, 765 N.Y.S.2d 104 (App. Div. 2003).

2. **Warnings and other barriers.** Would you favor a rule that permitted spring guns if there were a large, clear warning sign? How about electrified fences or trained attack dogs? In deciding how to structure a rule on this subject, should you consider the possibility that a child or a police officer with a warrant might enter and be killed or grievously wounded if deadly force were permissible?

3. **Defense of property versus crime prevention.** Some states have legislation that protects against criminal and civil liability when an individual is using force, even deadly force, to prevent specific, enumerated crimes. For example, crime prevention defense statutes in both Texas and Arizona shield a defendant from liability when the defendant uses deadly force to prevent burglary, among other crimes. *See* TEX. CIV. PRAC. & REM. CODE ANN. § 83.001 (West 2008); TEX. PENAL CODE ANN. § 9.42 (West 2008); ARIZ. REV. STAT. §§ 13–411 & 13–413 (2008). For a discussion of the tension between crime prevention statutes and traditional defense of property defenses, *see State v. Thomason*, 783 P.2d 809 (Ariz. Ct. App. 1989).

———————

BROWN v. MARTINEZ, 361 P.2d 152 (N.M. 1961). Plaintiff, a 15-year-old boy, and two other boys visited the defendant's garden patch for the purpose of stealing watermelons. On the next night, the boys returned to the defendant's farm for the same purpose. Hearing the boys in the patch, defendant came out of his house with a rifle, and called to the boys to get out. Seeing two boys running toward the southwest corner of the property, defendant fired the gun toward the southeast to scare them. However, plaintiff was in the southeast corner of the property and the bullet struck him in the back of the left leg. The trial court dismissed the plaintiff's claim. *Held*, reversed and remanded for a determination of damages. "Our examination of the authorities convinces us that the question of the reasonableness of resort to firearms to prevent a trespass or to prevent commission of an unlawful act not amounting to a felony is one of law for the court, and that such conduct is not excusable.

Dean Prosser in his Handbook of the Law of Torts, states the rule thus:

> "The reasonableness of the force used is usually a question of fact for the jury. But as in the case of self-defense, the law has marked out certain limitations. The force used must be of a kind appropriate to the defense of the property. A push in the right direction may be proper where a slap in the face is not. *And, since the law has always placed a higher value upon human safety than upon mere rights in*

property, it is the accepted rule that there is no privilege to use any force calculated to cause death or serious bodily injury where only the property is threatened. The defendant may use the force reasonably necessary to overcome resistance and expel the intruder, and if in the process his own safety is threatened, he may defend himself, and even kill if necessary but in the first instance a mere trespass does not justify such an act.'' (Emphasis ours.)

There is no suggestion in the proof here that appellee in any way felt his safety was threatened. Accordingly, under the facts as proven and found, the appellee acted improperly and is liable for injuries caused in using a gun in the manner he did, and with such unfortunate consequences, in order to drive away trespassers on his property, or to protect his watermelons, or to scare the intruders.''

NOTES

1. **Was the defendant's act privileged?** Did the defendant perform any unprivileged act? Does the law of transferred intent help the plaintiff here?

2. **Recapture of chattels.** Defending possession is one thing; using force to regain possession is something else. If a thief runs out of a store with a valuable electronic calculator, the store detective is privileged to recapture it if he does so immediately or in hot pursuit. Once possession has been lost, however, the detective cannot forcibly recapture it from the thief a week later. The store instead will be forced to sue or to invoke criminal processes. Why is this the rule? Perhaps the case of *Auto Owners Insurance Co. v. Grier*, 593 S.E.2d 804 (N.C. 2004), provides a clue. Grier was a laundromat and car wash owner who had money and keys taken by Fields. Grier chased Fields but did not catch him. He then got in his van in an attempt to bring Fields to the police. Spotting Fields walking alongside a street, "Grier pulled his gun, jumped out of his van, grabbed Fields by the jacket and told him he was taking Fields back to [the store] to await the police.'' Grier held his gun on Fields as police were called. Fields struggled and Grier fired his gun, striking Fields in the hand and leg. In Fields' suit against him, Grier claimed self-defense. But the court rejected this defense since the amount of force used was unreasonable, and since Grier was the one who escalated the violence. The court concluded that he should have called the police. Would a defense of repossession of chattels have worked any better than the defense of self-defense?

3. **Repossession of consumer goods.** Similarly, one cannot use force in the repossession of consumer goods such as automobiles, even though the buyer is in default. The car seller may repossess the car from the defaulting buyer only if he can do so peaceably; indeed, the buyer may defend his possession with reasonable force.

4. **Repossession of land.** Many courts, operating under statutes, invoke similar rules when the owner of land has lost or given up possession: he must seek recovery in the courts, not by use of force, even by the use of reasonable force. The cases are divided, however, and some permit the owner

with right to possession to use force, limited always to reasonable force. *See* DOBBS ON TORTS § 80 (2000).

E. DISCIPLINE

Some states refuse to permit children to sue their parents for torts. *See* Chapter 14. Where children are permitted to sue parents, parents still enjoy a privilege to discipline, and to use force and confinement to do so. The limits of this force are ill-defined. The Restatement says parents may use reasonable force as they reasonably believe necessary. *See* RESTATEMENT (SECOND) OF TORTS § 147 (1965).

People who are in charge of a child not their own also enjoy a similar privilege. Teachers and school bus drivers are the most obvious examples. However, it may be that the teacher would not enjoy the same latitude for punishment that courts would recognize in a parent. Suppose a child is spanked by her parent for misbehavior and again by her teacher for additional misbehavior. Apart from local school board regulations affecting corporal punishment, what factors should a court consider in determining whether either the parent or the teacher is liable in tort?

What if "to calm him down" a teacher holds down on the floor a twelve-year-old child who has Asperger's syndrome? What if an 8-year-old with attention deficit disorder and mild mental retardation is repeatedly locked in a "seclusion room" by herself when she misbehaves at school? Some false imprisonment lawsuits have arisen from those sorts of teacher responses.

REFERENCES: DOBBS ON TORTS §§ 93–94 (2000); HARPER, JAMES & GRAY, LAW OF TORTS § 3.20 (3d ed. 2006).

F. OBSERVING PRIVILEGES

Many common law privileges have the effect of resolving the issues in the case into matters of reasonableness and degree. In self-defense, the issue is frequently whether the defendant reasonably believed that defense was necessary and then whether he used the amount of force reasonable to cope with the apparent threat. In the case of schoolroom punishment, teachers, being privileged to inflict some punishment, are liable only if they go too far. In false imprisonment cases a defendant might be privileged to detain for investigation for a short time, but not for long. All such cases involve matters of reasonableness and hence matters of degree.

Notice how those cases differ from cases in which a defendant commits a "kissing battery"—he kissed the plaintiff, a stranger, or touched the plaintiff in a private place. This is an offensive battery and it is no defense to say the touching did not last long, that the force used was minimal, or that the injury was not great. Thus in common law actions, there are cases in which "degree" is not important, and other cases in which, because the issue of privilege is injected, degree becomes quite significant.

§ 2. THE SPECIAL CASE OF CONSENT

Austin cooked a continental dinner for a new acquaintance, Berwyn, served in candlelight and accompanied by excellent French wines. After dinner the couple sat on the sofa listening to *Traviata* and sipping Benedictine and Brandy. The moment came, as it must in every scene of this sort, in which Austin drew closer and with parted lips looked in Berwyn's eyes. A kiss was imparted and Austin's hand caressed Berwyn's neck. Suddenly, to the surprise of everyone, there was a snap as a vertebra in Berwyn's neck broke.

This vignette illustrates several problems about the surprisingly complex "defense" of consent, but also suggests some common sense answers to some of those problems.

1. Berwyn testified: "I never consented to be touched at all, and in fact I was revolted at the idea." If the trier of fact believes this testimony, does it show there was no consent?

2. Was there anything to show there *was* consent?

3. Berwyn's lawyer argued to the trial judge: "Berwyn certainly did not consent to a broken vertebra even if there was consent to a kiss." What do you think of this argument?

4. Is consent really a "defense"? What practical matter would turn on the answer to this?

5. Common sense answers to these questions should suggest several legal principles. Could you state them?

NOTE: RELATIONSHIP OF THE PARTIES

In real cases lawyers would want to know a great deal more about the facts. Would it impact the analysis if Berwyn had kissed Austin on the cheek when Austin arrived? What if Berwyn had kissed Austin on the lips? What if Berwyn worked for Austin and was told that the dinner was a meeting to discuss a potential promotion? Specific facts like these might be relevant to the issue of apparent consent. Maybe Austin can take it that consent is given by silence in some relationships but not in others. Maybe in some cases a person has no capacity to consent and the actor knows it. Suppose you are sedated and while sedated give "consent" to an operation. If the doctor knows you are heavily sedated should the doctor believe you have manifested consent? There may be some situations in which the power relationships between the parties affect the issue of consent.

———

ROBINS v. HARRIS, 769 N.E.2d 586 (Ind. 2002). As described by the appellate court in *Robins v. Harris,* 740 N.E.2d 914, 917 (Ind. Ct. App.

2000), plaintiff Tammy Robins was a female inmate at a county jail and defendant Michael Soules was a new corrections officer on the third shift. According to Soules, when he met Robins she and another inmate, Martha Custer, flashed him by lifting up their shirts and exposing their breasts. Later that evening, Soules ordered a lock down, requiring all inmates to stay in their cells. Soules first summoned Custer out of her cell and upon her return then summoned Robins. He grabbed Robins by the arm and brought her into the shower room where she performed fellatio on him. Robins filed suit, alleging battery. Soules originally denied the allegations but two days later admitted to the sexual contact and resigned his position. He subsequently pled guilty to misdemeanor official misconduct in exchange for dismissal of a felony charge. In the tort action, Soules claimed he was not liable and raised an affirmative defense of consent. The court of appeals held that several parties were potentially subject to liability and that the inmate's alleged consent to the sexual contact was no defense. In the Indiana Supreme Court, "affirmed except as to the availability of the consent defense to the claim of battery," on which point the majority issued no opinion.

Sullivan, J. dissenting: "[T]he Court of Appeals said: 'We also note that consent is not available has a defense to Robins's sexual assault claim. Under I.C. § 35–44–1–5(b), a [jailer] may not claim consent as a defense for sexual misconduct with a detainee. Given Robins's general lack of autonomy as an inmate, it would be incongruous to withhold the defense of consent in the criminal context but to allow Soules the defense in a civil claim.' I agree with this analysis. Our Legislature has made a public policy determination that the position of authority a jailer holds over a prisoner dictates that there be no exception for consent in our criminal law to the rule against sexual contact between jailer and prisoner. Our state's civil law should further the public policy objective the Legislature has adopted in the criminal context."

NOTES

1. **Power relationships.** Should consent be an available defense when the relationship between the plaintiff and the defendant is inherently unequal as in the situation of jailer and prisoner? What about relationships that involve lesser power imbalances? For example, some state statutes forbid all sexual contact between mental health professionals and their patients. Under these statutes, the patient's consent is not legally effective to bar a claim against the therapist. What of a relationship between a pastor and parishioner? *See Wende C. v. United Methodist Church*, 827 N.E.2d 265 (N.Y. 2005).

2. **Employers.** What about duress? Should employers be permitted to claim that an employee who is dependent for a job, wage increase, or promotion, consented to sexual intercourse? *See Reavis v. Slominski*, 551 N.W.2d 528 (Neb. 1996) (claim against employer based on sexual contact after an office New Year's eve party). Federal statutes against employment discrimination forbid sexual harassment of employees. Employer conduct might count

as a violation of those statutes, which are usually considered in advanced courses. You should be aware, however, that the damages awards under those statutes may be less attractive to the plaintiff in some instances than the common law awards. In addition, when plaintiffs sue under those statutes, an issue similar to the consent issue might be raised: courts would ask whether the employer's advances were "welcome" or not.

3. **Capacity to consent: minors.** State legislatures and the common law recognize that minors present special circumstances to be considered in a defense based on consent. Although courts are split, it is generally assumed that minors may consent to a number of touchings appropriate to their age. Probably two eight-year-olds can effectively consent to a football game in which touching is inevitable. Older minors can consent to more serious touchings, such as routine medical attention. The hospital emergency room that administers first aid to a 16-year-old with a broken arm is presumably protected from any claim of battery if the teenager consents. But there are cases that do raise special problems in the consent of minors.

4. **Consent to major surgery.** There are few cases involving a minor's consent to major surgery that do not involve an urgent need. Suppose a 17-year-old asks a doctor to perform cosmetic surgery on his nose. Should the right to consent or refuse consent lie with his parents? What if the operation is a risky one that could cause death or serious debility?

5. **Consent to abortion.** The Supreme Court has held that states may not regulate a woman's right to control her own body, and that this means she is free to have at least certain abortions without restriction. *See Roe v. Wade*, 410 U.S. 113 (1973). This right extends even to minor women, so that the states are not free to prescribe a blanket restriction of abortions to consenting minors. *Planned Parenthood of Central Missouri v. Danforth,* 428 U.S. 52 (1976). However, states can require notification to parents of a proposed abortion, but must leave room for a minor's abortion when the minor is fully capable of consenting and also when an abortion is needed because of the minor's life or health. *See Ayotte v. Planned Parenthood of Northern New England*, 546 U.S. 320 (2006). Some states have codified a minor's right to consent to medical treatment of STD's, abortion and family planning services. *See* HAW. REV. STAT. § 577A–2 (2008).

6. **Consent to intercourse.** Do minors have the requisite capacity to consent to sexual contact? Many states impose criminal liability for sexual conduct with a minor; the minor's consent is ineffective and provides no defense. Should the minor's consent also be an ineffective defense in a tort context? *Compare Christensen v. Royal Sch. Dist. No. 160*, 124 P.3d 283 (Wash. 2005) (yes, a child cannot meaningfully consent to sexual contact) and *Bjerke v. Johnson,* 742 N.W.2d 660 (Minn. 2007) (child's consent to sexual contact no bar to child's tort claim) *with Cynthia M. v. Rodney E.*, 279 Cal.Rptr. 94 (Ct. App. 1991) (no, a minor should not be allowed to consent to an illegal act and then collect damages for it). Should it matter to the availability of the consent defense whether the minor's consent was given to a same-aged peer or to the minor's much-older teacher? Should it matter what the actual age of the consenting child is? *See C.C.H. v. Philadelphia Phillies, Inc.*, 940 A.2d 336 (Pa. 2008) (holding in the case of an 11-year-old child, that

consent of a child to intercourse was not a defense for tort purposes below the age of 13).

  7. **Incapacity to consent: adults.** Incapacity of an adult is usually established only by showing that the adult could not manage his own affairs, or, in consent cases, that he did not understand the nature and character of the act. In *Saucier ex rel. Mallory v. McDonald's Rests. of Mont., Inc.*, 179 P.3d 481 (Mont. 2008), an employee who was mentally retarded engaged in a sexual relationship with her manager at McDonald's for nearly two months. In a suit against McDonald's and the manager, a neuropsychologist opined that "while [plaintiff] has the ability to seek out or reject sexual advances, she possesses an "extremely limited capacity" to appreciate the consequences attendant to a sexual relationship." The Montana Supreme Court held that a genuine issue of material fact remained as to plaintiff's ability to consent. Summary judgment on the battery claim was denied.

  ASHCRAFT v. KING, 278 Cal.Rptr. 900 (Ct. App. 1991). In 1983, a 16-year-old woman consented to an operation on the condition that any blood transfusions required would be made only from family-donated blood. The family donated blood for this purpose, but this blood was not used. Instead, the transfusions used blood from the general supplies on hand at the hospital. The blood was infected with HIV and after the operation the patient tested positive for AIDS. The reasons for the patient's insistence on family-donated blood were not clear. *Held,* the patient states a claim for battery, since the transfusions exceeded the consent given.

NOTE: EXCEEDING THE SCOPE
OF CONDITIONAL CONSENT

  Many cases of "medical battery" involve allegations that the doctor exceeded the scope of the patient's consent. For example, in *Duncan v. Scottsdale Medical Imaging, Ltd.*, 70 P.3d 435 (Ariz. 2003), a patient who was about to get a magnetic resonance imaging (MRI) exam from the defendant needed a painkiller as part of that procedure. Duncan, the patient, allegedly told the nurse that she would accept only demerol or morphine, and the nurse assured her that only one of those particular drugs would be administered. On the day of the MRI, however, another nurse informed Duncan that she would be receiving a synthetic drug that was similar to demerol and morphine. Duncan objected strenuously and urged the nurse to call her doctor. After the nurse assured her "that the medication had been changed to morphine" Duncan finally agreed to the procedure. In fact, Duncan was injected with the synthetic drug, and suffered serious complications including vocal cord dysfunction, vomiting, severe headache, and post-traumatic stress syndrome. Duncan sued for battery. Held, Duncan's "general authorization of an injection does not defeat her battery claim because her consent was limited to certain drugs.... The relevant inquiry here is not whether the patient consented to an injection; the issue is whether the patient consented to receive the specific drug that was administered." The scope of consent issue is not limited to medical situations. *See Peters v. Rome City School District*, 747 N.Y.S.2d 867 (N.Y.A.D. 2002) (addressing parental consent to put a learning-disabled second grader in a time-out room at school when the parents were unaware of the poor conditions and small size of the room).

KENNEDY v. PARROTT, 90 S.E.2d 754 (N.C. 1956). The plaintiff consented to an appendectomy by the defendant, Dr. Parrott. During the operation, the doctor found some enlarged cysts on her left ovary and punctured them. After the operation, the plaintiff developed phlebitis in her leg. She sued the doctor for battery on the theory that the phlebitis was proximately caused by the unauthorized extension of the appendectomy. She testified that Dr. Parrott told her that while he was puncturing the cysts, he had cut a blood vessel, causing her to develop blood clots. The trial judge entered a nonsuit for the defendant at the conclusion of the plaintiff's testimony. *Held*, affirmed. "[Some] courts, though adhering to the fetish of consent, express or implied, realize that 'The law should encourage self-reliant surgeons to whom patients may safely entrust their bodies, and not men who may be tempted to shirk from duty for fear of a lawsuit.'

"In major internal operations, both the patient and the surgeon know that the exact condition of the patient cannot be finally and definitely diagnosed until after the patient is completely anesthetized and the incision has been made. In such case the consent—in the absence of proof to the contrary—will be construed as general in nature and the surgeon may extend the operation to remedy any abnormal or diseased condition in the area of the original incision whenever he, in the exercise of his sound professional judgment, determines that correct surgical procedure dictates and requires such extension of the operation originally contemplated. This rule applies when the patient is at the time incapable of giving consent, and no one with authority to consent for him is immediately available."

NOTES

1. **Emergencies.** The ordinary rule—that it is battery when a doctor treats a patient without the patient's consent, or in excess of the scope of a patient's consent—may not apply when the doctor must act in an emergency and obtaining consent is not possible. In *Miller v. HCA, Inc.*, 118 S.W.3d 758 (Tex. 2003), parents sued doctors for battery when the doctors resuscitated their premature infant without their consent. The child would die without immediate treatment. Should a battery claim lie on those facts?

2. **Is *Kennedy v. Parrott* correct?** What if the doctor knew or should have known that cysts were often found on such occasions, but did not mention this to the patient ahead of time? At times a surgeon may seek the

patient's general consent to additional procedures. In *Hoofnel v. Segal*, 199 S.W.3d 147 (Ky. 2006), a patient had signed a general consent form which consented to the removal of her ovaries and left the physician free to perform all medically necessary procedures. However, the patient had previously denied consent to removal of her uterus. What result when the surgeon removed the patient's uterus? Courts often say that the specific controls the general. However, in this case the general consent protected the surgeon because the unwanted removal of the uterus was medically necessary to complete the very operation to which the plaintiff had consented. What if the plaintiff consented to an operation by Dr. A, but it was performed by Dr. B? *See Vitale v. Henchey*, 24 S.W.3d 651 (Ky. 2000) and *Meyers v. Epstein*, 232 F. Supp. 2d 192 (S.D.N.Y. 2002) (holding that a surgeon who operates without explicit consent commits a battery).

3. **Substituted consent.** In a *Kennedy* situation to what extent should hospital personnel try to obtain the consent of relatives? What if an adult patient, preparing for an operation, signs a form saying he refuses to accept a blood transfusion for religious reasons. Once on the operating table, the doctor believes he needs a transfusion and calls the patient's mother for permission, which she grants. When sued by the patient for battery, the doctor claims that the patient had once said he would "consider" a transfusion. Can we say that this patient impliedly consented to substituted consent by his mother? *See Harvey v. Strickland*, 566 S.E.2d 529 (S.C. 2002) said it is a jury question. Could a parent effectively consent to a medical experiment to be performed upon her child when the child is healthy and will derive no health benefit from the experiment? *See Grimes v. Kennedy Krieger Institute, Inc.*, 782 A.2d 807 (Md. 2001).

4. **Standards for substituted consent.** Substituted consent is almost a sub-specialty in itself. When someone is appointed as guardian for a person who is incompetent or unable to give or withhold consent, should the guardian make the decision (a) in the best interests of the patient or (b) on the basis of what the patient herself would do if she were competent?

5. **Incompetence to give or withhold consent.** What if a person is intoxicated at the time of emergency treatment—should the doctor be required to obtain consent? In *Miller v. Rhode Island Hospital*, 625 A.2d 778 (R.I. 1993) the plaintiff had consumed many, many drinks before he was in an automobile collision. The trauma team at the emergency room, fearing internal bleeding, insisted on performing a peritoneal lavage. When plaintiff objected, doctors strapped him to a gurney, anesthetized him and performed the lavage. The plaintiff sued for battery. The court thought that competence to consent (or refuse consent) should be measured by the plaintiff's ability to understand the condition, nature and effect of the proposed treatment or its rejection. When the plaintiff was unable to understand the nature of the treatment due to his intoxication, doctors could dispense with the consent requirement.

DOE v. JOHNSON, 817 F.Supp. 1382 (W.D. Mich. 1993). Plaintiff Jane Doe alleged: Earvin Johnson, Jr. transmitted human immunodeficiency virus (HIV) to her through consensual sexual contact. Johnson knew or should have known that he had a high risk of being infected with HIV because of his promiscuous lifestyle. Nevertheless, he did not warn Doe of this high risk or inform her that he did in fact have HIV. Nor did he use a condom. Doe suffers from HIV now and will develop AIDS. On motion to dismiss the battery claim, *held*, motion denied. One who knows he has a venereal disease and knows that his sexual partner does not know of his infection, commits a battery by having sexual intercourse.

NOTES

1. **STDs.** Where the defendant knows he has a sexually transmitted disease but neither warns his sexual partner nor provides any protection, several cases have imposed liability. *E.g., Hogan v. Tavzel,* 660 So.2d 350 (Fla. Dist. Ct. App. 1995) (genital warts not revealed). What if the defendant neither knows nor has reason to know that he is infected with a sexually-transmitted disease, and infects his partner. Does the partner's consent to intercourse bar a battery claim? *See, e.g., McPherson v. McPherson,* 712 A.2d 1043 (Me. 1998). In *Doe v. Johnson,* can you say that the defendant had the intent to touch in a harmful or offensive way? Remember to distinguish intent from negligence. Is it relevant that Johnson claimed to have had unprotected sex with more than 2,000 partners?

2. **Consent procured by fraud.** Courts recognize that, in a general way, consent procured by fraud is no consent at all. The nurse's misrepresentation to the patient in *Duncan v. Scottsdale Medical Imaging, Ltd.,* 70 P.3d 435 (Ariz. 2003), discussed above, was yet another reason why the consent was held invalid in that case. Do you see how the outcome in *Doe v. Johnson* could be characterized as consent procured by fraud? If induced by false information, consent may not be valid even if one voluntarily participates in the touching. *See Hackett v. Fulton County Sch. Dist.,* 238 F. Supp. 2d 1330 (N.D. Ga. 2002) (rejecting defendant's consent claim on the basis that consent was obtained under fraudulent circumstances when high school teacher invited students to participate in a "college scholarship program," which was a ruse for sexual abuse).

3. **Avoiding the effect of consent.** If the plaintiff manifests consent only because plaintiff relies upon the defendant's misrepresentation or simply mistaken facts, can we say that the consent is always nullified and the plaintiff is always permitted to recover? No. *See Taylor v. Johnston,* 985 P.2d 460 (Alaska 1999). To avoid the effect of a manifested consent, the plaintiff's mistake must be "about the nature and quality of the invasion intended by the conduct." Prosser & Keeton § 18. Mistakes or misrepresentations about collateral matters such as price or timing do not nullify the consent. *See* DOBBS ON TORTS § 100 (2000).

4. **Consent to crime.** A and B agree to have an illegal boxing match. Each is injured. Some courts have said that the consent to illegal acts is ineffective. Under this rule, A and B could sue each other for battery, on the

ground that one cannot consent to a crime. On the other hand, when it seemed to suit their purposes, courts readily switched to the rule that no one can found a cause of action on an illegal act. Under this view, courts would sometimes bar the victim who participated in crime. *E.g., Castronovo v. Murawsky*, 120 N.E.2d 871 (Ill. App. Ct. 1954) (victim died, allegedly as the result of illegal and wholly negligent abortion, no recovery).

The Restatement rejects any flat view that consent is ineffective; it provides that consent IS generally effective and neither A nor B is liable to the other. In spite of this general rule, however, the Restatement also takes the position that a statute might make some act a crime for the very reason that the victims all too often are induced to consent by pressures against which the legislature wishes to protect, and that in such a case the expression of consent is ineffective. Suppose a statute makes it unlawful to hire a child under 15 for work near industrial machinery. Should the child's consent be a bar? What about consent to take illegal drugs? To incest? *See* RESTATEMENT (SECOND) OF TORTS § 892C (1979).

5. **Revocation of consent.** Subject only to the slightest qualification, the plaintiff can revoke consent at any time by communicating the revocation to the defendant. *See* DOBBS ON TORTS § 104 (2000).

———————

PROBLEM

Payton v. Donner

Lisa Payton suffered from an abscessed tooth. Before the source of her pain was discovered, doctors prescribed painkiller drugs. She gradually became addicted. When supplies dried up from normal medical sources she found Dr. William Donner, a medical doctor in his seventies, who was willing to prescribe for her claimed "pain." He also provided her ordinary medical treatment, referring her to a specialist on one occasion and ordering X-rays on another. After providing the drugs to Payton for many months, Donner forced her to admit that she was addicted. Thereafter, he refused to give her the drugs unless she would engage in sexual touchings. Although she resisted this for a while, she was unable to find other sources and eventually agreed to the exchange of sexual contact for the drugs.

A police investigation eventually broke up this arrangement. Payton underwent treatment for her addiction and is now drug-free. However, she suffers remorse and shame. She would have been free of her addiction sooner if Donner had properly referred her to a rehabilitation center. She may have medical expenses resulting from her addiction and from her relationship with Dr. Donner.

You represent Lisa Payton. Can you establish a prima facie case based on materials covered so far in the course? You can forecast that Donner will attempt to defend on the ground of consent. Do you think you can mount an argument based on legal rules or policies to overcome that defense?

§ 3. PRIVILEGES NOT BASED ON PLAINTIFF'S CONDUCT

The "privileges" seen so far have been grounded largely in the plaintiff's conduct or apparent conduct. We now see privileges created by courts for reasons of policy.

1. *Arrests and searches.* As you would expect, officers are privileged to enter land to execute a search or arrest warrant. But they are not privileged to invite the news media to cover their heroics, *see Wilson v. Layne,* 526 U.S. 603, (1999) (sustaining claim for civil rights violation). And, except in Florida, the news media have no independent privilege to enter to cover news in the absence of the landowner's consent. *See* DOBBS ON TORTS § 96 (2000).

2. *Public rights.* A user of a public utility or common carrier has the "privilege" to enter appropriate portions of the premises; in other words, the utility cannot deny the right of the public generally to patronize it. *See* RESTATEMENT (SECOND) OF TORTS § 191 (1965). This much was common law. Since the 1960s federal and some state statutes, known as public accommodations laws, have required that places open generally to the public cannot exclude would-be patrons on the basis of such considerations as race or gender. *See* 42 U.S.C.A. § 2000a. This might be expressed by saying not only that one has a right to patronize, say, a restaurant, but also that one is privileged to enter for that purpose and cannot be held as a trespasser. Another privilege of this kind is the privilege to enter land to reclaim goods of one's own, as for example, goods washed up on the plaintiff's land. Finally, very limited authority supports a privilege to exercise free speech rights by entering shopping center malls open to the public and campaigning on public issues there. *See Robins v. Pruneyard Shopping Ctr.,* 592 P.2d 341 (Cal. 1979).

3. *Necessity.* Perhaps the most interesting privileges are those of public and private necessity.

SUROCCO v. GEARY

3 Cal. 69 (1853)

MURRAY, CHIEF JUSTICE, delivered the opinion of the Court.

This was an action, commenced in the court below, to recover damages for blowing up and destroying the plaintiffs' house and property, during the fire of the 24th of December, 1849.

Geary, at that time Alcalde of San Francisco, justified, on the ground that he had the authority, by virtue of his office, to destroy said building, and also that it had been blown up by him to stop the progress of the conflagration then raging.

It was in proof, that the fire passed over and burned beyond the building of the plaintiffs', and that at the time said building was destroyed, they were engaged in removing their property, and could, had they not been prevented, have succeeded in removing more, if not all of their goods.

The cause was tried by the court sitting as a jury, and a verdict rendered for the plaintiffs, from which the defendant prosecutes this appeal under the Practice Act of 1850.

The only question for our consideration is, whether the person who tears down or destroys the house of another, in good faith, and under apparent necessity, during the time of a conflagration, for the purpose of saving the buildings adjacent, and stopping its progress, can be held personally liable in an action by the owner of the property destroyed....

The right to destroy property, to prevent the spread of a conflagration, has been traced to the highest law of necessity, and the natural rights of man, independent of society or civil government. "It is referred by moralists and jurists to the same great principle which justifies the exclusive appropriation of a plank in a shipwreck, though the life of another be sacrificed; with the throwing overboard goods in a tempest, for the safety of a vessel; with the trespassing upon the lands of another, to escape death by an enemy. It rests upon the maxim, Necessitas inducit privilegium quod jura privata."

The common law adopts the principles of the natural law, and places the justification of an act otherwise tortious precisely on the same ground of necessity.

This principle has been familiarly recognized by the books from the time of the saltpetre case, and the instances of tearing down houses to prevent a conflagration, or to raise bulwarks for the defense of a city, are made use of as illustrations, rather than as abstract cases, in which its exercise is permitted. At such times, the individual rights of property give way to the higher laws of impending necessity.

A house on fire, or those in its immediate vicinity, which serve to communicate the flames, becomes a nuisance, which it is lawful to abate, and the private rights of the individual yield to the considerations of general convenience, and the interests of society. Were it otherwise, one stubborn person might involve a whole city in ruin, by refusing to allow the destruction of a building which would cut off the flames and check the progress of the fire, and that, too, when it was perfectly evident that his building must be consumed....

The counsel for the respondent has asked, who is to judge of the necessity of the destruction of property?

This must, in some instances, be a difficult matter to determine. The necessity of blowing up a house may not exist, or be as apparent to the owner, whose judgment is clouded by interests, and the hope of saving his property, as to others. In all such cases the conduct of the individual must be regulated by his own judgment as to the exigencies of the case. If a building should be torn down without apparent or actual necessity, the parties concerned would undoubtedly be liable in an action of trespass. But in every case the necessity must be clearly shown. It is true, many cases of hardship may grow out of this rule, and property may often in such cases be destroyed, without necessity, by irresponsible persons, but this difficulty would not be obviated by making the parties responsible in every case, whether the necessity existed or not.

The legislature of the State possess the power to regulate this subject by providing the manner in which buildings may be destroyed, and the mode in which compensation shall be made; and it is to be hoped that something will be done to obviate the difficulty, and prevent the happening of such events as those supposed by the respondent's counsel.

In the absence of any legislation on the subject, we are compelled to fall back upon the rules of the common law.

The evidence in this case clearly establishes the fact, that the blowing up of the house was necessary, as it would have been consumed had it been left standing. The plaintiffs cannot recover for the value of the goods which they might have saved; they were as much subject to the necessities of the occasion as the house in which they were situate; and if in such cases a party was held liable, it would too frequently happen, that the delay caused by the removal of the goods would render the destruction of the house useless.

The court below clearly erred as to the law applicable to the facts of this case. The testimony will not warrant a verdict against the defendant.

Judgment reversed.

WEGNER v. MILWAUKEE MUTUAL INS. CO., 479 N.W.2d 38 (Minn. 1991). Two suspected felons were believed to be selling narcotics at a certain location. The police staked out the address, but the felons spotted police and fled in their cars. The felons then abandoned their car, separated and fled on foot. One suspect entered the house of Harriet G. Wegner and hid in the front closet. Wegner's granddaughter and her fiancé fled the premises and notified the police. A police "SWAT" team surrounded the house and, a few hours later, fired 25 rounds of chemical munitions or "tear gas" into the house. The tear gas broke virtually every window in the house. In addition, police cast three "flash-bang" grenades into the house to confuse the suspect. The police then entered the home and apprehended him. The tear gas and flash-bang grenades caused extensive damage to the Wegner house. Wegner sued the City of Minneapolis to recover damages. In conjunction with a trespass claim against the City, Wegner asserted that the police department's actions constituted a compensable taking under Minn. Const. art. I, § 13. The lower courts held that any "taking" of property was justified and non-compensable under the doctrine of public necessity. *Held*, reversed and remanded for a calculation of damages.

"The Restatement (Second) of Torts § 196 describes the doctrine [of necessity] as follows: One is privileged to enter land in the possession of another if it is, or if the actor reasonably believes it to be, necessary for the purpose of averting an imminent public disaster.... We are not inclined to allow the city to defend its actions on the grounds of public necessity under the facts of this case. We believe the better rule, in situations where an innocent third party's property is taken, damaged or destroyed by the police in the course of apprehending a suspect, is for the municipality to compensate the innocent party for the resulting damages. The policy considerations in this case center around the basic notions of fairness and justice. At its most basic level, the issue is whether it is fair to allocate the entire risk of loss to an innocent homeowner for the good of the public. We do not believe the imposition of such a burden on the innocent citizens of this state would square with the underlying principles of our system of justice. Therefore, the City must reimburse Wegner for the losses sustained." The takings clause in the Minnesota Constitution, which provides that "Private property shall not be taken, destroyed or damaged for public use without just compensation, first paid or secured," requires compensation because "capturing a dangerous suspect was for a public use within the meaning of the [Minnesota] constitution."

NOTES

1. **Public benefit.** The central idea of justice behind the constitutional provisions is that individuals should not be forced to bear public burdens alone. If the public benefits from a burden it imposes upon others, it should pay. *See Armstrong v. United States*, 364 U.S. 40 (1960). Similar ideas have been advanced to justify imposing tort liability upon government.

2. **Who pays as a policy matter?** If it is right to say that the government should be required to pay when it forces an individual citizen to produce a benefit for the public, is the principle rightly applied in *Wegner*? In *Customer Co. v. City of Sacramento*, 895 P.2d 900 (Cal. 1995) the California Court, on facts somewhat like those in *Wegner,* held that the city was not liable for damage done by police in apprehending an armed suspect, saying that compensation was required only with taking of property for public improvements, such as highways or parks. Some other states have followed this analysis, holding that police destruction or seizure of property is not a constitutional "taking." *See, e.g., Eggleston v. Pierce County*, 64 P.3d 618 (Wash. 2003); *Kelley v. Story County Sheriff*, 611 N.W.2d 475 (Iowa 2000); *Sullivant v. City of Oklahoma City*, 940 P.2d 220 (Okla. 1997). As a matter of principle, which view is preferable, that the public should pay for the benefits it receives at the expense of individuals? Or that the public should not pay?

3. **Scope of principle.** How far would the *Wegner* principle go? Suppose the government forces all children to be vaccinated. This is for the good of everyone and the only way to stop disease. However, in rare cases the vaccinated child will suffer a serious reaction that may cause brain damage or even death even though no one is at fault. If a child is injured in such a case, should she be permitted to recover from the government on the ground that

the government exacted a benefit for society as a whole by forcing the child to accept the risks of the vaccination? In *Lapierre v. Attorney–General of Quebec*, 16 D.L.R.4th 554 (Can. 1985) the court rejected the claim that the government should be liable for injuries from compulsory vaccination. Distinguish: (a) government intentionally imposes harm, as in *Wegner*; (b) government intentionally imposes a *risk* that is not substantially certain to injure any particular or identifiable persons.

4. **Insurance.** Compare *Wegner* to *Surocco*. Might *Surocco* be justified today on the ground that fire insurance is commonly purchased by all landowners and that it is a cheap and efficient way of dealing with the loss by fire? Why might that be cheaper than torts suits?

PLOOF v. PUTNAM, 71 A. 188 (Vt. 1908). The defendant owned an island in Lake Champlain. The plaintiff, with his wife and two children, were sailing a sloop on the lake when a violent tempest arose. To avoid destruction of the sloop and injury to himself and his family, the plaintiff moored the boat at the defendant's dock. The defendant, through his servant, unmoored the boat. The sloop and its contents were destroyed and the people in it injured. The plaintiff claimed that unmooring the sloop was a trespass to it and that the defendant had a duty to permit the sloop to remain moored there. *Held,* for the plaintiff. "There are many cases in the books which hold that necessity . . . will justify entries upon land and interferences with personal property that would otherwise have been trespasses. . . . If one have a way over the land of another for his beasts to pass, and the beasts, being properly driven, feed the grass by morsels in passing, or run out of the way and are promptly pursued and brought back, trespass will not lie. A traveler on a highway who finds it obstructed from a sudden and temporary cause may pass upon the adjoining land without becoming a trespasser because of the necessity. An entry upon land to save goods which are in danger of being lost or destroyed by water or fire is not a trespass. . . . One may sacrifice the personal property of another to save his life or the lives of his fellows. . . . It is clear that an entry upon the land of another may be justified by necessity for mooring the sloop."

VINCENT v. LAKE ERIE TRANSPORTATION CO.
124 N.W. 221 (Minn. 1910)

O'BRIEN, J. The steamship Reynolds, owned by the defendant, was for the purpose of discharging her cargo on November 27, 1905, moored to plaintiff's dock in Duluth. While the unloading of the boat was taking place a storm from the northeast developed, which at about 10 o'clock P.M., when the unloading was completed, had so grown in violence that the wind was then moving at 50 miles per hour and continued to increase during the night. There is some evidence that one, and perhaps two, boats were able to enter the harbor that night, but it is plain that navigation was practically suspended from the hour mentioned until the morning of the 29th when the storm abated, and during that time no master would have been justified in attempting to navigate his vessel, if he could avoid doing so. After the discharge of the cargo the Reynolds signaled for a tug to tow her from the dock, but none could be obtained because of the severity of the storm. If the lines holding the ship to the dock had been cast off, she would doubtless have drifted away; but, instead, the lines were kept fast, and as soon as one parted or chafed it was replaced, sometimes with a larger one. The vessel lay upon the outside of the dock, her bow to the east, the wind and waves striking her starboard quarter with such force that she was constantly being lifted and thrown against the dock, resulting in its damage as found by the jury, to the amount of $500.

We are satisfied that the character of the storm was such that it would have been highly imprudent for the master of the Reynolds to have attempted to leave the dock or to have permitted his vessel to drift away from it.... Nothing more was demanded of them than ordinary prudence and care, and the record in this case fully sustains the contention of the appellant that, in holding the vessel fast to the dock, those in charge of her exercised good judgment and prudent seamanship....

The appellant contends by ample assignments of error that, because its conduct during the storm was rendered necessary by prudence and good seamanship under conditions over which it had no control, it cannot be held liable for any injury resulting to the property of others, and claims that the jury should have been so instructed. An analysis of the charge given by the trial court is not necessary, as in our opinion the only question for the jury was the amount of damages which the plaintiffs were entitled to recover, and no complaint is made upon that score.

The situation was one in which the ordinary rules regulating property rights were suspended by forces beyond human control, and if, without the direct intervention of some act by the one sought to be held liable the property of another was injured, such injury must be attributed to the act of God, and not to the wrongful act of the person sought to be charged. If during the storm the Reynolds had entered the harbor, and while there had become disabled and been thrown against the plaintiffs' dock, the plaintiffs could not have recovered. Again, if while attempting to hold fast to the dock the lines had parted, without any negligence, and the vessel carried against some other boat or dock in the harbor, there would be no liability upon her owner. But here those in charge of the vessel deliberately and by their direct efforts held her in such a position that the damage to the dock resulted, and, having thus preserved the ship at the expense of the dock, it seems to us that her owners are responsible to the dock owners to the extent of the injury inflicted....

In Ploof v. Putnam, 71 Atl. 188, the Supreme Court of Vermont held that where, under stress of weather, a vessel was without permission moored to a private dock at an island in Lake Champlain owned by the defendant, the plaintiff was not guilty of trespass, and that the defendant was responsible in damages because his representative upon the island unmoored the vessel, permitting it to drift upon the shore, with resultant injuries to it. If, in that case, the vessel had been permitted to remain, and the dock had suffered an injury, we believe the shipowner would have been held liable for the injury done.

Theologians hold that a starving man may, without moral guilt, take what is necessary to sustain life; but it could hardly be said that the obligation would not be upon such person to pay the value of the property so taken when he became able to do so. And so public necessity, in times of war or peace, may require the taking of private property for public purposes; but under our system of jurisprudence compensation must be made.

Let us imagine in this case that for the better mooring of the vessel those in charge of her had appropriated a valuable cable lying upon the dock. No matter how justifiable such appropriation might have been, it would not be claimed that, because of the overwhelming necessity of the situation, the owner of the cable could not recover its value.

This is not a case where life or property was menaced by any object or thing belonging to the plaintiff, the destruction of which became necessary to prevent the threatened disaster. Nor is it a case where, because of the act of God, or unavoidable accident, the infliction of the injury was beyond the control of the defendant, but is one where the defendant prudently and advisedly availed itself of the plaintiffs' property for the purpose of preserving its own more valuable property and the plaintiffs are entitled to compensation for the injury done.

Order affirmed.

LEWIS, J. I dissent. . . . In my judgment, if the boat was lawfully in position at the time the storm broke, and the master could not, in the exercise of due care, have left that position without subjecting his vessel to the hazards of the storm, then the damage to the dock, caused by the pounding of the boat, was the result of an inevitable accident. . . .

I am of the opinion that one who constructs a dock to the navigable line of waters, and enters into contractual relations with the owner of a vessel to moor at the same, takes the risk of damage to his dock by a boat caught there by a storm, which event could not have been avoided in the exercise of due care, and further, that the legal status of the parties in such a case is not changed by renewal of cables to keep the boat from being cast adrift at the mercy of the tempest.

NOTES

1. **The role of fault.** Is *Vincent* contrary to *Van Camp v. McAfoos*? After all, the court here recognizes that the captain was not at fault, yet liability is imposed.

2. **Necessity to take a life?** The driver of a school bus with twenty children on board is coming down a mountain road. On her left is a sheer

precipice. On her right is solid rock. As the bus picks up speed, a car coming up the hill traveling very fast appears in the bus' lane. It is now clear that the driver must act. If she stays where she is, a collision will ensue. If she turns left, she will take the children over the cliff. She can turn right before gaining any more speed, but if she does so she will certainly strike two children waiting at the bus stop. This would kill the two children or seriously maim them, but it will probably save most of those on the bus. On the rationale of *Vincent* would the driver be liable for the deaths of the two children? Professor George Christie, in *The Defense of Necessity Considered from the Legal and Moral Points of View*, 48 DUKE L.J. 975 (1999), analyzes the positions of a number of philosophers. He himself thinks that an intentional killing to save a greater number of lives is not privileged.

3. **Contractual rights.** Presumably the shipowner and dock owner made some consensual arrangement about the use of the dock. If the shipowner had the right to continued use of the dock under that arrangement, can it be said that by renewing the lines he took any benefit he was not entitled to?

4. **An economic perspective.** Does it matter whether courts adopt a legal rule that requires a boat owner to pay for damage to the dock or a rule that does not require such payment? It might not matter to whether the parties achieve an efficient allocation of resources. In his 1960 article entitled, *The Problem of Social Cost*, 3 J. OF LAW AND ECON. 1, Ronald Coase explained why. Parties can bargain around the legal rule in order to reach an efficient allocation of resources, regardless of the court-determined legal rule. Imagine for example that the boat is worth $500. If it goes out in the storm its full value will be lost. If it stays tethered to the dock, it will cause $1000 of damage to the dock. Given those damage estimates, the efficient allocation of resources would be to forgo the value of the boat rather than cause greater injury to the dock. Of course, the parties will reach this efficient result— letting the boat go—if the boat owner has to pay for damage done to the dock. In that scenario, the owner would face the choice of incurring a $500 loss or a $1000 loss, and would let the boat go in order to incur the lesser loss. However, if the boat owner does not have to pay for the damage to the dock, might the owner chose a $1000 loss to the dock owner rather than a $500 cost of the boat owner's own? Perhaps not. Given the opportunity to bargain, the dock owner could pay the boat owner an amount of money between $500 and $1000 to let the boat go and both parties would be better off. At times, however, the legal rule may indeed matter to whether the parties reach the efficient result. When barriers to bargaining are high, such as significant transaction and information costs, the parties may not be able to bargain effectively. In addition, the legal rule may matter a great deal to the parties themselves. The distribution of legal entitlements will affect the distribution of wealth between them. Under the rule that requires the boat owner to pay for damage, the owner will have a $500 loss from letting the boat go. If the boat owner is not required to pay for damage, the boat owner will at worst have no loss, and at best have a gain of $500.

REFERENCES: DOBBS ON TORTS §§ 107–109 (2000); HARPER, JAMES & GRAY, LAW OF TORTS § 1.22 (3d Ed. 2006).

TOPIC B

THE SCHEME OF NEGLIGENT WRONGS

■ ■ ■

SUBTOPIC 1. THE PRIMA FACIE CASE FOR NEGLIGENCE

CHAPTER 5

DUTY

■ ■ ■

SUBCHAPTER A. THE FAULT BASIS OF LIABILITY

§ 1. NEGLIGENCE AND FAULT

OLIVER W. HOLMES, THE COMMON LAW

(1881 Howe ed. 1963 pp. 76–78)

The general principle of our law is that loss from accident must lie where it falls, and this principle is not affected by the fact that a human being is the instrument of misfortune. But relatively to a given human being anything is accident which he could not fairly have been expected to contemplate as possible, and therefore to avoid. In the language of the late Chief Justice Nelson of New York: "No case or principle can be found, or if found can be maintained, subjecting an individual to liability for an act done without fault on his part.... All the cases concede that an injury arising from inevitable accident, or, which in law or reason is the same thing, from an act that ordinary human care and foresight are unable to guard against, is but the misfortune of the sufferer, and lays no foundation for legal responsibility." ...

A man need not, it is true, do this or that act,—the term act implies a choice,—but he must act somehow. Furthermore, the public generally profits by individual activity. As action cannot be avoided, and tends to the public good, there is obviously no policy in throwing the hazard of what is at once desirable and inevitable upon the actor.

The state might conceivably make itself a mutual insurance company against accidents, and distribute the burden of its citizens' mishaps among its members. There might be a pension for paralytics, and state aid for those who suffered in person or estate from tempest or wild beasts. As between individuals it might adopt the mutual insurance principle *pro tanto*, and divide damages when both were in fault, as in the *rusticum judicium* of the admiralty, or it might throw all loss upon the actor irrespective of fault. The state does none of these things, however, and the prevailing view is that its cumbrous and expensive machinery ought not to be set in motion unless some clear benefit is to be derived from disturbing the status quo. State interference is an evil, where it cannot be shown to be a good. Universal insurance, if desired, can be better and more cheaply accomplished by private enterprise. The undertaking to redistribute losses simply on the ground that they resulted from the defendant's act would not only be open to these objections, but, as it is hoped the preceding discussion has shown, to the still graver one of offending the sense of justice. Unless my act is of a nature to threaten others, unless under the circumstances a prudent man would have foreseen the possibility of harm, it is no more justifiable to make me indemnify my neighbor against the consequences, than to make me do the same thing if I had fallen upon him in a fit, or to compel me to insure him against lightning.

§ 2. INSTITUTIONS AND ELEMENTS OF NEGLIGENCE

A. SOME INSTITUTIONS OF NEGLIGENCE PRACTICE

Intentional torts were defined in highly structured ways. In effect, the law of intentional torts prohibited specific acts like intentional touchings or intentional confinement of another person. The tort broadly called negligence is not defined by naming specific forbidden acts. Instead, negligence may be any conduct that creates an unreasonable risk of harm to others. It is actionable as a tort when that risk comes to fruition in actual harm. Before we explore the detailed meanings of negligence, we must recognize several important legal institutions or problems that condition negligence law. These are in no sense merely a general background; they are practices we must have in mind when we try to understand what it really means to impose liability for negligence.

1. Litigation finance—the attorney fee. As we know from Chapter 1, each party must pay his or her own attorney. This has led to the contingent fee, under which the plaintiff may retain an attorney without payment of any fee unless the plaintiff wins the case. If the plaintiff wins, the attorney will share in the recovery, usually between 25% to 50%. In large time-consuming cases, large awards for pain and suffering or for punitive damages are required if an attorney is to take the case, for otherwise the attorney won't be paid enough to make the case economically feasible.

2. Liability insurance. Although liability insurance for automobiles may be compulsory, the policy limit—the sum available to pay for injuries—is likely to be too low to cover serious injury.

3. The role of settlement. The number of personal injury trials is small. However, the number of personal injuries is large. The volume of routine negligence claims in, say, auto accidents, is vast. Almost all injury claims are settled without trial. To come up with a reasonable estimate of a case's settlement value, lawyers for each side must determine what facts will be proved if the case goes to court and what legal rules will affect the outcome. Accordingly, lawyers must know the rules and also how they are likely to be applied in court. Although lawyers approach the cases as adversaries, they must make neutral, balanced judgments about how the case will appear to the judge and jury. The lawyer who relies on a rule that represents injustice or bad policy may find that the judge will reject the rule or that the jury will find a way not to apply it. Accordingly, lawyers and students must make careful evaluation of the rules announced in cases.

B. ASSESSING RESPONSIBILITY

So far as tort law is built on fault such as negligence, it clearly attempts to assess responsibility for one's actions. On closer inspection, assessing fault turns out to be a difficult, time-consuming, and expensive task. Assessing legal responsibility requires the consideration of a number of important matters, including:

1. Fault. Intentionally harming another person is surely fault. But what is negligence? What about intentionally driving a car at 70 m.p.h.? Should we examine motives, states of mind, or merely external conduct? What if the defendant is in a hurry? Or does not understand the risk?

2. Causation. A person who causes no harm is not legally responsible, no matter how bad his act. Imagine that defendant drives 90 m.p.h., but does not strike anyone. Plaintiff is offended, but not harmed. This will not suffice in the case of negligence, since actual damages is an element of the plaintiff's case.

3. Fixing the scope of responsibility. A person is not legally responsible for every harm that occurs because of his negligence, though the rule might be otherwise with intentional torts. Suppose Jim, who has promised to babysit at 7:00 p.m., is negligent in coming late. The parents, concluding that Jim would soon be there, leave the child alone. While the child is alone, he burns himself. Jim is undoubtedly negligent and responsible for something. In a sense he has caused the harm, since if he had not been late, the child would not have been burned. The law may well decide, however, that the injury was not within the scope of Jim's responsibility.

4. A duty to take responsibility. In many instances it will be possible to find that a defendant has failed to behave reasonably, that his conduct has caused harm, and that the harm caused is the very kind that was risked by his negligent conduct. Yet not every problem is the defendant's responsibility. Suppose you know your neighbor fails to watch his toddler and consequently that there is a risk the child will run into the street and be injured. You *could* watch the child when you are not busy, but perhaps you should be free to decide that for yourself. If so, we will say you are under no duty to the child, even if a reasonable person would have tried to avoid injury to him.

C. LEGAL ELEMENTS OF A NEGLIGENCE CLAIM

Drawing on the important considerations just discussed, courts have developed a general formula for the negligence claim. To receive compensation, the plaintiff must allege and prove facts establishing five elements:

(1) The defendant owed the plaintiff a legal duty;

(2) The defendant, by behaving negligently, breached that duty;

(3) The plaintiff suffered actual damage;

(4) The defendant's negligence was an actual cause of this damage; and

(5) The defendant's negligence was a "proximate cause" of this damage.

Different courts may state these required elements in slightly different ways, but the differences are matters of style, not substance. All courts require the plaintiff to sustain the burden of proving each of the five elements. All courts also agree that if the plaintiff fails to meet the burden of proving any one of them, the plaintiff cannot recover. In the following materials, we explore each of these elements in turn.

SUBCHAPTER B. DUTY AND BREACH
§ 3. THE GENERAL DUTY OF CARE: THE PRUDENT PERSON STANDARD

The duty owed by all people generally—the standard of care they owe—is to exercise the care that would be exercised by a reasonable and prudent person under the same or similar circumstances to avoid or minimize risks of harm to others. Since no one tries to avoid risks that cannot be identified or harms that cannot be foreseen as a possibility, the reasonable person exercises care only about the kinds of harm that are foreseeable to reasonable people and risks that are sufficiently great to require precaution.—DOBBS ON TORTS § 117 (2000).

STEWART v. MOTTS

654 A.2d 535 (Pa. 1995)

MONTEMURO, JUSTICE. . . .

The sole issue presented before us is whether there exists a higher standard of "extraordinary care" for the use of dangerous instrumentalities over and above the standard of "reasonable care" such that the trial court erred for failing to give an instruction to the jury that the Appellee should have used a "high degree of care" in handling gasoline. Because we believe that there is but one standard of care, the standard of "reasonable care," we affirm.

The pertinent facts of this case are simple and were ably stated by the trial court:

On July 15, 1987, Plaintiff, Jonathon Stewart, stopped at Defendant, Martin Motts' auto repair shop and offered assistance to the Defendant in repairing an automobile fuel tank. In an effort to start and move the car with the gasoline tank unattached, the Plaintiff suggested and then proceeded to pour gasoline into the carburetor. The Defendant was to turn the ignition key at a given moment. While the exact sequence of events was contested, the tragic result was that the car backfired, caused an explosion and resulted in Plaintiff suffering severe burns to his upper body.

[In Stewart's suit against Motts, the plaintiff asked the judge to instruct the jury in part "that gasoline due to its inflammability, is a very dangerous substance if not properly handled. . . . With an appreciation of such danger, and under conditions where its existence reasonably should have been known, there follows a high degree of care which circumscribes the conduct of everyone about the danger. . . ." The judge refused to so instruct and the jury returned a verdict for the defendant.]

We begin our discussion by reaffirming the principle that there is but one standard of care to be applied to negligence actions involving dangerous instrumentalities in this Commonwealth. This standard of care is "reasonable care" as well stated in the Restatement (Second) of Torts: "The care required is always reasonable care. The standard never varies, but the care which it is reasonable to require of the actor varies with the danger involved in his act and is proportionate to it. The greater the danger, the greater the care which must be exercised. . . ." Restatement (Second) of Torts § 298 comment b (1965). . . .

Properly read, our cases involving dangerous agencies reaffirm these well accepted principles found in the Restatement. In *Konchar v. Cebular*, 333 Pa. 499, 3 A.2d 913 (1939) . . . we recognized that the question of the plaintiff's contributory negligence was to be determined using the reasonable care standard in light of the particular circumstances of the case. One such circumstance, we acknowledged, was that gasoline, a dangerous substance, was involved requiring that the reasonably prudent person exercise a higher degree of care under these circumstances. Taken in context, our statement that the plaintiff was under a "high duty of care" did nothing more than reaffirm the general principle that the care employed by a reasonable man must be proportionate to the danger of the activity.

[The court reviewed other cases and concluded:] We do not believe that these cases created a heightened or extraordinary standard of care above and beyond the standard of reasonable care for handling dangerous agencies. When we referred to a "higher degree of care" in these cases, we were not creating a second tier of "extraordinary care" over and above ordinary or reasonable care. Instead, we were simply recognizing the general principle that under the reasonable care standard, the level of care must be proportionate to the danger involved. Our use of the language "higher degree of care" merely stated the common sense conclusion that the use of a dangerous agency would require the reasonably prudent person to exercise more care. . . .

In summation, this Commonwealth recognizes only one standard of care in negligence actions involving dangerous instrumentalities—the standard of reasonable care under the circumstances. It is well established by our case law that the reasonable man must exercise care in proportion to the danger involved in his act.

With these principles in mind we must next examine the jury instructions in this case. The trial judge explained to the jury that negligence is "the absence of ordinary care which a reasonably prudent person would exercise in the circumstances here presented." The trial judge further explained: "It is for you to determine how a reasonably prudent person would act in those circumstances. Ordinary care is the care a reasonably prudent person would use under the circumstances presented in this case. It is the duty of every person to use ordinary care not only for his own safety and the protection of his property, but also to avoid serious injury to others. What constitutes ordinary care varies according to the particular circumstances and conditions existing then and there. The amount of care required by law must be in keeping with the degree of danger involved. . . ."

We find that this charge, when read as a whole, adequately instructed the jury. The charge informed the jury that the proper standard of care was "reasonable" or "ordinary" care under the circumstances in accordance with the law of this Commonwealth. The charge properly instructed the jury that the level of care required changed with the circumstances. The charge also informed the jury that the level of care required increased proportionately with the level of danger in the activity. We find nothing in this charge that is confusing, misleading, or unclear. From these instructions, the jury had the tools to examine the circumstances of the case and determine that the defendant was required to exercise a "higher degree of care" in using the dangerous agency of gasoline. . . .

For the reasons set forth above, we affirm the order of the Superior Court.

NOTES

1. **The general standard of care.** *Stewart* applies the general standard of care for negligence cases. When a plaintiff sues a defendant on a negligence theory, the defendant is held to the standard of care that would be exercised by a reasonable person under the same or similar circumstances as the defendant was in at the time of the alleged negligence.

2. **Dangerous instrumentalities: The orthodox view.** *Stewart* also states the orthodox view for negligence cases involving the use of dangerous instrumentalities: (a) the standard of care remains the reasonable and prudent person standard, but (b) if the foreseeable danger is high, the reasonable person will ordinarily exercise a greater degree of care than if the foreseeable danger is low. *E.g., Butler v. Acme Mkts., Inc.,* 426 A.2d 521 (N.J. Super. Ct. App. Div. 1981), *aff'd,* 445 A.2d 1141 (N.J. 1982). The *standard* thus remains the same whether danger is high or low. What changes with the danger is the *amount of care* that a reasonable person would take. *E.g., Purtle v. Shelton,* 474 S.W.2d 123 (Ark. 1971) (trial judge in hunting-injury case was correct to refuse to instruct the jury that the defendant should have used a "high degree of care commensurate with the dangers involved"; "The duty enunciated in an instruction should be ordinary care under the circumstances, and the contention that the circumstances dictate a high degree of caution should be left to arguments of counsel.").

3. **Departures from the orthodox view.** Courts do not always observe the orthodox view; some have held instead that when the danger is greater, the standard itself is higher. *See Wood v. Groh,* 7 P.3d 1163 (Kan. 2000); DOBBS ON TORTS §§ 128 & 303 (2000) (citing cases).

4. **Judge and jury.** Why does it matter whether the standard itself changes as the degree of foreseeable danger rises? What impact might an instruction based on such a conception have on the jury?

BJORNDAL v. WEITMAN

184 P.3d 1115 (Or. 2008)

BALMER, J. . . .

Plaintiff was driving east on Highway 22 in Linn County and looking for her father, whose car had broken down along the highway. Defendant had been following plaintiff for approximately 20 minutes, and there was no evidence that defendant was following too closely during that time. Plaintiff then spotted her father ahead on the right side of the road. Defendant testified that he had watched plaintiff's father, who was waving his hands and gesturing, for two seconds and then, assuming "that there was some sort of emergency situation, a hazard, or something that we needed to be aware of and looked—I did glance to my left and I scanned the horizon [for about a second] to try and identify what this possible hazard or emergency was." Defendant testified that, when he returned his eyes to the road ahead of him, he noticed that plaintiff, who was driving a van, had rapidly decelerated or was in the process of decelerating. He estimated that plaintiff slowed from a speed of 50 miles per hour to 10 miles per hour within one second. Defendant testified that he then applied his brakes and, seeing that there was no oncoming traffic, decided to steer to his left to pass plaintiff on her left. Plaintiff, however, had planned to turn left because she had been told that there was a snowpark on the left side of the highway where she could stop. As she slowed to make the left turn, she signaled and steered to the left. Defendant testified that he did not see plaintiff's left turn signal until after the van started to move to the left and at that point he was unable to avoid colliding with plaintiff's van.

Plaintiff brought this negligence action against defendant, seeking damages for her injuries and medical expenses arising out of the collision. The case was tried to a jury. Defendant requested, and the trial court gave, the "emergency instruction" as set forth in Oregon Uniform Civil Jury Instruction 20.08:

> "People who are suddenly placed in a position of peril through no negligence of their own, and who are compelled to act without opportunity for reflection, are not negligent if they make a choice as a reasonably careful person placed in such a position might make, even though they do not make the wisest choice."

Plaintiff properly excepted to that instruction. The jury returned a special verdict in which it found that defendant had not been negligent in the operation of his motor vehicle.

Plaintiff appealed, arguing that the trial court had erred in giving the emergency instruction. Plaintiff first asserted that the instruction was improper because the evidence established that any "emergency" had been created by defendant. Plaintiff's second argument was that it always is error for a trial court to give an emergency instruction because that instruction is an inaccurate statement of negligence law and constitutes an improper comment on the evidence. . . .

Plaintiff . . . argues that the emergency instruction misstates Oregon negligence law. The trial court here, before giving the emergency instruction quoted above, gave the standard negligence instruction set out in Uniform Civil Jury Instruction 20.02:

> "The law requires every person to use reasonable care to avoid harming others. Reasonable care is the degree of care and judgment used by reasonably careful people in the management of their own affairs to avoid harming themselves or others.
>
> "In deciding whether a party used reasonable care, consider the dangers apparent or reasonably foreseeable when the events occurred. Do not judge the party's conduct in light of subsequent events; instead, consider what the party knew or should have known at the time.
>
> "A person is negligent, therefore, when that person does some act that a reasonably careful person would not do, or fails to do something that a reasonably careful person would do under similar circumstances."

Plaintiff asserts that the foregoing general negligence instruction correctly states that a person is negligent if the person fails to use reasonable care and that it then elaborates on some of the considerations relevant to determining "reasonable care." But plaintiff points out that the emergency instruction, in contrast, tells the jury that a person is "*not* negligent" if the person "make[s] such a choice as a reasonably careful person placed in such a position *might* make, *even though* [the person did] *not make the wisest choice.*" (Emphases added.) As we explain below, that instruction appears to modify the general standard of care as described in the negligence instruction by making negligence turn, in part, on whether a person makes one of many choices a reasonably careful person "might" make, by introducing the concept of "wisest choice," and by attempting to define the legal standard for negligence in part by describing what is "not negligent."

A person is negligent if the person fails to exercise reasonable care, a standard that is measured by what a reasonable person of ordinary prudence would, or would not, do in the same or similar circumstances. The emergency instruction, however, tells the jurors that, notwithstanding the instruction that a person must exercise reasonable care, if there was an emergency, they nevertheless may conclude that the person whose actions are at issue was "*not* negligent" (emphasis added), even if the person made a choice that is not the "wisest choice," as long as it was a choice a "reasonably careful person" in those circumstances "might" make. Jurors would understandably view that instruction as permitting them to find a defendant "not negligent," even when the defendant makes an "unwise" choice. To be sure, the reasonable care standard does not *always* require a defendant to make the "wisest choice." But neither does it mean that a defendant was "not negligent" simply because the defendant's "unwise choice" was made in the context of an emergency. . . .

Parties may of course introduce evidence, and may argue about, the "emergency" nature of the circumstances in which the parties acted and whether or not various "choices" of conduct, wise or not, were available. The *existence* of "emergency" circumstances in vehicle accident cases-sudden actions by other drivers, unexpected weather events, roadway hazards—is indisputably appropriate for a jury to consider in determining whether a person has used reasonable care in attempting to avoid harming others. But this court has never articulated the *legal* standard of negligence as turning on those considerations. Rather, the negligence standard focuses on whether a person acted with reasonable care to avoid harm to others, in light of all the circumstances, including any "emergency." Thus, the general negligence standard embodied in Uniform Civil Jury Instruction 20.02 encompasses any legitimate concerns about "emergency" circumstances, without introducing misleading concepts of the extent to which a "choice" available to the person was "unwise," "wise," "wiser," or "wisest." Moreover, the negligence instruction already refers to facts that may create an emergency situation when it speaks of the "dangers apparent or reasonably foreseeable when the events occurred" and the "circumstances" that are to be considered in determining whether a person used reasonable care. UCJI 20.02.[3] As we stated in *Evans v.*

---

3. In citing the uniform negligence instruction, we do not mean to suggest that that instruction is the best of all possible negligence instructions. A trial judge may craft a more specific instruction on negligence that is appropriate in a particular case, as long as it accurately states the law.

General Telephone, "the usual instruction on negligence sufficiently covers what a reasonably prudent person would do under all circumstances, including those of sudden emergency."

We therefore conclude that the emergency instruction incorrectly stated the law and was likely to confuse the jury as to the correct legal standard to apply. When an instruction gives "the jury the wrong legal rule to apply[,]" and thus permits the jury to reach a legally incorrect result, this court consistently has held that the error substantially affects a party's rights. *Wallach v. Allstate Ins. Co.,* 344 Or. 314, 322, 180 P.3d 19 (2008). That is the case here. The erroneous jury instruction substantially affected plaintiff's rights, and the judgment must be reversed. . . .

NOTES

1. Is the rule for "emergencies" as stated in *Bjorndal* consistent with the rule for dangerous instrumentalities as articulated in *Stewart*?

2. Is the *fact* of emergency irrelevant under the rule enunciated in *Bjorndal*? If you represented a defendant in such a case, could you use that fact in determining what sum to offer in settlement, or in what to say to the jury in closing argument?

3. Several courts have now said that the idea behind the emergency instruction is adequately covered by the instruction defining the reasonable care standard and that the separate emergency instruction should never be given. *See Lyons v. Midnight Sun Transportation Services, Inc.,* 928 P.2d 1202 (Alaska 1996) ("We believe that the sudden emergency instruction is a generally useless appendage to the law of negligence. With or without an emergency, the standard of care a person must exercise is still that of a reasonable person under the circumstances."); DOBBS ON TORTS § 131 (2000). In such a state, what should the judge do about the plaintiff's proffered instruction on commensurate care or care in keeping with the danger?

4. Other courts have stopped just short of wholesale condemnation of separate emergency instructions, although most at least recognize that they are rarely appropriate and merely duplicate general standard-of-care instructions. *See, e.g., Willis v. Westerfield,* 839 N.E.2d 1179 (Ind. 2006) ("The emergency is simply one of the circumstances to be considered. . . .").

5. What constitutes an "emergency" remains a relevant question in those states that still allow emergency instructions in some cases. The usual definition is a sudden, unexpected and unforeseen happening or condition that calls for immediate action, and that was not created by the party seeking the instruction. *See, e.g., Herr v. Wheeler,* 634 S.E.2d 317 (Va. 2006).

6. Following up the ideas about how the standard of care should affect jury instructions, consider whether a lawyer could make a principled objection to an instruction that told the jury, "The defendant is not liable for an unavoidable accident." *See Fry v. Carter,* 825 A.2d 1042 (Md. 2003).

7. Allen drives at a speed within the speed limit in a residential area. A number of children are playing soccer on a vacant lot. They appear to range in age from about 6 to about 15. Allen does not slow down. Baker, an 8-year-old,

runs into the street after the ball, and Allen is unable to stop in time. He would have avoided impact had he driven 5 miles per hour slower. What is the standard of care? Should the judge give any special instruction?

SHEPHERD v. GARDNER WHOLESALE, INC., 256 So.2d 877 (Ala. 1972). Plaintiff Roxie Shepherd tripped over a raised concrete slab in the sidewalk in front of defendant's business. Shepherd suffered from cataracts, leaving her with 20/100 vision in one eye and 20/80 in the other. "[A] person with impaired vision is not required to see what a person with normal vision can see. Such would be impossible, and one is not guilty of negligence by using the public sidewalks with the physical inability to see what a person with normal vision can see. A person laboring under a physical disability such as defective vision is not required to exercise a higher degree of care to avoid injury than is required of a person under no disability. Ordinary care in the case of such a person is such care as an ordinarily prudent person with a like infirmity would have exercised under the same or similar circumstances."

NOTES

1. **Role of physical impairments.** *Shepherd* reflects the rule on the role of physical impairments, disabilities, or limitations in setting the standard of care in negligence cases. The newest Restatement provides that "The conduct of an actor with physical disability is negligent only if it does not conform to that of a reasonably careful person with the same disability." RESTATEMENT (THIRD) OF TORTS: LIABILITY FOR PHYSICAL HARM § 11(a) (Proposed Final Draft No. 1, 2005). What if the general rule were otherwise?

2. **Effect of the physical impairment rule.** Is the rule an advantage for the physically disabled, or does the rule actually cut both ways? What if a person is blind, gets into a car and drives, and causes an accident because he cannot see. Posit that a sighted person would not have caused the accident at all. Does the physical impairment rule free the blind person from liability on those facts? What, exactly, is the standard of care on such facts? See RESTATEMENT (THIRD) § 11, cmt. *b* (P.F.D. No. 1, 2005); *Cf. Roberts v. State*, 396 So.2d 566 (La. Ct. App. 1981) (blind man knocked over the plaintiff in a crowded post office).

3. **Old age.** Cases hold that old age is not taken into account in setting the standard of care. What if old age produces particular physical disabilities, however, such as an inability to move quickly? Should that be taken into account?

4. **Exceptional physical ability.** Suppose, instead of having a physical infirmity, the actor has strength and agility not possessed by normal persons, or that the actor's reaction time is exceptionally good. How would you express the standard of care owed by such a person? How might *Shepherd* contribute to your analysis?

5. **Intoxication.** What is to be done about an intoxicated person? Suppose one is wildly intoxicated, but drives in a perfect way. Injury results, though the driving is flawless. Presumably the law should not attempt to judge the ultimate worth or character of persons, but should judge conduct instead. The general rule is that an intoxicated person owes the same care as a sober person, and that if his overt conduct would be negligence in a sober person, it is also negligence in a drunken one. What can be made of this? Can it be reconciled with the rule that one considers physical impairments as one of the circumstances? Is it possible that in the case of voluntary intoxication the risk is taken when intoxicants are consumed rather than later, when the driver speeds?

6. **Sudden incapacitation.** Courts have uniformly held that where a person's alleged negligence is caused by a sudden physical incapacitation that is not foreseeable, there should be no liability. The standard of care, of course, is that of a reasonable and prudent person under the same or similar circumstances. Thus, for example, if a reasonable and prudent person would have had no notice of the sudden seizure or heart attack, and that incapacitation caused the conduct that led to the plaintiff's injury, the defendant is not legally responsible. RESTATEMENT (THIRD) § 11, cmt. *d* (P.F.D. No. 1, 2005). Many courts place the burden of proving sudden incapacitation on the defendant. *See, e.g., Roman v. Estate of Gobbo*, 791 N.E.2d 422 (Ohio 2003) (driver of vehicle died from sudden heart attack and caused accident). What if a person has a serious medical condition and has been warned not to drive by doctors but does so anyway, suffers a seizure and causes an accident. How does the standard of care work in that case?

CREASY v. RUSK

730 N.E.2d 659 (Ind. 2000)

SULLIVAN, JUSTICE. . . .

In July, 1992, Lloyd Rusk's wife admitted Rusk to the Brethren Healthcare Center ("BHC") because he suffered from memory loss and confusion and Rusk's wife was unable to care for him. Rusk's primary diagnosis was Alzheimer's disease. Over the course of three years at BHC, Rusk experienced periods of anxiousness, confusion, depression, disorientation, and agitation. Rusk often resisted when staff members attempted to remove him from prohibited areas of the facility. On several occasions, Rusk was belligerent with both staff and other residents. In particular, Rusk was often combative, agitated, and aggressive and would hit staff members when they tried to care for him. . . .

On May 16, 1995, Creasy and another certified nursing assistant, Linda Davis, were working through their routine of putting Rusk and other residents to bed. Creasy knew that Rusk had been "very agitated and combative that evening." By Creasy's account:

> [Davis] was helping me put Mr. Rusk to bed. She was holding his wrists to keep him from hitting us and I was trying to get his legs to put him to bed. He was hitting and kicking wildly. During this time,

he kicked me several times in my left knee and hip area. My lower back popped and I yelled out with pain from my lower back and left knee.

. . . Rusk moved for summary judgment and the trial court granted his motion. Creasy appealed. The Court of Appeals reversed, holding "that a person's mental capacity, whether that person is a child or an adult, must be factored [into] the determination of whether a legal duty exists." . . .

[T]he generally accepted rule in jurisdictions other than Indiana is that mental disability does not excuse a person from liability for "conduct which does not conform to the standard of a reasonable man under like circumstances." Restatement (Second) of Torts § 283B; accord Restatement (Third) of Torts § 9(c) (Discussion Draft Apr. 5, 1999) ("Unless the actor is a child, the actor's mental or emotional disability is not considered in determining whether conduct is negligent."). People with mental disabilities are commonly held liable for their intentional and negligent torts. No allowance is made for lack of intelligence, ignorance, excitability, or proneness to accident. See Restatement (Second) of Torts § 283B cmt. c.

Legal scholars and authorities recognize that it is "impossible to ascribe either the volition implicit in an intentional tort, the departure from the standard of a 'reasonable' person which defines an act of ordinary negligence, or indeed any concept of 'fault' at all to one who . . . is by definition unable to control his [or her] own actions through any exercise of reason." Anicet v. Gant, 580 So.2d 273, 275 (Fla.Dist.Ct.App. 1991) (citations omitted). Rather, the Restatement rule holding people with mental disabilities liable for their torts was founded upon public policy considerations.

The public policy reasons most often cited for holding individuals with mental disabilities to a standard of reasonable care in negligence claims include the following.

(1) Allocates losses between two innocent parties to the one who caused or occasioned the loss. . . .

(2) Provides incentive to those responsible for people with disabilities and interested in their estates to prevent harm and "restrain" those who are potentially dangerous. . . .

(3) Removes inducements for alleged tortfeasors to fake a mental disability in order to escape liability. . . .

(4) Avoids administrative problems involved in courts and juries attempting to identify and assess the significance of an actor's disability. As a practical matter, it is arguably too difficult to account for or draw any "satisfactory line between mental deficiency and those variations of temperament, intellect, and emotional balance."

(5) Forces persons with disabilities to pay for the damage they do if they "are to live in the world." A discussion draft for the Restatement (Third) of Torts rephrases this policy rationale and concludes: "[I]f a

person is suffering from a mental disorder so serious as to make it likely that the person will engage in substandard conduct that threatens the safety of others, there can be doubts as to whether this person should be allowed to engage in the normal range of society's activities; given these doubts, there is nothing especially harsh in at least holding the person responsible for the harms the person may cause by substandard conduct." Restatement (Third) of Torts § 9 cmt. e (Discussion Draft April 5, 1999)....

Since the 1970s, Indiana law has strongly reflected policies to deinstitutionalize people with disabilities and integrate them into the least restrictive environment. National policy changes have led the way for some of Indiana's enactments in that several federal acts either guarantee the civil rights of people with disabilities or condition state aid upon state compliance with desegregation and integrationist practices. See, e.g., Individuals with Disabilities Education Act, 20 U.S.C. § 1400 et seq. (1994) (requiring that children with disabilities receive a free appropriate public education in the least restrictive environment in states that accept allocated funds) (originally enacted in 1975 as the Education for All Handicapped Children Act, P.L. 94–142 (amending the state education grant program under the 1970 Education for the Handicapped Act, P.L. 91–230; requiring states to provide a free appropriate public education to all children with disabilities in order to receive state grant funds)); Americans with Disabilities Act, 42 U.S.C. § 12132 (1994), and implementing regulation 28 C.F.R. § 35.130(d) (1999) (providing that a public entity shall administer services, programs, and activities in the most integrated setting appropriate to the needs of qualified individuals with disabilities); Fair Housing Act, 42 U.S.C. § 3604 (1994) (prohibiting discrimination based on "handicap" in the sale or rental of a dwelling).

These legislative developments reflect ... a determination that people with disabilities should be treated in the same way as non-disabled persons.

[T]he Restatement rule may very well have been grounded in a policy determination that persons with mental disabilities should be institutionalized or otherwise confined rather than "live in the world." It is clear from our recitation of state and federal legislative and regulatory developments that contemporary public policy has rejected institutionalization and confinement for a "strong professional consensus in favor of ... community treatment ... and integration into the least restrictive ... environment." ... We observe that it is a matter of some irony that public policies favoring the opposite ends—institutionalization and confinement on the one hand and community treatment and integration into the least restrictive environment on the other–should nevertheless yield the same common law rule: that the general duty of care imposed on adults with mental disabilities is the same as that for adults without mental disabilities.

. . . We hold that a person with mental disabilities is generally held to the same standard of care as that of a reasonable person under the same circumstances without regard to the alleged tortfeasor's capacity to control or understand the consequences of his or her actions.

[The court held, however, that one employed to take care of a patient known to be combative because of Alzheimer's disease has no complaint for injuries sustained in doing so. As to such a caretaker the duty of care is a one-way street, from caretaker to patient, not the other way around. Hence Rusk was not liable on these facts.]

NOTES

1. **Other cases.** *Accord*, that the objective standard of care applies but that a mentally disabled person, involuntarily hospitalized, does not owe a duty of care to his professional caregiver and hence is not liable for negligence or recklessness causing the caregiver harm, *Berberian v. Lynn*, 845 A.2d 122 (N.J. 2004). Cases like *Arias v. State*, 755 N.Y.S.2d 223 (Ct. Cl. 2003), that state a subjective standard for mentally deficient plaintiffs seem to be in reality cases based on the limited duty a confined disabled person owes to his caregiver. However, *Hofflander v. St. Catherine's Hospital, Inc.*, 664 N.W.2d 545 (Wis. 2003), clearly states a subjective standard for situations like the one in *Creasy v. Rusk*.

2. **"Defense" vs. "standard of care."** Sometimes insanity is discussed as a possible "defense," but it seems clear that the underlying issue is about the standard of care, not about defenses. The view of the Third Restatement § 11(c) (P.F.D. No. 1, 2005), the Second Restatement § 283B (1965), and the prevailing orthodoxy, is that neither insanity nor mental deficiency relieves the actor from liability, and that his conduct must conform to the general standard of care of a reasonable person under similar external circumstances.

3. **Mental and psychological limitations.** Low intelligence and other mental or psychological limitations are treated the same way. Durfee is a sane man of low intelligence. He has never connected the danger of fire with his storage of rags, newspapers and paint thinner in his garage. A fire originates in his garage and spreads to his neighbor's house. The jury will be instructed that Durfee is held to the care of a reasonable and prudent person. He does not escape liability because he did "the best he could do," or because he behaved as well as others of similar intelligence.

4. **Contributory negligence.** The common law called a plaintiff's negligence "contributory negligence" and held that it barred the plaintiff's recovery completely. In most states today, contributory negligence of a plaintiff operates to reduce the plaintiff's recovery of damages, but does not necessarily bar all recovery. The focus of contributory negligence is often on the idea that the plaintiff should take reasonable care for herself, not on her failure to take care for others. In any event, the difference is a slight one, and the usual assumption is that the standard of care is the same, whether the issue is one of negligence or one of contributory negligence. RESTATEMENT (THIRD) OF TORTS: LIABILITY FOR PHYSICAL HARM § 3, cmt. *a* (P.F.D. No. 1, 2005);

RESTATEMENT (THIRD) OF TORTS, APPORTIONMENT OF LIABILITY § 3, cmt. *a* (2000). Some thinkers say that the objective standard of reasonable care should not apply to the plaintiff's conduct—in other words, should not apply to the contributory negligence issue. Can you formulate an argument for or against this view?

5. **Considering rationales.** Are the rules of liability for insane and mentally deficient persons based upon justice? Deterrence?

6. **Consistency?** Are the rules for mental disability at odds with the rules for physical disability? Can you harmonize or justify the difference in the law's treatment of these two situations? What about a mental disability that clearly springs from a physical disability—such as mental retardation that results from cerebral palsy? Should that condition be taken into account in setting the standard of care? *See, e.g., Burch v. American Family Mutual Ins. Co.*, 543 N.W.2d 277 (Wis. 1996).

7. **Persons with superior knowledge.** What is to be done about a person with superior knowledge or mental ability, who can appreciate and act on some risk which reasonable and prudent persons, not having the special knowledge, would ignore?

HILL v. SPARKS, 546 S.W.2d 473 (Mo. Ct. App. 1976). Wayne Sparks was an operator of earth-moving machinery and had several seasons experience with a machine known as an earth scraper. At an exhibit of such machines he drove one, instructing his sister to stand on a ladder on the machine. It hit a mound of dirt and, because of its large rubber tires, bounced back. Sparks' sister was thrown forward in front of the left wheel and was run over before Sparks could stop the machine. She died almost instantly. This is an action for her death. "[Sparks], as an operator, with several seasons experience with earth scrapers, was familiar with the propensities of such machines.... He had heard decedent's husband, upon observing a boy riding on the scraper ladder during the demonstration, tell a Liberty Equipment employee to get the boy off the scraper because if he fell he would fall right under the wheel. Despite his knowledge and experience, appellant directed his sister to ride as a passenger on the ladder while he operated the machine.... 'The standard of the reasonable man requires only a minimum of attention, perception, memory, knowledge, intelligence, and judgment in order to recognize the existence of the risk. If the actor has in fact more than the minimum of these qualities, he is required to exercise the superior qualities that he has in a manner reasonable under the circumstances.' 2 Restatement of Torts (2d) § 289.... The evidence in this case presented an issue submissible to the jury of whether ... appellant met the requisite standard of care."

NOTES

1. A high school sports coach has received special courses dealing with injured students. Would the standard of care require the coach of a small high

school team to use this special knowledge in deciding whether to keep an injured player in a football game? *See Cerny v. Cedar Bluffs Junior/Senior Pub. Sch.*, 628 N.W.2d 697 (Neb. 2001), *on appeal after remand*, 679 N.W.2d 198 (Neb. 2004).

2. With babies, sudden infant death syndrome (SIDS) is a small risk. Allowing babies to sleep stomach down multiplies the risk—the risk is at least double, maybe as much as 12 times as great as the risk of having them sleep on their backs. Should one who operates a daycare center for infants know about the danger of letting small babies sleep in a prone position? If a baby dies from SIDS after the daycare center has placed her on her stomach to sleep, would the plaintiff need some kind of testimony to show that the daycare center should have known the risk? What if the daycare center admits that it knew about a recommendation of the American Academy of Pediatrics against prone sleeping because of the risk of SIDS associated with it? *LePage v. Horne*, 809 A.2d 505 (Conn. 2002).

3. A medical doctor's special training will certainly be taken into account where the doctor is a defendant in a medical malpractice case, a situation we address at length in Chapter 13. But what if a doctor is a plaintiff in a lawsuit, claiming an injury caused by another doctor's negligence in failing to diagnose the plaintiff's condition when the plaintiff was a patient? Should the plaintiff's special knowledge and training be taken into account in determining whether he was contributorily negligent in failing to tell the defendant doctor about all of his symptoms? *See Jackson v. Axelrad*, 221 S.W.3d 650 (Tex. 2007).

ROBINSON v. LINDSAY

598 P.2d 392 (Wash. 1979)

UTTER, CHIEF JUSTICE.

An action seeking damages for personal injuries was brought on behalf of Kelly Robinson who lost full use of a thumb in a snowmobile accident when she was 11 years of age. The petitioner, Billy Anderson, 13 years of age at the time of the accident, was the driver of the snowmobile. After a jury verdict in favor of Anderson, the trial court ordered a new trial.

The single issue on appeal is whether a minor operating a snowmobile is to be held to an adult standard of care. The trial court failed to instruct the jury as to that standard and ordered a new trial because it believed the jury should have been so instructed. We agree and affirm the order granting a new trial.

The trial court instructed the jury under WPI 10.05 that:

In considering the claimed negligence of a child, you are instructed that it is the duty of a child to exercise the same care that a reasonably careful child of the same age, intelligence, maturity, training and experience would exercise under the same or similar circumstances.

Respondent properly excepted to the giving of this instruction and to the court's failure to give an adult standard of care. . . .

The current law in this state is fairly reflected in WPI 10.05, given in this case. In the past we have always compared a child's conduct to that expected of a reasonably careful child of the same age, intelligence, maturity, training and experience. This case is the first to consider the question of a child's liability for injuries sustained as a result of his or her operation of a motorized vehicle or participation in an inherently dangerous activity.

Courts in other jurisdictions have created an exception to the special child standard because of the apparent injustice that would occur if a child who caused injury while engaged in certain dangerous activities were permitted to defend himself by saying that other children similarly situated would not have exercised a degree of care higher than his, and he is, therefore, not liable for his tort. Some courts have couched the exception in terms of children engaging in an activity which is normally one for adults only. *See, e.g., Dellwo v. Pearson*, 259 Minn. 452, 107 N.W.2d 859 (1961) (operation of a motorboat). We believe a better rationale is that when the activity a child engages in is inherently dangerous, as is the operation of powerful mechanized vehicles, the child should be held to an adult standard of care.

Such a rule protects the need of children to be children but at the same time discourages immature individuals from engaging in inherently dangerous activities. Children will still be free to enjoy traditional childhood activities without being held to an adult standard of care. Although accidents sometimes occur as the result of such activities, they are not activities generally considered capable of resulting in "grave danger to others and to the minor himself if the care used in the course of the activity drops below that care which the reasonable and prudent adult would use. . . ." *Daniels v. Evans*, 107 N.H. 407, 408, 224 A.2d 63, 64 (1966).

Other courts adopting the adult standard of care for children engaged in adult activities have emphasized the hazards to the public if the rule is otherwise. We agree with the Minnesota Supreme Court's language in its decision in *Dellwo v. Pearson*, supra:

> Certainly in the circumstances of modern life, where vehicles moved by powerful motors are readily available and frequently operated by immature individuals, we should be skeptical of a rule that would allow motor vehicles to be operated to the hazard of the public with less than the normal minimum degree of care and competence.

Dellwo applied the adult standard to a 12-year-old defendant operating a motor boat. Other jurisdictions have applied the adult standard to minors engaged in analogous activities. [The court cited cases in which the minor had been operating a tractor, a motorcycle, a minibike and an automobile.]

The operation of a snowmobile likewise requires adult care and competence. Currently 2.2 million snowmobiles are in operation in the United States. Studies show that collisions and other snowmobile accidents claim hundreds of casualties each year and that the incidence of accidents is particularly high among inexperienced operators.

At the time of the accident, the 13-year-old petitioner had operated snowmobiles for about 2 years. When the injury occurred, petitioner was operating a 30–horsepower snowmobile at speeds of 10–20 miles per hour. The record indicates that the machine itself was capable of 65 miles per hour. Because petitioner was operating a powerful motorized vehicle, he should be held to the standard of care and conduct expected of an adult.

The order granting a new trial is affirmed.

HUDSON–CONNOR v. PUTNEY, 86 P.3d 106 (Or. Ct. App. 2004). The 14-year-old defendant allowed an 11-year-old boy to operate the defendant's golf cart. The boy hit the accelerator when he meant to hit the brake. As a result, the cart ran directly into the plaintiff, breaking her leg. She required surgery. *Held*, the defendant's conduct is not to be judged under the adult standard of care because (1) there was no evidence that adult skills were required and (2) there was no evidence that golf carts were normally operated only by adults. "[T]he level of skill and judgment required to perform an activity safely increases in proportion to the danger" posed by the activity. A golf cart that moves at a maximum of 12 miles per hour is not inherently dangerous and does not require adult skills. Since operation of a golf cart is not an adult activity, neither is entrustment of the cart to another minor an adult activity.

NOTES

1. **General rule for children.** *Robinson* reflects the general rule: a child accused of negligence is held to the standard of care of a reasonably careful child of the same age, intelligence and experience. DOBBS ON TORTS § 124 (2000). Is this purely subjective?

2. **Tests and policies for the adult standard.** Is it possible that neither the "inherently dangerous" test nor the "adult activity" test captures the essence of the result courts are seeking? Suppose an adult rides on a snowmobile with an operator he knows to be 10 years of age. Would it be reasonable to demand and expect an adult standard of care of the child? RESTATEMENT (THIRD) OF TORTS: LIABILITY FOR PHYSICAL HARM § 10, cmt. *f* (P.F.D. No. 1, 2005). This issue will arise again in the next chapter. What is your opinion at this point? Should children be held only to the child standard when they are engaged in "carefree" activities appropriate to their development but to the adult standard when they engage in dangerous activities usually engaged in only by adults?

3. **Application of the adult standard.** Alaska extended the adult standard to cover a 14-year-old's decision to permit another minor to drive the

car with deadly results. *Ardinger v. Hummell,* 982 P.2d 727 (Alaska 1999). Meager authority has imposed the adult standard when a minor uses fire- arms. *See Goss v. Allen,* 360 A.2d 388 (N.J. 1976). Otherwise, courts have imposed the adult standard almost exclusively in cases of minors operating motorized vehicles. So a 12-year-old might be held to an adult standard while operating a motor boat, but a 17-year-old held only to a child standard while operating a bicycle. In *Strait v. Crary,* 496 N.W.2d 634 (Wis. Ct. App. 1992), a 16-year-old drinking passenger attempted to climb out the window of a moving truck. He fell out and suffered a broken leg. The court used the child standard in determining whether he was guilty of contributory negligence.

4. **The rule of sevens.** A few courts still say that minors over 14 are presumed capable of negligence, those between seven and 14 presumed incapable of it, and those below seven are incapable of negligence as a matter of law. Indiana has held that all children over the age of 14 are held to an adult standard of care, no matter what they are doing. *Penn Harris Madison School Corp. v. Howard,* 861 N.E.2d 1190 (Ind. 2007) (17-year-old "flying" during a rehearsal of Peter Pan, using a device he himself had invented).

5. **Trial problems.** (a) Prior to *Robinson,* the adult standard had not been applied to children in Washington. What made the lawyers think of raising that issue? (b) Why did the judge first refuse to tell the jury that children might be held to an adult standard and then, after the trial was over, hold that his earlier ruling was wrong? Did he simply change his mind or was there a calculated risk involved?

6. **Very young children.** The rule of sevens is not so common now, but most states hold that children of very young years, three and under, are simply incapable of negligence. The Third Restatement, § 10(b), provides that children under five are incapable of negligence.

Suppose a six-year-old boy runs alongside a moving train, trying to catch it, falls, and has his legs severed. Is he incapable of contributory negligence as a matter of law? Presumed incapable? Or merely subject to the subjective child standard of care? Which choice leaves it to a jury to decide?

§ 4. SPECIFICATION OF PARTICULAR STANDARDS OR DUTIES

MARSHALL v. SOUTHERN RAILWAY CO., 62 S.E.2d 489 (N.C. 1950). Plaintiff was driving at night on a paved road about 30 feet wide. Defendant's railroad trestle above the road was supported by large tim- bers, which narrowed the road to about 15 feet under the trestle. As plaintiff approached this, a car came toward him with bright lights on and plaintiff ran into the trestle supports. The trial judge sustained defen- dant's motion for nonsuit at the end of the plaintiff's evidence. *Held,* affirmed. "[I]t is manifest from the evidence that plaintiff failed to exercise due care at the time and under the circumstances of his inju- ry. . . . It is a general rule of law, even in the absence of statutory requirement, that the operator of a motor vehicle must exercise ordinary care, that is, that degree of care which an ordinarily prudent person would exercise under similar circumstances. And in the exercise of such duty it is incumbent upon the operator of a motor vehicle to keep a reasonably careful lookout and to keep same under such control at night as to be able to stop within the range of his lights.''

NOTE

Is the court here saying that plaintiff was guilty of contributory negligence ''as a matter of law,'' that is, that there is no room for reasonable jurors to differ about this conclusion? Or is it saying that there is a rule of law that one must be able to stop within the range of one's lights, whether or not a reasonable person would be able to do so? What's the difference?

CHAFFIN v. BRAME

64 S.E.2d 276 (N.C. 1951)

ERVIN, JUSTICE.

[Plaintiff was driving about 40 miles an hour at night on a paved highway 18 feet wide. A car approached driven by one Garland, who refused to dim his headlights. Plaintiff, blinded by the lights, ran into a truck left unlighted and blocking the entire right lane. Plaintiff sued the person responsible for the truck, who argued that the plaintiff was guilty of contributory negligence as a matter of law. The trial court, however, permitted the case to go to the jury, which returned a verdict for the plaintiff.] To sustain his position, the defendant invokes the long line of cases beginning with Weston v. Southern R. Co., 194 N.C. 210, 139 S.E. 237, and ending with Marshall v. Southern R. Co., 233 N.C. 38, 62 S.E.2d 489, declaring either expressly or impliedly that ''it is negligence as a matter of law to drive an automobile along a public highway in the dark at such a speed that it can not be stopped within the distance that objects can be seen ahead of it.''

. . . ''Few tasks in trial law are more troublesome than that of applying the rule suggested by the foregoing quotation to the facts in particular cases. The difficulty is much enhanced by a tendency of the bench and bar to regard it as a rule of thumb rather than as an effort to express in convenient formula for ready application to a recurring factual situation the basic principle that a person must exercise ordinary care to avoid injury when he undertakes to drive a motor vehicle upon a public highway at night. The rule was phrased to enforce the concept of the law that an injured person ought not to be permitted to shift from himself to another a loss resulting in part at least from his own refusal or failure to see that which is obvious. But it was not designed to require infallibility of the nocturnal motorist, or to preclude him from recovery of compensation for an injury occasioned by collision with an unlighted obstruction whose presence on the highway is not disclosed by his own headlights or by any other available lights. When all is said, each case must be decided according to its own peculiar state of facts. This is true because the true and ultimate test is this: What would a reasonably prudent person have done under the circumstances as they presented themselves to the plaintiff?''

It thus appears that the cases invoked by the defendant enunciate no mere shibboleth. They simply apply to the factual situations involved in them the fundamental truth that the law charges every person with the duty of exercising ordinary care for his own safety....

When the plaintiff's evidence is taken in the light most favorable to him, it reasonably warrants these inferences: The plaintiff was keeping a proper lookout and driving at a reasonable speed as he traveled southward along Route 18. On being partially and temporarily blinded by the glaring lights of Garland's approaching automobile, the plaintiff reduced the speed of his car, and proceeded with extreme caution. The plaintiff exercised due care in adopting this course of action instead of bringing his car to a complete stop because he reasonably assumed that Garland would seasonably dim his headlights in obedience to the law, and thus restore to the plaintiff his full normal vision. The plaintiff had no reason whatever to anticipate or expect that the defendant's truck had been left standing on the traveled portion of the highway ahead of him without lights or warning signals until his car came within 30 feet of it. He did everything possible to avert the collision just as soon as the truck became visible.

This being true, we cannot hold that the plaintiff was guilty of contributory negligence as a matter of law....

There is in law no error.

NOTES

1. In many cases, a court will conclude, on the particular facts of the case, that the plaintiff (or sometimes the defendant) was negligent "as a matter of law." This phrase means that the court concludes, on the facts, that reasonable persons could not find otherwise and accordingly directs a verdict for the opposing party on this issue. There are other cases, fewer in number, in which the court, having reached such a conclusion on the facts of the case, generalizes it and states it as a legal rule for all cases. Notice how the court in *Marshall v. Southern Railway Co.* states the range-of-lights rule.

2. Almost all rules of this kind have come to grief, or have caused it. Holmes once took the view that it was contributory negligence not to stop, look and listen at a railroad crossing and that, if vision was impaired, one might be expected to get out of the car and walk to the edge of the track to assess the danger. *Baltimore & O.R. Co. v. Goodman*, 275 U.S. 66 (1927). Cardozo was later able gently to push this decision aside, pointing to some of the injustices that could result. "Illustrations such as these," he said, "bear witness to the need for caution in framing standards of behavior that amount to rules of law. The need is the more urgent when there is no background of experience out of which the standards have emerged. They are then, not the natural flowering of behavior in its customary forms, but rules artificially

developed and imposed from without." *Pokora v. Wabash Railway*, 292 U.S. 98 (1934).

3. Is there a pattern in *Marshall* and *Chaffin* on the one hand and *Goodman* and *Pokora* on the other?

MARTIN v. HERZOG, 126 N.E. 814 (N.Y. 1920). Defendant, driving at night, crossed over the center line on a curve and struck a buggy occupied by decedent, causing his death. In a wrongful death action the defendant contended that decedent was negligent in driving without lights. A statute provided in part: "Every vehicle on wheels whether stationary or in motion, while upon any public street ... shall have attached thereto a light or lights to be visible from the front and from the rear from one hour after sunset to one hour before sunrise.... A person violating the provisions of this section shall be guilty of a misdemeanor punishable by a fine not to exceed ten dollars." The trial judge charged the jury that decedent's violation of the statute could be considered as evidence of contributory negligence but not as negligence in itself. The jury found for the plaintiff. The Appellate Division reversed for new trial. In the Court of Appeals, by Cardozo, J., held, the Appellate Division is affirmed. "We think the unexcused omission of the statutory signals is more than some evidence of negligence. It is negligence in itself.... Yet the jurors were instructed in effect that they were at liberty in their discretion to treat the omission of lights either as innocent or as culpable. They were allowed to 'consider the default as lightly or gravely' as they would. They might as well have been told that they could use a like discretion in holding a master at fault for the omission of a safety appliance prescribed by positive law for the protection of a workman. Jurors have no dispensing power, by which they may relax the duty that one traveler on the highway owes under the statute to another."

NOTES

1. **Kinds of statutes covered by the negligence per se rule.** Negligence per se is not applicable to all statutes. First, the doctrine applies only to statutes that declare conduct unlawful but are silent as to civil liability— statutes that either do not expressly provide for civil liability or which "cannot be readily interpreted as impliedly creating a private right of action. RESTATEMENT (THIRD) OF TORTS: LIABILITY FOR PHYSICAL HARM § 14, cmt. *b* & *c* (P.F.D. No. 1, 2005). Where a statute itself provides for civil liability, creating a private right of action, the court must simply apply it. For example, a statute might provide that generators of hazardous wastes must dispose of them only in certain permitted ways, and that a person injured by unpermitted disposal has a statutory cause of action for damages against the waste generator. *See, e.g., Hickle v. Whitney Farms, Inc.,* 64 P.3d 1244 (Wash. 2003) (applying REV. CODE OF WASH. § 70.95.240). Or a statute could provide that the owner or keeper of a dog that damages the property or person of another

must pay compensation to the person whose property or person is harmed. *See, e.g., Auster v. Norwalk United Methodist Church*, 943 A.2d 391 (Conn. 2008) (applying CONN. GEN. STAT. § 22–357). To take another example, the federal civil rights statute, 42 U.S.C. § 1983, expressly creates a private right of action for persons whose rights are violated by particular defendants. *See* Chapter 1 § 5, *supra*. In such cases the court simply applies and enforces the statutory right.

In a negligence per se case, by contrast, the legislature has neither expressly nor impliedly provided for civil liability. For example, a statute might set a speed limit for vehicles on the highway, prescribing a criminal penalty for violation, but not mentioning anything at all about the liability of a violator to someone harmed by a crash caused by speeding. In that case, the negligence per se doctrine comes into play.

2. **The rule's effect on the duty of care.** The position taken by Cardozo in *Martin v. Herzog* is the one followed by the Restatement and most courts, namely, that the unexcused violation of such statutes is, subject to some qualifications, "negligence per se." This means that violation of the statute—even though the statute itself does not say this—actually determines the actor's negligence. Said another way, when a court applies the negligence per se rule to a statute, the statute itself supplants the usual common law standard of care, and violation of the statute establishes breach. *See* RESTATEMENT (THIRD) § 14 (P.F.D. No. 1, 2005).

3. **Jurisdictional variations.** Some states makes violation of such a statute some *evidence of negligence* that may be considered by the jury, rather than regarding the statute as setting the standard of care. *See,* e.g., WASH. REV. CODE § 5.40.050; *Brooks v. Lewin Realty III, Inc.,* 835 A.2d 616 (Md. 2003); *Kalata v. Anheuser–Busch Cos., Inc.,* 581 N.E.2d 656 (Ill. 1991); *Praus v. Mack,* 626 N.W.2d 239 (N.D. 2001). This would be the statutory parallel to cases like *Chaffin v. Brame, supra. See* Massachusetts Superior Court Civil Practice Jury Instructions 2.2.2. This puts the ultimate decision on the negligence issue with the jury. California's rule is different still: Evidence Code § 669 says that when a statute applies and a person has violated it, the failure of that person to exercise due care is presumed. The burden is then placed upon the violator to rebut that presumption. The California approach is perhaps only subtly different from the majority per se rule, given the availability of excuses in most states. Legally acceptable excuses are addressed near the end of this Chapter.

4. **Statutory instruments covered by the rule.** Courts usually apply the negligence per se rule to violations of city ordinances and even to violations of administrative regulations as well as to state and federal statutes. A few, however, hold that violation of an ordinance or administrative regulation is merely some evidence of negligence. *See Chambers v. St. Mary's Sch.,* 697 N.E.2d 198 (Ohio 1998) (violation of administrative codes is not negligence per se, only some evidence of negligence); *Elliott v. City of New York,* 747 N.E.2d 760 (N.Y. 2001) (violation of ordinances is evidence of negligence only).

O'GUIN v. BINGHAM COUNTY

122 P.3d 308 (Idaho 2005)

TROUT, JUSTICE.

Frank and Leslie O'Guin, acting as individuals and as legal guardians of Frank O'Guin Jr. (the O'Guins), appeal the district court's grant of summary judgment in favor of Bingham County, Bingham County Commissioners and Bingham County Public Works, (collectively the County). Because the district court erred in its determinations regarding the negligence *per se* claim, we reverse the grant of summary judgment.

On July 7, 1999, Shaun and Alex O'Guin were killed while playing at the Bingham County landfill. Apparently, a section of the pit wall collapsed and crushed the children. Their older brother, Frank Jr., initially discovered their bodies at the bottom of the pit. Earlier that day, the children had been eating lunch at Ridgecrest Elementary School as part of a summer lunch program. As they started walking home, the children went through an unlocked gate at the back of the schoolyard and through a privately owned empty field. The empty field is situated between the landfill and the schoolyard. The border between the empty field and the landfill was unobstructed. At the time of the children's death, the landfill was open to the public one day a week. It was closed on the day the children were killed and no landfill employees were present on the site.

[The O'Guins sued the County for negligence, claiming among other things that the County was negligent *per se*, relying on Idaho statutes and federal regulations. The trial court granted the County's motion for summary judgment, and the O'Guins appealed.]

Generally, the question of whether a duty exists is a question of law, over which we exercise free review. Negligence *per se,* which results from the violation of a specific requirement of law or ordinance, is a question of law, over which this Court exercises free review.

The dispute in this case focuses on the duty or standard of care the County owed to the O'Guin children. . . . In Idaho, it is well established that statutes and administrative regulations may define the applicable standard of care owed, and that violations of such statutes and regulations may constitute negligence *per se*. A court may adopt 'as the standard of conduct of a reasonable man the requirements of a legislative enactment or an administrative regulation. The effect of establishing negligence *per se* through violation of a statute is to conclusively establish the first two elements of a cause of action in negligence. Negligence *per se* lessens the plaintiff's burden only on the issue of the 'actor's departure from the standard of conduct required of a reasonable man.' " *Ahles v. Tabor,* 136 Idaho 393, 395, 34 P.3d 1076, 1078 (2001) (quoting Restatement (Second) of Torts § 288, cmt. b (1965)). Thus, the elements of duty and breach are taken away from the jury.

In order to replace a common law duty of care with a duty of care from a statute or regulation, the following elements must be met: (1) the statute or regulation must clearly define the required standard of conduct; (2) the statute or regulation must have been intended to prevent the type of harm the defendant's act or omission caused; (3) the plaintiff must be a member of the class of persons the statute or regulation was designed to protect; and (4) the violation must have been the proximate cause of the injury.

As to the first element, the district court found, and we agree, that the statute and regulations in this case clearly define the County's standard of conduct.... These regulations require the County to fence or otherwise block access to the landfill when an attendant is not on duty. The Legislature has specifically declared it to be "unlawful" to fail to comply with the landfill rules. In this case, the record reveals that on July 7, 1999, some of the landfill boundaries were not fenced or blocked. There is also evidence that the landfill was closed and no attendant was on duty on July 7, 1999. Therefore, the district court was correct that the regulations clearly define the County's required standard of conduct, and the County failed to meet that standard.

The second element asks whether the death of the O'Guin children is the type of harm the statute and regulations were intended to prevent. Idaho Code Section 39–7401(2) states:

> [I]t is the intent of the legislature to establish a program of solid waste management which complies with 40 CFR 258 and facilitates the incorporation of flexible standards in facility design and operation. The legislature hereby establishes the solid waste disposal standards and procedures outlined herein and a facility approval process for the state of Idaho, the political subdivisions thereof, and any private solid waste disposal site owner in order to facilitate the development and operation of solid waste disposal sites, to effect timely and responsible completion of statutory duties and to ensure protection of human health and the environment, to protect the air, land and waters of the state of Idaho.

This section demonstrates the legislature's desire to ensure the "protection of human health" in the "development and operation of solid waste disposal sites." It also makes specific reference to 40 C.F.R. § 258.... Section 258.25 of the Code of Federal Regulations states "[o]wners or operators of all municipal solid waste landfill units must control public access ... by using artificial barriers, natural barriers, or both, as appropriate to protect human health." ... "[P]rotection of human health" ... certainly includes possible injury or death to people on the facility grounds. Operators of a landfill have a duty not only to prevent illegal dumping and unauthorized vehicular traffic, but to control public access as well.

     ... These statutes and rules demonstrate that the Legislature intended to safeguard both human health and safety. The injury to the safety of the O'Guin children is the type of harm the Idaho statute and regulations were intended to prevent because the children's deaths relate directly to control of public access and protection of human health and safety.

As to the third element, the O'Guin children are members of the class of persons the regulations were designed to protect. The regulations state "[u]nauthorized vehicles and persons shall be prohibited access to the site." As trespassers, the O'Guin children were certainly "unauthorized persons" and the regulations do not differentiate between the unauthorized person who comes to the landfill to dump improper materials and the unauthorized person who comes to the landfill to play. Furthermore, the regulations require the landfill "be fenced or otherwise blocked to access when an attendant is not on duty." This regulation demonstrates the connection between the requirement that the landfill perimeter be fenced or blocked and the protection of persons whose access is unauthorized. Therefore, the regulations controlling access were designed to protect the human health and safety of the unauthorized person who comes to a landfill when an attendant is not on duty and the O'Guin children fit within that category.

Finally, as to the fourth element, there is at least a disputed issue of fact created by an affidavit in the record, as to whether the County's violation of the statute and regulations resulted in the O'Guin children's deaths.

After concluding the regulations established a duty and that the County had breached that duty, the district court held "the O'Guins' allegations of negligence *per se* do not change the duty owed by the County to trespassers." This was error. There was no need for the district court to look to the common law duty owed to trespassers once it determined the statutory duty applied. Liability may become established upon proof that the violation of the statute caused the injuries of the plaintiff and the plaintiff's subsequent damages. A statute that adequately defines the required standard of care "supplants the reasonable person standard encompassed in the concept of ordinary negligence." *Ahles,* 136 Idaho at 395, 34 P.3d at 1078....

... Standing alone, the regulations in this case are sufficient to satisfy the duty element for a negligence *per se* action. The O'Guins' use of statutory obligations to establish the County's duty under a negligence *per se* action replaces the common law duty of landowners to trespassers.... The district court's grant of summary judgment is vacated and the case remanded for further proceedings....

JUSTICE EISMANN, Dissenting.

I cannot concur in the majority opinion because the regulations cited therein as supporting a claim of negligence *per se* were clearly not intended to prevent the type of harm involved in this case....

The majority opinion relies upon IDAPA 58.01.06.005.02 and 40 C.F.R. 258.25 as providing the applicable standard of care. Neither of those regulations is intended to prevent trespassers from injuring themselves through an accident at a landfill. They are intended to prevent trespassers from dumping or salvaging materials that may be harmful to health or the environment. . . .

The concern is illegal dumping of wastes that are dangerous to human health and the environment. The word "health" is not normally construed to include freedom from accidents. Rather, it simply means "freedom from disease or abnormality." The majority can reach its conclusion only by redefining the word "health" to include "safety." Such redefinition is not supported either by Idaho law or by the federal regulations. . . .

The [federal] regulation only requires barriers to prevent "unauthorized vehicular traffic and illegal dumping of wastes." The required barriers need not be able to keep out trespassing pedestrians who may accidentally injure themselves at the landfill. . . . [T]he regulation was not intended to require municipal solid waste disposal facilities to fence out trespassing pedestrians. . . .

NOTES

1. **The class of persons and type of harm tests.** As the Idaho court explains in *O'Guin*, a threshold requirement for a statute to be given per se effect is that the injured person must be in a class of persons that the statute is designed to protect, and the type of harm that the actor's conduct causes must be a type that the statute is designed to protect against. These requirements are fairly uniform from state to state. *See* RESTATEMENT (THIRD) § 14 (P.F.D. No. 1, 2005). As California's high court puts it, the negligence per se rule "arises from a tortfeasor's failure to exercise due care in violation of a statute designed to protect a class of persons, of which the injured party is a member, from the type of injury sustained." *Ramirez v. Nelson*, 188 P.3d 659 (Cal. 2008). *See* DOBBS ON TORTS § 137 (2000).

2. **Judicial applications of the class of persons and type of harm tests.** As you might glean from the *O'Guin* case, there is a good deal of flexibility built in to the determination of whether the injured person is in the protected class and whether the type of harm that occurred is of the same type that the statute was designed to protect against. One problem is that legislatures, especially state legislatures, rarely specify such matters.

3. **Statutes intended to protect the public at large.** One might think that if a court determines that the class protected by a statute is the public at large, the plaintiff will always fit within it. But many courts have held that a statute that does not create a duty to an identifiable class—a subset of the general public, in other words—cannot be given per se effect. *See, e.g., Pehle v. Farm Bureau Life Ins. Co.*, 397 F.3d 897 (10th Cir. 2005). *See* DOBBS ON TORTS § 142 (2000).

4. **Making the determination.** How does the court in *O'Guin* determine who is in the protected class, and what types of harm the statute was designed to protect against? How do we know whether the majority or the dissent is correct about what the legislature intended?

5. **Judicial adoption theory of statutes and the class of person and harm rules.** *Must* the court consider legislative purpose to protect a certain class of persons or to protect against a certain type of harm? Remember that the statutes used in negligence per se cases do not themselves create, either expressly or impliedly, tort causes of action. Many courts would agree, therefore, with the statement that the fact the legislature has enacted such a statute "does not necessarily mean that the courts must adopt it as a standard of civil liability. Decisions regarding the proper civil standard of conduct rest with the courts. Thus, the courts must ultimately decide whether they will adopt a statutory standard to define the standard of reasonable persons in specific circumstances." *Rains v. Bend of the River*, 124 S.W.3d 580 (Tenn. Ct. App. 2003).

If, as the *Rains* court also said, the court is free to adopt the standard as one that reflects what reasonable people would do, what difference does it make that the legislature wrote the particular statute narrowly? To think about this, suppose the statute provides that heavy machinery used at construction sites must automatically make back-up noises when in reverse gear, and that the statute is for the protection of workers at the job site. If the machine in violation of the statute backs over an unsuspecting architecture student who is on the premises to be shown how a building is constructed, he has no negligence per se claim. *Cf.* Restatement (Second) of Torts § 286, illus. 1 (1965). Yet the contractor violated the statute. It would have cost him no more to have complied with it for the purpose of protecting everyone than for the purpose of protecting workers on the job. Besides this, the legislature might have thought back-up beepers were needed "because of danger to workers," without really intending to exclude the possibility of saving other persons as well. These things might suggest that the class of person/class of risk rule should not be used to limit liability. But they might also suggest that the courts should use very large classifications, or, conceivably, that statutory violations should be treated in all cases as merely evidence of negligence. In *Scott v. Matlack, Inc.*, 39 P.3d 1160 (Colo. 2002), the court faced a federal statute and regulations specifying workplace safety practices required for the benefit of the employer's employees. The court held that the safety regulations could be admitted in evidence to show industry safety customs not only for employees—the class of persons protected by the statute—but also for independent contractors on the work site.

6. **The "defining the standard of conduct" requirement.** Why does the *O'Guin* court say that a statute cannot be given negligence per se effect unless it "clearly defines the required standard of conduct?" Could any statute be given per se effect if it did not? *See, e.g., Rains v. Bend of the River*, 124 S.W.3d 580 (Tenn. Ct. App. 2003) (Federal Gun Control Act "does not contain a clearly defined standard of conduct" and thus cannot be given per se effect); *Hurst v. Ohio Dep't of Rehabilitation and Corrections*, 650 N.E.2d 104 (Ohio 1995) (statute inapplicable where it defines the obligation only in "abstract or general terms").

7. **Rejecting statutory standards that impose new duties.** "[T]he defendant in most negligence per se cases already owes the plaintiff a pre-existing common law duty to act as a reasonably prudent person, so that the statute's role is merely to define more precisely what conduct breaches that

duty." *Perry v. S.N.,* 973 S.W.2d 301 (Tex. 1998). When the statute creates a wholly new obligation and does not in itself purport to create a new cause of action, courts tend to give the statute no tort law effect at all. That was the case in *Perry*, where the statute required people to report known cases of child abuse. Since no common law obligation of this sort existed, and the statute did not purport to create a new cause of action, the court denied recovery to children whose abuse might have been avoided if a timely report had been made.

8. **The "causation" requirement.** Many cases say that the negligence per se rule does not impose liability for violation of a statute unless violation is a "proximate" or legal cause of the plaintiff's harm, but on analysis, this should work out to produce the same results produced by the class of person/ type of harm rules. Proximate cause is considered in Chapter 8.

9. **Licensing statutes.** Should courts adopt licensing statutes as standards of care? Perhaps the most famous case on this topic is *Brown v. Shyne*, 151 N.E. 197 (N.Y. 1926). The plaintiff alleged that the defendant held himself out to practice medicine, that his treatments paralyzed her, and that he had no license to practice medicine. The New York Court of Appeals held that the plaintiff could not get to the jury on this allegation but would instead be required to allege and prove negligence by ordinary means. A few cases apply the negligence per se rule to particular licensing statutes, or find limited exceptions. *See Kizer v. Harper,* 561 S.E.2d 368 (W.Va. 2001).

10. **Common law negligence.** Be sure to notice that the plaintiff can claim negligence on ordinary common law principles even if the statute has no effect. That is, the standard of care "defaults" back to the reasonable and prudent person standard where the statute is held not to supplant it.

IMPSON v. STRUCTURAL METALS, INC.

487 S.W.2d 694 (Tex. 1972)

GREENHILL, JUSTICE.

[The driver of defendant's truck attempted to pass a car within 100 feet of an intersection; the car turned left into the intersection and was struck by the truck. This is an action for injury to some passengers in the car and death of another. A statute prohibits passing within 100 feet of an intersection. The trial judge held that, the jury having found that the defendant passed within 100 feet of the intersection, negligence was established as a matter of law. Accordingly he entered judgment for the plaintiffs. The Texas Court of Appeal held that since defendant had offered some excuses, the negligence issue had to be submitted to the jury. The plaintiffs bring this appeal.]

[T]he problem here is to decide what excuses or justifications are legally acceptable. In *Phoenix*, the excuse was a tire blowout. In *Hammer*, it was that because of the wet streets, the defendant's bus unavoidably skidded out of control. In *Christy*, the contention was that it was simply impossible for the truck driver to stop within the prescribed distance from the railroad track. In none of these cases has this court addressed itself to the legal sufficiency of the excuse.

The Restatement of Torts, Second (1965), deals with this problem in a new section, 288A. It states that an excused violation of a legislative enactment is not negligence. While the section expressly says that the list of excusable situations given is not intended to be exclusive, it lists five categories. They are:

"(a) the violation is reasonable because of the actor's incapacity;

"(b) he neither knows nor should know of the occasion for compliance;

"(c) he is unable after reasonable diligence or care to comply;

"(d) he is confronted by an emergency not due to his own misconduct;

"(e) compliance would involve a greater risk of harm to the actor or to others."

Under category (a), "incapacity," could come cases where the violator was too young, or did not have the mental capacity, to be charged with negligence. It might include a blind man who unknowingly walks a red light (though he may be contributorily negligent for other reasons), or a driver who is rendered physically incapable because of a heart attack. Under category (b) could come cases where a night driver has a tail light go out unexpectedly and without his knowledge. Under category (c), "unable after reasonable diligence or care to comply," could come cases involving impossibility, as in Christy v. Blades. Under category (d), "emergency not due to his own misconduct," could come cases in which there is an unexpected failure in the steering or braking system; a blowout of a tire which is reasonably thought to be in good condition; a sudden confrontation with blinding dust or smoke on the highway. It could include driving on the left side of the highway to avoid striking a darting child, and similar situations. Finally, the illustration given by the Restatement for category (e), "greater risk of harm," is one in which the law requires people to walk facing traffic, but due to particular circumstances, it would involve greater risk to walk upon that side. The above are intended merely as illustrations of a principle and are recognized to be dictum here. But we do approve of the general treatment of legally acceptable excuses as set out in the Restatement, Second.

[The defendant sought to excuse its violation of the statute by pointing to evidence that the driver had forgotten the existence of the intersection in question; that the sign marking the intersection was small; that there were no lines in the road to indicate "no passing"; and that he was watching the car ahead, which was partly off the road on the right, rather than watching for the intersection sign.]

All of the above matters fall within the realm of ordinary care,–or lack of care. The driver made his move deliberately, with knowledge of the law and with at least notice of the presence of the highway intersection. There was no impossibility, no reason for any particular hurry, no emergency, and no incapacity. The problem of greater risk of harm is not involved. If there was an emergency, it was only after the statutory violation had begun, and was due in large part to his own deliberate conduct.

In view of the evidence offered, the trial court correctly determined that there was no evidence offered of any legally acceptable excuse or justification. It was, in law, an unexcused violation. The finding, therefore, that the driver violated the statute intended as a safety measure and the finding of proximate cause entitled the plaintiffs to a judgment.

[On motion for rehearing the court remanded the case solely for consideration of certain issues about damages.]

NOTES

1. In a number of extreme cases, courts that ordinarily recognize the per se rule have held that statutory violation was excused. This has been the holding, for example, where the statute required good brakes, but the brakes suddenly failed without the driver's fault.

2. The Restatement Third has reworked and clarified the list of excuses from the Restatement Second quoted in *Impson*. It now provides that a violation of a statute is "excused and not negligent" if (a) the violation is reasonable in light of the actor's childhood, physical disability, or physical incapacitation; (b) the actor exercises reasonable care in attempting to comply with the statute; (c) the actor neither knows nor should know of the factual circumstances that render the statute applicable; (d) the actor's violation of statute is due to the confusing way in which the requirements of the statute are presented to the public; or (e) the actor's compliance with the statute would involve a greater risk of physical harm to the actor or to others than noncompliance. RESTATEMENT (THIRD) OF TORTS: LIABILITY FOR PHYSICAL HARM § 15 (P.F.D. No. 1, 2005).

3. **Implications.** If excuses are limited to those formulated by the Restatement, might the effect be a kind of strict liability? On the other hand, if excuses are not limited, is the negligence per se rule in effect scuttled? In *Alarid v. Vanier*, 327 P.2d 897 (Cal. 1958) the court said: "In our opinion the correct test is whether the person who has violated a statute has sustained the burden of showing that he did what might reasonably be expected of a person of ordinary prudence, acting under similar circumstances, who desired to comply with the law." What effect, if any, does such an approach give to the statute?

4. **Child's standard in negligence per se cases.** Which prevails when a child violates a statute, the child standard of care or the statutory standard? In other words, does the negligence per se rule apply to children? In *Bauman v. Crawford*, 704 P.2d 1181 (Wash. 1985), the court said: "We hold that a minor's violation of a statute does not constitute proof of negligence per se, but may, in proper cases, be introduced as evidence of a minor's negligence." Why would holding children to the statutory standard be such a bad idea, especially where they are engaged in childish activities like walking across a street or riding a bicycle?

5. **Non–Excuses.** Case law, and the Restatement (Third) recognize that negligence per se has been applied, typically and traditionally, only to "unexcused" statutory violations, a formulation we saw *in Martin v. Herzog, supra.* Is it a valid excuse for a person to say that he did not agree with the statute's provisions? Or to argue that he was ignorant of the law? Or what if the violator can prove that people customarily violate the statutory provisions? No is the answer to all of these questions. *See* RESTATEMENT (THIRD) § 15, cmt. *a* (P.F.D. No. 1, 2005).

PROBLEM

Lind v. Maigret

Driving his car on a mountain highway, Maigret hit a fog bank and slowed. A large boulder rolled down the hillside and struck the rear of Maigret's car from the side. The impact spun Maigret's car around. Maigret did not react skillfully. He went into a state of shock when he felt the impact, gripping the steering wheel and closing his eyes. When his car came to a stop, the engine was stalled. He was unable to start it. The car was projecting across most of one lane of traffic in fairly thick fog. At this point it was hit by a truck driven by Lind. That impact caused serious injury to Lind. A statute provided that "no person shall stop, park, or leave standing any vehicle, whether attended or unattended, upon the roadway." Another statute provided that "Every person driving a motor vehicle shall exercise care for the safety of others at all times."

Lind has proposed negligence per se instructions to the judge, who asks you, as Maigret's counsel, whether you have any objections or views on the subject. What is your position based on authority in this section?

CHAPTER 6

NEGLIGENCE: BREACH OF DUTY

■ ■ ■

§ 1. ASSESSING REASONABLE CARE BY ASSESSING FORESEEABLE RISKS AND COSTS

Once the court determines that the defendant owed the plaintiff a duty, and what that duty is—usually the duty of reasonable care—the question for the jury is whether the defendant breached that duty by failing to exercise the requisite quantum of care. The defendant who breaches the duty of care is negligent.

Negligence is overt conduct that creates unreasonable risks that a reasonable person would avoid. The risk of harm is unreasonable when a reasonable and prudent person would foresee that harm might result *and* would avoid conduct that creates the risk. Conduct may include a failure to act if action is required, but a mere state of mind is not conduct. If the defendant daydreams but drives properly in all respects, he might be careless in the lay sense, but he is not legally negligent. Analysis of unreasonable risk leads us to consider, among other things, whether alternative conduct would have avoided the harm.

As the New Jersey Supreme Court has explained, "To act non-negligently is to take reasonable precautions to prevent the occurrence of foreseeable harm to others. What precautions are 'reasonable' depends upon the risk of harm involved and the practicability of preventing it." *Weinberg v. Dinger*, 524 A.2d 366 (N.J. 1987).

———

Legal professionals think of intentional torts as contrasting with negligence. However, an intentional *act*, as opposed to an intentional *harm*, is not necessarily an intentional tort. For example if you intentionally drive at a very high speed you may be taking an unreasonable risk; if so, you'd be negligent. What else would be necessary to show you were chargeable with an intentional tort rather than negligence?

———

PROBLEM

Brown v. Stiel

The Stiel Company, a construction contractor, decided to build a building for its own use. It provided an architect with the basic design elements, and plans were drawn which Stiel then followed in building. Stiel chose a design in which the major structural components were steel. It rejected a design based on poured concrete in favor of steel beams because the steel beam construction was, in the particular situation, much cheaper and quicker. However, as Stiel knew, the kind of steel beam construction proposed generally caused or was associated with accidents which caused death or serious injury. In fact, it was known that for a building the size of Stiel's, three workers or others would be killed or paralyzed or otherwise seriously injured. The concrete building also involved predictable injuries; but, for a building this size, the prediction for such injury was that only one person would be injured. Stiel nevertheless chose the riskier steel construction because of time and cost differences.

There was a collapse of some steel beams and John White, an employee of Stiel who had done steel work for many years, fell to the ground and suffered a broken back and permanent paralysis from the neck down. The same collapse dropped a steel beam on Billy Brown, a delivery person for a nearby deli. Billy Brown was on the premises bringing an order for the supervising architect when the beam fell. Brown lost a leg as a result of the building's collapse.

NOTES

1. Did Stiel Co. commit an intentional tort? Consider whether this case differs from a case in which A throws a brick from the roof of a building into a crowd below.

2. Suppose a court holds that no intentional tort is shown in this problem. Even so, maybe Stiel ought to pay for the harm done as a matter of justice or social policy. If certain costs are more or less inevitable in a business, maybe those costs should be regarded as a cost that business should bear as a part of its overhead. If a construction company expects that its own construction vehicles will periodically collide and sustain damage, it will budget for this cost and charge sufficient amounts to cover this cost as well as all others. Should the same be done when it comes to human costs?

3. Workers' compensation statutes proceed upon the theory that work-connected injuries may generally be regarded as a part of the employer's cost of doing business—the human "breakage," analogous to broken plates in a restaurant. Since such losses are more or less inevitable in a statistical sense, the employer simply budgets for them—charging sufficiently for its work to cover the costs.

4. Is there any justification for holding Stiel liable to White for workers' compensation but not holding Stiel liable to Brown?

5. Assuming that Brown cannot recover workers' compensation from Stiel because he was not an employee, and that he cannot recover from the

deli because the statute did not cover businesses with very few employees, would Brown nevertheless have an action under common law tort theory? Consider the introductory comments about negligence as well as the cases that follow.

PIPHER v. PARSELL

930 A.2d 890 (Del. 2007)

HOLLAND, JUSTICE.

The plaintiff-appellant, Kristyn Pipher ("Pipher"), appeals from the Superior Court's judgment as a matter of law in favor of the defendant-appellee, Johnathan Parsell ("Parsell"). Pipher argues that the Superior Court erred when it ruled that, as a matter of law, Parsell was not negligent. We agree and hold that the issue of Parsell's negligence should have been submitted to the jury.

On March 20, 2002, around 6 p.m., Pipher, Parsell and Johnene Beisel ("Beisel"), also a defendant, were traveling south on Delaware Route 1 near Lewes, Delaware, in Parsell's pickup truck. All three were sitting on the front seat. Parsell was driving, Pipher was sitting in the middle, and Beisel was in the passenger seat next to the door. They were all sixteen-years-old at the time.

As they were traveling at 55 mph, Beisel unexpectedly "grabbed the steering wheel causing the truck to veer off onto the shoulder of the road." Parsell testified that Beisel's conduct caused him both shock and surprise. Although Beisel's conduct prompted him to be on his guard, Parsell further testified that he did not expect Beisel to grab the wheel again. Nevertheless, his recognition of how serious Beisel's conduct was shows he was aware that he now had someone in his car who had engaged in dangerous behavior.

Parsell testified that he did nothing in response to Beisel's initial action. Approximately thirty seconds later, Beisel again yanked the steering wheel, causing Parsell's truck to leave the roadway, slide down an embankment and strike a tree. Pipher was injured as a result of the collision.

Pipher's testimony at trial was for the most part consistent with Parsell's testimony. Pipher recalled that the three occupants in the vehicle were talking back and forth and that the mood was light as they drove south on Route 1. She also testified that after Beisel yanked the steering wheel for the first time, Parsell was able to regain control of the truck. According to Pipher, despite the dangerous nature of the conduct, Parsell and Beisel just laughed about it like it was a joke. Pipher testified she felt that Beisel grabbed the steering wheel a second time because Parsell "laughed it off" the first time.

At trial, Parsell acknowledged that he could have taken different steps to try to prevent Beisel from grabbing the steering wheel a second time. First, Parsell acknowledged, he could have admonished Beisel not to touch the steering wheel again. Second, he acknowledged that he could have pulled over to the side of the road and required Beisel to get into the back seat. Third, Parsell acknowledged that he could have warned Beisel that he would put her out of the vehicle.

The trial judge concluded that, as a matter of law, Parsell had no duty to do anything after Beisel yanked the wheel the first time because it would be reasonable for the driver to assume that it would not happen again. The trial judge also ruled that (1) there was no negligence in failing to discharge the dangerous passenger and (2) that failing to admonish the dangerous passenger was not negligence. . . .

A driver owes a duty of care to her or his passengers because it is foreseeable that they may be injured if, through inattention or otherwise, the driver involves the car she or he is operating in a collision. Almost forty-five years ago, this Court held that a minor who operates a motor vehicle on the highways of Delaware will be held to the same standard of care and "must accord his [or her] own passengers the same diligence and protection which is required of an adult motorist under similar circumstances." . . .

Pipher argues that after Beisel grabbed the steering wheel initially, Parsell was on notice that a dangerous situation could reoccur in the truck. Pipher further argues that once Parsell had notice of a possibly dangerous situation, he had a duty to exercise reasonable care to protect his passengers from that harm. Finally, Pipher concludes that Parsell was negligent when he kept driving without attempting to remove, or at least address, that risk. . . .

In general, where the actions of a passenger that cause an accident are not foreseeable, there is no negligence attributable to the driver. But, when actions of a passenger that interfere with the driver's safe operation of the motor vehicle are foreseeable, the failure to prevent such conduct may be a breach of the driver's duty to either other passengers or to the public. Under the circumstances of this case, a reasonable jury could find that Parsell breached his duty to protect Pipher from Beisel by preventing Beisel from grabbing the steering wheel a second time.

The issue of Parsell's alleged breach of duty to Pipher, the foreseeability of Beisel's repeat conduct, and the proximate cause of Pipher's injuries were all factual determinations that should have been submitted to the jury. Accordingly, the judgment of the Superior Court, that was entered as a matter of law, is reversed. This matter is remanded for further proceedings in accordance with this opinion.

NOTES

1. Would the trial court have been correct in ruling that there was no breach of duty as a matter of law if Beisel had caused the accident the first time he grabbed the wheel? Why would that be a different case? *Cf. Brown v. Mobley,* 488 S.E.2d 710 (Ga. Ct. App. 1997) (no evidence that eventual conduct of intoxicated passenger should have been anticipated).

2. What facts should the jury consider on remand on the issue of whether Parsell breached a duty to Pipher? Can you state the strongest arguments for both the plaintiff and the defendant on this issue?

3. Foreseeability of harm (both the likelihood of harm and its severity) plays a number of roles in negligence law. Some courts hold that foreseeability of harm is necessary for a duty of care to exist at all, but other courts and the Restatement (Third) strongly disagree. *Compare, e.g., Tarasoff v. Regents of University of California*, 551 P.2d 334 (Cal. 1976) (foreseeability of harm is the "major factor" in a duty analysis), *with* RESTATEMENT (THIRD) § 7, cmt. j (P.F.D. No. 1, 2005) (positing that a focus on foreseeability of harm on the duty issue usurps the jury's function to decide as a factual matter whether a duty was breached). We will see much more of this debate in coming chapters. There is no disagreement, however, that foreseeability of harm is central to the issue of whether a person's conduct fell below the standard of reasonable care.

NOTE: ASSESSING THE LANGUAGE
OF FORESEEABILITY AND RISK

Focus for a moment, not on the ideas, principles, or rules, but on the *language* courts often use to express themselves about negligence and how we must read and understand that language.

"Courts often use the term 'foreseeable' as a shorthand expression. They might say, for example, that a defendant is negligent if harm was foreseeable. Such statements should not ordinarily be taken in a literal way. Harm is a foreseeable consequence of almost all acts, but courts definitely do not mean that *all* acts are negligent. Courts are likely to use the term 'foreseeable' to mean that harm was not only foreseeable but also too likely to occur to justify risking it without added precautions. Similarly, courts sometimes speak about some harms as more foreseeable than others, which can be understood to mean that the risk or probability of harm is greater in some cases than in others. Along the same lines, when courts say that harm is unforeseeable, they may mean that although harm was actually foreseeable on the facts of the case, a reasonable person would not have taken action to prevent it because the risk of harm was low, and harm was so improbable that a reasonable person would not have taken safety precautions. Put differently, to say that harm was unforeseeable often seems to mean only that the foreseeable harm was not probable enough to require precaution, meaning ultimately that the defendant's conduct was not unreasonably risky." 1 DOBBS ON TORTS § 143 (2001).

Consider the court's language in *Romine v. Village of Irving*, 783 N.E.2d 1064 (Ill. App. Ct. 2003). Police officers ejected two unruly, intoxicated people from a fair, knowing that those people were from out of town. Once ejected, the intoxicated people drove their car negligently, causing injuries to the plaintiff. The plaintiff included the police officers in the suit for damages on the ground that the police officers should have arrested the intoxicated persons to prevent their dangerous driving. The court said that police officers could not foresee criminal acts in general and in particular drunken driving by intoxicated persons they ejected from a fair. Can either of these statements be taken literally? Surely police can foresee criminal activity in general—after all, they are hired to prevent it and to arrest its perpetrators. And intoxicated driving seems not only foreseeable but as the court itself said, all too common. So what might the court have been trying to say when it used the "foreseeability" locution?

INDIANA CONSOLIDATED INSURANCE CO. v. MATHEW

402 N.E.2d 1000 (Ind. Ct. App. 1980)

HOFFMAN, JUDGE.

Appellant Indiana Consolidated Insurance Company seeks review of the finding that Robert D. Mathew (Mathew) did not act in a negligent manner so as to be liable for damages done to his brother's garage when a Toro riding lawnmower that Mathew was starting caught fire. Appellant insured the garage and premises under a homeowner's insurance policy and is pursuing this claim against Mathew by virtue of its subrogation rights.[1]

[T]he facts favorable to Mathew disclose that on May 1, 1976 Mathew's brother was out of town for the weekend. The two brothers lived across the street from each other and took turns mowing both lawns. In the late afternoon Mathew decided to mow both lawns and went to his brother's garage where a twelve horsepower Toro riding lawnmower was stored. The mower was approximately eight years old, was kept in good mechanical condition, and had required only minor tune-ups and belt replacements for the rotary mower assembly. Mathew pulled the mower away from the side wall of the garage and after checking the gas gauge filled the lawnmower approximately three-fourths full with gasoline using a funnel. He then went back across the street to his home for approximately twenty minutes. Upon returning to the garage Mathew started the lawnmower. However, he noticed a flame in the engine area under the hood and immediately shut the engine off. He opened the hood and saw a flame four to five inches tall under the gas tank. Using some clean towels Mathew tried to snuff out the flame but was unsuccessful. He could find no other means to extinguish the fire. The flames continued to grow and the machine began spewing gasoline, so he ran to his home to call the fire department. Here turned to find the garage totally engulfed in flames.

At trial Mathew testified that he was afraid to try to push the flaming machine outside the garage for fear that the tank would explode in his face.

Indiana Consolidated brought this action against Mathew alleging that he breached a duty owed to his brother to exercise due care in starting the lawnmower and therefore stands liable for the damages

---

1. [Editors' note.] A fire insurer or collision insurer who pays its insured's loss "stands in the shoes" of the insured for the purpose of suing any tortfeasor whose tortious acts caused the loss.

resulting from his negligence. After a bench trial the court below entered the following finding, to-wit:

> The Court having heretofore taken this matter under advisement and having considered the evidence introduced in the trial of this cause and being sufficiently advised, now enters Findings as follows: The Court now finds ... that there is no evidence of negligence on the part of the defendant, Robert D. Mathew, and that the plaintiff should take nothing by its complaint.

> IT IS THEREFORE ORDERED, ADJUDGED AND DECREED BY THE COURT that the plaintiff, Indiana Consolidated Insurance Company, take nothing by its complaint; and Judgment is entered for and on behalf of the defendant, Robert D. Mathew. Costs of this action are taxed to the plaintiff.

On appeal appellant contends that the judgment is contrary to law because Mathew was negligent in filling the gas tank, in starting the mower in an enclosed area, and in failing to push the flaming mower out of the garage. The standard by which Mathew's conduct is to be measured is whether he exercised the duty to use due care in operating the mower that an ordinary prudent man would exercise under the same or similar circumstances.

The record amply supports the finding that Mathew did not act in a negligent manner in filling the gas tank. He testified that he did so carefully, with the use of a funnel. He did not fill the tank full, and he was adamant in his belief that he did not spill any gasoline. He hypothesized that even had any gas been spilled it would have evaporated in the cool air during the twenty-minute period before he started the mower. Appellant is merely asking this Court to reweigh the evidence in regard to any gasoline spillage due to Mathew's admission on cross-examination that he could have spilled some fuel. The trier of fact resolved this issue in favor of Mathew, finding that he exercised due care in fueling the mower, and it must remain undisturbed upon appeal. Appellant is again reminded that any conflicts in testimony when appeal from a negative judgment is taken must be resolved in favor of the appellee.

Appellant's contention that Mathew should be held liable for the act of negligently starting the mower inside the garage is also without merit. It cannot seriously be contended that the evidence shows that Mathew acted other than a reasonably prudent man in pulling the mower out into an open area of the garage and starting it. The mower was a riding type that was of considerable weight and size. Garages are designed to permit the starting of motorized vehicles such as automobiles and are commonly used for such purpose. That this particular mower would catch fire at this particular time was not reasonably foreseeable. As one is not required to anticipate that which is unlikely to happen, the trial court did not err in determining that Mathew was not negligent in starting the mower inside the garage.

Appellant's further allegation that Mathew negligently failed to push the flaming mower out of the garage area is refuted by the evidence that the machine was spewing gasoline and that he was afraid for his safety should the tank explode. Mathew therefore chose to leave and summon help from the local fire department. One who is confronted with a sudden emergency not of his own making is not chargeable with negligence if he acts according to his best judgment. The sudden emergency doctrine requires the person so confronted to do that which an ordinary prudent man would do under like circumstances. Mathew's course of action can be deemed an exercise of ordinary prudence. The law values human life above property. Greater risk of one's person is justified to save life than is reasonable in protecting property. If Mathew had tried to push the riding mower ten feet into an open area the machine might have exploded and caused much graver damage to his person than was suffered by the destruction of the garage. Contrary to appellant's position several jurisdictions have ruled that one may be deemed negligent in voluntarily risking life or serious injury for the purpose of saving mere property. . . .

The judgment is not contrary to law and is therefore affirmed.

NOTES

1. Precisely what permitted the trial court to find that the defendant was not negligent?

2. Does it matter to the analysis that the alternative conduct proposed by the defendant imposes costs or burdens on third parties? For example, what if a child fell on wet grass while participating in a relay race at defendant's camp? See *Fintzi v. New Jersey YMHA–YWHA*, 765 N.E.2d 288 (N.Y. 2001).

3. A woman fell while taking off her shoes before going through airport security, and sued the Transportation Safety Administration (TSA) for negligence in not providing her a chair. The record showed that "of the thousands of passengers passing through the security screening measures at the airport prior to plaintiff's injury, no similar incidents had occurred." The trial court granted summary judgment for the defendant, holding there was no breach of duty. In light of *Piper* and *Mathew*, how would you analyze this issue on appeal? *See Barnes v. United States*, 485 F.3d 341 (6th Cir. 2007).

STINNETT v. BUCHELE

598 S.W.2d 469 (Ky. Ct. App. 1980)

BREETZ, JUDGE.

This is a tort action filed by an employee against his employer for injuries sustained during the course and scope of his employment. The lower court granted summary judgment to the employer on the ground that there was no showing that the injury was caused by the negligence of the employer. We affirm.

The accident which gave rise to this suit was also the subject of a workmen's compensation claim. The Workmen's Compensation Board denied benefits because the employee, being employed in agriculture, was exempt from the coverage of the Workmen's Compensation Act. We have today, by separate and non-published opinion, affirmed the board in that regard. . . .

Earl S. Buchele is a practicing physician in Hardinsburg, Kentucky. He hired Alvin Stinnett as a farm laborer in January 1976. In September of that year Mr. Stinnett undertook to repair the roof on a barn located at one of Dr. Buchele's farms known as the Cloverport Farm. The repairs were to consist of nailing down the edges of the roof that had been loosened by the wind and painting the roof with a coating. Stinnett was severely injured when he fell from the roof while applying the coating with a paint roller.

Stinnett urges in his brief to this court that Dr. Buchele was negligent for failing to comply with occupational and health regulations and also for his failure to provide a safe place to work. Dr. Buchele denies both of those assertions, and, additionally, argues that Stinnett was contributorily negligent as a matter of law. We do not reach the issue of contributory negligence. . . .

Nor do we find any evidence to be submitted to the jury that Dr. Buchele was negligent in failing to provide Stinnett with a safe place to work. We agree with Stinnett when he states that Dr. Buchele had the obligation to furnish him:

> . . . a place reasonably safe having regard for the character of work and reasonably safe tools and appliances for doing the work. The measure of duty is to exercise ordinary or reasonable care to do so. The standard is the care exercised by prudent employers in similar circumstances.

We also agree with the sentence immediately preceding the quotation from that same opinion: "An employer's obligation to its employee is not the frequently impossible duty of furnishing absolutely safe instrumentalities or place to work."

Although we may consider that painting a barn roof is dangerous work, we cannot say that Dr. Buchele can be held liable for failing to provide a safe place to work solely because he asked Stinnett to work on the roof. We hold, therefore, that there was no showing of any negligence on the part of Dr. Buchele arising solely out of the fact that he had asked Stinnett to paint the barn roof.

Stinnett next argues . . . that a reasonable and prudent employer would have provided safety devices of some kind even though not required to by force of statute or regulation and that the question whether Dr. Buchele measured up to the standards of an ordinarily careful and prudent employer is one for the jury. . . . The liability of the employer:

> . . . rests upon the assumption that the employer has a better and more comprehensive knowledge than the employees, and ceases to be applicable where the employees' means of knowledge of the dangers to

be incurred is equal to that of the employer. 53 Am. Jur. 2d, Master and Servant, § 160.

Stinnett had been in the painting business with his brother-in-law for two years before he began working for Dr. Buchele. Although the record is not clear whether Stinnett, his brother-in-law or both did the painting, they did paint a church steeple and an undetermined number of barn roofs. On occasion safety belts and safety nets had been used while painting the barn roofs. Stinnett was injured on a Sunday. Dr. Buchele was not present and he did not know that Stinnett was going to work on the barn roof on that particular day. Dr. Buchele had, however, purchased the material that Stinnett was applying to the roof when he fell. Stinnett did not ask Dr. Buchele to procure a safety net nor did he check to see if one was available. He admitted he could have used a safety rope around his waist but he did not think any were available. . . .

In short, we find no evidence of negligence on the part of Dr. Buchele to submit to a jury.

NOTES

1. **Workers' compensation.** Although workers' compensation statutes have been adopted everywhere, they do not include all workers within their benefits. Statutes may exclude agricultural employees, domestic employees and casual employees, for example. One special case is that of the worker on interstate railroads. Under the Federal Employers Liability Act, 45 U.S.C.A. §§ 51 *et seq.*, called FELA, these workers have expanded tort rights, but no workers' compensation. Workers not covered by compensation laws must, like Mr. Stinnett, seek recovery under the tort system.

2. **Social vs. individual responsibility for injuries.** Even if Dr. Buchele was not at fault and this was simply an accident, Mr. Stinnett was still injured. Persons in this position may not be able to work at all and may have substantial medical needs. Apart from human sympathy, is there any reason to consider this as a social problem rather than as Mr. Stinnett's individual problem? If there are social problems represented in injury cases and society ought to respond in some fashion, does that indicate that Dr. Buchele as an individual ought to bear any of Mr. Stinnett's loss?

3. **Expecting the plaintiff to care for himself.** How could the court have concluded that Dr. Buchele was not negligent? Was it not foreseeable that Stinnett might fall off the roof if he did not have safety equipment? Compare *Stinnett* with *Lowery v. Echostar Satellite Corp.*, 160 P.3d 959 (Okla. 2007). *In Lowery*, a customer of a satellite TV company was injured when she fell off the roof of her garage while attempting to repair her satellite dish. She claimed the company was negligent in exposing her to the risks of falling off the roof by refusing to repair the dish and instead insisting that she should make the minor repairs herself, even over her protestations that she was inexperienced and did not want to climb the roof. She was actually talking with the company's customer service department on her cordless phone when she fell. The court affirmed the trial court's grant of summary judgment for the company, concluding that there was no evidence that the company "was

in a superior position to protect her," such as by knowing of some danger of harm beyond those normally presented by climbing up on any roof. The court said it was "beyond good sense" to hold otherwise.

Consider how the courts in *Stinnett* or *Lowery* would have ruled if the plaintiff had suffered from serious dementia, likely to forget where he or she was, and the defendant knew it. *See Daniels v. Senior Care, Inc.*, 21 S.W.3d 133 (Mo. Ct. App. 2000).

4. **The obviousness of danger.** "[T]he obviousness of a risk may make the likelihood of its materializing so slight that there is no need to try to eliminate the risk." *Halek v. United States*, 178 F.3d 481 (7th Cir. 1999). Is that an explanation for the *Stinnett* holding? The *Lowery* court, *supra* Note 3, referred more than once in its discussion to "the obvious risks of climbing onto a rooftop." You may think this principle is sometimes misapplied. For instance, you might seriously doubt whether a railroad flatcar blocking a crossing at night creates a risk so obvious that no precaution is needed, yet an Illinois court held that the flatcar gave its own warning. *Malcome v. Toledo, Peoria & W. Ry. Corp.*, 811 N.E.2d 1199 (Ill. App. Ct. 2004). If that is a distortion of a fair principle, however, the principle itself might still be sound. That is, perhaps it is not unreasonable to fail to take action to lessen a risk to someone that is so patently obvious that the other person can be relied upon to avoid it on his own.

5. **Expecting care by third persons.** If parents accompany a child to a backyard party and know of the swimming pool there, can the host reasonably think the risk of injury to the child is low in spite of the dangers of a pool? Why? *Herron v. Hollis*, 546 S.E.2d 17 (Ga. Ct. App. 2001). What if the parents do not know the host has a pool that can be reached by a small child? *Cf. Perri v. Furama Restaurant, Inc.*, 781 N.E.2d 631 (Ill. App. Ct. 2002) ("If parents or caregivers are unaware of a particular danger, it is reasonably foreseeable that they will fail to prevent a minor child from encountering that danger. Thus, while defendant was certainly entitled to rely on the adults in plaintiffs' group to protect their children from dangers of which the adults were or should have been aware, defendant is not absolved of its duty ... simply because Jordan was accompanied by his parents."). What if a parent and her three-year-old child visit the defendant's house, and the child is injured when he pulls over an empty bookcase? Would the defendant be liable? *See Foss v. Kincade*, 746 N.W.2d 912 (Minn. Ct. App. 2008) (no liability for failing to protect a child visiting in the company of a parent from the dangers posed by ordinary household objects).

BERNIER v. BOSTON EDISON CO.

403 N.E.2d 391 (Mass. 1980)

KAPLAN, JUSTICE.

About 2:30 p.m., May 24, 1972, the plaintiffs Arthur Bernier, Jr., and Patricia J. Kasputys, then eighteen and fifteen years old, were let out of school and, after going to Kasputys's house, sauntered to an ice cream parlor on Massachusetts Avenue in Lexington Center, one of the town's major shopping areas. A half hour later, Alice Ramsdell entered her 1968

Buick Skylark automobile parked, pointed east, on the south side of Massachusetts Avenue (which here runs west-east), in the last metered space about fifteen to twenty feet short of where the avenue meets Muzzey Street, a one-way street beginning at the avenue and running south. No traffic signals were posted at the junction with Muzzey Street.

As Ramsdell started her car, she noted, checking her rear-view and side-view mirrors, that there was a car—later identified as a Cadillac convertible driven by John Boireau—some seventy-five feet behind her. She wanted to make a right turn on Muzzey Street. Just before pulling out, Ramsdell observed that the Cadillac was much closer to her than before. Boireau, too, wished to turn right onto Muzzey Street. As there were no cars ahead of her before the intersection, Ramsdell thought she could make the turn before the Cadillac interfered.

As Ramsdell was pulling left slightly away from the curb, Boireau passed her traveling (as he said) about five miles an hour. Whether Ramsdell's car then "bolted" out and struck Boireau's car as he was negotiating the right turn, or Boireau turned into Ramsdell's car as the two attempted to make the turn, was the subject of conflicting testimony. So, too, the estimates of Ramsdell's speed on impact with Boireau varied from five to thirty miles an hour. Both drivers said they recognized the trouble and braked, but not before a minor collision occurred some ten to fifteen feet into the Muzzey Street intersection, Boireau's right front fender being slightly dented by contact with Ramsdell's left front fender.

What might have been a commonplace collision turned into a complicated accident. On impact, Ramsdell, a woman of sixty-nine, hit her head against her steering wheel and suffered a bloody nose. She testified she "lost complete control of that car." Dazed, she unknowingly let her foot slip from the power brake to the gas pedal. In the result, after veering right around Boireau's car and perhaps slowing slightly, she accelerated across the remaining twenty feet of Muzzey Street, bounced to the south sidewalk, about nine feet wide, of Massachusetts Avenue, and moved about fifty-five feet down the sidewalk. On this passage the car scraped the front of a camera store, hit and levelled a parking meter, struck and damaged extensively the right rear section of a Chevrolet Chevelle automobile (the third parked car beyond Muzzey Street), knocked down an electric light pole owned by the defendant Boston Edison Company (Edison), and struck the plaintiffs who had left the ice cream parlor and were walking side by side west, into the face of the oncoming car. There was much confusion at trial whether, after hitting the meter and car, Ramsdell first hit the pole and then the plaintiffs, or first the plaintiffs and then the pole, but no one denied she hit all three. The car came to a stop two to three feet over the stump of the pole with its left wheels in the gutter and its right wheels on the sidewalk, and in contact with the Chevelle.

The electric light pole, when hit, fell away from Ramsdell's car toward the east, struck a Volkswagen automobile parked along Massachusetts Avenue (the fourth car from Muzzey Street), and came down across the legs of Bernier. Boireau was able with help to lift the pole off Bernier. Bernier's thighs and left shin bone were broken, the latter break causing a permanently shortened left leg; and he had other related injuries. Kasputys lay within two feet of the pole further in from the curb than Bernier. There was no eyewitness testimony that she had been struck by the pole. She was unconscious and vomiting. She suffered a skull fracture on the right side of her head where pieces of metal and length of wire were found imbedded, and developed permanent pain in her left lower leg.

[Bernier and Kasputys sued Ramsdell, Boireau, and Edison. The claims against Edison alleged that it had negligently designed, selected, constructed and maintained the pole. The jury found against Ramsdell and Edison. Edison appeals.]

[T]he gravamen of the plaintiffs' case, as it appeared at trial, was that Edison had failed through negligence to design a pole that was accommodated reasonably to foreseeable vehicular impacts so as to avoid pedestrian injuries, and that the continued use of the pole created an unreasonable risk of such injuries.

As designer or codesigner of the pole and in control of its maintenance, Edison "must anticipate the environment in which its product will be used, and it must design against the reasonably foreseeable risk attending the product's use in that setting." Certainly the evidence showed that a risk of automobiles colliding with Edison poles—in particular No. 6 poles—was not only foreseeable but well known to the company. About 100 to 120 Edison poles a year were knocked down in such collisions in Edison's "Northeast Service Center" which included Lexington.... A so-called "knock down truck" worked steadily replacing downed poles in the district and installing new ones, and there were estimates by employees that in their years of field work they had replaced "thousands" of Edison poles. One employee said he had been personally involved in replacing at least a hundred poles of the type involved in the accident at bar.

As in the case of vehicles, design should take into account "foreseeable participation in collisions". And for the speeds to be encountered and consequences entailed in collisions, one analyzes the whole "setting." This was a busy shopping area with heavy pedestrian and vehicular traffic.

... Edison installed this No. 6 pole on February 3, 1949. It was of reinforced concrete, twenty-six feet nine inches in height, and ran from an eight inch base to a 5–3/8 inch top diameter. Four anchor bolts held it to a base that extended 4–2/3 feet below the surface. The pole was hollow, allowing for feeder wires to come from an underground cable up to the luminaire. Implanted in the concrete shaft were six vertical steel rods, each .375 (3/8) inch thick. Total weight of the pole and luminaire structure was 1,200 pounds.

What precautions were taken in the design to guard against the risk of pedestrian injury through collapse of a No. 6 pole upon impact by a vehicle? According to the evidence, the problem was not seriously adverted to.... Overall, the major considerations in Edison's design of poles (including their materials) seemed to be cost, adaptability to Edison's existing system of power supply and connecting apparatus, and capacity of Edison employees to install the poles safely.[2]

... To begin with, since injuries might be serious (as the present case indeed indicated), the likelihood of accidents need not be high to warrant careful consideration of safety features.

The plaintiffs' major witness concerning design safety was Howard Simpson, who had a doctorate in engineering and practiced as a consulting structural engineer. His qualifications as an expert on the strength of reinforced concrete were unchallenged. In his opinion, the concrete of the thickness specified for No. 6 poles lacked "ductility," the quality which would allow a pole, when struck by a car, to absorb part of the impact and bend without breaking. No. 6 would shatter when hit with sufficient force; indeed, one of the Edison supervisors testified about No. 6 that the concrete "all crumbles at the point of impact." As the exposed steel rods could not then support the weight of the pole, it would fall. As to the force sufficient to break No. 6 in this fashion, Simpson testified that the pole would succumb to a 1968 Buick Skylark with a passenger, spare tire, and full gas tank going as slowly as six m.p.h. A medium-sized truck weighing 10,000 pounds could level No. 6 when traveling at 1.5 m.p.h.

Simpson went on to say that the strength of the pole could have been substantially improved by using steel rods of larger diameter or by placing steel "hoops" or "spirals" perpendicular to those vertical rods. In his opinion the latter device would have enabled the pole to withstand the impact of the Buick at 11 m.p.h.—an important advance, as a car going 9 m.p.h. has an energy considerably greater than that at 6 m.p.h. Such hoops and spirals had been in use since the early 1900's in columns for buildings. Simpson calculated the cost per pole of the hoops at $5.75 and the spirals at $17.50.

We should add here that there was evidence from Edison employees of the existence of other pole-types, possibly of greater strength, that would at least have warranted comparison by Edison with the No. 6 pole in respect to safety values. Various metal poles (aluminum and steel) might have deserved such study. Edison's own No. 26, of prestressed concrete, designed in 1968, might have been an improvement....

Edison argues that a finding of negligence here left it in the grip of a "polycentric" problem. If it chose to protect pedestrians by using stronger poles, motorists might be more seriously injured when they hit poles which did not break. If it chose to protect motorists, pedestrians would claim recovery when poles fell on them. No designer or owner, Edison added, is required to make or use a product wholly accident-free. There is

---

2. It is fair to mention, however, that one engineer thought metal poles might have been passed over because they would tend to become electrified when downed and subject pedestrians to shock. Another thought pedestrian safety was adequately handled by having a reputable manufacturer fabricate the poles. There was some indication that Edison did not install so-called "breakaway" poles in areas such as Lexington Center because of danger to pedestrians.

some disingenuousness in this argument as the evidence shows Edison paid scant attention in the design of the No. 6 pole to the safety either of motorists or pedestrians. But we think there is nothing in the argument to relieve Edison of a duty to take precautions against knock-downs by cars, and it would seem reasonable for Edison to consider pedestrian safety with particular seriousness. Persons in a car are protected by a metal and glass shield sometimes three times as heavy as the pole's entire weight; pedestrians are exposed. Whether drivers are hurt any less by impact at similar speeds with poles that topple than with poles that bend rather than fall is unknown to us and apparently to Edison as well. To be sure, many more cars will hit poles than poles will hit pedestrians, but a six m.p.h. threshold for cars, and less for trucks, seems little protection indeed.

. . . Here the jury could rationally find negligence of design and maintenance. They could find that the vehicular speed at which No. 6 would topple was grievously low, creating an unacceptable risk of grave injury to persons at the scene (who in shopping areas such as Lexington Center might be numerous). The impact resistance of the pole could have been improved by relatively minor alterations available at the time and not inconveniencing Edison or the public, or possibly by the use of another type of pole with greater resistance. In balancing all the pertinent factors, the jury made a judgment as to the social acceptability of the design. . . .

Judgments affirmed.

NOTES

1. What factors are important to the court's belief that negligence was proved?

2. Do you have a good idea just how risky it was to use these poles? How much benefit was there in using these poles? To whom did the benefit, if any, flow? Suppose falling poles will cause one pedestrian injury per year in Boston, on the order of a broken leg, and sturdier poles will cause two fractured skulls per year in Boston when motorists collide. What if the motorist's injuries are caused in part by fault on the part of the motorist but the pedestrian injuries all involve non-faulty pedestrians?

3. Is fault easy to assess here? Should we apportion some responsibility to Boston Edison, some to Mrs. Ramsdell? If the negligent actors are liable only for a portion of the harm, does that dilute the deterrent effect?

4. What difference does it make to the negligence analysis if the defendant's conduct has social utility or value? In *Parsons v. Crown Disposal Co.*, 936 P.2d 70 (Cal. 1997), the plaintiff was thrown from the horse he was riding when the defendant's garbage truck, operating in a normal manner, startled the horse with loud noises. Affirming a summary judgment for the defendant, the court said that the main factor in the case is the social value of defendant's conduct. Because garbage collection activity is a vital public service and a matter of high social utility. the defendant is not negligent merely because he uses a machine that produces noises necessary to its

regular operation, even though fright of horses might be foreseeable. *See also, e.g., Giant Food, Inc. v. Mitchell*, 640 A.2d 1134 (Md. 1994) (defendant's attempted "hot pursuit" recovery of stolen property did not expose other store customers to any unreasonable risk of harm; the "degree of risk of harm to invitees must be weighed against the privilege" to protect one's property); *Cf. Gooden v. City of Talladega*, 966 So.2d 232 (Ala. 2007) (police officer not negligent for engaging in a high-speed chase where the speeding motorist posed "a clear and immediate threat to the safety of other motorists").

UNITED STATES v. CARROLL TOWING CO.

159 F.2d 169 (2d Cir. 1947)

L. HAND, CIRCUIT JUDGE.

[Proceedings in admiralty involving several different entities interested in the collision and sinking of a barge, the Anna C. The Conners company owned the barge, which was loaded with flour. Grace Line employees, operating the Carroll Towing Company tug, negligently caused the Anna C to break adrift. She was carried by wind and tide against a tanker, whose propeller broke a hole in her bottom. Conners' bargee was not on board, and the damage was not reported to anyone. Had there been a bargee there, the Grace Line employees, who had pumps available, could have saved the Anna C; as it was, she careened, dumped her cargo of flour, and sank. The court first held that Grace Line and Carroll Towing were liable, and then considered whether the absence of a bargee on board the Anna C was negligence that reduced recovery to Conners.]

It appears from the foregoing review that there is no general rule to determine when the absence of a bargee or other attendant will make the owner of the barge liable for injuries to other vessels if she breaks away from her moorings. . . . It becomes apparent why there can be no such general rule, when we consider the grounds for such a liability. Since there are occasions when every vessel will break from her moorings, and since, if she does, she becomes a menace to those about her; the owner's duty, as in other similar situations, to provide against resulting injuries is a function of three variables: (1) The probability that she will break away; (2) the gravity of the resulting injury, if she does; (3) the burden of adequate precautions. Possibly it serves to bring this notion into relief to state it in algebraic terms: if the probability be called P; the injury, L; and the burden, B; liability depends upon whether B is less than L multiplied by P: i.e., whether $B < PL$. Applied to the situation at bar, the likelihood that a barge will break from her fasts and the damage she will do, vary with the place and time; for example, if a storm threatens, the danger is greater; so it is, if she is in a crowded harbor where moored barges are constantly being shifted about. On the other hand, the barge must not be the bargee's prison, even though he lives aboard; he must go ashore at times. . . . In the case at bar the bargee left at five o'clock in the afternoon of January 3rd, and the flotilla broke away at about two o'clock in the afternoon of the following day, twenty-one hours afterwards. The bargee had been away all the time, and we hold that his fabricated story was affirmative evidence that he had no excuse for his absence. At the locus in quo—especially during the short January days and in the full tide of war activity—barges were being constantly "drilled" in and out. Certainly it was not beyond reasonable expectation that, with the inevitable haste and bustle, the work might not be done with adequate care. In such circumstances we hold—and it is all that we do hold—that it was a fair requirement that the Conners Company should have a bargee aboard (unless he had some excuse for his absence), during the working hours of daylight.

NOTES

1. As we have seen, many cases approve risk-utility balancing to determine negligence, although very often in a form less structured than the formula Judge Hand advanced. *See also, e.g., Doe Parents No. 1 v. State, Dep't of Educ.*, 58 P.3d 545 (Haw. 2002); DOBBS ON TORTS § 144 (2000 & Supp.).

2. We have also seen in this section that the party asserting negligence first identifies some specific act of negligence, by pointing to what the defendant did or did not do and identifying some specific safer conduct that might have been pursued. If the alternative conduct was safer, the court will want to know how much safer and something about its costs. What was the specific alternative conduct Judge Hand was considering in *Carroll Towing?*

3. Suppose that, by not having a bargee on board at all times, the barge would break loose and cause damage to itself or others about once a year, and that the average damage would be $25,000. Suppose also that the cost of keeping a bargee on board at all times to prevent this would be an average of $30,000 a year. Judge Hand seems to say this would be a case of no negligence, and Judge Posner says this is correct because the function of the fault system is to impose liability rules that will bring about "efficient" or cost-justified rules of safety. A rule that required the barge owner to spend $30,000 to save $25,000 would be inefficient and not cost-justified. *See* Richard A. Posner, *A Theory of Negligence*, 1 J. LEG. STUDIES 29, 32 (1972).

4. Consider the hypothetical variation of *Carroll Towing* given in Note 3. Where does probability come in? The answer is that it is built into the "average." Suppose that the probability is that the barge without a full-time bargee will break loose once every *other* year with the damage of $25,000. The probability of harm is reduced, and this will be reflected in a new average—$12,500 instead of $25,000. Try working this out the other way—by supposing that the barge will break loose *twice* a year. Would it then be negligent not to have a full-time bargee?

5. In the light of this kind of thinking, reconsider the *Brown v. Stiel* problem. Does the *Carroll Towing* formula assist in structuring your analysis? Does the test's utility wane where the the defendant's conduct risked physical injury or death rather than just property damage?

6. Judge Hand says in *Carroll Towing* that "the owner's duty ... is a function of three variables...." Does it seem to you that he is really assuming a *duty* of reasonable care and then addressing the question of *breach* of that duty? The Third Restatement says that the major factors in analyzing whether conduct is negligent are "the foreseeable likelihood that the person's conduct will result in harm, the foreseeable severity of any harm that may ensue, and the burden of precautions to eliminate or reduce the risk of harm." See RESTATEMENT (THIRD) OF TORTS: LIABILITY FOR PHYSICAL HARM § 3 (Proposed Final Draft No. 1, 2005).

NOTE: APPLYING THE RISK–UTILITY FORMULA

1. *Estimating risks.* Everything we do carries *some* risk. In applying the Hand formula, how do we know the degree of risk attributable to the defendant's activity? One answer might be that Hand was not proposing a formula into which actual numbers could be substituted for the "algebra." Instead, Hand might have been proposing only a model, an indication about the nature of the decision or estimate we need to make. Do the cases preceding *Carroll Towing* suggest that courts were estimating costs or benefits of the defendant's conduct compared to some supposedly safer alternative?

2. *Estimating costs or benefits.* How do you *know* how much a safety precaution would cost or how much the activity benefits people? Almost any activity has *some* benefit and almost any safety precaution has *some* costs, although one safety precaution—a warning of danger—is usually almost costless, so that under *Carroll Towing* a warning might be due even if the danger is small. *See* RESTATEMENT (THIRD) OF TORTS § 18 (P.F.D. No. 1, 2005). It is often much easier to reduce costs and benefits to numbers than it is to do the same for risks. That is so because many costs can be identified in dollar-numbers. Benefits can also be identified in dollar-numbers by asking about the earnings, savings, or increase in capital value effected by the activity.

3. *The forgotten gopher hole.* As you leave your house one morning, on the way to try a tort case, you observe that a burrowing animal has dug a hole in your yard, very close to the sidewalk. Recognizing that the hole is a risk to anyone who might step off the sidewalk, you make a mental note to fill the hole or barricade it as soon as you get home. At the end of a long, hard day before a hostile jury, an irascible judge, and an unappreciative client, you have forgotten the hole. You plop in front of the television. In the meantime, the plaintiff, a neighbor on his way to bring you a misdelivered copy of *Torts Illustrated*, steps off the sidewalk in the dark, and breaks his ankle as he falls in the hole. Are you negligent? Does *Carroll Towing* help you decide?

4. *The putative memory requirement.* Courts sometimes hold the actor to memory of dangerous conditions that he knew about in the recent past, even though the ordinary prudent person will no doubt sometimes forget. *See* Mark Grady, *Why Are People Negligent? Technology, Non– Durable Precautions, and the Medical Malpractice Explosion*, 82 NW. U. L.

REV. 293 (1988); *but cf.* RESTATEMENT (SECOND) OF TORTS § 289 (1965) (memory of the reasonable person is required). Would such a rule help decide the case of the gopher hole? Could it possibly be consistent with the *Carroll Towing* formula?

5. *Costs of memory.* An engineer fails to blow a whistle at a crossing, and a collision with a car results. Blowing a whistle is cost-free, so it sounds as if the *Carroll Towing* formula could readily be applied: there is at least some risk in failing to sound the whistle and it costs nothing to do it; therefore, failure to do it is negligent. But from the railroad's point of view, the actual cost of preventing the engineer's inattention might be very high indeed. The railroad might be required to design a computer-controlled system to make the whistle blow, or to pay for a second engineer to help remind the first that whistles are important. This cost might be very great indeed. *See* Izhak Englard, *The System Builders: A Critical Appraisal of Modern American Tort Theory*, 9 J. LEG. STUDIES 27 (1980). How would lawyers, judges, and juries ever really know how much the costs would be?

6. *Costs of information.* The actor only needs to consider those risks that would be taken into account by a reasonable person. This is why courts discuss whether harm is "foreseeable"; they limit liability to cases in which the actor can recognize a risk or danger. Suppose the railroad above could reduce the speed of its trains by five miles an hour and thereby save an average of $25,000 a year in injury costs. Suppose this would cost the railroad only $10,000. It will be more efficient in this case to reduce the speed. But suppose the railroad does not know this and cannot find out without spending a great deal of money to make a study. Suppose the railroad doesn't even realize that it could find out? Information about the existence and degree of risk is itself an item of cost. Can you apply the *Carroll Towing* formula to such a case?

7. *Variable probabilities and costs.* Look back at *Indiana Consolidated Ins. Co. v. Mathew*. What if leaving the burning mower in the garage created a 90% probability of fire damage to the garage of about $10,000 and no more, but a 5% probability of fire totally destroying the house at a loss of $100,000, a 4% probability of a fire spread that would cause losses of more than a million dollars, and a 1% probability of no harm. Does it seem preposterous to say that the jury should somehow factor all this in to its negligence decision?

8. What is the proper scope of *Carroll Towing*'s risk-utility formula? Professor Latin points out that many routine cases involve nothing more than mistake and momentary inattention. Howard Latin, *"Good" Warnings, Bad Products, and Cognitive Limitations*, 41 U.C.L.A. L. REV. 1193 (1994). If he is right, and if normative rules should be based upon realistic assessment behavioral patterns, should *Carroll Towing*'s formula be discarded for routine automobile accidents? Where does the formula work best?

NOTE: EVALUATING THE RISK–UTILITY ASSESSMENT

1. *What values?* What values or tort goals does the risk-utility assessment foster? Since everything we do carries some degree of risk, one argument for a risk-utility assessment is that it provides deterrence in the "right" amount. Relatedly, it maximizes community resources, for the community is richer if its members do not spend $10 to save someone else $5.

2. Although economically oriented lawyers often like the risk-utility formula as Hand expressed it in *Carroll Towing*, there has been a strong current of objection to it so far as it emphasizes wealth or money. One approach says that basic liberties—freedom of action and security—are primary and take precedence over considerations of wealth. Under this approach, security from harm would be weighed against freedom of action, one basic liberty against another, but losses of liberty would not be offset by increases in wealth. *See* Gregory C. Keating, *Reasonableness and Rationality in Negligence Theory,* 48 STAN. L. REV. 311, 383 (1996). But don't losses or gains in wealth—costs or benefits under the *Carroll Towing* formula—represent freedom of action?

3. *Alternatives to the risk-utility formula?* If you reject a weighing of risks and utilities, costs and benefits, how could you judge whether the defendant is negligent? Consider: Juries could judge (1) intuitively that "it seems negligent to me"; (2) solely by statutory prescriptions such as speed limits; (3) by hard-and-fast rules developed by judicial prescriptions, like the rule that you are always negligent if you drive so that you cannot stop within the range of your vision; (4) by custom of the community or the business involved; (5) by a moral rule that imposes liability if the defendant did anything more risky than he would have done to prevent the same harm to himself or his own property. How does the *Carroll Towing* formula stack up among the alternatives?

4. Is the risk-utility assessment a matter of policy or a matter of justice? If policy, what policy? On the risk-utility balance generally, *see* DOBBS ON TORTS §§ 144–146 (2000).

§ 2. ASSESSING RESPONSIBILITY WHEN MORE THAN ONE PERSON IS NEGLIGENT

Many tort cases involve at least two tortfeasors who contribute to the harm done. To analyze and evaluate such cases properly, we need to understand as clearly as possible that liability of one person does not necessarily exclude liability of another. Equally, we need to understand how responsibility is apportioned—that is, who will pay what for damages caused. We deal with more advanced issues about this topic later on. For now, we can set out the structure of apportionment you should have in mind as we begin to read negligence cases.

In considering the rules set out in this section, you might want to have in mind a case like *Bernier v. Boston Edison Co.*, covered in the last section. Suppose that the jury found Mrs. Ramsdell to be chargeable with 20% of the fault and Boston Edison with 80%.

(1) Comparative fault. If Mrs. Ramsdell had been injured and sued Boston Edison, the rules in most states would allow her to recover, but with her damages reduced in proportion to her fault. The plaintiff's recovery is not ordinarily reduced to reflect her fault when the defendant is guilty of an intentional tort, but they are nowadays generally reduced in negligence and strict liability cases. The idea is that each faulty party must bear his or her share of the losses. The defendant's liability is correspondingly reduced so that he pays less than all of the plaintiff's damages. In some cases, the plaintiff actually recovers nothing at all, even though the defendant is also negligent in a substantial way.

(2) Apportionment among defendants. What would happen in the suits by Bernier and Kasputys against Boston Edison and Ramsdell if those defendants were chargeable with 80% and 20% of the fault respectively? Since both are negligent, it looks as if both should share in payments to the plaintiff. Ideally, then, Boston Edison would pay 80% of the damages for Bernier's permanently shortened leg and Kasputys' permanent pain and other injuries. Correspondingly, Ramsdell would pay 20% of those damages. Tort law recognizes this ideal by adopting one of two systems to accomplish it. One of these systems, called the joint and several liability system, also tries to accommodate some other ideals.

(3) Joint and several liability. "Joint and several liability" sounds mysterious. Joint and several liability means that the plaintiff can enforce her tort claim against either tortfeasor. She can actually obtain a judgment against both, but she cannot collect more than her full damages. Although it looks as if Kasputys had very substantial damages indeed, let's suppose for convenience that her damages came to $10,000. Under the rule of joint and several liability, the plaintiff might enforce that judgment entirely against either Boston Edison or against Ramsdell. But that is not the end of the story.

(4) Contribution. If Boston Edison paid the entire judgment of $10,000, it would be paying more than its fair share of the damages relative to Ramsdell. Under the joint and several liability system, most states would allow Boston Edison to obtain *contribution* from Ramsdell so as to make its payment proportional to its fault. Under today's rules, if Ramsdell's fault were 20% of the whole and Boston Edison's fault were 80%, Boston Edison should recover contribution from Ramsdell equal to 20% of the damages, $2,000. What is the net cost to Boston Edison after recovery of contribution? Do the rules of joint and several liability plus the rules of contribution carry out the goals of tort law?

Example of Joint and Several Liability With Contribution

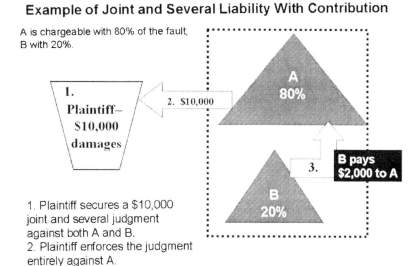

A is chargeable with 80% of the fault, B with 20%.

1. Plaintiff secures a $10,000 joint and several judgment against both A and B.
2. Plaintiff enforces the judgment entirely against A.
3. A obtains contribution from B.

In the diagram, the plaintiff is not at fault and recovers all her losses resulting from the injury. Defendant A, although initially liable for all the losses, eventually recoups contribution from B. The net result is that A, who is chargeable with 80% of the fault, ultimately pays 80% of the plaintiff's damages, and B, with 20% of the fault, pays 20%. The principle applies, of course, without regard to the amount of the damages.

(5) **Insolvent or immune tortfeasors.** Suppose hypothetically that Mrs. Ramsdell had no insurance and no personal assets from which Kasputys could collect a judgment. Or suppose that Mrs. Ramsdell for some reason was immune to tort liability. (As bad as it sounds, it is true that some wrongdoers are free to commit torts without any liability.) On these suppositions, the joint and several liability rule means that the plaintiff would recover her damages from Boston Edison but that as a practical matter Boston Edison could not recover contribution, either because Mrs. Ramsdell had an immunity or because she had no assets with which to pay contribution. The joint and several liability system, then, in effect requires the solvent tortfeasor, Boston Edison, to pick up and pay the insolvent, uninsured, or immune tortfeasor's share. In such a case, the law's ideal—payment proportioned to fault—is not achieved. What other important goal is being accommodated by the joint and several liability system?

(6) **Several liability and comparative fault apportionment among tortfeasors.** An alternative scheme of apportionment has been enacted in a substantial number of states. We'll call it several liability, proportionate share liability, or comparative fault liability. In the several or proportionate share systems, the trier of fact makes a comparative fault

apportionment of liability. This several liability system differs from joint liability in that no tortfeasor is liable for more than his proportionate share. On our hypothetical assumptions about *Bernier*, the plaintiffs there would collect only 80% of their damages from Boston Edison in a several liability system, because Boston Edison's fault was only 80% of the whole set of faults. Thus contribution is not needed. The plaintiff would have to take her chances on collecting the remaining 20% from Mrs. Ramsdell. If Mrs. Ramsdell for any reason could not pay, the plaintiffs would bear 20% of their own losses.

B Cannot Pay His Share

(7) Evaluating the two systems for apportioning loss. When tortfeasor A is fully insured and tortfeasor B has neither insurance nor assets, which system is more consistent with tort goals, the joint and several liability system or the comparative apportionment system?

(8) Recapping. This is a lot of specialized information to absorb at one time. Maybe the best recap is to try your hand at applying the rules for sharing damages liabilities. Suppose:

(a) Patricia, a single mother often up at night with her child, is sleepy while driving to work. Dunn, driving a truck, attempts to cross the street in front of Patricia. Patricia was probably slow in hitting her brakes. She broadsided Dunn's truck. Dunn wasn't injured but Patricia was. The jury finds that Dunn's fault was 90%, Patricia's 10%, and that her damages come to $10,000. What amount of money must Dunn (or his liability insurance company) pay under the rules followed in most states?

(b) Agatha and Bert are each driving a car. Both are negligent and they collide in a city intersection. The force of the collision causes Bert to lose control. Consequently, his car strikes a pedestrian, Paul. Paul's injury results in medical expense, loss of wages, and pain. The jury assesses his damages at $100,000 and finds that Agatha's negligence was 75% of the whole, while Bert's was only 25%. (i) In a joint and several liability system, suppose that both Agatha and Bert are insured for liability or otherwise able to pay, but Paul enforces the judgment solely against Bert. What does Bert pay and what contribution rights does he have? (ii) If Agatha is insolvent and uninsured, what is Bert's position in a joint and several liability system? (iii) In a several liability system with comparative fault apportionment?

§ 3.   PROVING AND EVALUATING CONDUCT

The plaintiff must prove each element of the case by a preponderance of the evidence, that is, by the greater weight of the evidence. Negligence, for example, must be shown to be more probable than not. The trier of facts, in other words, must reasonably believe that the probability of negligence exceeds one-half. *See* David Kaye, *Probability Theory Meets Res Ipsa Loquitor*, 77 Mich. L. Rev. 1456, 1467 (1979).

A.   PROVING CONDUCT

SANTIAGO v. FIRST STUDENT, INC.

839 A.2d 550 (R.I. 2004)

Per Curiam. . . .

[Defendant operates a school bus. The plaintiff alleged that in 1997, when she was in the eighth grade and being transported on one of defendant's busses, it collided with a car at an intersection the plaintiff cannot now identify.]

When plaintiff was deposed as part of pretrial discovery in this case, she testified that she could not remember the street or the neighborhood where the accident occurred. She also admitted that she "could [not] find [the] street today if [she] wanted to." The plaintiff did, however, offer a brief description of her recollection of the events. She remembered that the bus was driving on a one-way street approaching a stop sign. According to plaintiff, she saw the unidentified vehicle approaching the intersection, coming toward the bus from the right. She was then jerked forward when the bus driver applied the brakes and the bus collided with the unidentified vehicle. As a result of the collision, plaintiff says, the right side of her face hit the seat in front of her. Police did not respond to the accident and, consequently, there is no police report describing the incident.

Admitting that she did not see the collision occur, plaintiff was unable to offer any details about it. She was unable to say whether the unidentified car had a stop sign. She did not know whether the bus was damaged or the extent of the damage to the other vehicle, other than that its side mirror was knocked off. . . .

[The trial judge granted summary judgment for the defendant.]

Reviewing the evidence in the light most favorable to plaintiff, we must accept her assertion that she was injured in an accident. To assign negligence to defendant based on the evidence in the record, however, would impermissibly cross the line from reasonable inference and venture into the realm of rank speculation. The plaintiff admitted that she did not see how the collision occurred. Although she testified that a stop sign controlled the flow of traffic coming from the bus's direction, she does not allege that the bus driver failed to stop at the sign as directed. The plaintiff is unable to describe any actions on the part of the driver of the unidentified vehicle or unidentified bus driver relating to the accident. Indeed, there is no evidence of the interaction between the bus and the unidentified car, except that the two vehicles collided. Furthermore, plaintiff can provide no other witnesses capable of offering a meaningful description of the accident.

. . . The plaintiff attempts to justify a lack of evidence to support her case by pointing to the nature of the accident. . . . The fact that the plaintiff's case may be extremely difficult to prove, however, does not relieve her of the burden of presenting sufficient evidence to demonstrate the existence of a material question of fact. The plaintiff has not met that burden in this case and the defendant, therefore, is entitled to judgment as a matter of law.

[Affirmed.]

NOTES

1.   In *Gift v. Palmer*, 141 A.2d 408 (Pa. 1958), the defendant was driving on a street 30 feet wide in clear weather. No cars were parked on the side. He ran into a three-year-old child in the street. No one saw how the child got in the street and no one saw the impact itself. The plaintiff asserts a claim on behalf of the child. Is the evidence sufficient to get the plaintiff to the jury on the negligence issue?

2.   Could a reasonable person listen to the proof in the *Gift* and *Santiago* cases and state exactly how the defendant should have altered his conduct to make it safer?

UPCHURCH v. ROTENBERRY

761 So.2d 199 (Miss. 2000)

PITTMAN, PRESIDING JUSTICE, for the Court. . . .

On the night of October 5, 1992, the decedent, Timothy Adam Upchurch, was riding in the passenger seat of Teresa Rotenberry's car while Rotenberry was driving. Adam was the only passenger in the car. The car was traveling west on Highway 182 in Oktibbeha County, Mississippi when Rotenberry lost control of her vehicle. Upchurch claims Teresa left the road suddenly without warning, causing injuries and damages to the decedent that resulted in his death. [The plaintiff sued for the wrongful death of her son. The jury found for the defendant. The plaintiff moved for Judgment N.O.V. The trial court denied the motion and this appeal followed.]

[There were no eyewitnesses except Rotenberry. One expert, Rosenhan, however, testified from evidence at the scene that Rotenberry's vehicle traveled in a straight line from the point it left the road to the point it hit the tree 160 feet away, that there were no scuff or skid marks, and that the vehicle's speed when it hit the tree was 60 mph.]

The speed the vehicle was traveling when it struck the tree, as well as, whether the vehicle left any marks either on the roadway or the area between leaving the road and striking the tree is . . . disputed in this case. Rotenberry's expert, Thomas Shaeffer, testified that there were tire marks which began on the road and proceeded off the road, through the grass, and down toward the tree. Shaeffer identified these marks as yaw marks. Shaeffer defines yaw marks as a mark a tire makes when it is still rotating but not traveling in the direction that it is oriented. . . .

On direct examination, Shaeffer testified that the car was traveling approximately 25 to 35 mph when it hit the tree. However, on cross examination, Shaeffer testified that the car was going 42 to 50 mph when it made impact with the tree.

Rotenberry introduced into evidence photographs to corroborate the conclusions of Shaeffer. . . .

Shaeffer also testified that he observed small pebbles wedged between the rim and tire on both the front left and rear left wheels of the vehicle. This is additional evidence that the vehicle made an extreme right hand turn. All of the evidence presented at trial by Shaeffer was consistent with the vehicle making an evasive maneuver to the right in order to avoid an object on the roadway. Shaeffer's final determination was that the car struck the tree and flipped over on its top, which undoubtedly caused additional damage to the vehicle.

Rotenberry testified as an adverse witness. Throughout the discovery proceedings and at the trial itself, Rotenberry testified that she could not remember the events leading up to the accident including a two-day period just prior to the accident. However, on November 13, 1992 (about 5 weeks after the accident), Rotenberry did sign a written statement detailing the accident. In this statement, Rotenberry testified that a large animal, either a deer or a dog, ran across the road and into her lane ultimately causing her to leave the road. . . .

In her brief, Upchurch raises the issue that Kirk Rosenhan, plaintiff's expert, testified that he smelled alcohol on the defendant at the accident scene. However, on direct [cross?] examination of Rosenhan the following exchange occurred.

Q. Did you get close to Teresa Rotenberry?

A. Not really.

Q. Did you get close enough to smell her?

A. No, I didn't.

Q. Did you smell any odor of intoxicant on her?

A. Uh, not on her. . . .

On redirect examination after an overnight recess, Rosenhan changed his testimony to say that he had not been specific as to the driver of the vehicle the day before and that he did smell alcohol on the driver the night of the accident. The above exchange, however, makes it clear that Rosenhan was perfectly specific on direct examination in denying that he smelled alcohol on Rotenberry at the scene of the accident. It is noteworthy that Rosenhan did testify on direct examination that he smelled alcohol in the area. Also, the presence of beer in the car is not disputed in the facts of this case.

Larry Guyton, a trooper with the Mississippi Highway Patrol, also testified for the plaintiff. Officer Guyton testified that he arrived on the scene after Rotenberry had been taken away by ambulance. Officer Guyton spoke to Rotenberry by telephone in her hospital room two days after the accident, October 7th, and again on October 8th. Rotenberry was able to remember the accident at this point. She appeared alert during the conversation. Officer Guyton testified that Rotenberry told him that she was traveling westbound on Highway 182 near Starkville when she saw an animal coming into her lane from the opposite side of the road. She swerved to the right to avoid hitting the animal. In Officer Guyton's opinion, Rotenberry appeared to be telling him the truth.

Further, Officer Guyton testified on direct examination that Rotenberry told him that she had two beers earlier in the evening at a place called "The Landing" on Highway 182 near Starkville. On cross examination, however, Officer Guyton testified that Rotenberry did not tell him about drinking beer or about being at The Landing. He just asked her how the accident occurred, and she told him. Further, he stated that he did not put anything in his accident report concerning drinking or about being at The Landing. He continued by testifying that Rotenberry had not told him anything different than what was in his report. . . .

[T]his Court concludes that reasonable and fairminded jury members could reach different conclusions. Consequently, the jury verdict stands, and the motion for JNOV is denied.

This Court will not intrude into the realm of the jury by determining the credibility of a witness and making findings of fact. The jury is the judge of the weight of the evidence and the credibility of the witnesses. Through her statement and the testimony of other witnesses, Rotenberry offered evidence explaining the events of that tragic night. The jury considered this evidence, weighed it, and found in favor of Rotenberry. . . .

This Court has been even more specific regarding the realm of the jury concerning the credibility of witnesses in stating:

> The demeanor or bearing, the tone of voice, the attitude and appearance of the witnesses, all are primarily for inspection and review by the jury. The jury not only has the right and duty to determine the truth or falsity of the witnesses, but also has the right to evaluate and determine what portions of the testimony of any witness it will accept or reject; therefore, unless it is clear to this Court that the verdict is contrary to the overwhelming weight of the credible testimony, this court will not set aside the verdict of a jury.

... According to its duty, the jury concluded that Rotenberry acted reasonably in swerving to the right to avoid an animal and that she did not have time to avoid a tree which lay only 160 feet (or slightly over 53 yards) from where Rotenberry left the road. The jury makes such fact determinations, not this Court. . . .

The resolution of disputed facts such as this is a duty that devolves upon the jury sitting as finders of fact. They are charged with listening to the witnesses, observing their demeanor, and coming to their own conclusions of which evidence they find more credible. Our system of jurisprudence has determined that citizen jurors, employing their native intelligence and collective life experiences, are best qualified to make those judgments. Absent some clear indication that the jurors in a particular case somehow ignored that duty, neither the trial court, nor this Court reviewing the record on appeal, are permitted to interfere in the conclusions reached by these jurors.

NOTES

The Process of Determining Fault

1. **Small physical limitations—fault or not?** Lawyers often find it difficult to obtain facts necessary for an assessment of fault. One reason is that injuries are often caused by tiny miscalculations, hard for the actor to appreciate and almost impossible for a jury to understand at a later date. For instance, a car traveling at 50 m.p.h. travels about 75 feet per second. The time for drivers to react to an emergency, such as a child darting into the road, varies considerably. About half of all drivers take nearly a second to respond, but some take two seconds. *See* LEON ROBERTSON, INJURIES, CAUSES, CONTROL STRATEGIES AND PUBLIC POLICY 42 (1983). If a driver hits a child 100 feet from the point of observation, a reaction time for hitting the brakes of one second might have been sufficient to avoid the impact, but a reaction time of two seconds would not. Or again, what about the fact that a driver may lose part of her field of vision as she gets older—and with no way to be aware of this? Studies seem to indicate that loss of visual field is commonly associated with auto injuries, yet the topic does not come up in the cases. See *id.* at 62.

2. **Accuracy of testimony.** A second problem in obtaining facts for making a judgment about fault lies with the accuracy of testimony. A very considerable body of information indicates that witnesses are generally inaccurate in a number of particulars. Part of this lies in perception of events, which is especially difficult if they occur quickly, only once, and with violence or stress. *See* ELIZABETH LOFTUS, EYEWITNESS TESTIMONY (1979).

3. **Using traffic rules to test "fault."** A social scientist studying the process of settling tort claims in automobile accident cases has said that, in practice, evaluation of claims consists chiefly in discovering traffic violations and that though "formal tort law" concerns issues of duty, foreseeability, reasonable care and a "fine weighing" of negligence, in most auto cases a traffic violation is the central issue. H. LAURENCE ROSS, SETTLED OUT OF COURT 20 (2d Ed. 1980). If this is so, is it merely a result of the negligence per se rule? *See* RESTATEMENT (THIRD) OF TORTS: LIABILITY FOR PHYSICAL HARM § 14, cmt.

d (Proposed Final Draft No. 1, 2005) ("[T]he conduct of motorists is extensively dealt with by statutes and regulations; accordingly, in most highway-accident cases, findings of negligence depend on ascertaining which party has violated the relevant provisions of the state's motor-vehicle code."). Does this make it any more or any less important to find out exactly what the conduct was?

4. **Changing safety environments.** As some of these paragraphs show, the process of determining fault in tort cases is difficult at best. This leads to the idea that if you try to deal with vehicle safety after injury has occurred, you must look for fault, but that if you try to prevent accidents before they occur, you might try to change the environment. For example, roads may be better designed or signals more visible. Another approach to automobile safety left the tort system altogether. This sought to require auto makers to provide safer automobiles. This approach required regulations to be issued by the National Highway Traffic Safety Administration. Many have concluded that this approach has not been very successful. *See* JERRY MASHAW & DAVID HARFST, THE STRUGGLE FOR AUTO SAFETY (1990). Does that leave us to rely upon uncertain estimates of fault?

The Credibility Rule

5. **Jury role.** Credibility of witnesses is almost always a question for the jury, and almost never a question for the judge. Standard instructions tell the juries to determine credibility of witnesses for themselves, considering factors such as the witnesses' demeanor and other factors mentioned in *Upchurch. See,* e.g., ILL. PATTERN JURY INSTRUCTIONS-CIVIL § 1.01, ¶ 4 (2007 ed.).

6. **Lawyers' roles.** What is the role of the lawyers in this? Would you expect simply to gather favorable witnesses together, put their testimony on, and quit? What else *could* you do?

7. **Credibility and directed verdicts.** Given the credibility rule, should the plaintiff be entitled to a directed verdict in her favor if the defendant puts on no evidence at all, or if his evidence does not contradict the plaintiff's? In *Dorn v. Leibowitz*, 127 A.2d 734 (Pa. 1956), a pedestrian testified she crossed with the light, and was struck by a truck after she had taken five steps into the crosswalk. The defendant offered no testimony except that of a police officer, who did not contradict the plaintiff in any substantial way. The court held that the plaintiff was not entitled to a directed verdict or "binding instructions" in her favor, since her credibility was for the jury even though she was not contradicted. Some courts take the view that if the plaintiff offers testimony that is not only uncontradicted, but is clear and self-consistent, a directed verdict for the party having the burden of proof— usually the plaintiff—is permissible. *See, e.g., Trevino v. Kent County*, 936 S.W.2d 488 (Tex. App. 1996). But, as you may readily imagine, there are few cases that meet such requirements.

––––––––––

FORSYTH v. JOSEPH, 450 P.2d 627 (N.M. Ct. App. 1968). Decedent was an occupant of a car struck by the Villa truck. The trial court found

Villa to be negligent, partly because of excessive speed. There was evidence that Villa skidded 129 feet before the impact. *Held*, affirmed. "The speed limit was 55 miles per hour. The court found he was exceeding this speed and was traveling at the rate of 55 miles per hour at the point of impact. These findings are supported by the evidence. Even Villa testified that his speed 'at the point of impact' was 55 miles per hour. In addition thereto, we have the skid marks to which reference is above made, the force of the impact which knocked the Joseph vehicle about 20 or 25 feet and spun it about 90 degrees, and the continued momentum of Villa's vehicle, which carried it through the fence and into the open field where it came to a rest."

NOTES

1. **Circumstantial evidence.** Circumstantial evidence—which is to say evidence of one fact that permits an inference of another fact—is often the most important evidence in tort cases. Almost all negligence cases involve at least some factual inferences. The inference may, of course, assist the defendant rather than the plaintiff. What inference would you draw if the proof showed defendant stopped his car in 33 feet?

2. **An alert.** Perhaps Villa did not literally mean he was traveling 55 at the point of impact. What else might he have meant? What is the responsibility of the lawyer about such a matter? Notice that Villa's admission was considered against him.

3. **Judge and jury.** Questions of fact and questions of credibility are for the jury to decide. What about *inferences* of fact, such as those involved in *Forsyth*? The answer is that the jury is also the decision maker as to inferences, provided there is room for reasonable persons to draw or reject those inferences. Judges may sometimes declare that any given inference is one that reasonable people cannot draw on the facts of the case. If different inferences are possible, however, or if some reasonable persons would draw an inference of fact and others not, the jury must decide the matter. *Cf.* RESTATEMENT (THIRD) § 8(b) (P.F.D. No. 1, 2005) ("When, in light of all the facts relating to the actor's conduct, reasonable minds can differ as to whether the conduct lacks reasonable care, it is the function of the jury to make that determination."). This means that "[i]f the evidence adduced at trial is conflicting on a material point, or if reasonable persons may draw different conclusions from the evidence, or if a conclusion is dependent on the weight the fact finder gives to the testimony, a judge may not substitute his or her conclusion for that of the jury merely because he or she would have reached a different result." *McGuire v. Hodges*, 639 S.E.2d 284 (Va. 2007).

4. **Evidence to assist in drawing inferences.** In many instances one might reject an inference of fact simply for lack of knowledge. Suppose the evidence is that the defendant left skid marks of 137 feet, and that his car was at a complete stop at the end of the marks. Do you know how fast he was going? What evidence could be introduced to assist a judge or jury in drawing an inference about speed?

NOTE: WITNESSES' OPINIONS AS TO FACTS
AND FACTUAL INFERENCES

1. *Non-expert opinion.* Witnesses are not usually permitted to give opinions on "ultimate" issues that are reserved for jury decision in the case. For example, a witness would not be permitted to testify, "In my opinion, the defendant was negligent." The witness is required instead to state facts within his knowledge, for instance, "I saw the defendant run the red light." A few statements that might be classed as opinions are permitted, however, as a kind of shorthand or summing up of direct experience. An eyewitness may be permitted to estimate speed, distance, or intoxication, for example. It would be difficult to express any more accurately the facts on which it is based, and juries are likely to understand that the impression or estimate is no more than that.

The opinion rule reinforces the lawyer's active role in litigation. The lawyer must investigate, or obtain an investigation that produces detailed and convincing facts, and must maintain the initiative in the courtroom by presenting these facts effectively.

2. *Expert opinion.* Experts are usually allowed to give expert opinion or conclusions within the field of their expertise, provided the testimony is likely to be helpful to the jury on an issue in the case. For example, an orthopedic surgeon, examining a plaintiff who has tingling in the fingers and pain in the shoulder and neck, may infer that the patient suffers from some impingement on a nerve in the 6–7 cervical interspace of the neck. Although the surgeon may explain to the jury how she inferred the existence of an impingement, it would not be helpful to recapitulate large segments of a medical education.

For this and similar reasons, expert opinion often seems the most or only practical method of establishing certain facts, and it is usually admitted on medical issues. In the same way, investigating officers are usually allowed to give opinions about speed, distance, direction, and point of impact from evidence at the scene of a motor vehicle collision. But even this simple kind of testimony may be excluded if it is not helpful to the jury or the jury can readily determine the issue by interpreting the facts for themselves. In other words, expert testimony is not needed, and may not be admissible at all, where the issues on which the expert is going to opine are within the "common knowledge" of lay jurors. *See, e.g., District of Columbia v. Shannon,* 696 A.2d 1359 (D.C. 1997) (issue of the kind of care required of those who maintain playgrounds); *Hammons Inc. v. Poletis,* 954 P.2d 1353 (Wyo. 1998) (jury could draw inferences about why a towel bar pulled out of a wall without expert testimony).

Expert opinion testimony raises serious issues. One very common problem is that experts often differ. One expert may testify that in her opinion the plaintiff suffers a serious paralysis that is irremediable, while another may testify that in his opinion the plaintiff is not injured at all or, if injured, will recover speedily. Juries have little basis for resolving such conflicts of opinion except on the basis of a feeling that one expert is more impressive than another—which perhaps suggests one of the reasons why courts are reluctant about opinion testimony in the first place.

A second problem with expert testimony is that the witness may not in fact be an expert at all with respect to his particular testimony; or that the expert may be an expert in some sense but still offer an opinion that is only speculation.

Another problem with expert testimony is that it may overwhelm the jury. Experts are often prestigious by reason of their professional status, and some are more or less professional witnesses whose presence and demeanor may be highly impressive. The seemingly independent status of the expert witness may suggest a disinterested appraisal, which may lend this testimony even more weight in the jury's mind, though in fact some experts become quite partisan.

NOTE

Should we be skeptical about our ability to resolve disputes by judging negligence? Chance plays a big role in determining whether you will recover if you are injured. As *Upchurch* shows, there may be no witness to the event other than the defendant himself; the evidence may be conflicting; and witnesses on your side may be unappealing personalities and disliked by jurors, while witnesses on the other side may be pleasant and convincing.

B. EVALUATING CONDUCT

PROBLEM

Kibler v. Maddux

You have been retained by the parents of Tommy Kibler, 4 years of age, to bring suit for Tommy's injuries. On January 6, Linda Rodriguez called Mrs. Kibler and invited Tommy to come play with her son, also 4, at her house. It was rainy and Mrs. Kibler dressed him in a slicker and took him to the Rodriguez home about 2:30. She asked Mrs. Rodriguez to call when she was ready for Tommy to come home, saying she would pick him up rather than let him cross the street alone. She had trained him to wait for her at the curb. About 4:00, Mrs. Rodriguez called and told Mrs. Kibler she would dress Tommy in his slicker and take him to the curb where Mrs. Kibler would meet him. It was anticipated that Mrs. Kibler would arrive slightly before or at the same time as Tommy, but she slipped and fell on her slippery sidewalk and walked rather slowly and painfully. Tommy arrived at the curb and waited for his mother, looking in the direction she was to come from.

In the meantime, Irene Maddux was proceeding north on Spruce Street driving her car. She arrived at the crest of a slope and at that point she could see Tommy standing at the curb in his yellow slicker about 400–500 yards away. She proceeded on towards that point, driving at 20 m.p.h. because of the rain, slippery roads and gathering dusk. She watched Tommy constantly as she approached. When she reached a point she thinks was about 15 feet from Tommy, he suddenly ran out in front of her. It later became clear that he had waited somewhat longer for his mother than he expected to, and that when he saw her coming, he ran toward her. Maddux hit the brakes and also swerved to the right, but her left front fender struck Tommy and knocked him about 30 feet, causing some considerable injury.

Both sides have taken depositions and all the facts stated above are established. Defendant Maddux has moved for summary judgment on the basis of these admitted or established facts. How do you evaluate your case? What arguments can you make?

NOTES

1. In many cases, as in *Kibler*, it is possible to point to more than one act or omission that might constitute negligence. On occasion, lawyers fail to perceive their best claims of negligence and argue only the most obvious. Suppose the trial judge decided to hold a brief oral argument on the defendant's motion for summary judgment, and you have an opportunity to state in what respects Ms. Maddux could be found negligent by the trier. Would your primary argument be that she was driving too fast considering the weather?

2. Courts are reluctant to decide negligence cases on summary judgment motions. Why is this? "An inherently normative issue ... is not generally susceptible to summary judgment: the evidence requires that a jury balance the [safety precautions] against the nature and extent of the risk." *Little v. Liquid Air Corp.*, 952 F.2d 841 (5th Cir. 1992). In other words, juries are often called upon to decide not merely bare facts but also to make normative evaluations of the conduct involved.

THOMA v. CRACKER BARREL OLD COUNTRY STORE, INC.

649 So.2d 277 (Fla. Dist. Ct. App. 1995)

KAHN, JUDGE. . . .

After eating breakfast at the Cracker Barrel, Thoma took three or four steps away from her table when her left foot slid out from under her, causing her to fall. The fall occurred in a common aisle, near the passage from the kitchen to the restaurant. When Thoma got up, she noticed an area 1 foot by 2 feet containing drops of clear liquid. She claims to have slipped on this liquid. Thoma was in the restaurant about thirty minutes before her accident. During that time, she saw no one drop anything on the floor in the area where she fell. [In Thoma's suit against the restaurant, the trial court granted defendant's motion for summary judgment.]

Mr. Leonard McNeal was the only known witness to the fall. He arrived at breakfast about 15 minutes before the accident. His seat was some 12 to 15 feet away from where Thoma fell. McNeal described the area as "a normal area where waitresses would frequently go in and out (the kitchen) door." McNeal felt sure he saw waitresses carrying beverage pitchers in that area. He did not see any Cracker Barrel customers carrying drinks in the area, nor did he see anyone drop or spill anything.

Cracker Barrel's manager, Mr. Charlie Gray, inspected the area of the fall and saw no foreign substance whatever on the floor. According to Mr. Gray, the Cracker Barrel is not a buffet restaurant and he would not expect customers to get up and walk around with food or drinks.

To recover for injuries incurred in a slip and fall accident, the plaintiff must show that the premises owner either created a dangerous condition or had actual or constructive knowledge of a dangerous condition. Notice of a dangerous condition may be established by circumstantial evidence, such as evidence leading to an inference that a substance has been on the floor for a sufficient length of time such that in the exercise of reasonable care the condition should have become known to the premises owner.

We have recently reversed a defense summary judgment in a similar case, Gonzalez v. Tallahassee Medical Center, Inc., 629 So.2d 945 (Fla. 1st DCA 1993). In that case, Gonzalez slipped and fell on a liquid substance that looked like water, but could have been "syrup or Sprite." Her grandson testified that … the fall occurred near a soda drink dispenser set out for customer use and in an area where the cashier had a clear view. The grandson was in the cafeteria ten to fifteen minutes before the accident and did not hear or see anyone spill a liquid in the area of the fall. While we declined to speculate on what a jury might do with those facts, we held that inferences arose which "could establish the length of time the dangerous condition had been present on the floor, a critical element in proving that appellee, through the exercise of ordinary care, should have known of the condition."

In the present case, Thoma and McNeal took their breakfast at a location near where Thoma eventually fell. Despite their proximity, neither Thoma nor McNeal saw anyone drop or spill anything. The area of the fall was in clear view of Cracker Barrel employees, since they traversed it regularly on their way in and out of the kitchen. If a jury were to believe Thoma's description of the liquid as covering an area 1 foot by 2 feet, it might also be convinced that Cracker Barrel employees, in the exercise of due diligence, should have noticed the liquid before the accident. No one except Cracker Barrel employees were seen to carry food or beverage in the area of the fall, and the manager of the restaurant would not have expected customers to move around carrying food or drinks.

Cracker Barrel notes that "common sense" suggests "a plethora" of reasonable inferences other than the inferences urged by appellants. We certainly agree with this observation, but take issue with the suggestion that the existence of other possible inferences requires affirmance of the summary judgment in favor of Cracker Barrel. It will be for a jury to determine whether a preponderance of the evidence supports the inferences suggested by Thoma.

Reversed and Remanded.

NOTES

1. **Three common theories of liability.** Lawyers have developed several means of attempting to prove a defendant's negligence when the plaintiff slips on foreign substances in the defendant's place of business. The plaintiff can show negligence on the part of the defendant by proving either that: (a) The defendant created and failed to take reasonable actions to abate the hazard, as where a waiter spills sauce on the floor; (b) the defendant did not directly create the condition but discovered or should have discovered a condition created by others (often called "constructive notice") and failed to take reasonable steps to prevent injury from that condition; or (c) the defendant's mode or method of business operations made it foreseeable that others would create a dangerous condition, and the defendant failed to take reasonable measures to discover and remove it, as where a grocery's bean bin is constructed so that customers will regularly cause loose beans to fall on the floor.

The "mode of operation" theory has gathered momentum in recent years with the rise of self-service stores. *See, e.g., Kelly v. Stop and Shop, Inc.*, 918 A.2d 249 (Conn. 2007) (finding that at least 22 states have adopted such a rule or some variation of it); *Sheehan v. Roche Bros. Supermarkets, Inc.*, 863 N.E.2d 1276 (Mass. 2007).

2. **Evidence that defendant should have discovered.** How do you prove that the defendant should have discovered a foreign substance spilled on the floor by a customer? The chief method approved by the courts is to show that the substance has been there for a relatively long time. The jury is then permitted to conclude that a reasonable person should have discovered and remedied it. When such proof is presented, courts may say that the defendant was on constructive notice of the danger, meaning only that he should have discovered it. Getting evidence of this kind may be difficult, and when the evidence shows instead that some hazard was only present for a brief period of time, the plaintiff will have failed to prove constructive notice. *See, e.g., Wal–Mart Stores, Inc. v. Spates*, 186 S.W.3d 566 (Tex. 2006) (evidence that an empty plastic six-pack ring was on the floor near a store employee for 30 to 45 seconds before plaintiff tripped on it was insufficient as a matter of law to prove constructive notice).

3. **Evaluating reasonableness.** The main focus of this segment of the book is the evaluation of conduct. If we infer that the okra has been on the floor for an hour, we are left with the problem of evaluating the defendant's conduct. In some cases you might doubt whether courts or juries really have any way of saying that a reasonable and prudent store operator would have discovered a clear liquid on the floor within 15 minutes. On this issue consider: (a) The plaintiff can show the volume of customer traffic in the area where she fell. Would that be relevant to show that inspections by the storekeeper should have been more frequent? *See Jones v. Brookshire Grocery Co.*, 847 So.2d 43 (La. Ct. App. 2003). (b) Can the risk-utility test be applied in evaluating the restaurant's conduct in *Thoma?* Could you evaluate the conduct as negligent or not by considering the consumer's reasonable expectations instead?

4. **Judicial help for the plaintiff.** Clearly slip-and-fall plaintiffs have serious proof problems. Some courts have developed corollary rules to help the plaintiff a little. In *Ortega v. Kmart Corp.*, 36 P.3d 11 (Cal. 2001), the court suggested leeway for the plaintiff when it said: "Whether a dangerous condition has existed long enough for a reasonably prudent person to have discovered it is a question of fact for the jury, and the cases do not impose exact time limitations. Each accident must be viewed in light of its own unique circumstances." The Alaska high court has held that "factfinders can best ascertain whether the proprietor of a grocery store acted reasonably in maintaining the store's premises considering all of the circumstances," expressly making any of the three common theories described in Note 1 above a factor, but not a required element, in a plaintiff's case. *Edenshaw v. Safeway, Inc.*, 186 P.3d 568 (Alaska 2008). In *Blair v. West Town Mall*, 130 S.W.3d 761 (Tenn. 2004), the court seemed to say that a defendant might be found to be negligent because "a pattern of conduct, a recurring incident, or a general or continuing condition indicating the dangerous condition's existence," was proved. Isn't there a big leap from knowledge that dangerous conditions such as spills may occur to the conclusion that the defendant should have known about the spill that caused the plaintiff's injury? A few courts have gone even further, shifting the burden of proof to the shopkeeper to exculpate itself once the plaintiff has shown a fall due to a foreign substance. *Lanier v. Wal–Mart Stores, Inc.*, 99 S.W.3d 431 (Ky. 2003).

WAL–MART STORES, INC. v. WRIGHT, 774 N.E.2d 891 (Ind. 2002). A woman slipped on a puddle of water in the outdoor garden area of a Wal–Mart store. She sued for her injuries, alleging that Wal–Mart was negligent in the maintenance, care and inspection of the premises. The parties stipulated to the admission of a number of Wal–Mart's employee documents assembled as a "Store Manual." Several of the provisions detailed procedures for dealing with spills and other floor hazards. At the end of the trial, the plaintiff tendered a jury instruction that said: "You may consider the violation of any rules, policies, practices and procedures contained in these manuals and safety handbook along with all of the other evidence and the Court's instructions in deciding whether Wal–Mart was negligent. The violation of its rules, policies, practices and procedures are a proper item of evidence tending to show the degree of care recognized by Wal–Mart as ordinary care...." The trial judge gave the instruction over Wal–Mart's objection. The jury found for the plaintiff, reducing her damages for her own comparative fault.

Held, the instruction was improper and the verdict must be reversed. "[Y]ou can set standards for yourself that exceed ordinary care and the fact that you've done that shouldn't be used, as this [instruction] says, as evidence tending to show the degree that you believe is ordinary." Wal–Mart's "rules and policies may exceed its view of what is required by ordinary care in a given situation. Rules and policies in the Manual may have been established for any number of reasons having nothing to do with safety and ordinary care, including a desire to appear more clean and neat to attract customers, or a concern that spills may contaminate merchandise. The law has long recognized that failure to follow a party's precautionary steps or procedures is not necessarily failure to exercise ordinary care.... 1 Dan B. Dobbs, The Law of Torts § 165 (2000). We think this rule is salutary because it encourages following the best practices without necessarily establishing them as a legal norm." The instruction is also erroneous for suggesting that jurors could apply "Wal-Mart's subjective view—as evidenced by the Manual—rather than an objective standard of ordinary care."

NOTE

Why does the court believe that not giving internal safety rules the force of legal norms "encourages following the best practices"?

DUNCAN v. CORBETTA, 577 N.Y.S.2d 129 (App. Div. 1991). "The plaintiff William C. Duncan was injured when he began to descend a wooden exterior stairway at the defendant's residence and the top step collapsed. The court erred by precluding the plaintiffs' expert from testifying that it was common practice to use pressure-treated lumber in the construction of such stairways, even though the nonpressure-treated lumber used was permissible under the applicable building code. Proof of a general custom and usage is admissible because it tends to establish a standard by which ordinary care may be judged even where an ordinance prescribes certain minimum safety requirements which the custom exceeds. However, no significant prejudice resulted from the error. The plaintiffs failed to establish that the defendant had a role in the design or construction of the stairway." Judgment for defendant affirmed.

NOTES

1.   **General rule.** Evidence that the defendant violated customary safety precautions of the relevant community is usually sufficient to get the plaintiff to the jury. The Restatement (Third) says that a person's "departure from the custom of the community, or of others in like circumstances, in a way that increases the risk" is evidence of that person's negligence "but does not require a finding of negligence." RESTATEMENT (THIRD) OF TORTS: LIABILITY FOR PHYSICAL HARM § 13(b) (P.F.D. No. 1, 2005).

2.   **Customary statutory violations.** In *Duncan v. Corbetta* the court was willing to say that a defendant who complied with all the safety requirements of a statute might still be negligent if he failed to follow a safety custom. What if a litigant who failed to comply with a statute or ordinance wants to introduce evidence that the law is customarily violated, that is, that custom tends to show that violation is reasonable conduct? Judges generally disfavor such a use of custom evidence. *See e.g., Robinson v. District of*

Columbia, 580 A.2d 1255 (D.C. App. 1990) (rejecting party's argument that it was reasonable to disobey traffic law by jaywalking outside the marked crosswalk, as allegedly shown by "common practice of pedestrians at the location of the accident").

3. **What custom proves.** Existence of a safety custom might conceivably prove a number of different things. It might, for example, prove that harm was foreseeable, which is to say that the activity was recognizably risky; it might prove that the defendant knew or should have known of the risk; and it might prove that the risk was an "unreasonable" one unless the customary precaution is taken, or at least that it was unreasonable in the opinion of the community in general. As Justice Holmes famously put it in *Texas & Pacific Ry. v. Behymer,* 189 U.S. 468 (1903), "what usually is done may be evidence of what ought to be done, but what ought to be done is set by the standard of reasonable prudence, whether it is usually complied with or not." Even if it proved none of these things, however, custom might prove at least one thing, namely that a safety precaution was feasible.

4. **Custom other than safety custom.** What if the custom is well-established and even widespread, but there is no evidence whether the custom arose from safety considerations or from convenience? In *Levine v. Russell Blaine Co.,* 7 N.E.2d 673 (N.Y. 1937), the plaintiff injured her hand on a rough, bristly rope for which defendant was responsible. There was an infection and later the arm had to be amputated. The plaintiff sought to introduce evidence that by custom the rope supplied should have been a smooth one. The court said:

> A smoother rope might have advantages other than greater safety. Its customary use might be due to these advantages, and might not show a general recognition that risk of injury would arise from use of a rougher rope. Proof of such custom or practice would then be insufficient, standing alone, to show negligence … but the chain of proof might, in this case, have been completed if evidence of customary use of a different rope had been supplemented by expert evidence explaining how and why one kind of rope may cause a foreseeable risk of injury which others customarily avoid.

5. **Safety manuals.** Could a plaintiff introduce into evidence safety manuals or codes promulgated by private or governmental organizations to show that the defendant, in failing to follow such manuals or codes, fell below the standard of reasonable care? Many courts have allowed such evidence. *See, e.g., McComish v. DeSoi,* 200 A.2d 116 (N.J. 1964) (holding that safety codes were admissible as evidence of what was customarily done, although they did not set the standard of care). Some safety codes prepared by trade associations or industry groups have been adopted by statute or ordinance. Many city ordinances, for example, adopt a building or electrical code prepared by industry. In such a case, the privately prepared safety code takes on the force of a statute or ordinance and is not only admissible but may set the standard of care.

THE T.J. HOOPER

60 F.2d 737 (2d Cir. 1932)

L.   HAND, CIRCUIT JUDGE.

The barges No. 17 and No. 30, belonging to the Northern Barge Company, had lifted cargoes of coal at Norfolk, Virginia, for New York in March, 1928. They were towed by two tugs of the petitioner, the "Montrose" and the "Hooper,"and were lost off the Jersey Coast on March tenth, in an easterly gale. The cargo owners sued the barges under the contracts of carriage; the owner of the barges sued the tugs under the towing contract, both for its own loss and as bailee of the cargoes; the owner of the tug filed a petition to limit its liability. All the suits were joined and heard together, and the judge found that all the vessels were unseaworthy; the tugs, because they did not carry radio receiving sets by which they could have seasonably got warnings of a change in the weather which should have caused them to seek shelter in the Delaware Breakwater en route. He therefore entered an interlocutory decree holding each tug and barge jointly liable to each cargo owner, and each tug for half damages for the loss of its barge. The petitioner appealed, and the barge owner appealed and filed assignments of error. . . .

[Radio broadcasts gave forecasts of coming heavy weather. Reasonable masters would have put in at a safe harbor had they received the broadcasts. The masters of these tugs did not receive the broadcasts] because their private radio receiving sets, which were on board, were not in working order. These belonged to them personally, and were partly a toy, partly a part of the equipment, but neither furnished by the owner, nor supervised by it. It is not fair to say that there was a general custom among coastwise carriers so to equip their tugs. One line alone did it; as for the rest, they relied upon their crews, so far as they can be said to have relied at all. An adequate receiving set suitable for a coastwise tug can now be got at small cost and is reasonably reliable if kept up; obviously it is a source of great protection to their tows. Twice every day they can receive these predictions, based upon the widest possible information, available to every vessel within two or three hundred miles and more. Such a set is the ears of the tug to catch the spoken word, just as the master's binoculars are her eyes to see a storm signal ashore. Whatever may be said as to other vessels, tugs towing heavy coal laden barges, strung out for half a mile, have little power to maneuver, and do not, as this case proves, expose themselves to weather which would not turn back stauncher craft. They can have at hand protection against dangers of which they can learn in no other way.

Is it then a final answer that the business had not yet generally adopted receiving sets? There are, no doubt, cases where courts seem to make the general practice of the calling the standard of proper diligence; we have indeed given some currency to the notion ourselves. Indeed in most cases reasonable prudence is in fact common prudence; but strictly it is never its measure; a whole calling may have unduly lagged in the adoption of new and available devices. It never may set its own tests, however persuasive be its usages. Courts must in the end say what is required; there are precautions so imperative that even their universal disregard will not excuse their omission. But here there was no custom at all as to receiving sets; some had them, some did not; the most that can be urged is that they had not yet become general. Certainly in such a case we need not pause; when some have thought a device necessary, at least we may say that they were right, and the others too slack.... [H]ad [the tugs] been properly equipped, they would have got the Arlington reports. The injury was a direct consequence of this unseaworthiness.

Decree affirmed.

NOTES

1. In *Elkerson v. North Jersey Blood Center,* 776 A.2d 244 (N.J. Super. Ct. App. Div. 2001), a man died, allegedly as a result of receiving a transfusion of blood tainted with hepatitis. In the suit against the blood bank that had supplied the blood, the plaintiff's evidence showed that a better test was available to detect hepatitis. But evidence also showed that no blood banks used the better test. The trial judge instructed the jury that the defendant was to be judged by the standard practice of the blood banking industry at the relevant time. So instructed, the jury found that the defendant was not negligent. If you represented the plaintiff, what proposition would you assert in your brief on appeal?

2. Earlier decisions sometimes held that (a) evidence of custom was wholly inadmissible; or (b) on the contrary, custom represented the sole standard of care. As *The T.J. Hooper* would suggest, these older rules are largely obsolete. *See* RESTATEMENT (THIRD) § 13(a) (P.F.D. No. 1, 2005) ("An actor's compliance with the custom of the community, or of others in like circumstances, is evidence that the actor's conduct is not negligent but does not preclude a finding of negligence.") However, some courts are still cautious about admitting custom evidence, lest the jury treat it as a standard of care. *Jones v. Jitney Jungle Stores of Am., Inc.,* 730 So.2d 555 (Miss. 1998).

3. If you have reservations about the risk-utility rule of *Carroll Towing,* how about using custom as the standard of care and the test of negligence?

§ 4. PROVING UNSPECIFIED NEGLIGENCE: THE SPECIAL CASE OF RES IPSA LOQUITUR

"Some circumstantial evidence is very strong, as when you find a trout in the milk." H.D. THOREAU, JOURNAL, *November 11, 1850* (B. Torrey, ed. 1906).

A. ORIGINS AND BASIC FEATURES

BYRNE v. BOADLE

2 H. & C. 722, 159 Eng. Rep. 299 (Exch. 1863)

[Plaintiff gave evidence that he was walking in Scotland Road when he lost all recollection. Witnesses testified that a barrel of flour fell on him. The defendant's shop was adjacent and the barrel appeared to have fallen or to have been dropped from the shop. The trial judge "nonsuited" the plaintiff, taking the view that the plaintiff had put on no evidence of negligence. The plaintiff's attorney then sought review in a higher court by obtaining a "rule nisi to enter the verdict for the plaintiff...." What follows includes a portion of the argument by Charles Russell for the defendant before Barons Channell, Bramwell, Pigott and Chief Baron Pollock of the Exchequer Court.]

Charles Russell now showed cause. First, there was no evidence to connect the defendant or his servants with the occurrence.... Surmise ought not to be substituted for strict proof when it is sought to fix a defendant with serious liability. The plaintiff should establish his case by affirmative evidence.

Secondly, assuming the facts to be brought home to the defendant or his servants, these facts do not disclose any evidence for the jury of negligence. The plaintiff was bound to give affirmative proof of negligence. But there was not a scintilla of evidence, unless the occurrence is of itself evidence of negligence. There was not even evidence that the barrel was being lowered by a jigger-hoist as alleged in the declaration. [POLLOCK, C.B. There are certain cases of which it may be said res ipsa loquitur, and this seems one of them. In some cases the Courts have held that the mere fact of the accident having occurred is evidence of negligence, as, for instance, in the case of railway collisions.] On examination of the authorities, that doctrine would seem to be confined to the case of a collision between two trains upon the same line, and both being the property and under the management of the same Company. Such was the case of Skinner v. The London, Brighton and South Coast Railway Company (5 Exch. 787), where the train in which the plaintiff was ran into another train which had stopped a short distance from a station, in consequence of a luggage train before it having broken down. In that case there must have been negligence, or the accident could not have happened. Other cases cited in the textbooks, in support of the doctrine of presumptive negligence, when examined, will be found not to do so. Amongst them is Carpue v. The London and Brighton Railway Company (5 Q.B. 747), but there, in addition to proof of the occurrence, the plaintiff gave affirmative evidence of negligence, by showing that the rails were somewhat deranged at the spot where the accident took place, and that the train was proceeding at a speed which, considering the state of the rails, was hazardous.... Later cases have qualified the doctrine of presumptive negligence. In Cotton v. Wood (8 C.B.N.S. 568), it was held that a Judge is not justified in leaving the case to the jury where the plaintiff's evidence is equally consistent with the absence as with the existence of negligence in the defendant. In Hammack v. White (11 C.B.N.S. 588, 594), Erle, J., said that he was of opinion "that the plaintiff in a case of this sort was not entitled to have the case left to the jury unless he gives some affirmative evidence that there has been negligence on the part of the defendant." [Pollock, C.B. If he meant that to apply to all cases, I must say, with great respect, that I entirely differ from him. He must refer to the mere nature of the accident in that particular case. Bramwell, B. No doubt, the presumption of negligence is not raised in every case of injury from accident, but in some it is. We must judge of the facts in a reasonable way; and regarding them in that light we know that these accidents do not take place without a cause, and in general that cause is negligence.] The law will not presume that a man is guilty of a wrong. It is consistent with the facts proved that the defendant's servants were using the utmost care and the best appliances to lower the barrel with safety. Then why should the fact that accidents of this nature are sometimes caused by negligence raise any presumption against the defendant? There are many accidents from which no presumption of negligence can arise. [Bramwell, B. Looking at the matter in a reasonable way it comes to this—an injury is done to the plaintiff, who has no means of knowing whether it was the result of negligence; the defendant, who knows how it was caused, does not think fit to tell the jury.] Unless a plaintiff gives some evidence which ought to be submitted to the jury, the defendant is not bound to offer any defense. This plaintiff cannot, by a defective proof of his case, compel the defendant to give evidence in explanation. [Pollock, C.B. I have frequently observed that a defendant has a right to remain silent unless a prima facie case is established against him. But here the question is whether the plaintiff has not shewn such a case.] In a case of this nature, in which the sympathies of a jury are with the plaintiff, it would be dangerous to allow presumption to be substituted for affirmative proof of negligence.

Littler appeared to support the rule, but was not called upon to argue.

Pollock, C.B. We are all of opinion that the rule must be absolute to enter the verdict for the plaintiff. The learned counsel was quite right in saying that there are many accidents from which no presumption of negligence can arise, but I think it would be wrong to lay down as a rule that in no case can presumption of negligence arise from the fact of an accident. Suppose in this case the barrel had rolled out of the warehouse and fallen on the plaintiff, how could he possibly ascertain from what cause it occurred? It is the duty of persons who keep barrels in a warehouse to take care that they do not roll out, and I think that such a case would, beyond all doubt, afford prima facie evidence of negligence. A barrel could not roll out of a warehouse without some negligence, and to say that a plaintiff who is injured by it must call witnesses from the warehouse to prove negligence seems to me preposterous. [The other Barons concurred.]

NOTES

1. Consider how res ipsa loquitur evidence differs from ordinary circumstantial evidence. Using *Byrne* as a model, can you state exactly what *Byrne* has permitted that has not been permitted in earlier decisions?

2. The judges in *Byrne*, which is more or less the original res ipsa loquitur case, repeatedly recurred to the common sense interpretation of the facts before them—the accident, they felt, "spoke for itself," and what it said was that the defendant must have been negligent. Suppose you are driving behind a large truck and trailer; the spare tire somehow comes out of the cradle beneath the trailer and crashes through your windshield, causing you injury. Is that enough to show negligence? *McDougald v. Perry,* 716 So.2d 783 (Fla. 1998).

3. Modern courts have developed rules for the application of res ipsa loquitur. States differ as to their particular requirements. Traditionally, in order for res ipsa to apply, the plaintiff has to show three things: (1) the accident which produced a person's injury was one which ordinarily does not happen in the absence of negligence, (2) the instrumentality or agent which caused the accident was under the exclusive control of the defendant, and (3) the circumstances indicated that the untoward event was not caused or contributed to by any act or neglect on the part of the injured person. *See, e.g., Eaton v. Eaton*, 575 A.2d 858 (N.J. 1990). The Restatement (Second) refined this traditional test, providing that a plaintiff must prove: (1) the event is of a kind which ordinarily does not occur in the absence of negligence; (2) other responsible causes, including the conduct of the plaintiff and third persons, are sufficiently eliminated by the evidence; and (3) the indicated negligence is within the scope of the defendant's duty to the plaintiff. RESTATEMENT (SECOND) OF TORTS § 328D (1965). Are these requirements materially different from each other? The Restatement (Third) offers still another formulation—that negligence can be inferred when the accident causing harm is a type that "ordinarily happens because of the negligence of the class of actors of which the defendant is the relevant member." RESTATEMENT (THIRD) OF TORTS: LIABILITY FOR PHYSICAL HARM § 17 (Proposed Final Draft No. 1, 2005). We should expect variation in local verbalization of the rules, but always remember that a different verbalization may be intended to express substantially the same ideas.

NOTE: PROCEDURAL INCIDENTS AND EFFECTS OF RES IPSA LOQUITUR

1. *Sufficiency of evidence issue.* The application of res ipsa loquitur means that, on the negligence issue, the plaintiff will survive a motion for directed verdict and get to the jury, which can then decide the case either way.

2. *Instructing on res ipsa.* If the plaintiff has adduced evidence from which the jury could conclude that the elements of res ipsa loquitur are present, then trial judges commonly give a res ipsa loquitur instruction to the jury. The instruction "merely tells the jury that if they do find the

existence of these elements then they may draw the inference of negligence," not that they must do so. *K–Mart Corp. v. Gipson*, 563 N.E.2d 667, 670 (Ind. Ct. App. 1990).

3. *Permissible inference effect.* Most courts hold that res ipsa creates a permissible inference that the jury may draw if it sees fit, and further that res ipsa does not shift the burden of persuasion from the plaintiff. Thus even if the defendant introduces no evidence at all, the jury may reject the inference and bring in a verdict for the defendant.

4. *Abnormally strong inferences of negligence.* To say that the inference of negligence is merely permitted, not required, is to say that the plaintiff who makes out a permissible inference case would not be entitled to a directed verdict. But could there be cases so strong that the permissible inference becomes a mandatory inference so that the trial judge would direct a verdict after all? In *Morejon v. Rais Constr. Co.*, 851 N.E.2d 1143 (N.Y. 2006) (dictum), the court said that "when the plaintiff's circumstantial proof is so convincing and the defendant's response is so weak that the inference of defendant's negligence is inescapable," it would be proper for the trial court to grant summary judgment or a directed verdict for the plaintiff in a res ipsa case. This occurred in *Quinby v. Plumsteadville Family Practice, Inc.*, 907 A.2d 1061 (Pa. 2006), where a quadriplegic patient fell off an examination table at the doctor's office and subsequently died. The court found that no reasonable jury could believe that this occurred for any reason other than the defendant's leaving the patient unattended and unrestrained. We see another example in *De Leon Lopez v. Corporacion Insular de Seguros*, 931 F.2d 116 (1st Cir. 1991), where two women gave birth to twins in the University Hospital at Puerto Rico Medical Center. The hospital somehow switched one twin from each set, so that each mother went home with two children, but only with one of her own. The mistake was discovered after a year and a half. The court thought that occasions for directing a verdict for the plaintiff were "hen's-teeth rare"; the court nevertheless affirmed such a ruling.

5. *The presumption effect.* A small number of courts say that res ipsa loquitur is *not* merely a common sense assessment of evidence which permits an inference of fault, but that, instead, it creates a "presumption" of negligence. The term "presumption" can be used loosely or can have technical meanings, explored in the course in evidence. Courts usually enforce one of two possible effects when a presumption of negligence applies:

(a) The jury is told that, once the presumption applies, the defendant has the burden of showing he is *not* negligent; OR

(b) The judge will direct a verdict for the plaintiff unless the defendant produces some evidence that he was not negligent. CAL. EVID. CODE § 646(b) is an example; it defines res ipsa as "a presumption affecting the burden of producing evidence." (How *much* evidence the defendant must produce is another disputed matter.)

Sometimes courts describe the presumption as (a) shifting the *burden of persuasion* or (b) shifting the *burden of production* (meaning production of evidence), or the burden of going forward with evidence. *See* DOBBS ON TORTS § 152 (2000) (describing presumptions and their effects). How would you compare or contrast the permissible inference approach to res ipsa?

6. *Rebuttal by defendant.* Suppose the defendant does in fact offer proof about his conduct. What does this do to the res ipsa loquitur inference? Can the plaintiff still get to the jury? Suppose in *Byrne* the defendant had proved that a trucker loading the flour had negligently dropped it. Suppose instead that the defendant proved it did everything normally, exercised all precautions about the flour storage, and cannot understand why the injury took place? Would the results be different under these two versions of the defendant's proof?

B.   IS NEGLIGENCE MORE PROBABLE THAN NOT?

KOCH v. NORRIS PUBLIC POWER DISTRICT, 632 N.W.2d 391 (Neb. App. 2001). Defendant's high-voltage line broke and fell, starting a fire that did considerable damage to the plaintiff's property. The weather was sunny and dry, and winds at 40 mph were ordinary. There was some inconclusive evidence that the line might have been shot by a bullet, but other evidence suggests that a bullet did not cause the line to fall. *Held,* the plaintiff may rely on res ipsa loquitur. "[P]ower lines do not normally fall without fault on behalf of the company that maintains them and that res ipsa loquitur is applied in the absence of a substantial, significant, or probable explanation. . . . It seems clear that power lines should be built and maintained so they do not fall without the intervention of nature or a person and that therefore if a line falls without explanation, it must have been negligently constructed or maintained."

COSGROVE v. COMMONWEALTH EDISON CO., 734 N.E.2d 155 (Ill. App. Ct. 2000). On a stormy night, the electric company's power lines were seen to be sparking in the alley behind the plaintiffs' house. At some point the power line was seen to fall. A few hours after the sparking was noticed, a fire occurred in the alley. Evidence indicated that a leak in a buried gas line was ignited by the sparks. The fire injured the plaintiffs. *Held,* the plaintiff cannot rely on res ipsa loquitur as to the electric company but can rely on it as to the gas company. "Other forces [besides negligence] may cause a downed power line, such as wind, lightning, storm, or an animal chewing through the wire." But a "ruptured gas line feeding a fire does not ordinarily occur in the absence of negligence. Gas mains are buried beyond the reach and interference of the general public, and the probability is great that breaks therein are occasioned by defects in the pipes or improper utilization thereof. In the ordinary course of events, gas explosions and fires do not occur; when one does occur, an inference of fault is justifiable. This inference may be explained or rebutted. However, even if the gas company is blameless, its superior knowledge of the facts at hand and its responsibility to the community create a duty to come forward and make an explanation.''

NOTES

1. **Judging probabilities.** In determining the probabilities that the defendant was somehow negligent, judges draw on their common experience in life, rarely on actual data. See *Eversole v. Woods Acquisition, Inc.,* 135 S.W.3d 425 (Mo. Ct. App. 2004). The reasoning in *Koch* and *Cosgrove* is fairly typical. And once the trial judge believes jurors have the common life experience to make the judgment, the question will be passed to the jury for its verdict.

2. **Common knowledge.** To invoke res ipsa loquitur, the plaintiff must first show that negligence is more probable than not, or as commonly expressed, that the event does not ordinarily occur without negligence of someone. But how do we know the probabilities? In some cases, judges believe juries lack sufficient knowledge or experience to conclude that negligence is more probable than not. In such instances, judges direct verdicts for the defendant. *E.g., Scott v. James,* 731 A.2d 399 (D.C. App. 1999) (stressing jury's lack of knowledge of chemistry). In situations like *Byrne v. Boadle,* however, judges believe that common knowledge and general experience of jurors permit (but do not require) them to think that, more likely than not, the defendant was negligent.

3. **Res ipsa and "ordinary accidents."** If res ipsa applies only when a permissible inference arises that the event would not ordinarily occur without negligence, does that mean that res ipsa is inapplicable to "ordinary accidents" that often occur without negligence? Some courts have said just that. *See, e.g., Linnear v. Centerpoint Energy Entex/Reliant Energy,* 966 So.2d 36 (La. 2007). Might this be the reason why courts have usually held res ipsa loquitur inapplicable to slip-and fall cases? *See* DOBBS ON TORTS § 155 (2000) (where a plaintiff falls on a slippery substance on defendant's premises "the possibilities are too strong that the defendant was not responsible for placing the substance there and that he did not have time to discover it and make it safe, so specific evidence on these points is usually required"). A few courts have said res ipsa could apply to such cases, however. *See, e.g., Morris v. Wal– Mart Stores, Inc.,* 330 F.3d 854 (6th Cir. 2003) (applying Tennessee law).

4. **The case of rear-end collisions.** The driver of a stopped forward car is struck from behind by a car driven by the defendant. In the absence of special reasons to say otherwise, is this a res ipsa loquitur case? Or should we say instead that the defendant was either following too closely, or driving too fast, or failing to keep a reasonable lookout? Some courts address rear-end collisions through the terminology of res ipsa loquitur, but others address the rear-end collision as indicating specific negligence, permitting or requiring the jury to find that the defendant was following too closely or driving too fast in the absence of some explanation. *E.g., Garnot v. Johnson,* 387 S.E.2d 473 (Va. 1990). Georgia courts take a different view, holding that proof that the plaintiff's car was rear-ended is not sufficient to permit an inference that the defendant who drives into the plaintiff's forward car was negligent. *See Davis*

v. Sykes, 593 S.E.2d 859 (Ga. Ct. App. 2004). Courts also recognize that once a rear-end collision creates an inference or presumption of negligence, the defendant may adduce evidence that rebuts it. Would proof that the car ahead stopped suddenly rebut the presumption or inference? *Clampitt v. D.J. Spencer Sales,* 786 So.2d 570 (Fla. 2001). What about proof that the car ahead was accelerating from a stoplight and then suddenly stopped for no reason? *Eppler v. Tarmac Am., Inc.,* 752 So.2d 592 (Fla. 2000). Or that the defendant struck an unforeseeable icy patch that prevented a stop?

WARREN v. JEFFRIES

139 S.E.2d 718 (N.C. 1965)

PER CURIAM.

Terry Lee Enoch, a six-year-old child, was injured when a wheel of defendant's Chevrolet automobile ran over his body, and from these injuries he died. Plaintiff instituted this action to recover for his alleged wrongful death. From judgment of involuntary nonsuit entered at the close of plaintiff's evidence, plaintiff appeals.

Plaintiff's evidence, taken as true for the purposes of this appeal, discloses these facts:

Defendant drove to Terry's home to see Terry's father and parked his car in the yard. Terry's father was not at home and defendant went in the house and waited for his return. The car was left standing on an incline. During the time there were in and around the house about a dozen children, including Terry; their ages ranged from 18 months to 20 years. The car remained parked for about an hour prior to the accident, and during this interval no one had gone to the car or touched it for any purpose. One of the children needed shoe polish and defendant gave Terry's mother the keys to his automobile so she could drive it to a store for the polish. She and five children, including Terry, started to the car. It was raining and Terry didn't want to wear his glasses; he gave them to his mother and she went back in the house to put them up. The five children (eldest, 20 years) got in the rear seat of the car; it was a 4–door sedan, and none of them got in the front seat. They did not touch any of the control mechanisms of the car. Terry was the last to get in and when he "closed the door something clicked in the front and ... the car started rolling" backwards in the direction of a large ditch. One of the older children opened the door and told the others to jump out. All jumped out, Terry first. When he jumped out he fell, and the front wheel ran over his chest.

The mother's graphic description of her son is so typical of an alert and active little boy that it is worthy of preservation. "He was full of fun at all times, he never was still unless he was asleep, he was either laughing or playing or doing something to let you know he was around. One thing I remember, the lady I worked for give (sic) him a little puppy and he was crazy about this little dog...."

Plaintiff alleges defendant was negligent in that (1) he failed to set the hand brake, (2) failed to engage the transmission, and (3) neglected to maintain adequate brakes as required by G.S. § 20–124. There is no evidence as to the condition of the brakes, whether the hand brake had been set, or whether the car was in gear. Apparently the car was not examined after the accident. What caused it to make a "clicking" sound and begin rolling backwards is pure speculation. The doctrine of *res ipsa loquitur* is not applicable.

Affirmed.

NOTES

1. **Questioning *Warren*.** Testimony, which the jury could believe, excluded the possibility of tampering by the children. Why, then, isn't *Warren v. Jeffries* a res ipsa case like any other case of a car inexplicably going off the road? Is there an explanation for the accident that would *not* involve negligence of the defendant?

2. **Inferences from plaintiff's failure to offer available proof?** Would it have helped the plaintiff to put on evidence that the car was examined immediately after the accident by a qualified mechanic and that the examination revealed nothing throwing light on the occurrence? Did the court in effect draw an inference against the plaintiff for failure to introduce some such testimony? In *Lawson v. Mitsubishi Motor Sales of America, Inc.*, 938 So.2d 35 (La. 2006), the court held that res ipsa was inappropriate where plaintiffs' experts had tampered with material evidence in a car-crash case, preventing the discovery of "direct evidence [that] would have been available to prove or disprove the plaintiff's theory" of the accident. For res ipsa to apply, the court said, "plaintiffs need to sufficiently exclude inference of . . . the responsibility of others besides defendant in causing the accident."

3. **Judge Posner's bus example.** Consider also *Howard v. Wal–Mart Stores, Inc.*, 160 F.3d 358 (7th Cir. 1998). In that case, Judge Posner discussed a hypothetical case in which the plaintiff was struck by a bus. At that location, 51% of all buses are owned by company A and 49% by company B. Does the plaintiff make out a case against A by showing these facts plus negligence and causation? "If the 51/49 statistic is the plaintiff's only evidence, and he does not show that it was infeasible for him to obtain any additional evidence, the inference to be drawn is not that there is a 51 percent probability that it was a bus owned by A that hit the plaintiff. It is that the plaintiff either investigated and discovered that the bus was actually owned by B (and B might not have been negligent and so not liable even if a cause of the accident, or might be judgment-proof and so not worth suing), or that he simply has not bothered to conduct an investigation. If the first alternative is true, he should of course lose; and since it may be true, the probability that the plaintiff was hit by a bus owned by A is less than 51 percent and the plaintiff has failed to carry his burden of proof. If the second alternative is true—the plaintiff just hasn't conducted an investigation—he still should lose. A court shouldn't be required to expend its scarce resources of time and effort on a case until the plaintiff has conducted a sufficient investigation to make

reasonably clear that an expenditure of public resources is likely to yield a significant social benefit. This principle is implicit in the law's decision to place the burden of producing evidence on the plaintiff rather than on the defendant.''

4. **Inferences against a defendant for failing to explain?** In some cases, the defendant or his witnesses appear to have extensive knowledge of relevant facts, but never offer any testimony about them. Courts sometimes permit the trier of fact to draw inferences against the defendant in this situation. The trier may be permitted to find that the evidence was not produced because it would have been adverse to the defendant, and then may be permitted to treat the case as if adverse evidence had in fact appeared. In other cases, the defendant's questionable handling of evidence may be used by the court to bolster the plaintiff's res ipsa argument. *See, e.g., DeBusscher v. Sam's East, Inc.*, 505 F.3d 475 (6th Cir. 2007) (portable basketball goal on display in store fell on plaintiff; fact that defendant sent the goal to the claims department without checking the ballast level showed that "evidence of the true explanation for the accident was more readily accessible" to the defendant).

5. **Defendant's superior knowledge.** Sometimes courts say or imply that res ipsa cannot be invoked unless the defendant has superior knowledge. *See, e.g., Pacheco v. Ames*, 69 P.3d 324 (Wash. 2003); *DeBusscher v. Sam's East, Inc.*, 505 F.3d 475 (6th Cir. 2007) (Michigan law). But if res ipsa is a matter of assessing the probability that defendant is negligent, is superior knowledge by the defendant really necessary? Suppose the defendant runs off the road in a car, injures the plaintiff and has amnesia. The plaintiff, on the other hand, remembers everything she saw in perfect, horror-stricken detail. No res ipsa?

6. **Specific evidence of negligence.** If a plaintiff relies on res ipsa loquitur and the defendant comes forward with an explanation that the accident was caused by something other than defendant's negligence, then the jury might well decide the case against the plaintiff. *See* RESTATEMENT (THIRD) § 17, cmt. *g* (P.F.D. No 1, 2005). What if the plaintiff relies on res ipsa loquitur, but also produces specific evidence of the defendant's negligence? Under the traditional rule, the plaintiff could not do that. The more modern approach does allow a plaintiff to put on proof of the defendant's particular negligent conduct while relying on res ipsa loquitur in the alternative—as long as the specific evidence does not provide a "complete explanation" of the accident. *Widmyer v. Southeast Skyways, Inc.*, 584 P.2d 1 (Alaska 1978) (allowing res ipsa in an air-crash case); *see also, e.g., Clinkscales v. Nelson Securities, Inc.*, 697 N.W.2d 836 (Iowa 2005) (allowing res ipsa theory in a restaurant grease-fire case).

Why would res ipsa loquitur not be needed when the plaintiff's evidence provides a complete explanation of what occurred? *See Conner v. Menard, Inc.*, 705 N.W.2d 318 (Iowa 2005) ("[T]he doctrine does not apply when there is direct evidence as to the precise cause of the injury and all of the facts and circumstances attending the occurrence.... [T]his is because, when direct evidence is presented, the underlying reason frequently advanced for application of the res ipsa doctrine is not present: the chief evidence of the true cause of plaintiff's injury is practically inaccessible to plaintiff but accessible to defendant."). Should the plaintiff be unhappy that he cannot rely on res ipsa loquitur?

7. **Res ipsa, probability, and experts.** "[W]hen no fund of common knowledge would enable a layperson to reasonably draw such a conclusion, the plaintiff may present expert testimony that such an event usually does not occur without negligence," and the fact that experts for the defendant offer conflicting opinions does not rule out res ipsa loquitur. *Lowrey v. Montgomery Kone, Inc.,* 42 P.3d 621 (Ariz. Ct. App. 2002); *accord, States v. Lourdes Hosp.,* 792 N.E.2d 151 (N.Y. 2003) (emphasizing that the defendant may adduce evidence that tends to rebut the inference and that the jury makes the ultimate decision whether to draw the inference or not). But no expert will be needed where a lay jury can decide the issue based on common knowledge. *See, e.g., Jerista v. Murray,* 883 A.2d 350 (N.J. 2005) (automatic door suddenly closed on plaintiff).

C. ATTRIBUTING THE FAULT TO DEFENDANT RATHER THAN OTHERS

GILES v. CITY OF NEW HAVEN

636 A.2d 1335 (Conn. 1994)

Katz, Associate Justice.

The defendant Otis Elevator Company (defendant) appeals from the Appellate Court's determination that the trial court should not have granted the defendant's motion for a directed verdict in an action by the plaintiff, an elevator operator, to recover for the defendant's negligent failure to inspect, maintain and repair an elevator compensation chain that caused the plaintiff to sustain personal injuries. The Appellate Court concluded that the plaintiff had presented sufficient evidence to warrant presentation of the question of negligence under the doctrine of res ipsa loquitur to the jury. We affirm the judgment of the Appellate Court. . . .

[T]he Appellate Court reviewed the record and concluded that the trial court could reasonably have considered the following facts in deciding whether the doctrine of res ipsa loquitur applied. "For fourteen years, the plaintiff was an elevator operator for one of three elevators in the Powell Building in New Haven. On the date her injuries were sustained, the elevator she was operating was ascending from the first floor to the twelfth floor when its compensation chain became hooked on a rail bracket located on the wall of the elevator shaft. The plaintiff was not able to control the movement of the chain from the interior of the cab. Once hooked, the chain then tightened up and broke free from two bolts securing it to the underside of the cab. The cab began to shudder and shake, and the plaintiff struck her head and shoulder against the walls of the cab. The chain then fell to the bottom of the elevator shaft with a loud crash, which frightened the plaintiff. Upon hearing the crash, the plaintiff, fearing for her safety, reversed the direction of the elevator a sit was approaching the twelfth floor. She directed the elevator to the nearest floor, the eleventh, where she jumped from the cab sustaining additional injuries. At the time the plaintiff received her injuries, the defendant had along standing exclusive contract with the building owner to maintain and inspect the elevator and its component parts. The elevator was installed by the defendant approximately sixty-one years before the accident. . . .

"[William] Hendry, [the defendant's district maintenance supervisor] testified that the normal sway of a compensation chain is approximately one to two inches, and in order for the chain to get hooked on a rail bracket it must sway at least eighteen inches. He further testified that for the chain to sway eighteen inches there must be some misoperation of the elevator, such as rapid reversals of direction. . . . [Plaintiff testified] that the crash of the compensation chain as it hit the bottom of the elevator shaft occurred before she reversed the direction of the cab." . . .

Before the Appellate Court the parties agreed that . . . the accident would not have occurred unless someone had been negligent. The parties were, however, in disagreement about whether the plaintiff had made a case for the jury with respect to the second and third conditions of the doctrine, namely, control of the elevator by the defendant and the absence of responsibility for the accident on the part of the plaintiff.

The defendant challenges the application of the res ipsa loquitur doctrine to this case because in its view the plaintiff failed to demonstrate that the defendant had exclusive control over the elevator. Specifically, the defendant argues that because plaintiff operated the elevator and controlled its movement and its chain's sway, she could not benefit from the doctrine notwithstanding defendant's own duty to maintain and inspect the elevator and to warn of any dangerous propensity. We disagree. . . .

[I]n describing the extent of the defendant's control of the use of the instrumentality [that caused the event], we have never held that any use whatsoever of the instrumentality by the plaintiff would automatically preclude application of res ipsa loquitur. So restrictive an interpretation would substantially undermine the efficacy of the doctrine. Rather, our previous discussions of use were meant to reflect the idea of management and control, factors that help to limit the application of the res ipsa loquitur doctrine to those situations in which the defendant's negligence was more probably than not the cause of the plaintiff's injuries. The plaintiff's actual use of the instrument, therefore does not, in and of itself bar application of the doctrine.

The growing trend in res ipsa loquitur jurisprudence is not to apply the "control" condition in such a way that renders it "a fixed, mechanical and rigid rule. 'Control,' if it is not to be pernicious and misleading, must be a very flexible term. It may be enough that the defendant has the right or power of control, and the opportunity to exercise it. . . . It is enough that the defendant is under a duty which he cannot delegate to another. . . ." W. Prosser & W. Keeton, supra, § 39, p. 250.

"The point of requiring control by the defendant is, as indicated by Prosser, to provide the basis for an inference that whatever negligence was involved may properly be charged to the defendant...."

In many jurisdictions, courts now deemphasize the role of exclusive control as a condition of res ipsa loquitur, even though their earlier decisions included such a requirement. "Exclusive control is merely one way of proving a defendant's responsibility. 'He may be responsible, and the inference may be drawn against him, where he shares the control with another.' Restatement (Second) of Torts § 328D, comment g...." If the jury could reasonably find that defendant's control was sufficient to warrant an inference that the defendant was more likely responsible for the incident than someone else, even in the absence of proof of absolute exclusivity and control over the instrumentality by the defendant, the trial court must allow the jury to draw that inference.

... In this case, the parties agree that the defendant was in control of the maintenance and repair of the elevator and its parts, and that the operation of the elevator by the operator was tantamount to its use. The defendant, however, seeks to distinguish the components of the elevator from their mechanical function by arguing that, although it controlled the elevator chain, it did not control the chain's sway. Although by operating the elevator the plaintiff may have diminished the exclusivity of the defendant's control, a jury could find that her conduct did not strip the defendant of control or responsibility for the chain and its condition, which resulted in the excessive sway....

Although Hendry explained that there was no reason to inspect the compensation chain and that he believed the accident had been caused by multiple rapid direction reversals, the plaintiff was not required to prove the absence of such reversals in order to avail herself of the res ipsa loquitur inference.

[The court found, finally, that Connecticut's adoption of comparative negligence compels the conclusion that res ipsa can apply to a case even where the plaintiff's negligence contributed to the injury, citing cases from seven other states which have also so held.]

The Appellate Court properly upheld the plaintiff's claim that the trial court should not have granted the defendant's motion for a directed verdict. Pursuant to the doctrine of res ipsa loquitur as we have refined its conditions in this opinion, the plaintiff was entitled to have a jury consider her claim that the defendant's negligence was the cause of her personal injuries.

The judgment of the Appellate Court is affirmed.

NOTES

1. **Verbal obeisance to the control rule.** Many courts routinely list the defendant's exclusive control over the instrumentality of harm as one of the elements the plaintiff must prove to establish a res ipsa loquitur case.

However, in many cases courts apply the rule loosely, so that the plaintiff can get to the jury on res ipsa loquitur even when she did not truly have exclusive control.

2. **Contemporary view of control rule.** *Giles* reflects a contemporary view of the control rule, perhaps one that makes the words used to express the rule correlate with the application or outcome. Thus "control" is only one way of establishing the important point that the negligence was probably that of the defendant, not that of someone else. It is enough if, control or no control, instrument or no instrument, the defendant was one of the persons who was probably negligent. *See Harder v. F.C. Clinton, Inc.*, 948 P.2d 298 (Okla. 1997); *Errico v. LaMountain*, 713 A.2d 791 (R.I. 1998).

3. **Absurd control arguments?** At one time, the control rule was taken quite literally. In *Kilgore v. Shepard Co.*, 158 A. 720 (R.I. 1932), the plaintiff sat down on a chair in defendant's store. It collapsed and she was injured. The court rejected this res ipsa loquitur on the ground that the defendant was not in exclusive control of the chair, the plaintiff herself being in "control" when she sat upon it. In line with *Giles*, courts today apply res ipsa to cases of injury resulting from taking a seat on chairs, bar stools and even bleachers. *E.g., Trujeque v. Service Merch. Co.*, 872 P.2d 361 (N.M. 1994).

In *Aldana v. School City of East Chicago*, 769 N.E.2d 1201 (Ind. Ct. App. 2002) a bus with child passengers went off the clear, dry highway, then fishtailed back on two wheels, throwing passengers against and under seats. Oncoming traffic prudently stopped and no other vehicle was involved. The defendant argued that res ipsa loquitur was inapplicable because the road, "which was part of the instrumentality, was not within the control of the driver" and in particular that there were some holes in the road. How should the court respond?

4. **Instrumentalities accessible to the public.** When, as in *Giles*, an instrumentality is more or less accessible to the public, numerous persons may have interfered with the instrumentality, so the defendant is not literally in exclusive control. Nevertheless, *Giles* is not alone in invoking res ipsa loquitur in public accessibility cases. On the other hand, New York has invoked the control rule to defeat res ipsa loquitur in the case of a plaintiff who was thrown to the ground when his shoe was caught in an escalator. *Ebanks v. New York City Transit Auth.*, 512 N.E.2d 297 (N.Y. 1987).

5. **Exploding bottle cases.** Under a liberal formulation of the control requirement, the plaintiff might show that any fault in the case was attributable to the defendant merely by excluding other causes. Suppose the plaintiff buys a soft drink from a grocery, takes it home, and suffers an injury when the bottle "explodes." The bottler obviously was not in control at the time of injury. Nor do we know when the negligence was likely to have occurred. The grocer or a customer might well have dropped the bottle, causing a chip for which the bottler is not responsible. In a leading case, *Escola v. Coca Cola Bottling Co.*, 150 P.2d 436 (Cal. 1944), the California Supreme Court held that the plaintiff could use res ipsa loquitur by showing that the defendant had control at the time of the probable negligence, and that this could be shown by excluding the negligence of others. Thus the plaintiff might show that the

bottle had not been subjected to any unusual treatment in the grocery store, and on making such proof would be permitted to use res ipsa loquitur. As the New York Court of Appeals put it in a non-bottling case, "the exclusive control requirement is thus subordinated to its general purpose, that of indicating that it *probably* was the defendant's negligence which caused the accident." *Corcoran v. Banner Super Mkt., Inc.*, 227 N.E.2d 304 (N.Y. 1967).

6. **Eliminating the plaintiff's fault.** Courts have often said that the plaintiff must show that she herself was not at fault or did not contribute to the injury. In retrospect, this looks like a specific instance of the control rule and shares its purpose. If so, then the real point is to show that the fault was at least in part attributable to the defendant. If this is right, the control rule and its subsidiary rule about plaintiff-fault merely point to evidence that will be important but not conclusive. Is *Giles* consistent with this view?

7. **Effect of comparative fault systems.** Some courts apparently assume that the plaintiff-fault rule was a rule of contributory negligence. These courts have concluded that, with the advent of comparative fault, under which any contributory negligence will reduce but not bar the plaintiff's claim, the plaintiff-fault limit on res ipsa should be abolished or modified. *E.g., Cox v. May Dep't Store Co.*, 903 P.2d 1119 (Ariz. Ct. App. 1995).

COLLINS v. SUPERIOR AIR–GROUND AMBULANCE SERVICE, INC., 789 N.E.2d 394 (Ill. App. Ct. 2003). Laura Collins, an elderly, bedridden woman who was unable to speak, lived with her daughter, Eva. Eva admitted her to Alden Wentworth Rehabilitation and Health Care Center for five days while the daughter was out of town. An ambulance service, Superior, transported Laura to Alden and returned her home after five days. When Laura was returned home, Eva discovered that she was suffering. A doctor quickly confirmed that Laura was (a) dehydrated and (b) had a broken leg. Suit was brought by Laura against both Superior and Alden. After Laura died, the suit was continued by Laura's estate. The estate relied upon res ipsa loquitur. "Superior argues that, because there were two defendants, plaintiff cannot, and does not, plead that it was Superior alone that controlled the instrumentality of the injury, a requirement necessary for a successful cause of action for *res ipsa loquitur.* However, this requirement frustrates the essence of *res ipsa loquitur,* which allows proof of negligence by circumstantial evidence when the direct evidence concerning the cause of injury is primarily within the knowledge and control of the defendant.... Under these specific facts, we conclude that where there are only two defendants who had consecutive control over plaintiff, and either one could have caused plaintiff's injuries, and both are named in the complaint, the complaint is sufficient for pleading purposes to raise the inference of negligence under the doctrine of *res ipsa loquitur.*"

NOTES

1. **The special problem of multiple actors.** Res ipsa loquitur does not ordinarily assist the plaintiff when two or more defendants are in control of the relevant instrumentality at different times. In such a case of serial or consecutive control, the occurrence of injury does not usually tend to show which defendant was negligent, much less that both were. *See Novak Heating & Air Conditioning v. Carrier Corp.*, 622 N.W.2d 495 (Iowa 2001). That is, where two or more defendants have been in serial control, "further information is typically needed in order to establish that any one of [them] was probably the negligent party," and the burden of coming forward with that information is on the plaintiff. RESTATEMENT (THIRD) § 17, cmt. *f* (P.F.D. No. 1, 2005).

2. **The vehicular collision example.** The plaintiff proves his automobile was struck by defendant's and that he, plaintiff, was injured. Is this a res ipsa loquitur case? When there are two moving vehicles there seems no basis for deciding that the driver of one is more likely at fault than the other, or so the cases say. Is the case any different if the plaintiff is not one of the drivers but is instead a pedestrian injured by flying debris from a collision between A and B? The traditional answer has been no. *See* Fleming James, *Proof of Breach in Negligence Cases*, 37 VA. L. REV. 179, 209–12 (1951).

3. **Questioning *Collins*.** In the light of the preceding paragraphs, how can we explain *Collins*? Is it more likely than not that both defendants were negligent? Cf. RESTATEMENT (SECOND) § 17, cmt. *f* (P.F.D. No. 1, 2005) ("If two parties have an ongoing relationship pursuant to which they share responsibility for a dangerous activity, and if an accident happens establishing the negligence of one of the two, imposing res ipsa loquitur liability on both is proper."). Some of the complications of multiple actor cases are considered in Chapter 13 in connection with the use of res ipsa loquitur in medical malpractice cases.

PROBLEM

Chang v. Grey's Department Stores, Inc., et al.

Janice Chang ascended the escalator in Grey's Department Store when her jacket lodged between the escalator's moving handrail and stationery guide. This caused her to be thrown down violently and dragged to the top of the escalator, resulting in serious physical injuries. Before the accident, Chang noticed nothing unusual about the escalator. Her jacket was not unusual and she was riding the escalator in a normal manner. She did not see how her jacket became caught under the handrail.

Grey's Department store owns the escalator, but contracts with Presley Elevator Co. to maintain it. Just two weeks prior to the accident, Presley had inspected the escalator and had found no maintenance was required.

You represent Chang and wish to recover against Grey's or Presley, or both. Do you have a res ipsa loquitur case? Or must you do further investigation? What lines of investigation, if any, would you pursue?

REFERENCES ON RES IPSA LOQUITUR: DOBBS ON TORTS §§ 154–161 (2000); HARPER, JAMES & GRAY, THE LAW OF TORTS §§ 19.5–19.12 (2d Ed. 1986 & Supp.).

CHAPTER 7

HARM AND CAUSATION IN FACT

■ ■ ■

§ 1. ACTUAL HARM

The third element of a negligence prima facie case is that the plaintiff must suffer legally cognizable harm, frequently referred to as actual damages. The plaintiff who proves that the defendant's conduct was negligent, but fails to show that actual damage resulted from it, will lose the case.

RIGHT v. BREEN

890 A.2d 1287 (Conn. 2006)

KATZ, J.

In May, 2000, the plaintiff had stopped his automobile at a red traffic light when it was struck from behind by a vehicle driven by the defendant. There was minor damage to the plaintiff's vehicle, but no physical injuries were reported at the accident scene. Thereafter, the plaintiff brought this action, alleging that, as a result of the defendant's negligence, he had suffered bodily injury leading to both economic and noneconomic damages[1]....

[At trial, plaintiff presented evidence that his injuries resulted from the collision. The defendant, however, presented evidence that the injuries resulted from the plaintiff's five previous automobile accidents]. Using a verdict form provided by the plaintiff, the jury returned a verdict of zero economic damages and zero noneconomic damages....

The plaintiff then filed motions to set aside the verdict and for additur, arguing that, under Connecticut case law, he was entitled to at least nominal damages because he had suffered a technical legal injury that admittedly had been caused by the defendant. The defendant objected to the motions, arguing that ... although she had admitted to causing the collision, she had denied the causal relationship between the collision and the plaintiff's alleged injuries. The trial court granted the plaintiff's motions, setting aside the jury's verdict and awarding the plaintiff $1,

---

1. Neither the plaintiff's complaint nor his amended complaint sought recovery for the damage done to his automobile.

194

based upon the abundant appellate case law cited. [The trial court also awarded plaintiff $467.10 in costs as the prevailing party].

The defendant appealed from the judgment of the trial court.... [Although the Appellate Court described the Connecticut Supreme Court's prior precedents, which apparently required an award of nominal damages] as "inconsistent and troubling," it observed that it was not at liberty to overrule or discard [those] precedents and, accordingly, affirmed the trial court's judgment.... This certified appeal followed....

The defendant contends that, because causation and actual injury are essential elements of a negligence claim, a plaintiff's claim of negligence must fail entirely if he cannot establish these elements....

The plaintiff responds that there is no need to revisit [a prior case which holds that defendant's admission of liability establishes a technical legal injury which entitles the plaintiff to damages] because [of] General Statutes § 52–195(b)[2].... Specifically, the plaintiff contends that, by filing an offer of judgment of $1 under § 52–195, a defendant may protect herself from an award of costs based on a technical legal injury and a consequent award of nominal damages. We agree with the defendant that a plaintiff must establish all of the elements of a negligence claim, including causation and actual injury, in order to recover and, therefore, the technical legal injury concept does not apply to a negligence action....

Connecticut common law requires proof of actual damages to support a cause of action sounding in negligence.... [N]one of our cases has held that a plaintiff may prevail in a negligence action without alleging and proving actual damage.... [T]his was the rule at common law...No contrary authority is cited and the common law rule, ancient as it may be, has been approved by contemporary commentators.

Although the rule making actual damage an element of a cause of action in negligence may have originated in the common law distinction between trespass and trespass on the case, we are not inclined to obliterate the distinction between intentional and unintentional conduct in terms of legal consequences which it serves to implement. Where the plaintiff's right has been intentionally invaded, its vindication in a court of law and the award of nominal and even exemplary damages serves the policy of deterrence in a real sense. It is difficult to imagine what purpose would be furthered by permitting anyone who is jostled in a crowd or otherwise suffers some unintended contact with his person or injury to his dignity to set in motion the judicial machinery necessary for a recovery of nominal damages. That judges and juries have more important business to occupy them is as true today as it was in ancient times when the rule

---

2. General Statutes § 52–195 addresses offers of judgment and provides in subsection (b) that, "[u]nless the plaintiff recovers more than the sum named in the offer of judgment, with interest from its date, he shall recover no costs accruing after he received notice of the filing of such offer, but shall pay the defendant's costs accruing after he received notice. Such costs may include reasonable attorney's fees in an amount not to exceed three hundred fifty dollars." [Statutory amendments changed this to "offers of compromise" rather than "judgment".]

originated. There is nothing arcane about the wisdom of not cluttering the courts with trivia. . . .

This court clarified our common law to reflect the different treatment accorded to intentional and negligent acts-allowing recovery of nominal damages where a plaintiff's right intentionally has been invaded, but allowing recovery only upon proof of causation and of actual damages where a plaintiff's right negligently has been invaded. [The court then overruled its prior case law.] . . .

[C]onduct that is merely negligent, without proof of an actual injury, is not considered to be a significant interference with the public interest such that there is any right to complain of it, or to be free from it.

The judgment of the Appellate Court is reversed and the case is remanded to that court with direction to reverse the judgment of the trial court . . . and to modify the order of costs accordingly.

NOTES

1. **Nominal damages.** Nominal damages are damages in name only—usually $1 or six cents. Remember that attorneys for plaintiffs are normally paid only if they win and then by a percentage of the recovery. Would you take a case if your contingent fee could only amount to 40% of one dollar? In personal injury cases the market—that is, the attorney's financial incentives—will exclude nominal damages claims from the courts. The issue normally arises, then, because the plaintiff and her attorney hope to prove substantial damages but fail to convince judge or jury.

2. **What counts as legally cognizable harm?** Suppose the defendant causes impermanent bodily changes in the plaintiff without pain. For example, suppose the plaintiff, a male cancer patient, proves that the defendant, a hospital, negligently administered a labor-inducing drug, which may have caused a change in blood pressure or heart rate. If the plaintiff proved nothing else on the issue of harm or damages, should the trial judge direct a verdict for the defendant? *See Dailey v. Methodist Med. Ctr.,* 790 So.2d 903 (Miss. Ct. App. 2001). Or suppose the defendant's drug causes users' hearts to take longer to ''reset'' for the next heartbeat, but this causes neither pain nor symptoms nor permanent harm? *Searfoss v. Johnson & Johnson Co.,* 847 A.2d 766 (Pa. Super. Ct. 2004) (Table; Text at 2004 WL 792789).

3. **Damages recoverable in a personal injury case.** Recall the elements of damages from Chapter 1—past and future medical expenses, loss of wages or earning capacity, pain and suffering (including emotional harm), and damages for any other specifically-identifiable harm, such as special expenses necessary to travel for medical care. Punitive damages are generally *not* recoverable unless a cause of action for compensatory or nominal damages is established and then only if the defendant has a bad state of mind, variously described as willful, wanton, reckless, or malicious.

4. **Statutory offer of judgment or compromise.** Statutes like the one mentioned in *Right* are designed to encourage defendants to make settlement offers. For the defendant, filing notification of an offer of judgment

or compromise can make good sense. If the plaintiff does not recover a judgment that exceeds the amount of the defendant's offer, the defendant may not be required to pay certain costs of the plaintiff and may be entitled to recover some costs of its own from after the time the offer was made. The statutes may help plaintiffs get more viable settlement offers from defendants. Plaintiffs, however, face greater financial risk if they don't accept what can sometimes be very low offers.

§ 2. CAUSE IN FACT

The fourth element of a negligence prima facie case is cause in fact, also called actual cause or factual causation. The plaintiff must prove, not only that she suffered legally recognized harm, but that the harm was in fact caused by the defendant. Cause in fact is a very simple concept in the great number of cases.

A. THE BUT–FOR TEST OF CAUSATION

HALE v. OSTROW

166 S.W.3d 713 (Tenn. 2005)

E. Riley Anderson, J. . . .

On May 27, 1998, plaintiff Shirley Hale ("Ms. Hale") was walking home from a bus stop in Memphis, Tennessee. She had taken a different bus than usual and so was walking a route along a sidewalk that she did not normally travel. As she proceeded south on Mississippi Boulevard, a busy street, she noticed that the sidewalk ahead was blocked. Bushes protruding from 1073 Mississippi Boulevard had overgrown the sidewalk and had grown around a telephone pole located on the sidewalk, blocking Ms. Hale's way. Ms. Hale determined that she had to leave the sidewalk and enter the street in order to bypass the obstruction. She noticed that the sidewalk was "crumbled." As she left the sidewalk, but before she reached the bushes, Ms. Hale looked into the street to check for traffic. As she looked up, she tripped over a chunk of concrete and fell into the street. Ms. Hale's left hip was crushed in the fall, and she required extensive medical care.

The bushes that had overgrown the sidewalk were located in front of 1073 Mississippi Boulevard. That property, a vacant lot, was owned by the defendants Max Ostrow, Erwin Ostrow, and Rose Ostrow (collectively, "the Ostrows" or "defendants"). The crumbled sidewalk, and the spot where Ms. Hale actually fell, were located in front of 1063 Mississippi Boulevard. That property was not owned by the defendants.

Ms. Hale filed suit against the Ostrows [as well as the other property owner and the City of Memphis. The Ostrows moved for summary judgment on the ground that Ms. Hale's "injury was caused by the defective sidewalk, not by the overgrown bushes." The trial court granted summary judgment which the Court of Appeals affirmed. The Tennessee

Supreme Court reviewed each of the five elements of the plaintiff's negligence claim. Its discussion of causation began as follows].

As we often recite, a negligence claim requires proof of two types of causation: causation in fact and proximate cause. Causation in fact and proximate cause are distinct elements of negligence, and both must be proven by the plaintiff by a preponderance of the evidence. Cause in fact and proximate cause are ordinarily jury questions, unless the uncontroverted facts and inferences to be drawn from them make it so clear that all reasonable persons must agree on the proper outcome.

The defendant's conduct is the cause in fact of the plaintiff's injury if, as a factual matter, it directly contributed to the plaintiff's injury. In a case such as this one, we must ask whether the plaintiff's injury would have happened "but for" the defendants' act. If not, then the defendants' conduct is a cause in fact of the plaintiff's injury. It is not necessary that the defendants' act be the *sole* cause of the plaintiff's injury, only that it be *a* cause.

Viewing the facts in the light most favorable to Ms. Hale, there is a genuine issue of material fact as to whether the overgrown bushes on the Ostrows' property were a cause in fact of her injury. Ms. Hale stated in her deposition that the bushes had completely overgrown the sidewalk, that she determined that she could not bypass the bushes on the sidewalk, and that she therefore decided to leave the sidewalk and step into the street. As she did so, she looked up to check for traffic and tripped over the broken sidewalk. But for the bushes overgrowing the sidewalk, Ms. Hale would not have looked up to check for traffic, as she would not have needed to step into the street. Might she nevertheless have tripped over the concrete and suffered the same injury? Indeed she might have. Given that the evidence on summary judgment must be viewed in the light most favorable to the plaintiff, however, the issue of causation, as well as the allocation of comparative fault, are determinations of fact to be made by the jury. . . .

[W]e reverse the decisions of the trial court and the Court of Appeals granting summary judgment to the defendants.

SALINETRO v. NYSTROM

341 So. 2d 1059 (Fla. Dist. Ct. App. 1977)

[Anna Salinetro was in an auto accident and underwent a medical examination in connection with back injuries sustained. Dr. Nystrom made x-rays of her lower back and her abdominal areas.]

PER CURIAM.

Although unknown to her, Anna was approximately four-six weeks pregnant at the time; however, neither Dr. Nystrom nor his receptionist or his x-ray technician inquired whether or not she was pregnant or the date of her last menstrual period. Thereafter, upon suspecting she was pregnant, on December 12 Anna visited her gynecologist, Dr. Emilio Aldereguia, who, after running some tests, confirmed her pregnancy. In January Dr. Aldereguia learned that Dr. Nystrom had taken x-rays of Anna's pelvis and advised her to terminate her pregnancy because of possible damage to the fetus by the x-rays. Anna underwent a therapeutic abortion and the pathology report stated that the fetus was dead at the time of the abortion. Thereafter, Anna filed the instant lawsuit against Dr. Nystrom for medical malpractice. . . .

After the presentation of all the evidence on Anna's behalf, Dr. Nystrom moved for a directed verdict on the ground she failed to make a prima facie case of medical malpractice. The trial judge granted the motion and entered judgment for Dr. Nystrom. . . .

Assuming arguendo that Dr. Nystrom's conduct fell below the standard of care in failing to inquire of Anna whether she was pregnant or not on the date of her last menstrual period, this omission was not the cause of her injury. Anna herself testified that even if asked about being pregnant, she would have answered in the negative. Anna further testified to the effect that being a few days late with her menstrual period was not unusual and did not indicate to her that she may have been pregnant at the time she went to Dr. Nystrom; that six days prior thereto she had visited Dr. Aldereguia, and he had found no evidence that she was pregnant. We further note that simply because Anna was late with her menstrual period would not in and of itself mean that she was pregnant because further tests were required to ascertain whether she was pregnant. Thus, this point is without merit.

NOTES

1. **But-for as a hypothetical or counterfactual test.** "Determining causation always requires evaluation of hypothetical situations concerning what might have happened, but did not. . . . [T]he very idea of causation necessarily involves comparing historical events to a hypothetical alternative." *Viner v. Sweet*, 70 P.3d 1046, 1053 (Cal. 2003). The but-for rule thus requires the judge or jury to imagine an alternate scenario that never happened, that is, to imagine what *would* have happened without the defendant's negligence. Do you see any problems with this?

2. **The alternate scenarios in *Hale* and *Salinetro*.** The *Hale* court raised uncertainty about what the alternate scenario in that case might have been. Would Ms. Hale have tripped over the concrete and suffered the same injury even without the bush that blocked the sidewalk? If so, what result on her negligence claim? For actual cause, the harm must not have occurred absent the negligent conduct. *See Jordan v. Jordan*, 257 S.E.2d 761 (Va. 1979) (defendant backed out of the driveway without looking in her rearview mirror, however, her husband was squatting behind the rear bumper where he wouldn't have been seen even if she had looked). The *Salinetro* court felt the causation issue did not warrant review by the jury. However, is there any scenario under *Salinetro* in which the fetus might have been saved? Could the

plaintiff have asserted a different act of negligence that would lead to a different conclusion about but-for causation?

3. **Actual and proximate cause**. In *Hale,* the court discusses actual cause and, later in the opinion, proximate cause. Some courts lump both concepts together under the term proximate cause. *Hale* noted that the appellate court used the but-for concept of actual cause but the label "proximate cause." Confusion between the two concepts is distressingly common. Conceptually, actual cause—sometimes called cause in fact—is very different from proximate cause. The orthodox thinking is that the actual cause issue is truly a factual issue in the sense that it does not entail policy decisions. Proximate cause is primarily a policy judgment. Plaintiff must prove both types of causation. Consequently, a decision against the plaintiff on the cause in fact issue will bar the plaintiff's claim altogether, however, a decision favorable to the plaintiff on the actual cause issue does not mean that the plaintiff will win the case. As noted in *Hale,* even when the plaintiff has proved that the negligence caused actual harm, the plaintiff must go further and convince the judge and the trier of fact that the defendant not only caused harm but that as a matter of principle or policy should be liable for it.

4. **Res ipsa loquitur and but-for cause.** Does res ipsa loquitur always assist the plaintiff on causal as well as on negligence issues? Suppose a surgeon leaves sponges in the plaintiff's abdomen after an operation and this is regarded as a res ipsa loquitur case. This causes some harm, for which the surgeon would then be liable. But suppose the plaintiff claims the sponges caused stomach cancer. Will there be a causal issue that will require proof even though this is a res ipsa loquitur case?

B. PROBLEMS WITH AND ALTERNATIVES TO BUT–FOR TESTS

NOTE: LIABILITY OF TWO OR MORE PERSONS

1. *Two persons causing separate or divisible injuries.* Under the but-for rule, more than one actor's conduct can be causal. In some cases, tortfeasor A may cause a broken arm while tortfeasor B causes a broken leg. So far as the two injuries are separate, liability can be apportioned by causation. Each tortfeasor will be liable for the harms that tortfeasor caused and no more.

2. *Two persons causing a single indivisible injury.* In some injuries, however, both tortfeasors' conduct contributes to a single injury. Suppose A negligently runs into a horse and then negligently leaves the carcass on the highway where it might cause a second accident. B then negligently runs into the carcass, causing injury to his passenger, P. But-for A's negligence, the second collision would not have occurred, as there would have been no horse on the road. But-for B's negligence, the second collision would not have occurred because he would have stopped or taken evasive action to avoid hitting it. Both A and B are but-for causes of the plaintiff's single injury and both are subject to liability. *See also Spann v. Shuqualak Lumber Co. Inc.*, 990 So.2d 186 (Miss. 2008) (emissions from

lumber company caused dense fog for which company can be actual cause of collision along with drivers who were potentially at fault in the accident). How do we assign liability for harm to the tortfeasors in these multiple defendant cases? The question is which fault-apportionment rule to use, joint and several liability with possible contribution, or proportionate fault liability. When contribution is based on the relative fault of the tortfeasors, both these systems are forms of a fault-apportionment approach.

3. *Glancing back.* Before we go on, glance back at the two preceding paragraphs to see how simple they really are. If we can say that A caused only a broken arm and B only a broken leg, we can simply apportion liability to causes. A is liable only for the broken arm because he caused that harm and no other. But conversely, if an indivisible injury is caused in fact by two or more persons, we cannot apportion liability by causation. We must use some form of fault apportionment.

4. *Some defendants not a but-for cause of all injury.* Now suppose that C, a doctor, negligently makes both injuries worse, so that each break takes a week longer to heal than necessary. Can you work out (a) who is causally responsible for the broken arm and its delayed healing? (b) how joint and several liability would apply or not to the claims arising from the broken arm? Here is a start: A is a but-for cause of the broken arm. He is likewise a but-for cause of the delayed healing, isn't he? The doctor, C, is not a but-for cause of the broken arm but is a but-for cause of the added harm. How would joint and several liability work?

5. *Liability without but-for causation.* Under some circumstances a defendant is liable for harm to the plaintiff even though the defendant's negligent or illegal conduct was not a but-for cause of the harm. This is the case with *respondeat superior* liability: the telephone company is liable for its driver's on-the-job negligent driving that causes the plaintiff's injury. Such liability is not based upon the telephone company's negligence at all, but on the idea that, as a matter of policy, it should be liable for its employee's harmful torts. The same idea applies to partners in some circumstances, each being liable for the other's act. Analogously, those who act in a conspiracy or "in concert" to cause harm are all liable for the harm caused, even though only one of the conspirators is a direct cause of harm. At least one person must be a but-for cause of harm in such cases. If he is, the others are liable because they are deemed responsible for his acts. These paragraphs show that two or more persons can be but-for causes and thus liable in some degree for the same harm. (The amount of liability depends upon whether the state follows joint and several liability or proportionate share liability.) What is to be said about but-for cause if the independent acts of either A or B would be sufficient to cause harm even if the other had not acted at all?

LANDERS v. EAST TEXAS SALT WATER DISPOSAL CO.

248 S.W.2d 731 (Tex. 1952)

CALVERT, JUSTICE.

[Plaintiff owned a small lake, which he had cleaned and stocked with fish at considerable expense. He alleged that on or about April 1 the pipe lines of the East Texas Salt Water Disposal Company broke and some 10 to 15 thousand barrels of salt water flowed over his land and into the lake, killing the fish and causing other damages. He alleged that the other defendant, Sun Oil Company, on or about the same day also caused large quantities of salt water and also oil to flow into his lake, killing the fish. He alleged that each defendant was negligent.]

Did the plaintiff in his pleading allege facts which, if established by evidence, made the defendants jointly and severally liable for plaintiff's damages? From the face of the petition it appears that there was no concert of action nor unity of design between the defendants in the commission of their alleged tortious acts, an absence said by the court in the case of Sun Oil Co. v. Robicheaux, Tex. Com. App., 23 S.W.2d 713, 715, to be determinative of the non-existence of joint liability. In that case the rule was thus stated:

"The rule is well established in this state, and supported by almost universal authority, that an action at law for damages for torts cannot be maintained against several defendants jointly, when each acted independently of the others and there was no concert or unity of design between them. In such a case the tort of each defendant is several when committed, and it does not become joint because afterwards its consequences, united with the consequences of several other torts committed by other persons in producing damages. Under such circumstances, each tortfeasor is liable only for the part of the injury or damages caused by his own wrong; that is, where a person contributes to an injury along with others, he must respond in damages, but if he acts independently, and not in concert of action with other persons in causing such injury, he is liable only for the damages which directly and proximately result from his own act, and the fact that it may be difficult to define the damages caused by the wrongful act of each person who independently contributed to the final result does not affect the rule."....

The rule of the *Robicheaux* case, strictly followed, has made it impossible for a plaintiff, though gravely injured, to secure relief in the nature of damages through a joint and several judgment by joining in one suit as defendants all wrongdoers whose independent tortious acts have joined in producing an injury to the plaintiff, which, although theoretically divisible, as a practical matter and realistically considered is in fact but a single indivisible injury. As interpreted by the Courts of Civil Appeals the rule also denies to a plaintiff the right to proceed to judgment and satisfaction against the wrongdoers separately because in such a suit he cannot discharge the burden of proving with sufficient certainty, under pertinent rules of damages, the portion of the injury attributable to each defendant.... In other words, our courts seem to have embraced the philosophy, inherent in this class of decisions, that it is better that the injured party lose all of his damages than that any of several wrongdoers should pay more of the damages than he individually and separately caused. If such has been the law, from the standpoint of justice it should not have been; if it is the law now, it will not be hereafter. The case of Sun Oil Co. v. Robicheaux is overruled. Where the tortious acts of two or more wrongdoers join to produce an indivisible injury, that is, an injury which from its nature cannot be apportioned with reasonable certainty to the individual wrongdoers, all of the wrongdoers will be held jointly and severally liable for the entire damages and the injured party may proceed to judgment against any one separately or against all in one suit....

There is, of course, no joint liability for damages for the loss of trees and grass killed by the salt water escaping from the pipe line owned by East Texas Salt Water Disposal Company before such water entered the lake....

ANDERSON v. MINNEAPOLIS, ST. PAUL & SAULT STE. MARIE RAILWAY

179 N.W. 45 (Minn. 1920)

LEES, C....

[Plaintiff's property was burned by a fire in October 1918. Plaintiff's proof tended to show that the fire was one set by defendant's engine in August, which smoldered until, in October, it swept east and burned the plaintiff's place. Defendant, however, offered proof tending to show that there were other fires sweeping east towards plaintiff's property and that these fires might have originated from other and perhaps non-negligent causes. The trial judge instructed in part: "If you find that other fires not set by one of the defendant's engines mingled with one that was set by one of the defendant's engines, there may be difficulty in determining whether you should find that the fire set by the engine was a material or substantial element in causing plaintiff's damage. If it was, the defendant is liable; otherwise, it is not...." The jury, so charged, found for the plaintiff.]

The following proposition is stated in defendant's brief and relied on for a reversal:

"If plaintiff's property was damaged by a number of fires combining, one being the fire pleaded, and the others being to no responsible origin, but of such sufficient or superior force that they would have produced the damage to plaintiff's property, regardless of the fire pleaded, then defendant was not liable."

This proposition is based upon Cook v. M., St. P. & S.S.M. Ry. Co., 98 Wis. 624, 74 N.W. 561, 40 L.R.A. 457, 67 Am. St. Rep. 830.... The Supreme Court of Michigan has referred to it as good law. The Supreme Court of Idaho says the opinion is logical and well reasoned, but the discussion is in a large measure theoretical and academic. Judge Thompson, in his work on Negligence (volume 1, § 739), says that the conclusion reached is so clearly wrong as not to deserve discussion. If the Cook Case merely decides that one who negligently sets a fire is not liable if another's property is damaged, unless it is made to appear that the fire was a material element in the destruction of the property, there can be no question about the soundness of the decision. But if it decides that if such fire combines with another of no responsible origin, and after the union of the two fires they destroy the property and either fire independently of the other would have destroyed it, then, irrespective of whether the first fire was or was not a material factor in the destruction of the property, there is no liability, we are not prepared to adopt the doctrine as the law of this state. If a fire set by the engine of one railroad company unites with a fire set by the engine of another company, there is joint and several liability, even though either fire would have destroyed plaintiff's property. But if the doctrine of the Cook Case is applied, and one of the fires is of unknown origin, there is no liability. G. S. 1913, § 4426, leaves no room for the application of a rule which would relieve a railroad company from liability under such circumstances. Moreover, the reasoning of the court in McClellan v. St. P., M. & M. Ry. Co., 58 Minn. 104, 59 N.W. 978, leads to the conclusion that, regardless of the statute, there would be liability in such a case. We therefore hold that the trial court did not err in refusing to instruct the jury in accordance with the rule laid down in the Cook Case. In the foregoing discussion we have assumed, although it is doubtful, that the evidence was such that a foundation was laid for the application of the rule, if it was otherwise applicable.

NOTES

1. **The but-for test applied to *Landers*.** Apply the but-for test to *Landers*. How does that test work if you believe the two bodies of salt water entered the plaintiff's lake at the same time? How does it work if you believe that one body of salt water reached the lake first?

2. **The but-for test applied to *Anderson*.** Apply the but-for test to *Anderson*. Must you conclude that neither fire was an actual cause of the harm done to the plaintiff's property? But-for the defendant's fire, would the plaintiff have avoided harm?

3. **"Duplicative" causation.** Professor Richard Wright works out a modified and more complicated version of the but-for rule. Applying his rule, he draws a distinction between "preempted cause" and "duplicative cause." If each of the two fires in *Anderson* was sufficient to burn the plaintiff's

property and would have done so regardless of the other fire, the two fires are "duplicative" causes. Professor Wright thinks cause should be defined in such a way that we would recognize the defendant's fire as a cause even if some other fire would have burned the property anyway, and applies the same idea to all duplicative cause cases. *See* Richard Wright, *Causation in Tort Law*, 73 CAL. L. REV. 1735 (1985). Wright recognizes, however, that a straight but-for rule would not get this result.

4. **"Preemptive" causation.** Professor Wright's "preempted cause" category is illustrated by a case in which one tortfeasor poisons the victim's tea. Just as the victim puts the tea to his lips, the other tortfeasor shoots him dead. Death would have followed from the poison even if the second tortfeasor had fired no shot at all, just as one fire would have burned the plaintiff's property even if no other fire had existed. But the two cases are not alike under Professor Wright's test. The victim died of a gunshot wound, not poison. The poisoner is not a cause. Is this *Landers*?

5. **Substantial factor.** In *Anderson* the court approved a jury instruction that allowed the jury to find actual causation if the defendant's fire was a "material or substantial element" in the harm done. Where the but-for test seems to produce clearly wrong results, as in the duplicative cause cases, the substantial factor test has been widely accepted. "[I]f two or more causes concur to bring about an event, then cause-in-fact is established by the 'substantial factor' test.... [W]hen either the 'but for' or 'substantial factor' test [is] satisfied, a party has established that the other party's conduct was the cause-in fact of an injury." *Busta v. Columbus Hosp. Corp.*, 916 P.2d 122, 135 (Mont. 1996).

6. **Substantial factor as the exception.** Is it clear that the "but for" test governs *except* in cases of concurrent independent causes, each of which would suffice by itself to cause the harm done to the plaintiff? *Viner v. Sweet*, 70 P.3d 1046 (Cal. 2003), so holds. According to *Joshi v. Providence Health Sys. of Oregon Corp.*, 149 P.3d 1164 (Or. 2006), the but-for test applies in most cases and the substantial factor test is reserved for cases like *Anderson* in which the conduct of each of two or more tortfeasors is sufficient to cause the harm. The court suggests the substantial factor test could be appropriate in a few other contexts as well.

7. **Substantial factor: Broad dicta.** At times courts say that the substantial factor test applies whenever "multiple causes of injury are present." *Palermo v. Port of New Orleans*, 951 So.2d 425 (La. Ct. App. 2007). Of course, this needn't be so. The but-for test works well in many multiple defendant cases, as in the case of tortious conduct by two actors, each of which is necessary to the harm but neither of which is sufficient to produce it. An example would be the case of the dead horse negligently left in the road and the negligent driver who runs into it. Both of the defendants are but for causes of the harm to the passenger who is injured in the resulting car accident. Is it a problem if more than one actor is considered an actual cause of harm under the but-for test? The but-for test may lead to more neutral, factual judgments about actual cause. Is substantial factor a test or measure of anything at all?

8. **The Third Restatement's formulation.** Without using the "substantial factor" terminology, the Physical Harm Restatement provides that if tortious conduct of one tortfeasor, A, fails the but-for test only because there is another set of conduct also sufficient to cause the harm, A's conduct is still a cause in fact or factual cause. RESTATEMENT (THIRD) OF TORTS: LIABILITY FOR PHYSICAL HARM § 27 (Proposed Final Draft No. 1, 2005).

9. **Indivisible injury with numerous defendants.** A and B, each acting negligently, separately cause injury to the plaintiff. As a practical matter, the plaintiff cannot show how much of the injury was caused by A and how much by B. Under traditional rules, A and B are jointly and severally liable. Does this work when a large number of defendants contribute to harm? Suppose the plaintiff was exposed at work to various identified products of 55 different defendants, that toxins from these products entered his body, and "that each toxin that entered his body was a substantial factor in bringing about, prolonging, or aggravating" cancer. Would such facts sufficiently show causation? *See Bockrath v. Aldrich Chem. Co., Inc.*, 980 P.2d 398 (Cal. 1999). If your answer is "yes," what exactly is left to be decided in the case, if anything?

10. **Divisible vs. indivisible injury.** In *Landers,* if one body of salt water entered the lake at the same time as the other, but the salt water from the Salt Water Disposal Company alone damaged the grass on one side of the lake, would liability for damage to the grass be apportioned in a different way than would liability with respect to the lake? With respect to the damage to the lake, would it matter if we learn these additional facts: (1) the water disposal company released twice as much salt water as the oil company, but (2) the oil company, though releasing less salt water, was far more negligent than the water disposal company?

NOTE: INCREASED RISK SHOWING CAUSATION

Suppose the defendant negligently constructs stairs that are too steep and negligently fails to light them. The plaintiff falls down them in the dark and is injured. Can you say the condition of the premises was a cause of the plaintiff's harm? After all, the plaintiff might fall for many reasons. Many cases are like this, often when the defendant fails to provide a safety measure. The defendant negligently fails to have a lifeguard on duty at a motel. A child drowns. Would a lifeguard have saved the child? In many cases like this, courts permit juries to find that the defendant's negligent act or omission was a cause in fact of the plaintiff's harm. Can we say those cases represent a principle or rule that when the defendant negligently creates a risk of the very harm that befell the plaintiff, causation is established, or at least that an inference of causation is permitted? In *Zuchowicz v. United States,* 140 F.3d 381, 390–91 (2d Cir. 1998), Judge Calabresi, a most eminent torts scholar, referring to opinions of Cardozo and Traynor, said:

> [T]hey stated that: if (a) a negligent act was deemed wrongful *because* that act increased the chances that a particular type of accident would occur, and (b) a mishap of that very sort did happen, this was enough to support a finding by the trier of fact that the negligent behavior

caused the harm. Where such a strong causal link exists, it is up to the negligent party to bring in evidence denying *but for* cause and suggesting that in the actual case the wrongful conduct had not been a substantial factor.

Courts often decide cases without mentioning the inference of causation drawn from increased risk. In *McGuire v. Hodges,* 639 S.E.2d 284 (Va. 2007), a thirty-month-old child was found floating in a pool. The pool was fenced but had a gate that lacked a proper latching device. The homeowner argued that plaintiff failed to show how the child accessed the pool and thus the jury's verdict was based on "conjecture and speculation." However, the court held that the circumstantial evidence in the case was sufficient to support the jury's verdict for the plaintiff. "Testimony at trial described an unlocked gate, secured only by a chain, which the young boy was attempting to open shortly before he was found floating in the pool.... The only evidence directly supporting as fact that the gate was well secured at the time of the drowning was the testimony of [the homeowner]," which the "jury was free to discredit." Similarly, in *Yount v. Deibert,* 147 P.3d 1065 (Kan. 2006), boys playing with fire inside a house that was later engulfed in flames created an inference of causation for the jury to consider.

PROBLEM

Tillo v. Eagle

Darlene Tillo gave birth to a child, Desiree, who was unusually large. Darlene Tillo suffered gestational diabetes. This, along with Desiree's size, contributed to a difficult delivery. Tillo's obstetrician, Dr. Josephine Kendrick, was negligent in estimating Desiree's size and in employing improper surgical procedures during delivery. As a result of Kendrick's negligence, Desiree suffered trauma in delivery and hypoxia, insufficient oxygen supply to cells and tissues. These conditions would or did cause brain damage and severe retardation.

Immediately after birth, Desiree was seen by a pediatrician, Dr. Eagle. Dr. Eagle was negligent in dealing with two conditions Desiree suffered, hyperbilirubinemia and excessively high hematocrit levels. Either of these conditions could ultimately cause damage to the brain and severe retardation unless it was properly treated. The conditions were not properly treated. Desiree is permanently and severely retarded. Care and treatment costs for her lifetime, not to mention other damages, will be very high.

Rules of law (including rules of causation) are often most important not because they dictate the final outcome but because they tell lawyers what kind of evidence to look for and what kind of arguments may be acceptable. You represent Dr. Eagle. What questions would you ask of him or of experts that would help clarify causal issues?

C. PROOF: WHAT WAS CAUSED?

Liability for negligence attaches only when actual cause links the defendant's negligence to the plaintiff's injury. Consequently, how we define plaintiff's injury and defendant's negligence can be important parts of the causation question.

In *Dillon v. Twin State Gas & Electric Co.*, 163 A. 111 (N.H. 1932), the defendant's negligence in failing to insulate a wire caused a 14-year-old boy to be electrocuted just as he slipped off of a bridge and was about to fall into a river in which he would have been killed or seriously injured. Did the electrocution cause the loss of the boy's whole life, or simply the loss of a few additional minutes of it?

SUMMERS v. TICE

199 P.2d 1 (Cal. 1948)

CARTER, JUSTICE.

Each of the two defendants appeals from a judgment against them in an action for personal injuries. Pursuant to stipulation the appeals have been consolidated.

Plaintiff's action was against both defendants for an injury to his right eye and face as the result of being struck by bird shot discharged from a shotgun. The case was tried by the court without a jury and the court found that on November 20, 1945, plaintiff and the two defendants were hunting quail on the open range. Each of the defendants was armed with a 12 gauge shotgun loaded with shells containing 7–1/2 size shot. . . . The view of defendants with reference to plaintiff was unobstructed and they knew his location. Defendant Tice flushed a quail which rose in flight to a ten foot elevation and flew between plaintiff and defendants. Both defendants shot at the quail, shooting in plaintiff's direction. At that time defendants were 75 yards from plaintiff. One shot struck plaintiff in his eye and another in his upper lip. Finally it was found by the court that as the direct result of the shooting by defendants the shots struck plaintiff as above mentioned and that defendants were negligent in so shooting and plaintiff was not contributorily negligent. . . .

The one shot that entered plaintiff's eye was the major factor in assessing damages and that shot could not have come from the gun of both defendants. It was from one or the other only.

It has been held that where a group of persons are on a hunting party, or otherwise engaged in the use of firearms, and two of them are negligent in firing in the direction of a third person who is injured thereby, both of those so firing are liable for the injury suffered by the third person, although the negligence of only one of them could have caused the injury. Both drivers have been held liable for the negligence of one where they engaged in a racing contest causing an injury to a third person. These cases speak of the action of defendants as being in concert as the ground of decision, yet it would seem they are straining that concept and the more reasonable basis appears in Oliver v. Miles, supra. There two persons were hunting together. Both shot at some partridges and in so doing shot across the highway injuring plaintiff who was traveling on it. The court stated they were acting in concert and thus both were liable. The court then stated: "We think that . . . each is liable for the resulting injury to the boy, although no one can say definitely who actually shot him. *To hold otherwise would be to exonerate both from liability, although each was negligent, and the injury resulted from such negligence.*" . . .

When we consider the relative position of the parties and the results that would flow if plaintiff was required to pin the injury on one of the defendants only, a requirement that the burden of proof on that subject be shifted to defendants becomes manifest. They are both wrongdoers negligent toward plaintiff. They brought about a situation where the negligence of one of them injured the plaintiff, hence it should rest with them each to absolve himself if he can. The injured party has been placed by defendants in the unfair position of pointing to which defendant caused the harm. If one can escape the other may also and plaintiff is remediless. Ordinarily defendants are in a far better position to offer evidence to determine what one caused the injury. . . .

Cases are cited for the proposition that where two or more tortfeasors acting independently of each other cause an injury to plaintiff, they are not joint tortfeasors and plaintiff must establish the portion of the damage caused by each, even though it is impossible to prove the portion of the injury caused by each. In view of the foregoing discussion it is apparent that defendants in cases like the present one may be treated as liable on the same basis as joint tortfeasors, and hence the last cited cases are distinguishable inasmuch as they involve independent tortfeasors.

In addition to that, however, it should be pointed out that the same reasons of policy and justice [which] shift the burden to each of defendants to absolve himself if he can—relieving the wronged person of the duty of apportioning the injury to a particular defendant—apply here where we are concerned with whether plaintiff is required to supply evidence for the apportionment of damages. If defendants are independent tortfeasors and thus each liable for the damage caused by him alone, and, at least, where the matter of apportionment is incapable of proof, the innocent wronged party should not be deprived of his right to redress. The wrongdoers should be left to work out between themselves any apportionment. Some of the cited cases refer to the difficulty of apportioning the burden of damages between the independent tortfeasors, and say that where factually a correct division cannot be made, the trier of fact may make it the best it can, which would be more or less a guess, stressing the factor that the wrongdoers are not in a position to complain of uncertainty. . . .

The judgment is Affirmed.

NOTES

1. **The harm caused.** One tortfeasor in *Summers* caused the harm to the plaintiff's eye. What harm did the other tortfeasor cause? In a recent hunting case, a hunter shot at a deer. Another member of his hunting party then shot in the same direction and injured a person from another group. Even though the first hunter's bullet did not hit the injured plaintiff, the court found that the first hunter also could be liable to the plaintiff if 1) his shooting was negligent and 2) it was reasonably foreseeable that shooting in that direction would encourage his companion to shoot that way negligently too. *See Hellums v. Raber,* 853 N.E.2d 143 (Ind. Ct. App. 2006).

2. **Harm by one of seven.** In *State v. CTL Distribution, Inc.,* 715 So.2d 262 (Fla. Dist. Ct. App. 1998), one or more truckers spilled a hazardous substance when making deliveries of that substance at a certain business. The state environmental agency sued the seven truckers who delivered the substance. It proved that one of them, CTL, had once spilled the substance and argued that *Summers v. Tice* would authorize liability for all seven. How would you rule if you were the judge?

3. **Aggravation of an existing injury.** In *Canada v. McCarthy,* 567 N.W.2d 496 (Minn. 1997), a two-year-old child suffered from lead poisoning before July. After July, the defendant subjected her to additional lead exposure that enhanced the injury, but the plaintiff cannot prove the amount of the enhancement. If *Summers* is appealing when two defendants are negligent, would it apply by analogy to a single defendant aggravating an existing injury?

LORD v. LOVETT

770 A.2d 1103 (N.H. 2001)

NADEAU, J. . . .

The plaintiff suffered a broken neck in an automobile accident on July 22, 1996, and was treated at the Lakes Region General Hospital by the defendants. She contends that because the defendants negligently misdiagnosed her spinal cord injury, they failed both to immobilize her properly and to administer steroid therapy, causing her to lose the opportunity for a substantially better recovery. She alleges that she continues to suffer significant residual paralysis, weakness and sensitivity.

Upon learning that the defendants intended to move to dismiss at the close of the plaintiff's case, the trial court permitted the plaintiff to make a pre-trial offer of proof. She proffered that her expert would testify that the defendants' negligence deprived her of the opportunity for a substantially better recovery. She conceded, however, that her expert could not quantify the degree to which she was deprived of a better recovery by their negligence. [The trial court dismissed the action on the ground that lost opportunity was not a recognized theory.]

The loss of opportunity doctrine, in its many forms, is a medical malpractice form of recovery which allows a plaintiff, whose preexisting injury or illness is aggravated by the alleged negligence of a physician or health care worker, to recover for her lost opportunity to obtain a better degree of recovery. See King, *"Reduction of Likelihood" Reformulation and Other Retrofitting of the Loss-of-a-Chance Doctrine,* 28 U. Mem. L.Rev. 491, 492–93 (1998).

Generally, courts have taken three approaches to loss of opportunity claims.

The first approach, the traditional tort approach, is followed by a minority of courts. According to this approach, a plaintiff must prove that as a result of the defendant's negligence, the plaintiff was deprived of at least a fifty-one percent chance of a more favorable outcome than she actually received. [Here and throughout the opinion, the court cites the King article, *supra.*] Once the plaintiff meets this burden, she may recover damages for the entire preexisting illness or condition.

Under this approach, a patient whose injury is negligently misdiagnosed, but who would have had only a fifty percent chance of full recovery from her condition with proper diagnosis, could not recover damages because she would be unable to prove that, absent the physician's negligence, her chance of a better recovery was at least fifty-one percent. If, however, the patient could establish the necessary causal link by establishing that absent the negligence she would have had at least a fifty-one percent chance of a better outcome, not only would the patient be entitled to recover, but she would be awarded damages for her entire injury. This approach has been criticized as yielding an "all or nothing" result.

The second approach, a variation of the traditional approach, relaxes the standard of proof of causation. The causation requirement is relaxed by permitting plaintiffs to submit their cases to the jury upon demonstrating that a defendant's negligence more likely than not "increased the harm" to the plaintiff or "destroyed a substantial possibility" of achieving a more favorable outcome.

Under this approach, the patient would not be precluded from recovering simply because her chance of a better recovery was less than fifty-one percent, so long as she could prove that the defendant's negligence increased her harm to some degree. The precise degree required varies by jurisdiction. Some courts require that the defendant's negligence increase the plaintiff's harm by any degree, while other courts require that the increase be substantial. As in the traditional approach, once the plaintiff meets her burden, she recovers damages for the entire underlying preexisting condition or illness rather than simply the loss of opportunity. This approach "represents the worst of both worlds [because it] continues the arbitrariness of the all-or-nothing rule, but by relaxing the proof requirements, it increases the likelihood that a plaintiff will be able to convince a jury to award full damages."

Under the third approach, the lost opportunity for a better outcome is, itself, the injury for which the negligently injured person may recover. As with the second approach, a plaintiff may prevail even if her chances of a better recovery are less than fifty-one percent. The plaintiff, however, does not receive damages for the *entire* injury, but just for the lost opportunity.

In other words, if the plaintiff can establish the causal link between the defendant's negligence and the lost opportunity, the plaintiff may recover that portion of damages actually attributable to the defendant's negligence.

Under this approach, "[b]y defining the injury as the loss of chance . . ., the traditional rule of preponderance is fully satisfied."

We agree with the majority of courts rejecting the traditional "all-or-nothing" approach to loss of opportunity cases, and find the third approach most sound. The third approach permits plaintiffs to recover for the loss of an opportunity for a better outcome, an interest that we agree should be compensable, while providing for the proper valuation of such an interest.

> [T]he loss of a chance of achieving a favorable outcome or of avoiding an adverse consequence should be compensable and should be valued appropriately, rather than treated as an all-or-nothing proposition. Preexisting conditions must, of course, be taken into account in valuing the interest destroyed. When those preexisting conditions have not absolutely preordained an adverse outcome, however, the chance of avoiding it should be appropriately compensated even if that chance is not better than even.

King, *Causation, Valuation, and Chance in Personal Injury Torts Involving Preexisting Conditions and Future Consequences*, 90 Yale L.J. 1353, 1354 (1981).

Accordingly, we hold that a plaintiff may recover for a loss of opportunity injury in medical malpractice cases when the defendant's alleged negligence aggravates the plaintiff's preexisting injury such that it deprives the plaintiff of a *substantially* better outcome. . . .

Finally, defendant Lovett argues that we should not recognize the plaintiff's loss of opportunity injury because it is intangible and, thus, is not amenable to damages calculation. We disagree.

First, we fail to see the logic in denying an injured plaintiff recovery against a physician for the lost opportunity of a better outcome on the basis that the alleged injury is too difficult to calculate, when the physician's own conduct has caused the difficulty. Second, "[w]e have long held that difficulty in calculating damages is not a sufficient reason to deny recovery to an injured party." Third, loss of opportunity is not inherently unquantifiable. A loss of opportunity plaintiff must provide the jury with a basis upon which to distinguish that portion of her injury caused by the defendant's negligence from the portion resulting from the underlying injury. This can be done through expert testimony just as it is in aggravation of pre-existing injury cases. . . .

[A concurring opinion is omitted.]

Reversed and remanded.

NOTES

1. **The preponderance test.** Remember that the plaintiff must prove each element of her case by a preponderance of the evidence. This means the "greater weight" of the evidence—more likely than not. Translated to numbers, this traditional rule would require plaintiff to persuade the trier that the probabilities are greater than 50% that each element is established. Some courts insist that this rule should preclude a recovery when a patient dies after her physician's misdiagnosis increases her chance of death, but when she had only a 50–50 chance of living anyway. *E.g., Fennell v. Maryland Hosp. Ctr., Inc.*, 580 A.2d 206 (Md. 1990).

2. **Relaxed causation tests.** Some courts, either by their words or their deeds, have eased the plaintiff's burden of proof in cases when a physician causes the loss of a chance of 50% or less. In this group, courts permit juries to award full damages, as if the plaintiff had proved causation by a preponderance of the evidence. *See, e.g., Hamil v. Bashline*, 392 A.2d 1280 (Pa. 1978).

3. **Duty-to-try analysis.** A similar but more striking approach appeared in *Gardner v. National Bulk Carriers, Inc.*, 310 F.2d 284 (4th Cir. 1962). Gardner, a seaman on board a ship at sea, was called to stand watch at 11:30, but he could not be found. He had last been seen five or six hours earlier. The ship notified the Coast Guard but did not attempt to return to those areas of the sea where, at any time during the five hours, he might have fallen overboard. In a suit for Gardner's death, the defendant argued that actual cause had not been shown, since a search probably could not have found a man who had gone overboard hours earlier. But the Fourth Circuit held that the duty of the captain was to make every reasonable effort. "It was less than a duty to rescue him, but it was a positive duty to make a sincere attempt at rescue. . . . [C]ausation is proved if the master's omission destroys the reasonable possibility of rescue." The court apparently envisioned full liability for the seaman's death.

4. **Quantified value-of-the-chance approach.** Still another approach is to say that causal rules are not changed. Instead, the defendant's duty of care is broad enough not merely to protect the plaintiff against injury or loss of life, but also to protect the plaintiff against loss of substantial *chances*. If the *chance* of survival was 40% and the defendant's negligence more likely than not eliminated that *chance,* then the defendant would be liable for the loss he has caused—the chance. In damages, this is presumably 40% of the damages for which the defendant would be liable if he caused death.

5. **Damages under the quantified approach when some items of damages are proved by a preponderance of the evidence.** Imagine that a patient dies soon after a physician negligently fails to treat the patient, and

that this negligence certainly caused the patient to undergo unnecessary pain and also to lose a 40% chance of surviving. Wouldn't the damages for the pain be 100% for that item? *See* Todd S. Aagaard, *Identifying and Valuing the Injury in Lost Chance Cases*, 96 MICH. L. REV. 1335 (1998).

6. **What *must* be proved by a preponderance of the evidence under quantified approach.** Under the lost chance rule, are there some things that still *must* be proved by a preponderance of the evidence, that is, under a more-likely-than-not standard? What if the plaintiff proved that there was a 40% chance that the patient had a 30% chance? *See Alphonse v. Acadian Ambulance Servs., Inc.*, 844 So.2d 294 (La. Ct. App. 2003); *Alberts v. Schultz*, 975 P.2d 1279 (N.M. 1999).

7. **Reducing damages to reflect probability where causation is more likely than not.** "If the patient in our example was entitled to 25 percent of his full damages because he had only a 25 percent chance of survival, he should be entitled to 75 percent of his damages if he had a 75 percent chance of survival—not 100 percent of his damages on the theory that by establishing a 75 percent chance he proved injury by a preponderance of the evidence. He proves injury in both cases, but in both cases the injury is merely probabilistic and must be discounted accordingly." *Doll v. Brown*, 75 F.3d 1200, 1206 (7th Cir. 1996) (Posner, J.). *See also* John Makdisi, *Proportional Liability: A Comprehensive Rule to Apportion Tort Damages Based Probability*, 67 N.C. L. REV. 1063 (1989) (supporting general use of lost chance or probabilistic causation). How would this change the "normal" rules of causation? How would juries determine these percentages?

8. **Recent cases.** The value-of-the-chance theory has gained substantial support in recent years, primarily as a result of a 1981 article, Joseph H. King, Jr., *Causation, Valuation and Chance in Personal Injury Torts*, 90 YALE L. J. 1353 (1981). The Massachusetts Supreme Court gave a recent ringing endorsement to the theory in *Matsuyama v. Birnbaum*, 890 N.E.2d 819 (Mass. 2008). The court wrote "the loss of chance doctrine views a person's prospects for surviving a serious medical condition as something of value." It then joined the many courts it listed that have previously endorsed the theory. The court also listed a number of courts that have rejected the lost-chance theory. Michigan does so by statute, at least in medical malpractice cases. Another case that rejected the claim, *Smith v. Parrott*, 833 A.2d 843 (Vt. 2003), noted the policy argument that lost chance recoveries could elevate "the price of malpractice insurance and health care costs in general, as doctors are forced to practice 'defensive' medicine."

Evaluating the Approaches

9. **Deterrence.** Which rule (if any) seems to provide the most appropriate deterrence? Take a look at the hypothetical facts and table below.

Three Cancer Patients

Each patient has a 1/3 or 33.33% chance of survival if properly treated. The defendant negligently treats each one and all three die. In each case, damages for wrongful death would have been $100,000 if the negligence is treated as a cause of the harm. We cannot in fact know which one would have lived had proper treatment been provided, but the overwhelming likelihood is that one would have lived. An omniscient trier of fact would know which one (line four).

	Recovery	Total Liability
Traditional rule	$0.0	$0.0
Relaxed causation	$100,000 each	$300,000
Lost chance	$33,333.33 each	$100,000
Omniscient trier	$100,000 to one estate	$100,000

10. **Limits on lost chance liability?** Do you think that value-of-the-chance would create limitless tort cases? David A. Fischer, *Tort Recovery for Loss of a Chance,* 36 WAKE FOREST L. REV. 605 (2001) explores the question whether any rationale for lost chance recovery would also function to limit the lost chance recovery to appropriate cases. He believes case-by-case decision will be required. To that end, you might think that courts could appropriately limit the lost chance recovery to cases in which the defendant owed a duty to maximize the plaintiff's chances. That would certainly cover physicians who are hired for the very purpose of maximizing chances. In fact, courts so far have applied value of the chance reasoning mainly to physician-patient cases. *See Hardy v. Southwestern Bell Tel. Co.,* 910 P.2d 1024 (Okla. 1996) (refusing to extend loss-of-chance theory "beyond the established boundary of medical malpractice").

———

ALEXANDER v. SCHEID, 726 N.E.2d 272 (Ind. 2000). The plaintiff's physician ordered an X-ray. The radiologist reported that it showed a "density . . . in the upper lobe" of her lung and concluded that "comparison with old films would be of value." In breach of the standard of care, the defendant did not follow up on this information. The mass grew but was not discovered until the plaintiff went to another doctor months later. By this time she was suffering from advanced cancer that had metastasized. The probability of her long-term survival was significantly reduced because of the delay. The trial court granted the defendant's motion for summary judgment and the Court of Appeals affirmed. In the Supreme Court of Indiana, *held,* reversed and remanded. "We think that loss of chance is better understood as a description of the injury than as either a term for a separate cause of action or a surrogate for the causation element of a negligence claim. If a plaintiff seeks recovery specifically for what the plaintiff alleges the doctor to have caused, i.e., a decrease in the patient's probability of recovery, rather than for the ultimate outcome, causation is no longer debatable. Rather, the problem becomes one of identification and valuation or quantification of that injury.... A number of jurisdictions allow recovery for negligence that has 'increased the risk of harm,' even where the full ramifications of the defendant's actions are not yet known.... More specifically, many jurisdictions have recognized a decrease in life expectancy as a cognizable injury.... [W]e hold that JoAnn may maintain a cause of action in negligence for this increased risk of harm, which may be described as a decreased life expectancy or the diminished probability of long-term survival. Here, we also have an injury that often accompanies a delay in diagnosis—the invasion of healthy tissue by a tumor or other growth. Accordingly, this case does not present the issue whether a plaintiff must have incurred some physical injury as a result of the defendant's negligence in order to recover for an increased risk of harm. Some courts have concluded, particularly in the loss of chance context, that the loss must be 'substantial' before it is compensable. We see no obvious method of quantifying that test. Because we measure damages by probabilizing the injury, the likelihood that plaintiffs will bring claims for trivial reductions in chance of recovery seems small. If, in the future, we face a volume of insignificant claims, perhaps such a rule will become necessary. For now, we are content to rely on basic economics to deter resort to the courts to redress remote probabilities or insubstantial diminutions in the likelihood of recovery."

DILLON v. EVANSTON HOSPITAL, 771 N.E.2d 357 (Ill. 2002). A catheter was inserted into the plaintiff's body in the course of a medical procedure. As planned, it was removed, except that a portion broke off and remained in her body. Neither her doctor nor the hospital so advised her. Much later, she discovered that the remaining portion had worked its way in two pieces into her heart, one part floating freely in the heart, the other with its tip embedded in the wall of the right ventricle. In the plaintiff's suit against doctor and hospital, the jury found for the plaintiff and awarded damages for past and future pain and suffering and also damages for increased risk of future harm. *Held*, judgment for plaintiff on increased risk is permissible, but the case is reversed for more adequate instruction. "[T]heories of lost chance of recovery and increased risk of future injury have similar theoretical underpinnings." However, the trial judge's instruction on the increased risk damages requires reversal because it failed to require (a) evidence of increased risk of future harm and (b) damages proportioned to the probability that the risks of future harm would materialize.

NOTES

1. **Present injury.** In an Illinois case subsequent to *Dillon*, the defendant negligently caused a car accident with a pregnant woman. The woman required x-rays and medication which doctors told her could cause disabilities in the fetus. Because of these risks and risks to her own health from

continuing the pregnancy—a pelvic bone fracture which could not be fixed during a pregnancy—she elected to terminate the pregnancy. The Illinois Supreme Court denied recovery under its wrongful death act on the ground that the fetus' increased risk of future harm was not a present injury for which the fetus could have brought an action for damages against the defendant. The court distinguished Dillon on the ground that the catheter embedded in plaintiff's heart was a present injury. See *Williams v. Manchester,* 888 N.E.2d 1 (Ill. 2008).

2. **Small risks.** Where the plaintiffs had only slight exposure to asbestos and only a small increased risk of future harm, Louisiana held there could be no recovery for the increased risk. *Bonnette v. Conoco, Inc.,* 837 So.2d 1219 (La. 2003). Professor King concludes that the courts are divided on whether to apply the loss of chance approach to future consequences that may not in fact ever occur. Joseph H. King, Jr., *"Reduction of Likelihood" Reformulation And Other Retrofitting of The Loss-of-a-Chance Doctrine,* 28 U. MEM. L. REV. 491 (1998).

AN END NOTE

Causation in fact has proven to be a difficult topic. From a moral or normative point of view, would it be wrong to hold a defendant liable when he has committed negligent acts but, fortuitously, has not caused harm? From the point of view of deterring unsafe conduct, would liability without causation be a good idea? *See* Margaret A. Berger, *Eliminating General Causation: Notes Towards a New Theory of Justice and Toxic Torts,* 97 COLUM. L. REV. 2117 (1997). Consider this possible rule for liability without proof of causation: The defendant is liable without proof that his conduct caused legal harm if, but only if

(1) the defendant has acted negligently; and

(2) the negligence created an identifiable risk; and

(3) the plaintiff was one of the persons subjected to that risk; and

(4) the plaintiff actually suffered harm of the kind risked by the defendant.

REFERENCES: On actual cause generally, see DOBBS ON TORTS §§ 166–179 (2000); David W. Robertson, *The Common Sense of Cause in Fact,* 75 TEX. L. REV. 1765, 1780 (1997); HARPER, JAMES & GRAY, THE LAW OF TORTS § 20.2 (2d Ed. 1986 & Supp.). Besides articles cited in this section, see also the philosophically-oriented symposium, *Causation in the Law of Torts,* 63 CHI-KENT L. REV. 397 (1987).

CHAPTER 8

NEGLIGENCE: THE SCOPE OF RISK OR "PROXIMATE CAUSE" ELEMENT

■ ■ ■

§ 1. THE PRINCIPLE: SCOPE OF RISK

The final element that a plaintiff must prove in a negligence case is that the defendant's negligent conduct was, in traditional language, "a proximate cause" of the plaintiff's harm. This is an issue of fact for the jury. Proximate cause determinations involve case-specific inquiries into whether the defendant should be held legally responsible to the plaintiff. Even when the defendant was negligent and in fact caused harm to the plaintiff, the defendant is not liable if the harm actually resulting was not the kind of harm that led to a finding of negligence in the first place.

Why would it be either just or good policy to hold that a defendant is not liable for harm he has, in fact, negligently caused? Suppose that the defendant is Dr. Dayden, a surgeon who performed a vasectomy operation upon Mr. Fallow some years ago. Because the vasectomy was negligently performed, Mr. Fallow sired a child, William. William, when he reached the age of six, set fire to the plaintiff's garage. The plaintiff has now sued William, Mr. Fallow, and Dr. Dayden. The plaintiff can show that Dr. Dayden negligently performed the vasectomy and that his negligence in fact was one of the causes of William's conception and birth. The plaintiff can also show that since his garage would not have been burned but for William's existence, Dr. Dayden's negligence in the vasectomy operation was a cause in fact of that harm.

Probably all lawyers would agree that the surgeon is not liable for the burning of the garage. The reasons for this outcome may be expressed in different ways. Many judicial opinions are likely to emphasize "causation," the attenuated causal link between the surgeon's negligence and the harm ultimately done by William. Yet while causation is often the conventional locution, the underlying idea seems to be more precise and more principled: Liability for negligence is liability for the unreasonable risks the defendant created, not for reasonable risks or for those that were unforeseeable. We don't think a vasectomy is negligently performed because it might cause a fire, so the fire loss was outside the risks that led us to think Dr. Dayden was negligent.

However judges express themselves on proximate cause issues, ask yourself in each case whether the reason for relieving the defendant of liability was merely one of practicality or policy. Or is it a moral reason, grounded in justice of limiting liability to harms for unreasonable risks?

MEDCALF v. WASHINGTON HEIGHTS CONDOMINIUM ASS'N, INC.

747 A.2d 532 (Conn. App. Ct. 2000)

Mihalakos, J. . . .

[T]he plaintiff and a friend, Deborah Michelson, arrived at 1633 Washington Boulevard in Stamford at approximately 9 p.m. to visit a friend, Tracy Skiades. The defendant Washington Heights Condominium Association, Inc., is a Connecticut corporation comprised of the unit owners of the premises. The defendant Professional Property Management Company, Inc., is the managing agent in control of the operation, management and repair of the premises.

The plaintiff parked her car in the street level parking lot and walked to the lobby doors. The lighting in the parking lot was dim. She picked up the intercom outside the lobby and called Skiades. The intercom was answered by Skiades' brother-in-law, who told Skiades that the plaintiff was downstairs. Skiades then attempted to let the plaintiff into the lobby by using the electronic buzzer system. The system failed to work, and Skiades told the plaintiff that she would come down and let her in. Before Skiades could admit her, the plaintiff was attacked by a man, later identified as Kenneth Strickler. She suffered injuries as a result of the attack.

The jury, in response to interrogatories presented to it, returned a verdict for the plaintiff on only the following count of the complaint: "[failure to] maintain the building telephone security intercom communication system in working order so as to allow the plaintiff, and other persons entering the building, to contact others within the building; and for those persons within the building to electronically open the front lobby doors."

The defendants claim that the court improperly denied their motion for a directed verdict. We agree. . . .

The second component [of a negligence action] is proximate cause. Proximate cause establishes a reasonable connection between an act or omission of a defendant and the harm suffered by a plaintiff. The Connecticut Supreme Court has defined proximate cause as "[a]n actual cause that is a substantial factor in the resulting harm. . . . The substantial factor test reflects the inquiry fundamental to all proximate cause questions, that is, whether the harm which occurred was of the same general nature as the foreseeable risk created by the defendant's negligence." Proximate cause is a question of fact to be decided by the trier of fact, but it becomes a question of law when the mind of a fair and reasonable person could reach only one conclusion. Lines must be drawn determining how far down the causal continuum individuals will be held liable for the consequences of their actions.... This line is labeled proximate cause....

The defendants could not have reasonably foreseen that a malfunctioning intercom system might provide a substantial incentive or inducement for the commission of a violent criminal assault on their property by one stranger upon another.

We rule that, as a matter of law, the jury could not reasonably have found that the assault on the plaintiff and the resultant injury were within the foreseeable scope of risk created by the defendants' failure to maintain the intercom system. Therefore, the plaintiff failed to establish the necessary causal relationship.

The judgment is reversed and the case is remanded with direction to render judgment for the defendants.

NOTES

1. **The Restatement's rule.** "An actor's liability is limited to those physical harms that result from the risks that made the actor's conduct tortious." RESTATEMENT (THIRD) OF TORTS: LIABILITY FOR PHYSICAL HARM § 29 (Proposed Final Draft No. 1, 2005). Is the Restatement compatible with *Medcalf*?

2. ***Medcalf* and but-for causation.** The claim in *Medcalf* seems to be that if the buzzer had worked properly, the plaintiff would have been admitted when she rang and would thus have avoided the attack. On that assumption, is it clear that the defendant is a but-for cause of the plaintiff's harm and that the issue in *Medcalf* is not about causation in this sense?

3. **Two ways of stating the elements of the plaintiff's case.** We have been careful in this book to state the cause in fact element separately from the scope of risk or proximate cause element. However, many courts conflate the two by saying that the term proximate cause includes both cause in fact and foreseeability components. While these two different formulations cover the same ground, the latter approach risks confusion: when a court speaks of "proximate cause," it may not be clear whether the court means the cause in fact component, or the foreseeability component. We aim to avoid this confusion by keeping the two elements separate.

4. **Formulations of the principle.** Take a few minutes to consider the idea that the harm that occurred to the plaintiff must be of the "same general nature as the foreseeable risk created by the defendant's negligence." Evaluate the following as alternative statements of the idea. (1) Liability must be rejected unless a reasonable person would have reasonably foreseen and avoided harm of the same general kind actually suffered by the plaintiff. (2) The defendant who negligently creates a risk to the plaintiff is subject to liability when that risk or a similar one results in harm, but not when some entirely different risk eventuates in an entirely different harm.

5. **Applying the rule in *Medcalf*.** Look at the facts in *Medcalf* itself. Ask yourself what kind of harm or risk the defendant negligently created. Some kind of risk or foreseeable harm makes us think the defendant was negligent. Was it the harm that transpired? A similar case is *Benaquista v. Municipal Housing Authority*, 622 N.Y.S.2d 129 (App. Div. 1995) where the defendant failed to maintain an intercom and the apartment owner was injured walking downstairs to admit a visitor.

ABRAMS v. CITY OF CHICAGO, 811 N.E.2d 670 (Ill. 2004). The plaintiff, suing for herself and the estate of her deceased child, alleged that the defendant was negligent in failing to send an ambulance to take her to the hospital for delivery of the child when her contractions were 10 minutes apart. As a result of this failure, a friend took her in a car. The friend drove through a red light, horn sounding, and was struck by Gregory Jones, driving at 75 m.p.h. Jones had been drinking and using cocaine. The plaintiff was left in a coma for two weeks and her child died. The trial court dismissed the claim on the ground that the defendant's failure to provide an ambulance was not a proximate cause of the injuries. The intermediate court reversed. On review, *held*, the intermediate court erred, and the trial court's judgment of dismissal is affirmed. "[W]e conclude as a matter of law that the City could *not* have reasonably anticipated that a refusal to send an ambulance when labor pains are 10 minutes apart would likely result in plaintiff's driver running a red light at the same time that a substance-impaired driver was speeding through the intersection on a suspended license. Millions of women in labor make it safely to the hospital each year by private transportation.... While all traffic accidents are to some extent remotely foreseeable, this is not the kind of harm that was sufficiently foreseeable...."

Notes

1. **Step 1: Identifying the risks that called for more care.** "I'd better send an ambulance to this caller, otherwise she might use a private car which would be in a collision." Would a reasonable dispatcher ever think that? If your answer is no, maybe you've decided that the risks created by the failure to dispatch an ambulance did not include car collisions. In that case, the plaintiff's injury and the child's death would not be within the scope of the risk we would have in mind when we said the defendant was negligent, so the conclusion is, "no proximate cause."

2. **Answering the scope of risk question.** Scope of risk analysis poses the question but does not decide it. Could reasonable people think that, after all, negligent failure to send an ambulance for a pregnant woman might easily result in speeding to the hospital because of the delay? If the answer to that question is "yes," then proximate cause would be a question for the judgment of the jury on the foreseeability issue.

3. **Examples.** Try the idea on some other facts.

(a) Defendant negligently pollutes a bay with oil. One risk is that the oil will cling to docks and have to be cleaned off. Fire is not a foreseeable risk, however, because everyone involved reasonably believes that the oil cannot catch fire on the cold waters of the bay. Their belief, though reasonable, proved wrong and by a fluke, the oil caught fire and burned the plaintiff's docks. If the scope of risk rule enunciated and applied in *Medcalf* controls here, can the plaintiff recover? *Overseas Tankship (U.K.) Ltd. v. Mort's Dock & Eng'g Co. Ltd. (The Wagon Mound),* [1961] A.C. 388 (Privy Council 1961).

(b) Last year, the plaintiff received a blood transfusion. Blood was supplied by the defendant blood bank, ABO. Neither ABO nor anyone else at that time knew that blood could carry an obscure disease, tortosis, much less any way to test for it. However, ABO and other blood banks knew that blood could carry a devastating disease, contractosis, and that blood could readily be tested for that disease. No such test was made. The blood received by the plaintiff carried tortosis, from which the plaintiff now suffers. If ABO had screened the blood for contractosis, it would have found signs of that disease and would have rejected the blood for that reason. If ABO was negligent in not screening for contractosis is it liable to the plaintiff for tortosis?

(c) Defendant installed a fire alarm system in a customer's premises, but negligently managed the system and negligently transmitted a false fire alarm. A fire engine was dispatched to deal with the supposed fire. The engine's brakes failed because of the city's negligent maintenance and the engine crashed into a tree, causing injuries to the firefighters. The defendant argued that the brake failure "introduced a risk not merely of a different degree, but of a different kind." Is the defendant liable to the firefighters? *Lodge v. Arett Sales Corp.,* 717 A.2d 215 (Conn. 1998).

4. **Policy or justice: the risk rule or not.** Maybe the scope of risk rule as articulated in *Medcalf* is wrong. It relieves a faulty defendant at the expense of the innocent plaintiff, doesn't it? For this reason, older cases sometimes held that the defendant would be liable, even for unforeseeable harms, so long as they were "direct" and no new tort by someone else intervened. This view is rarely applied today, although many proximate cause cases involve more than one cause of harm. We deal pointedly with these "intervening cause" cases in section 2(c) below.

5. **Policy or justice: justification for the risk rule.** If the scope of the risk rule is right, what exactly is its justification? Consider: (1) The rule is purely pragmatic. Liability must stop somewhere. The but-for causation test would leave people exposed to continuous liability as long as they lived. (2) The risk rule is just or at least logical. If liability is imposed only for negligence and negligence creates only a risk of harm A, then liability should be limited to harm A. Any other result would be a species of strict liability, that is, liability for harms as to which the defendant created no unreasonable risks. *See* DOBBS ON TORTS § 181 (2000).

PALSGRAF v. LONG ISLAND RAILROAD CO.

162 N.E. 99 (N.Y. 1928)

CARDOZO, C.J.

Plaintiff was standing on a platform of defendant's railroad after buying a ticket to go to Rockaway Beach. A train stopped at the station, bound for another place. Two men ran forward to catch it. One of the men reached the platform of the car without mishap, though the train was already moving. The other man, carrying a package, jumped aboard the car, but seemed unsteady as if about to fall. A guard on the car, who had held the door open, reached forward to help him in, and another guard on the platform pushed him from behind. In this act, the package was dislodged, and fell upon the rails. It was a package of small size, about fifteen inches long, and was covered by a newspaper. In fact it contained fireworks, but there was nothing in its appearance to give notice of its contents. The fireworks when they fell exploded. The shock of the explosion threw down some scales at the other end of the platform many feet away. The scales struck the plaintiff, causing injuries for which she sues. [The case was submitted to a jury, which returned a verdict for the plaintiff. The Appellate Division affirmed the judgment for the plaintiff.]

The conduct of the defendant's guard, if a wrong in its relation to the holder of package, was not a wrong in its relation to the plaintiff, standing far away. Relatively to her it was not negligence at all. Nothing in the situation gave notice that the falling package had in it the potency of peril to persons thus removed. Negligence is not actionable unless it involves the invasion of a legally protected interest, the violation of a right. "Proof of negligence in the air, so to speak, will not do." "Negligence is the absence of care, according to the circumstances." The plaintiff, as she stood upon the platform of the station, might claim to be protected against intentional invasion of her bodily security. Such invasion is not charged. She might claim to be protected against unintentional invasion by conduct involving in the thought of reasonable men an unreasonable hazard that such invasion would ensue. These, from the point of view of the law, were the bounds of her immunity, with perhaps some rare exceptions.... If no hazard was apparent to the eye of ordinary vigilance, an act innocent and harmless, at least to outward seeming, with reference to her, did not take to itself the quality of a tort because it happened to be a wrong, though apparently not one involving the risk of bodily insecurity, with reference to some one else....

The risk reasonably to be perceived defines the duty to be obeyed, and risk imports relation; it is risk to another or to others within the range of apprehension. This does not mean, of course, that one who launches a destructive force is always relieved of liability, if the force, though known to be destructive pursues an unexpected path. "It was not necessary that the defendant should have had notice of the particular method in which an accident would occur, if the possibility of an accident was clear to the ordinarily prudent eye." Some acts, such as shooting are so imminently dangerous to any one who may come within reach of the missile however unexpectedly, as to impose a duty of provision not far from that of an insurer. Even today, and much oftener in earlier stages of law, one acts sometimes at one's peril. Under this head, it may be, fall certain cases of what is known as transferred intent, an act willfully dangerous to A resulting by misadventure in injury to B. Talmage v. Smith, 101 Mich. 370, 374, 59 N.W. 656, 45 Am. St. Rep. 414. These cases aside, wrong is defined in terms of the natural or probable, at least when unintentional. The range of reasonable apprehension is at times a question for the court, and at times, if varying inferences are possible, a question for the jury. Here, by concession, there was nothing in the situation to suggest to the most cautious mind that the parcel wrapped in newspaper would spread wreckage through the station. If the guard had thrown it down knowingly and willfully, he would not have threatened the plaintiff's safety, so far as appearances could warn him. His conduct would not have involved, even then, an unreasonable probability of invasion of her bodily security. Liability can be no greater where the act is inadvertent. . . .

The law of causation, remote or proximate, is thus foreign to the case before us. The question of liability is always anterior to the question of the measure of the consequences that go with liability. If there is no tort to be redressed, there is no occasion to consider what damage might be recovered if there were a finding of a tort. We may assume, without deciding, that negligence, not at large or in the abstract, but in relation to the plaintiff, would entail liability for any and all consequences, however novel or extraordinary. There is room for argument that a distinction is to be drawn according to the diversity of interests invaded by the act, as where conduct negligent in that it threatens an insignificant invasion of an interest in property results in an unforeseeable invasion of an interest of another order, as, e.g., one of bodily security. Perhaps other distinctions may be necessary. We do not go into the question now. The consequences to be followed must first be rooted in a wrong.

The judgment of the Appellate Division and that of the Trial Term should be reversed, and the complaint dismissed, with costs in all courts.

ANDREWS, J. (dissenting.) . . .

[1: Duty runs to the world at large and negligence toward one is negligence to all]

The result we shall reach depends upon our theory as to the nature of negligence. Is it a relative concept—the breach of some duty owing to a particular person or to particular persons? Or where there is an act which unreasonably threatens the safety of others, is the doer liable for all its proximate consequences, even where they result in injury to one who would generally be thought to be outside the radius of danger? This is not a mere dispute as to words. We might not believe that to the average mind the dropping of the bundle would seem to involve the probability of harm to the plaintiff standing many feet away whatever might be the case as to the owner or to one so near as to be likely to be struck by its fall. If, however, we adopt the second hypothesis, we have to inquire only as to the relation between cause and effect. We deal in terms of proximate cause, not of negligence. . . .

But we are told that "there is no negligence unless there is in the particular case a legal duty to take care, and this duty must be one which is owed to the plaintiff himself and not merely to others." Salmond Torts (6th Ed.) 24. This I think too narrow a conception. Where there is the unreasonable act, and some right that may be affected there is negligence whether damage does or does not result. That is immaterial. Should we drive down Broadway at a reckless speed, we are negligent whether we strike an approaching car or miss it by an inch. The act itself is wrongful. It is a wrong not only to those who happen to be within the radius of danger, but to all who might have been there—a wrong to the public at large. . . .

It may well be that there is no such thing as negligence in the abstract. "Proof of negligence in the air, so to speak, will not do." In an empty world negligence would not exist. It does involve a relationship between man and his fellows, but not merely a relationship between man and those whom he might reasonably expect his act would injure; rather, a relationship between him and those whom he does in fact injure. If his act has a tendency to harm some one, it harms him a mile away as surely as it does those on the scene. . . .

In the well-known Polemis Case, [1921] 3 K.B. 560, Scrutton, L.J., said that the dropping of a plank was negligent, for it might injure "workman or cargo or ship." Because of either possibility, the owner of the vessel was to be made good for his loss. The act being wrongful, the doer was liable for its proximate results.[1] . . .

The proposition is this: Every one owes to the world at large the duty of refraining from those acts that may unreasonably threaten the safety of others. Such an act occurs . . . Unreasonable risk being taken, its consequences are not confined to those who might probably be hurt. . . .

[2: Liability is limited by proximate cause, not by defining the scope of duty or negligence]

The right to recover damages rests on additional considerations. The plaintiff's rights must be injured, and this injury must be caused by the negligence. We build a dam, but are negligent as to its foundations. Breaking, it injures property down stream. We are not liable if all this happened because of some reason other than the insecure foundation. But, when injuries do result from our unlawful act, we are liable for the consequences. It does not matter that they are unusual, unexpected,

---

1. The facts that made these statements significant were probably known to many of Judge Andrews' readers. Workers on deck negligently caused a wooden plank to fall into the hold, no doubt risking injury to workmen below, to goods, or even to the ship, but not foreseeably risking a fire. Nevertheless, the wood somehow sparked a fire that destroyed the ship and those responsible for the workmen's negligence were held liable for this startling result.

unforeseen, and unforeseeable. But there is one limitation. The damages must be so connected with the negligence that the latter may be said to be the proximate cause of the former.

[3: Proximate cause is determined by several factors, not by the scope of the defendant's negligence]

These two words have never been given an inclusive definition. What is a cause in a legal sense, still more what is a proximate cause, depend in each case upon many considerations, as does the existence of negligence itself. Any philosophical doctrine of causation does not help us. A boy throws a stone into a pond. The ripples spread. The water level rises. The history of that pond is altered to all eternity. It will be altered by other causes also. Yet it will be forever the resultant of all causes combined. Each one will have an influence. How great only omniscience can say. You may speak of a chain, or, if you please, a net. An analogy is of little aid. Each cause brings about future events. Without each the future would not be the same. Each is proximate in the sense it is essential. But that is not what we mean by the word. Nor on the other hand do we mean sole cause. There is no such thing.

Should analogy be thought helpful, however, I prefer that of a stream. The spring, starting on its journey, is joined by tributary after tributary. The river, reaching the ocean, comes from a hundred sources. No man may say whence any drop of water is derived. Yet for a time distinction may be possible. Into the clear creek, brown swamp water flows from the left. Later, from the right comes water stained by its clay bed. The three may remain for a space, sharply divided. But at last inevitably no trace of separation remains. They are so commingled that all distinction is lost.

As we have said, we cannot trace the effect of an act to the end, if end there is. Again, however, we may trace it part of the way. A murder at Serajevo may be the necessary antecedent to an assassination in London twenty years hence. An overturned lantern may burn all Chicago. We may follow the fire from the shed to the last building. We rightly say the fire started by the lantern caused its destruction.

A cause, but not the proximate cause. What we do mean by the word "proximate" is that, because of convenience, of public policy, of a rough sense of justice, the law arbitrarily declines to trace a series of events beyond a certain point. This is not logic. It is practical politics. Take our rule as to fires. Sparks from my burning haystack set on fire my house and my neighbor's. I may recover from a negligent railroad. He may not. Yet the wrongful act as directly harmed the one as the other. We may regret the line was drawn just where it was, but drawn somewhere it had to be. We said the act of the railroad was not the proximate cause of our neighbor's fire. Cause it surely was. The words we used were simply indicative of our notions of public policy. Other courts think differently. But somewhere they reach the point where they cannot say the stream comes from any one source....

There are some hints that may help us. The proximate cause, involved as it may be with many other causes, must be, at the least, something without which the event would not happen. The court must ask itself whether there was a natural and continuous sequence between cause and effect. Was the one a substantial factor in producing the other? Was there a direct connection between them, without too many intervening causes? Is the effect of cause on result not too attenuated? Is the cause likely, in the usual judgment of mankind, to produce the result? Or, by the exercise of prudent foresight, could the result be foreseen? Is the result too remote from the cause, and here we consider remoteness in time and space.... Clearly we must so consider, for the greater the distance either in time or space, the more surely do other causes intervene to affect the result. When a lantern is overturned, the firing of a shed is a fairly direct consequence. Many things contribute to the spread of the conflagration—the force of the wind, the direction and width of streets, the character of intervening structures, other factors. We draw an uncertain and wavering line, but draw it we must as best we can....

Once again, it is all a question of fair judgment, always keeping in mind the fact that we endeavor to make a rule in each case that will be practical and in keeping with the general understanding of mankind....

In fairness he would make good every injury flowing from his negligence. Not because of tenderness toward him we say he need not answer for all that follows his wrong. We look back to the catastrophe, the fire kindled by the spark, or the explosion. We trace the consequences, not indefinitely, but to a certain point. And to aid us in fixing that point we ask what might ordinarily be expected to follow the fire or the explosion.

This last suggestion is the factor which must determine the case before us. The act upon which defendant's liability rests is knocking an apparently harmless package onto the platform. The act was negligent. For its proximate consequences the defendant is liable. If its contents were broken, to the owner; if it fell upon and crushed a passenger's foot, then to him; if it exploded and injured one in the immediate vicinity, to him also.... Mrs. Palsgraf was standing some distance away. How far cannot be told from the record—apparently 25 or 30 feet, perhaps less. Except for the explosion, she would not have been injured. We are told by the appellant in his brief, "It cannot be denied that the explosion was the direct cause of the plaintiff's injuries." So it was a substantial factor in producing the result—there was here a natural and continuous sequence—direct connection. The only intervening cause was that, instead of blowing her to the ground, the concussion smashed the weighing machine which in turn fell upon her. There was no remoteness in time, little in space. And surely, given such an explosion as here, it needed no great foresight to predict that the natural result would be to injure one on the platform at no greater distance from its scene than was the plaintiff. Just how no one might be able to predict. Whether by flying fragments, by broken glass, by wreckage of machines or structures no one could say. But injury in some form was most probable.

Under these circumstances I cannot say as a matter of law that the plaintiff's injuries were not the proximate result of the negligence. That is all we have before us. The court refused to so charge. No request was made to submit the matter to the jury as a question of fact, even would that have been proper upon the record before us.

NOTES

1. **Integrating *Palsgraf* and *Medcalf*.** Reading *Palsgraf* and *Medcalf* together, we can say that the defendant is liable only for harms within the scope of the risks he negligently created. More specifically, that the defendant is liable only (a) for types of injuries foreseeably risked by his negligence and (b) to classes of persons foreseeably risked by his negligence. In other words, the defendant is not liable unless a reasonable person in defendant's circumstances should have foreseen that his conduct risked injuries of the same general type that occurred to a general class of persons of which the plaintiff is within.

2. **Jury role.** Scope of risk is a matter that must necessarily be determined on the facts of each case. Consequently, when the question is about the scope of the risk, the question is usually one for the jury so long as reasonable people could differ. Why did Cardozo, then, refuse to permit a jury to decide foreseeability in *Palsgraf*?

3. **What is the class of persons?** To what class of persons should the guard have foreseen injury in *Palsgraf*? Was Mrs. Palsgraf within that class? Modern cases often free a defendant from liability where the plaintiff is not within a class foreseeably risked by the negligent conduct. *See, e.g., Mellon Mortgage Co. v. Holder*, 5 S.W.3d 654 (Tex. 1999) (woman raped in defendant Mellon's parking garage by a policeman who had pulled her over several blocks away was "not a member of [a] class ... that Mellon could have reasonably foreseen would be the victim of a criminal act in its garage).

4. **"Foreseeability."** If a reasonable person would foresee no harm to anyone as a result of his actions we do not need to reach the proximate cause issue. Why not?

5. **Cardozo's duty/negligence locution compared to proximate cause language.** In *Palsgraf*, Cardozo seemed concerned with scope of risk but did not invoke the concept of proximate cause by that name. Instead, he concluded that "[r]elatively to her it was not negligence at all," because no harm to her was foreseeable. Although expressed in terms of duty or negligence, the rule is identical to one that asserts the defendant's conduct is not a proximate cause when the defendant could not foresee harm to persons situated like the plaintiff.

6. **Andrews: Rejecting the duty/negligence locution.** Judge Andrews, dissenting, tried to establish two points. First, he argued that a person who is negligent to *any* class of persons is negligent to everyone who is in fact injured. He rejected Cardozo's effort to deal with the issue as one of duty or negligence. Instead, for Andrews, the issue became one of proximate cause.

7. **Andrews: The limited role of foreseeability in proximate cause determinations.** Andrews' second point was that proximate cause was *not* a matter of foreseeability alone. For Andrews, proximate cause was a matter of a host of factors. Since it was not foreseeability alone that determined proximate cause for Andrews, he would not allow the railroad to escape liability for its supposed negligence merely because no reasonable person would expect the package to cause harm to someone a distance away.

8. **Adopting a scope of risk or foreseeability approach.** When courts are concerned with the scope of risk question, they have often adopted Andrews' proximate cause locution but Cardozo's foreseeability test. The result is that decisions on proximate cause today almost always emphasize foreseeability in some form as a limitation on liability. They are thus scope of risk cases. Only a few cases continue to reflect some affinity with Andrews' view that liability could be imposed for types of harm or to classes of person who were not reasonably foreseeable victims, and even these may find policy reasons against liability beyond the scope of the risk in particular cases. *See Fandrey v. American Family Mut. Ins. Co.*, 680 N.W.2d 345 (Wis. 2004).

9. **Duty vs. breach vs. proximate cause.** Cardozo invoked a scope of risk rule, but expressed it by saying either that the railroad was not negligent toward Mrs. Palsgraf or by saying it owed her no duty of care. Some courts today use "no duty" or "limited duty" terminology in adjudicating scope of risk questions based on foreseeability, saying a defendant owes no duty of care if the type of harm is not foreseeable. *See Wiener v. Southcoast Childcare Ctrs., Inc.*, 88 P.3d 517 (Cal. 2004); *Valcaniant v. Detroit Edison Co.*, 679 N.W.2d 689 (Mich. 2004). However, courts also invoke the "no duty" expression when liability is ruled out for entirely different reasons, not associated with foreseeability. We will see these other "no duty" and "limited duty" considerations in several chapters beginning with Chapter 12.

10. **Was the defendant negligent at all?** Could Cardozo have just as easily said that the defendant was not negligent at all, towards anyone?

NOTE: THE RESCUE DOCTRINE

How does the risk rule work in this kind of case: Defendant negligently creates a risk to *A*. *B*, who was not subject to the risk or who escaped it, attempts to rescue *A* and is hurt in the process. Defendant, having created a risk to *A*, is liable to him. Is he also liable to *B*? *Palsgraf* might lead one to answer that he is not, or that the issue would turn on whether rescue would be foreseeable in the particular situation at the time defendant was guilty of negligence. Judge Cardozo's own answer, however, was otherwise.

In *Wagner v. International Railway*, 133 N.E. 437 (N.Y. 1921) the railway permitted passengers to stand in between the cars while the train was moving over a high trestle. One of them fell off into a gorge as the train rounded a curve. The plaintiff attempted to climb down to locate the victim, who was his cousin. In the course of this attempt, the plaintiff himself was injured. Cardozo, speaking in his Delphic manner, held that the railway was liable to the rescuer. "Danger invites rescue," he said, suggesting, perhaps, that rescue is foreseeable or is foreseeable as a matter of law. But he added a few sentences later: "The wrongdoer may not have foreseen the coming of a deliverer. He is accountable as if he had." The latter statement might be read as rejecting any criterion of foreseeability, or it might be read to mean only that a reasonable person would have foreseen rescue, whether the defendant subjectively foresaw it or not.

Whatever Cardozo meant, the cases have generally agreed that the rescuer can recover from the defendant whose negligence prompts the rescue. *See, e.g., Clinkscales v. Nelson Securities, Inc.*, 697 N.W.2d 836 (Iowa 2005). The rule includes cases in which the defendant negligently injures or endangers himself and the plaintiff is injured in attempting a rescue. *See Sears v. Morrison,* 90 Cal.Rptr.2d 528 (Ct. App. 1999).

Try applying the rescue doctrine to these cases: (A) Dorothy Lambert was in an accident, allegedly caused by a tortfeasor's negligence. Her husband, over a block away in an office, heard of the accident; he rushed out to reach his wife, slipped on a patch of ice, and was injured. Is the tortfeasor liable to the husband as a rescuer? *Lambert v. Parrish*, 492 N.E.2d 289 (Ind. 1986). (B) Defendant ran over a small child. Police officers came to the scene. One gave aid to the child while the second helped in controlling a crowd and the child's hysterical parent. While so engaged, the second officer collapsed and suffered a fatal heart attack. Is the defendant liable to the officer's survivors or estate because the officer was a rescuer? *Snellenberger v. Rodriguez,* 760 S.W.2d 237 (Tex. 1988).

NOTE: VIOLATION OF STATUTE AND "PROXIMATE CAUSE"

As we saw in Chapter 5, in most states violation of a non-tort statute is "negligence per se," but this rule is conditioned upon a finding that the statute was designed to protect against the kind of harm that occurred and also to protect the class of persons of which the plaintiff is a member.

A well-known and very clear example of this is *Larrimore v. American National Insurance Co.*, 89 P.2d 340 (Okla. 1939). A statute forbade laying out poisons. The defendant provided a rat poison to its tenant, a coffee shop. The coffee shop put the poison near the coffee burner. The plaintiff was injured when she lit the burner, because the poison exploded due to its phosphorous content. The trial judge, as trier of fact, found for the defendant. The Supreme Court of Oklahoma affirmed, commenting:

> It is not enough for a plaintiff to show that the defendant neglected a duty imposed by statute. He must go further and show that his injury was caused by his exposure to a hazard from which it was the purpose of the statute to protect him. . . . Those only to whom [the statutory] duty is due and who have sustained injuries of the character its discharge was designed to prevent can maintain actions for its breach.

The court is stating the fundamental scope of risk rule as applied to a statutory liability, isn't it?

§ 2. ASSESSING THE SCOPE
OF THE RISK

A. IS HARM OUTSIDE THE SCOPE OF THE RISK BECAUSE OF THE MANNER IN WHICH IT OCCURS?

HUGHES v. LORD ADVOCATE

[1963] A.C. 837 (H.L.)

[Post Office employees were working on an underground telephone cable in Edinburgh, Scotland. At 5:00 they took a tea break, leaving unguarded an open manhole, covered with a tent and surrounded by kerosene lanterns. Two boys, 8 and 10 years old, found the unguarded site, tied one of the lanterns to a rope they found, and descended into the manhole. They came back up without mishap, but once back on top, they knocked or dropped the lantern into the hole. The accepted reconstruction of what happened next was that the lantern broke and that, quite unforeseeably, some of the kerosene vaporized. This gaseous form of the kerosene came into contact with the flame of the lantern and there was a large explosion, followed by a raging fire. Hughes, the eight year old, fell into the manhole as a result of the explosion and suffered severe burns, some of them on his fingers as he tried to climb out by holding to the heated metal ladder. He brought an action against the Lord Advocate of Scotland, as representative of the Post Office. The courts of Scotland held in favor of the Lord Advocate on the grounds that though burns were foreseeable, the vaporization of the kerosene and the explosion were not.]

LORD REID. . . . I am satisfied that the Post Office workmen were in fault in leaving this open manhole unattended and it is clear that if they had done as they ought to have done this accident would not have happened. It cannot be said that they owed no duty to the appellant. But it has been held that the appellant cannot recover damages. . . .

[T]here could be a case where the intrusion of a new and unexpected factor could be regarded as the cause of the accident rather than the fault of the defender. But that is not this case. The cause of this accident was a known source of danger, the lamp, but it behaved in an unpredictable way. . . . This accident was caused by a known source of danger, but caused in a way which could not have been foreseen, and, in my judgment, that affords no defense. I would therefore allow the appeal.

LORD GUEST. . . . In dismissing the appellant's claim the Lord Ordinary and the majority of the judges of the First Division reached the conclusion that the accident which happened was not reasonably foreseeable. . . . Concentration has been placed in the courts below on the explosion which, it was said, could not have been foreseen because it was caused in a unique fashion by the paraffin forming into vapour and being ignited by the naked flame of the wick. But this, in my opinion, is to concentrate on what is really a non-essential element. . . .

[B]ecause the explosion was the agent which caused the burning and was unforeseeable, therefore the accident, according to them, was not reasonably foreseeable. In my opinion, this reasoning is fallacious. An explosion is only one way in which burning can be caused. Burning can also be caused by the contact between liquid paraffin and a naked flame. In the one case paraffin vapour and in the other case liquid paraffin is ignited by fire. I cannot see that these are two different types of accident. They are both burning accidents and in both cases the injuries would be burning injuries. Upon this view the explosion was an immaterial event in the chain of causation. It was simply one way which burning might be caused by the potentially dangerous paraffin lamp. . . .

LORD PEARCE. . . . Did the explosion create an accident and damage of a different type from the misadventure and damage that could be foreseen? In my judgment it did not. The accident was but a variant of the foreseeable. . . . [It] would be, I think, too narrow a view to hold that those who created the risk of fire are excused from the liability for the damage by fire because it came by way of explosive combustion. The resulting damage, though severe, was not greater than or different in kind from that which might have been produced had the lamp spilled and produced a more normal conflagration in the hold.

I would therefore allow the appeal.

DOUGHTY v. TURNER MANUFACTURING CO., LTD., [1964] 1 Q.B. 518 (C.A. 1963). Defendant's manufacturing process involved use of two vats of molten liquid maintained at 800 degrees centigrade, into which metal parts were immersed. Covers made of asbestos and cement were set beside the vat, to be put on as needed to conserve heat. Such covers had been used in this process in England and in the United States for over 20 years. A worker knocked one of the covers into the molten liquid. The cover sank without causing a splash. After one or two minutes the molten liquid erupted and injured the plaintiff, who was standing nearby. Thereafter experiments indicated that a compound of asbestos and cement would undergo a chemical change when subjected to temperatures over 500 degrees centigrade, so that hydrogen and oxygen in the material would combine to form water. The water at this temperature would turn to steam and produce an explosion or eruption. The trial judge held in favor of the plaintiff, finding negligence on the part of the worker in knocking the cover into the vat. *Held*, appeal allowed, judgment for defendants. LORD PEARCE: "The evidence showed that splashes caused by sudden immersion . . . were a foreseeable danger which should be carefully avoided. The falling cover might have ejected the liquid by a splash, and in the result it did eject the liquid, though in a more dramatic fashion." Therefore, the plaintiff's counsel argued, the accident was "merely a variant of foreseeable accidents by splashing. . . . [I]t would be quite unrealistic to describe this accident as a variant of the perils from splashing. The cause of the accident, to quote Lord Reid's words, was 'the intrusion of a new and unexpected factor.' There was an eruption due to chemical changes underneath the surface of the liquid as opposed to a splash caused by displacement from bodies falling on to its surface. In my judgment, the reasoning in Hughes v. Lord Advocate cannot be extended far enough to cover this case." HARMON, L.J. "In my opinion the damage here was of an entirely different kind from the foreseeable splash." DIPLOCK, L.J.: "The first risk . . . is that if [the cover] is allowed to drop on to the hot liquid in the bath with sufficient momentum it may cause the liquid to splash on to persons. . . . The second risk is that if it becomes immersed in a liquid the temperature of which exceeds 500 degrees centigrade, it will disintegrate and cause an under-surface explosion which will eject the liquid. . . . There is no room today for mystique in the law of negligence. It is the application of common morality and common sense to the activities of the common man." The plaintiff's attorney relied on Hughes v. Lord Advocate where the plaintiff's burns were more serious than they would have been expected to be. "But they were the direct consequence of the defendant's breach of duty and of the same kind as could reasonably have been foreseen, although of unforeseen gravity. But in the present case the defendants' duty owed to the plaintiff in relation to the only foreseeable risk, that is of splashing, was to take reasonable care to avoid knocking the cover into the liquid or allowing it to slip in such a way as to cause a splash which would injure the plaintiff. Failure to avoid knocking it into the liquid . . . was of itself no breach of duty to the plaintiff."

NOTES

1. There is obviously much room for judicial judgment in characterizing the risks that are foreseeable, but how do we explain *Doughty*? The court says it is applying the general principle expressed in *Hughes*. Is the type of harm that occurred in *Doughty* different from what was risked by the defendant's conduct? Where the harm occurs in some bizarre, unforeseeable manner, is that irrelevant to judging whether the type of harm was foreseeable?,

2. In *Darby v. National Trust*, [2001] P.I.Q.R. 27 (C.A., Civ.), a healthy adult man drowned in a murky pond on the grounds of a large English estate owned by the National Trust and held open for recreational use. The plaintiff (the man's wife and estate) sued the National Trust, claiming that it was negligent in failing to prevent swimming in the pond, either by posting signage or by providing in-person warnings by rangers. The plaintiff relied in part on an expert witness who testified that the ponds on the estate were particularly unsuited for swimming because of the risk of swimmers contracting Weils disease, "an unpleasant and occasionally fatal condition transmitted from rats' urine." The judges of the English Court of Appeal held that the defendant was not liable, one of them concluding, "Unpleasant though Weils disease, I have no doubt, is, it was not the kind of risk or damage which Mr Darby suffered, and any duty to warn against Weils disease, cannot, in my judgment, support a claim for damages resulting from a quite different

cause." If one risk of swimming in this murky pool was death (perhaps from Weils disease), and death did in fact occur (albeit from drowning), is the court making liability turn on the way that the death occurred?

3.   Some courts do appear to require foreseeability of many details about the manner in which an injury occurred. In such cases the negligent defendant escapes responsibility even when he should have foreseen the precise injury that occurred, because he could not foresee the precise *manner* in which it occurred. In *Morguson v. 3M Co.,* 857 So.2d 796 (Ala. 2003), the defendants manufactured a heart-lung machine, but its design left it possible that it would be wrongly connected with potentially deadly results. That in fact happened in an operation on the decedent; the perfusionist set it up so the blood flowed the wrong way and the patient died. The court focused on the fact that although the machine's design made misconnection and death foreseeable, the perfusionist's later specific acts in failing to check the connection then falsely claiming he had, were not. That was enough to hold that the defendant was not responsible.

B.   IS HARM OUTSIDE THE SCOPE OF THE RISK BECAUSE ITS EXTENT IS UNFORESEEABLE?

HAMMERSTEIN v. JEAN DEVELOPMENT WEST, 907 P.2d 975 (Nev. 1995). Plaintiff, about 70 years of age, was a guest at defendant's hotel. As the hotel knew, he was a diabetic. Walking up and down stairs was bad for him, but there were no rooms on the ground floor and besides there was an elevator. In the early morning hours a fire alarm went off. Elevators were locked and plaintiff had to walk down from the fourth floor. In doing so he twisted his ankle. Much later, on returning to his room, he found a blister on his foot. This eventually became a gangrenous infection probably because of his diabetes, which interferes with circulation in the lower extremities. There was in fact no fire and the fire alarm system had gone off without a fire on numerous occasions but had never been corrected. *Held,* summary judgment for defendant was error. "It should have been foreseeable to Nevada Landing that if its fire alarm system was unreasonably faulty, harm to a certain type of plaintiff, i.e., one of its guests, could result. Also, this particular variety of harm, injuring an ankle or foot on the way down a stairwell, is a foreseeable variety of harm in this circumstance. The extent of the infection on Hammerstein's leg may not have been foreseeable, but the underlying injury should have been."

NOTES

1.   **The thin skull rule.** The term "thin skull" or "eggshell skull" is widely used in tort law in reference to some variant on the following facts. Defendant negligently strikes the plaintiff. The blow is such that a normal person would suffer only slight injury, such as a bruise. The plaintiff, however, has an unusually thin skull, a fact the defendant does not know. As a result of the minor blow, the plaintiff suffers terrible injuries. If the defendant is in fact guilty of tort—that is, if he was negligent or guilty of

intentional harm—then the fact that the harm was much worse than anyone would have expected does not limit his liability. This is the thin skull rule. It is often generalized by saying that the defendant "takes the plaintiff as he finds her," that is, with whatever extra damages the plaintiff might have because the plaintiff has a "thin skull," or has diabetes, or is pregnant, or suffers hemophilia, or is otherwise pre-disposed to suffer more. A leading case is *McCahill v. New York Transportation Co.*, 94 N.E. 616 (N.Y. 1911). There the defendant ran into the plaintiff, who suffered a broken thigh. In the hospital he began to suffer delirium tremens, from which he died. This resulted only because of a pre-existing alcoholic condition. The defendant took the plaintiff as it found him and was held liable for his death.

2. **Nuances of the rule.** The thin skull cases do not impose liability without fault. The defendant's act must have been one that would cause some harm to a normal person, or the defendant must have been at fault because he knew or should have known of the plaintiff's susceptible condition. The thin skull rule merely holds that the defendant does not escape liability for the unforeseeable personal reactions of the plaintiff, once negligence or intentional fault is established. Nor does the thin skull rule shift the burden of proof to the defendant; the plaintiff must prove by a preponderance of the evidence that the defendant actually caused the plaintiff harm—that may, in this case, have aggravated a pre-existing condition. *See, e.g., Rowe v. Munye*, 702 N.W.2d 729 (Minn. 2005). The defendant would be liable in such a case for newly-caused harms, including the aggravation, but not for the pre-existing injury or condition itself. Does *Dillon v. Twin States Electric Co.*, *supra* Chapter 7, help explain this?

3. **A broader principle.** The thin skull rule may reflect a broader principle, and indeed that is the way the court in *Hammerstein* articulated its holding: a defendant may be liable for the full extent of a plaintiff's harm, even where the extent of that harm was unforeseeable, where the other elements of a prima facie case are established. In a famous English case, *Smith v. London & South Western Railway*, L.R. 6 C.P. 14 (1870), a judge articulated the principle quite well:

> If a man fires a gun across a road where he may reasonably anticipate that persons will be passing, and hits someone, he is guilty of negligence, and liable for the injury he has caused; but if he fires in his own wood, where he cannot reasonably anticipate that any one will be, he is not liable to any one whom he shoots, which shews that what a person may reasonably anticipate is important in considering whether he has been negligent; but if a person fires across a road when it is dangerous to do so and kills a man who is in the receipt of a large income, he will be liable for the whole damage, however great, that may have resulted to his family, and cannot set up that he could not have reasonably expected to have injured any one but a labourer.

The principle is well-settled. *See* RESTATEMENT (THIRD) § 29, cmt. *p* (P.F.D. No. 1, 2005). Is it consistent with the scope-of-risk rule?

C. IS HARM OUTSIDE THE SCOPE OF THE RISK BECAUSE IT RESULTS MOST DIRECTLY FROM AN ACT OF AN INTERVENING PERSON OR FORCE?

1. INTRODUCTION: SCOPE OF RISK AND NATURAL AND CONTINUOUS SEQUENCE

Imagine this case: Tortfeasor A leaves an unlighted excavation in the sidewalk. Tortfeasor B negligently jostles the plaintiff, causing him to fall into the excavation.

"The proximate cause of an injury is that which, in a natural and continuous sequence, unbroken by any efficient intervening cause, produces an injury, and without which the injury would not have occurred."

These words and others very similar have been used in literally hundreds of American cases. They have done quite a bit to obscure issues and principles. For one thing, courts have recognized repeatedly, and we ourselves have seen, that there may be many tortfeasors who are all liable and thus all proximate causes. When judges speak of "the" proximate cause rather than "a" proximate cause, they may be pushing the jury to an unconscious bias against finding both tortfeasors liable. *See, e.g., Holmes v. Levine*, 639 S.E.2d 235 (Va. 2007) (holding that a jury instruction that the plaintiff had to prove that defendant's negligence was "*the* proximate cause of the death of [decedent]" was reversible error, where evidence supported that there could be other proximate causes of the death).

When tortfeasors act in sequence, the first tortfeasor often argues that the second tortfeasor is an "intervening cause" that "supersedes" his liability entirely. Courts often use metaphorical rather than principled language here: a superseding cause breaks the causal chain.

The emphasis on intervening causes and causal chains has obscured the more fundamental scope-of-risk principle: An intervening act of some second tortfeasor should relieve the first tortfeasor of liability only when the resulting harm is outside the scope of the risk negligently created by the first tortfeasor. In other words, an "intervening cause that lies within the scope of the foreseeable risk, or has a reasonable connection to it, is not a superseding cause." *Fancyboy v. Alaska Village Elec. Co-op., Inc.*, 984 P.2d 1128 (Alaska 1999). *See also Winschel v. Brown*, 171 P.3d 142 (Alaska 2007) (reversing a summary judgment for defendant on superseding cause grounds, stating that "proximate cause requires only that the general kind of harm be foreseeable for an actor's conduct to be considered the proximate cause of plaintiff's injuries").

Look back at *Medcalf*. The plaintiff's injury resulted directly from the act of her attacker, an intervening tortfeasor, not the landlord who negligently left the buzzer in disrepair. The *Medcalf* court made no special point about intervening actors and didn't need to. Instead it went directly to the general principle—defendants should be liable for risks or harms they negligently created but not others. But when courts emphasize intervening cause, they often make no direct mention of the general scope of risk principle. They instead put the weight of their discussion on intervening causes. Are they talking the language of intervening cause but in fact carrying out the scope of risk principle, or some distorted version of it?

2. INTENTIONAL OR CRIMINAL INTERVENING ACTS

WATSON v. KENTUCKY & INDIANA BRIDGE & RAILROAD, 126 S.W. 146 (Ky. 1910). Defendant railroad negligently derailed a gasoline tank car and it sprung a leak. A man named Duerr threw a match into the area; an explosion resulted, causing the plaintiff injury. *Held*, if Duerr acted "for the purpose of causing the explosion," the railroad would not be liable. "[I]f the intervening agency is something so unexpected or extraordinary as that [the railroad] could not or ought not to have anticipated it, he will not be liable, and certainly he is not bound to anticipate the criminal acts of others by which damage is inflicted and hence is not liable therefor."

NOTES

1. A view common in the 19th and early 20th centuries was that the deliberate infliction of harm by a "moral being," who was adequately informed, free to act, and able to choose, would "supersede" the negligence of the first actor. *See* H.L.A. HART & A.M. HONORE, CAUSATION IN THE LAW 129 (1962). This reasoning sometimes pops up in modern cases. *See, e.g., Alston v. Advanced Brands and Importing Co.*, 494 F.3d 562 (6th Cir. 2007) (holding that parents of minor children who were harmed by drinking alcohol lacked standing to sue the manufacturer and importer of the beverages because "the causal connection between the defendants' [acts] and the plaintiff's alleged injuries is broken by the intervening criminal acts of the third-party sellers and the third-party underage purchasers.... A crime is an independent action.") On the history of proximate cause thinking, see Patrick J. Kelley, *Proximate Cause in Negligence Law: History, Theory, and the Present Darkness*, 69 WASH. U. L. Q. 49, 78–81 (1991).

2. *Watson* itself was repudiated in *Britton v. Wooten*, 817 S.W.2d 443 (Ky. 1991) where the court said that if the defendant negligently created the increased risk of fire or its spread the defendant could be held responsible. In *Craig v. Driscoll*, 813 A.2d 1003 (Conn. 2003), the court said this: "The scope of the risk analysis of proximate cause similarly applies where ... the risk of harm created by the defendant's negligence allegedly extends to an intervening criminal act by a third party.... [C]riminal acts may in themselves be foreseeable, and so within the scope of the created risk."

3. In determining whether intervening criminal conduct is foreseeable and thus within the scope of the risk, courts sometimes say that the plaintiff's burden of showing foreseeability is "heightened" or that the "the foreseeability of the risk be more precisely shown" in such cases. *See District of Columbia v. Beretta, U.S.A., Corp.*, 847 A.2d 1127 (D.C. 2004). Certainly courts continue to conclude that intervening criminal conduct was unforesee-

able to a reasonable person in particular cases. This conclusion will bar the plaintiff's recovery against a negligent defendant whether the result is explained by saying "no proximate cause" or "no duty." *See Wiener v. Southcoast Childcare Ctrs., Inc.,* 88 P.3d 517 (Cal. 2004) (defendant child care organization had four-foot fence, but Steven Abrams intentionally drove through it and into a group of children with his Cadillac, killing two and injuring others; *held,* his intentional act was unforeseeable, hence the defendant owed no duty of care with respect to it).

4. In *Hines v. Garrett,* 108 S.E. 690 (Va. 1921), the defendant railroad went past the plaintiff's station without stopping. The plaintiff was required to get off and walk back through an area which, as the railroad knew, was especially dangerous. Criminals in the dangerous area did in fact attack the plaintiff. She sued the railroad. The court imposed liability. Here is what is said: "We do not wish to be understood as questioning the general proposition that no responsibility for a wrong attaches whenever an independent act of a third person intervenes.... [But] this proposition does not apply where the very negligence alleged consists of exposing the injured party to the act causing the injury."

5. A landlord leasing apartments to women fails to control access to the landlord's copy of keys to the apartments and fails to maintain records of access. Someone used the landlord's keys to gain entrance to the plaintiff's apartment. The intruder raped the plaintiff. In the plaintiff's suit against the landlord, the defendant argued that the intruder was a superseding cause. The court said, quoting the RESTATEMENT (SECOND) OF TORTS § 449, cmt. *b:* "[t]he happening of the very event the likelihood of which makes the actor's conduct negligent and so subjects the actor to liability cannot relieve him from liability." *Tenney v. Atlantic Assocs.,* 594 N.W.2d 11 (Iowa 1999). Was the court accepting or rejecting the defendant's argument?

6. A strange decision is *Doe v. Linder Construction Co.,* 845 S.W.2d 173 (Tenn. 1992). The defendant developer of a planned united development retained copies of keys to the plaintiff's unit, with labels. He negligently allowed two workers on the premises access to the keys and they used them to enter the unit and rape the plaintiff. In the plaintiff's suit against the developer, the trial court granted summary judgment for defendants on the ground that the criminal act of the rapists was an independent intervening act that broke the causal chain. The Supreme Court of Tennessee affirmed. "[T]he acts of rape were criminal acts of which the defendants had no warning and which they had no reason to believe would occur.... [I]f the injury was not reasonably foreseeable, then the criminal act of the third party would be a superseding, intervening cause of the harm, relieving the [defendants] from liability." What *do* you foresee as a danger if you leave a woman's house key available for any worker at a large construction project? The *Linder* decision was roundly attacked in Leslie Bender, *Is Tort Law Male?: Foreseeability Analysis and Property Managers' Liability for Third Party Rapes of Residents,* 69 CHI.-KENT L. REV. 313 (1993).

DELANEY v. REYNOLDS

825 N.E.2d 554 (Mass. App. Ct. 2005)

[Plaintiff Delaney began to live with Defendant Reynolds, a police officer. The two lived at Reynolds's house. Reynolds routinely stored his gun, loaded and unlocked, in the bedroom. Reynolds knew that Delaney knew where he kept his gun. Reynolds also knew that Delaney was depressed and had substance abuse problems. One night Delaney smoked crack cocaine and was drinking heavily. Reynolds ordered her to move out of his house. While packing her belongings, Delaney took Reynolds's loaded gun from the bedroom. She went down the stairway towards the living room in which Reynolds was sitting, aimed the gun at the window, and pulled the trigger twice. The gun did not fire. Delaney then ran back up the stairs, pursued by Reynolds. When they reached the bedroom Delaney put the gun under her chin and pulled the trigger. This time the gun went off, seriously injuring her. In Delaney's suit against Reynolds for negligence, Reynolds claimed that Delaney's intentional act of attempting suicide was a superseding cause of her injuries. The trial judge agreed and granted Reynolds's motion for summary judgment.]

... Delaney, if she is to prevail on her claim, [must] prove that Reynolds was negligent and that his negligence was a proximate cause of her injury. As explained, "negligent conduct is the proximate cause of an injury ... [if] the injury to the plaintiff was a foreseeable result of the defendant's negligent conduct." ... This formulation is not altered when the original negligent act is followed by an independent act or event that actively operates in bringing about a plaintiff's injury, that is, a so-called intervening cause. Where the intervening occurrence was foreseeable by a defendant, the causal chain of events remains intact and the original negligence remains a proximate cause of a plaintiff's injury....

[Reviewing the case law leads] to the question whether, as matter of law, suicide is such an extraordinary event as not to be reasonably foreseeable. To date, reported decisions in which a defendant's antecedent negligence has been considered as a legal cause of a plaintiff's death by suicide have eschewed specific discussion of the foreseeability of suicide as a break in the chain of causation. Rather, it appears to be the historical view that a purposeful act of suicide, rather than any antecedent negligence, will be deemed the legal cause of a decedent's injury unless the defendant's negligence rendered the decedent unable to appreciate the self-destructive nature of the suicidal act or, even if able to appreciate the nature of the act, unable to resist the suicidal impulse.... Cases from other jurisdictions discussing the policies underlying this traditional rule cite to (1) the historic notion that suicide is an immoral or culpable act; (2) the reluctance to impose a duty to protect others from harm; (3) the inordinate burden of being one's brother's keeper and the too-great magnitude of imposing a burden to foresee and prevent a suicide; or (4) the unforeseeability of an intentionally self-destructive act.

Other jurisdictions have more recently gone beyond the traditional and often categorical basis for treating suicide as an intervening and superseding cause of injury and have considered various nontraditional circumstances as relevant to the issue of foreseeability. A review of these cases as well as our more recent holdings reveals that we have not limited our analysis of like cases to an ironclad rule, subject to ... limited exceptions ..., that suicide or an intentionally self-inflicted injury constitutes an intervening and superseding cause as matter of law....

[The trial judge ruled that Delaney intended to kill herself and thus her action was a superseding cause of her own harm as a matter of law. Delaney argues that whether she intended to kill herself was a contested issue of fact, given that the gun had misfired twice before she shot herself. We agree with her argument.]

Even were the jury to find that Delaney intended to commit suicide when she turned Reynolds's gun on herself with an intentional suicidal or self-injurious purpose, we think it should also be open to Delaney to show and the jury to find that the risk that she would handle or use Reynolds's gun in a manner so as to cause intentional injury to herself was foreseeable and that his failure to secure his gun was a proximate cause of her injury. See *Sarna v. American Bosch Magneto Corp.*, 195 N.E. 328 (Mass. 1935) (jury could properly find causation where decedent's act of meddling with tank containing poisonous gas could be expected when defendant abandoned tank in location where people came to salvage metal)....

Judgment reversed.

NOTES

1. Most states continue to follow the traditional rule—where a plaintiff intentionally attempts to commit or commits suicide, that act is a superseding cause of plaintiff's harm, freeing the defendant from any liability for negligence .. *See, e.g., Sindler v. Litman*, 887 A.2d 97 (Md. Ct. Spec. App. 2005) (citing cases from several jurisdictions). Some courts, following the lead of Restatement (Second) § 455, have recognized two main exceptions to this traditional rule: (1) where the defendant's tortious conduct induces a mental illness or an "uncontrollable impulse" in the plaintiff (or decedent) from which the suicide attempt (or suicide) results; and (2) where there is a special relationship between the two parties, that presumes or includes knowledge by the defendant of plaintiff's risk of committing suicide. *Johnstone v. City of Albuquerque*, 145 P.3d 76 (N.M. Ct. App. 2006); *Cook v. Shoshone First Bank*, 126 P.3d 886 (Wyo. 2006). A smaller number of states follow the approach adopted in *Delaney* and use a foreseeability test on a case-by-case basis. Which rule is preferable?

2. Do the suicide cases turn as much on the scope of the defendant's duty to the plaintiff as on the scope of risks created? *See* DOBBS ON TORTS § 195 (2000).

3. NEGLIGENT INTERVENING ACTS

DERDIARIAN v. FELIX CONTRACTING CORP.

414 N.E.2d 666 (N.Y. 1980)

COOKE, CHIEF JUDGE.

[Defendant Felix Contracting Corp. was installing an underground gas main, and for this purpose had excavated most of the eastbound lane of traffic. Felix engaged Bayside Pipe Coaters to seal the mains. Bayside had a kettle of liquid enamel, boiling to 400 degrees at the job site. Derdiarian worked for Bayside and was in charge of the kettle. Against Derdiarian's wishes, Felix insisted that he set up the kettle on the west side of the excavation, that is, facing the oncoming, eastbound traffic. Felix protected against this oncoming traffic by a single wooden horse barricade and by use of a single flagman.

[James Dickens was driving eastbound on Oak Street when he suffered a seizure and lost consciousness. Dickens was under treatment for epilepsy and had neglected to take his medication at the proper time. His car crashed through a single wooden horse-type barricade and struck the plaintiff, throwing him into the air. He was "splattered over his face, head and body with 400 degree boiling hot liquid enamel from a kettle struck by the automobile.... Although plaintiff's body ignited into a fire ball, he miraculously survived the incident."

[The jury found in favor of the plaintiff against Dickens, against Felix, and against Consolidated Edison. The Appellate Division affirmed. Only the claim against Felix is involved here.]

To support his claim of an unsafe work site, plaintiff called as a witness Lawrence Lawton, an expert in traffic safety. According to Lawton, the usual and accepted method of safeguarding the workers is to erect a barrier around the excavation. Such a barrier, consisting of a truck, a piece of heavy equipment or a pile of dirt, would keep a car out of the excavation and protect workers from oncoming traffic. The expert testified that the barrier should cover the entire width of the excavation. He also stated that there should have been two flagmen present, rather than one, and that warning signs should have been posted advising motorists that there was only one lane of traffic and that there was a flagman ahead.

Following receipt of the evidence, the trial court charged the jury, among other things, that it could consider, as some evidence of negligence, the violation of a Mount Vernon ordinance. The ordinance imposed upon a construction "permittee" certain safety duties. Defendant Felix now argues that plaintiff was injured in a freakish accident, brought about solely by defendant Dickens' negligence, and therefore there was no causal link, as a matter of law, between Felix' breach of duty and plaintiff's injuries.

The concept of proximate cause, or more appropriately legal cause, has proven to be an elusive one, incapable of being precisely defined to cover all situations. This is, in part, because the concept stems from policy considerations that serve to place manageable limits upon the liability that flows from negligent conduct. Depending upon the nature of the case, a variety of factors may be relevant in assessing legal cause. Given the unique nature of the inquiry in each case, it is for the finder of fact to determine legal cause, once the court has been satisfied that a prima facie case has been established. To carry the burden of proving a prima facie case, the plaintiff must generally show that the defendant's negligence was a substantial cause of the events which produced the injury. Plaintiff need not demonstrate, however, that the precise manner in which the accident happened, or the extent of injuries, was foreseeable (Restatement, Torts 2d, § 435, subd. 2).

Where the acts of a third person intervene between the defendant's conduct and the plaintiff's injury, the causal connection is not automatically severed. In such a case, liability turns upon whether the intervening act is a normal or foreseeable consequence of the situation created by the defendant's negligence. If the intervening act is extraordinary under the circumstances, not foreseeable in the normal course of events, or independent of or far removed from the defendant's conduct, it may well be a superseding act which breaks the causal nexus. Because questions concerning what is foreseeable and what is normal may be the subject of varying inferences, as is the question of negligence itself, these issues generally are for the fact finder to resolve.

There are certain instances, to be sure, where only one conclusion may be drawn from the established facts and where the question of legal cause may be decided as a matter of law. Those cases generally involve independent intervening acts which operate upon but do not flow from the original negligence. Thus, for instance, we have held that where an automobile lessor negligently supplies a car with a defective trunk lid, it is not liable to the lessee who, while stopped to repair the trunk, was injured by the negligent driving of a third party. (Ventricelli v. Kinney System Rent A Car), [45 N.Y.2d 950, 411 N.Y.S.2d 555, 383 N.E.2d 1149 (1978)]. Although the renter's negligence undoubtedly served to place the injured party at the site of the accident, the intervening act was divorced from and not the foreseeable risk associated with the original negligence. And the injuries were different in kind than those which would have normally been expected from a defective trunk. In short, the negligence of the renter merely furnished the occasion for an unrelated act to cause injuries not ordinarily anticipated.

By contrast, in the present case, we cannot say as a matter of law that defendant Dickens' negligence was a superseding cause which interrupted the link between Felix's negligence and plaintiff's injuries. From the evidence in the record, the jury could have found that Felix negligently failed to safeguard the excavation site. A prime hazard associated with such dereliction is the possibility that a driver will negligently enter the work site and cause injury to a worker. That the driver was negligent, or even reckless, does not insulate Felix from liability. Nor is it decisive that the driver lost control of the vehicle through a negligent failure to take medication, rather than a driving mistake. The precise manner of the event need not be anticipated. The finder of fact could have concluded that the foreseeable, normal and natural result of the risk created by Felix was the injury of a worker by a car entering the improperly protected work area. An intervening act may not serve as a superseding cause, and relieve an actor of responsibility, where the risk of the intervening act occurring is the very same risk which renders the actor negligent.

[Affirmed].

NOTES

1. Is *Derdiarian* consistent with the scope of the risk principle? The defendant could foresee some kind of harm from a motor vehicle entering the excavation and that is what happened. The precise manner in which the injury came about, as we know from *Hughes,* does not necessarily matter.

2. Once again, think about whether the manner in which the injury came about ever matters to the analysis of reasonable foreseeability. Suppose on facts like *Derdiarian* the injury occurs because an airplane crashes into the excavation. Try working that out under a scope of risk analysis.

3. In *Malolepszy v. State of Nebraska*, 729 N.W.2d 669 (Neb. 2007), the plaintiff was injured in an accident in a highway construction zone when another driver drove his vehicle from the shoulder into the lane in which the plaintiff was driving. The plaintiff sued the State, alleging it negligently failed to follow "fundamental safety principles when routing traffic" through the construction site. The trial court granted the State's motion for summary judgment on the ground that the second driver's action was a superseding cause of the plaintiff's injury, saying that the State could not have foreseen that a driver in that position "would negligently enter an oncoming lane of traffic without yielding to traffic in that lane." Affirming, the Supreme Court said that "the State was not bound to anticipate that a vehicle stopped along the shoulder of the road would suddenly pull out in front of oncoming traffic." The second driver's negligence was thus "an efficient intervening cause" freeing the State from liability. If the State was negligent for failing to do such things as post warning signs and provide an adequate reentry lane, what are the kinds of risks that such conduct creates?

4. Many, many cases use foreseeability in some fashion when there are intervening causes, but, like *Derdiarian* and *Malolepszy*, often speak of foreseeability of the intervening cause itself rather than foreseeability of the general result. *See, e.g., Summy v. City of Des Moines*, 708 N.W.2d 333 (Iowa 2006); *Contois v. Town of West Warwick*, 865 A.2d 1019 (R.I. 2004). Is this the risk rule coupled with a tendency to describe the risk by describing the mechanism that brings the risk about?

5. "Foreseeable intervening forces are within the scope of the original risk, and hence of the defendant's negligence. The courts are quite generally agreed that intervening causes which fall fairly in this category will not supersede the defendant's responsibility. Put another way, an intervening force which falls squarely within the scope of the original risk will not

supersede the defendant's responsibility." *Estate of Long ex rel. Smith v. Broadlawns Medical Center,* 656 N.W.2d 71 (Iowa 2003).

Try applying the logic: If the defendant airplane manufacturer negligently designs airplane cockpit doors so that terrorists can take over and crash the plane, could the designer who is found to be negligent possibly claim that the terrorism was an unforeseeable and therefore superseding cause? *See In re Sept. 11 Litigation,* 280 F. Supp. 2d 279 (S.D.N.Y. 2003). If it is negligent to leave your loaded gun out where it might be stolen and used feloniously, can the thief's act of taking and using the gun to kill be a superseding cause? *Heck v. Stoffer,* 786 N.E.2d 265 (Ind. 2003). If it is negligent to leave your unlocked loaded gun in a shoebox on a closet shelf, is your child's act of taking the gun out, playing with it, and accidentally shooting his friend a superseding cause of that other child's death? *Adames v. Sheahan,* 880 N.E.2d 559 (Ill. App. Ct. 2007).

6. In *Charles v. Lavergne,* 412 So.2d 726 (La. Ct. App. 1982), the plaintiff and a crew of workers were splicing a new electric cable to an old one on a pole near a highway. To permit this, a long length of cable lay across the road and was attached to the pole on which the plaintiff was working. Defendant drove his truck loaded with 48,000 pounds of rice across the cable. The cable bounded off the pavement and became entangled in the rear axle. This pulled the cable taut and broke the pole, causing the plaintiff to fall to the ground. He suffered injuries to his back, neck, leg and arm. The trial judge gave judgment for the defendant on the ground that he was under a duty to slow down "to avoid striking the workers" and that "this duty did not encompass the particular risk of the cable becoming entangled in the axle of the truck and causing the pole to break and throw the plaintiff to the ground." On appeal this was affirmed. "[W]e do not believe that the risk and harm caused in this case were within the scope of the protection afforded by the breach of any duty by the defendant." Is this inconsistent with *Derdiarian*? Would the Louisiana court have reached a different result if it had characterized the duty as the New York court did in *Derdiarian*? "A prime hazard," the New York court said there, was "that a driver will negligently enter the work site and cause injury to a worker."

VENTRICELLI v. KINNEY SYSTEM RENT A CAR, INC.

383 N.E.2d 1149, *modified,* 386 N.E.2d 263 (N.Y. 1978)

[Defendant Kinney leased plaintiff a car with a defective trunk lid that did not close satisfactorily. Kinney unsuccessfully attempted a repair. While the car was parked on Mott Street, the plaintiff and a passenger were attempting to slam the lid shut. One Maldonado was parked several car lengths behind the plaintiff. His car suddenly "jumped ahead" and ran into the plaintiff. The jury awarded plaintiff $550,000 for his injuries. The Appellate Division reversed and dismissed as to Kinney.]

MEMORANDUM.

Order of the Appellate Division affirmed, with costs. Proximate cause and foreseeability are relative terms, "nothing more than a convenient formula for disposing of the case" (Prosser, Law of Torts [4th ed.], § 43, p. 267). In writing of the "orbit of the duty," Chief Judge Cardozo said "[t]he range of reasonable apprehension is at times a question for the court, and at times, if varying inferences are possible, a question for the jury." (Palsgraf v. Long Is. R.R. Co., 248 N.Y. 339, 345, 162 N.E. 99, 101). So it is with proximate cause and foreseeability.

Although the negligence of the automobile renter, defendant Kinney, is manifest, and was, of course, a "cause" of the accident, it was not the proximate cause. "What we do mean by the word 'proximate' is that, because of convenience, of public policy, of a rough sense of justice, the law arbitrarily declines to trace a series of events beyond a certain point." (Palsgraf v. Long Is. R.R. Co., 248 N.Y. 339, 352, 162 N.E. 99, 103, supra [Andrews, J., dissenting]). The immediately effective cause of plaintiff's injuries was the negligence of Maldonado, the driver of the second car, in striking plaintiff while he was standing behind his parked automobile. That Kinney's negligence in providing an automobile with a defective trunk lid would result in plaintiff's repeated attempts to close the lid was reasonably foreseeable. Not "foreseeable," however, was the collision between vehicles both parked a brief interval before the accident. Plaintiff was standing in a relatively "safe" place, a parking space, not in an actively traveled lane. He might well have been there independent of any negligence of Kinney, as, for example, if he were loading or unloading the trunk. Under these circumstances, to hold the accident a foreseeable consequence of Kinney's negligence is to stretch the concept of foreseeability beyond acceptable limits (see Prosser, Law of Torts [4th ed.], pp. 267–270; Restatement, Torts 2d, § 435, subd. 2).

FUCHSBERG, JUDGE (dissenting)....

Ample was the proof that, to the knowledge of the rental company, the trunk door on the automobile it furnished to the plaintiff had a penchant for flying open so as to obstruct the operator's view while the vehicle was moving. Given these facts, it was not only foreseeable, but a most reasonable rather than a remote expectation, that a driver confronted by such an emergency would alight and promptly proceed to the rear of the car to attempt to secure the lid manually so that he might continue on his way without further danger to others and himself. The seemingly ineluctable consequence was to expose the driver to the danger of being struck by another vehicle while he was positioned behind the trunk. On these facts, it could readily be found, as the jury apparently did here, that the choice between the alternatives—the danger from the obstruction of the driver's view from the vehicle and the danger of being struck while engaged in the act of removing the danger—was thrust on the plaintiff by Kinney's negligence. Of course, whether in making the choice he did plaintiff himself was negligent similarly raised a factual issue within the province of the jury....

NOTES

1. The plaintiff in *Ventricelli* is injured trying to minimize a risk created by the the rental company. Why, then, can't the plaintiff win here? Is the intervening fault of Mr. Maldonado somehow less foreseeable than the intervening act of Mr. Dickens in the *Derdiarian* case?

2. Is the fact that the plaintiff in *Ventricelli* was not left in a "position of danger" by the rental company's negligence a sufficient way to distinguish the case from *Derdiarian*? Is the "position of danger" analysis merely a variant of the scope-of-risk rule?

3. Defendant negligently injures Plaintiff, who is then taken to a hospital for treatment. Is the Defendant liable for any subsequent negligence in medical treatment? While you might see this as a "position of safety" for the plaintiff, virtually all courts agree that when a defendant causes harm to a person, that defendant will also be liable for any "enhanced harm" caused by the later negligent provision of aid, including negligent medical treatment. *See* RESTATEMENT (THIRD) § 35 (P.F.D. No. 1, 2005). Courts have even extended the medical-treatment rule to other risks resulting from efforts to assist an injured person. *See, e.g., Anaya v. Superior Court*, 93 Cal.Rptr.2d 228 (Ct. App. 2000) ("Obviously, if the original tortfeasor is liable for injuries or death suffered during course of the treatment of injuries suffered in the accident, the original tortfeasor is liable for injuries or death suffered during transportation of the victim to a medical facility for treatment of the injuries resulting from the accident.") Is this rule consistent with the more general scope-of-risk rule?

MARSHALL v. NUGENT

222 F.2d 604 (1st Cir. 1955)

MAGRUDER, J.

[Plaintiff was a passenger in Harriman's car. There was ice and hard-packed snow on the highway. As Harriman topped a hill, he saw a truck coming toward him, partly in his lane. Harriman went off the road. The driver stopped to help pull the car back on the road. This effort partly blocked the road again, so the plaintiff walked toward the top of the hill to flag any approaching motorists. Before he could reach the top, Nugent drove over the hill, saw the truck blocking the road, and attempted to avoid it. He skidded into the plaintiff, Marshall. The plaintiff sued both Nugent and the truck driver. The jury found against the truck driver, who appeals urging that he was not a proximate cause.]

To say that the situation was created by the defendant's culpable acts constituted "merely a condition," not a cause of plaintiff's harm, is to indulge in mere verbiage, which does not solve the question at issue, but is simply a way of stating the conclusion, arrived at from other considerations, that the causal relation between the defendant's act and the plaintiff's injury is not strong enough to warrant holding the defendant legally responsible for the injury.

The adjective "proximate," as commonly used in this connection, is perhaps misleading, since to establish liability it is not necessarily true that the defendant's culpable act must be shown to have been the next or immediate cause of the plaintiff's injury. . . .

[S]peaking in general terms, the effort of the courts has been, in the development of this doctrine of proximate causation, to confine the liability of a negligent actor to those harmful consequences which result from the operation of the risk, or of a risk, the foreseeability of which rendered the defendant's conduct negligent.

Of course, putting the inquiry in these terms does not furnish a formula which automatically decides each of an infinite variety of cases. Flexibility is still preserved by the further need of defining the risk, or risks, either narrowly, or more broadly, as seems appropriate and just in the special type of case.

Regarding motor vehicle accidents in particular, one should contemplate a variety of risks which are created by negligent driving. There may be injuries resulting from a direct collision between the carelessly driven car and another vehicle. But such direct collision may be avoided, yet the plaintiff may fall and injure himself in frantically racing out of the way of the errant car. . . . Or the plaintiff may faint from intense excitement stimulated by the near collision, and in falling sustain a fractured skull. . . . This bundle of risks could be enlarged indefinitely with a little imagination. In a traffic mix-up due to negligence, before the disturbed waters have become placid and normal again, the unfolding of events between the culpable act and the plaintiff's eventual injury may be bizarre indeed; yet the defendant may be liable for the result. In such a situation, it would be impossible for a person in the defendant's position to predict in advance just how his negligent act would work out to another's injury. Yet this in itself is no bar to recovery.

When an issue of proximate cause arises in a borderline case, as not infrequently happens, we leave it to the jury with appropriate instructions. . . .

Exercising that judgment on the facts in the case at bar, we have to conclude that the district court committed no error in refusing to direct a verdict for the defendant Socony on the issue of proximate cause. . . .

Plaintiff Marshall was a passenger in the oncoming Chevrolet car, and thus was one of the persons whose bodily safety was primarily endangered by the negligence of Prince, as might have been found by the jury, in "cutting the corner" with the Socony truck in the circumstances above related. In that view, Prince's negligence constituted an irretrievable breach of duty to the plaintiff. Though this particular act of negligence was over and done with when the truck pulled up alongside of the stalled Chevrolet without having actually collided with it, still the consequences of such past negligence were in the bosom of time, as yet unrevealed.

If the Chevrolet had been pulled back onto the highway, and Harriman and Marshall, having got in it again, had resumed their journey and had had a collision with another car five miles down the road in which Marshall suffered bodily injuries, it could truly be said that such subsequent injury to Marshall was a consequence in fact of the earlier delay caused by the defendant's negligence, in the sense that but for such delay the Chevrolet car would not have been at the fatal intersection at the moment the other car ran into it. But on such assumed state of facts, the courts would no doubt conclude, "as a matter of law," that Prince's earlier negligence in cutting the corner was not the "proximate cause" of this later injury received by the plaintiff. That would be because the extra risks to which such negligence by Prince had subjected the passengers in the Chevrolet car were obviously entirely over; the situation had been stabilized and become normal, and, so far as one could foresee, whatever subsequent risks the Chevrolet might have to encounter in its resumed journey were simply the inseparable risks, no more and no less, that were incident to the Chevrolet's being out on the highway at all. But in the case at bar, the circumstances under which Marshall received the personal injuries complained of presented no such clear-cut situation....

NOTES

1. A phrase once used was "termination of the risk." In *Pittsburg Reduction Co. v. Horton*, 113 S.W. 647 (Ark. 1908), a boy named Copple found explosive dynamite caps that the defendant had negligently left in a place where children could be expected to pick them up. Copple kept them at home and his mother knew of them. A week later he traded them to a 13-year-old boy, Jack Horton. Horton lost a hand while playing with them. The court thought that Mrs. Copple's knowing tolerance of the shells "broke the causal connection" and that the defendant which had negligently scattered them around for the children to find would not be liable. "Charlie Copple's parents having permitted him to retain possession of the caps, his further acts in regard to them must be attributable to their permission and were wholly independent of the original negligence of appellants." Commentators have suggested that this is an example of a "terminated risk." Defendant's conduct created a risk but the risk so created was no longer existent. How do you have to describe the risk if this view is taken? Is the termination of the risk idea consistent with the risk principle?

2. The termination of the risk idea emphasizes that the plaintiff had reached a position of "apparent safety." In *Horton* this would be because one could presumably believe that a mother, having actually discovered the caps, would confiscate them or otherwise provide for safety. But this was not because somehow the defendant's fault had terminated; the defendant had no reason to think the caps had been put in the protective custody of the mother.

3. But if *Horton* is wrong, liability must end somewhere. What would you suggest?

4. Defendant leaves keys in his car. The car is stolen by a group of teenaged boys. Several hours and a hundred miles later, the driver runs down

a pedestrian. The pedestrian, unable to locate or collect from the boys, sues the defendant. Is the defendant negligent in leaving the keys in the car? If so, should the theft by the boys supersede the defendant's liability? What elements are most important here? The intended, intervening criminal act? The scope of the risk created by one leaving the keys in the car? The "termination" of the risk?

5. Sometimes courts resolve scope of risk issues involving intervening causes by saying that if the defendant's negligence "merely furnished a condition by which the injury was possible and a subsequent independent act caused the injury, the existence of such condition is not the proximate cause of injury." *Sturdevant v. Kent*, 322 P.2d 408 (Okla. 1958). Statements like this seem to add nothing to a sound analysis of scope of risk, and indeed courts that use such verbiage seldom pursue any analysis of foreseeability. In *Sheehan v. City of New York*, 354 N.E.2d 832 (N.Y. 1976), a transit authority bus stopped illegally in the driving lane to allow passengers to board or alight. At that point a city sanitation truck crashed into the bus, injuring the plaintiff, a bus passenger. Holding in favor of the bus company, the court concluded that the admitted negligence of the sanitation truck driver was "the sole proximate cause of the injuries, and that the continued presence of the bus in the traveling lane at the time it was struck merely furnished the condition or occasion for the occurrence of the event rather than one of its causes." Is this, as the *Marshall* court said, "mere verbiage," or is there something more to this "condition, not a cause" concept?

PROBLEM

Wolfe v. Gramlich, Inc.

Your client, Gramlich Corp., is being sued by Louis Wolfe on a negligence theory. The following facts are not disputed. Gramlich, as part of its business, maintained a large tank for storing tar. It negligently allowed the tar to spill over, so that it flowed from its premises onto an area where plaintiff, a 9-year-old boy, and other children often played.

One day, plaintiff walked into the tar to such depth that his feet were covered up to his ankles. When he returned to his house, his parents saw the tar on his feet and began to remove it by taking the child into the middle of the back yard and using a solvent which is regarded as a safe product for removing tar from skin. While the parents were so engaged, a second child ran into their yard and unexpectedly exploded a cap from a cap-pistol, creating a spark that ignited the fumes from the solvent and resulted in serious burns to plaintiff's legs.

Gramlich's general counsel believes that it might be able to move for summary judgment on the ground that its actions, even if negligent, were not a proximate cause of Wolfe's injuries. She has asked you, as outside counsel, to advise her on the strengths and weaknesses of such a motion.

AN END NOTE: THE FUTURE OF PROXIMATE CAUSE OR SCOPE OF RISK ANALYSIS

Proximate cause rules arose before the full development of the joint and several liability system coupled with contribution. Those rules also arose before the development of comparative fault systems. As we will begin to see in the next chapter, comparative fault systems are capable of apportioning liability among many tortfeasors, imposing greater liability upon those who are more at fault. Proximate cause rules, on the other hand, are all-or-nothing rules. In the intervening cause situation, the first actor may escape liability altogether, while the second bears the whole burden. That is surely as appropriate as it ever was when it is clear that the second defendant created an entirely new and different risk. When the judge merely feels that the second actor is much more at fault, it may be that proximate cause/superseding cause analyses are counterproductive and that comparative fault rules, with each tortfeasor liable for some portion of the damages, may provide the best solution.

Several courts have now said that superseding cause analyses are to be abandoned as confusing and duplicating the basic foreseeability/scope of risk rules. *See Barry v. Quality Steel Prods., Inc.,* 820 A.2d 258 (Conn. 2003); *Control Techniques, Inc. v. Johnson,* 762 N.E.2d 104 (Ind. 2002); *Torres v. El Paso Elec. Co.,* 987 P.2d 386 (N.M. 1999), *limited in Herrera v. Quality Pontiac,* 73 P.3d 181 (N.M. 2003). Do you regard this as a step toward resolving more cases by allocating liability according to fault rather than on an all-or-nothing basis? This is a point to bear in mind as we look at comparative fault apportionment of responsibility in the next chapter.

REFERENCES: On legal or proximate cause generally see DOBBS ON TORTS §§ 180–197 (2000); HARPER, JAMES & GRAY, THE LAW OF TORTS §§ 20.4–20.6 (2d Ed. 1986 & Supp.); C. MORRIS & C. MORRIS, TORTS, 158–201 (2d Ed. 1980).

SUBTOPIC 2. DEFENSES

■ ■ ■

About Defenses

A plaintiff who proves every element of a prima facie case for negligence will survive a directed verdict and get her claim to the jury. Nevertheless, her recovery may be defeated or reduced if the defendant mounts a successful affirmative defense. The defendant has the burden of proving affirmative defenses. This chapter and the two that follow examine the major affirmative defenses.

The defenses covered in this subtopic are the traditional ones. Legislatures may create other and narrow defenses for particular cases. Such defenses must be found in local statutes. Many other impediments to the plaintiff's recovery exist but are not necessarily affirmative defenses. Among these are rules that reduce or eliminate a defendant's duty of care and those that provide for complete immunity from tort liability. In addition, procedural impediments applied to particular claims like medical malpractice may vastly reduce the number of successful suits. Finally, among the partial defenses enacted by some legislatures are damages caps, limiting liability in particular cases. All of these appear in later chapters.

CHAPTER 9

CONTRIBUTORY/COMPARATIVE FAULT

■ ■ ■

§ 1. CONTRIBUTORY NEGLIGENCE: THE COMMON LAW RULE

BUTTERFIELD v. FORRESTER

11 East. 60, 103 Eng. Rep. 926 (1809)

This was an action on the case for obstructing a highway, by means of which obstruction the plaintiff, who was riding along the road, was thrown down with his horse, and injured, & c. At the trial before Bayley J. at Derby, it appeared that the defendant, for the purpose of making some repairs to his house, which was close by the road side at one end of the town, had put up a pole across this part of the road, a free passage being left by another branch or street in the same direction. That the plaintiff left a public house not far distant from the place in question at 8 o'clock in the evening in August, when they were just beginning to light candles, but while there was light enough left to discern the obstruction at 100 yards distance: and the witness, who proved this, said that if the plaintiff had not been riding very hard he might have observed and avoided it: the plaintiff however, who was riding violently, did not observe it, but rode against it, and fell with his horse and was much hurt in consequence of the accident; and there was no evidence of his being intoxicated at the time. On this evidence Bayley J. directed the jury, that if a person riding with reasonable and ordinary care could have seen and avoided the obstruction; and if they were satisfied that the plaintiff was riding along the street extremely hard, and without ordinary care, they should find a verdict for the defendant: which they accordingly did. [The plaintiff sought a "rule" which would have granted him a new trial.]

BAYLEY J. The plaintiff was proved to be riding as fast as his horse could go, and this was through the streets of Derby. If he had used ordinary care he must have seen the obstruction; so that the accident appeared to happen entirely from his own fault.

LORD ELLENBOROUGH C.J. A party is not to cast himself upon an obstruction which has been made by the fault of another, and avail himself of it, if he do not himself use common and ordinary caution to be in the right. In cases of persons riding upon what is considered to be the wrong side of the road, that would not authorize another purposely to ride up against them. One person being in fault will not dispense with another's using ordinary care for himself. Two things must concur to support this action, an obstruction in the road by the fault of the defendant, and no want of ordinary care to avoid it on the part of the plaintiff. [The new trial was refused.]

NOTES

1. **Contributory negligence.** After *Butterfield v. Forrester*, the courts developed the rule of contributory negligence as a complete, all-or-nothing defense. Even relatively minor failure of the plaintiff to exercise ordinary care for her own safety would completely bar recovery. This remained true even if the defendant's negligence was extreme, so long as it fell short of a reckless or wanton act.

2. **Justifying *Butterfield*.** It is important, for reasons that will later become apparent, to identify the several grounds on which the result in *Butterfield v. Forrester* might be justified.

(a) *The fault principle.* If liability is to be based upon fault and the defendant mulcted because his fault causes harm, should the same fault principle compel the faulty plaintiff to lose his case entirely?

(b) *Proximate cause.* Could *Butterfield v. Forrester* be understood as applying some view of proximate cause in which the plaintiff is treated as a superseding cause? Test this idea. Imagine that a child, standing near the obstruction, had been injured when the horse fell. Would the defendant, if negligent, have been liable for that?

(c) *Negligence.* Granted that the defendant owed the plaintiff a duty of care, was that duty breached? Formulate an argument that the defendant's conduct was not negligent at all. Try to draw on specific cases or hypotheticals for a principle or general idea that furthers the defendant's argument.

3. **Origin of the rule.** Why do you think the contributory negligence rule developed in such a stringent fashion? Rules often develop from social and economic needs or assumptions. But sometimes a rule develops from a conceptual failure, that is, because legal professionals are unable at the moment to put together a coherent or logical idea about what a rule ought to be. Does the contributory negligence rule reflect social or economic standards or merely a conceptual failure?

4. **Avoiding the bar to recovery.** In several situations courts found reasons not to apply the contributory negligence defense. When an exception applied, the plaintiff made a full recovery in spite of her own fault. It was still an all-or-nothing system, but when an exception applied it was "all" rather than "nothing" for the plaintiff. We will look at these exceptions and how they fare under modern comparative negligence law in §§ 3–5 below.

§ 2. ADOPTING AND APPLYING COMPARATIVE FAULT RULES

NEW YORK MCKINNEY'S CIV. PRAC. LAW § 1411

In any action to recover damages for personal injury, injury to property, or wrongful death, the culpable conduct attributable to the claimant or to the decedent, including contributory negligence or assumption of risk, shall not bar recovery, but the amount of damages otherwise recoverable shall be diminished in the proportion which the culpable conduct attributable to the claimant or decedent bears to the culpable conduct which caused the damages.

WISCONSIN STAT. ANN. § 895.045

Contributory negligence does not bar recovery in an action by any person or the person's legal representative to recover damages for negligence resulting in death or in injury to person or property, if that negligence was not greater than the negligence of the person against whom recovery is sought, but any damages allowed shall be diminished in the proportion to the amount of negligence attributed to the person recovering. . . .

NOTES

1. **Adoption of comparative fault rules.** The Federal Employers' Liability Act (FELA), 45 U.S.C. § 53, was promulgated in 1906 to facilitate claims against interstate railroads by workers injured on the job. It adopted a comparative negligence system as one of its major provisions. Another federal statute, the Jones Act, applied the FELA rules to seafaring workers. Only a handful of states adopted comparative fault systems until a wave of change occurred after the late 1960s. As of the early 21st century, only Alabama, North Carolina, Maryland, Virginia, and the District of Columbia have failed to adopt comparative fault rules. In those jurisdictions, the plaintiff's contributory fault remains a complete bar.

2. **Pure vs. modified comparative fault.** The approach represented by the New York statute, *supra*, is called pure comparative fault. The approach represented by the Wisconsin statute is called modified comparative fault.

3. **Jury role in attributing fault percentages.** How much fault is attributable to each party? If the evidence permits reasonable people to differ, this is a "fact" question, not a question of law. Attribution of fault percentages is necessarily a rough approximation even though it is expressed in mathematical terms. The jury is usually told, in effect, to treat all of the fault in the case as 100% and to then find the percentage of fault attributable to each person.

4. **Applying the rules.** Suppose four cars, driven by P, B, C and D all collide. P is guilty of 5% of the negligence, B 10%, C 40% and D 45%. P has damages of $100,000. What does P recover?

5. **Information to the jury.** Should the jury be told how its comparative fault findings will impact an award of damages? In *Sollin v. Wangler*, 627 N.W.2d 159 (N.D. 2001), Dale Wangler, who was attempting to load a 1200–pound bale of straw into a grinder, dropped it on Richard Sollin, causing serious injuries. The jury assigned 50% of the fault to Sollin, the plaintiff, and 50% to Wangler, the defendant. It then awarded Sollin $100,000 in damages and Wangler $8,000. The trial judge did not answer the jury's question—"is the of fault going to determine damage awards?" The North Dakota comparative fault statute barred plaintiffs from recovering if their fault was "as great as the combined fault of all other persons." Because plaintiff's fault was as great as defendant's fault, the trial court dismissed with prejudice the plaintiff's claim. The North Dakota Supreme Court rejected "the blindfold rule" and held that the jury should have been informed of the legal consequences of its verdict. The court wrote, "The jury's lack of knowledge does not eliminate sympathy and bias, but merely insures that the jury makes its decision in greater ignorance."

6. **Two types of modified comparative fault systems.** Notice the two types of modified comparative fault represented by the Wisconsin statute on the one hand and the North Dakota statute, from *Sollin* in note 5, on the other. In Wisconsin what would a plaintiff recover in a two-party collision if his damages were $10,000 and his fault 50%? In North Dakota, what result?

WASSELL v. ADAMS

865 F.2d 849 (7th Cir. 1989)

POSNER, CIRCUIT JUDGE.

The plaintiff, born Susan Marisconish, grew up on Macaroni Street in a small town in a poor coal-mining region of Pennsylvania—a town so small and obscure that it has no name. She was the ninth of ten children, and as a child was sexually abused by her stepfather. After graduating from high school she worked briefly as a nurse's aide, then became engaged to Michael Wassell, also from Pennsylvania. Michael joined the Navy in 1985 and was sent to Great Lakes Naval Training Station, just north of Chicago, for basic training. He and Susan had decided to get married as soon as he completed basic training. The graduation was scheduled for a Friday. Susan, who by now was 21 years old, traveled to Chicago with Michael's parents for the graduation. The three checked into a double room at the Ron–Ric motel, near the base.... The Ron–Ric is a small and inexpensive motel that caters to the families of sailors at the Great Lakes Naval Training Station a few blocks to the east. The motel has 14 rooms and charges a maximum of $36 a night for a double room. The motel was owned by Wilbur and Florena Adams, the defendants in the case.

Four blocks to the west of the Ron–Ric motel is a high-crime area: murder, prostitution, robbery, drugs—the works. The Adamses occasionally warned women guests not to walk alone in the neighborhood at night. They did not warn the Wassells or Susan. [The plaintiff stayed on in the motel after the Wassels left; she was to look for an apartment because

Michael was to be stationed there permanently.] She spent most of Sunday in her room reading the newspaper and watching television. In the evening she went to look at an apartment. Upon returning to her room at the motel, she locked the door, fastened the chain, and went to bed. She fell into a deep sleep, from which she was awakened by a knock on the door. She turned on a light and saw by the clock built into the television set that it was 1:00 a.m. She went to the door and looked through the peephole but saw no one. Next to the door was a pane of clear glass. She did not look through it. The door had two locks plus a chain. She unlocked the door and opened it all the way, thinking that Michael had come from the base and, not wanting to wake her, was en route to the Adamses' apartment to fetch a key to the room. It was not Michael at the door. It was a respectably dressed black man whom Susan had never seen before. He asked for "Cindy" (maybe "Sidney," she thought later). She told him there was no Cindy there. Then he asked for a glass of water. She went to the bathroom, which was at the other end of the room . . . to fetch the glass of water. When she came out of the bathroom, the man was sitting at the table in the room. (The room had a screen door as well as a solid door, but the screen door had not been latched.) He took the water but said it wasn't cold enough. He also said he had no money, and Susan remarked that she had $20 in her car. The man went into the bathroom to get a colder glass of water. Susan began to get nervous. She was standing between the bathroom and the door of her room. She hid her purse, which contained her car keys and $800 in cash that Michael had given her. There was no telephone in the room. There was an alarm attached to the television set, which would be activated if someone tried to remove the set, but she had not been told and did not know about the alarm, although a notice of the alarm was posted by the set. The parking lot on which the motel rooms opened was brightly lit by floodlights.

A few tense minutes passed after the man entered the bathroom. He poked his head out of the doorway and asked Susan to join him in the bathroom, he wanted to show her something. She refused. After a while he emerged from the bathroom—naked from the waist down. Susan fled from the room, and beat on the door of the adjacent room. There was no response. The man ran after her and grabbed her. She screamed, but no one appeared. The motel had no security guard; the Adamses lived in a basement apartment at the other end of the motel and did not hear her screams.

The man covered Susan's mouth and dragged her back to her room. There he gagged her with a wash cloth. He raped her at least twice (once anally). These outrages occupied more than an hour. Eventually Susan persuaded the rapist to take a shower with her. After the shower, she managed to get out of the bathroom before he did, dress, and flee in her car. To save herself after the rapes, she had tried to convince him that she liked him, and had succeeded at least to the extent that his guard was down. The Adamses' lawyer tried halfheartedly to show that she had consented to the rapes, but backed off from this position in closing argument.

The rapist was never prosecuted; a suspect was caught but Susan was too upset to identify him. There had been a rape at the motel several years previously (a sailor had opened the door of his room to two men who said they were "the management," and the men raped his wife). There had also been a robbery, and an incident in which an intruder kicked in the door to one of the rooms. These were the only serious crimes committed during the seven years that the Adamses owned the motel.

Susan married Michael, but the rape had induced post-trauma stress that has, according to her testimony and that of a psychologist testifying as her expert witness, blighted her life. She brought this suit against the Adamses on January 21, 1986. It is a diversity suit that charges the Adamses with negligence in failing to warn Susan or take other precautions to protect her against the assault. The substantive issues are governed by the law of Illinois. A jury composed of four women and three men found that the Adamses had indeed been negligent and that their negligence had been a proximate cause of the assault, and the jury assessed Susan's damages at $850,000, which was the figure her lawyer had requested in closing argument. But in addition the jury found that Susan had been negligent too—and indeed that her negligence had been 97 percent to blame for the attack and the Adamses' only 3 percent. . . . [T]he jury awarded Susan only $25,500 in damages. This happens to be approximately the midpoint of the psychologist's estimate—$20,000 to $30,000—of the expense of the therapy that the psychologist believes Susan may need for her post-traumatic stress. . . .

Susan Wassell's counsel argues that the jury's verdict "reflected a chastened, hardened, urban mentality—that lurking behind every door is evil and danger, even if the guest is from a small town unfamiliar with the area." He takes umbrage at the defendants' argument that Susan's "antennae" should have been alerted when she didn't see anyone through the peephole. He rejects the metaphor, remarking unexceptionably that human beings do not have antennae and that this case is not a Kafka story about a person who turned into an insect (i.e., is not *The Metamorphosis*). He points out that a person awakened from a deep sleep is not apt to be thinking clearly and that once Susan opened the door the fat was in the fire—if she had slammed the door in the rapist's face he might have kicked the door in, as had happened once before at this motel, although she didn't know that at the time. The Adamses' counsel argued to the jury (perhaps with the wisdom of hindsight) that Susan's "tragic mistake" was failing to flee when the man entered the bathroom. Susan's counsel insists that Susan was not negligent at all but that, if she was, she was at most 5 percent responsible for the catastrophe, which, he argues, could have been averted costlessly by a simple warning from the Adamses. To this the Adamses' counsel replies absurdly that a warning would have been costly—it might have scared guests away! The loss of business from telling the truth is not a social loss; it is a social gain. . . .

The old common law rule barring the contributorily negligent plaintiff from recovering any damages came eventually to seem too harsh. That is why it has been changed in most jurisdictions, including Illinois. It was harsh, all right, at least if one focuses narrowly on the plight of individual plaintiffs, but it was also simple and therefore cheap to administer. The same cannot be said for comparative negligence, which far from being simple requires a formless, unguided inquiry, because there is no method- ology for comparing the causal contributions of the plaintiff's and of the defendant's negligence to the plaintiff's injury. In this case, either the plaintiff or the defendants could have avoided that injury. It is hard to say more, but the statute requires more—yet without giving the finder of facts any guidance as to how to make the apportionment.

We have suggested in previous cases that one way to make sense of comparative negligence is to assume that the required comparison is between the respective costs to the plaintiff and to the defendant of avoiding the injury. If each could have avoided it at the same cost, they are each 50 percent responsible for it. According to this method of comparing negligence, the jury found that Susan could have avoided the attack at a cost of less than one thirty-second the cost to the Adamses. Is this possible?

It is careless to open a motel or hotel door in the middle of the night without trying to find out who is knocking. Still, people aren't at their most alert when they are awakened in the middle of the night, and it wasn't crazy for Susan to assume that Michael had returned without telling her, even though he had said he would be spending the night at the base. So it cannot be assumed that the cost ... to the reasonable person who found himself or herself in her position ... was zero, or even that it was slight. As innkeepers (in the increasingly quaint legal term), the Adamses had a duty to exercise a high degree of care to protect their guests from assaults on the motel premises. And the cost to the Adamses of warning all their female guests of the dangers of the neighborhood would have been negligible. Surely a warning to Susan would not have cost the Adamses 32 times the cost to her of schooling herself to greater vigilance.

But this analysis is incomplete. It is unlikely that a warning would have averted the attack. Susan testified that she thought the man who had knocked on the door was her fiance. Thinking this, she would have opened the door no matter how dangerous she believed the neighborhood to be. The warning that was not given might have deterred her from walking alone in the neighborhood. But that was not the pertinent danger. Of course, if the Adamses had told her not to open her door in the middle of the night under any circumstances without carefully ascertaining who was trying to enter the room, this would have been a pertinent warning and might have had an effect. But it is absurd to think that hoteliers are required to give so obvious a warning, any more than they must warn guests not to stick their fingers into the electrical outlets. Everyone, or at least the average person, knows better than to open his or her door to a stranger in the middle of the night. The problem was not that Susan thought that she should open her bedroom door in the middle of the night to anyone who knocked, but that she wasn't thinking clearly. A warning would not have availed against a temporary, sleep-induced lapse.

Giving the jury every benefit of the doubt, ... we must assume that the jury was not so muddle-headed as to believe that the Adamses' negligence consisted in failing to give a futile warning. Rather, we must assume that the jury thought the Adamses' negligence consisted in failing to have a security guard, or telephones in each room, or alarms designed to protect the motel's patrons rather than just the owners' television sets. (The Adamses did, however, have an informal agreement with the local police that the police would cruise through the parking lot of the Ron–Ric whenever they drove down the street at night—and this was maybe three or four times a night.) The only one of these omitted precautions for which there is a cost figure in the record was the security guard. A guard would have cost $50 a night. That is almost $20,000 a year. This is not an enormous number. The plaintiff suggests that it would have been even lower because the guard would have been needed only on busy nights. But the evidence was in conflict on whether the Sunday night after a Friday graduation, which is the night that Susan was attacked, was a busy night. And the need for a security guard would seem to be greater, the less busy rather than the busier the motel; if there had been someone in the room adjacent to Susan's, she might have been saved from her ordeal. In any event the cost of the security guard, whether on all nights or just on busy nights—or just on unbusy nights—might be much greater than the monetary equivalent of the greater vigilance on the part of Susan that would have averted the attack....

If we were the trier of fact, persuaded that both parties were negligent and forced to guess about the relative costs to the plaintiff and to the defendants of averting the assault, we would assess the defendants' share at more than 3 percent. But we are not the trier of fact, and are authorized to upset the jury's apportionment only if persuaded that the trial judge abused his discretion in determining that the jury's verdict was not against the clear weight of the evidence. We are not so persuaded. It seems probably wrong to us, but we have suggested an interpretation of the evidence under which the verdict was consistent with the evidence and the law. And that is enough to require us to uphold the district judge's refusal to set aside the verdict.

Affirmed.

Nᴏᴛᴇs

1. **A caution.** It may be difficult to reach the central issues decided by the *Wassell* court. The facts themselves are likely to generate strong feelings of anger, sympathy and frustration that somehow the victim is blamed for the outrage of another. On the other hand, some readers may feel that it is by no means clear that the defendant motel owners were themselves negligent.

2. **Comparing fault.** What conduct was alleged to have been negligent on the part of the motel owners? On the part of the plaintiff? If a reasonable jury could find that both parties failed to use reasonable care, how should the parties' negligence be compared?

3. **Comparing fault by comparing costs of safety.** Do you estimate the amount of negligence and contributory negligence by comparing costs of non-negligent conduct for each party? That is the approach Judge Posner took. Under Judge Posner's approach, what percentages of negligence on the part of each party would he find if each could have avoided the harm by expending $100?

4. **Costs of achieving safety.** Judge Posner seems to compare the costs of having a security guard on all nights or just on busy or unbusy nights, with "the monetary equivalent of the greater vigilance on the part of Susan that would have averted the attack." Should the motel's yearly cost for increased security be compared with the greater vigilance of one potential victim? Judge Posner seems to think the plaintiff would have had "costs" in avoiding the injury. Could those costs be reasonably quantified? Would it matter to the cost comparison whether the defendant was at fault for not giving a warning (cost free) or for failing to have a security guard?

5. **Where reasonable care by one party eliminates the need for care by the other.** In a fraud and misrepresentation case against a lawyer— concededly a different kind of case from *Wassell*—Judge Posner had this to say about contributory negligence:

> Due care is the care that is optimal given that the other party is exercising due care. It is not the higher level of care that would be optimal if potential tort victims were required to assume that the rest of the world was negligent. A pedestrian is not required to exercise a level of care (e.g., wearing a helmet or a shin guard) that would be optimal if there were no sanctions against reckless driving. Otherwise drivers would be encouraged to drive recklessly, and knowing this pedestrians would be encouraged to wear helmets and shin guards. The result would be a shift from a superior method of accident avoidance (not driving recklessly) to an inferior one (pedestrian armor).... The law normally does not require duplicative precautions unless one is likely to fail or the consequences of failure ... would be catastrophic.

Greycas, Inc. v. Proud, 826 F.2d 1560, 1566 (7th Cir. 1987). How does this kind of analysis work, if at all, in a case like *Wassell*?

6. **Harm to self versus harms to others.** Should the plaintiff's fault be considered at all in a case in which that fault poses no risk to the defendant? The risks involved in a negligence action are often risks to others' safety. However, in comparative fault, the risks may be only to the plaintiff and not to others. Because of this difference in risk, some scholars have argued that the concepts of negligence and contributory negligence should be kept separate. *See* Gary T. Schwartz, *Contributory and Comparative Negligence: A Reappraisal,* 87 YALE L.J. 697 (1978). In addition, some courts have suggested that plaintiff fault be judged by a different, subjective standard. *See Dodson v. South Dakota Dept. of Human Svcs.,* 703 N.W.2d 353 (S.D. 2005) (jury should have been instructed to evaluate plaintiff's contributory negli-

gence in light of her own mental capacity). However, the Restatement Third of Torts treats risks to self and others in the same way. RESTATEMENT (THIRD) OF TORTS: LIABILITY FOR PHYSICAL HARM § 3 cmt. *b* (Proposed Final Draft No. 1, 2005).

7. **Where the parties are under different standards of care.** Can comparative fault judgments be any more difficult to make than they were in *Wassell*? Maybe. Consider the difficulties that would arise if the plaintiff and defendant were operating under different duties or standards of care, a possibility we'll see in Chapter 12. If both plaintiff and defendant are negligent, how would you compare the fault of the defendant who owed the highest degree of care with the fault of the plaintiff who owed only ordinary care? In *Aguallo v. City of Scottsbluff,* 678 N.W.2d 82 (Neb. 2004), the court seemed to say that the trier should estimate the deviation of the plaintiff from her ordinary care standard, then estimate the deviation of the defendant from his special standard of care, then compare the two deviations. How would the trier do that?

8. **Apportioning the unknown fault in res ipsa loquitur cases.** How is apportionment of fault to proceed in a res ipsa case involving a plaintiff's comparative negligence? The Connecticut court in *Giles v. City of New Haven,* 636 A.2d 1335 (Conn. 1994), said that the judge, after determining that the requirements of res ipsa were sufficiently met to send the case to the jury on that theory, "should thereafter instruct the jury to compare the negligence of the plaintiff, if any, with that of the defendant to decide what percentages to attribute to each party." How is the jury to assign a percentage of fault to each when the defendant's negligence is not known? Is res ipsa loquitur simply not well suited to the proportional system of comparative fault?

9. **Apportioning fault by an "equitable and just" approach.** Maine has a comparative negligence rule radically different from most. Instead of requiring the jury to reduce the plaintiff's damages in proportion to the plaintiff's relative fault, the statute requires the jury to make a reduction it considers to be equitable and just. In *Pelletier v. Fort Kent Golf Club,* 662 A.2d 220 (Me. 1995), the jury found that the defendant was more negligent than the plaintiff and that the plaintiff suffered $250,000 in damages. Yet the award was only $40,000. The court held this was within the jury's discretion. It is obvious that the jury could not have made its reduction on the basis of proportional fault, since on that basis the plaintiff would have recovered something more than $125,000. If the verdict was not based on any legal rule, what might have motivated to the jury? Do you think the *Wassell* jury would have brought in a different verdict under the Maine statute?

RESTATEMENT (THIRD) OF TORTS, APPORTIONMENT OF LIABILITY

(2000)

§ 8. FACTORS FOR ASSIGNING SHARES OF RESPONSIBILITY

Factors for assigning percentages of responsibility to each person whose legal responsibility has been established include

(a) the nature of the person's risk-creating conduct, including any awareness or indifference with respect to the risks created by the conduct and any intent with respect to the harm created by the conduct; and

(b) the strength of the causal connection between the person's risk-creating conduct and the harm.

a. Assigning shares of responsibility. The factfinder assigns comparative percentages of "responsibility" to parties and other relevant persons whose negligence or other legally culpable conduct was a legal cause of the plaintiff's injury. The factfinder does not assign percentages of "fault," "negligence," or "causation."

"Responsibility" is a general and neutral term. Assigning shares of "fault" or "negligence" can be misleading because some causes of action are not based on negligence or fault. Assigning shares of "causation" wrongly suggests that indivisible injuries jointly caused by two or more actors can be divided on the basis of causation. Assigning shares of "culpability" could be misleading if it were not made clear that "culpability" refers to "legal culpability," which may include strict liability.

Of course, it is not possible to precisely compare conduct that falls into different categories, such as intentional conduct, negligent conduct, and conduct governed by strict liability, because the various theories of recovery are incommensurate. However, courts routinely compare seemingly incommensurate values, such as when they balance safety and productivity in negligence or products liability law. "Assigning shares of responsibility" may be a less confusing phrase because it suggests that the factfinder, after considering the relevant factors, assigns shares of responsibility rather than compares incommensurate quantities. Nevertheless, the term "comparative responsibility" is used pervasively by courts and legislatures to describe percentage-allocation systems.

b. Causation and scope of liability. Conduct is relevant for determining percentage shares of responsibility only when it caused the harm and when the harm is within the scope of the person's liability.

c. Factors in assigning shares of responsibility. The relevant factors for assigning percentages of responsibility include the nature of each person's risk-creating conduct and the comparative strength of the causal connection between each person's risk-creating conduct and the harm. The nature of each person's risk-creating conduct includes such things as how unreasonable the conduct was under the circumstances, the extent to which the conduct failed to meet the applicable legal standard, the circumstances surrounding the conduct, each person's abilities and disabilities, and each person's awareness, intent, or indifference with respect to the risks. The comparative strength of the causal connection between the conduct and the harm depends on how attenuated the causal connection is, the timing of each person's conduct in causing the harm, and a comparison of the risks created by the conduct and the actual harm suffered by the plaintiff.

One or more of these factors may be relevant for assigning percentages of responsibility, even though they may not be a necessary element proving a particular claim or defense. However, these factors are irrelevant even to apportionment if there is no causal connection between the referenced conduct and the plaintiff's injuries. See Comment b. It should be noted that the mental-state factors in this Section may be considered for apportioning responsibility even if they are not themselves causally connected to the plaintiff's injury, as long as the risk-creating conduct to which they refer is causally connected to the injury.

NOTES

1. **The Restatement factors.** Is the Restatement correct in inviting the trier to consider mental states of the parties and the strength of causal connections as well as the unjustified risks they created? Is this just an elaborate version of Maine's "equitable and just" apportionment?

2. **Comparing fault and causation.** Think back to *Anderson* from Chapter 7. In that case salt water from an oil company and salt water from a disposal company killed the fish in the lake. Imagine that the oil company dumped twice as much salt water as the disposal company, and that the salt water was twice as concentrated, and therefore harmful. However, suppose also that an expert testified that it was somewhat more likely that the salt water from the disposal company reached the lake first. In addition, there was testimony that the disposal company knew with substantial certainty that the salt water would enter the lake, while the oil company should have known of the unreasonable risk. Is the Restatement formula helpful here? Would the Restatement factors have been helpful to the jury or to the appellate court in *Wassell*?

§ 3. ALL-OR-NOTHING JUDGMENTS AFTER COMPARATIVE FAULT

1. *No plaintiff negligence.* Comparison of plaintiff and defendant fault is only at issue when both parties are negligent. If the plaintiff is not negligent, or if her negligence is not the actual or proximate cause of the harm. No comparison is necessary. *See Harmon v. Washburn,* 751 N.W.2d 297 (S.D. 2008) (as a matter of law plaintiff was not negligent to pass another car on a bridge in a legal passing zone so that trial court should not have permitted comparison).

2. *Plaintiff negligence that is not the actual cause of injury.* Suppose the plaintiff is negligent because she is walking a dog she can't control. She then trips on the sidewalk. However, there is no evidence that she tripped on the sidewalk because she couldn't control the dog. Her negligence does not reduce her damages any more than it would make her liable for the defendant's injuries. *See Townsend v. Legere,* 688 A.2d 77 (N.H. 1997). *See also Pavlou v. City of New York,* 868 N.E.2d 186 (N.Y. 2007) (worker operated a crane with an excess load, but a crack in the crane made it unsafe to operate with any load).

3. *Plaintiff injury that is not within the scope of the risk created by plaintiff's negligence.* It is also possible that the plaintiff's fault will be disregarded because the injury suffered was not within the risk created by that fault. Consider: a house guest negligently blunders onto a dark patio. He is negligent because he is unfamiliar with the place and he might easily trip or fall into the swimming pool. Instead he is struck by his host's runaway car which crashes through the back gate. *See* Dan B. Dobbs, *Accountability and Comparative Fault*, 47 LA. L. REV. (1987). *See also Estate of Moses ex rel. Moses v. Southwestern Virginia Transit Management Co.*, 643 S.E.2d 156 (Va. 2007), reinstating a jury verdict for the plaintiff on the ground that it was within the province of the jury to decide whether the pedestrian's negligence—crossing in the middle of the street when the street looked clear—was a proximate cause of the accident in which he was hit by a bus.

4. *No defendant negligence.* The same all-or-nothing result will obtain if the defendant is not negligent, or if the defendant's negligence is not the actual or proximate cause of the plaintiff's harm. When an element of plaintiff's prima facie case against the defendant fails, comparative fault is irrelevant and the plaintiff recovers nothing.

5. *Sorting claims into all-or-nothing or comparative elements.* Under the old regime of contributory negligence, a court could say the plaintiff was at fault, or that the defendant's conduct was not an actual or legal cause of the plaintiff's harm, and the result would be the same whichever view the court took—no recovery for the plaintiff. With the adoption of comparative fault, you really need to know whether you are talking about fault or actual or proximate cause because the effects can now be quite different.

6. *Reasonable care by the defendant in light of plaintiff fault?* What if the defendant doctor fails to diagnose a medical-expert patient who failed to give the doctor the information needed to make an accurate diagnosis. Is this a case of the plaintiff's comparative fault or the defendant's non-negligence? On similar facts, see *Juchniewcz v. Bridgeport Hosp.*, 914 A.2d 511 (Conn. 2007).

7. *Plaintiff's fault as a superseding cause of the harm.* Typically, when both plaintiff and defendant are at fault, the court will leave the apportionment of responsibility to the jury. However, in some cases, courts disclaim plaintiff's recovery altogether on superseding cause grounds. In *Exxon Co., U.S.A. v. Sofec, Inc.*, 517 U.S. 830 (1996), an Exxon tanker broke away from moorings owned by one defendant and operated by another. The captain managed to get the tanker safely past a number of perils nearby and safely out to sea. But once he reached safety, he neglected to get a fix on his position and he ran aground. The ship was substantially destroyed. Exxon claimed that the owner and operator of the moorings were responsible for the breakaway. The Court held that even if that were so, the captain's negligence in failing to fix his position once he had reached a position of relative safety was a superseding cause. So

Exxon could recover nothing, even though admiralty law, which governed the case, uses pure comparative fault to divide damages.

Similarly, in *Wright v. New York City Transit Authority*, 633 N.Y.S.2d 393 (N.Y. App. Div. 1995), a passenger was injured when he entered an unlocked subway motorman's cab and stuck his head outside the cab window of the moving train. The court held as a matter of law that the plaintiff passenger's conduct was a superseding cause that broke the causal connection between his injuries and the Transit Authority's asserted negligence in leaving the cab unlocked.

Is this analysis right? According to Professor Dobbs, *Wright* "is arguably the very kind of case that ought to be left to comparative fault allocation, because the case must rely on the plaintiff's fault rather than on the limited scope of the risk created by the defendant." DOBBS ON TORTS § 196, at 489 n.4 (2000).

On the superseding cause topic, *see* Michael D. Green, *The Unanticipated Ripples of Comparative Negligence: Superseding Cause in Products Liability and Beyond*, 53 S.C. L. REV. 1103 (2002) (criticizing *Sofec* unless it is construed quite narrowly); *and* Paul T. Hayden, *Butterfield Rides Again: Plaintiff's Negligence as Superseding or Sole Proximate Cause in Systems of Pure Comparative Responsibility*, 33 LOYOLA L.A. L. REV. 887 (2000).

8. *Causal apportionment of separate injuries.* Comparative fault reductions may also be inappropriate when the plaintiff and the defendant cause separate injuries. Suppose the plaintiff negligently crashes her car into a tree, sustaining multiple injuries. Dr. Dann's negligent treatment causes paralysis of her legs, which appropriate medical treatment could have avoided. The physician in such a case is liable for his enhancement of the plaintiff's injury, but he is not liable for the initial injury itself. Of course, if the plaintiff and defendant cause indivisible injuries the result would be different.

9. *The mitigation of damages rule.* The avoidable consequences or mitigation of damages rule traditionally required the plaintiff to minimize her damages by reasonable efforts and expenses. If a plaintiff whose foot was bruised by the defendant's negligence could avoid loss of the foot by taking antibiotics, she might be expected to do so. If she unreasonably refused and lost the foot as a result, she would not be allowed to recover for loss of the foot, although of course she would be permitted to recover for the bruise.

This is not a rule of comparative fault. Instead, it simply excluded all recovery for a particular item of harm when the court concluded either that the defendant was not a but-for cause of that harm or that the harm was outside the scope of the risk negligently created by the defendant. When the plaintiff failed to take the prescribed antibiotics, some courts might treat the loss of her foot as if it were caused entirely by the plaintiff's fault. Such courts would not compare fault of the plaintiff in failing to take antibiotics with fault of the defendant in causing the injury in the first place. Instead, they would simply exclude liability for loss of the foot.

Automatic exclusion of all recovery in the foot example looks like an attempt to make a causal apportionment. If so, it seems wrong, because the defendant in that case is clearly a but-for cause of the foot's loss and because the foot's loss also seems to be within the scope of the risk the defendant created. Perhaps with cases like this in mind, the Restatement specifically follows some statutes by converting avoidable consequences or minimizing damages cases to comparative fault cases. The plaintiff in the foot case would probably be at fault in failing to take prescribed antibiotics and in computing damages, and thus her fault would be compared with the defendant's fault. RESTATEMENT (THIRD) OF TORTS, APPORTIONMENT OF LIABILITY § 3, cmt. *b* (2000).

§ 4. ALLOCATING FULL RESPONSIBILITY TO THE DEFENDANT IN THE INTERESTS OF POLICY OR JUSTICE

BEXIGA v. HAVIR MANUFACTURING CORP.

290 A.2d 281 (N.J. 1972)

PROCTOR, J.

This is a products liability case. Plaintiff John Bexiga, Jr., a minor, was operating a power punch press for his employer, Regina Corporation (Regina), when his right hand was crushed by the ram of the machine, resulting in the loss of fingers and deformity of his hand. His father, John Bexiga, Sr., brought this suit against Havir Manufacturing Corporation (Havir), the manufacturer of the machine.... The trial court dismissed the action at the close of the plaintiffs' case. The Appellate Division affirmed....

The particular operation John, Jr. was directed to do required him to place round metal discs, about three inches in diameter, one at a time by hand on top of the die. Once the disc was placed on the die it was held there by the machine itself. He would then depress the foot pedal activating the machine and causing the ram to descend about five inches and punch two holes in the disc. After this operation the ram would ascend and the equipment on the press would remove the metal disc and blow the trimmings away so that the die would be clean for the next cycle. It was estimated by John, Jr. that one cycle as described above would take approximately 10 seconds and that he had completed about 270 cycles during the 40 minutes he operated the machine. He described the accident as follows:

> Well, I put the round piece of metal on the die and the metal didn't go right to the place. I was taking my hand off the machine and I noticed that a piece of metal wasn't in place so I went right back to correct it, but at the same time, my foot had gone to the pedal, so I tried to take

my hand off and jerk my foot off too and it was too late. My hand had gotten cut on the punch, the ram.

Plaintiffs' expert, Andrew Gass, a mechanical engineer, testified the punch press amounted to a "booby trap" because there were no safety devices in its basic design and none were installed prior to the accident. . . .

Gass described two "basic types" of protective safety devices both of which were known in the industry at the time of the manufacture and sale. One was a push-button device with the buttons so spaced as to require the operator to place both hands on them away from the die areas to set the machine in motion. The other device was a guardrail or gate to prevent the operator's hands from entering the area between the ram and die when the machine was activated. These and other safety devices were available from companies specializing in safety equipment. . . .

Because of our disposition of the case it is necessary to consider defendant's contention that John, Jr. was contributorily negligent as a matter of law. Neither court below decided this issue. . . . [I]n negligence cases the defense has been held to be unavailable where considerations of policy and justice dictate. . . . We think this case presents a situation where the interests of justice dictate that contributory negligence be unavailable as a defense to either the negligence or strict liability claims.

The asserted negligence of plaintiff—placing his hand under the ram while at the same time depressing the foot pedal—was the very eventuality the safety devices were designed to guard against. It would be anomalous to hold that defendant has a duty to install safety devices but a breach of that duty results in no liability for the very injury the duty was meant to protect against. We hold that under the facts presented to us in this case the defense of contributory negligence is unavailable.

[Reversed and remanded.]

NOTES

1. *Bexiga* **and comparative fault.** Should the principle in *Bexiga* apply after adoption of comparative fault? On the problem of allocating risks entirely to the defendant or the defendant's special duty to protect even a negligent plaintiff, see DOBBS ON TORTS § 200 (2000).

2. **Defendant's undertaking to protect the plaintiff.** In *McNamara v. Honeyman*, 546 N.E.2d 139 (Mass. 1989), Decedent, who was mentally ill, hanged herself while confined in a state hospital. In a suit for her death, the trial judge rendered a judgment in favor of the plaintiffs against the Commonwealth. Although the court held that mentally ill people "can be comparatively negligent in some circumstances," it nevertheless held that "there can be no comparative negligence where the defendant's duty of care includes preventing the self-abusive or self-destructive acts that caused the injury." Courts have reached different conclusions. *See, e.g., Joseph v. State*, 26 P.3d 459 (Alaska 2001) (a jailer owes a duty of care to one in custody to prevent

foreseeable suicide, but the jury will be permitted to consider the fault of the person committing suicide and allocate damages accordingly). Should the defendant's responsibility include protecting a plaintiff not only when she is exercising care, but also from her own negligence?

3. **Plaintiff negligence that occasioned the need for treatment.** What if a plaintiff's negligence occasions the need for defendant's services? In *Mercer v. Vanderbilt University*, 134 S.W.3d 121 (Tenn. 2004), the plaintiff was driving with an estimated blood alcohol level of .20% when he caused a car accident. Several days later, to facilitate a CT scan, he was given a paralytic drug that made him temporarily ventilator dependent. Three portable oxygen tanks were attached to the ventilator. No one checked the ventilator, and the plaintiff stopped breathing. The patient was resuscitated after a code was called, but suffered severe and permanent brain damage. The trial court allowed the jury to compare plaintiff's and defendant's fault. The Tennessee Supreme Court held, however, that the plaintiff's antecedent negligence could not be considered. "[M]ost jurisdictions have held that a patient's negligence that provides only the occasion for medical treatment may not be compared to that of a negligent physician." Quoting another court for the rationale, the court stated, "It would be anomalous to posit, on the one hand, that a health care provider is required to meet a uniform standard of care in its delivery of medical services to all patients, but permit, on the other hand, the conclusion that, where a breach of that duty is established, no liability may exist if the patient's own pre-injury conduct caused the illness or injury which necessitated the medical care." The court agreed that "patients who may have negligently injured themselves are nevertheless entitled to subsequent non-negligent medical treatment and to an undiminished recovery if such subsequent non-negligent treatment is not afforded."

The Restatement approves of the result in cases like *Mercer,* but argues that the result cannot be explained on foreseeability/scope of risk grounds. RESTATEMENT (THIRD) OF TORTS, APPORTIONMENT § 7, cmt. *h* (2000). Can you see a basis for the Restatement's position?

4. **Statutes to protect vulnerable plaintiffs.** Statutes sometimes impose a duty upon the defendant to protect plaintiffs who are vulnerable or disabled. Minor workers in dangerous occupations may be so protected by statutes. Similarly, a statute that requires school buses to remain stopped until school children have crossed the road is a recognition that the children may not exercise care to protect themselves when they cross. The school bus driver who violates such a statute may be denied the right to raise contributory negligence of the child as a defense. *See Van Gaasbeck v. Webatuck Cent. Sch. Dist. No. 1*, 234 N.E.2d 243 (N.Y. 1967). Would these be situations in which to impose a *Bexiga* duty upon the defendant?

5. **Nonreciprocal risks and known disability.** One characteristic that unites these cases is that the defendant imposes a risk upon the plaintiff, but that the plaintiff's fault imposes no similar risk upon the defendant. In other words, the risks are not reciprocal or mutual. Contrast the ordinary automobile collision case in which each driver is acting negligently, thus creating risks to others as well as to self.

Maybe *Bexiga* and similar cases suggest that the plaintiff's vulnerability rightly plays a part in determining responsibility, but only in certain cases. The plaintiff's disability or vulnerability might be especially important if (1) the defendant knows of the plaintiff's disability which prevents or inhibits the plaintiff's care for himself; and (2) the plaintiff's risky conduct endangers himself but not others. Consider the following cases.

Case 1. A mentally disabled adult, John Clay, works for a farmer, Johnson. Johnson took Clay as a foster child, an arrangement made with the welfare department. Johnson put him to work with machinery on the farm, and explained his duties, but did not explain the dangers. Clay put his hand in a grinder and it was severely injured. A reasonable person would have perceived the risk and would not have put a hand in the grinder. Clay did not adequately perceive the risk because of his mental limitations. In Clay's suit against Johnson, the defense was contributory negligence.

Case 2. Kincheloe, a child of 12, is driving a car on a rural road. His neighbor, Davis, was driving in excess of the speed limit in the opposite direction, approaching Kincheloe. He recognized Kincheloe and knew he was inclined to take his father's car and pull dangerous stunts. Nevertheless, Davis did not slow down. Kincheloe pulled over in Davis' lane, and Davis was unable to avoid collision because of his speed. Both Davis and Kincheloe were injured. In Kincheloe's claim against Davis, contributory negligence of Kincheloe was pleaded as a defense.

Case 3. Paulin, a mentally disabled adult, walked down a rural road in the pre-dawn hours. He walked on the right side and wore dark clothes. Dalrymple was driving in the same direction. As he neared Paulin, a car came from the opposite direction and Dalrymple dimmed his lights. He never saw Paulin until the last minute. He struck Paulin, who was seriously injured. Contributory negligence was the defense in Paulin's claim against Dalrymple.

Case 4. Perez and Dittman were both speeding as they traveled south on a public highway. Perez, who was 13, attempted to pass Dittman on a curve. At the same time Dittman lost control and began to skid over to his left. The two cars collided at this point. Each driver was injured. Contributory negligence is pleaded.

These examples might suggest that you agree with the principle in *Bexiga*, but might think that application of the principle to more concrete cases is debatable.

6. **Policy factors in allocation of risks to the defendant.** One article that examines cases in which courts bar plaintiff fault defenses after the shift from contributory negligence to comparative fault concludes that court-created limits are grounded in identifiable and consistent issues of principle or policy. The policies involved when judges limit comparative fault defenses include: plaintiff incapacity (plaintiff lacks total or partial capacity for self care); structural safety (due to systemic differentials in knowledge, experience or control, the defendant can be expected to take better care of plaintiff's safety than can the plaintiff herself); role definition (defendant's obligation is to care for even a negligent plaintiff because of defendant's responsibilities as a professional rescuer); process values (litigating the comparative fault defense would harm litigants, create unmanageable litigation,

or produce statements of relative fault where such statements are problematic); fundamental values (a determination of comparative fault would encroach on fundamental, sometimes constitutional values); and autonomy and self risk (plaintiff's conduct risked only harm to self and as such receives more latitude for plaintiff choice). *See* Ellen M. Bublick, *Comparative Fault to the Limits*, 56 VAND. L. REV. 977 (2003). Are any of these policies at issue in the cases here?

CHRISTENSEN v. ROYAL SCHOOL DISTRICT NO. 160

124 P.3d 283 (Wash. 2005)

ALEXANDER, C.J. . . .

[Steven Diaz, a 26-year-old teacher engaged in sexual activity with his 13-year-old middle-school student Leslie Christensen. The sexual activity occurred in Diaz's classroom. Diaz claimed that Leslie voluntarily participated in the relationship.]

Leslie and her parents brought suit against Diaz, the Royal School District (the District), and Principal Andersen. . . . In their complaint, they claimed that Diaz sexually abused Leslie. Damages were also sought against the District and Andersen based on the allegation that the District and its principal, Andersen, were negligent in hiring and supervising Diaz.

In a responsive pleading, the District and Andersen asserted an affirmative defense that Leslie's voluntary participation in the sexual relationship with Diaz constituted contributory fault. . . Leslie moved for partial summary judgment on this issue, seeking to strike the affirmative defense. The trial court deferred ruling on the motion pending an answer from this court to the certified question [can contributory fault be assessed against a 13-year-old victim of sexual abuse for her participation in the relationship]. . . .

The existence of a legal duty is a question of law and "depends on mixed considerations of logic, common sense, justice, policy, and precedent."

The District and Andersen argue that contributory fault applies in this case because Leslie had a duty to protect herself against sexual abuse by an adult, a duty she allegedly ignored by voluntarily engaging in a sexual relationship with Diaz. . . .

The District and Andersen contend that contributory fault applies because "Washington has a long history of holding children responsible for their comparative negligence" and that Leslie had a duty to protect herself against sexual abuse but failed to do so. In support of this contention, they cite several cases where contributory fault has been applied against a child. Although the District and Andersen correctly pointed out that Washington does apply contributory fault and the duty of protecting oneself to children in some instances, the cases that they cite are not germane to our inquiry, as none involve sexual abuse. The act of sexual abuse is key here. As indicated above, our public policy is directed to protecting children from such abuse. . . .

[The court discussed the idea that a claim of contributory negligence was barred because the acts of sexual molestation were intentional, even though the contributory negligence was being alleged by a negligent rather than an intentional tortfeasor.]

Our conclusion that the defense of contributory negligence should not be available to the Royal School District and Principal Anderson is in accord with the established Washington rule that a school has a "special relationship" with the students in its custody and a duty to protect them "from reasonably anticipated dangers." The rationale for imposing this duty is on the placement of the student in the care of the school with the resulting loss of the student's ability to protect himself or herself. . . .

[B]ecause we recognize the vulnerability of children in the school setting, we hold, as a matter of public policy, that children do not have a duty to protect themselves from sexual abuse by their teachers. Moreover, we conclude that contributory fault may not be assessed against a 13-year-old child based on the failure to protect herself from being sexually abused when the defendant or defendants stand in a special relationship to the child and have a duty to protect the child. *See* Ellen M. Bublick, *Comparative Fault to the Limits,* 56 VAND. L. REV. 977, 1004 (2003). Andersen and the District had a clear duty to protect students in their custody, and this duty encompassed the obligation to supervise and control Diaz. . . .

[In response to defendant's allegation that when asked about the sexual relationship by the principal, Leslie did not disclose it, the court said:] we have not said in this opinion that the school district should be precluded from defending on the basis that it was not negligent. The fact that it may not, under Washington law, assert that the 13-year-old child was contributorily negligent should not bar it from claiming at trial that it was careful in hiring and supervising the child's teacher and, thus, was without negligence. If, indeed, the District was thwarted in its efforts to ascertain if Leslie Christensen was abused by her teacher, that fact would likely be relevant on the issue of its alleged negligence. . . .

The child, in our view, lacks the capacity to consent to the sexual abuse and is under no duty to protect himself or herself from being abused. An opposite holding would, in our judgment, frustrate the over-arching goals of prevention and deterrence of child sexual abuse. . . .

SANDERS, J., dissenting. . . .

Washington law holds minors responsible for contributory negligence in many contexts. The majority dismisses these cases because they do not involve sexual conduct. I fail to see why a minor can be contributorily negligent for driving a snowmobile but cannot be contributorily negligent in a negligence action relating to sexual misconduct. Generally contributory negligence is a question of fact for the jury.

But under the majority's rule, a 15-year-old girl can seduce a male teacher, and then sue the school district for damages knowing she cannot be found contributorily negligent in the school district suit as a matter of law.... [T]his provides a powerful incentive to engage in sexual misconduct. We are deceiving ourselves if we think children are unable to understand the risks and potential rewards. Perhaps some are not, but that is why a jury determines this question as a matter of fact in each case.... I see no reason to deviate from our standard rule on contributory negligence for minors in negligence cases involving sexual activity.

The majority appeals to a school's duty to protect students. Well and good. However, merely because a school must protect the children in its care does not relieve the students of any personal responsibility for their own conduct. Children should not be allowed to take advantage of the school's duty by forcing it to pay damages for injuries invited by the student or injuries which the district could have prevented *but for* obstruction by the student. Such a rule is inequitable and excuses all manner of mischief....

This school district *did* take steps to protect the female student. School officials met with the girl and her parents to determine if anything untoward was occurring with the teacher. The girl, however, allegedly lied about her involvement with the teacher, thwarting the school district's efforts to protect her. She may be below the age of consent, but not below the age of honesty. Yes, school districts must protect their students, but students must cooperate. If a student undermines school officials' actions to protect her, she must bear at least some of the fault for resulting injury. If the girl lied, this is contributory negligence on her part and a proper defense for the school district....

[A separate dissent is omitted.]

NOTES

1. **The plaintiff's "no duty" expression.** The Restatement provides that in light of principle or policy, plaintiffs (like defendants) might sometimes have "no-duty" to act reasonably in self protection. RESTATEMENT (THIRD) OF TORTS, APPORTIONMENT § 7, cmt. *h* (2000). If a plaintiff has no duty to protect herself by the use of reasonable care, she can not be charged with contributory negligence in failing to do so. The no duty language is infelicitous in one respect, since "duty" refers to an obligation enforceable by suit. The point of using no duty language, however, is to draw attention to a parallel set of rules that relieve defendants of liability for negligent conduct. For instance, we will see in Chapter 12 that landowners frequently do not owe a duty of reasonable care to trespassers. That means the landowner is free to be negligent toward trespassers. The idea of a plaintiff no-duty rule is that the same approach should be taken to protect the interests of the plaintiff.

2. **No duty of a child to guard against sexual abuse by an adult.** What policy interests might be served by the Washington Supreme Court's plaintiff no-duty rule? Child sexual activity with an adult could be treated like

any other potential contributory negligence by a child. When immature plaintiffs are confronted with involvement in adult activity, might child safety be promoted by placing greater responsibility on the more mature and experienced party? Or as the dissent argues, will a no-duty rule encourage plaintiffs to engage in sexual misconduct? In some ways, the no-duty rule in *Christensen* parallels the doctrine that requires children to use extra care when engaged in adult activities that pose risk to others. When engaged in adult activities that risk the children's own safety, others may owe extra care to them. Ellen M. Bublick, *Comparative Fault to the Limits,* 56 VAND. L. REV. 977 (2003).

3. **Failure to disclose sexual contact.** The dissent makes much of a contested fact that the plaintiff, when asked by school officials if she was being sexually abused, did not reveal the truth. Would it be relevant, either to a no-duty rule or to a reasonable care analysis, if research shows that fewer than 50% of adolescents ever reveal sexual abuse to anyone at all, and that those who reveal abuse usually reveal it only to a best friend or parent? R.J.R. Levesque, *Sex Differences in the Experience of Child Sexual Victimization,* 9 J. OF FAM. VIOLENCE 357–369 (1994).

4. **Effect of no-duty rules.** The *Christensen* court struck the defendant's contributory fault defense. As the court made clear, the plaintiff still may not win her claim. Why would the plaintiff want a situation in which she either recovers fully or not at all—are there process considerations? Might an attorney for the child plaintiff ever want a court to permit a contributory negligence defense in a case like *Christensen*?

LEROY FIBRE CO. v. CHICAGO, MILWAUKEE & ST. PAUL RAILWAY CO.

232 U.S. 340 (1914)

[The plaintiff owned land abutting the defendant's railroad. He stacked flax on the land for use in his manufacturing business. He alleged that the railroad negligently emitted sparks and coals that set fire to and destroyed the flax. The closest stacks were about 75 feet from the tracks. The defendant argued that the plaintiff was contributorily negligent in stacking the combustible flax so near the railroad. The jury, charged on the contributory negligence defense, found for the defendant.]

MR. JUSTICE MCKENNA delivered the opinion of the Court:

That one's uses of his property may be subject to the servitude of the wrongful use by another of his property seems an anomaly. It upsets the presumptions of law, and takes from him the assumption, and the freedom which comes from the assumption, that the other will obey the law, not violate it. It casts upon him the duty of not only using his own property so as not to injure another, but so to use his own property that it may not be injured by the wrongs of another. . . .

The legal conception of property is of rights. When you attempt to limit them by wrongs, you venture a solecism. If you declare a right is subject to a wrong, you confound the meaning of both. It is difficult to deal with the opposing contention. There are some principles that have axiomatic character. The tangibility of property is in its uses, and that the uses by one owner of his property may be limited by the wrongful use of another owner of his is a contradiction. . . .

[The Court held that the contributory negligence defense presented no question for the jury.]

So ordered.

MR. JUSTICE HOLMES, partially concurring. . . .

[A]s a general proposition people are entitled to assume that their neighbors will conform to the law; that a negligent tort is unlawful in as full a sense as a malicious one, and therefore that they are entitled to assume that their neighbors will not be negligent. . . .

If a man stacked his flax so near to a railroad that it obviously was likely to be set fire to by a well-managed train, I should say that he could not throw the loss upon the railroad by the oscillating result of an inquiry by the jury whether the road had used due care.

NOTES

1. **Trying the shoe on the other foot again.** Suppose the flax caught fire and the fire foreseeably spread to burn down the shelter for abused children next door. Would the flax owner have no responsibility? If he does have responsibility to the shelter but not for any share of his own loss is something wrong? Or should we say that risks that threaten oneself are quite different from those that threaten others?

2. **Property law vs. tort law.** One way to look at this problem is to recognize that property law, emphasizing the owner's right to use property as she pleases, is sometimes at odds with negligence law, which emphasizes the safety of conduct and judges safety case by case after the event has occurred. Both approaches represent important values in our culture. How should we determine which prevails? William Powers, Jr., *Border Wars,* 72 TEX. L. REV. 1209 (1994). *See also* RESTATEMENT (THIRD) OF TORTS, APPORTIONMENT OF LIABILITY § 3, cmt. *d* (2000).

3. **Plaintiff's rights or entitlements not based on rights to possession of tangible property.** Some of the discourse on this topic is framed in terms of the plaintiff's rights or entitlements. The plaintiff may be entitled to use her property even if in doing so she is in danger of harm by the defendant's negligence. Similarly, the plaintiff might have entitlements not grounded in tangible property. She might be entitled to, say, use the public streets although they are dangerous or shop for groceries at night although rape or robbery is an ever present possibility. If she had such an entitlement, then under *LeRoy Fibre* she could not be charged with contributory negligence merely because she shopped at night.

4. **Determining plaintiff entitlements.** How should courts decide what entitlements a plaintiff has beyond those arising from ownership of

tangible property? Can we identify any principle? Consider *Brandon v. County of Richardson*, 624 N.W.2d 604 (Neb. 2001), where a rape victim reported a rape to the sheriff, who also knew that the rapists were dangerous and might murder Brandon if there was no police protection. The sheriff did not protect Brandon and the rapists did in fact commit murder. Should the estate's recovery against the sheriff be reduced on the ground that Brandon was negligent in reporting the rape after the rapists warned Brandon not to do so? Does Brandon, on analogy to *LeRoy Fibre*, have an entitlement to report crime to the police even if it is risky?

Is a plaintiff guilty of contributory negligence for wearing expensive jewelry in a neighborhood that has a high crime rate? In *Isik Jewelry v. Mars Media, Inc.*, 418 F. Supp. 2d 112 (E.D.N.Y. 2005), the music artist Albert Johnson, known as "Prodigy," left a video shoot wearing jewelry valued at over $100,000. He was robbed at gunpoint as he walked across the street to get some water from a convenience store. In a bailment action, the court examined whether Johnson failed to use reasonable care. The court found that Johnson was not negligent as a matter of law. Could the conclusion be said to reflect an entitlement by the plaintiff?

One scholar has argued that in light of freedom and equality considerations, citizens should have no duty to shape their conduct around pervasive rape and fear of rape in society. *See* Ellen M. Bublick, *Citizen No-duty Rules: Rape Victims and Comparative Fault,* 99 Cᴏʟᴜᴍ. L. Rᴇᴠ. 1413 (1999). Would such a no-duty rule have changed the outcome in *Wassell*?

5. **Entitlements vs. case by case adjudication of plaintiff fault.** Do we need entitlements decided by a judge like those in *Mercer, Christensen, LeRoy Fibre* or *Brandon*? Do you think it would suffice instead to judge contributory fault case by case in light of the plaintiff's rights and legitimate interests? For example, couldn't we rely upon courts to hold as a matter of ordinary analysis of contributory fault that a woman is definitely not guilty of contributory fault merely because she shops late at night? If you think juries might be unreliable when it comes to deciding issues of contributory fault, would you expect judges to be more trustworthy in formulating entitlements in advance?

§ 5. TRADITIONAL EXCEPTIONS TO THE CONTRIBUTORY NEGLIGENCE BAR

Cases that allocate full responsibility to the defendant even after a shift to comparative fault may draw on traditional exceptions to the contributory negligence bar. To what extent are these doctrines still necessary?

A. THE RESCUE DOCTRINE

"The rescue doctrine is a rule of law holding that one who sees a person in imminent danger caused by the negligence of another cannot be charged with contributory negligence" unless the rescuer acted recklessly. *Ouellette v. Carde*, 612 A.2d 687 (R.I. 1992). In *Ouellette*, the defendant was pinned in a closed garage under a car he had been fixing. There was gasoline all over the floor. Defendant called a friend for help but when the friend activated the electric garage door opener to rescue him, the gas ignited and she was badly burned. She sued the defendant who asked for a comparative negligence instruction. The trial court denied the instruction and the jury found for the plaintiff without reduction in damages. The award was upheld on appeal under the rescue doctrine.

After the advent of comparative fault, some courts leave the allocation of fault between the defendant and the rescuer plaintiff to the jury. *See Govich v. North American Systems, Inc.*, 814 P.2d 94 (N.M. 1991).

B. LAST CLEAR CHANCE OR DISCOVERED PERIL

In the traditional system that barred all recovery for contributory negligence, courts allowed the negligent plaintiff a full recovery when the plaintiff was left in a helpless position by his own negligence and the defendant, who had the last clear chance to avoid injury, negligently inflicted it anyway. *See* RESTATEMENT (SECOND) OF TORTS §§ 479, 480 (1965).

The doctrine first appeared in *Davies v. Mann*, 10 M. & W. 546, 152 Eng. Rep. 588 (Exch. 1842). In that case the plaintiff had left his ass fettered in the road eating grass. The defendant negligently drove a team and wagon down the hill and ran over the animal, which, being fettered, was unable to move. The court held that the plaintiff's contributory negligence was no defense. Baron Parke said that "unless [the plaintiff] might, by the exercise of ordinary care, have avoided the consequences of the defendant's negligence, he is entitled to recover," stressing that if the rule were otherwise, "a man might justify the driving over goods left on a public highway, or even a man lying asleep there. . . ."

The last clear chance doctrine held that if the defendant discovered or should have discovered the plaintiff's peril, and could reasonably have avoided it, the plaintiff's earlier negligence would neither bar nor reduce the plaintiff's recovery. A slightly less generous version, called the discovered peril doctrine, applied these rules only if the defendant actually did discover the plaintiff's peril. The plaintiff could not invoke these doctrines unless the plaintiff was helpless; if he could extricate himself from danger at any time, the defendant did not have the last chance to avoid injury and the negligent plaintiff would be barred entirely.

In states that have adopted comparative fault systems, the last clear chance and discovered peril doctrines have been discarded, mostly on the grounds that they were attempts to aid the plaintiff in a harsh system and not needed once comparative fault rules apply. HENRY WOODS & BETH DEERE, COMPARATIVE FAULT § 8.3 (3d ed. 1996). Occasionally, courts still face last clear chance arguments. In *Penn Harris Madison School Corp. v. Howard*, 861 N.E.2d 1190 (Ind. 2007), the Indiana Supreme Court considered the applicability of the last clear chance doctrine to actions against a governmental entity to which the state's comparative fault statute did not apply. The court held that in appropriate circumstances, the last clear chance rule would still apply to cases involving contributory negligence. However, the defense was not applicable on the facts of that case.

Should the last clear chance doctrine be retained in a modified comparative fault system? Would the fact that the defendant had the last chance still be relevant in determining relative fault? On both points see DOBBS ON TORTS § 207 (2000).

C. DEFENDANT'S RECKLESS OR INTENTIONAL MISCONDUCT

Contributory negligence was historically no defense to an intentional tort. By extension of this idea, courts also held that contributory negligence was no defense to willful, wanton or reckless torts, defined as involving "utter indifference to or conscious disregard for the safety of others." Such torts border on intentional wrongdoing because they involve a bad state of mind, as well as risky conduct. Under this rule the plaintiff charged with contributory negligence was allowed a full recovery against a reckless or wanton defendant.

Once comparative negligence rules are adopted, should courts discard the old rule and simply let the jury apportion fault between plaintiff and defendant, even when the defendant is guilty of reckless conduct? When he is guilty of an intentional tort?

The Restatement of Apportionment § 1 calls for application of comparative fault rules to all claims for personal injury, death, and harms to tangible property. That includes suits against an intentional tortfeasor. At the same time, the Restatement of Apportionment takes "no position" on the question whether a plaintiff's comparative fault reduces recovery against an intentional tortfeasor. ID., cmt. *c*.

Should comparative apportionment have a role in either of these cases?

Case 1. Defendant strikes the plaintiff. When sued, he argues that the plaintiff was guilty of contributory negligence because she provoked the attack.

Case 2. A negligently provides B with keys to A's car, knowing that B is dangerous, in a rage at P, and might attack her. B intentionally runs down P. After P recovers fully against A, A seeks contribution from B.

D. PLAINTIFF'S ILLEGAL ACTIVITY

BARKER v. KALLASH, 468 N.E.2d 39 (N.Y. 1984). The plaintiff, 15 years old, was making a pipe bomb from a pipe filled with powder he said was from firecrackers sold by a nine-year-old defendant. It exploded, he was injured and sued the 9-year-old, his parents and everyone else in sight. *Held*, no recovery. A distinction must be drawn between lawful activities regulated by statute, in which case violation of the statute is negligence or contributory negligence under the rule in *Martin v. Herzog*, and those activities that are prohibited. When "the plaintiff's injury is a direct result of his knowing and intentional participation in a criminal act he cannot seek compensation for the loss, if the criminal act is judged to be so serious an offense as to warrant denial of recovery. . . . Thus a burglar who breaks his leg while descending the cellar stairs, due to the failure of the owner to replace a missing step cannot recover compensation from his victims." Though plaintiff could not be criminally convicted, he does not escape this rule. He "was not a toddler. And building a bomb is not such an inherently innocuous activity that it can reasonably be presumed to be a legally permissible act by an average 15 year old." Nor does the comparative negligence statute relieve the plaintiff here. In referring to "culpable conduct" the statute does not allow a recovery here with diminution of damages. The rule that bars the plaintiff here is not the contributory negligence rule but a rule of public policy that courts should not aid one who engages in a substantial violation of law. Two judges dissented.

NOTES

1. **Context.** Would it matter whether the firecrackers were sold to the plaintiff by a nine-year-old child or by an adult? Would any other facts make a difference?

2. **Illegal activity.** Does any illegal activity by the plaintiff bar a claim? In *Winschel v. Brown*, 171 P.3d 142 (Alaska 2007), the trial court granted summary judgment for defendant because the plaintiff was illegally riding his ATV on a bicycle path when he was injured. The Alaska Supreme Court disagreed. This illegal activity did not preclude recovery because the crime was not "serious." However, the crime could be given "significant weight" in fixing the percentage of comparative fault. What result when the illegal activity was defrauding various doctors to obtain Oxycontin? *See Price v. Purdue Pharma Co.*, 920 So.2d 479 (Miss. 2006).

3. **Commentary.** Joseph H. King, Jr., *Outlaws and Outlier Doctrines: The Serious Misconduct Bar in Tort Law*, 43 Wm. & Mary L. Rev. 1011 (2002), attacks the serious misconduct bar as a frustration of tort law goals and the comparative negligence structure, as a doctrine unpredictable and selective in application, and as an invitation to judges to apply the moral flavor of the month. Should plaintiffs guilty of serious misconduct be allowed to present their cases to the jury and see what percentages of responsibility juries assign?

REFERENCES: Contributory and comparative negligence generally: Dobbs on Torts §§ 198–210 (2000); Comparative negligence: Victor Schwartz, Comparative Negligence (3d Ed. 1994); Henry Woods & Beth Deere, Comparative Fault (3d Ed. 1996 & Supp.); Arthur Best et al., Comparative Negligence (1992 and Later Dates, 3 Vols.).

CHAPTER 10

ASSUMPTION OF THE RISK

■ ■ ■

§ 1. CONTRACTUAL OR EXPRESS ASSUMPTION OF THE RISK

BOYLE v. REVICI, 961 F.2d 1060 (2d Cir. 1992). Cecelia Zyjewski was diagnosed by several physicians as having cancer. They all recommended immediate surgery. However, she consulted Dr. Revici, who purported to treat cancer, but not by any method accepted by the medical profession and not by surgery. Instead, he administered medications. He expressly told her that his medications were not approved by the FDA and that he could offer no guarantees. She also understood that his therapy was non-standard. Nevertheless she put herself in his care. Her condition deteriorated quickly and within a year, Zyjewski died. This diversity suit was brought under New York law. The trial court submitted the case to the jury on comparative fault instructions and the jury found for the plaintiff, but reduced damages for Zyjewski's comparative fault. Even after reduction, the verdict came to over $1.3 million. The defendant appealed, arguing that the plaintiff was barred by an express assumption of the risk. *Held*, under governing New York law, the jury should have been instructed on express assumption of the risk; it may find that Zyjewski expressly assumed the risk and is barred from recovery even though there was no written document at all.

NOTE

"In appropriate situations, the parties to a transaction should be able to agree which of them should bear the risk of injury, even when the injury is caused by a party's legally culpable conduct. That policy is not altered or undermined by the adoption of comparative responsibility. Consequently, a valid contractual limitation on liability, within its terms, creates an absolute bar to a plaintiff's recovery from the other party to the contract. A valid contractual limitation on liability does not provide an occasion for the factfinder to assign a percentage of responsibility to any party or other person...." RESTATEMENT (THIRD) OF TORTS: APPORTIONMENT OF LIABILITY § 2, cmt. *b* (2000).

TUNKL v. REGENTS OF UNIVERSITY OF CALIFORNIA, 383 P.2d 441 (Cal. 1963). Tunkl brought this action for injuries received allegedly as a result of the negligence of the hospital operated by defendant. Tunkl was admitted to the hospital on condition that he execute a release, absolving the defendants "from any and all liability for the negligent or wrongful acts or omissions of its employees. . . ." The validity of this release was submitted to the jury, which found it to be valid and the trial court entered judgment for the defendants. *Held*, reversed. "While obviously no public policy opposes private, voluntary transactions in which one party, for a consideration, agrees to shoulder a risk which the law would otherwise have placed upon the other party, the above circumstances pose a different situation. In this situation the releasing party does not really acquiesce voluntarily in the contractual shifting of the risk, nor can we be reasonably certain that he receives an adequate consideration for the transfer. Since the service is one which each member of the public, presently or potentially, may find essential to him, he faces, despite his economic inability to do so, the prospect of a compulsory assumption of the risk of another's negligence. . . . From the observance of simple standards of due care in the driving of a car to the performance of the high standards of hospital practice, the individual citizen must be completely dependent upon the responsibility of others. . . . We cannot lightly accept a sought immunity from careless failure to provide the hospital service upon which many must depend."

NOTES

1. On the strength of *Boyle*, would New York reject California's *Tunkl* decision? *See Ash v. New York University Dental Center,* 564 N.Y.S.2d 308 (App. Div. 1990).

2. In California, the plaintiffs were allowed to enroll their almost-four-year-old in the defendant's child care program only if the parents signed a release absolving the defendant of liability for negligence and also agreeing to indemnify the defendant if for any reason the defendant were held liable in spite of the release. The plaintiffs' child was subjected to sexual contact by another child, whose propensities in that respect were allegedly known to the defendant. In determining whether the release is valid as a bar to the claim, is it relevant that the demand for child care in California far exceeds the supply? Why or why not? *See Gavin W. v. YMCA of Metro. Los Angeles,* 131 Cal. Rptr.2d 168 (Ct. App. 2003).

MOORE v. HARTLEY MOTORS

36 P.3d 628 (Alaska 2001)

FABE, CHIEF JUSTICE. . . .

Gayle Moore and her husband bought a Suzuki four-wheel ATV in May 1993 from Suzuki, Arctic Cat Motor Sports. At the time of the sale, the salesperson offered the Moores a $50 rebate upon completion of an

ATV rider safety class. On October 23, 1993, the Moores attended an ATV rider safety class held on the property of Hartley Motors, Inc. James Croak instructed the class using the curriculum of the ATV Safety Institute. Before starting instruction, Croak requested that all participants sign a consent form and release. Moore signed the consent form and release.

[During the class, Moore was thrown from her ATV when it struck a rock obscured by high grass.]

Moore brought suit in July 1995 against Hartley Motors, the dealer that sold the Moores their ATV, ATV Safety Institute, and Jim Croak. She alleged that the defendants negligently failed to provide a safe ATV rider training course and location, and negligently concealed the fact that the course was unsafe.... The superior court granted summary judgment to the defendants.

[The court first held that the release was supported by consideration.] In *Municipality of Anchorage v. Locker,* we evaluated whether an exculpatory release should be invalidated as against public policy. In *Locker,* we concluded that a limited liability clause in a contract for an advertisement in the yellow pages was unconscionable and void as against public policy. We relied upon *Tunkl v. Regents of the University of California* in identifying the factors for review in invalidating an exculpatory provision on public policy grounds....

Of particular relevance to this case is the type of service performed and whether the party seeking exculpation has a decisive advantage in bargaining strength because of the essential nature of the service. Here, the ATV safety course, although perhaps providing a desirable opportunity for an ATV driver, is not an essential service, and therefore the class providers did not have a "decisive advantage of bargaining strength" in requiring the release for participation in the class. Moore had a choice whether to take the class or not, and chose to sign the release in order to participate. The release in this circumstance does not present a violation of public policy.

Other courts have upheld exculpatory releases for activities similar to ATV riding where the activities themselves were not regulated by statute....

Even if there was no genuine issue of material fact regarding a misrepresentation [as to safety of the course], the trial court erred in failing to consider the scope of the release signed by Moore. Moore agreed to release the ATV Safety Institute and all other organizations and individuals affiliated with the ATV safety class from liability, loss, and damages "including but not limited to all bodily injuries and property damage arising out of participation in the ATV RiderCourse." But the release does not discuss or even mention liability for general negligence. Its opening sentences refer only to unavoidable and inherent risks of ATV riding, and nothing in its ensuing language suggests an intent to release ATVSI or Hartley Motors from liability for acts of negligence unrelated to those inherent risks. Based on this language, we conclude that Moore released ATVSI and Hartley Motors only from liability arising from the inherent risks of ATV riding and ordinary negligence associated with those inherent risks. As we noted in *Kissick v. Schmierer,* an exculpatory release can be enforced if "the intent to release a party from liability for future negligence" is "conspicuously and unequivocally expressed." However, underlying the ATV course release signed by Moore was an implied and reasonable presumption that the course is not unreasonably dangerous.

Moore claims that she was injured when she fell off her ATV after riding over a rock obscured by tall grass. We assume the truth of this assertion for purposes of reviewing the superior court's summary judgment order. Moore asserts that the course on which the class operated was set up in such a way that she had to ride into the grass and that this posed an unnecessary danger.

The allegedly improper course layout may be actionable if the course posed a risk beyond ordinary negligence related to the inherent risks of off-road ATV riding assumed by the release. As we have explained in the context of skiing, "[i]f a given danger could be eliminated or mitigated through the exercise of reasonable care, it is not a necessary danger" and is therefore not an inherent risk of the sport.

We have described an "unreasonable risk" as one for which "the likelihood and gravity of the harm threatened outweighed the utility of the ... conduct and the burden on the [defendant] for removing the danger." If the course was designed or maintained in such a manner that it increased the likelihood of a rider encountering a hidden rock, then the course layout may have presented an unnecessary danger; holding an ATV safety class on an unnecessarily dangerous course is beyond the ordinary negligence released by the waiver. Holding a safety class on an unreasonably risky course may give rise to liability even if encountering rocks is generally an inherent risk of ATV riding. Moreover, the fact that the course was geared towards novice ATV riders may also affect the level of care required of ATVSI and Hartley Motors to reduce unnecessary dangers and unreasonable risk.

... Here, Moore presented facts that could support a finding that the ATV safety course was laid out in an unnecessarily dangerous manner that was not obvious to novice ATV riders and therefore not within the scope of the release. Thus, it was error to grant summary judgment.

[Reversed and remanded.]

NOTES

1. While people may contractually waive their right to sue for damages caused by the ordinary negligence of others, such preinjury releases are unenforceable if they offend public policy, or if they are unclear or ambiguous. *See, e.g., Pearce v. Utah Athletic Foundation,* 179 P.3d 760 (Utah 2008);

Cohen v. Five Brooks Stable, 72 Cal.Rptr.3d 471 (Ct. App. 2008). Even if a release passes these two tests, the court must determine whether the risk that caused the injury was within the scope of the release. Only if the answer to that question is yes will the release bar the plaintiff's claim. *See, e.g., Thompson v. Hi Tech Motor Sports, Inc.*, 945 A.2d 368 (Vt. 2008) (waiver of liability for injuries on test drive on one of dealership's motorcycles, while not facially invalid, covered only injuries caused by inherent risks of riding, not those caused by dealer's negligence).

2.   Do the cases, taken together, sufficiently indicate when public policy would permit or reject contractual assumptions of the risk? "Public policy" is often a case-specific inquiry. States continue to strike down preinjury releases on a number public policy grounds. *See, e.g., Yang v. Voyagaire Houseboats, Inc.*, 701 N.W.2d 783 (Minn. 2005) (likening a houseboat rental company to an innkeeper providing a "public service," thus rendering release invalid); *Rothstein v. Snowbird Corp.*, 175 P.3d 560 (Utah 2007) (skier's waiver of right to sue ski resort for negligence invalidated in light of state statute immunizing ski resorts from suits based on injuries resulting from inherent risks of skiing); *Hojnowski v. Vans Skate Park*, 901 A.2d 381 (N.J. 2006) (public policy prevents parent of a minor child from releasing minor child's potential tort claims arising out of use of a commercial recreational facility); *Brown v. Soh*, 909 A.2d 43 (Conn. 2006) (exculpatory agreements in the employment context offend public policy). *See also* DOBBS ON TORTS § 213 (2000).

3.   Most courts have held that a contractual assumption of the risk clause barring recovery for recklessly or intentionally caused injury would offend public policy. *See, e.g., City of Santa Barbara v. Superior Court*, 161 P.3d 1095 (Cal. 2007) (majority of states hold that public policy precludes enforcement of a release that would shelter aggravated misconduct). Should a general clause purporting to waive "all liability" be enforceable to bar a negligence claim if the plaintiff fails to prove recklessness on the defendant's part? *See Moore v. Waller*, 930 A.2d 176 (D.C. 2007).

4.   When the defendant is the only person who can provide reasonable safety, should he be permitted to shift the responsibility to another by contract? *See Hanks v. Powder Ridge Restaurant Corp.*, 885 A.2d 734 (Conn. 2005); *Reardon v. Windswept Farm, LLC*, 905 A.2d 1156 (Conn. 2006)

5.   Releases in recreational activities are usually upheld as long as they are clear and unambiguous. *See Pearce, supra* Note 1 (citing cases from many jurisdictions). Do such releases encourage recreation and athletic activity? How? Should courts encourage economic activity by allowing *every* business to demand a release before it will sell you its goods or services?

§ 2. IMPLIED ASSUMPTION OF THE RISK

DAN B. DOBBS,
THE LAW OF TORTS § 214

(2000)

Most agreements in everyday life are tacit, not expressed. No logical reason prevents parties from tacitly or impliedly consenting or agreeing to a shift of responsibility to the plaintiff. The traditional assumed risk rules found such tacit consent when the plaintiff, knowing of the risk and appreciating its quality, voluntarily chose to confront it. For instance, if the plaintiff accepted dangerous employment, he was once held to have assumed the risk of employment dangers, including the employer's negligence. Holdings like this gave the doctrine of implied assumption of risk a bad name, and courts gradually modified such holdings....

As Prosser pointed out, the driver of an automobile cannot reasonably believe that the jaywalking plaintiff is consenting to the driver's negligence. The jaywalker assuredly confronts a known risk and does so voluntarily, but voluntary confrontation of the risk does not communicate any release of the driver from the duties of ordinary care. Instead, the jaywalker is simply negligent. His negligence is to be judged under comparative fault rules....

BETTS v. CRAWFORD, 965 P.2d 680 (Wyo. 1998). The plaintiff worked for the defendants as a housekeeper for several hours a week. She occasionally had to pick up children's items on the stairs. One day when she was carrying bundled sheets to be laundered, she tripped over some items left on the stairs, fell down the stairs, and suffered serious injuries. The defendants asked the trial judge to instruct that "A servant assumes all of the risks and dangers pertaining to his employment which are known to him, or discoverable by the exercise of ordinary care ... even though said risks are directly attributable to his master's negligence...." The trial court rejected this and instead instructed the jury that homeowners must use reasonable care to avoid injury to those permitted on the premises, that an employer had a duty to furnish a safe place to work, that all persons owed a duty of ordinary care, and that comparative fault applied. The jury found for the plaintiff, reducing her damages 15% for her own fault. The defendants appeal, claiming error in failing to give the assumed risk instruction. *Held,* judgment for plaintiff affirmed. "[T]here is no distinction between contributory negligence and assumption of risk when raised as a defense to an established breach of duty." Assumed risk is now merged into the comparative negligence system.

NOTES

1. **Traditional implied assumption of risk.** Implied assumption of the risk was once a complete defense to negligence liability. Where the plaintiff knew of the risk, appreciated its danger, and voluntarily confronted it, the plaintiff could take nothing. Only a few states continue to follow such a broad all-or-nothing rule today. *See, e.g., Morgan State University v. Walker*, 919 A.2d 21 (Md. 2007) (barring negligence claim by woman who walked across icy parking lot knowing it was slippery); *Crews v. Hollenbach*, 751 A.2d 481 (Md. 2000) (barring negligence claim by gas-company foreman against defendants who caused a gas leak); *Rickey v. Boden*, 421 A.2d 539 (R.I. 1980) (barring negligence claim by elevator operator injured when she fell on a narrow stairway in defendant's building while walking to a coffee-break area). Yet many people would no doubt agree that either contractually-expressed consent or unexpressed but genuine consent to, or preference for, the defendant's conduct should bar the plaintiff's claim entirely. If so, does that mean that the traditional rule was right? What about Prosser's jaywalker? *See* Kenneth W. Simons, *Reflections on Assumption of Risk*, 50 U.C.L.A. L. REV. 481 (2002).

2. ***Betts* as a contemporary view.** Recall that the New York statute on comparative fault (Chapter 9, § 2), specifically provides that "assumed risk" is to be treated as comparative fault. The American Law Institute takes the same position, pointing out that if the plaintiff is reasonable in facing a risk, she is not negligent, but that when she unreasonably confronts a known risk, her negligence in doing so reduces her recovery of damages. RESTATEMENT (THIRD) OF TORTS: APPORTIONMENT OF LIABILITY § 3, cmt. *c* (2000). The point is judicially recognized as well. *E.g., Green v. Mid Dakota Clinic*, 673 N.W.2d 257 (N.D. 2004).

3. **Important qualifications of the rule.** The Restatement's position is subject to two important explanations. First, if the defendant reasonably believes that the plaintiff has accepted the risk, the defendant may not be negligent at all in relying on the plaintiff to achieve safety. In that case, the defendant would not be liable at all. This has long been a familiar idea to users of this casebook. Second, as reflected in the Note following *Boyle, supra* Section 1, the Restatement does recognize a separate and complete defense based on "contractual" (more commonly called "express") assumption of the risk.

AVILA v. CITRUS COMMUNITY COLLEGE DISTRICT

131 P.3d 383 (Cal. 2006)

WERDEGAR, J. . . .

Jose Luis Avila, a Rio Hondo Community College (Rio Hondo) student, played baseball for the Rio Hondo Roadrunners. On January 5, 2001, Rio Hondo was playing a preseason road game against the Citrus Community College Owls (Citrus College). During the game, a Roadrunners pitcher hit a Citrus College batter with a pitch; when Avila came to bat in the top of the next inning, the Citrus College pitcher hit him in the head with a pitch, cracking his batting helmet. Avila alleges the pitch was an intentional "beanball" thrown in retaliation for the previous hit batter or, at a minimum, was thrown negligently.

Avila staggered, felt dizzy, and was in pain. The Rio Hondo manager told him to go to first base. Avila did so, and when he complained to the Rio Hondo first base coach, he was told to stay in the game. At second base, he still felt pain, numbness, and dizziness. A Citrus College player yelled to the Rio Hondo dugout that the Roadrunners needed a pinch runner. Avila walked off the field and went to the Rio Hondo bench. No one tended to his injuries. As a result, Avila suffered unspecified serious personal injuries.

Avila sued both schools, his manager, the helmet manufacturer, and various other entities and organizations. Only the claims against the Citrus Community College District (the District) are before us. [The District demurred, claiming it owed no duty of care to Avila. The trial court sustained the demurrer and dismissed the action. The Court of Appeal reversed.]

. . . [T]he existence and scope of a defendant's duty is an issue of law, to be decided by a court, not a jury. When the injury is to a sporting participant, the considerations of policy and the question of duty necessarily become intertwined with the question of assumption of risk.

The traditional version of the assumption of risk doctrine required proof that the plaintiff voluntarily accepted a specific known and appreciated risk. The doctrine depended on the actual subjective knowledge of the given plaintiff and, where the elements were met, was an absolute defense to liability for injuries arising from the known risk

California's abandonment of the doctrine of contributory negligence in favor of comparative negligence led to a reconceptualization of the assumption of risk. In *Knight v. Jewett*, 834 P.2d 696 (Cal. 1992), a plurality of this court explained that there are in fact two species of assumption of risk: primary and secondary. Primary assumption of the risk arises when, as a matter of law and policy, a defendant owes no duty to protect a plaintiff from particular harms.[6] Applied in the sporting context, it precludes liability for injuries arising from those risks deemed inherent in a sport; as a matter of law, others have no legal duty to eliminate those risks or otherwise protect a sports participant from them. Under this duty approach, a court need not ask what risks a particular plaintiff subjectively knew of and chose to encounter, but instead must evaluate the fundamental nature of the sport and the defendant's role in or relationship to that sport in order to determine whether the defendant owes a duty to protect a plaintiff from the particular risk of harm. A majority of this court has since embraced the *Knight* approach.

---

6. Secondary assumption of the risk arises when the defendant still owes a duty of care, but the plaintiff knowingly encounters the risks attendant on the defendant's breach of that duty. We deal here with an issue of primary, not secondary, assumption of the risk.

Here, the host school's role is a mixed one: its players are coparticipants, its coaches and managers have supervisorial authority over the conduct of the game, and other representatives of the school are responsible for the condition of the playing facility. We have previously established that coparticipants have a duty not to act recklessly, outside the bounds of the sport, and coaches and instructors have a duty not to increase the risks inherent in sports participation; we also have noted in dicta that those responsible for maintaining athletic facilities have a similar duty not to increase the inherent risks, albeit in the context of businesses selling recreational opportunities. . . . [The host school also owes a duty to participants, both home and visiting players, "at a minimum, not [to] increase the risks inherent in the sport."]

We consider next whether Avila has alleged facts supporting breach of the duty not to enhance the inherent risks of his sport. Though it numbers them differently, Avila's complaint in essence alleges four ways in which the District breached a duty to Avila: by (1) conducting the game at all; (2) failing to control the Citrus College pitcher; (3) failing to provide umpires to supervise and control the game; and (4) failing to provide medical care. The District's demurrer was properly sustained if, and only if, each of these alleged breaches, assumed to be true, falls outside any duty owed by the District and within the inherent risks of the sport assumed by Avila.

With respect to the first of these, conducting the game, Avila cites unspecified "community college baseball rules" prohibiting preseason games. But the only consequence of the District's hosting the game was that it exposed Avila, who chose to participate, to the ordinary inherent risks of the sport of baseball. Nothing about the bare fact of the District's hosting the game enhanced those ordinary risks, so its doing so, whether or not in violation of the alleged rules, does not constitute a breach of its duty not to enhance the ordinary risks of baseball. Nor did the District owe any separate duty to Avila not to host the game.

The second alleged breach, the failure to supervise and control the Citrus College pitcher, is barred by primary assumption of the risk. Being hit by a pitch is an inherent risk of baseball. The dangers of being hit by a pitch, often thrown at speeds approaching 100 miles per hour, are apparent and well known: being hit can result in serious injury or, on rare tragic occasions, death. [Since 1920, at least eight batters in organized baseball have been killed by pitches.] Being *intentionally* hit is likewise an inherent risk of the sport, so accepted by custom that a pitch intentionally thrown at a batter has its own terminology: "brushback," "beanball," "chin music." In turn, those pitchers notorious for throwing at hitters are "headhunters." Pitchers intentionally throw at batters to disrupt a batter's timing or back him away from home plate, to retaliate after a teammate has been hit, or to punish a batter for having hit a home run. Some of the most respected baseball managers and pitchers have openly discussed the fundamental place throwing at batters has in their sport. . . .

It is true that intentionally throwing at a batter is forbidden by the rules of baseball. (See, e.g., Off. Rules of Major League Baseball, rule 8.02(d); National Collegiate Athletic Assn., 2006 NCAA Baseball Rules (Dec.2005) rule 5, § 16(d), p. 62.) But even when a participant's conduct violates a rule of the game and may subject the violator to internal sanctions prescribed by the sport itself, imposition of *legal liability* for such conduct might well alter fundamentally the nature of the sport by deterring participants from vigorously engaging in activity that falls close to, but on the permissible side of, a prescribed rule. It is one thing for an umpire to punish a pitcher who hits a batter by ejecting him from the game, or for a league to suspend the pitcher; it is quite another for tort law to chill any pitcher from throwing inside, i.e., close to the batter's body—a permissible and essential part of the sport—for fear of a suit over an errant pitch. For better or worse, being intentionally thrown at is a fundamental part and inherent risk of the sport of baseball.[11] It is not the function of tort law to police such conduct.

In *Knight, supra,* we acknowledged that an athlete does not assume the risk of a coparticipant's intentional or reckless conduct "totally outside the range of the ordinary activity involved in the sport." Here, even if the Citrus College pitcher intentionally threw at Avila, his conduct did not fall outside the range of ordinary activity involved in the sport. The District owed no duty to Avila to prevent the Citrus College pitcher from hitting batters, even intentionally. Consequently, the doctrine of primary assumption of the risk bars any claim predicated on the allegation that the Citrus College pitcher negligently or intentionally threw at Avila. . . .

The third way in which Avila alleges the District breached its duty of care, by failing to provide umpires, likewise did not increase the risks inherent in the game. Baseball may be played with umpires, as between professionals at the World Series, or without, as between children in the sandlot. Avila argues that providing umpires would have made the game safer, because an umpire might have issued a warning and threatened ejections after the first batter was hit. Whatever the likelihood of this happening and the difficulty of showing causation, the argument overlooks a key point. The District owed a duty not to increase the risks inherent in the sport, not a duty to decrease the risks. While the provision of umpires might-*might*-have reduced the risk of a retaliatory beanball, Avila has alleged no facts supporting imposition of a duty on the District to reduce that risk.

[Avila's final allegation, that the District breached a duty to him by failing to provide medical care after he was injured, fails because (1) the district did not cause his injury; (2) he was not helpless and (3) his own Rio Hondo coaches and trainers were present to assist him.]

---

11. The conclusion that being intentionally hit by a pitch is an inherent risk of baseball extends only to situations such as that alleged here, where the hit batter is at the plate. Allegations that a pitcher intentionally hit a batter who was still in the on-deck circle, or elsewhere, would present an entirely different scenario.

For the foregoing reasons, we reverse the judgment of the Court of Appeal.

NOTES

1. The *Avila* court says that primary implied assumption of risk arises when the plaintiff impliedly assumes those risks that are *inherent* in a particular activity. How did the court determine that being struck by a pitched ball is an inherent risk in baseball? *Cf. Bjork v. Mason*, 92 Cal.Rptr.2d 49 (Ct. App. 2000) (water skier assumed inherent risks of sport, but those did not include dangers arising from the defendant's defective equipment and frayed ropes).

2. What, exactly, is the relationship between primary assumption of risk and the scope of a defendant's duty? A leading case on this point is *Sunday v. Stratton Corp.*, 390 A.2d 398 (Vt. 1978). Plaintiff was a paying patron at the defendant's ski resort. Although the evidence was that the defendant provided a very smooth novice trail, on which the plaintiff skied, his ski struck a small bush that was concealed by snow. The plaintiff's injuries resulted in permanent quadriplegia and he recovered a verdict and judgment of one and one-half million dollars. The court affirmed. The defendant argued that "brush was an inherent danger of the sport." This, said the court, "is the equivalent of, and better put as, a claim that defendant owed plaintiff no duty with respect thereto, sometimes referred to as 'primary' assumption of risk.' ... Where primary assumption of risk exists, there is no liability to the plaintiff, because there is no negligence on the part of the defendant to begin with; the danger to plaintiff is not one which defendant is required to extinguish or warn about; having no duty to begin with, there is no breach of duty to constitute negligence." But here, the court held, "While skiers fall, as a matter of common knowledge, that does not make every fall a danger inherent in the sport. If the fall is due to no breach of duty on the part of the defendant, its risk is assumed in the primary sense, and there can be no recovery. But where the evidence indicates existence or assumption of duty and its breach, that risk is not one 'assumed' by the plaintiff. What he then 'assumes' is not the risk of injury, but the use of reasonable care on the part of the defendant."

3. Should it matter in *Avila* that the act of throwing a "bean ball" is a violation of baseball's rules? In a well-known case from New York, *Turcotte v. Fell*, 502 N.E.2d 964 (N.Y. 1986), plaintiff Turcotte, a professional jockey who had once won the Triple Crown on Secretariat, was thrown from his horse during a race and rendered a paraplegic. Turcotte claimed that another rider, Fell, was negligent and had engaged in "foul riding" that caused his injury. New York racing rules prohibited the acts of "foul riding" allegedly engaged in by Fell. Affirming a grant of summary judgment for Fell, the court held, "If a participant [in a professional sports event] makes an informed estimate of the risks involved in the activity and willingly undertakes them, then there can be no liability if he is injured as a result of those risks." In such a case the plaintiff can be said to have "consented" to encounter the risks posed by the activity. "Plaintiff's 'consent' is not constructive consent; it is actual consent implied from the act of electing to participate in the activity." Plaintiff's claim

was completely barred, even where the defendant's act violated racing rules, because plaintiff, as a professional rider, "clearly understands the usual incidents of competition." The court distinguished the kind of "bumping and jostling" involved in the case and "flagrant infractions unrelated to the normal method of playing the game and done without any competitive purpose."

4. Is a complete-bar rule consistent with modern comparative negligence rules?

5. A growing number of courts now say that "personal injury cases arising out of an athletic event must be predicated on reckless disregard of safety." *Gauvin v. Clark*, 537 N.E.2d 94 (Mass. 1989) (applying recklessness standard to two hockey participants). That is, where one sports participant sues another for an injury sustained during the sport, the plaintiff must prove that the defendant acted recklessly or worse. *See* DOBBS ON TORTS § 215 (2000). Looking back at *Avila*, how does this limited duty relate to the inherent risks of the sport?

6. Should such a limited duty apply in all sports-participant cases? What if your ping-pong opponent becomes enraged and strikes you with the paddle? Would you distinguish amateur from professional sports? Contact from non-contact sports? Several courts have now applied the limited-duty rule to amateur golfers. *See, e.g., Shin v. Ahn*, 165 P.3d 581 (Cal. 2007); *Yoneda v. Tom*, 133 P.3d 796 (Haw. 2006); *Bowman v. McNary*, 853 N.E.2d 984 (Ind. Ct. App. 2006).

7. Rather than distinguishing between contact and non-contact sports, for example, does it make more sense to focus on the reasonable expectations of the parties? In a case involving a collision of skiers, allegedly the result of negligence, one court thought that the duty of care should turn on the parties' reasonable expectations. As to skiing, the court thought "the expectations of skiers to be that fellow participants in the sport will conduct themselves in a manner befitting the dangerous potentialities attendant with the sport. Thus, skiers will expect that other skiers will follow the rules and generally accepted practices of the sport of skiing." *Jagger v. Mohawk Mountain Ski Area, Inc.*, 849 A.2d 813 (Conn. 2004).

8. State legislatures sometimes enact special statutes intended to protect some particular group of defendants. For instance: "A person who takes part in the sport of skiing accepts as a matter of law the dangers inherent in that sport insofar as they are obvious and necessary." N.M. STAT. § 24–15–10(B). A number of statutes contain similar provisions. Suppose you are injured skiing on the defendant's slopes because the operator has left a dangerous, pointed stake just covered by the snow. Have you assumed the risk that the defendant has been negligent in this way? In other words, is the defendant's negligence an inherent risk of the sport? If not, then does the statute only mean that the defendant is not liable without negligence? *See, e.g., Jagger, supra* Note 7 (saying a state statute "provides that a skier assumes the risk of those hazards over which an operator has no control or over which an operator cannot reasonably act so as to ameliorate the potentiality of harm."); *Cecere v. Loon Mountain Recreation Corp.*, 923 A.2d 198 (N.H. 2007) (construing a

state statute to mean that "an injury caused by an inherent risk cannot have been negligently caused").

9. Primary assumption of risk or limited duty rules are routinely applied to bar claims by spectators injured by risks inherent in the game, such as the risk of a spectator's being hit in the face by a hockey puck, or on the head by a foul ball. *See, e.g., Hurst v. East Coast Hockey League, Inc.*, 637 S.E.2d 560 (S.C. 2006); *Sciarrotta v. Global Spectrum*, 944 A.2d 630 (N.J. 2008).

NOTE: BEYOND THE SPORTS CONTEXT

1. *Testing the limits: Assumption of risk by criminals.* Many cases in this section involve sports, but implied assumption of risk or no-duty rules sweep more broadly than that. How far might it go? Would a criminal mugger, for instance, "assume the risk" that the police officer might shoot him when lesser force would be more appropriate? New York allowed the mugger to recover in *McCummings v. New York City Transit Authority*, 613 N.E.2d 559 (N.Y. 1993). Can you square this result with the limited duty (or assumed risk) applied by the same court in *Turcotte*, discussed in Note 3 above? Can you square it with the same court's rule that a criminal cannot recover for injury sustained as a direct result of a serious criminal act? *Barker v. Kallash*, 468 N.E.2d 39 (N.Y. 1984) (Chapter 9.)

2. *Thinking about alternative locutions.* In *Washington Metropolitan Area Transit Authority v. Cross*, 849 A.2d 1021 (D.C. App. 2004), a passenger on the defendant's bus fell when the bus allegedly lurched forward then suddenly braked. The trial judge instructed the jury that "a common carrier ... is not liable for sudden starts, stops, jerks or jars which are no more than the necessary or usual incidence of the operation of the vehicle. *Passengers assume such risks as part of their travel.*" Can you think of a more straightforward way to instruct the jury without mentioning assumed risk?

3. *Re-categorizing the old "assumed risk" defense.* How can you determine in a particular case whether the old "assumed risk" should be treated as contributory fault (with damages reduction) or as a fact showing no-duty/no-negligence? Suppose plaintiff and defendant are rural neighbors, far from medical help. Plaintiff's spouse or partner is injured and needs immediate medical attention, but plaintiff's car is not available. Defendant's car could be used, but it is in a mechanical condition dangerous to the driver. Should defendant refuse permission to use the car? If he explains the risks and permits its use, but its bad condition causes an injury to the plaintiff, would the plaintiff be entitled to recover, with a reduction for contributory fault? Or would the plaintiff be denied all recovery?

REFERENCES: DOBBS ON TORTS §§ 211–215 (2000); HARPER, JAMES & GRAY, THE LAW OF TORTS § 21.0 (2d Ed. 1986 & Supp.).

Chapter 11

Defenses Not on the Merits

■ ■ ■

§ 1. STATUTES OF LIMITATION

Statutes of limitation are not peculiar to tort law. Almost every kind of claim must be brought within a period of time specified by statutes of limitation. If the claim is brought later, it is barred by the statute, even though it is otherwise a legitimate claim. The traditional statute of limitations serves at least two distinct purposes. One is to bar "stale" claims, the presentation of which might be unfair or costly because evidence is lost or subtly altered with time. A second is to permit both personal and business planning and to avoid the economic burden that would be involved if defendants and their insurance companies had to carry indefinitely a reserve for liability that might never be imposed. The time limit for tort claims may vary depending on the tort. The period is often short in cases of libel or slander, but in cases of personal injury the statute in most instances will allow the plaintiff two or three years in which to bring his action. Once the action is properly brought, the statute of limitations has no other function. It does not, for example, require *trial* by any certain time, only the commencement of the action.

The traditional analysis of statutes requires the action to be brought within the statutory period after the claim "accrues." When the claim accrues, starting the ticking of the limitations period clock, is often a contested issue.

CRUMPTON v. HUMANA, INC.

661 P.2d 54 (N.M. 1983)

H. Vern Payne, C.J.

This is a frivolous appeal. We also note that there is a strong indication in the record that counsel for the appellant ineptly and perhaps negligently handled his client's case. Counsel for the appellant failed to file suit before the applicable statute of limitations had run. We are disappointed when members of our State Bar betray the trust and confidence of their clients by engaging in careless and unprofessional practice.

On February 8, 1979, Wanda Crumpton underwent surgery at Llano Estacado Medical Center in Hobbs. She alleged that she sustained injuries to her neck and legs when an attending nurse attempted to lower her hospital bed on February 11, 1979. Her suit was filed more than three years later on February 15, 1982. The trial court granted a motion for summary judgment on the ground that the suit was barred by the three-year statute of limitations....

Crumpton argues that her injury was not ascertainable until some time after the accident occurred. Further, she contends that the statute of limitations should have been tolled during the time the parties were negotiating.

These arguments are entirely without merit. In her deposition, Crumpton plainly testified that her injuries occurred on February 11, 1979. She also testified that she is still having problems in her shoulders, legs and sides which she attributed to the February 11, 1979 incident. Crumpton offers no evidence to contradict the fact that the alleged negligent act and injury occurred simultaneously on February 11, 1979. In our view, the fact that she had continuing treatments and hospitalizations after the injury does not necessarily make the date of the injury unascertainable.

... [T]he statute of limitations commences running from the date of injury or the date of the alleged malpractice....

Crumpton cites no authority for her argument that the statute of limitations should be tolled during the time when the parties were negotiating a settlement. The record indicates that defendants did not fraudulently lead Crumpton to believe that the case would be settled at some future date. In fact, the record indicates that in May 1981, defendants sent Crumpton a letter wherein defendants made a final offer for a compromise settlement of the case.

Accordingly, we affirm the trial court's grant of summary judgment against Crumpton. Because we determine this appeal to be frivolous and entirely without merit, costs and attorneys fees are to be borne by appellants.

NOTES

1. Attorneys responsible for failure to file a meritorious suit (or a defense) in time are subject to liability to the client for malpractice. What would you do to be sure you never filed a late claim, answer, or motion? Sometimes the client is late in consulting an attorney. Why might a client delay?

2. Suppose the defendant physician is actually a state employee entitled to invoke a short statute of limitations, but he presents himself to patients of a private clinic as an employee of that clinic. A longer statute of limitations applies to private doctors. Is the physician estopped to assert the shorter

statute of limitation because of the appearance he created? *See Hagen v. Faherty,* 66 P.3d 974 (N.M. Ct. App. 2003).

SHEARIN v. LLOYD, 98 S.E.2d 508 (N.C. 1957). Defendant, a surgeon, performed an operation to remove plaintiff's appendix in July, 1951. Plaintiff returned for checkups, complaining of pain near the incision. Defendant repeatedly told the plaintiff he would be all right and that it would take time "to heal up and get tough." In November, 1952, the defendant admitted that something was wrong. X-rays showed a "sponge" had been left in the abdomen. This was removed in November, 1952, but in December "a knot" in the incision "rose up and bursted." Defendant dressed this, but another knot occurred in January, 1953, and another in May. In the fall of 1953 defendant told plaintiff he was doing all he could to kill the infection but that plaintiff needed another operation. Plaintiff then ended his relations with the defendant and commenced this action for negligence in November, 1955. There was a three-year statute of limitations. The trial judge granted defendant's motion for non-suit. *Held,* affirmed. A cause of action accrues so as to start the running of the statute of limitations as soon as the right to institute an action arises. "It is inescapable that plaintiff's cause of action accrued on July 20, 1951, when defendant closed the incision without first removing the lappack.... Defendant's failure thereafter to detect or discover his own negligence in this respect did not affect the basis of his liability therefor."

NOTES

1. **The rule in *Shearin*.** The *Shearin* case reflects the rule generally followed at the time it was decided. In a sense the rule was "logical." The idea was that the statute of limitations must begin running when the plaintiff can sue on a claim, since, if he can sue, the claim must have "accrued." Legally speaking, a plaintiff injured like the plaintiff in *Shearin* could sue on his claim when the incision was closed. Factually speaking, he could not do so, but that inability was not the result of any legal rule, only of his own ignorance. Thus, legally, he could sue at that time and the claim must have accrued.

2. **Adopting the discovery rule.** Such a result is obviously harsh, and beginning in the 1960s a number of states changed the rule. North Carolina itself changed the rule by statute. N.C. GEN. STAT. § 1–52(16). Many changed it by judicial decision. They adopted instead the "discovery rule." In most states, the discovery rule delays the accrual of the claim until (1) all the elements of the tort are present; and (2) the plaintiff discovers, or a reasonable person should discover, both the injury and defendant's role in causing it. The discovery rule treats the cause of action as accruing when in *fact* the plaintiff could reasonably sue. This avoids the harsh result of *Shearin*, but it substitutes a good deal of uncertainty, since discovery will depend upon the highly individualized facts of each case. It also injects a normative issue— when plaintiff *should* have discovered the injury and its likely cause.

3. **Continuous treatment.** A growing number of states have adopted a rule that delays the start of the statute of limitations until the medical treatment for which the patient consulted the physician has been concluded. *See, e.g., Harrison v. Valentini*, 184 S.W.3d 521 (Ky. 2006). Suppose a radiologist reading an x-ray fails to detect cancer on an x-ray and reports a clean bill of health to the primary physician. Months later he reads a new x-ray but this time is not negligent. Does the second reading indicate continuous treatment so that the statute starts then? *Cf. Montgomery v. South County Radiologists, Inc.*, 49 S.W.3d 191 (Mo. 2001).

4. **Concealment.** What result would you expect if the doctor deliberately conceals negligent treatment from the patient? *See Florida Dep't of Health & Rehab. Serv. v. S.A.P.*, 835 So.2d 1091 (Fla. 2002).

SCHIELE v. HOBART CORP.

587 P.2d 1010 (Or. 1978)

HOLMAN, JUSTICE.

[Plaintiff, a meat wrapper, developed serious lung problems, allegedly from using defendant's machine. The trial court gave summary judgment for defendant on the ground that the two-year statute of limitations had run.]

[P]laintiff began work as a meat wrapper at Fred Meyer in Portland, Oregon, in November of 1948. She worked in that capacity from 1948 through March of 1974. In May or June of 1972 Fred Meyer purchased and installed defendant Hobart's meat wrapping machine which allegedly incorporated defendant Dayton Electric's ventilator. The machine used a hot wire to cut the polyvinyl chloride meat wrapping film allegedly manufactured by defendant Borden Chemical. In December of 1972 plaintiff began using the new meat wrapping machine during a considerable part of her work day. Prior to this time, plaintiff had been in good health. Soon after beginning use of the machine, she began to experience a variety of health problems, more specifically, nausea, dizziness, choking, coughing, and difficulty catching her breath. Almost from the outset, plaintiff associated these problems with the fumes which the machine generated as its hot wire cut the polyvinyl chloride meat wrapping film.

Between January of 1973 and October of 1973, plaintiff's condition worsened. Her choking and coughing increased. She began to cough at night and experienced pain in her lungs. In the summer of that year she began to cough up quantities of white sputum at night. While at work she experienced coughing spells six to eight times a day which forced her to walk out to a breezeway to get air. She complained about the problems to her employer's manager but nothing was done.

Between October of 1973 and January of 1974, plaintiff's condition continued to deteriorate. She experienced fatigue, shortness of breath, and a burning sensation in her eyes, in addition to the symptoms previously described. To facilitate breathing at night, plaintiff elevated her head with two or three pillows.

In January of 1974, plaintiff noted that her lungs were more sore than usual. During the latter part of January and the first part of February 1974, the pain became almost constant. Plaintiff put in her last day at work on March 12, 1974. Almost immediately thereafter she was hospitalized for pulmonary pneumonia. After testing and x-rays during March 1974, plaintiff's doctors informed her on or about April 15, 1974, that her illness was possibly due to her exposure to polyvinyl chloride fumes on the job.

Plaintiff filed her complaint in this action on March 8, 1976....

Plaintiff contends that the statute of limitations did not begin to run until plaintiff was informed by a physician of the nature of her disease or injury and its possible cause. Since this did not occur until April of 1974 she argues that her March 8, 1976 filing fell within the limitation period. Defendants argue that the limitation period began to run when plaintiff first became aware of her symptoms and their cause. Since she first associated her symptoms with the fumes prior to March 8, 1974, defendants believe the two-year limitation period had expired by the time plaintiff initiated her action.

[The court here discussed earlier decisions involving long exposure to silica dust.]

These cases stand for the proposition that the statute of limitations on claims involving negligent infliction of an occupational disease does not begin to run until the plaintiff knows, or as a reasonably prudent person should know, that he has the condition for which his action is brought and that defendant has caused it. Plaintiff's actionable condition in this case is alleged to be her *permanent injuries*. However, it still remains to be determined exactly what type of knowledge plaintiff must have before it should be said that she knew or should have known of her condition. Plaintiff argues that the statute of limitations did not begin to run until her physician diagnosed her disease and identified its source. We agree that the acquisition of such information from a physician would undoubtedly start the period running. However, we reject plaintiff's contention that nothing short of a positive diagnosis by a physician will have this effect. A plaintiff whose condition has not yet been diagnosed by a physician can have or, in the exercise of reasonable care, could have access to information which requires or would require a reasonable person to conclude she is being seriously or permanently injured.

On the other hand, we reject defendants' claim that knowledge of symptoms and their causal relationship to defendants' actions in and of itself initiates the running of the statute. We do not believe the legislature intended that the statute be applied in a manner which would require one to file an action for temporary sickness or discomfort or risk the loss of a right of action for permanent injury.

The statute of limitations begins to run when a reasonably prudent person associates his symptoms with a serious or permanent condition and at the same time perceives the role which the defendant has played in inducing that condition. Of course, one's condition may deteriorate to the point where a delay in seeking medical attention is no longer reasonable and to further such delay would be to charge the individual with any knowledge which a medical examination would otherwise have disclosed.

If knowledge of the occupational disease, its symptoms, and its causes is widespread among persons similarly situated to plaintiff, then we hold that plaintiff, as a reasonable person, should have recognized her condition for what it was and brought the action within the applicable period of limitation following the onset of the symptoms. However, defendants have made no showing that there was any prevalent knowledge concerning the dangers of the fumes from polyvinyl chloride. This is an extremely close case, but we believe we cannot say as a matter of law that a reasonably prudent person would have apprehended more than two years prior to the commencement of plaintiff's action that she was being seriously or permanently injured. Many persons would probably have realized the seriousness of their condition and have gone to a doctor, but not everyone goes to a doctor with the same degree of alacrity. We cannot, therefore, say as a matter of law that anyone who is optimistic about his condition's taking a turn for the better is unreasonable. . . .

The trial court's grant of summary judgment is reversed and the case is remanded for trial.

NOTES

1. **Different times for starting the statutory clock.** The *Schiele* problem obviously parallels the *Shearin* problem. Some courts made the statute begin to run from the time of the first exposure or first negligent act. Others used a last exposure or termination of employment trigger. Still others have adopted the discovery rule.

2. **What counts as discovery?** Exactly what discovery ought to count? Is it a discovery that "something is wrong"? That something is wrong and it was caused by defendant? That the defendant was or might be negligent? In *United States v. Kubrick*, 444 U.S. 111 (1979), the plaintiff had an operation in a VA hospital and thereafter suffered a hearing loss. In 1969 he discovered that this probably resulted from antibiotics administered in the post-operative care, but it was not until much later that someone suggested that the hospital may have been negligent in administering the antibiotics. The Supreme Court held that the statute began to run in 1969 when he was aware of the injury and possible cause of it, even though he was not then aware of possible negligence.

In *Walk v. Ring*, 44 P.3d 990 (Ariz. 2002), the court rejected *Kubrick's* bright-line rule. The *Walk* court thought that the question was whether the plaintiff knew facts that would put a person of reasonable diligence on notice, either that she had a potential suit against the defendant or that she should investigate further. In some cases, discovery of injury and the defendant's causal connection would put the plaintiff on notice, but in others it would not, or it would be a jury question. The *Walk* case involved a plaintiff who knew she suffered injury after dental work but did not initially think the dentist was at fault. Only when she discovered that other dentists thought he was at fault did the statute begin to run.

Somewhat similarly, Connecticut has said that the statute runs from the time injury is or should have been discovered, but that "injury" means *actionable injury*. In turn, actionable injury means an injury caused by negligence. So the statute would not commence to run until the plaintiff discovered or should have discovered all the elements of a cause of action, including *both* the defendant's negligence *and* the defendant's causal link to the injury,, or at least reason to investigate those issues. *Lagassey v. State,* 846 A.2d 831 (Conn. 2004).

In California, the discovery rule similarly "delays accrual until the plaintiff has, or should have, inquiry notice of the cause of action," which means the discovery of "a factual basis for a cause of action." Thus excusable ignorance of a "generic element of the cause of action" will delay accrual. But because the identity of the defendant is not an element, the plaintiff's ignorance of that fact does not delay accrual. *Fox v. Ethicon Endo–Surgery, Inc.*, 110 P.3d 914 (Cal. 2005).

3. **The jury's role.** As *Schiele* indicates, and as the cases in Note 2 imply, the discovery rule will often produce an issue of fact with respect to whether a reasonable person would have discovered sufficient facts to start the limitations clock. *See also, e.g., Murtha v. Cahalan,* 745 N.W.2d 711 (Iowa 2008); *T.R. v. Boy Scouts of America,* 181 P.3d 758 (Or. 2008). Does this feature of the discovery rule undercut the purposes of having statutes of limitation in the first place?

4. **Statutes limiting the discovery rule.** The Oregon court, which decided *Schiele,* has also said that the discovery rule must be found in the statute itself, not judicially created. *Gladhart v. Oregon Vineyard Supply Co.,* 26 P.3d 817 (Or. 2001). Beyond this, some statutes have been adopted to provide special protections for health care professions and others and one kind of these specifically eliminates the discovery rule altogether. The statutes may be unconstitutional under state constitutions in some states but they are perfectly constitutional in others. *See Martin v. Richey,* 711 N.E.2d 1273 (Ind. 1999) (unconstitutional as applied to plaintiff); *Aicher v. Wisconsin Patients Comp. Fund,* 613 N.W.2d 849 (Wis. 2000).

5. **Statutes adopting the discovery rule.** The discovery rule is especially appealing for victims of toxic torts, the effects of which may not appear for many, many years or even for generations. A federal statute creates certain liabilities in connection with disposal or release of hazardous substances. The federal statute goes on to add that in cases brought under *state* law for personal injury or property damage, the state must give the plaintiff the benefit of the discovery rule. The state must also toll the statute of limitations for minors until they reach majority, and toll the statute for incompetents until they become competent or have a guardian appointed. 42 U.S.C.A. § 9658.

NOTE: LATENT POTENTIAL HARM

Partial Injury, Latent Potential

Shearin v. Lloyd turns in part on the notion that a tort occurs when harm is done and the related notion that the statute of limitations begins to run when the tort occurs, not when the plaintiff learns of it. If the plaintiff knows of the tort, one would imagine at first glance that the statute of limitations presents no problem to the plaintiff. But suppose a tort occurs and the plaintiff knows it, yet the plaintiff wishes to postpone suit because he believes damages may become much worse than they are at present. It is perfectly possible to claim and recover damages that will occur in the future, but under traditional rules this can be done only if the proof shows such damages to be more likely than not. If the plaintiff sues now to stay within the statute of limitations, he will avoid that problem; but he will be limited to damages he can presently prove. The *res judicata* rules will prevent a second suit later on. If he waits to see whether damages will become much worse, he will eventually run into the statute of limitations problem.

In *Hagerty v. L. & L. Marine Services, Inc.*, 788 F.2d 315 (5th Cir. 1986), Hagerty was drenched with dripolene, a carcinogen. He had some dizziness and leg cramps, and stinging in the extremities, all of which disappeared after showers. He undergoes regular medical checkups because of the cancer threat, but he does not presently have cancer and cancer is not "more likely than not." But his present fear of future cancer is real. Consider the options for the court:

(1) Adopt a view similar to that in *Lord v. Lovett*, Chapter 7, § 2. This would allow the plaintiff to recover now for any actual injury, plus all possible future injuries that might result from it, but future injuries would be reduced to reflect their probability. For example, if future cancer appearing in ten years is a 40% probability and would, if it occurs, impose damages of $100,000, the plaintiff would recover $40,000. This is the "enhanced risk" or reduced chance recovery.

(2) Reject the enhanced risk recovery, allow present actual damages only, but with present damages including the mental anguish or suffering resulting from the plaintiff's fear of future cancer.

(3) Reject the enhanced risk and fear claims, allow the plaintiff to recover what he can prove in actual damages, and bar any future claims under *res judicata* rules.

(4) Reject enhanced risk recovery but allow present damages and leave open the possibility for a second suit if substantially different kinds of damage occur. This would allow recovery for cancer if it later develops.

The *Hagerty* court adopted the fourth option. This eliminates the dilemma created by the statute of limitations on the one hand and the *res judicata* rules on the other. A growing number of cases support some such view. *See Mauro v. Raymark Indust., Inc.*, 561 A.2d 257 (N.J. 1989) ("neither the statute of limitations nor the single-controversy doctrine will bar a toxic tort plaintiff's timely damage claim instituted after discovery of a causally-related disease"); *Pustejovsky v. Rapid–American Corp.*, 35 S.W.3d 643 (Tex. 2000) (settlement of asbestosis claim did not bar suit for asbestos-induced cancer, mesothelioma); *Sopha v. Owens–Corning Fiber-*

glas Corp., 601 N.W.2d 627 (Wis. 1999) (diagnosis of non-malignant asbestos-related injury does not trigger statute of limitations with respect to a claim for distinct, later-diagnosed asbestos-related malignancy; nor does doctrine of claim preclusion apply). Will such a view work for all kinds of cases?

Exposure without Symptoms

Suppose the plaintiff is exposed to a toxin in sufficient quantities to raise the possibility of future harm that could occur in ten, twenty or thirty years. But suppose also that the plaintiff has no present symptoms at all. You might think that in this kind of case there is no problem. There is no statute of limitations to confront because the plaintiff merely waits until injury occurs and then sues. However, the plaintiff exposed to chemical poisons in her water or gases in the air she breathes may have two present "injuries" without symptoms. First, the plaintiff may have fear of future harm and that fear may itself poison her life. Second, the plaintiff may have medical expense because continuous medical monitoring is important to minimize future harm by early detection.

Some decisions have treated the non-symptomatic exposure as a tort and have said, with *Hagerty*, that the plaintiff could recover now for the costs of medical monitoring and that an additional suit could be brought later if cancer or other serious disease actually occurs. A landmark case is *Ayers v. Jackson Twp.*, 525 A.2d 287 (N.J. 1987). *See also Meyer ex rel. Coplin v. Fluor Corp.*, 220 S.W.3d 712 (Mo. 2007) (citing cases from a dozen other jurisdictions supporting such a theory). Other courts have rejected claims for medical monitoring damages in the absence of proven physical injury. *See, e.g., Paz v. Brush Engineered Materials, Inc.*, 949 So.2d 1 (Miss. 2007); *Henry v. Dow Chemical Co.*, 701 N.W.2d 684 (Mich. 2005)

Are you willing to say that any exposure, even though not accompanied by symptoms, is a tort for which damages can be recovered?

––––––––––

McCOLLUM v. D'ARCY, 638 A.2d 797 (N.H. 1994). The plaintiff, fifty years old, sued her parents, now in their eighties, alleging childhood sexual abuse ending more than thirty-five years earlier. She alleged that she repressed all memory of the abuse from the time it occurred until recent flashbacks triggered by attending a "therapy workshop on child abuse." *Held*, if these allegations are true, the statute of limitations will be tolled under the discovery rule, so the trial court properly rejected the defendants' motion to dismiss. Defendants can, however, still argue that the plaintiff discovered or should have discovered the facts earlier.

DOE v. MASKELL, 679 A.2d 1087 (Md. 1996). The two plaintiffs were students at a parochial high school in the late 1960s and early 1970s. They filed suit in 1994 alleging that during their high school years, they were physically, sexually, and psychologically abused by the school chaplain.

Plaintiffs claimed that at some point they had "ceased to recall the abuse ... due to a process they term 'repression.' Both plaintiffs began to 'recover' memories of this abuse in 1992." Both sides put on expert testimony about "whether there is a difference between forgetting and repression." *Held*, the claims are barred by Maryland's three-year statute of limitations. "After reviewing the arguments on both sides of the issue, we are unconvinced that repression exists as a phenomenon separate and apart from the normal process of forgetting.... Therefore we hold that the mental process of repression of memories of past sexual abuse does not activate the discovery rule."

NOTES

1. **Reality of childhood sexual abuse.** Scientists and psychologists agree that childhood sexual abuse is real. Sometimes it is inflicted upon quite young children by parents, grandparents, or others in positions of trust and authority. It is often extremely harmful to ordinary emotional development.

2. **Disputes about repression.** Scientists and therapists often stringently differ about the existence of repression and the accuracy of "recovered" memory. Those who approach the problem as scientists seeking data tend to deny or doubt the supposed "repression." Those who approach the problem as therapists, not surprisingly, adhere to the concept of repression and vigorously support claims of childhood sexual abuse. The conflict presents a difficult problem for the law because the emotional stakes are high. Sexual abuse sometimes causes severe problems to the victim, but false claims of sexual abuse have also caused severe problems to those accused. For an observer whose only agenda is to do justice, it is sometimes a chicken and egg problem—did the sexual abuse cause the plaintiff's psychological problems or did the psychological problems cause false allegations of sexual abuse? The problem is aggravated because there is a small industry devoted to convincing those with emotional troubles that their problems result from sexual abuse whether they remember it or not. As a result, some plaintiffs who see therapists may be talked into "remembering" abuse that never occurred. Some therapists may even hypnotically induce or "implant" false memories.

3. **Choosing up your experts.** Was the *Doe v. Maskell* court right to take sides with one group of experts against another group? In *Doe v. Roe*, 955 P.2d 951 (Ariz. 1998), the Arizona Court believed the other set of "experts." The court said that repression exists and also that it furnishes a ground for invoking the discovery rule. Is this how it should work—one group of "experts" controls the law in Arizona, while another controls the law in Maryland? What else could be done? In *Doe v. Creighton,* 786 N.E.2d 1211 (Mass. 2003), the court did not discuss the repression debate at all, but held that the plaintiff would be required to show that she sued within the statutory period after a reasonable person would have learned of her abuse and connected it with the emotional problems for which she sues. Under this objective test, the plaintiff's "[p]ersonal traits unrelated to the tort, such as cultural background and educational history, are not relevant to the reasonableness inquiry."

4. **The logical problems behind repression.** If a court accepts the idea of repression in general, should that toll the statute of limitations for the particular plaintiff? The Arizona Court in *Doe v. Roe, supra,* said:

> A victim whose memory is inaccessible lacks conscious awareness of the event and thus cannot know the facts giving rise to the cause. The policy behind the discovery rule is thus served by application to repressed memory cases involving childhood sexual abuse and is, we believe, logically appropriate given that the intentional act of the tortfeasor caused both the damage and the repression of memory. To hold otherwise would be to effectively reward the perpetrator for the egregious nature of his conduct and the severity of the resulting emotional injury.

In order to decide the statute of limitations questions, did the court assume that the defendant was in fact guilty?

5. **Rejecting the discovery rule in "repression" cases.** A few courts, without overtly rejecting the idea of repression, have rejected the discovery rule in childhood sexual abuse claims. *See Lemmerman v. Fealk,* 534 N.W.2d 695 (Mich. 1995) (the rule should apply only when the defendant inflicts tangible harm that can be judged by an objective standard); *Dalrymple v. Brown,* 701 A.2d 164 (Pa. 1997) (discovery rule uses objective, not subjective standard in determining whether plaintiff was reasonably diligent in discovering harm; discovery rule applies only when the nature of the injury itself is such that no amount of vigilance will permit discovery).

6. **Memory intact but other psychological impediments to suit.** Some judicial decisions would apply the discovery rule when the plaintiff is aware of the abuse but not aware of its connection to her emotional injury or the amount of harm done to her. *E.g., McCreary v. Weast,* 971 P.2d 974 (Wyo. 1999) (alleging 20 years of sexual abuse). Some statutes appear to provide for the same result. *E.g.,* N.J. STAT. ANN. § 2A:61B–1. But some courts have held that if the victim retained her memory of the abuse, the discovery rule has no application, even though the plaintiff was unable to understand that the abuse caused her emotional problems. *E.g., Clay v. Kuhl,* 727 N.E.2d 217 (Ill. 2000); *see also Colosimo v. Roman Catholic Bishop of Salt Lake City,* 156 P.3d 806 (Utah 2007) (statute of limitations is tolled only when a plaintiff completely represses all memory of sexual abuse, not simply when the victim cannot causally connect present injuries to the past abuse).

7. **Statutes.** Some states have passed statutes liberalizing the statute of limitations in cases of childhood sexual abuse. *E.g.,* IOWA CODE ANN. § 614.8A; MONT. CODE ANN. § 27–2–216; WASH. REV. CODE § 4.16.340; UTAH CODE ANN. § 78–12–25.1. In 2007, Delaware abolished the statute of limitations entirely for such cases. 10 DEL. CODE ANN. § 8145. If you were in the legislature, what provisions would you want to see in a liberalizing statute?

NOTE: TOLLING FOR DISABILITIES

Tolling for disabilities. The discovery rule is not the only avenue of relief for the late-suing plaintiff. Statutes of limitation may be tolled so that the clock is not running while the plaintiff is under a disability such as minority or mental incompetence. State laws generally toll the statute of limitations on a child's injury claim until the child has reached the age of majority, usually 18. Thus if the statutory period is two years and the injured child sued within two years after reaching majority, the suit would be timely. Some state courts have held that legislating otherwise violates their constitution. *See Piselli v. 75th Street Med.*, 808 A.2d 508 (Md. 2002); *Sands ex rel. Sands v. Green*, 156 P.3d 1130 (Alaska 2007). Other courts have upheld legislative restrictions on minority tolling against constitutional attack. *See, e.g., Christiansen v. Providence Health System of Oregon Corp.*, 184 P.3d 1121 (Or. 2008).

Minority is a type of legal disability, but the law recognizes other types as well for tolling purposes. In the sexual abuse cases, the plaintiff sometimes claims tolling because he or she was of unsound mind when the tort was committed or at least during the time in which suit could otherwise have been brought.

For purposes of commitment to an institution, an individual might be deemed of unsound mind if he is a danger to himself or others. In the statute of limitations context, however, unsound mind usually means that the individual is unable to manage his or her business affairs or estate, or to comprehend his or her legal rights or liabilities. *Ellis v. Estate of Ellis*, 169 P.3d 441 (Utah 2007); *Doe v. Roe*, 955 P.2d 951 (Ariz. 1998); *Basham v. Hunt*, 773 N.E.2d 1213 (Ill. App. Ct. 2002). Thus no matter what the psychological impediments to suit, the victim cannot have the benefits of tolling for unsound mind if he can manage his daily affairs by working, buying food, writing checks or the like. State statutes sometimes explicitly set forth the requirements for tolling on account of disability, and of course courts apply such statutes unless they are constitutionally infirm. *See Ballinger v. Thompson*, 118 P.3d 429 (Wyo. 2005) (holding that imprisonment does not toll the statute because no Wyoming statute lists it as a ground for tolling).

Grace periods. Tolling is a true time-out, time not counted on the statute of limitations period. A number of legislatures have now replaced time-out tolling with a grace period. A grace period merely extends the statute of limitations; it does not stop the clock. Some statutes provide hardly any grace at all. For example, Michigan provides that if a child under 13 suffers injury to reproductive organs, she must sue before her fifteenth birthday. MICH. COMP. L. ANN. § 600.5851(8).

In *Callahan v. State*, 464 N.W.2d 268 (Iowa 1990), a four-year-old child, "deaf and cerebral palsied," was sexually abused for three years in a state school. By the time his mother discovered the facts he had been out of the school for more than two years. The state pleaded the two-year statute of limitations. Instead of tolling the statute for minority, the court held that the cause of action would not begin to run until the mother discovered or should have discovered the facts. Given the familiar repression by victims of childhood sexual abuse, the court thought the trier could find the suit to be timely.

DASHA v. MAINE MEDICAL CENTER, 665 A.2d 993 (Me. 1995). Defendant erroneously diagnosed the plaintiff as having a fatal brain tumor. On that diagnosis, surgery plus radiation to the brain would prolong life for a short time and the plaintiff opted for that treatment. The treatment itself allegedly caused severe brain damage and the plaintiff became incompetent. Two years after the misdiagnosis and treatments, another physician reviewed the diagnosis and discovered that it was erroneous. The plaintiff's original problem had been a relatively benign tumor not calling for such treatments. His guardian sued, but by this time it was more than three years after the original misdiagnosis. Under Maine's legislation, the discovery rule did not apply. Nor did tolling for mental incapacity work because the plaintiff was mentally sound at the time of the misdiagnosis. The plaintiff argued that, nonetheless, the defendant should be equitably estopped from pleading the statute of limitations, since the defendant's own fault had caused the incapacity as well as the injury. *Held,* no equitable estoppel applies. "[E]stoppel may be used to prevent the affirmative defense of the statute of limitations if the elements of estoppel are present.... The gist of an estoppel barring the defendant from invoking the defense of the statute of limitations is that the defendant has conducted himself in a manner which actually induces the plaintiff not to take timely legal action on a claim. The plaintiff thus relies to his detriment on the conduct of the defendant by failing to seek legal redress while the doors to the courthouse remain open to him."

"The stipulated facts of this case do not meet the elements of equitable estoppel. First, MMC made no affirmative misrepresentation, as required to support the application of equitable estoppel. Although a claim of equitable estoppel can be supported by an act of negligence that is the equivalent of fraud, the misdiagnosis by MMC is not the equivalent of fraud sufficient to support the assertion of equitable estoppel. Dasha relied on the misdiagnosis to seek radiation treatments, but he did not rely on a representation of MMC to decide to forego seeking legal redress."

NOTES

1. "The elements of an equitable estoppel claim are 1) a delay in filing an action that is induced by the defendant; 2) the defendant misled the plaintiff; and 3) the plaintiff must have acted on the information in good faith to the extent that he failed to pursue his action in a timely manner." *Archuleta v. City of Rawlins,* 942 P.2d 404 (Wyo. 1997).

2. If a defendant prevented suit by physical force or threats, he might be estopped from pleading the statute of limitations as a defense. *See John R. v. Oakland Unified School Dist.,* 769 P.2d 948 (Cal. 1989) (child molester); *Ortega v. Pajaro Valley Unified Sch. Dist.,* 75 Cal.Rptr.2d 777 (Ct. App. 1998) (same).

3. Some courts have distinguished equitable estoppel, fraudulent concealment, and equitable tolling, on the ground that the first two involve some misconduct by the defendant while the latter does not. With equitable tolling,

a court may decide to toll the statute simply because "despite all due diligence [the plaintiff] is unable to obtain vital information bearing on his claim." *Valdez v. United States*, 518 F.3d 173 (2d Cir. 2008). Does this give the court more flexibility than would a simple application of the discovery rule?

NOTE: LIMITATIONS NOT BASED ON ACCRUAL

1. The traditional rule seen in *Shearin*, though modified by the discovery rule, remained one based on accrual of a cause of action. The shift to the discovery rule was merely a shift in the legal definition of "accrual." There are at least two forms of limitation not based on accrual, both of which are significant.

2. *The notice bar.* In certain instances a statute or ordinance may require that the plaintiff give notice to the defendant of his claim a specified number of days before filing a legal action. This is commonly required in the cases of actions against public entities, such as cities. Similarly, "retraction statutes" in some states require a plaintiff to demand a retraction before suing for libel. Under the notice statutes and to a lesser extent under the retraction statutes, it may be impossible to file a legal action in any effective way until the notice requirement has been met. If notice must be given 30 days before filing the action, the net effect is that the statute of limitations is shortened by 30 days—that is, the plaintiff who gives the required notice 15 days before the statute of limitations has run cannot file the legal action in time, since it will be necessary to wait 30 days after notice in order to sue, and at that time the statute will have run.

3. *The pre-accrual bar: "statutes of repose."* In the latter part of the 20th century, a new kind of statute was adopted for certain kinds of cases. For instance, the North Carolina legislature, in effect overruling *Shearin*, provided that claims for personal injury and physical damage to property "shall not accrue until bodily harm to the claimant or physical damage to his property becomes apparent or ought reasonably to have become apparent.... Provided that no cause of action shall accrue more than ten years from the last act or omission of the defendant giving rise to the cause of action." N.C. GEN. STAT. § 1–52(16). The proviso could obviously bar a claim before it accrues. For example, if a doctor negligently administers a drug which causes no harm for 15 years, the cause of action would not accrue until harm was done, but the statute would have run ten years after the doctor's "last act." A number of states have enacted statutes of this kind, usually aimed at providing protection for some special group. Products manufacturers, doctors, architects, engineers, and construction contractors have been singled out in some instances to receive the benefits of this pre-accrual bar or statute of "ultimate repose."

One line of attack on this sort of statute questions its constitutionality, usually on the basis of state constitutional provisions. Some courts have held such statutes unconstitutional, but others have upheld them. Much may depend on the exact wording of the particular state constitution. A narrower attack aims to persuade courts that the statute does not apply in the particular case. For instance, a contractor who builds a defective building that causes harm twelve years after it is completed may be protected by the statute, but the current owner who fails to repair or maintain the building may not be. *See Davenport v. Comstock Hills–Reno,* 46 P.3d 62 (Nev. 2002).

HOERY v. UNITED STATES

64 P.3d 214 (Colo. 2003)

JUSTICE BENDER delivered the Opinion of the Court. . . .

[The Tenth Circuit certified questions of Colorado law to the Supreme Court of Colorado. This opinion is answering those questions.]

[In 1993, the Hoery family bought a residence with a groundwater well. The property is seven blocks north of Lowry Air Force Base, where, it turned out, the United States had been dumping trichloroethylene (TCE) and other toxic substances, creating underground plumes of toxic chemicals that migrated underneath Hoery's property. Some chemicals remain there and others continue to migrate to areas underneath the Hoery's land, even though the United States quit dumping toxic chemicals in 1994. Hoery brought suit against the United States in 1998. The District Court dismissed on the ground that the statute of limitations had run. Federal law determines when the claim accrues. If the tort is "permanent" the claim accrues when the plaintiff learned or should have learned of injury, but if the tort is "continuing" the claim continues to accrue.] In this event, plaintiff's recovery is limited to the statute of limitations period dating back from when plaintiff's complaint was filed. . . .

The typical trespass or nuisance is complete when it is committed; the cause of action accrues, and the statute of limitations beings to run at that time. But in cases, for example, when the defendant erects a structure or places something on or underneath the plaintiff's land, the defendant's invasion continues if he fails to stop the invasion and to remove the harmful condition. In such a case, there is a continuing tort so long as the offending object remains and continues to cause the plaintiff harm. . . .

For continuing intrusions—either by way of trespass or nuisance— each repetition or continuance amounts to another wrong, giving rise to a new cause of action. The practical significance of the continuing tort concept is that for statute of limitation purposes, the claim does not begin to accrue until the tortious conduct has ceased.

We recognized claims for continuing torts in *Wright,* 40 Colo. 437, 91 P. 43. In *Wright,* the plaintiff's house was adjacent to the defendant's slaughterhouse. We held that the harmful noises and stenches emanating from the slaughterhouse to the plaintiff's property constituted a continuing nuisance. We reasoned that the defendant was liable until the "nuisance was abated and the cause of damage removed." The plaintiff's claim was not barred by the statute of limitations because "the continuing of a trespass or nuisance from day to day is considered in law a several trespass on each day." In other words, for statute of limitations purposes, a claim would only accrue once the defendant abated the nuisance and removed the cause of damage. . . .

Colorado courts have embraced the concept of "permanent trespass and nuisance" to distinguish those unique factual situations—primarily in the context of irrigation ditches and railway lines—where the trespass or nuisance would and should continue indefinitely.

For example, in *Middelkamp,* the defendant built an irrigation ditch in loose, porous soil. As a result of the loose soil, water seeped through the bottom and sides of the ditch, causing flooding damage to plaintiff's adjacent properties. We found that the irrigation ditch, as a permanent improvement, was distinguishable from the abatable nuisance we analyzed in *Wright* (house adjacent to cattle slaughterhouse).

We reasoned that irrigation ditches were intended to be permanent structures and seep by necessity. Because the irrigation ditches were permanent, the seepage would continue indefinitely absent extraordinary measures.

Even if the seepage was abatable, we declined to require it for defendants who lawfully constructed irrigation ditches because they represented a class of enterprises "so vital to the future development of our state." The practical impact of the *Middelkamp* decision was that an action to recover for present and future damages would accrue when the lands were first visibly affected.

In addition to irrigation ditches, we have applied the concept of permanent tort to the construction and maintenance of railway lines. . . . Similar to the context of irrigation ditches, defendants who lawfully constructed and maintained railway lines represented an enterprise that was vital to the future development of the state. . . .

[W]e agree with Hoery that the ongoing presence and continued migration of toxic chemicals originally emanating from Lowry constitute a continuing trespass and nuisance and decline to extend the permanent tort concept of the irrigation ditch cases to the facts alleged here. . . .

Pursuant to the fundamental principles of tort law, the United States's failure to act, or its omissions, can be the basis for tortious conduct. . . .

These continuing property invasions are not dependent upon whether the United States still releases TCE into the ground. We decline to hold, as urged by the United States, that its wrongful conduct has ceased and that the contamination of Hoery's property represents only the product of that prior conduct. . . .

The irrigation ditch cases do not change our conclusion. In those cases, we held that defendants lawfully constructed permanent improvements that would and should continue indefinitely. Indeed, such defendants represented an enterprise that was vital to the development of our state. The record does not indicate that the continued migration or ongoing presence of toxic pollution plumes underneath Hoery's residential property will or should continue indefinitely. Rather, the record at this stage of the litigation indicates that the contamination is not permanent— that is, it is remediable or abatable. Although the United States did not address the factual issue, Hoery's expert opined under oath that Hoery's property could be remediated.

We also note that the continued contamination does not benefit the development of our state. In contrast to our policy supporting our holding that the seepage from irrigation ditches constituted a permanent property invasion, there exists no sound public policy supporting the classification of contamination from the release of toxic chemicals as a permanent property invasion. One basis for classifying a property invasion as permanent is whether public policy favors the continuation of the invasion. *See* Dan B. Dobbs, *Law of Torts* § 57 (2000). . . .

Here, we find that public policy favors the discontinuance of both the continuing migration and the ongoing presence of toxic chemicals into Hoery's property and irrigation well. Under Colorado law, a tortfeasor's liability for continuing trespass and nuisance creates a new cause of action each day the property invasion continues. Hence, the alleged tortfeasor has an incentive to stop the property invasion and remove the cause of damage.

[Justice Kourlis dissented. Among other things he said: "It seems to me that resting a tort law distinction on the question of whether public policy would champion the defendant or the plaintiff is unwise."]

NOTES

1. **Divergent judicial opinion.** The results in the cases on this difficult topic are not always consistent or easy to summarize. Some cases refuse to treat the tort as continuing if the defendant's conduct causing the intrusion has ceased. *See Boudreaux v. Jefferson Island Storage & Hub, LLC,* 255 F.3d 271 (5th Cir. 2001) (salt water injected in defendant's own land migrated; if actionable as a trespass, the statute of limitations begins running at the time of the defendant's conduct and the trespass is not continuing merely because the effects continue).

2. **Effects of classifying as permanent.** To classify an intrusion as permanent is to create three effects. First, the cause of action accrues when the intrusion first occurs, or at least when the plaintiff discovered or should have discovered it. Second, the classification affects damages. For a permanent intrusion, the plaintiff who is not barred by the statute of limitations recovers all damages, present and future. Third, the suit is res judicata and the plaintiff cannot sue again later. Once the defendant has satisfied the judgment, he has in effect bought the right to continue the intrusion.

3. **Effects of classifying as continuing or temporary.** To classify an intrusion as continuing or temporary is to say that since the intrusion can be abated (by court order if necessary), each day's intrusion is like a new cause of

action. If the statute has run on the first day's intrusion, it has not necessarily run on second day's intrusion. In that case the plaintiff could sue for the second day's intrusion and those coming afterwards. Commensurately, however, damages are limited; the plaintiff does not recover the first day's damages, since the statute has run on that cause of action. Nor does the plaintiff recover all future damages, only those up to the time of trial. And because each day's intrusion represents a new cause of action and damages recovered are limited, the plaintiff can sue again and again if the defendant's acts continue.

4. **Incentives.** If you want to give an incentive to the defendant to abate the nuisance or trespass, which classification would most likely do the job? Which classification if you want to permit the defendant to continue the intrusion and pay damages, in effect to buy the right to intrude or pollute?

5. **Factors in classification.** "Classification as permanent or temporary is partly a matter of fact and partly a matter of policy seemingly governed by a number of factors. The most significant factors favoring a classification as temporary seem to be: (1) the invasion can in fact be terminated or abated; (2) the cost of termination is not wasteful or oppressive; (3) no privilege or public policy favors a continuation of the invasion; (4) incentive to abate the invasion can be provided by permitting repeated suits for damages as they accrue; and (5) the plaintiff prefers temporary damages; (6) overall, it is not just to permit the defendant to acquire the permanent right to invade the plaintiff's interests in land by paying market price for that right against the plaintiff's wishes." 1 DOBBS ON TORTS § 57 (2000). Is this pretty much in accord with *Hoery*?

6. **Scope of the problem.** Is the problem in *Hoery* and these notes limited to intrusions upon land or could it arise when the plaintiff is repeatedly subjected to toxic chemicals in the air while he is in a public place or on another's land?

7. **Years of abuse as one tort or many?** In *Feltmeier v. Feltmeier,* 798 N.E.2d 75 (Ill. 2003), the defendant husband began to abuse the plaintiff wife physically and emotionally from early in their marriage until sometime after the marriage was dissolved eleven years later. The abuse was a regular pattern of the marriage. Some of the acts of abuse constituted batteries; some constituted slander. Probably some constituted false imprisonment. After dissolution of the marriage, the plaintiff wife sued for intentional infliction of emotional distress, a tort requiring outrageous misconduct, covered in Chapter 19. But most acts of abuse here had occurred well outside the limitations period, some more than eleven years before suit. The court dealt with this by saying that the repeated nature of the abuse was part of the basis for finding outrageous misconduct and that the whole pattern of abuse should be treated as one large tort. As a matter of logic based on traditional legal rules, when should the statute begin to run? As a matter of policy or fairness, when should the statute begin to run? *Feltmeier* said it began to run at the time of the defendant's last injury suffered or the last tortious act. What about a case in which plaintiffs sued a Roman Catholic archdiocese for negligent supervision of priests who allegedly molested them over several years? Should the statute of limitations on such a claim begin to run only when the abuse ends,

or should each individual act trigger a limitations period? In *John Doe 1 v. Archdiocese of Milwaukee*, 734 N.W.2d 827 (Wis. 2007), the court held that the statute of limitations began to run at the time of the last incident of molestation.

NOTE: POLICY AND SOLUTIONS

Certainty. The statute of limitations as traditionally construed and applied provided one of those benefits one often longs for in law—certainty. After the stated period, a defendant could be sure that no suit would be filed. How important is the certainty? Insurers, concerned over the potential for losses indefinitely into the future under the discovery rule, may be required to escalate premiums, or even cease to provide coverage. Something like this did happen in medical malpractice insurance at one time. The "long tail" on the cause of action provides added protection for the few plaintiffs who need it, but costs to all doctors may be very high and ultimately it may be patients who pay.

Testimonial accuracy. One pillar of the statute of limitations is the idea that testimony will be lost altogether or will cease to be accurate over time. This might be especially true in some cases but not necessarily true in others. Do we need a certain rule like the statute to deal with testimonial accuracy? For instance, in some cases the defendant admits the acts in question. Where this occurs or there is good corroboration, and where the defendant cannot show that witnesses on his behalf have become unavailable, do we need the fixed statutory period?

Alternatives. How should these concerns be balanced? Is there any alternative that will help protect injured plaintiffs while preserving a bright-line termination of the claim? Would you favor any of the following?

The statute begins running when injury is first inflicted, but the plaintiff who fails to file within the time limits:

(a) can still recover, but only for limited, pecuniary losses and not for pain and suffering; or can recover only those damages accrued before the statute ran.

(b) can still recover, but only from the government, which will pay him rather than see an injustice done, but which will not demand payment from the defendant.

(c) can still recover and there should be no limitation; defendants should be held liable to defend at any time and, if they are tortfeasors, to pay as well.

(d) cannot recover, but may purchase his own accident, health, or income interruption insurance, and may be provided for in that way.

REFERENCE: DOBBS ON TORTS §§ 216–223 (2000).

§ 2. PREEMPTION AND COMPLIANCE WITH STATUTE

MILLER v. WARREN, 390 S.E.2d 207 (W.Va. 1990). The plaintiffs awoke in their motel room to find it filled with smoke. They attempted to get out, but the door was too hot to touch. They suffered serious burns before they were rescued. In a suit against the motel, the plaintiffs asserted that the motel should have had smoke alarms in the rooms. The fire code did not require such alarms, however. The trial judge instructed the jury: "The Court instructs the jury that compliance with the fire codes under the law meets the standard of care and duty required of the defendant as it relates to the installation or lack of installation of safety devices unless other circumstances appear which would require additional care in order to comply with the requirements to use ordinary care in attendant circumstances." The jury, so instructed, found for the defendant. *Held*, reversed and remanded for new trial. "Failure to comply with a fire code or similar regulation constitutes prima facie negligence, if an injury proximately flows from the non-compliance and the injury is of the sort the regulation was intended to prevent. [But] [c]ompliance with a regulation does not constitute due care per se. Compliance with the appropriate regulations is competent evidence of due care, but not conclusive evidence of due care. If the defendants knew or should have known of some risk that would be prevented by reasonable measures not required by the regulation, they were negligent if they did not take such measures. It is settled law that a statute or regulation merely sets a floor of due care. Circumstances may require greater care, if a defendant knows or should know of other risks not contemplated by the regulation."

NOTES

1. Courts traditionally agree that compliance with statute or regulation is not a defense. Statutory requirements usually reflect a minimum standard of care, not a maximum obligation. Compliance with statute, like compliance with custom, is some *evidence* of reasonable care, even though it is not conclusive. See RESTATEMENT (THIRD) OF TORTS: LIABILITY FOR PHYSICAL HARM § 16 (Proposed Final Draft No. 1, 2005).

2. Some kinds of federal regulation are deemed to "preempt" the field, so that any state regulation of the same field is ineffective. This is a complicated subject, of most importance in the area of products liability. Accordingly, we deal with it in greater detail in Chapter 24. The basis of this doctrine is the Supremacy Clause of Article VI of the U.S. Constitution, which makes federal law supreme over state law. If the intent to preempt state law is the "clear and manifest purpose of Congress" in enacting a particular law or regulation, *CSX Transportation, Inc. v. Easterwood*, 507 U.S. 658 (1993), then state laws that conflict with those federal provisions simply cannot be enforced. The effect is to displace tort law and leave the plaintiff without a remedy where the defendant has complied with federal regulations. *See*

Norfolk Southern Railway Co. v. Shanklin, 529 U.S. 344 (2000) (where railroad crossing warnings are constructed with federal funds, no state tort action permitted).

3. The federal government regulates the kind of headlights required on railroad trains. This regulation has been held to preempt the field, so that state regulation is not permitted. The plaintiff is struck by a railroad train, the engine of which complies with the federal headlight regulation. The plaintiff attempts to prove, in his state tort law suit, that better lights were available, that a prudent person would have used them on the engine, and that had they been used, the collision could have been avoided. If state tort law permitted this proof, would that be the same as "regulating" the railroad as to a federally-preempted matter? The court so held in *Marshall v. Burlington Northern, Inc.,* 720 F.2d 1149 (9th Cir. 1983). Is there any practical way in which this is different from saying that compliance is a defense?

4. Even if the defendant has *violated* federal regulations, they may be given preclusive effect. *See, e.g., Henning v. Union Pacific Railroad Co.,* 530 F.3d 1206 (10th Cir. 2008). In such a situation the plaintiff is left to federal remedies only. But because Congress often does not provide a federal remedy for those aggrieved by a regulatory violation, a plaintiff may be left without any legal recourse at all. *See* Robert L. Rabin, *Poking Holes in the Fabric of Tort: A Comment,* 56 DePaul L. Rev. 293 (2007). Does this produce a situation where businesses would prefer more, rather than less, federal regulation?

PART 3

LIMITING OR EXPANDING THE DUTY OF CARE ACCORDING TO CONTEXT OR RELATIONSHIP

■ ■ ■

"Duty" can be a confusing word in tort cases. Courts often use the term to describe a standard or measure of one's obligation. For instance, the normal duty is the duty to use the care of the reasonable, prudent person under the same or similar circumstances, but other standards or duties can be used. For example, in some cases the actor is under a strict duty to protect the plaintiff, meaning that he is liable even if he is not at fault. At the other end of the spectrum, there are cases in which the defendant owes no duty at all. In between there are several possible duties that demand more or less than ordinary care under the reasonable person standard. In many cases landowners owe people on the land only the duty to avoid wilful or wanton injury. So the term duty usually refers to a *standard* or general principle that measures the defendant's obligations to the plaintiff. A *standard* can have general application beyond the facts of the particular case.

As already observed, however, courts sometimes use the term duty as a way of talking about what particular acts are required by the exercise of ordinary care. For instance, a court might say that defendant had "a duty to stop, look, and listen before crossing a railroad track." When a court uses the term duty in this way it is not setting a *standard* for cases generally; it is reaching a *conclusion* about the particular case or stating a very specific rule that cannot be generalized beyond the facts. You will see courts using the term duty in both ways. The aim of this Part, however, is to talk about duty in the first sense, as a standard. In this sense, duties (or standards) range from the very demanding to the very lenient.

TOPIC A

LIMITING DUTIES ACCORDING TO CLASS OR STATUS OF THE PARTIES

■ ■ ■

CHAPTER 12

CARRIERS, HOST-DRIVERS AND LANDOWNERS

■ ■ ■

§ 1. CARRIERS AND HOST-DRIVERS

DOSER v. INTERSTATE POWER CO., 173 N.W.2d 556 (Iowa 1970). Defendant's bus was involved in an automobile accident and a bus passenger was injured. The evidence was that the automobile turned left in front of the bus and the defendant argued that the plaintiff had not shown negligence. " 'A carrier of passengers for hire must exercise more than ordinary diligence for their protection. Its duty stops just short of insuring their safety. It is bound to protect its passengers as far as human care and foresight will go and is liable for slight negligence.' ... [T]he high degree of care must be exercised in *foreseeing*, as well as in *guarding against*, danger. Plaintiff made a prima facie case by showing she was injured while a passenger on the bus by a collision between the bus and the automobile. This cast upon defendants the burden to show their freedom from negligence in causing the collision.... Given the high degree of care demanded of common carriers and the factual situation presented, we hold the court was correct in submitting the various specifications of negligence to the jury.''

NOTES

1. Many courts have now rejected the traditional higher standard of care reflected in *Doser* in favor of the general negligence standard based upon reasonable care under all the circumstances. *Lowrey v. Montgomery Kone, Inc.,* 42 P.3d 621 (Ariz. Ct. App. 2002); *Bethel v. New York City Transit Auth.,* 703 N.E.2d 1214 (N.Y. 1998). Others retain the higher standard. *See, e.g., Todd v. Mass Transit Admin.,* 816 A.2d 930 (Md. 2003) ("A common carrier owes its passengers the highest degree of care to provide safe means and methods of transportation for them.").

2. What is a "common carrier" and what is the rationale for a higher duty? In *Speed Boat Leasing, Inc. v. Elmer,* 124 S.W.3d 210 (Tex. 2003), the court explained that "those in the business of carrying passengers and goods who hold themselves out for hire by the public" owe "that degree of care

which would be exercised by a very cautious and prudent person.... The rationale for holding common carriers to a higher standard is that passengers should feel safe when traveling." The court noted that the higher standard had been applied in Texas to railroads, buses, airplanes, taxis, street cars, and other vehicles. Some states have a very broad conception of what a "common carrier" is. California's high court held in *Gomez v. Superior Court*, 113 P.3d 41 (Cal. 2005), that Disneyland was a common carrier in a suit over a death on the Indiana Jones ride.

ALA. CODE § 32–1–2

The owner, operator or person responsible for the operation of a motor vehicle shall not be liable for loss or damage arising from injuries to or death of a guest while being transported without payment therefor in or upon said motor vehicle, resulting from the operation thereof, unless such injuries or death are caused by the wilful or wanton misconduct of such operator, owner or person responsible for the operation of said motor vehicle.

NOTES

1. Some guest statutes state the standard as "gross negligence," others as "wilful or wanton misconduct." There are variations of these two basic forms. The wilful, wanton standard may be construed to require not merely extremely negligent conduct, but also a bad state of mind. Litigation under these statutes was often on the question whether a jury case had been made on the statutory gross negligence or wilful misconduct standard.

2. The guest statutes also raised some less obvious issues, notably those associated with the question, "Who is a guest?" Problems arise if the "guest" is injured in entering or leaving the car, for example, and also if the "guest" is paying a part of the cost of travel, or is providing non-monetary assistance to the driver.

3. Guest statutes were the product of a specific time, the late 1920s and the 1930s, and began to decline in the 1970s. In *Brown v. Merlo*, 506 P.2d 212 (Cal. 1973), the court held that the California guest statute was unconstitutional as a denial of equal protection under state law, partly because it treated guests and non-guests differently without any rational reason for doing so. The guest statute does not prevent collusion between host and guest because if they wish to collude they can testify that the passenger paid for the ride. The statute is not explicable as a means of encouraging hospitality because hospitality is extended to others who are not barred, and because in any event it is difficult to see why a "hospitable" host should be free to be negligent toward a guest. After *Brown* a good many other courts adopted similar reasoning under their own state constitutions. Legislatures, too, repealed many guest statutes. In 1985, the Texas Supreme Court offered this count: "of the twenty-nine states which originally enacted guest statutes, only Texas and four other states still have such statutes." It then promptly reduced the

number by holding the Texas statute unconstitutional. *Whitworth v. Bynum*, 699 S.W.2d 194 (Tex. 1985). Nebraska narrowly upheld its guest statute against constitutional attack by a 4–3 vote in *Le v. Lautrup*, 716 N.W.2d 713 (Neb. 2006).

4.   The era of the guest statutes is largely over. Why bother to consider them? One reason is that guest statutes set up a limited legal duty that closely resembles some others we will see in this chapter. Consider as you proceed whether your evaluation of the guest statutes should reflect your evaluation of other limited duty cases. Consider also whether the constitutional considerations would be the same when we come to other cases of limited duties, starting with the landowners' rules.

§ 2.   LANDOWNERS' DUTIES TO TRESPASSERS, LICENSEES, INVITEES, AND CHILDREN

GLADON v. GREATER CLEVELAND REGIONAL TRANSIT AUTHORITY

662 N.E.2d 287 (Ohio 1996)

Greater Cleveland Regional Transit Authority ("RTA") appeals from a jury verdict awarding Robert M. Gladon $2,736,915.35 in damages arising from RTA's operation of a rapid transit train.

Gladon purchased a passenger ticket and boarded an RTA rapid transit train at Terminal Tower after attending a Cleveland Indians' night game with friends. During the baseball game, Gladon consumed about five 16–ounce beers. He left his friends at the stadium in search of a restroom, and ended up traveling alone on the RTA trains. [H]e mistakenly exited the train at the West 65th Street Station and, once on the platform, was chased and attacked by two unknown males. Gladon testified that he remembered being "rolled up in a ball" on the tracks but he could not recall if he had jumped onto the tracks or had been pushed onto the tracks. While there, however, he did recall being kicked in the head.

While Gladon lay on the tracks with his legs draped over the rail, an RTA rapid train approached the West 65th Street Station. Mary Bell, the train's operator, had the train in braking mode when she observed first a tennis shoe and then Gladon's leg on the tracks. The operator pulled the cinestar, or control handle, back and hit the "mushroom," or emergency brake. Unfortunately, the train struck Gladon causing him serious and permanent injuries.

Gladon sued RTA and the operator alleging negligence in the security of RTA's premises and in the operation of the train. Specifically, Gladon alleged that the operator was negligent by failing to bring the train to a stop "after the point she perceived or should have perceived the Plaintiff's peril prior to her striking the Plaintiff." The trial court granted RTA summary judgment as to the negligent security claim and the case proceeded to trial on the negligent operation claim.

The trial court overruled RTA's motion for a directed verdict at the close of Gladon's case-in-chief. The court instructed the jury that "as a matter of law that the only evidence produced by either side indicates that the plaintiff was an invitee." The court further informed the jury that "the driver of a rapid transit car with the right of way must use ordinary care. Therefore, to avoid colliding with a person found on the tracks, the defendant is required to use ordinary care to discover and to avoid danger." . . .

COOK, JUSTICE. . . .

In Ohio, the status of the person who enters upon the land of another (i.e., trespasser, licensee, or invitee) continues to define the scope of the legal duty that the landowner owes the entrant. Invitees are persons who rightfully come upon the premises of another by invitation, express or implied, for some purpose which is beneficial to the owner.

The status of an invitee is not absolute but is limited by the landowner's invitation. "The visitor has the status of an invitee only while he is on part of the land to which his invitation extends—or in other words, the part of the land upon which the possessor gives him reason to believe that his presence is desired for the purpose for which he has come. If the invitee goes outside of the area of his invitation, he becomes a trespasser or a licensee, depending upon whether he goes there without the consent of the possessor, or with such consent."

. . . RTA's invitation to Gladon to use their premises did not extend to the area on or near the tracks. In fact, Gladon acknowledged that RTA did not permit the public in the area on or near the tracks. . . .

Gladon contends that he retained his invitee status because there was no evidence that he "intentionally or purposely entered upon the track area." According to the Restatement, "so far as the liability of the possessor of the land to the intruder is concerned, however, the possessor's duty, and liability, will be the same regardless of the manner of entry, so long as the entry itself is not privileged."

In determining whether the person is a trespasser within the meaning of this section, the question whether his entry has been intentional, negligent or purely accidental is not material, except as it may bear on the existence of a privilege. . . .

The illustration employed by the Restatement to explain the duties owed to a trespasser is remarkably similar to Gladon's situation. "Without any negligence on his part A, standing on the platform of a subway station of the X Company, slips and falls onto the tracks. While there he is run over by the train of X Company, and injured. A is a trespasser, and the liability to him is determined by the rules stated in sections 333 and 336, notwithstanding the accidental character of his intrusion."

Furthermore, whether Gladon was privileged to enter the tracks is immaterial. A person privileged to enter the land is owed the same duties as a licensee. Because the duties owed to a licensee and trespasser are the same, whether Gladon was privileged to enter the land does not change the standard of care RTA owed to him.

. . . Because Gladon then became either a licensee or a trespasser for purposes of determining the duty RTA owed to him, the trial court erred in instructing the jury that he was an invitee as a matter of law.

[A] landowner owes no duty to a licensee or trespasser except to refrain from willful, wanton or reckless conduct which is likely to injure him. Furthermore, a railroad owes no duty to anticipate or prevent the presence of licensees or trespassers.

When a trespasser or licensee is discovered in a position of peril, a landowner is required to use ordinary care to avoid injuring him. The duty to exercise ordinary care arises after the landowner "knows, or from facts within his knowledge should know or believe," that a trespasser or licensee is on the land.

Having instructed the jury as a matter of law that Gladon was an invitee, the trial court assigned RTA a duty of ordinary care "to discover and to avoid danger." These instructions erred in two respects. First, the instructions imposed upon RTA a duty to use ordinary care to discover Gladon's presence. To the contrary, RTA was under no duty to anticipate trespassers and could only be liable for injuries resulting from willful or wanton conduct. Second, the instructions imposed upon RTA a duty to use ordinary care to avoid injuring Gladon prior to the operator's discovery of him. Rather, RTA's duty to use ordinary care to avoid injuring Gladon did not arise until RTA knew or should have known that Gladon was on the tracks. Whether the operator knew or should have known a person was on the tracks upon observing the tennis shoe remains a question for the jury.

Given that the instructions were erroneous and prejudicial, we reverse the judgment of the court of appeals and remand this cause for a new trial.

RTA owed Gladon no duty except to avoid injuring him by willful or wanton conduct prior to discovering Gladon on the tracks. Willful conduct " 'involves an intent, purpose or design to injure.' " Wanton conduct involves the failure to exercise " 'any care whatsoever toward those to whom he owes a duty of care, and his failure occurs under the circumstances in which there is great probability that harm will result.' "

At trial, Gladon produced evidence that the tracks were wet when the operator traveled eastbound toward the West 65th Street platform. The testimony of the operator indicates that she had the train in braking mode as she traveled through a dark area near the platform with her high beams on at an estimated 20 m.p.h. Generally, the speed limit in that area is 25 m.p.h., but when a train is going to pass rather than stop at a platform, the permitted speed is 5 m.p.h.

Gladon also presented RTA regulations which require operators to operate the trains on sight, within the range of vision, at all times, and to anticipate changes in the range of vision. . . .

Viewing these facts in the light most favorable to Gladon, we find that in this trial reasonable minds could have reached different conclusions regarding whether the speed of the train at the time the operator approached the West 65th platform meets the wanton standard in light of the operator's duty to adjust the train's speed to her range of vision and to the known track conditions. Therefore, the trial court did not err in overruling RTA's motions for a directed verdict or judgment notwithstanding the verdict.

RTA owed Gladon a duty to use reasonable care to avoid injuring Gladon after the operator discovered Gladon on the tracks. Here, again, the RTA contends that Gladon failed to produce evidence of a breach of that duty.

Viewing these facts presented in this trial in the light most favorable to Gladon, reasonable minds could have reached different conclusions as to whether the operator exercised ordinary care. First, the point at which this duty arose remains a question for the jury. Reasonable minds could have reached different conclusions regarding whether the operator should have known a person was on the tracks when she saw the tennis shoes. Second, when the operator did realize a person was on the tracks, she was not sure whether she pulled the cinestar all the way back to the maximum braking mode before she hit the "mushroom" when she observed Gladon's legs on the tracks. Furthermore, the operator testified that she was not sure whether she hit the "mushroom" before or after the train struck Gladon. . . .

Judgment reversed and cause remanded. [Dissenting and concurring opinions are omitted.]

NOTES

1. **The traditional classifications.** About half of the states continue to follow the traditional common-law rules when an entrant sues the landowner or occupier (which includes a renter or anyone who is on the land acting on the possessor's behalf) for injuries suffered on the land. This traditional scheme classifies entrants as either trespassers, licensees, or invitees. A *trespasser* is any person who has no legal right to be on another's land and enters the land without the landowner's consent. An *invitee* is any person on the premises (1) at least in part for the pecuniary benefit of the landowner (a "business invitee") or (2) who is on premises held open to the general public (a "public invitee"). A *licensee* is someone who is on the land with permission, but with a limited license to be there; it is not inaccurate to say that a licensee is someone who is neither a trespasser nor an invitee.

2. **Classifying social guests.** Notice that the traditional definition of invitee would exclude social guests in a home. Indeed, social guests are

considered licensees in the traditional view, because they are not present for the pecuniary benefit of the landowner. A few states have now broadened the definition of invitee to include social guests. *See Burrell v. Meads,* 569 N.E.2d 637 (Ind. 1991). Is that a good idea?

3. **Changing categories.** Can a person who is on the land with permission and some business purpose (thus an invitee) become a trespasser on the same property? What if a shopper in a department store goes into a closed door marked "Employees Only" and is injured when he trips over a box. Does *Gladon* provide guidance on this point?

4. **Duty owed to invitees.** Landowners and occupiers owe a duty of reasonable care to invitees. There are many specific common-law rules about what this entails, but all such rules are merely specific applications of the general duty of care that we explored earlier in the course.

5. **Duty owed to trespassers and licensees.** (a) As *Gladon* indicates, under the traditional view, landowners do not owe a duty of reasonable care to either trespassers or licensees. Instead, the landowner owes only the duty to avoid intentional, wanton, or wilful injury. That statement, however, is usually applied only when the landowner has not discovered or received notice of imminent danger to the entrant. (The Restatement Second uses the term "has reason to know," meaning that the defendant is aware of some specific fact, like the shoe on the track in *Gladon*, that directly shows the danger. The "should have known" language of reasonable care would not suffice.) Besides the protection of the landowner's limited duty, he may enjoy a privilege—a privilege to use reasonable force to expel the trespasser, for example, or to defend his property. A California statute immunizes landowners for negligent-ly causing injuries to persons committing a felony on the property. *See* CAL. CIV. CODE § 847. In *Calvillo–Silva v. Home Grocery,* 968 P.2d 65 (Cal. 1998), this was construed to protect the landowner who actively inflicts harm so long as it is not wilful or wanton.

(b) If the landowner discovers both the presence of the entrant *and* the fact that he is about to encounter a danger, the situation is different. In that case, some courts might say that the landowner who fails to act reasonably in the face of this known danger to an entrant (by trying to warn him, for example), is then guilty of wilful or wanton misconduct. Others might say with the *Gladon* court that in such a situation the landowner owes a duty of reasonable care (which may be expressed more specifically as a duty to warn him of the danger). The two ways of addressing this situation thus appear to come down to the same bottom-line, with liability in either case for failing to act with reasonable care in light of the known situation.

(c) Some courts impose a duty of care upon landowners who have not discovered the actual presence of a trespasser, provided the landowner knows trespassers frequently use a limited area. *See, e.g., Humphrey v. Glenn,* 167 S.W.3d 680 (Mo. 2005).

6. **Conditions versus activities.** Even in a state that follows the traditional classification scheme, a landowner will often be held to a duty of reasonable care in carrying out affirmative acts such as driving on his private roads, once he knows a trespasser is present. In the case of licensees, the landowner is said to owe duty of reasonable care to all licensees in carrying

out activities on the land. Thus the wilful-wanton rule protecting landowners is mainly addressed to *conditions* on the land, such as a dangerous non-obvious excavation, a dangerous electrical connection, a hidden step, or a rotten railing that may give way. Not all courts draw this distinction with any meaningful degree of precision, however. Does the *Gladon* court appear to do so?

7. **Hazards originating on adjacent land.** What if an entrant on the defendant's land is injured by a hazard originating on adjacent land? In *Galindo v. Town of Clarkstown*, 814 N.E.2d 419 (N.Y. 2004), a storm caused a large tree adjacent to the defendant's property to lean precariously over his driveway. The defendant warned various work crews and city officials over the next few days, but nothing was done. One morning the tree fell on a car in the defendant's driveway, killing its occupant. The court rejected liability, holding that "an owner owes no duty to warn or protect others from a defective or dangerous condition on neighboring premises, unless the owner had created or contributed to it." Does this rule make sense? Could the defendant in this case have hired a crew to remove the tree from the neighboring property before it fell?

8. **Duties to persons outside the land.** Persons who are injured while on the public way or on adjoining property outside the landowner's land are not "entrants" at all and thus do not, of course, fit within any of the three categories. Where a natural condition on the land creates a risk to persons outside the land, the cases may be moving toward a duty of ordinary care. *See, e.g., Hale v. Ostrow*, 166 S.W.3d 713 (Tenn. 2005) (overgrown bushes that obstructed sidewalk). Some courts impose a duty only where a natural condition on the land actually extends onto the adjacent property. *See, e.g., Williams v. Davis*, 974 So.2d 1052 (Fla. 2007) (overgrown foliage obstructed motorists' view of intersection).

BENNETT v. STANLEY

748 N.E.2d 41 (Ohio 2001)

PFEIFER, J.

In this case we are called upon to determine what level of duty a property owner owes to a child trespasser. We resolve the question by adopting the attractive nuisance doctrine set forth in Restatement of the Law 2d, Torts (1965), Section 339....

When Rickey G. Bennett, plaintiff-appellant, arrived home in the late afternoon of March 20, 1997, he found his two young daughters crying. The three-year-old, Kyleigh, told him that "Mommy" and Chance, her five-year-old half-brother, were "drowning in the water." Bennett ran next door to his neighbors' house to find mother and son unconscious in the swimming pool. Both died.

The Bennetts had moved next door to defendants-appellees, Jeffrey and Stacey Stanley, in the fall of 1996. The Stanleys had purchased their home the previous June. At the time of their purchase, the Stanleys' property included a swimming pool that had gone unused for three years.

At that time, the pool was enclosed with fencing and a brick wall. After moving in, the Stanleys drained the pool once but thereafter they allowed rainwater to accumulate in the pool to a depth of over six feet. They removed a tarp that had been on the pool and also removed the fencing that had been around two sides of the pool. The pool became pond-like: it contained tadpoles and frogs, and Mr. Stanley had seen a snake swimming on the surface. The pool contained no ladders, and its sides were slimy with algae.

Rickey and Cher Bennett ... rented the house next to the Stanleys. The houses were about one hundred feet apart. There was some fencing with an eight-foot gap between the two properties. The Stanleys were aware that the Bennetts had moved next door and that they had young children. They had seen the children outside unsupervised. Stacey Stanley had once called Chance onto her property to retrieve a dog. The Stanleys testified, however, that they never had any concern about the children getting into the pool. They did not post any warning or "no trespassing" signs on their property. . . .

Kyleigh told her father that she and Chance had been playing at the pool on the afternoon of the tragedy. The sheriff's department concluded that Chance had gone to the pool to look at the frogs and somehow fell into the pool. His mother apparently drowned trying to save him.

[Bennett sued the Stanleys on a negligence theory, specifically alleging "that appellees' pool created an unreasonable risk of harm to children who, because of their youth, would not realize the potential danger." The trial court granted the Stanleys' motion for summary judgment, finding that because the decedents were trespassers, the only duty owed to them was "to refrain from wanton and wilful misconduct." Because the complaint alleged only a violation of ordinary care, the trial court found for the Stanleys as a matter of law. The appeals court affirmed.]

Ohio has long recognized a range of duties for property owners vis-a-vis persons entering their property. A recent discussion of Ohio's classification system can be found in *Gladon v. Greater Cleveland Regional Transit Auth.* ... Today, we face the issue of whether child trespassers should become another class of users who are owed a different duty of care.

This court has consistently held that children have a special status in tort law and that duties of care owed to children are different from duties owed to adults:

"[T]he amount of care required to discharge a duty owed to a child of tender years is necessarily greater than that required to discharge a duty owed to an adult under the same circumstances. This is the approach long followed by this court and we see no reason to abandon it. 'Children of tender years, and youthful persons generally, are entitled to a degree of care proportioned to their inability to foresee and avoid the perils that they may encounter. * * * The same discernment and foresight in discovering defects and dangers cannot be reasonably expected of them, that

older and experienced persons habitually employ; and therefore the great-
er precaution should be taken, where children are exposed to them.' " *Di
Gildo v. Caponi* (1969), 18 Ohio St.2d 125, 127, 47 O.O.2d 282, 283, 247
N.E.2d 732, 734.

Recognizing the special status of children in the law, this court has
even accorded special protection to child trespassers by adopting the
"dangerous instrumentality" doctrine [which] imposes upon the owner or
occupier of a premises a higher duty of care to a child trespasser when
such owner or occupier actively and negligently operates hazardous machinery or other apparatus, the dangerousness of which is not readily
apparent to children. . . .

Despite the fact that in premises liability cases a landowner's duty is
defined by the status of the plaintiff, and that children, even child
trespassers, are accorded special protection in Ohio tort law, this court has
never adopted the attractive nuisance doctrine. The doctrine as adopted by
numerous states is set forth in Restatement of the Law 2d, Torts (1965),
Section 339:

> "A possessor of land is subject to liability for physical harm to
> children trespassing thereon caused by an artificial condition upon
> land if:

> "(a) the place where the condition exists is one upon which the
> possessor knows or has reason to know that children are likely to
> trespass, and

> "(b) the condition is one of which the possessor knows or has reason
> to know and which he realizes or should realize will involve an
> unreasonable risk of death or serious bodily harm to such children,
> and

> "(c) the children because of their youth do not discover the condition
> or realize the risk involved in intermeddling with it or in coming
> within the area made dangerous by it, and

> "(d) the utility to the possessor of maintaining the condition and the
> burden of eliminating the danger are slight as compared with the risk
> to children involved, and

> "(e) the possessor fails to exercise reasonable care to eliminate the
> danger or otherwise to protect the children."

This court has never explicitly rejected the Restatement version of the
doctrine, which was adopted in 1965. Instead, Ohio's tradition in this area
of the law is based upon this court's rejection in 1907 of the "turntable
doctrine" in *Wheeling & Lake Erie RR. Co. v. Harvey* (1907), 77 Ohio St.
235, 83 N.E. 66. In *Harvey,* this court held . . . that "[i]t is not the duty of
an occupier of land to exercise care to make it safe for infant children who
come upon it without invitation but merely by sufferance."

The "turntable doctrine" was a somewhat controversial doctrine
wherein railroads could be liable to children for injuries suffered on

unguarded railroad turntables. The theory of liability was established in *Sioux City & Pacific RR. Co. v. Stout* (1873), 84 U.S. (17 Wall.) 657, 21 L.Ed. 745, and had been adopted by many states as of 1907. The burning question for many years was whether to apply the doctrine to non-turntable cases. Many of the states that adopted the turntable doctrine refused to apply it to cases not involving turntables.

However, the theory of liability has evolved since 1907. The Restatement of the Law, Torts (1934) and Restatement of the Law 2d, Torts (1965) removed legal fictions and imposed balancing factors to consider on behalf of landowners. Ohio's refusal to recognize the turntable doctrine in 1907 was not a serious anomaly at the time; today, our failure to adopt the attractive nuisance doctrine is. Ohio is one of only three states that have not either created a special duty for trespassing children or done away with distinctions of duty based upon a person's status as an invitee, licensee, or trespasser. . . .

Adopting the attractive nuisance doctrine would be merely an incremental change in Ohio law, not out of line with the law that has developed over time. It is an appropriate evolution of the common law. While the present case is by no means a guaranteed winner for the plaintiff, it does present a factual scenario that would allow a jury to consider whether the elements of the cause of action have been fulfilled.

We therefore use this case to adopt the attractive nuisance doctrine contained in Restatement of the Law 2d, Torts (1965), Section 339. In doing so, we do not abandon the differences in duty a landowner owes to the different classes of users. In this case we simply further recognize that children are entitled to a greater level of protection than adults are. We remove the "distinctions without differences" between the dangerous instrumentality doctrine and the attractive nuisance doctrine. Whether an apparatus or a condition of property is involved, the key element should be whether there is a foreseeable, "unreasonable risk of death or serious bodily harm to * * * children." Restatement, Section 339(b).

The Restatement's version of the attractive nuisance doctrine balances society's interest in protecting children with the rights of landowners to enjoy their property. Even when a landowner is found to have an attractive nuisance on his or her land, the landowner is left merely with the burden of acting with ordinary care. A landowner does not automatically become liable for any injury a child trespasser may suffer on that land.

The requirement of foreseeability is built into the doctrine. The landowner must know or have reason to know that children are likely to trespass upon the part of the property that contains the dangerous condition. Moreover, the landowner's duty "does not extend to those conditions the existence of which is obvious even to children and the risk of which should be fully realized by them." *Id.* at Comment *i*. Also, if the condition of the property that poses the risk is essential to the landowner, the doctrine would not apply:

"The public interest in the possessor's free use of his land for his own purposes is of great significance. A particular condition is, therefore, regarded as not involving unreasonable risk to trespassing children unless it involves a grave risk to them which could be obviated without any serious interference with the possessor's legitimate use of his land."

We are satisfied that the Restatement view effectively harmonizes the competing societal interests of protecting children and preserving property rights. In adopting the attractive nuisance doctrine, we acknowledge that the way we live now is different from the way we lived in 1907, when *Harvey* was decided. We are not a rural society any longer, our neighbors live closer, and our use of our own property affects others more than it once did.

Despite our societal changes, children are still children. They still learn through their curiosity. They still have developing senses of judgment. They still do not always appreciate danger. They still need protection by adults. Protecting children in a changing world requires the common law to adapt. Today, we make that change. . . .

[Reversed and remanded. Concurring and dissenting opinions omitted.]

NOTES

1. **The "attractive nuisance" rule.** As *Bennett* explains, the so-called "attractive nuisance" doctrine, with its special rules for child trespassers, is widely accepted in the states today. Are you convinced that the policy rationales behind it are sound?

2. **Tender years.** The special child trespasser rules apply only to children who, because of their tender years, are foreseeably unlikely to appreciate the dangers and to avoid them. Thus the "attractive nuisance" doctrine applies mainly to children of grade school age or younger and only rarely to teenagers. *See, e.g., Racine v. Moon's Towing*, 817 So.2d 21 (La. 2002) (doctrine inapplicable to two trespassers, one 14 and one 15, because they were "clearly old enough to know what they were doing was wrong").

3. **Injury caused by something other than the "attractive nuisance."** What if the young child is injured by something on the property that is different from the "nuisance" that attracted the child in the first place? Can you formulate arguments based on policy that would support liability nonetheless? *See Henson ex rel. Hunt v. International Paper Co.*, 650 S.E.2d 74 (S.C. 2007).

4. **Common hazards.** Some courts have said that "common hazards," such as fire and pools of water cannot be considered attractive nuisances and the trespassing child who drowns in the stock pond is entitled to no protection from the landowner. The better explanation for many of these cases may be that there is a duty of care owed, but that given the importance of stock ponds and the difficulty of fencing them, the duty is not breached, which is to say the defendant is not negligent. This explanation is supported by the fact that

even in states that announce a "common hazard" rule, recovery is sometimes allowed for swimming pool deaths and for injuries by hidden burning embers.

O'SULLIVAN v. SHAW

726 N.E.2d 951 (Mass. 2000)

LYNCH, J.

The plaintiff seeks to recover for injuries he sustained when he dived, headfirst, into the shallow end of a swimming pool owned by the defendants and located on their residential property. His complaint alleges that the defendants were negligent in allowing visitors to dive into the shallow end of the pool and in failing to warn of the danger associated with this activity. A judge in the Superior Court allowed the defendants' motion for summary judgment, reasoning that diving into the shallow end of a swimming pool is an open and obvious danger which was known to the plaintiff, and that the defendants therefore did not owe the plaintiff a duty of care. . . .

The pool in question is an in-ground type, measuring eighteen feet in width by thirty-six feet in length, with both shallow and deep ends. The bottom of the pool is level in the shallow end, for approximately ten feet of the pool's length, after which it slopes gradually toward the deep end, the sides of which are tapered. When filled to capacity, the pool is four feet deep at its shallowest point and eight feet at its deepest. There are no markers, either in the pool or on its exterior surround, to indicate the pool's depth at various points along its length or to demarcate the separation of its shallow and deep ends. However, a diving board is affixed to the exterior of the pool at its deep end. The pool's interior is covered with a vinyl liner and there is no underwater lighting, so that the bottom of the pool is not visible at night. . . .

[T]he plaintiff suffered injuries to his neck and back when he dived into the shallow end of the pool. At the time, he was attempting, in racing dive fashion, to clear the ten-foot expanse of the shallow end and surface in the deep end, but he entered the water at too steep an angle and struck his head on the pool bottom, resulting in a fracture of his cervical vertebrae. By his own admission, the plaintiff knew that he could be injured if he were to hit his head on the bottom of the pool when diving, and his purpose in trying to clear the shallow end was to avoid the sort of accident that occurred. The plaintiff's injury caused immediate paralysis in his lower extremities and required a two-day stay in the hospital, but the paralysis was not permanent. . . .

[I]t is well established in our law of negligence that a landowner's duty to protect lawful visitors against dangerous conditions on his property ordinarily does not extend to dangers that would be obvious to persons of average intelligence. Landowners are relieved of the duty to warn of open and obvious dangers on their premises because it is not reasonably foreseeable that a visitor exercising (as the law presumes) reasonable care for his own safety would suffer injury from such blatant hazards. Stated otherwise, where a danger would be obvious to a person of ordinary perception and judgment, a landowner may reasonably assume that a visitor has knowledge of it and, therefore, "any further warning would be an empty form" that would not reduce the likelihood of resulting harm.

The plaintiff argues on appeal that the open and obvious danger rule was implicitly abolished by the comparative negligence statute, which expressly abolishes "the defense of assumption of risk," because, he maintains, the former is a corollary of the latter. Accordingly, he argues, the judge erred in concluding that the defendants owed no duty to the plaintiff due to the obvious nature of the risk, for it properly belongs to a jury to decide the issue of the defendants' liability by applying statutorily mandated principles of comparative fault. We reject this argument.

. . . Assumption of risk, along with contributory negligence, was an affirmative defense to negligence for which the defendant bore the burden of proof at trial. A plaintiff assumed the risk of harm when he voluntarily exposed himself to a known danger which had been caused by the defendant's negligence; the focus of the inquiry was thus on the plaintiff's own carelessness or negligence in failing to avoid a hazard which he knew about and appreciated. By contrast, the open and obvious danger doctrine arises in connection with the separate issue of a defendant's duty to protect others from dangerous conditions about which the defendant knows or should know. Rather than evaluating a particular plaintiff's subjective reasonableness or unreasonableness in encountering a known hazard, the inquiry is an objective one that focuses, instead, on the reasonableness of the defendant's conduct: it presumes a plaintiff's exercising reasonable care for his own safety and asks whether the dangerous condition was, objectively speaking, so obvious that the defendant would be reasonable in concluding that an ordinarily intelligent plaintiff would perceive and avoid it and, therefore, that any further warning would be superfluous.

Thus, the superseded common-law defense of assumption of risk goes to a plaintiff's failure to exercise due care for his own safety, whereas the open and obvious danger rule concerns the existence of a defendant's duty of care, which the plaintiff must establish as part of his prima facie case before any comparative analysis of fault may be performed. . . . [W]e conclude that the Legislature's express abolition of "the defense of assumption of risk" does not alter the plaintiff's burden in a negligence action to prove that the defendant owed him a duty of care in the circumstances, and thus leaves intact the open and obvious danger rule, which operates to negate the existence of a duty of care.

. . . The remaining issue concerns whether the judge, in granting summary judgment for the defendants, correctly concluded that the open and obvious danger rule obviated any duty to warn the plaintiff not to dive headfirst into the shallow end of the defendants' swimming pool. Plain common sense, bolstered by the weight of authority in other jurisdictions where this issue has been addressed, convince us that this conclusion is indisputably correct. . . .

Judgment affirmed.

NOTES

1. **Open and obvious danger.** At one time, courts routinely held that the landowner was not liable for injuries even to an invitee which were caused by an open and obvious danger. Some courts still say this. *General Motors Corp. v. Hill,* 752 So.2d 1186 (Ala. 1999). The idea was frequently expressed, as in *O'Sullivan,* by saying the landowner owed no duty to protect from obvious dangers. *See Bucki v. Hawkins,* 914 A.2d 491 (R.I. 2007) (also suggesting that a person injured by an open and obvious hazard is the sole cause of his own harm).

2. **Contributory negligence/assumed risk.** Some courts interpreted the rule against liability for open and obvious dangers as a rule based upon contributory negligence or assumed risk, imputing fault to the plaintiff in such cases as a matter of law. With the coming of comparative fault, some of these courts now reject the flat rule against recovery. The fact that danger should have been obvious to the plaintiff then figures as fault with reduction in damages. *E.g., Brooks v. K–Mart Corp.,* 964 P.2d 98 (N.M. 1998).

3. **No duty—or no negligence?** Under the mainstream theory, adopted in *O'Sullivan,* the obvious danger rule is not a matter of contributory negligence or assumed risk. It is instead a no duty rule, created by judges as a matter of policy. Yet the theory is that if the danger was obvious, the invitee could avoid it and thus protect himself, so that the landowner would foresee no harm. Under that theory, wouldn't it be more accurate to say that the landowner was under a duty of care, but that a duty of care is not breached— the landowner is not negligent—when no harm is foreseeable? *See Shaw v. Petersen,* 821 P.2d 220 (Ariz. Ct. App. 1991); *Stinnett v. Buchele,* 598 S.W.2d 469 (Ky. Ct. App. 1980).

4. **Harm foreseeable in spite of obvious danger.** If you see the issue as one of negligence rather than duty, the trier of fact will decide whether the risk of harm was in fact foreseeable to the defendant even if the danger is obvious. *E.g., Louis v. Louis,* 636 N.W.2d 314 (Minn. 2001) (swimming pool slide). How is that possible? Consider two kinds of cases:

a. A landowner is constructing his own house and has not yet put a railing on a second-floor balcony. A painter (an invitee) accidentally steps off the balcony and falls while he is working. *Hale v. Beckstead,* 116 P.3d 263 (Utah 2005). Or suppose the landowner operates a bar at the top of a long, dangerous flight of steps that furnish the only means of egress. Is a fall foreseeable? *Fulmer v. Timber Inn Rest. & Lounge, Inc.,* 9 P.3d 710 (Or. 2000).

b. A utility customer must cross an obvious patch of ice to pay her utility bill. Unless she does so immediately, power will be cut off in her home in the dead of winter. If the utility is negligent in failing to sand the ice, is it foreseeable that someone exercising her right to enter will be injured?

Look back at *O'Sullivan* and see whether you think it leaves room for liability in such cases. If so, could the plaintiff's damages be reduced for comparative fault?

5. **Children and "open and obvious" hazards.** Should it matter whether a person injured by what looks to an adult like an obvious hazard is a child of tender years? Recall the special standard of care for children, and the attractive nuisance doctrine. Do the policies behind those doctrines suggest an answer? *See Bragan v. Symanzik*, 687 N.W.2d 881 (Mich. Ct. App. 2004); *see also Grant v. South Roxana Dad's Club*, 886 N.E.2d 543 (Ill. App. Ct. 2008).

6. **Natural conditions: Snow and ice.** Some courts follow a rule that landowners owe no duty, not even to an invitee, with respect to dangers created by natural accumulations of snow and ice. The rule does not relieve the landowner of liability for dangers created by the landowner's activities that make the ice more dangerous.

7. **The rescue doctrine and "open and obvious" hazards.** A patron in a bar sees that a gas leak has caused a fire that endangers other people and property. He rushes in to suppress the fire and is burned. Should the bar owner be able to argue that his recovery should be barred because the hazard was "open and obvious"? *Clinkscales v. Nelson Securities, Inc.*, 697 N.W.2d 836 (Iowa 2005).

§ 3. THE FIREFIGHTER'S RULE

MINNICH v. MED–WASTE, INC.
564 S.E.2d 98 (S.C. 2002)

JUSTICE PLEICONES.

[A federal District Court certified a question to the Supreme Court of South Carolina, asking whether the firefighter's rule barred a claim for injury to emergency professionals.] The District Court made the following factual findings:

Jeffrey Minnich ("Plaintiff") was employed by the Medical University of South Carolina ("MUSC") as a public safety officer. While working in this capacity, Plaintiff assisted in loading medical waste from the premises of MUSC onto a tractor-trailer truck owned by Defendant Med–Waste, Inc. Plaintiff noticed the unoccupied truck begin to roll forward, toward a public street. Plaintiff ran to the truck, jumped inside, and stopped the truck.

Plaintiff alleges he suffered serious injuries, proximately caused by the acts or omissions of the defendants' employees, for which he seeks to recover damages. The defendants assert that Plaintiff's claims are barred by the firefighter's rule. The firefighter's rule is a common law doctrine that precludes a firefighter (and certain other public employees, including police officers) from recovering against a defendant whose negligence caused the firefighter's on-the-job injury. . . .

Finding no definitive answer to the certified question in the case law of this state, we examine the various rationales advanced in support of the rule, and its applications and limitations in other states.

The common law firefighter's rule originated in the case of *Gibson v. Leonard*, 143 Ill. 182, 32 N.E. 182 (Ill.1892). There, the Illinois Supreme Court held that a firefighter who entered private property in the performance of his job duties was a licensee, and as such, the property owner owed the firefighter a duty only to "refrain from willful or affirmative acts which are injurious." Practically, this meant that a firefighter, injured while fighting a blaze on private property, could not recover tort damages from the property owner whose ordinary negligence caused the fire.

A number of courts reason that police officers and firefighters, aware of the risks inherent in their chosen profession, have assumed those risks. As such, the firefighter or police officer should not be allowed to recover when injured as a result of confronting these known and accepted risks.

A third rationale advanced is public policy.... First, injuries to firemen and policemen are compensable through workers' compensation. It follows that liability for their on-the-job injuries is properly borne by the public rather than by individual property owners. Second, firemen and policemen, unlike invitees or licensees, enter at unforeseeable times and at areas not open to the public. In such situations, it is not reasonable to require the level of care that is owed to invitees or licensees.

Still other courts reason that the public fisc pays to train firefighters and police officers on the ways to confront dangerous situations, and compensates them for doing so. If these public employees were permitted to bring suit against the taxpayers whose negligence proximately caused injury, the negligent taxpayer would incur multiple penalties in exchange for the protection provided by firefighters and police officers.

Not only have courts been unable to agree on a consistent rationale for the rule, they have not been able to agree on the proper parameters for the rule. A number of courts which recognize the firefighter's rule as a viable defense to negligence claims allow recovery for willful and wanton conduct resulting in injury. As one court observed, "a tortfeasor who acts wilfully and wantonly is so culpable that the fireman's rule ought not to preclude the injured officer from suing the egregiously culpable wrongdoer." *Miller v. Inglis*, 223 Mich.App. 159, 567 N.W.2d 253 (1997).

Courts have allowed police officers and firefighters to recover for injuries resulting from an act of negligence unrelated to the specific reason for which the officer or firefighter was originally summoned. As stated by the Supreme Court of New Jersey:

> The core of the "fireman's rule" is that a citizen's ordinary negligence that occasioned the presence of the public safety officer shall not give rise to liability in damages for the injuries sustained by the officer in the course of the response to duty.... The corollary of the rule is that independent and intervening negligent acts that injure the safety officer on duty are not insulated....

More recently, a number of state legislatures have acted to limit or abolish the firefighter's rule. For instance ... the Virginia legislature passed a statute providing that:

An owner or occupant of real property containing premises normally open to the public shall, with respect to such premises, owe to firefighters ... and law-enforcement officers who in the performance of their duties come upon that portion of the premises normally open to the public the duty to maintain the same in a reasonably safe condition or to warn of dangers thereon of which he knows or has reason to know, whether or not such premises are at the time open to the public.

An owner or occupant of real property containing premises not normally open to the public shall, with respect to such premises, owe the same duty to firefighters ... and law-enforcement officers who he knows or has reason to know are upon, about to come upon or imminently likely to come upon that portion of the premises not normally open to the public....

Va.Code Ann. § 8.01–226 (Michie 2001). [The court also discussed statutes from California, Florida, Minnesota, New Jersey, New York and Nevada, some of which effectively abolished the rule altogether.]

... [T]hose jurisdictions which have adopted the firefighter's rule offer no uniform justification therefor, nor do they agree on a consistent application of the rule. The legislatures in many jurisdictions which adhere to the rule have found it necessary to modify or abolish the rule. The rule is riddled with exceptions, and criticism of the rule abounds.

Against this backdrop, we answer the certified question in the negative. South Carolina has never recognized the firefighter's rule, and we find it is not part of this state's common law. In our view, the tort law of this state adequately addresses negligence claims brought against non-employer tortfeasors arising out of injuries incurred by firefighters and police officers during the discharge of their duties. We are not persuaded by any of the various rationales advanced by those courts that recognize the firefighter's rule. The more sound public policy—and the one we adopt—is to decline to promulgate a rule singling out police officers and firefighters for discriminatory treatment.

CERTIFIED QUESTION ANSWERED.

NOTES

1. **The firefighter's rule.** As *Minnich* indicates, the states disagree on the merits of the firefighter's rule. Most states, however, continue to apply it in some form, and a number have adopted or reaffirmed it recently. *See, e.g., Fordham v. Oldroyd*, 171 P.3d 411 (Utah 2007); *Espinoza v. Schulenburg*, 129 P.3d 937 (Ariz. 2006); *Farmer v. B & G Food Enters., Inc.*, 818 So.2d 1154 (Miss. 2002). Certainly most states continue to hold that a firefighter who is injured in fighting a fire has no claim against the negligent fire-setter.

2. **Assumed risk/no duty.** In those states which still adhere to the firefighter's rule, the exclusion of firefighters from the negligence system is often explained by saying that the firefighter assumed the risk. This could

hardly be assumed risk in the sense of contributory fault; it is not negligent to fight fires in a professional way. So the firefighter's rule, though explained in terms of assumed risk, is merely another way of saying "it is appropriate to find that the defendant owes no duty of care." *Neighbarger v. Irwin Indust, Inc.*, 882 P.2d 347 (Cal. 1994).

3. **No duty/public policy.** "No duty" in turn reflects judicial notions of appropriate policy. The *Minnich* court finds the policy rationales unconvincing. Other courts have reached the opposite conclusion. *See Moody v. Delta W., Inc.*, 38 P.3d 1139 (Alaska 2002) ("The Firefighter's Rule reflects sound public policy.") What do you think?

4. **Expansions.** The earliest cases applying the firefighter's rule were anchored in premises liability law, and applied only to firefighters. But in many states it has been vastly expanded. First, the rule has been applied outside the land as well as on it. *See, e.g., Pinter v. American Family Mut. Ins. Co.*, 613 N.W.2d 110 (Wis. 2000) (applying rule to bar a negligence action by an emergency medical technician injured during a car-crash rescue); *Moody, supra* Note 3. Likewise, in most states the rule is no longer limited to firefighters; it has been applied to police officers, EMTs, and even lifeguards. *E.g., Sobanski v. Donahue*, 792 A.2d 57 (R.I. 2002) (police); *Pinter, supra* (EMTs); *City of Oceanside v. Superior Court,* 96 Cal.Rptr.2d 621 (Ct. App. 2000) (lifeguard). Maybe the operative category is not firefighters but publicly-employed professional risk-takers or public safety officers. What will courts do with public building inspectors injured in buildings they inspect? *See* DOBBS ON TORTS § 287 (2000).

5. **Private rescuers.** The firefighter's rule has no application to private individuals who may undertake assistance at a fire. On the contrary, private persons are considered heroic and it is said under one branch of the "rescue doctrine" that it is not contributory negligence or assumed risk to render assistance in a physical emergency. "The extent of the risk which the volunteer is justified in assuming under the circumstances increases in proportion to the imminence of the danger. . . ." *Moravec v. Moravec*, 343 N.W.2d 762 (Neb. 1984) (plaintiff injured in fighting a fire could recover from homeowner who negligently set it). Some courts have said expressly that the firefighter's rule is "an exception to the rescue doctrine." *Espinoza v. Schulenberg, supra* Note 1.

6. **Privately-employed professional rescuers.** In a leading California case, *Neighbarger v. Irwin Industries, Inc.*, 882 P.2d 347 (Cal. 1994), the court concluded that the firefighter's rule had no application to a professional firefighter/safety officer who was privately employed. The plaintiff, a plant safety officer, was therefore permitted to pursue his claim against a negligent outsider who caused a fire in the plant.

7. **Off-duty professional rescuers.** If the rescuer in the case is a professional, but off-duty at the time, some courts have held that the firefighter's rule has no application. See *Espinoza v. Schulenberg, supra* Note 1. Several other states use a multi-factor test going to the issue of whether the rescuer was acting in a "professional capacity" at the time.

8. **Wrongdoing not covered by the rule.** Courts agree that the firefighter's rule does not protect all wrongdoers.

(1) Most courts hold that it does not foreclose suit against an intentional or wilful wrongdoer. *Baldonado v. El Paso Natural Gas Co.*, 176 P.3d 277 (N.M. 2008).

(2) At least in some jurisdictions, it does not foreclose suit for injuries arising from violation of a fire-safety statute or ordinance. *See, e.g., Mullen v. Zoebe, Inc.*, 654 N.E.2d 90 (N.Y. 1995).

(3) It does not foreclose suit for harms resulting from risks not inherent in the job the officer has undertaken or risks the officer was not paid to assume. One specific effect is that the firefighter's rule applies to prohibit a firefighter from recovering only for injuries caused by the "misconduct which created the risk which necessitated his presence." *Lipson v. Superior Court of Orange County,* 644 P.2d 822 (Cal. 1982). *See also Ruffing v. Ada County Paramedics,* 188 P.3d 885 (Idaho 2008); *Moody v. Delta Western, Inc.*, 38 P.3d 1139 (Alaska 2002).

Example 1. The officer may recover against a defendant who negligently increases a risk to the officer after the officer's presence is known. This specific rule is statutory in California. *See* CAL. CIV. CODE § 1714.9; *but see Calatayud v. State,* 959 P.2d 360 (Cal. 1998) (fellow officer's negligence after plaintiff-officer's presence is known is not actionable in spite of the statute).

Example 2. A traffic officer stops A. While the officer is on the roadside issuing a speeding ticket to A, B, driving another car, negligently strikes him. B is not free of all responsibility on the ground that the officer assumes risks inherent in traffic work. Rather, B's negligence, not being conduct that drew the officer to the location in the first place, is not protected by the firefighter's rule. *Harris–Fields v. Syze,* 600 N.W.2d 611 (Mich. 1999). The same point can be illustrated by the case of a firefighter injured by the homeowner's attack dogs; dog danger was not part of the reason for the firefighter's presence, hence he may pursue his claim for the dog bites. Cf. *Wiley v. Redd,* 885 P.2d 592 (Nev. 1994) (police officer). Put in broader terms, dog danger was not one of the risks inherent in the job and not a risk the public officer was paid to face. *See* DOBBS ON TORTS § 286 (2000).

§ 4. ADOPTING A REASONABLE CARE STANDARD FOR LANDOWNERS

ROWLAND v. CHRISTIAN
443 P.2d 561 (Cal. 1968)

PETERS, JUSTICE.

[Plaintiff was a social guest in Miss Christian's apartment. The porcelain handle of a bathroom faucet broke in his hand and severed tendons and nerves. Miss Christian had known the handle was cracked and had in fact reported it to her lessors, but, though she knew plaintiff was going to the bathroom, she gave him no warning. These facts were established by affidavit and the trial judge gave summary judgment for the defendant.]

Section 1714 of the Civil Code provides: "Everyone is responsible, not only for the result of his willful acts, but also for an injury occasioned to another by his want of ordinary care or skill in the management of his property or person, except so far as the latter has, willfully or by want of ordinary care, brought the injury upon himself. . . ." This code section, which has been unchanged in our law since 1872, states a civil law and not a common law principle. . . .

One of the areas where this court and other courts have departed from the fundamental concept that a man is liable for injuries caused by his carelessness is with regard to the liability of a possessor of land for injuries to persons who have entered upon that land. It has been suggested that the special rules regarding liability of the possessor of land are due to historical considerations stemming from the high place which land has traditionally held in English and American thought, the dominance and prestige of the landowning class in England during the formative period of the rules governing the possessor's liability, and the heritage of feudalism. (2 Harper and James, The Law of Torts, supra, p. 1432.)

The departure from the fundamental rule of liability for negligence has been accomplished by classifying the plaintiff either as a trespasser, licensee, or invitee and then adopting special rules as to the duty owed by the possessor to each of the classifications. . . .

[The court here reviewed the trespasser-licensee-invitee rules and a number of cases which it said created exceptions, complexity and confusion.]

Complexity can be borne and confusion remedied where the underlying principles governing liability are based upon proper considerations. Whatever may have been the historical justifications for the common law distinctions, it is clear that those distinctions are not justified in the light of our modern society and the complexity and confusion which has arisen is not due to difficulty in applying the original common law rules—they are all too easy to apply in their original formulation—but is due to the attempts to apply just rules in our modern society within the ancient terminology.

Without attempting to labor all of the rules relating to the possessor's liability, it is apparent that the classifications of trespasser, licensee, and invitee, the immunities from liability predicated upon those circumstances, and the exceptions to those immunities, often do not reflect the major factors which should determine whether immunity should be conferred upon the possessor of land. Some of those factors, including the closeness of the connection between the injury and the defendant's conduct, the moral blame attached to the defendant's conduct, the policy of preventing future harm, and the prevalence and availability of insurance bear little, if any relationship to the classification of trespasser, licensee and invitee and the existing rules conferring immunity.

Although in general there may be a relationship between the remaining factors and the classifications of trespasser, licensee, and invitee, there are many cases in which no such relationship may exist. Thus, although the foreseeability of harm to an invitee would ordinarily seem greater than the foreseeability of harm to a trespasser, in a particular case the opposite may be true. The same may be said of the issue of certainty of injury. The burden to the defendant and consequences to the community of imposing a duty to exercise care with resulting liability for breach may often be greater with respect to trespassers than with respect to invitees, but it by no means follows that this is true in every case. In many situations, the burden will be the same, i.e., the conduct necessary upon the defendant's part to meet the burden of exercising due care as to the invitees will also meet his burden with respect to licensees and trespassers. The last of the major factors, the cost of insurance, will, of course, vary depending upon the rules of liability adopted, but there is no persuasive evidence that applying ordinary principles of negligence law to the land occupier's liability will materially reduce the prevalence of insurance due to increased cost or even substantially increase the cost. . . .

A man's life or limb does not become less worthy of protection by the law nor a loss less worthy of compensation under the law because he has come upon the land of another without permission or with permission but without a business purpose. Reasonable people do not ordinarily vary their conduct depending upon such matters, and to focus upon the status of the injured party as a trespasser, licensee or invitee in order to determine the question whether the landowner has a duty of care, is contrary to our modern social mores and humanitarian values. The common law rules obscure rather than illuminate the proper consideration which should govern determination of the question of duty. . . .

It may be noted that by carving further exceptions out of the traditional rules relating to the liability to licensees or social guests, other jurisdictions reach the same result. . . .

The Judgment is Reversed.

TRAYNOR, C. J., and TOBRINER, MOSK and SULLIVAN, J. J., concur.

BURKE, JUSTICE (dissenting).

I dissent. In determining the liability of the occupier or owner of land for injuries, the distinctions between trespassers, licensees and invitees have been developed and applied by the courts over a period of many years. They supply a reasonable and workable approach to the problems involved, and one which provides the degree of stability and predictability so highly prized in law. The unfortunate alternative, it appears to me, is the route taken by the majority in their opinion in this case; that such issues are to be decided on a case by case basis under the application of the basic law of negligence, bereft of the guiding principles and precedent which the law has heretofore attached by virtue of the relationship of the parties to one another.

Liability for negligence turns upon whether a duty of care is owed, and if so, the extent thereof. Who can doubt that the corner grocery, the large department store, or the financial institution owes a greater duty of care to one whom it has invited to enter its premises as a prospective customer of its wares or services than it owes to a trespasser seeking to enter after the close of business hours and for a nonbusiness or even an antagonistic purpose? I do not think it unreasonable or unfair that a social guest (classified by the law as a licensee, as was plaintiff here) should be obliged to take the premises in the same condition as his host finds them or permits them to be. Surely a homeowner should not be obliged to hover over his guests with warnings of possible dangers to be found in the condition of the home (e.g., waxed floors, slipping rugs, toys in unexpected places, etc., etc.) . . . .

McComb, J., concurs.

Notes

1. This is the first decision to abolish the categories and substitute the general duty of reasonable care. California was also the first state to hold guest statutes unconstitutional. *Brown v. Merlo*, 506 P.2d 212 (Cal. 1973). Is there any logical relation between the two decisions?

2. By 2008, about half of the states had either included social guests in the invitee category or had completely or partly abolished the categories, with the result that all or most non-trespassing entrants upon land are entitled to reasonable care under the circumstances.

3. Many courts have retained the limited-duty-to-trespassers rules even though they have dropped the licensee-invitee distinction. *See Bennett v. Napolitano,* 746 A.2d 138 (R.I. 2000) (citizen in park after it was closed for the night was a trespasser to whom reasonable care was not owed). The Third Restatement takes the position that all entrants are owed a duty of reasonable care, except in "exceptional cases," then provides that land possessors owe "flagrant trespassers" only a duty not to intentionally, willfully or wantonly injure them. RESTATEMENT (THIRD) OF TORTS: LIABILITY FOR PHYSICAL AND EMOTIONAL HARMS § 52(a) (Council Draft No. 8, 2008).

4. Some recent decisions have continued to affirm all the traditional limited duty categories. *See, e.g., Pinnell v. Bates*, 838 So.2d 198 (Miss. 2002) (also listing other states). Iowa, which may be poised to abandon the licensee-invitee distinction, reaffirmed all categories in a case involving a trespassing adult, saying that "we remain unconvinced that the rights of property owners have so little value in today's society that those rights should be diminished in favor of persons trespassing on another's land." *Alexander v. Medical Assocs. Clinic*, 646 N.W.2d 74 (Iowa 2002).

5. In a state that has abolished all of the categories, the duty of general care has been held to apply to child trespassers as well, thus eliminating those special rules. *See, e.g., Morse v. Goduti*, 777 A.2d 292 (N.H. 2001).

SCURTI v. CITY OF NEW YORK, 354 N.E.2d 794 (N.Y. 1976). A 14-year-old boy was electrocuted in a railroad yard after crawling through a hole in the fence. There was evidence that the fence was part of a city park and the city and others were joined as defendants. New York had previously abolished the trespasser-licensee-invitee distinctions and had adopted the standard of reasonable care.

"Under the standard of reasonable care ... the factors which sustained the landowner's immunity and inspired the exceptions under prior law will no longer be considered decisive. But, as indicated, most of them have some probative value.... The fact that the injury occurred on the defendant's property is certainly a relevant circumstance in assessing the reasonableness of defendant's conduct. The defendant has a right to use his property and to develop it for his profit and enjoyment. That often means that he must conduct dangerous activities or permit dangerous instruments and conditions to exist on the premises. However under those circumstances he must take reasonable measures to prevent injury to those whose presence on the property can reasonably be foreseen. Whether the threat is posed by a dangerous condition or a dangerous activity is of little significance in itself. It may have some bearing on the effort required to prevent the injury, but that depends on the facts of the particular case. In this connection it is important to note that the elimination of the immunity conferred by prior law should not pose an unreasonable burden on the use of the property since all that is now required is the exercise of reasonable care under the circumstances. The defendant can always show that it would have been unduly burdensome to have done more.... The fact that the plaintiff entered without permission is also a relevant circumstance. It may well demonstrate that the plaintiff's presence was not foreseeable at the time and place of the injury.... This does not mean that every case involving injury on private property raises a factual question for the jury's consideration. In any negligence case the court must always determine as a threshold matter whether the facts will support an inference of negligence.... However, in this particular case the question of reasonableness of the parties' conduct cannot be resolved as a matter of law."

NOTES

1. When the categories have been abolished, the landowner is still not liable unless he is negligent. *E.g., Senkus v. Moore*, 535 S.E.2d 724 (W.Va. 2000). Do you believe there are any situations that cannot be justly resolved by applying the prudent person standard? Can you give an example?

2. How would you characterize what the *Scurti* court is doing with the plaintiff's trespasser status? What do you think of its reasoning? In *Louis v. Louis*, 636 N.W.2d 314 (Minn. 2001), the court said that after the abolition of the common-law distinctions, an entrant's status as an invitee or a licensee was no longer controlling, but that it remained "one element among many to be considered in assessing the landowner's duty to use reasonable care for the safety of persons invited on the premises." Do you agree with that approach?

3. The Kansas Supreme Court has now accepted a reasonable care standard for licensees, but back in 1982, in *Britt v. Allen County Community*

Junior College, 638 P.2d 914 (Kan. 1982), it strongly reaffirmed its commitment to the traditional approach. It quoted at length from Carl S. Hawkins, *Premises Liability After Repudiation of the Status Categories: Allocation of Judge and Jury Functions*, [1981] UTAH L. REV. 15 (1981). Among other points the court made by reference to Professor Hawkins were these: (1) A survey of 80 cases in jurisdictions that abolished the status categories showed that in 30 of them judges ruled for defendants as a matter of law; (2) in most of the cases surveyed, the outcome would be the same under either the *Rowland* rule or the traditional status-of-entrant analysis. (3) Professor Hawkins agreed with an earlier article by Professor James Henderson, arguing in effect that "structure" was needed to fix the limits of liability and that a reasonable prudent person rule would be merely a conduit funneling all cases to the jury room.

4. If the result is the same whether or not the status categories are used, what considerations would dictate your choice of one approach over the other? Does the conceptual "conduit" argument conflict with the findings that even under the *Rowland* approach a high percentage of plaintiffs still suffered directed verdicts?

5. Will new problems arise in the jurisdictions abolishing the status categories? What should be done with the firefighter's rule in jurisdictions that have abolished both the status categories and the assumed risk doctrine?

§ 5. RECREATIONAL USES: RE–CREATION OF THE STATUS CATEGORIES

1. *Recreational use statutes*. Most states have now passed statutes dealing with "recreational users" on private land and waters. The gist of these is to retain the landowners' special immunities as to any non-paying recreational user. The Michigan statute, MICH. COMP. L. ANN. § 324.73301, imposes liability only for "gross negligence or willful and wanton misconduct of the owner, tenant or lessee." It applies to "a person who is on the lands of another without paying ... a valuable consideration for the purpose of fishing, hunting, trapping, camping, hiking, sightseeing, motorcycling, snowmobiling, or any other outdoor recreational use, with or without permission." The original statute has been expanded to similarly restrict the redress available to invitees on a farm to buy produce.

California's recreational use statute provides:

> An owner of any estate in real property ... owes no duty of care to keep the premises safe for entry or use by others for any recreational purpose or to give any warning of hazardous conditions, uses of, structures, or activities on such premises to persons entering for such purpose, except as provided in this section.

CAL. CIV. CODE § 846. A duty of due care is owed under this section to those who have paid to enter and also those who are "expressly invited rather than merely permitted." Otherwise liability is only for "willful or malicious failure to guard or warn against a dangerous condition, use, structure or activity." Recreational purpose is defined to include many of the activities mentioned in the Michigan statute and others, such as sport parachuting, spelunking, and even "viewing or enjoying historical, natural, archaeological, natural, or scientific sites."

2. *Theory of the statutes.* Although the motives for the statutes were undoubtedly associated with a desire to protect private landowners from suits and judgments, the *theory* erected for these statutes was that they were being enacted to limit liability in order to encourage landowners to make land available for recreation in a world becoming increasingly crowded. Citing this rationale, states have generally held that that a governmental entity is not protected by these statutes, since a public entitity "needs no incentive to perform this traditional function." *Bronsen v. Dawes County*, 722 N.W.2d 17 (Neb. 2006) (citing cases from other jurisdictions). Most courts have also held that the recreational use statutes do not abrogate a landowner's duty of care to private guests, as opposed to members of the general public who are on the land for recreational purposes. *Estate of Gordon–Couture v. Brown*, 876 A.2d 196 (N.H. 2005) (guest of landowner drowned at private birthday party held for landowner's daughter).

3. *Constitutionality.* Could recreational use statutes be upheld in states that have already ruled guest statutes to be unconstitutional? Remember that one reason given for automobile guest statutes was that they would encourage hospitality. That sounds a great deal like the encouragement supposedly offered by recreational use statutes. We have seen that the California Court found the guest statute to be unconstitutional and that the hospitality purpose did not save it, since not all non-paying persons were treated alike. Interestingly enough, recreational use statutes have been upheld against constitutional attack. *E.g., Lostritto v. Southern Pac. Transp. Co.*, 140 Cal.Rptr. 905 (Ct. App. 1977).

4. *Scope of recreational use statutes.* Many statutes leave much to be interpreted and fail to provide solutions for some obvious problems. Court interpretations of similar statutes are often quite diverse.

(a) Sometimes the interpretive difficulty relates to the place where the injury takes place. For example, in *Liberty v. State, Dept. of Transp.*, 148 P.3d 909 (Or. 2006), the statute was held not to apply to property owners that permitted members of the public to use their property as a means of access to another property that was used for a recreational purpose. In *Wilson v. Kansas State University*, 44 P.3d 454 (Kan. 2002), the statute was applied to a case in which the plaintiff was going to the bathroom in a football stadium, on the reasoning that the stadium itself fit the broad definition of open areas for recreational use. In *Rexroad v. City of Springfield*, 796 N.E.2d 1040 (Ill. 2003), the court found the statute inapplicable to an injury suffered on a parking lot adjacent to a high school football field; the "character of the property in question," not the activity (walking across to a recreational area), is determinative. What about injury on a dam that created a recreational-use lake? *See Stone v.*

York Haven Power Co., 749 A.2d 452 (Pa. 2000) (statutory immunity covers lake but not dam).

(b) At other times the interpretive difficulty relates to what the plaintiff was doing at the time of the injury, that is, whether the use was truly "recreational." For example, in *Crichfield v. Grand Wailea Co.,* 6 P.3d 349 (Haw. 2000), the plaintiff was injured when she was on hotel lands both for recreational purposes and to eat lunch at the hotel as a business invitee. The court found the statute did not protect the hotel where the plaintiff had business as one of her purposes. By contrast, in *Ali v. City of Boston,* 804 N.E.2d 927 (Mass. 2004), the plaintiff was injured while riding his bike across a park merely to get home. He sued the city for negligently maintaining a gate in the park. The defendant raised the recreational use statute as a defense. The plaintiff argued that he was injured while using the park for a "nonrecreational purpose." The court held that the plaintiff's subjective intent was irrelevant, and that liability should not turn on precisely what someone was doing in a recreational area: "It matters not that the plaintiff's purpose was transportation, or that the student's purpose is to learn, or that the financial analyst's purpose is to work. What matters is that they are engaging in recreational pursuits permitted in the park."

§ 6. LESSORS

PAGELSDORF v. SAFECO INSURANCE CO.

284 N.W.2d 55 (Wis. 1979)

CALLOW, JUSTICE.

[Mahnke owned a two-story, two-family duplex. The upper unit was rented to the Blattners and had two balconies. The railing on one had been replaced, but the one in question was the original wooden railing, composed of 2 x 4s parallel to the floor and 2 x 2 spacers perpendicular to the floor. This was secured by nails to upright 4 x 4s at each end. Mr. Blattner left his family and thereafter Mrs. Blattner moved her children out and made arrangements for her brothers to remove her furniture. The brothers secured the aid of Pagelsdorf in moving heavier items. Pagelsdorf lowered a box spring down over the side of the balcony. When he placed his hands on the railing to straighten up afterwards, the railing gave way and he fell to the ground. He claims for the injuries he suffered in the fall. Inspection showed that the railing assembly had dry rot and would not hold well, but this had not been apparent to the eye. There was evidence that the defendant-lessor had contracted to keep the premises in repair, but also evidence, seemingly accepted by the jury, that this was limited to repair of known or reported defects. The trial judge charged the jury that Mahnke owed no duty to discover dangers of which he was unaware, and the jury found for the defendant.]

[W]ith certain exceptions, a landlord is not liable for injuries to his tenants and their visitors resulting from defects in the premises. The general rule of nonliability was based on the concept of a lease as a conveyance of property and the consequent transfer of possession and control of the premises to the tenant.

There are exceptions to this general rule of nonliability. The landlord is liable for injuries to the tenant or his visitor caused by a dangerous condition if he contracts to repair defects, or if, knowing of a defect existing at the time the tenant took possession, he conceals it from a tenant who could not reasonably be expected to discover it. Additionally, the general rule is not applicable where the premises are leased for public use, or are retained in the landlord's control, or where the landlord negligently makes repairs. The rule of nonliability persists despite a decided trend away from application of the general rule and toward expansion of its exceptions.

None of the exceptions to the general rule are applicable to the facts of this case. The premises were not leased for public use, nor was the porch within Mahnke's control, nor did he negligently repair the railing. The plaintiffs argue that Mahnke contracted to repair defects; but according to Mrs. Blattner's testimony, Mahnke's promise extended only to items the Blattners reported as being in disrepair.... Finally, the concealed-defect exception does not apply because there was no evidence that the dry rot existed in 1969 when the Blattners moved in....

Therefore, if we were to follow the traditional rule, Pagelsdorf was not entitled to an instruction that Mahnke owed him a duty of ordinary care. We believe, however, that the better public policy lies in the abandonment of the general rule of nonliability and the adoption of a rule that a landlord is under a duty to exercise ordinary care in the maintenance of the premises.

... Issues of notice of the defect, its obviousness, control of the premises, and so forth are all relevant only insofar as they bear on the ultimate question: Did the landlord exercise ordinary care in the maintenance of the premises under all the circumstances?

Judgment reversed and cause remanded for proceedings consistent with this opinion.

NOTES

1. **Applying the rule.** Will the plaintiff in *Pagelsdorf* necessarily prevail under the new rule adopted by the court?

2. **The traditional rule: lease as conveyance**. The traditional view is that a lease is a conveyance of land. The lessee is the "owner" of the land in question for the period of the lease, and the lessor has no more responsibility for the upkeep of the land than any other person who conveys land. *See, e.g., Benham v. Morton & Furbish Agency*, 929 A.2d 471 (Me. 2007). A corollary rule is that the landlord owes no more to the tenant's guests than he owes to the tenant himself. Note that even under the traditional rule, a landlord might be liable on a contract theory for failure to repair defects, or on a tort

theory for such things as failing to repair latent defects the landlord knows about, or doing repairs negligently. *See* Jean C. Love, *Landlord's Liability for Defective Premises: Caveat Lessee, Negligence, or Strict Liability?*, 1975 WIS. L. REV. 19

3. **Changing concepts of leases.** *Pagelsdorf* and several other decisions have departed from the traditional rules by imposing upon the landlord the duty to exercise ordinary care to the tenant or those on the premises by virtue of the tenant's rights. *See e.g., Childs v. Purll*, 882 A.2d 227 (D.C. 2005) (basing duty on housing code provisions); *Favreau v. Miller*, 591 A.2d 68 (Vt. 1991). In *Antwaun A. v. Heritage Mutual Insurance Co.*, 596 N.W.2d 456 (Wis. 1999), the court held that a landlord who did not actually know of lead paint used in his buildings but who was notified of peeling paint in a building constructed before lead paint was banned, was under a specific duty to test for lead. Some states abrogate the common law rule for leases only for residential leases, retaining the traditional rule for commercial leases. *See, e.g., Lucier v. Impact Recreation, Ltd.*, 864 A.2d 635 (R.I. 2005) (commercial landlord not liable for skateboarder's injuries at commercial skate park operated by landlord's tenant).

4. **Implied warranty of habitability.** Courts now often recognize a new liability—an implied warranty of habitability. This could conceivably impose strict liability, but courts have reserved the implied warranty theory for breach of contract damages. They insist that personal injury claims are best adjudicated under the law of negligence. *See Antwaun A., supra* Note 2.

5. **Statutory duties of landlords.** Further, many statutes now set standards or impose liability for specific defects, such as the knowing use of lead-based paint that poisons a tenant's child, *see Gore v. People's Savings Bank*, 665 A.2d 1341 (Conn. 1995), or a failure to disclose lead-based paint the lessor should have discovered on reasonable inspection, *Benik v. Hatcher,* 750 A.2d 10 (Md. 2000). However, some courts have held that a building owner's violation of a building code by failure to have handrails on stairs or the like is not negligence per se unless the owner knew or should have known that the building was constructed in violation of code. *Bills v. Willow Run I Apartments,* 547 N.W.2d 693 (Minn. 1996) (tenant injured); *Lamm v. Bissette Realty, Inc.,* 395 S.E.2d 112 (N.C. 1990) (invitee injured).

PROBLEMS

Paton v. Missouri & Atlantic Railway

Paton lived in a small rural house adjacent to a railroad track. A friend of his, Talbot, lived on the other side of the track. The two men sometimes met at or near the track and drank together in the evenings. One evening in July they met at the track and began drinking. Sometime later Talbot awoke and realized that a train was approaching. He did not see Paton in the dark and the train's light was not bright. After the train passed, however, he found Paton near the track. The lower part of his right leg had been severed by the passing train. Paton's lawyer showed: (1) the engineer of the train said he kept a lookout but never saw Paton or anyone on the track, (2) the train was moving slowly and could have stopped within a very short distance, and (3) the headlight was out of repair and fell short of standards prescribed by a regulatory agency. Although all states would recognize a duty on the part of railroads to keep a reasonable lookout at public crossings, only a few states impose a duty of lookout for trespassers along the track. *If Paton's injury did not occur in a state requiring a lookout for trespassers, did the railroad owe him any duty?*

Christie v. Embry Corp.

Christie, a girl of 11 years, entered a garbage dump maintained by the Embry Corporation on its own land. She was looking for any kind of old toys or comic books. Walking on what appeared to be a solid surface, she suddenly sank through and was burned on hot embers below. In her action against Embry Corp., she proved that in past times Embry had had to call the fire department to put out fires that spontaneously flared in the dump. She also proved that other children often went there looking for comics and toys, that there was no fence, and that there were many houses nearby. This was all the proof. *Can she get to the jury?*

Paget v. Owen

Paget asked Owen for permission to enter Owen's large farm to fish in one of the ponds. Owen agreed to this. Owen believed from the location involved, that Paget intended to take the north road on Owen's property. The north road had been undermined by flooding of a creek, though Owen did not know this. The south road had also been undermined by flooding of a different creek, and Owen was well aware of this. Paget drove into the farm land to fish the next day. Although the road appeared to be safe, it caved in where it had been undermined by the flooding. Paget's car overturned and he was injured. *Did Owen breach any duty? Does it matter which road Paget took?*

In re Claims of Picklesimer, Patrick and Plangent

The facts our law firm has after an initial interview with our client, Herman Picklesimer, are as follows:

Picklesimer was driving in a generally southerly direction on highway 101 in an area with which he was only vaguely familiar. It was about 7:30 at night and dark. The road bends slightly to the right about a mile south of the town of Roan. The road also is rising slightly at this point, with the result that headlights are aimed slightly upward. At the point where the road bends to the right, a private unpaved road on the property of James P. Dalzell continues straight ahead. There are no markers, signs, reflectors or other indicators of the curve. Mr. Picklesimer says that there was not even any center stripe and that the road was black. The result of all this was that with his lights forced slightly upward by the road grade, he did not appreciate the fact that it bent to the right. He continued straight until he dropped off the highway and headed downhill on the Dalzell private road. At this point he realized his error, and tried to steer back onto the road, but this compounded the problem and he turned his car over.

According to the police report a car driven by James Patrick was proceeding northerly on the same road at the same time and place. Patrick became confused or at least he tried to react when—according to him—Mr. Picklesimer crossed the road in his path as he proceeded straight onto the Dalzell property. Patrick steered to his left, lost control in the gravel on his left side (the west side) of the road and crashed into a tree some distance from the road. His passenger, Blanche Plangent, suffered head wounds when she hit the windshield. Patrick himself was also injured.

Picklesimer was not aware of any of this. He apparently suffered a concussion and certainly he was confused. He wandered away from the highway on Dalzell's land. He has no recollection of this, but the police report and emergency room report indicate that in the dark he fell into an excavation on Dalzell's land. This was not lighted or marked in any way. In this he broke his hip. He is 68 years old and there were complications in the hospital when a nurse, misreading the doctor's drug order, gave the wrong drug, which in turn created complications when Mr. Picklesimer was under anesthetic. He has emerged with a slight speech impairment, though at this stage we are not sure whether this is psychological or whether it is a result of the hospital mishap. The doctor is Dr. Daniel Doubs and the nurse is Mr. Paul Hadini. The hospital was the Murphy Medical Center in the town of Roan.

We should outline our basic claims and the probable defenses and prepare to investigate as needed.

GENERAL REFERENCES: DOBBS ON TORTS §§ 231–241 (landowners generally); §§ 284–287 (firefighter's rule) (2000); GLEN WEISSENBERGER & BARBARA MCFARLAND, THE LAW OF PREMISES LIABILITY (3d ed. 2001); JOSEPH PAGE, THE LAW OF PREMISES LIABILITY (2d ed. 1988).

CHAPTER 13

DUTIES OF MEDICAL AND OTHER PROFESSIONALS

■ ■ ■

§ 1. TRADITIONAL DUTIES OF HEALTH CARE PROVIDERS IN TRADITIONAL PRACTICE

Medical malpractice suits are negligence suits with some special rules. The special rules derive in part from the professional setting of the doctor-patient relationship. Ordinarily, the malpractice claim must be asserted by a patient. The doctor's acceptance of the patient represents an undertaking of care by the doctor.

But couldn't a physician undertake a duty of care to a person who is not the doctor's patient? Suppose a doctor, on behalf of a potential employer, examines a non-patient potential employee and fails to notice cancer on an X-ray. Consider what care, if any, you think the doctor has undertaken to the potential employee. In this era of increasingly-complex health care provider relationships, whether a doctor has undertaken a duty of care is sometimes contested.

When a doctor-patient relationship is found to exist, what standard of care applies?

WALSKI v. TIESENGA
381 N.E.2d 279 (Ill. 1978)

KLUCZYNSKI, JUSTICE.

[Defendants operated to remove plaintiff's thyroid. A well-recognized risk of a thyroidectomy is that the recurrent laryngeal nerves, which run through the thyroid, may be damaged, with resulting loss of voice. One solution to the problem is to locate the nerves and segregate them before removal of the thyroid. In this case, however, there was a great deal of scar tissue present as a result of earlier operations and treatments and the defendants, instead of locating the nerve, made a wide cut so as to avoid the area where the nerve was thought to be. In fact they cut the nerve and plaintiff's vocal chords are paralyzed. The trial court directed a verdict for the defendants and the intermediate appellate court affirmed.]

Dr. David M. Berger testified as an expert witness on plaintiff's behalf.... His direct testimony concerning acceptable procedures for thyroid surgery was that "in my feeling the standards by which I feel are acceptable practice, one must identify and preserve the recurrent laryngeal nerves on all occasions." On cross-examination Dr. Berger testified that there are always options available in surgery but that in his own mind it was not a proper option to skirt the left recurrent laryngeal nerve. He stated he could not testify generally but only "on the basis of my own opinion as to what I consider a proper option." When asked on cross-examination if there existed a contemporary school of surgeons that will skirt the nerve when they encounter a host of adhesions, Dr. Berger responded that "in the institutions in which I trained that is not the teaching. And I can't speak for other institutions or other areas of training. I can only speak for my own." Defense counsel read a quotation to Dr. Berger from a medical textbook which indicated that there existed a certain amount of controversy in the medical community concerning deliberate exposure of the laryngeal nerve. The quotation concluded with the remark that the situation remained one in which each surgeon will find the approach which suits him best. Dr. Berger indicated that he did not fully agree with that statement, but indicated the decision whether or not to expose the nerve depends on the surgeon and the technique and care he uses. Dr. Berger stated that "[e]verybody who is a certified surgeon doesn't use the same methods, obviously."

One element of a cause of action for medical malpractice is proof of the standard of care by which the defendant physician's conduct is to be measured.... [T]he appellate decisions in this State have held that the plaintiff in a medical malpractice action generally must establish the standard of care through expert testimony. The plaintiff must then prove that, judged in the light of these standards, the doctor was unskillful or negligent and that his want of skill or care caused the injury to the plaintiff. Generally, expert testimony is needed to support a charge of malpractice because jurors are not skilled in the practice of medicine and would find it difficult without the help of medical evidence to determine any lack of necessary scientific skill on the part of the physician. However, in those situations where the physician's conduct is so grossly negligent or the treatment so common that a layman could readily appraise it, the appellate decisions indicate that no expert testimony is necessary.... A requirement that the standard of care be established through expert testimony except where the common knowledge of laymen is sufficient to recognize or infer negligence is broadly recognized throughout the country....

Plaintiff here had the burden of establishing that the defendant doctors were guilty of malpractice. She failed, however, to introduce evidence of the standard of care to which the defendants were bound to adhere. Plaintiff's expert, Dr. Berger, testified only concerning his own personal preference for isolating the laryngeal nerve under the facts presented to him in the hypothetical question. He at no time testified that there was a generally accepted medical standard of care or skill which required the identification of the laryngeal nerve under the circumstances. . . .

The appellate courts have held that the testimony of the defendant doctor may be sufficient to establish the standard of care, but it is apparent that the defendants' testimony here did not indicate a standard at variance with their actual conduct. Dr. Tiesenga testified that because of prior surgery on and treatment of plaintiff's thyroid, it would have been unwise to attempt to isolate her laryngeal nerve. The better practice, according to Dr. Tiesenga's testimony, was to skirt the area where the nerve might possibly be. Dr. Walsh concurred. When confronted with a statement from a recognized treatise that the first step in performing a thyroidectomy is to expose and identify the recurrent laryngeal nerve, Dr. Tiesenga agreed with the statement only as a general proposition. He testified that where there has been prior surgery and treatment, it is not always good practice to follow the procedure indicated in the treatise. . . .

It is insufficient for plaintiff to establish a prima facie case merely to present testimony of another physician that he would have acted differently from the defendant, since medicine is not an exact science. It is rather a profession which involves the exercise of individual judgment within the framework of established procedures. Differences in opinion are consistent with the exercise of due care. . . .

For the above reasons the judgment of the appellate court is affirmed.

NOTES

1. **Medical "standards."** The medical standard discussed in the opinions seldom sounds like a "standard" comparable to the standard of the reasonable prudent person. The term standard suggests a measure or benchmark of some generality. Medical "standards" almost always reflect particular customs or procedures used under very particular circumstances, like the "wide-cut" procedure in *Walski*. The medical "standard" is understood as a rule for the very circumstances involved in the plaintiff's case. "The standard of care is determined by the care customarily provided by other physicians, it need not be scientifically tested or proven effective: what the average qualified physician would do in a particular situation *is* the standard of care." *Palandjian v. Foster*, 842 N.E.2d 916 (Mass. 2006) (appropriate question was whether other doctors would have ordered an endoscopy for the patient given the patient's family history of gastric cancer, not whether the patient's risk of gastric cancer was in fact increased).

2. **Sufficiency of testimony.** In *Heinrich v. Sweet,* 308 F.3d 48 (1st Cir. 2002), the plaintiff's attorney attempted to establish breach of the medical standard of care by asking the expert whether the defendant physician had acted "appropriately or inappropriately, responsibly or irresponsibly," in his treatments of the patients. The expert answered, "inappropriately." Can the plaintiff get to the jury on the duty and breach issue based on this testimony?

3. **Jury instructions.** If the proof is sufficient to get the plaintiff to the jury, the instructions must reflect the medical, not the ordinary care, standard. Instructions often state that the physician must possess the learning, skill and ability of other physicians, must exercise reasonable care in the use of this knowledge and skill and must use his or her best judgment in the care of the patient. It is common also to hear the trial judge emphasize the defense side of the case by telling the jury that the physician is not liable for an honest mistake or bona fide error or that the physician is not expected to be infallible or that he does not guarantee results. These instructions have come under attack by plaintiffs' lawyers as unduly emphasizing the defendant's side of the case or as misleading the jury. The "honest mistake" and "no guarantee" instructions have been rejected in a number of cases. *See Nestorowich v. Ricotta,* 767 N.E.2d 125 (N.Y. 2002) (error in judgment instruction proper only when physician is choosing among medically acceptable procedures); *McKinnis v. Women & Infants Hosp. of R.I.,* 749 A.2d 574 (R.I. 2000).

4. **Expert medical testimony.** Expert medical testimony is usually required to establish the medical standard of care. If the plaintiff furnishes no such testimony, or it is inadequate to show the standard, the judge will direct a verdict for the defendant. *See, e.g., Toogood v. Rogal,* 824 A.2d 1140 (Pa. 2003). In a few obvious cases, as where the surgeon amputates the wrong limb, expert testimony is not required. What if a doctor orders blood to be given to a patient who had made it clear that he did not want a blood transfusion for religious reasons? Would expert testimony be required on that malpractice claim? *Campbell v. Delbridge,* 670 N.W.2d 108 (Iowa 2003).

5. **Purposes of expert testimony.** Expert testimony may be crucial to several aspects of the plaintiff's case—the standard of care, the doctor's departure from that standard and evidence that the doctor's action or inaction was a direct cause of the plaintiff's harm. When expert testimony is necessary, can the plaintiff prove his case through cross-examination of the defendant doctor along with introduction of excerpts from medical treatises? In *Smith v. Knowles,* 281 N.W.2d 653 (Minn. 1979), both mother and child died of toxemia of pregnancy. Plaintiff, the husband and father of the decedents, claimed that diagnosis and treatment should have commenced earlier. However, plaintiff called no independent medical experts. Instead, he chose to prove his case through his cross-examination of the treating doctor and the introduction of excerpts from several recognized medical treatises. Although the evidence was admissible and minimally sufficient to establish the standard of care, it was not sufficient show that the doctor breached that standard of care or that the doctor's breach was the actual cause of the deaths.

6. **More than one medical "standard" or practice.** Suppose that among doctors in the relevant medical community, the majority believe that human bite wounds should not be closed with stitches. But suppose that some doctors believe to the contrary, that the wound should be stitched and treated with antibiotics. A patient suffers serious infection when his doctor closes the wound. What is the standard? "Where competent medical authority is divided, a physician will not be held responsible if in the exercise of his judgment he followed a course of treatment advocated by a considerable number of recognized and respected professionals in his given area of expertise." *Sinclair v. Block,* 633 A.2d 1137 (Pa. 1993). What if the defendant says his practices

represent a medical standard or school of thought even though no one else in the profession agrees? *See Yates v. University of W.Va. Bd. of Trustees*, 549 S.E.2d 681 (W.Va. 2001).

7. **Rejecting *T.J. Hooper*.** Medical standards are not to be found in an authoritative book. For the most part, the medical standard of care is the practice of the relevant medical community. Does the medical standard rule reject the rule about custom in *T.J. Hooper*?

8. **Rejecting reasonable care.** Medical standards will often reflect reasonable care. Notice that under the reasonable person standard, a professional practitioner would be obliged to exercise the skill and use all the knowledge he actually has, even if that is more skill or knowledge than other people have. So the medical care standard is not different from the reasonable person standard in this respect.

But the medical standard might require *less* care than the reasonable person standard. To see why, suppose Dr. Berger had testified that, as a matter of scientific fact, the risk of severing the nerve is doubled when the wide cut procedure is used as compared to the nerve identification procedure and that there are no corresponding advantages to the wide cut procedure. That testimony seems to be important under a *Carroll Towing* or reasonable care standard, because it shows an increase of risk. But it does not seem relevant at all, much less determinative, under the medical standard, because it does not address what doctors actually do.

Is it fair to say that a customary standard can also require *more* care than the reasonable person standard in some instances? What result if the medical standard of care is to perform a procedure despite a lack of scientific evidence suggesting that the procedure is generally beneficial? See *Palandjian v. Foster*, 842 N.E.2d 916 (Mass. 2006).

9. **Accepting reasonable care standards**. A few decisions have indicated that in extreme cases, the reasonable person standard might be used. *See United Blood Serv's, Div. of Blood Sys., Inc. v. Quintana*, 827 P.2d 509 (Colo. 1992); *Helling v. Carey*, 519 P.2d 981 (Wash. 1974) (cheap, efficient test for glaucoma should be given with ophthalmic exam even if that was not the practice of the medical community). Professor Peters' study concludes that 12 cases have shifted to the reasonable care standard and that a number of others have implicitly done so. *See* Philip G. Peters, Jr., *The Quiet Demise of Deference to Custom: Malpractice Law at the Millennium*, 57 WASH. & LEE L. REV. 163 (2000). Logically, the shift implies that testimony about medical custom would no longer be necessary. Some cases like *Helling v. Carey, supra*, are in accord with that, but it remains to be seen whether all those courts adopting reasonable care will go that far against long-standing tradition.

10. **Non-medical negligence of health care providers.** Suppose that you, as a hospital patient, slip and fall because the hospital left a slippery substance on the floor. Would you be required to prove the standard of care for hospitals by expert testimony? *See Self v. Executive Comm. of Ga. Baptist Convention*, 266 S.E.2d 168 (Ga. 1980) (not a claim of medical malpractice, no requirement of expert testimony). Do you need expert testimony in this case: a doctor knows a patient is dangerous but fails to warn his coworkers. *Powell v. Catholic Med. Ctr.*, 749 A.2d 301 (N.H. 2000)?

11. **Apology.** The defendant might conceivably admit before trial that he violated the appropriate standard of care. If he does so, evidence of this admission can be introduced to show the standard and its breach. Suppose the defendant, after an operation turns out badly, says "I made a mistake, that should not have happened." Would that suffice to show the standard? *Fossett v. Board of Regents of Univ. of Neb.,* 605 N.W.2d 465 (Neb. 2000). Some recent state statutes permit physicians to apologize to patients for mistakes without risk that the apology will be used in court. *See* Marilyn Wei, *Doctors, Apologies, and the Law: An Analysis and Critique of Apology Laws,* 40 J. Health L. 107 (2007) (listing a dozen such recent laws). Is this a help to injured patients? To doctors? *Compare* Aaron Lazare, *The Healing Forces of Apology in Medical Practice and Beyond,* 57 DePaul L. Rev. 251(2008), *with* Lee Taft, *Apology Subverted: The Commodification of Apology,* 109 Yale. L. J. 1135 (2000).

VERGARA v. DOAN

593 N.E.2d 185 (Ind. 1992)

Shepard, Chief Justice.

Javier Vergara was born on May 31, 1979, at the Adams Memorial Hospital in Decatur, Indiana. His parents, Jose and Concepcion, claimed that negligence on the part of Dr. John Doan during Javier's delivery caused him severe and permanent injuries. A jury returned a verdict for Dr. Doan and the plaintiffs appealed. The Court of Appeals affirmed. Plaintiffs seek transfer, asking us to abandon Indiana's modified locality rule. We grant transfer to examine the standard of care appropriate for medical malpractice cases.

In most negligence cases, the defendant's conduct is tested against the hypothetical reasonable and prudent person acting under the same or similar circumstances. In medical malpractice cases, however, Indiana has applied a more specific articulation of this standard. It has become known as the modified locality rule: "The standard of care ... is that degree of care, skill, and proficiency which is commonly exercised by ordinarily careful, skillful, and prudent [physicians], at the time of the operation and in similar localities." Appellants have urged us to abandon this standard, arguing that the reasons for the modified locality rule are no longer applicable in today's society. We agree.

The modified locality rule is a less stringent version of the strict locality rule, which measured the defendant's conduct against that of other doctors in the same community. When the strict locality rule originated in the late 19th century, there was great disparity between the medical opportunities, equipment, facilities, and training in rural and urban communities. Travel and communication between rural and urban communities were difficult. The locality rule was intended to prevent the inequity that would result from holding rural doctors to the same standards as doctors in large cities.

With advances in communication, travel, and medical education, the disparity between rural and urban health care diminished and justification for the locality rule waned. The strict locality rule also had two major drawbacks, especially as applied to smaller communities. First, there was a scarcity of local doctors to serve as expert witnesses against other local doctors. Second, there was the possibility that practices among a small group of doctors would establish a local standard of care below that which the law required. In response to these changes and criticisms, many courts adopted a modified locality rule, expanding the area of comparison to similar localities. . . .

Use of a modified locality rule has not quelled the criticism. Many of the common criticisms seem valid. The modified locality rule still permits a lower standard of care to be exercised in smaller communities because other similar communities are likely to have the same care. We also spend time and money on the difficulty of defining what is a similar community. The rule also seems inconsistent with the reality of modern medical practice. The disparity between small town and urban medicine continues to lessen with advances in communication, transportation, and education. In addition, widespread insurance coverage has provided patients with more choice of doctors and hospitals by reducing the financial constraints on the consumer in selecting caregivers. . . . Many states describe the care a physician owes without emphasizing the locality of practice. Today we join these states and adopt the following: a physician must exercise that degree of care, skill, and proficiency exercised by reasonably careful, skillful, and prudent practitioners in the same class to which he belongs, acting under the same or similar circumstances. Rather than focusing on different standards for different communities, this standard uses locality as but one of the factors to be considered in determining whether the doctor acted reasonably. Other relevant considerations would include advances in the profession, availability of facilities, and whether the doctor is a specialist or general practitioner.

. . . Plaintiff was permitted to present his expert witness, Dr. Harlan Giles, even though he was from Pittsburgh, Pennsylvania (not Decatur or a similar locality). Dr. Giles testified regarding his experience and knowledge of the standard of care in communities similar to Decatur and in hospitals similar in size to Adams County Memorial Hospital. He testified that in his opinion, considering all the factors incident to the pregnancy and birth of Javier Vergara, the standard of care required Dr. Doan to have delivered the baby by cesarean section. He stated that this opinion was based on the standard of care as it existed in 1979 in Decatur or similar communities. He also testified that the failure to have either an anesthesiologist or a qualified nurse anesthetist present at the delivery was a breach of the national standard of care for hospitals the size of Adams County Memorial and smaller. Evidently the jury disagreed with Dr. Giles and found Dr. Doan's conduct reasonable under the circumstances.

We regard our new formulation of a doctor's duty as a relatively modest alteration of existing law. It is unlikely to have changed the way this case was tried. We are satisfied that an instruction without the locality language would not lead a new jury to a different conclusion.

Therefore, we hold that giving instruction 23 was harmless and does not require reversal. . . .

NOTES

1. **The local medical standard and problems of testimony.** Adoption of a local standard means that only a local physician, or one who knows what the local standard is, can testify against the defendant-doctor. What problems does this raise for the plaintiff? In *Robinson v. LeCorps,* 83 S.W.3d 718 (Tenn. 2002) the defendant practiced in Nashville, Tennessee, and the plaintiff's expert was from Johnson City, Tennessee. The expert testified that the defendant violated the national standard, and that the national standard was "the same as the recognized standard of acceptable professional practice as it would be in Nashville, Tennessee." The court, bound by a statutory locality rule, affirmed a dismissal of the claim because the testimony did not meet that rule. One reason: the expert did not specify a basis for his opinion. The court may also have thought that a statement that the standard "would be" the same was not good enough, perhaps meaning that the testimony should have been "is the same."

2. **The national medical standard.** It is sometimes argued that adoption of a standard like *Vergara's* would be unfair to doctors in small towns, who might not have the latest equipment. Would a national medical standard be likely to require a small-town doctor to own CT scan technology? What about the reasonable person standard? In *Hall v. Hilbun,* 466 So.2d 856 (Miss. 1985) the Mississippi Court adopted a national standard which governs the physician's care and skill, but not the particular resources available to that physician. If you were a small-town doctor without equipment, what would you do about a patient who needed a CT scan?

NOTE: SPECIALISTS

1. *Specialists.* The medical profession is organized to a large extent (as the legal profession is not) around recognized specialties. Examples include orthopedics, internal medicine, obstetrics and gynecology, and radiology. Medical specialization usually entails several years of study following medical school and success in an examination administered by the "board" which certifies specialists.

2. *The local standard.* Specialists are held to the standard of their specialties; thus an orthopedic surgeon is held to a higher standard in setting a fracture than is a family practitioner. It is often assumed or held that the relevant medical community for them is the community of specialists, not a geographical community. *Wall v. Stout,* 311 S.E.2d 571 (N.C. 1984).

3. *Non-specialist expert testimony.* Could a family practitioner testify against an orthopedic surgeon? Could an obstetrician testify against a radiologist? The answer logically ought to be "yes—provided the witness knows the relevant standard and can state it." Some courts exclude such testimony, others admit it, and still others admit it where the two specialties share common standards or procedures. See DOBBS ON TORTS § 246 (2000). In *Staccato v. Valley Hosp.*, 170 P.3d 503 (Nev. 2007), the court held that an emergency-room physician could testify as an expert about the appropriate standard of care for intermuscular injections even though the defendant in the case was a nurse.

NOTE: NON–MEDICAL PRACTITIONERS

1. *Standard.* Non-medical practitioners such as chiropractors and podiatrists, are permitted to practice according to their schools of belief. They are subject to the standards of the school they profess, not to medical standards. What if a naturopath diagnoses tonsilitis in a child and prescribes orange juice, but in fact the child has diphtheria and dies of it? Should a Christian Scientist practitioner, whose religion opposes medical treatment, be liable for treating a child with prayer when known and readily available medical treatment can save the child's life? In *Lundman v. McKown,* 530 N.W.2d 807 (Minn. Ct. App. 1995), a child whose mother was a Christian Scientist died when the mother called in a Christian Science practitioner instead of a medical doctor. The practitioner would be held to the standard he professes—healing by prayer—in the case of an adult. Would it be different with a child? Is there a limit? In *Guerrero v. Smith,* 864 S.W.2d 797 (Tex. App. 1993) the plaintiff alleged that a "homeopathic physician" injected the plaintiff's vagina with compounds not approved for human use, used unsterile instruments, and directed the plaintiff to drink her own urine, with horrible consequences. Does he escape responsibility on the ground that all this is within the homeopathic standard?

2. *Referral.* Medical practitioners must refer their patients to specialists when the standard of care so requires. When a *non*medical practitioner recognizes or should recognize that a patient has a medical problem, some courts hold that they must refer the patient to a medical doctor. *Kerkman v. Hintz,* 418 N.W.2d 795 (Wis. 1988), however, held that referral is not required or even logically permissible. It is enough, the *Kerkman* court said, that the chiropractor cease treating a condition that lies outside his school of work. What about a church counselor who believes that the word of God is the only counseling anyone requires and for that reason does not refer a suicidal young man to different professional help? *Nally v. Grace Cmty. Church of the Valley*, 763 P.2d 948 (Cal. 1988). What about a medical health care provider who morally opposes a needed abortion—must he advise the patient that an abortion is available and where? *Cf. Brownfield v. Daniel Freeman Marina Hosp.*, 256 Cal.Rptr. 240 (Ct. App. 1989) (rape victim, duty to refer for pregnancy prevention supported in dictum).

NOTE: OTHER PROFESSIONALS

1. *Nurses.* Courts now seem to assume that nurses are held to the standard of nurses in a similar practice. *Fein v. Permanente Med. Group,* 695 P.2d 665 (Cal. 1985).

2. *Hospitals.* The present view seems to be that, in performing their own duties, hospitals owe a duty of reasonable care under national standards fixed by the Joint Commission on Accreditation of Hospitals. *See* DOBBS ON TORTS § 254 (2000).

3. *Pharmacists.* The rule in most states is that pharmacists owe their clients no duty to warn of side effects, that the physician has prescribed an excessive dosage, or that a drug is counter-indicated, even though the patient may be seriously injured if the prescription is filled. *See Allberry v. Parkmor Drug, Inc.,* 834 N.E.2d 199 (Ind. Ct. App. 2005). In these jurisdictions, the pharmacist is liable only if he voluntarily undertakes to give appropriate warnings and negligently fails to do so. *Cottam v. CVS Pharmacy,* 764 N.E.2d 814 (Mass. 2002). However, some courts have held that a pharmacist owes a duty to warn when serious contraindications are present or the drugs prescribed carry inherent risk. In *Powers v. Thobhani,* 903 So.2d 275 (Fla. Dist. Ct. App. 2005), the patient's neurologist had prescribed several different contraindicated drugs in rapid succession and the 46-year-old patient ultimately died of a drug overdose. *See also, Happel v. Wal–Mart Stores, Inc.,* 766 N.E.2d 1118 (Ill. 2002) (holding that a pharmacist has a duty to warn when she knows that a prescription is dangerous due to the patient's particular allergies).

4. *Other callings, occupations or activities.* Courts often state the prudent person standard of care by referring to the care that should be exercised by a reasonable person in the defendant's occupation or status as a shorthand way of referring to the circumstances. A court's reference to a reasonable and prudent dog owner is not meant to establish a different standard of care for dog owners. But consider a blood bank whose tests for infection in donated blood are up to the standard of the industry but are dangerously and needlessly inadequate. Is the claim of a victim of tainted blood so much like a medical malpractice claim that the professional standard should be used? *See Elkerson v. North Jersey Blood Ctr.,* 776 A.2d 244 (N.J. Super. Ct. App. Div. 2001).

5. *Architects, engineers, accountants and lawyers.* When courts refer to the standard for members of learned professions or skilled trades, however, reference to the custom or standard of the profession itself may be more than a way of loosely stating that the professional setting is part of the "circumstances" in a reasonable person standard. The result is that expert testimony may be required, not merely to establish a risk, but to establish that the risk was a violation of professional standards. For instance, in *Rentz v. Brown,* 464 S.E.2d 617 (Ga. Ct. App. 1995), the court insisted that the standard of care for building contractors was the care and skill employed by other contractors under similar circumstances and that expert testimony was required to show that standard. Similar rules

standards apply to both accountants and lawyers. *E.g., Simko v. Blake*, 532 N.W.2d 842 (Mich. 1995).

6. *Educational malpractice.* Educators may commit intentional torts (for example by an unprivileged spanking) or negligent torts (for example by failure to remove a dangerous condition on the school ground). In such cases the rules of intentional tort and the standard of the prudent person seem to govern. When the alleged educational malpractice is the product of training, testing, promotion, failure, or classification of the student, the courts have not merely provided the protective professional standard. Instead they have said there is little duty or none at all. *Ross v. Creighton Univ.*, 957 F.2d 410 (7th Cir. 1992); *Peter W. v. San Francisco Unified School District*, 131 Cal.Rptr. 854 (Ct. App. 1976); *Hoffman v. Board of Educ. of N.Y.*, 400 N.E.2d 317 (N.Y. 1979). However, in *Sain v. Cedar Rapids Community School District*, 626 N.W.2d 115 (Iowa 2001), the court recognized that analysis was required to determine whether a duty should be imposed. In that case, the plaintiff alleged that, as a high school student, he received erroneous information from a guidance counselor, the effect of which was to deprive him of a college scholarship that he would have obtained otherwise. These allegations, if proven, would make out a good claim.

HIRPA v. IHC HOSPITALS, INC., 948 P.2d 785 (Utah 1997). A patient in active labor at a hospital became unresponsive and her hands began to spasm. Her physician broadcast a "Code Blue" over the hospital intercom. Dr. Daines responded, entering the delivery room and taking over. Seventeen minutes later, the patient was dead. The surviving spouse sued Daines and others involved in a federal court. Daines moved for summary judgment. He invoked a statute covering medical providers: "No person licensed under this chapter ... who in good faith renders emergency care at the scene of the emergency, shall be liable for any civil damages as a result of any acts or omissions by such person in rendering the emergency care." The federal court certified questions to the state court. One question asked whether the statute applied. *Held*, the statute applies. This was an emergency. The statute is intended to encourage aid without fear of liability, so the location of the emergency in a hospital instead of a roadside is irrelevant, so long as the physician had no preexisting duty to aid. It has no application, however, when the physician already had a duty to aid the patient, for in that case he needs no encouragement. Whether the doctor was under a preexisting duty to the patient could depend upon the doctor-patient relationship, his contractual duty to respond, hospital rules or other factors.

NOTES

1. **Liability for gross negligence.** A milder version of the Good Samaritan statute leaves open the possibility of liability for gross negligence,

or for wanton conduct or intentional wrongdoing. *See, e.g.,* N.C. Gen. Stat. § 20–166(d). The North Carolina statute applies to any person, not merely to health care providers.

2. **Emergency care.** Should a Good Samaritan statute apply to protect an on-call physician who negligently treats a hospital patient in the emergency department? *See Washington v. Clark,* 550 S.E.2d 671 (Ga. Ct. App. 2001). Would such a statute protect a surgeon who performs emergency surgery with an expectation of remuneration? *See Chamley v. Khokha,* 730 N.W.2d 864 (N.D. 2007) (no). Some states have other special statutes favoring physicians who act in an emergency. For example, a state may require clear and convincing evidence—not merely a preponderance of the evidence—when the alleged malpractice occurs in connection with labor or delivery. *See* Ariz. Rev. Stat. § 32–1473 (protecting both physician and the health care facility). A major study of preventable medical errors found that "High error rates with serious consequences are most likely to occur in intensive care units, operating rooms, and emergency departments." Institute of Medicine, To Err Is Human: Building a Safer Healthy System (2000). Does that fact make legislation protecting doctors more necessary or more troubling?

3. **Scope of immunity.** The scope of immunity granted by Good Samaritan Acts varies. The New Jersey Supreme Court wrote in *Velazquez v. Jiminez,* 798 A.2d 51 (N.J. 2002), "All fifty states and the District of Columbia have now enacted some form of Good Samaritan legislation. . . . The country's Good Samaritan statutes broadly can be classified as falling into one of three categories: those that expressly exclude hospital care; those that expressly include hospital care; and those, like New Jersey's, that contain no explicit provision one way or the other." The court stated that its Good Samaritan statute was designed "to encourage the rendering of medical care to those who would not otherwise receive it, by physicians who come upon such patients by chance, without the benefit of the expertise, assistance, equipment or sanitation that is available in a hospital or medical setting." Thus it did not extend immunity to physicians in the hospital setting. According to the court, in the hospital context "physicians' contracts, hospital protocols, ethical rules, regulatory standards and physicians' personal relationships" make it unlikely that, without immunity, physicians would stand by and allow patients to die.

4. **Need for immunity.** The court in *Velazquez* believed that the roadside accident is the kind of case for which the immunity is designed. Was there ever any need for immunity in such a case or wouldn't ordinary negligence rules protect the physician unless the physician imposes unreasonable risks even in the light of the emergency?

References: Dobbs on Torts §§ 242–246 (2000); Harper, James & Gray, The Law of Torts § 17.1 (3d Ed. 2007).

§ 2. RES IPSA LOQUITUR

STATES v. LOURDES HOSPITAL

792 N.E.2d 151 (N.Y. 2003)

CIPARICK, J.

[The court first reviewed the facts of the case concerning plaintiff Kathleen States. States underwent surgery for removal of an ovarian cyst. States believes that during the operation the anesthesiologist negligently hyperabducted her right arm beyond a 90–degree angle for an extended period of time, causing right thoracic outlet syndrome and reflex sympathetic dystrophy. The New York Court of Appeals had previously determined that res ipsa loquitur was available in simple medical malpractice cases which required no expert. In this case, the court was called upon to answer "whether expert testimony can be used to educate the jury as to the likelihood that the occurrence would take place without negligence where a basis of common knowledge is lacking."]

At the close of discovery, defendant moved for summary judgment on the ground that there was no direct evidence that the plaintiff's arm was hyperabducted during surgery and no evidence of any other negligence. Conceding the absence of direct evidence of negligence, plaintiff opposed the motion, submitting expert medical opinion that her injuries would not have occurred in the absence of negligence. Plaintiff claimed this testimony could be used by a jury in support of a res ipsa loquitur theory.

[The trial court denied defendant's motion for summary judgment and permitted plaintiff to rely on the expert medical opinion to support the conclusion that the injury would not have occurred in the absence of negligence. A divided Appellate Division reversed before this appeal was taken] . . . .

Under appropriate circumstances, the evidentiary doctrine of res ipsa loquitur may be invoked to allow the factfinder to infer negligence from the mere happening of an event. Res ipsa loquitur, a doctrine of ancient origin (*see Byrne v Boadle,* 2 H & C 722, 159 Eng. Rep. 299 [1863]), derives from the understanding that some events ordinarily do not occur in the absence of negligence. . . .

Defendant contends that res ipsa loquitur cannot apply here because, in order to establish the first prerequisite—that the occurrence would not take place in the absence of negligence—plaintiff must rely on expert medical opinion, and the doctrinal foundation of res ipsa loquitur can only lie in everyday experience. Therefore, when expert testimony is necessary to provide the basis for concluding that the event would not occur in the absence of negligence, the matter is outside the ken of a layperson and res ipsa loquitur is inapplicable.

In the circumstances presented, we conclude that expert testimony may be properly used to help the jury "bridge the gap" between its own common knowledge, which does not encompass the specialized knowledge and experience necessary to reach a conclusion that the occurrence would not normally take place in the absence of negligence, and the common knowledge of physicians, which does. . . .

In an increasingly sophisticated and specialized society such as ours, it is not at all surprising that matters entirely foreign to the general population are commonplace within a particular profession or specially trained segment of society. . . .

Notwithstanding the availability of expert testimony to aid a jury in determining whether an event would normally occur in the absence of negligence, expert opinion of course does not negate the jury's ultimate responsibility as finder of fact to draw that necessary conclusion. The purpose of expert opinion in this context is to educate the jury, enlarging its understanding of the fact issues it must decide. However, the jury remains free to determine whether its newly-enlarged understanding supports the conclusion it is asked to accept. . . .

Applying the foregoing principles to the facts of this case, we conclude that defendant's motion for summary judgment was properly denied by Supreme Court. The jury should be allowed to hear from plaintiff's experts in order to determine whether this injury would normally occur in the absence of negligence. Likewise, defendant must be given an opportunity to rebut the assertion with competent expert evidence to show, for example, that the injury complained of is an inherent risk of the procedure and not totally preventable with the exercise of reasonable care. . . .

NOTES

1. **Common knowledge.** The normal basis for medical res ipsa loquitur is that, as a matter of common knowledge, the plaintiff's injury is more likely than not to have resulted from negligence. The clearest cases are those in which instruments or towels are left in the patient's abdomen after surgery and those in which injury is inflicted upon a part of the body not being treated. "It is within the common knowledge and experience of a layperson to determine that an individual does not enter the hospital for gallbladder surgery and come out of surgery with an ulnar nerve injury to the left arm." *Wick v. Henderson,* 485 N.W.2d 645 (Iowa 1992). Another case decided along similar lines is *Szydel v. Markman,* 117 P.3d 200 (Nev. 2005). There the plaintiff sued on a res ipsa theory over a needle left inside her left breast after a breast lift. The court found that the allegations fit within the common knowledge exception and thus no expert was required. Similarly, in *Quinby v. Plumsteadville Family Practice, Inc.,* 907 A.2d 1061 (Pa. 2006), a quadriplegic patient who was left unattended on an examining table fell and sustained injuries which ultimately lead to his death. The court held that the res ipsa question did not require expert testimony because "Defendants' positioning and securing of Decedent, a quadriplegic, on an examination table," was "a non-complex medical scenario."

2. **Expert testimony.** Expert testimony is "frequently necessary" in a medical malpractice case brought on a res ipsa theory. RESTATEMENT (THIRD) OF

TORTS: LIABILITY FOR PHYSICAL HARMS § 17, cmt. *c* (Proposed Final Draft No. 1, 2005). As indicated in *States v. Lourdes*, expert testimony can be used in most jurisdictions to fill the role of common knowledge. Thus an expert who cannot pinpoint negligence can nevertheless testify that the injury is one that, in the common knowledge of experts, is likely to occur only because of negligence. *See Seavers v. Methodist Med. Ctr. of Oak Ridge,* 9 S.W.3d 86 (Tenn. 1999).

3. **When is an instruction proper?** To reinforce the site of a hernia, a surgeon places a surgical mesh in the body. The mesh will be incorporated into the body as tissues grow into it. But the mesh becomes infected without fault of the surgeon and a second surgery is required. In this second surgery, the surgeon removes the mesh that has not been incorporated into the body but leaves the rest. Further infection occurs and a third surgery is required. One expert testified that the standard of care was violated by leaving any mesh in the body. Others testified to the contrary, that the standard of care required the surgeon to leave the parts of the mesh that had been incorporated. The trial judge submitted the case to the jury with a res ipsa loquitur instruction. Right or wrong? *Kenyon v. Miller,* 756 So.2d 133 (Fla. Dist. Ct. App. 2000).

4. **Abandonment.** Courts agree that a patient may terminate the doctor-patient relationship, but that neither a doctor nor a hospital can abandon a patient before treatment is completed. Would expert testimony be required to show breach of duty if the doctor walked out in the middle of an operation? What if the doctor, leaving town, arranged for coverage by another doctor for his hospitalized patient?

YBARRA v. SPANGARD

154 P.2d 687 (Cal. 1944)

GIBSON, CHIEF JUSTICE.

This is an action for damages for personal injuries alleged to have been inflicted on plaintiff by defendants during the course of a surgical operation. The trial court entered judgments of nonsuit as to all defendants and plaintiff appealed.

On October 28, 1939, plaintiff consulted from Dr. Tilley, who diagnosed his ailment as appendicitis, and made arrangements for an appendectomy to be performed by defendant Dr. Spangard at a hospital owned and managed by defendant Dr. Swift. Plaintiff entered the hospital, was given a hypodermic injection, slept, and later was awakened by Drs. Tilley and Spangard and wheeled into the operating room by a nurse whom he believed to be defendant Gisler, an employee of Dr. Swift. Defendant Dr. Reser, the anesthetist, also an employee of Dr. Swift, adjusted plaintiff for the operation, pulling his body to the head of the operating table and, according to plaintiff's testimony, laying him back against two hard objects at the top of his shoulders, about an inch below his neck. Dr. Reser then administered the anesthetic and plaintiff lost consciousness. When he awoke early the following morning he was in his hospital room attended by defendant Thompson, the special nurse, and another nurse who was not made a defendant.

Plaintiff testified that prior to the operation he had never had any pain in, or injury to, his right arm or shoulder, but that when he awakened he felt a sharp pain about half way between the neck and the point of the right shoulder. He complained to the nurse, and then to Dr. Tilley, who gave him diathermy treatments while he remained in the hospital. The pain did not cease but spread down to the lower part of his arm, and after his release from the hospital the condition grew worse. He was unable to rotate or lift his arm, and developed paralysis and atrophy of the muscles around the shoulder. He received further treatments from Dr. Tilley until March, 1940, and then returned to work, wearing his arm in a splint on the advice of Dr. Spangard.

[Medical evidence for the plaintiff established that his problem resulted from some trauma, pressure or strain applied between his shoulder and neck.]

Plaintiff's theory is that the foregoing evidence presents a proper case for the application of the doctrine of *res ipsa loquitur*, and that the inference of negligence arising therefrom makes the granting of a nonsuit improper. Defendants take the position that, assuming that plaintiff's condition was in fact the result of an injury, there is no showing that the act of any particular defendant, nor any particular instrumentality, was the cause thereof. . . .

The present case is of a type which comes within the reason and spirit of the doctrine more fully perhaps than any other. The passenger sitting awake in a railroad car at the time of a collision, the pedestrian walking along the street and struck by a falling object or the debris of an explosion, are surely not more entitled to an explanation than the unconscious patient on the operating table. Viewed from this aspect, it is difficult to see how the doctrine can, with any justification, be so restricted in its statement as to become inapplicable to a patient who submits himself to the care and custody of doctors and nurses, is rendered unconscious, and receives some injury from instrumentalities used in his treatment. Without the aid of the doctrine a patient who received permanent injuries of a serious character, obviously the result of someone's negligence, would be entirely unable to recover unless the doctors and nurses in attendance voluntarily chose to disclose the identity of the negligent person and the facts establishing liability. If this were the state of the law of negligence, the courts, to avoid gross injustice, would be forced to invoke the principles of absolute liability, irrespective of negligence, in actions by persons suffering injuries during the course of treatment under anesthesia. But we think this juncture has not yet been reached, and that the doctrine of *res ipsa loquitur* is properly applicable to the case before us. . . .

The argument of defendants is simply that plaintiff has not shown an injury caused by an instrumentality under a defendant's control, because he has not shown which of the several instrumentalities that he came in contact with while in the hospital caused the injury; and he has not shown that any one defendant or his servants had exclusive control over any particular instrumentality. Defendants assert that some of them were not the employees of other defendants, that some did not stand in any permanent relationship from which liability in tort would follow, and that in view of the nature of the injury, the number of defendants and the different functions performed by each, they could not all be liable for the wrong, if any.

We have no doubt that in a modern hospital a patient is likely to come under the care of a number of persons in different types of contractual and other relationships with each other. For example, in the present case it appears that Drs. Swift, Spangard and Tilley were physicians or surgeons commonly placed in the legal category of independent contractors; and Dr. Reser, the anesthetist, and defendant Thompson, the special nurse, were employees of Dr. Swift and not of the other doctors. But we do not believe that either the number or relationship of the defendants alone determines whether the doctrine of *res ipsa loquitur* applies. Every defendant in whose custody the plaintiff was placed for any period was bound to exercise ordinary care to see that no unnecessary harm came to him and each would be liable for failure in this regard. Any defendant who negligently injured him, and any defendant charged with his care who so neglected him as to allow injury to occur, would be liable. The defendant employers would be liable for the neglect of their employees; and the doctor in charge of the operation would be liable for the negligence of those who became his temporary servants for the purpose of assisting in the operation.

In this connection, it should be noted that while the assisting physicians and nurses may be employed by the hospital, or engaged by the patient, they normally become the temporary servants or agents of the surgeon in charge while the operation is in progress, and liability may be imposed upon him for their negligent acts under the doctrine of respondeat superior. Thus a surgeon has been held liable for the negligence of an assisting nurse who leaves a sponge or other object inside a patient, and the fact that the duty of seeing that such mistakes do not occur is delegated to others does not absolve the doctor from responsibility for their negligence.

It may appear at the trial that, consistent with the principles outlined above, one or more defendants will be found liable and others absolved, but this should not preclude the application of the rule of *res ipsa loquitur*. The control at one time or another, of one or more of the various agencies or instrumentalities which might have harmed the plaintiff was in the hands of every defendant or of his employees or temporary servants. This, we think, places upon them the burden of initial explanation. Plaintiff was rendered unconscious for the purpose of undergoing surgical treatment by the defendants; it is manifestly unreasonable for them to insist that he identify any one of them as the person who did the alleged negligent act.

The other aspect of the case which defendants so strongly emphasize is that plaintiff has not identified the instrumentality any more than he has the particular guilty defendant. Here, again, there is a misconception which, if carried to the extreme for which defendants contend, would unreasonably limit the application of the *res ipsa loquitur* rule. It should be enough that the plaintiff can show an injury resulting from an external force applied while he lay unconscious in the hospital; this is as clear a case of identification of the instrumentality as the plaintiff may ever be able to make.

An examination of the recent cases, particularly in this state, discloses that the test of actual exclusive control of an instrumentality has not been strictly followed, but exceptions have been recognized where the purpose of the doctrine of *res ipsa loquitur* would otherwise be defeated. Thus, the test has become one of right of control rather than actual control. In the bursting bottle cases where the bottler has delivered the instrumentality to a retailer and thus has given up actual control, he will nevertheless be subject to the doctrine where it is shown that no change in the condition of the bottle occurred after it left the bottler's possession, and it can accordingly be said that he was in constructive control. Escola v. Coca Cola Bottling Co., 24 Cal.2d [453], 150 P.2d 436. . . .

In the face of these examples of liberalization of the tests for *res ipsa loquitur*, there can be no justification for the rejection of the doctrine in the instant case. . . .

We do not at this time undertake to state the extent to which the reasoning of this case may be applied to other situations in which the doctrine of *res ipsa loquitur* is invoked. We merely hold that where a plaintiff receives unusual injuries while unconscious and in the course of medical treatment, all those defendants who had any control over his body or the instrumentalities which might have caused the injuries may properly be called upon to meet the inference of negligence by giving an explanation of their conduct.

The judgment is reversed.

NOTES

1. **Exclusive control.** Most courts, in accord with *Ybarra* and the Second Restatement, have held that "exclusive control" is no longer a strict requirement in res ipsa cases, no matter the context. *See, e.g., Kelly v. Hartford Cas. Ins. Co.*, 271 N.W.2d 676 (Wis. 1978) (interpreting the control requirement to preclude use of a res ipsa instruction "where the injury can reasonably be attributed to a pre-existing condition, an allergic reaction or some other frailty in the plaintiff," any of which would indicate that the apparent cause of the injury was something other than the defendant's negligence); *Giles v. City of New Haven*, 636 A.2d 1335 (Conn. 1994) (holding that control is a flexible term that most courts have de-emphasized).

2. **Likelihood that defendant caused the harm.** Can it be said in *Ybarra* that any particular defendant is more likely than not the person whose negligence caused the harm? Then how can res ipsa loquitur apply at all?

REFERENCES: DOBBS ON TORTS § 249 (2000); HARPER, JAMES & GRAY, THE LAW OF TORTS § 19.7 (3d ed. 1995).

§ 3.   INFORMED CONSENT

SCHLOENDORFF v. SOCIETY OF NEW YORK HOSPITAL, 105 N.E. 92 (N.Y. 1914). Cardozo, J.: "Every human being of adult years and sound mind has a right to determine what shall be done with his own body; and a surgeon who performs an operation without his patient's consent commits an assault, for which he is liable in damages."

HARNISH v. CHILDREN'S HOSPITAL MEDICAL CENTER

439 N.E.2d 240 (Mass. 1982)

O'CONNOR, JUSTICE.

The plaintiff underwent an operation to remove a tumor in her neck. During the procedure, her hypoglossal nerve was severed, allegedly resulting in a permanent and almost total loss of tongue function.

The plaintiff's complaint charges the defendant physicians and hospital with misrepresentation and negligence in failing to inform her before surgery of the risk of loss of tongue function. The complaint alleges that the purpose of the operation was cosmetic, that the loss of tongue function was a material and foreseeable risk of the operation, and that, had the plaintiff been informed of this risk, she would not have consented to the operation. There is no claim that the operation was negligently performed.

[A medical malpractice tribunal, which functions to screen malpractice claims against physicians, held that the plaintiff's proof was inadequate and on this basis the trial judge dismissed the action.]

. . . "There is implicit recognition in the law of the Commonwealth, as elsewhere, that a person has a strong interest in being free from nonconsensual invasion of his bodily integrity. . . . In short, the law recognizes the individual interest in preserving 'the inviolability of his person.' One means by which the law has developed in a manner consistent with the protection of this interest is through the development of the doctrine of informed consent." "[I]t is the prerogative of the patient, not the physician, to determine . . . the direction in which . . . his interest lie." Every competent adult has a right "to forego treatment, or even cure, if it entails what for him are intolerable consequences or risks however unwise his sense of value may be in the eyes of the medical profession." Knowing exercise of this right requires knowledge of the available options and the risks attendant on each. We hold, therefore, that a physician's failure to divulge in a reasonable manner to a competent adult patient sufficient information to enable the patient to make an informed judgment whether to give or withhold consent to a medical or surgical procedure constitutes professional misconduct and comes within the ambit of G.L. c. 231, § 60B.

... Communication of scientific information by the trained physician to the untrained patient may be difficult. The remotely possible risks of a proposed treatment may be almost without limit. The patient's right to know must be harmonized with the recognition that an undue burden should not be placed on the physician. These interests are accommodated by the rule that we adopt today, that a physician owes to his patient the duty to disclose in a reasonable manner all significant medical information that the physician possesses or reasonably should possess that is material to an intelligent decision by the patient whether to undergo a proposed procedure. The information a physician reasonably should possess is that information possessed by the average qualified physician or, in the case of a specialty, by the average qualified physician practicing that specialty. What the physician should know involves professional expertise and can ordinarily be proved only through the testimony of experts. However, the extent to which he must share that information with his patient depends upon what information he should reasonably recognize is material to the plaintiff's decision. "Materiality may be said to be the significance a reasonable person, in what the physician knows or should know is his patient's position, would attach to the disclosed risk or risks in deciding whether to submit or not to submit to surgery or treatment." The materiality determination is one that lay persons are qualified to make without the aid of an expert. Appropriate information may include the nature of the patient's condition, the nature and probability of risks involved, the benefits to be reasonably expected, the inability of the physician to predict results, if that is the situation, the irreversibility of the procedure, if that be the case, the likely result of no treatment, and the available alternatives, including their risks and benefits. The obligation to give adequate information does not require the disclosure of all risks of a proposed therapy, or of information the physician reasonably believes the patient already has, such as the risks, like infection, inherent in any operation.

Many jurisdictions have adopted the rule that a physician must disclose to his patient only such information as is customarily disclosed in similar circumstances. We think that the better is the one we adopt today. The customary practice standard overlooks the purpose of requiring disclosure, which is protection of the patient's right to decide for himself.

We recognize that despite the importance of the patient's right to know, there may be situations that call for a privilege of nondisclosure. For instance, sound medical judgment might indicate that disclosure would complicate the patient's medical condition or render him unfit for treatment. Where that it is so, the cases have generally held that the physician is armed with a privilege to keep the information from the patient.... The physician's privilege to withhold information for therapeutic reasons must be carefully circumscribed, however, for otherwise it might devour the disclosure rule itself. "The privilege does not accept the paternalistic notion that the physician may remain silent simply because divulgence might prompt the patient to forego therapy the physician feels the patient really needs" (footnotes omitted). *Canterbury v. Spence*, supra at 789. A full discussion of the privilege is neither required nor attempted here, because the burden of proving it must rest with the physician, and thus the question of privilege is inappropriate to the directed verdict standard. . . .

We turn to the question of causation. "An unrevealed risk that should have been made known must materialize, for otherwise the omission, however unpardonable, is legally without consequence." Whether the alleged undisclosed risk materialized is a medical question appropriate to the tribunal's inquiry. At trial, the plaintiff must also show that had the proper information been provided neither he nor a reasonable person in similar circumstances would have undergone the procedure. Such proof, not relating to medical questions, is not appropriate to the tribunal's inquiry.

[The court found that one of the defendants was only an assistant in the operation and had no duty to give the plaintiff information, and that the hospital itself was not liable.]

The judgment as to the defendants Muliken and Holmes is reversed. The judgment as to defendants Gilman and Children's Hospital Medical Center is affirmed.

So Ordered.

————————

WOOLLEY v. HENDERSON, 418 A.2d 1123 (Me. 1980). Defendant operated on the plaintiff's back but because of an abnormality in the spine, he got the wrong interspace between the vertebrae. He also inadvertently tore part of the tissue encasing the spinal cord, which resulted in a number of medical problems for the plaintiff. A tear of this kind is a normal risk of this procedure, but the doctor had not informed the plaintiff. The trial court instructed the jury that the plaintiff was entitled only to disclosures of risks that would be made by a reasonable medical practitioner. The jury found in favor of the defendant. *Held*, affirmed. The standard of disclosure is that of the reasonable medical practitioner and this will ordinarily require expert medical testimony. This rule is justified (1) because this is professional malpractice and the professional standard must be used, (2) because there might be therapeutic reasons for withholding information, and (3) because since the plaintiff must produce medical testimony on other issues, this will add very little burden. The plaintiff in informed consent cases must also prove causation by the objective test, that is, that a reasonable person would have refused the treatment had full information been given, and that the plaintiff herself would have refused it.

MARSINGILL v. O'MALLEY, 128 P.3d 151 (Alaska 2006). Plaintiff Marsingill suffered acute abdominal discomfort late one evening and called the defendant Dr. O'Malley, who had removed a staple from her stomach approximately four months earlier. After Ms. Marsingill described her symptoms, Dr. O'Malley told her that he could not accurately diagnose her condition over the phone and recommended that she go to the emergency room. Marsingill asked what would happen at the emergency room and Dr. O'Malley explained that the doctors on duty would likely order x-rays and insert a nasogastric tube to relieve the abdominal pressure. Ms. Marsingill knew from previous experience that the insertion of a nasogastric tube is an unpleasant procedure. She ended the call saying that she felt better and disregarded Dr. O'Malley's recommendation to go to the emergency room. As a result, she suffered serious and permanent injury, including brain damage and partial paralysis. Marsingill sued Dr. O'Malley, alleging that he negligently failed to inform her of the risks associated with waiting to seek medical treatment. A jury found in favor of Dr. O'Malley. On appeal, Marsingill objected to Dr. O'Malley's introduction of trial testimony from four doctors who testified that they "would have behaved similarly to Dr. O'Malley and that Marsingill had all the information she needed to make an intelligent and informed decision." Marsingill argues the doctors' testimony about the general standard of care for physician disclosures and what a reasonable patient would want to know should be inadmissible; a physician's opinion concerning information the physician thinks important is not directly relevant to establish what a reasonable patient would deem to be important. *Held*, "Marsingill's arguments on this point are unpersuasive." Alaska courts "have rejected the traditional 'professional standard in the field' approach in favor of 'the modern trend' of case law, which 'measure [s] the physician's duty of disclosure by what a reasonable patient would need to know in order to make an informed and intelligent decision.' " Nevertheless, "the doctors who testified in this case had extensive experience interacting with patients. . . . [T]heir testimony concerning the amount and kinds of information that patients generally want in late night phone calls was relevant to establish whether Dr. O'Malley gave Marsingill as much information as a reasonable patient would want to know. In addition, their testimony was relevant to show what a reasonable doctor is likely to think a patient might want to know."

NOTES

1. **Negligence vs. battery theory.** As we saw in Chapter 4, courts today recognize a battery claim against a doctor who operates when the plaintiff has not consented at all to that procedure. Some courts also treat cases of consent without appropriate information or informed consent claims as battery cases. *See Montgomery v. Bazaz–Sehgal*, 798 A.2d 742 (Pa. 2002). The usual approach, however, is to treat informed consent claims under negligence, not battery rules. *See Mole v. Jutton*, 846 A.2d 1035 (Md. 2004) (collecting cases).

2. **Practical consequences of the theory.** Use of a negligence approach is important for a number of reasons. The defendant doctor's liability

insurance might not cover battery, an intentional tort. Also, negligence rules might make the doctor's duty to disclose depend upon the disclosure the medical community would make, which might require expert testimony. Many courts, like the *Woolley* court, have so held. Further, an informed consent claim may be subject to special statutory limits or conditions for recovery.

3. **Professional standard or the "patient rule"?** Beginning in the early 1970s a series of major decisions retained the negligence theory of informed consent but rejected the requirement of proof from the medical community. These cases, including *Cobbs, Canterbury* and *Wilkinson*, all cited in *Harnish*, held that the standard was "materiality" of the information. In the absence of statutory directive, most of the recent major decisions have taken this view. *See, e.g., Carr v. Strode,* 904 P.2d 489 (Haw. 1995); *Jaskoviak v. Gruver,* 638 N.W.2d 1 (N.D. 2002) (but also finding sufficient expert testimony). How different is a standard that requires disclosure of information material to the patient's treatment decision, versus information that a reasonable doctor would provide? In *Marsingill*, the Alaska Supreme Court thought these two standards were basically indistinguishable.

4. **Causation.** Most courts have required an "objective" test of causation. This means that the plaintiff cannot recover merely by showing that she herself would have refused the injury-causing operation had she been fully informed. She will have to go further and show that a reasonable person would also have refused it. Is this requirement because the courts are reluctant to permit a jury to believe the plaintiff's testimony on this point? If so, what happened to the usual rule that the jury is the sole judge of credibility? Or is the "objective" test of causation intended merely to limit protection to reasonable patients? Is that what autonomy is about—matching other people's expectations of reasonableness? Several courts have sought a compromise, saying that the issue is to be judged by the reasonable person standard in the light of the plaintiff's personal fears and religious beliefs. *Ashe v. Radiation Oncology Assocs.,* 9 S.W.3d 119 (Tenn. 1999).

5. **Incompetent patients and life-saving treatment.** The informed consent rules imply that the patient may refuse treatment. May a physician treat a competent patient over her objection if the treatment is required to save her life? *Shine v. Vega,* 709 N.E.2d 58 (Mass. 1999) (no); *Harvey v. Strickland,* 566 S.E.2d 529 (S.C. 2002) (no). Can a dying patient refuse treatment that would save her fetus? "What we distill from the cases . . . is that every person has the right, under the common law and the Constitution, to accept or refuse medical treatment. This right of bodily integrity belongs equally to persons who are competent and persons who are not. Further, it matters not what the quality of a patient's life may be; the right of bodily integrity is not extinguished simply because someone is ill, or even at death's door. To protect that right against intrusion by others—family members, doctors, hospitals, or anyone else, however well-intentioned—we hold that a court must determine the patient's wishes by any means available, and must abide by those wishes unless there are truly extraordinary or compelling reasons to override them. When the patient is incompetent, or when the court is unable to determine competency, the substituted judgment procedure must be followed." *In re A.C.,* 573 A.2d 1235 (D.C. 1990). Does the right to refuse life-saving treatment mean that the patient would also have a right to

assistance in committing suicide? *Krischer v. McIver,* 697 So.2d 97 (Fla. 1997) ("Forty-five states that recognize the right to refuse treatment or unwanted life-support have expressed disapproval of assisted suicide").

WLOSINSKI v. COHN, 713 N.W.2d 16 (Mich. Ct. App. 2005). Michael Wrobel suffered kidney failure during his senior year in high school. After researching various medical facilities and their kidney transplant success rates, Michael and his family selected William Beaumont Hospital for treatment. In pre-operative consultations, Dr. Steven Cohn allegedly represented his kidney transplant success rate as "good". The plaintiff, Michael's mother, donated a kidney in an effort to save her son, and Dr. Cohn performed the transplant surgery. Michael experienced severe postoperative complications, resulting in the removal of his new kidney, which ultimately led to his death. Plaintiff's expert inferred medical incompetence by testifying that five out of seven kidney transplants that Dr. Cohn had performed in the months leading up to Michael's surgery had failed. The plaintiff contends that Dr. Cohn owed a duty to Michael to disclose his failure rate before obtaining consent to the procedure. *Held,* "[t]he doctrine of informed consent requires a physician to warn a patient of the risks and consequences of a medical procedure. By itself, Dr. Cohn's success rate was not a risk related to the medical procedure.... [W]e simply hold that defendants, as a matter of law, did not have a duty to disclose Dr. Cohn's statistical history of transplant failures to obtain the decedent's informed consent."

ARATO v. AVEDON, 858 P.2d 598 (Cal. 1993). Mr. Arato was diagnosed with cancer. Doctors performed surgery, but the cancer was a kind that was overwhelmingly likely to cause death in a short time. Although Arato had indicated to his doctor that he wanted to know the truth, his doctor did not tell him that death in a short time was statistically almost certain. Instead, the doctor recommended some post-operative treatments that had been experimentally successful with some other forms of cancer and that the doctors hoped would help Mr. Arato. The treatments were not successful. Mr. Arato's survivors claimed against the doctor. They said he should have told Mr. Arato that his chances were slim to none because that information would have been relevant to his decision to accept the treatments and that, living in a false hope, Mr. Arato had failed to arrange his economic affairs, a failure that led to business and tax losses. The jury found for the defendants. The Court of Appeal reversed for error in instructions. *Held,* the Court of Appeal is reversed. "Patient sovereignty" or autonomy is an extreme. It was not error to leave to the jury the question whether all material information about risks had been given. Furthermore, the doctor had no duty to disclose statistical life expectancy information because it was not information about risks of the procedures. As to relevant information that is not about risks, the standard of disclosure is the "standard of practice within the medical community."

Since expert physicians testified that the standard was NOT to reveal this kind of information voluntarily, there could be no liability for failure to give informed consent. As to Mr. Arato's written request to be told the truth, "a patient may validly waive the right to be informed, [but] we do not see how a request to be told the 'truth' in itself heightens the duty of disclosure imposed on physicians as a matter of law."

Notes

1. **Physician and procedure success rates.** Suppose a surgeon has little experience with the proposed brain surgery or a record of bad results. Must he inform his patient? *Johnson v. Kokemoor*, 545 N.W.2d 495 (Wis. 1996) held that the patient was entitled to information from her surgeon that more experienced brain surgeons were available and had substantially better success rates than inexperienced surgeons. *See* Aaron D. Twerski & Neil B. Cohen, *The Second Revolution in Informed Consent: Comparing Physicians to Each Other*, 94 Nw. U. L. Rev. 1 (1999) (discussing and supporting a duty to disclose risks about the particular provider). Can the *Wlosinski* court's holding be justified on the ground that a reasonable patient would not have cared about the five out of seven failure rate, or is there some other issue at work? If doctors must disclose success rates, will doctors fudge their records? Reject high-risk patients to establish a better set of statistics? *See* Lynn M. LoPucki, *Twerski and Cohen's Second Revolution: A Systems/Strategic Perspective*, 94 Nw. U. L. Rev. 55 (1999). What if the procedure itself is generally unsuccessful? *See Williamson v. Amrani*, 152 P.3d 60 (Kan. 2007) (holding that expert testimony was necessary to determine whether the lack-of-success rate of recommended back surgery was something a reasonable medical practitioner would have disclosed to the patient).

2. **What information must a doctor disclose to a patient?** *Harnish* tells us that "a physician owes to his patient the duty to disclose in a reasonable manner all significant medical information that the physician possesses or reasonably should possess that is material to an intelligent decision by the patient whether to undergo a proposed procedure." Whether information is material to an intelligent decision by the patient is a jury question. *See Miller–McGee v. Washington Hosp. Center*, 920 A.2d 430 (D.C. 2007) (jury must decide whether doctor owed duty to inform patient of risks of lacerations from forceps-assisted vaginal delivery). Would a doctor be required to disclose to the patient that he might minimize the risk of an AIDS infection from a blood transfusion by donating his own blood in advance of the operation? *See Doe v. Johnston*, 476 N.W.2d 28 (Iowa 1991). Suppose the doctor for an 81-year-old woman with a broken hip thinks surgery with screws to hold it together is a bad idea because of her age. He never informs her that without surgery she will probably never walk again. He prescribes bed rest only and in fact she is never able to walk thereafter. Did the doctor breach a duty of providing information? *Matthies v. Mastromonaco*, 733 A.2d 456 (N.J. 1999).

3. **Physician experience.** What if the surgeon merely represents that he has extensive experience in performing a highly risky operation when in fact he has much more limited experience? *See Howard v. University of Med.*

& *Dentistry of N.J.*, 800 A.2d 73 (N.J. 2002). Some states apply to physicians state consumer protection acts which forbid unfair and deceptive practices. In *Williamson v. Amrani*, 152 P.3d 60 (Kan. 2007), the court held that a doctor's false representation that a generally unsuccessful back surgery procedure would likely relieve the patient's pain counted as an unfair and deceptive act.

4. **Physician impairment.** Georgia says that a physician owes no duty to inform a patient of the physician's own cocaine use, *Albany Urology Clinic, P.C. v. Cleveland*, 528 S.E.2d 777 (Ga. 2000), so the patient has neither an informed consent claim nor a battery claim when the doctor treats him without the patient's knowledge of the impairment. A little authority goes the other way on such matters as chronic alcohol abuse or AIDS infection. *See* DOBBS ON TORTS § 251 (2000).

5. **Conflict of interest.** What about disclosure of the doctor's financial interest? In *Moore v. Regents of the University of California*, 793 P.2d 479 (Cal. 1990) the patient claimed that the physicians and hospital withdrew blood ostensibly in the course of treatment. They developed a "cell line" that could be used efficiently to produce a commercial product of great value. None of this was mentioned to the patient. The court refused to permit the plaintiff to pursue a conversion claim, but it said that the physician was under a fiduciary duty to disclose some of the facts to the patient. Is this an informed consent case or something different?

6. **Emergencies.** In an emergency, would failure to obtain informed consent at all be a breach of duty? In *Stewart–Graves v. Vaughn,* 170 P.3d 1151 (Wash. 2007), a neonatologist began resuscitation efforts on an infant without a heartbeat, and continued until, 24 minutes later, the baby was revived. The child was severely and permanently disabled. The court recognized an exception to the informed consent rule. It held that no duty to obtain consent exists "in emergency situations where immediate action is necessary for the protection of life." Consent in such a case would be implied. Should the result be different if the state recognizes a parent's right to discontinue extraordinary measures?

7. **Research performed upon humans.** Suppose no treatment is involved—a researcher wishes to perform experiments upon healthy human beings. Would you expect informed consent rules to be more demanding or less? *See Grimes v. Kennedy Krieger Inst., Inc.,* 782 A.2d 807 (Md. 2001). If the rules of informed consent are more demanding, you may have to distinguish between experiment ("research") and therapy or medical practice. What if a hospital sets a hospital-wide rule tripling the then-standard dose of an antibiotic, regardless of what the patient's doctor prescribed for the patient's individual treatment? *See Ancheff v. Hartford Hosp.,* 799 A.2d 1067 (Conn. 2002).

8. **Damages.** Knowledge about risks and choices is necessary if patients are to participate in decisions about their bodies. Maybe courts should allow some kind of dignitary damages if the patient is deprived of the right to "vote" on the operation with appropriate knowledge, even if the patient would have given consent if she had been fully informed. What do you think? See *Lugenbuhl v. Dowling*, 701 So.2d 447 (La. 1997) (permitting damages for deprivation of self-determination); *cf. Provenzano v. Integrated Genetics*, 22 F.

Supp. 2d 406 (D.N.J. 1998) (negligently depriving mother of opportunity to terminate pregnancy because fetus suffered serious disease).

***

TRUMAN v. THOMAS, 611 P.2d 902 (Cal. 1980). Rena Truman consulted Dr. Thomas as her doctor over a six year period. She died of cervical cancer, which could have been discovered and successfully treated by a pap smear given early enough. Dr. Thomas did repeatedly advise her to have the pap smear, but never warned her of the purpose or of the dangers of not having one. In an action for her death, the trial judge refused to instruct the jury on the failure to disclose the dangers of refusing the pap smear and the jury found for the defendant doctor. On appeal, *held*, reversed. "If a patient indicates that he or she is going to *decline* the risk-free test or treatment, then the doctor has the additional duty of advising of all material risks of which a reasonable person would want to be informed.... [A] jury could reasonably conclude that Dr. Thomas had a duty to inform Mrs. Truman of the danger of refusing the test because it was not reasonable for Dr. Thomas to assume that Mrs. Truman appreciated the potentially fatal consequences of her conduct."

BROWN v. DIBBELL, 595 N.W.2d 358 (Wis. 1999). After conference with the defendant doctors, Mrs. Brown underwent a double mastectomy with some unfortunate results. She sued on an informed consent theory. The jury found that Dr. Dibbell was not negligent in performing surgery but that he was negligent in obtaining Ms. Brown's consent to surgery. The jury also found that a reasonable patient in Ms. Brown's circumstances, if adequately informed, would have refused to undergo the surgery that was performed. Finally, the jury found that Mrs. Brown was chargeable with 50% of the negligence for failing to exercise care for her own health. The plaintiff argued on appeal that it was error for the trial judge to submit the issue of contributory negligence. *Held,* affirming the Court of Appeals, a new trial is required to correct various errors in instruction. As to the plaintiff's comparative fault, the defense may be invoked in an informed consent action. Specifically, a patient may be chargeable with comparative fault for failing to give truthful and complete family history when it is material. But a patient may ordinarily trust the doctor's information and except in a most unusual case could not be charged with fault for failure to ascertain the truth or completeness of the information presented by the doctor or to seek independent advice.

REFERENCES: DOBBS ON TORTS §§ 250–251 (2000); HARPER, JAMES & GRAY, THE LAW OF TORTS § 17.1, pp. 627–40 (3d ed. 2007).

§ 4. CHANGING MEDICINE, CHANGING LAW

A. THE MEDICAL MALPRACTICE "CRISIS"

The Institute of Medicine, in a comprehensive study of medical errors, estimated that at least 44,000 and perhaps as many as 98,000 people die each year in hospitals as a result of preventable medical errors. The Institute concluded that more people die from medical errors than from motor vehicle accidents, breast cancer or AIDS. Common errors include adverse drug events, wrong-site surgery, and mistaken patient identities. To illustrate these problems, the study mentioned a patient who died of a chemotherapy overdose, another who had the wrong leg amputated, and another, a child, who died during minor surgery because of a drug mix-up. The IOM estimated the total cost of preventable medical errors (including the expense of additional care necessitated by the errors, lost income and household productivity, and disability) at between $17 billion and $29 billion per year. According to the IOM, the know-how already exists to prevent many of these mistakes. Consequently, it set a strategy to significantly reduce these errors. *See* INSTITUTE OF MEDICINE, TO ERR IS HUMAN: BUILDING A SAFER HEALTHY SYSTEM (2000).

Despite the large number of medical errors, there has been a public outcry against medical malpractice litigation. Medical costs have increased enormously in the last generation. The cost of insurance for doctors has also increased. In some instances and in some years it has been difficult for doctors to procure liability insurance.

Some people have pointed the finger at lawyers: costs go up and insurance becomes expensive or impossible to get because greedy lawyers bring too many malpractice suits (and courts permit judgments against doctors). This kind of talk can be misleading for several reasons:

(1) Existing empirical evidence does not support claims that medical malpractice payouts are increasing significantly, let alone increasing at a staggering rate. For example, several studies looked at all settled and litigated medical malpractice claims in Texas during a time of "crisis." Although insurance premium costs had gone up dramatically during the time period, the costs of paid and settled malpractice claims remained largely stable. Bernard Black, Charles Silver, David A. Hyman & William M. Sage, *Stability, Not Crisis: Medical Malpractice Claims Outcomes in Texas, 1998–2002*, 2 J. EMPIRICAL LEGAL STUD. 207, 210 (2005). Moreover, headlines about large jury awards may be misleading because the vast majority of verdicts are not paid at their full value. In Texas, 75% of plaintiffs who received jury awards over $25,000 received payouts of less than their full award, with mean reductions of 29%. As the value of the award increased, so did the percentage reduction. For plaintiffs whose award was valued at over 2.5 million dollars, 98% received a reduced award with an average cut of 56%. *See* David A. Hyman, et al., *Do Defendants Pay What Juries Award? Post–Verdict Haircuts in Texas Medical Malpractice Cases, 1988–2003*, 4 J. EMPIRICAL. LEG. STUD. 3 (2007). Insurance policy limits act as an effective cap on recovery. In a study of 9,389 closed claims, 98.5% were resolved with payments at or below policy limits. In the few instances in which doctors did draw on their own assets, their personal contributions were relatively small, with only 10 of those contributions exceeding $300,000. For more comprehensive analysis, *see* Kathryn Zeiler, et al., *Physicians' Insurance Limits and Malpractice*

Payments: Evidence from Texas Closed Claims, 1990–2003, 36 J. LEGAL STUD. 9 (2007).

(2) The concern that doctors are particularly vulnerable defendants has not been borne out by empirical data. At least in some locales, plaintiffs prevail against medical doctors in only about one claim in five that is submitted to a jury. *See* Deborah Jones Merritt & Kathryn Ann Barry, *Is the Tort System in Crisis? New Empirical Evidence,* 60 OHIO ST. L.J. 315, 358 (1999). Also, study of medical malpractice claims suggests that weak claims are not being paid. A study of over 1400 closed claims concluded that medical errors in fact existed in about 60% of the claims. Most of the claims that did *not* involve medical error by the investigators were *not* paid. David M. Studdert, et al., *Claims, Errors, and Compensation Payments in Medical Malpractice Litigation,* 354 NEW ENG. J. MED. 2024 (2006). Reviewing a large number of studies, one scholar concluded that across the many studies, "Plaintiffs who received substandard care generally obtained compensation; plaintiffs who received proper care generally did not; and plaintiffs whose care quality was uncertain wound up in between." *See David A. Hyman & Charles Silver, Medical Malpractice Litigation and Tort Reform: It's the Incentives Stupid*, 59 VAND. L. REV. 1085, 1097 (2006).

(3) As to increases in insurance costs, this has been partly a result of investment cycles. Insurers invest premium monies until they are needed to make payouts under the policy. These investments produce large incomes that help make the payments required by the policy. When investment income is down, premium income must go up if the insurer is to pay. So to some extent, the insurer and the insured are subject to the fluctuations of the market, and increased costs to the doctors reflect this as well as other factors. But premium increases were less than the increase of doctors' incomes, *see* 1 BARRY R. FURROW, THOMAS L. GREANEY, SANDRA H. JOHNSON, TIMOTHY S. JOST, & ROBERT L. SCHWARTZ, HEALTH LAW 517 (1995), and insurance costs are not high enough to explain the vehement attacks on the law. *See* Patrick Hubbard, *The Physicians' Point of View Concerning Medical Malpractice: A Sociological Perspective on the Symbolic Importance of "Tort Reform,"* 23 GA. L. REV. 295 (1989).

(4) Costs of medical treatment have gone up for a number of reasons not associated with lawsuits. These include the costs of new equipment and buildings and increased technology, and an increase in the pool of elderly. In addition, an increase in the pool of patients who do not pay for services received may also add to costs, which must be borne by other patients or by public funds.

B. STATUTORY RESPONSES

The medical profession had sought favorable legislation before the insurance crisis—the Good Samaritan statutes, for example—but the insurance problem prompted even more demands for special rules. In at least two different crises, many states passed statutes attempting to relieve the insurance problem for health care providers, either directly or indirectly. The exact package of provisions varies from state to state, but most states have adopted one or more of the kinds of provisions listed below.

(1) *Substantive Changes:*

(a) The plaintiff must prove actual negligence, or, more explicitly, res ipsa loquitur may not be used against a health care provider, or may not be used in traditional cases. In *Larsen v. Zarrett,* 498 N.W.2d 191 (N.D. 1993), the court interpreted a statute to forbid the use of res ipsa loquitur against a surgeon when the plaintiff awoke from an operation with an injury to a separate, previously healthy, portion of her body.

(b) The standard of care must be local or statewide, not national.

(c) Statutes of repose and statutes of limitation have an absolute outside limit even when the patient cannot discover the negligence for many years.

(d) No malpractice claim may be based on a contract unless the contract is in writing.

(e) Informed consent claims are limited or discouraged.

(2) *Remedial Changes:*

(a) State statutes limit damages and many include absolute caps on recovery.

(b) Joint and several liability is limited.

(c) Periodic payment plans are provided for large damage awards.

(3) *Procedural Changes.*

The statutes have imposed various procedural changes. One type of statute excludes testimony of experts who do not meet some arbitrary test. In *Endorf v. Bohlender*, 995 P.2d 896 (Kan. Ct. App. 2000), the court held that a statute required the trial judge to exclude testimony of a qualified expert who was Medical Director of a major hospital and who taught at the University of Arizona because he spent only 25% of his time in actual clinical work, devoting the rest to teaching and administration. In Virginia, a statute excluded all the plaintiff's experts in a suit based on a nursing home's failure to prevent a fracture and the doctors' failure to diagnose it. One witness with more than 20 years' experience as head of a major emergency department, was excluded because he was not actually dealing with fractures in his current practice. Another, who would have testified about how the nursing home failed to prevent the resident's fracture, was excluded because her experience was in a hospital, not a nursing home and thus had not recently engaged in the procedures at issue. *Perdieu v. Blackstone Family Practice Ctr., Inc.*, 568 S.E.2d 703 (Va. 2002). Another type of statute may require the plaintiff to submit her claim to arbitration or screening panels before suing or permit contracts between patient and medical provider to require arbitration in lieu of tort claims. In *Engalla v. Permanente Medical Group, Inc.*, 938 P.2d 903 (Cal.

1997), you can read about the terrible delays, seemingly intentionally produced by a gigantic HMO. Still another provision requires the plaintiff to give notice of intent to sue and then forbids suit for a waiting period after that, with complex effects on the statute of limitations. *See Hillsborough County Hosp. Auth. v. Coffaro*, 829 So.2d 862 (Fla. 2002).

(4) *Insurance Changes.*

A fourth group of changes does not directly affect tort law; these attempt to facilitate insurance coverage.

What injuries fall under the statutes? Not all claims that occur in a health care setting are medical malpractice claims that garner the special statutory protections. A failure of life support systems, resulting from a power outage in the aftermath of Hurricane Katrina was not. *LaCoste v. Pendleton Methodist Hosp., LLC*, 966 So.2d 519 (La. 2007) (death from failed power system). A failure to protect the patient from fire is not. *Cf. Taylor v. Vencor, Inc.*, 525 S.E.2d 201 (N.C. 2000). The issue depends upon statutory wording and the court's own conception of policy. In *Rome v. Flower Memorial Hospital*, 635 N.E.2d 1239 (Ohio 1994), the court found injuries covered by the medical malpractice statute when the plaintiff, allegedly improperly secured to a tilting radiology table, slipped off and injured her head when the table was tipped up. This was medical malpractice because it was "ancillary" to an X-ray procedure that was medical in nature.

C. STATE CONSTITUTIONAL CHALLENGES TO STATUTORY REFORM

Plaintiffs can challenge medical malpractice statutes, like other tort reform legislation, under state constitutional guarantees. Statutes impeding medical malpractice claims have been challenged under state constitutional open access to courts provisions. In *Zeier v. Zimmer, Inc.*, 152 P.3d 861 (Okla. 2006), the Oklahoma Supreme Court examined a state statute which required that plaintiffs filing medical malpractice actions attach an affidavit attesting that a qualified expert had been consulted and had issued an opinion sufficient to deem the claim meritorious. The court held that the affidavit requirement, which front-loaded litigation costs and disproportionately reduced claims by low-income litigants, was a monetary barrier to suit that violated state constitutional guarantees of open access to the courts. The affidavit requirement also violated the state constitutional prohibition against special laws. In this case the unlawful differential treatment was between victims alleging negligence generally and victims alleging medical negligence.

Under another state constitutional clause, the "right to a remedy" clause, the Oregon Supreme Court struck down a statutory cap on damage awards. In *Clarke v. Oregon Health Sciences University*, 175 P.3d 418 (Or.

2007), the plaintiff, a minor patient who was deprived of oxygen after heart surgery, challenged two statutes that together greatly diminished her recovery. One statute capped recovery from a public entity and the other required substitution of the public entity, not its employees, as the sole defendant. Estimates of the economic damages for plaintiff's lifetime exceeded $12 million. Yet under the statutes, the maximum award available was $200,000. The court held that the statute confining claims against the public entity to $200,000 was constitutional with respect to the public entity, which would have been entitled to sovereign immunity at the common law. However, the elimination of a cause of action against public employees or agents violates the remedy clause because the substituted remedy against the public body "is an emasculated version of the remedy that was available at common law."

However, some courts have been cautious about striking down state statutes. For example, in *Ledbetter v. Hunter,* 842 N.E.2d 810 (Ind. 2006), the plaintiff raised a statutory challenge under the state constitution's privileges and immunities clause. Under this provision, the state legislature could not "grant to any citizen, or class of citizens, privileges or immunities, which, upon the same terms, shall not equally belong to all citizens." The statute challenged in *Ledbetter* required minors injured by medical malpractice before age six to file suit within two years of an injury or by their eighth birthday at the latest. Plaintiff contended that the legislation unconstitutionally subjected to differential treatment two classes of minors—those injured by medical negligence and those injured by other types of negligence. However, the *Ledbetter* court held that the differentiation could be justified based on the legislature's rationale for the legislation—that it *could* prevent a reduction in health care services. This rationale was valid even though "neither the insurance carriers nor the health care associations could produce a single document showing that a change in the disability provision for minors in medical malpractice cases would have any adverse effect on the cost of insurance, the availability of health care services, or the ability to defend malpractice claims." The court left the matter to the legislature, suggesting that the lack of evidence "may well provide powerful support for legislative reconsideration of the challenged minor limitation period."

D. THE MEDICAL MALPRACTICE REALITY

Whether any kind of crisis justifies the limitations on patients' rights or not, the underlying reality of preventable injury remains. The committee responsible for the Institute of Medicine's study (composed of health care professionals) concluded that the aim should be "to make errors costly to health care organizations and providers, so they are compelled to take action to improve safety." *See* INSTITUTE OF MEDICINE, TO ERR IS HUMAN: BUILDING A SAFER HEALTHY SYSTEM 3 (2000). Does this sound like *Carroll Towing*?

The committee recognized that individuals are responsible for errors, but emphasized that safety would be best improved by designing the health care system so that errors are prevented or minimized (much as highway and vehicle design has minimized the harms from driver error). For example, equipment can be simplified and standardized and drugs that look or sound alike can be given distinctively different names or packaging.

Unlike those who emphasized "crisis" and costs of insurance, the Institute of Medicine recognizes the overwhelming prevalence of medical malpractice (or preventable errors) and emphasizes the need for patient safety. It also adopts one tort-law goal: making errors costly enough to discourage them. Yet it does not emphasize tort law solutions. It wants design and management solutions. If the Institute of Medicine is on the right track, should tort law wither away, or would it retain an important role? Does it matter whether tort law provides effective deterrence? Two scholars who canvassed evidence bearing on the connections between malpractice exposure, error reporting, and health care quality, concluded: "Some evidence, such as the Harvard Medical Practice Study and the history of anesthesia safety, shows that the quality of health care improves as the risk of being sued rises. No evidence shows that malpractice lawsuits cause the quality of health care to decline. Nor does any rigorous evidence show that fear of malpractice lawsuits discourages error reporting—to the contrary, the historical record suggests that liability risk has encouraged providers to discuss treatment risks with patients. . . . Thus, there is no foundation for the widely held belief that fear of malpractice liability impedes efforts to improve the reliability of health care delivery systems. Health care error rates are higher than they should be not because providers fear malpractice liability, but because providers have defective incentives and norms [to produce safety]." David A. Hyman & Charles Silver, *The Poor State of Health Care Quality in the U.S.: Is Malpractice Liability Part of the Problem or Part of the Solution?*, 90 CORNELL L. REV. 893, 893 (2005).

E. MEDICAL COSTS, CONTAINMENT EFFORTS AND TORT STANDARDS

Fee for service system and over-utilization of medical services. Until very recently, people who received services of doctors or hospitals paid a fee for the service rendered. If services were greater, the fee was greater. If the patient could not pay the fee, chances were good that the patient would not get the service needed. Insurance plans first simply provided for payment of the medical costs, whatever they were. This led to over-utilization of medical services, either because patients demanded more extensive services (like testing, or longer hospital stays, for example) or because doctors and hospitals provided more. Neither doctor nor patient had economic incentives to keep costs down. As health concerns increased, governments and private employers added many potential patients through government payments or private insurance. Over-utilization became an even more significant cost.

Managed care strategies. One solution to over-utilization is managed care. A variety of Managed Care Organizations (MCOs) have sprung up, including Health Maintenance Organizations (HMOs) and other systems under which a provider accepts a flat fee or premium and guarantees to provide all needed medical services described in the agreement.

The Medicare form. Another form of managed care is the Medicare DRG system. Hospital admittees covered by Medicare are classified in Diagnostic Related Groups. Depending on the group and some related factors, Medicare will pay the hospital a predetermined amount, no more, no less. What are the economic incentives for the hospital with a Medicare patient? Suppose Medicare pays for a four-day hospital stay. Does the hospital have any economic incentive to discharge the patient one day early? Incentives are similar for HMOs. In the case of hospitals, is there an incentive to overadmit patients at the same time there is an incentive to provide less than optimum care? *See* Timothy S. Jost, *Policing Cost Containment: The Medicare Peer Review Organization Program*, 14 UNIV. PUGET SOUND L. REV. 483 (1991). In an attempt to address some of these defective safety incentives, Medicare has announced some recent changes to its reimbursement policies. For example, hospitals will not be reimbursed for extra time and costs associated with repairing their own failures such as allowing patients to develop pressure sores.

Utilization review. Insurance and MCO arrangements provide strategies that work somewhat like DRGs. These are generically called utilization review. In many instances "review" is a misleading word because the review will take place *before* medical service is delivered or concurrently with that service. The pre-certification or concurrent review will tell the health care provider such as a hospital exactly what the insurer will pay for. That might be a four-day hospital stay or none at all. In such cases utilization review sets the economic incentive for the health care provider. If insurance will pay only for a four-day hospital stay, the hospital may discharge the patient at the end of four days.

Liability for denial of coverage. One possibility suggested by these changes in the way medical service is delivered and financed is that an insurer whose utilization review is negligent might be held liable to the patient who gets limited medical care as a result of the refusal to pay. Several cases have now said that a provider could be held liable for wrongful refusal to authorize payment in advance. *See Wilson v. Blue Cross of S. Calif.*, 271 Cal.Rptr. 876 (Ct. App. 1990) (suicide by patient whose hospitalization for depression was terminated); *McEvoy v. Group Health Co-op. of Eau Claire*, 570 N.W.2d 397 (Wis. 1997) (an HMO's bad faith breach of contract is a common law tort, not a medical malpractice claim subject to the malpractice rule); *Long v. Great W. Life & Annuity Ins. Co.*, 957 P.2d 823 (Wyo. 1998) (Kafkaesque stonewalling by health insurer, tortious breach of contract claim with punitive damages would be authorized).

Other liabilities of MCOs.

(a) Suppose an MCO permits its physicians to prescribe only Drug X for a given medical problem, but Drug Y is regarded by all other physicians in the community as the drug of choice because Drug X has side effects that can be harmful. A physician limited to Drug X prescribes it for his patient, who faints while driving and crashes into a child. Does the MCO bear any responsibility, either to the injured patient or to the child? *See McKenzie v. Hawai'i Permanente Med. Group, Inc.,* 47 P.3d 1209 (Haw. 2002).

(b) If an MCO has information about risks of an approved physician or statistics about success rates of its physicians, must it disclose that information to patients? What if an HMO knows that a surgeon has a low success rate and is a drug addict? Aaron D. Twerski and Neil B. Cohen, in *The Second Revolution in Informed Consent: Comparing Physicians to Each Other,* 94 Nw. U. L. Rev. 1 (1999), argue that MCOs should be under a duty to disclose provider risk information they actually have in usable form.

(c) Suppose it is reasonable for an HMO to assign no more than 3,500 patients to a single physician. The HMO assigns more, say 4,000 or 5,000, or knows that the physician has a thousand other patients from his non-HMO practice. Is there a risk that the physician will be forced to rely inappropriately on telephone interviews instead of physical exams or that he will not have time to bring good judgment to bear on the patient's complaint? If so, would the HMO be responsible? *Jones v. Chicago HMO Ltd. of Ill.,* 730 N.E.2d 1119 (Ill. 2000).

Federal preemption. Many plaintiffs are members of MCO's by virtue of their employment. Employer-provided health care providers are regulated by the Employee Retirement Income Security Act of 1974, commonly known as ERISA. Such plaintiffs may face an insurmountable barrier in suing their MCO for negligence in handling coverage decisions. In *Aetna Health Inc. v. Davila,* 542 U.S. 200 (2004), the Supreme Court held all such claims to be preempted by the comprehensive federal scheme set up by section 502(a) of the Act, 29 U.S.C. § 1132(a). That section provides that "A civil action may be brought—(1) by a participant or beneficiary— ... (B) to recover benefits due to him under the terms of his plan, to enforce his rights under the terms of the plan, or to clarify his rights to future benefits under the terms of the plan." The Court held that "if an individual brings suit complaining of a denial of coverage for medical care, where the individual is entitled to such coverage only because of the terms of an ERISA-regulated employee benefit plan, and where no legal duty (state or federal) independent of ERISA or the plan terms is violated, then the suit falls 'within the scope of' ERISA 502(a)." Any such claim brought in state court would be "completely preempted" by ERISA. In the two consolidated cases under consideration, since "respondents complain only about the denials of coverage promised under the terms of ERISA-regulated employee benefit plans," they could not maintain a suit on a state-law negligence theory at all. The Court did not address purely medical decisions, as opposed to coverage decisions.

F. MANDATORY EMERGENCY TREATMENT AND SCREENING

42 U.S.C.A. § 1395dd

§ 1395dd. Examination and treatment for emergency medical conditions and women in labor.

(a) Medical screening requirement

In the case of a hospital that has a hospital emergency department, if any individual (whether or not eligible for benefits under this subchapter) comes to the emergency department and a request is made on the individual's behalf for examination or treatment for a medical condition, the hospital must provide for an appropriate medical screening examination within the capability of the hospital's emergency department, including ancillary services routinely available to the emergency department, to determine whether or not an emergency medical condition ... exists.

(b) Necessary stabilizing treatment for emergency medical conditions and labor

(1) In general

If any individual (whether or not eligible for benefits under this subchapter) comes to a hospital and the hospital determines that the individual has an emergency medical condition, the hospital must provide either—

(A) within the staff and facilities available at the hospital, for such further medical examination and such treatment as may be required to stabilize the medical condition, or

(B) for transfer of the individual to another medical facility in accordance with subsection (c) of this section....

(c) Restricting transfers until individual stabilized

(1) Rule

If an individual at a hospital has an emergency medical condition which has not been stabilized ... the hospital may not transfer the individual unless—

(A)(i) the individual (or a legally responsible person acting on the individual's behalf) after being informed of the hospital's obligations under this section and of the risk of transfer, in writing requests transfer to another medical facility,

(ii) a physician (within the meaning of section 1395x(r)(1) of this title) has signed a certification that based upon the information available at the time of transfer, the medical benefits reasonably expected from the provision of appropriate medical treatment at another medical facility outweigh the increased risks to the individual and, in the case of labor, to the unborn child from effecting the transfer ... and

(B) the transfer is an appropriate transfer (within the meaning of paragraph (2)) to that facility. . . .

NOTES

1. **Physician liability?** Notice that this federal statute is directed to hospitals, not doctors. Could physicians nonetheless be liable under it? On what grounds?

2. **Private right of action.** Must the violation of the statute be a cause of the plaintiff's harm? Subsection (d) of the statute provides that "Any individual who suffers personal harm as a direct result of a participating hospital's violation of a requirement of this section may, in a civil action against the participating hospital, obtain those damages available for personal injury under the law of the State in which the hospital is located, and such equitable relief as is appropriate."

3. **Labor.** The statute treats childbirth and labor as an emergency. An earlier version of the statute used the phrase "active labor" instead of "labor," which gave rise to its popular name as the Emergency Medical Treatment and Active Labor Act (EMTALA).

4. **Screening and treatment duties.** Notice the curious shift in the statutory "comes to" language. In subsection (a), which sets up the screening requirement, the statute speaks of an individual who "comes to the emergency department." But in subsection (b), which sets up the treatment and stabilization requirement, the statute speaks of an individual who "comes to a hospital." The Ninth Circuit examined the "comes to the hospital" requirement in *Arrington v. Wong,* 237 F.3d 1066 (9th Cir. 2001). In that case, an ambulance transporting a heart attack patient received direction from the hospital to take the patient to a different hospital, five miles away. On an appeal that considered the EMTALA claim, the court grappled with the ambiguous statutory language. In considering at which point a hospital becomes obligated to screen and stabilize a patient, the court ultimately deferred to the Department of Health and Human Services which interprets the statute to include all hospital property. In addition, the non-hospital owned ambulance was covered by EMTALA because of a regulation that a hospital may not deny emergency vehicles hospital access unless the hospital "is in diversionary status." Next step: suppose that the plaintiff comes to the hospital for an emergency that requires screening, which the hospital provides. It then admits the patient to the hospital as a regular in-patient. Would the hospital's duty to stabilize be terminated once the patient has been admitted?

LEWELLEN v. SCHNECK MEDICAL CENTER

2007 WL 2363384 (S.D. Ind.)

JOHN DANIEL TINDER, J. . . .

Plaintiff Kevin Lewellen is a registered nurse anesthetist in Paris, Tennessee, who made a terrible mistake on June 8, 2003. After a weekend visit with his cousin in Greenwood, Indiana, Lewellen began the roughly

350 mile journey home with a drink of scotch.... [T]hree hours later his blood alcohol content would be nearly four times the legal limit and he would be heading to the hospital, afterwards to jail.

Lewellen's bad judgment caught up with him somewhere in Jackson County, Indiana.... [H]is vehicle left the road, rolled once, and ended up in a ditch....

When Troopers Roger Drew and Rick Hudson of the Indiana State Police arrived at the accident site, paramedics were already there placing Lewellen on a stretcher and loading him into an ambulance....

According to [Schneck] hospital records, Defendant Amanda Davis, a nurse in the Emergency Department, admitted Lewellen to the hospital shortly after 3:00 p.m. She did an initial assessment and noted on Lewellen's chart that he had been in a motor vehicle accident. After this initial assessment, Defendant John M. Reisert, a doctor on duty, examined Lewellen. Reisert noted that Lewellen was complaining of lower back pain and his lumbar spine was tender. Reisert ordered x-rays of Lewellen's lumbar and cervical spine to determine whether Lewellen had fractured his back in the accident....

[X-rays were taken. The quality of the x-rays was poor. There was a dispute in the record as to whether the poor quality was because Lewellen was in significant pain and unable to turn on his side or whether he was "uncooperative [and] made threats to staff."] Trooper Drew backs Lewellen's version [of events] by stating that Lewellen was nothing but cooperative when he observed him....

Before the last of Lewellen's x-rays had even printed, at 4:07 p.m., Davis informed Lewellen that Reisert was discharging him. This was less than one hour after Lewellen had been admitted to the hospital. Lewellen refused to sign the consent to discharge, pleaded with Davis that he was in tremendous pain and begged to talk to the doctor. Nurse Davis told Trooper Drew ... that Lewellen was not cooperating in the discharge and asked if Drew would sign the discharge. Drew refused....

Lewellen was insistent that he was in great pain and that the hospital had not examined him sufficiently. Drew asked Nurse Davis about Lewellen's pain and asked if the hospital was really done examining him. Nurse Davis responded that Lewellen was fine, he was just drunk....

Lewellen was in too much pain to stand or walk.... Drew explained to Lewellen that once the hospital had discharged him he had no choice but to transport Lewellen to jail....

[As Lewellen was discharged] the last of Lewellen's x-rays came off the printer. Lewellen contends that Dr. Reisert did not even bother to look at these x-rays before deciding to discharge him.... At some point, whether before or after Lewellen was discharged, Reisert wrote on the ER chart that the x-rays revealed no fracture and that Lewellen's lack of cooperation caused the films to be of poor quality....

[T]wo hours after being discharged from the hospital, Defendant Dr. John F. Alexander, a radiologist at Schneck, looked at Lewellen's x-rays as part of a second read quality control process. His report mentions the poor quality of the x-rays and blames Lewellen's lack of cooperation, but Alexander admitted in his deposition that he had no reason to believe that that was the case. The report also states that... a fracture "cannot be completely excluded" because the lateral view of the lumber spine was not diagnostic, meaning that it was not clear enough to be useful. According to protocol, if the radiologist notices something that the ER physician missed, the radiologist needs to communicate with the ER physician. From the record, it appears that Alexander contacted no one.

Yet there was something seriously wrong with Lewellen. He had a burst fracture in his spine that was damaging his spinal nerves while he was being held in the Jackson County Jail. Over the course of the night, Lewellen started to notice neurological systems like numbness in his lower body. Despite the fact that Alexander and Reisert claim not to be able to tell if there was a fracture from Lewellen's x-rays, several other doctors who have looked at them say that a fracture can be seen. These include Alexander's boss, Dr. Staib....

Around 9:00 p.m. Officer McPherson went back to Lewellen's holding cell to check on another inmate. He saw Lewellen crying in pain and noticed that Lewellen had urinated all over himself.... McPherson left the cell to call the jail nurse, who ... instructed McPherson to give Lewellen some Tylenol. Unsatisfied, McPherson called Schneck's Emergency Department directly. He spoke with Defendant Sharon Duffield who said ... that someone had re-reviewed the x-ray and found an abnormality.... Despite notifying McPherson that there was an abnormality in his x-ray, Duffield told McPherson not to bring Lewellen back to the hospital and did not give any instructions as to a proper treatment.

Officer McPherson was so upset with the nurse's response that he contacted the jail commander imploring him to get medical help for Lewellen.... This was done and an ambulance was called to pick up Lewellen.

Before the ambulance arrived, McPherson went back to the holding cell to tell Lewellen that medical help was being secured. He noticed blood on the wall of the cell and looked at Lewellen, finding a deep laceration on his arm that had not been treated in any way. The cut still had grass and dirt in it.

At 1:00 a.m., June 9, 2003, Lewellen arrived back at Schneck. A CT scan of his spine performed at Schneck revealed that during the night Lewellen spent in jail, a fragment of bone from the burst fracture had displaced and was impinging on his spinal column....

Despite [an] operation, Lewellen suffered from permanent neurological defects as a result of this injury. Lewellen cannot urinate or defecate on his own; he suffers from some sexual dysfunction. Dr. Schwartz [the surgeon] believes that had Lewellen been properly treated on June 8,

2003, instead of discharged, he "more likely than not [ ] would have remained neurologically intact."

Plaintiff presents a claim against Schneck under the Emergency Medical Treatment and Active Labor Act ("EMTALA"). Schneck argues that it should receive summary judgment on this claim. . . .

The Emergency Medical Treatment and Active Labor Act (EMTALA) was passed to combat the problem of "patient dumping;" that is, the practice of transferring or discharging indigent or non-insured patients while their emergency conditions worsen. There are two requirements for certain federally-funded hospitals under EMTALA. First, a hospital "must provide for an appropriate medical screening examination within the capability of the hospital's emergency department . . . to determine whether or not an emergency medical condition . . . exists." Second, if an emergency medical condition is detected by this screening, the patient may not be discharged until he or she has received a stabilizing treatment or transferred when certain criteria are met. The statute authorizes a patient harmed by a hospital's failure to adhere to either of these two requirements to sue the hospital.

A hospital is only required to stabilize an emergency medical condition that they actually know about. Schneck claims that it performed an appropriate medical screen and thus that the stabilization requirement was not triggered. . . . If Schneck fulfilled the screening requirement, then the stabilization claim necessarily fails too because the stabilization requirement was not triggered. If Schneck did not fulfill the screening requirement, it is liable and there is no need to analyze the stabilization requirement separately.

EMTALA is not a national medical malpractice statute imposing a standard of care on hospital emergency rooms. A hospital that conducts an appropriate medical screen yet fails to detect, or misdiagnoses, an emergency medical condition—even if negligent and liable under medical malpractice—is not liable under EMTALA.

"EMTALA aims at disparate treatment." Therefore, a patient must show that he was treated differently from other patients. . . .

[A] hospital satisfies EMTALA's "appropriate medical screening" requirement if it provides a patient with an examination comparable to the one offered to other patients presenting similar symptoms, unless the examination is so cursory that it is not "designed to identify acute and severe symptoms that alert the physician of the need for immediate medical attention to prevent serious bodily injury."

Defendants correctly point out that Plaintiff presented no evidence that the screen performed on him differed from any other patient's screen. However, a reasonable jury could conclude that the screen performed was so cursory that it was not designed to identify acute and severe symptoms and thus did not meet the requirements of EMTALA. In its brief, Schneck barely argues Reisert's screen was more than cursory. Schneck argues only that Reisert did *something* and found Lewellen had a normal neurological exam. Defendants claim: "Based upon his examination, Dr. Reisert brought to bear on the case his medical judgment and concluded Mr. Lewellen could be safely discharged."

But according to the evidence presented by the Plaintiffs, the x-rays ordered by Dr. Reisert were being printed off as Lewellen was being discharged. A jury could conclude that either Dr. Reisert did not even bother to look at them or looked at them so casually that he missed what two other physicians said was obvious: that the x-rays demonstrate that Lewellen had a burst fraction in his spine. If Reisert did not study the x-rays how could his screen be designed to identify acute and severe symptoms? Lewellen's stay at the hospital was alarmingly brief considering he was in a motor vehicle accident and complaining of severe back pain so bad he could not stand or sit in a chair correctly. Lewellen still had a bleeding gash in his arm with grass and dirt in it when he arrived at prison. The court is mindful that EMTALA's screening requirement means something more than an inadvertent failure to follow the regular screening process in a particular case. But this scenario is so grave that a jury could conclude that rather than a negligent deviation from normal practice, the screening requirement was simply not met. For this reason, Schneck's motion for summary judgment will be DENIED.

NOTES

1. **Screening.** *Lewellen* notes that "EMTALA is not a national medical malpractice statute imposing a standard of care on hospital emergency rooms." However, the case imposes some standard of care, doesn't it? What screening is "appropriate"? Federal courts fear that tests based upon negligence would turn the statute into a federal medical malpractice statute. One idea is that disparate screening—providing better screening to some patients than others—would be a violation of the appropriate screening requirement. *Power v. Arlington Hosp. Ass'n*, 42 F.3d 851 (4th Cir. 1994). If that is right, would it also be right to say that the screening is appropriate whenever it is of the same quality provided all other individuals? What if the screening is simply negligent?

2. **Unpublished opinions.** The opinion in *Schneck* is an unpublished decision. Unpublished decisions are controlling authority to the parties in the litigation. However, in many jurisdictions they are of no precedential value to other cases. The rules about citing unpublished opinions are in flux and vary by jurisdiction. Most jurisdictions do not permit attorneys to cite these decisions as precedent in later cases. Some jurisdictions allow citation as long as a copy of the opinion is attached to the party's brief. A relatively new federal rule of appellate procedure—FRAP 32.1(a)—allows for citation to unpublished opinions issued on or after January 1, 2007. Why might a court issue an unpublished opinion? According to a standard note inserted in the *Schneck* case, the decision is unpublished because "the discussion [in the case] is not sufficiently novel to justify commercial publication." Should the *Schneck* decision have been published to be used as precedent in later suits

alleging EMTALA violations based on inadequate screening? Over 75% of federal appellate court decisions are not published. Commentators have taken different views about whether the large volume of unpublished opinions is necessary for the smooth functioning of courts, or a worrisome problem of unaccountable precedent either on the whole or in particular cases which seem not to fit within the formal criteria for an unpublished decision. For an overview see Stephen Wasby, *Publication (or Not) of Appellate Court Rulings: An Evaluation of Guidelines*, 2 SETON HALL CIR. REV. 41 (2005).

3. **Treatment and stabilization.** In *Roberts v. Galen of Virginia, Inc.*, 525 U.S. 249 (1999), the Supreme Court said that liability may be imposed under the stabilization requirement even if the hospital had no bad motive, such as a motive to dump patients who had no insurance. The Court did not decide whether motive played a part in liability for screening failures.

4. **Coordinating with or trumping state law.** Could state-law limits on health-care claims also limit EMTALA claims? In *Smith v. Richmond Memorial Hospital*, 416 S.E.2d 689 (Va. 1992), the court said that the state-law pre-suit notice of claim requirement had no application to suits brought under the federal EMTALA statute. But in *Hardy v. New York City Health & Hospitals Corp.*, 164 F.3d 789 (2d Cir. 1999), the court asserted that by authorizing damages measured by state-law damages rules, EMTALA meant to exclude claims that would be barred altogether under state law because of the plaintiff's failure to give notice of claim within 90 days of the occurrence.

Would you distinguish the pre-suit notice requirement in *Hardy* from a state's statutory cap on damages for health care injury? In *Barris v. County of Los Angeles*, 972 P.2d 966 (Cal. 1999), the California Supreme Court applied the state's damages cap to an EMTALA claim.

Suppose that, under state law, a hospital is completely immune from all tort liability and therefore liable for zero damages. Would an EMTALA claim be barred? *Root v. New Liberty Hosp. Dist.*, 209 F.3d 1068 (8th Cir. 2000).

5. **Lowering the state-law standard of care for indigents.** Should the medical standard of care be lowered when patients cannot pay? *See* James A. Henderson & John A. Siliciano, *Universal Health Care and the Continued Reliance on Custom in Determining Medical Malpractice*, 79 CORNELL L. REV. 1382 (1994).

G. STRICT AND LIMITED LIABILITY PROPOSALS

A number of scholars have suggested that health care providers should be strictly liable for some kinds of untoward medical events. *See* Barry Furrow, *Defective Mental Treatment: A Proposal for the Application of Strict Liability to Psychiatric Services*, 58 B.U.L. REV. 391 (1978); Clark C. Havinghurst, *"Medical Adversity Insurance"—Has Its Time Come?*, 1975 DUKE L.J. 1233. With strict liability, the damages award might be limited; pain and suffering damages might be excluded, for example. For this reason, it might even be cheaper for doctors or hospitals to pay every injured patient than to defend legal actions. *See* Jeffrey O'Connell, *Offers That Can't Be Refused: Foreclosure of Personal Injury Claims by Defen-*

dants' Prompt Tender of Claimants' Net Economic Losses, 77 Nw. U. L. Rev. 589 (1982).

The American Law Institute's Reporter's Study of Enterprise Liability for Personal Injury (ALI 1991) suggested: (1) eliminating individual doctor liability in favor of hospital liability when injury results from the practice of a hospital-affiliated doctor; (2) limiting pain and suffering damages, with some other adjustments in damages awards; (3) awarding attorney fees to the prevailing plaintiff (since pain and suffering recoveries, from which such fees might have been paid, would be limited or barred). It also supported a strict liability or no-fault plan when the patient and hospital agreed.

One strict liability plan is actually in use. In Virginia, obstetricians contribute to a fund which pays for the pecuniary needs of infants who suffer brain damage at birth. No pain and suffering award is made. VA. CODE § 38.2–5001. *See* Peter H. White, Note, *Innovative No–Fault Tort Reform for An Endangered Specialty*, 74 VA. L. REV. 1487 (1988).

REFERENCES: BARRY R. FURROW, THOMAS L. GREANEY, SANDRA H. JOHNSON, TIMOTHY S. JOST & ROBERT L. SCHWARTZ, HEALTH LAW (2 vols. 1995).

§ 5. NURSING HOMES, LONG–TERM CARE AND ELDER ABUSE

HORIZON/CMS HEALTHCARE CORP. v. AULD

985 S.W.2d 216 (Tex. App. 1999)

DIXON W. HOLMAN, JUSTICE. . . .

In August 1994, Martha Hary, age 76, became a resident at the nursing home. The case was tried upon allegations that beginning in December 1994, the nursing home neglected to provide Martha with medical care and treatment within the acceptable standard of care. . . . At trial, Auld asserted that while a resident at the nursing home between mid-December 1994 and August 1995, and because of substandard nursing care, Martha's body developed pressure sores, some of which deteriorated to a condition described as Stage IV, where the tissue overlying a person's bone rots away and leaves the bone exposed. Auld asserted that Martha suffered contractures in all extremities and that the nursing home did not provide Martha all of the wound care treatments and pressure relieving devices that had been ordered. Auld contended that the care administered for Martha's pressure sores was painful, including surgical excision of foreign matter and all dead and devitalized tissue in the wounds, a procedure known as debridement. On August 6, 1995, Martha was taken from the nursing home to Fort Worth's Osteopathic Hospital where she was treated for 10 days. After her discharge from the hospital, Martha spent the remaining year of her life at a facility that is not a party to this suit. She died August 9, 1996. . . .

. . . The jury found that the nursing home's negligence proximately caused Martha's injury and found $2,371,000 as actual damages [a sum later adjusted by agreement to $2,370,941.71]. That sum includes $1,750,000 for physical pain and mental anguish, $150,000 for disfigurement, $250,000 for impairment, and $221,000 for medical care. The jury did not find that Martha's injuries resulted from malice, but found the nursing home grossly negligent.... The jury found $90,000,000 as exemplary damages.

[Much of the courts's opinion on appeal is devoted to the application of statutes capping damages. Actual damages of $2,371,000 were capped to leave the plaintiff $1,541,203.13 including an award for interest. Punitive damages were capped at four times the uncapped actual damages for a total of $9,483,766.92.]

The nursing home does not complain that either the jury finding of $90,000,000 in punitive damages or the court's reduction of that sum to $9,483,766.92 is excessive....

[The nursing home argued that the trial judge erred in admitting into evidence the written investigation reports made by investigators for the Texas Department of Human Services to determine compliance with state licensing requirements and federal and state Medicaid requirements.] The nursing home argues that the survey reports merely measure the extent of the home's compliance with contractual and regulatory standards, not whether it has negligently deviated from the standard of medical care necessary for patients.

After the defense rested its case, a hearing was held out of the jury's presence where Auld offered as rebuttal evidence thirteen state "survey reports" labeled exhibit 22, pages A through M, covering the period from September 1, 1994 to December 31, 1995. For most of that time, Martha resided at the home. Auld's exhibit list identifies exhibit 22 as "certified copies of Texas Department of Human Services, Long Term Care Records, Vendor 498–51, Heritage Western Hills Nursing Home." ...

Both the opening statement to the jury by the nursing home's attorney, and the eventual testimony of the nursing home's witnesses about a good quality of care given to Martha, opened the door to the admission of exhibit 22 and the use of its contents as impeachment material. The trial court observed:

> Well, your witnesses have testified that no patient ever failed to have the basic care. So, if there is an incident [recorded within exhibit 22] showing that a patient failed to have basic care, it is at least impeachment if it goes to the issues that are the basis of this case....

Because exhibit 22 is (and was presented to the trial court as) a certified copy of a record of a public agency, it is not inadmissible hearsay. Moreover, evidence of a defendant's subjective knowledge of the peril his conduct creates is admissible to prove gross negligence, which was an issue at this trial. The information contained in exhibit 22 confirms the nursing home's knowledge of the conditions in the home that adversely affected Martha's care and showed that the state did bring those conditions to the home's knowledge in a timely manner with regard to Martha's stay at the home. . . .

[W]e conclude that the trial court did not abuse its discretion by admitting exhibit 22. . . .

[The nursing home argued that the compensatory damages award was excessive.] Our review of all the evidence reveals that at trial, Auld established that (1) four basic nursing interventions were necessary to prevent Martha from developing pressure sores and contractures on her body; (2) the first intervention required that Martha be turned and repositioned regularly; (3) the second intervention required that Martha receive adequate nutrition; (4) the third intervention required that, as an incontinent patient, Martha's skin be kept clean and dry; (5) the fourth intervention required that to stimulate blood flow to the skin and prevent contractures, Martha's joints should have been treated with a passive range of motion exercises; (6) in the beginning of Martha's stay at the nursing home, she received those types of care which kept pressure sores and contractures from developing on her body; (7) from mid-December 1994 until she was taken from the nursing home on August 6, 1995, Martha did not receive those types of nursing care; (8) during the latter time-period, Martha's body was not turned or repositioned during approximately 210 eight-hour shifts, totaling 1,680 hours; (9) that during the same period of months, Martha was not fed regularly and missed 238 meals; (10) that during the same period of months, Martha was not given incontinent care during approximately 216 eight-hour shifts, totaling 1,728 hours; (11) during that period of months, no range of motion exercises were administered to Martha; (12) the nursing home's current and past employees admitted that its records (flow sheets) for Martha accurately reflected these deficiencies, and they testified that they had no reason to doubt the records' accuracy; (13) that between mid-December 1994 and August 1995, Martha's body developed between nine and 12 pressure sores, at least four of which deteriorated to Stage IV, and she also developed contractures in all of her extremities; (14) after Martha developed the pressure sores, the nursing home did not furnish all of the wound-care treatments and pressure-relieving devices that were ordered for her; (15) those conditions resulted in painful wound care and debridement; (16) when she was taken from the nursing home to the hospital, the hospital personnel considered her condition to be terminal due to the pressure sores, contractures, infection, and malnutrition; (17) that those conditions caused her to have to undergo painful treatments at the hospital; and (18) the injuries she suffered while at the nursing home caused her severe physical pain, mental anguish, physical impairment, and physical disfigurement, which lasted until her death nearly a year after she left the nursing home. Auld carried her burden to prove and secure jury findings that the nursing home proximately caused Martha's injuries.

. . . The evidence is both legally and factually sufficient to support the jury's findings of damages for physical pain and mental anguish, disfigurement, and impairment. We overrule the nursing home's third issue.

. . . Finding no reversible error, we affirm the trial court's judgment. . . .

Notes

1. **Subsequent case history.** This case was affirmed in the Texas Supreme Court except on the issue of prejudgment interest, which that court held was capped by a statute. The punitive damage award was allowed to stand. *Horizon/CMS Healthcare Corp. v. Auld,* 34 S.W.3d 887 (Tex. 2000).

2. **Extent of elder abuse.** A federally funded study indicates that around half a million elders are abused every year in their own homes, usually by their adult children or spouses. *Sieniarecki v. State,* 756 So.2d 68 (Fla. 2000), upholding the constitutionality of Florida's criminal punishment, gives a graphic and upsetting description.

3. **Nursing homes.** Nursing homes range from mom-and-pop outfits with a few beds to giant corporate enterprises, some of which can take in or lose billions in any given year. Horizon/CMS, the defendant in *Auld*, showed total operating revenues of $1,753,084,000 ($1.75 Billion) in its 1996 annual report filed with the Securities and Exchange Commission. Manor Care, Inc., itself a subsidiary of Health Care and Retirement Corp., is another chain. It reported assets of $2,280,866,000 at the end of 1999 and revenue for the year of $2,135,345,000. According to a company profile, the President and CEO has an annual salary of $1,600,000.

4. **Nursing home finance.** A high percentage of nursing home residents are on Medicaid. Their social security income, if any, plus Medicaid pays the nursing home. Medicaid pays only to the extent that nursing home care is needed and to the extent that the resident cannot himself pay the costs. Distinguish Medicare. Medicare pays for covered items without regard to the beneficiary's wealth or income, but it does not cover basic custodial care in a nursing home, only some special items. The two programs together, administered by the Centers for Medicare and Medicaid Services (CMS), directly pay nursing homes for care provided. These programs have thus helped create the big chain nursing home industry.

5. **Under-reporting of abuse.** Abuse and neglect in care facilities ranges from physical and sexual attacks on residents to systematic neglect as seen in the *Auld* case. The amount of abuse is enormous, but it is hard to document its exact extent because residents are often incompetent or too afraid to report it.

6. **Affordability for the lawyer.** Even when a resident or outsider reports deficiencies in care and injury, a tort action is often impractical. In the *Horizon/Auld* case, actual physical harm was discovered and Horizon's own records helped document its neglect. But in most cases, family members (if any) may not discover the harm or its cause. The nursing home records may not document the abuse. If a suit is brought, the patient may make a poor

witness. Actual damages may be quite limited in many cases: the nursing home may have inflicted pain and misery, but its neglect does not deprive the resident of an active life; if the nursing home hastens death, it does not hasten it by very much. Lawyers can hardly afford to take cases that will require enormous investments of time to recover small damages, so many of these claims may be rejected by lawyers or possibly settled cheaply without suit. *See* 1 Barry R. Furrow, et al., HEALTH LAW §§ 1–2 (1995). Independent claims by family members for emotional distress might help make up for these problems, but such claims are likely to be rejected under special rules that tend to limit emotional distress claims. *See Moon v. Guardian Postacute Serv., Inc.*, 116 Cal.Rptr.2d 218 (Ct. App. 2002) (plaintiff not close enough relative); *Ess v. Eskaton Prop's, Inc.*, 118 Cal.Rptr.2d 240 (Ct. App. 2002) (sister of nursing home victim was not "present" when victim was sexually attacked, no emotional distress claim). These circumstances make punitive damages especially important in nursing home cases—first to provide an appropriate level of deterrence, since ordinary damages may be small, and second to encourage lawyers to bring suits they could not afford to try without a fee based on punitive recoveries.

7. **Access to courts.** Nursing homes may include arbitration agreements in admission papers, requiring residents to forgo their right to seek redress through the courts. The Federal Arbitration Act may validate such agreements if the nursing home participates in interstate commerce. Although some courts have held that receipt of Medicaid funds shows interstate commerce and thus validates the jurisdiction-ousting arbitration agreement, *Bruner v. Timberlane Manor Limited Partnership*, 155 P.3d 16 (Okla. 2006), held otherwise. Another possibility, not considered there, is that state rules applicable to contracts generally are enforceable and might conceivably hold the arbitration agreement to be invalid as a contract of adhesion and unenforceable under general contract rules.

8. **Standard of care and coverage by medical malpractice statutes.** If a victim's survivors manage to identify abuse and bring suit, does the medical standard of care control and do the medical malpractice reforms statutes apply to present further obstacles to suit? Suppose the nursing home does not provide adequate nutrition, doesn't provide the patient the pain medication prescribed by a doctor, or doesn't wash or clean a helpless patient. Is that really a matter of health care as distinct from ordinary negligence? *See Integrated Health Care Services, Inc. v. Lang–Redway*, 840 So.2d 974 (Fla. 2002) (action under statute specifying nursing home duties not subject to special requirements of "medical malpractice" claims). But in *Richard v. Louisiana Extended Care Centers, Inc.*, 835 So.2d 460 (La. 2003), the caretaker of a 92-year-old woman sued the nursing home operator for negligence and intentional torts for severe head injuries she suffered either in a fall or perhaps a beating. The court held that because the facility was a "qualified health care provider" under the medial malpractice statute, all claims against it must be brought under the statute. This meant that the nursing home operator would get the benefit of a medical review panel and a limitation on liability that would not be accorded for common-law claims.

What about unnecessary chemical or physical restraint—could the plaintiff recover without expert professional testimony about the standard of care on the ground that the defendant has committed a battery or false imprison-ment? *See Roberson v. Provident House,* 576 So.2d 992 (La. 1991) (battery).

9. **Res ipsa loquitur.** Since the nursing home has a large measure of control over the relatively helpless (sometimes totally helpless) resident, would res ipsa loquitur apply to establish negligence when the resident has bedsores? What if the resident suffers injury because she ingests the wrong medicine? *Harder v. F.C. Clinton, Inc.,* 948 P.2d 298 (Okla. 1997) (doctrine applied though defendant denied providing the medicine, which was not prescribed for the resident at all).

10. **Using regulations to prove a standard of care and/or breach.** Long-term care facilities like nursing homes are regulated both by state and federal law. CMS regulations can conceivably be put in evidence as standards to which the facility must conform. For example, one regulation provides that "Each resident must receive and the facility must provide the necessary care and services to attain or maintain the highest practicable physical, mental, and psychosocial well-being, in accordance with the comprehensive assess-ment and plan of care." Other regulations provide many more specific standards. For example, the facility must ensure that "(1) A resident who enters the facility without pressure sores does not develop pressure sores unless the individual's clinical condition demonstrates that they were un-avoidable; and (2) A resident having pressure sores receives necessary treat-ment and services to promote healing, prevent infection and prevent new sores from developing." 42 C.F.R. § 483.25. In *In re Conservatorship of Gregory,* 95 Cal.Rptr.2d 336 (Ct. App. 2000), understaffing of a nursing home led to injuries. Although suit was brought under state law, the trial court instructed the jury on federal regulatory standards. This was upheld on appeal.

11. **Inspection or survey reports.** In *Horizon/CMS v. Auld, supra,* the court admitted into evidence the reports of state inspections. These reflect annual surveys made by the states pursuant to federal standards. Failure to meet federal standards (deficiencies) are noted in standardized ways. In the *Auld* case, admission of the survey evidence showed that Horizon knew of its own violations. This might create a basis for punitive damages. Conversely, if the trial judge does not admit such evidence in the case, the plaintiff will have no claim for punitive damages unless she can show the nursing home's malice or recklessness by some other means.

12. **Elder abuse, residents' rights statutes.** Some states have creat-ed statutory tort claims for elders against caregivers under specified circum-stances. In *Health Facilities Management Corp. v. Hughes,* 227 S.W.3d 910 (Ark. 2006), although the jury concluded that medical malpractice and wrong-ful death claims were not satisfied, it did find a violation of the residents' rights statute. In that case the resident, Ms. Smith, "was sometimes found lying in urine for extended periods of time. As a result of not being properly belted into her wheelchair, she suffered a fractured tibia when she was almost in a van accident. She further suffered a urinary tract infection and developed pressure sores and sepsis. In addition, she developed contractures due to the home's failure to provide range-of-motion exercises." The court therefore upheld the jury's $700,000 verdict. California's statute, the Elder Abuse and

Dependent Adult Civil Protection Act, in effect says that neglect such as failure to provide nourishment or abuse such as sexual assault is actionable. Does this add anything to ordinary tort law? The statutes may advance the rights of patients in other ways. The Washington statute permits the prevailing victim to recover attorney fees. REV. CODE WASH. § 74.34.200. The California statute also permits the victim to recover attorney fees, although only if the plaintiff proves oppression, recklessness, or malice by clear and convincing evidence as well as the abuse or neglect itself. *See* CAL. WELF. & INST. CODE § 15657. Such proof then permits the plaintiff to avoid limitations that would apply to medical malpractice claims. *See Delaney v. Baker*, 971 P.2d 986 (Cal. 1999). This includes avoiding the special medical malpractice procedural requirements for an award of punitive damages. *Covenant Care, Inc. v. Superior Court*, 86 P.3d 290 (Cal. 2004). In states where pain and suffering damages do not survive the death of the victim, the elder abuse statute may permit the pain claim to survive. *Guardianship of Denton*, 945 P.2d 1283 (Ariz. 1997).

NOTE: REGULATION OR FINANCIAL PARTNERSHIP?

Nursing homes, like much of the rest of the health care industry, are largely financed through Medicare or Medicaid payments. The Health Care Financing Administration authorizes Medicaid payments to certified care providers. Although CMS indisputably issues regulations, that is more or less incidental to the business of managing Medicare/Medicaid. In theory, CMS can enforce its standards by terminating payments, but in practice its aim is to deliver health care or long-term care and in that sense it is in a kind of partnership with nursing facilities. If a nursing home fails to meet standards, you might expect that CMS would simply terminate the nursing home as a certified provider. This has occasionally happened. *See N. Health Facilities, Inc. v. United States*, 39 F.Supp.2d 563 (D. Md. 1998). However, elimination of a nursing home at a time when the elderly population is increasing may be unwise in the long term and certainly is likely to disrupt the lives of all the present residents. Given the widespread deficiencies among nursing homes, the dilemma may be like that presented to child protective workers—movement from one bad home may turn out to be movement to another that is just as bad or worse. Besides this, CMS is not designed as a regulatory agency and not imbued with regulatory zeal. It is a financing agency. In consequence, the regulations may sometimes help lawyers seeking to establish a standard of care, but they may not do the job of preventing abuse in the first place.

NOTE: THE FALSE CLAIMS ACT AND QUI TAM ACTIONS

False claims. Social control of nursing home abuse may come about in another way. Federal prosecutors, who are in no way connected with CMS, are charged with prosecuting crimes of all sorts. Under the Federal False Claims Act, any one who knowingly presents a false claim against the United States is criminally liable and also liable for a civil fine and treble damages. 18 U.S.C. § 287 & 31 U.S.C. § 729. If a nursing facility presented a claim for Medicaid reimbursement for services it did not deliver, this would be a false claim and it could be criminally and civilly liable under the False Claims Act. Could it also be liable if it presented a claim for Medicaid or Medicare payments when its care did not meet standards? Maybe companies seeking Medicaid reimbursement from the government impliedly certify that they have complied with regulatory standards. If they in fact provide the kind of "care" the court found was provided for Martha Hary in the *Auld* case, wouldn't that be a false claim?

Qui tam. The question takes on added importance because of a bounty-hunter provision in the False Claims Act. This provision permits private citizens to sue on behalf of the government for False Claims Act violations. The government can then take over the lawsuit or not, but even if it does, the private plaintiff who brought suit in the government's name is paid a percentage of the recovery. These private citizen actions are called qui tam actions, from the first words of a Latin phrase used in common law actions to describe the plaintiff—one who sues for the king as well as for himself. The question here is whether federal prosecutors or a qui tam plaintiff could recover treble damages under the False Claims Act on proof that the facility sought reimbursement for woefully substandard care. A few such cases have been settled in favor of the government. At least one such implied certification claim has received judicial approval. *United States ex rel. Aranda v. Community Psychiatric Ctrs. of Okla., Inc.*, 945 F.Supp. 1485 (W.D. Okla. 1996). But other courts have denied a similar claim. *United States ex rel. Swan v. Covenant Care, Inc.*, 279 F. Supp. 2d 1212 (E.D. Cal. 2002); *United States ex rel. Mikes v. Straus*, 84 F. Supp. 2d 427 (S.D.N.Y. 1999).

Refocusing. One problem about nursing home abuse or neglect is that it may not be discovered at all. Nursing home residents are elderly and expected to die within a short period anyway. Unless the resident has close family members who monitor her condition, neither mistreatment nor neglect is likely to be known. A second problem is affordability of suit. When nursing home abuse and negligence are discovered, suit may not be feasible because expected damages awards will often not pay for the time the lawyer must invest. The result is underdeterrence on one side and under- or no-compensation on the other. This section reflects three ways in which courts or legislatures can deal with the affordability problem. Which is the best? Should all three be available?

§ 6.   INTENTIONAL TORTS AND SEXUAL HARASSMENT BY PROFESSIONALS

The focus of this chapter is on negligent, not intentional, torts. But some torts that appear to be intentional in some sense, may be treated as negligent torts for one purpose or another. The characterization of the tort as one based upon negligence or one based upon battery often becomes important in determining whether the defendant's liability insurance will cover the case.

A. SEXUAL BATTERY OR EXPLOITATION OF PATIENTS, PARISHIONERS, OR CLIENTS

When a health care provider is guilty of sexual harassment of a patient, two issues aside from the merits may become dominant: (1) Will his liability insurance policy cover intentional misconduct? (2) Is his conduct covered by medical malpractice statutes so that he gets whatever special benefits those statutes provide in his jurisdiction?

(1) On the first question, you could guess that insurers dislike covering criminal misconduct, but more to the point they are likely to exclude coverage for non-professional conduct. Yet non-professional sexual harassment may arise rather directly from the physician patient relationship. In that case, the court may hold that the policy provides coverage that will pay for the harasser's legal liability. That was the result in *St. Paul Fire & Marine Insurance Co. v. Shernow*, 610 A.2d 1281 (Conn. 1992). In that case, a female patient of a dentist alleged that the dentist administered nitrous oxide and that she lost consciousness. Regaining consciousness, she realized that the dentist's tongue was in her mouth and that her breasts felt painful. She resisted and the dentist turned up the nitrous oxide. On regaining consciousness again, she found the dentist on top of her. Again he turned up the gas. Although the insurance policy excluded coverage for battery, the court held that battery was so mixed with negligent professional treatment—too much gas—that the policy covered all of the dentist's liability.

(2) Does a malpractice statute with its special rules cover a sexual attack or harassment claim against a health care provider? In *Hagan v. Antonio*, 397 S.E.2d 810 (Va. 1990), a female plaintiff sued a male doctor alleging that in the course of a medical examination he improperly played with her breasts and made sexual remarks. The doctor defended on the ground that the plaintiff had failed to give the special pre-suit notice required by the statute. The plaintiff argued that the statute only covered claims based on health care or professional services rendered, and that the acts complained of were not such professional services. The court held, however, that the doctor was protected by the notice requirement because the alleged act "stemmed from, arose from, and was 'based on' the performance of a physical examination." The court thought rape would be distinguishable.

B. EXPLOITATION OF THE CONSENTING PATIENT, PARISHIONER, OR CLIENT

Many professionals appear to engage in consensual sexual relationships with patients or clients. The problem is especially common with therapists such as psychologists, psychiatrists, or analysts. A number of states have enacted statutes that permit the patient to recover, at least under some circumstances, for injury suffered as a result of sexual contact with the therapist, regardless of consent. CAL. CIV. CODE § 43.93 (b) (if there is therapeutic deception); ILL. COMP. STAT. ANN. 140/2 (even after treatment if the patient was emotionally dependent or the therapist practiced deception); MINN. STAT. § 148A.02 (similar); WIS. STAT. ANN. § 895.70 (regardless of emotional dependence or deception).

Even apart from the statutes, the patient's consent may not be a defense if it is less-than-informed or the therapist manipulates the patient. If consent is no defense, is the claim against the therapist a claim for battery, so that the therapist's liability insurance does not protect the therapist and does not provide a source of funds for the victim? Patients attempt to avoid the battery trap by asserting that the therapist has negligently mishandled the "transference" phenomenon. That is, that the therapist mishandled the well-known tendency of patients to develop sexual, romantic, or dependent relationships with their therapists. Sexual relationships with patients in therapy is regarded as a way of negligently mishandling transference and "[c]ourts have uniformly regarded mishandling of transference as malpractice or gross negligence." *Simmons v. United States*, 805 F.2d 1363 (9th Cir. 1986). This reasoning converts a battery into negligence.

Therapist exploitation cases also incidentally call into question the professional standard of care. Although the American Psychiatric Association states that sexual contact with patients is unethical, many therapists of various persuasions do in fact engage in sexual relations with patients. *See* Linda Jorgenson, Rebecca Randles & Larry Strasburger, *The Furor over Psychotherapist-patient Sexual Contact: New Solutions to an Old Problem*, 32 WM. & MARY L. REV. 645 (1991). If the "custom of the industry" is to take advantage of the relationship to engage in sexual relations with patients, can the therapist be held liable after all?

Clergy sexual exploitation. What if a clergyperson exploits the pastoral relationship with parishioners to engage in sexual relationships that prove emotionally harmful? A number of these cases hold in favor of the allegedly exploitive clergy, sometimes advancing the view that religious freedom protects the clergy and their churches from liability for sexually exploitive behavior. *See Pritzlaff v. Archdiocese of Milwaukee*, 533 N.W.2d 780 (Wis. 1995); *cf. Byrd v. Faber*, 565 N.E.2d 584 (Ohio 1991) (considerations based in First Amendment impose requirement of more specific pleading when church is sued for negligent hiring); *but cf. Malicki v. Doe*, 814 So.2d 347 (Fla. 2002) (rejecting First Amendment protections for church charged in the complaint with negligently hiring or retaining a priest who foreseeably would commit sexual batteries); *Olson v. First Church of the Nazarene*, 661 N.W.2d 254 (Minn. Ct. App. 2003) (church could be held vicariously liable for pastor's misconduct without any First Amendment problem since the theory of liability turned only on a "scope of employment" issue). Courts tend to say that there is no such tort as clergy malpractice or clergy breach of fiduciary duty. *Schieffer v. Catholic Archdiocese of Omaha*, 508 N.W.2d 907 (Neb. 1993). A similar result may be reached even when the priest or minister is functioning as a counselor to his parishioner. *Bladen v. First Presbyterian Church of Sallisaw*, 857 P.2d 789 (Okla. 1993). The *Bladen* court thought that the claim would lie against a member of the clergy only upon a showing that he misused the transference mechanism or breached a fiducial duty. A few cases go the other way, holding the clergyman responsible for sexual exploitation of a parishioner. *See F.G. v. MacDonell*, 696 A.2d 697 (N.J. 1997). A little authority supports the parishioner when she claims negligence of the religious body itself in hiring or supervising clergy, or breach of a fiducial duty that might occur when the religious body does not seek to prevent or ameliorate the effects of priestly sexual behavior with vulnerable parishioners. *See Doe v. Evans*, 718 So.2d 286 (Fla. Dist. Ct. App. 1998) (fiduciary relationship arises when church through its clergy holds itself out as qualified to engage in marital counseling and a counseling relationship arises); *Moses v. Diocese of Colorado*, 863 P.2d 310 (Colo. 1993).

Lawyers. Suppose a lawyer counsels a client about divorce. The lawyer induces the client to engage in sexual activity. How does this compare or contrast with similar scenarios in the case of therapists and clergy? The American Bar Association's ethics rules for lawyers now makes having sex with a current client a disciplinary infraction under most circumstances. *See* ABA Model Rules of Prof. Conduct 1.8(j). Prior to the ABA's decision on this issue, a few states had already adopted disciplinary rules to the same effect. *See* Cal. Rules of Prof. Conduct 3–120. Note that these rules do not create tort causes of action, but provide the basis for disciplinary sanction by state bars.

CHAPTER 14

FAMILY MEMBERS AND CHARITIES

■ ■ ■

NOTE: IMMUNITIES

The kind of defendants encountered in Chapters 12 and 13—landowners and health care professionals—usually obtain special protections from liability because courts limit the duties they owed to something less than the duty of reasonable care. In Chapters 14 and 15, defendants such as family members, charities, and governmental entities are granted similar protections, but the locution is slightly different. Here courts say that these defendants are immune from tort suits or tort liability. The difference between a no-duty rule and an immunity rule, if a difference exists at all, is minuscule. In short, the immunity rules are quite similar to the limited duty rules except that they tended in their original form to be absolute and without exception.

§ 1. FAMILY MEMBERS

A. THE TRADITIONAL FAMILY IMMUNITIES

Spouses. The common law took the view that upon marriage the wife lost her legal identity, which was merged with that of the husband. The logical result of this conception was, of course, that the spouses could not sue each other. See Carl W. Tobias, *Interspousal Tort Immunity in America*, 23 GA. L. REV. 359 (1989) (giving complete history of immunity).

Parent and child. There was no such conceptual reason to bar suits between parents and children. The parent-child immunity was introduced rather casually in *Hewellette v. George*, 9 So. 885 (Miss. 1891) with the unadorned argument that family harmony would not permit such actions. "[S]o long as the parent is under obligation to care for, guide, and control, and the child is under reciprocal obligation to aid and comfort and obey, no such action as this can be maintained." Other states followed this decision and it became mainstream law.

Scope and exceptions. (1) Property interests. Children were allowed, however, to sue parents to protect property, and after the Married Women's Property Acts spouses were also allowed to sue for such property torts as conversion.

(2) Relationship terminated. The parental immunity terminated when the child reached the age of majority, or when the child was emancipated (that is, recognized as self-supporting, or married). Some states have held that the parent-child relationship might also be terminated when the parent dies—with the result that the parent's estate could be sued though the parent could not be. Missouri once held that the immunity did not protect the non-custodial parent. *Fugate v. Fugate*, 582 S.W.2d 663 (Mo. 1979). By contrast, Connecticut held that a divorced father who had visitation rights without physical custody retained the parental immunity. *Ascuitto v. Farricielli*, 711 A.2d 708 (Conn. 1998).

(3) Intentional torts. Even in states that held a spouse or parents immune from negligent torts, liability was often imposed for intentional torts. *See, e.g., Lusby v. Lusby*, 390 A.2d 77 (Md. 1978) (no immunity where wife alleged husband raped her at gunpoint); *Hurst v. Capitell*, 539 So.2d 264 (Ala. 1989) (no immunity for sexual abuse of child).

(4) Family injury from violation of duty owed to larger class. Nor did the immunity apply where family members were involved only fortuitously in an injury-causing event; that is, the injury and the family relationship in no way intersected. For example, if a teenage daughter negligently drives a car and strikes a pedestrian in the cross-walk, the fact that he turns out to be her father would not bar recovery. *Schenk v. Schenk*, 241 N.E.2d 12 (Ill. App. Ct. 1968). Put differently, the immunity may be limited to cases in which the parental conduct involves discretion in discipline or supervision, and does not apply to ordinary negligent accidents. *See Cates v. Cates*, 619 N.E.2d 715 (Ill. 1993).

Rationale. Two reasons predominate as justifications for the family immunities: (1) To permit suits between family members would be to encourage fraud and collusion; and (2) to permit suits of this kind would be to interfere with the family, and disrupt family harmony or unity.

Put baldly, the two main reasons for the immunity seem to have little force. Can these reasons be fleshed out? If liability insurance covers the defendant spouse, there is, no doubt, a tendency of the insured spouse, with the approval of the other, to assert fault. What may be an ordinary home accident, with no witnesses, may become a case of "negligence" quite readily. And even if it is negligence, there is the probability that both spouses will share in some sense in the recovery. This obviously does not square with ordinary notions of accountability, because the faulty party, far from paying, would share in payment by his insurer.

In the case of parent-child actions, there was obviously some notion at one time that these would interfere with "discipline," and that if the child could sue, the parent's appropriate authority would be disrupted by judicial interference. This argument perhaps has little appeal today, especially if, as is often the case, the parent encourages the child's tort action in order to tap insurance funds. If there is no insurance, the danger is not fraud but misallocation of family funds. If a child recovers $100,000 from a parent, the parent may be unable to meet other obligations within the family, so that one child may enjoy relative riches while others are unable to receive any of the ordinary benefits of childhood. As these comments suggest, the two arguments of fraud and harmony can be expanded quite a bit. Is further elaboration of these arguments possible? When the arguments are fully developed, do you find them convincing?

Rejection of the immunities. By the end of the 1970s a majority of courts had abolished the spousal immunity, though sometimes only as to motor vehicle collisions. *See, e.g., Ellis v. Estate of Ellis*, 169 P.3d 441 (Utah 2007) (holding that Married Women's Act abrogates immunity for all claims); *Waite v. Waite*, 618 So.2d 1360 (Fla. 1993) (complete abrogation of immunity). South Carolina has not only rejected spousal immunity but has said that the immunity would be contrary to natural justice and public policy. For this reason, if one South Carolina spouse negligently injured the other in a state that retained the immunity, the injured spouse would be permitted to sue in South Carolina. *Boone v. Boone*, 546 S.E.2d 191 (S.C. 2001).

What, besides a legal immunity, might deter an abused spouse from suing and what should be done about it? *See* Jennifer Wriggins, *Domestic Violence Torts*, 75 S. CAL. L. REV. 121 (2001).

The courts have been a bit slower in abolishing the parent-child immunity, but it appears that a majority have now done so. *See, e.g., Broadbent v. Broadbent*, 907 P.2d 43 (Ariz. 1995) (abolishing immunity and applying ordinary duty of reasonable care). Some states have abolished the immunity only for special groups of cases, such as those arising out of intentional torts, sexual abuse, motor vehicle accidents, or the conduct of a family business. *E.g., Henderson v. Woolley*, 644 A.2d 1303 (Conn. 1994) (immunity does not bar child's claim for sexual abuse)

Where the immunities have been generally abolished, a whole set of new problems arises, centered primarily now on the question of duty and negligence.

GOLLER v. WHITE, 122 N.W.2d 193 (Wis. 1963). Goller was a foster child living in White's home under an arrangement with the Milwaukee County Welfare Department. White permitted Goller, who was 12 years old, to ride on the draw bar of White's tractor without warning him of protruding bolts on the wheels. These caught Goller's trouser leg and caused injury for which he sues. The trial court entered summary judgment for the defendant. *Held*, reversed and remanded. Courts generally have held that a foster parent or one who stands in loco parentis can claim the parental immunity. The existence of insurance in a particular case offers no ground for an exception to the immunity. But "the wide prevalence of liability insurance in personal injury actions [is] a proper element to be considered in making the policy decision of whether to abrogate parental immunity in negligence actions.... [T]he existence of insurance tends to negate any possible disruption of family harmony and discipline." The immunity should be abrogated "except in these two situations: (1) where the alleged negligent act involves an exercise of parental authority over the child; and (2) where the alleged negligent act involves an exercise of ordinary parental discretion with respect to the provision of food, clothing, housing, medical and dental services, and other care."

COMMERCE BANK v. AUGSBURGER, 680 N.E.2d 822 (Ill. App. Ct. 1997). The Illinois Department of Children and Family Services arranged for placement of a three-year-old with foster parents, the defendants here. The defendants allegedly confined the child "in an enclosed space described as the 'upper half of a divided shelf of a wooden cabinet inside a bedroom closet at [their] home with the door closed' and did not supervise or monitor her; as a result, she died of asphyxia and hyperthermia." *Held,* dismissal affirmed. The plaintiff did not allege an intentional tort. Illinois has limited the immunity to cases of parental discretion but "parental discretion in the provision of care includes maintenance of the family home, medical treatment, and supervision of the child." The defendant's conduct, though severe, was the very kind to be protected under this standard.

NOTES

1. ***Goller.*** Many states follow the *Goller* limited-immunity formula, which effectively bars most children's claims of negligent parental supervision. The Restatement Second of Torts § 895F (1979), approved *Goller* but phrased the rule in terms of a parental privilege for exercising discipline and parental discretion. Are you happy with the application of *Goller* in *Commerce Bank v. Augsburger*?

2. **The reasonable person standard.** Some courts have gone beyond *Goller* saying that parents may be liable to children under a reasonable person (or "reasonable parent") standard. *See Broadbent v. Broadbent,* 907 P.2d 43 (Ariz. 1995); *Anderson v. Stream*, 295 N.W.2d 595 (Minn. 1980); *Gibson v. Gibson*, 479 P.2d 648 (Cal. 1971). Does this demand too much of parents, or fail to recognize their important role in making decisions about care of children?

3. **Immunity in negligent supervision cases.** Other courts have moved in the opposite direction, holding parents owe no legally-enforceable duty to supervise their children. As New York's court explained, "Each child is different, as is each parent; as to the former, some are to be pampered while some thrive on independence; as to the latter, some trust in their children to use care, others are very cautious. Considering the different economic, educational, cultural, ethnic and religious backgrounds which must prevail, there are so many combinations and permutations of parent-child relationships that may result that the search for a standard would necessarily be in vain—and properly so. . . . [P]arents have always had the right to determine how much independence, supervision and control a child should have, and to best judge the character and extent of development of their child." *Holodook v. Spencer,*

350 N.Y.S.2d 199 (App. Div. 1973), *quoted with approval on appeal*, 324 N.E.2d 338 (N.Y. 1974). *See also Shoemake v. Fogel, Ltd.*, 826 S.W.2d 933 (Tex. 1992). Thus in *Holodook* there was no liability when a parent failed to control a small child who ran into the street and was struck by a car. New York has at times carried the "inadequate supervision" category to great lengths. In *Nolechek v. Gesuale*, 385 N.E.2d 1268 (N.Y. 1978) the court held that when a father provided a motorcycle to his teenage son, who was blind in one eye and had impaired vision in the other, it was only a case of "parental supervision," in the same way that decision to monitor a child's play is.

HOPPE v. HOPPE, 724 N.Y.S.2d 65 (App. Div. 2001). "The infant plaintiff was entrusted by his father, the defendant herein, with a hammer and a container of nails which contained an 'explosive nail gun cartridge.' He was injured when he struck the cartridge with the hammer, causing the cartridge to explode. [T]he Supreme Court correctly denied his motion for summary judgment dismissing the complaint. While a child may not sue a parent for negligent supervision, the infant plaintiff possesses a cognizable claim that his injuries were proximately caused by the defendant's alleged breach of a duty of care owed to the world at large, one that exists outside of, and apart from, a family relationship. 'The duty not to negligently maintain explosives is a duty owed to all and is not simply a duty emanating from the parent-child relationship.' "

NOTES

1. **Applications.** A father, knowing his child cannot swim, leaves him alone in the swimming pool. The child is found at the bottom of the pool and rescued, but he suffers brain damage from lack of oxygen. In a suit by the child's guardian against the father, what results (a) under *Goller*; (b) under a reasonable person standard; or (c) under New York's rule?

2. **Foster parents, step-parents, and those standing *in loco parentis*.** Notice that the defendants in *Goller* and *Augsburger* were foster parents. Courts are somewhat divided as to whether foster parents are entitled to parental immunity. *See, e.g., Nichol v. Stass,* 735 N.E.2d 582 (Ill. 2000) (granting immunity to foster parents except for acts in violation of regulations, criminal acts, or child neglect). Some courts have given step-parents the same immunity as parents. *See, e.g., Zellmer v. Zellmer,* 188 P.3d 497 (Wash. 2008). Still others suggest that anyone who stands *in loco parentis* (in the parent's shoes) should share the parental immunity. *See, e.g., Smith v. Smith*, 922 So.2d 94 (Ala. 2005) (saying that a non-parent stands in such a role when he or she "assumes the obligations incident to parental status" and "voluntarily performs the parental duties to generally provide for the child"). Are such extensions in line with the policies behind the parental immunity in the first place?

§ 2.   CHARITIES

Traditional rule. Beginning in the mid-nineteenth century, in response to an English decision, most American states adopted the view that charities were not liable in tort. This included virtually all "non-profit" organizations, such as hospitals, the Boy Scouts, the YWCA and many others, of which, however, hospitals were by far the most important. The idea initially was that tort liability would divert trust funds from their intended charitable purpose.

Exceptions. This rule followed a development that is by now familiar. First a number of exceptions were developed, with varying emphasis and acceptance in each state:

(1) The charity was not exempt from liability as to non-trust funds. Charities would be liable to the extent that insurance or other free funds were available to pay the judgment.

(2) Some jurisdictions had phrased the rule by saying that the charity would not be liable for the negligence of its servants. Thus the hospital would not be liable for the negligence of the orderly who left a slippery substance on the floor. However, the view was developed that the charity could somehow act "itself" rather than through agents or servants if it acted through its top administrators. In this view, if the hospital administrator had been negligent in hiring a dangerous orderly who was likely to and did attack patients, the hospital would not enjoy an immunity. This is sometimes called "administrative negligence."

(3) The charity could not claim the immunity against those who paid for its services. So, for example, a hospital could not claim an immunity as to a paying patient, but could as to a "charity" patient.

(4) The charity could not claim an immunity as to its collateral commercial activities. Thus the YMCA ski trip, for which fees were charged, would not be protected by an immunity.

(5) Intentional or "reckless" torts were not protected by the immunity in some states.

General abolition of immunity, with some dissenters. The Restatement Second of Torts § 895E (1979) states the rule that there is no charitable immunity, and most states have abolished it entirely, some by statute and some by judicial decision. However, some states retain the immunity, causing litigation over exceptions or over factors in a complicated analysis to determine whether the immunity applies in a particular case. *See, e.g., O'Connell v. State*, 795 A.2d 857 (N.J. 2002); *George v. Jefferson Hosp. Ass'n,* 987 S.W.2d 710 (Ark. 1999). A few states have retained the charitable immunity for negligent torts, but not for willful or wanton acts. *See, e.g., Cowan v. Hospice Support Care, Inc.*, 603 S.E.2d 916 (Va. 2004). The statutes of some states abolish the immunity only as to particular charities such as hospitals. *See, e.g.,* S.C. CODE § 44–7–50 (abolishing immunity as it relates "to hospitals and other medical facilities"). What issues might this limited abolition of immunity raise in South Carolina?

Other statutes abolish charitable immunity but cap damages in cases where the tort involved activities in furtherance of charitable purposes. *See, e.g.,* MASS. GEN. LAWS ANN. 231 § 85K ($20,000 cap). Does that kind of statute raise concerns?

Individuals engaged in charitable activities. The traditional charitable immunity protected the charity itself in its form as a trust or corporation, but did not protect individuals who were engaged in its activities. A number of contemporary statutes provide some kind of limitation on the duty of various individuals associated with charities or even with individual charitable acts. We have already seen one example-the medical Good Samaritan statutes. Some others are ridiculously specific in identifying the specially privileged or protected group. An Illinois statute lowers the standard of care for volunteers who coach or umpire in non-profit sports programs. 745 ILL. STATS. § 80/1 (liability only if conduct falls substantially below standard). Although such statutes are highly specific, there are a number of them and various sports programs are singled out for protection.

A much broader protection for individuals and organizations comes with statutes protecting donors of food to non-profit organizations. *E.g.,* CAL. CIV. CODE § 1714.25. Broader yet, some states have enacted statutes protecting all volunteers who assist non-profit corporations. The federal Congress has also enacted such a statute. The federal statute begins by providing absolute immunity for volunteers who work for non-profit corporations, then recognizes some exceptions. See 42 U.S.C.A. § 14503 (a)(3). An interesting twist on this statute is that it protects volunteers working for any non-profit organization that escapes income taxes under the Revenue Code, 26 U.S.C.A. § 501(c). That includes a number of organizations you might not think of as charities. The Chamber of Commerce is one example.

GENERAL REFERENCE: DOBBS ON TORTS §§ 279–281 (2000) (family immunities); §§ 282–283 (2000) (charitable immunity).

CHAPTER 15

GOVERNMENTAL ENTITIES AND OFFICERS

■ ■ ■

§ 1. TRADITIONAL IMMUNITIES AND THEIR PASSING

1. *Governmental tort immunity.* The English common law said "The King can do no wrong," an ambiguous statement that ultimately was taken to mean that one could not sue government in tort. This idea was carried over to America and perpetuated even after the American Revolution, with the result that the federal government and the states were immune from tort actions. This immunity extends to all their agencies unless statutes provide otherwise. On rare occasions it may even protect government contractors following government specifications, a point covered in Chapter 24. In addition to this general "sovereign immunity" of the federal and state governments, the Eleventh Amendment of the United States Constitution has been construed to immunize states from being sued in federal court.

2. *Taking of property.* One important qualification to the governmental immunity is that under the due process clauses of the Fifth and Fourteenth Amendments of the United States Constitution, neither state nor federal governments may "take" private property for public purposes without just compensation.

3. *Municipal immunity.* Municipalities and other local entities are not "sovereigns." Rather, they are corporations chartered by the sovereign. They were traditionally accorded immunity nonetheless, but over the years, courts freely created various exceptions. Municipalities were and are of course liable for takings of property. But additionally, courts made them liable for nuisances such as unsanitary garbage dumps, and for torts committed in the course of proprietary activities, as distinct from governmental activities. For example, a city might be liable for negligence in the operation of a city-owned electrical company. Cities were also held liable in many states for negligent failure to maintain streets properly.

4. *Abolishing state and municipal immunity.* New York waived its sovereign immunity in 1929, a waiver that later was interpreted to apply

as well to municipal immunities. *Bernardine v. City of New York*, 62 N.E.2d 604 (N.Y. 1945). Most states lagged behind for many years, but in the 1960s and 1970s, both courts and legislatures acted to abolish or limit the immunity of states and municipalities. Today most states have enacted statutes that abolish the state's immunity to at least some extent. We cover immunities under state law in more detail in section 3 of this Chapter.

5. *Abolishing federal immunity.* The federal government's immunity from tort suit eventually became a nuisance to the Congress because citizens who were denied access to courts often sought a recovery from their Congressperson via a "private bill" awarding compensation. Such bills consumed a good deal of Congressional time. To minimize time loss, Congress finally passed the Federal Tort Claims Act (FTCA) in 1946, in effect turning over many such claims to the judicial process. As we will see in the next section, the FTCA waived the federal government's immunity from tort suits, but did not do so completely.

§ 2.   THE FEDERAL TORT CLAIMS ACT

A.   THE GENERAL STRUCTURE OF THE FTCA

UNITED STATES v. OLSON

546 U.S. 43 (2005)

JUSTICE BREYER delivered the opinion of the Court.

The Federal Tort Claims Act (FTCA or Act) authorizes private tort actions against the United States "under circumstances where the United States, if a private person, would be liable to the claimant in accordance with the law of the place where the act or omission occurred." 28 U.S.C. § 1346(b)(1). We here interpret these words to mean what they say, . . . [a]nd we reverse a line of Ninth Circuit precedent permitting courts in certain circumstances to base a waiver simply upon a finding that local law would make a "state or municipal entity" liable.

In this case, two injured mine workers (and a spouse) have sued the United States claiming that the negligence of federal mine inspectors helped bring about a serious accident at an Arizona mine. The Federal District Court dismissed the lawsuit in part upon the ground that their allegations were insufficient to show that Arizona law would impose liability upon a private person in similar circumstances. The Ninth Circuit, in a brief *per curiam* opinion, reversed this determination. It reasoned from two premises. First, where "unique governmental functions" are at issue, the Act waives sovereign immunity if "a state or municipal entity would be [subject to liability] under the law [. . .] where the activity occurred." Second, federal mine inspections being regulatory in nature are such "unique governmental functions," since "there is no private-sector analogue for mine inspections." The Circuit then held that Arizona law would make "state or municipal entities" liable in the circumstances alleged; hence the FTCA waives the United States' sovereign immunity. We disagree with both of the Ninth Circuit's legal premises.

The first premise is too broad, for it reads into the Act something that is not there. The Act says that it waives sovereign immunity "under circumstances where the United States, if a *private person*," not "the United States, if a state or municipal entity," would be liable. Our cases have consistently adhered to this "private person" standard. In *Indian Towing Co. v. United States,* 350 U.S. 61, 64 (1955), this Court rejected the Government's contention that there was "no liability for negligent performance of 'uniquely governmental functions.' " It held that the Act requires a court to look to the state-law liability of private entities, not to that of public entities, when assessing the Government's liability under the FTCA "in the performance of activities which private persons do not perform." . . .

The Ninth Circuit's second premise rests upon a reading of the Act that is too narrow. The Act makes the United States liable "in the same manner and to the same extent as a private individual under *like circumstances.*" 28 U.S.C. § 2674 (emphasis added). As this Court said in *Indian Towing,* the words "like circumstances" do not restrict a court's inquiry to the *same circumstances,* but require it to look further afield. The Court there considered a claim that the Coast Guard, responsible for operating a lighthouse, had failed "to check" the light's "battery and sun relay system," had failed "to make a proper examination" of outside "connections," had "fail[ed] to check the light" on a regular basis, and had failed to "repair the light or give warning that the light was not operating." These allegations, the Court held, were analogous to allegations of negligence by a private person "who undertakes to warn the public of danger and thereby induces reliance." It is "hornbook tort law," the Court added, that such a person "must perform his 'good Samaritan' task in a careful manner."

The Government in effect concedes that similar "good Samaritan" analogies exist for the conduct at issue here. It says that "there are private persons in 'like circumstances' " to federal mine inspectors, namely "private persons who conduct safety inspections." Reply Brief for United States 3. . . . [As we said in *Indian Towing,*] private individuals, who do not operate lighthouses, nonetheless may create a relationship with third parties that is similar to the relationship between a lighthouse operator and a ship dependent on the lighthouse's beacon. The Ninth Circuit should have looked for a similar analogy in this case.

Despite the Government's concession that a private person analogy exists in this case, the parties disagree about precisely which Arizona tort law doctrine applies here. We remand the case so that the lower courts can decide this matter in the first instance. The judgment of the Ninth Circuit is vacated, and the case is remanded for proceedings consistent with this opinion.

NOTES

1. **Some key conditions of the waiver.** The FTCA is a broad waiver of sovereign immunity, but the statute itself contains a number of conditions. For example, before filing a suit in court the plaintiff must submit the claim to the government agency involved; suit is not permitted until the agency has refused payment or has delayed over six months in making a decision on it. Courts lack jurisdiction over suits filed prematurely. *See, e.g., Turner v. United States*, 514 F.3d 1194 (11th Cir. 2008). The statute also specifies that cases may be brought only in federal court, not state court. Neither side may have a jury; all FTCA trials are bench trials.

2. **Governing law.** Although FTCA claims against the government must be brought in federal court, the substantive law that governs claims under the FTCA is *not* federal law. Instead, the FTCA itself requires the court to follow the law of the state in which the alleged tort occurred. 28 U.S.C.A. § 1346(b)(1). As you can see from *Olson*, this means that the outcome of a particular FTCA case may vary depending on the state in which the tort occurred.

3. **Specific statutory exceptions for particular activities.** The statute itself lays out a number of specific instances in which the government is not liable, that is, in which the immunity is retained. One set of exceptions retains the immunity for specific governmental activities (combatant activities of the military and delivery of mail, for example) and for all claims arising in foreign countries. These exceptions have typically been read broadly, in favor of immunity. *See, e.g., Sosa v. Alvarez–Machain*, 542 U.S. 692 (2004) (holding that the "foreign country" exception bars all claims against the federal government based on any injury suffered in a foreign country, no matter where the alleged tortious act or omission giving rise to that injury occurred).

4. **Specific statutory exceptions for particular torts.** Another set of provisions in the statute retains the government's immunity for a number of specific torts, mostly those of a dignitary or economic kind. These include those "arising out of" assault, battery, false imprisonment, malicious prosecution, abuse of process, libel, slander, misrepresentation and interference with contract. Suppose the government negligently hires a man who has a propensity to commit sexual assaults or to molest children. The man uses his government job to take advantage of a child. The government usually escapes liability in such cases because the claim "arises out of" assault or battery, even though the legal basis of the claim is that the government is negligent in hiring without adequate investigation, or negligent in supervision. *See, e.g., LM v. United States*, 344 F.3d 695 (7th Cir. 2003).

The immunity for assault, battery, and the like does have two significant limitations. First, if an off-duty employee commits a battery, the government might be liable for its negligence in fostering the risk. For example, it might be liable for its negligence in permitting an employee to take a government rifle off-duty. *Sheridan v. United States*, 487 U.S. 392 (1988). But this rationale does not appear to apply to *on*-duty employees. Second, under the statute itself, the government may be liable for the assault, battery, or false imprisonment if it is committed by "investigative or law enforcement officers."

5. **Judicially-established exceptions.** The Court has construed the statute to permit liability of the government only for the negligent or other "wrongful" acts of government employees. Strict liability, even when a private individual would be strictly liable, is not permitted. *See Laird v. Nelms*, 406 U.S. 797 (1972). However, Congress can still appropriate funds directly to compensate for harm without fault. *See Land v. United States*, 29 Fed. Cl. 744 (1993). A second and more important judicially-created exception is considered next.

B. THE *FERES* RULE

BROOKS v. UNITED STATES, 337 U.S. 49 (1949). Two brothers named Brooks were in the armed forces but were on furlough. While driving on a public road, their vehicle was struck by a negligently driven army truck. One man was killed, the other injured. The government as defendant argued that it should be immune from negligence liability when the injured persons were members of the armed forces. *Held*, the government has no such immunity. "[W]e are dealing with an accident which had nothing to do with the Brooks' army careers, injuries not caused by their service except in the sense that all human events depend upon what has already transpired." Congress authorized a suit for "any claim." It created 12 exceptions, but none applies here. The FTCA "excludes claims arising out of combatant activities of the military or naval forces, or the Coast Guard, during time of war. . . . [S]uch exceptions make it clear to us that Congress knew what it was about when it used the term 'any claim.' It would be absurd to believe that Congress did not have the servicemen in mind in 1946, when this statute was passed. The overseas and combatant activities exceptions make this plain."

FERES v. UNITED STATES, 340 U.S. 135 (1950). Three consolidated cases, heard together. In *Feres* the decedent was killed in a barracks fire while he was on active duty in the service of the United States. The claim alleges negligence. In *Jefferson* the plaintiff underwent an abdominal operation while he was in the army. Eight months later, after he was discharged, a doctor removed a towel 30 inches long and 18 inches wide from his abdomen. It was marked "Medical Department U.S. Army." The third case, *Griggs*, claimed that army surgeons were responsible for the death of a soldier on active duty. *Held*, all these claims are barred because injuries received were "incident to service." The FTCA makes no specific exception for service-connected injuries to members of the armed forces, but the Act as a whole was not intended to impose unprecedented liability upon the government. There are three reasons for this conclusion. (1) Although private persons do practice medicine and cause fires, no private persons operate armies. So government liability would find no private-law analogue. (2) The FTCA invokes the tort law of the state where the injury occurred. This would subject the unique government-to-soldier relationship to the varied laws of the states. (3) The armed forces provide substantial compensation in the form of pensions or otherwise. These can operate, like state workers' compensation laws, as a substitute for tort liability.

NOTES

1. **Applications.** Although the *Feres* rule's contours are less than distinct, it has been broadly construed to bar claims by active military personnel. *See, e.g., Kitowski v. United States*, 931 F.2d 1526 (11th Cir. 1991) (military trainer brutally held a recruit under water until he died); *United States v. Stanley*, 483 U.S. 669 (1987) (government conducted LSD experiments upon serviceman without informing him of risks; held to be "incident to service"). It also applies to bar claims brought for violation of Constitutional rights rather than for violation of state tort law. *Chappell v. Wallace*, 462 U.S. 296 (1983).

2. **Extending the rationales.** Long after *Feres* itself was decided, the Court began to emphasize a fourth reason for the immunity, insisting that a suit by a service person would somehow interfere with military discipline. Military discipline is given an extremely broad meaning. In *United States v. Johnson*, 481 U.S. 681 (1987), a Coast Guard pilot, flying under the control of a civilian FAA controller, was killed in a crash. The surviving spouse asserted that the FAA was negligent in causing the death. The Court applied the *Feres* immunity, partly because "a suit based upon service-related activity necessarily implicates the military judgment and decisions" and "military discipline involves not only obedience to orders, but more generally duty and loyalty to one's service and to one's country. Suits brought by service members against the Government for service-related injuries could undermine the commitment essential to effective service and thus have the potential to disrupt military discipline in the broadest sense of the word."

3. **Spouses and children.** *Feres* does not bar a recovery by a spouse or child of a person in the armed forces if the spouse or child is directly injured. Common examples of recovery by spouses or children are those involving medical malpractice in military hospitals.

Suppose, however, that the army subjects a serviceman to inoculations or exposure to radioactive materials that result in birth defects in his or her children. Can the children recover for the harms done to them? *See Minns v. United States*, 155 F.3d 445 (4th Cir. 1998) (Gulf War inoculation causing birth defects, *Feres* bars children's claim because it had its genesis in injury to service person and would implicate military discipline); *Hinkie v. United States*, 715 F.2d 96 (3d Cir. 1983) (exposure of service personnel to radioactive materials, children injured by genetic damage to parent are barred by *Feres*). There are a number of similar cases.

4. **"Incident to service."** *Feres* formally covers only those injuries that are "incident to service," seemingly on the assumption that the policy reasons advanced for rejecting liability more or less automatically apply when injury is incident to service and do not apply otherwise. Service members injured while on furlough, for example, are not injured incident to service. *See, e.g., Schoenfeld v. Quamme*, 492 F.3d 1016 (9th Cir. 2007). A soldier injured while on leave but still on active duty, however, is injured incident to service. *See, e.g., McConnell v. United States*, 478 F.3d 1092 (9th Cir. 2007) (*Feres* barred claim for death of Air Force pilot killed while waterskiing on Air Force base). Judge Calabresi has attempted to make the rationale for *Feres* more coherent by emphasizing analysis of "incident to service." If the injury

is not incident to service, no military discipline issue arises. Likewise, if it is not incident to service, the fact that military benefits are paid looks like an analogy to a civilian employer's voluntary provision of health benefits rather than an analogy to workers' compensation payments that would protect the employer from a tort suit. Incident to service thus becomes central in determining whether *Feres* bars the claim. *See Taber v. Maine,* 67 F.3d 1029 (2d Cir. 1995).

C. THE DISCRETIONARY OR BASIC POLICY IMMUNITY

WHISNANT v. UNITED STATES
400 F.3d 1177 (9th Cir. 2005)

BETTY B. FLETCHER, CIRCUIT JUDGE.

[Plaintiff-appellant Lorrin Whisnant worked for a company that provided seafood to the commissary on a Naval base. The commissary is operated by a government agency, DeCA. DeCA regulations require periodic safety inspections, but DeCA employees are allowed to decide how and when to conduct such inspections. The base contracts out maintenance work to Johnson Controls. Johnson Controls inspections showed in June, 1997, that mold had accumulated in the meat department of the commissary. Over the next three years, several employees and customers became ill. Tests conducted in October 2000 proved that toxic molds were present, and government closed the meat department shortly thereafter.]

As a result of his exposure to the mold prior to the closure of the meat department, Whisnant contracted pneumonia, and experienced headaches, swollen glands, sore throat, persistent cough, and other health problems. [He sued the government under the FTCA for damages for its negligence in allowing workers and customers to come into contact with the mold despite known health hazards.] The government moved to dismiss ... on the ground that Whisnant's suit was barred by the discretionary function exception to the FTCA, 28 U.S.C. § 2680(a) (providing that the FTCA shall not apply to "[a]ny claim ... based upon the exercise or performance or the failure to exercise or perform a discretionary function or duty on the part of a federal agency or an employee of the Government, whether or not the discretion involved be abused"). The district court granted the motion to dismiss. . . .

As the district court correctly noted, the Supreme Court has prescribed a two-part test for determining the applicability of the discretionary function exception. *See United States v. Gaubert,* 499 U.S. 315, 322–25 (1991); *Berkovitz v. United States,* 486 U.S. 531, 536–37 (1988). Courts are to ask first whether the challenged action was a discretionary one—i.e., whether it was governed by a mandatory statute, policy, or regulation. If the action is not discretionary, it cannot be shielded under the discretionary function exception. Second, courts ask whether the challenged action is of the type Congress meant to protect—i.e., whether the action involves a decision susceptible to social, economic, or political policy analysis. It is the government's burden to demonstrate the applicability of the discretionary function exception.

Application of the first prong is straightforward in Whisnant's case. No statute, policy, or regulation prescribed the specific manner in which the commissary was to be inspected or a specific course of conduct for addressing mold. The parties are in agreement on this point.

The dispute in this case concerns the application of the second *Gaubert/Berkovitz* prong. We have recently remarked upon the difficulty of charting a clear path through the weaving lines of precedent regarding what decisions are susceptible to social, economic, or political policy analysis. Government actions can be classified along a spectrum, ranging from those "totally divorced from the sphere of policy analysis," such as driving a car, to those "fully grounded in regulatory policy," such as the regulation and oversight of a bank. But determining the appropriate place on the spectrum for any given government action can be a challenge.

We begin by noting the lines of analysis that are foreclosed. Specifically, the Supreme Court has rejected two categorical approaches to this area of law. First, the applicability of the exception does not depend on whether the relevant decision was made by an individual at the "operational" or "planning" level. Second, actions that are regulatory or "uniquely governmental" in nature are not automatically covered by the exception by virtue of that designation.

A review of circuit precedent reveals two trends in the law that bear particularly on Whisnant's case. First, a dominant theme in our case law is the need to distinguish between design and implementation: we have generally held that the *design* of a course of governmental action is shielded by the discretionary function exception, whereas the *implementation* of that course of action is not. Second, and relatedly, matters of scientific and professional judgment—particularly judgments concerning safety—are rarely considered to be susceptible to social, economic, or political policy.

Thus, for example, in a suit alleging government negligence in the design and maintenance of a national park road, we held that designing the road without guardrails was a choice grounded in policy considerations and was therefore shielded under the discretionary function exception, but maintaining the road was a safety responsibility not susceptible to policy analysis. Similarly, in a suit alleging government negligence in the design and construction of an irrigation canal, we held that the decision not to line the canal with concrete was susceptible to policy analysis, but the failure to remove unsuitable materials during construction was not.... And in an action for the death of a prospective logger "trying out" for a job with a government contractor at a logging site under the management of a government agency, we held that while the government's authorization of the contract was protected under the discretionary function exception, the government's failure to monitor and ensure safety at the work site was not....

Under these principles, Whisnant's suit is not barred by the discretionary function exception. Whisnant does not allege that the government was negligent in designing its safety inspection procedures; rather, he charges that the government was negligent in following through on those procedures to safeguard the health of employees and customers of the Bangor commissary. Like the government's duties to maintain its roads in safe condition, to ensure the use of suitable materials in its building projects, and to monitor the safety of its logging sites, the government's duty to maintain its grocery store as a safe and healthy environment for employees and customers is not a policy choice of the type the discretionary function exception shields. Cleaning up mold involves professional and scientific judgment, not decisions of social, economic, or political policy. Indeed, the crux of our holdings on this issue is that a failure to adhere to accepted professional standards is not susceptible to a policy analysis. Because removing an obvious health hazard is a matter of safety and not policy, the government's alleged failure to control the accumulation of toxic mold in the Bangor commissary cannot be protected under the discretionary function exception.

The government argues that implementation of the DeCA regulations regarding health and safety required employees "to balance the agency's goal of occupational safety against such resource constraints as costs and funding." In addressing government negligence in the implementation of safety precautions, we have several times rejected this precise argument.... [I]n *O'Toole v. United States,* we held that the discretionary function exception did not apply to a claim for private property damage resulting from the government's failure to maintain an irrigation ditch on its own property.... [W] explained:

> The danger that the discretionary function exception will swallow the FTCA is especially great where the government takes on the role of a private landowner. Every slip and fall, every failure to warn, *every inspection and maintenance decision* can be couched in terms of policy choices based on allocation of limited resources.... Were we to view inadequate funding alone as sufficient to garner the protection of the discretionary function exception, we would read the rule too narrowly and the exception too broadly.

Like the plaintiffs in *O'Toole,* Whisnant is alleging that government negligence in the maintenance of its own property caused his injuries. Following *O'Toole,* then, we decline to permit the government to use the mere presence of budgetary concerns to shield allegedly negligent conduct from suit under the FTCA. To hold otherwise would permit the discretionary function exception to all but swallow the Federal Tort Claims Act....

[T]he question of *how* the government is alleged to have been negligent is critical. If Whisnant were claiming that the government was negligent in electing to employ contractors rather than doing the work itself, or in designing its safety regulations, then his claim would most likely be barred; instead, he is claiming that the government negligently ignored health hazards that were called to its attention, and so his claim is not barred. Because it failed to recognize the import of this distinction, the district court mischaracterized Whisnant's allegations and thereby erred in dismissing his action.

While the government has discretion to decide how to carry out its responsibility to maintain safe and healthy premises, it does not have discretion to abdicate its responsibility in this regard. When it does so, the discretionary function exception cannot shield the government from FTCA liability for its negligent conduct. . . .

In this case, Whisnant has alleged negligence in the implementation, rather than the design, of government safety regulations, and the governmental decisions Whisnant claims were negligent concerned technical and professional judgments about safety rather than broad questions of social, economic, or political policy. Therefore, the discretionary function exception to the FTCA does not bar Whisnant's suit.

We reverse the district court's dismissal of the action and remand for further proceedings consistent with this opinion.

NOTES

1. **Purposes of the discretionary immunity.** Why did Congress retain federal immunity for discretionary functions? In *United States v. Varig Airlines*, 467 U.S. 797 (1984), the Court explained that the discretionary immunity "marks the boundary between Congress' willingness to impose tort liability on the United States and its desire to protect certain governmental activities from exposure to suit by private individuals." Discretionary immunity is designed "to prevent judicial 'second-guessing' of legislative and administrative decisions grounded in social, economic, and political policy through the medium of an action in tort." Other courts have said that the immunity's purpose is in "keeping the judiciary out of the business of reviewing policy judgments by government employees." *Shuler v. United States*, 531 F.3d 930 (D.C. Cir. 2008). Why prevent the judiciary from passing on the legality of the policy-based actions of the other branches of government?

2. **Planning-level versus operational-level decisions.** Courts once routinely drew immunity lines according to whether government decisions were made at the "planning level," in which case they immune, or at the "operational level," in which case they were not. But in *United States v. Gaubert*, 499 U.S. 315 (1991), the Court said, "It is the nature of the conduct, rather than the status of the actor, that governs whether the discretionary function exception applies in a given case." Thus a low-level government employee might select a course of action that would be considered discretionary, or a higher-level official might merely implement a policy, which would not be immunized from liability. But where higher-ups are exercising "judgment," the discretionary function immunity is likely to be found.

3. **"Maintenance" as discretionary?** The *Whisnant* court draws a distinction between the design of a policy (discretionary) and its implementation (not discretionary). Does this mean that the government's failure to

maintain property or buildings, for example, would never be protected by discretionary immunity? In *Terbush v. United States*, 516 F.3d 1125 (9th Cir. 2008), the court said that "matters of routine maintenance are not protected . . . because they generally do not involve policy-weighing decisions or actions." But the court added that "sometimes 'maintenance' is far from routine and may involve considerable discretion that invokes policy judgment." Especially where maintenance decisions require a federal agency "to prioritize among its repairs," or choose between maintenance and doing something else entirely, such decisions may implicate policy concerns. *Id.*

4. **Funding decisions as discretionary.** Is it relevant to a determination of the scope of discretionary immunity that a challenged governmental decision was based partially on fiscal concerns? Does the *Whisnant* court say it is not? *Cf. Merando v. United States*, 517 F.3d 160 (3d Cir. 2008) (suit against government for failing to find and remove a dead tree that fell on plaintiffs in national park).

5. **Where the government makes no conscious decision.** In some cases, the government pursues a course of action without having made any conscious decision, either of policy or otherwise. Occasionally courts have said that in such cases the discretionary immunity has no application, since no discretion was exercised. *Cf. Dube v. Pittsburgh Corning*, 870 F.2d 790 (1st Cir. 1989). But in *Gaubert*, *supra* Note 2, the Supreme Court used this language: "The focus of the inquiry is not on the agent's subjective intent in exercising the discretion conferred by statute or regulation, but on the nature of the actions taken and on whether they are susceptible to policy analysis." Does this language mean that immunity does not depend on whether the government actually made any conscious decision?

LOGE v. UNITED STATES, 662 F.2d 1268 (8th Cir. 1981). A federal agency licensed a drug company to manufacture a live-virus oral polio vaccine. A risk of such vaccines is that either a recipient or a person who comes in contact with "shed" virus could develop polio. Recognizing that risk, the agency promulgated regulations pertaining to the safety and potency of these strains, and required drug manufacturers to prove their product's conformity to these regulations before getting a license to manufacture. Mrs. Loge was exposed to the virus and rendered a paraplegic after a doctor inoculated her infant son. She filed an FTCA action alleging that the government was negligent (1) in not requiring the drug manufacturer to comply with the government's own regulations and (2) in licensing at all, or in licensing without additional safety regulations. *Held*, the first set of allegations state a claim under applicable state law and are not barred by the discretionary function immunity. The government "has no discretion to disregard the mandatory regulatory commands pertaining to criteria a vaccine must meet before licensing its manufacture or releasing a particular lot of vaccine for distribution to the public." However, "[i]nsofar as the Loges' amended complaint alleged that the government was negligent in promulgating or failing to promulgate regulations that would ensure the safety of live, oral poliovirus vaccines and properly protect susceptible persons such as Mrs. Loge, the district court correctly found that such actions by the government were discretionary functions and therefore immune from suit under FTCA."

NOTES

1. **Immunity for legislative inaction.** If a court could impose liability when Congress fails to enact safety legislation, courts, not elected members of the political branch, would have ultimate legislative control. Why would this be a problem?

2. **Violation of regulations.** Where there is a professional standard of safety incorporated in federal regulations, the government's violation of that standard is not discretionary and is actionable, according to *Loge*. This is somewhat anomalous, since the FTCA explicitly invokes *state* law as the basis of tort liability, and since the regulation is a federal one. How does this work?

3. **A case example.** A camper falls off an unmarked and unfenced cliff in a campground on government property managed by the Army Corps of Engineers. A federal regulation requires the government to manage its resources so as to "provide the public with safe and healthful recreational opportunities." The Army Corps' written safety plan for the area includes an instruction that "dangerous terrain conditions, such as drop-offs, etc., will be properly marked or fenced." What is the relevance of the safety plan and regulation, and on what basis could the government be held liable in such a case? *Navarette v. United States*, 500 F.3d 914 (9th Cir. 2007).

§ 3. IMMUNITIES UNDER STATE LAW

In our system of government, the states are sovereigns, too, subject only to the limitations of the United States Constitution. At one time the states claimed sovereign immunity on the same basis as did the federal government. Most states now have now enacted tort claims statutes that provide for at least a partial waiver of sovereign immunity. As a matter of structure, most states follow the federal model (often copying from the FTCA) and waive the tort immunity generally, retaining it in particular, specified situations. A smaller, but still significant number work in reverse, retaining the immunity generally but abolishing it in particular, specified situations. Both kinds of statutes do retain substantial blocks of immunity for the states. A small number retain virtually complete immunity. Most states have special procedural rules and remedial restrictions on tort claims against the state. *See* DOBBS ON TORTS § 268 (2000).

Municipalities within the states are sometimes covered under state tort claims statutes, so that municipal immunity parallels state government immunity. Other states have separate immunity rules for municipalities.

While generalization is difficult, a number of important issues recur in tort litigation against state and local entities under state law. Some of these issues parallel those faced in FTCA actions against the federal government; others are more or less unique to the non-federal setting—in part because of the different functions for which different levels of government are typically responsible.

RISS v. CITY OF NEW YORK

240 N.E.2d 860 (N.Y. 1968)

[Linda Riss was terrorized for months by a rejected suitor, one Pugach. He threatened to kill or maim her if she did not yield to him. She repeatedly sought protection from law enforcement officers. Eventually she became engaged to another man. At a party celebrating the event, she received a phone call warning her that it was her "last chance." She again called police, but nothing seems to have been done. The next day Pugach carried out his threat by having a person hired for the purpose to throw lye in Linda's face. She was blinded in one eye, lost a good portion of her vision in the other and suffered permanent scarring of her face. This is her action against the City of New York for failure to provide police protection. The trial court dismissed the complaint at the end of all the evidence and the Appellate Division affirmed.]

BREITEL, JUDGE.

This appeal presents, in a very sympathetic framework, the issue of the liability of a municipality for failure to provide special protection to a member of the public who was repeatedly threatened with personal harm and eventually suffered dire personal injuries for lack of such protection. . . .

It is necessary immediately to distinguish those liabilities attendant upon governmental activities which have displaced or supplemented traditionally private enterprises, such as are involved in the operation of rapid transit systems, hospitals, and places of public assembly. Once sovereign immunity was abolished by statute the extension of liability on ordinary principles of tort law logically followed. To be equally distinguished are certain activities of government which provide services and facilities for the use of the public, such as highways, public buildings and the like, in the performance of which the municipality or the State may be liable under ordinary principles of tort law. The ground for liability is the provision of the services or facilities for the direct use of members of the public. In contrast, this case involves the provision of a governmental service to protect the public generally from external hazards and particularly to control the activities of criminal wrongdoers.

The amount of protection that may be provided is limited by the resources of the community and by a considered legislative-executive decision as to how those resources may be deployed. For the courts to proclaim a new and general duty of protection in the law of tort, even to those who may be the particular seekers of protection based on specific hazards, could and would inevitably determine how the limited police resources of the community should be allocated and without predictable limits. This is quite different from the predictable allocation of resources and liabilities when public hospitals, rapid transit systems, or even highways are provided.

Before such extension of responsibilities should be dictated by the indirect imposition of tort liabilities, there should be a legislative determination that that should be the scope of public responsibility.

It is notable that the removal of sovereign immunity for tort liability was accomplished after legislative enactment and not by any judicial arrogation of power. It is equally notable that for many years, since as far back as 1909, in this State, there was by statute municipal liability for losses sustained as a result of riot. Yet even this class of liability has for some years been suspended by legislative action, a factor of considerable significance. When one considers the greatly increased amount of crime committed throughout the cities, but especially in certain portions of them, with a repetitive and predictable pattern, it is easy to see the consequences of fixing municipal liability upon a showing of probable need for and request for protection. To be sure these are grave problems at the present time, exciting high priority activity on the part of the national, State and local governments, to which the answers are neither simple, known, or presently within reasonable controls. To foist a presumed cure for these problems by judicial innovation of a new kind of liability in tort would be foolhardy indeed and an assumption of judicial wisdom and power not possessed by the courts.

Nor is the analysis progressed by the analogy to compensation for losses sustained. It is instructive that the Crime Victims Compensation and "Good Samaritan" statutes, compensating limited classes of victims of crime, were enacted only after the most careful study of conditions and the impact of such a scheme upon governmental operations and the public fisc. And then the limitations were particular and narrow.

For all of these reasons, there is no warrant in judicial tradition or in the proper allocation of the powers of government for the courts, in the absence of legislation, to carve out an area of tort liability for police protection to members of the public. Quite distinguishable, of course, is the situation where the police authorities undertake responsibilities to particular members of the public and expose them, without adequate protection, to the risks which then materialize into actual losses (Schuster v. City of New York, 5 N.Y.2d 75,180 N.Y.S.2d 265,154 N.E.2d 534).

Accordingly, the order of the Appellate Division affirming the judgment of dismissal should be affirmed.

DeLONG v. COUNTY OF ERIE, 457 N.E.2d 717 (N.Y. 1983). At 9:29 Mrs. DeLong called the 911 emergency number covering all cities and towns in Erie County, New York. She reported that someone was attempting to break in and gave her address. The "complaint writer" assured her someone would come right away. Since her own local police station in the town of Kenmore was only a block and a half away, assistance might have been readily available except for the fact that the complaint writer sent officers to an address in Buffalo instead of Kenmore. When the officers found "no such address," the complaint writer dropped the call as a "fake." In the meantime the burglar gained entrance and at 9:42 Mrs. DeLong was seen running from the house bleeding. She collapsed and died of stab wounds. A jury found for the plaintiff in a wrongful death action. *Held*, affirmed. Where police refuse assistance, there is an issue of how to allocate public resources and it should be left to the executive and legislative branches. But in this case "the decision had been made by the municipalities to provide a special emergency service...." There is, as defendants argue, a "familiar rule," that public entities are not liable for "negligence in the performance of a governmental function, including police and fire protection, unless a special relationship existed between the municipality and the injured party...." But here there is a special relationship between the city and the caller. The "victim's plea for assistance was not refused." The special relationship between the defendants and the caller required the defendants "to exercise ordinary care in the performance of a duty it has voluntarily assumed."

NOTES

1. In considering *Riss*, remember that New York had earlier abolished the state's sovereign immunity. Judge Breitel was obviously concerned about allocation of public resources by way of tort judgments. But *any* tort judgment against the city would allocate resources, including a judgment based on a city bus driver's negligence. Does the distinction between tort suits against the police department and those against the bus authority hold up?

2. Judge Breitel did not really say why the police in *Riss* refused assistance. He seemed to assume, however, that there was a professional reason bearing on resource allocation. Suppose that was not the case; suppose the police simply did not follow sound procedure, or made a clerical mistake and failed to record Miss Riss' call. Would the result be different?

3. The *DeLong* court stresses that a "special relationship" formed between the city and the victim because her plea for assistance was accepted, not refused. Would the case have come out differently, then, had the county negligently managed the entire 911 system and not answered any calls at all for several hours? Is it important whether the operator's assurances to the caller induced her reliance? *See Pelaez v. Seide*, 810 N.E.2d 393 (N.Y. 2004).

4. Can *DeLong* be seen as resting not on a "special relationship," but rather on the fact that no professional judgment at all was involved, only an operational mistake?

5. Does a "resource allocation" rationale for retaining immunity sweep too broadly? In *Zelig v. County of Los Angeles*, 45 P.3d 1171 (Cal. 2002), the court held that the county was not liable to the estate of a woman who was

killed by her husband in the county courthouse despite the county's knowledge that she was coming to court, that her husband had threatened her, and that he was under a court order not to bring guns into her presence. The court stressed that its holding, whether "expressed as a limitation on duty or as a form of governmental immunity," rested on the notion that "the level of police protection is an allocative question best left to the political branches." In *Barillari v. City of Milwaukee*, 533 N.W.2d 759 (Wis. 1995), the city was held immune from liability for the killing of a woman by her estranged boyfriend even though he had earlier sexually assaulted her and police had promised to protect her and to arrest him at a specific time when he was expected to come to her house. They failed to arrest him and did not tell her that he was still at large. Days later he murdered her and killed himself. The police "decisions" were discretionary, said the court: "The nature of law enforcement requires moment-to-moment decision making and crises management, which, in turn, requires that the police department have the latitude to decide how to best utilize law enforcement resources."

HARRY STOLLER AND CO. v. CITY OF LOWELL

587 N.E.2d 780 (Mass. 1992)

[The plaintiff's five brick buildings were destroyed by a fire which started on the sixth floor of one of them. A sprinkler system was in place and had been tested two days earlier. Firefighters, in violation of accepted practice, chose not to use it, fighting the fire with hoses instead. All five buildings and their contents were destroyed. After a jury awarded the plaintiff $785,000, the trial judge granted judgment NOV for the defendant under the state's statutory discretionary immunity. *Held*, reversed.]

WILKINS, J.

This court has declined to apply the discretionary function exception to a variety of governmental acts. A police officer deciding whether to remove from the roadways a motorist, known to be intoxicated, is not making a policy or planning judgment. A physician employed by a city is not engaged in a discretionary function, within the meaning of § 10(b), in her treatment of a patient in a hospital emergency room.... The failure to provide sufficient information to enable a person to protect his property against the conduct of a client of the Department of Mental Health does not involve the exercise of choice regarding public policy and planning but rather the carrying out of previously established policies or plans....

There are aspects of firefighting that can have an obvious planning or policy basis. The number and location of fire stations, the amount of equipment to purchase, the size of the fire department, the number and location of hydrants, and the quantity of the water supply involve policy considerations, especially the allocation of financial resources. In certain situations, firefighting involves determinations of what property to attempt to save because the resources available to combat a conflagration are or seem to be insufficient to save all threatened property. In such cases, policy determinations might be involved, and application of the discretionary function exception would be required.

The case before us is different. The negligent conduct that caused the fire to engulf all the plaintiff's buildings was not founded on planning or policy considerations. The question whether to put higher water pressure in the sprinkler systems involved no policy choice or planning decision. There was a dispute on the evidence whether it was negligent to fail to fight the fire through the buildings' sprinkler systems. The firefighters may have thought that they had a discretionary choice whether to pour water on the buildings through hoses or to put water inside the buildings through their sprinkler systems. They certainly had discretion in the sense that no statute, regulation, or established municipal practice required the firefighters to use the sprinklers (or, for that matter, to use hoses exclusively). But whatever discretion they had was not based on a policy or planning judgment. The jury decided that, in exercising their discretion not to use the buildings' sprinkler systems, the Lowell firefighters were negligent because they failed to conform to generally accepted firefighting practices. When the firefighters exercised that discretion, policy and planning considerations were not involved. Therefore, the discretionary function exception does not shield the city from liability. . . .

NOTES

1. As you can see from all of the cases in this section, courts are reluctant to second-guess fire and police departments in their decisions not to act. In line with *Riss*, New York has held that the fire department's failure to enforce a fire safety rule was not actionable on behalf of someone who suffered a fire loss that could have been avoided, and this was true even though the city had actual notice of the danger. *Motyka v. City of Amsterdam*, 204 N.E.2d 635 (N.Y. 1965). How then can we explain *Harry Stoller and Co.*? A few courts have imposed liability for failure to provide enforcement of fire safety laws. *Adams v. State*, 555 P.2d 235 (Alaska 1976). And statutes may impose a duty to enforce criminal law for the protection of potential victims, such as those subject to domestic violence. *See Roy v. City of Everett*, 823 P.2d 1084 (Wash. 1992).

2. Can you argue that where the governmental function is to provide safety or exercise care, the government has no discretion to act unsafely? *See* DOBBS ON TORTS § 270, at 721 (2000). Would the following cases support such an argument? *Brantley v. Department of Human Resources*, 523 S.E.2d 571 (Ga. 1999): A decision to leave a two-year-old child unattended in a swimming pool was not a policy decision but one of routine child care. No immunity was warranted. *Tadros v. City of Omaha*, 694 N.W.2d 180 (Neb. 2005): A city's decision to set a particular number of seconds on a crosswalk signal. No immunity. What about a school that fails to take any steps at all when one student is threatened by another? *See L.W. v. McComb Separate Mun. Sch. Dist.*, 754 So.2d 1136 (Miss. 1999).

3. Many states' statutes contain discretionary immunity provisions, although state-court interpretations are not always identical those seen in the

FTCA case law. *See, e.g., Commonwealth v. Sexton*, 256 S.W.3d 29 (Ky. 2008) (state was immune from suit over failure to inspect and remove dead tree, since such activity was not "ministerial"); *Schroeder v. St. Louis County*, 708 N.W.2d 497 (Minn. 2006) (county has discretionary immunity where there has been a "planning-level decision" but not where there has been an "operational-level" decision; here a decision to permit gravel road graters to operate against traffic was a planning-level decision); *Garrison v. Deschutes County*, 48 P.3d 807 (Or. 2002) (discretionary immunity determined by looking at whether "the decision is the result of a choice among competing policy considerations, made at the appropriate level of government").

4.   A number of state statutes allow governmental entities to be sued when harm results from a defect in government property. *See, e.g., Bonanno v. Central Contra Costa Transit Auth.*, 65 P.3d 807 (Cal. 2003) (location of a bus stop). This often extends to negligently-maintained traffic lights or signage. The government will face liability for failure to correct the problem where that failure is a cause of harm. See, e.g., *Twomey v. Commonwealth*, 825 N.E.2d 989 (Mass. 2005) (traffic sign obscured by bushes); *Hensley v. Jackson County*, 227 S.W.3d 491 (Mo. 2007) (downed stop sign); *Fickle v. State*, 735 N.W.2d 754 (Neb. 2007) (malfunctioning traffic light). Would you expect liability where the suit alleged a negligent failure to install a traffic signal at an intersection? *See Kohl v. City of Phoenix*, 160 P.3d 170 (Ariz. 2007).

5.   High-speed police chases produce a good deal of litigation when innocent bystanders are injured. *See* DOBBS ON TORTS § 272, at 730 (2000). What is the best way to handle such cases? Some states provide a specific complete immunity, often by statute. *See, e.g., Colvin v. City of Gardena*, 15 Cal.Rptr.2d 234 (Ct. App. 1992). Others judge the case according to an ordinary negligence analysis, taking into account the importance of the particular arrest attempt and the degree of risk the chase imposes or does not impose upon others. *See, e.g., Gooden v. City of Talladega*, 966 So.2d 232 (Ala. 2007). Some lower the standard of care so that liability is permitted only when the police officer has acted recklessly or worse. *See, e.g., City of Winder v. McDougald*, 583 S.E.2d 879 (Ga. 2003).

In some cases, courts engage in a discretionary immunity analysis. What constitutes "discretion" in this context is a contested issue. For example, in *Pletan v. Gaines*, 494 N.W.2d 38 (Minn. 1992), the court found "official immunity," which "involves the kind of discretion which is exercised on an operational rather than a policymaking level. . . . The decision to engage in a car chase and to continue the chase involves the weighing of many factors. . . . It is difficult to think of a situation where the exercise of significant, independent judgment and discretion would be more required." But in *Clark v. South Carolina Dept. of Public Safety*, 608 S.E.2d 573 (S.C. 2005), the court held that a law enforcement officer may not invoke discretionary immunity "for the decision on whether to begin or continue the immediate pursuit of a subject." For the discretionary immunity to attach, the *Clark* court said, the "governmental entity must prove its employees, faced with alternatives, actually weighed competing considerations and made a conscious choice," utilizing "accepted professional standards appropriate to resolve the issue." Might discretionary immunity attach to a policy decision to allow police officers to run red lights, but not to the officer's individual decision to do so during a chase? *See Smith v. Burdette,* 566 S.E.2d 614 (W.Va. 2002).

6. The decision to release a dangerous person from custody, such as a violent mental patient or a violent criminal, is typically regarded as "discretionary," both in state and federal cases. *E.g., Payton v. United States,* 679 F.2d 475 (5th Cir. 1982). Some states provide specific statutory immunity. *See, e.g.,* CAL. GOV. CODE § 845.8 (no liability for "parole or release of a prisoner"). A few courts impose liability for a negligent or reckless release. *See Faile v. South Carolina Dep't of Juvenile Justice,* 566 S.E.2d 536 (S.C. 2002) (no discretionary immunity if officer who placed violent juvenile back with his parents did so with gross negligence); *Grimm v. Arizona Bd. of Pardons & Paroles,* 564 P.2d 1227 (Ariz. 1977). However, even where the *decision to release* is immunized, a number of cases impose a duty of care on government officials to *supervise* parolees. *See, e.g., Starkenburg v. State,* 934 P.2d 1018 (Mont. 1997). Other states limit such a duty to those situations where officials knew or should have known that the parolee posed a danger to a particular individual or identifiable group. *State Dept. of Corrections v. Cowles,* 151 P.3d 353 (Alaska 2006). *Cf. Osborn v. Mason County,* 134 P.3d 197 (Wash. 2006) (no duty to warn of offender's release where victim was not "foreseeable" and there was no reliance); *Thompson v. County of Alameda,* 614 P.2d 728 (Cal. 1980) (no duty to warn of the release of an inmate "who has made nonspecific threats of harm directed at nonspecific victims").

NOTE: THE PUBLIC DUTY DOCTRINE

1. The public duty doctrine is formally different from discretionary immunity. The public duty doctrine holds that public entities and officers are not liable to individuals for failure to carry out a duty, even a statutory duty, owed to the public at large rather than to particular individuals or groups. *See, e.g., DeSmet v. County of Rock Island,* 848 N.E.2d 1030 (Ill. 2006). For example, some courts hold that a public entity is not liable for a police officer's failure to arrest a drunk driver who, left free, drunkenly injures or kills others. *Ezell v. Cockrell,* 902 S.W.2d 394 (Tenn. 1995). Perhaps the most important effect of the doctrine is that statutes commanding action by public entities or officers are frequently construed to impose public duties only, so that no private person can recover for a public officer's failure to enforce the statute. *See, e.g., Ware v. City of Chicago,* 873 N.E.2d 944 (Ill. App. Ct. 2007) (no duty to enforce building code in case involving collapse of porch).

2. The public duty doctrine can differ from the discretionary immunity not only in adopting the language of duty but also in recognizing that the duty may be narrowed and liability imposed if the officer or entity takes affirmative action that endangers the plaintiff or if the duty becomes individualized because of a special relationship with the plaintiff. *See, e.g., Eklund v. Trost,* 151 P.3d 870 (Mont. 2006) (special duty owed to pedestrian injured in high speed chase). In other words, the traditional rule about nonaction: the officer is not liable for failure to arrest a drunk, but he is liable if he himself causes injury by driving negligently. *See Hetzel v. United States,* 43 F.3d 1500 (D.C. Cir. 1995). This is essentially a specific

application of rules about nonaction, explored in more depth in Chapter 16.

3. In *Caulfield v. Kitsap County,* 29 P.3d 738 (Wash. App. Ct. 2001) the county undertook to provide home care for a profoundly disabled adult with multiple-sclerosis but failed take any steps to do so. Horrible injuries resulted to the plaintiff, who could not feed or turn himself. The county argued it had no duty, but the court said that the public duty doctrine did not apply partly because one "exception arises where (1) there is direct contact or privity between the governmental agency and the plaintiff 'which sets the latter apart from the general public, and (2) there are express assurances given by a public official [or agency], which (3) gives rise to justifiable reliance on the part of the plaintiff.' "

4. In addition, a statute might create a special duty to a particular group rather than to the public at large. In that case, the court may conclude that the statutory duty is not merely a duty owed to the public at large. For example, a statute creating a specific duty to protect victims of domestic violence may be construed to impose a duty to a special group, so that a failure to provide the protection required will be actionable. *See Calloway v. Kinkelaar,* 659 N.E.2d 1322 (Ill. 1995) (liability for willful or wanton misconduct of the police in failing to protect).

5. In spite of what has been said above, a number of courts have verbally identified the public duty doctrine with discretionary immunity. For instance, Rhode Island expresses the doctrine in terms of discretionary immunity by saying that it "shields the state and its political subdivisions from tort liability arising out of discretionary governmental actions that by their nature are not ordinarily performed by private persons." Stated this way, the doctrine sounds like a discretionary immunity that could protect affirmative action as well as a failure to act. Yet Rhode Island also recognizes that a special relationship between public officer and individual plaintiff may eliminate the immunity. *See Schultz v. Foster–Glocester Reg'l Sch. Dist.,* 755 A.2d 153 (R.I. 2000).

6. Do we need a public duty doctrine? If it is a matter of construing the statute, it is not a doctrine at all but merely a matter of construing each statute as it arises. If it is independent of the legislature's intent, why should courts add this additional immunity to the discretionary immunity that already exists?

PROBLEM

Claims of Picklesimer, et al.

[Memo from partner in charge of the case.]

Since the initial memo [Chapter 12 § 6, *supra*], I have talked with an engineer who says that the highway design at the point of the accident was dangerous. He is quite specific. The highway appears to be a state highway rather than a local road. Can we sue the state for this, assuming the testimony really does support the claim of negligence? Would it matter whether we claimed (1) failure to mark the road, (2) failure to provide warning signs, (3) the design of the curve or the slope? Also, would our claim against Dalzell prejudice a claim against the state or vice versa?

§ 4. OFFICERS

STATE v. SECOND JUDICIAL DISTRICT COURT, COUNTY OF WASHOE, 55 P.3d 420 (Nev. 2002). A 14-month-old girl had serious medical problems. Based on allegations that she was neglected, the state removed her from her biological parents' care. While in the care of her foster parents, a 15-year-old babysitter fed her a hot dog and the girl choked and died. The biological mother sued the state, individual state employees, and others. The defendants argued that they were absolutely immune in the same way that judges and legislators would be for injuries caused in the course of their work. The trial court refused to dismiss the plaintiff's claim. *Held,* affirmed. "State employees engaged in child protective services are entitled to quasi-judicial immunity when they provide information to the court (*e.g.,* reports, case plans, testing evaluations and recommendations) pertaining to a child who is or may become a ward of the State. . . . When a state agency or its employees provide their decision-making expertise to the court, they act as an arm of the court and are entitled to absolute quasi-judicial immunity. However, once the court makes a decision ratifying the recommendations of the state agency (*e.g.,* placement in foster care, need for further medical evaluation, etc.), the state agency and its employees are no longer acting as an arm of the court. Rather, their function in carrying out the order of the court falls within the executive branch of government and pursuant to their statutory duties. Specifically, quasi-judicial immunity does not apply to state agencies or their employees for the day-to-day management and care of their wards." Thus in this case, the defendants are not entitled to quasi-judicial immunity against an allegation of negligence for their conduct after the district court's order made the child a ward of the state.

NOTES

1. **Absolute immunity for judicial and legislative officers.** Judicial and legislative officers are traditionally given absolute immunity under the common law, so long as they are acting with jurisdiction and in their judicial or legislative capacity. The rule applies both to state and federal officers. Thus both state and federal judges are absolutely immune in their judicial work. The immunity also applies whether the claim is based on ordinary state tort law or on federal civil rights claims.

2. **Quasi-judicial immunity.** As the *County of Washoe* case indicates, this absolute immunity may extend to people who are not actually "officers," but this extension is not absolute. In *Butz v. Economou*, 438 U.S. 478 (1978), the Court listed three factors that could support extending absolute judicial immunity to non-judicial officers: (1) whether the official in question performed functions sufficiently comparable to those of officials who have tradi-

tionally been afforded absolute immunity at common law; (2) whether the likelihood of harassment or intimidation by personal liability was sufficiently great to interfere with the official's performance of his or her duties; and (3) whether procedural safeguards exist in the system that would adequately protect against unconstitutional conduct by the official.

3. **Further extending the quasi-judicial immunity.** Some courts have gone further than the Nevada court in *County of Washoe* by protecting pre-and post-adjudication decisions by social workers. In *Beltran v. Santa Clara County*, 514 F.3d 906 (9th Cir. 2008), the court said that social workers had absolute immunity when they make "quasi-prosecutorial" decisions such as to institute dependency proceedings or to remove a child from parents, but no absolute immunity for investigatory conduct.

VAUGHN v. RUOFF

253 F.3d 1124 (8th Cir. 2001)

VIETOR, SENIOR DISTRICT J. . . .

The summary judgment record discloses the following facts, which are either undisputed or viewed in a light most favorable to the Vaughns. Margaret and Kevin Sr. are married and have children. Margaret has been diagnosed as mildly retarded. On August 19, 1993, Margaret gave birth to the couple's first child, a daughter named Leta. Leta was born with various health problems that required ongoing medical care. On October 27, 1993, the Missouri Division of Family Services ("MDFS") took custody of Leta, finding that the Vaughns failed to maintain a sanitary home and could not demonstrate an ability to rear her properly.

After Leta's birth, Ruoff, the social service worker assigned to the Vaughns' case, counseled Margaret on birth control options. Margaret agreed to be and was injected with Depo Provera, a prescription medication contraceptive delivered intravenously. Margaret, however, became pregnant again. On August 19, 1994, Margaret gave birth to the couple's second child, a son named Kevin Jr. On August 26, 1994, MDFS took custody of Kevin Jr., finding unsanitary home conditions and an inability on the part of the Vaughns to rear him properly.

While Margaret was pregnant with Kevin Jr., Ruoff broached the subject of sterilization with the Vaughns. The same day as, but after, Kevin Jr.'s birth, and while Margaret was still in the hospital, Ruoff told Margaret that if she got her "tubes tied, that [she] would have [her] kids back in two to three weeks." Ruoff also told both Margaret and Kevin Sr. that "if [he] or [Margaret] would get sterilized, [their] chances of getting the kids back would be really great." Margaret then agreed to a tubal ligation, and Ruoff scheduled the procedure for October 3, 1994. [Ruoff made all the arrangements and the ligation was performed as scheduled.] On December 28, 1994, MDFS informed the Vaughns that it would recommend termination of their parental rights to both Leta and Kevin Jr.

Ruoff argues that she is entitled to qualified immunity on the Vaughns' due process claims. Qualified immunity analysis initially asks the following two questions: (1) was there a deprivation of a constitutional right, and, if so, (2) was the right clearly established at the time of the deprivation?...

We begin by determining whether Margaret possessed a protected liberty interest under the Fourteenth Amendment. U.S. Const. amend. XIV, § 1 ("[N]or shall any State deprive any person of life, liberty, or property, without due process of law...."). It is clear that she did because a personal decision relating to procreation or contraception is a protected liberty interest. All persons, including the mentally handicapped, possess this liberty interest.

The next issue is whether Ruoff's conduct violated Margaret's due process rights. We hold that it did. Before the State may deprive an individual of a protected liberty interest, the Due Process Clause requires the State to provide certain procedural protections [including notice and opportunity to be heard before termination of the liberty interest.]

Ruoff disputes that she deprived Margaret of her protected liberty interest.... [W]e conclude that the evidence could support a finding that Ruoff coerced Margaret into submitting to sterilization. A jury could reasonably find that Ruoff's comments about getting the two children back implied that the children would not be returned to the Vaughns if they did not agree to sterilization. A jury could properly conclude from such a finding that Margaret's sterilization decision was not voluntary but rather was coerced, and this, we hold, implicates due process concerns.

It is undisputed that Margaret was not given any procedural protections before the sterilization occurred. Ruoff argues that even without procedural protections, the sterilization was justified. It is true that involuntary sterilization is not always unconstitutional if it is a narrowly tailored means to achieve a compelling government interest.... It does not follow, however, that the State can dispense with procedural protections, coerce an individual into sterilization, and then after the fact argue that it was justified. If it did, it would invite conduct, like that alleged in this case, that is ripe for abuse and error.... Sterilization results in the irreversible loss of one of a person's most fundamental rights, a loss that must be preceded by procedural protections. Ruoff's conduct violated Margaret's Due Process Clause right to be free from coerced sterilization without appropriate procedures.

The last issue is whether the unconstitutionality of Ruoff's alleged conduct was clearly established at the time it occurred. We hold that it was. To be clearly established, the right's contours "must be sufficiently clear that a reasonable official would understand that what [s]he is doing violates that right." There is no requirement that "the very action in question has previously been held unlawful," but rather, "in the light of pre-existing law the unlawfulness must be apparent." We subscribe to a broad view of the concept of clearly established law, and we look to all available decisional law, including decisions from other courts, federal and state, when there is no binding precedent in this circuit. Even in the complete absence of any decisions involving similar facts, a right can be clearly established if a reasonable public official would have known her conduct was unconstitutional.

We have not found any cases with facts similar to those in this case. This does not, however, carry the day for Ruoff. Numerous pre-1994 cases show that minimum procedures regularly precede state compelled sterilizations, and some clearly establish that pre-sterilization procedures are constitutionally required. Furthermore, any reasonable social worker—indeed, any reasonable person, social worker or not—would have known that a sterilization is compelled, not voluntary, if it is consented to under the coercive threat of losing one's children, and hence unconstitutional.

The district court did not err in denying qualified immunity to Ruoff on the Vaughns' due process claims. We affirm.

NOTES

1. Distinguish the two questions in this case: (a) Was a constitutional right violated? And (b) Was the right established before the defendant acted?

2. The claimed coercion is relevant to both questions, isn't it? On the constitutional right itself, suppose the Family Services department in fact would keep the children unless it could be assured that the parents would have no more children and that such a decision would be within its constitutional power. In that case, wouldn't it be in fact desirable to reveal the agency's standards to citizens affected by them?

3. The constitutional right itself takes us a bit afield; our concern is with the qualified immunity. As the court in *Vaughn* says, that turns on whether the constitutional right was established clearly enough that a reasonable official would understand that her conduct violated that right. But how could Ruoff have known that revealing the department's standards would count as coercion unless she also knew that those standards were themselves unconstitutional?

4. When state or local executive officers are sued under federal civil rights laws, federal courts apply a qualified immunity. They sometimes characterize it as a good faith immunity, but that is misleading, because the test is objective rather than subjective. That is, the officer can be held liable in spite of his personal good faith if a reasonable officer would have known that the plaintiff's constitutional rights were impaired by the action in question. *Harlow v. Fitzgerald*, 457 U.S. 800 (1982). Conversely, though, the officer is immune if decisions at the time he acted had not established the right the plaintiff now asserts. *See, e.g., Burella v. City of Philadelphia*, 501 F.3d 134 (3d Cir. 2007) (immunity for police officers where there was no clearly established due process right to the enforcement of restraining orders).

5. What if a state or local executive branch officer is sued under state law? Under the common law, state or local officers did not share the sovereign immunity of the states themselves. If their conduct is characterized by the

court as ministerial, something about which they have no choice or discretion, they may be held liable for torts. *E.g., Morway v. Trombly*, 789 A.2d 965 (Vt. 2001) (operating a snow plow is ministerial and operator is personally liable if he is negligent). If their acts are characterized as discretionary, they are protected by a qualified immunity, that is, by an immunity destructible by improper purpose or "malice." These tests leave much room for litigation. Instead of a discretionary immunity, some states now (a) remove some or all of the immunity but provide indemnity to the officer for cost of defense and amount of any judgment against him; *see, e.g.,* N.J. STAT. ANN. § 59:10–1; or (b) grant a very broad immunity and leave the plaintiff a direct claim against the state for the officer's torts. *See Martin v. Brady,* 802 A.2d 814 (Conn. 2002).

NOTE: FEDERAL EXECUTIVE BRANCH OFFICERS

Suits under federal law. Section 1983 has no application to federal officers unless they happen to be acting under color of state law. There is no statute comparable to § 1983 granting a claim against federal officers acting under color of *federal* law. However, in *Bivens v. Six Unknown Named Agents of Federal Bureau of Narcotics,* 403 U.S. 388 (1971), the Court held that federal officers could be sued for constitutional violations directly under the Constitution. There is no general absolute immunity in such cases. The federal officer has a qualified immunity, which is lost only if (1) the facts alleged show that the officer violated a constitutional right, and (2) the right was so clearly established that a reasonable official would have known the conduct violated the constitution. *See, e.g., Lombardi v. Whitman,* 485 F.3d 73 (2d Cir. 2007).

Suits under state law. Where the federal officer is sued under *state* law, older authority afforded an absolute immunity for discretionary decisions, an immunity not destroyed by malice or improper purpose. This was true not only with judicial officers acting within their jurisdiction and with members of Congress doing legislative business, but also with executive officers acting within the "outer perimeter" of the scope of their duties. *Barr v. Matteo,* 360 U.S. 564 (1959). This may still be the law. The clearest case for the plaintiff against a federal officer is therefore the claim that he violated the federal Constitution rather than state law. This would invoke the rules stated in the above paragraph.

The FTCA immunity. If a plaintiff claims that the federal officer was negligent in a case where no discretion is involved, the officer is given an immunity by the Federal Tort Claims Act (FTCA), leaving the plaintiff's sole claim against the government as an entity. The FTCA, pursuant to an amendment known as the Westfall Act, now explicitly provides that when the plaintiff sues a federal employee, the attorney general may certify that the acts of the employee were within the scope of his federal employment. When such a certificate is presented to the court, the court must dismiss the suit against the allegedly negligent employee. The plaintiff may proceed against the United States alone, subject to all the limitations of the FTCA. *Osborn v. Haley,* 549 U.S. 225 (2007).

Suppose the plaintiff is injured by a negligent U.S. federal agent in Italy or Colombia. The attorney general presents a certificate that the employee was within the scope of employment at the time. Since the United States retains immunity for negligent acts committed outside this country, has Congress deprived the plaintiff of her claim both against the government and the individual tortfeasor? *United States v. Smith*, 499 U.S. 160 (1991) (yes). Any doubts about the justice, policy, or constitutionality of this statute? The Supreme Court has left the plaintiff a tiny possibility: the plaintiff can seek judicial review of the attorney general's determination. *Gutierrez de Martinez v. Lamagno*, 515 U.S. 417 (1995). If the court concludes that the attorney general was wrong and that the federal employee was not within the scope of his employment, then the plaintiff could sue the employee because the Westfall Act's immunity would not apply.

§ 5. STATE AND MUNICIPAL LIABILITY UNDER § 1983

Although state and municipal immunities have been widely abrogated or limited, considerable immunity remains, as the cases in preceding sections show. These immunities lead plaintiffs to assert federal civil rights claims against states and municipalities in hopes of avoiding any immunity.

State liability under § 1983. The Eleventh Amendment, as construed, provides that citizens cannot subject states to federal court suits against their will. In addition, the Supreme Court has held that states are not "persons" who can be sued under § 1983. *Will v. Michigan Dep't of State Police*, 491 U.S. 58 (1989). Although state officers may be sued for acts done in the course of their official duties, a judgment against the officer cannot serve as a basis for reaching the state's funds. *See Hafer v. Melo*, 502 U.S. 21 (1991).

Liability of municipalities under § 1983. It is now settled that municipalities are "persons" who may be liable under § 1983. There are two peculiarities about this, however. First, the municipality is liable only if the right is violated because of some "policy" or custom of the municipality. *Monell v. Department of Social Serv.*, 436 U.S. 658 (1978). It is not liable, in other words, for the casual derelictions of the police officer on the beat, but is liable for denial of a due process hearing to accused employees. Second, the municipality, unlike the officer, is not entitled to a good faith defense. *Owen v. City of Independence*, 445 U.S. 622 (1980).

NAVARRO v. BLOCK

72 F.3d 712 (9th Cir. 1995)

PREGERSON, CIRCUIT JUDGE....

At 10:30 p.m. on August 27, 1989, Maria Navarro was celebrating her birthday with her relatives and friends in her home in East Los Angeles when she received a telephone call from the brother of her estranged husband, Raymond Navarro, warning her that Raymond was on his way to her house to kill her and any others present.

Maria immediately dialed 911 to request emergency assistance. She told the 911 dispatcher that she had just received a warning that her estranged husband was on his way to kill her, that she believed that he was in fact on his way to kill her, and that he was under a restraining order.

When Maria stated that her estranged husband had not yet arrived, but that she believed he would definitely come to her house, the dispatcher responded, "O.K., well, the only thing to do is just call us if he comes over there. . . . I mean, what can we do? We can't have a unit sit there to wait and see if he comes over."

Fifteen minutes after the 911 call, Raymond Navarro entered through the rear of Maria Navarro's house, shot and killed Maria Navarro and four other people, and injured two others.

[The Navarros filed suit against Los Angeles County and the Sheriff, who handled 911 calls. The trial court granted summary judgment for the defendants on all claims.]

Under Monell v. Dept. of Social Services, 436 U.S. 658, 691 (1978), municipalities may not be held liable under 42 U.S.C. § 1983 "unless action pursuant to official municipal policy of some nature caused a constitutional tort." The Supreme Court made clear that in addition to an official policy, a municipality may be sued for "constitutional deprivations visited pursuant to governmental 'custom' even though such custom has not received formal approval through the [governmental] body's official decisionmaking channels."

Proof of random acts or isolated events is insufficient to establish custom. But a plaintiff may prove "the existence of a custom or informal policy with evidence of repeated constitutional violations for which the errant municipal officials were not discharged or reprimanded." Once such a showing is made, a municipality may be liable for its custom "irrespective of whether official policy-makers had actual knowledge of the practice at issue."

The Navarros claim that the County carried out a policy and practice of not treating 911 requests for assistance relating to domestic violence as "emergency" calls. The Navarros rely primarily on the deposition of Helen Pena, the 911 dispatcher who answered Maria Navarro's call. In her deposition, Helen Pena testified that it was the practice of the Sheriff's Department not to classify domestic violence 911 calls as Code 2 or "emergency procedure" calls. Ms. Pena also testified that dispatchers were not instructed to treat domestic violence calls as emergencies, that there were no clearly delineated guidelines for responding to domestic violence calls, and that as such, the dispatchers were allowed to exercise unbridled discretion.

... Because there was no conclusive evidence that the Sheriff's Department has a policy of refusing to send a squad car to non-domestic crimes not yet in progress, or of only treating crimes in progress as emergencies, a practice of not treating domestic crimes as emergencies may have been the cause of the failure to send a squad car to assist Navarro.

... [T]he district court erred in concluding that there were no genuine issues of material fact as to whether the County had a policy or custom of not classifying domestic violence calls as an "emergency."

The County argues that even assuming that it had a policy of affording victims of domestic violence less police protection than other crime victims, there was no evidence that discrimination against women was a motivating factor behind the administration of the alleged policy.

The Equal Protection Clause of the Fourteenth Amendment states: "No State shall ... deny to any person within its jurisdiction the equal protection of the laws." Gender-based classifications must pass the "intermediate scrutiny" test, i.e., the classification "must serve important governmental objectives and must be substantially related to achievement of those objectives."

The Navarros contend that the County's custom of treating domestic violence 911 calls differently from non-domestic violence calls impermissibly discriminates against abused women. The custom of according different treatment to victims of domestic violence is gender-neutral on its face. However, it is well established that discriminatory application of a facially neutral law also offends the Constitution.

Nevertheless, a long line of Supreme Court cases make clear that the Equal Protection Clause requires proof of discriminatory intent or motive.

... In the present case ... aside from the conclusory allegation that the County's custom of not classifying domestic violence calls as an emergency discriminates against abused women, the Navarros have failed to offer any evidence of such invidious intent or motive.

Nevertheless, even absent evidence of gender discrimination, the Navarros' equal protection claim still survives because they could prove that the domestic violence/non-domestic violence classification fails even the rationality test. Unless a statute employs a classification that is inherently invidious (such as race or gender), or that impinges on fundamental rights, we exercise only limited review. At a minimum, however, the Supreme Court "consistently has required that legislation classify the persons it affects in a manner rationally related to legitimate governmental objectives." Although we may not substitute our personal notions of good public policy for those of the legislature, the rational-basis standard is "not a toothless one."

Because the district court did not review the rationality of the County's domestic violence/non-domestic violence classification, we remand for a proper determination.

The Navarros also contend that the Sheriff's failure to train dispatchers on how to handle 911 domestic violence calls, and to instruct dispatchers to treat such calls in the same manner as they treat non-domestic violence calls, amounts to deliberate indifference to the equal protection rights of abused women. However, the Navarros fail to offer any evidence to support these claims.... Accordingly, we affirm the district court's conclusion that the Navarros' deliberate indifference claim fails to survive summary judgment.

For the foregoing reasons, we (1) affirm the district court's conclusion that the Navarros have failed to provide sufficient evidence to defeat summary judgment on their claim of deliberate indifference to constitutional rights arising from a failure to train 911 dispatchers; and (2) reverse the district court's grant of summary judgment on the Navarros' equal protection claim because genuine issues of material fact remain as to whether the County had a custom of not classifying domestic violence 911 calls as "emergencies." On remand, if the Navarros prove the existence of a discriminatory custom against victims of domestic violence, the district court must review the rationality of such a custom.

AFFIRMED in part, and REVERSED and REMANDED in part.

NOTES

1. A city's failure to train can constitute a "deliberate indifference to the rights of persons with whom the police come into contact," that amounts to a city policy so that the *Monell* rule is satisfied. *City of Canton v. Harris*, 489 U.S. 378 (1989). However, the city is still not liable unless its policy is one that violates an identifiable constitutional right. *Collins v. City of Harker Heights*, 503 U.S. 115 (1992).

2. On remand of the *Navarro* case, the trial judge concluded that the sheriff's policy excluded domestic violence cases because they were usually cases of violence-not-in-progress and that it was rational to give not-in-progress cases a lower priority than cases in which violence had already begun. On second appeal, however, the Ninth Circuit held that, at the pleading stage, domestic violence calls could not be equated with not-in-progress calls because some domestic violence calls could involve violence in progress. "Nothing in the pleadings suggests that victims of domestic violence are less likely to suffer severe injury or death than are victims of other 9–1–1 emergency crimes." The case was remanded again "for a hearing to determine first, whether the city had a policy or custom of giving lower priority to domestic violence calls than to non-domestic violence calls, and second, if such a policy or custom exists, whether that policy or custom has a rational basis." *Fajardo v. City of Los Angeles*, 179 F.3d 698 (9th Cir. 1999).

3. Other domestic violence claims have not fared so well. In *Town of Castle Rock v. Gonzales*, 545 U.S. 748 (2005), a wife sued the city and police officers under § 1983 for failing to enforce a domestic abuse restraining order against her husband, claiming violation of Fourteenth Amendment Due

Process rights. The court held that she did not show a protected property interest in the enforcement of the restraining order, in part because state law did not make such enforcement mandatory. "[A] benefit is not a protected entitlement if government officials may grant or deny it in their discretion."

GENERAL REFERENCE: DOBBS ON TORTS §§ 260–278 (2000); LESTER S. JAYSON & ROBERT C. LONGSTRETH, HANDLING FEDERAL TORT CLAIMS (2007).

TOPIC B

RELATIONSHIPS OR THEIR ABSENCE: NONACTION, CONTRACT AND PROTECTION FROM OTHERS

■ ■ ■

CHAPTER 16

NONFEASANCE

■ ■ ■

§ 1. THE NO DUTY TO ACT RULE

"Dawson was standing at the window of his third-floor apartment when he saw a woman on the sidewalk below. The woman later proved to be Mrs. Perrera. A man approached her, took out a knife, and appeared to demand her purse. She resisted somewhat, and the man grabbed the purse. Dawson's telephone was within reach but he did not use it. The man did not depart after taking the woman's purse, but began some kind of verbal altercation. She tried to run, but he grabbed her and began to beat her. Dawson continued to watch as he beat her to death, perhaps as long a ten minutes. This is a wrongful death action brought by Perrera's family against Dawson. The allegation is that he could have prevented her death without danger to himself by calling 911. Taking this allegation to be true, the trial judge upheld Dawson's motion to dismiss the claim. We must affirm."

The "case" above is fictional but true to life and to legal traditions. Under the general common law rule, one person owes another no duty to take active or affirmative steps for the other's protection. A defendant is generally subject to liability for misfeasance (negligence in doing something active)—but not for nonfeasance (doing nothing). *See* RESTATEMENT (SECOND) OF TORTS § 314, Ill. (1965); DOBBS ON TORTS § 314 (2000). In this chapter, consider: (1) Is the distinction between misfeasance and nonfeasance meaningful? (2) If the distinction is useful, is it right to say that liability is not imposed for nonfeasance? (3) What are the exceptions to the no liability rule?

YANIA v. BIGAN

155 A.2d 343 (Pa. 1959)

BENJAMIN R. JONES, JUSTICE . . . .

On September 25, 1957, John E. Bigan was engaged in a coal strip-mining operation in Shade Township, Somerset County. On the property being stripped were large cuts or trenches created by Bigan when he

437

removed the earthen overburden for the purpose of removing the coal underneath. One cut contained water 8 to 10 feet in depth with side walls or embankments 16 to 18 feet in height; at this cut Bigan had installed a pump to remove the water.

At approximately 4 p.m. on that date, Joseph F. Yania, the operator of another coal strip-mining operation and one Boyd M. Ross went upon Bigan's property for the purpose of discussing a business matter with Bigan, and, while there, were asked by Bigan to aid him in starting the pump. Ross and Bigan entered the cut and stood at the point where the pump was located. Yania stood at the top of the cut's side walls and then jumped from the side wall—a height of 16 to 18 feet—into the water and was drowned.

Yania's widow, in her own right and on behalf of her three children, instituted wrongful death and survival actions against Bigan contending Bigan was responsible for Yania's death. [The trial judge sustained preliminary objections in the nature of demurrers.]

... Appellant initially contends that Yania's descent from the high embankment into the water and the resulting death were caused "entirely" by the spoken words and blandishments of Bigan delivered at a distance from Yania. The complaint does not allege that Yania slipped or that he was pushed or that Bigan made any *physical* impact upon Yania. On the contrary, the only inference deductible from the facts alleged in the complaint is that Bigan, by the employment of cajolery and inveiglement, caused such a *mental* impact on Yania that the latter was deprived of his volition and freedom of choice and placed under a compulsion to jump into the water. Had Yania been a child of tender years or a person mentally deficient then it is conceivable that taunting and enticement could constitute actionable negligence if it resulted in harm. However, to contend that such conduct directed to an adult in full possession of all his mental faculties constitutes actionable negligence is not only without precedent but completely without merit.

Lastly, it is urged that Bigan failed to take the necessary steps to rescue Yania from the water. The mere fact that Bigan saw Yania in a position of peril in the water imposed upon him no legal, although a moral, obligation or duty to go to his rescue unless Bigan was legally responsible, in whole or in part, for placing Yania in the perilous position. Restatement, Torts, § 314. Cf. Restatement, Torts, § 322.... The complaint does not aver any facts which impose upon Bigan legal responsibility for placing Yania in the dangerous position in the water and, absent such legal responsibility, the law imposes on Bigan no duty of rescue.

Recognizing that the deceased Yania is entitled to the benefit of the presumption that he was exercising due care and extending to appellant the benefit of every well pleaded fact in this complaint and the fair inferences arising therefrom, yet we can reach but one conclusion: that Yania, a reasonable and prudent adult in full possession of all his mental faculties, undertook to perform an act which he knew or should have known was attended with more or less peril and it was the performance of that act and not any conduct upon Bigan's part which caused his unfortunate death.

Order affirmed.

NOTES

1. **Nonfeasance versus misfeasance.** *Newton v. Ellis*, 5 El. & Bl. 115, 119 Eng. Rep. 424 (K.B. 1855), is perhaps the classic case attempting to draw a distinction between nonfeasance and misfeasance. The Local Board of Health contracted with defendant to dig certain wells in the road. Defendant did so, leaving unlighted excavations at night. The plaintiff's carriage was drawn into the unlighted hole and he was injured. Plaintiff sued the contractor, Ellis, who argued this was "nonfeasance" and thus no duty was owed. Lord Campbell reasoned, "The action is brought for an improper mode of performing the work. How can that be called a nonfeasance? It is doing unlawfully what might be done lawfully: digging improperly without taking the proper steps for protecting from injury.... Cases where the action has been for a mere nonfeasance are inapplicable: the action here is for doing what was positively wrong." This reasoning can apply in many situations. Suppose the defendant drives a car. When a bicycle appears in front of him he does nothing. In particular, he does not move his foot to the brake pedal. As a result he strikes the cyclist. Is this nonfeasance? Can we really set a standard for determining what is and what is not mere inaction?

2. **Characterizing conduct.** Are *Newton* and *Yania* essentially contrary to one another in the way they characterize conduct? Why is *Yania* not a case of one complex act, a case of enticing-without-aiding? Did Bigan do more than merely "maintain an existing circumstance," or did he do things that placed Yania at risk of harm?

3. **Is the distinction critical?** Is the nonfeasance/misfeasance distinction itself critical in reaching the right result in these cases? Suppose the *Yania* court had considered that, overall, Bigan's conduct showed affirmative action and that the failure to help Yania was merely one omission in the overall conduct that was, as a whole, affirmative. Would there then be any reasons left to deny liability?

4. **The *Rocha* case.** In *Rocha v. Faltys*, 69 S.W.3d 315 (Tex. App. 2002), Rocha attended a party at his college fraternity house at which beer was available. At 2:45 a.m., Rocha and a fraternity brother, Faltys, accompanied by three female students, went to a local swimming spot on a river. Rocha and Faltys climbed to the top of a cliff overlooking the river. Faltys dove in and (according to the plaintiffs) encouraged Rocha to do the same even though Rocha could not swim. Rocha dove in and drowned despite the efforts of Faltys and the others to save him. Rocha's parents sued Faltys and others for negligence. Affirming a summary judgment for Faltys, the court cited the basic nonfeasance rule and held that Faltys owed Rocha no duty. What about the argument that by taking Rocha to the top of the cliff and encouraging him to jump in, Faltys assumed a duty of care? The court rejected that argument, noting that "basic principle of legal responsibility

that individuals should be responsible for their own actions and should not be liable for others' independent misconduct." Simply taking an "adult man" to the top of a cliff does not create a dangerous situation giving rise to a duty, and "[n]one of the parties have identified any Texas case suggesting that an adult encouraging another adult to engage in a dangerous activity can give rise to a legal duty." If *Yania* is wrong, is *Rocha* wrong as well?

5. **Applying the rule.** How does the nonfeasance rule work in these two cases?

A. The Rockweit families camped together and used a communal firepit in the ground. Tynan was a friend at a nearby campground with its own firepit. She joined the Rockweits one evening. One of the Rockweits was an 18-month-old child, Anthony. Tynan and some others stayed up until 4:00 a.m. playing cards. No one took care to make sure the embers were safe. Hours later Anthony got up, slipped into the pit and was terribly burned. Is Tynan liable? *Rockweit v. Senecal*, 541 N.W.2d 742 (Wis. 1995).

B. The defendant operates a rapid transit system. At 5:00 a.m., personnel on one of its trains discover a man in the system warming room, either drunk or unconscious, possibly with blood nearby. They notify the company, which notifies security, which is too busy at the moment. On the next two rounds, the same personnel discover the same man, still there, still unconscious. They call again. Only after 10:00 a.m. does someone arrive, and at that time the man speaks briefly and is taken to the hospital where he dies soon thereafter. He had a closed head injury, not caused by the defendant, and could have been saved if he had been helped sooner. He may not have been a ticketed passenger. *Rhodes v. Illinois Cent. Gulf R.R.*, 665 N.E.2d 1260 (Ill. 1996).

6. **Rationales.** What are the rationales behind the nonfeasance rule? In *Stockberger v. United States*, 332 F.3d 479 (7th Cir. 2003), Judge Posner said this:

> Various rationales have been offered for the seemingly hardhearted common law rule: people should not count on nonprofessionals for rescue; the circle of potentially liable nonrescuers would be difficult to draw (suppose a person is drowning and no one on the crowded beach makes an effort to save him—should all be liable?); altruism makes the problem a small one and liability might actually reduce the number of altruistic responses by depriving people of credit for altruism (how would they prove they hadn't acted under threat of legal liability?); people would be deterred by threat of liability from putting themselves in a position where they might be called upon to attempt a rescue, especially since a failed rescue might under settled common law principles give rise to liability, on the theory that a clumsy rescue attempt may have interfered with a competent rescue by someone else.

Does *Yania* suggest further rationales?

§ 2. EXCEPTIONS, QUALIFICATIONS AND QUESTIONS

The nonfeasance rule has deep roots in Anglo–American jurisprudence, but has come under withering criticism for many decades. Many European countries impose an affirmative duty to rescue, often making a failure to rescue a criminal offense. *See* JULIE A. DAVIES & PAUL T. HAYDEN, GLOBAL ISSUES IN TORT LAW 120–29 (2008). A comment in the Second Restatement of Torts remarked that American decisions upholding the nonliability of those who declined an easy chance to rescue another from drowning "have been condemned by legal writers as revolting to any moral sense, but thus far they remain the law." RESTATEMENT (SECOND) OF TORTS § 314, cmt. *c*.

Not surprisingly, then, courts have developed a number of exceptions to the no-duty rule. Some of these seem less like "exceptions" and more like situations where there has been an affirmative act and not nonfeasance in the first place. *See* RESTATEMENT (THIRD) OF TORTS: LIABILITY FOR PHYSICAL HARM § 40 (Proposed Final Draft No. 1, 2005). First, if a person knows or has reason to know that his conduct, whether tortious or innocent, has caused harm to another person, he then has a duty to render assistance to prevent further harm. RESTATEMENT (SECOND) § 322. *See South v. National R.R. Passenger Corp.*, 290 N.W.2d 819 (N.D. 1980) (without fault, train struck plaintiff; train personnel then had duty to assist reasonably). If this duty is breached, what would the legally-cognizable harm be? Second, if a person has created an unreasonable risk of harm, even innocently, a duty of reasonable care arises to employ reasonable care to prevent the harm from occurring. RESTATEMENT (SECOND) § 321. For example, in *Pacht v. Morris*, 489 P.2d 29 (Ariz. 1971), the defendant innocently collided with a horse on the highway, killing it. If he does not exercise reasonable care to remove the horse or to provide some kind of effective warning, he would be subject to liability if a second driver is injured by hitting the horse or in trying to avoid hitting it.

Another exception may be found if a statute or ordinance requires a person to act affirmatively for the protection of another. In such a situation, a court may rely on that statute to find an affirmative duty to assist or protect that is enforceable in a tort action. *See* RESTATEMENT (THIRD) § 39; DOBBS ON TORTS § 133, at 311–12 (2000). *See, e.g., Brock v. Watts Realty Co.*, 582 So.2d 438 (Ala. 1991) (municipal ordinance that required landlords to maintain door locks created a duty to protect tenants from intruders). We consider other exceptions in the materials that follow.

WAKULICH v. MRAZ

751 N.E.2d 1 (Ill. App. Ct. 2001)

JUSTICE MCBRIDE delivered the opinion of the court. . . .

[Suit for the death of 16-year-old Elizabeth Wakulich. The plaintiff alleged that Michael and Brian Mraz, then 21 and 18 years old, provided a quart of Goldschlager alcohol and offered Elizabeth money as a prize if she could drink the entire bottle without losing consciousness or vomiting. Dennis Mraz, the father of the young men, was allegedly in the house and should have known these events.]

In the early morning hours of June 16, decedent, after drinking the Goldschlager, lost consciousness. According to the complaint, Michael and Brian then placed her in the downstairs family room, where they observed her vomiting profusely and making "gurgling" sounds. They later checked on her again, at which time they removed her vomit-saturated blouse and placed a pillow under her head to prevent aspiration. According to the complaint, Michael and Brian did not seek medical attention for decedent and actually prevented others present in the home from calling 911 or seeking other medical intervention. Later in the morning, Dennis ordered Michael and Brian to remove decedent from the home. They then took her to a friend's home. Later, decedent was taken to a hospital where she was pronounced dead.

[The complaint was dismissed for failure to state a cause of action on the ground that Illinois case law eliminated any liability of social hosts for providing alcohol. In this appeal the court held that "the allegations of peer pressure and offers of money in the instant case fail" to show an exception to the rule against social host liability.]

Plaintiff next maintains that she has pleaded sufficient facts to establish a cause of action based upon defendants' failure to exercise due care in voluntarily undertaking to care for plaintiff's decedent after she became unconscious. We agree.

"One who voluntarily undertakes to render services to another is liable for bodily harm caused by his failure to perform such services with due care or with such competence and skill as he possesses." . . .

Here, plaintiff has alleged that Michael and Brian voluntarily undertook affirmative steps to care for decedent and did so in a negligent manner. . . .

The viability of the voluntary undertaking counts . . . is not dependent on a duty created through the defendants' provision of alcohol to decedent but, rather, on the defendants having voluntarily undertaken to care for decedent after she became unconscious and having allegedly failed to exercise due care in the performance of that undertaking. . . .

Defendants maintain that none of their alleged acts indicate a voluntary assumption of any responsibility for decedent's health or well-being.

We disagree. Specifically, it was alleged that after decedent became unconscious, Michael and Brian carried her downstairs, placed her on a couch, observed her vomiting profusely and making gurgling noises, checked on her later, changed her vomit-saturated shirt, and placed a pillow underneath her head to prevent aspiration. The actions of Michael and Brian ... clearly demonstrated an undertaking concerning decedent's well-being. ... We find therefore, that plaintiff has sufficiently pled that defendants Michael and Brian voluntarily assumed a duty to care for decedent.

Defendants maintain that they were not negligent in discharging any responsibility they did undertake, that a finding that there was a duty in this case creates uncertainty as to how that duty may be adequately discharged, and that decedent's death was not the proximate result of any voluntary undertaking on their part. We are confident that a jury or other trier of fact is capable of determining whether defendants, having voluntarily undertaken to care for the decedent after she became unconscious and began to vomit and gurgle, performed that undertaking with due care. We also find that the complaint alleges various acts, including allegations that defendants Michael and Brian prevented other individuals from calling for emergency medical intervention, from which a jury could find the defendants acted negligently in discharging their voluntarily assumed duty, proximately leading to decedent's death.

[The trial court erred in dismissing the counts based on voluntary undertaking.]

NOTES

1. The Restatement Third of Torts recognizes in section 43 that an actor who undertakes to render services to another, when the actor knows or should know that those services will reduce the risk of harm to the other, has a duty to use reasonable care in rendering those services if the failure to exercise care would increase the risk of harm beyond which would have existed without the undertaking; or if the other person relies on the actor's using reasonable care in the undertaking.

2. Distinguish liability for positive acts—preventing others from calling for help in *Wukulich*—from liability for voluntary undertakings, that is, for breach of duties voluntarily assumed where no duty would otherwise exist. For example, most states thankfully place no duty on a passenger in a car to give the driver advice. But if the driver tells the passenger that he cannot see behind him while backing up, and the passenger affirmatively tells the driver that it is clear to back up, the passenger has a legal duty to use reasonable care in giving that advice. *See, e.g., Roos v. Morrison*, 913 So.2d 59 (Fla. Dist. Ct. App. 2005). What if hosts at a party volunteer to check guests for weapons, but then someone is shot? *See Rice v. White*, 874 N.E.2d 132 (Ill. App. Ct. 2007).

FARWELL v. KEATON

240 N.W.2d 217 (Mich. 1976)

LEVIN, JUSTICE.

[Richard Farwell, 18, and his friend David Siegrist, 16, waiting for a friend to finish work, had a few beers. When teenaged girls walked by, they attempted to engage in conversation without success. The girls complained to friends that they were being followed, and six boys chased Farwell and Siegrist back to a trailer lot. Siegrist escaped but Farwell was severely beaten. Siegrist found him under a car, put ice on his head and then drove around for two hours, stopping at drive-in restaurants. Farwell "went to sleep" in the back of the car and around midnight Siegrist drove him to his grandparents' home, where he left him in the back of the car after an attempt to arouse him. Farwell died three days later from the beating and there was evidence that prompt medical attention could have prevented this. The jury found for the plaintiff in an action for Farwell's death, but the Court of Appeals reversed on the ground that Siegrist had not assumed any duty to aid Farwell.]

Without regard to whether there is a general duty to aid a person in distress, there is a clearly recognized legal duty of every person to avoid any affirmative acts which may make a situation worse. "[I]f the defendant does attempt to aid him, and takes charge and control of the situation, he is regarded as entering voluntarily into a relation which is attended with responsibility. Such a defendant will then be liable for a failure to use reasonable care for the protection of the plaintiff's interests." Prosser, supra, § 56, pp. 343–344. . . .

Courts have been slow to recognize a duty to render aid to a person in peril. Where such a duty has been found, it has been predicated upon the existence of a special relationship between the parties; in such a case, if defendant knew or should have known of the other person's peril, he is required to render reasonable care under all the circumstances. . . .

Farwell and Siegrist were companions on a social venture. Implicit in such a common undertaking is the understanding that one will render assistance to the other when he is in peril if he can do so without endangering himself. Siegrist knew or should have known when he left Farwell, who was badly beaten and unconscious, in the back seat of his car that no one would find him before morning. Under these circumstances, to say that Siegrist had no duty to obtain medical assistance or at least to notify someone of Farwell's condition and whereabouts would be "shocking to humanitarian considerations" and fly in the face of "the commonly accepted code of social conduct." . . .

Farwell and Siegrist were companions engaged in a common undertaking; there was a special relationship between the parties. . . .

The Court of Appeals is reversed and the verdict of the jury reinstated.

NOTES

1. **Making matters worse.** Where the defendant discontinues aid, the Restatement Third section 44(b) imposes liability if the defendant, by acting unreasonably, has left the victim in a "worse position than existed before the defendant took charge." Section 324(b) of the Restatement Second said virtually the same thing, reflecting the vast majority of case law. *See, e.g., Krieg v. Massey*, 781 P.2d 277 (Mont. 1989). How does this stack up with the *Farwell* and *Wakulich* cases? Could it be said that Farwell would have been better off if Siegrist had shrugged his shoulders and walked home, leaving Farwell under the car, or that Elizabeth Wakulich would have been better off if the men had not put a pillow under her head?

2. **Duty to take charge reasonably.** Section 44(a) of the Restatement Third says that when a person voluntarily takes charge of an imperiled and helpless person, he has assumed a duty to take charge in a reasonable manner. Does that also explain the reasoning in *Farwell* and *Wakulich*? What if a helicopter rescue crew locates an injured woman stranded in a dangerous ice gorge from which, without such a rescue, she could not escape. The crew lowers a sling, and begins to haul her aboard. It then negligently reverses the ratchet and the sling drops into the gorge again, causing a further injury to the woman. Is the crew liable to the woman for the second injury? Why?

3. **Special relationship.** Are you convinced that a "special relationship" such as that between Farwell and Segrist triggered a duty of care independent of the "takes charge" exception? Section 40 of the Restatement Third recognizes seven kinds of formal relationships that place a defendant under a duty of reasonable care for the plaintiff's safety, including reasonable affirmative efforts to rescue. The relationships are those of (1) carrier-passenger, (2) innkeeper-guest, (3) landowner-lawful entrant; (4) employer-employee; (5) school-student; (6) landlord-tenant; and (7) custodian-person in custody. This represents a slight expansion of a similar list in the Restatement Second. The Restatement Third also explicitly states in a comment that the list is not exclusive and that courts may identify additional relationships that give rise to a duty to assist. Notice that not all of the "special relationship" cases will be true exceptions to the nonfeasance rules, since in some of them the defendant is already doing something affirmatively that should produce a duty of acting reasonably under the circumstances. But where the plaintiff and defendant are in a special relationship, the defendant will have a duty of reasonable care whether or not the defendant had anything to do with creating or increasing the risk of harm to the plaintiff. RESTATEMENT (THIRD) OF TORTS: LIABILITY FOR PHYSICAL HARM § 40, cmt. *c* (P.F.D. No. 1, 2005).

4. **Other determinate relationships.** What other preexisting relationships might generate a duty to act affirmatively when one party is in danger? What if a parent sees a child in danger? What if a sheriff takes no steps to protect a crime witness who is in terrible danger for reporting the crime?

5. **Indeterminate or ad hoc relationships.** In *Farwell* the two boys, Farwell and Siegrist, were not in any preexisting, recognized status with respect to each other. But they did have a relationship that was, for the

evening, special in the sense that people in general did not and could not share it. Is this enough to impose upon Siegrist a duty he would not have had if Siegrist had simply glanced out of a second story window and had seen the beating? Recall that in *Rocha v. Faltys*, 69 S.W.3d 315 (Tex. App. 2002), Rocha and Faltys were fellow fraternity members who drank at a party and went to a swimming hole where Rocha drowned. Does *Farwell* cause you to reassess that case, if you thought it was controlled by the reasoning in *Yania*?

PODIAS v. MAIRS

926 A.2d 859 (N.J. Super. Ct. App. Div. 2007)

PARRILLO, J.A.D. . . . .

In the evening of September 27, 2002 and early morning hours of September 28, eighteen-year-old Michael Mairs was drinking beer at the home of a friend Thomas Chomko. He eventually left with two other friends, defendants Swanson and Newell, both also eighteen years of age, to return to Monmouth University where all three were students. Mairs was driving. Swanson was in the front passenger seat and Newell was seated in the rear of the vehicle where he apparently fell asleep. It was raining and the road was wet.

At approximately 2:00 a.m., while traveling southbound in the center lane of the Garden State Parkway, Mairs lost control of the car, struck a motorcycle driven by Antonios Podias, and went over the guardrail. All three exited the vehicle and "huddled" around the car. Swanson saw Podias lying in the roadway and because he saw no movement and heard no sound, told Mairs and Newell that he thought Mairs had killed the cyclist. At that time, there were no other cars on the road, or witnesses for that matter.

Even though all three had cell phones, no one called for assistance. Instead they argued about whether the car had collided with the motorcycle. And, within minutes of the accident, Mairs called his girlfriend on Newell's cell phone since his was lost when he got out of the car. Swanson also used his cell phone, placing seventeen calls in the next one-and-one-half hours. Twenty-six additional calls were made from Newell's cell phone in the two-and-one-half hours after the accident, the first just three minutes post-accident and to Matawan, where Chomko resides. None of these, however, were emergency assistance calls. As Swanson later explained: "I didn't feel responsible to call the police." And Newell just "didn't want to get in trouble."

After about five or ten minutes, the trio all decided to get back in the car and leave the scene. Swanson directed, "we have to get to an exit." Upon their return to the car, Swanson instructed Mairs "not to bring up his name or involve him in what occurred" and "don't get us [Swanson and Newell] involved, we weren't there." The three then drove south on the parkway for a short distance until Mairs' car broke down. Mairs pulled over and waited in the bushes for his girlfriend to arrive, while Swanson and Newell ran off into the woods, where Newell eventually lost sight of

Swanson. Before they deserted him, Swanson again reminded Mairs that "there was no need to get [Swanson and Newell] in trouble ...." Mairs thought Swanson was "just scared" and that both defendants were concerned about Mairs "drinking and driving." Meanwhile, a motor vehicle operated by Patricia Uribe ran over Podias, who died as a result of injuries sustained in these accidents.... [The Administratrix of Podias' estate sued Mairs, Swanson and Newell. Plaintiff appeals from the trial court's grant of summary judgment in favor of Swanson and Newell.] ...

Ordinarily, mere presence at the commission of the wrong, or failure to object to it, is not enough to charge one with responsibility inasmuch as there is no duty to take affirmative steps to interfere. Because of this reluctance to countenance "inaction" as a basis of liability, the common law "has persistently refused to impose on a stranger the moral obligation of common humanity to go to the aid of another human being who is in danger, even if the other is in danger of losing his life." ...

Of course, exceptions are as longstanding as the rule. [Even those under no pre-existing duty may be liable if they voluntarily begin to assist and do so negligently.] ... Over the years, liability for inaction has been gradually extended still further to a limited group of relations, in which custom, public sentiment, and views of social policy have led courts to find a duty of affirmative action. Thus, a duty to render assistance may either be "contractual, relational or transactional." In New Jersey, courts have recognized that the existence of a relationship between the victim and one in a position to provide aid may create a duty to render assistance....

To establish liability, however, such relationships need not be limited to those where a pre-existing duty exists, or involving economic ties, or dependent on the actor's status as, for instance, a landowner or business owner. Rather, it may only be necessary "to find some definite relation between the parties [ ] of such a character that social policy justifies the imposition of a duty to act." [Keeton, et al., *Prosser and Keeton on Torts* § 56 at 374 (5th Ed.)]....

So too, even though the defendant may be under no obligation to render assistance himself, he is at least required to take reasonable care that he does not prevent others from giving it. In other words, there may be liability for interfering with the plaintiff's opportunity of obtaining assistance. And even where the original danger was created by innocent conduct, involving no fault on the part of the defendant, there may be a duty to make a reasonable effort to give assistance and avoid further harm where the prior innocent conduct has created an unreasonable risk of harm to the plaintiff. Indeed, one commentator has suggested that "the mere knowledge of serious peril, threatening death or great bodily harm to another, which an identified defendant might avoid with little inconvenience, creates a sufficient relation to impose a duty of action." *Prosser, supra,* § 56 at 377.

Actually, the extension of liability based on these and other "relational" features mirrors evolving notions of duty, which are no longer tethered to rigid formalisms or static historical classifications. This progression is not surprising. The assessment of duty necessarily includes an examination of the relationships between and among the parties. The fundamental question is whether the plaintiff's interests are entitled to legal protection against the defendant's conduct. In this regard, the determination of the existence of duty is ultimately a question of fairness and public policy, which in turn draws upon notions of fairness, common sense, and morality. . . .

[W]e are satisfied that the summary judgment record admits of sufficient facts from which a reasonable jury could find defendants breached a duty which proximately caused the victim's death. In the first place, the risk of harm, even death, to the injured victim lying helpless in the middle of a roadway, from the failure of defendants to summon help or take other precautionary measures was readily and clearly foreseeable. Not only were defendants aware of the risk of harm created by their own inaction, but were in a unique position to know of the risk of harm posed by Mairs' own omission in that regard, as well as Mairs' earlier precipatory conduct in driving after having consumed alcohol. Even absent any encouragement on their part, defendants had special reason to know that Mairs would not himself summon help, but instead illegally depart the scene of a hit-and-run accident, *N.J.S.A.* 39:4–129; *see also N.J.S.A.* 39:4–130, either intentionally or because of an inability to fulfill a duty directly owed the victim, thereby further endangering the decedent's safety.

Juxtaposed against the obvious foreseeability of harm is the relative ease with which it could have been prevented. All three individuals had cell phones and in fact used them immediately before and after the accident for their own purposes, rather than to call for emergency assistance for another in need. The ultimate consequence wrought by the harm in this case-death-came at the expense of failing to take simple precautions at little if any cost or inconvenience to defendants. Indeed, in contrast to Mairs' questionable ability to appreciate the seriousness of the situation, defendants appeared lucid enough to comprehend the severity of the risk and sufficiently in control to help avoid further harm to the victim. In other words, defendants had both the opportunity and ability to help prevent an obviously foreseeable risk of severe and potentially fatal consequence.

In our view, given the circumstances, the imposition of a duty upon defendants does not offend notions of fairness and common decency and is in accord with public policy, [which] encourages gratuitous assistance by those who have no legal obligation to render it. Simply and obviously, defendants here were far more than innocent bystanders or strangers to the event. On the contrary, the instrumentality of injury in this case was operated for a common purpose and the mutual benefit of defendants, and driven by someone they knew to be exhibiting signs of intoxication. Although Mairs clearly created the initial risk, at the very least the evidence reasonably suggests defendants acquiesced in the conditions that may have helped create it and subsequently in those conditions that further endangered the victim's safety. Defendants therefore bear some relationship not only to the primary wrongdoer but to the incident itself. It is this nexus which distinguishes this case from those defined by mere presence on the scene without more, and therefore implicates policy considerations simply not pertinent to the latter.

Even assuming no independent duty to take affirmative action, at the very least defendants were obligated, in our view, not to prevent Mairs from exercising his direct duty of care.... [A]t the very least defendants collaborated in, verbally supported, or approved his decision to leave the scene, and at most actively convinced Mairs to flee as a means of not getting caught.... The entire aftermath of the incident betrays an orchestrated scheme among the three to avoid detection not only by taking no action to prevent further harm to the victim, but by affirmatively abandoning the scene, practically guaranteeing his death....

We formulate today no rule of general application since the question of duty remains one of judicial balancing of the mix of factors peculiar to each case. We also stress the narrowness of the issue before us.... It is the degree of defendants' involvement, coupled with the serious peril threatening imminent death to another that might have been avoided with little effort and inconvenience, suggested by the evidence, that in our view creates a sufficient relation to impose a duty of action. Of course, it still remains a question of fact whether the primary wrongdoer was able to exercise reasonable care to summon emergency assistance or was prevented from doing so by defendants; whether, on the other hand, defendants knew or had reason to know that Mairs was unable or unwilling to do so, and thereafter were in a position to have influenced the outcome; whether the decision to abandon the victim was otherwise Mairs' alone or the result of encouragement, cooperation or interference from defendants; and finally, if the latter, whether the assistance was substantial enough to support a finding of liability. The facts here are certainly not such that all reasonable persons must draw the same conclusion. We cannot say that upon any version of the facts there is no duty.

Reversed and remanded.

NOTES

1. **Examining the disclaimer.** Why did the court insist it was "formulating no rule of general application?" Did it not articulate a rule about when a duty to assist will arise that could be applied in other cases?

2. **Other factors in *Podias*.** The ad hoc relationship in *Podias* is quite similar to the one found to be "special" in *Farwell*. But does *Podias* go further than *Farwell* in calling into question the entire nonfeasance rule?

DeSHANEY v. WINNEBAGO COUNTY DEPT. OF SOCIAL SERVICES*

489 U.S. 189 (1989)

CHIEF JUSTICE REHNQUIST delivered the opinion of the Court.

Petitioner is a boy who was beaten and permanently injured by his father, with whom he lived. The respondents are social workers and other local officials who received complaints that petitioner was being abused by his father and had reason to believe that this was the case, but nonetheless did not act to remove petitioner from his father's custody. Petitioner sued respondents claiming that their failure to act deprived him of his liberty in violation of the Due Process Clause of the Fourteenth Amendment to the United States Constitution. We hold that it did not.

[FACTS]

The facts of this case are undeniably tragic. Petitioner Joshua DeShaney was born in 1979. In 1980, a Wyoming court granted his parents a divorce and awarded custody of Joshua to his father, Randy DeShaney. The father shortly thereafter moved to Neenah, a city located in Winnebago County, Wisconsin, taking the infant Joshua with him. There he entered into a second marriage, which also ended in divorce.

The Winnebago County authorities first learned that Joshua DeShaney might be a victim of child abuse in January 1982, when his father's second wife complained to the police, at the time of their divorce, that he had previously "hit the boy causing marks and (was) a prime case for child abuse." Winnebago County Department of Social Services (DSS) interviewed the father, but he denied the accusations, and DSS did not pursue them further. In January 1983, Joshua was admitted to a local hospital with multiple bruises and abrasions. The examining physician suspected child abuse and notified DSS, which immediately obtained an order from a Wisconsin juvenile court placing Joshua in the temporary custody of the hospital. Three days later, the county convened an ad hoc "Child Protection Team"—consisting of a pediatrician, a psychologist, a police detective, the county's lawyer, several DSS caseworkers, and various hospital personnel—to consider Joshua's situation. At this meeting, the Team decided that there was insufficient evidence of child abuse to retain Joshua in the custody of the court. The Team did, however, decide to recommend several measures to protect Joshua, including enrolling him in a preschool program, providing his father with certain counselling services, and encouraging his father's girlfriend to move out of the home. Randy DeShaney entered into a voluntary agreement with DSS in which he promised to cooperate with them in accomplishing these goals.

Based on the recommendation of the Child Protection Team, the juvenile court dismissed the child protection case and returned Joshua to

---

* Headings are inserted by the editors for convenience of reference.

the custody of his father. A month later, emergency room personnel called the DSS caseworker handling Joshua's case to report that he had once again been treated for suspicious injuries. The caseworker concluded that there was no basis for action. For the next six months, the caseworker made monthly visits to the DeShaney home, during which she observed a number of suspicious injuries on Joshua's head; she also noticed that he had not been enrolled in school and that the girlfriend had not moved out. The caseworker dutifully recorded these incidents in her files, along with her continuing suspicions that someone in the DeShaney household was physically abusing Joshua, but she did nothing more. In November 1983, the emergency room notified DSS that Joshua had been treated once again for injuries that they believed to be caused by child abuse. On the caseworker's next two visits to the DeShaney home, she was told that Joshua was too ill to see her. Still DSS took no action.

In March 1984, Randy DeShaney beat 4-year-old Joshua so severely that he fell into a life-threatening coma. Emergency brain surgery revealed a series of hemorrhages caused by traumatic injuries to the head inflicted over a long period of time. Joshua did not die, but he suffered brain damage so severe that he is expected to spend the rest of his life confined to an institution for the profoundly retarded. Randy DeShaney was subsequently tried and convicted of child abuse.

[DUE PROCESS CLAIMS]

[Joshua and his mother filed this action against the county and its social services department, as well as some individual employees involved. They claimed rights under 42 U.S.C.A. § 1983 on the ground that the defendants denied due process to Joshua. The trial court granted summary judgment for the defendants. The Court of Appeals affirmed.]

The Due Process Clause of the Fourteenth Amendment provides that "[n]o State shall ... deprive any person of life, liberty, or property, without due process of law." Petitioners contend that the State deprived Joshua of his liberty interest in "free[dom] from ... unjustified intrusions on personal security," by failing to provide him with adequate protection against his father's violence. The claim is one invoking the substantive rather than procedural component of the Due Process Clause; petitioners do not claim that the State denied Joshua protection without according him appropriate procedural safeguards, but that it was categorically obligated to protect him in these circumstances.

But nothing in the language of the Due Process Clause itself requires the State to protect the life, liberty, and property of its citizens against invasion by private actors. The Clause is phrased as a limitation on the State's power to act, not as a guarantee of certain minimal levels of safety and security. It forbids the State itself to deprive individuals of life, liberty, or property without "due process of law," but its language cannot fairly be extended to impose an affirmative obligation on the State to ensure that those interests do not come to harm through other means. Nor does history support such an expansive reading of the constitutional text. Like its counterpart in the Fifth Amendment, the Due Process Clause of the Fourteenth Amendment was intended to prevent government "from abusing [its] power, or employing it as an instrument of oppression," Its purpose was to protect the people from the State, not to ensure that the State protected them from each other. The Framers were content to leave the extent of governmental obligation in the latter area to the democratic political processes.

. . . If the Due Process Clause does not require the State to provide its citizens with particular protective services, it follows that the State cannot be held liable under the Clause for injuries that could have been averted had it chosen to provide them.[3] As a general matter, then, we conclude that a State's failure to protect an individual against private violence simply does not constitute a violation of the Due Process Clause.

[THE ROLE OF SPECIAL RELATIONSHIPS]

Petitioners contend, however, that even if the Due Process Clause imposes no affirmative obligation on the State to provide the general public with adequate protective services, such a duty may arise out of certain "special relationships" created or assumed by the State with respect to particular individuals. Petitioners argue that such a "special relationship" existed here because the State knew that Joshua faced a special danger of abuse at his father's hands, and specifically proclaimed, by word and by deed, its intention to protect him against that danger. Having actually undertaken to protect Joshua from this danger—which petitioners concede the State played no part in creating—the State acquired an affirmative "duty," enforceable through the Due Process Clause, to do so in a reasonably competent fashion. Its failure to discharge that duty, so the argument goes, was an abuse of governmental power that so "shocks the conscience," as to constitute a substantive due process violation.

We reject this argument. It is true that in certain limited circumstances the Constitution imposes upon the State affirmative duties of care and protection with respect to particular individuals. In *Estelle v. Gamble*, 429 U.S. 97, 97 S.Ct. 285, 50 L.Ed.2d 251 (1976), we recognized that the Eighth Amendment's prohibition against cruel and unusual punishment, made applicable to the States through the Fourteenth Amendment's Due Process Clause, requires the State to provide adequate medical care to incarcerated prisoners. We reasoned that because the prisoner is unable "by reason of the deprivation of his liberty [to] care for himself, it is only just" that the State be required to care for him.

In *Youngberg v. Romeo*, 457 U.S. 307, 102 S.Ct. 2452, 73 L.Ed.2d 28 (1982), we extended this analysis beyond the Eighth Amendment setting, holding that the substantive component of the Fourteenth Amendment's Due Process Clause requires the State to provide involuntarily committed

---

3. The State may not, of course, selectively deny its protective services to certain disfavored minorities without violating the Equal Protection Clause. See *Yick Wo v. Hopkins*, 118 U.S. 356, 6 S.Ct. 1064, 30 L.Ed. 220 (1886). But no such argument has been made here.

mental patients with such services as are necessary to ensure their "reasonable safety" from themselves and others. As we explained, "[i]f it is cruel and unusual punishment to hold convicted criminals in unsafe conditions, it must be unconstitutional (under the Due Process Clause) to confine the involuntarily committed—who may not be punished at all—in unsafe conditions."

[INTERPRETING THE CASES]

But these cases afford petitioners no help. Taken together, they stand only for the proposition that when the State takes a person into its custody and holds him there against his will, the Constitution imposes upon it a corresponding duty to assume some responsibility for his safety and general well-being. The rationale for this principle is simple enough: when the State by the affirmative exercise of its power so restrains an individual's liberty that it renders him unable to care for himself, and at the same time fails to provide for his basic human needs—e.g., food, clothing, shelter, medical care, and reasonable safety—it transgresses the substantive limits on state action set by the Eighth Amendment and the Due Process Clause. The affirmative duty to protect arises not from the State's knowledge of the individual's predicament or from its expressions of intent to help him, but from the limitation which it has imposed on his freedom to act on his own behalf. In the substantive due process analysis, it is the State's affirmative act of restraining the individual's freedom to act on his own behalf—through incarceration, institutionalization, or other similar restraint of personal liberty—which is the "deprivation of liberty" triggering the protections of the Due Process Clause, not its failure to act to protect his liberty interests against harms inflicted by other means.[8]

The *Estelle–Youngberg* analysis simply has no applicability in the present case. Petitioners concede that the harms Joshua suffered did not occur while he was in the State's custody, but while he was in the custody of his natural father, who was in no sense a state actor. While the State may have been aware of the dangers that Joshua faced in the free world, it played no part in their creation, nor did it do anything to render him any more vulnerable to them. That the State once took temporary custody of Joshua does not alter the analysis, for when it returned him to his father's custody, it placed him in no worse position than that in which he would have been had it not acted at all; the State does not become the permanent guarantor of an individual's safety by having once offered him shelter. Under these circumstances, the State had no constitutional duty to protect Joshua.

[THE POSSIBLE ROLE OF STATE TORT LAW]

It may well be that, by voluntarily undertaking to protect Joshua against a danger it concededly played no part in creating, the State

---

8. Of course, the protections of the Due Process Clause, both substantive and procedural, may be triggered when the State, by the affirmative acts of its agents, subjects an involuntarily confined individual to deprivations of liberty which are not among those generally authorized by his confinement.

acquired a duty under state tort law to provide him with adequate protection against that danger. See Restatement (Second) of Torts § 323 (1965) (one who undertakes to render services to another may in some circumstances be held liable for doing so in a negligent fashion); see generally W. Keeton, D. Dobbs, R. Keeton, & D. Owen, Prosser and Keeton on the Law of Torts § 56 (5th ed. 1984) (discussing "special relationships" which may give rise to affirmative duties to act under the common law of tort). But the claim here is based on the Due Process Clause of the Fourteenth Amendment, which, as we have said many times, does not transform every tort committed by a state actor into a constitutional violation. A State may, through its courts and legislatures, impose such affirmative duties of care and protection upon its agents as it wishes. But not "all common-law duties owed by government actors were ... constitutionalized by the Fourteenth Amendment." Because, as explained above, the State had no constitutional duty to protect Joshua against his father's violence, its failure to do so—though calamitous in hindsight—simply does not constitute a violation of the Due Process Clause.

Judges and lawyers, like other humans, are moved by natural sympathy in a case like this to find a way for Joshua and his mother to receive adequate compensation for the grievous harm inflicted upon them. But before yielding to that impulse, it is well to remember once again that the harm was inflicted not by the State of Wisconsin, but by Joshua's father. The most that can be said of the state functionaries in this case is that they stood by and did nothing when suspicious circumstances dictated a more active role for them. In defense of them it must also be said that had they moved too soon to take custody of the son away from the father, they would likely have been met with charges of improperly intruding into the parent-child relationship, charges based on the same Due Process Clause that forms the basis for the present charge of failure to provide adequate protection.

The people of Wisconsin may well prefer a system of liability which would place upon the State and its officials the responsibility for failure to act in situations such as the present one. They may create such a system, if they do not have it already, by changing the tort law of the State in accordance with the regular law-making process. But they should not have it thrust upon them by this Court's expansion of the Due Process Clause of the Fourteenth Amendment.

Affirmed.

JUSTICE BRENNAN, with whom JUSTICE MARSHALL and JUSTICE BLACKMUN join, dissenting....

I would focus first on the action that Wisconsin has taken with respect to Joshua and children like him, rather than on the actions that the State failed to take.... [T]he fact of hospitalization was critical in *Youngberg* not because it rendered Romeo helpless to help himself, but because it separated him from other sources of aid that, we held, the State was obligated to replace. Unlike the Court, therefore, I am unable to see in Youngberg a neat and decisive divide between action and inaction.

... I would recognize, as the Court apparently cannot, that "the State's knowledge of [an] individual's predicament [and] its expressions of intent to help him" can amount to a "limitation of his freedom to act on his own behalf" or to obtain help from others. Thus, I would read *Youngberg* and *Estelle* to stand for the much more generous proposition that, if a State cuts off private sources of aid and then refuses aid itself, it cannot wash its hands of the harm that results from its inaction....

[Wisconsin's child-welfare system effectively excluded others from helping the child.]

In these circumstances, a private citizen, or even a person working in a government agency other than DSS, would doubtless feel that her job was done as soon as she had reported her suspicions of child abuse to DSS. Through its child-welfare program, in other words, the State of Wisconsin has relieved ordinary citizens and governmental bodies other than the Department of any sense of obligation to do anything more than report their suspicions of child abuse to DSS. If DSS ignores or dismisses these suspicions, no one will step in to fill the gap. Wisconsin's child-protection program thus effectively confined Joshua DeShaney within the walls of Randy DeShaney's violent home until such time as DSS took action to remove him. Conceivably, then, children like Joshua are made worse off by the existence of this program when the persons and entities charged with carrying it out fail to do their jobs.

It simply belies reality, therefore, to contend that the State "stood by and did nothing" with respect to Joshua....

I would allow Joshua and his mother the opportunity to show that respondents' failure to help him arose, not out of the sound exercise of professional judgment ... but from the kind of arbitrariness that we have in the past condemned.

... My disagreement with the Court arises from its failure to see that inaction can be every bit as abusive of power as action, that oppression can result when a State undertakes a vital duty and then ignores it.

JUSTICE BLACKMUN, dissenting.

Today, the Court purports to be the dispassionate oracle of the law, unmoved by "natural sympathy." But, in this pretense, the Court itself retreats into a sterile formalism which prevents it from recognizing either the facts of the case before it or the legal norms that should apply to those facts. As Justice Brennan demonstrates, the facts here involve not mere passivity, but active state intervention in the life of Joshua DeShaney— intervention that triggered a fundamental duty to aid the boy once the State learned of the severe danger to which he was exposed....

NOTES

1. **Conceptions of nonfeasance.** Perhaps a plaintiff cannot prevail in a § 1983 case by arguing that state inaction caused harm. *See Town of Castle Rock v. Gonzalez*, 545 U.S. 748 (2005) (failure to enforce restraining order not actionable). But was it really nonfeasance in *DeShaney*? Argue pro or con: (a) The officials took affirmative action to manage the case and then managed it in a negligent way. (b) The state "undertook" to provide protection and did not do so, with the result that it would be liable. (c) The officials established a special relationship with Joshua, either by the statutory enactments or otherwise.

2. **Bases for constitutional duties.** Can you identify the grounds for liability on constitutional grounds recognized in *DeShaney*?

3. **What about other special relationships?** "Custody" creates one kind of special relationship. *See, e.g., Jackson v. Schultz*, 429 F.3d 586 (6th Cir. 2005) (no "custody" and thus no special relationship between EMT's and man allegedly allowed to bleed to death from gunshot wounds). Would other relationships that would create a duty at common law also create a constitutional duty of state protection? For example, the common law recognizes that employers owe employees a reasonably safe place in which to work, and this may entail protecting them from injury by others. See DOBBS ON TORTS § 328 (2000). The Supreme Court, however, has flatly said that there is no Due Process right to a safe place in which to work. *Collins v. City of Harker Heights,* 503 U.S. 115 (1992).

4. **State-created danger.** Once a state officer takes affirmative action that creates a danger, *DeShaney* no longer stands as a barrier to recovery. A public entity takes custody of an abused child, then unaccountably returns her to her father's custody in spite of strong evidence that she will be abused by her father's friend. She is in fact abused. Is this *DeShaney,* or is this state-created danger? If it is a state-created danger case, in which the defendants have increased the risk of harm through an affirmative act, the defendants are under a constitutional duty to the plaintiff. That leaves the question whether the duty was breached by deliberate indifference or the like. *See, e.g. K.H. v. Morgan*, 914 F.2d 846 (7th Cir. 1990); *S.S. v. McMullen*, 225 F.3d 960 (8th Cir. 2000).

5. **A foreign perspective.** The European Convention on Human Rights, Article 3, provides: "No one shall be subjected to torture or to inhuman or degrading treatment or punishment." In *A. v. United Kingdom,* 27 E.H.R.R. 611 (1999), the European Court of Human Rights held that England violated this provision when a jury acquitted a child's stepfather, who had clearly delivered severe and repeated beatings. The Court thought that the Convention "requires [each country] to take measures designed to ensure that individuals within their jurisdiction are not subjected to torture or inhuman or degrading treatment or punishment, including such ill-treatment administered by private individuals. Children and other vulnerable individuals, in are entitled to State protection, in the form of effective deterrence, against such serious breaches of personal integrity." The court

required England to pay the child £10,000. Notice that the relevant text of the Convention and that of the United States Constitution are quite different.

6. **Beyond doctrine.** Are there practical considerations that would make you want to be cautious about imposing liability upon social workers who fail to intervene in family life?

GENERAL REFERENCES: DOBBS ON TORTS §§ 314–319 (2000); HARPER, JAMES & GRAY, THE LAW OF TORTS § 18.6 (3d ed. 2007).

CHAPTER 17

CONTRACT AND DUTY

■ ■ ■

In many instances, tort duties can be created, modified, or limited by contracts, informal undertakings, or even by mutual and reasonable expectations between the parties. Saying that a contract, undertaking or relationship may create tort duties means that liability will be determined under the rules of tort law and that tort damages will be appropriate if the plaintiff prevails.

§ 1. NONPERFORMANCE OF PROMISES

A. UNENFORCEABLE PROMISES

THORNE v. DEAS

4 Johns. (N.Y.) 84 (1809)

[The Thornes owned a one-half interest in a vessel called the Sea Nymph; and Deas, the defendant, owned the other one-half interest. The vessel sailed from New York bound for North Carolina and in two conversations on the subject, Deas assured one of the Thornes that he would procure insurance. He did not do so and the vessel was wrecked off the coast of Carolina. The Thornes brought this action against Deas, "on the case, for nonfeasance in not causing insurance to be made...." There was a verdict for the plaintiffs for one-half the value of the vessel, subject to the opinion of the court on the issue whether a recovery was proper.]

KENT, CH. J., delivered the opinion of the court:

The chief objection raised to the right of recovery in this case, is the want of a consideration for the promise. The offer on the part of the defendant to cause insurance to be effected, was perfectly voluntary. Will, then, an action lie when one party intrusts the performance of a business to another, who undertakes to do it gratuitously, and wholly omits to do it? If the party who makes this engagement enters upon the execution of the business and does it amiss, through the want of due care, by which damage ensues to the other party, an action will lie for this misfeasance. But the defendant never entered upon the execution of his undertaking, and the action is brought for the nonfeasance....

A short review of the leading cases will show that, by the common law a mandatory, or one who undertakes to do an act for another without reward, is not answerable for omitting to do the act, and is only responsible when he attempts to do it and does it amiss. In other words, he is responsible for a misfeasance but not for a nonfeasance, even though special damages are averred. Those who are conversant with the doctrine of *mandatum* in the civil law, and have perceived the equity which supports it, and the good faith which it enforces, may, perhaps, feel a portion of regret that Sir William Jones was not successful in his attempt to engraft this doctrine in all its extent, into the English law. I have no doubt of the perfect justice of the Roman rule.... But there are many rights of moral obligation which civil laws do not enforce, and are, therefore, left to the conscience of the individual, as rights of imperfect obligation....

Judgment for the defendant.

NOTES

1. Should a tort duty be created by nothing more than a promise to perform?

2. The Restatement of Contracts, in its famous § 90, puts forward the notion that a promise by defendant plus a reasonable reliance upon it by the plaintiff might operate as a kind of substitute for consideration in certain cases. Would that section eliminate the problem and permit the plaintiffs in *Thorne v. Deas* to recover?

3. In *Belhumeur v. Zilm*, 949 A.2d 162 (N.H. 2008), Mr. Belhumeur was attacked by wild bees that came from Mr. Zilm's bee-infested tree. Belhumeur sued Zilm for negligence, claiming that a duty arose from Zilm's promise to remove the tree combined with his obtaining bids to do the job. The court affirmed summary judgment for Zilm, reasoning that "obtaining estimates for the tree's removal was not enough of an affirmative undertaking to create a duty to actually remove it." Further, said the court, obtaining the estimates "did nothing to increase the risk of danger to Mr. Belhumeur or put him in any worse position than he was in before Mr. Zilm agreed to remove the tree. The risk of injury by the bees remained exactly the same before and after the estimates were obtained."

B.   ENFORCEABLE PROMISES

SPENGLER v. ADT SECURITY SERVICES, INC.

505 F.3d 456 (6th Cir. 2007)

BOYCE F. MARTIN, JR., CIRCUIT JUDGE.

Dwight Spengler appeals from the district court's dismissal of his tort claim on summary judgment. Spengler alleges that ADT is responsible for his mother's death by failing to dispatch an ambulance to her address after she pressed an ADT-issued emergency call button. Because the district court correctly held that this case sounds in contract and not in tort, we AFFIRM the holding of the district court.

On May 10, 2004, Dwight Spengler signed a residential services contract with ADT to install and monitor a security alarm at the home of Veronica Barker, his mother. The agreement included a portable call button alarm that Barker could activate when in distress. Due to cancer of the larynx and previous medical treatment of that condition, she could not speak. ADT therefore had instructions to call Plaintiff in the event of an alarm from Barker.

ADT received an alarm from Barker on October 26, 2005. Due to an error in the address that ADT gave to ambulance dispatchers in response to the alarm, emergency medical services were delayed in their arrival at Barker's residence by approximately sixteen minutes. By the time emergency personnel arrived, Barker's heart rhythm was asystolic. She never regained consciousness and later died in the hospital.

Spengler's lawsuit against ADT alleged that by providing an erroneous address to the dispatcher, ADT committed misfeasance, subjecting it to tort liability. The district court granted summary judgment for ADT on the tort claim, finding that ADT breached no duty independent of the parties' agreement. The court also granted summary judgment to Spengler, finding that ADT breached its contract, and limiting damages to the $500 amount stated in the parties' agreement. Spengler appealed, arguing that (1) the district court erred in finding that the case sounded in contract instead of tort, and (2) the limitation of liability clause is unconscionable and unenforceable.

. . . Although there was no choice-of-laws provision in the contract, the place of contracting, performance, and subject matter of the contract was in Michigan. Thus we apply Michigan law. Under Michigan law, in order for an action in tort to arise out of a breach of contract, the act must constitute (1) a breach of duty separate and distinct from the breach of contract, and (2) active negligence or misfeasance. The duty prong is the threshold inquiry.

The Michigan Supreme Court addressed the question of a tort arising out of a contract in *Hart v. Ludwig,* 79 N.W.2d 895 (Mich. 1956). The court held that where the only violation was that of a broken promise to perform a contract, and there existed no independent duty outside the contract, "liability, if any, must rest solely upon a breach of [the] contract." *Id.* at 897–98, quoting *Tuttle v. Gilbert Manfg. Co.,* 13 N.E. 465, 467 (Mass. 1887).

Similarly, ADT's obligation to promptly and correctly dispatch EMS emanated only from the contract, not Michigan common law, and thus no tort claim is available. Having found no independent duty, we need not determine whether ADT's actions constituted misfeasance or negligence.

Spengler also argues that the $500 limitation of liability clause contained in the parties' contract is unenforceable under the Michigan

Consumer Protection Act and unconscionable. These arguments, however, are raised for the first time before this court.... Because it is well-settled that issues not presented to the district court are not proper on appeal, we will not consider these issues now.

We therefore AFFIRM the judgment of the district court.

NOTES

1. **Critiquing *Spengler*.** Does the Michigan common law as applied in *Spengler* make any sense? RESTATEMENT (THIRD) OF TORTS: LIABILITY FOR PHYSICAL HARM § 42 (Proposed Final Draft No. 1, 2005) (which replaces RESTATEMENT (SECOND) § 323), states that an actor who undertakes to render services to another, when the actor knows or should know that the services will reduce the risk of physical harm to the other, owes a duty of reasonable care in carrying out that undertaking if (a) the failure to exercise care increases the risk of harm beyond that which would have existed without the undertaking, or (b) the other person relies on the undertaking. How might this provision have helped the plaintiff in *Spengler*?

2. **Distinguishing contract from tort.** The security contract in *Spengler* related to physical safety, and breach of the contract caused physical harm. Should that be enough to create a tort duty of care? *See* DOBBS ON TORTS §§ 319–20 (2000). In *Southwestern Bell Tel. Co. v. DeLanney*, 809 S.W.2d 493 (Tex. 1991), the court rejected tort liability where a telephone company failed to fulfill a contract to publish a Yellow Pages ad. "If the defendant's conduct—such as negligently burning down a house—would give rise to liability independent of the fact that a contract exists between the parties, the plaintiff's claim may also sound in tort. Conversely, if the defendant's conduct—such as failing to publish an advertisement—would give rise to liability only because it breaches the parties' agreement, the plaintiff's claim ordinarily sounds only in contract." How would this reasoning apply to *Spengler*?

GRIMES v. KENNEDY KRIEGER INSTITUTE, INC., 782 A.2d 807 (Md. 2001). To determine whether costly abatement of lead in rental houses was necessary for safety, researchers allegedly set up a study that placed some groups of children in houses with incomplete abatement of lead. The plaintiff children, whose parents were not fully informed, allegedly suffered elevated lead levels in their blood. The trial court dismissed the claim because defendant researchers owed no duty to the children. *Held,* reversed. A duty of care can be found on several grounds. One ground is that the contract between researchers and families calling for families to submit to blood sampling and researchers to test for lead, may be found to create a special relationship and attendant tort duties of care.

NOTES

1. **Tort duty from contract.** *Grimes* indicates that a contract can create tort duties that may extend beyond the contract's own terms. Does this make sense, or should the terms of the contract circumscribe the defendant's liability?

2. **Leases.** At one time, most courts applied the rule that a tenant could not bring a tort action against a lessor based on breach of an agreement to make repairs to the premises, even when personal injury resulted. *See, e.g., Leavitt v. Twin County Rental Co.*, 21 S.E.2d 890 (N.C. 1942) (damages for personal injury are "too remote" and "not within the contemplation of the parties"). Many states have now abrogated this rule by statute with respect to residential leases, and many courts have changed the rule for commercial leases as well. *See Mobil Oil Corp. v. Thorn*, 258 N.W.2d 30 (Mich. 1977). The Restatement (Second) § 357 provides that a lessor is subject to liability for physical harm to a lessee and others on the land with the lessee's permission caused by a condition of disrepair, if (1) the lessor has contracted to repair, (2) the disrepair creates an unreasonable risk, and (3) the lessor fails to exercise reasonable care to perform his contract. The Restatement (Third) says that a person in a "special relationship with another owes the other a duty of reasonable care with regard to risks that arise within the scope of the relationship." The relationship between a landlord and tenants is specifically listed. RESTATEMENT (THIRD) OF TORTS: LIABILITY FOR PHYSICAL HARM § 40 (P.F.D. No. 1, 2005). Could this broad provision support the recognition of a tort duty to fulfill a contractual obligation to repair if a tenant is injured by non-repair?

3. **Reassessing *Spengler*.** Does *Grimes* and the modern approach to landlord duties described in Note 2 further undermine the reasoning in *Spengler*?

4. **Expired contracts.** Might a contractual undertaking simply expire with the contract? *See Folsom v. Burger King*, 958 P.2d 301 (Wash. 1998) (security company owed no duty to workers who pushed the still-working alarm during a robbery but were ignored because defendant was not under a contractual obligation to respond and their failure to remove the alarm did not represent a voluntary assumption of a duty).

§ 2. PROMISES TO THIRD PERSONS

WINTERBOTTOM v. WRIGHT, 10 M. & W. 109, 152 Eng. Rep. 402 (Exch. Pl. 1842). Defendant was under contract with the Postmaster–General to supply coaches for use in delivering mail. The contract also called for the defendant to keep them in good repair. Plaintiff was the coachman on one of the coaches supplied by the defendant and was allegedly lamed for life when the coach broke down and he was thrown from his seat. He alleged that it broke down because the defendant neglected to perform the repair portion of his contract. *Held*, for the defendant. LORD ABINGER, C.B.: "Here the action is brought simply because the defendant was a contractor with a third person; and it is contended that thereupon he became liable to every body who might use the carriage.

If there had been any ground for such an action, there certainly would have been some precedent of it; but with the exception of actions against innkeepers, and some few other persons, no case of a similar nature has occurred in practice. That is a strong circumstance, and is of itself a great authority against its maintenance. It is however contended that this contract being made on the behalf of the public by the Postmaster–General, no action could be maintained against him, and therefore the plaintiff must have a remedy against the defendant. But that is by no means a necessary consequence—he may be remediless altogether. There is no privity of contract between these parties; and if the plaintiff can sue, every passenger, or even any person passing along the road, who was injured by the upsetting of the coach, might bring a similar action. Unless we confine the operation of such contracts as this to the parties who entered into them, the most absurd and outrageous consequences, to which I can see no limit, would ensue. Where a party becomes responsible to the public, by undertaking a public duty, he is liable, though the injury may have arisen from the negligence of his servant or agent. So, in cases of public nuisances, whether the act was done by the party as a servant, or in any other capacity, you are liable to an action at the suit of any person who suffers. Those, however, are cases where the real ground of the liability is the public duty, or the commission of the public nuisance. There is also a class of cases in which the law permits a contract to be turned into a tort; but unless there has been some public duty undertaken, or public nuisance committed, they are all cases in which an action might have been maintained upon the contract. Thus, a carrier may be sued either in assumpsit or case; but there is no instance in which a party, who was not privy to the contract entered into with him, can maintain any such action. The plaintiff in this case could not have brought an action on the contract; if he could have done so, what would have been his situation, supposing the Postmaster General had released the defendant? That would, at all events, have defeated his claim altogether. By permitting this action, we would be working this injustice, that after the defendant had done everything to the satisfaction of his employer, and after all matters between them had been adjusted, and all accounts settled on the footing of their contract, we should subject them to be ripped open by this action of tort being brought against him.''

ALDERSON, B.: ''The only safe rule is to confine the right to recover to those who enter into the contract: if we go one step beyond that, there is no reason why we should not go fifty.''

NOTE

It was once thought that *Winterbottom v. Wright* established a rule about privity, not a rule about nonfeasance. The result was that even if the defendant was guilty of affirmative negligence in performance of a contract, he would not be liable to third persons who were not parties to the contract. This was attacked, not only on grounds of injustice, but on the ground that

Winterbottom v. Wright was really only a nonfeasance case and that its rule should be applied only to cases of nonfeasance in the performance of a contract. Do you agree that it was a nonfeasance case?

H.R. MOCH CO. v. RENSSELAER WATER CO.

159 N.E. 896 (N.Y. 1928)

CARDOZO, C.J. The defendant, a waterworks company under the laws of this state, made a contract with the city of Rensselaer for the supply of water during a term of years. Water was to be furnished to the city for sewer flushing and street sprinkling; for service to schools and public buildings; and for service at fire hydrants, the latter service at the rate of $42.50 a year for each hydrant. Water was to be furnished to private takers within the city at their homes and factories and other industries at reasonable rates, not exceeding a stated schedule. While this contract was in force, a building caught fire. The flames, spreading to the plaintiff's warehouse near by, destroyed it and its contents. The defendant, according to the complaint, was promptly notified of the fire, "but omitted and neglected after such notice, to supply or furnish sufficient or adequate quantity of water, with adequate pressure to stay, suppress, or extinguish the fire before it reached the warehouse of the plaintiff, although the pressure and supply which the defendant was equipped to supply and furnish, and had agreed by said contract to supply and furnish, was adequate and sufficient to prevent the spread of the fire to and the destruction of the plaintiff's warehouse and its contents." By reason of failure of the defendant to "fulfill the provisions of the contract between it and the city of Rensselaer," the plaintiff is said to have suffered damage, for which judgment is demanded. A motion, in the nature of a demurrer, to dismiss the complaint, was denied at Special Term. The Appellate Division reversed by a divided court.

Liability in the plaintiff's argument is placed on one or other of three grounds. The complaint, we are told, is to be viewed as stating: (1) A cause of action for breach of contract within Lawrence v. Fox, 20 N.Y. 268; (2) a cause of action for a common-law tort, within MacPherson v. Buick Motor Co., 217 N.Y. 382, 111 N.E. 1050, L.R.A. 1916F, 696, Ann. Cas. 1916C, 440; (3) a cause of action for the breach of a statutory duty. These several grounds of liability will be considered in succession.

(1) We think the action is not maintainable as one for breach of contract.

No legal duty rests upon a city to supply its inhabitants with protection against fire. That being so, a member of the public may not maintain an action under Lawrence v. Fox against one contracting with the city to furnish water at the hydrants, unless an intention appears that the promisor is to be answerable to individual members of the public as well as to the city for any loss ensuing from the failure to fulfill the promise. No such intention is discernible here.... In a broad sense it is true that every city contract, not improvident or wasteful, is for the benefit of the public. More than this, however, must be shown to give a right of action to a member of the public not formally a party. The benefit, as it is sometimes said, must be one that is not merely incidental and secondary. It must be primary and immediate in such a sense and to such a degree as to bespeak the assumption of a duty to make reparation duty to the individual members of the public if the benefit is lost. The field of obligation would be expanded beyond reasonable limits if less than this were to be demanded as a condition of liability. A promisor undertakes to supply fuel for heating a public building. He is not liable for breach of contract to a visitor who finds the building without fuel, and thus contracts a cold. . . .

An intention to assume an obligation of indefinite extension to every member of the public is seen to be the more improbable when we recall the crushing burden that the obligation would impose. The consequences invited would bear no reasonable proportion to those attached by law to defaults not greatly different . . . . If the plaintiff is to prevail, one who negligently omits to supply sufficient pressure to extinguish a fire started by another assumes an obligation to pay the ensuing damage, though the whole city is laid low. A promisor will not be deemed to have had in mind the assumption of a risk so overwhelming for any trivial reward. . . .

(2) We think the action is not maintainable as one for a common-law tort.

"It is ancient learning that one who assumes to act, even though gratuitously, may thereby become subject to the duty of acting carefully, if he acts at all." The plaintiff would bring its case within the orbit of that principle. The hand once set to a task may not always be withdrawn with impunity though liability would fall if it had never been applied at all. A time-honored formula often phrases the distinction as one between misfeasance and nonfeasance. Incomplete the formula is, and so at times misleading. Given a relation involving in its existence a duty of care irrespective of a contract, a tort may result as well from acts of omission as of commission in the fulfillment of the duty thus recognized by law. What we need to know is not so much the conduct to be avoided when the relation and its attendant duty are established as existing. What we need to know is the conduct that engenders the relation. It is here that the formula, however incomplete, has its value and significance. If conduct has gone forward to such a stage that inaction would commonly result, not negatively merely in withholding a benefit, but positively or actively in working an injury, there exists a relation out of which arises a duty to go forward. Bohlen, Studies in the Law of Torts, p. 87. So the surgeon who operates without pay is liable, though his negligence is in the omission to sterilize his instruments; the engineer, though his fault is in the failure to shut off steam; the maker of automobiles, at the suit of some one other than the buyer, though his negligence is merely in inadequate inspection The query always is whether the putative wrongdoer has advanced to such a point as to have launched a force or instrument of harm, or has stopped where inaction is at most a refusal to become an instrument for good.

The plaintiff would have us hold that the defendant, when once it entered upon the performance of its contract with the city, was brought into such a relation with everyone who might potentially be benefitted through the supply of water at the hydrants as to give to negligent performance, without reasonable notice of a refusal to continue, the quality of a tort.... We are satisfied that liability would be unduly and indeed indefinitely extended by this enlargement of the zone of duty. The dealer in coal who is to supply fuel for a shop must then answer to the customers if fuel is lacking. The manufacturer of goods, who enters upon the performance of his contract, must answer, in that view, not only to the buyer, but to those who to his knowledge are looking to the buyer for their own sources of supply. Everyone making a promise having the quality of a contract will be under a duty to the promisee by virtue of the promise, but under another duty, apart from contract, to an indefinite number of potential beneficiaries when performance has begun. The assumption of one relation will mean the involuntary assumption of a series of new relations, inescapably hooked together....

(3) We think the action is not maintainable as one for the breach of a statutory duty....

NOTES

1. *Winterbottom v. Wright* reasoned in the language of privity but might be best understood as a nonfeasance case. *Moch* reasoned in part in the language of nonfeasance, but could it be best understood as a privity case?

2. Maybe *Moch* is not a nonfeasance case at all. Did the defendant not operate a water company and operate it badly? How would the case have been handled if the defendant had caused the pressure to fall by (a) failing to read its own instruments? (b) failing to open a valve? (c) opening the wrong valve?

3. If the problem in *Moch* is not nonfeasance, consider this: *Moch* was decided the same year as *Palsgraf*. Is it plausible to treat *Moch* as a scope-of-duty problem rather than a nonfeasance problem? You could ask (a) what persons are within the defendant's promised protection? and (b) what risks are within the promised protection? Such an approach would delineate the duty by asking about the scope of the promise or undertaking rather than by asking about foreseeability, but otherwise it would sound pretty much like a basic proximate cause approach.

4. Another possibility is that the court is simply afraid of potentially unlimited liability and will arbitrarily mark a limit to that liability. In *Strauss v. Belle Realty Co.*, 482 N.E.2d 34 (N.Y. 1985), the defendant, an electrical utility, was grossly negligent in permitting an electrical failure and general blackout over a large urban area for a long period of time. The 77-year-old plaintiff had a contract with the utility for electrical service in his apartment. When the electricity failed, the plaintiff could not get running water, which depended upon electrical pumps. On the second day of the blackout, he went to the basement of the building in an attempt to obtain water, to be carried up to his apartment. He fell in the darkened basement and sustained injury.

Although the plaintiff was a utility customer for service in his apartment, he had no contract with the utility for electrical service in the basement; the basement was a common area covered by the landlord's contract for electrical service. The Court held that the utility was not liable even though its negligence was "gross." However, other victims of the blackout who had contracted directly with the utility for electrical services were allowed to recover in similar circumstances. The court did not characterize the defendant's conduct as nonfeasance. Instead it emphasized its fear of unlimited liability and frankly invoked privity as an implement of judicial policy to "limit the legal consequences of wrongs to a controllable degree."

5. One kind of risk covered by contracts is economic. A breach of contract may cause financial loss but not physical injury. Most of Cardozo's examples in *Moch* were like this. But suppose a contract promise is intended to protect against physical injury. Would there by any need to worry about extended liability in the examples Cardozo gives? Did Cardozo overlook the fact that *Moch* was a physical harm case and that his concerns about extensive economic liability were misplaced?

6. Is it possible to interpret the "intent of the parties" without resorting to an automatic rule based on privity? In *Libbey v. Hampton Water Works Co.*, 389 A.2d 434 (N.H. 1978), the court in a *Moch*-type case observed: "Water companies are in business to supply water, not to extinguish fires. Their rates reflect this assumption; they are uniform, not varying with the greater or lesser inherent danger in given areas." This kind of reasoning suggests that even one in privity might be denied recovery for some consequential damages if those damages did not represent harms against which the parties were contracting. Compare the contemplation-of-the-parties rule of *Hadley v. Baxendale*, as to which see DAN DOBBS, THE LAW OF REMEDIES §§ 12.4(4)–12.4(7) (1992).

PALKA v. SERVICEMASTER MANAGEMENT SERVICES CORP., 634 N.E.2d 189 (N.Y. 1994). Palka was a nurse employed by Ellis Hospital. Ellis had contracted with Servicemaster to manage maintenance operations at the hospital. Before that, the hospital had conducted its own safety inspections of such things as fans mounted on walls. After Servicemaster took over, the hospital left all such programs to Servicemaster. Servicemaster did not exercise reasonable care with respect to wall-mounted fans and one of them fell on the plaintiff. She sued Servicemaster. *Held:* (1) safety of such items as wall-mounted fans was within the scope of the contract obligation; and (2) Servicemaster was under a duty to the plaintiff, a non-contracting party. Palka "proved not only that Servicemaster undertook to provide a service to Ellis Hospital and did so negligently, but also that its conduct in undertaking that particular service placed Palka in an unreasonably risky setting greater than that, had Servicemaster never ventured into its hospital servicing role at all." "[U]nlike our decisions in Moch Co. v. Rensselaer Water Co. and Strauss v. Belle Realty Co., the instant case presents this array of factors:

reasonably interconnected and anticipated relationships; particularity of assumed responsibility under the contract and evidence adduced at trial; displacement and substitution of a particular safety function designed to protect persons like this plaintiff; and a set of reasonable expectations of all the parties. These factors, taken together, support imposition of liability against this defendant in favor of this plaintiff."

NOTES

1. **"Third party beneficiaries."** Some courts use the language of contract law in explaining the imposition of a tort duty. For example, in *Doe ex rel. Doe v. Wright Sec. Services, Inc.*, 950 So.2d 1076 (Miss. App. 2007), a student named Jim was sexually assaulted by another student in the restaurant restroom at a school bus stop. Jim sued Wright, the security company hired by the school district, claiming negligence. Reversing a summary judgment for Wright, the court said a tort duty may extend to "third party beneficiaries of a contract," and that here, "one purpose of Wright's contract with [the District] was to prevent violence or altercations among the alternative school students." This "shows as a matter of law that Wright owed a duty to minimize risks to Jim's safety."

2. **Some effects of shifting a duty.** If A by contract or other understanding shifts his duty to the plaintiff to B, any one or more of three distinct results might follow: (a) Plaintiff is entitled to the same care to which she was entitled from A; (b) B is subjected to a duty he did not have before; and (c) A may or may not be relieved of the duty A owed to the plaintiff before the contract. The Restatement attempts to deal with some problems in this setting under the doctrines of proximate cause. RESTATEMENT SECOND OF TORTS § 452(2) (1965). Very commonly, when A contractually shifts responsibility to B, the contract also provides that if A is held liable for B's acts, A will be entitled to indemnity from B.

3. **Implied contract–transfer of control.** Duty might be shifted from A to B without a formal or express contract. For example, suppose a landowner hires a contractor to build on the land. While the contractor is at work, it is in control and owes duties of care commensurate with that control, even though no contract articulates such a duty. When the contractor completes the project and returns the improved land back to the landowner, the landowner assumes the duty of care, even as to danger created by the contractor.

4. **Shifting a duty as reasonable care.** Are there not some occasions in which a defendant can exercise reasonable care by arranging for someone else to exercise that care? Can the defendant arrange for the *plaintiff* to provide the care needed?

5. **Allocating responsibility.** In *Alder v. Bayer Corp.*, 61 P.3d 1068 (Utah 2002), the defendant manufactured a system for developing x-rays. The defendant re-installed the machine in the hospital's new mammography suite. Both the hospital and the defendant knew that the fumes would be dangerous if ventilation was not adequate, but neither assured appropriate ventilation. As a result, technicians working with the machine allegedly developed serious

conditions, including, in one case, cognitive deficits. How should a court go about allocating responsibility? In the absence of a tacit or explicit understanding between defendant and hospital, should both be subject to liability? Neither? What if the contract allocated all responsibility to the hospital but the defendant knew the hospital was not going to check or improve ventilation?

PAZ v. STATE OF CALIFORNIA

994 P.2d 975 (Cal. 2000)

CHIN, J. . . .

[Osborne, which runs north and south, dead-ends at Foothill Boulevard. Stoneman Corporation was developing condos and other residential projects near that intersection. As a condition of granting a permit for the development, the city required Stoneman to install traffic signals and road markings. Stoneman hired Jennings for engineering, and in 1989 Jennings hired KOA to design and install the signals. In 1991, the signals still had not been installed, in part due to KOA's delay in seeking permits from the state. The intersection was already dangerous because of road angles and obscured sight lines; a number of accidents had occurred there. In 1991, the signals still not installed, the plaintiff, riding a motorcycle in a westerly direction on Foothill, crashed into a car that had been headed south on Osborne and was in the process of turning left or east onto Foothill. The plaintiff sued a number of defendants, including the state and its transportation department, the city, Stoneman and KOA. He alleged that they were negligent in failing to get the traffic signals installed. The trial court granted summary judgment in favor of KOA and Stoneman. The Court of Appeals reversed.]

In this court, plaintiff reiterates his claim that defendants negligently discharged a contractual obligation to install traffic signals. Plaintiff asserts that timely installation of the signals would have alleviated the allegedly dangerous condition of obstructed sight lines at the intersection, and hence prevented his collision with Trafton's car. Thus, plaintiff's claim necessarily is grounded in the negligent undertaking theory of liability articulated in section 324A.

Section 324A reads:

> One who undertakes, gratuitously or for consideration, to render services to another which he should recognize as necessary for the protection of a third person or his things, is subject to liability to the third person for physical harm resulting from his failure to exercise reasonable care to [perform] his undertaking, if
>
> > (a) his failure to exercise reasonable care increases the risk of such harm, or
> >
> > (b) he has undertaken to perform a duty owed by the other to the third person, or

(c) the harm is suffered because of reliance of the other or the third person upon the undertaking.

. . . In assessing the applicability of section 324A here, we assume for the sake of discussion that defendants undertook the tasks they are alleged to have performed negligently. . . . Similarly, we assume that defendants' agreement to install traffic control signals for the City constituted an undertaking "to render services to another which [defendants] should recognize as necessary for the protection of [third persons]. . . ."

However, the negligent undertaking theory of liability requires more than simply establishing defendants' undertaking to another. . . . In this case, none of these three conditions for section 324A liability are present.

The evidence fails to support an inference that defendants' conduct increased the risk of physical harm to plaintiff beyond that which allegedly existed at the intersection. Plaintiff alleged that the intersection was dangerous because of restricted sight lines. However, nothing in the record suggests that defendants did anything that increased the risk to motorists that allegedly existed because of these sight lines. Instead, defendants simply did not succeed in completing—before plaintiff's collision—a project that might have reduced the preexisting hazard at the intersection. In this instance, where the record shows that nothing changed but the passage of time, a failure to alleviate a risk cannot be regarded as tantamount to increasing that risk. . . .

Neither the record nor the law shows any basis for satisfying the second alternative condition required for section 324A liability. In agreeing to the traffic signal installation condition, Stoneman (and by extension KOA) did not undertake to perform a duty that the City owed to plaintiff. As our cases and statutes establish, cities generally have no affirmative duty to install traffic control signals. . . .

Finally, plaintiff did not submit, and the record does not contain, any evidence that he was harmed because either he or the City relied on defendants' timely installation of traffic control signals. The only reasonable inferences available from the record are to the contrary. The City and Stoneman did not make a contract to install the traffic signals. Instead, the City only made the signals a condition of Stoneman's condominium development project. If Stoneman had abandoned the development project—a decision that real property developers may face if financing becomes uncertain or if litigation entangles a project—Stoneman would not have been obliged to install the traffic signals at all. Thus, imposing the traffic signal installation as a condition of development did not give the City a basis for relying on the installation's being completed at any time before the condominium project's completion.

The fact that the City was not relying on defendants to complete traffic signal installation within any particular time is further demonstrated by the City's own conduct in the matter. [T]he City did not apply for its own encroachment permit, necessary to operate and maintain the signals, for more than two months after Caltrans stopped KOA's work on the project just days before it would have been completed. . . .

[Remanded with instructions to enter judgment for KOA and Stoneman.]

Concurring Opinion by MOSK, J. . . .

This is therefore not a case in which a developer breached an obligation to install traffic improvements before commencing the operation of a commercial or residential development. Under such circumstances, a municipality may be said to rely upon a developer's timely installation of the traffic signal, and the developer could accordingly be held liable for harm resulting from its negligent delay based on that reliance. (Rest.2d Torts, § 324A, subd. (c).) Thus, I do not understand the majority as foreclosing liability for negligent delay when a developer has breached a legal obligation to install a traffic improvement by a certain time or under a certain condition.

Dissenting Opinion by GEORGE, C.J. . . .

[The city could be found to have a duty to make the intersection safer. Hence KOA was undertaking to perform the city's duty.]

Second, . . . I believe the developer owed a duty to the users of the intersection under the third condition of section 324A, because in these circumstances the city (and the neighborhood residents who repeatedly had lobbied the city for the installation of a traffic signal at the intersection) reasonably relied upon the developer's undertaking to install the traffic signal[1] . . . .

Once a developer has made a commitment to install a needed safety measure as a condition of obtaining a development permit and goes ahead with work under the permit . . . the local entity and the public reasonably anticipate that the safety measure in question will be provided by the developer within a reasonable period of time. Thus, under these circumstances the public entity would have no reason to expend its own funds or to seek to impose a similar requirement upon some other entity, absent some indication from the developer that it does not intend to fulfill its responsibility under the permit. . . .

NOTES

1. **Increased risk—increase over what?** Consider the increased risk clause in § 324A. Does that clause mean that liability is appropriate if the risk is greater than it would have been had the defendant performed his contract? Or must it be greater than it would have been if there were no contract at all? Can you tell whether Justice Chin has a view about that? RESTATEMENT (THIRD) OF TORTS § 43 (Proposed Final Draft No. 1, 2005), intended to replace § 324A,

---

1. Although there is no evidence in this case that plaintiff was aware of, or relied upon, the developer's commitment to install a traffic signal, under section 324A the relevant reliance may be either by the injured person or by the entity for which the developer undertakes to render the service, here, the city. . . .

resolves this ambiguity by proving that a duty of care is owed on increased risk grounds if the failure to exercise reasonable care increases the risk of harm beyond that which would have existed without the undertaking.

2. **A model for increased risk cases?** In an omitted portion of the opinion, Justice Chin gave an example of increased danger based upon *Thirion v. Fredrickson & Watson Construction Co.,* 14 Cal.Rptr. 269 (Ct. App. 1961). In that case the plaintiff lost control when his car struck loose gravel on a highway. The jury could find (a) that the defendant contractor had not begun work on the portion of the highway where the plaintiff lost control, but (b) he had conducted his operations on a different part of the road so as to cause loose gravel to be deposited outside the work area. The jury could also find that this gravel was a cause of the plaintiff's injury. Liability was held to be proper. If this case is the only model for increased risk, isn't it clear that there was no increased risk in *Paz? Cf. Fung v. Japan Airlines Co., Ltd.,* 880 N.E.2d 845 (N.Y. 2007) (no duty owed by snow-plow contractor to motorists where plowing pursuant to contract "could not be said to have created or exacerbated a dangerous condition").

3. **Increased risk and reliance.** A 14-year-old boy walking to the bus stop in pre-dawn hours was struck and killed by a truck. The streetlight near which the boy was struck was not operative. His mother sued the streetlight company for negligence. The trial court found no duty. But the court in *Clay Electric Cooperative, Inc. v. Johnson,* 873 So.2d 1182 (Fla. 2003), reversed and remanded on both the "increased risk" and "reliance" issues. When the company undertook to maintain the streetlights, the court said, it should have foreseen that proper maintenance was necessary for the protection of children who walked to the bus in the early morning hours before school. Do cases like this place too great a burden on defendants?

§ 3.   ACTION AS A PROMISE
OR UNDERTAKING

FLORENCE v. GOLDBERG

375 N.E.2d 763 (N.Y. 1978)

JASEN, JUDGE.

[A mother took her 6-year-old child to school each day for two weeks, during which time the city police had stationed a guard at a street crossing. The mother, having observed this protection, ceased to take the child to school. On the day in question the crossing guard regularly assigned there called in sick. Departmental regulations called for sending a substitute if possible and, if not, to cover the most dangerous crossings. No substitute was sent and the principal of the school was not notified. The child was struck at the unguarded crossing and suffered severe brain damage. The plaintiffs recovered against the city and those responsible for operation of the car. The city appeals.]

[A] municipality cannot be held liable for failure to furnish adequate police protection. This duty, like the duty to provide protection against fire, flows only to the general public. (Riss v. City of New York, 22 N.Y. 2d 579, 583, 293 N.Y.S.2d 897, 899, 240 N.E.2d 860, 861. . . .)

[T]here is little question that the police department voluntarily assumed a particular duty to supervise school crossings. . . .

Significantly, the duty assumed by the police department was a limited one: a duty intended to benefit a special class of persons—viz., children crossing designated intersections while traveling to and from school at scheduled times. Thus, the duty assumed constituted more than a general duty to provide police protection to the public at large. Having witnessed the regular performance of this special duty for a two-week period, the plaintiff infant's mother relied upon its continued performance. To borrow once more from Chief Judge Cardozo, "[i]f conduct has gone forward to such a state that inaction would commonly result, not negatively merely in withholding a benefit, but positively or actively in working an injury, there exists a relation out of which arises a duty to go forward." (Moch Co. v. Rensselaer Water Co., 247 N.Y. at p. 167,159 N.E. at p. 898, supra). Application of this principle to the present case leads unmistakably to the conclusion that the police department, having assumed a duty to a special class of persons, and having gone forward with performance of that duty in the past, had an obligation to continue its performance. Had the police department not assumed a duty to supervise school crossings, plaintiff infant's mother would not have permitted her child to travel to and from school alone. The department's failure to perform this duty placed the infant plaintiff in greater danger than he would have been had the duty not been assumed, since the infant's mother would not have had reason to rely on the protection afforded her child and would have been required, in her absence, to arrange for someone to accompany her child to and from school.

[The court found that there was also proof that the city was negligent in failing to provide a guard.]

The order of the Appellate Division should be affirmed, with costs.

KIRCHER v. CITY OF JAMESTOWN, 543 N.E.2d 443 (N.Y. 1989). The plaintiff was entering her car in a drug store parking lot when a man, Blanco, accosted her. She screamed. Karen Allen and Richard Skinner heard the screams and saw Blanco force her into the car. Allen and Skinner gave chase, but lost sight of the car in heavy traffic. While trying to catch up to the car, they saw a police officer, Carlson. They explained what they had seen and gave him the car's description and license number. He promised to "call in," but in fact Carlson never even reported the incident. Meanwhile, Blanco repeatedly raped and beat the plaintiff, fracturing her larynx and inflicting other brutal injuries. In the Court of Appeals, *held*, the plaintiff cannot recover.

(1) A city is not held liable for negligent exercise of government functions unless it is in a special relationship with the claimant. "Nevertheless, where a municipality voluntarily undertakes to act on behalf of a particular citizen who detrimentally relies on an illusory promise of protection offered by the municipality, we have permitted liability because in such cases the municipality has by its conduct determined how its resources are to be allocated in respect to that circumstance and has thereby created a 'special relationship' with the individual seeking protection."

(2) Liability on this ground requires the municipality to be in "direct contact" with the claimant and requires justifiable reliance by the claimant upon the municipality's affirmative undertaking. Although Allen and Skinner were in direct contact with police, the plaintiff was not, so the direct contact requirement is not fulfilled.

(3) The reliance requirement is not fulfilled, either. "[T]he helpless and isolated plaintiff could not even communicate with the police, much less rely on any promise of protection the police might have offered. Yet, although plaintiff's failure to rely can be directly attributed to her dire circumstances, this does not, as the dissenters urge, provide a justification for ignoring the reliance requirement altogether."

NOTES

1. **Action as undertaking.** The issue in many cases is whether the defendant's conduct counted as an undertaking at all. The insurer for a manufacturing plant regularly inspects it for safety. The insurer makes recommendations for increased safety and adjusts its premium charges based on what it finds. It should have discovered a danger that cost the lives to two employees. Could a jury find that by its inspections, the insurer undertook a duty to use care for the benefit of employees? *See Schoenwald v. Farmers Coop Ass'n of Marion,* 474 N.W.2d 519 (S.D. 1991) (no); *Hodge v. United States Fid. & Guar. Co.,* 539 So.2d 229 (Ala. 1989) (yes). *Cf. Fackelman v. Lac d'Amiante du Quebec, LTEE,* 942 A.2d 127 (N.J. Super. Ct. App. Div. 2008) (insurer performed industrial hygiene studies for company; held, no duty to warn employees of danger from asbestos exposure because insurer did not thereby assume responsibility for workplace safety).

In *Florence* is it clear that the city's actions counted as undertakings because they seemed to promise continued protection for the children?

2. **Reliance and discriminatory enforcement.** If *Florence* requires reliance in order to justify recovery, is that desirable? What about a child whose parents never knew of the presence of a guard? Or a child both of whose parents knew there was no guard but neither of whom could take the child to school because they both worked? Is there anything wrong with permitting a recovery for the Florence boy but not for the child of non-relying parents?

3. **Why is reliance necessary?** The requirement of reliance works even more dramatically to deny a recovery in *Kircher.* In addition, that case

reflects New York's more recent additional "direct contact" requirement. Why require either on the facts of *Kircher*? Can you have no special relationship without reliance? Was the city making some careful calculation about its limited resources when the officer failed even to report as he promised?

4. **Why is undertaking relevant?** Turn to a different problem with "undertakings." The idea that "undertaking" may create a duty that did not otherwise exist is generally recognized but profoundly uncertain. First consider why an undertaking might be relevant to the question of the defendant's duty. Would it show: (a) a special relationship, established by the undertaking itself; (b) affirmative action, not mere nonfeasance; (c) the equivalent of a promise from which a tort duty might arise if there is consideration or reliance? *See, e.g., State Auto Ins. Cos. v. B.N.C.*, 702 N.W.2d 379 (S.D. 2005) (discussing duty of care owed by daughter who undertook to watch her father's home while he was on vacation).

NOTE: CONTENT AND SCOPE OF DUTY
DERIVED FROM "UNDERTAKINGS"

1. *Scope of duty imposed by undertaking.* Many courts would agree that "the scope of any duty assumed depends upon the nature of the undertaking." *Delgado v. Trax Bar & Grill*, 113 P.3d 1159 (Cal. 2005). What is undertaken in the following cases?

A. A mother, seeing the crossing guards in the afternoon, assumes that the school has undertaken to provide crossing safety before and after school and thus allows her child to walk to school unaccompanied the next morning. There are no crossing guards and the child is struck in a crosswalk by a motorist. The school has never provided guards in the morning. Did it (a) undertake to provide crossing safety and do it negligently? or (b) undertake to provide afternoon guards only? In *Jefferson County School District R–1 v. Gilbert*, 725 P.2d 774 (Colo. 1986), the court took the narrower view, that the school had assumed the duty to provide afternoon guards only.

B. A landlord provides door buzzers and an intercom system in the tenant's apartment building. She is raped by a third party who accosted her first on the sidewalk outside the front gate of the building, then took her to the back of the building. She sues the landlord for failure to provide greater security. She argues that the landlord's provision of the buzzers and intercom constituted a voluntary undertaking to provide security. In *Bourgonje v. Machev*, 841 N.E.2d 96 (Ill. App. Ct. 2005), the court held that the door buzzers and intercom did not constitute such an undertaking, on the facts. The main safety benefit was to the residents inside the building, not to "persons outside the premises."

C. An elderly Alzheimer's patient is attacked and bitten by fire ants in her bed in a nursing home. She dies, and her heirs sue many defendants, including the construction company that built the nursing home and two landscaping companies. All three of the companies had contracts with the nursing home: The construction company contracted to build, according to plaintiffs, a "safe facility." The first landscaper had a maintenance contract which required it to maintain the lawn and shrubbery, and sprayed insecticide pursuant to that contract. But that contract terminated one month before the fire ant attack. The second landscaper had a similar contract, but it included providing "ant bed control." Against which defendant do the plaintiffs have the strongest case? Should they succeed against any? *Rein v. Benchmark Constr. Co.*, 865 So.2d 1134 (Miss. 2004).

2. *Scope and breach.* The scope of the duty is important in determining whether it was breached. The defendant contracts with a hospital to provide "rodent sanitation services." Thereafter, the plaintiff, who was a hospital patient, was injured when a rat ran across her feet, causing her to fall into a bathtub. Did the defendant breach its duty to provide rodent sanitation services? *See Hill v. James Walker Mem. Hosp.*, 407 F.2d 1036 (4th Cir. 1969).

3. *Content of duty.* Granted that the defendant's undertaking creates a duty and that it is limited to persons and harms within the risk, what is the content or measure of the duty? Is it a general duty of due care? Or is it a specific duty to do whatever the contract or undertaking calls for? If the latter, is it an absolute duty, a case of strict liability, or only a duty to make reasonable effort to perform? Should this be determined by what the promisor promised? *See, e.g., Sall v. T's, Inc.*, 136 P.3d 471 (Kan. 2006) (examining golf course's policy on warning golfers of lightning to determine content of duty); *South v. McCarter*, 119 P.3d 1 (Kan. 2005) (construing lease agreement).

GENERAL REFERENCE: DOBBS ON TORTS §§ 319–321 (2000).

CHAPTER 18

THE DUTY TO PROTECT FROM THIRD PERSONS

▪ ▪ ▪

§ 1. DEFENDANT'S RELATIONSHIP WITH THE PLAINTIFF

ISEBERG v. GROSS

879 N.E.2d 278 (Ill. 2007)

JUSTICE BURKE delivered the judgment of the court, with opinion:

In this interlocutory appeal, plaintiffs, Mitchell Iseberg (Iseberg) and his wife, Carol, seek reversal of the order dismissing with prejudice count I of their third amended complaint, brought against defendants, Sheldon Gross (Gross) and Henry Frank (Frank). In count I, plaintiffs alleged that Gross and Frank were negligent because they failed to warn Iseberg that a former mutual business partner, Edward Slavin (Slavin), had made threats against Iseberg's life. Slavin later acted on his threats and shot Iseberg, rendering him a paraplegic....

[Slavin and Gross started a business in 1995 under the name Vernonshire Auto Laundry Group, Inc. (VAL). Shortly afterward, Gross contacted Iseberg, a lawyer and real estate broker, who was in the process of acquiring land to develop into a strip mall. Frank and Iseberg formed a corporation, LFD, in order to complete that transaction. In 1996, VAL and LFD formed a partnership, with each company contributing funds to purchase the land. The purchase was made and title to the land was placed in a land trust, with VAL and LFD each owning 50%. A dispute arose among the partners and the partnership was dissolved, leaving VAL with sole ownership of the property. Much time passed and because the property did not sell, Slavin lost his entire investment. Plaintiffs alleged that Slavin became mentally unbalanced and that he focused his anger on Iseberg. Slavin told Gross several times that he wanted to harm Iseberg, once saying that he wanted to kill Iseberg and then commit suicide. Gross told Frank about these threats, but neither of them told Iseberg. In early 2000, Slavin rang the doorbell at Iseberg's home and shot him four times when he answered the door.]

... Because of the procedural posture of this case, the only issue before us is whether a legal duty existed.... What we must decide is whether Iseberg and defendants stood in such a relationship to one another that the law imposed on defendants an obligation of reasonable conduct for the benefit of Iseberg. Under common law, the universally accepted rule, articulated in section 314 of the Restatement (Second) of Torts, and long adhered to by this court, is that a private person has no duty to act affirmatively to protect another from criminal attack by a third person absent a "special relationship" between the parties. Historically, there have been four "special relationships" which this and other courts have recognized, namely, common carrier-passenger, innkeeper-guest, business invitor-invitee, and voluntary custodian-protectee. When one of these special relationships exists between the parties and an unreasonable risk of physical harm arises within the scope of that relationship, an obligation may be imposed on the one to exercise reasonable care to protect the other from such risk, if the risk is reasonably foreseeable, or to render first aid when it is known that such aid is needed. The existence of one of these four "special relationships" has typically been the basis for imposing an affirmative duty to act where one would not ordinarily exist.

In the case at bar, plaintiffs do not allege that one of the above-listed "special relationships" existed.... Instead, plaintiffs ask us to find, as did the dissenting appellate justice, that the facts alleged in the third amended complaint, viewed in a light most favorable to them, are sufficient to bring this case within an exception to the no-affirmative-duty rule. [Specifically, plaintiffs argue (1) that a duty to warn Iseberg of Slavin's threats arose because at the time of the shooting Iseberg was an agent of both Gross and Frank, and alternatively (2) that the court should abandon the requirement of a "special relationship."]

[On the agency argument, courts have found that a principal may have a duty to warn an agent if the principal knows of "an unreasonable risk involved in the employment, if the principal should realize that it exists and that the agent is likely not to become aware of it, thereby suffering harm." Here, however, the allegations in the complaint fail to establish the existence of a principal-agent relationship between defendants and Iseberg at the time of Iseberg's injury. Further, the complaint fails to allege that the risk of harm to Iseberg arose "from the particular nature" of the alleged agency relationship.]

[Plaintiffs also] contend that our recent case law demonstrates that the "special relationship" doctrine has been eroded in this state and that "the evolution of our case law has clearly been away from the formulaic application of the special relationship doctrine." Plaintiffs argue that the "special relationship" doctrine, in particular, and the no-duty rule, in general, are "antiquated" and out of step with contemporary societal morals. Thus, according to plaintiffs, the existence of an affirmative duty to warn or protect, particularly in situations where the parties are not strangers, should be a policy determination, made on a case-by-case basis, upon consideration of factors commonly used to determine the existence of a duty in ordinary negligence situations, *i.e.,* the reasonable foreseeability of the injury; the likelihood of the injury; the magnitude of the burden of guarding against the injury; and the consequences of placing that burden on the defendants. Plaintiffs urge us to abandon the "special relationship" framework for determining whether to impose an affirmative duty to protect against third-party attacks and to find a duty in the case at bar by applying the above four-factor negligence test. . . .

[Cases cited by plaintiffs are easily distinguishable.] Further, we can find no case in which this court has recognized an affirmative duty, based upon consideration of the four factors cited by plaintiffs, in the absence of a special relationship. Rather, the special relationship doctrine has been cited by this court in a number of recent cases, indicating our continued adherence to its general principles. . . .

Plaintiffs' only remaining argument for abandoning the "special relationship" doctrine is that the doctrine and the no-duty rule, in general, are antiquated and out of step with today's morality. While it is true that the no-duty rule has suffered criticism from a number of legal scholars, criticism of the rule is not new. Legal pundits have assailed the rule, citing its lack of social conscience, for as long as it has existed. . . . Contrary to plaintiffs' assertions, the no-affirmative-duty rule, as a common law tort principle, has been retained in every jurisdiction. . . . Thus, given the wide acceptance of the no-duty rule and the "special relationship" doctrine, it cannot be said that they are "antiquated" or "outmoded." . . . In *Rhodes,* we said, "the impracticality of imposing a legal duty to rescue between parties who stand in no special relationship to each other would leave us hesitant to do so." That statement is no less true today.

. . . The no-affirmative-duty rule and the "special relationship" doctrine stand as the law of this state. Accordingly, an affirmative duty to warn or protect against the criminal conduct of a third party may be imposed on one for the benefit of another only if there exists a special relationship between them. In the case at bar, no such relationship existed between the defendants and Iseberg. Nor was it shown that a principal-agent relationship existed between the parties which gave rise to a duty to warn. . . . For these reasons, we affirm the judgment of the appellate court.

Notes

1. **Special relationships.** The Second Restatement's list of special relationships has been widely applied, as the *Iseberg* court noted. Is it wrong for a court to apply the list literally? In *Hills v. Bridgeview Little League Association,* 745 N.E.2d 1166 (Ill. 2000), the court held that the possessor of a Little League ball park had no duty to prevent brutal and extended attacks by coaches of one team on a coach of the other team. "The playing field on which the attack on John Hills took place was not a business open to the general public. The only people permitted on the field at the time of the game were the two teams and the umpires." *See also Parish v. Truman,* 603 P.2d 120

(Ariz. Ct. App. 1979) (finding no duty to protect a social guest from third-party harm in the defendant's house on the ground that he was merely a licensee).

The Third Restatement's section 40 broadens the list to include employer-employee, school-student, and landlord-tenant, and changes the "business invitor-invitee" item to "a business or other possessor of land that holds its premises open to the public with those who are lawfully on the premises." Is this still too narrow? In *Grimes v. Kennedy Krieger Institute, Inc.*, 782 A.2d 807 (Md. 2001), the court recognized that a special relationship and concomitant tort duties might arise form a contract between the parties, from statute regulating their dealings, from the superior knowledge of one of them, and even, perhaps, from international law (the Nuremberg Code). In any event, special relationships are determined by the courts from the facts, not necessarily from a preconceived list.

2. **Why such a requirement?** Do you think the plaintiffs in *Iseberg* were correct in their argument that any "special relationship" requirement could be abandoned in favor of utilizing a more general test of duty, at least where the parties are not complete strangers? If that test were applied to the *Iseberg* facts, how would it work?

3. **Necessary, but not sufficient?** Is it enough to trigger a duty that the plaintiff and defendant are in a special relationship, or is more required? *See, e.g., Bjerke v. Johnson*, 742 N.W.2d 660 (Minn. 2007) (duty to protect another person from harm will be found if there is a special relationship and the risk is foreseeable); *Taboada v. Daly Seven, Inc.*, 626 S.E.2d 428 (Va. 2006) (even where the plaintiff and defendant are in a special relationship, "there is no liability when the defendant neither knows of the danger of an injury to the plaintiff from the criminal conduct of a third party nor has reason to foresee that danger").

4. **Employers and employees.** The *Iseberg* court rejected the plaintiffs "agency" argument on the complaint's factual allegations. Does an employer owe a duty of reasonable care to protect its employees from third parties? The Third Restatement adds employer-employee as a special relationship, as noted in Note 1, *supra*. The Second Restatement's § 314B recognizes such a duty, but only if the employee "comes into a position of imminent danger" and the employer knows it. *Accord, Dupont v. Aavid Thermal Tech., Inc.*, 798 A.2d 587 (N.H. 2002). A further requirement is that the risks of harm by a third person must arise within the scope of the employment relationship itself. *See* RESTATEMENT (SECOND) OF TORTS § 314A; RESTATEMENT (SECOND) OF AGENCY §§ 471 & 521(1); *accord, MacDonald v. Hinton*, 836 N.E.2d 893 (Ill. App. 2005).

5. **Duty to protect plaintiffs against negligent acts by third parties.** We focus in this section of the book mainly on whether a duty exists to protect a plaintiff from a criminal act by a third person. The special relationship rules apply much the same way, however, even in cases where the plaintiff alleges that the defendant failed to protect her from the *negligence* of a third party. *See, e.g., Marshall v. Burger King Corp.*, 856 N.E.2d 1048 (Ill. 2006). Both the Second and Third Restatements are in accord. *See* RESTATEMENT (SECOND) OF TORTS §§ 314A & 344; RESTATEMENT (THIRD) OF TORTS: LIABILITY FOR PHYSICAL HARM §§ 19 & 40 (Proposed Final Draft No. 1, 2005).

6. **Nonfeasance.** Is a special relationship required only where the plaintiff alleges that the defendant failed to act, or does it apply even when the defendant has acted and created a risk of harm?

POSECAI v. WAL–MART STORES, INC.

752 So.2d 762 (La. 1999)

Mᴀʀᴄᴜs, Jᴜsᴛɪᴄᴇ. . . .

[On July 20, 1995, Mrs. Posecai shopped at Sam's Club, then returned to her car in Sam's parking lot. It was not dark, but a man hiding under her car grabbed her ankle and pointed a gun at her. He robbed her of jewels worth about $19,000 and released her. Mrs. Posecai sued Sam's, claiming it was negligent in failing to provide security guards in the parking lot. The courts below assessed almost $30,000 in damages against Sam's. Evidence showed that Sam's was adjacent to but was not in a high-crime area. From 1989 to 1995, there were three robberies on Sam's premises. But during the same period, there were 83 predatory offenses at 13 businesses in the same block at Sam's.]

A threshold issue in any negligence action is whether the defendant owed the plaintiff a duty. Whether a duty is owed is a question of law. In deciding whether to impose a duty in a particular case, the court must make a policy decision in light of the unique facts and circumstances presented. The court may consider various moral, social, and economic factors, including the fairness of imposing liability; the economic impact on the defendant and on similarly situated parties; the need for an incentive to prevent future harm; the nature of defendant's activity; the potential for an unmanageable flow of litigation; the historical development of precedent; and the direction in which society and its institutions are evolving. . . .

Other jurisdictions have resolved the foreseeability issue in a variety of ways, but four basic approaches have emerged. The first approach, although somewhat outdated, is known as the specific harm rule. According to this rule, a landowner does not owe a duty to protect patrons from the violent acts of third parties unless he is aware of specific, imminent harm about to befall them. Courts have generally agreed that this rule is too restrictive in limiting the duty of protection that business owners owe their invitees.

More recently, some courts have adopted a prior similar incidents test. Under this test, foreseeability is established by evidence of previous crimes on or near the premises. The idea is that a past history of criminal conduct will put the landowner on notice of a future risk. Therefore, courts consider the nature and extent of the previous crimes, as well as their recency, frequency, and similarity to the crime in question. This approach can lead to arbitrary results because it is applied with different standards regarding the number of previous crimes and the degree of similarity required to give rise to a duty.

The third and most common approach used in other jurisdictions is known as the totality of the circumstances test. This test takes additional factors into account, such as the nature, condition, and location of the land, as well as any other relevant factual circumstances bearing on foreseeability. As the Indiana Supreme Court explained, "[a] substantial factor in the determination of duty is the number, nature, and location of prior similar incidents, but the lack of prior similar incidents will not preclude a claim where the landowner knew or should have known that the criminal act was foreseeable." The application of this test often focuses on the level of crime in the surrounding area and courts that apply this test are more willing to see property crimes or minor offenses as precursors to more violent crimes. In general, the totality of the circumstances test tends to place a greater duty on business owners to foresee the risk of criminal attacks on their property and has been criticized "as being too broad a standard, effectively imposing an unqualified duty to protect customers in areas experiencing any significant level of criminal activity."

The final standard that has been used to determine foreseeability is a balancing test, an approach which has been adopted in California and Tennessee. This approach was originally formulated by the California Supreme Court in Ann M. v. Pacific Plaza Shopping Center in response to the perceived unfairness of the totality test. The balancing test seeks to address the interests of both business proprietors and their customers by balancing the foreseeability of harm against the burden of imposing a duty to protect against the criminal acts of third persons. The Tennessee Supreme Court formulated the test as follows: "In determining the duty that exists, the foreseeability of harm and the gravity of harm must be balanced against the commensurate burden imposed on the business to protect against that harm. In cases in which there is a high degree of foreseeability of harm and the probable harm is great, the burden imposed upon defendant may be substantial. Alternatively, in cases in which a lesser degree of foreseeability is present or the potential harm is slight, less onerous burdens may be imposed." Under this test, the high degree of foreseeability necessary to impose a duty to provide security, will rarely, if ever, be proven in the absence of prior similar incidents of crime on the property.

We agree that a balancing test is the best method for determining when business owners owe a duty to provide security for their patrons. The economic and social impact of requiring businesses to provide security on their premises is an important factor. Security is a significant monetary expense for any business and further increases the cost of doing business in high crime areas that are already economically depressed. Moreover, businesses are generally not responsible for the endemic crime that plagues our communities, a societal problem that even our law enforcement and other government agencies have been unable to solve. At the same time, business owners are in the best position to appreciate the crime risks that are posed on their premises and to take reasonable precautions to counteract those risks.

... The greater the foreseeability and gravity of the harm, the greater the duty of care that will be imposed on the business. A very high degree of foreseeability is required to give rise to a duty to post security guards, but a lower degree of foreseeability may support a duty to implement lesser security measures such as using surveillance cameras, installing improved lighting or fencing, or trimming shrubbery....

In the instant case, there were only three predatory offenses on Sam's premises in the six and a half years prior to the robbery of Mrs. Posecai. The first of these offenses occurred well after store hours, at almost one o'clock in the morning.... Two years later, an employee of the store was attacked in the parking lot and her purse was taken, apparently by her husband.... It is also relevant that Sam's only operates during daylight hours and must provide an accessible parking lot to the multitude of customers that shop at its store each year....

We conclude that Sam's did not possess the requisite degree of foreseeability for the imposition of a duty to provide security patrols in its parking lot....

NOTES

1. **Applying *Posecai.*** How does the balancing test in *Posecai* work in these cases: (a) The plaintiff is attacked in a mall parking lot and claims the mall owners should have provided better lighting. (b) The plaintiff is attacked in a mall which had security guards but scheduled the guards' rounds negligently so they were not covering the attack area appropriately; (c) The plaintiff leases space in an underground parking garage. She is sexually attacked at her car. The garage's surveillance cameras do not work; some of the lights are out; the place is deteriorating; there is a smell of urine. No crimes of personal violence have been committed in the garage though plenty of other crimes have been committed nearby. *Sharon P. v. Arman,* 989 P.2d 121 (Cal. 1999).

2. **Business creating or enhancing risks.** Suppose a business creates or enhances risks that third persons will attack customers. Suppose a business sells items or brands that are especially coveted by violent people, so that the business itself attracts violence. What if it merely maintains a large, unguarded parking garage? In *Stewart v. Federated Department Stores, Inc.,* 662 A.2d 753 (Conn. 1995) the court imposed liability upon a retail store for the murder of a customer in the store's parking garage. The court thought that the unguarded garage, constantly filled with customers laden with packages, was an "invitation" to violence. What if the business is merely located in a remote setting and stays open late? Does that make an abduction and rape actionable? *Rogers v. Burger King Corp.,* 82 P.3d 116 (Okla. Ct. App. 2003).

3. **Imminent harm known.** Early cases involved landowners who were present when their invitees were subjected to some imminent threat of harm from others. For instance, in *Greco v. Sumner Tavern, Inc.,* 128 N.E.2d 788

(Mass. 1955) the defendant knew that a man had been drinking in the defendant's tavern all day and causing "trouble." About 10:00 that night he attacked and seriously injured another customer. The tavern owner was held liable for negligence in failing to deal with the situation. Some recent cases also find a duty owed to invitees where harm is either imminent or when some physical altercation has already begun on the premises. *See, e.g., Morris v. De La* Torre, 113 P.3d 1182 (Cal. 2005); *Haupt v. Sharkey*, 832 N.E.2d 198 (Ill. App. Ct. 2005). Would knowledge of imminent harm, without a special relationship between plaintiff and defendant, suffice as a trigger of duty? *See Corinaldi v. Columbia Courtyard, Inc.*, 873 A.2d 483 (Md. Ct. Spec. App. 2005).

4. **Prior similar incidents approach.** Gradually, a number of began to impose liability when attacks by third persons were foreseeable and the business failed to take reasonable steps to protect those on its premises. The usual basis for finding foreseeability in these cases is that there were previous crimes on the premises or nearby. *See, e.g., Nallan v. Helmsley–Spear, Inc.*, 407 N.E.2d 451 (N.Y. 1980). Predictably, what looks like a simple matter of evidence about foreseeability became something of a rule of law for some judges, so that if no similar incidents had occurred on or near the premises, crime was deemed unforeseeable and the business would not be under any duty to take reasonable steps to protect its visitors. *See, e.g., Liszewski v. Target Corp.*, 374 F.3d 597 (8th Cir. 2004) (applying Missouri law). You can expect litigation over what counts as a similar incident. *See, e.g., Surles ex rel. Johnson v. Greyhound Lines, Inc.*, 474 F.3d 288 (6th Cir. 2007) (evidence of prior incidents involving passengers assaulting drivers or attempting to grab the driver or the steering wheel on a moving bus was properly admitted in case involving a passenger's armed attack on a bus driver); *Sturbridge Partners, Ltd. v. Walker*, 482 S.E.2d 339 (Ga. 1997) (knowledge of burglaries might mean that rape is foreseeable).

In *L.A.C. v. Ward Parkway Shopping Center Co.*, 75 S.W.3d 247 (Mo. 2002), the plaintiff alleged that she had been raped in a shopping mall. She sued the owners-operators and the company that had contracted to provide security. There was a good deal of evidence about crimes in the mall and its parking areas, of which the defendant were seemingly well aware. Reversing a summary judgment for defendant, the court said, "Foreseeability does not require identical crimes in identical locations. Violent crimes against women, particularly, serve sufficient notice to reasonable individuals that other violent crimes, including sexual assault or rape of women, may occur. Defendants argue that incidents involving 'escaping suspects, verbal and physical altercations, robbery and indecent acts' are not sufficiently similar to the rape that is alleged to have occurred here. This is not realistic. These are precisely the type of criminal acts that would put reasonable and prudent people on notice that precautions should be taken...."

5. **Totality of circumstances approach.** Instead of requiring prior similar incidents to show foreseeability, courts more recently have treated foreseeability as a fact question to be determined like other facts from any relevant circumstances. Some courts have labeled this the totality of circumstances rule. Recent major examples of this view can be found in *Monk v. Temple George Associates, LLC*, 869 A.2d 179 (Conn. 2005); *Delta Tau Delta,*

Beta Alpha Chapter v. Johnson, 712 N.E.2d 968 (Ind. 1999) and *Clohesy v. Food Circus Supermarkets, Inc.*, 694 A.2d 1017 (N.J. 1997) ("Generally, our tort law, including products liability, does not require the first victim to lose while subsequent victims are permitted to at least submit their cases to a jury.").

6. **Balancing approach.** The balancing approach postulates that the defendant may have no duty to deal with even foreseeable harm. *See, e.g., Sakiyama v. AMF Bowling Ctrs., Inc.*, 1 Cal.Rptr.3d 762 (Ct. App. 2003) (no duty owed to an attendee at an all-night "rave" at defendant's facility, despite foreseeability that attendees would use illegal drugs and drive home in fatigued state). The idea got its impetus from *Ann M. v. Pacific Plaza Shopping Center*, 863 P.2d 207 (Cal. 1993). In that case, the plaintiff, working in a store at a strip mall, was accosted by a man in her place of work, held at knife point, and raped. She sued the mall, claiming it should have had security guards. The court said: "Foreseeability, when analyzed to determine the existence or scope of a duty, is a question of law to be decided by the court. . . . [T]he social costs of imposing a duty on landowners to hire private police forces are also not insignificant. For these reasons, we conclude that a high degree of foreseeability is required in order to find that the scope of a landlord's duty of care includes the hiring of security guards." Given this test, the court held that the shopping mall was not liable in that case for failing to have security guards. *See also Wiener v. Southcoast Childcare Centers, Inc.*, 88 P.3d 517 (Cal. 2004) (utilizing balancing test, holding no duty on the part of a day care center to guard against a criminal act by man who intentionally drove his car through a fence at the center; the driver's "brutal criminal attack was unforeseeable").

7. **Duty versus breach.** As summarized by the Tennessee Court, the balancing test works this way: "In determining the duty that exists, the foreseeability of harm and the gravity of harm must be balanced against the commensurate burden imposed on the business to protect against that harm." *McClung v. Delta Square Ltd. P'ship*, 937 S.W.2d 891 (Tenn. 1996). This sounds like the risk-utility balance for determining negligence, doesn't it? Does it matter that many courts have used it in determining duty rather than breach of duty? In *Staples v. CBL & Associates*, Inc., 15 S.W.3d 83 (Tenn. 2000), Justice Holder argued in a concurring opinion that unless the question was so clear that reasonable people could not differ, the balancing should be done by the jury as part of its decision on the negligence issue, not by judges. In *Delta Tau Delta, supra* Note 6, the Indiana court rejected the balancing test on the ground that it put the question of reasonable precautions in the hands of judges. "We believe that this is basically a breach of duty evaluation and is best left for the jury to decide."

8. **Negligence and causation.** In all these cases, the plaintiff must prove not only a duty but also negligence and causation. Would better lighting avoid nighttime attacks? Always, never, or sometimes? In *Shadday v. Omni Hotels Management Corp.*, 477 F.3d 511 (7th Cir. 2007), a guest in a luxury hotel in Washington, D.C., was raped in the elevator by another guest. Should the plaintiff prevail in a negligence suit alleging inadequate security by offering evidence that there had been 637 criminal acts in the surrounding

neighborhood in the three years preceding the attack, none involving guest-on-guest violence? What problems do you see for such a claim?

MARQUAY v. ENO

662 A.2d 272 (N.H. 1995)

HORTON, JUSTICE....

The plaintiffs are three women who were students in the Mascoma Valley Regional School District. In separate complaints filed in the district court, each plaintiff alleges that she was exploited, harassed, assaulted, and sexually abused by one or more employees of the school district. According to the complaints, Lisa Burns was sexually abused by Brian Erskine, a high school teacher, beginning in her sophomore year and continuing beyond graduation.... [Other plaintiffs made similar allegations about Michael Eno, a sports coach, and Brian Adams, a teacher.] Each plaintiff also alleges that a host of school employees, including other teachers, coaches, superintendents, principals and secretaries either were aware or should have been aware of the sexual abuse....

[The plaintiffs sued the district and its allegedly abusing employees. The federal district court certified a number of questions to this Court.]

I.   RELATIONSHIP OF STATUTORY VIOLATION TO CIVIL LIABILITY

The first certified question asks whether RSA 169–C:29, which, under penalty as a misdemeanor, requires that any person "having reason to suspect that a child has been abused or neglected shall report the same [to the State]," creates a private right of action in favor of abused children against those who have violated the statute's reporting requirement....

At first glance, our cases appear to be inconsistent on this issue. Everett v. Littleton Construction Co., 94 N.H. 43, 46 A.2d 317 (1946), instructs that "the violation of a penal statute is an actionable wrong only when the Legislature expressly so provides ..., or when the purpose and language of the statute compel such inference...." We have also held, however, that "[t]he breach of a statutory duty results in liability ... when the plaintiff is in a class the statute is designed to protect and the injury is of the type that the statute is intended to prevent."

The apparent inconsistency in our jurisprudence arises from a failure to distinguish two distinct bases of civil liability: (1) statutorily expressed or implied causes of action; and (2) negligence per se. The former, recognized in Everett, is the principle that whether or not the common law recognizes a cause of action, the plaintiff may maintain an action under an applicable statute where the legislature intended violation of that statute to give rise to civil liability. The doctrine of negligence per se, on the other hand, provides that where a cause of action does exist at common law, the standard of conduct to which a defendant will be held may be defined as that required by statute, rather than as the usual reasonable person standard. The doctrine of negligence per se, however, plays no role in the creation of common law causes of action. Thus, in many cases, the common law may fail to recognize liability for failure to perform affirmative duties that are imposed by statute. . . .

We hold that the reporting statute does not support a private right of action for its violation because we find no express or implied legislative intent to create such civil liability. First, we note that where the legislature has intended that civil liability flow from the violation of a statute, it has often so provided. Where, as here, civil liability for a statutory violation would represent an abrupt and sweeping departure from a general common law rule of nonliability, we would expect that if the legislature, which is presumed to recognize the common law, intended to impose civil liability it would expressly so provide. Here there was no expressed intent. Nor can we divine any implied intent.

We now turn to the negligence per se question. . . . [U]se of a statute to establish the standard of care is limited to situations where a common law cause of action exists, and then, only if the statute is "applicable." Whether a statutory standard is applicable depends, in part, on whether the type of duty to which the statute speaks is similar to the type of duty on which the cause of action is based. Because the duty to which the statute speaks—reporting of abuse—is considerably different from the duty on which the cause of action is based—supervision of students—we hold that a violation of the reporting statute does not constitute negligence per se in an action based on inadequate supervision of a student.

II. COMMON LAW CAUSES OF ACTION

The plaintiffs argue that all school district employees have a common law duty to protect students whom they know or should know are being sexually abused by another school employee. We hold that some employees owe such a duty while others do not. The duty owed by some defendants is based on their relationship to the students; for other defendants the duty derives from their relationship to the alleged abusers.

As a general rule, a person has no affirmative duty to aid or protect another. Such a duty may arise, however, if a special relationship exists. The plaintiffs argue that a special relationship exists between educators and school children, imposing a duty upon educators to protect students whom they know or should know are being sexually abused by another school employee.

"One who is required by law to take or who voluntarily takes the custody of another under circumstances such as to deprive the other of his normal opportunities for protection is under a . . . duty to the other." Restatement (Second) of Torts § 314A at 118 (1965). "[A] child while in school is deprived of the protection of his parents or guardian. Therefore, the actor who takes custody . . . of a child is properly required to give him the protection which the custody or the manner in which it is taken has deprived him." Id. § 320 comment b at 131. We agree with the majority of courts from other jurisdictions that schools share a special relationship with students entrusted to their care, which imposes upon them certain duties of reasonable supervision. The scope of the duty imposed is limited by what risks are reasonably foreseeable. . . .

Major factors influencing our conclusion that a special relationship exists between schools and students include the compulsory character of school attendance, the expectation of parents and students for and their reliance on a safe school environment, and the importance to society of the learning activity which is to take place in public schools. For these reasons, we conclude that "the social importance of protecting the plain-tiff[s'] interest outweighs the importance of immunizing the defendant from extended liability."

School attendance impairs both the ability of students to protect themselves and the ability of their parents to protect them. It is this impairment of protection from which the special relationship between school and student arises and from which the duty of supervision flows. We decline, however, to accept the plaintiffs' argument that every school employee shoulders a personal duty simply by virtue of receiving a paycheck from the school district. Instead, the duty falls upon those school employees who have supervisory responsibility over students and who thus have stepped into the role of parental proxy. Those employees who share such a relationship with a student and who acquire actual knowl-edge of abuse or who learn of facts which would lead a reasonable person to conclude a student is being abused are subject to liability if their level of supervision is unreasonable and is a proximate cause of a student's injury.

While the impairment of protection creates an affirmative duty, it also circumscribes the limits of that duty. Thus the existence of a duty is limited to those periods when parental protection is compromised. That is not to say that employees with a special relationship to a student may not be liable for injuries that occurred off school premises or after school hours, if the student can show that the employee's negligent acts or omissions, within the scope of his or her duty, proximately caused injury to the student. This is a question for the jury.

We note that the principal or superintendent rarely has primary supervisory authority over a student. Because, however, it is the school to which parents turn over custody of their children and from which they expect safety and because the superintendent and principal are charged with overseeing all aspects of the school's operation, we hold that a duty of supervision is owed to each student. Where the principal or superinten-dent knows or should know that a particular school employee poses a threat to a student, entrustment of the student to the care of that employee will not satisfy the duty of reasonable supervision.

[Employees with supervisory powers of hiring and firing might be liable for negligent hiring or retention of a person they knew or should have known was an abuser.] While we held in section I that the reporting statute is not applicable in an action based on negligent supervision, we hold that it is applicable in a negligent hiring or retention action. Accordingly, under these circumstances, failure to report abuse in accordance with the statute could give rise to liability, provided the plaintiff can show that reporting would have prevented the subsequent abuse.

Remanded.

NOTES

1. **Liability of the abusers.** In *Marquay,* the plaintiffs claimed at-school sexual abuse by employees of the school. The actual abusers are no doubt liable. In fact, if the coach is a public-school employee, his molestation of a student might even count as a violation of § 1983, on the ground that molestation is an infringement of a liberty interest protected by the due process clause, and, so far as it is a sexual harassment, it is also a denial of equal protection. *Doe v. Taylor Independent School Dist.,* 975 F.2d 137 (5th Cir. 1992).

2. **Vicarious liability.** Employers (including school districts) are normally liable for the torts of their employees, provided the torts are committed within the scope of their employment. When the employee is acting for purely personal reasons, the employer's liability may be doubtful. *See* Chapter 22, *infra.*

3. **Primary liability of schools.** When the school officials know or should know of abuse or harassment by teachers or coaches, the officials seem to be in violation of their duty of care if they do nothing about the abuse. *Marquay* seems to support that rule. In addition, the United States Supreme Court has held that a student states a civil rights claim if school officials do nothing about sexual harassment by a sports coach. *Franklin v. Gwinnett County Public Schools,* 503 U.S. 60 (1992). *See also Gebser v. Lago Vista Indep. Sch. Dist.,* 524 U.S. 274 (1998) (setting forth requirements for claim based on teacher's sexual harassment of student).

4. **Child-abuse reporting statutes.** Every state has some kind of child abuse reporting statute. Most courts hold that a statutory reporting requirement does not affect tort law. *E.g., Perry v. S.N.,* 973 S.W.2d 301 (Tex. 1998). Some courts appear to accept a negligence claim based on a reporting statute. *See, e.g., Yates v. Mansfield Bd. of Educ.,* 808 N.E.2d 861 (Ohio 2004); *Landeros v. Flood,* 551 P.2d 389 (Cal. 1976). As a common law matter, any duty to report child abuse would ordinarily be based upon a special relationship, either with the child or with the abuser. *See Berry v. Watchtower Bible and Tract Society of New York, Inc.,* 879 A.2d 1124 (N.H. 2005).

5. **Student-on-student violence.** Could school officials be held liable for failing to protect one student from another? Many courts have said yes. In *Mirand v. City of New York,* 637 N.E.2d 263 (N.Y. 1994), one student threatened to kill another after a perceived slight. The victim of this threat told teachers about it and tried to report it to security officers, but could not find one. As school was ending, a group of students attacked the threatened student with a hammer and knives. She prevailed in her suit against the school. "Schools are under a duty to adequately supervise the students in their charge and they will be held liable for foreseeable injuries proximately

related to the absence of adequate supervision." The care owed is that which
" 'a parent of ordinary prudence would observe in comparable circumstances.'
The duty owed derives from the simple fact that a school, in assuming
physical custody and control over its students, effectively takes the place of
parents and guardians." The school knew of the threat and also knew that
security was needed. Yet no security was present and no steps had been taken
to deal with the death threat. *Query:* Did the duty in *Mirand* arise because of
the school's relationship to the injured student, or its relationship to the
attackers? Does it matter?

YOUNG v. SALT LAKE CITY SCHOOL DISTRICT, 52 P.3d 1230
(Utah 2002). Eric Young, an elementary school student, was riding his
bike to a mandatory after-school Parent–Teacher–Student meeting at the
school. He reached the crosswalk leading directly to the school. A parked
car allegedly obscured the vision of approaching drivers and those using
the cross walk. Young was struck in the crosswalk. He sued the school
after settling with the driver. He claimed that the school should have
informed the city of dangerous parking conditions, supplied a crossing
guard, or provided flashing warning lights. *Held,* the school owed its
student no duty of protection. "[W]hen a school district lacks custody, it
has no protective obligation and no special relationship exists." The school
did not have custody here. "First, Young's elementary school had adjourned for the day, and he had been released into the care of his
parents.... Second, Young's injury did not occur on premises within the
District's control.... Lastly, at the time he sustained his injury, Young
was not participating in a curricular, or extra-curricular, school-sponsored
event; he was simply *in the process of traveling* to such an event."

NOTES

1. The *Young* court stressed that the injury took place off school
grounds and after the school day had ended. How important do you think
these facts are? What if the injury had occurred during dismissal, immediately
after school? *See Jerkins ex rel. Jerkins v. Anderson*, 922 A.2d 1279 (N.J.
2007) (in case involving child hit by car during dismissal, *held,* educators owe
duty of care). Or does such timing really matter? In *Fazzolari v. Portland
School District No. 1J*, 734 P.2d 1326 (Or. 1987), Judge Linde wrote that "the
school's duty is not based on ownership of property but on its relation to the
student," and that this duty exists "apart from any general responsibility not
unreasonably to expose people to a foreseeable risk of harm." The plaintiff in
Fazzaroli, a 15-year-old student, was attacked long before school started, after
having been dropped off by her mother at 6:50 a.m. The school argued that
whatever duty it owed to its students was limited to the school day. To that
argument, Judge Linde said that no such bright-line rule existed; testimony
indicated that custodians opened the school before that time, and that some
teachers and students were present for other activities. A fact-finder could

conclude that "a sensible school administration would take some precautions, if not to provide supervision, then at least to warn students and their parents about its absence before a designated hour."

2.   What role does "custody" play in establishing a duty? Does it imply a kind of reliance?

3.   Even if a school owed a duty of reasonable care to a student, would that duty be breached if the injury was unforeseeable? *See Edson v. Barre Supervisory Union #61*, 933 A.2d 200 (Vt. 2007) (high school student left school secretly and without authorization and was murdered off campus).

NOTE: DUTIES OF COLLEGES

1.   *College temptations and stress.* Courts have generally refused to impose upon universities any duty to protect or guide new students with respect to the pleasures and dangers of sex, alcohol, drugs, or even overstudy. *See Beach v. University of Utah*, 726 P.2d 413 (Utah 1986); *Wilson v. Continental Ins. Cos.*, 274 N.W.2d 679 (Wis. 1979).

2.   *Risks of attacks.* Consider whether the college owes a duty of care to its students in these cases.

    A.   One evening an underage sorority member attended a number of parties hosted by other Greek houses at her college. The college provided employees to supervise at some of the fraternity parties. The young woman became so intoxicated that she fell from a fire escape. *Coghlan v. Beta Theta Pi Fraternity*, 987 P.2d 300 (Idaho 1999). Or suppose a college has rules against drinking parties in dorms, but does not enforce them. A college woman is sexually assaulted by several college football players after she and some of the players attend a drinking party in their dorm. *Tanja H. v. Regents of the Univ. of Calif.*, 278 Cal.Rptr. 918 (Ct. App. 1991).

    B.   A prisoner applied for admission to a state university and was admitted upon his release. The university knew he was a prisoner when he applied but not much else. The new student, with a ten-year history of heroin addiction and a string of arrests, made friends with three other students and shared an apartment with them. He then seriously injured one of his roommates, raped another, and murdered the third. *Eiseman v. State*, 511 N.E.2d 1128 (N.Y. 1987).

    C.   A college assigns a student to practicum work at a dangerous location. The college knows the danger but it neither warns the student, arranges a different practicum, nor provides protection. The student—an adult—is abducted from the practicum site, robbed, and sexually assaulted. *Nova Southeast Univ., Inc. v. Gross*, 758 So.2d 86 (Fla. 2000). What if the student knows of the danger before she is attacked?

FUNCHESS v. CECIL NEWMAN CORP., 632 N.W.2d 666 (Minn. 2001). Decedent was killed by intruders who gained access to his apartment, according to some of the evidence, because the outside security door was not working properly and because the decedent opened his apartment door to see who buzzed him, an act required because the intercom wasn't working properly. The landlord had covenanted in the lease to provide security and to make prompt repairs. *Held,* the landlord was under no duty of care to the tenant with respect to these attacks. (1) One generally owes no duty to protect others from third persons; the landlord-tenant relationship is not by itself sufficient to change that rule, in part because the landlord is in no position to protect from criminal attack. (2) Was provision of security measures (the security door, intercom) an undertaking of a duty? "Courts in other states are divided on whether a landlord's provision of security measures can give rise to liability for harm to tenants that results from a failure to maintain those measures. We are not inclined to establish a rule that would discourage landlords from improving security. Transforming a landlord's gratuitous provision of security measures into a duty to maintain those measures and subjecting the landlord to liability for all harm occasioned by a failure to maintain that security would tend to discourage landlords from instituting security measures for fear of being held liable for the actions of a criminal.... Assuming the security door was malfunctioning, Newman/Gravzy still provided the security against criminal attack that Haynes could reasonably expect. The security guard was performing his duty...." (3) Did the lease covenant provide a basis for a duty? "Funchess did not plead breach of contract in her complaint, nor did she argue breach of contract as a separate legal theory before the district court or the court of appeals. We will not consider such a claim now."

NOTES

1. The court based its decision on duty, but might the case have also posed some causal issues? The plaintiff does not claim that the tenant reported the equipment failures or asked for repair. Repair may or may not have prevented the harm. If you think the plaintiff might have lost on other grounds, does it make any difference that the court rested on a no-duty argument?

2. What did the court mean by saying the landlord was in no position to protect from third persons? Could it not have protected here by properly maintaining its own security equipment?

3. Is the court's argument that liability predicated upon undertaking or assumed duty would lead landlords to provide NO security factually sound? Would such an idea lead logically to courts never finding duties based on their voluntary assumption? And why is the lease merely a matter of contract, and not a form of undertaking or assumed duty that is enforceable in tort?

4. In a leading case, *Kline v. 1500 Massachusetts Ave. Apartment Corp.*, 439 F.2d 477 (D.C. Cir. 1970), the plaintiff leased one of 585 apartments in

the defendant's building. At that time, there were several forms of protection against intrusion, including a doorman. Seven years later, there was no doorman and other forms of protection had also been withdrawn, although assaults, larcenies and robberies against tenants in the common hallways had increased. Plaintiff was attacked and injured by an intruder in the hallway. The court held that the landlord was under a duty to protect tenants against attacks by third persons. Among other things, the court emphasized (a) the control of the landlord over common passageways and the tenant's lack of power to control them or to protect themselves there; (b) the special character of the modern urban multiple-unit lease; (c) the notice of the landlord that the tenants were being subjected to crimes against their persons. The court added: "[T]he applicable standard of care in providing protection for the tenant is that standard which this landlord himself was employing . . . when the appellant became a resident. . . ." The court said that the precise protections need not be kept, but that the same relative degree of security had to be maintained. Should this duty extend to commercial leases as well? *Compare Doe v. Dominion Bank of Wash.*, 963 F.2d 1552 (D.C. Cir. 1992) (yes) *with Doe v. Grosvenor Properties (Hawaii) Ltd.*, 829 P.2d 512 (Haw. 1992) (no).

5. If the lessor itself brings in dangerous third persons, as tenants or as visitors to tenants, the case may seem a relatively easy one for imposition of a duty. What if the lessor leases an office in a commercial building to a mental health clinic which does a major business in seeing violent criminals on parole and one of these "clients" of the mental health clinic attacks another tenant? *Samson v. Saginaw Prof. Bldg., Inc.*, 224 N.W.2d 843 (Mich. 1975).

6. Many cases impose a duty of reasonable care on landlords to maintain common areas in a reasonably safe condition for tenants. *See, e.g., Scully v. Fitzgerald*, 843 A.2d 1110 (N.J. 2004) (landlord kept common, open storage area in messy condition where co-tenants discarded cigarette butts, causing fire that damaged plaintiff's property); *Evers v. FSF Overlake Assocs.*, 77 P.3d 581 (Okla. 2003) (applying the rule in a case in which fumes from a co-tenant's apartment reached the plaintiff's apartment through a common ventilation system).

7. Suppose the plaintiff is not the tenant but a guest of the tenant. Does the landlord owe the plaintiff a duty of care while he is rightfully in the parking lot provided by the landlord or in other portions of the premises in the possession and control of the landlord? *Martinez v. Woodmar IV Condo. Homeowners Assoc., Inc.*, 941 P.2d 218 (Ariz. 1997) (duty of care owed to tenant's guest to protect from attacks in common areas).

8. Suppose a landlord negligently creates or enhances a risk that someone will criminally attack the plaintiff. Someone does attack the plaintiff but he cannot be found or has no funds. Recall that in states that have abolished joint and several liability, the rule is that each tortfeasor is liable only for his own proportionate fault share. What do you think the landlord's share would be as compared to the rapist? Should several liability states return to the joint and several liability rule for this kind of case? This point is considered in more detail in Chapter 25, but you may wish to have the problem in mind as you review the preceding cases and examine those that follow.

§ 2. DEFENDANT'S RELATIONSHIP WITH DANGEROUS PERSONS

DUDLEY v. OFFENDER AID & RESTORATION OF RICHMOND, INC., 401 S.E.2d 878 (Va. 1991). Spencer was a convicted felon with a long, active career in crime. In prison he engaged in vicious beatings of new inmates and set fires; psychologists warned that he was a potential security problem. Because of his violence and for other reasons, he was not eligible to serve any part of his term in a halfway house. Nevertheless, he was permitted to live in one, operated by a private organization. He repeatedly violated rules there, including rules about prompt return from outside work. Security was "practically nonexistent" and Spencer was permitted to leave without much control. He was unaccounted for at 7:00 p.m. During that night he broke into an apartment nearby, bound Davis, beat and raped her, then strangled her to death. In an action against the operator of the halfway house, the trial court sustained the defendant's demurrer. *Held,* reversed and remanded. Under the general rule one owes no duty to control the conduct of a third person for the benefit of the plaintiff. However, if the defendant is in a special relationship to either the plaintiff or the third person, the defendant is under a duty of care. The halfway house, upon receiving Spencer, became a custodian in charge. The defendant's duty ran not only to victims that might be identified in advance but to all those who are "directly and foreseeably exposed to risk of bodily harm" from the defendant's negligence. The decedent was within the area of danger.

NOTES

1. **"Custody."** Is strict "custody" required to invoke the duty of care imposed in *Dudley*? Suppose: (a) A parole officer does not warn the parolee's employer that the parolee is a high-risk sexual offender. *Schmidt v. HTG, Inc.,* 961 P.2d 677 (Kan. 1998). (b) DSS, a child protection agency of the state, takes custody of JH, then places him in a foster home without revealing to the foster parents that JH might molest children. JH made inappropriate sexual touchings of a neighbor child while JH was in foster care. Would DSS be subject to liability? *E.P. v. Riley,* 604 N.W.2d 7 (S.D. 1999). (c) An employer knows that Employee #1 is on parole from a previous conviction for attempted sexual battery on a child. Is the employer under a duty to warn Employee #2 about this criminal background, when the employer also knows that Employee #1 is going to babysit Employee #2's child at Employee #2's home after work? *K.M. v. Publix Super Markets, Inc.,* 895 So.2d 1114 (Fla. Dist. Ct. App. 2005).

2. **A duty to control spouses or family members?** Consider: A wife knows her husband has a history of sexual misconduct with young children and might invite neighborhood girls to go swimming in the family pool while she is away. Has she any duty to warn anyone? What if she told neighbors it would be safe for the girls to swim? On similar facts, *see Pamela L. v. Farmer,*

169 Cal.Rptr. 282 (Ct. App. 1980). *Compare J.S. v. R.T.H.*, 714 A.2d 924 (N.J. 1998) (duty of care exists) *with D.W. v. Bliss*, 112 P.3d 232 (Kan. 2005) (no duty). In *Eric J. v. Betty M.*, 90 Cal.Rptr.2d 549 (Ct. App. 1999) the court held that parents and brothers of a repeated offender, paroled on child molesting charges, had no duty to warn the molester's new woman friend that her son might be in danger even though the boy was taken to the home of some of them and molested here. What if an adult man, known by his family to be an habitual drunk driver, crashes his car into the plaintiff. Would an action lie against his parents or his brother for failing to control him? Does it matter that just prior to the accident his parents had signed him out of "some sort of institution" related to his drinking? *Bebry v. Zanauskas*, 841 A.2d 282 (Conn. Ct. App. 2004).

3. **A duty to control tenants?** A landlord leases an apartment to a man who, after moving in, sometimes fires a gun from the back yard. The landlord does nothing about it. Subsequently the tenant kills a 10-year-old girl, who, while standing in her own yard, was struck by a bullet fired from the apartment building's yard. Did the landlord owe the victim a duty? In *Rosales v. Stewart*, 169 Cal.Rptr. 660 (Ct. App. 1980), the court said where the lessor has control over a danger from the tenant, he is under a duty of care, though he is not liable if there is no control. "In effect ... the landlord is under a duty to third persons to do all that he legally can to get rid of a dangerous condition *on the leased premises*, even if it means getting rid of the tenant." What about the decision to rent to a dangerous person in the first place? For example, what if a landlord suspects that a prospective tenant is a gang member? Should there be a duty not to rent to that person? *See Castaneda v. Olsher*, 162 P.3d 610 (Cal. 2007). Or suppose a prospective tenant tells a prospective landlord that he has a vicious dog. Should the landlord refuse to lease the premises to him? *Strunk v. Zoltanski*, 468 N.E.2d 13 (N.Y. 1984), holds that the landlord is under a duty to take reasonable precautions to protect others from injury by the dog. What reasonable precautions? Might they turn on the degree of control the landlord could exert? *See Klitzka v. Hellios*, 810 N.E.2d 252 (Ill. App. Ct. 2004). In *Smaxwell v. Bayard*, 682 N.W.2d 923 (Wis. 2004), the court decided that the common-law liability of landlords for negligence associated with tenants' dogs must be limited to situations where the landlord was also the owner or keeper of the dog. What if the same landlord leases premises to a tenant who carries on drug trafficking activities there and the landlord knows it? *Muniz by Gonzales v. Flohern, Inc.*, 570 N.E.2d 1074 (N.Y. 1991).

4. **A duty to control employees?** Could an employer be liable for negligently hiring a dangerous person? *See, e.g., Spencer v. Health Force, Inc.*, 107 P.3d 504 (N.M. 2005); *Munroe v. Universal Health Serv., Inc.*, 596 S.E.2d 604 (Ga. 2004). Or for negligently failing to supervise an employee who might cause harm? *See, e.g., Seguro v. Cummiskey*, 844 A.2d 224 (Conn. App. Ct. 2004) (tavern owner failed to control employee's drinking on the job; employee crashed car into plaintiff's vehicle). Does liability turn on exactly what the employer knew about the employee, and what act the employee actually committed? *See Keller v. Koca*, 111 P.3d 445 (Colo. 2005) (male employee who was known to have fondled and made suggestive remarks to female employees

brought a child into the workplace when it was closed and sexually assaulted her).

NOTE: A DUTY TO CONTROL CHILDREN?

1. *Basic limits.* Remember that parents are not liable for a child's torts merely on the basis of the parental relationship alone. Nor are they liable for failure to control a child merely because the child is known to be rough. Parents are liable only for failing to control some specific dangerous habit of a child of which the parent knows or should know in the exercise of reasonable care.

2. *Normal children.* Are parents responsible if they leave a teen-aged son alone at home while they are out of town and he has irresponsible sex with a teen-aged girl? *McNamee v. A.J.W.,* 519 S.E.2d 298 (Ga. Ct. App. 1999). Would a parent have a duty of reasonable care to control a child riding a bike in a crowd? *Compare Crisafulli v. Bass,* 38 P.3d 842 (Mont. 2001) (overruling an earlier no-duty decision) *with Buono v. Scalia,* 843 A.2d 1120 (N.J. 2004) (father's decision was a valid exercise of parental authority, thus he was immune from suit).

3. *Children known to be violent.* In *Dinsmore–Poff v. Alvord,* 972 P.2d 978 (Alaska 1999), plaintiffs' decedent was murdered by defendants' 17-year-old son. The son had a long history of emotional disturbance and violence. In fact, he had been arrested once for shooting a boy. The parents did not impose curfews or search his belongings. The son used a gun to kill his victim. The court absolved the parents. It said: "plaintiff must show more than a parent's general notice of a child's dangerous propensity. A plaintiff must show that the parent had reason to know with some specificity of a present opportunity and need to restrain the child to prevent some imminently foreseeable harm."

Williamson v. Daniels, 748 So.2d 754 (Miss. 1999) absolved the mother of a 15-year-old boy who shot the plaintiff in the chest. Since the mother was not aware of this specific kind of misconduct in the past, she was not responsible. It thought liability "would pose the risk of transforming parents from care givers and disciplinarians into the jailors and insurers of their minor children," and that "this is a role most parents are ill equipped to take on."

In one astonishing case the "child"—a teenager with a history of aggressive, anti-social behavior—began beating a woman with a hammer. He demanded she remove her clothes. A daughter ran for the phone; he began beating her with a hammer, then began to saw off an ear of his original victim. His parents were well aware of a long history of serious behavior. Psychiatrists had recommended that the boy be treated. The parents were not liable. Apparently the theory was that they could not have foreseen the particular type of violence. *Parsons v. Smithey,* 504 P.2d 1272 (Ariz. 1973); *see also Popple v. Rose,* 573 N.W.2d 765 (Neb. 1998) (parents knew teenaged son was violent but did not know it would take the form of a sexual assault upon children he was babysitting; parents under no duty to warn).

What if the parent or the parent's domestic partner knows that a ten-year-old child has a propensity for sexually abusing younger females and knows also that a four-year-old girl is playing in the home? *Gritzner v. Michael R.*, 611 N.W.2d 906 (Wis. 2000).

4. *Is ability to control important?* Some courts stress parents' inability to control their children's behavior as a reason not to impose a duty of care. This may be because the "child" is older, see *Grover v. Stechel*, 45 P.3d 80 (N.M. Ct. App. 2002) (mother's only "control" over adult son who stabbed the plaintiff was financial), or because the parent at issue was a non-custodial parent at the time of the incident, *see K.H. v. J.R.*, 826 A.2d 863 (Pa. 2003) (child shot another with a BB gun given to him by non-custodial parent).

TARASOFF v. REGENTS OF UNIVERSITY OF CALIFORNIA

551 P.2d 334 (Cal. 1976)

TOBRINER, JUSTICE.

On October 27, 1969, Prosenjit Poddar killed Tatiana Tarasoff. Plaintiffs, Tatiana's parents, allege that two months earlier Poddar confided his intention to kill Tatiana to Dr. Lawrence Moore, a psychologist employed by the Cowell Memorial Hospital at the University of California at Berkeley. They allege that on Moore's request, the campus police briefly detained Poddar, but released him when he appeared rational. They further claim that Dr. Harvey Powelson, Moore's superior, then directed that no further action be taken to detain Poddar. No one warned plaintiffs of Tatiana's peril.

Concluding that these facts set forth causes of action against neither therapists and police involved, nor against the Regents of the University of California as their employer, the superior court sustained defendant's demurrers to plaintiffs' second amended complaints without leave to amend. This appeal ensued.

Plaintiffs' complaints predicate liability on two grounds: defendants' failure to warn plaintiffs of the impending danger and their failure to bring about Poddar's confinement.... Defendants, in turn, assert that they owed no duty of reasonable care to Tatiana and that they are immune from suit....

In analyzing this issue, we bear in mind that legal duties are not discoverable facts of nature, but merely conclusory expressions that, in cases of a particular type, liability should be imposed for damage done. As stated in Dillon v. Legg (1968) 68 Cal. 2d 728, 734, 69 Cal. Rptr. 72, 76, 441 P.2d 912, 916: "The assertion that liability must ... be denied because defendant bears no 'duty' to plaintiff 'begs the essential question whether the plaintiff's interests are entitled to legal protection against the defendant's conduct.... [Duty] is not sacrosanct in itself, but only an expression of the sum total of those considerations of policy which lead the law to say that the particular plaintiff is entitled to protection.' (Prosser, Law of Torts [3d ed. 1964] at pp. 332–333.)"

In the landmark case of Rowland v. Christian (1968) 69 Cal. 2d 108, 70 Cal. Rptr. 97, 443 P.2d 561, Justice Peters recognized that liability should be imposed "for an injury occasioned to another by his want of ordinary care or skill" as expressed in Section 1714 of the Civil Code. Thus, Justice Peters, quoting from Heaven v. Pender (1883) 11 Q.B.D. 503, 509 stated: " 'whenever one person is by circumstances placed in such a position with regard to another ... that if he did not use ordinary care and skill in his own conduct ... he would cause danger of injury to the person or property of the other, a duty arises to use ordinary care and skill to avoid such danger.' "

We depart from "this fundamental principle" only upon the "balancing of a number of considerations"; major ones "are the foreseeability of harm to the plaintiff, the degree of certainty that the plaintiff suffered injury, the closeness of the connection between the defendant's conduct and the injury suffered, the moral blame attached to the defendant's conduct, the policy of preventing future harm, the extent of the burden to the defendant and consequences to the community of imposing a duty to exercise care with resulting liability for breach, and the availability, cost and prevalence of insurance for the risk involved."

The most important of these considerations in establishing duty is foreseeability. As a general principle, a "defendant owes a duty of care to all persons who are foreseeably endangered by his conduct, with respect to all risks which make the conduct unreasonably dangerous." As we shall explain, however, when the avoidance of foreseeable harm requires a defendant to control the conduct of another person, or to warn of such conduct, the common law has traditionally imposed liability only if the defendant bears some special relationship to the dangerous person or to the potential victim. Since the relationship between a therapist and his patient satisfies this requirement, we need not here decide whether foreseeability alone is sufficient to create a duty to exercise reasonable care to protect a potential victim of another's conduct....

Although plaintiffs' pleadings assert no special relation between Tatiana and defendant therapists, they establish as between Poddar and defendant therapists the special relation that arises between a patient and his doctor or psychotherapist. Such a relationship may support affirmative duties for the benefit of third persons. Thus, for example, a hospital must exercise reasonable care to control the behavior of a patient which may endanger other persons. A doctor must also warn a patient if the patient's condition of medication renders certain conduct, such as driving a car, dangerous to others....

Defendants contend, however, that imposition of a duty to exercise reasonable care to protect third persons is unworkable because therapists cannot accurately predict whether or not a patient will resort to violence. In support of the argument amicus representing the American Psychiatric Association and other professional societies cites numerous articles which indicate that therapists, in the present state of the art, are unable reliably to predict violent acts; their forecasts, amicus claims, tend consistently to overpredict violence, and indeed are more often wrong than right. Since predictions of violence are often erroneous, amicus concludes, the courts should not render rulings that predicate the liability of therapists upon the validity of such predictions. . . .

We recognize the difficulty that a therapist encounters in attempting to forecast whether a patient presents a serious danger of violence. Obviously we do not require that the therapist in making that determination, render a perfect performance; the therapist need only exercise "that reasonable degree of skill, knowledge, and care ordinarily possessed and exercised by members of [that professional specialty] under similar circumstances." Within the broad range of reasonable practice and treatment in which professional opinion and judgment may differ, the therapist is free to exercise his or her own best judgment without liability; proof, aided by hindsight, that he or she judged wrongly is insufficient to establish negligence. . . .

Amicus contends, however, that even when a therapist does in fact predict that a patient poses a serious danger of violence to others, the therapist should be absolved of any responsibility for failing to act to protect the potential victim. In our view, however, once a therapist does in fact determine, or under applicable professional standards reasonably should have determined, that a patient poses a serious danger of violence to others, he bears a duty to exercise reasonable care to protect the foreseeable victim of that danger. While the discharge of this duty of due care will necessarily vary with the facts of each case, in each instance the adequacy of the therapist's conduct must be measured against the traditional negligence standard of the rendition of reasonable care under the circumstances. As explained in Fleming and Maximov, The Patient or His Victim: The Therapist's Dilemma (1974), 62 Cal. L. Rev. 1025, 1067: ". . . the ultimate question of resolving the tension between the conflicting interest of patient and potential victim is one of social policy, not professional expertise. . . . In sum, the therapist owes a legal duty not only to his patient, but also to his patient's would-be victim and is subject in both respects to scrutiny by judge and jury." . . .

The risk that unnecessary warnings may be given is a reasonable price to pay for the lives of possible victims that may be saved. We would hesitate to hold that the therapist who is aware that his patient expects to attempt to assassinate the President of the United States would not be obligated to warn the authorities because the therapist cannot predict with accuracy that his patient will commit the crime.

Defendants further argue that free and open communication is essential to psychotherapy; that "Unless a patient . . . is assured that . . . information [revealed by him] can and will be held in utmost confidence, he will be reluctant to make the full disclosure upon which diagnosis and treatment . . . depends." The giving of a warning, defendants contend, constitutes a breach of trust which entails the revelation of confidential communications.

We recognize the public interest in supporting effective treatment of mental illness and in protecting the rights of patients to privacy, and the consequent public importance of safeguarding the confidential character of psychotherapeutic communication. Against this interest, however, we must weigh the public interest in safety from violent assault. The Legislature has undertaken the difficult task of balancing the countervailing concerns. In Evidence Code section 1014, it established a broad rule of privilege to protect confidential communications between patient and psychotherapist. In Evidence Code section 1024, the Legislature created a specific and limited exception to the psychotherapist-patient privilege: "There is no privilege . . . if the psychotherapist has reasonable cause to believe that the patient is in such mental or emotional condition as to be dangerous to himself or to the person or property of another and that disclosure of the communication is necessary to prevent the threatened danger."[13]

We realize that the open and confidential character of psychotherapeutic dialogue encourages patients to express threats of violence, few of which are ever executed. Certainly a therapist should not be encouraged routinely to reveal such threats; such disclosures could seriously disrupt the patient's relationship with his therapist and with the persons threatened. To the contrary, the therapist's obligations to his patient require that he not disclose a confidence unless such disclosure is necessary to avert danger to others, and even then that he do so discreetly, and in a fashion that would preserve the privacy of his patient to the fullest extent compatible with the prevention of the threatened danger. (See Fleming & Maximov, *The Patient or His Victim: The Therapist's Dilemma* (1974), 62 CAL. L. REV. 1025, 1065–1066.)

The revelation of a communication under the above circumstances is not a breach of trust or a violation of professional ethics; as stated in the Principles of Medical Ethics of the American Medical Association (1957), section 9: "A physician may not reveal the confidence entrusted to him in

---

13. Fleming and Maximov note that "White [section 1024] supports the therapist's less controversial *right* to make a disclosure, it admittedly does not impose on him a *duty* to do so. But the argument does not have to be pressed that far. For if it is once conceded . . . that a duty in favor of the patient's foreseeable victims would accord with general principles of tort liability, we need no longer look to the statute for a source of duty. It is sufficient if the statute can be relied upon . . . for the purposes of countering the claim that the needs of confidentiality are paramount and must therefore defeat any such hypothetical duty. In this more modest perspective, the Evidence Code's 'dangerous patient' exception may be invoked with some confidence as a clear expression of legislative policy concerning the balance between the confidentiality values of the patient and the safety values of his foreseeable victim." (Emphasis in original.) Fleming & Maximov, *The Patient or His Victim: The Therapist's Dilemma* (1974), 62 CAL. L. REV. 1025, 1063.

the course of medical attendance ... *unless he is required to do so by law or unless it becomes necessary in order to protect the welfare of the individual or of the community.*" (Emphasis added.) We conclude that the public policy favoring protection of the confidential character of patient-psychotherapist communications must yield to the extent to which disclosure is essential to avert danger to others. The protective privilege ends where the public peril begins.

Our current crowded and computerized society compels the interdependence of its members. In this risk-infested society we can hardly tolerate the future exposure to danger that would result from a concealed knowledge of the therapist that his patient was lethal. If the exercise of reasonable care to protect the threatened victim requires the therapist to warn the endangered party or those who can reasonably be expected to notify him, we see no sufficient societal interest that would protect and justify concealment. The containment of such risks lies in the public interest. For the foregoing reasons, we find that plaintiffs' complaints can be amended to state a cause of action against defendants Moore, Powelson, Gold, and Yandell and against the Regents as their employer, for breach of a duty to exercise reasonable care to protect Tatiana....

Turning now to the police defendants, we conclude that they do not have any such special relationship to either Tatiana or to Poddar sufficient to impose upon such defendants a duty to warn respecting Poddar's violent intentions. Plaintiffs suggest no theory, and plead no facts that give rise to any duty to warn on the part of the police defendants absent such a special relationship....

[The court held that the decision not to warn was not a basic policy decision and that there was therefore no immunity.]

[Dissenting opinions omitted.]

NOTES

1. **Scope.** Consider whether, given a *Tarasoff* duty, therapists will be liable in every case in which a patient causes harm after making a threat. On what facts would a therapist be counted as reasonably prudent even if he fails to warn after a threat is made?

2. ***Tarasoff* and *Thompson*.** Four years after issuing *Tarasoff*, the California Court decided *Thompson v. County of Alameda*, 614 P.2d 728 (Cal. 1980). In that case, the court refused to impose liability upon a county which had released a dangerous criminal who was threatening to kill some unnamed child. When released on furlough, he did in fact kill a 5-year-old child. Can *Thompson* and *Tarasoff* be squared? The *Thompson* court suggested a possibility: "In those instances in which the released offender poses a predictable threat of harm to a named or readily identifiable victim ... a releasing agent may well be liable for failure to warn such persons." *See also State Dep't of Corrections v. Cowles*, 151 P.3d 353 (Alaska 2006) (state owed duty to exercise care in supervising parolees only where officials knew or should know that the

parolee posed a danger to a particular person or identifiable group of persons); *Osborn v. Mason County*, 134 P.3d 197 (Wash. 2006) (citing *Thompson*, holding county owed no duty to warn of sex offender's presence where victim was "unforeseeable"). Does this reasoning suggest that if Poddar had shown a clear and strong probability that he would kill a number of small children, or old women, the psychiatrist would not owe any duty to later victims? Is the *Thompson* reasoning sound? The Wisconsin Court thought there was "no legitimate policy" for the *Thompson* limitation on the duty of care. *Schuster v. Altenberg*, 424 N.W.2d 159 (Wis. 1988).

3. **Accepting the *Tarasoff* duty.** Many states have adopted some sort of *Tarasoff* duty by statute. In addition, almost all courts that have considered the issue have accepted such a duty. Many of these states have added the *Thompson* qualification—that is, a duty to warn will exist, but only where the patient communicates a threat to an identifiable person. *See, e.g., Robinson v. Mount Logan Clinic, LLC*, 182 P.3d 333 (Utah 2008) (no duty to warn police officer called to transport suidal patient who attacked attacked officer during transport); *Doe v. Marion*, 645 S.E.2d 245 (S.C. 2007) (no duty to warn future foreseeable victims of patient's predilection for child molestation, where patient did not specifically threaten an identifiable person); *DeJesus v. United States*, 479 F.3d 271 (3d Cir. 2007) (no duty to warn wife of patient's violent tendencies where no particularized threat was made); *Munstermann v. Alegent Health–Immanuel Medical Center*, 716 N.W.2d 73 (Neb. 2006) (no duty to warn patient's girlfriend unless patient communicated threat of physical violence to a readily identifiable victim); *Campbell v. Ohio State Univ. Medical Center*, 843 N.E.2d 1194 (Ohio 2006) (applying statute).

4. **Rejecting or modifying *Tarasoff*.** A few courts have rejected *Tarasoff*. *See, e.g., Nasser v. Parker,* 455 S.E.2d 502 (Va. 1995). Others draw distinctions between negligence in diagnosis, commitment, release, and failure to warn those endangered, rejecting some of those duties. *See Gregory v. Kilbride,* 565 S.E.2d 685 (N.C. App. 2002) (no duty to warn, duty to use care in commitment); *compare Thapar v. Zezulka*, 994 S.W.2d 635 (Tex. 1999) (no duty to warn potential victim) *with Texas Home Mgmt., Inc. v. Peavy,* 89 S.W.3d 30 (Tex. 2002) (no duty to diagnose or treat for protection of third persons, but a duty to use care to *control* one in custody for protection of foreseeably endangered third persons). Some courts find a duty to warn not on a *Tarasoff* theory, but rather on the basis of a promise made to the victim. *Long v. Broadlawns Med. Ctr.,* 656 N.W.2d 71 (Iowa 2002) (mental health center failed to notify wife of husband's release, after promise to do so).

5. **Extending *Tarasoff*.** California expanded the *Tarasoff* cuty in *Hedlund v. Superior Court of Orange County,* 669 P.2d 41 (Cal. 1983), holding that the defendant owed a duty not only to the direct victim of a threatened beating but also to her son, who was emotionally upset at seeing his mother attacked. Does a counselor owe a duty to warn about a patient's suicide threat? In *Eisel v. Board of Education of Montgomery County,* 597 A.2d 447 (Md. 1991), the court held that public-school counselors were under a duty to use reasonable means to attempt to prevent the suicide of a student once they were on notice of suicidal intent. But California refused to recognize a therapist's duty to protect a suicidal patient in *Bellah v. Greenson,* 146 Cal.Rptr. 535 (Ct. App. 1978).

6. **Doctors' warnings to patients.** Should a doctor owe a duty to warn a patient of the effects of a drug or treatment the doctor has administered? For example, what if a doctor knows that a patient's driving might be impaired, but does not tell the patient that? The patient then causes a wreck, injuring the plaintiff. *See McKenzie v. Hawai'i Permanente Medical Group, Inc.*, 47 P.3d 1209 (Haw. 2002) (doctor owes a duty to warn his own patient of the dangers of driving while on a prescribed medication unless the patient himself could be expected to know the risk); *accord, Taylor v. Smith*, 892 So.2d 887 (Ala. 2004); *Burroughs v. Magee*, 118 S.W.3d 323 (Tenn. 2003). *Cf. Hardee v. Bio–Medical Applications of South Carolina, Inc.*, 636 S.E.2d 629 (S.C. 2006) (dialysis center owed duty to motorists to warn patient that dialysis treatment could make it dangerous for him to drive). *Contra, Lester v. Hall*, 970 P.2d 590 (N.M. 1998); *Schmidt v. Mahoney*, 659 N.W.2d 552 (Iowa 2003); *Weigold v. Patel*, 840 A.2d 19 (Conn. App. 2004). Or what if the patient has a communicable disease. Is there a duty to tell the patient how to avoid infecting others? *See DiMarco v. Lynch Homes—Chester County, Inc.*, 583 A.2d 422 (Pa. 1990) (yes; duty exists to protect persons other than the patient). Would there be a similar duty to tell a patient not to drive because her eyesight is poor? Why might that be different? *See Witthoeft v. Kiskaddon*, 733 A.2d 623 (Pa. 1999). Are these cases easier than *Tarasoff*?

7. **Doctors' warnings to non-patients.** Should a doctor owe a duty to warn a non-patient of a risk posed by the patient's health condition? Suppose T has AIDS or is at risk for AIDS because he received a blood transfusion from a contaminated batch and D knows it. D also knows that T is about to marry P or has regular sexual relations with P. Should D advise P? Legislatures have enacted strong medicine for that kind of case: Doctors, health care providers, blood suppliers may be prohibited from revealing that a person has AIDS or even that he is at risk. See *Santa Rose Health Care Corp. v. Garcia*, 964 S.W.2d 940 (Tex. 1998). A California statute permits the doctor to disclose a positive test for AIDS to anyone reasonably believed to be a spouse, sexual partner or needle-sharer, but the doctor is not permitted to disclose any information that will identify the patient. In any event the doctor is not required to make disclosure to a non-patient. CAL. HEALTH & SAFETY CODE § 199.25.

New York's courts have held that a physician owes a non-patient no duty of care, unless the physician's treatment of the patient is the cause of the non-patient's harm. *McNulty v. City of New York*, 792 N.E.2d 162 (N.Y. 2003). Thus where a doctor inoculates a patient with a polio vaccine that may spread the virus to family members, the doctor *does* owe a duty to those non-patients. *Tenuto v. Lederle Labs.*, 687 N.E.2d 1300 (N.Y. 1997). But where a patient has hepatitis C and the doctors fail to warn the patient's daughter that the disease was contagious, despite knowing that the daughter was caring for the patient, no duty existed. *Candelario v. Teperman*, 789 N.Y.S.2d 133 (App. Div. 2005). Is this inconsistent with *Tarasoff*?

BRIGANCE v. VELVET DOVE RESTAURANT, INC.

725 P.2d 300 (Okla. 1986)

HODGES, JUDGE.

[The defendant, the Velvet Dove Restaurant, served alcohol to a group of minors, including one Jeff Johnson. Defendant's employees knew Jeff Johnson drove the group to the restaurant. The plaintiffs alleged that alcohol served by the defendant caused Johnson to become intoxicated or increased his earlier intoxication and that this in turn caused a one-car accident in which the plaintiff Shawn was injured. The trial court dismissed the claim.]

At common law a tavern owner who furnishes alcoholic beverages to another is not civilly liable for a third person's injuries that are caused by the acts of an intoxicated patron. Such rule is principally based upon concepts of causation that, as a matter of law, it is not the sale of liquor by the tavern owner, but the voluntary consumption by the intoxicated person, which is the proximate cause of resulting injuries, so that the tavern owner is therefore not liable for negligence in selling the liquor.

In recent years, many states have retreated from the common law rule of nonliability for a liquor vendor regarding it as antiquated and illogical. Several states with dram shop laws have also recognized a new common law right of action against a vendor of liquor. Many of the jurisdictions which now recognize a civil right of action do so on the theory enunciated in Rappaport v. Nichols, 31 N.J. 188, 156 A.2d 1 (1959):

"When alcoholic beverages are sold by a tavern keeper to a minor or to an intoxicated person, the unreasonable risk of harm ... to members of the traveling public may readily be recognized and foreseen; this is particularly evident in current times when traveling by car to and from the tavern is so commonplace and accidents resulting from drinking are so frequent."

As shown by the modern trend, the old common law rule of nonliability has been changed by judicial opinion: "Inherent in the common law is a dynamic principle which allows it to grow and to tailor itself to meet changing needs...."

... The development of the law of torts is peculiarly a function of the judiciary. Because duty and liability are matters of public policy they are subject to the changing attitudes and needs of society....

Appellees assert that we are not free to change the common law because the Legislature has expressly spoken in this area by its 1959 repeal of Oklahoma's dram shop act and its failure to reenact such provision since that time. We are not persuaded by this argument. The dram shop act was not selectively repealed for it was repealed when intoxicants were legalized in 1959. Because the Legislature has failed to act to impose civil liability, for reasons unknown, does not unequivocally demonstrate legislative intent. To hold otherwise, would be indulging in a type of psychoanalysis of the Legislature. We simply cannot conclude that statutory silence is here indicative of legislative intent to bar the cause of action before us.

We also cannot accede to the view urged by appellees that this area of law is better dealt with by the Legislature. We find that on the basis of the clear trend in this area we are free to establish a civil cause of action by an injured third person against a commercial vendor of liquor for on the premises consumption. In rendering the opinion of Vanderpool v. State, 672 P.2d 1153, 1157 (Okla.1983), which modified the common law doctrine of governmental immunity, this Court stated in response to the oft-expressed view that if the doctrine is to be abrogated such should be done by the Legislature and not the courts of this State: "But having come to the conclusions that the judicially recognized doctrine of governmental immunity in its present state under the case law is no longer supportable in reason, justice or in light of the overwhelming trend against its recognition, our duty is clear. Where the reason for the rule no longer exists, that alone should toll its death knell."

We believe the application of the old common law rule of a tavern owner's nonliability in today's automotive society is unrealistic, inconsistent with modern tort theories and is a complete anachronism within today's society.

The automobile is a constant reminder of a changed and changing America. It has made a tremendous impact on every segment of society, including the field of jurisprudence. In the "horse and buggy" days the common law may not have been significantly affected by the sale of liquor to an intoxicated person. The common law of nonliability was satisfactory. With today's car of steel and speed it becomes a lethal weapon in the hands of a drunken imbiber. The frequency of accidents involving drunk drivers are commonplace. Its affliction of bodily injury to an unsuspecting public is also of common knowledge. Under such circumstances we are compelled to widen the scope of the common law.

We, thus, hold that one who sells intoxicating beverages for on the premises consumption has a duty to exercise reasonable care not to sell liquor to a noticeably intoxicated person. It is not unreasonable to expect a commercial vendor who sells alcoholic beverages for on the premises consumption to a person he knows or should know from the circumstances is already intoxicated, to foresee the unreasonable risk of harm to others who may be injured by such person's impaired ability to operate an automobile.

... A commercial vendor for on the premises consumption is under a common law duty to exercise ordinary care under the circumstances. We reach our conclusion in accordance with other courts finding a common law duty, relying on the general rule expressed in Restatement (Second) of Torts § 308 (1965):

"It is negligence to permit a third person to use a thing or to engage in an activity which is under the control of the actor, if the actor knows or should know that such person intends or is likely to use the thing or to conduct himself in the activity in such a manner as to create an unreasonable risk of harm to others."

And, Restatement (Second) of Torts § 390 (1965):

"One who supplies . . . a chattel for the use of another whom the supplier knows or has reason to know to be likely because of his youth, inexperience or otherwise to use it in a manner involving unreasonable risk of physical harm to himself and others . . . is subject to liability for physical harm resulting to them."

Even if a commercial vendor for on the premises consumption is found to have breached its duty, a plaintiff must still show the illegal sale of alcohol led to the impairment of the ability of the driver which was the proximate cause of the injury and there was a causal connection between the sale and a foreseeable ensuing injury. . . .

. . . Ordinarily the question of causation in a negligent tort case is one of fact for the jury and becomes one of law only when there is no evidence from which the jury could reasonably find a causal nexus between the negligent act and the resulting injuries. . . .

In adopting a new rule of liability which creates a civil cause of action, we specifically hold that the law hereby established will be applied prospectively to all causes of action occurring from and after the date the mandate issues herein [except that the rule of liability also applies to the parties in this case. Reversed and remanded.]

NOTES

1. **The negligent entrustment analogy.** The *Brigance* court cited with approval two sections of the Restatement Second that deal with what is commonly called "negligent entrustment." The thrust of this body of law is that a person in control of a chattel owes a responsibility not to entrust that chattel to a person whom the entruster knows or should know is apt to use it in a dangerous way. Once that duty of care is imposed, the negligent entrustment case is just like any other negligence case, with the same elements. *See* DOBBS ON TORTS § 330 (2000); RESTATEMENT (THIRD) OF TORTS: LIABILITY FOR PHYSICAL HARM § 19, cmt. e. (P.F.D. No. 1, 2005). Most cases involve products that could be operated by the entrustee, such as cars, guns, or cigarette lighters. *See, e.g., Morin v. Moore*, 309 F.3d 316 (5th Cir. 2002) (making an AK–47 automatic rifle accessible to a dangerous person invested in Nazi ideology); *Ardinger v. Hummell*, 982 P.2d 727 (Alaska 1999) (furnishing automobile to 15-year-old). A negligent entruster may be liable not only to third persons injured by the entrustee, but also to the entrustee himself.

2. **Provision of alcohol as negligent entrustment.** Is the court's use of the negligent entrustment rules sound as a matter of logic and policy? Some courts have been willing to test the boundaries. For example, in *Vince v.*

Wilson, 561 A.2d 103 (Vt. 1989), the court held that the plaintiff, injured in an accident with an incompetent driver, stated a claim against the driver's great aunt who provided money to buy the car knowing that her grand-nephew was a substance abuser who had failed the driver's test many times. In *West v. East Tennessee Pioneer Oil Co.*, 172 S.W.3d 545 (Tenn. 2005), the court held that a convenience store could be held liable on a negligent entrustment theory when its clerk sold gasoline to a clearly intoxicated motorist and helped him pump the gas.

3. **The traditional approach to alcohol-sales cases.** Courts traditionally denied the kind of liability imposed in *Brigance* on the ground that the alcohol provider was not a proximate cause of harm done by the drinker. Some courts or legislatures still reject liability even for providing alcohol to minors or intoxicated persons. *See Prime v. Beta Gamma Chapter Pi Kappa Alpha,* 47 P.3d 402 (Kan. 2002); *Wegleitner v. Sattler,* 582 N.W.2d 688 (S.D. 1998) (legislative no-liability rule). Would the plaintiff have a better case if the defendant, instead of providing alcohol to a drinker, had left it where it could be stolen by teenagers? *See Dettmann v. Kruckenberg,* 613 N.W.2d 238 (Iowa 2000).

4. **Rulings as a matter of law.** Scope of risk is usually decided case by case, often by the jury but in any event on the facts peculiar to the case. In the alcohol provider cases, however, judges made a rule of law for all cases: the provider's fault was *never* a proximate cause. Would it make more sense to say that this was a no-duty rule? Are there any policy bases for exculpating the seller of alcohol? What if the server cannot be sure whether a customer is intoxicated?

5. **Fixing responsibility.** The common law has expressed in many ways a strong belief that each individual should be responsible for his or her own actions. Not only does this imply, for some judges, that one is not responsible for the acts of others, but it implies that responsibility should not be shared. Thus courts had some difficulty in imposing joint and several liability upon multiple wrongdoers. If the last actor was an intentional wrongdoer, the feeling at one time apparently was that he and only he should be liable. To impose joint liability would lighten his burden and thus diminish his accountability. What arguments can you mount against this kind of outlook? Relatedly, you'll want to remember why the plaintiff is suing the alcohol provider.

6. **Suits by the drinker.** In a state that allows for some alcohol-provider liability, does the provider owe a duty of care to the drinker himself, or only to third persons who may be injured? Some courts have said the duty runs to the drinker as well as to others. *See, e.g., Mann v. Shusteric Enterp., Inc.,* 683 N.W.2d 573 (Mich. 2004) (allowing premises liability action by patron who fell in bar's parking lot after being served liquor illegally by bar). However, most appear to hold that the adult drinker is responsible for his own injury and the provider owes him nothing. *See, e.g., Bridges v. Park Place Entn't,* 860 So.2d 811 (Miss. 2003); *Cf. Lydia v. Horton,* 583 S.E.2d 750 (S.C. 2003) (intoxicated entrustee cannot sue for negligent entrustment, both on grounds of public policy and because the intoxicated plaintiff's fault is greater

than that of the entruster as a matter of law). If a duty of care is owed to the drinker himself, why is this not a *Bexiga* situation?

7. **Liability of social hosts.** Not surprisingly, some courts willing to impose liability upon sellers of alcohol are not willing to impose liability upon social hosts who provide alcohol with the same results. *Reynolds v. Hicks*, 951 P.2d 761 (Wash. 1998). Nevertheless, a few courts have approved of such liability, especially where the host has knowingly provided alcohol to minors. See, e.g., *Nichols v. Progressive Northern Ins. Co.*, 746 N.W.2d 220 (Wis. 2008); *Marcum v. Bowden*, 643 S.E.2d 85 (S.C. 2007); *Martin v. Marciano*, 871 A.2d 911 (R.I. 2005); *Hickingbotham v. Burke*, 662 A.2d 297 (N.H. 1995) (liability if social host is reckless).

8. **Scope of risk, redux.** Even where a duty is owed by an alcohol provider, the defendant might still avoid liability in some cases because the injury is outside the scope of the risk—or, if you prefer, is not a proximate result of the breach. Suppose the provider supplies alcohol to an obviously intoxicated person, who drives safely to a friend's house where he falls asleep smoking a cigarette. The cigarette causes a fire and the friend's house burns down. Liability?

NOTE: DRAM SHOP STATUTES

1. The traditional view is a statute regulating sales of alcohol—for example, a statute prohibiting sales to minors or intoxicated persons—does not create a private cause of action. *Robinson v. Matt Mary Moran, Inc.*, 525 S.E.2d 559 (Va. 2000). Now, however, many states have adopted statutes called dram shop statutes or civil damage acts that do not merely impose criminal penalties; instead, they expressly impose civil liability upon the dispenser of alcohol. There are many variations. Some statutes impose liability only for certain kinds of sales, such as sales to minors or intoxicated persons. Others require a higher showing than mere negligence. *See, e.g., Nunez v. Carrabba's Italian Grill, Inc.*, 859 N.E.2d 801 (Mass. 2007) (holding that statute, which requires proof of the seller's "willful, wanton or reckless" conduct, does not apply when alcohol is furnished to a minor). Some statutes apply only to those who sell alcohol for consumption on the premises, as opposed to stores selling packaged liquor. *See, e.g., Snodgras v. Martin & Bayley, Inc.*, 204 S.W.3d 638 (Mo. 2006) (upholding such a statute against constitutional attack). The dram shop statute may be the exclusive remedy, barring all common law claims, so the plaintiff must meet the terms of the statute. *See, e.g., Delta Airlines, Inc. v. Townsend*, 614 S.E.2d 745 (Ga. 2005). Some dram shop statutes seem to create a kind of strict liability upon the provider of alcohol. *See, e.g.*, 235 ILL. COMP. STAT. 5/6–21 (granting civil cause of action to any person injured by an intoxicated person against any person licensed to sell liquor who caused such intoxication, with no proof of fault required).

2. At the other extreme, legislators in some states have immunized alcohol providers for negligence, even where they have served drunken customers who are likely to drive. *See, e.g.*, TENN. CODE ANN. § 57–10–101

et seq.; WIS. STAT. ANN. 125.035. Idaho's statute bars claims by passengers injured in cars being driven by intoxicated drivers. *See McLean v. Maverik Country Stores, Inc.*, 135 P.3d 756 (Idaho 2006) (rejecting constitutional attack).

3.   Some states have refused to impose civil liability in the *absence* of a dram shop statute, saying that such a decision should be for the legislature alone. *See, e.g., Shea v. Matassa*, 918 A.2d 1090 (Del. 2007). Does that represent good policy in this area of law?

PROBLEMS

1.   A railroad, trying to clear its track after a derailment, works an employee more than 24 hours with no substantial rest. When the employee finally heads home, he falls asleep at the wheel and crashes into the plaintiff's car. Since the employee is not "on the job," the employer is not vicariously liable. Is the employer liable for negligence?

2.   The defendant, a physician, prescribed anabolic steroids for a patient. The patient's reaction to the drug or its dosage was to become extremely aggressive and hostile to those around him. After his behavior led his wife to leave the house out of fear, the physician talked to him and concluded he was safe and so advised the wife. The wife then went back to the house to get her clothes, taking a friend with her. The patient shot the friend, causing injury. In prescribing for the patient, did the physician owe any duty to protect third persons? Assume you are in a jurisdiction that recognizes the rule in *Brigance*.

3.   Defendant owned a pistol, which he left in his bedroom. He had a safe on the premises but did not keep the pistol there. While defendant was out of town, his daughter invited guests to the house. One of them stole the pistol and used it later in a robbery, killing decedent in the process. The estate sues the defendant alleging that he negligently failed to secure the pistol.

REFERENCES: DOBBS ON TORTS §§ 322–32 (2000); HARPER, JAMES & GRAY, THE LAW OF TORTS § 18.7 (3d Ed. 2007).

TOPIC C

LIMITING DUTIES
TO PROTECT AGAINST
SPECIAL TYPES OF HARM

■ ■ ■

Judicial attitudes about tort liabilities depend in part upon the relationships of the parties, but also in part upon the kind of harm the plaintiff claims.

In the absence of special relationships, courts are most receptive to tort claims when the defendant has risked and the plaintiff has suffered physical harm to person or property. What tort cases do *not* involve physical harms? First, cases of stand-alone economic harm. For instance, defendant negligently provides the plaintiff with information that leads the plaintiff to purchase property. The information proves unreliable and the plaintiff takes a financial loss on the purchase. Second, cases of stand-alone emotional harm or distress. For instance, the defendant negligently provides the plaintiff with information that makes the plaintiff believe her child has been injured. Before the plaintiff discovers that the information is false, she suffers great emotional harm.

Several different torts besides the tort of negligence address emotional interests. Physical torts like battery, assault and false imprisonment obviously have protection of emotional interests as one component. Defamation (libel and slander), malicious prosecution, the right to privacy, and even the tort called nuisance likewise protect emotional interests involved in reputation, seclusion, and the use and enjoyment of land.

The three chapters that follow consider how courts treat the undifferentiated negligence claims for emotional harm or loss generally, in prenatal injury cases, and in wrongful death cases.

CHAPTER 19

EMOTIONAL HARM

■ ■ ■

A plaintiff who establishes a tort claim for personal injury, or a claim based on trespassory torts like battery, assault, or false imprisonment, is always entitled to recover for any pain and suffering proven as well as for any pecuniary damages. In such cases, emotional harm, when proven, is recoverable as a species of pain and suffering if not as some separate item of damage. Such recoveries are often called parasitic damages. They represent the damages recoverable for some other tort, not for a stand-alone claim of emotional distress. This chapter is concerned primarily with stand-alone claims for distress.

SUBCHAPTER A. INTENTIONAL AND RECKLESS HARMS

§ 1. INTENTIONAL INFLICTION OF EMOTIONAL DISTRESS

RESTATEMENT (THIRD) OF TORTS: LIABILITY FOR PHYSICAL AND EMOTIONAL HARM § 45

Tentative Draft No. 5 (2007)

An actor who by extreme and outrageous conduct intentionally or recklessly causes severe emotional disturbance to another is subject to liability for that emotional disturbance and, if the emotional disturbance causes bodily harm, also for the bodily harm.

Comment: . . .

g. Actor's intent. To recover under this Section, a plaintiff must prove that the defendant intended to cause severe emotional disturbance to the plaintiff or acted with reckless disregard of whether the plaintiff would suffer such harm. An actor intends severe emotional disturbance when the actor acts with the purpose of causing severe emotional disturbance or acts knowing that severe emotional disturbance is substantially certain to result. An actor acts recklessly when the actor knows of the risk of severe emotional disturbance (or knows facts that make the risk obvious) and fails to take a precaution that would eliminate or reduce the risk even though the burden is slight relative to the magnitude of the risk, thereby demonstrating the actor's indifference.

Courts uniformly hold that reckless conduct, not just intentional conduct, can support a claim for intentional infliction of emotional disturbance. In this sense, the scienter requirement for this tort is more expansive than, for example, battery. Three rationales support this. First, and most important, to recover for intentional infliction of emotional disturbance, a plaintiff must prove that the defendant's conduct was extreme and outrageous. An actor who commits a battery does not *necessarily* act in an extreme and outrageous manner. Indeed, recklessness entails balancing the risk of harm with the difficulty of preventing it; that balancing can result in a reckless actor's being more culpable than another actor who satisfies the intent requirement only because emotional harm was substantially certain to occur, regardless of the burden of avoiding that harm. Second, unlike battery, the resulting harm must satisfy the "severe" threshold. Third, if an actor's state of mind fails to satisfy the intent requirement for battery, the injured person might still be able to prove negligence, but a person who cannot recover for intentional infliction of emotional disturbance usually faces substantial obstacles to recovering on a negligence theory. See §§ 46–47. Thus, courts have good reason to include cases of recklessness within the tort of intentional infliction of emotional disturbance.

GTE SOUTHWEST, INC. v. BRUCE, 998 S.W.2d 605 (Tex. 1999). Several employees of GTE working under Morris Shields alleged that over a period of years, Shields engaged in a pattern of grossly abusive, threatening, and degrading conduct, regularly using the harshest vulgarity, verbally threatening and terrorizing them. He would physically charge at the employees, put his head down, ball his hands into fists, and walk quickly toward or lunge at the employees, stopping very close to their faces. A number of witnesses testified that Shields frequently yelled and screamed at the top of his voice, and pounded his fists when requesting the employees to do things. There was testimony that he often called one employee into his office and kept her standing there up to thirty minutes while he simply started at her. He required employees to vacuum their own offices daily despite the availability of regular janitorial services. A jury found for plaintiffs in their suit for intentional infliction of emotional distress. *Held*, affirmed.

"Generally, insensitive or even rude behavior does not constitute extreme and outrageous conduct. Similarly, mere insults, indignities, threats, annoyances, petty oppressions, or other trivialities do not rise to the level of extreme and outrageous conduct. In determining whether certain conduct is extreme and outrageous, courts consider the context and the relationship between the parties.... Shields's ongoing acts of harassment, intimidation, and humiliation and his daily obscene and vulgar behavior, which GTE defends as his 'management style,' went beyond the bounds of tolerable workplace conduct.... Occasional malicious and abusive incidents should not be condoned, but must often be tolerated in our society. But once conduct such as that shown here becomes a regular pattern of behavior and continues despite the victim's objection and attempts to remedy the situation, it can no longer be tolerated. It is the severity and regularity of Shields's abusive and threatening conduct that brings his behavior into the realm of extreme and outrageous conduct."

NOTES

1. **History of the tort.** The American Law Institute recognized an independent tort based on intentional infliction of mental distress in the Restatement of Torts in 1948. The Restatement (Second) § 46 first employed the "extreme and outrageous conduct" standard and courts widely adopted it. One early kind of case involved intentional or reckless interference with a dead body. Such cases still arise. In *Travelers Insurance Co. v. Smith,* 991 S.W.2d 591 (Ark. 1999), an insurer refused to pay insurance due for the decedent's funeral until an autopsy was performed, then insisted that someone else arrange and pay for the autopsy. The result was that the funeral was so delayed that the body could not be viewed. The court upheld a jury verdict for the plaintiff.

2. **Markers of outrage.** Determining whether conduct is "extreme and outrageous" is a fact-sensitive, case-by-case inquiry. *See, e.g., Almy v. Grisham,* 639 S.E.2d 182 (Va. 2007). Perhaps the most common fact patterns, however, involve conduct that is (a) repeated or carried out over a period of time, (b) an abuse of power by a person with some authority over the plaintiff, or (c) directed at a person known to be especially vulnerable. Which pattern does *GTE v. Bruce* fit?

3. **Repeated conduct.** A single request for sexual contact might be offensive but is usually not sufficiently outrageous. *See Jones v. Clinton,* 990 F.Supp. 657 (E.D. Ark. 1998). On the other hand, repeated and harassing requests for sexual attention can be outrageous. *Samms v. Eccles,* 358 P.2d 344 (Utah 1961). *See also Riske v. King Soopers,* 366 F.3d 1085 (10th Cir. 2004) (two years of supervisor sending flowers anonymously with suggestive messages and following plaintiff around at work making suggestive remarks). Similarly, a creditor is not outrageous in demanding payment of an overdue debt, but numerous demands for payment of a debt not due may be actionable. *George v. Jordan Marsh Co.,* 268 N.E.2d 915 (Mass. 1971).

4. **Abuse of power.** Abuse of power by the defendant takes many forms. It might involve employers and employees, or public officials and those in a subordinate position. *See, e.g., Brandon v. County of Richardson,* 624 N.W.2d 604 (Neb. 2001) (sheriff crudely questioning rape victim soon after rape); *Taylor v. Metzger,* 706 A.2d 685 (N.J. 1998) (sheriff using racial slur against female officer). Not all courts find these lines easy to draw, however.

See, e.g., Washington v. Mother Works, Inc., 197 F.Supp.2d 569 (E.D. La. 2002) (supervisor ridiculing employee with racial slurs held not to go beyond "mere insult," thus not "outrageous"). What if an employee repeatedly yells at his employer at work, makes false police reports about his employer, and threatens to sue him? What do you see as the main weakness in the employer's suit for intentional infliction of emotional distress? *Langeslag v. KYMN Inc.*, 664 N.W.2d 860 (Minn. 2003).

5. **Knowledge of plaintiff's vulnerability.** This pattern may be seen as a subset of the abuse-of-power pattern, or it could constitute a more specific version of it. *See, e.g., MacDermid v. Discover Financial Services*, 488 F.3d 721 (6th Cir. 2007) (allegations stated claim against credit card company for repeated threats of legal action against woman known by them to have mental problems); *Liberty Mut. Ins. Co. v. Steadman*, 968 So.2d 592 (Fla. Dist. Ct. App. 2007) (insurance company's conduct was outrageous where it denied and delayed paying for treatment, knowing claimant had limited life expectancy); *Doe v. Corporation of Pres. of Church of Jesus Christ of Latter–Day Saints*, 167 P.3d 1193 (Wash. Ct. App. 2007) (affirming jury verdict for plaintiff where church bishop acted with knowledge of teenaged church member's peculiar susceptibility to emotional distress).

6. **Exercising legal rights.** Cases and the Restatement emphasize that a person cannot be held liable for this tort merely for exercising a legal right, even where he is substantially certain that it will cause emotional distress— such as filing for a divorce, or firing an at-will employee, or seeking to collect a debt. RESTATEMENT (THIRD) § 45, cmt. *d*. But a person is not "immunized from liability if the conduct goes so far beyond what is necessary to exercise that right that it is extreme and outrageous." Id.

7. **Intent to do what?** Can you tell from the black-letter of Restatement § 45 what the object of the defendant's intent must be? Does Comment *g* clarify that?

8. **Causation.** A plaintiff must prove a sufficient causal link between the defendant's conduct and the plaintiff's distress. This is usually thought to mean actual causation, meaning that the plaintiff must show that but for the defendant's outrageous conduct, the severe distress would not have occurred. *See* RESTATEMENT (THIRD) § 45, cmt. *j*. How can a jury know this? What if plaintiff is surrounded by a circle of men who threaten him with the most severe bodily reprisals unless he gives up his job or joins the garbage haulers association? Would you be more convinced by expert psychiatric testimony than by a detailed recitation of the threats? *See Miller v. Willbanks*, 8 S.W.3d 607 (Tenn. 1999); *see also Brandon v. County of Richardson*, 624 N.W.2d 604 (Neb. 2001). Some courts insist on expert testimony in some cases, as where a lay jury could not determine the cause of the plaintiff's distress otherwise. *See, e.g., Powell v. Grant Medical Ctr.*, 771 N.E.2d 874 (Ohio Ct. App. 2002) (defendant injured plaintiffs' mother's dead body; grief over the injury and over the mother's death were inextricably intertwined).

9. **Severity of emotional distress.** Although severe distress can be proved without showing physical symptoms, courts really insist that the distress must be severe or even debilitating. *See* DOBBS ON TORTS § 306 (2000). Take an example. You give blood at the blood bank, which then sends you a

letter saying your blood had tested positive for syphilis and that the test had been confirmed. You are upset, your spouse is upset and worried, you feel your character is on the line, you both go into counseling and get new blood tests (proving the blood bank wrong). In *Fisher v. American Red Cross Blood Services*, 745 N.E.2d 462 (Ohio Ct. App. 2000), the court held that these facts did not show severe distress. Is this a useful requirement, or should a plaintiff be allowed to recover damages for non-severe distress provably caused by a defendant's "extreme and outrageous" behavior?

10. **Overlap with other tort claims.** The Restatement (Third) § 45, in comment *a*, explains that the intentional infliction tort "originated as a catchall to permit recovery when an existing tort claim was unavailable but in the narrow instances in which an actor's conduct exceeded all permissible bounds of a civilized society." Did some of the supervisor's actions in *GTE v. Bruce* constitute other intentional torts? Should a plaintiff be allowed to bring a claim for intentional infliction of emotional distress if a claim for battery or assault is stated as well? On a different note altogether, consider whether courts should permit an intentional infliction claim to proceed if the intentional infliction is accomplished solely by acts that would count as a battery and if the battery claim is barred by a shorter statute of limitations. *See, e.g., Dickens v. Puryear*, 276 S.E.2d 325 (N.C. 1981); *Winkler v. Rocky Mountain Conference of the United Methodist Church*, 923 P.2d 152 (Colo. Ct. App. 1995).

11. **Statutes.** State and federal statutes may come into play to provide causes of action for plaintiffs who might otherwise be limited to common-law recovery for intentional infliction of emotional distress. (A) Statutes sometimes provide causes of action for discrimination against persons suffering from disability. A federal statute has been held to create a cause of action for a disabled person who was denied an airline flight because of her disability. Most of the $80,000 recovery was for emotional harm. *Tallarico v. Trans World Airlines, Inc.*, 881 F.2d 566 (8th Cir. 1989). (B) Sometimes sexual harassment can be redressed under federal or state anti-discrimination statutes. If the sexual harassment is not a battery but instead consists of verbal harassment such as repeated demands for sexual conduct, could the victim claim damages on a theory of intentional or reckless infliction of distress? In *Ford v. Revlon, Inc.*, 734 P.2d 580 (Ariz. 1987) the plaintiff recovered $10,000 in compensatory and $100,000 in punitive damages from the employer who knew of continuous physical and verbal harassment by the plaintiff's superior, but refused to interfere with it. (C) Federal statutory law of employment discrimination most commonly protects economic rights rather than rights in emotional tranquility. Since the 1991 Civil Rights Act, plaintiffs in some employment discrimination cases can recover limited emotional harm damages. The statutes are usually covered in advanced courses in employment law.

NOTE: FIRST AMENDMENT CONSIDERATIONS

1. *First Amendment and public figures.* The First Amendment to the U.S. Constitution forbids state or federal interference with free speech. What counts as "speech" is a complicated subject. Sometimes intentional or even merely negligent misstatements of fact might be grounds for

recovery on a libel or slander theory, in spite of the First Amendment. (There is more on the First Amendment and libel in Chapter 32.) In general, however, statements not understood to be factual—opinions and satire, for example—are protected. Public figures in particular may be denied tort recovery based on such "speech," since it is especially important to preserve the right of discussion about public affairs.

2. *The First Amendment and religion.* Another clause of the First Amendment protects free exercise of religion and another prevents the government from supporting religion. Can courts uphold emotional distress claims based on the defendant's promulgation of "false" or distressing religious doctrine? *See Tilton v. Marshall*, 925 S.W.2d 672 (Tex. 1996). Suppose a religious group threatens a member or former member with divine retribution under frightening circumstances. If the member is severely distressed, would she have a claim or would the courts hesitate to interfere this much with religion? In *Molko v. Holy Spirit Association for the Unification of World Christianity,* 762 P.2d 46 (Cal. 1988) a threat of divine retribution was not actionable, but the plaintiff's claim that the church fraudulently induced the plaintiffs "into an atmosphere of coercive persuasion" could go to the jury as an intentional infliction of mental distress. What about a plaintiff distressed because of church-ordered "shunning?" *See Sands v. Living Word Fellowship*, 34 P.3d 955 (Alaska 2001). Or what if the plaintiff's emotional distress results from church members' "laying hands" on her to combat "evil forces"? *Pleasant Glade Assembly of God v. Schubert*, 264 S.W.3d 1 (Tex. 2008). How about a plaintiff who claims that a church and its members tried to influence his brain-injured brother to move out of his house by telling him that the plaintiff "was an instrument of Satan, was under the influence of Satan, or was Satan," and that the brother's "salvation, and spiritual and emotional health was at risk" if he continued to live with the plaintiff? *Checkley v. Boyd,* 14 P.3d 81 (Or. Ct. App. 2000).

HOMER v. LONG

599 A.2d 1193 (Md. Ct. Spec. App. 1992)

WILNER, CHIEF JUDGE.

[The plaintiff alleged: He and his wife had been married many years when she was hospitalized for depression. While she was hospitalized, her therapist used confidential information and took advantage of her dependent, needy and vulnerable condition to seduce her. His wife's personality changed and he and his wife were ultimately divorced. The plaintiff here sues the therapist, among other things for intentional or reckless infliction of distress.]

. . . Mr. Homer alleged that [the conduct alleged] was intentional and reckless, and . . . we must accept the premise as pleaded by Mr. Homer. Whether, for purposes of this tort, the conduct is extreme and outrageous depends, at least in part, on the context in which it is viewed. Intrinsically, of course, it is extreme and outrageous; as noted, it violates clear standards set by the medical community itself. But the essence of the requirement is that the conduct must not simply be extreme and outrageous from the perspective of society at large, or from the perspective of someone else, but must be so as to the plaintiff. Outrageous conduct directed at A does not necessarily give B a cause of action.

There is no doubt that Dr. Long's conduct, as alleged, would be extreme and outrageous as to Ms. Homer, who, so far at least, has not chosen to complain of it. And ... had Mr. Homer also been a patient of Dr. Long, it could be regarded as outrageous to him as well.... But that is not the case here.

There are situations in which conduct directed principally at one person has been regarded as extreme and outrageous as to another, but normally the other person must be present to witness the conduct in order to recover. Restatement (Second) of Torts § 46, which defines the tort in question, states, in subsection (2): "Where such conduct is directed at a third person, the actor is subject to liability if he intentionally or recklessly causes severe emotional distress (a) to a member of such person's immediate family who is present at the time, whether or not such distress results in bodily harm, or (b) to any other person who is present at the time, if such distress results in bodily harm."

Comment 1 explains the presence requirement: "Where the extreme and outrageous conduct is directed at a third person, as where, for example, a husband is murdered in the presence of his wife, the actor may know that it is substantially certain, or at least highly probable, that it will cause severe emotional distress to the plaintiff. In such cases the rule of this Section applies...." [Prosser and Keeton note:] "Ordinarily recovery in such cases is limited to plaintiffs who are not only present at the time, but are known by the defendant to be present, so that the mental effect can reasonably be anticipated by the defendant. The distinction between the wife who sees her husband shot down before her eyes, and the one who hears about it five minutes later, may be a highly artificial one; but an argument in justification is the obvious necessity of drawing a line somewhere short of the widow who learns of the decease ten years afterward, when the genuineness and gravity of her distress may very reasonably be doubted."

The requirement of presence has been relaxed by some courts in particularly compelling circumstances, as, for example, where a parent sued the defendant for sexually molesting or kidnaping the plaintiff's child....

We see no reason not to apply the general rule, for the pragmatic reason noted in the Restatement and by Prosser and Keeton. The emotional and economic trauma likely to arise from the seduction of one's spouse is not limited to the case where the seducer is the spouse's therapist. The conduct may be just as outrageous and the harm may be just as great where the seducer is a neighbor, a good friend, a relative, an employee or business associate of the plaintiff, or indeed anyone in whom the plaintiff has imposed trust or for whom he or she has special regard. . . .

NOTES

1. **Transferred intent?** Why doesn't transferred intent work with intentional infliction of emotional distress? Should it apply to this cause of action?

2. **What "presence" means.** Can presence mean something other than witnessing the bad act? Some courts have extended the definition rather than creating exceptions. *See, e.g., Bevan v. Fix*, 42 P.3d 1013 (Wyo. 2002) (children who did not actually witness attacks on their mother were "present" if they could show "sensory and contemporaneous" awareness).

3. **Exceptions to the presence requirement.** Does the presence requirement represent good policy? *See, e.g., Reid v. Pierce County*, 961 P.2d 333 (Wash. 1998) (barring claim where plaintiffs were not present while defendants used autopsy photos of their relatives for their own purposes). The *Homer* court notes that some exceptions exist. *See also Bettis v. Islamic Republic of Iran*, 315 F.3d 325 (D.C. Cir. 2003) (plaintiffs did not have to be present while their family member was kidnapped and tortured in order to state a claim). In *Hatch v. Davis*, 147 P.3d 383 (Utah 2006), the court commented that exceptions should be reserved for "rare cases," but that they might be based upon such factors as (1) the relationship of the target of the conduct to the plaintiff; (2) the relationship between the person committing the conduct and the plaintiff; and (3) the egregiousness of the conduct. Further, the court added, "a plaintiff must establish that the conduct was undertaken, in whole or in part, with the intention of inflicting injury to the absent plaintiff." If that latter item is a requirement, then isn't the presence requirement irrelevant anyway?

SUBCHAPTER B. NEGLIGENT INFLICTION OF DISTRESS OR EMOTIONAL HARM
§ 2. FRIGHT OR SHOCK FROM RISKS OF PHYSICAL HARM

A. EMOTIONAL HARM DIRECTLY INFLICTED ON THE PLAINTIFF

MITCHELL v. ROCHESTER RAILWAY CO., 45 N.E. 354 (N.Y. 1896). In the spring of 1891, in Rochester, New York, the plaintiff was in the street about to board a street railway car when the defendant drove a team of horses at her. By the time the horses were stopped, the plaintiff found herself standing between the team, although never touched by them. The plaintiff suffered shock and a miscarriage as a result. The New York Court of Appeals held (1) there could be no recovery for fright alone and (2) as a corollary there could be no recovery for consequences of fright, even physical consequences like the miscarriage. Without a "physical injury," the negligence of the defendant would not be a proximate cause.

NOTES

1. **Parasitic damages.** By requiring physical injury preceding the emotional harm, the *Mitchell* court was rejecting a stand-alone claim for negligent infliction of emotional distress, as did all courts at the time. Instead, the court was applying the traditional rule for emotional harm as parasitic damages: If the defendant negligently causes physical injury to the plaintiff, the plaintiff can recover all damages that result, including damages for pain, suffering, and emotional harm. *See, e.g., Hagen Ins., Inc. v. Roller*, 139 P.3d 1216 (Alaska 2006) (distinguishing parasitic or "derivative" damages from stand-alone emotional harm claim). So if horses had actually run into Mitchell, causing some small physical harm, she would ordinarily recover not only for that harm but for any immediately ensuing emotional harm as well.

2. **The fright or shock pattern.** Notice that *Mitchell* involved a very definite pattern: (a) the defendant's negligent acts put the plaintiff at immediate risk of a personal injury at a very definite time and place and (b) the plaintiff's reaction to that risk was fright and shock. *Mitchell* was not, for example, a case in which the defendant merely used words nor one in which the plaintiff suffered depression or anger, humiliation, or long-term sense of loss.

NOTE: DEVELOPMENT OF A STAND–ALONE CLAIM

1. *Impact.* The first step away from *Mitchell* and towards allowing a stand-alone negligent infliction claim was a small one. Courts began to drop the requirement of a preceding physical injury and substituted a requirement of "physical impact," even if it caused no physical injury at all. (Notice that *Mitchell* also required an "impact.") A handful of states retain the impact requirement today, with variations. *See, e.g., Steel Technologies, Inc. v. Congleton*, 234 S.W.3d 920 (Ky. 2007) (also holding that emotional distress must be *caused by* the physical impact or injury); *Atlantic Coast Airlines v. Cook*, 857 N.E.2d 989 (Ind. 2006); *Lee v. State Farm Mut. Ins. Co.*, 533 S.E.2d 82 (Ga. 2000). Florida follows the impact rule but has crafted narrow exceptions, such as when the defendant has violated a duty of confidentiality. *Florida Dept. of Corrections v. Abril,* 969 So.2d 201 (Fla. 2007).

Most states have abandoned the impact rule. In *Battalla v. State,* 176 N.E.2d 729 (N.Y. 1961), the New York Court overruled *Mitchell* entirely, observing that although some claims might be fraudulent, that would also be the case if the plaintiff could claim emotional harm after showing a slight impact. Some speculative claims might be brought, the court said, but the solution to that is to deny those claims and not to exclude the entire class.

2. *Physical manifestation of objective symptoms.* Other states adopted a different condition: The plaintiff can recover only if she produces evidence of some objective physical manifestation of the shock or fright occurring after the events in question. This approach, too, retains some limited currency today. *See Brueckner v. Norwich Univ.,* 730 A.2d 1086 (Vt. 1999).

Some courts have modified or diluted the requirement rather than rejecting it completely. A number have said that the emotional injury must be medically diagnosable as an emotional disorder, but not necessarily reflected in observable physical manifestations. *Paz v. Brush Engineered Materials, Inc.,* 949 So.2d 1 (Miss. 2007); *Hegel v. McMahon,* 960 P.2d 424 (Wash. 1998); *Johnson v. Ruark Obstetrics & Gynecology Assocs., P.A.,* 395 S.E.2d 85 (N.C. 1990); *Hamilton v. Nestor,* 659 N.W.2d 321 (Neb. 2003) (no recovery, however, since no showing of "severe" distress). *See also Sullivan v. Boston Gas Co.,* 605 N.E.2d 805 (Mass. 1993) (requiring "objective corroboration of the emotional distress alleged").

Many states have abolished this requirement altogether. *See, e.g., Molien v. Kaiser Foundation Hospitals,* 616 P.2d 813 (Cal. 1980) (reasoning that the genuineness of emotional injury can be found in the facts of each case without such a rule). Other states have abolished the requirement in particular situations, *see Clark v. Estate of Rice,* 653 N.W.2d 166 (Iowa 2002), or when facts provide some special guarantee that the harm is genuine. *Doe Parents No. 1 v. State, Dept. of Educ.,* 58 P.3d 545 (Haw. 2002); *Johnson v. State,* 334 N.E.2d 590 (N.Y. 1975).

3. *Zone of danger.* Other states developed a different rule that allows recovery only where the defendant's negligence placed the plaintiff in danger of physical injury, and because of that danger the plaintiff suffered emotional harm. *See, e.g., AALAR, Ltd. v. Francis,* 716 So.2d 1141 (Ala. 1998). The zone of danger rule is more fully explored in the *Grube* case and its Notes, below.

4. *Combinations.* States may combine the rules described above (and others) in myriad ways. *See, e.g., Willis v. Gami Golden Glades, LLC,* 967 So.2d 846 (Fla. 2007) (plaintiff may recover either by showing impact or by proving that emotional distress is manifested in physical injury); *Catron v. Lewis,* 712 N.W.2d 245 (Neb. 2006) (plaintiff who fails to show impact or physical injury must be in zone of danger); *Atlantic Coast Airlines v. Cook,* 857 N.E.2d 989 (Ind. 2006) (plaintiff must show impact, and if the impact is "slight," must also show that the emotional distress is not "speculative, exaggerated, fictitious, or unforeseeable"); *Perrotti v. Gonicberg,* 877 A.2d 631 (R.I. 2005) (plaintiff must be in zone of danger, and must also suffer emotional harm "accompanied by physical symptomatology"); *Siegel v. Ridgewells, Inc.,* 511 F.Supp.2d 188 (D.D.C. 2007) (plaintiff must either suffer impact, or be within zone of danger, and must prove "verifiable" emotional distress) (D.C. law).

5. *The Restatement Third approach.* Section 46 of the Restatement (Third) of Torts: Liability for Physical and Emotional Harm (T.D. No. 5,

2007), provides that a person whose negligent conduct causes "serious emotional disturbance" to another is liable if (a) the defendant's negligence places plaintiff in "immediate danger of bodily harm," *or* (b) the negligence occurs (1) in the performance of particular categories of undertakings, such as caring for and disposing of dead bodies, or (2) in connection with a relationship in which the defendant is in a position of power or authority over the plaintiff, or "in which serious emotional disturbance is otherwise likely." How does this formulation appear to relate to the other approaches discussed above?

6. *Questions.* What result in the following cases, if you are in an "impact" state, a "physical manifestations" state, a "zone of danger" state, or a state that chooses to adopt the new Restatement rule?

(a) Defendant negligently performed surgery upon the plaintiff in such a way that the plaintiff lost the use or her right hand. She suffers periodic depression and a deep sense of loss, especially on bowling nights, but has no physical symptoms of the depression.

(b) Defendant, angry with a domestic partner, fired a pistol at random in an upscale restaurant. No one was hit, but one shot narrowly missed the plaintiff, breaking the back of his chair. The plaintiff was not touched and suffered no physical injury but wakes up with nightmares every night and has been unable to complete his college courses.

(c) Defendant negligently drove his car into the plaintiff's car, scratching the car but not physically touching or harming the plaintiff. Shortly thereafter, the plaintiff broke out in sweats and rashes, then fainted, all provably a result of the fright or shock.

B. EMOTIONAL HARM RESULTING FROM INJURY TO ANOTHER

1. THE EMOTIONAL DISTRESS CLAIM

GRUBE v. UNION PACIFIC RAILROAD

886 P.2d 845 (Kan. 1994)

DAVIS, JUSTICE. . . .

Ernest A. Grube was employed by Union Pacific Railroad Company (Union Pacific). This case arose when the train he was operating as engineer collided with an automobile trapped upon a railroad crossing outside Lawrence. One of the occupants in the automobile died and two others suffered serious injury as a result of the collision. [Grube claimed against his employer, the railroad,] seeking damages for negligent infliction of emotional injury with accompanying physical manifestations.

Grube saw the trapped car before the collision. He remembers the driver of the vehicle, a young man, looking at the approaching engine with an expression of shock, fright, or fear. Grube sustained no physical injury as a result of the collision, but when the train eventually stopped, he ran back to the accident scene attempting to render aid. He felt the pulse of the driver and touched the deceased, attempting to find a pulse. At the accident scene, Grube exhibited physical manifestations of his emotional distress; he became physically ill and, as he testified, he "threw up ... [and] that's when it started hitting me." Grube further testified that he had no thoughts of fear of personal injury at the time of the accident but was reacting and not thinking at the time and merely doing his job. The other employee in the cab of the engine with Grube, however, ducked down before impact out of fear of possible explosion at the time of impact.

[The jury returned a verdict for Grube in the sum of $121,500.]

Section 1 of FELA provides in pertinent part: "Every common carrier by railroad ... shall be liable in damages to any person suffering injury [or death] while he is employed by such carrier ... for such injury or death resulting in whole or in part from the negligence of any of the officers, agents, or employees of such carrier, or by reason of any defect or insufficiency, due to its negligence, in its cars, engines, appliances, machinery, track, roadbed, works, boats, wharves, or other equipment." 45 U.S.C. § 51.

Kansas law is clear in its requirements that a plaintiff demonstrate some physical impact/injury in order to recover for negligent inflection of emotional distress. The United States Supreme Court has made clear, however, that federal common law governs such claims under FELA....

[In Consolidated Rail Corporation v. Gottshall, 114 S.Ct. 2396, 129 L.Ed.2d 427 (1994), the Supreme Court discussed] the concern the courts have experienced with the recognition of a cause of action for emotional injury when not related to any physical trauma. One such concern is that these claims "may inundate judicial resources with a flood of relatively trivial claims, many of which may be imagined or falsified, and that liability may be imposed for highly remote consequences of a negligent act."

A more significant concern was that "[e]motional injuries may occur far removed in time and space from the negligent conduct that triggered them." There are no necessary limits on the number of persons who might suffer emotional injury because of the negligent act. Thus, many courts note that recognition of this cause of action raises the real possibility of "nearly infinite and unpredictable liability for defendants."

[The Gottshall Court] concluded that the zone of danger test best harmonized all concerns: "We believe that allowing recovery for negligently inflicted emotional injury as provided for under the zone of danger test best harmonizes these considerations. Under this test, a worker within the zone of danger of physical impact will be able to recover for emotional injury caused by fear of physical injury to himself, whereas a worker outside the zone will not...."

Grube acknowledges that he expressed no fear at the time of the collision, but argues that the zone of danger test adopted by the Supreme

Court does not require a contemporaneous expression of such fear. He points out that many times people react to dangerous situations automatically and only later come to the realization of the danger they were in at the time of the peril. This point is well taken, and we do not believe that the zone of danger test adopted in Gottshall necessarily requires that there be fear for one's personal safety expressed contemporaneously with the collision. However, fear for one's safety is an essential element of the zone of danger test and must be expressed at or near the time of the danger in order for plaintiff to prevail in the action.

The problem with Grube's position is that the record fails to establish that Grube expressed fear for his own personal safety at any time. His fear was for the youth whose face he saw before impact and whose face he touched afterwards. As a result of this fear, Grube became physically ill immediately after the collision. There is ample evidence to establish that Grube experienced his severe emotional problems because of his concern about the lawsuit and his involvement in an accident in which a man died and others were injured. We also agree that the entire damages may include emotional distress resulting from concern or fear for the safety of another person as long as plaintiff establishes that he or she suffered imminent apprehension of physical harm. In both instances, however, essential elements for recovery under the zone of danger test are that plaintiff be within the zone of danger and suffer imminent apprehension of physical harm which causes or contributes to the emotional injury. In this case, Grube failed to establish that he feared for his personal safety at any time. His emotional injury did not result from fear of his personal safety but rather from his experiences relating to others affected by the impact.

Grube nevertheless argues that the physical impact he experienced at the point of collision brings him within the zone of danger test. . . . As we understand Grube's argument, he contends that he was thrown against the console in the cab of the engine at the time of the collision and sustained physical impact. Thus, according to his contention, he falls within the physical impact test as well as within the zone of danger test because of the physical impact he sustained.

Grube was pushed against the console of the engine because of the emergency braking of the train at the time of the collision. However as Union Pacific points out, there was no evidence that this action caused Grube any physical or emotional injuries. He suffered no bruises or abrasions as a result of the impact. . . .

We therefore reverse the judgment of the trial court and enter judgment for the defendant, Union Pacific.

NOTES

1. **Original denial of "bystander" claims.** The classic case of emotional harm resulting from injury to another was an extension of the fright

and shock pattern. A mother watches in horror as a car strikes her child. The mother's fear and shock is much like the fear and shock in *Mitchell*, but it is fear for her child rather than for herself. Courts originally denied these claims altogether. A court that retains the impact rule might continue to deny such a claim. *See Lee v. State Farm Mut. Ins. Co.*, 533 S.E.2d 82 (Ga. 2000) (unless mother is herself impacted at the same time).

2. **Zone of danger "exception."** Courts eventually recognized the zone of danger exception discussed in *Grube*. Applying *Grube*'s formulation to the mother-and-child case, if the mother were actually within the zone of danger, she could claim for the emotional distress of seeing her child injured by the defendant's negligence, at least if part of her fear was fear for her own safety. *See Engler v. Illinois Farmers Ins. Co.*, 706 N.W.2d 764 (Minn. 2005) (holding that a plaintiff within the zone of danger who reasonably feared for her own safety could recover for the distress of witnessing serious bodily injury to a person in a "close relationship" with her). Other courts, however, would say that the zone of danger rule disallows any emotional distress damages that are not based on fear for the plaintiff's own safety. *See, e.g., Lukowski v. CSX Transportation, Inc.*, 416 F.3d 478 (6th Cir. 2005) (recognizing that *Grube* is the only FELA case suggesting that once the plaintiff proves fear for his own safety, he may also recover for the distress of seeing another injured). The implication of the latter view is that the zone of danger test would continue to disallow "bystander" claims.

DILLON v. LEGG, 441 P.2d 912 (Cal. 1968). A mother and infant sister saw a vehicle strike Erin Lee Dillon, a young child, as she crossed the road, causing her death. The mother and sister sued the driver for negligent infliction of emotional distress. The trial court granted defendant's motion for judgment on the mother's claim because she was not in the zone of danger, but denied the motion as it pertained to the sister, because she might have been. *Held*, reversed. "The instant case exposes the hopeless artificiality of the zone-of-danger rule.... [T]o rest upon the zone-of-danger rule when we have rejected the impact rule becomes even less defensible." The only reason for the zone-of-danger rule "lies in the fact that one within it will feel the danger of impact." While dropping this requirement may invite some fraudulent claims, this does not "justify a wholesale rejection of the entire class of claims." A defendant might owe a duty to protect not only the injured person but those who might foreseeably suffer emotional harm because of the injury. Courts should henceforth take into account three factors in determining foreseeability: "(1) Whether plaintiff was located near the scene of the accident as contrasted with one who was a distance away from it. (2) Whether the shock resulted from a direct emotional impact upon the plaintiff from the sensory and contemporaneous observance of the accident, as contrasted with learning of the accident from others after its occurrence. (3) Whether plaintiff and the victim were 'closely related.' " In this case, "the presence of all the above factors indicates that plaintiff has alleged a sufficient prima facie case."

THING v. La CHUSA, 771 P.2d 814 (Cal. 1989). Maria Thing, hearing that her son had been struck by an automobile, rushed to the scene. She found her bloody and unconscious child lying in the road. She believed him to be dead. She neither saw nor heard the accident. She sued for emotional distress. *Held*, she cannot recover. *Dillon*'s foreseeability test, limited only by guidelines rather than by rules, has left too much uncertainty in the law and too much room for unlimited expansion of liability. "We conclude, therefore, that a plaintiff may recover damages for emotional distress caused by observing the negligently inflicted injury of a third person if, but only if, said plaintiff: (1) is closely related to the injury victim [defined elsewhere as 'closely related by blood or marriage ... relatives residing the same household, or parents, siblings, children and grandchildren of the victim']; (2) is present at the scene of the injury producing event at the time it occurs and is then aware that it is causing injury to the victim; and (3) as a result suffers serious emotional distress—a reaction beyond that which would be anticipated in a disinterested witness and which is not an abnormal response to the circumstances."

NOTES

1. **Bystander recoveries.** Most states have followed either *Dillon* or *Thing* (or some variation of them), and now allow plaintiffs to recover damages for the emotional distress of seeing another person injured or killed by a negligent defendant. *See* RESTATEMENT (THIRD) OF TORTS: LIABILITY FOR PHYSICAL AND EMOTIONAL HARM § 47, cmt. *a*, Reporters' Note (T.D. No. 5, 2007) (listing states).

2. **Sensory perception.** The plaintiff's sensory perception of some sudden, injury-producing event when it happens or at least shortly thereafter is important as a factor under *Dillon* or as a strict rule under *Thing*. Many courts have denied recovery on this ground. *See, e.g., Bird v. Saenz*, 51 P.3d 324 (Cal. 2002) (requiring that a plaintiff be contemporaneously aware of negligent conduct and causation, denying recovery to family members who witnessed their mother's death in the hospital but not the medical acts that caused it); *Fernandez v. Walgreen Hastings Co.*, 968 P.2d 774 (N.M. 1998) (witnessing the results of a misfilled prescription); *Finnegan v. Wisconsin Patients Comp. Fund*, 666 N.W.2d 797 (Wis. 2003) (witnessing the results of medical malpractice).

3. **Delayed perception.** The clear case for recovery is one in which the plaintiff actually sees an injury as it occurs. A parent who does not see the event itself but only sees the injured child later, in the hospital, is likely to be denied recovery. *Roitz v. Kidman*, 913 P.2d 431 (Wyo. 1996). What about all the times in between? Isn't it true, as the court said in *Gates v. Richardson*, 719 P.2d 193 (Wyo. 1986), that "the immediate aftermath may be more shocking than the actual impact"? So imagine that a family member arrives at the scene of the injury immediately afterwards. That would not suffice under a rigid application of the *Thing* rules. *See, e.g., Ra v. Superior Court*, 64

Cal.Rptr.3d 539 (Ct. App. 2007) (woman heard loud noise and turned around to see husband holding his head; not "contemporaneous awareness" of his injury). Some courts, however, allow recovery where the plaintiff arrived at the scene of injury shortly thereafter, before there is a material change in the situation. *See Eskin v. Bartee*, 262 S.W.3d 727 (Tenn. 2008) (allowing claim by mother who saw her young child "lying in a pool of blood in his school's driveway minutes after he had been struck by an automobile"); *Smith v. Toney*, 862 N.E.2d 656 (Ind. 2007) ("The scene viewed by the claimant must be essentially as it was at the time of the incident, the victim must be in essentially the same condition as immediately following the incident, and the claiming must not have been informed of the incident before coming upon the scene."); *Colbert v. Moomba Sports, Inc.*, 176 P.3d 497 (Wash. 2008) (accepting the rule but denying recovery because plaintiff did not meet its requirements). Notice that a state that uses *Dillon*-like factors as opposed to *Thing*-like elements is far more likely to view matters more flexibly. *See, e.g., Rodriguez v. Cambridge Housing Auth.*, 823 N.E.2d 1249 (Mass. 2005) (allowing bystander claim by child who saw mother after she had been attacked).

4. **Close relationship.** Whether courts use the rules as guidelines or as elements, they usually insist upon a close relationship—usually a close family relationship—between the plaintiff and the injured person. In *Grotts v. Zahner*, 989 P.2d 415 (Nev. 1999), the court denied recovery to a fiancee who witnessed the fatal injury of the man she was engaged to marry. Does this limitation make sense given the purposes behind the rules themselves? New Hampshire allowed a fiancee to recover in *Graves v. Estabrook*, 818 A.2d 1255 (N.H. 2003), saying that unmarried cohabitants who have a "relationship that is stable, enduring, substantial, and mutually supportive ... cemented by strong emotional bonds and provid[ing] a deep and pervasive emotional security" are "closely related" for this purpose. Does making a right to recover turn on "subjective emotional connection of the parties" create too much uncertainty, as dissenters charged? *See St. Onge v. MacDonald*, 917 A.2d 233 (N.H. 2007) (noting that the determination had to be made on a case-by-case basis, affirming judgment that a non-cohabitating girlfriend of six months was not in a close relationship with plaintiff); *see also Smith v. Toney*, 862 N.E.2d 656 (Ind. 2007) (discussing problems with not having a bright-line rule).

5. **Beyond the family?** What about a "bystander" who is really a participant in the events, say a co-worker who attempts to rescue the primary victim but is forced to watch his horrible death instead? In *Michaud v. Great Northern Nekoosa Corp.*, 715 A.2d 955 (Me. 1998), the plaintiff, a diver, attempted to rescue another diver whose leg was trapped deep underwater and who watched as surface chains pulled him up, tearing his body apart. Similarly, in *Hislop v. Salt River Project Agricultural Improvement & Power Dist.*, 5 P.3d 267 (Ariz. Ct. App. 2000), the primary victim was burned alive allegedly as a result of the defendant's negligence; the plaintiff pulled the burning man from the trench where he was engulfed with flames. Both courts denied recovery. If the rescuer or would-be rescuer is not in a sufficiently close relationship, what about a plaintiff who, because of the defendant's negligence, becomes the unwilling trigger of harm to another? In *Kallstrom v. United States*, 43 P.3d 162 (Alaska 2002), the defendant negligently placed a

pitcher that appeared to be fruit juice on a kitchen counter; the pitcher actually contained caustic lye. The plaintiff poured a glass for a child, who suffered horrible injuries. The court rejected the plaintiff's claim for emotional harm. Are such limitations sensible?

6. **Combining the rules.** States that have adopted special "bystander rules" apply them only to bystanders, of course—only to those claiming to have suffered emotional distress from witnessing an injury to someone else. That means that if the plaintiff is not a "bystander" at all—what some states would call a "direct victim"—a separate set of rules (as seen above in Part A of this Section) would apply. *See, e.g., Jarrett v. Jones*, 258 S.W.3d 442 (Mo. 2008) (bystander limitations not applicable to truck driver who was direct victim of car driver's negligence). Which "separate rules" apply depend, of course, on the state. *See, e.g., Helsel v. Hoosier Ins. Co.*, 827 N.E.2d 155 (Ind. Ct. App. 2005) (impact rule applies to direct victims, special bystander rules to bystanders); *Jablonowska v. Suther*, 948 A.2d 610 (N.J. 2008) (zone of danger rule applies to direct victims, special bystander rules to bystanders). The possible variations, while not endless, are certainly large.

BURGESS v. SUPERIOR COURT, 831 P.2d 1197 (Cal. 1992). The plaintiff, Julia Burgess, was given prenatal care by her obstetrician, Gupta, who also delivered her child, Joseph. During Burgess' labor, Gupta diagnosed a prolapsed cord, which meant that the child would receive insufficient oxygen. Burgess was aware of this and of the urgent comings and goings thereafter. She knew when she was sedated for the cesarean that followed that something was wrong with the child. By the time the child was taken by cesarean, he had been deprived of oxygen for a lengthy period. He suffered permanent brain damage. Joseph brought suit against Gupta and the hospital. Julia asserted a separate claim for her own emotional distress. *Held,* the *Thing* rules do not apply. California recognizes two classes of emotional harm cases: In the first, the plaintiff is a bystander; in the second, the plaintiff is a "direct victim." A plaintiff who was in some kind of preexisting relationship with the defendant is a "direct victim," and the bystander rules are inapplicable to such a plaintiff. A "direct victim's" case is based on a breach of duty "assumed by the defendant or imposed on the defendant as a matter of law, or that arises out of a relationship between the two." Liability in this class of cases is not unlimited; it is limited by the relationship established by the parties themselves. Both parties here understood that the physician owes a duty to the pregnant woman, not merely to the fetus alone. If the mother were treated as a bystander, the physician would have an incentive to sedate her, so that she would not see or hear injury and thus would be defeated by the *Thing* rules.

NOTES

1. The fright and shock cases normally involve strangers, that is, persons who had no particular relationship that might affect duties. Any number of people might be frightened by runaway horses and, if you add the possibility of liability to bystanders, even more. *Burgess* is important because it recognizes that some claims are asserted against a defendant who has at least implicitly undertaken to protect the plaintiff and that such cases might call for quite different rules. *See* Dan B. Dobbs, *Undertakings and Special Relationships in Claims for Negligent Infliction of Emotional Distress*, 50 ARIZ. L. REV. 49 (2008).

2. The *Burgess* perception is that relationships (including implicit agreements between the parties) are important in determining the duties owed. Suppose that a mother, who is a doctor's patient, and a father, who is not, both suffer emotional harm as a result of the doctor's negligent treatment of their child but neither is a witness to the events causing harm? In a jurisdiction applying both *Thing* and *Burgess,* the mother would presumably recover under *Burgess. Cf. Pierce v. Physicians Ins. Co. of Wisconsin, Inc.*, 692 N.W.2d 558 (Wis. 2005) (refusing to apply bystander rules to mother who sued after her child was stillborn, on the rationale that she was a "participant"); *Ryan v. Brown*, 827 N.E.2d 112 (Ind. Ct. App. 2005) (mother was "directly involved" and thus could satisfy Indiana's "modified impact rule," making her a "direct victim"). But the father, who was not the doctor's patient, would presumably come under the *Thing* rules and would be barred because he was not actually present when the injury occurred. *Cf. Carey v. Lovett*, 622 A.2d 1279 (N.J. 1993). Wyoming has recognized a negligent emotional distress claim in a case involving two sisters who were negligently separated at birth by a hospital in 1954. In *Larsen v. Banner Health System*, 81 P.3d 196 (Wyo. 2003), the court said that "in the limited circumstances where a contractual relationship exists for services that carry with them deeply emotional responses in the event of breach," and that breach causes severe emotional distress, an action will lie.

2. THE LOSS OF CONSORTIUM CLAIM

The loss of consortium claim is quite different from the emotional harm claim in its origin. In the earlier common law, the master of an apprentice had a claim against the tortfeasor when the apprentice was injured, since the master would lose the services of the apprentice and might still be bound to provide him with food and housing. The claim had a firm economic basis in such cases. By the 17th century, the idea was carried over to permit a husband to recover from the tortfeasor when the wife was injured, on analogy, then all too true, to the master-servant relationship. Originally the claim was for loss of services, but it gradually expanded to take in non-economic losses such as loss of society and sexual relations.

"The concept of consortium includes not only loss of support or services, it also embraces such elements as love, companionship, affection, society, sexual relations, solace and more." *Millington v. Southeastern Elevator Co., Inc.*, 239 N.E.2d 897 (N.Y. 1968). After 1950, courts began to permit the wife to recover for loss of consortium when the husband was injured, thus putting the marital partners on an equal footing in this respect. In doing so, they often emphasized the non-financial side of the claim.

Emphasis on the intangible losses inflicted upon one person when another person is injured brings up the latent comparison to the bystander mental distress claim. Is the claim not one for a species of mental distress or emotional losses? The difference may lie in judicial attitudes. In the emotional distress claim, courts traditionally emphasized an acute moment-shock or fright. With the consortium claim, they recognize legal harm in a chronic, ongoing sense of loss. If emotional distress is the emotional equivalent of a stab wound, then loss of consortium is the emotional equivalent of carrying a large pack all day or living all your life in a cramped room. But both involve intangible and real losses in quality of life.

BOUCHER v. DIXIE MEDICAL CENTER

850 P.2d 1179 (Utah 1992)

HALL, CHIEF JUSTICE: . . .

Daniel Boucher, the eighteen-year-old son of James and Torla Boucher, was admitted into Dixie Medical Center with a severely injured right hand. He underwent surgery and lapsed into a coma during the postoperative recovery period. He remained in a coma for ten days before awakening as a severely brain-damaged quadriplegic who will need extensive care for the rest of his life. The Bouchers were present at the hospital and observed their son's condition both before and after he awoke from the coma.

[The Boucher parents claimed damages for (1) negligent infliction of mental distress and (2) loss of their child's consortium or society, in addition to the claim of Daniel Boucher himself. The trial court dismissed the complaint. The Supreme Court in this opinion concluded that the Boucher parents could not recover for negligent infliction of mental distress because they were not in the zone of danger. The court then considered the loss of consortium claim as follows.]

The Bouchers' second claim presents an issue of first impression in this court: Should Utah judicially adopt a cause of action that allows the parents of a tortiously injured adult child to recover for loss of the child's consortium?

Loss of consortium claims are based on the recognition of a legally protected interest in personal relationships. Accordingly, if one member of the relationship is tortiously injured the noninjured party has a cause of action to recover for damage to their relational interest, i.e., the loss of the injured party's " 'company, society, co-operation, [and] affection.' " In the instant case, we are asked to recognize a right of recovery based on the relationship between parents and their adult son. For the reasons set forth below, we decline to adopt such an approach.

A review of the case law reveals little support for the adoption of a cause of action for the loss of filial consortium. At common law, the father of a tortiously injured child did have a cause of action to recover the value of the child's loss of services and the medical expenses incurred on the child's behalf. However, this action was based on a father's right to his minor children's services and a father's obligation to pay his minor children's medical expenses. This right of recovery, therefore, did not extend beyond these two elements of damages, nor did it extend to injuries involving adult or emancipated children.

These common law principles have undergone some modification. However, no widely accepted development has occurred that allows recovery in cases involving adult children, nor has any widely accepted development occurred that allows recovery for the loss of a child's society and affection.

Indeed, the majority of jurisdictions that have addressed the issue have declined to recognize a cause of action for loss of filial consortium.... Furthermore, our research reveals only one jurisdiction that has expressly recognized the specific right the Bouchers urge this court to adopt: a judicially created right to recover for the loss of an adult child's consortium.

[But Utah's Married Woman's Act had been construed to abolish the claim of spousal consortium.] [A]llowing recovery for the loss of an adult child's consortium and denying recovery for the loss of a spouse's consortium would lead to anomalous results. In many instances, the marital relationship is closer and more involved than the relationship between parents and their adult children and therefore should be granted greater or equal protection. However, ... we cannot recognize a filial consortium claim and extend the same right of recovery to a plaintiff who suffers a loss of consortium because his or her spouse has been tortiously injured. The adoption of the Bouchers' claim, therefore, would invite inequitable applications of the consortium doctrine....

[C]onsortium claims have the potential for greatly expanding the liability that can flow from one negligent act, and courts that have adopted consortium claims have been unable to develop rational limits on this liability.... [T]he recognition of consortium claims may [also impact] the cost and availability of insurance. Finally, given these concerns and the fact that the legislature has previously acted in this area, ... the legislature is the appropriate body to determine if Utah should recognize consortium claims....

Furthermore, we do not find the Bouchers' arguments persuasive. They claim that because they have reorganized their lives in order to undertake the care of their son, they should be able to recover personally from the parties responsible for their son's condition. However, the expense incurred for Daniel Boucher's nursing care is recoverable as part of the damages in Daniel Bouchers' own suit. Even the jurisdictions that allow recovery for loss of consortium would not allow the Bouchers to recover for the nursing care they have provided, because to do so would be to allow a double recovery.

The Bouchers also contend that because Utah allows recovery for the loss of society and affection in wrongful death cases, it is logical to extend this theory of damages to cases involving nonfatal injuries.

However, we view wrongful death cases as distinguishable from consortium cases. In wrongful death cases, the party that suffers the actual physical injury has no cause of action and the legislature has prescribed the parties who have a right to recover for the loss of the deceased's society and affection. Therefore, there is no danger of expansive liability and no need for the judiciary to attempt to fashion rational limits on relational interests. Indeed, we rejected a similar argument in Hackford. . . .

We decline to adopt a cause of action that allows the parents of a tortiously injured adult child to recover for the loss of consortium. The trial court, therefore, did not err in dismissing the Bouchers' claims of negligent infliction of emotional distress and loss of filial consortium.

Affirmed. [Concurring and dissenting opinion omitted.]

NOTES

1. **Spousal consortium claims.** When one spouse is injured in a way that tends to diminish the ability of the partners to take pleasure in each other's company—in conversation, sports, travel, sexual relations, or any other pleasures of life—the other spouse has a loss-of-consortium claim. "[P]rior to the accident, the Alexanders spent most of their time together, enjoying walking, gardening, and fishing." As a result of injury to one spouse, "they no longer engage in their outdoor activities, and instead spend much of their time watching television." That was evidence of lost consortium. *Wal-Mart Stores, Inc. v. Alexander,* 868 S.W.2d 322 (Tex. 1993).

Should the non-injured spouse have a lost-consortium claim if the injured spouse suffers no physical harm but does suffer a severe and compensable emotional injury? *See Barnes v. Outlaw,* 964 P.2d 484 (Ariz. 1998).

2. **Derivative nature of spousal consortium claims.** Consortium claims are traditionally said to derive from the claim of the physically injured spouse. A derivative claim can rise no higher than the claim from which it is derived. *E.g., Wine–Settergren v. Lamey,* 716 N.E.2d 381 (Ind. 1999). For example, the contributory negligence of the injured spouse will bar or reduce the consortium claim just as it will bar or reduce the injured spouse's claim. Some cases, however, hold that the claim is independent and not affected by the fault of the physically injured victim or even by his release. *E.g., Hardy v. St. Clair,* 739 A.2d 368 (Me. 1999) (husband's release in advance and indemnity agreement did not bar wife's consortium claim).

3. **A child's claim for loss of parental consortium.** In 1980, Massachusetts permitted a claim by a child for loss of parental consortium following a serious injury to a father. *Ferriter v. Daniel O'Connell's Sons, Inc.,* 413 N.E.2d 690 (Mass. 1980). A good number of other courts have accepted the idea. *E.g., United States v. Dempsey,* 635 So.2d 961 (Fla. 1994). In *Rolf v. Tri State Motor Transit Co.,* 745 N.E.2d 424 (Ohio 2001), the court upheld a claim in favor of adult children living apart from a father whose cognitive and basic bodily functions were seriously impaired. A number of other contemporary cases, however, continue to reject any such extension of liability. *E.g., Harrington v. Brooks Drugs, Inc.,* 808 A.2d 532 (N.H. 2002); *Mendillo v. Board of Educ. of Town of East Haddam,* 717 A.2d 1177 (Conn. 1998).

4. **The parents' claim for loss of a child's society and companionship.** Earlier common law gave the father a claim for loss of a child's services under some circumstances, but this was usually a reflection of the fact that the father was entitled to a child's earnings and to actual work around the house. Otherwise, parents of an injured child have not generally been allowed a recovery for intangible harm such as loss of society or companionship. *E.g., Vitro v. Mihelcic,* 806 N.E.2d 632 (Ill. 2004). *Roberts v. Williamson,* 111 S.W.3d 113 (Tex. 2003). A few courts, however, have allowed the parents' claim. In most of these, the child was severely injured or comatose and some of the courts emphasized that the injury was total and permanent, or even that it was closely similar to death. *E.g., United States v. Dempsey,* 635 So.2d 961 (Fla. 1994). There are a few statutes on point as well.

5. **Basis of the general rule.** Grounds for denying a child's recovery for loss of parental consortium have included the points made in *Boucher.* It has also been argued that if children can recover such losses, then there is no principled basis for excluding recovery by siblings, grandparents, and others. In addition, some judges have professed great deference to the legislative branch on this claim. They have also said that damages could readily be magnified by the number of children in a family, with resulting high costs in liability insurance, and that the return for the increased insurance costs would be quite low since a child might become rich on the award, but would remain nonetheless a child deprived of parental guidance.

6. **Unmarried cohabitants.** Up until 1994, courts pretty consistently rejected consortium claims by unmarried consorts. *See Elden v. Sheldon,* 758 P.2d 582 (Cal. 1988). But some courts have now allowed such claims. *See Dunphy v. Gregor,* 642 A.2d 372 (N.J. 1994); *Lozoya v. Sanchez,* 66 P.3d 948 (N.M. 2003); *see also Surette v. Islamic Republic of Iran,* 231 F.Supp.2d 260 (D.D.C. 2002) (allowing recovery of "solatium" as a matter of federal common law) What about gay or lesbian partnerships? Vermont's civil union statute treats formalized same-sex unions like marriage. *See* 15 VT. STAT. §§ 1204(a) & 1204(e) (2). California provides by statute that domestic partners are "entitled to recover damages for negligent infliction of emotional distress to the same extent that spouses are entitled to do so" CAL. CIV. CODE § 1714.01, but domestic partners must ordinarily be of the same sex. *See* CAL. FAM. CODE § 297. What about a consortium claim by someone who married the injured person after the injury occurred? *See Owens–Illinois, Inc. v. Cook,* 872 A.2d 969 (Md. 2005); *Trombley v. Starr–Wood Cardiac Group, PC,* 3 P.3d 916 (Alaska 2000).

7. **Consortium and the *Dillon–Thing* rules.** Most courts that permit bystander recovery for mental distress do so under either the constraints of the zone of danger rule or those imposed by the *Dillon–Thing* rules. Notice that the consortium claim relies solely upon the relationship of the plaintiff and the injured person and on proof of actual loss of services or society. Why the difference? Could a marital partner ever recover both under the general mental distress claim and consortium?

8. **Animals.** Consider how the rules of this and the preceding section would apply if your cat, dog, or horse is negligently treated. Suppose you see the defendant nearly run over your cat; alternatively, he actually does injure or kill it. *Cf. Fackler v. Genetzky,* 595 N.W.2d 884 (Neb. 1999) (vet not liable for emotional distress when he negligently destroyed a race horse). Courts have generally rejected emotional distress liability based upon either breach of contract or negligent damage to property. *See Erlich v. Menezes,* 981 P.2d 978 (Cal. 1999); *Rabideau v. City of Racine,* 627 N.W.2d 795 (Wis. 2001); *Kennedy v. Byas,* 867 So.2d 1195 (Fla. Dist. Ct. App. 2004).

§ 3. DUTIES OF CARE TO PROTECT EMO- TIONAL WELL–BEING INDEPENDENT OF PHYSICAL RISKS

WASHINGTON v. JOHN T. RHINES CO., 646 A.2d 345 (D.C. 1994). "Mrs. Washington contracted with appellee John T. Rhines Company ('Rhines'), a funeral home in the District of Columbia, to prepare, embalm, and dress Mr. Washington's body. Pursuant to the agreement, Rhines also transported the casket containing the body to National Airport. From there it was shipped to a funeral home in El Paso, Texas, for an open-casket memorial service and eventual burial in El Paso National Cemetery." Mrs. Washington alleged that "when the casket arrived in El Paso on June 25, it was discovered that the clothing and the inside of the shipping case were drenched with fluid; there was an offensive odor of embalming and body fluids; there were extreme skin slips, blisters, and discolorations on several parts of the body; the body had begun to turn green and was rapidly decomposing; there was swelling in the face and neck areas; and a catheter tube which had been inserted in the deceased's body during his hospitalization had not been removed." In her claim for emotional distress damages, *held,* the trial court properly dismissed the complaint. Since the plaintiff was not in a zone of danger, she cannot claim negligent infliction of emotional distress.

NOTES

1. Good or bad, the zone of danger test is comprehensible when the plaintiff claims emotional harm based on danger of physical harm to herself or others. Does it make any logical sense at all when the plaintiff's claim is not based on a physical danger to a live person?

2. What if a hospital negligently loses the body of a patient who has died there? What if a hospital negligently permits the plaintiff's newborn baby to

be abducted from the hospital? New York has allowed the plaintiff's negligent infliction claim in the first case but denied it in the second. *Lando v. State,* 351 N.E.2d 426 (N.Y. 1976); *Johnson v. Jamaica Hosp.,* 467 N.E.2d 502 (N.Y. 1984). Is this sensible? Consider a third New York case: The plaintiff, a woman wishing to have a child uses the services of a fertility clinic. The clinic properly achieves in vitro fertilization but it mistakenly implants the resulting embryo in the body of another woman, who bears the child. The plaintiff gains custody of the child, but sues the clinic for emotional distress. *Perry–Rogers v. Obasaju,* 723 N.Y.S.2d 28 (App. Div. 2001).

3.   Reconsider *Burgess v. Superior Court.* Would a court following the idea in that case expect the mortuary to act with reasonable care for the very purpose of protecting the emotional well-being of the family? In *Christensen v. Superior Court,* 820 P.2d 181 (Cal. 1991), the plaintiffs alleged that defendant mortuaries and crematories had contracted to provide dignified burials or cremations, but that they in fact harvested various human organs from the remains of deceased persons and sold them. Saying the context was "unique," the California Supreme Court held the defendants had "assumed a duty to the close relatives ... for whose benefit they were to provide funeral and/or related services." So if the plaintiffs were aware that the services were being performed, they could recover damages, even though they learned about the indignities only from news media.

4.   In *Guth v. Freeland,* 28 P.3d 982 (Haw. 2001) a morgue left a body unrefrigerated with resulting decomposition similar to that described in *Washington.* Family members sued for negligent infliction of emotional distress, but the trial court dismissed the claim because Hawai'i had a statute, in line with the usual common law rule, forbidding emotional distress recovery resulting from harm to property. On appeal, the Supreme Court of Hawai'i held that a body was not property, so the statute did not apply. The court also said that "those who are entrusted with the care and preparation for burial of a decedent's body have a duty to exercise reasonable care"-a duty owed to immediate family members who are aware of, and for whose benefit, the funeral or similar services are being performed.

HEINER v. MORETUZZO, 652 N.E.2d 664 (Ohio 1995). Defendants tested the plaintiff for AIDS, but, according to allegations accepted as true, negligently and erroneously reported to the plaintiff that she was infected with that disease. They then did a re-test and erroneously confirmed the diagnosis and recommended a specialist in that disease. In fact the plaintiff later discovered that the diagnosis was wrong. She sued for negligent infliction of distress. *Held,* the plaintiff has no claim. "[T]he claimed negligent diagnosis never placed appellant or any other person in real physical peril, since appellant was, in fact, HIV negative.... [W]e hold that Ohio does not recognize a claim for negligent infliction of serious emotional distress where the distress is caused by the plaintiff's fear of a nonexistent physical peril."

NOTES

1. **Extending *Heiner*.** Ohio reaffirmed and extended *Heiner* in *Dobran v. Franciscan Medical Center*, 806 N.E.2d 537 (Ohio 2004). The defendant gathered an irreplaceable tissue sample for a cancer test on the plaintiff and then lost it. The plaintiff feared that his cancer would metastasize, and that this fear was caused by the defendant's negligent act. The court, affirming a defense summary judgment, stressed that the plaintiff never faced an actual physical peril since his cancer has not, in fact, ever metastasized.

2. **Negligent misdiagnosis.** Florida, a holdout for the old impact rule, denied recovery in a negligent misdiagnosis-of-AIDS case where there was no impact. *R.J. v. Humana of Fla., Inc.*, 652 So.2d 360 (Fla. 1995). Some other courts have upheld a right to recover in such misdiagnosis cases. *Baker v. Dorfman*, 239 F.3d 415 (2d Cir. 2000); *Chizmar v. Mackie*, 896 P.2d 196 (Alaska 1995); *Bramer v. Dotson*, 437 S.E.2d 773 (W.Va. 1993); *Doe v. Arts*, 823 A.2d 855 (N.J. Super. 2003). cf. *Molien v. Kaiser Foundation Hosp's.*, 616 P.2d 813 (Cal. 1980) (wife misdiagnosed as having venereal disease, leading to emotional distress of husband).

3. **Other misinformation cases.** Misinformation—like the misdiagnosis of AIDS—seldom creates a direct risk of physical harm, so it is not surprising that courts steeped in the tradition of the physical risk cases have produced mixed results when the plaintiff suffers emotional harm as the result of receiving erroneous information. If lawyers argue the *Burgess* idea, would this change?

4. **Death messages.** One kind of misinformation is treated as special in some courts. This is the message, usually carried by telegraph, erroneously announcing the death of a close relative. One group of cases has long permitted the plaintiff to recover for emotional harm in such cases. *E.g., Johnson v. State*, 334 N.E.2d 590 (N.Y. 1975).

5. **Information about the plaintiff.** When the plaintiff's emotional distress arises because the defendant has communicated information about the plaintiff rather than because the defendant has communicated information to the plaintiff, courts have almost never dealt with the claim as one for negligence, but have considered invasion of privacy, libel, slander, or malicious prosecution rules instead. These claims are covered in later chapters.

BOYLES v. KERR, 855 S.W.2d 593 (Tex. 1993). Dan Boyles, then 17, secretly videotaped his sexual intercourse with 19-year-old Susan Kerr. The tape also included comments made by Boyles' friends. Boyles then showed the tape on several occasions to various friends. Kerr claimed negligent infliction of emotional distress resulting from the tape, its showing, and the gossip that ensued. *Held*, there is no general duty to avoid negligent infliction of distress. Texas will not recognize a cause of action for emotional distress except where the defendant creates a risk of physical harm. Thus bystander recovery is permissible under the rules of

Dillon v. Legg. Some courts recognize a claim for serious or severe distress, but that standard is inadequate. "It is difficult to imagine how a set of rules could be developed and applied on a case-by-case basis to distinguish severe from nonsevere emotional harm. Severity is not an either/or proposition; it is rather a matter of degree. Thus, any attempt to formulate a general rule would almost inevitably result in a threshold requirement of severity so high that only a handful would meet it, or so low that it would be an ineffective screen. A middle-ground rule would be doomed, for it would call upon courts to distinguish between large numbers of cases factually too similar to warrant different treatment. Such a rule would, of course, be arbitrary in its application." [*Quoting* Richard N. Pearson, *Liability to Bystanders for Negligently Inflicted Emotional Harm—A Comment on the Nature of Arbitrary Rules*, 34 U. FLA. L. REV. 477, 511 (1982).]

NOTES

1. **Relationships.** The *Kerr* majority said it would recognize a duty based upon special relationships of the parties, and cited the telegraphic death message cases and dead body cases as examples. But it went on to say, without much discussion, that there was no such relationship in this case. Is that right? If the phrase "betrayal of confidence" comes to mind, it surely suggests an important relationship was involved. Even if so, however, it does not necessarily suggest that negligence is the proper basis for liability.

2. **Intentional infliction.** (a) While Boyles' acts were intentional as well as reprehensible, it does not look as if he intended to inflict distress unless you think Boyles intended that Kerr would discover the taping. So it is not clear that the plaintiff could succeed on an intentional infliction claim. Sometimes, however, courts confuse the intentional acts with intent to cause distress and hold that an intentional tort is made out in cases similar to *Boyles. Williams v. City of Minneola*, 619 So.2d 983 (Fla. Dist. Ct. App. 1993).

(b) If Kerr had won on an intentional infliction theory, she might have collected little, since the defendants' insurance policies probably covered negligent but not intentional torts.

3. **Privacy.** Mental distress is often part of the harm associated with a number of torts that do not entail physical harms, or even risks of physical harms. For example, invasion of privacy, under some circumstances, can be a tort. Some invasions of privacy produce mental distress damages. *Boyles* might have been brought as a privacy invasion claim in some jurisdictions. *See Fontaine v. Roman Catholic Church of Archdiocese of New Orleans*, 625 So.2d 548 (La. Ct. App. 1993) (allegation: a priest sexually abused a 17-year-old and later published photographs in a magazine and circulated video tapes; a privacy invasion claim is stated). But the privacy claim would be undesirable to the plaintiff if the defendant's liability insurance did not cover privacy claims.

CAMPER v. MINOR, 915 S.W.2d 437 (Tenn. 1996). Camper was driving a cement truck. Jennifer Taylor, age 16, had been stopped at a stop sign, but suddenly pulled out in front of the plaintiff. "The vehicles collided, and Ms. Taylor was killed instantly. Camper exited his truck moments after the crash, walked around the front of his vehicle, and viewed Ms. Taylor's body in the wreckage from close range." Camper sued her estate, claiming negligent infliction of emotional distress, in the form of a post-traumatic stress syndrome. *Held:* (1) The physical manifestation or injury rule will no longer be followed; (2) Negligent infliction of emotional distress claims should be analyzed under the general negligence approach, that is, no differently from any other negligence case. "[T]he plaintiff must present material evidence as to each of the five elements of general negligence-duty, breach of duty, injury or loss, causation in fact, and proximate, or legal, cause-in order to avoid summary judgment. [T]o guard against trivial or fraudulent actions, the law ought to provide a recovery only for serious or severe emotional injury. A serious or severe emotional injury occurs where a reasonable person, normally constituted, would be unable to adequately cope with the mental stress engendered by the circumstances of the case. Finally, we conclude that the claimed injury or impairment must be supported by expert medical or scientific proof."

NOTES

1. **End of the evolutionary line?** *Camper* appears to discard all the constraining rules for negligent infliction of emotional distress cases. Other courts have also moved in this direction. *See, e.g. Carrol v. Allstate Ins. Co.,* 815 A.2d 119 (Conn. 2003); *Sacco v. High Country Independent Press, Inc.,* 896 P.2d 411 (Mont. 1995). The Connecticut court in *Carrol* explained that a plaintiff must prove "that the defendant should have realized that its conduct involved an unreasonable risk of causing emotional distress." An appellate court interpreting *Carrol* affirmed a plaintiff's verdict in *Murphy v. Lord Thompson's Manor, Inc.,* 938 A.2d 1269 (Conn. App. Ct. 2008), where a wedding business negligently cancelled a bride's wedding date reservation. The court held that defendant's actions created an unreasonable risk of causing the bride emotional distress. Does such a case go too far?

2. **New constraints.** In discarding the older constraining rules, the *Camper* court substituted some new requirements—a severe emotional injury and expert medical proof. *See also Sacco, supra* Note 1 (requiring "serious or severe" emotional harm and suggesting that expert testimony would often be helpful to prove that); *Carrol, supra* Note 1 (requiring proof of distress "serious enough that it might result in illness or bodily harm). Do such requirements fulfill the purposes of the earlier constraints we've seen in this Chapter?

3. **Bystanders.** In a state that discards special rules for "direct" victims, are there still reasons to retain special rules for bystanders? Many states have retained bystander rules even after dropping special rules other-wise. *See, e.g., Burgess v. Superior Court,* 831 P.2d 1197 (Cal. 1992) (retaining *Thing* rule for bystanders). *Cf.* RESTATEMENT (THIRD) OF TORTS: LIABILITY FOR

PHYSICAL AND EMOTIONAL HARM § 47 (T.D. No. 5, 2007). Others have dropped all constraining rules, even for bystanders. *See, e.g., Wages v. First National Insurance Co.*, 79 P.3d 1095 (Mont. 2003).

§ 4. TOXIC EXPOSURES: FEAR OF FUTURE HARM: LIMITS ON RECOVERY?

POTTER v. FIRESTONE TIRE & RUBBER CO.

863 P.2d 795 (Cal. 1993)

BAXTER, JUSTICE. . . .

[Firestone operated a tire manufacturing plant near Salinas. It contracted with Salinas Disposal Service and another company for disposal of industrial wastes in a class II sanitary landfill operated by the City. Class II landfills prohibit disposal of toxic substances because of the danger that they will leach into the groundwater. In addition, the disposal service prohibited solvents, oils and other substances. Firestone assured the service that no such waste would be sent to the landfill. For a while official plant policy required proper disposal of hazardous wastes in a Class I landfill, but that program was costly. A production manager, sent to California from Firestone's Akron, Ohio to make the plant more profitable, became angered over the costs of the hazardous waste disposal program. As a consequence, Firestone's hazardous waste materials were once again deposited and these materials included serious toxins.]

[The plaintiffs, including the Potters, lived near the landfill. They discovered that toxic chemicals had contaminated their domestic water wells. At least two of the chemicals, benzene and vinyl chloride, are known human carcinogens and others are strong suspects. The plaintiffs sued Firestone on theories that included negligent infliction of emotional distress. The trial court awarded $269,500 for psychiatric illnesses and the cost of treating them, $142,975 for the cost of medical monitoring of the plaintiffs, and punitive damages of $2.6 million. The court of appeal modified the judgment in some respects, but affirmed the main elements.]

[The Supreme Court of California raised the possibility that if the plaintiffs had suffered harm to their cells or their immune systems, that might constitute physical injury and that if so, emotional distress damages could be recovered as parasitic to a recovery for that harm. But it concluded that there was not enough evidence in the record to pass on that question.]

We next determine whether the absence of a present physical injury precludes recovery for emotional distress engendered by fear of cancer. . . .

Our reasons for discarding the physical injury requirement in Molien remain valid today and are equally applicable in a toxic exposure case. That is, the physical injury requirement is a hopelessly imprecise screening device. . . .

We next consider whether recovery of damages for emotional distress caused by fear of cancer should depend upon a showing that the plaintiff's fears stem from a knowledge that there is a probable likelihood of developing cancer in the future due to the toxic exposure. This is a matter of hot debate among the parties and amici curiae. . . .

A carcinogenic or other toxic ingestion or exposure, without more, does not provide a basis for fearing future physical injury or illness which the law is prepared to recognize as reasonable. The fact that one is aware that he or she has ingested or been otherwise exposed to a carcinogen or other toxin, without any regard to the nature, magnitude and proportion of the exposure or its likely consequences, provides no meaningful basis upon which to evaluate the reasonableness of one's fear. For example, nearly everybody is exposed to carcinogens which appear naturally in all types of foods. . . .

[W]e would be very hard pressed to find that, as a matter of law, a plaintiff faced with a 20 percent or 30 percent chance of developing cancer cannot genuinely, seriously and reasonably fear the prospect of cancer. Nonetheless, we conclude, for the public policy reasons identified below, that emotional distress caused by the fear of a cancer that is not probable should generally not be compensable in a negligence action. . . .

[A]ll of us are potential fear of cancer plaintiffs, provided we are sufficiently aware of and worried about the possibility of developing cancer from exposure to or ingestion of a carcinogenic substance. The enormity of the class of potential plaintiffs cannot be overstated; indeed, a single class action may easily involve hundreds, if not thousands, of fear of cancer claims.

With this consideration in mind, we believe the tremendous societal cost of otherwise allowing emotional distress compensation to a potentially unrestricted plaintiff class demonstrates the necessity of imposing some limit on the class. Proliferation of fear of cancer claims in California in the absence of meaningful restrictions might compromise the availability and affordability of liability insurance for toxic liability risks.

A second policy concern that weighs in favor of a more likely than not threshold is the unduly detrimental impact that unrestricted fear liability would have in the health care field. As amicus curiae California Medical Association points out, access to prescription drugs is likely to be impeded by allowing recovery of fear of cancer damages in negligence cases without the imposition of a heightened threshold. To wit, thousands of drugs having no known harmful effects are currently being prescribed and utilized. New data about potentially harmful effects may not develop for years. If and when negative data are discovered and made public, however, one can expect numerous lawsuits to be filed by patients who currently have no physical injury or illness but who nonetheless fear the risk of adverse effects from the drugs they used. Unless meaningful restrictions are placed on this potential plaintiff class, the threat of numerous large, adverse monetary awards, coupled with the added cost of insuring against such liability (assuming insurance would be available), could diminish the availability of new, beneficial prescription drugs or increase their price beyond the reach of those who need them most. . . .

A third policy concern to consider is that allowing recovery to all victims who have a fear of cancer may work to the detriment of those who sustain actual physical injury and those who ultimately develop cancer as a result of toxic exposure. That is, to allow compensation to all plaintiffs with objectively reasonable cancer fears, even where the threatened cancer is not probable, raises the very significant concern that defendants and their insurers will be unable to ensure adequate compensation for those victims who actually develop cancer or other physical injuries. . . .

A fourth reason supporting the imposition of a more likely than not limitation is to establish a sufficiently definite and predictable threshold for recovery to permit consistent application from case to case. . . .

Finally, while a more likely than not limitation may foreclose compensation to many persons with genuine and objectively reasonable fears, it is sometimes necessary to "limit the class of potential plaintiffs if emotional injury absent physical harm is to continue to be a recoverable item of damages in a negligence action." . . .

Unless an express exception to this general rule is recognized: in the absence of a present physical injury or illness, damages for fear of cancer may be recovered only if the plaintiff pleads and proves that (1) as a result of the defendant's negligent breach of a duty owed to the plaintiff, the plaintiff is exposed to a toxic substance which threatens cancer; and (2) the plaintiff's fear stems from a knowledge, corroborated by reliable medical or scientific opinion, that it is more likely than not that the plaintiff will develop the cancer in the future due to the toxic exposure. Under this rule, a plaintiff must do more than simply establish knowledge of a toxic ingestion or exposure and a significant increased risk of cancer. The plaintiff must further show that based upon reliable medical or scientific opinion, the plaintiff harbors a serious fear that the toxic ingestion or exposure was of such magnitude and proportion as to likely result in the feared cancer.

[But] we hold that a toxic exposure plaintiff need not meet the more likely than not threshold for fear of cancer recovery in a negligence action if the plaintiff pleads and proves that the defendant's conduct in causing the exposure amounts to "oppression, fraud, or malice" as defined in Civil Code section 3294, which authorizes the imposition of punitive damages. Thus, for instance, fear of cancer damages may be recovered without demonstrating that cancer is probable where it is shown that the defendant is guilty of "despicable conduct which is carried on by the defendant with a willful and conscious disregard of the rights or safety of others."
. . .

In our view, Firestone's conduct brings this case within the "oppression, fraud or malice" exception for recovery of fear of cancer damages. . . .

[The court held similarly that the more likely than not threshold need not be met in an intentional infliction claim. It remanded for reconsideration but not necessarily denial of punitive damages. It approved the award of medical monitoring costs without regard to whether future cancer was more likely than not. Three judges concurred and dissented.]

NOTES

1. Notice that *Potter* is a kind of stranger case, in the sense that the defendant was in no contractual relationship with the plaintiffs. So it would be difficult to treat Firestone like a doctor or other professional who might be viewed as undertaking a special duty to the patient under *Burgess*.

2. Notice also that the court emphasized heavily its concern with mass torts. Given the mass tort element and the stranger element, would the California Court impose a similar more-likely-than-not rule, or any other special limiting rule when (a) the defendant is in a special relationship with the plaintiff and (b) the threat of mass exposure is not present?

3. A Nebraska judge expressed doubt that *Potter* could be properly applied to AIDS needle-stick cases. She said: "I am puzzled as to how the principles enunciated in *Potter* ..., driven by fear of cancer-related issues, became grafted in toto into the California jurisprudence regarding fear of AIDS. The course and profiles of cancer and AIDS are markedly different, and the fear of cancer due to generalized exposure and fear of AIDS due to a discrete event are not fungible." *Malena v. Marriott Int'l, Inc.*, 651 N.W.2d 850 (Neb. 2002) (Miller–Lerman, J., concurring).

NORFOLK & WESTERN RAILWAY v. AYERS, 538 U.S. 135 (2003). The plaintiffs brought a Federal Employers Liability Act suit against the railroad, their employer, alleging that the employer had negligently exposed them to asbestos and that they contracted asbestosis as a result. Asbestosis is a non-cancerous scarring of the lungs which causes shortness of breath and fatigue. The plaintiffs also claimed mental anguish based on their fear of developing cancer. The trial court permitted the plaintiffs to introduce evidence that, given their medical histories as smokers, the asbestosis significantly increased their risk of developing cancer and instructed the jury that although the plaintiffs could not recover for the possibility of cancer, they could recover for fear of developing it. The jury awarded damages to the plaintiffs, which, because damages were not specified for each item of harm, might have included awards for fear of developing cancer. *Held,* affirmed. Ginsburg, J.: "[O]ur decisions ... describe two categories: Stand-alone emotional distress claims not provoked by any physical injury, for which recovery is sharply circumscribed by the zone-of-danger test; and emotional distress claims brought on by a physical injury, for which pain and suffering recovery is permitted.... A plaintiff suffering bodily harm need not allege physical manifestations of her mental anguish. [Restatement Second of Torts § 456, cmt. *c*.] 'The plaintiff must of course present evidence that she has suffered, but otherwise her emotional distress claims, in whatever form, are fully recoverable.' D. Dobbs, Law of Torts 822 (2000). . . . Once found liable for 'any bodily harm,' a negligent actor is answerable in damages for emotional disturbance 'resulting from the bodily harm *or from the conduct which causes it.*' Restatement § 456(a)." The physically harmed plaintiff need not prove physical symptoms of his emotional distress, only that the emotional distress is both genuine and serious.

Kennedy, J., joined by three other Justices, dissenting: (1) Many companies have been bankrupted by asbestos litigation; awards of emotional harm damages like these will exhaust funds of asbestos defendants so that nothing will be available to compensate those who later suffer actual cancers resulting from asbestos exposures. (2) In any event "I do not think the brooding, contemplative fear the respondents allege can be called a direct result of their asbestosis. Unlike shortness of breath or other discomfort asbestosis may cause, their fear does not arise from the presence of disease in their lungs. Instead, the respondents' fear is the product of learning from a doctor about their asbestosis, receiving information (perhaps at a much later time) about the conditions that correlate with this disease, and then contemplating how these possible conditions might affect their lives."

NOTE: RECOVERY IN "NO EXPOSURE" CASES

1. Plaintiffs in almost all states who seek substantial damages for emotional harm for fear of contracting some disease have an incentive to plead their cases as involving actual physical injury, with the emotional distress as a parasitic element of damages. What if a plaintiff is stuck with a needle, suffering "minimal physical injury," and then suffers "anxiety and mental suffering occasioned by his or her fear of testing HIV positive and contracting AIDS, absent a showing of actual exposure to blood or body fluid infected with HIV?" In *Hartwig v. Oregon Trail Eye Clinic,* 580 N.W.2d 86 (Neb. 1998), the court concluded that this was a "simple negligence" case, not involving any separate claim of negligent infliction of emotional distress and thus not subject to any of its special rules.

2. What counts as a physical injury that will allow the plaintiff to claim emotional harm as parasitic damages? In *Temple–Inland Forest Products Corp. v. Carter,* 993 S.W.2d 88 (Tex. 1999) two workers were exposed to extensive asbestos dust for weeks before the defendant told them what it was. The doctor said they had been physically injured by inhalation of the dust, but that injury was producing no present symptoms. On the other hand, the likelihood that they would suffer asbestos-related diseases in the future was greatly increased. The court acknowledged the rule that physical injury warrants mental distress recovery, but held that at least in the case of asbestos, where future disease was highly uncertain, recovery for emotional distress would not be allowed. Although the court acknowledged that the fear was both real and reasonable, it also

said that claimants would be overcompensated if it turned out no disease eventuated.

3.　When the plaintiff is actually exposed to HIV, recovery for the resulting distress does not seem to be a problem even if the plaintiff suffers no physical harm. *See John & Jane Roes, 1–100 v. FHP, Inc.,* 985 P.2d 661 (Haw. 1999). Recovery is limited to harms inflicted in the window of anxiety, that is, to the time before testing indicates to a high probability that HIV infection is unlikely. *See Ornstein v. New York City Health & Hosp. Corp.,* 881 N.E.2d 1187 (N.Y. 2008). However, emotional harm in this period might conceivably cause permanent emotional harm for which damages should be assessed.

4.　Many courts have required "actual exposure," meaning that there must be a channel of exposure and also a virus or toxin must be shown to exist. *See, e.g., Majca v. Beekil,* 701 N.E.2d 1084 (Ill. 1998); *Carroll v. Sisters of Saint Francis,* 868 S.W.2d 585 (Tenn. 1993); *Coca–Cola Bottling Co. v. Hagan,* 813 So.2d 167 (Fla. Dist. Ct. App. 2002). But several state high courts have permitted recovery in no-exposure cases. *See, e.g., Chizmar v. Mackie,* 896 P.2d 196 (Alaska 1995) (misdiagnosis of AIDS); *Faya v. Almaraz,* 620 A.2d 327 (Md. 1993) (doctor with AIDS infection); *South Cent. Reg'l Med. Ctr. v. Pickering,* 749 So.2d 95 (Miss. 1999) (unsafe disposal of instruments); *Williamson v. Waldman,* 696 A.2d 14 (N.J. 1997). Some judges in the former camp fear that ignorant people would flood the courts with claims based upon unfounded fears unless the exposure rules were adopted. Why not simply require reasonable fear?

REFERENCE: DOBBS ON TORTS §§ 302–16 (2000).

CHAPTER 20

PRENATAL HARMS

■ ■ ■

§ 1. PRENATAL AND PRECONCEPTION INJURY

REMY v. MacDONALD

801 N.E.2d 260 (Mass. 2004)

GREANEY, J.

This case presents the issue whether a child, born alive, can maintain a cause of action in tort against her mother for personal injuries incurred before birth because of the mother's negligence. The plaintiff seeks to recover damages based on the alleged negligence of her mother, the defendant Christine MacDonald, in connection with a two-car automobile accident that occurred when the plaintiff was in utero. [At the time of the accident in 1999, MacDonald was 32 weeks pregnant with the plaintiff. The plaintiff was born by emergency caesarian section four days later. She continues to suffer from multiple breathing difficulties associated with her premature birth. The plaintiff claims that her mother's negligent driving caused the accident that led to the plaintiff's premature birth and subsequent related injuries. The trial court granted summary judgment for the defendant.]

In order to succeed on a claim of negligence, a plaintiff first must establish that the defendant owed a legal duty of care. We must decide whether a pregnant woman owes a legal duty of care to her unborn child to refrain from negligent conduct that may result in physical harm to that child. If no such duty exists, a claim of negligence cannot be brought.

Whether a duty exists is a question of common law, to be determined by "reference to existing social values and customs and appropriate social policy." As a general principle of tort law, every actor has a duty to exercise reasonable care to avoid physical harm to others. There are a limited number of situations, however, in which the other legal requirements of negligence may be satisfied, but the imposition of a precautionary duty is deemed to be either inadvisable or unworkable. This is such a case.

The [trial] judge ruled that the defendant did not owe a duty of care to the unborn plaintiff. In his memorandum of decision, the judge noted that no Massachusetts appellate court has recognized the existence of such a duty. Guiding himself by cases in other jurisdictions, the judge reasoned that, due to a "unique symbiotic relationship" between a mother and her unborn child, the judicial creation of such a duty, in this case, could raise a multitude of problematic issues, as well as potentially invade the personal choice of pregnant women. We, essentially, agree.

We begin by taking judicial notice of the fact that, during the period of gestation, almost all aspects of a woman's life may have an impact, for better or for worse, on her developing fetus. A fetus can be injured not only by physical force, but by the mother's exposure, unwitting or intentional, to chemicals and other substances, both dangerous and nondangerous, at home or in the workplace, or by the mother's voluntary ingestion of drugs, alcohol, or tobacco. A pregnant woman may place her fetus in danger by engaging in activities involving a risk of physical harm or by engaging in activities, such as most sports, that are generally not considered to be perilous. A pregnant woman may jeopardize the health of her fetus by taking medication (prescription or over-the-counter) or, in other cases, by not taking medication. She also may endanger the well-being of her fetus by not following her physician's advice with respect to prenatal care or by exercising her constitutional right not to receive medical treatment.

Recognizing a pregnant woman's legal duty of care in negligence to her unborn child would present an almost unlimited number of circumstances that would likely give rise to litigation. Courts would be challenged to refine the scope of such a duty, including the degree of knowledge expected of a mother in order to pinpoint when such a duty would arise (e.g., at the point of pregnancy; at the point of awareness of pregnancy; or at the point of awareness that pregnancy is a possibility) or the particular standard of conduct to which a reasonably careful pregnant woman, in a single case, should be held. There is no consensus on if and when a duty such as the one sought by the plaintiff should be imposed, and there is considerable debate with respect to a mother's civil liability for injuries to her unborn fetus, including disagreement over whether the rights of the child should supersede the legal rights of the mother. No set of clear existing social values and customs exist, and no settled social policy can be identified, to justify the maintenance of the present lawsuit.

[The court discussed two appellate court decisions, one in Illinois and one in Texas, that have declined to recognize a mother's duty of care toward her unborn child.]

There are three appellate decisions in jurisdictions that have allowed a claim brought against one's mother for negligently inflicted prenatal injuries. See *National Cas. Co. v. Northern Trust Bank,* 807 So.2d 86, 87 (Fla.App. 2002) (permitting claims only in context of motor vehicle accidents, up to limit of insurance); *Grodin v. Grodin,* 301 N.W.2d 869 (Mich.

App. 1980) (permitting claim based on mother's ingestion of drug that caused child, when born, to develop discolored teeth); *Bonte v. Bonte,* 616 A.2d 464 (N.H.1992) (permitting claim based on mother's failure to use reasonable care in crossing street). These decisions uniformly were premised on the assumption that, because an unborn child, after birth, may recover for prenatal injuries negligently inflicted by another, and because parental immunity had been abolished in those jurisdictions, logic demands that a child's mother should bear the same liability for injurious, negligent conduct to a fetus as would any third party. The courts undertook no serious analysis of the unique relationship between a pregnant woman and the fetus she carries. The courts also failed to address the collateral social and other impacts of the imposition of a legal (as opposed to a moral) obligation that would hold a pregnant woman to a standard of care towards her unborn child. Because it is on these considerations that our decision rests, we find these cases unpersuasive.

The plaintiff contends that her mother, as the operator of a motor vehicle, had an existing duty of care that extended to all other persons to operate her automobile in a reasonably careful and prudent manner, and argues that, based on this existing duty, there is no legal reason, particularly in the context of motor vehicle negligence, to distinguish between an unborn fetus and a child already born. We do not agree.

This court has recognized the right of a plaintiff to maintain an independent cause of action for prenatal injuries sustained as the result of the negligence of another. See *Payton v. Abbott Labs,* 437 N.E.2d 171 (Mass. 1982) (allowing claim against drug manufacturer for prenatal injuries caused by mother's ingestion of drug). "If the tortious conduct and the legal causation of the harm can be satisfactorily established, there may be recovery for any injury occurring at any time after conception." *Id.,* quoting Restatement (Second) of Torts, § 869 comment d (1979)....

It is true that, had the plaintiff been injured while MacDonald was a passenger in an automobile negligently operated by another, the plaintiff (whether or not she survived) would have been able to recover damages against the operator of the vehicle. There is also no question that, had the plaintiff been born at the time of the accident, even if only one hour of age, she would have been able to recover against MacDonald for injuries sustained as a result of her mother's negligence. See *Stamboulis v. Stamboulis,* 519 N.E.2d 1299 (Mass. 1988) ("no absolute curtain of immunity protects a parent who negligently causes injury to his or her minor child").... There is nothing in our statutes or case law, however, that addresses the situation before us.

We reject the plaintiff's argument that a rule permitting a child to recover for negligent injuries inflicted before birth by the child's mother could be restricted solely to a viable fetus claiming negligence in an automobile accident. Massachusetts law provides that there is nothing special about injuries incurred in automobile accidents that sets them apart from other negligently caused injuries, and the limitation sought by the plaintiff would be inconsistent with that law. The presence of automobile liability insurance does not create liability where none previously existed. Further, and more importantly, there is no meaningful way to limit such a rule to automobile accidents cases. It would be only a matter of time before the rule could be extended to a myriad of situations that would make pregnant women liable to their viable fetuses for all manner of allegedly negligent conduct.

We agree with the general principle expressed in Restatement (Second) of Torts § 869 (1979), that "[o]ne who tortiously causes harm to an unborn child is subject to liability to the child for the harm if the child is born alive." The quoted language emphasizes that it is not just a pregnant woman alone who may be harmed by the tortious act of a third party, but also the fetus, whose injuries become apparent at its birth. There is nothing in the Restatement text, or in comments to the text, to indicate that the drafters of § 869 intended to suggest a legal right, never before recognized in law, for a fetus to bring a claim of negligence against its own mother.... We have said that "[t]he evolution of the law of negligence has always required courts to make hard (and often fine) distinctions, and to assess and determine, in considering the existence of a duty, contemporary attitudes and public policy." *Cyran v. Ware*, 597 N.E.2d 1352 (Mass. 1992). We conclude that there are inherent and important differences between a fetus, in utero, and a child already born, that permits a bright line to be drawn around the zone of potential tort liability of one who is still biologically joined to an injured plaintiff.

Judgment affirmed.

NOTES

1. **Traditional rule.** A pregnant woman is injured by defendant's negligence. She herself may have a claim for her injury. If the fetus is also injured is there an additional claim? Suppose, for example, a physician negligently prescribes a drug to the mother and the child is born with serious defects. In *Dietrich v. Northhampton*, 138 Mass. 14 (1884), Justice Oliver Wendell Holmes took the view that there could be no action. The opinion suggested the absence of precedent, "remoteness," and the logical problem of injuring a being "before he became a person," but gave little justice or policy reasoning.

2. **Contemporary rules: Child born alive.** The *Dietrich* decision held sway for many years. Judicial reversals began shortly after the end of World War II and today most courts allow a tort claim by the child if the child is born alive. Some courts have insisted that the child must also be viable—capable of living independent of the mother—at the time of the injury. But that requirement seems strikingly unrelated to the reality of suffering after a live birth and most have rejected it. *See, e.g., Gonzales v. Mascarenas*, 190 P.3d 826 (Colo Ct. App. 2008) (listing states); *Leighton v. City of New York*, 830 N.Y.S.2d 749 (App. Div. 2007).

3. **Contemporary rules: Child not born alive but viable at injury.** Most courts passing on the question now appear to hold that a wrongful death

action is allowable when a fetus is stillborn, at least when the fetus was viable at the time of injury. *See, e.g., Pino v. United States,* 183 P.3d 1001 (Okla. 2008). A few states disagree. *See Shaw v. Jendzejec,* 717 A.2d 367 (Me. 1998).

4. **Contemporary rules: Child not born alive and not viable at injury or thereafter.** Most courts reject liability if the fetus was not born alive and was never viable at any time. *See, e.g, Santana v. Zilog,* Inc., 95 F.3d 780 (9th Cir. 1996); *Crosby v. Glasscock Trucking Co.,* Inc., 532 S.E.2d 856 (S.C. 2000); *cf. Bolin v. Wingert,* 764 N.E.2d 201 (Ind. 2002) (denying wrongful death recovery under a born-alive standard, but 10–week fetus would not in fact have been viable). However, a few cases have supported liability under wrongful death statutes for loss of a fetus that was never viable. *Wiersma v. Maple Leaf Farms,* 543 N.W.2d 787 (S.D. 1996); *Farley v. Sartin,* 466 S.E.2d 522 (W.Va. 1995). Cf. *Nealis v. Baird,* 996 P.2d 438 (Okla. 1999) (allowing recovery if fetus had "an instant of life outside the womb"); *66 Federal Credit Union v. Tucker,* 853 So.2d 104 (Miss. 2003) (allowing recovery if fetus was sufficiently developed to move in the womb).

5. **Emotional distress damages.** States are hardly uniform in their rules about recovery of stand-alone negligently-inflicted emotional distress. *See* Chapter 19, §§ 2 & 3. Should a mother be allowed to recover emotional distress damages for the negligently-caused death of a fetus when she has suffered no physical injury? The court in *Broadnax v. Gonzalez,* 809 N.E.2d 645 (N.Y. 2004), allowed such a claim. In *Sheppard–Mobley v. King,* 830 N.E.2d 301 (N.Y. 2005), the court held that *Broadnax* did not allow emotional distress recovery by the mother if the child was born alive, because in such a case the child herself can bring a medical malpractice action for physical injuries. Even where the fetus is not born alive, is there a risk of duplicative recovery if the mother sues for her own emotional harm and as a beneficiary for damages in a wrongful death suit? *See Smith v. Borello,* 804 A.2d 1151 (Md. 2002).

6. **Parental liability: Some hard questions.** Should courts hold a mother liable to her child for ingesting dangerous substances while pregnant? Or for failing to get appropriate pre-natal care? *See Stallman v. Youngquist,* 531 N.E.2d 355 (Ill. 1988); *Chenault v. Huie,* 989 S.W.2d 474 (Tex. App. 1999) (child suffering permanent and serious harm because of mother's use of cocaine during pregnancy). Do you agree with the *Remy* court's reasons for refusing to recognize a duty of care on the facts before it? Does a woman's right to decide whether to terminate a pregnancy during the first trimester as established in *Roe v. Wade,* 410 U.S. 113 (1973), bear on tort liability for an injury inflicted during that period?

RENSLOW v. MENNONITE HOSPITAL, 367 N.E.2d 1250 (Ill. 1977). When plaintiff's mother was 13 years of age, defendants negligently transfused her with Rh-positive blood. This was incompatible with her own blood, though she had no knowledge of this at the time. Years later when she became pregnant she discovered that her blood had become sensitized by this negligent transfusion. As a result of this her child, the plaintiff, was born jaundiced and suffering from hyperbilirubinemia. She has suffered various damages for which she here sues. The trial judge dismissed the claim because plaintiff had not been conceived at the time of the alleged negligence. *Held*, the plaintiff states a claim for relief. Although foreseeability alone does not establish a duty, a duty of care may be owed to one who may be foreseeably harmed, even if the person is unknown or is remote in time or place. The defendants argue a need for an end of liability somewhere and "raise the specter of successive generations of plaintiffs complaining against a single defendant for harm caused by genetic damage done an ancestor," but the judiciary "will effectively exercise its traditional role of drawing rational distinction, consonant with current perceptions of justice, between harms which are compensable and those which are not."

ALBALA v. CITY OF NEW YORK, 429 N.E.2d 786 (N.Y. 1981). Ruth Albala underwent an abortion at Bellevue Hospital during which her uterus was perforated. The plaintiff Jeffrey Albala was born some four years later. This action on his behalf claims he suffered brain damage as a result of the doctor's negligence in perforating his mother's uterus. *Held*, this does not state a claim. Although harm of this kind was foreseeable, foreseeability alone does not establish a duty to the plaintiff. And although New York recognizes prenatal injury claims, those cases are not controlling here because in those cases "there are two identifiable beings within the zone of danger each of whom is owed a duty independent of the other and each of whom may be directly injured." Were liability established in this case, it would be difficult to preclude liability "where a negligent motorist collides with another vehicle containing a female passenger who sustains a punctured uterus ... and subsequently gives birth to a deformed child," and the "staggering implications are manifest.... [R]ecognition of a cause of action under the circumstances of this case would have the undesirable impact of encouraging the practice of 'defensive medicine.' A physician faced with the alternative of saving a patient's life by administering a treatment involving the possibility of adverse consequences to later conceived off-spring of that patient would, if exposed to liability of the magnitude considered in this case, undoubtedly be inclined to advise against treatment rather than risk the possibility of having to recompense a child born with a handicap." This would place "physicians in a direct conflict between their moral duty to patients and the proposed legal duty to those hypothetical future generations outside the immediate zone of danger."

Notes

1. Suppose that, in 1970, D builds a defective building. At the time there is no other building around, though it is foreseeable that others will be built. In 1992 another building is completed adjacent to D's building. D's building, because of its defect, collapses and causes harm to the new building. Should New York allow a recovery if *Albala* is still recognized authority in that state?

2. A number of manufacturers once marketed a drug, DES, for use by pregnant women. The drug turned out to cause cancers and a number of other problems for the daughters of the women who ingested the drug. In several ways, New York has recognized that the manufacturer of the drug would be liable to the DES daughter. *E.g., Hymowitz v. Lilly & Co.*, 539 N.E.2d 1069 (N.Y. 1989). Is that inconsistent with *Albala*? What if it is a DES granddaughter rather than a DES daughter who suffers? *See Enright v. Eli Lilly & Co.*, 570 N.E.2d 198 (N.Y. 1991).

3. A number of cases are in accord with *Renslow* on various facts. *E.g., Lynch v. Scheininger*, 744 A.2d 113 (N.J. 2000); *see* DOBBS ON TORTS § 290 (2000). In a state that follows *Renslow*, Defendant negligently injures Christine Taylor in an auto accident. She requires hospitalization and operations twenty-five times as a result and still suffers some deformity of pelvic bones. Seven years later she gives birth to a child, whose head is damaged because during gestation it was shaped by the deformed pelvic bones. If the court would impose liability under *Renslow*, would it also impose liability on these facts? *Taylor v. Cutler*, 703 A.2d 294 (N.J. Super. Ct. App. Div. 1997), *aff'd*, 724 A.2d 793 (N.J. 1999).

§ 2. WRONGFUL LIFE, BIRTH, OR CONCEPTION

CHAFFEE v. SESLAR

751 N.E.2d 773 (Ind. Ct. App. 2001)

[Dr. Chaffee performed a medical procedure upon the plaintiff at her request to prevent conception of children. The procedure was not successful and the plaintiff bore a healthy child. She claims here for the cost of rearing the child. Dr. Chaffee in effect moved to strike claims for costs of child-rearing. The trial court rejected this motion and Dr. Chaffee appealed.]

We note initially that the United States Constitution protects the right of privacy including one's rights to family planning and birth control. The United States Supreme Court has provided that the right to choose not to have a child is at the "very heart" of a group of constitutionally protected choices, including the decisions relating to marriage, family relationships, child rearing and education. . . .

[W]e believe that the phrase "wrongful pregnancy," like the phrase "wrongful birth," does nothing but creates confusion and implies that Indiana recognizes a prenatal tort which is separate and distinct from other medical malpractice causes of action. Therefore, we will treat Seslar's claim as any other medical malpractice case and will disregard the label or term "wrongful pregnancy." . . . Medical malpractice actions are no different from other kinds of negligence actions regarding the elements which must be proven by a plaintiff. . . . If the plaintiff proves the elements of negligence, she is entitled to all damages naturally flowing from the healthcare provider's breach of duty. . . .

Three views have emerged regarding whether and to what extent a plaintiff may recover the costs associated with rearing an unplanned child, these being: (1) the full recovery rule—the parent may recover all costs of rearing the child; (2) the benefit rule—the parent may recover the cost of rearing the child offset by the benefits the parent will incur as a result of having the child; and (3) the no recovery rule—the parent may not recover the costs of rearing the child.... [The court counted 31 states in this category.]

We believe that child-rearing expenses are available to Seslar if she carries her burden of proof at trial that these damages are a natural and probable consequence of the healthcare provider's breach.... Seslar is faced with the cost of raising the unplanned child. Child-rearing expenses are the costs Seslar was attempting to avoid by undergoing the sterilization procedure. Seslar sought to prevent conception and the birth of the normal, healthy child resulted from the healthcare provider's breach. The healthcare provider's sole purpose in performing the procedure was to comply with Seslar's wishes to prevent conception. Certainly the costs associated with raising a child are foreseeable ... We believe that child-rearing expenses are a natural and probable consequence of the healthcare provider's breach....

However, it has been asserted that child-rearing damages should be prohibited because these expenses are too speculative. We reject this argument. Juries are often called upon to make more complex damage assessments in other medical malpractice actions such as those involving pain and suffering and mental anguish. Furthermore, damages are often awarded for future care and medical treatment in the personal injury context but are not considered speculative despite the fact that the money may not be needed or utilized for such care and treatment in the future. Moreover, there are means by which child-rearing expenses may be calculated, such as economic demographers, government studies, actuarial and insurance company statistics, and population studies. Such costs are easily understandable and appreciated by the average citizen through their own experience of raising children....

It has been argued that the birth of a healthy, normal child cannot constitute a legal harm for which damages are recoverable.... Moreover, it has been expounded that child-rearing damages should not be recoverable because society places such high value on human life that the birth of a normal, healthy child cannot be a legal wrong for which damages may be recovered. This concept embodies the belief that the sanctity of human life would be undermined if child-rearing damages are recoverable against a healthcare provider for the negligent performance of a sterilization procedure....

We believe that a parent's injury is not the birth of her child, but rather is the invasion of her interest in the financial security of her family and the attendant desire to limit her family size, and the deprivation of her right to limit procreation. Also, the sanctity of life is more undermined by a parent being financially unable to provide the basic necessities of life than allowing the recovery of child-rearing expenses. Therefore, we reject these policy arguments for denying child-rearing expenses. . . .

It has been argued the award of child-rearing damages will harm the emotional health of the unplanned child. . . . Parents who attempt to prove that the burdens of the unplanned child outweigh his "worth" will be encouraged to deny the child's "value" to them. Upon learning that another is providing his upbringing, the child may feel unwanted, an "emotional bastard."

We refuse to subscribe to this argument for limiting damages. A parent does not seek damages because he or she does not love or want to keep the unplanned child, rather because the healthcare provider's negligence has resulted in the imposition of financial burdens which the parent desired to avoid. . . .

[The court then considered whether the plaintiff must "mitigate" damages under the avoidable consequences rule.] The only forms of mitigation available to a parent in a claim of "wrongful pregnancy" are abortion and adoption. It has been asserted that by a parent failing to mitigate, he or she admits that they are accepting all the obligations of raising the child, including the costs such as child-rearing expenses. We believe that the requirement of considering an abortion or placing the child up for adoption is unreasonable. We see no reason why a parent who is threatened by future harm by a tortious act should subject herself to emotional or physical pain of a different kind in order to prevent future harm.

Furthermore, the choice of abortion or adoption is a personal and private choice involving deeply religious and moral convictions. Moreover, requiring mitigation of damages in a claim of "wrongful pregnancy" would affront the United States Supreme Court's protection of procreation decisions under the Constitutional right of privacy. Therefore, we hold that neither abortion nor adoption is an ordinary or reasonable measure in the law relating to mitigation of damages.

However, we believe that healthcare provider is entitled to present evidence to limit the amount of the recovery of child-rearing damages by the benefits resulting from the child's birth. . . . Damages are to be reduced only to the extent that the benefit received by the plaintiff is the "same interest" that was harmed by the defendant's tort. In addition, benefit can offset the damage only to the extent that it is equitable. Also, a tortfeasor should not be permitted to force a benefit on the plaintiff against the plaintiff's will . . . . . we refuse to articulate the benefits, if there are in fact any, that may be offset against child-rearing damages recovered as a result of a healthcare provider's negligent performance of a sterilization procedure which ultimately results in the birth of a normal, healthy child. We merely provide that a healthcare provider should not be precluded from presenting this type of mitigation evidence to the fact finder as in any other negligence claim.

NOTES

1. **"Wrongful conception" cases.** Although the Indiana court in *Chaffee* disclaimed the label, the case may be classified as a "wrongful conception" claim. As in *Chaffee*, such claims usually allege that the defendant physician failed to prevent conception because he negligently performed a sterilization procedure on the father or the mother. The child in such cases is normally healthy, but the parents, who had attempted to avoid pregnancy and childbirth, will now face financial costs because of the defendant's negligence. In addition, if they were emotionally unable to care for children, they will almost certainly have increased emotional difficulties. Was the *Chaffee* court right to recognize such a claim? Some legislatures have forbidden courts to entertain these claims. *See Thibeault v. Larson*, 666 A.2d 112 (Me. 1995).

2. **"Wrongful birth" cases.** In a typical "wrongful birth" case, a doctor has negligently failed to diagnose a genetic difficulty, with resulting physical harm to the fetus and economic and emotional harm to the parents. Often the parents argue that but for the doctor's negligence, they would have chosen to abort the fetus. Many courts have now upheld such claims. *See, e.g., Lininger v. Eisenbaum*, 764 P.2d 1202 (Colo. 1988); *Smith v. Cote*, 513 A.2d 341 (N.H. 1986); *Thornhill v. Midwest Physician Ctr.*, 787 N.E.2d 247 (Ill. App. Ct. 2003). Similarly, a physician who learns from genetic screening that any child conceived in the future is at risk may owe a duty to inform the prospective parents. *See Didato v. Strehler*, 554 S.E.2d 42 (Va. 2001). A few courts reject the wrongful birth claim entirely. *E.g., Etkind v. Suarez*, 519 S.E.2d 210 (Ga. 1999). A number of state statutes prohibit wrongful birth claims.

3. **Possible causal difficulties.** Does a wrongful birth claim present intrinsic causal problems, when the case may rest on the parents testifying that the fetus would have been aborted had they been non-negligently informed of problems? The court in *Wilson v. Kuenzi*, 751 S.W.2d 741 (Mo. 1988), thought so: "The percentage of women who under pressure refuse to consider abortion, whether for reasons of religious belief, strong motherly instincts, or for other reasons, is sometimes astounding. It would seem that testimony either more verifiable based upon experience or more verifiable by some objective standard should be required as the basis for any action for substantial damages." Is the court right about this, or should credibility determinations simply be left to the trier of fact?

4. **Wrongful life.** There is no support in the cases for a general wrongful life claim, as distinct from a wrongful birth or wrongful conception claim. The child, in other words, cannot recover for being born. However, several courts have permitted the child to recover the cost of extraordinary care in his own name.

5. **Emotional distress damages.** Some courts have been reluctant to award damages for emotional harm in wrongful birth cases. Where such damages are recoverable, would the plaintiff be required to show she was in the zone of danger or that she suffered physical injury from her emotional

distress? Or can the plaintiff state an ordinary tort claim with emotional distress as parasitic damage? Dan B. Dobbs, Law of Remedies § 8.2 (1992). In *Bader v. Johnson*, 732 N.E.2d 1212 (Ind. 2000), the court held that so-called wrongful birth actions were merely medical malpractice actions, that general rules of negligence applied, and that all damages proximately caused by the defendant's negligence would be recoverable.

6. **Damages for child-rearing costs.** Many courts recognizing a wrongful birth claim allow recovery for some of the expenses of rearing the now-impaired child. Recovery is usually limited, however, to the "extraordinary" expenses over and above ordinary child-rearing expenses. Some states have limited the available damages to the expenses of pregnancy and delivery. *See Schirmer v. Mt. Auburn Obstetrics & Gynecology Assocs., Inc.*, 844 N.E.2d 1160 (Ohio 2006). The *Shirmer* court pointed to the "underlying but critical fact" that in such cases the mother is claiming she would have terminated the pregnancy, making "unimpaired life never a possibility in this situation." Does computing "extraordinary" child-rearing expenses require the trier of fact to assess the relative merits of "being versus nonbeing," as the *Shirmer* court concluded?

7. **Damages in wrongful conception cases: The healthy but unwanted child.** In wrongful conception cases, most courts have allowed recovery for the mother's pain in pregnancy, and medical costs of pregnancy, abortion, or birth, as well as any lost wages during this period. However, most courts have denied recovery for the cost of rearing the healthy child. "The parents of a normal, healthy child whom they now love have not suffered any injury or damage," the Kentucky Court said bluntly. *Schork v. Huber*, 648 S.W.2d 861 (Ky. 1983). Other courts have emphasized similar ideas, and have said that the damages are speculative or out of proportion to the defendant's fault, or that the avoidable consequences rule would require the plaintiff-mother to have an abortion or put the child up for adoption. Did the *Chaffee* court address these arguments convincingly? A number of other recent decisions have framed rules permitting recovery even in healthy-child cases. *E.g., Zehr v. Haugen*, 871 P.2d 1006 (Or. 1994); *Marciniak v. Lundborg*, 450 N.W.2d 243 (Wis. 1990).

References: (1) Prenatal injury, Dobbs on Torts § 288–289 (2000); Harper, James & Gray, The Law of Torts § 18.3 (3d Ed. 2007); (2) Preconception negligence, Dobbs on Torts § 290; (3) Wrongful life, birth or conception: Dobbs on Torts §§ 291–293.

Chapter 21

Death

■ ■ ■

"In a civil Court, the death of a human being could not be complained of as an injury...."

> —Lord Ellenborough in *Baker v. Bolton*, 1 Camp. 493, 170 Eng. Rep. 1033 (1808).

———

Lord Ellenborough's statement meant or came to mean three separate things:

(1) If an injured person died before receiving judgment against the defendant, his cause of action died with him; put differently, the cause of action did not survive the death of the plaintiff.

(2) If an injured person remained alive after injury but the defendant died before a judgment was rendered against him, the plaintiff's cause of action died as well; put differently, the plaintiff's cause of action did not survive the death of the defendant.

(3) There was no separate cause of action on behalf of those who were dependent upon the deceased person.

In most states all of these rules have been changed; in all states one or more have been changed.[1] The first two rules have been changed by statutes generally known as "survival" statutes, because they provide that the cause of action survives the death of the plaintiff or the defendant or both. The third rule has been changed by statutes usually called "wrongful death" statutes, or "Lord Campbell's" Acts after the sponsor of the first such legislation.

Subject to a minor exception in federal maritime law, wrongful death and survival claims are entirely statutory. Statutes are amended from time to time and many have idiosyncratic elements. Lawyers must always

———

1. A number of federal statutes also allow for death recoveries in some form. *See, e.g.*, the Federal Employers' Liability Act, 45 U.S.C.A. § 51 (employees of interstate railroads); the Jones Act, 46 U.S.C.A. § 688 (employees at sea); the Death on the High Seas Act, 46 App. U.S.C.A. § 761 (deaths more than one maritime league from shore); the National Vaccine Compensation Program, 42 U.S.C.A. § 300aa–15(a) (deaths caused by vaccinations). Some cases have permitted recoveries for death under the basic federal civil rights statute, 42 U.S.C.A. § 1983.

consult the governing statute and should expect to find local variations in the general scheme described in this chapter.

WEIGEL v. LEE

752 N.W.2d 618 (N.D. 2008)

CROTHERS, JUSTICE.

[Darlyne Rogers died shortly after being admitted to a "regular" room in a hospital despite being critically ill. Her adult children (collectively "the Weigels") sued Dr. Lane Lee and the hospital (collectively "Lee") pursuant to the North Dakota wrongful death statute. The complaint sought damages for the Weigels' own emotional distress and loss of consortium. After a series of motions, orders, and reconsiderations, the trial court dismissed the Weigels' entire case. Ultimately the trial court reasoned that under *Butz v. World Wide, Inc.*, 492 N.W.2d 88 (N.D. 1992), children do not have a cause of action for either loss of parental consortium or for their own emotional distress damages. The court further suggested that the Weigels could bring only a claim for the emotional distress suffered by Rogers before her death.]

. . . The district court erred by blending three distinct claims for tortious conduct. At various points in its orders, the district court discussed (1) loss of consortium claims arising out of personal injury actions, (2) survival actions and (3) wrongful death actions. This Court and North Dakota's statutes distinguish between these three claims, as we explain below.

[Historically, a loss of consortium claim was available only to husbands whose wives were injured.] In *Hastings,* this Court acknowledged both spouses' right to recover for loss of consortium, but refused to extend this type of recovery to children who suffer the loss of a parent's consortium. Nonetheless, this is not the basis of the Weigels' action, and as this Court importantly clarified in *Hastings,* the inability of children to recover for loss of consortium arising out of personal injury to a parent "should not be construed to prohibit recovery where a parent dies and recovery is allowed under the Wrongful Death Act."

The distinction between loss of consortium in personal injury and in wrongful death actions is important here because Lee argues this Court's decision in *Butz* indicates a decedent's children are not entitled to damages in a wrongful death action. Lee misapplies *Butz. Butz* was not a claim under the wrongful death act because the tortious conduct resulted in severe injury, not in death. . . . Because *Butz* does not address claims made under the wrongful death statutes, it is not applicable to the Weigels' claim.

Second, N.D.C.C. § 28–01–26.1 provides for survival actions: "No action or claim for relief, except for breach of promise, alienation of affections, libel, and slander, abates by the death of a party or of a person who might have been a party had such death not occurred." For example, in *Nodak Mut. Ins. Co. v. Stegman,* 647 N.W.2d 133 (N.D. 2002), an individual was seriously injured in an automobile accident. He underwent hospital treatment, but died approximately two weeks later. This Court stated, "Clearly a personal injury action existed on behalf of [the injured party] against [the tortfeasor] for various damages, including the medical expenses occasioned by the accident, and that action survived [the injured party's] death." Survival statutes "are remedial in nature, and are intended to permit recovery by the representatives of the deceased for damages the deceased could have recovered had he lived.... A survival action merely continues in existence an injured person's claim after death as an asset of his estate." Although they could have, the Weigels' complaint indicates they are not seeking damages on Rogers' behalf as part of a survival action. Instead, the Weigels brought a wrongful death action for their own injuries: "The Plaintiffs have sustained mental and emotional anguish as a result of the Defendants' negligence and their mother's death. Furthermore, the Plaintiffs have been denied the society, comfort, counsel and companionship of Darlyne Rogers, all to their injury and damage."

Third, N.D.C.C. ch. 32–21 provides for wrongful death actions. The Weigels offer the wrongful death act as the legal basis for their claim. We conclude the Weigels are entitled to seek compensation for Rogers' wrongful death for the reasons stated below.

There was no wrongful death claim at common law. Early wrongful death statutes severely limited compensable damages. Generally, only pecuniary losses were awarded, with no compensation available for mental anguish or loss of companionship. Contemporary wrongful death statutes tend to address a broader scope of injuries, including those considered non-pecuniary. Wrongful death actions are intended to compensate the survivors of the deceased for the losses they have sustained as a result of a wrongful killing. Dependent upon the specific statutory language, losses recoverable by survivors in wrongful death actions often include the prospective loss of earnings and contribution; prospective expenses; loss of services; loss of companionship, comfort, and consortium; and mental anguish and grief.

North Dakota's wrongful death act, N.D.C.C. ch. 32–21, provides:

"Whenever the death of a person shall be caused by a wrongful act, neglect, or default, and the act, neglect, or default is such as would have entitled the party injured, if death had not ensued, to maintain an action and recover damages in respect thereof, then and in every such case the person who, or the corporation, limited liability company, or company which, would have been liable if death had not ensued, shall be liable to an action for damages, notwithstanding the death of the person injured or of the tort-feasor, and although the death shall have been caused under such circumstances as amount in law to felony."

This statute is not a survival statute intended to increase the estate of the deceased, but its purpose is to give a measure of protection to those persons within a fixed degree of relationship to and dependency on the deceased because of actual injury sustained by them by reason of the wrongful killing of the deceased. Damages under the wrongful death act are based on the loss suffered by the beneficiaries, and not on the loss sustained by the decedent's estate. A jury determines the quantity of damages and "shall give such damages as it finds proportionate to the injury resulting from the death to the persons entitled to the recovery." N.D.C.C. § 32–21–02.

Compensable damages available in wrongful death actions are enumerated in N.D.C.C. § 32–03.2–04 [and specifically include both economic and non-economic damages. Included in the latter are mental anguish, emotional distress, and loss of consortium.]

Section 32–21–04, N.D.C.C., clarifies that intended recipients of damages under the wrongful death act are "the decedent's heirs at law." This Court has determined "heirs at law" for purposes of this statute are "those persons who by the laws of descent would succeed to the property of the decedent in case of intestacy, but in addition, that if members of a preferred class are precluded from recovery for reasons other than death those next entitled to inherit may be considered beneficiaries." A decedent's descendants are designated by the Uniform Probate Code to share in portions of the intestate estate and are therefore able to seek recovery of damages under the wrongful death act.

Persons entitled to recover damages under the wrongful death act should not be confused with persons statutorily authorized to bring an action. Section 32–21–03, N.D.C.C. [authorizes the following persons to bring an action, in the following order: "(1) The surviving husband or wife, if any; (2) The surviving children, if any; (3) The surviving mother or father; (4) A surviving grandparent; (5) The personal representative; (6) A person who has had primary physical custody of the decedent before the wrongful act."]

The distinction between persons eligible to seek damages from wrongful death actions and those entitled to bring such actions is important because the trial judge is charged with splitting the recovery among eligible heirs.... In specific wrongful death actions, overlap will likely exist between plaintiffs bringing the action under N.D.C.C. § 32–21–03 and those entitled to any damages. However, those with authority to bring the action do not have an absolute right to the damages recovered, and, instead, bring the action in a representative capacity for the exclusive benefit of the persons entitled to recover. The wrongful death act thus differentiates between the capacity to bring an action and the right to share in the damages recovered. Surviving children are eligible to bring a wrongful death action under N.D.C.C. § 32–21–03(2) if the decedent had no eligible spouse or if the spouse fails to bring an action for thirty days after the children made a demand. But this issue is separate from the children's ability to recover damages in a wrongful death action.

Because the wrongful death act does not exclude the decedent's children from parties entitled to damages and because the damages requested are permitted under N.D.C.C. § 32–03.2–04, the Weigels' claim should not have been dismissed.

[Reversed and remanded.]

NOTES

Wrongful Death Statutes

1. **Parties and procedure.** A wrongful death action, unlike a survival action, does not involve a claim by the estate. Any recovery does not pass through the estate, but instead goes directly to the survivors. The action is often brought by survivors of the decedent; frequently one of them acts as a kind of informal trustee, suing for all of them. In some states the court appoints a trustee, who formally brings the action on behalf of all appropriate beneficiaries. Very often statutes provide that this person is to be the personal representative of the estate. But where this is so, the personal representative is a trustee for the survivors entitled to recover, not the representative of the estate generally. This means that a personal representative, say the surviving husband of a deceased wife, may bring one suit for the estate—the survival action; and that he may also bring a separate death action for the appropriate survivors.

2. **Measures of damages for wrongful death.** Wrongful death statutes traditionally aimed to replace pecuniary losses that would be suffered by others because of the decedent's death. "Apart from relatively minor items such as funeral expense, most states measure economic loss by the loss of support to dependents. Some measure it differently, by the loss of projected lifetime savings of the deceased. The first measure is usually called loss-to-survivors or loss-to-dependents measure, while the second is called the loss-to-the estate measure." "[M]ost of the states which use the loss-to-the estate measure calculate the loss by determining the deceased's probable lifetime earnings and then deducting the expenses the decedent would have had in maintaining himself." DAN B. DOBBS, THE LAW OF REMEDIES §§ 8.3 (3) & 8.3 (4) (1993).

3. **Pecuniary emphasis; loss to survivors' measure.** Wrongful death statutes originally limited the recovery to pecuniary losses suffered by dependents or those who would inherit. For example, under the loss to survivors' measure of damages, children of a decedent might recover for loss of support they received in the form of housing, food, and clothing. If the deceased person would not have contributed to any beneficiary during his lifetime, damages would be small or nonexistent.

4. **Loss-to-estate measure.** The loss-to-estate measure might allow substantial damages even where the decedent was not contributing to the support of others. This measure would allow recovery for whatever sums the decedent would have earned and saved in her normal lifetime, even if she

were supporting no one. This would be helpful if decedent would have earned more than her self-support required. Under some circumstances might it lead to a zero award?

5. **Combining measures**. Several courts have now permitted death action plaintiffs to recover both the loss of support and a loss of inheritance. The loss of inheritance is essentially like the loss to the estate. The claimant must show that the decedent would have accumulated an estate (or an increase in his estate) and that the claimant would have inherited a share. When the claimants were receiving no support, as is often the case with adult children of the decedent, in such jurisdictions they could still recover for reasonably provable loss of inheritance. *See Schaefer v. American Family Mut. Ins. Co.,* 531 N.W.2d 585 (Wis. 1995).

6. **Non-earning decedents.** Children, spouses who do not work in the labor market, retired persons, and others whose earnings are small or nonexistent create still another problem under the wrongful death statutes. It would be difficult to say that wrongful death has reduced their ultimate estate and equally difficult to say that they were supporting other persons. Thus neither measure of wrongful death damages is adequate for non-working decedents. In such cases, non-pecuniary damages become all-important.

7. **Non-pecuniary claims generally.** At least three basic kinds of non-pecuniary loss might be claimed in death actions: (1) punitive damages; (2) damages for the mental anguish or grief of the survivors; (3) loss of consortium, which might include (a) loss of society or companionship, (b) loss of services, and (c) loss of guidance and care. As *Weigel* explains, claims like these were excluded under most original wrongful death statutes. The first two elements are generally rejected in wrongful death suits, though a few states permit their recovery. The third, loss of consortium, is usually recoverable. Courts stress that loss of consortium does not include emotional distress of the survivors, but that it does include a broad range of mutual benefits of family membership, including love, affection, care, companionship and the like. *See Reiser v. Coburn,* 587 N.W.2d 336 (Neb. 1998) (a zero award to parents of a young independent adult was inadequate, new trial required).

8. **Future losses.** Both the loss-to-survivors rule and the loss-to-the-estate rule require the court to estimate the earnings the decedent would have had but for the death. How many years would the decedent have lived to save money or make contributions to dependents? What would those earnings have been? These are difficult matters of proof and complicated by possible inflation and taxes. A discount must be made after all this to take into account the fact that the plaintiffs will recover all future losses now and can invest the sum at interest. *See generally* DOBBS, *supra* Note 2, § 8.5 (1993).

Survival Statutes

9. **Parties and procedure.** The plaintiff in a survival claim is the personal representative of the decedent's estate. The claim is a debt owed to the estate just as any other claim is, and any recovery is paid to the estate. The estate in turn pays the debts of the deceased person and the costs of administering the estate. If any funds are left, the estate pays those to heirs or the beneficiaries of the deceased's will.

10. **Survival of claim after plaintiff's death.** A tort victim might bring a suit to redress a tort, then die before the suit goes to judgment. In that case, the claim is "revived" and continued in the name of the personal representative. Or, the victim might die without having brought suit, so that the claim is brought by the personal representative in the first place. Either way, the claim is a survival action. It is a species of property which passes to the estate of the deceased person in the same way a share of stock or a bank account might pass.

11. **Survival of claim after defendant's death.** Survival statutes usually also provide for survival of the victim's claim after the defendant's death. In this setting, the living victim asserts the claim for all damages against the estate of the deceased tortfeasor. The case of the deceased victim is the more common one.

12. **Survival Damages.** Since the survival action continues the claim held by the decedent for damages accruing up until his death, it may include any medical expenses, wages lost before death, and pain and suffering resulting from the injury. In some states it may also include funeral expenses. Most states allow for the recovery of punitive damages in these cases, on a rationale that "if a wrongdoer may be punished if his victim lives, then surely he should not escape retribution if his wrongful act causes a death." *Smith v. Whitaker*, 734 A.2d 243 (N.J. 1999).

13. **Special classes of damages.** Survival statutes can create new kinds of damages. A few states authorize "loss of life" damages, designed "to compensate a decedent for the loss of the value that the decedent would have placed on his or her life." *See Durham v. Marberry*, 156 S.W.3d 242 (Ark. 2004). Such damages are available even if the decedent died instantly, since it is not identical to an award for pain and suffering. *Id.*

CHAVEZ v. CARPENTER, 111 Cal.Rptr.2d 534 (Ct. App. 2001). Altie Chavez, 24 years of age, was killed by a drunk driver, the defendant here, in August. Though unmarried, Altie was the father of a two-year-old daughter, Jazmyne. Jazmyne died from unrelated causes in September. Altie had lived with and perhaps contributed monetary support to his parents, Jose and Elsa. They brought suit for his death. Maria Garcia, Jazmyne's mother, brought suit on behalf of Jazmyne's estate. Held: (1) the statute permits recovery by heirs, but the parents cannot recover as heirs of Altie because parents cannot be heirs if the decedent's child survived him, which Jazmyne did; (2) the statute now permits recovery by parents who were "dependents"; this is a factual question to be addressed at trial; and (3) Jazmyne, as an heir, had a cause of action for the wrongful death of her father, Altie, and that cause of action survived her and may be pursued by her estate.

NOTES

1. **Contributions of the decedent.** If contributions of the decedent measure the damages, is there a risk that the defendant will have to pay more than he should?

2. **Survival of wrongful death claims.** Granted a primary claim for injury should survive to the injured person's estate, should the wrongful death claim also survive? Holding with the *Chavez* decision, the court in *Bemenderfer v. Williams*, 745 N.E.2d 212 (Ind. 2001), thought that the tortfeasor should not get a windfall merely because the wrongful death beneficiary dies before judgment is rendered in the wrongful death action. It also suggested that a refusal to recognize survival of the wrongful death action might give tortfeasors and their insurers "an incentive for tortfeasors and their insurers to stall litigation in the hopes that the beneficiary will die before judgment."

3. **Claims by non-custodial parents for a child's death.** What legal problems with the death of a minor child? Where parents of a minor child are divorced, and one of them has custody of the child and the other has only "visitation rights," should the non-custodial parent be denied any wrongful death recovery? *Compare Sindelar v. Leguia*, 750 A.2d 967 (R.I. 2000) (granting half of a wrongful death recovery to each parent), *with Carter v. Beaver*, 577 So.2d 448 (Ala. 1991) (giving entire award to custodial parent). What if part of the award or settlement is based on contributions the deceased would have made to support the non-custodial parent in later years, or on loss of consortium of the non-custodial parent?

4. **Stepchildren.** Most courts interpreting statutes that allow "heirs" or "children" to recover have held that stepchildren do not qualify. *See, e.g., Klossner v. San Juan County*, 605 P.2d 330 (Wash. 1980) (based on statute that failed to specify "stepchildren" or to define "children" as including "stepchildren"); *Steed v. Imperial Airlines*, 524 P.2d 801 (Cal. 1974) (stepchild not an "heir" under the statute). The California legislature responded to *Steed* by amending its Civil Procedure Code § 377 to provide that minors living with the decedent for six months or more and receiving more than half their support from decedent could recover for wrongful death.

5. **Unmarried cohabitants.** Under statutes that distribute damages to heirs, or to named categories, such as "surviving spouse" or "children," there is obviously no room for compensation to the surviving friend or lover. *See, e.g., Langan v. St. Vincent's Hosp. of New York*, 802 N.Y.S.2d 476 (App. Div. 2005) (surviving partner of same-sex civil union not a "surviving spouse" under statute). Vermont's statute specifically affords same-sex couples the same rights as married couples, specifically including the right to sue for wrongful death. *See* 15 VT. STAT. §§ 1204(a) & 1204(e)(2). A California statute provides that unmarried domestic partners have standing to sue for wrongful death. CAL. CIV. PROC. CODE § 377.60, but except for certain elderly persons, that includes only persons of the "same sex." *See* CAL. FAM. CODE § 297.

6. **Jury awards.** Along with distributional defects in the statutory wrongful death schemes, there are problems in jury awards. Studies show that

jurors award much larger sums to the female spouse of a male decedent than to the male spouse of a female decedent, even when their earnings are the same. *See* Goodman, Loftus, Miller & Greene, *Money, Sex, and Death: Gender Bias in Wrongful Death Damage Awards*, 25 L. & SOC'Y REV. 263 (1991). Female decedents are worth less? Or female survivors need more? Is the disparity justified under either hypothesis?

NOTE: DEFENSES

1. *Decedent's contributory negligence or assumed risk.* The rule under most death statutes is that the action could be brought for wrongful death only if the decedent could have sued had he lived. This language obviously means that the defendant is not liable unless he is guilty of conduct that would be tortious toward some individual.

It is sometimes argued, however, that the wrongful death action, always in theory a "new and independent action" for the protection of survivors, should be permitted in spite of the contributory negligence of the decedent. The survivors, it is argued, were guilty of no misconduct, and the defendant should not escape liability to these innocent victims of his wrongful conduct. Is this a sound argument? Most courts treat the decedent's contributory fault as a defense. *See Horwich v. Superior Court*, 980 P.2d 927 (Cal. 1999). In comparative fault systems, that means the damages in the wrongful death suit will be reduced by the percentage of fault attributable to the decedent. *E.g., Adamy v. Ziriakus*, 704 N.E.2d 216 (N.Y. 1998).

2. *Beneficiary's contributory negligence or assumed risk.* (a) *Survival claims.* Under survival statutes, the decedent's own claim is being pursued, not a claim for beneficiaries. This point is emphasized by the form of the claim, which is a suit by the estate of the decedent, with proceeds payable to the estate. The fact that an heir was guilty of contributory negligence will be of no direct relevance, even though the heir will inherit the estate, including the survival action recovery. However, in a joint and several liability system, the defendant may obtain contribution from the negligent heir, thus negating his recovery. The same result may be achieved in a several liability system in which each tortfeasor is responsible only for a percentage of damages equal to his percentage of fault.

(b) *Wrongful death claims.* If there was but one beneficiary, and he was guilty of contributory negligence, the common law rule barred his recovery for wrongful death. Where there were several beneficiaries, some guilty of contributory negligence and some not, a number of courts took the view that contributory negligence should not bar the entire death claim, but should bar only the claim of the negligent beneficiary. The comparative fault system seems to make this an easy case. Either by reducing damages or by contribution, the defendant can eliminate liability for the percentage share attributable to any negligent beneficiary. *See* DOBBS ON TORTS § 299 (2000).

3. *Statutes of limitations.* Albert Weinberg was exposed to asbestos from 1941 to 1948. In 1975 a mesothelioma, or lung cancer, was discover-

ed. This allegedly resulted from the asbestos exposure. Mr. Weinberg brought no action during his life and he died in 1977. Thereafter an action for his death was brought within two years. The death act prescribes two years from death as the limitation period. Is the claim nevertheless barred on the ground that no action for death can be brought unless the decedent could have maintained an action at the same time had he lived? Some courts have taken this view. *See Russell v. Ingersoll–Rand Co.*, 841 S.W.2d 343 (Tex. 1992); *Edwards v. Fogarty,* 962 P.2d 879 (Wyo. 1998); *Chomic v. United States*, 377 F.3d 607 (6th Cir. 2004) (Michigan law). But many cases hold that the statute begins running at the time of death and that the death claim is not barred even if the decedent would be barred had he lived. *E.g., Chapman v. Cardiac Pacemakers, Inc.*, 673 P.2d 385 (Idaho 1983).

4. *Discovery rule.* Courts are divided and uncertain whether the discovery rule applies in wrongful death actions. *See* DOBBS ON TORTS § 300. What if the decedent never discovered the defendant's tort and the family reasonably fails to discover it for four years after the decedent's death?

5. Try your hand: Given the logic and purpose of the survival claim, how should the statute of limitations work?

6. *Damages caps.* Many states have a statutory cap on noneconomic damages in medical malpractice cases. If a doctor's negligence results in a wrongful death, should the damages cap be applied in the wrongful death case? *See Jenkins v. Patel*, 684 N.W.2d 346 (Mich. 2004) (yes); *Bartholomew v. Wisconsin Patient's Compensation Fund*, 717 N.W.2d 216 (Wis. 2006) (no).

REFERENCE: DOBBS ON TORTS §§ 294–301 (2000).

PART 4

THE EBB AND FLOW OF COMMON LAW STRICT LIABILITY FOR PHYSICAL HARMS

▪ ▪ ▪

In the materials covered so far, fault has been the keynote concept in liability. We now consider three areas involving complete or partial strict liability.

In the last chapter in this part, Chapter 24, the topic is products liability. Products liability law sometimes (but not always) imposes liability without fault upon manufacturers and distributors of defective products, even when the manufacturer or distributor is not negligent.

In Chapter 23 we will see older forms of strict liability, those associated with certain problems of neighboring landowners and those associated with especially hazardous activities that tend to cause harm even when not carried out negligently.

In the first chapter in this part, Chapter 22, we renew acquaintance with an idea introduced at the very beginning of the course—vicarious liability, which can be perceived as a limited form of strict liability in which one person or entity is held legally responsible for the fault-based torts of another.

CHAPTER 22

VICARIOUS LIABILITY

■ ■ ■

§ 1. RESPONDEAT SUPERIOR AND SCOPE OF EMPLOYMENT

We recognized early in the course that employers could be held liable for the torts of certain employees, provided those torts were committed within the scope of employment. This principle of liability is often called vicarious liability or the *respondeat superior* principle.

What is meant by the limitation that torts must be committed within the scope of employment? To a large extent the answer to this question turns on a much larger one—why hold the employer liable at all? The employer is not personally at fault, so that his liability is in a sense a kind of strict liability. One case summarized the goals of vicarious liability succinctly as (a) the prevention of future injuries, (b) the assurance of compensation to victims, and (c) the equitable spreading of losses caused by an enterprise. *See Lisa M. v. Henry Mayo Newhall Mem. Hosp.*, 907 P.2d 358 (Cal. 1995).

RIVIELLO v. WALDRON, 391 N.E.2d 1278 (N.Y. 1979). Waldron, employed as a cook at the Pot Belly Pub, a Bronx bar and grill, was talking to a customer and flipping an open knife. This accidentally struck the customer in the eye, causing a loss of its use. The customer sued the bar owner. *Held*, the bar owner is liable; Waldron was within the scope of employment. The scope of employment was originally defined narrowly "on the theory that the employer could exercise close control over his employees during the period of their service." But "social policy has wrought a measure of relaxation of the traditional confines of the doctrine." Reasons for this are that "the average innocent victim, when relegated to the pursuit of his claim against the employee, most often will face a defendant too impecunious to meet the claim, and that modern economic devices, such as cost accounting and insurance coverage, permit most employers to spread the impact of such costs. So no longer is an employer necessarily excused merely because his employees, acting in furtherance of his interests, exhibit human failings and perform negligently or otherwise than in an authorized manner. Instead, the test has come to be whether the act was done while the servant was doing his master's work, no matter how irregularly, or with what disregard of instructions."

FRUIT v. SCHREINER, 502 P.2d 133 (Alaska 1972). Fruit, a life insurance salesman, was at a convention where his employer required him to be. This involved social as well as business events. After business activities were over one evening, he drove to a bar, hoping to find some colleagues, found none and drove back to the convention center. It was 2:00 a.m. He skidded and struck Schreiner, whose legs were crushed. *Held*, Fruit was within the scope of his employment. "The basis of *respondeat superior* has been correctly stated as the desire to include in the costs of operation inevitable losses to third persons incident to carrying on an enterprise, and thus distribute the burden among those benefitted by the enterprise.... Insurance is readily available for the employer so that the risk may be distributed among many like insured paying premiums and the extra cost of doing business may be reflected in the price of the product."

NOTES

1. The employer's vicarious liability does not exclude liability of the employee. The plaintiff may sue the employee directly, either alone or joined with the employer. If the employer is held liable because of the employee's negligence, the employer has a theoretical right to indemnity from the employee. That right is seldom asserted, partly because the employer's liability insurance is likely to protect both employer and employee. Are the New York and Alaska Courts in *Riviello* and *Fruit* giving the same reasons for expansive liability of an employer? Is either court simply using the theory that the employer represents a "deep pocket"?

2. The *Riviello* court notes that vicarious liability may be found even where the employee disregards the employer's instructions in committing the injurious act. The general rule is that "the employer's vicarious liability extends to the negligent, willful, malicious, or even criminal acts of its employees when such acts are committed within the scope of the employment." *Adames v. Sheahan*, 880 N.E.2d 559 (Ill. App. Ct. 2007); *see also Farmers Ins. Group v. County of Santa Clara*, 906 P.2d 440 (Cal. 1995). The "true test ... is whether at the time of the commission of the injury the employee was performing a service in the furtherance of his employer's business, not whether it was done in exact observance of the detail prescribed by the employer." *Ohio Farmers Ins. Co. v. Norman*, 594 P.2d 1026 (Ariz. Ct. App. 1979). Some courts find no vicarious liability where the act is "too little actuated by a purpose to serve the master." *See Doe v. Newbury Bible Church*, 933 A.2d 196 (Vt. 2007).

3. What reasons can you give for holding an employer liable for the employee's negligence in causing harm to others?

4. Is it clear that Fruit's employer got any benefit, actual or expected, in his trip to the bar?

NOTE: ENTERPRISE LIABILITY

As reflected in *Fruit*, the concept of enterprise liability is often close to the surface of any strict liability analysis. In his groundbreaking book, *The Costs of Accidents* (1970), Professor (now Judge) Guido Calabresi urged that tort law's principal function is to reduce the costs of accidents and the costs of avoiding them. We will see Calabresi's ideas in some more depth in Chapter 24, but some of his central conceptions are worth thinking about here.

One idea is that the price of goods and activities should accurately reflect the accident costs they cause. Holding an enterprise strictly liable for harms it causes facilitates this "internalization of costs," which in turn reduces the costs of accidents. How are accident costs reduced? Consumers are influenced by prices. If the price of a particular product or service actually reflects its total costs, including accident costs, the market will tend to favor the cheaper (safer) product or service. Companies will thus have an incentive to make their products and activities safer to compete in the marketplace. Do these ideas support holding an employer strictly liable for the torts of its employees, committed within the scope of employment?

How well does enterprise liability theory mix with accountability for fault? If there is a good reason to hold an employer strictly liable in these cases, why not hold all employers liable, regardless of employee negligence, when an act within the scope of employment causes harm?

NOTE: SERVING TWO MASTERS

1. *Borrowed servants.* Where one employer "loans" one of its employees to another employer and that employee negligently injures someone, which of the "employers" is vicariously liable? This problem is known as the "borrowed servant" situation. The Restatement (Third) of Agency suggests that liability depends upon which "employer is in the better position to take measures to prevent the injury suffered," looking at which employer "has a right to control an employee's conduct." RESTATE-MENT (THIRD) OF AGENCY § 7.03, cmt. *d(2)* (2006). The traditional approach is that the first employer is vicariously liable, while the "borrowing" employer is not, unless evidence leads to a different conclusion based on who has the right to "control" the servant. *See, e.g., Jones v. James Reeves Contractors, Inc.,* 690 So.2d 1166 (Miss. 1997). Some authority holds both employers liable if the employee is acting within the scope of his employment for both masters simultaneously. *See Kastner v. Toombs,* 611 P.2d 62 (Alaska 1980).

2. *Captain of the ship doctrine.* Suppose nurses are employed by a hospital. A surgeon is permitted to use a hospital for an operation and the hospital furnishes nurses. At the end of the operation, the doctor removes the sponges and the nurses count them. If the nurses negligently counted and sponges are allowed to remain in the body, is the doctor vicariously liable under the borrowed servant doctrine? A few cases have said that the

doctor is the "captain of the ship" or that the nurses have become the doctor's special employees. Others say it is a question of fact whether the doctor was actually giving directions and exercising control over the nurses.

3. *The police officer problem.* Suppose a full-time city police officer is working at the D–Mart Discount store as a security guard when he is off-duty. In the course of his work at D–Mart, he uses his police pistol to shoot the plaintiff after a scuffle. The plaintiff alleges that the shooting was negligent or alternatively that it was intentional and unprivileged. Can the plaintiff state a prima facie case against the city, D–Mart, or both? Be sure to distinguish the borrowed servant scenario. In formulating your answer, do you think it would matter whether police officers are always under a obligation, even when off-duty, to enforce the law as to violations occurring in their presence? *See Lovelace v. Anderson,* 785 A.2d 726 (Md. 2001); *White v. Revco Disc. Drug Ctrs., Inc.,* 33 S.W.3d 713 (Tenn. 2000).

NOTE: SERVING GRATUITOUSLY

1. We've been referring to employers and employees, or in the old language of the law, masters and servants. The relationship of master and servant can be established without payment or promise of payment. RESTATEMENT (THIRD) OF AGENCY §§ 1.01, cmt. *d* & 7.07(3)(b). However, that relationship is not established unless the putative servant submits himself to the control of the employer. ID. A church member might accept unpaid duties of delivering cookies to shut-ins for a church program. If the church expects him to act on its behalf and he submits to the church's directions, he is a servant. Absent an immunity, the church is therefore liable if he negligently runs someone down while delivering cookies. *Trinity Lutheran Church, Inc. of Evansville, Ind. v. Miller,* 451 N.E.2d 1099 (Ind. Ct. App. 1983).

2. What about the person who voluntarily assists another, without such submission? *See Austin v. Kaness,* 950 P.2d 561 (Wyo. 1997) (adult son feeding cats while parents were away does not become an agent, servant or employee of parents).

HINMAN v. WESTINGHOUSE ELECTRIC CO.

471 P.2d 988 (Cal. 1970)

PETERS, JUSTICE.

Plaintiff, a Los Angeles policeman, was standing on the center divider of a freeway inspecting a possible road hazard when he was struck by a car driven by Frank Allen Herman, an employee of defendant Westinghouse. As a result of the accident he received permanent injuries. The city paid his medical expenses and disability pension. [In a suit against Westinghouse, the jury found for the defendant.]

At the time of the accident, Herman was employed by Westinghouse as an elevator constructor's helper and was returning home from work from a job site. He had been working for Westinghouse for about four months. His work was assigned from the Westinghouse office. He did not go to the office before or after work but instead went from home directly to the job site and after work returned home from the job site. The particular job on which Herman was working was not completed at the time of the accident, and he would ordinarily return to the job site until the job was completed or he was told not to return.

The union contracts under which Herman worked provided for the payment of "carfare" and travel time in certain circumstances depending on the location of the job site in relation to the Los Angeles City Hall. As to this job, which was 15 to 20 miles from the city hall, Herman received an hour and a half per day as his roundtrip travel time and $1.30 for his travel expense. The employer had no control over the method or route of transportation used by Herman.

The trial judge refused instructions that Herman was acting within the scope of his employment at the time of the accident and instead instructed the jury that whether he was acting within the scope of his employment depended upon a number of factors including among others "whether his conduct was authorized by his employer, either expressly or impliedly; the nature of the employment, its object and the duties imposed thereby; whether the employee was acting in his discharge thereof; whether his conduct occurred during the performance of services for the benefit of the employer, either directly or indirectly, or of himself; whether his conduct, even though not expressly or impliedly authorized, was an incidental event connected with his assigned work...." [So instructed, the jury found that Herman was not within the scope of his employment and hence gave a verdict for Westinghouse.]

Although earlier authorities sought to justify the *respondeat superior* doctrine on such theories as "control" by the master of the servant, the master's "privilege" in being permitted to employ another, the third party's innocence in comparison to the master's selection of the servant, or the master's "deep pocket" to pay for the loss, "the modern justification for vicarious liability is a rule of policy, a deliberate allocation of a risk. The losses caused by the torts of employees, which as a practical matter are sure to occur in the conduct of the employer's enterprise, are placed upon that enterprise itself, as a required cost of doing business. They are placed upon the employer because, having engaged in an enterprise which will, on the basis of past experience, involve harm to others through the torts of employees, and sought to profit by it, it is just that he, rather than the innocent injured plaintiff, should bear them; and because he is better able to absorb them, and to distribute them, through prices, rates or liability insurance, to the public, and so to shift them to society, to the community at large." ...

Another leading authority also points out that the modern and proper basis of vicarious liability of the master is not his control or fault but the risks incident to his enterprise. "We are not here looking for the master's fault but rather for risks that may fairly be regarded as typical of or broadly incidental to the enterprise he has undertaken...."

Liability of the employer may not be avoided on the basis of the "going and coming" rule. Under the "going and coming" rule, an employee going to and from work is ordinarily considered outside the scope of employment so that the employer is not liable for his torts. The "going and coming" rule is sometimes ascribed to the theory that the employment relationship is "suspended" from the time the employee leaves until he returns or that in commuting he is not rendering service to his employer. Nevertheless, there are exceptions to the rule.

Thus in Harvey v. D & L Construction Co., the court reversed a nonsuit for the employer where it was shown that because of the remote site of the construction project, the employer had asked the employee to recruit other employees, one such employee was riding at the time of the accident, and the employer was furnishing the gas for the trip to the employee's home....

The above cases indicate that exceptions will be made to the "going and coming" rule where the trip involves an incidental benefit to the employer, not common to commute trips by ordinary members of the work force. The cases also indicate that the fact that the employee receives personal benefits is not determinative when there is also a benefit to the employer.

There is a substantial benefit to an employer in one area to be permitted to reach out to a labor market in another area or to enlarge the available labor market by providing travel expenses and payment for travel time. It cannot be denied that the employer's reaching out to the distant or larger labor market increases the risk of injury in transportation. In other words, the employer, having found it desirable in the interests of his enterprise to pay for travel time and for travel expenses and to go beyond the normal labor market or to have located his enterprise at a place remote from the labor market, should be required to pay for the risks inherent in his decision.

We are satisfied that, where, as here, the employer and employee have made the travel time part of the working day by their contract, the employer should be treated as such during the travel time, and it follows that so long as the employee is using the time for the designated purpose, to return home, the doctrine of *respondeat superior* is applicable. It is unnecessary to determine the appropriate rule to be applied if the employee had used the time for other purposes. We also need not decide now whether the mere payment of travel expenses without additional payment for the travel time of the employee ... reflects a sufficient benefit to the employer so that he should bear responsibility to innocent third parties for the risks inherent in the travel.

The facts relating to the applicability of the doctrine of *respondeat superior* are undisputed in the instant case, and we conclude that as a matter of law the doctrine is applicable and that the trial court erred in its instructions in leaving the issue as one of fact to the jury. . . .

NOTE

Hinman verbally accepted an enterprise liability theory of vicarious liability—that the cost of injuries inflicted by employees "are placed upon the employer because, having engaged in an enterprise which will, on the basis of past experience, involve harm to others through the torts of employees, and sought to profit by it, it is just that he, rather than the innocent injured plaintiff, should bear them." New Jersey has recently refused to consider this approach, giving heavy emphasis to control by and/or benefit to the employer instead. *See O'Toole v. Carr*, 815 A.2d 471 (N.J. 2003). Did *Hinman* itself really rely on the enterprise liability theory or did it turn mainly on the supposed benefit to the employer?

FAUL v. JELCO, INC., 595 P.2d 1035 (Ariz. Ct. App. 1979). Employee, a construction worker, lived in Winslow, but for the duration of the construction stayed during the week in a trailer near Oracle Junction. During the week he drove from the trailer to a "show up" location, and was then transported from there to the actual job site. He went home to Winslow one weekend, carrying with him the tools he was required to have on the job. Early on Monday, he drove back toward Oracle Junction and was only three miles away when he crossed the center line and struck the plaintiff's vehicle. He was paid an hourly wage. Because of the remote location of the job site he was "paid zone pay, an increased hourly wage, but no separate compensation for travel time, travel expenses or per diem living expenses. . . ." The trial judge granted summary judgment in favor of the employer. *Held*, affirmed. "As a general rule, an employee is not within the scope of employment while commuting to or from work. One exception to this rule is recognized when travel to and from work involves special hazards. . . . [But authority] rejects the claim that distance alone constitutes a special hazard. A second exception to the going and coming rule is the dual purpose doctrine. . . . The dual purpose exception applies when in addition to merely commuting, the employee performs a concurrent service for his employer that would have necessitated a trip by another employee if the commuting employee had not been able to perform it while commuting." But in this case he was carrying tools "solely for personal reasons." The plaintiff attempts to claim a dual purpose based on *Hinman v. Westinghouse Electric Co.*, supra, on the theory that it served the employer's purpose to "reach out" into distant labor markets. "Because *Hinman* adopted a risk justification for respondeat superior, in contrast to the control justification applied in Arizona, we are uncertain whether the *Hinman* rule would apply in Arizona. We need not decide that question, however, because the *Hinman* court restricts its holding to cases where the employer compensates the employee for both travel expenses and travel time. In this case, the employee was not directly compensated for either."

AHLSTROM v. SALT LAKE CITY CORP., 73 P.3d 315 (Utah 2003). Plaintiff was allegedly injured in a collision with a negligently-driven marked police vehicle. Ross, the officer driving it, was on her way home from work. Officers were permitted to use the marked cars coming and going if they paid a small fee and agreed to be on call on such occasions. On the vicarious liability of the city, the plaintiff argued the dual purpose exception. *Held,* partial summary judgment for the plaintiff on the vicarious liability issue was error. "The major premise of the 'going and coming' rule is that it is unfair to impose unlimited liability on an employer for conduct of its employees over which it has no control and from which it derives no benefit. This does not mean that if the employer derives *any* benefit or exercises *any* control over the conduct it will be liable. Rather, where an employee engages in conduct benefitting the employer or which is controlled by the employer, we weigh the benefit and control against the personal nature of the trip.... Although the City received some benefit from Ross's trip home from work on the day of her accident, the facts before the trial court were not sufficient to make that benefit the predominant purpose of Ross's trip.... There is no indication the City would have sent any one else on the trip had Ross not gone."

NOTES

1. **Exceptions to the going and coming rule.** Suppose the employer requires the employee to use her own car to visit clients as part of her work and that, after leaving the last client's office for the day and starting home, the employee negligently injures the plaintiff. Going and coming rule or a special exception? In *Carter v. Reynolds,* 815 A.2d 460 (N.J. 2003), the court said: "*[R]espondeat superior* has been held to apply to a situation involving commuting when: (1) the employee is engaged in a special errand or mission on the employer's behalf; (2) the employer requires the employee to drive his or her personal vehicle to work so that the vehicle may be used for work-related tasks; and (3) the employee is 'on-call.' "

2. **Factual variations.** Factual variations on the going and coming rule are numerous. For example, the employee might be on an off-premises lunch break when the tort is committed, or a police officer or firefighter who is off duty but "on call," or an employee on his day off but checking on information he will need on the job when he gets into a deadly drag race.

3. **Frolic and detour.** A special factual category involves the employee who, during working hours, goes to a place not associated with employment for a purpose not associated with employment. The employee is instructed to deliver furniture to a town 30 miles north. After she has driven on the road 15 miles she turns to the east, intending to drive two miles in that direction to have a beer with a friend. She has a collision at a point one mile from the highway where she was supposed to be. Was she outside the employment and on a "frolic of her own," or merely on a "detour?" If the court characterizes the departure as a "mere detour," as in cases of trivial departures from the

job, the employer will remain liable. If instead the court sees this as a frolic (as some courts say "a personal mission"), then there is no vicarious liability. *See Nulle v. Krewer*, 872 N.E.2d 567 (Ill. App. Ct. 2007).

4. **Reentry into employment.** Suppose the employee sees her friend and starts back to the main highway and has a second collision at the same spot, but this time headed back to work? At what point has the employee reentered employment? "First, the employee must have formulated an intent to act in furtherance of the employer's business; second, the intent must be coupled with a reasonable connection in time and space with the work in which he should be engaged." *Prince v. Atchison, Topeka & Santa Fe Ry.*, 395 N.E.2d 592 (Ill. App. Ct. 1979). *See also* Restatement (Third) of Agency § 7.07, cmt. *e* (2006) (a frolic ends "when an employee is once again performing assigned work and taking actions incidental to it," or when an employee "has taken action consistent with once again resuming work").

EDGEWATER MOTELS, INC. v. GATZKE

277 N.W.2d 11 (Minn. 1979)

Scott, Justice.

[Gatzke, a district manager for Walgreen's, stayed in plaintiff's motel while he was in Duluth, Minnesota supervising the opening of a Walgreen-owned restaurant. The motel was damaged by fire, allegedly the result of Gatzke's negligence while in his motel room. The motel's claim here is against both Gatzke and his employer.]

[Gatzke] lived at the Edgewater at the company's expense. While in Duluth, Gatzke normally would arise at 6:00 a.m. and work at the restaurant from about 7:00 a.m. to 12:00 or 1:00 a.m. In addition to working at the restaurant, Gatzke remained on call 24 hours per day to handle problems arising in other Walgreen restaurants located in his district. Gatzke thought of himself as a "24–hour-a-day man." He received calls from other Walgreen restaurants in his district when problems arose. He was allowed to call home at company expense. His laundry, living expenses, and entertainment were items of reimbursement. There were no constraints as to where he would perform his duties or at what time of day they would be performed. . . .

[Around midnight or after, Gatzke left the work with others on the job; some went to their hotel rooms, but Gatzke and Hubbard went to the Bellows restaurant for a drink.]

In about an hour's time Gatzke consumed a total of four brandy Manhattans, three of which were "doubles." While at the Bellows, Gatzke and Hubbard spent part of the time discussing the operation of the newly-opened Walgreen restaurant. Additionally, Gatzke and the Bellows' bartender talked a little about the mixing and pricing of drinks. The testimony showed that Gatzke was interested in learning the bar business because the new Walgreen restaurant served liquor.

Between 1:15 and 1:30 a.m. Gatzke and Hubbard left the Bellows and walked back to the Edgewater. Witnesses testified that Gatzke acted normal and appeared sober. Gatzke went directly to his motel room, and then "probably" sat down at a desk to fill out his expense account because "that was [his] habit from traveling so much." The completion of the expense account had to be done in accordance with detailed instructions, and if the form was not filled out properly it would be returned to the employee unpaid. It took Gatzke no more than five minutes to fill out the expense form.

While Gatzke completed the expense account he "probably" smoked a cigarette. The record indicates Gatzke smoked about two packages of cigarettes per day. A maid testified that the ash trays in Gatzke's room would generally be full of cigarette butts and ashes when she cleaned the room. She also noticed at times that the plastic wastebasket next to the desk contained cigarette butts.

After filling out the expense account Gatzke went to bed, and soon thereafter a fire broke out. Gatzke escaped from the burning room, but the fire spread rapidly and caused extensive damage to the motel. The amount of damages was stipulated by the parties at $330,360.

One of plaintiff's expert witnesses, Dr. Ordean Anderson, a fire reconstruction specialist, testified that the fire started in, or next to, the plastic wastebasket located to the side of the desk in Gatzke's room. He also stated that the fire was caused by a burning cigarette or match. After the fire, the plastic wastebasket was a melted "blob." Dr. Anderson stated that X-ray examination of the remains of the basket disclosed the presence of cigarette filters and paper matches.

[The jury found Gatzke to be guilty of 60% of the negligence and the motel guilty of the remainder. The trial judge concluded, however, that Gatzke was not within the scope of his employment, and rendered judgment N.O.V. for Walgreen's.]

To support a finding that an employee's negligent act occurred within his scope of employment, it must be shown that his conduct was, to some degree, in furtherance of the interests of his employer. This principle is recognized by Restatement, Agency 2d, § 235, which states:

> An act of a servant is not within the scope of employment if it is done with no intention to perform it as a part of or incident to a service on account of which he is employed.

Other factors to be considered in the scope of employment determination are whether the conduct is of the kind that the employee is authorized to perform and whether the act occurs substantially within authorized time and space restrictions. No hard and fast rule can be applied to resolve the "scope of employment" inquiry. Rather, each case must be decided on its own individual facts.

The initial question raised by the instant factual situation is whether an employee's smoking of a cigarette can constitute conduct within his scope of employment. This issue has not been dealt with by this court. The courts which have considered the question have not agreed on its resolution. A number of courts which have dealt with the instant issue have ruled that the act of smoking, even when done simultaneously with work-related activity, is not within the employee's scope of employment because it is a matter personal to the employee which is not done in furtherance of the employer's interest.

Other courts which have considered the question have reasoned that the smoking of a cigarette, if done while engaged in the business of the employer, is within an employee's scope of employment because it is a minor deviation from the employee's work-related activities, and thus merely an act done incidental to general employment.

For example, in Wood v. Saunders, a gas station attendant negligently threw his lighted cigarette across an automobile's fuel tank opening while he was filling the vehicle with gasoline. The court, in finding this act to be within the employee's scope of employment, stated:

> In the case at bar, there was no abandonment by the employee of the master's purposes and business while the employee was smoking and carrying the lighted cigarette. There was merely a combining by the employee, with the carrying out of the master's purposes, of an incidental and contemporaneous carrying out of the employee's private purposes. . . .

The question of whether smoking can be within an employee's scope of employment is a close one, but after careful consideration of the issue we are persuaded by the reasoning of the courts which hold that smoking can be an act within an employee's scope of employment. It seems only logical to conclude that an employee does not abandon his employment as a matter of law while temporarily acting for his personal comfort when such activities involve only slight deviations from work that are reasonable under the circumstances, such as eating, drinking, or smoking. . . .

We . . . hereby hold that an employer can be held vicariously liable for his employee's negligent smoking of a cigarette [if] he was otherwise acting in the scope of his employment at the time of the negligent act. . . . It appears that the district court felt that Gatzke was outside the scope of his employment while he was at the Bellows, and thus was similarly outside his scope of employment when he returned to his room to fill out his expense account. The record, however, contains a reasonable basis from which a jury could find that Gatzke was involved in serving his employer's interests at the time he was at the bar. Gatzke testified that, while at the Bellows, he discussed the operation of the newly-opened Walgreen's restaurant with Hubbard. Also, the bartender stated that on that night "[a] few times we [Gatzke and the bartender] would talk about his business and my business, how to make drinks, prices."

But more importantly, even assuming that Gatzke was outside the scope of his employment while he was at the bar, there is evidence from which a jury could reasonably find that Gatzke resumed his employment activities after he returned to his motel room and filled out his expense account. The expense account was, of course, completed so that Gatzke could be reimbursed by Walgreen's for his work-related expenses. In this sense, Gatzke is performing an act for his own personal benefit. However, the completion of the expense account also furthers the employer's business in that it provides detailed documentation of business expenses so that they are properly deductible for tax purposes. In this light, the filling out of the expense form can be viewed as serving a dual purpose; that of furthering Gatzke's personal interests and promoting his employer's business purposes. Accordingly, it is reasonable for the jury to find that the completion of the expense account is an act done in furtherance of the employer's business purposes.

Additionally, the record indicates that Gatzke was an executive type of employee who had no set working hours. He considered himself a 24-hour-a-day man; his room at the Edgewater Motel was his "office away from home." It was therefore also reasonable for the jury to determine that the filling out of his expense account was done within authorized time and space limits of his employment.

In light of the above, we hold that it was reasonable for the jury to find that Gatzke was acting within the scope of his employment when he completed his expense account. Accordingly, we set aside the trial court's grant of judgment for Walgreen's and reinstate the jury's determination that Gatzke was working within the scope of his employment at the time of his negligent act. . . .

NOTES

1. **Other issues?** Once the judges determined that Gatzke was acting within the time and place limits of his employment, was there any other issue? Does the issue resemble the issue of legal cause or scope of the risk?

2. **Temporary deviations.** The *Gatzke* court is not alone in finding that an employer may be held vicariously liable for an employee's actions in doing something "necessary to the comfort, convenience, health and welfare of the employee while at work, though strictly personal and not acts of service," as long as the employee is either "combining his own business with that of the employer, or attending to both at substantially the same time." *Farmers Ins. Group v. County of Santa Clara*, 906 P.2d 440 (Cal. 1995). *See also* RESTATEMENT (THIRD) OF AGENCY § 7.07, cmt. *d* (2006) ("Purely personal acts" such as "personal hygiene, smoking, and eating may be within the scope of employment because they are incidental to the employee's performance of assigned work."). Do you see adjudicative problems if that were not the rule?

LISA M. v. HENRY MAYO NEWHALL MEMORIAL HOSPITAL

907 P.2d 358 (Cal. 1995)

WERDEGAR, ASSOCIATE JUSTICE. . . .

[The plaintiff, 19-years-old and pregnant, was injured in a fall and sought treatment at Hospital's emergency room. At the direction of the examining physicians, ultrasound technician Bruce Wayne Tripoli performed obstetrical and upper-right-quadrant ultrasonic imaging examinations. Tripoli then, on the pretense that additional testing was appropriate, scanned the plaintiff's pubic area, and inserted the ultra sound wand and then his fingers into her vagina. When the plaintiff discovered from her obstetrician that this procedure was not proper, she sued Tripoli and the hospital. The trial court granted summary judgment to the defendant hospital; the Court of Appeal reversed.]

It is clear, first of all, that California no longer follows the traditional rule that an employee's actions are within the scope of employment only if motivated, in whole or part, by a desire to serve the employer's interests. (*See* Rest.2d Agency, § 228, subd. 1(c) [conduct must be "actuated, at least in part, by a purpose to serve the master"].)

In Carr, this court held a building contractor liable for injuries caused when an employee, angry at a subcontractor's employee for interfering in his work, threw a hammer at the other worker's head. We rejected the defendant's claim its employee was not acting within the scope of employment because he "could not have intended by his conduct to further" the employer's interests: "It is sufficient, however, if the injury resulted from a dispute arising out of the employment.... It is not necessary that the assault should have been made as a means, or for the purpose of performing the work he (the employee) was employed to do." ...

While the employee thus need not have intended to further the employer's interests, the employer will not be held liable for an assault or other intentional tort that did not have a causal nexus to the employee's work. "If an employee inflicts an injury out of personal malice, not engendered by the employment, the employer is not liable." ...

Because an intentional tort gives rise to respondeat superior liability only if it was engendered by the employment, our disavowal of motive as a singular test of respondeat superior liability does not mean the employee's motive is irrelevant. An act serving only the employee's personal interest is less likely to arise from or be engendered by the employment than an act that, even if misguided, was intended to serve the employer in some way....

Respondeat superior liability should apply only to the types of injuries that are "as a practical matter are sure to occur in the conduct of the employer's enterprise." The employment, in other words, must be such as predictably to create the risk employees will commit intentional torts of the type for which liability is sought.

In what has proved an influential formulation, the court in Rodgers v. Kemper Constr. Co., supra, 50 Cal.App.3d at page 618, 124 Cal. Rptr. 143, held the tortious occurrence must be "a generally foreseeable consequence of the activity." ... The Rodgers foreseeability test is useful "because it reflects the central justification for respondeat superior [liability]: that losses fairly attributable to an enterprise—those which foreseeably result from the conduct of the enterprise—should be allocated to the enterprise as a cost of doing business."

Was Tripoli's sexual battery of Lisa M. within the scope of his employment? The injurious events were causally related to Tripoli's employment as an ultrasound technician in the sense they would not have occurred had he not been so employed. Tripoli's employment as an ultrasound technician provided the opportunity for him to meet plaintiff and to be alone with her in circumstances making the assault possible. The employment was thus one necessary cause of the ensuing tort. But, as previously discussed, in addition to such "but for" causation, respondeat superior liability requires that the risk of the tort have been engendered by, "typical of or broadly incidental to," or, viewed from a somewhat different perspective, "a generally foreseeable consequence of," Hospital's enterprise.

At the broadest level, Hospital argues sex crimes are never foreseeable outgrowths of employment because they, unlike instances of nonsexual violence, are not the product of "normal human traits." ... We are not persuaded that the roots of sexual violence and exploitation are in all cases so fundamentally different from those other abhorrent human traits as to allow a conclusion sexual misconduct is per se unforeseeable in the workplace....

[A] sexual tort will not be considered engendered by the employment unless its motivating emotions were fairly attributable to work-related events or conditions. Here the opposite was true: a technician simply took advantage of solitude with a naive patient to commit an assault for reasons unrelated to his work. Tripoli's job was to perform a diagnostic examination and record the results. The task provided no occasion for a work-related dispute or any other work-related emotional involvement with the patient. The technician's decision to engage in conscious exploitation of the patient did not arise out of the performance of the examination, although the circumstances of the examination made it possible. "If ... the assault was not motivated or triggered off by anything in the employment activity but was the result of only propinquity and lust, there should be no liability."

... Tripoli's criminal actions, of course, were unauthorized by Hospital and were not motivated by any desire to serve Hospital's interests. Beyond that, however, his motivating emotions were not causally attributable to his employment. The flaw in plaintiff's case for Hospital's respondeat superior liability is not so much that Tripoli's actions were personally motivated, but that those personal motivations were not generated by or an outgrowth of workplace responsibilities, conditions or events.

Analysis in terms of foreseeability leads to the same conclusion....

In arguing Tripoli's misconduct was generally foreseeable, plaintiff emphasizes the physically intimate nature of the work Tripoli was employed to perform. In our view, that a job involves physical contact is, by itself, an insufficient basis on which to impose vicarious liability for a sexual assault....

Here, there is no evidence of emotional involvement, either mutual or unilateral, arising from the medical relationship. Although the procedure ordered involved physical contact, it was not of a type that would be expected to, or actually did, give rise to intense emotions on either side. We deal here not with a physician or therapist who becomes sexually involved with a patient as a result of mishandling the feelings predictably created by the therapeutic relationship but with an ultrasound technician who simply took advantage of solitude, access and superior knowledge to commit a sexual assault....

Plaintiff contends the battery in this case, like the police officer's rape of a detainee in Mary M. v. City of Los Angeles, supra, 54 Cal. 3d 202, 285 Cal. Rptr. 99, 814 P.2d 1341, "arose from an abuse of job-created authority." More accurately, Tripoli abused his position of trust, since he had no legal or coercive authority over plaintiff. Assuming an analogy can be fully maintained between authority and trust, Mary M. still provides less than compelling precedent for liability here. In Mary M., we held a police officer's assault was a generally foreseeable consequence of his position. "In view of the considerable power and authority that police officers possess, it is neither startling nor unexpected that on occasion an officer will misuse that authority by engaging in assaultive conduct." ...

While a police officer's assault may be foreseeable from the scope of his unique authority over detainees, we are unable to say the same of an ultrasound technician's assault on a patient. Hospital did not give Tripoli any power to exercise general control over plaintiff's liberty. He was not vested with any coercive authority, and the trust plaintiff was asked to place in him was limited to conduct of an ultrasound examination....

In reaching our conclusion we have consulted the three identified policy goals of the respondeat superior doctrine—preventing future injuries, assuring compensation to victims, and spreading the losses caused by an enterprise equitably—for additional guidance as to whether the doctrine should be applied in these circumstances. In this case, however, we have drawn no firm direction from consideration of the first two policy goals. [Hospital liability might induce precautionary measures but the impact might be destructive rather than beneficial. As to compensation for victims, hospital liability might entail consequential costs that are not clear.]

Third and finally, we attempt to assess the propriety of spreading the risk of losses among the beneficiaries of the enterprise upon which liability would be imposed. As Hospital points out, this assessment is another way of asking whether the employee's conduct was "so unusual or startling that it would seem unfair to include the loss resulting from it among other costs of the employer's business." For reasons already discussed, we conclude the connection between Tripoli's employment duties—to conduct a diagnostic examination—and his independent commission of a deliberate sexual assault was too attenuated, without proof of Hospital's negligence, to support allocation of plaintiff's losses to Hospital as a cost of doing business. Consideration of the respondeat superior doctrine's basis in public policy, therefore, does not alter our conviction that an ultrasound technician's sexual assault on a patient is not a risk predictably created by or fairly attributed to the nature of the technician's employment.

[The judgment of the Court of Appeals is reversed and the matter remanded for other proceedings. Concurring and dissenting opinions omitted.]

RODEBUSH v. OKLAHOMA NURSING HOMES, LTD., 867 P.2d 1241 (Okla. 1993). A nurses' aide at a long-term care facility slapped an elderly resident suffering from Alzheimer's disease. Investigation led the facility to conclude that the aide was intoxicated (it was before 7:30 in the morning). Further investigation showed he had a criminal record of battery with intent to kill. *Held,* the employer is vicariously liable. The employer is not ordinarily liable for the employee's assault upon others. However, this rule does not apply when "the act is one which is fairly and naturally incident to the business, and is done while the servant was engaged upon the master's business and [arises] from some impulse of emotion which naturally grew out of or was incident to the attempt to perform the master's business."

FAHRENDORFF v. NORTH HOMES, INC., 597 N.W.2d 905 (Minn. 1999). The plaintiff was placed temporarily in a group home. A counselor, Kist, was the only adult on a night shift and made sexual advances to her, touching her and speaking to her inappropriately. She sued the owner of the home. *Held,* vicarious liability is a jury question. Evidence indicated that "inappropriate sexual contact or abuse of power in these situations, although infrequent, is a well known hazard" in this kind of enterprise.

NOTES

1. **Caregivers.** Caregivers—those who have undertaken, at least implicitly, to care for the plaintiff who is relatively helpless—may be subject to some special rules of liability. That was most dramatically illustrated in *Ybarra, supra,* Ch. 13, but there are other examples in the traditional liability of innkeepers and carriers and in the rule applied in *Burgess,* supra Chapter 19. Should special obligations of caregivers also affect vicarious liability? Illinois provides by statute that owners and licensees of nursing homes "are liable to a resident for any intentional or negligent act or omission of their agents or employees which injures the resident." 210 ILL. COMP. STAT. 45/3–601. Should such statutes be extended to cover all caregivers?

2. **Two cases: Scout leaders and priests.** In *Lourim v. Swensen,* 977 P.2d 1157 (Or. 1999), the plaintiff alleged that when the plaintiff was a minor,

his Boy Scout leader (Swenson) sexually abused him. *Held*, the Boy Scout organization may be held vicariously liable. A jury could reasonably infer that Swenson's acts "were merely the culmination of a progressive series of actions that involved the ordinary and authorized duties of a Boy Scout leader," that Swenson's performance of his duties "was a necessary precursor to the sexual abuse and that the assaults were a direct outgrowth of and were engendered by conduct that was within the scope of Swensen's employment." Further, it could be inferred that "Swensen's contact with plaintiff was the direct result of the relationship sponsored and encouraged by the Boy Scouts, which invested Swensen with authority to decide how to supervise minor boys under his care."

Accord as to vicarious liability for alleged sexual abuse by a priest who gained the confidence of the minor and his family through pastoral attentions and who was initially focused on carrying out his duties: *Fearing v. Bucher*, 977 P.2d 1163 (Or. 1999) (as alleged, the priest's dutiful acts then led to the acts that injured the plaintiff).

Would these cases necessarily come out differently under the test articulated in *Lisa M.*? Would the Oregon court that decided these cases decide *Lisa M.* differently, do you think?

3. **Trust, authority, and incentive.** As recognized in the cases just discussed, an employee's job may provide a "peculiar opportunity and ... incentive for" misbehavior, which might support vicarious liability. The dissenting justices in *Lisa M.* advanced such a view. Justice Kennard wrote that the job of an ultrasound technician involves "intimate contact, inherent in the job," which put plaintiff in a particularly vulnerable position and "contributed to Tripoli's sexual arousal." Justice Mosk thought that Tripoli's "inspiration arose from the mise-en-scene established by the hospital." Where the employee is placed in a position of trust, such views may have particular force. Should vicarious liability be imposed in any of the following cases?

- A public school teacher arranges special sessions with a student, becoming a tutor and counselor. The teacher then threatens failing grades unless the student engages in sexual acts with the teacher. Should the school district be liable? *John R. v. Oakland Unified Sch. Dist.*, 769 P.2d 948 (Cal. 1989).

- A police officer arrests a woman who is apparently driving under the influence of intoxicants; he then offers kindness by taking her home. Once there, he rapes her. Is the city liable? *Mary M. v. City of Los Angeles*, 814 P.2d 1341 (Cal. 1991); *cf. Cockrell v. Pearl River Valley Water Supply Dist.*, 865 So.2d 357 (Miss. 2004) (officer attempted to kiss woman he had arrested).

- A church encouraged its priests to engage in marriage counseling. One of the priests engaged in illicit sexual activity with one of the marital partners he was counseling. Is the church itself liable for the harm done? *Destefano v. Grabrian*, 763 P.2d 275 (Colo. 1988); *Byrd v. Faber*, 565 N.E.2d 584 (Ohio 1991).

- An employee of a hospital's child daycare facility becomes upset when a baby under her care will not stop crying. The employee allows the infant to roll of a crib onto the floor then intentionally strikes the child's head against a shelf. Is the hospital vicariously liable? *Baker v. Saint Francis Hosp.*, 126 P.3d 602 (Okla. 2005).

- A patient, being tested for neurological problems at the defendant clinic, is told to squeeze an object with her hands behind her back. The object, she alleged, was a "body part" of the doctor. If the doctor employed by the clinic would be liable, is the clinic vicariously liable? *Buck v. Blum,* 130 S.W.3d 285 (Tex. App. 2004).

§ 2. EMPLOYERS WHO ARE NOT MASTERS

DISTRICT OF COLUMBIA v. HAMPTON

666 A.2d 30 (D.C. 1995)

TERRY, ASSOCIATE JUDGE:

[The District of Columbia's Department of Human Services (DHS) removed two-year-old Mykeeda Hampton from her mother's care on the ground that the mother was not properly caring for the child. DHS placed the child in the care of a foster parent, Geraldine Stevenson. Stevenson left Mykeeda with her two sons for over ten hours. During that time Mykeeda was beaten to death by the 12-year-old son. Mykeeda's mother brought this survival action asserting (1) that the DHS was negligent in selecting or supervising Stevenson as a foster parent and (2) that Stevenson was an agent of the DHS so that DHS or the District was vicariously liable. The jury found for the plaintiff. On appeal, the court first concluded that the evidence did not support the first argument, then addressed vicarious liability.]

The District also maintains that Geraldine Stevenson was not its agent but an independent contractor, and thus that any negligence on her part cannot be imputed to it under the doctrine of respondeat superior. . . .

As it relates to foster care, this is an issue of first impression for this court, and one that has not been addressed by many other courts. The trend of recent case law, however, seems to be that foster parents are not deemed to be agents or employees of state family service agencies. . . .

Whether a master-servant (or principal-agent) relationship exists in a given situation "depends on the particular facts of each case." The person asserting the relationship—in this case, Mrs. Hampton—has the burden of proof. This court has recognized several factors to be considered in determining whether such a relationship exists:

(1) the selection and engagement of the servant, (2) the payment of wages, (3) the power to discharge, (4) the power to control the servant's conduct, (5) and whether the work is part of the regular business of the employer.

We have often held, however, that of these five factors "the determinative factor" is usually the fourth: "the right to control an employee in the performance of a task and in its result, and not the actual exercise of control or supervision."

In analyzing the employer's right to control, this court has generally looked to the actual relationship between the parties and, if a written agreement existed between them, to the language of that agreement. For instance, in Safeway Stores, supra, there was evidence of several instances in which Safeway management gave instructions to store security guards, who in turn complied with those instructions. We said that "specific instances of actual control are evidence of the general right of Safeway to control [the security guard] in the performance of his duties." . . .

In this case there was very little testimony about the actual relationship between Mrs. Stevenson and the DHS social workers, and none suggesting that the District had a right to control Stevenson's daily performance of her foster care duties. The testimony of Maria Clark, the DHS social worker assigned to supervise Mykeeda's foster care, did not establish that Mrs. Stevenson took direction from Clark in caring for Mykeeda. For example, on one occasion Stevenson telephoned Clark and said that Mykeeda had developed bruises from being spanked by Stevenson and her son, and from using a plastic potty trainer. Clark testified that she did not go to the Stevenson home to check on Mykeeda, but assumed that Mykeeda "simply . . . bruised easily." . . . In fact, as the District points out, Mrs. Stevenson testified that she controlled many areas of her foster children's lives and that she was responsible for making all the day-to-day decisions about their care: what they would eat, what clothes they would wear, when they needed new clothes, when they would bathe, where they would spend their time, and how they would be disciplined. Without any evidence that DHS actually controlled the manner in which Mrs. Stevenson cared for Mykeeda, no reasonable juror could have found that Mrs. Stevenson was the District's agent.

Mrs. Hampton argues that the many rules and regulations concerning foster homes demonstrate that the District reserved the right to control a foster parent. The list of "basic requirements" for a foster home, implicitly gives the District the right to control such matters as the sleeping arrangements for a foster child, the temperature of the foster home, the diet of the foster child, and certain aspects of the foster parents' health. The District also reserves the right to inspect a foster home at any time. There are rules pertaining to the health care of a foster child, and a foster parent must obtain permission from DHS before taking a foster child on an out-of-town trip. Finally, the District has the right to remove a foster child from the foster home at any time and without prior notice.

These regulations obviously show that the District has the authority to dictate many aspects of a foster child's life in a foster home. But that does not establish that the foster parent is under the actual control of the District to a degree sufficient to make him or her the District's agent. To paraphrase what we said in Giles v. Shell Oil, "the right to inspect" and "the right to set standards by which [a foster parent performs her duties] are not indicia of control. They in no way indicate that [the District] had the right to control the day-to-day operation of the [foster home] or the day-to-day performance of [the foster parent]." For these reasons we hold that the evidence was insufficient to prove that Mrs. Stevenson was the District's agent, and that the trial court therefore erred in allowing Mrs. Hampton's respondeat superior claim to go to the jury.

[Judgment reversed for entry of judgment NOV.]

NOTES

1. **Employer's liability for torts of independent contractor.** Subject to limited exceptions, the rule is that the employer is not vicariously liable for the torts of an independent contractor. The issue arises most commonly in a business setting, in which one person (or business) hires another—the independent contractor—to do some particular work. For example, a sawmill might hire independent contractors who are in the business of cutting and hauling timber to perform those tasks, instead of using its own employees. When an injury is caused by the independent contractor while on the job, the sawmill itself will not be vicariously liable. *See Leaf River Forest Prods., Inc. v. Harrison*, 392 So.2d 1138 (Miss. 1981).

2. **Tests for status as independent contractor.** In determining whether an employee is a servant or an independent contractor, courts have, as in *Hampton,* emphasized the right to control details of the work as a sign that the employee is a servant. *See, e.g., Walderbach v. Archdiocese of Dubuque, Inc.*, 730 N.W.2d 198 (Iowa 2007). *See also* RESTATEMENT (THIRD) OF AGENCY § 7.07(3)(a) (2006). If the employer can only determine what is acceptable as the end result, that is a sign that the employee is an independent contractor. *See, e.g, Anderson v. PPCT Management Systems, Inc.*, 145 P.3d 503 (Alaska 2006). But control is vague and sometimes it just doesn't seem to matter. The medical group or hospital that employs a physician may have no right to control details of his treatment of patients—that would interfere with the doctor-patient relationship—yet remains vicariously responsible for his malpractice. *See Dias v. Brigham Med. Assocs., Inc.*, 780 N.E.2d 447 (Mass. 2002). In addition, control is only one factor. If the employee runs his own business and works for others as well as for the employer, he is not likely to be a servant. If he provides his own tools or uses special skills, that is also likely to indicate that he is an independent contractor. In many cases these rules are easy to apply. Consider: the employee is a house painter you hired to paint your house. After the house is painted he will paint somewhere else.

3. **Structuring relationships by contract.** Employers often attempt to structure relationships with employees so that employees will be considered independent contractors. A newspaper may contract with scores or hundreds of home delivery drivers and describe the drivers in the contract as independent contractors. If the newspaper has the right to terminate their services for no reason at all, should the contractual label, "independent contractor"

determine a driver's status? *See Zirkle v. Winkler*, 585 S.E.2d 19 (W.Va. 2003).

4. **Retained control.** Employees who are ordinarily independent contractors—general building contractors and their subcontractors, for example—may become "servants" if sufficient control is retained by the employer. Retained control may also show that the employer himself was negligent in not exercising the control he has to obtain appropriate safety.

PUSEY v. BATOR

762 N.E.2d 968 (Ohio 2002)

DOUGLAS, J. . . .

In April 1987, Wilson, on behalf of Greif Brothers, entered into a contract with Youngstown Security Patrol, Inc. ("YSP") to supply a uniformed security guard to "deter theft [and] vandalism" on Greif Brothers' property during specified hours. Wilson told YSP's owner and president, Carl Testa, that he wanted the security guard to periodically check the parking lot and the inside of the building. Other than those instructions, Wilson did not instruct Testa in the manner that YSP was to protect Greif Brothers' property.

The written security contract did not specify whether the guard was to be armed or unarmed, and Wilson and Testa both later testified that they never discussed the subject. [Wilson became aware later, however, that some guards were armed but never asked for unarmed guards.]

Bator was the guard assigned to Greif Brothers' property from 11:00 p.m., August 11 to 7:00 a.m., August 12, 1991. [He was not certified to carry a gun, but he kept one in his briefcase.] At approximately 1:00 a.m., Bator looked out through a window in the guard office and saw two individuals, later identified as Derrell Pusey and Charles Thomas, walking through Greif Brothers' parking lot. Bator used the radio in the office to inform a YSP guard on duty at another location that two people were on Greif Brothers' property.

[Bator first went outside without the gun, but when the men were first evasive and then became angry and called Bator a "mother fucker." Bator then went in and got the gun. When he revealed it to the men, Pusey made a quick movement. Bator thought he was reaching for a gun and Bator fired. The bullet struck Pusey in the back of his head. Another guard arrived, then the police.]

Derrell was transported to the hospital, where he died from his wound. Thereafter, plaintiff-appellant, Ethel Pusey, Derrell's mother, individually and as executor of Derrell's estate, filed a wrongful death and survivorship action against Bator, YSP, and Greif Brothers. YSP and Bator settled with Pusey soon after the jury trial began, leaving Greif Brothers as the only defendant.

[The trial court granted a directed verdict in favor of Greif Brothers. The Court of Appeals affirmed in a divided opinion.]

We find that, even when viewed in the light most favorable to Pusey, the evidence clearly established YSP's status as an independent contractor. Greif Brothers specified the result to be accomplished, *i.e.,* to deter vandals and thieves, but the details of how this task should be accomplished, with the exception noted above regarding periodic patrolling of the property, were left to YSP....

[A]n employer is generally not liable for the negligent acts of an independent contractor. There are, however, exceptions to this general rule, several of which stem from the nondelegable duty doctrine. Nondelegable duties arise in various situations [including] duties imposed on the employer that arise out of the work itself because its performance creates dangers to others, *i.e.,* inherently dangerous work. [In such cases the] employer may delegate the *work* to an independent contractor, but he cannot delegate the *duty*. In other words, the employer is not insulated from liability if the independent contractor's negligence results in a breach of the duty....

Work is inherently dangerous when it creates a peculiar risk of harm to others unless special precautions are taken....

To fall within the inherently-dangerous-work exception, it is not necessary that the work be such that it cannot be done without a risk of harm to others, or even that it be such that it involves a high risk of such harm. It is sufficient that the work involves a risk, recognizable in advance, of physical harm to others, which is inherent in the work itself.

The exception does not apply, however, where the employer would reasonably have only a general anticipation of the possibility that the contractor may be negligent in some way and thereby cause harm to a third party. For example, one who hires a trucker to transport his goods should realize that if the truck is driven at an excessive speed, or with defective brakes, some harm to persons on the highway is likely to occur. An employer of an independent contractor may assume that a careful contractor will take routine precautions against all of the ordinary and customary dangers that may arise in the course of the contemplated work.

The inherently-dangerous-work exception does apply, however, when special risks are associated with the work such that a reasonable man would recognize the necessity of taking special precautions. The work must create a risk that is not a normal, routine matter of customary human activity, such as driving an automobile, but is rather a special danger to those in the vicinity arising out of the particular situation created, and calling for special precautions....

We find that work such as YSP was hired to perform does create a peculiar risk of harm to others. When armed guards are hired to deter vandals and thieves it is foreseeable that someone might be injured by the inappropriate use of the weapon if proper precautions are not taken. Thus, such an injury is one that might have been anticipated as a direct or probable consequence of the performance of the work contracted for, if reasonable care is not taken in its performance. Also, the risk created is not a normal, routine matter of customary human activity, such as driving an automobile, but is instead a special danger arising out of the particular situation created and calling for special precautions. We therefore hold that when an employer hires an independent contractor to provide armed security guards to protect property, the inherently-dangerous-work exception is triggered such that if someone is injured by the weapon as a result of a guard's negligence, the employer is vicariously liable even though the guard responsible is an employee of the independent contractor.

We do not mean to suggest by the foregoing that we have determined that Derrell's death resulted from YSP's negligence. That issue is to be determined by a finder of fact. If the fact finder so finds, however, then, pursuant to our holding herein, Greif Brothers is liable for the damages even though the negligence was that of an employee of an independent contractor. . . .

Judgment reversed and cause remanded.

[COOK, J., joined by Judges Moyer and Stratton, concurred in the judgment only. Those judges thought that the inherent danger question could be answered as a matter of law in some cases, but that in others it would be a question of fact or a mixed question of fact and law.]

NOTES

1. **"Nondelegable" terminology.** When courts say a duty is nondelegable, they mean only that the person who hires an independent contractor does not escape liability under the independent contractor rules. The independent contractor himself is also liable for his own negligence.

2. **Inherent danger and peculiar risk.** Courts have widely adopted provisions of the Restatement (Second) of Torts on nondelegable duties. *See* RESTATEMENT (THIRD) OF AGENCY § 7.06, cmt. *a* (2006). The Restatement (Second) of Torts applies the nondelegable duty rule to inherently dangerous activities in its § 427 and also, in § 416, to cases of "peculiar risk." The two classes of cases are similar. Peculiar risk must be different in some way from ordinary risks, but it is difficult to discover what courts think the difference might be. Courts have held the duty nondelegable when poisons are sprayed and when explosives and strong acids are used—in other words, in cases of instrumentalities dangerous by nature. But courts have also applied the inherently dangerous rule in many fairly ordinary cases. A contractor sprays paint; some of it splatters on the plaintiff's property next door; an independent distributor hires door-to-door salesmen to sell the manufacturer's vacuum cleaners; one of them had a criminal record and assaulted a woman once in her home; a worker for an independent contractor turns over a tractor on a grassy slope. All these cases and others have been held to count as inherent danger or peculiar risk. *See* DOBBS ON TORTS § 337 (2000).

3. **Duties imposed by statutory instruments.** The Restatement (Second) of Torts § 424 recognizes that one who is required by specific statute to provide safety protections for others may not avoid ultimate responsibility for this statutory duty by use of an independent contractor. *See, e.g., Sanatass v.*

Consolidated Investing Co., 887 N.E.2d 1125 (N.Y. 2008) (nondelegable duty under state "scaffold law"). Would this cover ordinary safety statutes that say nothing of independent contractors? In *Maloney v. Rath*, 445 P.2d 513 (Cal. 1968), a car owner had her brakes overhauled by a competent mechanic. Nevertheless, three months later the brakes failed and the plaintiff was injured in the resulting collision. The court first held that the defendant was not liable on the negligence per se doctrine, since her failure to maintain brakes in the statutory working order was excused by her care. But it went on to hold that the defendant was liable because the duty to maintain brakes in safe working order was a nondelegable one. It relied in part on the Restatement's version of "inherently dangerous" instrumentalities (§ 423) and also on § 424. If this is inherent danger, is every auto repair within the nondelegable duty rule?

4. **Duties to maintain safety of land open to the public or chattels supplied for business use.** The Restatement (Second) of Torts § 425 would impose liability upon one who employs an independent contractor to maintain the safety of land held open to the public as a place of business, or a chattel supplied to others for business uses. One illustration involves a hotel which employs an independent plumber to install a shower. The plumber puts the wrong handles on the faucets with the result that a hotel guest is scalded. The hotel is liable. This rule was applied in *Valenti v. Net Properties Management, Inc.*, 710 A.2d 399 (N.H. 1998), where the court held that a mall owner may be vicariously liable for the negligence of independent contractors in maintaining the premises and placing safety mats at the entrance. The court emphasized that the owner could contract with independent contractors for indemnity and was in the best position to protect against risks. *Cf. Simon v. Safeway, Inc.*, 173 P.3d 1031 (Ariz. Ct. App. 2007) (landowner owed nondelegable duty to protect patron from torts committed by security guard hired to provide security on premises).

5. **Landowners and construction contractors.** Owners of even noncommercial property frequently hire independent contractors to perform construction, repair or other work. What if someone is injured on the property (a private home, for example) after the work is done and the owner resumes possession? Would be owner be liable? Most courts would say yes. If the landowner owes a duty to the injured person to maintain the property in a safe condition, that duty cannot be delegated to someone else. *See Otero v. Jordon Restaurant Enterprises*, 895 P.2d 243 (N.M. Ct. App. 1995) (relying on Restatement (Second) of Torts § 422). There is an exception for situations in which the contractor has done some work improperly and has negligently created a temporarily risky condition during construction. In that situation, the landowner is not liable unless he himself is at fault. *Id.*

At one time, most courts followed the "completed and accepted rule" under which the contractor would not be liable for injuries caused to third persons after completion of the work and acceptance by the owner, but most courts have abrogated that rule—leaving the contractor liable along with the owner. *See Dorrell v. South Carolina Dept. of Transp.*, 605 S.E.2d 12 (S.C. 2004); *Peters v. Forster*, 804 N.E.2d 736 (Ind. 2004).

6. **Nondelegable duty as open-ended policy.** "Nondelegable duty" expresses a policy or sense of justice for some particular but not perfectly identified kinds of cases. For instance, it might be possible to say that an operating surgeon should be liable for the negligence of nurses furnished by the hospital and to express that view by saying that the surgeon had a nondelegable duty rather than by saying that the nurses were borrowed servants. Should courts declare a nondelegable duty in these cases?

A. An employee of a home for disabled children sexually abuses a helpless patient. The court concludes that the employee, acting for personal gratification, was not within the scope of his employment. *Cf. Stropes v. Heritage House Childrens Ctr. of Shelbyville, Inc.*, 547 N.E.2d 244 (Ind. 1989).

B. A hospital nurse discovers that a patient about to have an operation has symptoms of a transient heart condition that would make administration of general anesthesia dangerous. The nurse makes a note in the computerized chart available to the anesthesiologist but does not personally convey the information. The anesthesiologist, following the medical standard of care, relies entirely upon the nurse to tell him personally and does not look up the chart immediately prior to anesthesia. He uses a general anesthesia, causing brain damage. Could a court say the duty to get full information is nondelegable? *See Breeden v. Anesthesia West, P.C.*, 656 N.W.2d 913 (Neb. 2003).

O'BANNER v. McDONALD'S CORP.

670 N.E.2d 632 (Ill. 1996)

Justice Harrison delivered the opinion of the court:

Reginald O'Banner brought an action in the circuit court of Cook County to recover damages for personal injuries he allegedly sustained when he slipped and fell in the bathroom of a McDonald's restaurant. In his complaint, O'Banner named as defendants McDonald's Corporation (McDonald's) and certain "unknown owners." McDonald's promptly moved for summary judgment on the grounds that the restaurant was actually owned by one of its franchisees and that it neither owned, operated, maintained, nor controlled the facility. . . .

The circuit court here entered summary judgment in favor of McDonald's based on the company's argument that it was merely the franchisor of the restaurant where O'Banner was injured and, as such, had no responsibility for the conditions that caused his accident. O'Banner challenged this conclusion in the appellate court by theorizing that even though McDonald's was a franchisor, it could nevertheless be held liable for the franchisee's negligence under principles of respondeat superior because there was sufficient evidence in the record to establish that the franchisee served as McDonald's actual agent. In the alternative, O'Banner contended that McDonald's could be vicariously liable for the acts and omissions of the franchisee based on the doctrine of apparent agency.

The appellate court rejected the actual agency theory based on the documentary evidence, but held that there remained genuine issues of material fact with respect to O'Banner's alternative theory of apparent agency. Accordingly, it reversed and remanded for further proceedings....

In the appeal before this court, the issue of actual agency has not been pursued. The sole question before us is whether the appellate court erred in reversing and remanding based on the theory of apparent agency....

Apparent agency, also known in Illinois as apparent authority, ... is based on principles of estoppel. The idea is that if a principal creates the appearance that someone is his agent, he should not then be permitted to deny the agency if an innocent third party reasonably relies on the apparent agency and is harmed as a result.

Under the doctrine, a principal can be held vicariously liable in tort for injury caused by the negligent acts of his apparent agent if the injury would not have occurred but for the injured party's justifiable reliance on the apparent agency. The fundamental obstacle to O'Banner's recovery in this case concerns this element of reliance. Even if one concedes that McDonald's advertising and other conduct could entice a person to enter a McDonald's restaurant in the belief it was dealing with an agent of the corporation itself, that is not sufficient. In order to recover on an apparent agency theory, O'Banner would have to show that he actually did rely on the apparent agency in going to the restaurant where he was allegedly injured.

No amount of liberal construction can alter the fact that the record before us is devoid of anything remotely suggesting that the necessary reliance was present here. The pleadings and affidavit submitted by O'Banner in the circuit court state only that he slipped and fell in the restroom of a McDonald's restaurant. They give no indication as to why he went to the restaurant in the first place. The fact that this was a McDonald's may have been completely irrelevant to his decision. For all we know, O'Banner went there simply because it provided the closest bathroom when he needed one or because some friend asked to meet him there.

If O'Banner had any basis to support his position, he was obliged to present it to the circuit court. He did not do so, and the time for substantiating any claim of reliance has passed. The appellate court was therefore wrong to reverse the circuit court's entry of summary judgment in McDonald's favor based on the apparent agency doctrine.

For the foregoing reasons, the judgment of the appellate court is reversed, the judgment of the circuit court is affirmed, and the cause is remanded to the circuit court for further proceedings consistent with this opinion. [A dissenting opinion is omitted.]

NOTES

1. **Meaning of reliance.** What does "reliance" mean in *O'Banner*—(a) the plaintiff in fact believed and believed reasonably that the restaurant was operated by McDonald's, *or* (b) that the plaintiff reasonably so believed *and* that would not have used the restroom had he know that it was operated by a franchisee? In a case involving the claim that doctors working in a hospital were apparent agents of the hospital, the court, quoting other authority, said that the reliance issue "simply focuses on the patient's belief that the hospital or its employees were rendering health care." *Burless v. West Va. Univ. Hosp's., Inc.*, 601 S.E.2d 85 (W.Va. 2004). Other courts have also focused on whether the patient is looking to the institution rather than the doctor for care. *Dewald v. HCA Health Services of Tennessee*, 251 S.W.3d 423 (Tenn. 2008); *Jackson v. Power*, 743 P.2d 1376 (Alaska 1987).

2. **Managed health care or HMOs.** Health maintenance organizations, usually corporations, are not physicians. Instead they are contractors who manage health care programs. In one type of HMO, the HMO hires its own doctors and they are its employees. In a second type, the HMO contracts with independent physicians to provide the services needed. Suppose you go to work for a law firm which has a health care program through an HMO of the second type. You select a physician from the approved list and he negligently injures you. Is the HMO vicariously liable? In *Petrovich v. Share Health Plan of Illinois, Inc.*, 719 N.E.2d 756 (Ill. 1999), the Illinois court held that the HMO was subject to vicarious liability on the same apparent agency theory it rejected in *O'Banner*. The court said the patient would be relying upon the HMO if the patient is not selecting a specific physician for some reason such as a prior relationship with that physician but merely because some physicians had to be selected from the list furnished. Is the court's concept of reliance the same as it was three years earlier in *O'Banner*?

PUCKREIN v. ATI TRANSPORT, INC.

897 A.2d 1034 (N.J. 2006)

JUSTICE LONG delivered the opinion of the Court.

In 1998, Kevin and Alecia Puckrein were killed when their automobile was struck by an unregistered and uninsured tractor-trailer with seriously defective brakes. The tractor-trailer was owned by ATI Transport, Inc., (ATI) and, at the time of the accident, had been transporting a load of glass residue for Browning–Ferris Industries of New York, Inc., (BFI–NY) from Brooklyn, New York, to an incinerator plant in Newark, New Jersey. BFI–NY actually had contracted with World Carting Corp., to transport the load and World Carting, in turn, had assigned its responsibilities to ATI.

[Plaintiffs sued a number of defendants, most of whom were judgment-proof. The trial judge granted summary judgment for BFI–NY on the ground that ATI and World Carting (which were related entities) were independent contractors. Plaintiffs appeal that ruling, arguing that BFI–NY should be liable for hiring an incompetent independent contractor. Specifically, plaintiffs argue that BFI–NY never checked to see if ATI/World Carting had adequate registration, insurance and other licenses, and should have known that in fact, ATI/World Carting did not have liability insurance at the time of the accident.]

There are ... exceptions to the general rule that principals are not liable for the actions of independent contractors.... [T]he incompetent contractor exception is at issue here.

... [T]o prevail against the principal for hiring an incompetent contractor, a plaintiff must show that the contractor was, in fact, incompetent or unskilled to perform the job for which he/she was hired, that the harm that resulted arose out of that incompetence, and that the principal knew or should have known of the incompetence....

BFI–NY argues that, even assuming it was aware that World Carting's trucks were uninsured and unregistered (and therefore uninspected), [it should be insulated] from liability because ... insurance, registration, and poor financial condition are not competency issues....

[T]he very job that BFI–NY hired World Carting/ATI to do was to haul waste and recyclables across state lines.... Clearly, under our law, the hauler's basic competency included, at a minimum, a valid driver's license, a valid registration certificate, and a valid liability insurance identification card. Without those, the hauler has no right to be on the road at all. BFI–NY's own witnesses agreed with that conclusion.

The allegations in this case strike at the heart of the competency issue in a trucking case. [L]icensing, registration, and insurance are, under our law, the *sine qua non* to the transport of goods on the roadways. Registration, concomitant to inspection, is a method of insuring the safety of vehicles that place the public at risk and insurance is the guarantee that innocent victims of errant truckers will be compensated. Thus, the core question here is not whether World Carting was competent to transport BFI–NY's loads upon the public highways—it was not. The question is whether BFI–NY violated its duty to use reasonable care in selecting a trucker and whether it knew or should have known of World Carting's incompetence.

We return to the principles relevant to the duty of inquiry. As noted, an employer may be charged with negligence in hiring an independent contractor where it is demonstrated that he should have known, or might by the exercise of reasonable care have ascertained, that the contractor was not competent. The extent of the inquiry obviously depends on the status of the principal and the nature of the task that the contract covers. For example ... a principal who hires a contractor to paint or pave or install electrical outlets need not inquire whether its pick-up trucks are inspected and insured. Likewise, a casual shipper of goods has a right to assume that the carrier is not conducting business in violation of the law.

On the contrary, a company whose core purpose is the collection and transportation of materials on the highways, has a duty to use reasonable care in the hiring of an independent trucker including a duty to make an inquiry into that trucker's ability to travel legally on the highways. At a minimum, BFI–NY was required to inquire whether its haulers had proper insurance and registration because without those items the hauler had no right to be on the road. Just as BFI–NY itself could not have transported products in unregistered and uninsured trucks, it was not free to engage an independent contractor that did so. . . .

Even if it could be proved that BFI–NY made reasonable inquiry of World Carting at the time of its original retention, its duty did not end there. By April 1998, World Carting's insurance certificate, on file with BFI–NY, had expired. Despite its continuing duty to inquire, BFI–NY never did so although it continued to allow World Carting's trucks to transport its glass residue. In other words, at a point after the original retention but before plaintiffs' accident, BFI–NY should have known that World Carting had become incompetent to transport its products. Yet, according to the record, BFI–NY continued to load World Carting and ATI trucks without evidence that they were competent to transport its products.

Under the circumstances, summary judgment in BFI–NY's favor should not have been granted. . . . [P]laintiffs' complaint against BFI–NY is reinstated, and the cause is remanded to the Law Division for further proceedings consistent with this opinion.

NOTES

1. **Selecting incompetent contractors.** As *Puckrein* indicates, it has long been true in virtually all states that a defendant cannot insulate itself from liability by selecting or retaining an incompetent independent contractor. *See* RESTATEMENT (THIRD) OF AGENCY § 7.05(1) (2006). The incompetence can take many forms—for example, the contractor does not know how to do the job, or is known to be a drunkard or someone with anger management problems. The situation in *Puckrein* involves a form of financial incompetence; the contractor's lack of insurance in this case left the contractor and its employees "judgment proof." This means that the persons harmed by the contractor's negligence had no way of getting money from the contractor. After *Puckrein*, the New Jersey court rejected a similar "uninsured means incompetent" argument in a case in which a workers' compensation insurer retained an uninsured doctor to conduct an independent medical examination on a claimant as part of the insurer's pre-approval of a treatment plan for a workplace injury. The court held that *Puckrein*'s holding rested on the legal requirement of insurance in that case, and said there was no such insurance requirement for doctors at the time of the negligent act. *Basil v. Wolf*, 935 A.2d 1154 (N.J. 2007). The court noted, however, that a recent change in the law, requiring all doctors to have malpractice insurance, means that from henceforth a doctor without insurance is indeed "incompetent."

2. **The employer's primary negligence.** The employer who is not vicariously liable for torts of an independent contractor is nevertheless liable for his own causal negligence. *See Hickle v. Whitney Farms, Inc.*, 64 P.3d 1244 (Wash. 2003) (negligent entrustment claim where defendants may have known that contractor was not properly disposing of hazardous substances). An employer is similarly primarily liable if it negligently hires, supervises or retains a dangerous or incompetent employee who harms the plaintiff, as long as the employer's negligence was a cause of the harm. *See, e.g., Foradori v. Harris*, 523 F.3d 477 (5th Cir. 2008). A plaintiff may pursue a defendant on grounds of both vicarious liability and negligent hiring, supervision or retention. *James v. Kelly Trucking Co.*, 661 S.E.2d 329 (S.C. 2008).

3. **"Corporate negligence."** Suppose a hospital permits a physician to admit her patients to the hospital for its care and to utilize its operating room and other resources. The physician is not in any sense employed by the hospital and the hospital is not vicariously liable. However, the hospital may be liable for its own "corporate negligence" if it allows incompetent or dangerous physicians to use its facilities. *See, e.g., Darling v. Charleston Cmty. Mem. Hosp.*, 211 N.E.2d 253 (Ill. 1965); *Insinga v. LaBella*, 543 So.2d 209 (Fla. 1989). The rule has been applied to an HMO that allegedly assigned an overload of patients to independent contractor physicians. *Jones v. Chicago HMO Ltd. of Ill.*, 730 N.E.2d 1119 (Ill. 2000). Some states have recognized a claim for "negligent credentialing" of doctors, which they analogized to negligent hiring claims. *See Larson v. Wasemiller*, 738 N.W.2d 300 (Minn. 2007).

§ 3. OTHER FORMS OF VICARIOUS RESPONSIBILITY

1. *Partnership.* L and N form a partnership to sell groceries. They agree to, and do, acquire a truck for deliveries. N negligently drives the truck while delivering groceries and Grogan is injured. N is liable personally. Is L also liable? If there were a distinct business entity known as the partnership, the partnership could be viewed as the employer. If that were the case, both N and the partnership would be liable, as in any other master-servant relationship. But a partnership is not a separate entity in the way a corporation is—and both partners are personally liable. Each partner can be seen as a general agent for the other partner or partners.

2. *Joint enterprise.* D, E and F, three salespersons who are selling for three different companies but who are not servants, discover they all intend to drive from Buffalo to Chicago at the same time. They decide to rent a single car, share expenses and share driving. While one of them, D, is driving, there is a collision with Grogan's car. D may have been negligent. Grogan is injured. If D is negligent, he is personally liable. Are E and F also liable?

Courts have imposed liability upon all members of a joint enterprise when persons outside the enterprise are injured. This is said to exist where there is (1) an agreement, express or implied, (2) there is a common purpose, (3) there is a community of interest and (4) there is equal right of control. These terms are sometimes interpreted liberally. The agreement need not be spelled out in words and it is enough if the parties had a tacit understanding. In some cases, however, courts have held or stated that a social venture will qualify if all the elements are present. Under this view three friends sharing expenses, having a common purpose and equal right to control, might all be liable if one of them drives negligently on a fishing trip. Is this sound or not?

When members of the enterprise itself are injured, the rule is different, and there is no imputation of negligence among the enterprisers themselves. Thus if A, B, and C are on a joint enterprise, and A drives negligently, causing an injury to B, B will have a claim against A for his negligence, but no claim against C based on imputation of A's fault to C.

3. *Concert of action, conspiracy, aiding and abetting.* An early basis for joint and several liability was much like the idea behind liability of one partner or joint enterpriser for the acts of another. Conspirators or those who act in concert to commit a tort or crime are partners, as it were, in an illegal or tortious enterprise. *See, e.g., Reilly v. Anderson*, 727 N.W.2d 102 (Iowa 2007) (front-seat passenger who attempted to steer and driver who was attempting to light a marijuana pipe were acting in concert when they wrecked the car, causing injuries to plaintiff). Aiders and abetters are in much the same position. In *Courtney v. Courtney*, 413 S.E.2d 418 (W.Va. 1991), the complaint alleged Maud supplied her son with alcohol and drugs even though she knew that when he used them he beat his wife. The court held the complaint stated a claim on behalf of the family victims. Suppose that, as A begins to beat the plaintiff, A's uncle B shouts "Kill him, kill him!" *Rael v. Cadena*, 604 P.2d 822 (N.M. 1979). Is B subject to liability?

4. *Tacit agreement to participate in a tort.* Drag racing is a classic example of action in concert. Two teenagers driving two different cars are stopped at a light. One guns his engine. The other does the same. When the light changes, they take off, rapidly gaining speed. One of them loses control and crashes into the plaintiff, but the other drives safely by. Is the other liable because he was acting in concert by tacitly agreed to the illegal activity? In *Nelson v. Nason*, 177 N.E.2d 887 (Mass. 1961) the court commented: "Direct testimony of an agreement to race was not required. . . . There was evidence of challenge and response in the speed and relative positions of the two automobiles." But in *Canavan v. Galuski*, 769 N.Y.S.2d 629 (App. Div. 2003), the court was unwilling to find a tacit agreement where a group of defendants, insulted online, gathered together to go to the Lewis house to "resolve" the matter. They found the plaintiff in the driveway. Someone, unidentified, hit the plaintiff from behind. The court thought "parallel activity" by the defendants, did not permit an inference of concert. It relied on authority holding that parallel *economic* activity by corporations in marketing their products was not evidence of conspiracy.

5. *Entrustment of vehicle.* Defendant, owner of a car, permits T to drive it. T is not a servant, partner, or joint enterpriser. If T drives negligently, will defendant be liable? There are at least five distinct situations:

(a) *Negligent entrustment.* Defendant may be liable for his own negligent entrustment of the car to one who is incompetent to drive. This is not vicarious liability but requires proof that defendant knew or should have known of the incompetence and that injury resulted from that incompetence. The entrustor is thus assigned a percentage of the responsibility under comparative fault rules, and his liability calculated according to that percentage. *See Ali v. Fisher,* 145 S.W.3d 557 (Tenn. 2004)

(b) *Owner in the car with right of control.* When the defendant permits another to drive, but himself remains in the car, as owner he retains some degree of legal control and he may be liable for failing to exercise that control. Again, this may reflect not vicarious liability but ordinary negligence. In some cases courts have emphasized the legal right of control even if he is not actually negligent. This view is probably on its way out. Thus "the mere presence of the owner in an automobile driven by another does not create any presumption of a master-servant relationship or joint enterprise." *Reed v. Hinderland,* 660 P.2d 464 (Ariz. 1983).

(c) *Ordinary bailment.* If the owner-defendant simply lends the car to a competent driver, so that there is a bailment, with neither actual nor legal right of control, there is no agency and no liability. This is the common law rule.

(d) *Owner consent statutes.* Statutes of several states make the individual owner liable for the negligence of the driver even in the case of a pure bailment, provided only that the owner consented to the use of the car. This kind of statute may give rise to litigation over whether the defendant actually consented to the use of the car and if so whether the driver went beyond the consent. Commercial lessors of vehicles may be subject to further regulation in many states. In *Murdza v. Zimmerman,* 786 N.E.2d 440 (N.Y. 2003), A leased to B who consented to C's use but not the use by others; C permitted D to drive in violation of the B's restriction. The court held that the restriction avoids B's liability, but A as lessor cannot take advantage of B's restriction on use. What if the lease requires the driver to have a valid contract and the lessee does not have one? *See Fojtik v. Hunter,* 828 A.2d 589 (Conn. 2003).

(e) *Family purpose doctrine.* This doctrine, invented by the courts, was that if a car was maintained for general family use, the legal owner would be liable for its negligent use by a member of the family. The effect was that the driver was treated as the servant of the owner. At the time the doctrine originated, it was typically applied to hold a husband or father liable for the negligent driving of a wife or child.

6. *Imputed contributory negligence.* (a) *The "both ways" rule.* M employs S as his servant. S, in the course and scope of employment, negligently drives M's car, causing a collision with T, who is also driving

negligently. M is liable to T under ordinary rules of vicarious liability. In M's own action against T for damages to his car, should S's negligence be imputed to M, reducing or even barring M's recovery? The two issues are distinct and, in one well-known decision, the Minnesota Court held that although M should be vicariously liable to T, there was no justification in barring M's own claim against T. *Weber v. Stokely–Van Camp, Inc.*, 144 N.W.2d 540 (Minn. 1966). But most courts have not followed this rule. Instead, they follow the rule that responsibility operates "both ways"—if M is liable vicariously for S's negligence, then M's recovery against T is either reduced or barred on the basis of S's negligence (depending on the particular state's approach to contributory negligence). The Restatement of Apportionment adopts this "both ways" rule. RESTATEMENT (THIRD) OF TORTS: APPORTIONMENT § 5 (1999).

(b) *Negligence of family members.* H, a husband and father, negligently drives his car. T, driving another car in a negligent way, collides with H. W and C, the wife and child of H, are injured in the collision and sue T. Can T defend on the ground that H's negligence is imputed to his wife and child? Older cases said so, but these decisions have now been condemned everywhere. *See LaBier v. Pelletier*, 665 A.2d 1013 (Me. 1995).

Although it is no longer true that a family member's fault will be imputed to another family member in the absence of an agency relationship, the same result may be achieved on other grounds. Consider for example the *Dillon v. Legg* case: if the child crossing the street is guilty of contributory negligence, will the child's mother be permitted to recover for mental distress? Or suppose a consortium claim by a wife: if her husband was guilty of contributory negligence, will the consortium claim be barred or reduced?

(c) *Bailments.* A car owner bails it to a bailee who drives negligently. As we saw above, the owner is not liable to a third person for the bailee's negligence. Is the owner prevented from a recovery against a negligent third person if the bailee is at fault? Again, courts once so held, and again this rule has largely disappeared. *See* DOBBS ON TORTS § 340 (2000).

CHAPTER 23

THE DEVELOPMENT OF COMMON LAW STRICT LIABILITY

■ ■ ■

§ 1. STRICT LIABILITY FOR TRESPASSORY TORTS AND THE ADVENT OF FAULT THEORY

After the Norman Conquest of England (about 1066), the kings of England gradually began to decide many disputes through their judges. But England was a feudal country with many local barons who also had courts and who wished to decide matters for themselves. Many boroughs or free cities also developed courts; there were even church courts. To the extent that the king's courts decided disputes, local power was diminished. Local interests naturally resisted.

Among the earliest disputes the king's ministers or agents decided were those affecting land title or possession. It was easy for the king to assert this power, since he was the tenant-in-chief in a feudal system and it was natural that he would assert the power to make ultimate decisions as to land title and possession. Gradually the "king's peace" became the subject of royal power as well, and the king's judges began to handle all cases of violent crime.

Crime and tort were not readily distinguished in the early Norman period, and the king's courts gradually developed the power to decide violent tort cases as well as purely criminal matters.

The king's power in civil cases was exercised when the Chancellor issued an original writ, the effect of which was to command the sheriff to bring the defendant to answer the plaintiff's claims in the king's courts. These writs reflected the "forms of action." The forms of action—that is to say, the types of cases which the king's courts could hear—were limited in number. The local authorities had exerted sufficient pressure to achieve a general recognition that the king's courts were not to recognize any new forms of action or writs, but were to act only in the kinds of cases represented by the writs that then existed. They made one exception— cases that were "similar" to those covered by the old writs.

Trespass. For a long time, the term "trespass" was sometimes used more or less as the equivalent of "tort," referring to acts of the defendant. *See* MORRIS ARNOLD, SELECT CASES OF TRESPASS FROM THE KING'S COURTS 1307–1399 (1985). Procedurally, however, the term referred to the main writ or form of action. The plaintiff could begin a claim by obtaining a writ of *Trespass*; many of the incidents of the proceeding, including the substantive rules, were determined by the writ chosen. The writ of *Trespass* could be used in any kind of case in which the plaintiff could show that defendant had directly applied physical force to person or property. It came to cover the torts we now think of as assault, battery, false imprisonment, trespass to land and trespass to chattels. The connection between these torts and crimes of violence is sufficiently obvious, but the writ was not limited to cases of intended violence. By the end of the 12th century trespass was recognized as a tort as well as a crime, so that damages could be recovered for any of the acts of force for which the writ of *Trespass* would lie.

One set of rules that went with the writ of *Trespass* told the plaintiff what he had to prove. He had only to prove (1) force and (2) direct application to person or property. Not only was it unnecessary for the plaintiff to show intent or fault, it was also unnecessary to show damages. In a famous assault case, *I de S et Ux v. W de S*, Y.B. Lib. Ass. f. 99, pl. 60. (1348), the defendant, apparently frustrated to find that the tavern was closed, beat on the door with a hatchet and when the plaintiff put her head out of the window, he "struck with the hatchet but did not hit the woman." The Inquest, an early form of the jury, said it seemed to them there was no harm, but the judge instructed them that "[t]here is harm done and a trespass for which [plaintiff] shall recover damages. . . ." Thus when the writ of *Trespass* could be used—whenever direct physical force was applied—there was not only strict liability, but there was a recovery of damages without proof of harm.

Case. We have said that the local interests were willing to recognize power in the king's courts to hear the old writs, such as *Trespass*, and also such other writs as involved "similar cases." This concession, which appeared as the Statute of Westminster II in 1285, is often said to be the source of the new writ, *Trespass on the (Similar) Case*, a writ developed by analogy to the writ of *Trespass*, but different from it. Whether the statute is the source of the new writ or not is much debated, *see* CECIL FIFOOT, HISTORY AND SOURCES OF THE COMMON LAW 66 ff. (1949). At any rate, the new writ, called *Trespass on the Case*, or simply *Case*, developed after that time and had a foothold in English jurisprudence by the 14th century.

Case covered instances in which the defendant's acts caused harm to the plaintiff, but in which the harm did not result "directly," or did not result from physical force. The classic examples suggest that if you throw a log and it hits the plaintiff, the proper writ is *Trespass*, since there is both force and direct injury. But if you throw a log and it lands in the road where the plaintiff later trips over it in the dark, the proper writ must be *Case*, the force having dissipated and the injury being indirect.

Primitive law tends to be formal, but the distinction between *Trespass* and *Case* had important practical consequences. In *Case,* some quality we would now call fault was required—negligence, for example. As we have seen, no fault was required if the writ of *Trespass* could be used.

Changes in the law. It is apparent from the very first cases in this book that the rules applied in medieval England have little or no place in modern law. How did the change occur?

WEAVER v. WARD

Hob. 134, 80 Eng. Rep. 284 (K.B. 1616)

Weaver brought an action of trespass of assault and battery against Ward. The defendant pleaded, that he was amongst others by the commandment of the Lords of the Council a trained soldier in London, of the band of one Andrews captain; and so was the plaintiff, and that they were skirmishing with their musquets charged with powder for their exercise in re militari, against another captain and his band; and as they were so skirmishing, the defendant casualiter & per infortunium & contra voluntatem suam, in discharging of his piece did hurt and wound the plaintiff, which is the same, & c. absque hoc, that he was guilty aliter sive alio modo. And upon demurrer by the plaintiff, judgment was given for him; for though it were agreed, that if men tilt or turney in the presence of the King, or if two masters of defence playing their prizes kill one another, that this shall be no felony; or if a lunatick kill a man, or the like, because felony must be done animo felonico: yet in trespass, which tends only to give damages according to hurt or loss, it is not so; and therefore if a lunatick hurt a man, he shall be answerable in trespass: and therefore no man shall be excused of a trespass (for this is the nature of an excuse, and not of a justification, prout ei bene licuit) except it may be judged utterly without his fault.

As if a man by force take my hand and strike you, or if here the defendant had said, that the plaintiff ran cross his piece when it was discharging, or had set forth the case with the circumstances, so as it had appeared to the Court that it had been inevitable, and that the defendant had committed no negligence to give occasion to the hurt.

NOTES

1.   Does the court recognize liability without fault? Under what circumstances, if any, could a defendant escape liability? Do the court's examples suggest that the absence of fault, by itself, would be sufficient to avoid liability?

2.   In the 1700s, the idea arose that the writ of *Trespass* with its strict liability could be used not only when injury was "direct," but also when the injury was the result of an "unlawful" act, such as an intentional harm. This might be important, because the plaintiff who chose the wrong writ lost his case. If the plaintiff chose *Trespass* and proved an unlawful harm but not a

direct one, he would lose, unless this second idea was accepted. And there was some degree of acceptance of this new idea, one result of which may have been to associate the writ of *Trespass* with unlawfulness or intentional harm, rather than with "direct" harm. *Cf. Vosburg v. Putney*, 50 N.W. 403 (Wis. 1891) (unlawfulness of schoolroom misbehavior sufficient for liability).

3. In the 1800s a third idea occurred. It was that if the plaintiff had damages and could show fault in the defendant, he could "waive the trespass," even where harm was direct. Having waived the trespass, he could use the writ of *Case*, which had certain procedural advantages in some instances. The effect was to give the plaintiff an option whenever he sustained direct harm and could make proof of fault and damages. Given proof of those items, he had no need to resort to the *Trespass* writ with its strict liability. There were even some advantages to *Case*. One of these was that, having the option to sue in *Case*, he would not lose for technical reasons—it would always be the right writ provided he could make the proof of fault and harm. If he chose *Trespass*, on the other hand, he might find himself out of court if the judges thought the harm to be "indirect" and thus unsuited for the Trespass writ. The upshot was that *Case* came to be commonly used and negligence was routinely proven even where the harm was direct.

These seemingly minor changes had a large impact on the practice of law; lawyers routinely used *Case* and proved fault and damages in many instances.

4. The exact details of this history, which is here much simplified, are debated. *See* E. F. Roberts, *Negligence: Blackstone to Shaw to ?*, 50 CORNELL L.Q. 191 (1965). In fact, our book-learning about earlier practices may be an inaccurate reflection of both the practices and the conceptions of earlier periods. Certainly other descriptions of the history could be given. *See* FRANK VANDALL, STRICT LIABILITY: LEGAL AND ECONOMIC ANALYSIS 1–6 (1989). Still, by 1850, there had been a considerable change in attitude in the profession, but the law on the books remained pretty much in line with notions held as far back as the 14th century—strict liability would be imposed for trespass, but some kind of fault had to be found if only *Case* would lie.

It is important to understand the conceptual shift in the way lawyers understood the writs. But there are more important questions. One of these is whether the lawyers of the time understood the change that was going on in their professional world, and whether we ourselves do today. Another is whether larger forces were and *are* at work, influencing a shift from strict liability to a fault standard, or possibly vice versa.

BROWN v. KENDALL

60 Mass. (6 Cush.) 292 (1850)

This was an action of trespass for assault and battery, originally commenced against George K. Kendall, the defendant, who died pending the suit, and his executrix was summoned in.

[Defendant Kendall was beating two fighting dogs, attempting to separate them with a four-foot stick. In the movement of dogs and men, he backed towards the plaintiff, raised the stick over his shoulder to strike the dogs and accidentally hit the plaintiff in the eye. The defendant requested the judge to instruct the jury, among other things, that if defendant was using ordinary care and the plaintiff was not, the plaintiff could not recover.]

The judge declined to give the instructions, as above requested, but left the case to the jury under the following instructions: "If the defendant, in beating the dogs, was doing a necessary act, or one which it was his duty under the circumstances of the case to do, and was doing it in a proper way; then he was not responsible in this action, provided he was using ordinary care at the time of the blow. If it was not a necessary act; if he was not in duty bound to attempt to part the dogs, but might with propriety interfere or not as he chose; the defendant was responsible for the consequences of the blow, unless it appeared that he was in the exercise of extraordinary care, so that the accident was inevitable, using the word inevitable not in a strict but a popular sense." . . .

The jury under these instructions returned a verdict for the plaintiff; whereupon the defendant alleged exceptions.

SHAW, C.J. This is an action of trespass, *vi et armis*,[1] brought by George Brown against George K. Kendall, for an assault and battery. . . .

It appears to us, that some of the confusion in the cases on this subject has grown out of the long-vexed question, under the rule of the common law, whether a party's remedy, where he has one, should be sought in an action of the case, or of trespass. This is very distinguishable from the question, whether in a given case, any action will lie. The result of these cases is, that if the damage complained of is the immediate effect of the act of the defendant, trespass *vi et armis* lies; if consequential only, and not immediate, case is the proper remedy. Leame v. Bray, 3 East, 593; Hugget v. Montgomery, 2 N.R. 446, Day's Ed. and notes.

In these discussions, it is frequently stated by judges, that when one receives injury from the direct act of another, trespass will lie. But we think this is said in reference to the question, whether trespass and not case will lie, assuming that the facts are such, that some action will lie. These dicta are no authority, we think, for holding, that damage received by a direct act of force from another will be sufficient to maintain an action of trespass, whether the act was lawful or unlawful, and neither wilful, intentional, or careless. In the principal case cited, Leame v. Bray, the damage arose from the act of the defendant, in driving on the wrong side of the road, in a dark night, which was clearly negligent if not unlawful. In the course of the argument of that case (p. 595), Lawrence, J., said: "There certainly are cases in the books, where, the injury being direct and immediate, trespass has been holden to lie, though the injury was not intentional." The term "injury" implies something more than damage; but, independently of that consideration, the proposition may be true, because though the injury was unintentional, the act may have been

---

1. *Vi et armis*: with force and arms, words used in certain trespass writs, originally designed to justify intervention of the King's Courts in the interest of the King's peace.—eds.

unlawful or negligent, and the cases cited by him are perfectly consistent with that supposition. So the same learned judge in the same case says (p. 597), "No doubt trespass lies against one who drives a carriage against another, whether done wilfully or not." But he immediately adds, "Suppose one who is driving a carriage is negligently and heedlessly looking about him, without attending to the road when persons are passing, and thereby runs over a child and kills him, is it not manslaughter? And if so, it must be trespass; for every manslaughter includes trespass"; showing what he understood by a case not wilful.

We think, as the result of all the authorities, the rule is correctly stated by Mr. Greenleaf, that the plaintiff must come prepared with evidence to show either that the intention was unlawful, or that the defendant was in fault; for if the injury was unavoidable, and the conduct of the defendant was free from blame, he will not be liable. 2 Greenl. Ev. §§ 85 to 92; Wakeman v. Robinson, 1 Bing. 213. If, in the prosecution of a lawful act, a casualty purely accidental arises, no action can be supported for an injury arising therefrom. Davis v. Saunders, 2 Chit. R. 639; Com Dig. Battery, A. (Day's Ed.) and notes; Vincent v. Stinehour, 7 Vern. 69. In applying these rules to the present case, we can perceive no reason why the instructions asked for by the defendant ought not to have been given; to this effect, that if both plaintiff and defendant at the time of the blow were using ordinary care, or if at that time the defendant was using ordinary care, and the plaintiff was not, or if at that time, both the plaintiff and defendant were not using ordinary care, then the plaintiff could not recover.

In using this term, ordinary care, it may be proper to state, that what constitutes ordinary care will vary with the circumstances of cases. In general, it means that kind and degree of care, which prudent and cautious men would use, such as is required by the exigency of the case, and such as is necessary to guard against probable danger. A man, who should have occasion to discharge a gun, on an open and extensive marsh, or in a forest, would be required to use less circumspection and care, than if he were to do the same thing in an inhabited town, village, or city....

We are not aware of any circumstances in this case, requiring a distinction between acts which it was lawful and proper to do, and acts of legal duty....

The court instructed the jury, that if it was not a necessary act, and the defendant was not in duty bound to part the dogs, but might with propriety interfere or not as he chose, the defendant was responsible for the consequences of the blow, unless it appeared that he was in exercise of extraordinary care, so that the accident was inevitable, using the word not in a strict but a popular sense. This is to be taken in connection with the charge afterwards given, that if the jury believed, that the act of interference in the fight was unnecessary (that is, as before explained, not a duty incumbent on the defendant), then the burden of proving extraordinary care on the part of the defendant, or want of ordinary care on the part of plaintiff, was on the defendant.

The court are of opinion that these directions were not conformable to law. If the act of hitting the plaintiff was unintentional, on the part of the defendant, and done in the doing of a lawful act, then the defendant was not liable, unless it was done in the want of exercise of due care, adapted to the exigency of the case, and therefore such want of due care became part of the plaintiff's case, and the burden of proof was on the plaintiff to establish it. 2 Greenl. Ev. §§ 85; Powers v. Russell, 13 Pick. 69, 76; Tourtellot v. Rosebrook, 11 Met. 460.

Perhaps the learned judge, by the use of the term extraordinary care, in the above charge, explained as it is by the context, may have intended nothing more than that increased degree of care and diligence, which the exigency of particular circumstances might require, and which men of ordinary care and prudence would use under like circumstances, to guard against danger. If such was the meaning of this part of the charge, then it does not differ from our views, as above explained. But we are of opinion, that the other part of the charge, that the burden of proof was on the defendant, was incorrect. Those facts which are essential to enable the plaintiff to recover, he takes the burden of proving. The evidence may be offered by the plaintiff or by the defendant; the question of due care, or want of care, may be essentially connected with the main facts, and arise from the same proof; but the effect of the rule, as to the burden of proof, is this, that when the proof is all in, and before the jury, from whatever side it comes, and whether directly proved, or inferred from circumstances, if it appears that the defendant was doing a lawful act, and unintentionally hit and hurt the plaintiff, then unless it also appears to the satisfaction of the jury, that the defendant is chargeable with some fault, negligence, carelessness, or want or prudence, the plaintiff fails to sustain the burden of proof, and is not entitled to recover.

New trial is ordered.

Notes

1. **A new departure?** It is generally thought that *Brown v. Kendall* marked the first clear articulation of the shift from strict liability for direct, forcible harms to a fault-based liability. Professor Gregory pointed out that although Chief Justice Shaw asserted that the rules of substantive tort law were the same for those injured directly and those injured indirectly, the evidence pointed to the contrary. *See* Charles Gregory, *Trespass to Negligence to Absolute Liability*, 37 VA. L. REV. 359, 366 (1951). Notice how some of the conceptual developments mentioned in the notes preceding this case figure in Shaw's opinion, for example, the question of "lawfulness."

2. **Procedural reform.** One of the larger forces that may have played some part in the shift to a negligence approach was the decay of the writ system and concomitant adoption of the Field Code of procedure in New York. The forms of action as reflected in the writs were not merely procedural

devices. The forms of action dictated the scope of the jurisdiction of the king's courts, the procedure to be followed and the substantive rules. For example, as we have seen, *Trespass* embodied a substantive notion that liability was strict where harm was direct and forcible. With the adoption of Code procedure and the decay of the forms of action, was there a blank slate for substantive rules?

3. **Subsidizing industry?** An injury that was forcible and direct in 1350 was often the result of violence. An injury that was forcible and direct after the steam engine and the railroad might be unintended. It might also be the product of a desirable development of economic resources. Would judges have favored a negligence system on the ground that strict liability associated with *Trespass* might smother infant industry? See Gregory, *supra* Note 1, at 368.

Protective legal rules may have been more significant in 1850 than they could be now. At least two important economic institutions now exist that did not exist in 1850. The first is liability insurance, which allows the industry (or anyone) to spread the costs of injury over a period of time, so that no single large disaster will necessarily wipe out the industry. The second is the development of a system of finance which permits relatively easy aggregations of capital through corporate enterprise, together with a central banking system and a series of money markets which permit the borrowing of capital. Without these devices, infant industry may indeed have needed all the help it could get. The most careful scholarship, however, seems to indicate that on the whole, the courts of the early 1800s were sympathetic to the injured victim and quite willing to use negligence law, or negligence law mixed with forms of older strict liability, to aid the injured. Gary T. Schwartz, *The Character of Early American Tort Law*, 36 U.C.L.A. L. Rev. 641 (1989). If this is correct, negligence became dominant in tort law for reasons that had little to do with a "subsidy" for infant industry.

4. **Universalizing principles.** The action on the *Case* often involved suits between persons who had a kind of special or contractual relationship, such as a suit by a farmer against a vet for failure to treat a horse properly. The special relationship or contract imposed a duty of affirmative action upon the provider-defendant, so he was liable for "neglect," hence our word "negligence" for the vast span of actions that arose from *Case*. The relationship of the parties set the duty to be observed. By his implicit undertaking, the vet agreed to use the care that other vets would use. As long as *Case* was limited to parties in some relationship, like carriers and passengers, or innkeepers and guests, duties of care were generated out of those particular relationships and the expectations that those relationships created. It was a kind of reasonable "consumer expectation" test of the duty owed. When *Case* was expanded to cover negligence suits between strangers—that is, between parties who had no contractual relationship—a universal standard was needed for the first time. That seems to appear in *Brown v. Kendall*.

Is it also possible that the scientific revolution and the new ability to state universal laws of the natural world encouraged legal thinkers to seek similarly universal principles of law. For whatever reason, negligence with its reasonable person standard became "the touchstone ... of a general theory of civil obligation." G. EDWARD WHITE, TORT LAW IN AMERICA 16 (1980).

REFERENCES: DOBBS ON TORTS §§ 14, 111–13 (2000); HARPER, JAMES & GRAY, LAW OF TORTS § 1.3 (3d ed. 1996).

§ 2.　STRICT LIABILITY AFTER *BROWN v. KENDALL*

A.　TRESPASSING ANIMALS

Under the writ of *Trespass*, the plaintiff could redress all direct harms, even if the defendant was not at fault; and under the writ of *Case*, he would redress indirect harms, provided they were the result of fault. But there was a period in which the only writ, or the dominant one, was *Trespass*. As an English legal historian has pointed out, a lawyer writing a book about torts in the late 14th century would have called the book "*Trespass*," because at the time tort law was embodied in *Trespass*; *Case* developed later. S. MILSOM, HISTORICAL FOUNDATIONS OF THE COMMON LAW 261 (1969). What was done with claims for indirect injury before the writ of *Case* was developed?

As it happened, some of them were treated as *Trespass* cases and strict liability seems to have been imposed. If the defendant owned cattle and drove them onto the plaintiff's land, the writ of *Trespass* would be proper, or at least it could be argued. Such an entry would be reasonably "direct," and it might also meet the later test of "unlawfulness." However, suppose that the defendant's cattle merely strayed, or broke loose from an enclosure, and that they then entered the plaintiff's land and did harm such as crop damage. In such an instance, there seems to be no "direct" connection between the defendant's conduct and the harm—he did not "act"—and consequently the writ of *Trespass* would be inappropriate. But *Case* had not been developed, so the choice was to dismiss the claim or to entertain it under the writ of *Trespass*. The courts seem to have chosen the latter course, and since *Trespass* carried with it the rule of strict liability, cattle trespass became a strict liability tort. This rule, having gained its foothold in *Trespass*, remained the same even after *Case* was developed. As another English historian has said, if the claims had arisen later in time, *Case* would have been available and would have been used, with the result, presumably, that liability would have been based on negligence. G. Williams, Liability for Animals 133 (1939).

The cattle cases were apparently thought of as a special category of liability. Not only did the rule of strict liability for cattle trespass survive the advent of *Case*, in some degree it also survived *Brown v. Kendall*. The "universal" fault formula in *Brown v. Kendall* found an exception in the cattle cases.

The rule for cattle included the barnyard beasts in general—cows, horses, sheep and others. It did not include pets, such as dogs, even though dogs might have important functions on a farm. There was also a special exception even as to cattle: if they strayed from a highway on which they were being driven, there was no strict liability for their trespass.

Under some cases and the earlier Restatement, strict liability for these barnyard animals did not apply to personal injury, only to "trespass" damage. But the newest Torts Restatement extends strict liability to any injury resulting from animal intrusion upon land that is a characteristic of such intrusion, which may include personal injuries. RESTATEMENT (THIRD) OF TORTS: LIABILITY FOR PHYSICAL HARM § 21 cmt. *g* (Proposed Final Draft No. 1, 2005).

Although strict liability for cattle trespass survived *Brown v. Kendall's* universal rule, conditions in America were not the same as those in England, and a number of states adopted quite different rules, especially where large open grazing was feasible and desirable. Thus the strict liability rule of the English common law was rejected and some other rule imposed in many American states, not because of the universal formula proposed in *Brown v. Kendall* but because of different economic needs. Conflicting land uses and needs generated statutory solutions in many states—some requiring the cattle owner to fence the cattle in, some requiring the garden owner to "fence the cattle out." It is now common to find statutes providing for a local option or a fencing district, so that a given county or other area may provide the rule best suited to its economy and geography.

The special strict liability rule for animal trespass, though sometimes changed by American states, served as a reminder that some forms of strict liability would survive *Brown v. Kendall*. The animal trespass cases are in fact quite similar in some ways to another instance which may involve strict liability—nuisance cases.

B.   NUISANCE

BAMFORD v. TURNLEY

3 B. & S. 66, 122 Eng. Rep. 27 (Exch. Ch. 1862)

[Plaintiff declared that the defendant made certain brick kilns on his own land and that these produced "unwholesome vapours, smokes, fumes, stinks and stenches," which proceeded to "enter in, spread and diffuse themselves over, upon, into, through and about" the plaintiff's house. They were "corrupted, offensive, unwholesome, unhealthy and uncomfortable: and thereby the plaintiff had been greatly annoyed and inconvenienced in the possession and enjoyment" and family and servants had become ill. At trial it appeared that defendant had indeed made bricks on his own land, though this was a temporary matter, intended to use the clay on his land for building his own house, and the kilns themselves were as far removed from the plaintiff's property as possible. The trial judge ruled that if the spot chosen for the kilns was "convenient and proper, and the burning of the bricks was, under the circumstances, a reasonable use by the defendant of his own land, the defendant would be entitled to a verdict,'' and on this basis judgment was entered for the defendant, which is now under review.]

[The judgment of ERLE, C.J. is omitted.]

BRAMWELL B. I am of opinion that this judgment should be reversed. The defendant has done that which, if done wantonly or maliciously, would be actionable as being a nuisance to the plaintiff's habitation by causing a sensible diminution of the comfortable enjoyment of it. This, therefore, calls on the defendant to justify or excuse what he has done. And his justification is this: He says that the nuisance is not to the health of the inhabitants of the plaintiff's house, that it is of a temporary character, and is necessary for the beneficial use of his, the defendant's land, and that the public good requires he should be entitled to do what he claims to do.

The question seems to me to be, Is this a justification in law,—and, in order not to make a verbal mistake, I will say,—a justification for what is done, or a matter which makes what is done no nuisance? ... The defendant has infringed the maxim Sic utere tuo ut alienum non laedas. Then, what principle or rule of law can he rely on to defend himself? It is clear to my mind that there is some exception to the general application of the maxim mentioned. The instances put during the argument, of burning weeds, emptying cess-pools, making noises during repairs, and other instances which would be nuisances if done wantonly or maliciously, nevertheless may be lawfully done. It cannot be said that such acts are not nuisances, because, by the hypothesis, they are; and it cannot be doubted that, if a person maliciously and without cause made close to a dwelling-house the same offensive smells as may be made in emptying a cesspool, an action would lie. Nor can these cases be got rid of as extreme cases, because such cases properly test a principle. Nor can it be said that the jury settle such questions by finding there is no nuisance, though there is. For that is to suppose they violate their duty, and that, if they discharged their duty, such matters would be actionable, which I think they could not and ought not to be. There must be, then, some principle on which such cases must be excepted. It seems to me that the principle may be deduced from the character of these cases, and is this, viz., that those acts necessary for the common and ordinary use and occupation of land and houses may be done, if conveniently done, without subjecting those who do them to an action. . . . There is an obvious necessity for such a principle as I have mentioned. It is as much for the advantage of one owner as of another; for the very nuisance the one complains of, as the result of the ordinary use of this neighbor's land, he himself will create in the ordinary use of his own, and the reciprocal nuisances are of a comparatively trifling character. The convenience of such a rule may be indicated by calling it a rule of give and take, live and let live.

Then can this principle be extended to, or is there any other principle which will comprehend, the present case? I know of none: it is for the defendant to shew it. None of the above reasoning is applicable to such a cause of nuisance as the present. It had occurred to me, that any not unnatural use of the land, if of a temporary character, might be justified; but I cannot see why it being of a temporary nature should warrant it. What is temporary,—one, five, or twenty years? . . .

But it is said that, temporary or permanent, it is lawful because it is for the public benefit. Now, in the first place, that law to my mind is a bad one which, for the public benefit, inflicts loss on an individual without compensation. But further, with great respect, I think this consideration misapplied in this and in many other cases. The public consists of all the individuals of it, and a thing is only for the public benefit when it is productive of good to those individuals on the balance of loss and gain to all. So that if all the loss and all the gain were borne and received by one individual, he on the whole would be a gainer. But whenever this is the case,—whenever a thing is for the public benefit, properly understood,— the loss to the individuals of the public who lose will bear compensation out of the gains of those who gain. It is for the public benefit there should be railways, but it would not be unless the gain of having the railway was sufficient to compensate the loss occasioned by the use of the land required for its site; and accordingly no one thinks it would be right to take an individual's land without compensation to make a railway. It is for the public benefit that trains should run, but not unless they pay their expenses. If one of those expenses is the burning down of a wood of such value that the railway owners would not run the train and burn down the wood if it were their own, neither is it for the public benefit they should if the wood is not their own. . . . [Likewise] unless the defendant's profits are enough to compensate [plaintiff's loss], I deny that it is for the public benefit he should do what he has done; if they are, he ought to compensate.

The only objection I can see to this reasoning is, that by injunction or by abatement of the nuisance a man who would not accept a pecuniary compensation might put a stop to works of great value, and much more than enough to compensate him. This objection, however, is comparatively of small practical importance. . . .

[The judgment of POLLOCK, C.B., is omitted.]

NOTES

1. **Characteristics or elements of nuisance cases.** The *Bamford* case reflects many elements of the typical private nuisance case as well as some of the concerns such cases generate. A private nuisance is said to involve an interference, not with possession, but with use and enjoyment. Nuisance cases thus do not involve entry of large physical forces onto the land, but instead typically involve air pollution, as in *Bamford*, or pollution of water, or "noise pollution," as where the defendant plays loud music in a quiet

neighborhood or flies airplanes too low. A few nuisances may be accomplished without any invasion, even of this microcosmic kind. A funeral parlor or a "halfway house" for convicts, if located in residential areas, may constitute a nuisance.

2. **Intent.** Was the nuisance in *Bamford* an intentional tort? Dean Page Keeton once suggested at least four distinct kinds of situations:

(a) Defendant knows that its conduct causes non-trespassory invasions and knows it causes substantial and significant annoyance.

(b) Defendant knows only that her conduct causes a non-trespassory invasion, and does not know or believe the invasion to be serious. E.g., defendant burns leaves in the fall.

(c) Defendant knows only that its conduct risks an invasion of the plaintiff's interests, but does not know that any invasion is certain. E.g., the defendant's polluted water seeps through the ground and fouls the plaintiff's wells some distance away.

(d) Defendant causes no physical invasion at all, even by microscopic particles. For example, defendant erects and operates a funeral establishment or a halfway house for convicts in a residential area.

Is it sufficient that the intent is only of the *Garratt v. Dailey* kind and the defendant has no actual purpose or desire to invade the plaintiff's interests? Is it sufficient that the defendant intends an invasion which will be annoying if he does not believe it will amount to the kind of serious annoyance the law will call a nuisance? What does Baron Bramwell say on these two questions?

3. **Negligence and strict liability.** Most cases of nuisance would fit with an intentional tort analysis, using *Garratt v. Dailey* intent. In a few, negligence might be found; this, too, would serve as a basis for liability. And courts have recognized, often in reliance on Restatement (Second) § 822(b), that strict liability for nuisance is possible where it would be imposed under other independent rules governing abnormally dangerous activities.

4. **Risk-utility analysis and custom.** Does Baron Bramwell use the risk-utility analysis in the same way that Judge Learned Hand used it in *Carroll Towing*? Does Bramwell use custom the same way that Hand used it in *The T. J. Hooper*?

NOTE: A SHORT SIDE TRIP—NUISANCES TODAY

This chapter has focused on strict liability, particularly on the way law changed to impose strict liability for certain activities. It is convenient here, however, to provide a brief sketch of contemporary nuisance law.

1. *Substantial invasion.* The invasion of the plaintiff's interest in use and enjoyment must be substantial. This is a matter of degree and a plaintiff's success will often turn on effective proof. Suppose the plaintiff in *Bamford* only occasionally got a few whiffs of smoke from the brick kiln. Would this be sufficient?

2. *Unreasonable invasion.* The invasion must be unreasonable, not in the sense that the defendant creates an unreasonable risk, but in the sense that given the time, place, and social expectations of the locale, it is unreasonable to expect the plaintiff to put up with the invasion without compensation. An intentional invasion may thus be permissible: defendant burns leaves in the fall, or operates a brick kiln that regularly causes odors, but not for long. Other intended invasions may be actionable as nuisances if it is unreasonable to expect the plaintiff to put up with them. But this raises the question: how would you prove something is "unreasonable" if not by proving unreasonably risky conduct? RESTATEMENT (SECOND) OF TORTS § 826 (1979) provides the traditional answer that the invasion is a nuisance if the gravity of the harm to the plaintiff "outweighs" the utility of the defendant's conduct. This would require a balancing of harm (not *risk* of harm) and utility of the conduct causing the invasion. But the Restatement adds another alternative test: If the defendant could compensate the plaintiff and all others whose interests are invaded by the defendant's conduct, and could still stay in business, then compensation should be made. The idea is that it would be unreasonable to permit the defendant's activity to continue without paying, and the invasion will be regarded as a nuisance.

3. *Proof bearing on reasonableness.* What proof would you try to find in favor of a plaintiff in an industrial nuisance case? Would you expect to be able to get any of the following types of proof admitted into evidence?

(a) The harm is very great; plaintiffs cannot sleep and the value of their property is diminished by fifty percent.

(b) The plaintiffs are using their property in accord with the traditional uses in the neighborhood.

(c) Defendant's industrial use is unusual in the neighborhood.

(d) The locality is not especially well adapted to the defendant's use; the industry could move.

(e) Plaintiffs began using the neighborhood for residential housing long before defendants moved the industry into the area.

See DOBBS ON TORTS § 465 (2000).

4. *Sensitive plaintiffs and sensitive land uses.* What if a plaintiff has a unique allergy and nearly dies of pulmonary disorders when defendant's factory begins operating nearby. No one else is troubled. Or the plaintiff uses the land for raising animals called sinks. These valuable animals become crazed by noise and eat each other when they hear children yelling. A neighbor with five children moves in across the street. The sinks kill and eat each other. The rule is that there is no nuisance unless the invasion would substantially and unreasonably affect normal persons and normal land uses. *See Johnson v. Knox County Partnership*, 728 N.W.2d 101 (Neb. 2007) (cattle-confinement facility in rural area). How does this compare with the thin skull rule? Or does it compare at all?

5. *Coming to the nuisance.* The fact that the plaintiff moved in next door to a nuisance is a significant fact in judging unreasonableness and hence in judging whether there is a nuisance at all. But no enterprise is allowed to create a noisome condition on its own land and insist that forever after anyone who comes into the area must be willing to tolerate such a condition. To permit this would be to allow an enterprise to condemn the land of others and to force a stasis on a dynamic and changing world. The fact that the plaintiff came to the nuisance is therefore only one factor to be considered in determining whether a nuisance exists. If the natural spread of a city brings it to the edge of the defendant's smelly feed lot, the lot, which was no nuisance at all when the area was devoted to farming, may become one when the area becomes suburban. On the other hand, the plaintiff who moves from Palm Springs to Bakersfield cannot complain about oil wells.

Another possibility when the plaintiff comes to the nuisance is that he has already been compensated for it. This is so because, if the nuisance is open and obvious, the plaintiff will probably have paid the former owner a smaller price because of the nuisance.

6. *Injunctions.* In many cases the nuisance claim results in a recovery of damages. In some cases, however, the plaintiff may seek and obtain an injunction against the nuisance. Sometimes an injunction may merely require an industrial polluter to experiment to find a pollution-solution, or to install the best available technology to reduce pollution, or to operate at hours that cause less disturbance. *Cf. Biglane v. Under the Hill Corp.*, 949 So.2d 9 (Miss. 2007) (affirming injunction that restricted a saloon's hours of operation). In other cases, the plaintiff may ask the court to enjoin the entire operation, on the ground that, no matter how it is operated, it will constitute a nuisance. *See, e.g., Burch v. Nedpower Mount Storm, LLC*, 647 S.E.2d 879 (W.Va. 2007) (wind farm facility near private homes). An injunction like that is occasionally granted, but it is obviously more extreme than a remedy that merely makes the industrial polluter pay the costs of its pollution. For example, an injunction against operation of a business might compel discontinuance of a product or service the public wants and needs; it would certainly throw employees out of work. For these reasons, courts balance public interests and the private interests of the parties, and at times exercise discretion not to grant an injunction even if a nuisance is clearly shown. In such cases, the plaintiff may recover damages instead. *See generally* 1 DAN DOBBS, THE LAW OF REMEDIES § 5.7 (2d ed. 1993).

7. *Public nuisances.* Suppose the defendant, an industrial enterprise, dumps wastes on its own ground. These percolate through the soil and pollute a river, a lake, and even estuarine waters. All these bodies of water are public property. If the fish are killed or the waters become unusable, does anyone have a claim? Conceivably, landowners adjacent to these waters would have a nuisance claim on the principles stated above if the pollution substantially diminished the use and enjoyment of their land. What about a non-landowner who fishes for sport and can no longer catch

fish because they are dead? Or one who fishes commercially and can no longer catch them for the same reason? If the pollution constitutes a public nuisance because it substantially interferes with public health, safety, or convenience, the rule is that any person who has damages different in kind from the public generally may recover damages for the nuisance. The claimant who loses commercial fishing profits may thus have "standing to sue" because the claimant's injury differs from that of the public at large. The plaintiff who merely fishes for sport may be denied recovery, since her damages are not so different from those of other persons. In some states, a concern for environmental protection or enhancement may lead to a wider standing on the part of individuals.

8. *Environmental and zoning laws.* The common law of nuisance leads directly to contemporary legislation and administrative regulations aimed at pollution. It also leads to zoning laws, designed to maximize appropriate land-use. Although it would be theoretically possible to import a great deal of environmental and land-use law into a torts course, those fields have become major specialties of their own. Consequently, the bulk of nuisance law today may be better developed in connection with courses in property, land use, environmental protection, and public health and safety.

Reconsider the question of strict liability for nuisance. Did *Brown v. Kendall* succeed in imposing a universal principle that liability was limited to cases of "fault?" Or is *Bamford* a strict liability case? One way of making *Bamford* comport with the fault regime of *Brown v. Kendall* is to find fault by finding intent. To do this, intent must be defined in the broad sense encountered in *Garratt v. Dailey*. But imagine a defendant who operates a useful industry. Imagine that it unavoidably pollutes, and that this causes diminished use and enjoyment to the plaintiff, a nearby landowner, who complains to the defendant in no uncertain terms. The defendant spends a great deal of money to reduce the pollution, but it is simply impossible. There may be *Garratt v. Dailey* intent in such a case, but would anyone besides a lawyer say there is fault? Perhaps "intent" was given some rather special definitions to make the law seem compatible with *Brown v. Kendall's* requirement of fault. Could you say that, realistically, however, pockets of strict liability remained even after *Brown v. Kendall?*

It is even possible that *Brown v. Kendall* merely wiped the slate clean of traditional forms of strict liability, only to permit other cases to write in new forms of strict liability. Consider the materials that follow.

RYLANDS v. FLETCHER
Exchequer: 3 Hurl & C. 774 (1865)
Exchequer Chamber: L.R. 1 Exch. 265 (1866)
House of Lords: L.R. 3 H.L. 330 (1868)

[Plaintiff operated a mine in the county of Lancaster. Defendants operated a mill in the vicinity, and had contractors build a reservoir or pond to supply water. The contractors did build such a pond, though in fact it was located immediately over some vertical shafts once used in mining. The shafts had been filled rather inadequately, but gave the appearance of solid earth. When the pond was filled with water, its weight caused the material in the shafts to give way, and the water flooded down the vertical shafts. From there it flowed through horizontal mine shafts of an intervening mine into the plaintiff's mine. This is an action by the plaintiff for damages caused by this flooding. A procedure was used in which an arbitrator stated a special case or found facts. The case was then considered in the Court of Exchequer, followed by review in the Exchequer Chamber and finally in the House of Lords. The style of the case is that used in the House of Lords.]

[IN THE COURT OF EXCHEQUER]

Bramwell, B. . . .

The plaintiff's right then has been infringed; the defendants in causing water to flow to the plaintiff have done that which they had no right to do; what difference in point of law does it make that they have done it unwittingly? I think none, and consequently that the action is maintainable. . . .

It is said there must be a trespass, a nuisance, or negligence. . . . But why is not this a trespass? Wilfulness is not material: Leame v. Bray (3 East, 593). Why is it not a nuisance? The nuisance is not in the reservoir, but in the water escaping. As in Backhouse v. Bonomi the act was lawful, the mischievous consequence is a wrong. . . .

Martin, B. . . .

First, I think there was no trespass. . . . I think the true criterion of trespass is laid down in the judgments in the former case, viz., that to constitute trespass the act doing the damage must be immediate, and that if the damage be mediate or consequential (which I think the present was), it is not a trespass. Secondly, I think there was no nuisance in the ordinary and generally understood meaning of that word, that is to say, something hurtful or injurious to the senses. The making a pond for holding water is a nuisance to no one. The digging a reservoir in a man's own land is a lawful act. . . . To hold the defendants liable would therefore make them insurers against the consequence of a lawful act upon their own land when they had no reason to believe or suspect that any damage was likely to ensue. . . .

[Pollock, C. B., agreed with Martin, B., that the facts found by the arbitrator were not a sufficient basis for relief.]

[IN THE EXCHEQUER CHAMBER]

May 14, 1866. Blackburn, J., read the following judgment of the court. . . .

We have come to the conclusion that the opinion of Bramwell, B., was right, and that the answer to the question should be that the plaintiff was entitled to recover damages from the defendants by reason of the matters stated in the Case....

What is the liability which the law casts upon a person who, like the defendants, lawfully brings on his land something which, though harmless while it remains there, will naturally do mischief if it escapes out of his land? It is agreed on all hands that he must take care to keep in that which he has brought on the land, and keep it there in order that it may not escape and damage his neighbor's, but the question arises whether the duty which the law casts upon him under such circumstances is an absolute duty to keep it in at his peril, or is, as the majority of the Court of Exchequer have thought, merely a duty to take all reasonable and prudent precautions in order to keep it in, but no more....

We think that the true rule of law is that the person who, for his own purposes, brings on his land, and collects and keeps there anything likely to do mischief if it escapes, must keep it in at his peril, and, if he does not do so, he is prima facie answerable for all the damage which is the natural consequence of its escape. He can excuse himself by showing that the escape was owing to the plaintiff's default, or, perhaps, that the escape was the consequence of vis major, or the act of God; but, as nothing of this sort exists here, it is unnecessary to inquire what excuse would be sufficient....

The case that has most commonly occurred, and which is most frequently to be found in the books, is as to the obligation of the owner of cattle which he has brought on his land to prevent their escaping and doing mischief. The law as to them seems to be perfectly settled from early times; the owner must keep them in at his peril, or he will be answerable for the natural consequences of their escape, that is, with regard to tame beasts, for the grass they eat and trample upon, although not for any injury to the person of others, for our ancestors have settled that it is not the general nature of horses to kick or bulls to gore, but if the owner knows that the beast has a vicious propensity to attack man he will be answerable for that too.... So in May v. Burdett, the court, after an elaborate examination of the old precedents and authorities, came to the conclusion that a person keeping a mischievous animal is bound to keep it secure at his peril....

As has been already said, there does not appear to be any difference in principle between the extent of the duty cast on him who brings cattle on his land to keep them in, and the extent of the duty imposed on him who brings on his land water, filth, or stenches, or any other thing which will, if it escape, naturally do damage, to prevent their escaping and injuring his neighbor. Tenant v. Goldwin [a case decided in 1704 and reported in a number of places, including 1 Salk. 21 and 360, 91 Eng. Rep. 20 and 314, 2 Ld. Raym, 1089, 92 Eng. Rep. 222, and 6 Mod. Rep. 311, 87 Eng. Rep. 1051] is an express authority that the duty is the same, and is to keep them in at his peril. [In that case the defendant had a privy on his land and formerly had it enclosed by a wall. By reason of the defendant's failure to repair the wall, the filth of the privy flowed into the plaintiff's cellar.]

In the report in 6 Mod. Rep. at p. 314, it is stated:

"And at another day per totam curiam the declaration is good, for there is a sufficient cause of action appearing in it, but not upon the word solebat. If the defendant has a house or office enclosed with a wall which is his, he is, of common right, bound to use it so as not to annoy another. . . . The reason here is, that one must use his own so as thereby not to hurt another, and as of common right one is bound to keep his cattle from trespassing on his neighbor, so he is bound to use anything that is his so as not to hurt another by such use. . . ."

No case has been found in which the question of the liability for noxious vapours escaping from a man's works by inevitable accident has been discussed, but the following case will illustrate it. Some years ago several actions were brought against the occupiers of some alkali works at Liverpool for the damage alleged to be caused by the chlorine fumes of their works. The defendants proved that they had, at great expense, erected a contrivance by which the fumes of chlorine were condensed, and sold as muriatic acid, and they called a great body of scientific evidence to prove that this apparatus was so perfect that no fumes possible could escape from the defendant's chimneys. On this evidence it was pressed upon the juries that the plaintiff's damage must have been due to some of the numerous other chimneys in the neighborhood. The juries, however, being satisfied that the mischief was occasioned by chlorine, drew the conclusion that it had escaped from the defendant's works somehow, and in each case found for the plaintiff. No attempt was made to disturb these verdicts on the ground that the defendants had taken every precaution which prudence or skill could suggest to keep those fumes in, and that they could not be responsible unless negligence were shown, yet if the law be as laid down by the majority of the Court of Exchequer it would have been a very obvious defense. [T]he uniform course of pleading in actions for such nuisances is to say that the defendant caused the noisome vapours to arise on his premises and suffered them to come on the plaintiff's without stating that there was any want of care or skill on the defendant's part; and that Tenant v. Goldwin showed that this was founded on the general rule of law that he whose stuff it is must keep it so that it may not trespass. There is no difference in this respect between chlorine and water; both will, if they escape, do damage, the one by scorching and the other by drowning, and he who brings them on his land must at his peril see that they do not escape and do that mischief.

. . . But it was further said by Martin, B., that when damage is done to personal property, or even to the person by collision, either upon land or at sea, there must be negligence in the party doing the damage to render him legally responsible. This is no doubt true. . . . but we think these cases distinguishable from the present. Traffic on the highways, whether by land or sea, cannot be conducted without exposing those whose persons or property are near it to some inevitable risk; and, that being so, those who go on the highway, or have their property adjacent to it, may well be held to do so subject to their taking upon themselves the risk of injury from that inevitable danger ... and it is believed that all the cases in which inevitable accident has been held an excuse for what prima facie was a trespass can be explained on the same principle, namely that the circumstances were such as to show that the plaintiff had taken the risk upon himself. But there is no ground for saying that the plaintiff here took upon himself any risk arising from the uses to which the defendants should choose to apply their land. He neither knew what there might be, nor could he in any way control the defendants. . . .

The view which we take of the first point renders it unnecessary to consider whether the defendants would or would not be responsible for the want of care and skill in the persons employed by them. We are of opinion that the plaintiff is entitled to recover. . . .

[IN THE HOUSE OF LORDS]

Lord Cairns, L.C. . . . .

The principles on which this case must be determined appear to me to be extremely simple. The defendants, ... might lawfully have used that close for any purpose for which it might, in the ordinary course of the enjoyment of land, be used, and if, in what I may term the natural user of that land, there had been any accumulation of water, either on the surface or underground, and if by the operation of the laws of nature that accumulation of water had passed off into the close occupied by the plaintiff, the plaintiff could not have complained that that result had taken place. If he had desired to guard himself against it, it would have lain on him to have done so. . . .

On the other hand, if the defendants, not stopping at the natural use of their close, had desired to use it for any purpose which I may term a non-natural use, for the purpose of introducing into the close that which, in its natural condition, was not in or upon it—for the purpose of introducing water, either above or below ground, in quantities and in a manner not the result of any work or operation on or under the land, and if in consequence of their doing so, or in consequence of any imperfection in the mode of their doing so, the water came to escape and to pass off into the close of the plaintiff, then it appears to me that that which the defendants were doing they were doing at their own peril. . . .

These simple principles, if they are well founded, as it appears to me they are, really dispose of this case. The same result is arrived at on the principles referred to by Blackburn, J., in his judgment in the Court of Exchequer Chamber. . . .

In that opinion, I must say, I entirely concur. Therefore, I have to move your Lordships that the judgment of the Court of Exchequer Chamber be affirmed, and that the present appeal be dismissed with costs.

LORD CRANWORTH.

I concur with my noble and learned friend in thinking that the rule of law was correctly stated by Blackburn, J., in delivering the opinion of the Exchequer chamber. If a person brings or accumulates on his land anything which, if it should escape, may cause damage to his neighbor, he does so at his peril. If it does escape and cause damage, he is responsible, however careful he may have been, and whatever precautions he may have taken to prevent the damage. In considering whether a defendant is liable to a plaintiff for damage which the plaintiff may have sustained, the question in general is, not whether the defendant has acted with due care and caution, but whether his acts have occasioned the damage. This is all well explained in the old case of Lambert and Olliot v. Bessey. The doctrine is founded on good sense, for when one person in managing his own affairs causes, however innocently, damage to another, it is obviously only just that he should be the party to suffer. He is bound sic uti suo ut non laedat alienum. This is the principle of law applicable to cases like the present, and I do not discover in the authorities which were cited anything conflicting with it. . . .

NOTES

1. **Trespass or nuisance alternatives?** Liability for trespass would not be imposed today unless the defendant or his employees intended to enter the plaintiff's land. Perhaps the English law of the 19th century was stricter. Professor Bohlen, who became the Reporter of the first Restatement of Torts, thought that a trespass theory would not work in *Rylands* because the injury was "indirect," since the water did not escape when it was first poured into the reservoir. He thought that a nuisance theory would not work because there was no continuous seeping or percolation and hence no "continuous injurious condition," which he took to be necessary in a nuisance case. Francis Bohlen, *The Rule in Rylands v. Fletcher*, 59 U. PA. L. REV. 298 (1911).

2. **Why strict liability in *Rylands*?** What is the scope of strict liability in *Rylands* and why is it imposed? Is *Rylands* merely a nuisance case? If so, does it go beyond the implications of *Bamford*?

3. **Special hazards in *Rylands*?** Does *Rylands* require any special hazard as a prerequisite to liability? Substances like dynamite may represent unusual hazards. Is water like that?

4. **Legitimate land uses endangering one another.** In one respect *Rylands* may be easy to understand. Suppose that thousands of acres of land in an agricultural area are devoted to farming Murg, a kind of grain that requires repeated aerial spraying. Into the midst of this great agricultural area move two new businesses: one is a beekeeper and one is a heavy industry. If, without fault, the aerial spraying of the Murg fields injures the bees or prevents them from finding usable pollen, should the beekeeper have a claim? If, without fault, the heavy industry discharges pollution that contaminates 3,000 acres of Murg growing in the fields, should the Murg owners have a claim?

5. **Does *Rylands* fit the inconsistent land uses pattern?** Cases like those just suggested, cases like *Rylands*, and most nuisance cases can be

thought of as instances of inconsistent land uses. Though there is nothing "wrong" with moving a factory to the country, if it presents dangers to existing investments through its pollution, perhaps the most economical thing to do is to protect those investments without regard to "fault." Does this describe *Rylands*? After all, coal can be mined and that resource exploited only in places where the coal lies, but one could build a millpond almost anywhere in a pluvial country.

6. **A test case.** To test this idea, imagine that the coal mine in *Rylands* somehow caused damage to the mill owner or to nearby farmers. Would strict liability have been imposed then? Take an actual case: Salt water is used in oil well drilling, and must be stored in ponds. If the oil well driller's salt water pond collapsed without the driller's fault, would the farmer whose fields were ruined have an action based on strict liability? In *Turner v. Big Lake Oil Co.*, 96 S.W.2d 221 (Tex. 1936), the court rejected strict liability on such facts. While the court said it repudiated *Rylands,* is the result one *Rylands* might actually support? How?

7. **Coming to the nuisance.** There are similar ideas in pure nuisance cases. Although one who "comes to the nuisance" is not necessarily barred from recovery, since a number of factors must be weighed in nuisance cases, it seems clear that one who moves a home to a factory district cannot successfully enjoin operation of the factories or even recover damages. Compare the situation of the beekeeper in Note 4. If the factory moves into a residential neighborhood, the situation is reversed and it may well be found to be a nuisance.

8. **Animals.** (a) *Trespassing Cattle*. We have already seen that most courts would apply strict liability for cattle trespasses, and that such liability might even include personal injury damages where those harms are characteristic of such intrusion. Thus being hurt trying to chase a bull off your property might give you a strict liability claim, but tripping over a goat sleeping on your land at night would not. *See* Restatement of the Law (Third), Torts: Liability for Physical Harm § 21 cmt. *g* (Proposed Final Draft No. 1, 2005).

(b) *Other animals generally*. As to other animals, such as dogs, the owner's liability is commonly regarded as a species of strict but limited liability. If, but only if, the owner knows of the dog's vicious propensity (to bite, for example) the owner is strictly liable for injuries resulting from that particular propensity. Id., § 23. This rule seems to apply to any kind of animal. *See, e.g., Bard v. Jahnke*, 848 N.E.2d 463 (N.Y. 2006) (owner of bull lacked knowledge of bull's vicious propensities; no strict liability). Statutes and ordinances often impose additional liabilities on dog owners, through leash laws or otherwise.

(c) *Wild animals*. A third category deals with animals often said to be "wild by nature." These include lions and tigers and bears that people have seen fit to import and exhibit. As to this category, the rule existing at the time of *Rylands* was that strict liability would be imposed for injuries connected with the wild characteristic of the animal, so that the person in charge would be held responsible in spite of all possible care. Restatement (Third) § 22 is in accord. Is this rule consistent with *Rylands* itself?

———

THOMALEN v. MARRIOTT CORP., 845 F.Supp. 33 (D. Mass. 1994). A Marriott Hotel in Westborough, Massachusetts, hosted a "Murder Mystery Weekend," in which a troupe of actors staged murder mystery entertainments. One member of the group, attempting to perform a fire-eating act, became engulfed in flames; another member ran to the stage to help but knocked over a can of lighter fluid. This ignited and caused burns to Belmont, a guest close to the stage. *Held*, the Marriott is not strictly liable. Massachusetts has adopted *Rylands v. Fletcher* strict liability, but since there was "no escape of a dangerous instrumentality from Marriott's property," that rule does not apply.

C. SLOUCHING TOWARD THE ABNORMAL DANGER CONCEPTION

SULLIVAN v. DUNHAM, 55 N.E. 923 (N.Y. 1900). In June of 1895, Annie E. Harten, 19-years-old, was on a public highway near Irvington, New York. Defendant was blasting to get rid of stumps. A stump thus blasted flew through the air and struck and killed Harten. In an action for her wrongful death, held, verdict for plaintiff was properly affirmed by the Appellate Division. Where blasting throws rocks or trees onto the lands of another, there is liability as a trespasser. Though one has the right to blast, the other has the right to the beneficial use of his property. In this case there is no trespass to property, but the same reasons apply to a trespass to person. If the injury had been indirect, from concussion and shaking of the earth, there would have been no liability, as that would not have been a trespass. Likewise, *semble*, if the injury had been the result of an accidental rather than an intentional explosion, there would be no liability. But where there is a direct and trespassory invasion of another's land or person, there is liability.

NOTES

1. Is this merely a rejection of *Brown v. Kendall* and a retention of the early common law rules of liability for "direct" harms?

2. If so, then one would expect that a blaster who causes damage by concussion would not be liable, and, as reflected in *Sullivan*, that in fact was the New York rule at the time.

3. It must be clear from the preceding paragraphs that New York had rejected *Rylands v. Fletcher*, since otherwise concussion damage would have been actionable if it resulted from "non-natural" activities. At this time, a number of other states took positions similar to that of *Sullivan*, and explicitly rejected *Rylands*, at least in name.

4. This left the law in a rather awkward state. There was in the first place a rather general acceptance that negligence, not "directness," had

become the basis of liability. In other words, *Brown v. Kendall* was largely accepted by American courts, and *Rylands* largely rejected. Yet there were pockets of strict liability, of which *Sullivan* is one example. And this strict liability was a difficult problem because it seemed to proceed, as in *Sullivan*, on the very grounds that had been rejected in *Brown v. Kendall*. Worse, perhaps, it distinguished between two claims that seemed morally indistinguishable—the injury from debris thrown up by a blaster and injury from the same blast but occurring through the medium of vibrations in the ground. In both cases, the defendant's act was the same and the plaintiff's injury equally real.

5.   This puzzle could be resolved by either rejecting *Brown v. Kendall* or by accepting *Rylands,* but neither of these options was palatable. Was there any other solution?

———

EXNER v. SHERMAN POWER CONSTRUCTION CO., 54 F.2d 510 (2d Cir. 1931). Defendant was blasting for a hydroelectric development at Bellows Falls, Vermont, about 935 feet from the plaintiff's dwelling and restaurant. There was a severe explosion which shook the house, throwing Mrs. Exner from her bed and damaging the property. There was a jury verdict for the plaintiff, based on violation of a statute. On appeal, *held,* affirmed. The statute was not intended to protect the class of which the plaintiff was a member, but the judgment for the plaintiff may be affirmed if this is a case of "absolute liability" at common law. "While the rule laid down by Blackburn, J., in *Rylands v. Fletcher*, has not been followed in America to the full extent of all its implications, and, at the outset its authority was impaired by [decisions in New Hampshire, New York and New Jersey], yet in the so-called 'blasting' cases an absolute liability, without regard to fault, has uniformly been imposed by the American courts wherever there has been an actual invasion of property by rocks or debris. . . .

"It is true that some courts have distinguished between liability for a common law trespass, occasioned by blasting, which projects rocks or debris upon the property or the person of the plaintiff, and liability for so-called consequential damages arising from concussion, and have denied liability for the latter where the blasting itself was conducted at a lawful time and place and with due care. Yet in every practical sense there can be no difference between a blasting which projects rocks in such a way as to injure persons or property and a blasting which, by creating a sudden vacuum, shatters buildings or knocks down people. . . .

"[T]he imposition of absolute liability is not out of accord with any general principles of law. . . . [I]n trespass, fault ordinarily remained a matter of no consequence, and even in cases of damage to the person the early decisions prior to Brown v. Kendall, seemed to have imposed liability where there was no negligence.

"... The extent to which one man in the lawful conduct of his business is liable for injuries to another involves an adjustment of conflicting interests. The solution of the problem ... has never been dependent upon any universal criterion of liability (such as 'fault') applicable to all situations. If damage is inflicted, there ordinarily is liability, in the absence of excuse. When, as here, the defendant, though without fault, has engaged in the perilous activity of storing large quantities of a dangerous explosive for use in his business, we think there is no justification for relieving it of liability, and that the owner of the business, rather than a third person who has no relation to the explosion, other than that of injury, should bear the loss."

NOTES

1. Would this same decision be reached under *Rylands v. Fletcher*?

2. When *Exner* was decided, *Rylands* was unpopular in the United States, at least by name. How, then, should one express the rule in *Exner*?

3. Professor Bohlen relied in part on *Exner* and on *Sullivan* in formulating the Restatement's rule. *Sullivan* was important in emphasizing that this form of strict liability was not limited to property. *Exner* and other cases, Bohlen thought, emphasized that the defendant carried on an activity that introduced an "unescapable danger into the community" and did so for his own profit. The First Restatement accordingly introduced a whole chapter on "Ultrahazardous Activities," which years later became the basis for the Second Restatement's rules.

NOTE: THE RESTATEMENTS' RULES OF STRICT LIABILITY

1. *The formulation.* Strict liability has been addressed in three succeeding Torts Restatements, each coming up with a different formulation. The most recent appears in the Third Restatement § 20(b) (P.F.D. No. 1, 2005), which provides for liability without proof of negligence if:

> (1) the defendant's activity creates a reasonably foreseeable and highly significant risk of physical harm even where reasonable care is exercised by all actors; and

> (2) the activity is not one of common usage.

2. *When plaintiff or others contribute to the activity.* In comments, the Third Restatement emphasizes an additional matter—that strict liability is appropriate where the activity causes harm "without meaningful contribution from the conduct of the victim or of any other actors." The victim is an uninvolved and innocent party who is doing nothing. *See Id.*, cmt. *e.* Contrast the situation that arose in *Pullen v. West*, 92 P.3d 584 (Kan. 2004). The plaintiff was helping with a fireworks display and suffered injury when struck by a fireworks rocket. The court rejected his strict liability claim because it said he participated in the activity. The court said he might still recover under negligence rules.

3. *Risks or harms avoidable by reasonable care.* Notice that if reasonable care would reduce risks to a less-than-significant-level, strict liability does not apply. What if risks would be less than significant only if both the defendant and its potential victims were to exercise reasonable care? The Third Restatement provides in § 20, comment *h*, that the defendant's activity is not "unavoidably dangerous" and therefore not a matter of strict liability if potential victims can "commonly succeed in avoiding injuries."

4. *The Second Restatement's factors.* The Second Restatement § 520, in contrast, dragged out a list of factors to be considered by the court in deciding the issue. Besides the high risk, inability to eliminate risk by ordinary care, and uncommon nature of the activity, the Second Restatement emphasized the activity's inappropriateness to the place where it is carried on; and the extent to which the activity's value to the community is outweighed by its dangerous attributes. These factors made strict liability sound a good deal like negligence and they have been dropped from the Third Restatement. However, location of an activity might still bear on the question of high risk.

5. Rylands *and abnormal danger.* The Restatements concentrate in part on high danger. *Rylands* emphasized the uncommon, or at least non-natural, nature of the defendant's activity, but otherwise seems tied to landowners (as the Restatements are not) and to involve no special kind of danger. Where did the idea of high danger come from?

6. *Justifications for strict liability.* Why impose strict liability? (a) When the defendant engages in abnormally dangerous activities, knowing that he will reap the gains from the activity but that others may be harmed because it cannot be made safe by reasonable care, perhaps there is a moral basis for liability. If a defendant were *certain* that harm would result, you can make a moral case for liability. Is it so clear that the same is true when the defendant is not substantially certain of harm but merely knows of the high risk? Notice that, right or wrong, this idea is not to deter the activity—after all, it is not negligent—but to make it "pay its own way." (b) The Third Restatement suggests in § 20, comment *b*, that it is difficult to prove that an entire activity (like driving or building dams) is negligent and that some kinds of activity may involve negligence that cannot be detected or proved; strict liability, it suggests, is a good response to such cases.

7. *Common usage.* If an activity is normal in the community—"a matter of common usage"—strict liability does not apply and liability is limited to negligence and intent. The common usage rule certainly serves to limit the application of strict liability, but is a principle behind it? The Third Restatement in § 20, comment *j*, suggests two possibilities—first that the reason for strict liability might to some extent represent a concern for the acceptability of the activity and that when it is common, that concern tends to disappear. Second, when an activity is common, its benefits are likely to be distributed widely in the community and the basis

for strict liability is stronger when benefits are concentrated among a few. *Cf.* Mark Geistfeld, *Should Enterprise Liability Replace the Rule of Strict Liability for Abnormally Dangerous Activities?*, 45 U.C.L.A. L. REV. 611 (1998). What do you think? If nuclear energy were not regulated by statutes, would you say that benefits of a nuclear power plant (a high risk activity) were concentrated among a few when electricity is distributed to virtually everyone?

REFERENCE: DOBBS ON TORTS § 346–47 (2000).

§ 3. STRICT LIABILITY TODAY

A. THE SUBJECTS OF STRICT LIABILITY

To what kinds of cases do the rules of nuisance, *Rylands v. Fletcher*, and "abnormally dangerous activities" apply? Is there a single rationale or principle that covers them all? Do the rationales for vicarious liability that we saw in Chapter 22 support the imposition of strict liability in these situations?

1. *Impoundments.* On the precise facts of *Rylands*—the sudden escape of ponded water—very few modern courts would impose strict liability. However, in two variants on the *Rylands* facts, strict liability may be imposed. The first is where the defendant impounds noxious substances that suddenly escape. *See, e.g., Cities Service Co. v. State*, 312 So.2d 799 (Fla. Dist Ct. App. 1975) (escape of billions of gallons of phosphate slimes from a mine); *State Dept. of Envtl. Prot. v. Ventron Corp.*, 468 A.2d 150 (N.J. 1983) (escape of 268 tons of mercury).

The second variation involves impounded liquids that do not escape suddenly, but merely percolate through the soil and contaminate a well or otherwise cause harm. These percolation cases almost always involve noxious impoundments, and may be traced to *Tenant v. Goldwin*, discussed in *Rylands*, *supra*, where the judges appeared willing to impose strict liability for the escape of filth from a privy. *See Yommer* v. *McKenzie*, 257 A.2d 138 (Md. 1969) (gasoline); *Iverson v. Vint*, 54 N.W.2d 494 (Iowa 1952) (molasses dumped in ditch, percolation into farmer's well, strict liability). Some of these cases can be explained on other grounds, for example, that there was *Garratt v. Dailey* intent, or that there was a species of fault in carrying on an activity in an inappropriate place. Can there really be any principle, other than a whimsical one, that distinguishes damage caused by sudden escape from damage caused by percolation?

2. *Hazardous wastes.* Beyond the situations mentioned above, activities involving toxic substances are good candidates for strict liability based on abnormal danger. In *T & E Industries, Inc. v. Safety Light Corp.*, 587 A.2d 1249 (N.J. 1991), a plant used radium that left its own ground contaminated. Later it sold the property, which eventually passed to the plaintiff. Upon discovery of the contamination in the property it had purchased, the plaintiff sued. The court held that seller would be strictly

liable not only to adjoining landowners who suffered harm, but also to purchasers like the plaintiff.

3. *The Superfund Act.* Statutes and regulations are now of central importance in environmental litigation, both public and private, and they must be studied with care by any practitioner dealing with hazardous waste cases. Some statutes envision that government will shoulder the primary task of cleaning up hazardous substances, but leave some room for private litigation as well. The "Superfund Act" provides a fund, derived in part from taxes on industry, for the government to use to clean up substances released into the environment. Representatives of the fund may sue the responsible industry for reimbursement. Liability is strict and applies not only to one who actually released the substance but also to owners of the contaminated land whether they released the substance or not. *See* 42 U.S.C.A. § 9607(a).

4. *Lateral support.* "Between adjacent landowners, the general principle ... is that each has an absolute property right to have his land laterally supported by the soil of his neighbor, and if either in excavating on his own premises so disturbs the lateral support of his neighbor's land as to cause it, in its natural state, by the pressure of its own weight, to fall away or slide from its position, the one so excavating is liable." *Prete v. Cray,* 141 A. 609 (R.I. 1928). Can this form of strict liability be explained on the Restatement's "abnormally dangerous activity" theory? How does it compare, if at all, with other cases, such as those involving percolation, that appear to regulate property rights of near neighbors? *Cf.* RESTATEMENT (SECOND) OF TORTS § 817 (1979).

The same rule is applied to "subjacent" support, that is, where an owner of minerals removes them so that the surface subsides. See ID. § 820.

5. *Blasting and explosives.* The trespass theory behind *Sullivan* eliminated strict liability recovery for concussion damage from blasting. Courts, including New York courts, have now rejected their own earlier decisions limiting liability to cases in which there was a physical "trespass." *See Spano v. Perini Corp.,* 250 N.E.2d 31 (N.Y. 1969). Most courts today apply strict liability to either blasting or storage of explosives; indeed blasting remains the paradigm of abnormally dangerous activity. Note that some courts do not see mere storage of explosives as abnormally dangerous. *Compare Yukon Equip., Inc. v. Fireman's Fund Ins. Co.,* 585 P.2d 1206 (Alaska 1978) with *Liber v. Flor,* 415 P.2d 332 (Colo. 1966).

6. *Nuclear energy.* (a) *Governmental liability.* Public entities have generally retained immunity as to strict liability claims. Thus, for example, the United States is not liable under the FTCA for damages resulting from sonic booms caused by its planes. *Laird v. Nelms,* 406 U.S. 797 (1972). In the absence of a specific statute providing for liability in particular cases, then, the United States would not be liable for nuclear accidents.

(b) *Private liability*. Private liability of utilities licensed to operate nuclear plants is a complex question because the field is heavily but not clearly regulated by federal statutes and rules. In the Price–Anderson Act, 42 U.S.C.A. § 2210, Congress provided for tort liability, limiting the total liability of private industry to about $560 million for any one incident. The government in effect provides an insurance policy to cover much of this liability. Some state law is imported into the federal claim, so long as the state law is not inconsistent with the federal rules provided. Strict liability was imposed on the operator of a nuclear facility that created plutonium and released it into the atmosphere in *In re Hanford Nuclear Reservation Lit.*, 497 F.3d 1005 (9th Cir. 2007).

7. *Other high-energy activities*. The strict liability seen in explosives cases carries over to closely analogous activities where enormous force is involved, including the testing of rockets, *Smith v. Lockheed Propulsion Co.*, 56 Cal.Rptr. 128 (Ct. App. 1967) (ground vibration damaged water well); the use of pile driving equipment, *Caporale v. C. W. Blakeslee & Sons, Inc.*, 175 A.2d 561 (Conn. 1961) ("intrinsically dangerous," strict liability for vibration damage); and even a "blow out" of an oil well in a populated area, *Green v. General Petroleum Corp.*, 270 P. 952 (Cal. 1928).

8. *Utilities*. Should strict liability apply to the transmission of natural gas or electricity? Should this decision be affected by the fact that public utilities are regulated industries with limited profit margin and also with a high ability to pass costs back to consumers? By the fact that gas and electricity are in common use? Courts have refused to apply strict liability to transmission of electrical power and to transmission of natural gas. *See* RESTATEMENT (THIRD) OF TORTS: LIABILITY FOR PHYSICAL HARM § 20, cmts. *h* & *j* (P.F.D. No. 1, 2005).

9. *Fireworks*. If a person is injured by a Fourth of July fireworks display, should strict liability apply? Are such displays like blasting? Or would you call them a matter of "common usage?" And can the risks of such displays be avoided through the use of reasonable care? *Compare Cadena v. Chicago Fireworks Mfg. Co.*, 697 N.E.2d 802 (Ill. App. Ct. 1998) *with Klein v. Pyrodyne Corp.*, 810 P.2d 917 (Wash. 1991).

10. *Poisons*. In *Loe v. Lenhardt*, 362 P.2d 312 (Or. 1961) strict liability was applied to crop-dusting activities. Might this be justified on a pure *Rylands v. Fletcher* rule, without resort to any "abnormally dangerous activity" rule? Courts have imposed strict liability for abnormally dangerous activity in pest control and fumigation cases. *Luthringer v. Moore*, 190 P.2d 1 (Cal. 1948); *Old Island Fumigation, Inc. v. Barbee*, 604 So.2d 1246 (Fla. Dist. Ct. App. 1992).

REFERENCE: DOBBS ON TORTS § 348 (2000).

B. SCOPE OF RISK LIMITATIONS

Under the Restatement (Second) of Torts § 519, the defendant is not strictly liable for *all* harms caused by his abnormally dangerous activity, but only those "the possibility of which makes the activity abnormally dangerous." This simply articulates the basic scope of risk rule we saw in connection with negligence, doesn't it? *See* RESTATEMENT (THIRD) OF TORTS: LIABILITY FOR PHYSICAL HARM § 29, cmt. *l* (P.F.D. No. 1, 2005); § 21, cmt. *g* ("strict liability is typically limited to those harms that result from the risks justifying strict liability").

Suppose a defendant engages in in blasting, but the harm that results is neither harm from propelled objects, as in *Sullivan*, nor harm from vibrations as in *Exner*. Instead the loud noises upset mother minks on nearby mink ranches and as a result they killed their kittens, resulting in loss to the breeder. This is not the kind of harm which led courts in the first place to consider blasting as abnormally dangerous, since it involves neither flying debris nor vibrations of the earth, and liability has been denied on facts like these. *See Foster v. Preston Mill Co.*, 268 P.2d 645 (Wash. 1954). *Cf. Indiana Harbor Belt Railroad Co. v. American Cyanamid Co.*, 916 F.2d 1174 (7th Cir. 1990) (toxic material leaked from railroad car, but not as a result of the inherent properties of the toxic material; no strict liability). This of course would not preclude liability for negligence or nuisance. *See Summit View, Inc. v. W. W. Clyde & Co.*, 403 P.2d 919 (Utah 1965).

So what role does foreseeability play? The Third Restatement § 20 comment *i*, suggests that a case for strict liability is "strengthened when the defendant has actual knowledge of the risky quality of the activity in which the defendant is engaging." In most cases of abnormally dangerous activities, of course, defendants do possess such knowledge. If a defendant "sincerely and reasonably believes" that his activity is not harmful, however, "there is inadequate reason to impose strict liability." Id. Not all courts have imposed strict liability when there was an intervening criminal act that caused the harm, but some have. See, e.g., *Yukon Equipment, Inc. v. Fireman's Fund Insurance Co.*, 585 P.2d 1206 (Alaska 1978) (imposing "absolute liability" on the defendant who stored explosives after criminals blew them up, saying that the purposes of strict liability would be undermined if there was "insistence that the precise details of the intervening cause be foreseeable").

In *Cambridge Water Co. Ltd. v. Eastern Counties Leather*, 1 All ER 53 (H.L. 1994) the defendant was a tannery. It used a common solvent, PCE, in its tanning process. Small amounts of this solvent were spilled from time to time and as it turned out, over the years at least 1,000 gallons, perhaps much more, made its way into the ground on the defendant's land. From here it progressed downward through fissures about 50 meters. At that point, it was obstructed by an impermeable rock below and it formed a pool, which in turn percolated down the aquifer 173 miles where it polluted the plaintiff's water well. The water produced was not shown to be dangerous, but it counted as unwholesome under government guidelines derived from World Health Organization standards and those of the European Economic Community. Cambridge stopped using the well and had the expense of constructing another elsewhere.

Official government agencies attempted to trace the pollution which was discovered in 1983. Between 1987 and 1989 scholarly or scientific papers were published and they have become the source material on behavior and characteristics of this type of solvent in groundwater; before that, little was known on the subject. "The only harm that could have been foreseen from a spillage was that somebody might have been overcome by fumes from a spillage of a significant quantity."

The plaintiff's only remaining claim by the time the case reached the House of Lords was based on *Rylands v. Fletcher*. The Law Lords took the occasion to suggest strongly that *Rylands* was merely a specific version of nuisance, one based on an isolated instance rather than repeated behavior or harm. They then concluded that foreseeability was required in nuisance cases even though they were also strict liability cases, saying, "It is not sufficient that the injury suffered by the respondents' vessels was the direct result of the nuisance if that injury was in the relevant sense unforeseeable."

From here Lord Goff of Chieveley went on to say that foreseeability was also required in *Rylands v. Fletcher* cases: "[F]oreseeability of damage of the relevant type should be regarded as a prerequisite of liability in damages under the rule." On these grounds, the House of Lords refused to impose strict liability, because, it said, the damage done was not of the type that was foreseeable.

C. AFFIRMATIVE DEFENSES TO STRICT LIABILITY CLAIMS

1. *Traditional rule.* The traditional rule, and the one adopted by the Second Restatement, is that contributory negligence as such is no defense to a strict liability claim. The defendant, not at fault at all, is held fully liable to a plaintiff who is guilty of negligence causing his own harm. At least a formal reason for this result can be found in the argument that since the defendant's liability is not based on negligence in the first place, that liability is not limited by contributory negligence of the plaintiff. Are you satisfied with this reasoning? The Second Restatement also takes the view that the plaintiff's "assumed risk," and also any contributory negligence in "knowingly" subjecting himself to risks of harm, *is* a defense. *See* RESTATEMENT (SECOND) OF TORTS § 524 (1977).

2. *Comparative responsibility and the Third Restatement.* The advent of comparative negligence (or "comparative responsibility," as the Restatement of Apportionment calls it) appears to call for a change in the traditional analysis. Recall that in Chapter 10, supra, we saw that the defense of assumption of risk is no longer a unified one, and it is not self-evident what the label means without examining its context. Suppose, for example, in a comparative negligence state, that the defendant is blasting near or on a highway. Adequate signs are posted but the plaintiff negligently fails to observe them, drives into the danger area and is hurt by falling rocks from a blast. Should the plaintiff recover without any reduction in damages, or should a jury be allowed to compare the plain-

tiff's contributory negligence with the defendant's non-negligent activity? The Restatement of Apportionment, in § 8, provides that in all cases involving physical injury, the fact finder should assign shares of responsibility to each party, regardless of the legal theory of liability. That is, the Apportionment Restatement says that juries can and should assign percentages of responsibility even where one party is strictly liable and the other negligent. Further, the Apportionment Restatement does not recognize assumption of risk as a separate defense. *Accord*, RESTATEMENT (THIRD) OF TORTS: LIABILITY FOR PHYSICAL HARM § 25, cmt. *e* (P.F.D. No. 1, 2005). Is this a workable system? Are there situations in which a plaintiff impliedly consents to encounter a known risk, and thus should not recover even after the adoption of comparative responsibility?

3. *Non-negligent activity by the plaintiff.* Are some activities by plaintiffs such that the plaintiff should be the sole risk-bearer? Suppose defendant utility operates high voltage lines, and that for some purposes this might be considered a strict liability activity. The plaintiff wears a pacemaker which controls his heartbeat and which is interfered with by substantial electrical activity. If neither plaintiff nor defendant is negligent, but the plaintiff's pacemaker is disrupted by the high voltage lines, should the plaintiff be entitled to recover for injury sustained? Compare the problem of the beekeeper who moves his operation into the Murg fields where spray is regularly used. How should the rule be expressed? *See* RESTATEMENT (SECOND) OF TORTS § 524A (1977).

REFERENCE: DOBBS ON TORTS §§ 350, 369 (2000).

CHAPTER 24

TORT LIABILITY
FOR DEFECTIVE PRODUCTS

■ ■ ■

SUBCHAPTER A.
DEVELOPING CORE CONCEPTS
§ 1. EVOLUTION OF LIABILITY THEORIES

Products liability law deals with the liabilities of those who manufacture or distribute harm-causing products. That law has undergone significant and sweeping change in the last several decades. Under today's law, those involved in commercial distribution of products are potentially liable for product-caused harm, both in the United States and many other countries. The basis and extent of such liability, however, continues to be debated. A plaintiff may claim on a contract theory for breach of warranty, or on tort theories of negligence, strict liability, or even fraud. Tort theories dominate in cases of physical harm to person or property, but they cannot be understood in isolation from the law of contract and warranty.

The "Citadel of Privity" and Its Fall

Negligence action—the privity requirement. The oldest products cases were brought on a negligence theory, some arising before negligence was regarded as a general theory or approach to tort liability. In these earlier cases, courts thought that the manufacturer's liability for an injury-causing product was derived from some kind of contractual undertaking to the purchaser. Since the basis for liability was not the general duty of reasonable care but the duty implicitly undertaken in a contract of sale, the manufacturer could liable only to buyers who were in privity of contract—that is, a manufacturer who did not sell directly to the injured plaintiff could not be sued at all by that person. This rule insulated most manufacturers from liability.

In a leading New York case, *Losee v. Clute*, 51 N.Y. 494 (1873), the defendant Clute allegedly manufactured a boiler in a negligent way and sold it to Saratoga Paper Company. The boiler exploded and damaged, not Saratoga Paper, but the plaintiff's nearby property. The Court of Appeals of New York, following the privity rule, held that the complaint was properly dismissed. Defendants "contracted with the company ... and when the boiler was accepted they ceased to have any further responsibility. . . ." Thus even active negligence was protected by the privity rule.

Courts did recognize exceptions for extreme cases. In *Thomas v. Winchester*, 6 N.Y. 397 (1852), the defendant mislabeled a jar of "belladonna, which is a deadly poison," and as a result the plaintiff, consuming it, became ill. Had the defendant sold the jar to the plaintiff, there would have been no privity problem. But the defendant had sold the jar to Aspinwall, who sold it to Ford, who sold it to the plaintiff. There was thus no privity between plaintiff and the defendant. Nevertheless, the Court concluded that where death or great bodily harm would be "the natural and almost inevitable consequence of the sale" under a false label, privity would not be required.

Finally, in 1916, the New York Court of Appeals decided the landmark case of *MacPherson v. Buick Motor Co.*, 111 N.E. 1050 (N.Y. 1916). In *MacPherson* the wheel on an automobile collapsed. The plaintiff, who had purchased the car from a retail dealer, was injured. He sued the manufacturer of the car. Since he had purchased from the retailer, not the manufacturer, there was no privity between plaintiff and defendant. Judge Cardozo, writing for the court, said:

> We hold, then, that the principle of *Thomas v. Winchester* is not limited to poisons, explosives, and things of like nature, to things which in their normal operation are implements of destruction. If the nature of a thing is such that it is reasonably certain to place life and limb in peril when negligently made, it is then a thing of danger. . . . If [the manufacturer] is negligent where danger is to be foreseen, a liability will follow.

Cardozo in effect substituted foreseeability for contract or undertaking and thus applied general negligence principles to a case involving a defective product. Notice that *MacPherson* was definitely not a strict liability case—it simply permitted the application of negligence law to the products setting.

Misrepresentation. *MacPherson*'s rejection of the privity requirement for a products-liability negligence case, while it came to be accepted everywhere, did not assist every plaintiff. Some plaintiffs were injured by products that were not negligently made, and some simply could not prove negligence. Inventive lawyers attempted other theories to assist injured clients. One result was that it came to be held that a manufacturer would be liable for injuries resulting from conditions of the product that were misrepresented, even without privity. In *Baxter v. Ford Motor Co.*, 12 P.2d 409 (Wash. 1932), the plaintiff lost his eye when his windshield broke on impact from a pebble. The manufacturer had described its windshields as shatterproof. This was sufficient for liability, even though the manufacturer had not sold the car directly to the plaintiff. The misrepresentation approach can still aid plaintiffs and might even produce punitive damages awards. *See Williams v. Philip Morris Inc.*, 92 P.3d 126 (Or. Ct. App.

2004) (on reconsideration after remand from the United States' Supreme Court) (tobacco industry statements about safety of smoking and industry research on safety, upholding $79 million in punitive damages).

Warranty. Another theory that plaintiffs could rely on when they could not prove negligence was *express warranty*. To take *Baxter*'s facts as an example, if Ford had sold the car to Baxter directly and had, as part of the contract, promised or guaranteed that the windshield was "shatter-proof," this would be an express warranty, a kind of contract. Contract liability is usually strict liability; that is, proving breach of contract does not require proving that the breaching party is at fault. This contract theory is not often available, however, because manufacturers rarely make express guarantees about their products' safety directly to purchasing consumers.

Thus plaintiffs' lawyers began to argue to courts that the sale of goods gave rise to an *implied warranty*. For example, the act of selling a bottle of milk—whether it is sold by a retailer or by a manufacturer—seems to imply that it is not a bottle of belladonna, and also that it is not contaminated with human toes, dead flies, or unspeakable viruses. In other words, it should meet some kind of normal expectation as to quality and safety. Over the years, courts came to reject the maxim *caveat emptor*—let the buyer beware—and to accept the idea of a warranty implicit in the act of sale. The Uniform Commercial Code Art. 2–314, which applies to any seller of goods, recognizes an implied warranty that goods are "fit for the ordinary purposes for which such goods are used"; and that they are as good as the seller claims they are.

The implied-warranty theory carries with it all the advantages and disadvantages of contract law—liability for breach is strict, but privity is required. While some courts created exceptions to the privity rule in cases involving such things as bad food and intimate products such as soaps, hair dyes and the like, these cases seemed to lack any underlying principle and they came to an evolutionary dead-end. About 1960, however, courts started off in an entirely new direction.

A leading case of the period was *Henningsen v. Bloomfield Motors, Inc.*, 161 A.2d 69 (N.J. 1960). *Henningsen* involved an automobile purchased by Mr. Henningsen as a present for his wife. The car's steering failed, and the car crashed into a wall. The Henningsens sued the retailer and the manufacturer. The manufacturer and dealer had provided in the purchase contract that there were no warranties except that defective parts would be replaced within certain time limits. Since Mrs. Henningsen was badly injured, this was not helpful. The New Jersey Court held that there was an implied warranty in addition to this express warranty, that it ran to the ultimate purchaser and not merely to the retailer, and that the disclaimer of liability would be ineffective to protect the manufacturer. *Henningsen,* in other words, did for warranty about the same thing that *MacPherson* did for negligence.

Warranty remains a viable theory today in many products cases. However, to a very large extent the warranty theory has been displaced, or at least supplemented, by a theory of strict liability in tort, divorced from any conception of warranty.

The Development of Strict Products Liability

Strict tort liability emerged as a leading theory for products cases in *Greenman v. Yuba Power Products, Inc.*, 377 P.2d 897 (Cal. 1963). In that case, plaintiff's wife bought him a power tool that caused him serious injuries. Claiming the tool was defective, he sued the retailer and manufacturer on the two grounds then available to him: negligence and warranty. Affirming a jury verdict against the manufacturer, the court reasoned that in the case of defective products, "the liability is not one governed by the law of contract warranties but by the law of strict liability in tort." Justice Traynor wrote that the purpose of strict liability "is to insure that the costs of injuries resulting from defective products are borne by the manufacturers that put such products on the market rather than by the injured persons who are powerless to protect themselves."

Greenman was strongly influential in the drafting of the Restatement Second of Torts § 402A, promulgated in 1964. Section 402A quickly gained wide acceptance in the courts. By the mid–1960s, then, the developing law of strict products liability was freed from the older logic of the warranty theory and thus from the privity limitation. Section 402A became the lodestar of products liability discussion and development for a whole generation or more. Its essential provisions were simple: (a) sellers were strictly liable for physical injuries to persons or property other than the product itself; this meant that the injured consumer could recover without proving fault; (b) privity rules were abolished; this meant that the injured consumer could recovery without privity; and (c) strict liability attached to products that were "defective" because they were unreasonably dangerous to the consumer; and (d) the consumer's reasonable expectations defined what counted as a defective product.

REFERENCES: DOBBS ON TORTS § 353 (2000); DAVID G. OWEN, PRODUCTS LIABILITY LAW §§ 1.1–1.3 (2d Ed. 2008).

§ 2. RATIONALES FOR STRICT PRODUCTS LIABILITY

Strict products liability may be justified on one or more of the rationales discussed below. What do you think of them?

1. *Consumer expectations.* Manufacturers implicitly represent that the products they make are safe and healthy, and consumers are justified in relying on that implicit representation.

2. *Enterprise liability or "loss spreading."* Manufacturers and commercial sellers of goods can more easily spread the costs that result from injuries caused by defective products, by raising prices or purchasing

insurance. Compensation is needed, and the most practical way to secure it is to have all consumers share the cost by paying more for the product. It has also been argued that strict liability justly imposes legal responsibility for injuries that are statistically associated with the enterprise of manufacturing and selling, making liability a cost of doing business that should be borne by someone other than injured individuals.

3. *Practicality.* Since a retailer in privity with the plaintiff may be held liable on warranty, and since if so held the retailer could have indemnity from the manufacturer, it would be cheaper to permit the plaintiff to sue the manufacturer directly. Another argument from "practicality" is that, since most defective products are that way because of negligence, imposing strict liability saves the legal system the time and expense of proving negligence.

4. *Fairness.* Another set of justifications stresses the basic *fairness* of a strict liability regime. First, because the manufacturer enjoys the advantages of sending its products into commerce, it should also take the disadvantages in the form of injury costs when the risks of such activity come to fruition. (On this argument, compare the reasons for the liability of a master for the torts of a servant.)

A second fairness-based justification is that the manufacturer imposes a special kind of risk—*nonreciprocal risks*—on the consumer. That is, the manufacturer imposes risks on the consumer that are quite different from any risks the consumer imposes on the manufacturer, and this fact justifies strict liability. George P. Fletcher developed the theory of nonreciprocal risks in a very influential article, *Fairness and Utility in Tort Theory*, 85 HARV. L. REV. 537 (1972). One example Fletcher uses of a nonreciprocal risk is the risk an airplane pilot imposes upon those on the ground. He imposes a risk of crashing into them but they impose no comparable risk upon him. To Fletcher, the crashing plane that causes ground damages represents a good case for strict liability in the absence of a defense.

Fletcher's theory attacks the fairness of risk-utility balancing commonly followed in analysis of negligence claims. In part, he does so by pointing to criminal law. No individual human being should suffer criminal sanctions for the sake of the common good. Similarly, no injured person should be required to give up a claim against the defendant merely because the defendant's activities are socially useful. If these activities are socially useful, they need not be prohibited, but they should be "taxed" by tort law to provide compensation for harms they cause. Fletcher recognizes that his theory will not lead inexorably to a predictable result. You would have to ask whether the defendant imposed a risk so excessive that it should be considered non-reciprocal. He doubts, however, whether the risk-utility balancing is any more certain. For some later Fletcherian ideas, see George P. Fletcher, *Corrective Justice for Moderns*, 106 HARV. L. REV. 1658 (1993) (Book Review of JULES COLEMAN, RISKS AND WRONGS (1992)).

5. *Deterrence.* If strict liability is imposed, manufacturers will tend to make products safer in order to avoid the increased costs resulting from liability. Liability of the manufacturer will drive the manufacturer to increase the price so as to cover the liability costs. As prices rise on unsafe products consumers will seek cheaper substitutes. These substitutes will usually be safer products; they are cheaper because they are not bearing the costs of tort liability. In addition, manufacturers, to avoid this loss of customers and the liability itself, will seek to find ways to make products more safe.

Guido Calabresi, in his 1970 book *The Cost of Accidents,* offered an economic analysis of the accident cost-reduction effects of strict liability. Much of his book is devoted to an idea he calls primary accident cost reduction or primary accident cost avoidance, focusing on reducing accident costs by reducing the number or severity of accidents themselves. This can be done in his view by using some combination of two major devices:

a. *Specific deterrence.* One way to reduce primary accident costs is to prohibit conduct that is excessively risky. This can be done by legislation or administrative regulation, for example. Specific prohibitions might be made because conduct is either "immoral" or because it does more harm than good. However, it is difficult to decide by political processes what risks are more harmful than useful. Calabresi believes that "the market" can make this judgment in a much better way.

b. *General deterrence.* This is a technical term and an economic notion. The idea is that if a given activity, such as driving, causes accidents, that activity could be made to pay the costs. Calabresi believes that if an activity is made to pay all the costs it really causes, this will in fact reduce accidents or the severity of accidents. Here's how. Suppose that convertibles are riskier than sedans, especially in turnover accidents. If manufacturers of convertibles had to pay all the costs of convertible injuries, they would raise the price of convertibles. Potential buyers will know comparative risks if the price of the convertibles reflect their true costs to society. Purchasers would not have to think about relative risks at all when they considered purchasing a convertible; they would have only to look at its price tag. Some people would buy the more expensive convertible even so. But others would reject it as too expensive. Even if they did not think about risks that were included in the price, their decision would be more informed because they would know the true costs of operating the convertible. Because a number of people would reject the more dangerous convertible, convertible-caused injuries would be reduced.

Athens and Sparta examples. Calabresi offered an example. He supposed that in Athens accident costs of an activity (like driving) were always charged to that activity so that insurance costs for an activity like driving would be higher than they would be otherwise. In Sparta, on the other hand, all injuries were compensated from general public funds raised by taxes. Taney is thinking of buying a second car. The costs of owning the second car would be $200 a year for operating plus another $200 for insurance. The alternative would be to take taxis occasionally, a cost of about $250 a year. In Athens he might reject the second car because its total cost, including the insurance which reflected accident costs, would be much greater than the cost of taxis. In Sparta, however, he would have no insurance costs, since injuries would be taken care of by public assistance. So his cost for the second car would be $200 a year as compared to taxis costing $250. He would buy the second car.

The Athens plan reduces accident costs by showing people like Taney the true cost of activities they are considering. The point is not that everyone would forgo the car, but that some people, getting the risk information through the price, would do so. Calabresi thought there was a second and maybe more important way that general deterrence would help reduce accident costs. He thought that it would encourage us to make activities safer if we knew the real costs of risks associated with them. If cars cause an average of $200 a year in accident costs but a new brake costing the equivalent of $50 a year can reduce those costs to $100, then Taney would install the new brake if he lived in Athens.

Cheapest cost avoider. Ideally, the costs of accidents should be borne by acts or activities that could avoid the accident costs most cheaply. A new car manufacturer might be a good choice, for example, if the manufacturer could add the $50 brake when it produces the car. If it is liable for car accidents, it will have the incentive to add the $50 brake.

The (Partial) Decline of Strict Products Liability

All of the arguments for broad strict products liability have been challenged, and as courts worked out the details of strict liability over a thirty-year period many critics asserted that strict liability for defectively-designed products was wrong in principle. Many states passed statutes in the 1980s limiting products liability cases in one respect or another as the criticisms reached critical mass.

A major turning point was the 1998 publication of the Restatement Third of Torts: Products Liability, which essentially retains strict liability only for products flawed in manufacture, and adopts a negligence standard or something very like it for design and warning defects. While the ultimate effect of the Products Restatement is uncertain, it has already proved influential and has sparked heated debate about whether, or to what extent, strict liability should be imposed. The Products Restatement itself does not focus on the various theories of liability, but rather on whether products are proven to be "defective."

References: Dobbs on Torts § 353 (2000); 1 Madden & Owen on Products Liability § 5:4 (3d ed. 2000).

§ 3. EXCLUDING STAND–ALONE ECONOMIC HARM

MOORMAN MFG. CO. v. NATIONAL TANK CO.

435 N.E.2d 443 (Ill. 1982)

THOMAS J. MORAN, JUSTICE.

[Plaintiff purchased from defendant a steel grain-storage tank for use in plaintiff's feed processing plant. About ten years later, a crack developed in one of the steel plates on the tank. The plaintiff sued on theories of strict tort liability, misrepresentation, negligent design, and express warranty.]

The tort law of products liability stems from the contract cause of action for breach of warranty. In MacPherson v. Buick Motor Co. (1916), 217 N.Y. 382,111 N.E. 1050, liability in negligence was imposed upon a manufacturer to an ultimate consumer without privity of contract. Subsequently, courts began to hold manufacturers liable for personal injuries without negligence; the theory generally utilized to reach the manufacturers was based upon the law of sales warranty. (See Prosser, The Assault Upon The Citadel, 69 Yale L.J. 1099,1126 (1960) (Prosser I).) However, recognition of the difficulties facing consumers with respect to items such as notice and privity led most courts to abandon the privity requirement in implied-warranty actions (see Prosser, The Fall of the Citadel, 50 Minn. L.Rev. 791 (1966) (Prosser II)) and to ultimately abandon the fiction of warranty in favor of strict liability in tort.

This State adopted the tort theory of strict liability in Suvada v. White Motor Co. (1965), 32 Ill.2d 612, 210 N.E.2d 182, to allow a plaintiff to recover from a manufacturer for personal injuries. Suvada, however, did not address the question of whether a consumer could recover under a strict liability in tort theory for solely economic loss. That issue was first addressed in Santor v. A & M Karagheusian, Inc. (1965), 44 N.J. 52, 207 A.2d 305. There, the plaintiff purchased, from a third-party seller, carpeting that had been manufactured by the defendant. After several months, unsightly lines began to appear on the surface of the carpeting. The Supreme Court of New Jersey held that the plaintiff could maintain a breach-of-warranty claim directly against the manufacturer despite the lack of privity between them. In dicta, the court went on to declare that although the strict liability in tort doctrine had been applied principally in connection with personal injuries, the responsibility of the manufacturer should be no different where damage to the article sold or to other property is involved. 44 N.J. 52, 66, 207 A.2d 305, 312. Several months later, in Seely v. White Motor Co. (1965) 63 Cal.2d 9,403 P.2d 145, 45 Cal.Rptr.17, the Supreme Court of California rejected the rationale by which the court in Santor imposed strict liability in tort for economic loss. In Seely, plaintiff purchased a truck manufactured by defendant. After he took possession, Seely discovered that the truck bounced violently. Nine months later, the truck overturned after brake failure, causing damage to the truck but no personal injury to Seely. Plaintiff had the damage repaired and subsequently stopped making his installment payments. Defendant repossessed the truck, at which time plaintiff sued on theories of breach of express warranty and strict tort liability, and sought damages for the repair of the truck, for money paid on the purchase price, and for profits lost by virtue of the truck's unsuitability for normal use. The court affirmed the trial court's award to Seely for money paid on the purchase price and for lost profits on the basis of express warranty. The court, however, went on to state that these economic losses are not recoverable under strict liability in tort. The court also declared, in reference to Santor, "Only if someone had been injured because the rug was unsafe for use would there have been any basis for imposing strict liability in tort." Thus, the court refused to expand the scope of its opinion in Greenman v. Yuba Power Products, Inc. (1963), 59 Cal.2d 57, 62, 377 P.2d 897, 900, 27 Cal. Rptr. 697, 700, which declared that a manufacturer is strictly liable in tort for a product that has a defect that causes injury to a person.

Subsequent to these two seminal cases in the area, some courts have held a manufacturer liable under the theory of strict liability in tort for solely economic losses. Most courts, however, have denied recovery under strict liability in tort for solely economic losses.... Contrary to the conclusion reached by the appellate court, we believe the language limiting section 402A to unreasonably dangerous defects resulting in physical harm to the ultimate user or consumer, or to his property, reflects sound policy reasons.

First, the law of sales has been carefully articulated to govern the economic relations between suppliers and consumers of goods. The framework provided by the UCC includes the parol evidence rule, implied warranties, express warranties, rules on disclaimers, notice requirements, limitations on the extent of a manufacturer's liability, and a statute of limitations. Although warranty rules frustrate just compensation for physical injury, they function well in a commercial setting. These rules determine the quality of the product the manufacturer promises and thereby determine the quality he must deliver.

We note, for example, section 2–316 of the UCC, which permits parties to a sales contract to limit warranties in any reasonable manner, or to agree that the buyer possesses no warranty protection at all. The parties may even agree to exclude the implied warranties of merchantability and fitness if they do so in writing, and may modify the implied warranty by clear and conspicuous language. Yet, a manufacturer's strict liability for economic loss cannot be disclaimed because a manufacturer should not be permitted to define the scope of its own responsibility for defective products. Thus, adopting strict liability in tort for economic loss would effectively eviscerate section 2–316 of the UCC.

Further, application of the rules of warranty prevents a manufacturer from being held liable for damages of unknown and unlimited scope. If a defendant were held strictly liable in tort for the commercial loss suffered by a particular purchaser, it would be liable for business losses of other purchasers caused by the failure of the product to meet the specific needs of their business, even though these needs were communicated only to the dealer. Finally, a large purchaser, such as plaintiff in the instant case, can protect itself against the risk of unsatisfactory performance by bargaining for a warranty. Or, it may choose to accept a lower purchase price for the product in lieu of warranty protection. Subsequent purchasers may do likewise in bargaining over the price of the product. We believe it is preferable to relegate the consumer to the comprehensive scheme of remedies fashioned by the UCC, rather than requiring the consuming public to pay more for their products so that a manufacturer can insure against the possibility that some of his products will not meet the business needs of some of his customers. . . .

We do hold, however, that when a product is sold in defective condition that is unreasonably dangerous to the user or consumer or to his property, strict liability in tort is applicable to physical injury to plaintiff's property, as well as to personal injury. When an unreasonably dangerous defect is present, such as the truck's nonfunctioning brakes in Seely, and physical injury does, in fact, result, then "[p]hysical injury to property is so akin to personal injury that there is no reason to distinguish them." This comports with the notion that the essence of a product liability tort case is not that the plaintiff failed to receive the quality of product he expected, but that the plaintiff has been exposed, through a hazardous product, to an unreasonable risk of injury to his person or property. On the other hand, contract law, which protects expectation interests, provides the proper standard when a qualitative defect is involved, i.e., when a product is unfit for its intended uses.

Plaintiff argues that economic loss is not sought in this case. It asserts in its brief that a product defect existed that posed an "extreme threat to life and limb, and to property of plaintiff and others, a defect which resulted in a sudden and violent ripping of plaintiff's tank, and which only fortunately did not extend the full height of the tank." Plaintiff further asserts that, because costs of repairs are not economic losses, consequential damages resulting from the loss of use of the tank during repairs does not constitute economic loss either.

"Economic loss" has been defined as "damages for inadequate value, costs of repair and replacement of the defective product, or consequent loss of profits—without any claim of personal injury or damage to other property . . ." (Note, Economic Loss in Products Liability Jurisprudence, 66 Colum. L. Rev. 917, 918 (1966)) (Economic Loss) as well as "the diminution in the value of the product because it is inferior in quality and does not work for the general purposes for which it was manufactured and sold." (Comment, Manufacturers' Liability to Remote Purchasers for "Economic Loss" Damages—Tort or Contract? 114 U.Pa.L.Rev. 539, 541 (1966).) These definitions are consistent with the policy of warranty law to protect expectations of suitability and quality.

The demarcation between physical harm or property damage on the one hand and economic loss on the other usually depends on the nature of the defect and the manner in which the damage occurred. . . .

We . . . hold that, where only the defective product is damaged, economic losses caused by qualitative defects falling under the ambit of a purchaser's disappointed expectations cannot be recovered under a strict liability theory. Here, count I of the complaint alleged that during the last few months of 1976 and the first few months of 1977, "a crack developed in one of the steel plates on the second ring of [the] tank; such crack was not discovered by plaintiff . . . until such tank was being emptied on or about August 24, 1977." This was not the type of sudden and dangerous occurrence best served by the policy of tort law that the manufacturer should bear the risk of hazardous products. . . .

Our conclusion that qualitative defects are best handled by contract, rather than tort, law applies whether the tort theory involved is strict liability or negligence. Tort theory is appropriately suited for personal injury or property damage resulting from a sudden or dangerous occurrence of the nature described above. The remedy for economic loss, loss relating to a purchaser's disappointed expectations due to deterioration, internal breakdown or nonaccidental cause, on the other hand, lies in contract. . . .

The policy considerations against allowing recovery for solely economic loss in strict liability cases apply to negligence actions as well. When the defect is of a qualitative nature and the harm relates to the consumer's expectation that a product is of a particular quality so that it is fit for ordinary use, contract, rather than tort, law provides the appropriate set of rules for recovery. . . .

[The Court also held that economic losses, though recoverable for intentional misrepresentations, were not recoverable for innocent representations, and that in this case the statute of limitations had run on the warranty claim.]

NOTES

1. **The economic loss rule.** Most courts, following California Supreme Court Justice Traynor's lead in *Seely v. White Motor Co.*, discussed in *Moorman*, have agreed that economic harm standing alone is recoverable only on the basis of contract or warranty. The effect is to allocate cases of non-physical harms to the law of warranty and cases of physical harms to persons or other property to the law of tort. The basic principle is easy to apply in many cases. For example, where a vacuum cleaner quits working without harming anyone or anything, the economic loss rule forbids a tort claim.

2. **What constitutes "separate property?"** This is not a difficult question in many cases. If the vacuum cleaner shorted out and burned down the house, a tort action would lie for the house-damage. But where the product that fails is arguably a part of something larger, and the entire

product is damaged or destroyed, line-drawing is not so simple. The Restatement provides that if the component is part of an "integrated whole," then no tort action can lie because the product is deemed to have damaged only itself. RESTATEMENT OF PRODUCTS LIABILITY § 21, cmt. *e* (1998). *Compare, e.g., State Farm Mut. Auto. Ins. Co. v. Ford Motor Co.*, 592 N.W.2d 201 (Wis. 1999) (barring tort claim where a car's faulty ignition caused the car to catch fire, destroying the car), *with Saratoga Fishing Co. v. J.M. Martinac & Co.*, 520 U.S. 875 (1997) (tort claim allowed against boat engine's manufacturer where engine caused fire that damaged other equipment on the boat) *and Gunkel v. Renovations, Inc.*, 822 N.E.2d 150 (Ind. 2005) (tort claim allowed for water damage to home caused by defective installation of separately-installed stone façade);

3. **A mini-problem.** Suppose that TankCo manufactures tanks for storing toxic chemicals. ChemCo purchases toxic chemicals for use in its factory and stores them in tanks it has purchased from TankCo. One of the tanks is defective and a leak occurs. The leak contaminated ChemCo's property and also adjoining property that belongs to the plaintiff. Is TankCo liable for the costs of cleaning up the contamination (a) incurred by ChemCo on its property? (b) incurred by the plaintiff for cleaning up its adjoining property?

4. **Present economic harm resulting from product's risk of future physical harm.** Suppose the defendant expressly or impliedly warrants the reasonable safety of a motor vehicle. After purchase, the plaintiffs discover that the vehicle is not so safe because the seats will tend to collapse on rear impact or because the braking system sometimes does not work properly. The result is that the plaintiffs vehicles are worth less than the plaintiffs paid or worth less than they would be if they had been as safe as warranted. Would the defendants be liable for adequately proven damages? *See Briehl v. General Motors Corp.*, 172 F.3d 623 (8th Cir. 1999); *Frank v. DaimlerChrysler Corp.*, 741 N.Y.S.2d 9 (App. Div. 2002); *Tietsworth v. Harley–Davidson, Inc.*, 677 N.W.2d 233 (Wis. 2004); DOBBS ON TORTS, § 483A (Supp. 2008).

SUBCHAPTER B.
ESTABLISHING A PRIMA FACIE CASE

Courts have recognized three types of product defects that may lead to liability: (1) Manufacturing defects (also called production flaws); (2) Design defects; and (3) Information defects. Perhaps the most crucial questions in products cases—and the focus of the Restatement of Products Liability—concern whether a product is "defective" in the first place, and what a plaintiff has to prove to establish such a defect.

§ 4. MANUFACTURING DEFECTS

LEE v. CROOKSTON COCA–COLA BOTTLING CO.

188 N.W.2d 426 (Minn. 1971)

ROGOSHESKE, JUSTICE.

[Plaintiff, a waitress in the Norman Steak House at Ada, Minnesota, was injured when a Coca–Cola bottle exploded in her hand. The trial judge refused to submit a claim based on strict tort liability, and the jury, apparently finding no negligence and no breach of warranty, returned a defendant's verdict. Plaintiff appeals, arguing that the court should have submitted jury instructions on the strict liability claim.]

[Evidence showed the bottle exploded in the plaintiff's hand, that it had not struck anything, that it had not been subjected to temperature extremes or mishandling.]

The rule of strict liability, as revised and adopted by the American Law Institute in 1964, is embodied in Restatement, Torts (2d) § 402A. It imposes liability, without proof of negligence or privity of contract, upon a manufacturer or seller for injury caused by a dangerously defective product. To recover under the rule, the injured party must present evidence, direct or circumstantial, from which the jury can justifiably find that (1) the product was in fact in a defective condition, unreasonably dangerous for its intended use; (2) such defect existed when the product left defendant's control; and (3) the defect was the proximate cause of the injury sustained.

The greatest difficulty in establishing liability under this rule is in proving that the product was defective and that the defect existed when the product left defendant's control. While in conventional tort terms no proof of negligence is necessary, in many cases proof of a defect may simply be a substitute word for negligence. Thus, strict liability does not mean that the defendant is held liable as an insurer of his product regardless of circumstances. As is true in negligence cases with respect to the mere fact of an accident, the mere fact of injury during use of the product usually is insufficient proof to show existence of a defect at the time defendant relinquished control.... Also, liability is not imposed where the injured party has not eliminated the probability that improper handling by intermediate parties might have caused the defect....

The narrow question presented here, however, is whether circumstantial evidence, the core of the res ipsa loquitur doctrine, is sufficient to take the case to the jury on the theory of strict liability as well as on the theory of negligence....

It surely must be conceded that circumstantial evidence of the type present in ... this case justifies submission of the issue of liability on the theory of res ipsa.... As testified to by defendant's expert, there are three fundamental causes of bottle failure: Thermo-shock, internal pressure, and external force. According to the expert's testimony, failure because of thermo-shock could only result from drastic changes in temperature applied to the outside of the bottle, such as would be produced by placing a bottle containing hot liquid in cold water. Failure caused by external force, of course, usually results from an impact, such as striking or dropping the bottle. Failure because of internal pressure due to excessive carbonation is ordinarily unlikely because the bottle is designed to withstand approximately four times the pressure created by the gas introduced, and after the carbonated liquid is added to the syrup mixture, any excessive carbonation is equalized by exposure to atmospheric pressure during the interval between carbonation and capping. The capacity of different bottles to withstand internal pressure varies, however, in part due to bottlers' customary reuse of bottles. Some bottles have been refilled for years and might have been subjected to "rough" handling numerous times, thereby increasing the probability that even though they are designed to withstand such handling, some could develop defects which would escape detection by the most careful bottler. This may be the only plausible explanation for the bottle's failure in this case, since there is uncontradicted evidence dispelling the probability that the failure was attributable to thermo-shock or external force. Absent expert opinion, as in a case of this type, circumstantial evidence may be the only available means of establishing a claim of either negligence or a defective product.

Under the theory of strict liability, the elements of proof as noted above are few and uncomplicated. The significant difference is that under strict liability the jury need not infer from the circumstantial evidence that defendant was negligent in order to impose liability. It is sufficient that the evidence establishes that the manufacturer placed a dangerously defective product on the market, knowing that it is to be used without inspection for defects. . . .

In short, under the theory of strict liability plaintiff should not be required to prove specifically what defect caused the incident, but may rely upon circumstantial evidence from which it can reasonably be inferred that it is more probable than not that the product was defective when it left defendant's control. . . .

The jury could properly have found on the evidence submitted that defendant was not causally negligent. This finding, of course, defeats plaintiffs' claim on the theory of negligence. As has been pointed out above, however, it would not necessarily preclude recovery under the theory of strict liability. Under instructions solely on negligence, a jury might conclude that the bottle was defective when it left defendant's control but that defendant was not liable because the defect did not result from negligence. Under instructions on strict liability, on the other hand, a finding that the bottle was defective when defendant put it on the market would *compel* a verdict *for plaintiffs*, absent the aforementioned defenses and without considering the question of negligence.

Thus, the trial court's refusal to submit plaintiffs' claim upon the theory of strict liability in tort must also be regarded as reversible error. The court's ruling deprived plaintiffs of a legitimate choice of theories on which to submit the case. Plaintiffs are entitled to attempt to prove their case on either or both theories—that defendant was negligent or that it put a dangerously defective product on the market.

It could be argued that the case in effect was submitted to the jury on strict liability, since the jury was instructed on implied warranty. Although strict liability in tort and in warranty are very similar, we cannot view the court's instructions as sufficient to constitute submission of the question of strict liability in tort to the jury. The jury was told that defendant warranted that the bottle of Coca–Cola "was reasonably fit for the ordinary and usual handling as it might reasonably anticipate in the exercise of reasonable care." This language falls short of conveying to the jury that if a defect existed in defendant's product when it left its control, defendant should be found liable for the injuries caused by such defect.

Reversed and new trial granted.

NOTES

1. **Manufacturing defects.** A manufacturing defect is "a physical departure from a product's intended design." RESTATEMENT OF PRODUCTS LIABILITY § 1, cmt. *a* (1998). In other words, a manufacturing defect can occur even if there is nothing at all wrong with the product's design. Manufacturing defects typically affect only a small percentage of a manufacturer's products in a particular product line.

2. **The consumer expectation test.** The Restatement Second of Torts § 402A in effect imposed strict liability when the product was defective and unreasonably dangerous. It tested defect/unreasonable danger by asking whether the product was dangerous beyond the contemplation of the consumer. This test is usually called the consumer expectation test.

3. **The Products Liability Restatement's test.** The Products Liability Restatement states the test differently. It provides that "a product contains a manufacturing defect when the product departs from its intended design even though all possible care was exercised in the preparation and marketing of the product." RESTATEMENT OF PRODUCTS LIABILITY § 2(a) (1998). How does the new Restatement's standard relate to the Second Restatement's "consumer expectation" standard?

4. **Retaining the consumer expectation test.** Many courts today continue to apply the consumer expectation test, the Restatement notwithstanding. *E.g., Potter v. Chicago Pneumatic Tool Co.,* 694 A.2d 1319 (Conn. 1997) (with other tests in some cases). Subject to qualification, the consumer expectation test is also widely used in the products liability law of countries in Europe, Asia, South America and elsewhere. *See* Mathias Reimann, *Liability for Defective Products at the Beginning of the Twenty-first Century: Emergence of a Worldwide Standard?*, 51 AM. J. COMP. LAW. 751, 768 (2003).

5. **Elements of a strict liability claim.** To prevail on a strict liability claim, the plaintiff must prove not only that the product was defective, and that the defect was an actual and proximate cause of plaintiff's harm, but also that the product was defective when it left the defendant's hands. This may not be easy to prove. As *Lee* shows, drawing inferences is often necessary to make the plaintiff's case.

6. **Inferences of cause and defect.** The Restatement of Products Liability § 3, provides that it may be inferred that a product defect existing at the time of sale or distribution caused plaintiff's harm when the event (a) was of a kind that ordinarily occurs as a result of product defect; and (b) was not solely the result of causes other than product defect. What does this remind you of?

7. **Applications.** In *Kerr v. Corning Glass Works*, 169 N.W.2d 587 (Minn. 1969), a Pyrex baking dish "exploded" when the plaintiff removed it from the oven. The Minnesota Court held this was not proof of a defect existing when the dish left the manufacturer's hands, since the explosion might have occurred because of subsequent damage. Does the Minnesota Court have a different attitude in *Lee*?

In a 1964 New Jersey case, the plaintiff, working for Ford, operated a grinding machine with a grinding disc produced by the defendant. The same disc had been on the grinder earlier when the machine was used by another employee. When the plaintiff used the machine, the disc snapped and struck him. The court held this did not suffice to prove that the disc was defective. Although a manufacturing flaw was possible, it was equally possible that mishandling would explain the accident. *Jakubowski v. Minnesota Mining & Mfg.*, 199 A.2d 826 (N.J. 1964). In a later New Jersey decision the plaintiff was driving a six-month-old Lincoln Continental. He heard a "gink" in the front and the steering mechanism locked. The car then collided with a tree. The trial judge refused to charge the jury that it could infer a defect, but this time the New Jersey Court held that proof was sufficient to permit a finding of defect. Although other causes were possible, a defect in the car when it left the manufacturer was deemed sufficiently probable. *Moraca v. Ford Motor Co.*, 332 A.2d 599 (N.J. 1975). Although the later cases from New Jersey and Minnesota are probably distinguishable from the earlier cases in those states, it is probably fair to say they represent a more relaxed attitude about the proof problem.

The rule remains, however, that the plaintiff must prove a defect in the product that existed when it left the defendant's hands, and this rule does continue to foreclose recovery if the plaintiff's proof is insufficient. What if a tire blows out after 30,000 miles, and subsequent investigation shows it has a nail in it. Does a permissible inference arise that a defect in the tire caused the blowout? *See Cooper Tire & Rubber Co. v. Mendez*, 204 S.W.3d 797 (Tex. 2006). And consider *Mixon v. Chrysler Corp.*, 663 S.W.2d 713 (Ark. 1984). The plaintiff, driving a year-old car with 30,000 miles on it, suddenly found he could not control it. The car went over an embankment. The brakes were checked afterward and no defect was found. The wreckage was then disposed of before it occurred to anyone to check the steering. The plaintiff then brought suit, claiming that the steering was defective. Given no further facts, can the defendant have a summary judgment?

8. **Proof of specific defect.** An inference of defect may arise even when the plaintiff fails to prove what aspect of the product was defective. RESTATEMENT OF PRODUCTS LIABILITY, § 3, cmt. *c.* Does that mean a jury could infer a defect when the plaintiff's car burst into flames while unattended in her garage even though the plaintiff cannot show whether the fire was caused by a defective fuel tank, electrical system, or something else?

9. **Defect and negligence.** The use of *res ipsa* analogies, as in *Lee,* suggests a similarity between strict liability and negligence, as does the "unreasonable danger" phrase. One difference, however, is that a negligence claim focuses on the defendant's conduct, while a strict products liability claim focuses on the product itself. Thus, as in *Lee,* a jury might find no negligence and still find a product defective. A defendant which has done the best anyone can do to produce a safe product is still liable for the inevitable defects that cause harm. But in the great bulk of cases, it can be inferred that negligence caused the manufacturing defect. Since this will so often be true, this kind of strict liability might be regarded as a "shortcut" to the same result a negligence rule would ordinarily achieve, but without the necessity of long, detailed trials over the fault issue. *See* Gary T. Schwartz, *Understanding Products Liability,* 67 CAL. L. REV. 435, 460–461 (1979). Under this view, strict liability differs from negligence because it is cheaper to use. But as to most defendants most of the time, it will add very little liability. What do you think of this analysis?

MEXICALI ROSE v. SUPERIOR COURT (CLARK v. MEXICALI ROSE), 822 P.2d 1292 (Cal. 1992). Clark ordered a chicken enchilada at the Mexicali Rose restaurant. He swallowed a one-inch chicken bone contained in the enchilada, sustaining a throat injury for which he sues. He claims negligence, breach of implied warranty, and strict tort liability.

Held, demurrer to the warranty and tort strict liability claims should be sustained. "If the injury-producing substance is natural to the preparation of the food served, it can be said that it was reasonably expected by its very nature and the food cannot be determined unfit or defective. A plaintiff in such a case has no cause of action in strict liability or implied warranty." The "defendants owe no duty to provide a perfect enchilada," but under this rule they may still be liable for negligence in preparing the food if that negligence is proved.

JUSTICE MOSK, dissenting: "The majority hold that processed food containing a sharp, concealed bone is fit for consumption, though no reasonable consumer would anticipate finding the bone. They declare in effect that the bone is natural to the dish, therefore the dish is fit for consumption. The majority never explain why this should be the rule, when it is universally held that in the analogous case of a sharp bit of wire in processed food, liability occurs under both the implied warranty of

fitness and the theory of strict liability for defective consumer products."
JUSTICE ARABIAN also dissented.

JACKSON v. NESTLE–BEICH, INC., 589 N.E.2d 547 (Ill. 1992). The
plaintiff allegedly broke a tooth on a hard pecan shell embedded in a
chocolate-covered pecan-caramel candy purchased in a sealed can and
manufactured by Nestle. Nestle moved for summary judgment on the
ground that the substance was natural to pecans, not foreign. *Held*,
affirming the intermediate appellate court's decision, "the foreign-natural
doctrine is unsound and should be abandoned." Instead, the consumer's
reasonable expectation is the test of defectiveness under the Second
Restatement's § 402A, cmt. *i*.

NOTE

Food products and consumer expectations. The Products Restatement provides that a harm-causing ingredient in a food product is a defect "if
a reasonable consumer would not expect the food product to contain that
ingredient." RESTATEMENT OF PRODUCTS LIABILITY § 7. Is the consumer expectations test particularly apropos in food cases? If the standard was simply
whether the food "departs from its intended design," which is the new
Restatement's general standard for manufacturing defects, would that mean
that if the seller of chicken enchiladas or nut-candies never even tried to
remove bones or shells there would be no strict liability, since in that case
there would be no departure from "intended design?", Most courts do not
follow the foreign-natural distinction in *Mexicali Rose* but rely on consumer
expectations instead. *See Schafer v. JLC Food Systems, Inc.*, 695 N.W.2d 570
(Minn. 2005) (calling the foreign-natural distinction "arbitrary").

§ 5.　DESIGN DEFECTS

LEICHTAMER v. AMERICAN MOTORS CO., 424 N.E.2d 568 (Ohio
1981). Plaintiffs were passengers in a Jeep driven by Paul Vance on an off-
road facility. Vance was negotiating hills and terraces when he overturned
the Jeep in a back-to-front flip over. The rollbar, attached to relatively
thin metal housing, displaced toward the passengers when the housing
collapsed. Vance and his wife were killed. The plaintiff Jeanne Leichtamer's legs were twisted through the front seat and she is now a paraplegic.
The plaintiffs sued claiming that, though Vance was negligent, their
injuries were enhanced because of the roll-bar's displacement. The jury
found for the plaintiffs, awarding $1 million in compensatory and $1
million in punitive damages to Jeanne and $100,000 compensatory and
$100,000 punitive to Carl Leichtamer. *Held*, affirmed. "Appellees did not
claim that there was any defect in the way the vehicle was manufactured
in the sense of departure by the manufacturer from design specifications.
The vehicle was manufactured precisely in the manner in which it was
designed to be manufactured. It reached Paul Vance in that condition and
was not changed.... [T]he vast weight of authority is in support of
allowing an action in strict liability in tort ... for design defects.... Strict

liability in tort has been applied to design defect 'second collision' cases. While a manufacturer is under no obligation to design a 'crash proof' vehicle, an instruction may be given on the issue of strict liability in tort if the plaintiff adduces sufficient evidence that an unreasonably dangerous product design proximately caused or enhanced plaintiff's injuries in the course of a foreseeable use.... [A] product may be found defective in design if the plaintiff demonstrates that the product failed to perform as safely as an ordinary consumer would expect when used in an intended or reasonably foreseeable manner.... A product will be found unreasonably dangerous if it is dangerous to an extent beyond the expectations of an ordinary consumer when used in an intended or reasonably foreseeable manner." Since the roll-bar was designed for a side roll-over only and not a back-to-front roll-over, and since the company knew it had not provided tests for this kind of hazard when it advertised the Jeep for off-the-road use, punitive damages were warranted.

NOTES

1. **Design defects.** Notice that the "defect" was the design, not a flaw of production. Design defects are difficult to define and identify. In addition, design defect claims threaten manufacturers in ways that production defect claims do not. If a product is flawed in manufacture, only a few products with flaws will be in circulation; but if a product is misdesigned, every one of the products represents a potential lawsuit against the manufacturer.

2. **Consumer expectations and unreasonable danger.** As noted in § 4 above, the Restatement Second's section 402A provides that a product would be considered defective if it was more dangerous than the ordinary consumer would expect. When applied to design defect cases, this test raises many difficult questions. Cars do not provide roll-bars built into the roof. Does the consumer expectation test help decide whether such cars are defective? Would it be enough to show a defect if you could prove that consumers had a general expectation that cars would be safe? Or would it be necessary to show that consumer experience led to specific design expectations? *See Soule v. General Motors Corp.*, 882 P.2d 298 (Cal. 1994) (requiring specific expectation based on everyday experience). Think about how consumer expectations might be proved in court. Consider: The ultimate safety (or the safety features) that reasonable consumers expect is established by (a) the plaintiff's testimony about her own expectations; (b) the jury's general knowledge about safety expectations; (c) expert testimony.

3. **Consumer expectations and obvious dangers.** Many commentators and courts consider the consumer expectation test of section 402A a "pro-plaintiff" test. But what if a product's danger is obvious? Wouldn't a plaintiff always lose such a case, because the product would not be "more dangerous than the ordinary consumer would expect?" *See Bourne v. Marty Gilman, Inc.*, 452 F.3d 632 (7th Cir. 2006); *Blue v. Environmental Engineering, Inc.*, 828 N.E.2d 1128 (Ill. 2005).

4. **Bystanders or strangers.** Suppose you are not using the product, but you are injured by it. You fall against an exercise machine and, quite

surprisingly, a part pierces your thigh, cutting blood vessels and damaging nerves. *See Jones v. Nordictrack, Inc.,* 550 S.E.2d 101 (Ga. 2001). Or a defective lighter as used by one child causes burns to another child. See *Hernandez v. Tokai Corp.,* 2 S.W.3d 251 (Tex. 1999). Or you inhale asbestos fibers unknowingly brought into the house on the clothes of a worker who was exposed to such toxic materials. *See Stegemoller v. ACandS, Inc.,* 767 N.E.2d 974 (Ind. 2002); *Lunsford v. Saberhagen Holdings,* 106 P.3d 808 (Wash. Ct. App. 2005). Courts impose liability in such cases, but how can a bystander have an expectation about the particular product's safety?

5. **Crashworthiness.** At one time, a defendant in a case like *Leichtamer* could prevail on an argument that if a product was used in an unintended way—like getting involved in a car crash—then that unintended use, not any defect, was the sole cause of the harm. Such a restrictive view is no longer followed; manufacturers are liable for harms caused by defective products that are put to "foreseeable uses," even if unintended by the manufacturer. See §§ 8 & 9, *infra.*

KNITZ v. MINSTER MACHINE CO.

432 N.E.2d 814 (Ohio 1982)

[Defendant manufactured a press which delivered 60 tons of force in pressing die halves together. It was originally activated with a two-hand button tripping device, so that the operator's hands were necessarily outside the danger area. This press, with the button tripping device, was sold by defendant to Toledo Die and Manufacturing Company. Toledo, however, also purchased an optional foot pedal tripping device and it was in use at the time of the injury. Plaintiff, the press operator for Toledo, found it necessary to move the foot pedal with her foot; in doing so, she leaned on the bottom portion of the die with her hand. Her foot accidentally activated the foot pedal and the press descended, amputating two fingers. There was another safety device, intended to physically pull back the operator's hands, but it was not attached. The trial judge gave summary judgment for the manufacturer.]

WILLIAM B. BROWN, JUSTICE.

The case presents us with the question of whether a motion for summary judgment pursuant to Civ. R. 56 should have been granted to appellee....

The focus of the inquiry in *Leichtamer* was what constituted a "defective condition unreasonably dangerous" as formulated by Section 402A of the Restatement of Torts. We adopted a variation of the familiar "consumer expectation test" of Comment *i* to Section 402: "A product is in a defective condition unreasonably dangerous to the user or consumer if it is more dangerous than an ordinary consumer would expect when used in an intended or reasonably foreseeable manner." This standard followed as a logical development from commercial warranty origins of strict liability in tort. It reflected "the commercial reality that '[i]mplicit in . . .

[a product's] presence on the market . . . [is] a representation that it [will] safely do the jobs for which it was built.' "

Unlike the factual setting in *Leichtamer*, there are situations in which "the consumer would not know what to expect, because he would have no idea how safe the product could be made." Such is the case *sub judice*. Difficulty could arise, for example, where the injured party is an innocent bystander who is ignorant of the product and has no expectation of its safety, or where a new product is involved and no expectation of safety has developed. Conversely, liability could be barred hypothetically where industrial workmen "gradually learn of the dangers involved in the machinery they must use to make a living and come to 'expect' the dangers." In such cases, the policy underlying strict liability in tort, requires that "a product may be found defective in design, even if it satisfies ordinary consumer expectations, if through hindsight the jury determines that the product's design embodies 'excessive preventable danger,' or, in other words, if the jury finds that the risk of danger inherent in the challenged design outweighs the benefits of such design."

Accordingly, we hold that a product design is in a defective condition to the user or consumer if (1) it is more dangerous than an ordinary consumer would expect when used in an intended or reasonably foreseeable manner, or (2) if the benefits of the challenged design do not outweigh the risk inherent in such design. Factors relevant to the evaluation of the defectiveness of the product design are the likelihood that the product design will cause injury, the gravity of the danger posed, and the mechanical and economic feasibility of an improved design. . . . [W]e conclude that appellant has made out genuine issues of fact of whether appellee's press design was defective by allowing accidental tripping of the foot pedal control and in failing to provide a point of operation guard when the foot pedal is operative. Specifically, appellant provided an affidavit of James J. McCarthy, a former safety engineer for General Motors Corporation, involved with analysis of machine accident potential. McCarthy's affidavit states, *inter alia*, that in his opinion the press is defective "because of inadequate guarding at the point of operation caused by failure to attach a barrier or interlock gate guard to prevent entry of the operator's hands into the danger area while the ram is descending . . . the press is defective because of inadequate guarding of the foot pedal of the foot switch to prevent inadvertent entry and tripping."

Notes

1. **Consumer expectations test.** When it comes to design defects, much authority now adopts the risk-utility test seen in *Knitz*, and that test will absorb our attention in the materials that immediately follow. However, it is important to remember that some courts still use the consumer expectations test, either alone or along with the risk-utility test. *See, e.g., Calles v. Scripto–Tokai Corp.*, 864 N.E.2d 249 (Ill. 2007); *Tran v. Toyota Motor Corp.*, 420 F.3d 1310 (11th Cir. 2005) (Florida law); *Green v. Smith & Nephew AHP,*

Inc., 629 N.W.2d 727 (Wis. 2001); *Soule v. General Motors Corp.*, 882 P.2d 298 (Cal. 1994). Some states have combined the two tests. To take a noteworthy example, the court in *Mikolajczyk v. Ford Motor Co.*, 2008 WL 4603565 (Ill.) said that where both parties argue a design-defect case based solely on consumer expectations, the jury should be instructed only on that test. However, "both the consumer-expectation test and the risk-utility test continue to have their place in the law of strict product liability based on design defect. Each party is entitled to choose its own method of proof, to present relevant evidence, and to request a corresponding jury instruction. If the evidence is sufficient to implicate the risk-utility test, the broader test, which incorporates the factor of consumer expectations, is to be applied by the finder of fact." Would the flip-side work, as well? In other words, would it be possible to amalgamate the two tests by saying that consumer expectation is the test, but what a consumer expects is affected by the balance of risks and utilities? *McCathern v. Toyota Motor Corp.*, 23 P.3d 320 (Or. 2001).

2. **The fundamental distinction.** The distinction between design defects and manufacturing defects is fundamental in American law. As *Knitz* shows, courts will often invoke a different set of rules for each type of defect. Yet many other countries make no such distinction but instead apply the same rules to each type of defect. *See* Mathias Reimann, *Liability for Defective Products at the Beginning of the Twenty-first Century: Emergence of a Worldwide Standard?*, 51 AM. J. COMP. LAW. 751 (2003); Jane Stapleton, *Bugs in Anglo–American Products Liability*, 53 S.C. L. REV. 1225 (2002).

3. **Risks and utilities balanced.** Risk-utility balancing, now often adopted for design defect claims, involves weighing the likelihood of harm, the gravity of the harm if it occurs, and the cost of preventing harm by using a different design. The cost of a different design would include any loss of benefits in the present design as well as any direct costs of the alternative design (such as production and marketing costs). In assessing the risk, the capacity of users to protect themselves would be of importance. These factors are discussed in a frequently cited passage by Dean John Wade in his article, *On the Nature of Strict Tort Liability for Products*, 44 MISS. L.J. 825 (1973).

4. **Judge and jury.** If reasonable people can differ on the evidence, the jury, not the judge, determines whether the product was defective under the risk-utility balance. *See Bryant v. Hoffmann–La Roche, Inc.*, 585 S.E.2d 723 (Ga. Ct. App. 2003).

5. **Restatement of Products Liability.** The Restatement says that a product is defective in design when the seller could have reduced or avoided the product's "foreseeable risks of harm" by "the adoption of a reasonable alternative design, and the omission of the alternative design renders the product not reasonably safe." RESTATEMENT OF PRODUCTS LIABILITY § 2(b). Comment *d* explains that this section "adopts a reasonableness ('risk-utility balancing') test as the standard for judging the defectiveness of product designs." Comment *g* states that consumer expectations "do not constitute an independent standard for judging" design defects, but that such expectations "may substantially influence or even be ultimately determinative on risk-utility balancing," since they relate to foreseeability and frequency of the risks of harm.

6. **Negligence disguised in strict liability?** (a) *Conduct vs. product focus.* Where the consumer expectation test is discarded and the risk-utility test is adopted to control liability for design defects, does all this sound like *Carroll Towing* and thus like a negligence analysis? Sometimes courts have tried to distinguish risk-utility balancing on a negligence theory from the same balancing in strict liability cases by saying negligence is about conduct of the manufacturer, while strict product liability is about quality of the product. *E.g., Dart v. Wiebe Mfg., Inc.,* 709 P.2d 876 (Ariz. 1985). Yet behind every product's quality or lack of quality is the defendant's conduct. Is the distinction illusory? As Judge Posner put it in *Mesman v. Crane Pro Services,* 409 F.3d 846 (7th Cir. 2005), "*Expressly* requiring proof of negligence in a design-defect case, as Indiana law does, though unusual really isn't much of a legal innovation, since 'defect' always implied something that should not have been allowed into the product—something, in other words, that could have been removed at a reasonable cost in light of the risk that it created."

(b) *Desperately seeking distinctions.* In *Connelly v. Hyundai Motor Co.,* 351 F.3d 535 (1st Cir. 2003), involving a death resulting from airbag deployment, the jury found negligence in design but no defect leading to strict liability. The court attempted to reconcile these findings by saying that the jury could have found a negligently designed airbag, yet could have consistently "rejected the strict liability count because it decided that, on balance, the benefit to the public of including the overly aggressive airbag system in the Sonata outweighed the danger caused by the airbag system (because the system saved many more lives than it took)." To reconcile the negligence finding with the no-strict-liability finding, is the court adopting a radical view that negligence does not involve risk-utility assessments?

(c) If you feel these distinctions are unpersuasive, consider whether you can find other and more reliable distinctions in any of the following materials.

BARKER v. LULL ENGINEERING CO., 573 P.2d 443 (Cal. 1978). Plaintiff, an inexperienced operator of a high-lift industrial loader, lifted a load of lumber 10–18 feet off the ground. The ground was uneven and the loader began to vibrate as if it were about to tip over. Responding to warning shouts of fellow workers, the plaintiff scrambled out of the loader. He was hit and seriously injured by lumber falling from the load. The loader had no protective canopy and no outriggers to steady it. "We hold ... that a product is defective in design (1) if the plaintiff demonstrates that the product failed to perform as safely as an ordinary consumer would expect when used in an intended or reasonably foreseeable manner or (2) if the plaintiff proves that the product's design proximately caused his injury and the defendant fails to prove ... that on balance the benefits of the challenged design outweigh the risk of danger inherent in such design."

NOTES

1. Notice that *Barker* shifts the burden of proof to the defendant to justify its design by pointing to a suitable risk-utility balance. Only a few courts have embraced the burden-shifting idea in design or failure to warn cases. *See Shanks v. Upjohn Co.*, 835 P.2d 1189 (Alaska 1992). The shift occurs quite easily. All the plaintiff must do is prove that the "design caused" harm. The burden of justifying the product's design then falls on the defendant. *See Mikolajczyk v. Ford Motor Co.*, 2008 WL 4603565 (Ill.) (expressly adopting *Barker*'s burden shift). If the defendant fails to prove that the benefits outweigh the risks of the design, the plaintiff will prevail. *Cf. Gonzalez v. Autoliv ASP, Inc.*, 64 Cal.Rptr.3d 908 (Ct. App. 2007) (reversing summary judgment for defendant where it adduced no evidence to refute plaintiff's showing). How does this differ from the usual negligence case?

2. In *Campbell v. General Motors Corp.*, 649 P.2d 224 (Cal. 1982), the plaintiff was a 62-year-old woman who was injured when thrown from her seat while riding on a city bus. She was sitting in the forward-most front-facing seat. The seats immediately behind the plaintiff had grab bars on them, so that if she had sat in one of them, she would have had something to hold onto. There was also a vertical bar in the aisle in front of the side seat immediately in front of the plaintiff, but she could not reach it from her own seat. After she settled with the city, she sued the manufacturer of the bus. *Held*, it can be fairly inferred that the bus' design "caused" the injury, thus she prevails under the second test in *Barker*. Would this proof suffice in an ordinary negligence case, do you think?

3. Strict liability under the consumer expectation test will not always be available under *Barker*, because California plaintiffs can choose the consumer expectation test only where the ordinary consumer, based on "everyday experience," could determine how safely a product would have performed in the injury-causing event that occurred. *Soule v. General Motors Corp.*, 882 P.2d 298 (Cal. 1994). The key factor is not the product's complexity, but whether "in the context of the facts and circumstances of its failure, the product is one about which the ordinary consumers can form minimum safety expectations." *McCabe v. American Honda Motor Co.*, 123 Cal.Rptr.2d 303 (Ct. App. 2002) (plaintiff allowed to proceed on consumer expectation test in case of non-deploying air bag). Illinois, which also follows the *Barker* model, has said that "Nothing in our past decisions, even when we have applied the risk-utility test, has signaled a rejection of the consumer-expectation test merely because a complex product was involved." *Mikolajczyk, supra* Note 1. Are you troubled by allowing a jury to assess the defectiveness of a complex design using the consumer expectation test?

HONDA OF AMERICA MFG., INC. v. NORMAN

104 S.W.3d 600 (Tex. App. 2003)

EVELYN V. KEYES JUSTICE . . . .

At approximately 2:00 a.m. on December 2, 1992, Karen attempted to back her car up to turn around, and she accidentally backed down a boat ramp into the water in Galveston Bay. Her passenger, Josel Woods, was not wearing a seatbelt and was able to get out of the car by crawling out the passenger side window. After escaping, Woods reached back into the sinking car to get her purse. Woods testified that Karen was calm and did not appear scared. As Woods was swimming to the ramp, she heard Karen say, "Help me. I can't get my seatbelt undone." Woods testified that, after she reached the ramp, she heard Karen yell to her again that she could not get out of her seatbelt.

A dive team located Karen's car at 8:53 a.m. All of the windows were rolled up, including the one Woods testified she had escaped through, and all the doors were closed. Karen's body was found in the back seat. An autopsy revealed Karen's blood-alcohol level was .17.

At the time of the accident, Karen's four-door 1991 Honda Civic was equipped with a two-point passive restraint system—an automatic seatbelt that was mechanically drawn up over the shoulder when the door was closed—supplemented with a manual lap belt. The automatic seatbelt fastened itself with no action on behalf of the occupant. Robert Hellmuth, a former National Highway Traffic Safety Administration employee, testified that, in 1990, all cars were required to have either a passive belt system or an air bag. Hellmuth also testified that a two-point passive restraint system was the most expensive seatbelt system in use at the time Karen's car was manufactured.

The shoulder belt on both front seats was attached to a "mouse" that ran along a rail above the door. When the door was closed, the mouse moved from its starting position, near the front of the car, along the length of the door and then part-way down the pillar between the front and back doors, pulling the belt over the shoulder of the driver. When the door was opened or the ignition was turned off, the mouse moved forward, allowing the occupant to get out of the car. The shoulder belt could be manually disengaged by pressing an emergency release button located at the juncture of the belt and the mouse.... If the car experienced rapid deceleration (such as that encountered here when the car hit the water) or substantial tilting of the vehicle, however, the belt's emergency locking retractor would engage, preventing spooling of the belt and holding the occupant in her seat....

[In their suit against Honda, the] Normans contend that the emergency locking retractor locked as Karen backed down the ramp and that she pulled on the door latch, causing the mouse to move and then stall and the seatbelt to pin her to her seat. Because she was pinned to the seat, Karen was unable to reach the emergency release button located over her left shoulder. The Normans argue that the evidence showed the seatbelt system was defectively designed because (1) the mouse was able to move even when the retractor was locked, allowing the seatbelt to pin an occupant in the seat; (2) the seatbelt, when fully extended, could not be released easily and rapidly by pressing the emergency release button; and (3) the emergency release button was improperly located, in that Honda failed to provide an easy and rapid way to get out of the seatbelt under conditions it knew would occur.

The jury found that Karen was 25% contributorily negligent [and damages were awarded to the parents.]

. . . A claimant not only must meet the proof requirements of the statute but must show, under the common law, that the product was defectively designed so as to be unreasonably dangerous, taking into consideration the utility of the product and the risks involved in its use.

. . . Honda argues that the Normans failed to meet their threshold statutory burden because they failed to prove there was a safer alternative design to the Honda's seatbelt restraint system. To prove a design defect, the Normans had to show, among other things, that (1) there was a safer alternative; (2) the safer alternative would have prevented or significantly reduced the risk of injury, without substantially impairing the product's utility; and (3) the safer alternative was both technologically and economically feasible when the product left the control of the manufacturer. . . . In addition, a plaintiff complaining of a design defect is required to show that "the safety benefits from its proposed design are foreseeably greater than the resulting costs, including any diminished usefulness or diminished safety"—that is, that the alternative design not only would have reduced the risk of harm in the instant case, but also would not, "under other circumstances, impose an equal or greater risk of harm." Thus, the Normans had to prove that an economically and technologically feasible alternative seat belt and release system was available and would have prevented or significantly reduced the risk of Karen's death without substantially reducing the utility to the "intended users" of the product— namely, all automobile drivers. If no evidence is offered that a safer design existed, a product is not unreasonably dangerous as a matter of law.

. . . Thomas Horton, a mechanical engineer, and Kenneth Ronald Laughery, a human factors expert, testified that there were three potential alternative seatbelt system designs: (1) the mouse could be on a timer; (2) the release button could be located on the hip level, as in Toyota cars; and (3) there could be two release buttons—one near the hip and one over the shoulder.

. . . Instead of the mouse stopping in its place and losing power, as allegedly occurred here, Horton suggested the mouse could have been programmed to reverse direction and return to its forward position, releasing tension on the belt. A timer could have been programmed so that, if the mouse did not travel its entire cycle within a certain period of time, it would reverse and return to its original position. Horton explained that it would have been "simple within the electronics" to have created such a system.

. . . The Normans argue that Horton testified that this design was feasible. He did not. Instead, he simply answered "yes" to the general question of whether, in his opinion, economically and technologically feasible designs were available at the time Honda manufactured Karen's car. Horton did not identify any such available design, nor did he discuss the economic or technological feasibility of such a hypothetical alternative design....

We conclude, based on the record, that the Normans failed to prove that a timer-controlled mouse was a safer alternative design to the seatbelt system in Karen's Honda.

The Normans contend that, because of her small frame, Karen positioned the driver's seat close to the steering wheel, which made it difficult, if not impossible, for her to activate the release button found over her left shoulder on the car frame.

The Normans argue that Kenneth Laughery testified that placing a release button over the left shoulder of the driver was not sufficient. Laughery testified that, before 1991, at the same time the Honda system in Karen's car was designed, Toyota was using a release mechanism in the form of a lever control at the lower right side of the driver that released the emergency locking retractor. The Normans argue that Laughery concluded that Honda could have adopted this as an alternative design, because it was technologically and economically feasible. In fact, Laughery testified as follows:

Q: And from your understanding was it economically and technologically feasible at the time that this product left the control of Honda by the application of existing or reasonably achievable scientific knowledge to have provided this [Toyota-type] alternative design?

A: Yeah. I—well, I know it was technologically feasible because I know it was done already. I don't know what the cost of it was, but at least it was judged to be economically feasible in the sense that it existed in other vehicles.

While the use of an alternative design by another manufacturer may establish technological feasibility, we have held that, as a matter of law, it does not establish economic feasibility. *Smith,* 23 S.W.3d at 477; *Jaimes v. Fiesta Mart,* 21 S.W.3d 301, 306 (Tex. App.1999). The existence of a technological advancement goes to technological feasibility, while the cost of applying that technology to a particular design goes to economic feasibility. Evidence of use in the marketplace alone is not sufficient to establish economic feasibility under Texas law. To establish economic feasibility, the plaintiff must introduce proof of the "cost of incorporating this technology."

... [E]ven if the Normans presented more than a scintilla of evidence from which the jury could reasonably have inferred that the Toyota passive-restraint system was technologically and economically feasible, they did not establish that the right hip release would have prevented or significantly reduced the risk of Karen's death without "under other circumstances, impos[ing] an equal or greater risk of harm." ... Tanahashi testified that Honda chose a release mechanism located over the driver's left shoulder, instead of one located by the driver's right hip, to make it easier for third parties outside the vehicle to free trapped drivers—who might be unconscious or immobile—in an emergency. Neither Thomas nor Tanahashi testified that the Toyota right hip release design would have saved more lives than the Honda system. . . .

We conclude, based on the record, that the Normans presented no evidence from which the jury could reasonably find that the Toyota hip-release design would have prevented or significantly reduced the risk of Karen's death without imposing an equal or greater risk of harm under all relevant circumstances. . . .

[The court also concluded that the Normans also failed to prove that a two-release button design "was technologically and economically feasible and thus a safer alternative design."]

We reverse and render a take-nothing judgment.

NOTES

1. **Burden of proof.** On the facts of the *Norman* case would the plaintiffs get their case to the jury under *Barker v. Lull*? Most courts do not follow *Barker*'s burden shifting. Can we therefore say that "strict product liability" for design defects is really only liability for negligence?

2. **Proof of a reasonable alternative design.** The Restatement rejects *Barker's* burden shifting and also requires the plaintiff to prove that a reasonable alternative design (RAD) was or reasonably could have been available at the time the product was sold or distributed. RESTATEMENT OF PRODUCTS LIABILITY § 2, cmt. *d*. A reasonable alternative design is not by itself enough; the evidence must also show that the product was unreasonably dangerous and foreseeably would cause harm similar to that suffered by the plaintiff. *See, e.g., Slisze v. Stanley–Bostitch,* 979 P.2d 317 (Utah 1999); *Grzanka v. Pfeifer,* 694 A.2d 295 (N.J. Super. Ct. App. Div. 1997).

3. **Contours of the reasonable alternative design.** "Throughout the twentieth century, the great majority of design defect cases have inovled proof by the plaintiff of a feasible alternative design—proof of some practicable, cost-effective, untaken design precaution that would have prevented the plaintiff's harm." DAVID G. OWEN, PRODUCTS LIABILITY LAW § 8.5, at 521 (2d Ed. 2008). As the *Norman* case explains, proving such a thing involves proof not only that an alternative design would have been safer, but also that the alternative design was feasible. In showing a design's feasibility, should it matter whether the design would be "acceptable to the market," that is, that people would actually purchase it? *See Rose v. Brown & Williamson Tobacco Corp.,* 855 N.Y.S.2d 119 (App. Div. 2008).

4. **The R.A.D. requirement: a middle ground?** Could you put the burden on the plaintiff to show a defect that is unreasonably dangerous under the risk-utility test *without* requiring proof of a reasonable alternative design? That's what the court did in *Vautour v. Body Masters Sports Industries, Inc.,* 784 A.2d 1178 (N.H. 2001). How would it be possible to prove a risk-utility balance showing the product was unreasonably dangerous without also proving that safer alternatives were available?

5. **Manifestly unreasonable designs.** The Products Restatement provides that in one narrow case, the jury might properly infer that safer and reasonably feasible alternative designs were available without explicit evidence. Section 2, cmt. *e*, suggests that the designs of some products are so "manifestly unreasonable" because of their negligible utility and high risk of danger, that defectiveness could be found even without proof of an alternative. It uses the dangerous toy gun as an example. Would a trampoline qualify, do you think? *See Parish v. ICON Health and Fitness, Inc.*, 719 N.W.2d 540 (Iowa 2006).

6. **Unidentified defect.** In *Jarvis v. Ford Motor Co.*, 283 F.3d 33 (2d Cir. 2002), a Ford Aerostar suddenly accelerated from a stopped position, hurling itself into trees even though the driver pumped the brakes. Plaintiff's experts thought that a short in the cruise control system caused the problem, but no physical evidence supporting this theory was ever found. The expert went on to explain reasonable ways in which Ford could have prevented uncontrolled acceleration resulting from such a short. Is this evidence sufficient to show a defect? Is the design manifestly unreasonable?

7. **Consumer expectation test eliminating the reasonable alternative design requirement.** The reasonable alternative design requirement is a product of the risk-utility analysis. Consequently, courts that still permit the plaintiff to prevail on a consumer expectation test must logically reject the reasonable alternative design requirement when the consumer expectation test is advanced as the ground of liability. *See, e.g., Delaney v. Deere & Co.*, 999 P.2d 930 (Kan. 2000); *Green v. Smith & Nephew AHP, Inc.*, 629 N.W.2d 727 (Wis. 2001).

8. **Plaintiff strategy.** Why would a plaintiff fail to adduce evidence of a reasonable alternative design? Even if the court does not require such proof, should a plaintiff who has evidence of a feasible alternative design introduce it? What might such evidence tend to prove? *See Kinser v. Gehl Co.*, 184 F.3d 1259 (10th Cir. 1999).

9. **What is an "alternative" design?** A most intriguing question arises when you try to figure out what counts as an alternative design. Suppose there are three drugs on the market that, by different chemical formulas, help avoid some painful symptom like heartburn or rashes. All do the job, although by different means. The defendant manufactures a fourth drug, based on still a fourth formula. The defendant's drug, however, has serious side effects for a substantial number of people. Should the existing drugs be considered as alternatives, on the ground that they have the same end function? Or should they NOT be considered as alternatives on the ground that, whatever their function, their chemical formulas are widely different?

The Restatement Third poses a different set of facts for this problem. It supposes that the defendant manufactures a toy gun that shoots hard pellets at high velocity, presumably very dangerous to those who might be in close range of a child playing with the toy. The defendant could have manufactured a toy gun that is not harmful, say one that fires soft gelatin pellets or ping pong balls. Would a ping-pong-ball gun be an alternative for the hard-pellet gun? It depends how you characterize the product. If you think the product is "toy guns capable of doing injury," the ping-pong-ball gun will not be an alternative. You might think the pellet gun was defective because it should not be marketed at all, but you would not think it defective because it fails to achieve the safety of a ping-pong-ball gun. *See* RESTATEMENT OF PRODUCTS LIABILITY § 2, cmt. *e.*

10. **Another middle ground?** Could you agree with the RAD requirement but disagree with its application in the *Norman* case?

McCARTHY v. OLIN CORP.

119 F.3d 148 (2d Cir. 1997)

MESKILL, CIRCUIT JUDGE. . . .

On December 7, 1993, Colin Ferguson boarded the Long Island Railroad's 5:33 p.m. commuter train departing from New York City and opened fire on the passengers. Six people, including Dennis McCarthy, were killed and nineteen others, including Kevin McCarthy and Maryanne Phillips, were wounded in the vicious attack. Ferguson was armed with a 9mm semiautomatic handgun, which was loaded with Winchester "Black Talon" bullets (Black Talons). The injuries to Dennis and Kevin McCarthy and Maryanne Phillips were enhanced by the ripping and tearing action of the Black Talons because, unfortunately, the bullets performed as designed. [The plaintiffs sued the manufacturer of the bullets, alleging the negligent manufacture, advertising and marketing of a product that was unreasonably designed and ultrahazardous, the making of an unreasonably dangerous product, and strict liability in tort. The trial judge dismissed the complaint, and plaintiffs appealed].

The Black Talon is a hollowpoint bullet designed to bend upon impact into six ninety-degree angle razor-sharp petals or "talons" that increase the wounding power of the bullet by stretching, cutting and tearing tissue and bone as it travels through the victim. The Black Talon bullet was designed and manufactured by Olin Corporation (Olin) through its Winchester division and went on the market in 1992. Although the bullet was originally developed for law enforcement agencies, it was marketed and available to the general public. In November 1993, following public outcry, Olin pulled the Black Talon from the public market and restricted its sales to law enforcement personnel. Colin Ferguson allegedly purchased the ammunition in 1993, before it was withdrawn from the market. . . .

[The Court first rejected plaintiff's request for certification to the New York Court of Appeals, then addressed the merits.]

Appellants' first argument is that Olin should be held strictly liable for their injuries because the Black Talon ammunition was defectively designed and the design and manufacture of the bullets were inherently dangerous.

. . . Appellants argue that the Black Talons were defectively designed because the expansion mechanism of the bullets, which causes ripping and tearing in its victims, results in enhanced injuries beyond ordinary bullets.

The district court rejected this argument because the expanding of the bullet was an intentional and functional element of the design of the product. We agree.

To state a cause of action for a design defect, plaintiffs must allege that the bullet was unreasonably dangerous for its intended use. "[A] defectively designed product is one which, at the time it leaves the seller's hands, is in a condition not reasonably contemplated by the ultimate consumer." This rule, however, is tempered by the realization that some products, for example knives, must by their very nature be dangerous in order to be functional. The very purpose of the Black Talon bullet is to kill or cause severe wounding. Here, plaintiffs concede that the Black Talons performed precisely as intended by the manufacturer and Colin Ferguson.

> Sadly it must be acknowledged that: [m]any products, however well-built or well-designed may cause injury or death. Guns may kill; knives may maim; liquor may cause alcoholism; but the mere fact of injury does not entitle the [person injured] to recover ... there must be something wrong with the product, and if nothing is wrong there will be no liability.

DeRosa v. Remington Arms Co., 509 F.Supp. 762, 769 (E.D.N.Y.1981) (under New York law, shotgun as designed by defendant was not unreasonably dangerous for its foreseeable use).

Appellants have not alleged that the bullets were defective. As a matter of law, a product's defect is related to its condition, not its intrinsic function. The bullets were not in defective condition nor were they unreasonably dangerous for their intended use because the Black Talons were purposely designed to expand on impact and cause severe wounding.

Appellants next argue that under the risk/utility test analysis applied by New York courts, appellee should be held strictly liable because the risk of harm posed by the Black Talons outweighs the ammunition's utility. The district court properly held that the risk/utility test is inapplicable "because the risks arise from the function of the product, not any defect in the product." There must be 'something wrong' with a product before the risk/utility analysis may be applied in determining whether the product is unreasonably dangerous or defective.

The purpose of risk/utility analysis is to determine whether the risk of injury might have been reduced or avoided if the manufacturer had used a feasible alternative design. However, the risk of injury to be balanced with the utility is a risk not intended as the primary function of the product. Here, the primary function of the Black Talon bullets was to kill or cause serious injury. There is no reason to search for an alternative safer design where the product's sole utility is to kill and maim. Accordingly, we hold that appellants have failed to state a cause of action under New York strict products liability law.

Appellants also argue that Olin should be held strictly liable because the Black Talon ammunition is "unreasonably dangerous per se." According to the appellants' theory, a product is unreasonably dangerous per se if a reasonable person would conclude that the danger of the product, whether foreseeable or not, outweighs its utility. As the district court held, this is essentially a risk/utility analysis, which we have refused to apply. Under New York's strict products liability jurisprudence, there is no cause of action for an unreasonably dangerous per se product. Thus, this claim was properly dismissed.

... The crux of appellants' negligence theory is that Olin negligently marketed and placed the Black Talon ammunition for sale to the general public. Appellants argue that because of the severe wounding power of the bullets, Olin should have restricted sales to law enforcement agencies, for whom the bullet was originally designed. They also argue that Olin should have known that their advertising, which highlighted the ripping and tearing characteristics of the bullet, would attract "many types of sadistic, unstable and criminal personalities," such as Ferguson....

New York courts do not impose a legal duty on manufacturers to control the distribution of potentially dangerous products such as ammunition. Accordingly, although it may have been foreseeable by Olin that criminal misuse of the Black Talon bullets could occur, Olin is not legally liable for such misuse. As the district court pointed out, appellants have not alleged that any special relationship existed between Olin and Ferguson. Here, Olin could not control the actions of Ferguson. "[I]t is unreasonable to impose [a] duty where the realities of every day experience show us that, regardless of the measures taken, there is little expectation that the one made responsible could prevent the ... conduct [of another]."

... To impose a duty on ammunition manufacturers to protect against criminal misuse of its product would likely force ammunition products—which legislatures have not proscribed, and which concededly are not defectively designed or manufactured and have some socially valuable uses—off the market due to the threat of limitless liability. Because Olin did not owe a legal duty to plaintiffs to protect against Colin Ferguson's horrible action, appellants' complaint does not state a cause of action for negligence and the claim was properly dismissed....

[Judgment affirmed. Dissenting opinion omitted.]

NOTES

1. **Considering what is defective.** Does the product in *McCarthy* have more than negligible social utility when marketed to the public? Does it present an extremely high danger? Why, then, is it not "defective?" If a product's "sole utility is to kill and maim," does it follow that it is not defective when it inflicts as much pain and possible?

2. **Black Talons under a consumer expectation test.** Would it help the plaintiff in *McCarthy* to show that the Black Talon is "defective" if the court accepted the consumer expectation test? Psychological studies show that

consumers, in judging what risks are acceptable, are influenced by factors unlike those entailed in risk-utility assessments. For instance, consumers in general appear to think a risk is high or a benefit is low according to their feelings unrelated to probability or even to actual harm that might be caused. The trustworthiness of the manufacturer might affect consumers' judgment about how risky or useful the product is, for example. This has led one commentator to suggest that since consumers dread some deaths more than others, the Black Talons might be judged defective on a revitalized consumer expectation test, based on expert studies of what risks consumers find unacceptable. Douglas A. Kysar, *The Expectations of Consumers,* 103 COLUM. L. REV. 1700, 1767, 1774 (2003). This idea was criticized in James A. Henderson, Jr. & Aaron D. Twerski, *Consumer Expectations' Last Hope: A Response to Professor Kysar,* 103 COLUM. L. REV. 1791 (2003). What do you think?

3. **Firearms: Design defect theories.** Plaintiffs have had limited success in design defect cases against gun manufacturers where properly-working guns were at issue. In *Halliday v. Sturm, Ruger & Co.,* 792 A.2d 1145 (Md. 2002), a three-year-old found a hidden handgun that had no safety lock. The child also found the separately hidden ammunition, loaded the gun, and accidentally killed himself. The highest court of Maryland, though also emphasizing the father's fault, held that the gun was simply not defective—it worked exactly as it was designed and intended to work and as any ordinary consumer would have expected it to work. *Smith v. Bryco Arms,* 33 P.3d 638 (N.M. Ct. App. 2001) marked a different view. A teenager bought a handgun and ammunition for $40. He removed the magazine and then let friends examine the gun. They believed that with the magazine removed, it was impossible to fire the gun. One of them pulled the trigger. In fact there was a bullet in the chamber, the gun fired, and the bullet struck the other teenager in the face. The court held that a jury could find the handgun defective because it lacked both a trigger lock and a visual indication that the chamber was loaded and because the jury could find that a mistaken belief that the gun was not loaded when the magazine was removed was foreseeable.

4. **Firearms: The new federal immunity.** In 2005 Congress passed the Protection of Lawful Commerce in Arms Act (PLCAA), 15 U.S.C.A. §§ 7901–7903, and President George W. Bush signed it into law. The PLCAA prohibits legal claims against manufacturers, distributors, dealers and import-ers of guns or ammunition "for the harm solely caused by the criminal or unlawful misuse of firearm products or ammunition products by others when the product functioned as designed and intended." The Act directed that any legal claims pending at the time of enactment "shall be immediately dis-missed." There are narrow exceptions, most notably where a manufacturer or seller (1) "knowingly violated a State or Federal statute applicable to the sale or marketing of the product, and the violation was a proximate cause of the harm for which relief is sought," or "aided, abetted or conspired with any other person" to sell guns or ammunition "knowing, or having reasonable cause to believe, that the actual buyer ... was prohibited from possessing or receiving" the product. The PLCAA withstood Constitutional attack in *District of Columbia v. Beretta U.S.A. Corp.,* 940 A.2d 163 (D.C. 2008), and *City of New York v. Beretta U.S.A. Corp.,* 524 F.3d 384 (2d Cir. 2008).

5. **Firearms: Other theories of liability.** Prior to the passage of the PLCAA, a few courts had permitted plaintiffs to proceed on defective or negligent marketing claims, as where the plaintiffs allege that manufacturers deliberately promote sales through channels likely to lead to purchases by criminals and insane persons who are prohibited from buying from regular retailers. *See Ileto v. Glock Inc.*, 349 F.3d 1191 (9th Cir. 2003); *City of Cincinnati v. Beretta U.S.A. Corp.*, 768 N.E.2d 1136 (Ohio 2002) (multiple theories including design defects and marketing to criminals so as to create a public nuisance).The PLCAA cuts off most tort cases involving firearms and ammunition, *see District of Columbia v. Beretta U.S.A. Corp.*, 940 A.2d 163 (D.C. 2008), but may leave room for some theories. *See, e.g., Smith & Wesson Corp. v. City of Gary*, 875 N.E.2d 422 (Ind. Ct. App. 2007) (allowing public nuisance action under PLCAA exception); *City of New York v. A–1 Jewelry & Pawn, Inc.*, 247 F.R.D. 296 (E.D.N.Y. 2007) (same); *contra, City of New York v. Beretta U.S.A. Corp.*, 524 F.3d 384 (2d Cir. 2008) (state criminal nuisance statute could not support a civil claim consistent with the PLCAA)

6. **Tobacco.** The liability of tobacco companies for smoking-related illnesses is a complex and changing subject. In design defect cases, the companies have usually prevailed in the higher courts, for a variety of reasons, although other theories have met with some success. In *Buckingham v. R.J. Reynolds Tobacco Co.*, 713 A.2d 381 (N.H. 1998), the court faced a claim by the estate of a woman who died from cancer caused by second-hand smoke. The court affirmed dismissal of the plaintiff's strict liability claim but reversed dismissal of her negligence claim. The court contemplated discovery by the parties to determine the extent to which the defendants know of their products' hazards, the defendants' expectations as to the use of their products and those who might be affected, causation, and any plaintiff contribution to her own injuries.

In November, 1998, several tobacco companies reached an historic settlement agreement with 46 states, agreeing to pay $206 billion over 25 years to compensate the states for the cost of treating Medicaid patients who have smoking-related illnesses. Four other states settled separately for another $40 billion. For a description and analysis of this agreement, see Hanoch Dagan & James J. White, *Governments, Citizens, and Injurious Industries*, 75 N.Y.U. L. REV. 354 (2000). The settlement agreement did not bar later suits by individuals, however. In July 2000, a Florida jury in a class action case against five tobacco companies awarded $145 billion in punitive damages, the largest jury verdict in U.S. history. *Engle v. R.J. Reynolds Tobacco Co.*, No. 94–8273 (Cir. Ct. Dade Co. 2000).

7. **Drugs: The old § 402A, comment *k*.** Section 402A of the Restatement Second, comment *k*, provided that some products "are quite incapable of being made safe in their intended and ordinary use," saying that this is often true with drugs. The Pasteur rabies vaccine is given as the prime example, a vaccine which "not uncommonly leads to very serious and damaging consequences," but which guards against a disease which "invariably leads to a dreadful death." Thus, according to comment *k*, such a product is neither defective nor *unreasonably* dangerous. The court in *Cochran v. Brooke*, 409 P.2d 904 (Or. 1966), quoted this comment with approval in affirming a directed verdict for the drug manufacturer in a case in which the plaintiff was

rendered almost blind as a result of taking a prescription drug for treatment of arthritis. Some courts still work out their products decisions in terms of the old § 402A, and hence apply comment *k* in drug and medical product cases.

8. **The Restatement of Products Liability § 6.** "The Products Restatement, by requiring foreseeable harm in all design defect claims, has made comment *k*'s special rules obsolete where the new Restatement is fully accepted." DOBBS ON TORTS § 359 (2000). Actually, the Products Restatement goes further than comment *k* by providing immunity in any cases where a reasonable health care provider who knows both the benefits and risks would prescribe the drug. RESTATEMENT OF PRODUCTS LIABILITY § 6 (1998). This seems to mean that manufacturers of drugs and related products need not exercise reasonable care under a risk-utility balance to make a safer drug. To get this protection, the drug must provide benefits in excess of harms, but it still need not be as safe as it could be with reasonable cost or effort. Courts have rejected this provision of the Restatement. *See, e.g., Bryant v. Hoffmann–La Roche, Inc.*, 585 S.E.2d 723 (Ga. Ct. App. 2003) (rejecting the Restatement's "stringent test" and asserting that no court had accepted it). *See* George W. Conk, *Is There a Design Defect in the Restatement (Third) of Torts: Products Liability?*, 109 YALE L.J. 1087 (2000) (arguing that the reasonable alternative design rule applied to other products should apply to drugs as well). Notice, however, that once safer drugs are *actually marketed* (presumably by the defendant's competitors), the reasonable health care provider would cease prescribing the defendant's drug. In that situation, the manufacturer might be liable. *See* James A. Henderson, Jr. & Aaron D. Twerski, *Drug Designs Are Different*, 111 YALE L.J. 151 (2001).

9. **Manufacturing flaws in drugs.** Strict liability may still apply to drugs and medical products if a *manufacturing flaw* is demonstrated. *Transue v. Aesthetech Corp.*, 341 F.3d 911 (9th Cir. 2003) (breast transplants covered by old § 402A, comment *k*, which exempts them from strict liability for design defects but does not exempt them from strict liability for manufacturing defects).

10. **Unknowable risks.** Should manufacturers ever be liable for harms that were unforeseeable at the time the product was distributed? You could imagine a system of strict liability that weighed all the actual risks of a product against its utilities, even though the risks were not known or knowable at the time the product was distributed. Such "superstrict liability" has some, albeit little, support in case law. *See, e.g., Sternhagen v. Dow Co.*, 935 P.2d 1139 (Mont. 1997) (pesticide manufacturers may be strictly liable, despite their lack of knowledge or reason to know at the time of marketing that their pesticides contained carcinogenic components). Also, some cases have supported strict liability when the danger was not actually unknowable but was "unforeseeable" in the sense that a reasonable person would not have recognized it. *See Ayers v. Johnson & Johnson Baby Products Co.*, 818 P.2d 1337 (Wash. 1991). In *Green v. Smith & Nephew AHP, Inc.*, 629 N.W.2d 727 (Wis. 2001), the court seemed to treat unforeseeable risk and unknowable risks alike. Does strict liability for unknowable or unforeseeable dangers discourage production of beneficial goods that consumers want? *See* Victor Schwartz, *The Death of "Super Strict Liability" Common Sense Returns to Tort Law*, 27 GONZ. L. REV. 179 (1992). The Restatement of Products Liability

rejects any liability for unknowable or unforeseeable risks in § 2(b), with respect to prescription drugs in particular in § 6. Foreign products liability law is similar on this point. *See* Jane Stapleton, *Bugs in Anglo–American Products Liability*, 53 S.C. L. REV. 1225, 1246–1247 (2002) (discussing the European Union's Directive on products liability with its escape clause).

11. **State of the art.** Statutes in many jurisdictions now provide a defense to the manufacturer if the product conformed to the "state of the art" at manufacture or sale. The terminology is ambiguous. The statutes presumably eliminate any liability for unknowable risk. Do they go further and make industry custom to produce unsafe products a defense? Iowa, which has such a statute, says not; state of the art in Iowa refers to safety measures that could be feasibly applied. In *Falada v. Trinity Industries, Inc.*, 642 N.W.2d 247 (Iowa 2002), defendant manufactured an ammonia tank that ruptured. Fumes killed Falada. The plaintiff admitted that the tank's design was state of the art, but claimed that the welding was defective or of bad workmanship. The defendant argued that if the tank's design was state of the art, the state of the art defense prohibits any claim based upon workmanship defects too. What outcome?

AN END NOTE: ADJUDICATION OF DESIGN DEFECTS

The limits of adjudication? Recent years have seen a shift, reflected in the Restatement of Products Liability and in some case law, away from strict liability for design defects. Much of the intellectual impetus for revision in the law of design defects cases originated in an article, *Judicial Review of Manufacturer's Conscious Design Choices: The Limits of Adjudication*, 73 COLUM. L. REV. 1531 (1973), written by Professor James Henderson, who served as one of the Restatement's two Reporters. In the article, he argued that rules of law must be so constructed that lawyers know what arguments can be constructed and what proof to adduce, and that when the issues are "polycentric," this is not possible. A polycentric problem is one in which there are many appropriate solutions, and in which each step in solving the problem involves a decision that affects the decision in later steps. The late professor Lon L. Fuller, in *Adjudication and the Rule of Law*, PROC. AM. SOC'Y INT. L. 1 (1960), gave several examples. In one example, the coach of a football team had to choose how to deploy the players. If one could equally play end or halfback, the decision to place him at end would also affect his decision about who played guard. The decision as to who played guard would affect other positions. Since there is no prescribed sequence for these decisions, and since each decision will affect the others, it would indeed be difficult for a lawyer to attempt to prove, say, that Dubbs should play guard and Henson should play end. Using this idea, Professor Henderson has developed the notion that design choices are polycentric and that they cannot be appropriately litigated in court. What is your own opinion? Can you back it up with argument?

Jury role. Some critics of products liability, like some manufacturers and insurers, view the jury with trepidation. Whether for these reasons or not, some jurists have argued that the judge should enter aggressively into the decision about what constitutes a design defect so that appropriate policy factors can be considered. *See* David A. Fischer, *Products Liability— Functionally Imposed Strict Liability*, 32 OKLA. L. REV. 93 (1979); Aaron Twerski, *Seizing the Middle Ground Between Rules and Standards in Design Defect Litigation: Advancing Directed Verdict Practice in Law of Torts*, 57 N.Y.U. L. REV. 521 (1982). The judge would not only weigh the evidence to decide whether it is sufficient to get to the jury on the risk-utility balance, but would also consider, for example, the polycentricity issue or the institutional capacity of courts to handle the litigation (Twerski) or the availability of insurance and the effect of increased prices that strict liability would bring (Fischer). Both would involve the judge more directly in policy-making decisions with the result that the jury's role would be diminished.

Social or economic factors. What social factors should be considered in judging a product to be defective? Saying that tobacco smoking is addictive and that it kills 350,000 persons annually, Professor Frank Vandall argues for "absolute" liability. This would have the effect, he says, of raising the price of smoking so that the cost of cigarettes would reflect their true costs to society. Increased price would drive some smokers to quit. He argues that non-smokers presently bear some of the costs of smoking because smoker's insurance pays some medical expenses and this drives up insurance costs for everyone and because if insurance does not pay the costs, welfare may, again with non-smokers sharing in the costs. Based on these and other arguments he develops a proposal for absolute liability with virtually no defenses. *See* Frank Vandall, *Reallocating the Costs of Smoking: The Application of Absolute Liability to Cigarette Manufacturers*, 52 OHIO ST. L. J. 405 (1991). Would any of his arguments be relevant in determining whether cigarettes were defective under present law?

Is there a products liability "crisis"? Tort reformers often point to products liability cases, especially design defect cases, as evidence of the tort system running amok. Empirical studies, however, tend to undercut this perception. Recently, two scholars published the results of a 12-year study of cases in Franklin County, Ohio (the city of Columbus and its suburbs). Among their findings: products claims accounted for less than four percent of civil jury verdicts in that period; plaintiffs prevailed in only one of five cases; and plaintiffs' verdicts were modest, with one-third falling under $100,000. Further, not a single plaintiff was awarded punitive damages in a products case in Franklin County over the 12-year period between 1985 and 1996. Deborah Jones Merritt & Kathryn Ann Barry, *Is the Tort System in Crisis? New Empirical Evidence*, 60 OHIO ST. L.J. 315 (1999). Does such data call into question the need for more restrictive rules in design cases, if that is what is occurring?

The validity of the distinction between design and manufacturing defects. Finally, some thinkers have questioned whether there is any sound policy or theoretical basis for distinguishing design defects from manufacturing defects. The two categories, with strict liability rules for manufacturing defect cases and negligence-based liability for design defects are not dictated by nature. And they may not even cover the field. Suppose commercially supplied blood is contaminated, not by manufacture, but at its source, because the donor has HIV. Is this alleged defect to be analyzed under the rules for manufacturing defect or the rules for design defects? *See* Jane Stapleton, *Bugs in Anglo–American Products Liability*, 53 S.C. L. Rev. 1225 (2002). More broadly, should we treat all products cases alike, either by requiring negligence in manufacturing flaw cases or by eliminating the negligence requirement in design defect cases? We could go even further, by imposing liability in cases like the Black Talon case. Could you mount arguments either way?

§ 6. WARNING OR INFORMATION DEFECTS

A. FOCUSING ON POINT-OF-SALE AND ON-PRODUCT WARNINGS

LIRIANO v. HOBART CORP.

170 F.3d 264 (2d Cir. 1999)

CALABRESI, CIRCUIT JUDGE:

[Luis Liriano was severely injured on the job when his hand was caught in a meat grinder manufactured by Hobart Corporation and owned by his employer, Super Associated. The meat grinder had been sold to Super with a safety guard, but the safety guard was removed while the machine was in Super's possession and was not on the meat grinder at the time of the accident. The machine bore no warning indicating that the grinder should be operated only with a safety guard attached.

[Liriano sued Hobart, who brought a third-party claim against Super. The only claim that went to the jury was Liriano's failure to warn claim. The jury found for Liriano, attributing a degree responsibility to all three parties. Hobart and Super appealed, arguing (1) that there was no duty to warn, and (2) that even if there had been a duty to warn, the evidence presented was not sufficient to allow the failure-to-warn claim to reach the jury. The federal court certified both questions to the New York Court of Appeals, which rejected appellants' first argument but declined to address the second, leaving it for this court.]

More than a hundred years ago, a Boston woman named Maria Wirth profited from an argument about obviousness as a matter of law that is very similar to the one Hobart urges today. See Lorenzo v. Wirth, 170 Mass. 596, 49 N.E. 1010 (1898). Wirth was the owner of a house on whose property there was a coal hole. The hole abutted the street in front of the house, and casual observers would have no way of knowing that the area around the hole was not part of the public thoroughfare. A pedestrian called Lorenzo fell into the coal hole and sued for her injuries. Writing for a majority of the Supreme Judicial Court of Massachusetts, Oliver Wendell

Holmes, Jr., held for the defendant. He noted that, at the time of the accident, there had been a heap of coal on the street next to the coal hole, and he argued that such a pile provided sufficient warning to passers-by that they were in the presence of an open hole. "A heap of coal on a sidewalk in Boston is an indication, according to common experience, that there very possibly may be a coal hole to receive it." And that was that.

It was true, Holmes acknowledged, that "blind men, and foreigners unused to our ways, have a right to walk in the streets," and that such people might not benefit from the warning that piles of coal provided to sighted Bostonians. But Holmes wrote that coal-hole cases were simple, common, and likely to be oft repeated, and he believed it would be better to establish a clear rule than to invite fact-specific inquiries in every such case. "In simple cases of this sort," he explained, "courts have felt able to determine what, in every case, however complex, defendants are bound at their peril to know." With the facts so limited, this was an uncomplicated case in which the defendant could, as a matter of law, rely on the plaintiff's responsibility to know what danger she faced.

Justice Knowlton disagreed. His opinion delved farther into the particular circumstances than did Holmes's opinion for the majority. In so doing, he showed that Lorenzo's failure to appreciate her peril might have been foreseen by Wirth and hence that Wirth's failure to warn might constitute negligence. He noted, for example, that the accident occurred after nightfall, when Lorenzo perhaps could not see, or recognize, the heap of coal for what it was. There was "a throng of persons" on the street, such that it would have been difficult even in daylight to see very far ahead of where one was walking. And the plaintiff was, in fact, a foreigner unused to Boston's ways. "[S]he had just come from Spain, and had never seen coal put into a cellar through a coal hole." In sum, the case was not the "simple" one that Holmes had made it out to be. What is more, none of the facts he recited was either unusual or unforeseeable by Wirth. "What kind of conduct is required under complex conditions, to reach the usual standard of due care, namely, the ordinary care of persons of common prudence, is a question of fact.... [and thus] a question for a jury." Even cases involving "obvious" dangers like coal holes, Knowlton believed, might not be resolvable as matters of law when viewed in the fullness of circumstances that rendered the issue less clear than it would be when posed in the abstract.

Holmes commanded the majority of the Supreme Judicial Court in 1898, but Knowlton's position has prevailed in the court of legal history. " '[T]he so-called Holmes view—that standards of conduct ought increasingly to be fixed by the court for the sake of certainty—has been largely rejected.... The tendency has been away from fixed standards and towards enlarging the sphere of the jury.' " Fowler V. Harper, Fleming James, Jr., & Oscar S. Gray, The Law of Torts § 15.3, at 358–59 n. 16 (2d ed.1986).

The courts of New York have several times endorsed Knowlton's approach and ruled that judges should be very wary of taking the issue of liability away from juries, even in situations where the relevant dangers might seem obvious.... [Even so] there have been situations in which New York state courts have deemed dangers to be sufficiently clear so that warnings were, as a matter of law, not necessary. See, e.g., ... Caris v. Mele, 134 A.D.2d 475, 476, 521 N.Y.S.2d 260, 261 (1987) (holding that there is no duty to warn of the danger of diving headfirst into an above-ground swimming pool only four feet deep).

... Liriano was only seventeen years old at the time of his injury and had only recently immigrated to the United States. He had been on the job at Super for only one week. He had never been given instructions about how to use the meat grinder, and he had used the meat grinder only two or three times. And ... the mechanism that injured Liriano would not have been visible to someone who was operating the grinder. It could be argued that such a combination of facts was not so unlikely that a court should say, as a matter of law, that the defendant could not have foreseen them or, if aware of them, need not have guarded against them by issuing a warning....

Nevertheless, it remains the fact that meat grinders are widely known to be dangerous.... [W]e might well be of two minds as to whether a failure to warn that meat grinders are dangerous would be enough to raise a jury issue.

But to state the issue that way would be to misunderstand the complex functions of warnings. As two distinguished torts scholars have pointed out, a warning can do more than exhort its audience to be careful. It can also affect what activities the people warned choose to engage in. See James A. Henderson, Jr., and Aaron D. Twerski, Doctrinal Collapse in Products Liability: The Empty Shell of Failure to Warn, 65 N.Y.U. L.Rev. 265, 285 (1990). And where the function of a warning is to assist the reader in making choices, the value of the warning can lie as much in making known the existence of alternatives as in communicating the fact that a particular choice is dangerous. It follows that the duty to warn is not necessarily obviated merely because a danger is clear.

To be more concrete, a warning can convey at least two types of messages. One states that a particular place, object, or activity is danger-ous. Another explains that people need not risk the danger posed by such a place, object, or activity in order to achieve the purpose for which they might have taken that risk. Thus, a highway sign that says "Danger–Steep Grade" says less than a sign that says "Steep Grade Ahead–Follow Suggested Detour to Avoid Dangerous Areas."

If the hills or mountains responsible for the steep grade are plainly visible, the first sign merely states what a reasonable person would know without having to be warned. The second sign tells drivers what they might not have otherwise known: that there is another road that is flatter and less hazardous. A driver who believes the road through the mountainous area to be the only way to reach her destination might well choose to drive on that road despite the steep grades, but a driver who knows herself to have an alternative might not, even though her understanding of the risks posed by the steep grade is exactly the same as those of the first driver. Accordingly, a certain level of obviousness as to the grade of a road might, in principle, eliminate the reason for posting a sign of the first variety. But no matter how patently steep the road, the second kind of sign might still have a beneficial effect. As a result, the duty to post a sign of the second variety may persist even when the danger of the road is obvious and a sign of the first type would not be warranted.

One who grinds meat, like one who drives on a steep road, can benefit not only from being told that his activity is dangerous but from being told of a safer way.... Given that attaching guards is feasible, does reasonable care require that meat workers be informed that they need not accept the risks of using unguarded grinders? Even if most ordinary users may—as a matter of law—know of the risk of using a guardless meat grinder, it does not follow that a sufficient number of them will—as a matter of law—also know that protective guards are available, that using them is a realistic possibility, and that they may ask that such guards be used. It is precisely these last pieces of information that a reasonable manufacturer may have a duty to convey even if the danger of using a grinder were itself deemed obvious.

... A jury could reasonably find that there exist people who are employed as meat grinders and who do not know (a) that it is feasible to reduce the risk with safety guards, (b) that such guards are made available with the grinders, and (c) that the grinders should be used only with the guards. Moreover, a jury can also reasonably find that there are enough such people, and that warning them is sufficiently inexpensive, that a reasonable manufacturer would inform them that safety guards exist and that the grinder is meant to be used only with such guards. Thus, even if New York would consider the danger of meat grinders to be obvious as a matter of law, that obviousness does not substitute for the warning....

Hobart [also] raises the issue of causation. It maintains that Liriano "failed to present any evidence that Hobart's failure to place a warning [on the machine] was causally related to his injury." Whether or not there had been a warning, Hobart says, Liriano might well have operated the machine as he did and suffered the injuries that he suffered. Liriano introduced no evidence, Hobart notes, suggesting either that he would have refused to grind meat had the machine borne a warning or that a warning would have persuaded Super not to direct its employees to use the grinder without the safety attachment.

[Hobart's argument] assumes that the burden was on Liriano to introduce additional evidence showing that the failure to warn was a but-for cause of his injury.... But Liriano does not bear that burden. When a defendant's negligent act is deemed wrongful precisely because it has a strong propensity to cause the type of injury that ensued, that very causal tendency is evidence enough to establish a prima facie case of cause-in-fact. The burden then shifts to the defendant to come forward with evidence that its negligence was not such a but-for cause.

We know, as a general matter, that the kind of negligence that the jury attributed to the defendant tends to cause exactly the kind of injury that the plaintiff suffered.... In such situations, rather than requiring the plaintiff to bring in more evidence to demonstrate that his case is of the ordinary kind, the law presumes normality and requires the defendant to adduce evidence that the case is an exception. Accordingly, in a case like this, it is up to the defendant to bring in evidence tending to rebut the strong inference, arising from the accident, that the defendant's negligence was in fact a but-for cause of the plaintiff's injury.

This shifting of the onus procedendi has long been established in New York. Its classic statement was made more than seventy years ago, when the Court of Appeals decided a case in which a car collided with a buggy driving after sundown without lights. See Martin v. Herzog, 228 N.Y. 164, 170, 126 N.E. 814, 816 (1920). The driver of the buggy argued that his negligence in driving without lights had not been shown to be the cause-in-fact of the accident. Writing for the Court, Judge Cardozo reasoned that the legislature deemed driving without lights after sundown to be negligent precisely because not using lights tended to cause accidents of the sort that had occurred in the case. The simple fact of an accident under those conditions, he said, was enough to support the inference of but-for causal connection between the negligence and the particular accident....

The words that Judge Cardozo applied to the buggy's failure to use lights are equally applicable to Hobart's failure to warn: "If nothing else is shown to break the connection, we have a case, prima facie sufficient, of negligence contributing to the result." ... See Guido Calabresi, Concerning Cause and the Law of Torts: An Essay for Harry Kalven, Jr., 43 U. Chi. L.Rev. 69 (1975).

... The district court did not err. We affirm its decision in all respects.

[Concurring opinion omitted.]

NOTES

Duty to Provide Information

1. **Information defects.** As indicated in *Liriano*, a manufacturer's failure to provide appropriate information about a product may make an otherwise safe product dangerous and defective. Warnings about dangers represent one important kind of information necessary for some products. Thus, a product becomes defective when the product's foreseeable risks of harm could have been reduced or avoided by the provision of a reasonable warning, and the omission of such a warning renders the product "not reasonably safe." RESTATEMENT OF PRODUCTS LIABILITY § 2(c).

2. **Warnings where equipment is initially safe.** The New York Court of Appeals had earlier rejected Hobart's argument that it owed no duty to warn as a matter of law, in *Liriano v. Hobart Corp.*, 700 N.E.2d 303 (N.Y. 1998). How could Hobart have a duty to warn about the dangers of operating its grinder without a guard when Hobart had equipped it with a guard?

3. **Functions of product information.** Necessary information to make a product reasonably safe may include directions for use, warnings, or some combination. Warnings may be needed either to alert users to risks that are not obvious, or to inform users of safer alternatives. All that seems acceptable enough. Should manufacturers be held to a further duty to provide all material information necessary to permit consumers to make an informed choice, on analogy to the duty of physicians in some informed consent cases? *See* DOBBS ON TORTS § 363 (2000).

4. **The duty to provide a risk-utility balanced warning.** Since the cost of giving a warning is usually rather small, it may be easy to conclude that the risk-utility balance always calls for a warning. Even so, some warnings simply are not needed. Should a manufacturer of safety glasses warn that they will break under the force of a five-pound sledge-hammer dropped from a height of seven feet? *American Optical Co. v. Weidenhamer*, 457 N.E.2d 181 (Ind. 1983). Should a pickup truck manufacturer be required to warn of the risks of riding unrestrained in the open cargo bed? *Josue v. Isuzu Motors Amer., Inc.*, 958 P.2d 535 (Haw. 1998). Should a BB gun manufacturer warn users that the gun could kill someone shot from close range? *Abney v. Crosman Corp.*, 919 So.2d 289 (Ala. 2005). Are consumers more likely to read a few important warnings, or a long list including warnings about trivial risks?

5. **Unknowable risks.** Some cases have supported the idea that a manufacturer might be liable for failure to warn of risks that were not only not known, but not knowable. This position (often called "superstrict liability") is firmly rejected in the Restatement of Products Liability, as seen in Note 1 above, and by the vast majority of courts. *See Vassallo v. Baxter Healthcare Corp.*, 696 N.E.2d 909 (Mass. 1998) ("The thin judicial support for a hindsight approach to the duty to warn is easily explained. The goal of the law is to induce conduct that is capable of being performed. This goal is not advanced by imposing liability for failure to warn of risks that were not capable of being known."). Might superstrict liability serve other goals?

Obvious Danger

6. **Obvious dangers and the no duty rule.** As the Restatement Third has it, "no duty exists" to warn of dangers that are obvious or should be obvious. RESTATEMENT OF PRODUCTS LIABILITY § 2, cmt. j; *accord, Mills v. Giant of Maryland, LLC*, 508 F.3d 11 (D.C. Cir. 2007); *Caterpillar, Inc. v. Shears*, 911 S.W.2d 379 (Tex. 1995). Is this merely the logical result of using a risk-utility balance and even more clearly dictated by a consumer expectation test? Some states have codified the rule. Michigan's statute, for example, provides that a "defendant is not liable for failure to warn of a material risk that is or should be obvious to a reasonably prudent product user or a material risk that is or should be a matter of common knowledge to persons in the same or

similar position as the person upon whose injury or death the claim is based in a product liability action." M.C.L. § 600.2948(2) (1996).

7. **Obvious dangers and comparative fault.** Distinguish the no duty rule from defenses based upon obvious danger. If the plaintiff is or should be actually aware of the specific danger and its magnitude, the defendant might avoid or limit liability under assumed risk or comparative negligence rules. (See § 8). Courts sometimes conflate the plaintiff fault issue with the defendant duty issue. In addition, courts may throw in proximate cause and "misuse" into the discussion. The straightforward explanation for most obvious danger problems, however, is simply that if the danger is foreseeably obvious in a significant degree, then the product is not defective at all for lack of a warning.

8. **Obvious danger and design defect.** A product that presents an obvious danger and thus provides its own warning, may still be defectively designed. Diving into a pool of unknown depth is obviously dangerous, so no warning for that is required. However, if the manufacturer should foresee that harm will befall users in spite of the obvious danger, the manufacturer may be liable for design defect if it could easily mark the depth and failed to do so. *See Camacho v. Honda Motor Co., Ltd.*, 741 P.2d 1240 (Colo. 1987) (a product can be unreasonably dangerous under the risk-utility test even if it is not more dangerous than the consumer expected; the consumer expectation test cannot be used to bar the plaintiff in such a case); *Uloth v. City Tank Corp.*, 384 N.E.2d 1188 (Mass. 1978) ("If a slight change in design would prevent serious, perhaps fatal, injury, the designer may not avoid liability by simply warning of the possible injury.").

9. **Obvious danger and consumer expectations.** If the danger is truly obvious, the product could seldom be defective under the consumer expectation test, since the consumer could not expect safety in the fact of obvious danger. What would the plaintiff's attorney argue in such a case? *See also Tabieros v. Clark Equip. Co.*, 944 P.2d 1279 (Haw. 1997) (open and obvious danger may prevent liability for failure to warn under consumer expectations test, but not necessarily under a risk-utility test).

Causation

10. **Causation in warning failure cases.** Suppose the plaintiff proves that the defendant failed to give a warning that was needed to make the product safe and that a safe warning would have been on the label of the product or on instructions accompanying it. Most case law says that unless the plaintiff would have read, understood and heeded the warning, the failure to warn cannot be a cause of the harm. But courts usually "presume" that the plaintiff would have read and heeded the warning, leaving it to the defendant to show otherwise if it can, a phenomenon known as the "heeding presumption." What result if the plaintiff admits that he did not read any of a product's accompanying instructions or warnings? Consider a different scenario: the defendant fails to give a warning, but the plaintiff was already intimately familiar with the danger. Does the plaintiff's knowledge of the danger go to the issue of defendant's duty, the issue of cause in fact, or

something else? *See Burke v. Spartanics, Ltd.*, 252 F.3d 131 (2d Cir. 2001) (facts similar to *Liriano* except the plaintiff knew the danger).

11.   **Shifting burden of proof on causation.** The *Liriano* court placed the burden on the defendant to prove that its negligent failure to warn was not a cause in fact of the plaintiff's harm, once the plaintiff proved that such failure "greatly increased the likelihood of the harm that occurred." How, if at all, does this approach differ from the "heeding presumption" mentioned above in Note 10? Can you compare *Liriano*'s burden-shifting approach to that in *Barker v. Lull*?

CARRUTH v. PITTWAY CORP., 643 So.2d 1340 (Ala. 1994). Seven family members were killed in a house fire. Their estates sued Pittway, a smoke-detector manufacturer, claiming that the deaths were caused by its negligence in providing insufficient installation instructions and warnings. Just two days before the fire, the victims' father had installed the smoke detector near a ceiling-wall junction. The device was accompanied by a seven-page pamphlet, set in small type. The pamphlet stated: "Dead air spaces are often . . . in the corners between ceilings and walls. Dead air may prevent smoke from reaching a detector." None of these statements was captioned by the words "warning," "caution," or "danger," as were other cautionary statements. The "dead air" statements were contained in a portion of the pamphlet that included numerous instructions and illustrations that together "could be viewed as confusing at best." A colored and highly visible diagram purported to show effective smoke detector locations, including the area immediately below a wall-ceiling junction. Ultimately, "from the pamphlet's format and print size, and the seemingly sufficient diagram on the box, a fair-minded person could reasonably infer that a user would be induced to only scan the pamphlet and thereby not get from the pamphlet the information about dead-air-space." A jury question was thus presented "as to whether the Pittway pamphlet provided a legally adequate warning about dead-air-space concerns."

Notes

1.   **Content or expression.** Warnings must be reasonably clear, and of sufficient force and intensity to convey the nature and extent of the risks to a reasonable person. "A manufacturer's techniques in promoting the product, inconsistencies or undue qualifications in stating the warning or directions, and depictions of uses that run counter to warnings may each nullify or dilute the warnings provided in printed literature. . . . When possible harm is severe, quite specific information may be required. A drug warning about possible blood clotting may disguise rather than reveal the possibility of a stroke." Dobbs on Torts § 364 (2000).

2.   **Form and location.** Can a warning be defective because it is in a form or location where it is not likely to be read? The father in *Carruth*

admitted that he did not read the instruction pamphlet "in depth." Why wasn't this enough to support a summary judgment for the defense?

3. **Nature and seriousness of harm.** Sometimes the warning must not only alert the user to danger and how to avoid it but also to the extent of harm that can result. In *Pavlik v. Lane Ltd./Tobacco Exporters International*, 135 F.3d 876 (3d Cir. 1998), the estate of a man who died from self-administered butane inhalation sued the distributor, claiming that the single warning on the can ("DO NOT BREATHE SPRAY") was inadequate. The court left it to the trier to determine whether a more specific warning would have averted the harm. What might such a warning have said? In *Benjamin v. Wal–Mart Stores, Inc.*, 61 P.3d 257 (Or. Ct. App. 2002), a Coleman heater carried this: "WARNING: FOR OUTDOOR USE ONLY. Never use inside house, camper, tent, vehicle or other unventilated or enclosed areas." Deceased used it in his tent while camping; the heater depleted the oxygen and the user died as a result. Was the warning adequate?

4. **Language of the warning.** If the warning must be reasonably clear, should it be presented in any language besides English? Suppose a manufacturer advertises in Spanish to buyers whose main or only language is Spanish. Should it even include symbols to help convey the message to non-readers? If a poison contains verbal warnings but no skull and crossbones or unhappy faces, is that adequate?

LEWIS v. LEAD INDUSTRIES ASSOCIATION

793 N.E.2d 869 (Ill. App. Ct. 2003)

[The plaintiffs are parents of children who may have been exposed to lead and may develop serious medical conditions as a result. They sue and propose a class action against (1) a trade association that promoted the use of lead pigments and (2) defendants who manufactured and marketed lead pigment for use in paint. Allegedly, none of the defendants warned anyone of the considerable danger of lead in paint, to which children could be easily exposed in living quarters where lead paint was used. The plaintiffs seek to recover the costs of regular medical monitoring or screening of the children needed to provide appropriate treatment promptly when medical problems are found. The plaintiffs' failure to warn and other similar claims were dismissed on the ground that causation was not alleged, because plaintiffs did not identify which manufacturer or manufacturers made the pigments that exposed the particular children involved.]

[Count VI, however, states a good claim for civil conspiracy.] [T]he plaintiffs alleged that the Manufacturing Defendants, acting in concert through LEAD [the trade association], conspired to: market, produce, and promote lead pigment for use in paint without regard to the dangerous properties and toxic effects of such paint; suppress research, regulation, and public dissemination of information concerning the dangerous properties and toxic effects of lead-based paint; and conceal from and/or mislead the public about the medical and scientific data which indicated that lead-based paint was potentially hazardous to the health and safety of children....

Civil conspiracy is the combination or two or more persons or entities for the purpose of accomplishing by concerted action either an unlawful purpose or a lawful purpose by unlawful means....

A cause of action for civil conspiracy exists only if one of the parties to the agreement commits some act in furtherance of the agreement, which is itself a tort. Thus, the gist of a conspiracy claim is not the agreement itself, but the tortious acts performed in furtherance of the agreement. It is only where means are employed, or purposes are accomplished, which are themselves tortious, that the conspirators who have not acted but have promoted the act will be held liable.... By identifying the defendants along with Eagle–Picher as the sole producers and promoters of lead pigment used in paint and further alleging that each was a party to the conspiratorial agreement, the plaintiffs have alleged both an agreement and tortious conduct in furtherance of the agreement. For the purposes of this claim, the fact that the plaintiffs may not be able to identify which of the defendants was the active tortfeasor that supplied the lead pigment used in the paint to which their children were exposed is not fatal.

The civil conspiracy theory has the effect of extending liability for a tortious act beyond the active tortfeasor to individuals who have not acted but have only planned, assisted, or encouraged the act. If the plaintiffs can prove, as they allege, that the sale and distribution of lead pigment for use in paint was tortious in nature, that the defendants and Eagle Picher were the sole suppliers and promoters of lead pigment, and that each was a party to the conspiratorial agreement, then it is of little consequence that the plaintiffs cannot establish which of the defendants actually supplied the lead pigment used in the paint to which any given child might have been exposed as each defendant would be liable regardless of which one was the active tortfeasor. We conclude, therefore that the circuit court erred in dismissing count VI of the plaintiffs' second amended complaint.

NOTE

Product combinations. Sidon manufactures multi-piece tire rims, which, allegedly, are inherently dangerous. Tyre manufactures tires that can be used only with multi-piece rims. Has Tyre any duty to warn users that the only use of its tires will entail danger from the rims? *See Rastelli v. Goodyear Tire & Rubber Co.*, 591 N.E.2d 222 (N.Y. 1992). Are the manufacturers conspirators if they don't warn?

NOTE: LEARNED INTERMEDIARIES AND SOPHISTICATED USERS

1. *Prescription drugs: The learned intermediary rule.* What warnings should accompany a prescription drug and to whom should the warnings be given? Many courts say the manufacturer must provide warnings only to the doctor who might prescribe, not directly to the patient. *See, e.g., Gourdine v. Crews*, 955 A.2d 769 (Md. 2008). When the manufacturer does

in fact give appropriate warning or information to the physician, it is said that the physician is a "learned intermediary" upon whom the manufacturer can properly rely, and the warning can be couched in terms the physician can understand, not necessarily terms the consumer would grasp. *See, e.g., Larkin v. Pfizer, Inc.*, 153 S.W.3d 758 (Ky. 2004); *Martin v. Hacker*, 628 N.E.2d 1308 (N.Y. 1993). And no warning at all is required if the physician already knows the danger. *Christopher v. Cutter Labs.*, 53 F.3d 1184 (11th Cir. 1995). In *Schaerrer v. Stewart's Plaza Pharmacy, Inc.*, 79 P.3d 922 (Utah 2003), the court said: "We extend the learned intermediary rule to exempt pharmacies from strict products liability when they properly fill a physician's prescription."

2. *Direct marketing of drugs.* If a drug manufacturer advertises its prescription drugs directly to consumers, does the learned intermediary doctrine apply to defeat a consumer's failure-to-warn claim? In *Perez v. Wyeth Laboratories., Inc.*, 734 A.2d 1245 (N.J. 1999), the defendant argued that it does, and that the physician's prescription of the drugs broke any causal link between its failure to warn consumers of harmful side effects and their resulting harm. The court rejected both arguments. Citing *Perez* with approval, the court in *State ex rel. Johnson & Johnson Corp. v. Karl*, 647 S.E.2d 899 (W.Va. 2007), rejected the learned intermediary doctrine entirely, calling its justifications "largely outdated and unpersuasive" given modern marketing techniques. The *Karl* court pointed out that while the learned intermediary doctrine first arose in 1925, the patient/doctor relationship was fundamentally changed in 1997 when television and radio advertising of drugs began. Note that not all courts agree that marketing undercuts the learned intermediary doctrine. *See, e.g., In re Norplant Contraceptive Prods. Liab. Litig.*, 165 F.3d 374 (5th Cir. 1999) (applying Texas law, holding that learned intermediary doctrine precluded manufacturer's duty to warn consumers, despite aggressive marketing to the public).

3. *The Restatement of Products Liability.* Restatement § 6(d) provides that warnings about the health risks of prescription drugs and medical devices must be given directly to consumers only when the manufacturer knows or had reason to know that the learned intermediary "will not be in a position to reduce the risks of harm in accordance with the instructions or warnings." When might this occur? Comment *e* gives as an example the administration of mass inoculation, where health care providers are not in a position to evaluate individualized risks of the vaccine. Patients should be directly warned in that situation, if such warnings are feasible and would be effective.

4. *Sophisticated users.* Similar rules apply to those who supply products to sophisticated users, meaning those users who are already aware or should be aware of the product's dangers, such as members of a trade or profession in which such knowledge is widespread. In such a case, the sophisticated users' knowledge of the product's dangers is the equivalent of prior notice. *See, e.g., Johnson v. American Standard, Inc.*, 179 P.3d 905 (Cal. 2008) (applying rule in case brought by air conditioning

technician against air conditioning equipment manufacturer for failure to warn to equipment's dangers). Is the "sophisticated user" rule merely a variant of the "open and obvious" rule? *See Mohr v. St. Paul Fire & Marine Ins. Co.*, 674 N.W.2d 576 (Wis. Ct. App. 2003).

5. *Suppliers of bulk goods.* Similarly, those who supply goods in bulk may be permitted to rely upon their buyers to use the goods properly and to pass on any appropriate warnings. For instance, a supplier of bulk chemicals to a manufacturer ordinarily need not try to warn ultimate users of the manufactured product. This means that the product is not defective for lack of a warning to the ultimate consumer. Although some courts treat this "defense" as a rule of law, *see* DOBBS ON TORTS § 366 (2000), others make it turn on the reasonableness of relying upon the particular buyer to pass warnings along to those who might be affected. In the latter view, the trier would consider the risks and utilities and the ease or difficulty of giving a warning directly to the user who might be affected. *See Ritchie v. Glidden Co.*, 242 F.3d 713 (7th Cir. 2001).

6. *Government as "learned intermediary?"* In *Macias v. State*, 897 P.2d 530 (Cal. 1995), the state of California sprayed the pesticide malathion over a large area in an attempt to control a Mediterranean fruit fly infestation. Federal regulations require certain label warnings on malathion, including warnings to flush with water if it touches the skin or eyes. The EPA required the state to inform the public of the precautions that would have been on a label, but the state did not do so. Fourteen-year-old Juan Macias was sprayed and was eventually rendered legally blind. In his suit against the manufacturers, Macias argued that they were aware of the state's failure to warn, and were aware that children were particularly susceptible and that blindness could result, but failed either to provide a warning themselves, or to persuade the state to do so. *Held*, the manufacturers were under no duty to warn the public nor to request the state to give warnings. "It was reasonable to rely on the state to convey required warnings.... To judicially impose a private duty to design and disseminate independent warnings in direct conflict with those formulated by the State would represent an unprecedented intrusion on the State's sovereign authority...." Are you convinced?

B. FOCUSING ON POST–SALE WARNINGS

COMSTOCK v. GENERAL MOTORS CORP., 99 N.W.2d 627 (Mich. 1959). Friend purchased a 1953 Buick Roadmaster. In 1954 the brakes suddenly failed, but Friend was able to avoid any harm. He took the car into the Ed Lawless Buick Company for repair, following closely behind another car, which he used as a bumper. He explained the problem, which as a matter of fact was not new to the company because General Motors began experiencing brake problems on that model almost immediately after its introduction. However, General Motors did not notify any of the purchasers. Instead it provided dealers with repair kits. When a 1953 Buick was brought in for any reason, the repair would be made to the brakes without disclosing the facts to the customer. As one witness said,

"It was a hush thing. They didn't want the public to know the brakes were bad and they were very alarmed." After Friend turned his brakeless car over to the dealer, an employee, knowing but forgetting that the car was without brakes, attempted to drive it to a service stall. Comstock was working behind another car. The driver was unable to stop the brakeless Buick and it crushed Comstock's right leg against the other car. In Comstock's action against General Motors as manufacturer of the brakeless car, *held*, "the facts in this case imposed a duty on defendant to take all reasonable means to convey effective warning to those who had purchased '53 Buicks with power brakes when the latent defect was discovered. . . . If [a] duty to warn of a known danger exists at point of sale, we believe a like duty to give prompt warning exists when a latent defect which makes the product hazardous to life becomes known to the manufacturer shortly after the product has been put on the market."

GREGORY v. CINCINNATI, INC., 538 N.W.2d 325 (Mich. 1995). Defendant designed and produced a sheet metal press in 1964. In 1986 the plaintiff was injured in using the press when the ram descended on his thumb, necessitating amputation. The plaintiff claimed a continuing duty to warn or recall and on this basis introduced evidence that in 1971, OSHA required safety devices that would have avoided the injury and evidence that such devices were developed after the press was made in 1964. The jury found for the plaintiff. *Held,* reversed and remanded for a new trial. The post-manufacture evidence was erroneously admitted. "Generally, before there can be any continuing duty—whether it be to warn, repair, or recall—there must be a defect or an actionable problem at the point of manufacture. If there is no defect or actionable problem at this point, then there can be no continuing duty to warn, repair, or recall. . . . In Michigan to date, the only post-manufacture duty imposed on a manufacturer has been the duty to warn when the defect existed at the point of manufacture, but for some reason was undiscoverable by both the manufacturer and the consumer at that time. Comstock, *supra*. However, we have never held that a manufacturer has a post-manufacture duty to repair or recall in this context, and have never held that any post-manufacture duties can arise from subsequently discovered knowledge unattributable to a defect at the time of manufacture." Comstock's duty to warn arose in "the unique context in which the manufacturer acknowledged the existence of a latent manufacturing defect, as evidenced by numerous failures and the offer to repair." In any event, the manufacturer has no duty to recall or repair. A duty to warn or even to recall might be found on the basis of a unique relationship between the parties, but otherwise such a duty will be recognized only if imposed by statute or regulation.

NOTES

1. **What's the point of a post-sale duty?** If a post-sale duty to warn arises only when the defendant was negligent in the first place, or when the

product was defective from the start, does a post-sale duty to warn become meaningless as a basis for legal action?

2. **Post-sale duty and the statute of limitations.** If the defect existed at the time of sale, when does the cause of action arise for failure to give a post-sale warning, if one is due? The answer may determine whether the statute of limitations has run. In *Land v. Yamaha Motor Corp.*, 272 F.3d 514 (7th Cir. 2001) the defendant manufactured a defectively designed boat— defective because the design created a risk that the boat would explode, as in fact has happened with at least 25 of boats manufactured to this design. The defendant knew of the defect and the danger but never warned. More than ten years after sale, one of these boats exploded, causing injury to the plaintiff. The state had a statute of limitations barring products actions brought more than 10 years from delivery to the consumer. The court held that a post-sale failure to warn could start a new cause of action only if "the defect in the product was not present at the time of the initial sale." Since the manufacturer here knew about the defect all along, the statute of limitations had run.

3. **Recognizing post-sale duties.** Courts are divided about post-sale duties and unsure how far to take them or where they could stop. On the one hand there is authority that if the danger is sufficient and the cost is limited, the manufacturer might even be obliged to provide a corrective device or make a repair itself. *See Gracyalny v. Westinghouse Elec. Corp.*, 723 F.2d 1311 (7th Cir. 1983). In some pharmaceutical cases, courts have even said that the manufacturer was under a duty to keep abreast of scientific developments and to warn the medical profession of newly discovered side effects. *See Schene- beck v. Sterling Drug, Inc.*, 423 F.2d 919 (8th Cir. 1970). If, in the course of "keeping abreast," the manufacturer is put on notice of possible dangers, this may require the manufacturer to institute further investigations or tests and studies of its own. *Barson v. E.R. Squibb & Sons, Inc.*, 682 P.2d 832 (Utah 1984).

4. **Rejecting post-sale duties.** On the other hand, some courts have firmly denied that there is any post-sale duty at all, even to give a warning. *See, e.g., Bragg v. Hi–Ranger*, Inc., 462 S.E.2d 321 (S.C. Ct. App. 1995) (approving instruction that "[A] manufacturer, ladies and gentlemen, has no duty to notify previous purchasers of its products about later developed safety devices or to retrofit those products if the products were non-defective under standards existing at the time of the manufacture or sale."). However, in *Couch v. Astec Industries Inc.*, 53 P.3d 398 (N.M. Ct. App. 2002), the court insisted that the rule was a narrow one: "The courts refusing to recognize post-sale duties generally do so because they believe such duties would inhibit manufacturers from developing innovative safety technology and improving their designs for fear of the expensive and onerous process required to find and warn all past purchasers of a product, or, even more costly, to retrofit the product.... [T]he policy reasons relied on by these courts are inapplicable. Here, there is no question that the technology of pull cords existed and was in use at the time Defendant manufactured the plant in question." Consequent- ly, the defendant owed a duty to provide a reasonable post-sale warning.

5. **Restatement of Products Liability.** The Restatement provides that a seller or distributor is obliged to give a post-sale warning when a reasonable person would do so. A reasonable person would give such a warning if he knew or should know that the product poses a substantial risk of harm; those to whom a warning might be given can be identified and assumed to be unaware of the risk; a warning can be effectively communicated; and the risk of harm outweighs the burden of giving a warning. RESTATEMENT OF PRODUCTS LIABILITY § 10. The reasonable person standard means that a jury instruction on post-sale duty to warn should tell the jury to consider any factors that make it burdensome for the manufacturer to provide a warning. *Lovick v. Wil–Rich*, 588 N.W.2d 688 (Iowa 1999). In *Lewis v. Ariens Co.*, 751 N.E.2d 862 (Mass. 2001), the court reiterated its support for a post-sale duty to warn, but held that, as a matter of law, no duty existed where the manufacturer could not feasibly identify the potential victim because he had purchased the product secondhand sixteen years after it was originally sold, and did not own the product until years after a duty to provide additional warnings arguably arose. "In these circumstances, he is a 'member of a universe too diffuse and too large for manufacturers or sellers of original equipment to identify.' "

6. **Successor corporations.** The Products Restatement also recognizes a limited post-sale duty on the part of a successor corporation that acquires the assets of a predecessor corporation to warn users about risks created by a product manufactured or sold by the predecessor. RESTATEMENT OF PRODUCTS LIABILITY § 13. Such a duty arises only where the successor has undertaken or agrees to provide repair or maintenance services on the product, and when it would be reasonable to provide such a warning. Courts adopting this rule have held that the successor corporation owes a duty to warn the end user "only if it has a reasonable means of doing so." *Tabor v. Metal Ware Corp.*, 168 P.3d 814 (Utah 2007).

7. **Statutory recall/repair duties.** Statutes or regulations may require post-sale warnings or repairs. Some standards for motor vehicles are set by federal regulation. If a manufacturer fails to comply with standards, the Secretary of Transportation may require the manufacturer to (a) give notice of the defect to purchasers and dealers and (b) to remedy the defect. 49 U.S.C.A. § 30118. The Consumer Products Safety Commission has the power to require a recall of dangerous products or to order their replacement. 15 U.S.C.A. § 2064 (d). The Restatement Third limits liability for failure to recall or repair to cases in which a recall obligation is imposed by statute or regulation or in which the manufacturer voluntarily undertakes a recall and fails to follow through in a reasonable way. RESTATEMENT OF PRODUCTS LIABILITY § 11.

REFERENCE: DOBBS ON TORTS §§ 363–68 (2000).

§ 7. SPECIAL ISSUES OF PROOF

BITTNER v. AMERICAN HONDA MOTOR CO., 533 N.W.2d 476 (Wis. 1995). The plaintiff, riding a three-wheeled, all terrain vehicle (ATV), suffered severe injuries when it overturned. The plaintiff sued the manufacturer asserting both negligence and strict product liability claims, in part because of the allegedly dangerous high-center-of-gravity design. The defendant introduced evidence (1) that injury rates associated with use of snowmobiles, mini-bikes and trail bikes were *less* than injury rates associated with ATVs; and (2) that injury rates of many sports, including scuba-diving and football, were much higher than rates associated with ATV use. From the first set of evidence, the defendant argued that because the recreational vehicles in question were similar in purpose to ATVs, the lower rate of injury suggested that ATV accidents were due to operator error. From the second set of evidence, the defendant argued that "if fewer individuals are injured riding ATVs than, for instance, playing football, then the risk of injury associated with ATV riding is reasonable." *Held,* the first set of evidence is admissible as tending to show operator error, but the second set of evidence is not admissible. Evidence of greater risks of activities that are generally acceptable is not relevant. "[T]he comparative risk evidence comparing ATV riding with dissimilar products and activities, such as sky diving, cannot be introduced, as Honda asserts, to demonstrate that ATVs are not unreasonably dangerous."

Nᴏᴛᴇs

1. **Similar accidents.** In design and information defect cases, evidence that a product either has or has not caused similar accidents is usually admissible as tending to show that the product was or was not defective, and that the defendant did or did not have notice of the danger. *See, e.g., Uniroyal Goodrich Tire Co. v. Martinez*, 977 S.W.2d 328 (Tex. 1998) (no error in admission of evidence of 34 other lawsuits against defendant involving similar product claims); *Spino v. John S. Tilley Ladder Co.*, 696 A.2d 1169 (Pa. 1997) (no abuse of discretion in the admission of testimony of company president that 100,000 of its ladders had been marketed in a 100-year period, without any prior claims against the company). However, when the plaintiff claims only a manufacturing flaw in the particular item, the safety history of the product line generally seems irrelevant. Does any of this sound like a basis for the *Bittner* court's ruling on the first set of evidence?

2. **Comparative risks and risk-utility weighing.** Consider the second set of evidence in *Bittner,* that the risks of injury in, say, football, were greater than the risks of injury in ATVs. If higher risks are acceptable in a variety of life's activities, would *Carroll Towing* or any form of risk-utility analysis suggest that the risk of ATVs would be a reasonable one? *Cf.* David A. Fischer, *Proportional Liability: Statistical Evidence and the Probability Paradox,* 46 Vᴀɴᴅ. L. Rᴇᴠ. 1201 (1993) (arguing that liability limited to a percentage of the plaintiff's damages, based on proportional causation, is undesirable because whenever the environment generally becomes more dangerous, the liability of individuals would be reduced).

NOTE: SUBSEQUENT REMEDIAL MEASURES

Suppose that a plaintiff is injured by the defendant's product or property. After the defendant learns of the injury, he repairs the property or modifies the product to make it safer. The rule in negligence cases is that evidence of the defendant's subsequent remedial measures is not admissible to show negligence. First, subsequent repairs or other safety measures (like warnings) do not say much if anything about whether the defendant should reasonably have perceived danger before the injury or whether a reasonable person would have recognized the need for safety measures. Second, coupled with this low relevance is high risk that the jury would treat subsequent repairs as an admission of negligence. Third, courts have speculated that if evidence of subsequent safety measures were admissible, some defendants might refuse to make needed changes lest their efforts be used against them in court.

A 1997 amendment to the Federal Rules of Evidence makes inadmissible evidence of remedial measures "taken after an injury or harm allegedly caused by an event," including such evidence offered to prove "a defect in the product, a defect in the product's design or a need for a warning or instruction." FED. R. EVID. 407. This rule applies only in federal court, and states are free to depart from it.

Some state courts do in fact hold that evidence of subsequent safety measures is admissible in strict liability products cases. A leading case is *Ault v. International Harvester Co.,* 528 P.2d 1148 (Cal. 1974); *see also Caprara v. Chrysler Corporation,* 417 N.E.2d 545 (N.Y. 1981) ("spirit of strict liability" and desire to aid plaintiff in proof make blanket exclusion in strict liability cases inappropriate); *Forma Sci., Inc. v. BioSera, Inc.,* 960 P.2d 108 (Colo. 1998) (such evidence should be admitted in strict liability design-defect cases, since its probative value outweighs any unfair prejudice to the manufacturer). Does the persuasive weight of these cases suffer in a state that adopts the Restatement of Products Liability, with its emphasis on risk-utility analysis and its rejection of strict liability for product defects?

Although in many jurisdictions, evidence of subsequent safety measures cannot be offered to prove negligence (and maybe not a product defect either), those subsequent safety efforts could at least indicate that a safer product is feasible. Such evidence has been admitted for that limited purpose. *Duchess v. Langston Corp.,* 769 A.2d 1131 (Pa. 2001) (where defendant put feasibility in issue, trial judge should admit evidence of subsequent remedial changes to show feasibility unless the evidence will be unduly prejudicial to the defendant).

MERCK & CO. v. GARZA

2008 WL 5169577 (Tex. App.)

Opinion by SANDEE BRYAN MARION, JUSTICE. . . .

At the time of his death on April 21, 2001, Leonel Garza was seventy-one years old and had a history of heart problems. On March 27, 2001, Mr. Garza visited his cardiologist, Dr. Michael Evans, because he had been experiencing "[i]ntermittent numbness, left arm pain and weakness that had started the day before and was occurring on and off over a 24–hour period." During this visit, Dr. Evans gave Mr. Garza a one-week sample supply of Vioxx to ease the pain in his arm. This was the first time Mr. Garza had taken Vioxx. Following his appointment with Dr. Evans, Mr. Garza underwent several tests, including an ultrasound of his neck to check blood circulation in the brain and a cardiolite stress test to check blood flow in the heart. On April 4, 2001, Mr. Garza returned to the doctor for the test results, this time seeing Dr. Evans' partner, Dr. Juan Posada. Because Mr. Garza's stress test showed a "mild abnormality," Dr. Posada recommended a cardiac catheterization, which Mr. Garza declined pending his next appointment with Dr. Evans. Although Dr. Posada does not recall giving Mr. Garza more Vioxx, Mr. Garza's wife testified that he did. On April 21, 2001, Mr. Garza died of a heart attack. Mrs. Garza and the Garzas' children (collectively, "the plaintiffs") sued Merck & Co., Inc. on design defect and marketing defect strict liability claims based upon allegations that Merck's prescription drug Vioxx caused Mr. Garza's death. This is an appeal from a jury verdict in favor of the plaintiffs.

On appeal, Merck raises a number of complaints, including challenges to the sufficiency of the evidence on causation. . . . Merck asserts the plaintiffs did not present legally sufficient evidence of a causal link between Mr. Garza's use of Vioxx and his fatal heart attack. Under both their marketing defect and design defect claims, plaintiffs were required to prove both general and specific causation. *See Merrell Dow Pharm., Inc. v. Havner,* 953 S.W.2d 706, 714–15 (Tex.1997). General causation asks whether a substance is capable of causing a particular injury in the general population; specific causation asks whether that substance caused a particular individual's injury. *Id.*

A. General Causation

On appeal, Merck insists the evidence is legally insufficient because the plaintiffs did not introduce into evidence at least two statistically significant scientific studies showing Vioxx at the same dose and duration as taken by Mr. Garza more than doubled the risk of heart attack. According to Merck, *Havner* requires experts to base their causation opinions on reliable epidemiological or other scientific evidence when, as here, there is no direct experimental evidence of causation. Merck views *Havner* as requiring that epidemiological studies show more than a doubling of the risk and that any study relied upon by a causation expert be statistically significant; *i.e.,* the study must have a confidence level of ninety-five percent that does not include a value of 1.0 or below. We do not construe *Havner* as narrowly as Merck, nor do we believe *Havner* established such a bright-line test for causation. Instead, the *Havner* Court "emphasize[d] that courts must make a determination of reliability from all the evidence. . . . Courts should allow a party, plaintiff or defen-dant, to present the best available evidence . . . and only then should a court determine from a totality of the evidence, considering all factors affecting the reliability of particular studies, whether there is legally sufficient evidence to support a judgment." In this case, plaintiffs relied on clinical trials to establish causation. . . .

Merck concedes clinical trials "are considered the best type of epidemiological evidence for determining the relationship between an agent and a disease or health outcome." At trial, the head of Merck's Department of Epidemiology, whom the plaintiffs called as an adverse witness, characterized clinical trials as "much more powerful that an epidemiology study." . . . To establish general causation, the plaintiffs were required to show that Vioxx is a substance capable of causing a particular injury in the general population. After reviewing the evidence and considering the appropriate standard of review for a legal sufficiency challenge, we conclude the plaintiffs carried their burden of presenting legally sufficient evidence to support a finding of general causation.

B. Specific Causation

To establish specific causation, plaintiffs may rely on studies showing an increased risk of their particular injury resulting from exposure to the substance at issue to raise a fact question on causation. *Havner*, 953 S.W.2d at 714–15. However, "if there are other plausible causes of the injury or condition that could be negated, the plaintiff must offer evidence excluding those causes with reasonable certainty." *Id.* at 720. On appeal, Merck focuses its argument on a single complaint: that the plaintiffs' evidence on specific causation is insufficient because plaintiffs' expert, Dr. Simonini, did not rule out, with reasonable certainty, the most plausible cause of Mr. Garza's heart attack, which was the progression of his preexisting cardiovascular disease.

At trial, Dr. Simonini conceded Mr. Garza had cardiac problems and was a "high-risk patient." Mr. Garza was seventy-one years old and overweight; he had already suffered one heart attack; he had had quadruple bypass surgery sixteen years before his death; he had high blood pressure and high cholesterol; and he had some diseased arteries. He had been smoking as much as two packs a day for almost forty years, and continued to smoke until his death but had decreased to only two or three cigarettes a day. Dr. Simonini admitted that continuing to smoke puts one at risk, even someone like Mr. Garza who was taking blood pressure and cholesterol medication, and smoking may reduce the benefits of any such medication. Dr. Simonini also conceded that the type of heart disease Mr. Garza had put him at risk for having another heart attack. Mr. Garza's autopsy revealed the "aorta shows stress of severe atherosclerotic disease," "extensive scarring and old fibrosis along the posterior lateral and anterior lateral segments of the heart and also along the ventricular septum," "severe atherosclerotic diseases of all coronaries," and "the bypass graft shows severe disease."

Despite Mr. Garza's history of heart problems, plaintiffs contend they excluded, with reasonable certainty, the possibility that his fatal heart attack was caused by his preexisting heart condition by establishing the following: Mr. Garza's two physical examinations, between March 27 and

April 4 of 2001, showed him to have "stable cardiac status" before he began taking Vioxx; his death was caused by two fresh occlusions (or clots) that occurred after he began taking Vioxx; the simultaneous formation of two clots is very rare without the introduction of a causative agent like Vioxx; and the formation of clots is the type of problem caused by Vioxx.

As support for their contention that Mr. Garza's heart condition was stable, plaintiffs point to Dr. Posada's notes following his April 4, 2001 examination of Mr. Garza in which he stated "stable cardiac status...." The result of Mr. Garza's stress test revealed the tip of Mr. Garza's heart did not get enough blood flow. However, Dr. Simonini noted this was "a very small area of the heart, and it was stable from [a previous test]." Dr. Simonini explained that the stress test revealed Mr. Garza's heart had only a "mild abnormality." Dr. Simonini said that sixty percent of Mr. Garza's heart emptied every time the heart squeezed and this fraction was within normal range and was a "good predictor of staying alive longer." Dr. Simonini characterized Mr. Garza's blood pressure as "good" and under control and his "bad" cholesterol was down, all because he was taking medication to control his blood pressure and cholesterol levels.

Plaintiffs also relied on Mr. Garza's autopsy, which revealed that Mr. Garza's heart attack was caused by the simultaneous formation of two clots in two of Mr. Garza's vein graphs from his bypass surgery. Plaintiffs contrast the autopsy results with the results of the stress test that showed blood flow to these same areas was good and there was no evidence of blockage. According to Dr. Simonini, the simultaneous formation of the two clots in two different arteries was a "rare" occurrence, and it would be difficult to explain why Mr. Garza suffered a heart attack within a few weeks of his stress test absent his taking Vioxx. However, if his taking Vioxx was added to the scenario, Dr. Simonini opined "then you have a causative effect" because "[y]ou have something that has been shown to cause clots, and now you could explain this—this simultaneous event of two vessels being blocked ... at the same time."

As part of their burden on specific causation, the plaintiffs were required to offer evidence excluding other causes of Mr. Garza's heart attack with reasonable certainty. We cannot conclude that Dr. Simonini's causation opinion, premised on Mr. Garza's "stable cardiac status" and the "rare" formation of the two blood clots, was little more than speculation or amounted to no evidence on this issue. Therefore, after reviewing the evidence and considering the appropriate standard of review for a legal sufficiency challenge, we conclude the plaintiffs carried their burden of presenting legally sufficient evidence to support a finding of specific causation....

[The judgment in favor of plaintiffs on the design defect claim must be reversed, however, because plaintiffs failed to present sufficient evidence of a feasible alternative design. Further, juror misconduct tainted the rest of the jury's verdict and the trial court erred in not granting

Merck's motion for a new trial. *Reversed as to the design defect claim; remanded for further proceedings on other claims.*]

NOTES

1. **General and specific causation.** A plaintiff in a products liability suit, just as in any other tort suit, must prove cause-in-fact. In some cases, however, such proof is not at all simple and is dependent on reliable expert testimony. In toxic-tort and many pharmaceutical cases, professionals speak of "general causation" (*i.e.*, that a particular substance or product is capable of causing a given disease) and "specific causation" (*i.e.*, that exposure to the substance or product actually caused the particular plaintiff's harm). To prove actual cause, a plaintiff may have to produce expert testimony on both of these issues. In some cases, proof of general causation will be sufficient to prove specific causation, but this is not always true. *See, e.g., Terry v. Caputo*, 875 N.E.2d 72 (Ohio 2007); *Aventis Pasteur, Inc. v. Skevofilax*, 914 A.2d 113 (Md. 2007); RESTATEMENT THIRD OF TORTS: LIABILITY FOR PHYSICAL HARM § 28, cmt. *c* (Proposed Final Draft No. 1, 2005). "General causation" seems an odd conception for lawyers. If a product is not capable of causing harm, how could it have caused the harm? And how can such a product be defective at all?

2. **Proof of dosage or exposure levels.** Suppose we know that the defendant's product *can* cause injury of the type suffered by the plaintiff and we know that the plaintiff was exposed to the product. Must the plaintiff prove (a) the level or dosage of her exposure and (b) that such a level is known to be sufficient to cause the harm she suffered? In *Alder v. Bayer Corp., AGFA Div.*, 61 P.3d 1068 (Utah 2002), the court said the plaintiff need not prove the level of exposure she had been subjected to, because (a) given that there was some exposure to toxins for which the defendant was responsible, the "victims' toxic symptoms are themselves evidence of harmful levels, at least as an issue of triable fact"; and (b) "common law tort doctrine declares that 'one who injures another takes him as he is'; if the defendant negligently caused exposure in some degree, then 'toxic level' becomes any level that is harmful to these specific plaintiffs." Would you criticize either of these reasons? Many courts would require more proof. *See, e.g., Borg–Warner v. Flores*, 232 S.W.3d 765 (Tex. 2007) (plaintiff must adduce "defendant-specific evidence relating to the approximate dose to which the plaintiff was exposed, coupled with evidence that the dose was a substantial factor in causing [plaintiff's] disease").

3. **Admissibility of expert testimony.** In *Garza*, the issue was about sufficiency of the plaintiff's expert proof. In many cases, however, the plaintiff may face an even greater initial hurdle in simply getting the expert testimony admitted into evidence. The Supreme Court considered admissibility of scientific evidence in federal court in *Daubert v. Merrell Dow Pharm's, Inc.*, 509 U.S. 579 (1993). Under the *Daubert* decision, scientific opinion can be admitted as evidence even though it is not generally accepted. However, the trial judge must decide that it will be "helpful" to the jury and that the opinion offered is "derived by the scientific method," that is, based on "good grounds" in the light of what is known and testable in future scientific studies. The trial judge must make "a preliminary assessment of whether the

reasoning or methodology underlying the testimony is scientifically valid" and whether it can be applied in the case. The judge should consider (a) whether the expert's theory or technique has been tested; (b) whether it has been subjected to peer review; (c) whether it has a known potential error rate; and (d) whether it is generally accepted. All these matters, however, are only factors; none is dispositive of the decision. The trial judge's wide discretion in admitting expert testimony (or not) was reaffirmed in *General Electric Co. v. Joiner*, 522 U.S. 136 (1997) (holding that such rulings were reviewed only for an abuse of discretion). And in *Kumho Tire Co., Ltd. v. Carmichael*, 526 U.S. 137 (1999), the Court extended *Daubert* to all expert testimony, not just "scientific" testimony. Rule 702 of the Federal Rules of Evidence was then amended to state the principles behind these decisions rather than a list of factors. The *Daubert* test has been said to be designed primarily to exclude "junk science," and should not be misused by a judge as a way to make a preliminary inquiry into the merits of the plaintiff's case. *985 Associates, Ltd. v. Daewoo Electronics America, Inc.*, 945 A.2d 381 (Vt. 2008) (reversing trial judge's decision to exclude expert testimony on causation, finding it met the *Daubert* test even if in the judge's view it did not satisfy the plaintiff's burden of proof on the merits of the case).

4. **State law differences.** For trials in state court, states are not controlled by federal evidence rules and are thus free to use their own standards for admissibility of expert testimony. The rule followed in federal courts, and most state courts, before *Daubert* was based on *Frye v. United States*, 293 F. 1013 (D.C. Cir. 1923). Many states continue to follow the *Frye* test, which requires that an expert's techniques must "generate results accepted as reliable within the scientific community generally," and are "sufficiently established to have gained general acceptance in the particular field in which it belongs." *Frye* has been characterized as an approach which "emphasizes counting scientists' votes, rather than on verifying the soundness of a scientific conclusion." *Parker v. Mobil Oil Corp.*, 857 N.E.2d 1114 (N.Y. 2006) (reaffirming New York's use of the *Frye* test rather than the *Daubert* test).

This means that unless the expert is using a novel and not-generally-accepted methodology, no special analysis is required to determine the admissibility of expert testimony. *See Roberti v. Andy's Termite & Pest Control, Inc.*, 6 Cal.Rptr.3d 827 (Ct. App. 2003) (expert, extrapolating from non-definitive animal studies, could offer opinion that pesticide caused child's autism); *Hayes v. Decker*, 822 A.2d 228 (Conn. 2003).

In *Donaldson v. Central Illinois Public Service Co.*, 767 N.E.2d 314 (Ill. 2002), the court in a toxic tort claim based on dumping of coal tar and negligent remediation permitted experts to testify and the jury to conclude that the tar probably caused the unusual appearance of rare cancers among near neighbors. Although no studies supported any findings one way or another about the role of coal tar in causing the rare cancers, coal tar was a known carcinogen. In light of the limited data, experts were permitted to "extrapolate" data about similar conditions, because the scientific community would itself use extrapolation when data is limited. Similarly, in *Castillo v. E.I. Du Pont de Nemours & Co., Inc.*, 854 So.2d 1264 (Fla. 2003), the plaintiff's mother, while pregnant, was covered with a toxic agricultural spray. The plaintiff suffered a birth defect. Experts were allowed to extrapolate the results of animal exposures to the chemical and to conclude that even less exposure to humans would result in the birth defect. Suppose an expert rules out other exposures and genetic causes. Would that strengthen the inference that the spray was the cause?

5. **Strategy: federal diversity jurisdiction.** Given the divergence between some of the state cases and some of the federal decisions, do you think federal diversity jurisdiction plays a big role in adjudication of products liability cases?

6. **Epidemiological and animal studies.** Two types of studies are often admitted through expert testimony on causation issues: epidemiological studies and animal studies. Epidemiology is the study of disease occurrence in humans, usually based on statistical methodology intended to show correlations or lack of correlations between disease and some other conditions. *See, e.g., Turpin v. Merrell Dow Pharmaceuticals, Inc.*, 959 F.2d 1349 (6th Cir. 1992). Animal studies are usually thought of as less reliable, because extrapolating toxicity on animals to humans is at best tricky. For a discussion of some of the key issues raised by the consideration of scientific evidence, *see* Michael D. Green, *Expert Witnesses and Sufficiency of Evidence in Toxic Substances Litigation: The Legacy of Agent Orange and Bendectin Litigation*, 86 Nw. U. L. Rev. 643 (1992); David H. Kaye, *Is Proof of Statistical Significance Relevant?*, 61 Wash.L. Rev. 1333 (1986).

7. **Legal vs. scientific purposes.** The Supreme Court in *Daubert* viewed science as a continuous inquiry, with answers always tentative and open to revision. More research, a better hypothesis, a different interpretation of data could all yield a different scientific picture. Judicial resolution of particular disputes, however, requires a final decision and a decision now, not one made after many years of further research. Does this difference between the goals and methods of science on the one hand and law on the other suggest anything about what law should do in toxic tort cases when the exact risk of the chemical in question cannot be determined? See Heidi Li Feldman, *Science and Uncertainty in Mass Exposure Litigation*, 74 Tex. L. Rev. 1 (1995).

8. **Experts and reasonable alternative design.** (a) In requiring reasonable alternative design evidence, the Products Restatement specifically asserts that the plaintiff is not required to build a prototype. RESTATEMENT OF PRODUCTS LIABILITY § 2, cmt. *f* (1998). *General Motors Corp. v. Sanchez*, 997 S.W.2d 584 (Tex. 1999) makes the same point. The court there said: "[P]laintiffs did not have to build and test an automobile transmission to prove a safer alternative design. A design need only prove 'capable of being developed.'" The expert's testimony about the engineering principles supporting his proposed design backed up his opinion that his design would be safer than G.M.'s actual design. *See also Sand Hill Energy, Inc. v. Ford Motor Co.*, 83 S.W.3d 483 (Ky. 2002), *judgment vacated for reconsideration on punitive damages*, 538 U.S. 1028 (2003).

(b) This principle, however, may be undermined by evidentiary rulings. Purporting to follow *Daubert* or subsequently promulgated evidence rules, some decisions have discarded the testimony of highly qualified experts on the ground that the expert had not built an alternatively designed product and tested it. *See Dhillon v. Crown Controls Corp.*, 269 F.3d 865 (7th Cir. 2001)

("Neither expert has actually designed a model of a forklift truck with a rear door. Nor has either performed any tests of such a model to see if it is both economically feasible and just as safe or safer than the model without the door."); *Colon v. BIC USA, Inc.,* 199 F. Supp. 2d 53 (S.D.N.Y. 2001) (expert's proposed safety lock improvement, based largely on the defendant's own existing patents and on well-accepted mechanical and electrical principles, was not acceptable because the expert had not actually "tested" the proposed alternative design). Under these cases, must the plaintiff lose a design defect claim if she can't afford to design, build, and test a new model?

REFERENCE: 1 MADDEN & OWEN ON PRODUCTS LIABILITY §§ 12:4–5 (3d Ed. 2000).

SUBCHAPTER C. DEFENSES AND DEFEATS
§ 8.   COMPARATIVE FAULT AND ASSUMPTION OF RISK

BOWLING v. HEIL CO.
511 N.E.2d 373 (Ohio 1987)

[Heil manufactured a dump hoist system which was installed on a dump truck owned by Rogers. Brashear borrowed the truck for personal use. He and Bowling delivered gravel to Bowling's residence and dumped it, but the truck bed would not return to the down position after the load had been dumped. Bowling leaned underneath over the truck chassis to see what was wrong. This put him underneath the upraised truck bed. In this posture he grabbed the control lever on the pump valve assembly and manipulated it. The truck bed rapidly descended upon him, killing him instantly. This is an action against Heil and various others involved in the hoist assembly and controls. The jury found that Bowling was guilty of contributory negligence but not assumed risk. Damages were assessed at $1.75 million. The trial court and the court of appeals treated Bowling's contributory negligence in different ways. The effect of contributory fault in a products strict liability case is the main issue before the Ohio Supreme Court in the discussion below.]

HERBERT R. BROWN, JUSTICE. . . .

Currently, two affirmative defenses based upon a plaintiff's misconduct are recognized. First, an otherwise strictly liable defendant has a complete defense if the plaintiff voluntarily and knowingly assumed the risk occasioned by the defect. Second, such a defendant is also provided with a complete defense if the plaintiff misused the product in an unforeseeable manner. The court of appeals below, construing Comment n to Section 402A, attempted to distinguish between negligent "affirmative action" by a plaintiff and negligent passive conduct by him in failing either to discover a defect or to guard against the possibility of its existence. The court held that although a plaintiff's passive contributory negligence provides no defense to a products liability action, his contributorily negligent "affirmative action" does provide a defense, and that such affirmative negligence should be compared by a jury to the fault of a strictly liable manufacturer of a defective product, in a manner similar to the principles of comparative negligence embodied in [the statute].

Comment n to Section 402A provides:

"Contributory negligence. * * * Contributory negligence of the plaintiff is not a defense when such negligence consists merely in a failure to discover the defect in the product, or to guard against the possibility of its existence. On the other hand the form of contributory negligence which consists in voluntarily and unreasonably proceeding to encounter a known danger, and commonly passes under the name of assumption of risk, is a defense under this Section as in other cases of strict liability. If the user or consumer discovers the defect and is aware of the danger, and nevertheless proceeds unreasonably to make use of the product and is injured by it, he is barred from recovery."

The court of appeals has carved out a middle ground, to wit: contributory negligence consisting of "affirmative action," theoretically located between a plaintiff's failure to discover or guard against a defect and his voluntary assumption of a known risk. There is no such middle ground. Comment n covers the entire spectrum of conduct which can be termed "contributory negligence," as applicable to products liability actions. That spectrum begins with a mere failure to discover a defect in a product, continues with a failure to guard against the existence of a defect, and concludes with an assumption of the risk of a known defect. "Affirmative action" by the plaintiff is not left uncovered. Failure to guard against a defect can be "affirmative action." Indeed such would describe the conduct of David Bowling in this case.

Under Comment n, either a plaintiff's contributory negligence amounts to a voluntary assumption of a known risk, or it does not. If it does, then that conduct provides an otherwise strictly liable defendant with a complete defense. If it does not, the contributory negligence of the plaintiff provides no defense.

In the case sub judice, the jury found that Bowling was contributorily negligent but that he had not assumed a known risk. Therefore, his contributory negligence did not provide Heil with a defense to appellant's strict liability claim . . . .

The definitive statement of the policy and goals underlying the application of strict liability in tort to cases involving defective products is provided in Comment c to Section 402A, at 349–350:

"On whatever theory, the justification for the strict liability has been said to be that the seller, by marketing his product for use and consumption, has undertaken and assumed a special responsibility toward any member of the consuming public who may be injured by it; that the public has the right to and does expect, in the case of products which it needs and for which it is forced to rely upon the seller, that reputable sellers will stand behind their goods; that public policy demands that the burden of accidental injuries caused by products intended for consumption be placed upon those who market them, and be treated as a cost of production against which liability insurance can be obtained; and that the consumer of such products is entitled to the maximum of protection at the hands of someone, and the proper persons to afford it are those who market the products."

Dean Prosser has expressed this idea in slightly different terms:

"The costs of damaging events due to defectively dangerous products can best be borne by the enterprisers who make and sell these products. Those who are merchants and especially those engaged in the manufacturing enterprise have the capacity to distribute the losses of the few among the many who purchase the products. It is not a 'deep pocket' theory but rather a 'risk-bearing economic' theory. The assumption is that the manufacturer can shift the costs of accidents to purchasers for use by charging higher prices for the costs of products."

Prosser & Keeton, Law of Torts (5th Ed.1984) 692–693, Section 98.

Under negligence principles, on the other hand, liability is determined (and, under R.C. 2315.19, apportioned) according to fault. In negligence, we seek to make the person or persons responsible for causing a loss pay for it. In other words, we "blame" the loss on the negligent party or parties because it was they who could have avoided the loss by conforming to due care. Conversely, in strict liability in tort we hold the manufacturer or seller of a defective product responsible, not because it is "blameworthy," but because it is more able than the consumers to spread that loss among those who use and thereby benefit from the product.

We recognize that strict liability cannot be absolutely divorced from traditional concepts of fault. In a sense we "blame" the loss on the manufacturer or seller because it introduced the defective product into the marketplace. However, it must be reemphasized that strict liability is at odds with traditional notions of due care. . . .

Comparative negligence or comparative fault has been applied in products liability cases by a number of courts, both in states that have comparative negligence statutes and in states where comparative negligence was judicially adopted. On the other hand, numerous courts have refused to apply comparative negligence principles to products liability cases.

We believe that the better-reasoned decisions are those that decline to inject a plaintiff's negligence into the law of products liability. We agree with the court's holding in Kinard v. Coats Co., Inc. (1976), 37 Colo. App. 555, 557, 553 P.2d 835, 837, which states:

" . . . Products liability under § 402A does not rest upon negligence principles, but rather is premised on the concept of enterprise liability for casting a defective product into the stream of commerce. * * * Thus, the focus is upon the nature of the product, and the consumer's reasonable expectations with regard to that product, rather than on the conduct either of the manufacturer or the person injured because of the product."

We agree with Justice Mosk of the California Supreme Court, who stated in his dissent in Daly v. General Motors Corp., supra:

"The defective product is comparable to a time bomb ready to explode; it maims its victims indiscriminately, the righteous and the evil, the careful and the careless. Thus when a faulty design or otherwise defective product is involved, the litigation should not be diverted to consideration of the negligence of the plaintiff. The liability issues are simple: was the product or its design faulty, did the defendant inject the defective product into the stream of commerce, and did the defect cause the injury? The conduct of the ultimate consumer-victim who used the product in the contemplated or fore-seeable manner is wholly irrelevant to those issues."

Therefore, when we search the decisions from other jurisdictions, we find no rationale which persuades us that comparative negligence or comparative fault principles should be applied to products liability actions.

Based upon the foregoing analysis, we hold that principles of comparative negligence or comparative fault have no application to a products liability case based upon strict liability in tort. Strict liability, in focusing on the product rather than the conduct of its manufacturer or seller, does not seek to apportion a loss among all persons who have caused or contributed to it. Rather, it seeks to spread the loss among all users of the product. The concept of comparative fault is fundamentally inapplicable.

We therefore reverse the judgment of the court of appeals with respect to its reduction of appellant's verdict by the thirty percent found by the jury to be attributable to contributory negligence. . . .

[A majority of the court supported the opinion, but one Justice concurred in the result and only part of the opinion, another wrote a separate concurring opinion, and a third dissented.]

NOTES

1. **Comparative fault reductions.** *Bowling* applies the traditional rule that some forms of contributory negligence of the plaintiff are not a defense to a strict liability claim. Some courts still hold these views. For example, in *Jett v. Ford Motor Co.*, 84 P.3d 219 (Or. Ct. App. 2004), the court insisted that "a plaintiff's incidental carelessness or negligent failure to discover or guard against a product defect is not an appropriate defense" to strict product liability claims. In *Daly v. General Motors Corp.*, 575 P.2d 1162 (Cal. 1978), the California Court rejected that view for products strict liability and applied comparative fault rules to reduce the plaintiff's recovery. The Restatement of Products Liability provides that whatever comparative responsibility system is used in a given state should apply to products liability claims as well. RESTATEMENT OF PRODUCTS LIABILITY § 17 (1998).

2. **Unreduced recoveries.** *Bowling* imports into strict products liability cases the traditional view of contributory negligence as applied in abnormal

danger cases, discussed in Chapter 23. Many other courts agree. Does the "time bomb" argument have any application in *Bowling* itself or could the plaintiff have protected himself by ordinary care?

3. **Causal apportionment.** Suppose the plaintiff's fault contributes to his injury and so does the defendant's defective product, but it is possible to say that the product caused a broken arm and the plaintiff's fault caused a broken leg. Would either *Bowling* or *Daly* foreclose a causal apportionment? But suppose that the injury is indivisible so that no causal apportionment is possible between the plaintiff and the defendant. In *Owens Corning Fiberglas Corp. v. Parrish,* 58 S.W.3d 467 (Ky. 2001) the plaintiff's smoking contributed to a lung disease and the defendant's defective product contributed to a different lung disease, both resulting in a shortness of breath. It was not possible to say how much of the plaintiff's ultimate injury resulted from the asbestosis. Consequently the court permitted the jury to use comparative fault to apportion responsibility. What result under *Bowling*?

4. **Misuse.** In a footnote the *Bowling* court said: "... In some sense, [product] misuse is an act of contributory negligence. Nonetheless, it remains a defense to a products liability action based upon strict liability in tort." No reason was given. Why should contributory negligence be a defense if it involves product misuse but not even a basis for reducing damages if it takes some other form? Is it because some misuse cases can be viewed as "no defect" cases?

5. **Discovered vs. undiscovered defect.** Many states that do allow a contributory fault defense in products cases restrict that defense at times. In *Hernandez v. Barbo,* 957 P.2d 147 (Or. 1998), the plaintiff was a mechanic whose hand was partially amputated when it contacted a saw blade. He sued the saw's sellers and others, claiming that the product was defective because the on/off switch was inconspicuous. Defendants argued that the plaintiff was contributorily negligent. *Held,* a plaintiff's recovery will not be reduced when his negligence consisted solely of failure to discover or guard against the product's defect. Many courts agree with this rule. Texas has said that "a duty to discover defects, and to take precautions in constant anticipation that a product might have a defect, would defeat the purposes of strict liability." *General Motors Corp. v. Sanchez,* 997 S.W.2d 584 (Tex. 1999). Does this distinction between failing to discover or guard against defects and other kinds of negligence make sense? Would it be better to formulate the rule by saying that a plaintiff is not negligent for trusting the defendant's product until there is some reason to distrust it?

6. **Obvious danger.** We have seen that a product is sometimes considered defective even when its danger is obvious and the plaintiff could be safe by taking the product's characteristics into account. In such a case, would a state adopting the Products Restatement's rule of comparative fault reduce the plaintiff's recovery? And would a court applying the *Bowling* rule allow full recovery?

7. **Assumed risk.** Recall that under the Restatement of Apportionment, assumption of risk is subsumed within the comparative responsibility rules, and is not regarded as a separate defense at all. *See* Chap. 9, § 2. Some states continue to agree with the *Bowling* court's view, however, that assumption of

risk is a complete defense to a strict products liability suit, even if contributory negligence is not. Ohio reaffirmed this view in *Carrel v. Allied Products Corp.*, 677 N.E.2d 795 (Ohio 1997). Should courts distinguish between a plaintiff's negligence and "assumption of the risk," or should all forms of plaintiff "misconduct" enter into the comparison?

8. ***Bexiga.*** If you would apply ordinary comparative negligence in products cases, maybe there are still cases in which you would not want to apply it. How would you feel about applying the comparative fault rule in *Bexiga*, Chapter 9, § 1? *Cf. Carrel, supra* Note 7 (assumption of risk defense not available when the plaintiff "is required to encounter the risk while performing normal job duties"). Or an eclectic approach in which you apply comparative fault where you think it would encourage safety by the plaintiff without removing safety incentives of the defendant? *See Cotita v. Pharma–Plast, U.S.A., Inc.*, 974 F.2d 598 (5th Cir. 1992) (nurse exposed to AIDS virus as a result of defectively capped needle, but nurse was himself negligent).

9. **Seatbelts.** The plaintiff occupies a vehicle that is defective because it is not reasonably safe in cases of collision. The door pops open and the plaintiff is ejected. Although the vehicle was defective, the plaintiff's injuries are much worse because he failed to wear an available seat belt. Many states have adopted statutes that prohibit this "seatbelt defense." DOBBS ON TORTS § 205 (2000). What instructions should be given to a jury about the plaintiff's failure to wear the belt in a jurisdiction that lacks such a statute and follows the *Bowling* rule?

10. **The firefighter's rule.** A firefighter is injured in a fire. The fire was caused by a defective product manufactured by the defendant. Does the firefighter's rule provide a defense to the product manufacturer? If so, what defense would it be? *Mignone v. Fieldcrest Mills*, 556 A.2d 35 (R.I. 1989) concluded that the rule was grounded in assumed risk and that the firefighter was completely barred from recovery. But *Hawkins v. Sunmark Industries, Inc.*, 727 S.W.2d 397 (Ky. 1986) held the manufacturer liable when its product made a fire worse. What if the product neither caused the fire nor made it worse, but injured the firefighter on the scene? Should that claim be barred? *See Stapper v. GMI Holdings, Inc.*, 86 Cal.Rptr.2d 688 (Ct. App. 1999) (injury caused by alleged design defect in garage door).

11. **Effect on deterrence.** Does taking a plaintiff's contributory negligence into account in a products liability case remove incentives from manufacturers to make their products safer? Is this a greater problem in those states that follow either modified comparative fault or the old contributory negligence rules, where barring a plaintiff entirely on negligence grounds is a very real possibility? Or is the newer approach of the Products and Apportionment Restatements a sound way to account for a plaintiff's own responsibility for causing injury?

REFERENCES: DOBBS ON TORTS § 369 (2000); OWEN, PRODUCTS LIABILITY LAW §§ 13.1–13.4 (2d Ed. 2008).

§ 9. DISTINGUISHING DEFENSES FROM FAILURE TO PROVE DEFECT: PROXIMATE CAUSE AND MISUSE

A. MISUSE, DEFECTIVENESS, AND COMPARATIVE FAULT/ASSUMED RISK

HUGHES v. MAGIC CHEF, INC.

288 N.W.2d 542 (Iowa 1980)

UHLENHOPP, JUSTICE....

Plaintiff Vincent E. Hughes was severely burned on March 9, 1976, when a stove manufactured by defendant Magic Chef, Inc., exploded in his mobile home. The propane gas tank which fueled the stove had run dry on March 7, 1976. After the propane tank was refilled that evening, two pilot lights on the top of the stove were re-lit but a third pilot light in the oven broiler cavity was not re-ignited. Experts testified that a resultant buildup of propane gas in the stove produced an explosion and fire when Hughes attempted to use the stove on the evening of March 9th....

Hughes and his wife Eileen brought this strict liability action against Magic Chef, alleging the stove was unreasonably dangerous in several respects. Magic Chef raised affirmative defenses of assumption of risk and misuse of product. The jury found for Magic Chef and the trial court overruled the Hugheses' motion for new trial. Hugheses then appealed....

A. As to Hughes' first argument, this court held in *Rosenau* that in an ordinary negligence case in which the defendant raises the issue of the plaintiff's own negligence, assumption of risk is not to be pled and submitted as a separate defense. Instead, the essential elements of assumed risk, if supported by substantial evidence, are to be included in the contributory negligence instruction. Separate instructions on those defenses might result in the jury's rendering inconsistent verdicts and in the trial court's over-emphasizing a particular aspect of a case.

Hughes' argument that the *Rosenau* reasoning applies equally to the products liability defenses of misuse of product and assumption of risk does not recognize the differing natures of those two issues. Misuse precludes recovery when the plaintiff uses this product "in a manner which defendant could not reasonably foresee." Assumption of risk is a defense to a strict liability action when the plaintiff has "voluntarily and unreasonably proceed[ed] to encounter a known danger...." The misuse of product doctrine has to do with the producer's responsibility in the first place; he has no liability at the outset if the product is misused. The assumption of risk doctrine has to do with the user's culpability; he bars himself from recovering if he voluntarily proceeds in the face of known danger. Although we recognize that in certain cases a plaintiff might have *both* used the product in a manner which the defendant could not reasonably foresee and voluntarily and unreasonably proceeded to encounter a known risk, we reject the idea that a plaintiff cannot do one without doing the other.

Despite our rejection of Hughes' attempt to apply *Rosenau* by analogy to this case, we agree with his basic contention that the trial court should not have given an instruction on misuse as a *defense* in this strict liability action. Misuse is not an affirmative defense but rather has to do with *an element of the plaintiff's own case.*

This conclusion departs somewhat from language in some of our prior products cases. Under that language the misuse issue may arise twice: first in connection with the plaintiff's prima facie case and again in connection with the defendant's affirmative defense.... [A]s part of his prima facie case, the plaintiff must establish that the product was unreasonably dangerous in a reasonably foreseeable use.

We have also said, however, that a defendant may defend a section 402A action by pleading and proving that the injured person misused the product, that is, he used it in a manner not reasonably foreseeable. The result of this prior language is that precisely the same issue—whether the product was used in a reasonably foreseeable manner—may be decisive both as to whether the plaintiff made a prima facie case and as to whether the defendant established an affirmative defense.

If we continued to treat misuse as an affirmative defense distinct and additional to the plaintiff's burden of proving that the product was used in reasonably foreseeable manner, we would create the potential for inconsistent jury findings in the same case. In addition we would create the possibility of a shifting burden of proof on the issue. The burden of proof regarding the use made of the product should not shift depending on the subtle distinction of whether the defendant offers evidence of misuse to rebut the plaintiff's evidence or instead offers it "to support an affirmative defense he is attempting to raise." ...

Misuse of product is no longer to be considered an affirmative defense in products liability actions but is rather to be treated in connection with the plaintiff's burden of proving an unreasonably dangerous condition and legal cause. Regardless of whether a defendant does or does not plead misuse of the product, the burden is on the plaintiff to prove that the legal cause of the injury was a product defect which rendered the product unreasonably dangerous in a reasonably foreseeable use....

B. Hughes' second challenge to the misuse instruction is that it erroneously held him to a "reasonableness" standard in the use of the product. The instruction directed the jury as follows:

> The Defendant asserts the affirmative defense that the Plaintiff Vincent Hughes misused the stove. The burden of proof is on the Defendant.

The Defendant claims that this Plaintiff knew, or ought reasonably to have known, of the existence of the pilot light in the oven area and that it was not lit after the service call by the Thermogas service man. The Defendant claims further that the Plaintiff took no action to relieve against this situation but instead attempted to utilize the oven or broiler on the second day thereafter and that such constituted a misuse of the stove by this Plaintiff.

If you find the Defendant has proved the above, that such action or failure to act on the part of the Plaintiff was not reasonably foreseeably [sic] by the Defendant, and further that such action or failure to act by the Plaintiff was the proximate cause of the accident, then the Plaintiff may not recover. . . .

If Hughes is correct that this misuse instruction imposes a "reasonableness" standard on his conduct the instruction is indeed erroneous, for in some situations negligent use of a product by a consumer is reasonably foreseeable by the producer and therefore is not "misuse" for liability purposes. To hold otherwise would interpose contributory negligence as a defense under the guise of misuse.

We find no necessity to resolve this issue, however, because the misuse instruction is objectionable on another ground; it gives undue emphasis, in such an instruction, to what Hughes personally knew or should have known.

If the ordinary user would reasonably be aware that use of a product in a certain way is dangerous, use of the product in that manner is less foreseeable by the producer than a use to which danger is not normally ascribed. But the ordinary user's awareness that use of the product in a certain manner is dangerous does not conclusively establish that such use is not reasonably foreseeable, for the defendant may in a given case reasonably foresee that a given product will be used by persons such as children who do not possess the knowledge of the ordinary user. Hence knowledge which can be reasonably attributed to the ordinary user is to be considered as a factor in determining whether the manner in which the plaintiff used the product was reasonably foreseeable.

The problem with the misuse instruction here is that it specifically directed the jury to consider what Hughes knew or ought reasonably to have known. What Hughes knew or should have known about the pilot light has slight relevance to the issue of whether Magic Chef should reasonably have foreseen the use to which the stove was put. The personal characteristics of users or, in this case, knowledge of users, becomes relevant to foreseeability of use only when the characteristics are attributable to a substantial group of users. By including a specific reference to what Hughes knew or should have known, the misuse instruction invited the jury to consider a matter of little relevance to the issue it had to resolve—whether Magic Chef should reasonably have foreseen that users would attempt to operate the stove after an interruption in gas service without first igniting all the pilot lights.

We thus hold that on retrial misuse is not to be treated in the jury instructions as an affirmative defense. Instead, the instructions with respect to the use to which the stove was put must place the burden of proof on Hughes to establish by a preponderance of the evidence that the use made of the stove was reasonably foreseeable by Magic Chef. Reference to knowledge reasonably attributable to the ordinary user may be made, but the instruction must make clear that such knowledge is one factor to be weighed in determining whether Hughes' manner of using the product was reasonably foreseeable by Magic Chef. If on retrial Hughes proves by a preponderance of the evidence that the use made of the stove was reasonably foreseeable and that the stove was unreasonably dangerous when so used, then he will have established the first element of his case; otherwise the case is over.

Reversed.

NOTES

1. **Misuse.** What does the *Hughes* Court think about unforeseeable misuse of a product that causes harm? (a) Unforeseeable misuse means the plaintiff is guilty of contributory negligence. (b) Unforeseeable misuse means the plaintiff assumed the risk. (c) Unforeseeable misuse means that, with respect to harms caused by the misuse and that would not have been caused by a properly used product, the product simply is not defective at all.

2. **Defendant strategy.** Suppose you are in a jurisdiction that considers plaintiffs' comparative fault in a products liability action to reduce recovery. If you represent the defendant would you rather establish (a) no defect or (b) plaintiff's fault? Why?

3. **Is misuse a "defense?"** Given the answer to the preceding question, can you establish firmly in your own mind whether it is accurate to say that misuse is a defense?

4. **Comparing contributory fault, assumed risk and no-defect.** How can you determine whether the plaintiff's conduct is "misuse" on the one hand or contributory fault or assumed risk on the other? Is it more important to distinguish one kind of act from another, or foreseeable uses from unforeseeable ones? Note that many courts apply comparative fault principles to products strict liability cases and also treat misuse as merely one form of comparative fault. *Chapman v. Maytag Corp.*, 297 F.3d 682 (7th Cir. 2002). Presumably this rule applies to foreseeable misuse only. Can you see why that might be so?

B. MISUSE, DEFECTIVENESS, AND PROXIMATE CAUSE

REID v. SPADONE MACHINE CO.
404 A.2d 1094 (N.H. 1979)

Grimes, Justice.

[Defendant manufactures a "guillotine-type" cutting machine for cutting blocks of molded plastic. A blade descends to a strike plate when two buttons are pressed by the operator's hands. Operators in the Davidson Rubber Company would cut blocks of plastic, then turn the block at right angles to cut it in the other direction.]

[There were several safety devices. Originally the machine could be operated only when activated by pressing two buttons simultaneously, thus requiring the operator's hands to be out of the blade area. However, some workers fashioned a bar so that both buttons could be pressed at once while one hand was free to turn the blocks of plastic. To avoid this danger, the defendant moved the switch to one side of the machine so that the operator would be required to walk to the side of the machine. The machine was intended as a one-person cutter, but some workers in Davidson Rubber Company would at times work together on this machine, one pushing the side-button and one turning the blocks of plastic after each cut. Plaintiff, doing this, reached under the blade without using the push-stick available and his co-worker pressed the buttons. Plaintiff lost three fingers and brings this action.]

[Davidson, the employer, knew of the two-person use and its danger, but did not stop it. In fact, the machine was so used ten per cent of the time, and even supervisors used it in that way.]

The trial court, . . . ruled over objection that defendant could not use as a defense Davidson's conduct as a superseding cause. [After the court denied various defense motions, the jury returned a general verdict for the plaintiff, and defendant appealed.]

The evidence supports a finding that the machine was defectively designed. Placement of the buttons on the side required the operator to leave the feeding area open while he actuated the blade. This could be found not only to permit, but actually to encourage, two-person operation. This condition, coupled with inadequate warnings against two-person use, could properly be found to have made the machine "unreasonably dangerous." . . .

When the buttons were moved to the side of the machine the danger from one-handed operation of the blade was diminished but the danger of two-person operation was increased. There was evidence that the danger created by a bar being placed across the buttons on the front could have been avoided, for example, by placing one button on each side facing out, thus requiring inward pressure in opposite directions. This design would have discouraged two-person use because the operator would have had to occupy the feeding area while pushing the buttons. In comparison, positioning the buttons to one side not only left open the feeding area for a second person, but required extra effort and time on the part of the single operator. The natural tendency being to save unnecessary effort and time, two-person use was facilitated. . . .

At trial, defendant sought to argue that Davidson's conduct, negligence, and misuse of the bail cutter was the sole proximate cause of plaintiff's injury. The position taken is not that plaintiff's damages should be apportioned by Davidson's comparative causation, but that plaintiff is not entitled to a verdict of any sort against the defendant, because Davidson's conduct and not the defendant's product was the sole proximate cause of the injury. Defendant contends that it is entitled to a new trial because the court committed reversible error in preventing the submission of this superseding cause argument to the jury. A careful consideration of the facts in the case, however, convinces us to the contrary.

The manufacturer or seller faced with an allegation of strict liability in tort for a defective design may have several defenses against liability, for example, product misuse or abnormal use, and what was formerly termed contributory negligence or unreasonable assumption of the risk

These defenses relate to the comparative fault of the plaintiff and are now classified as "plaintiff's misconduct." With respect to a non-party third person's conduct, however, the manufacturer's sole defense is that of total nonliability based upon the third person's conduct as a superseding cause. In the usual case, no reason of the law stands to prevent a defendant in a products liability action from arguing a third person's negligence or misuse of the product as the sole proximate cause of the plaintiff's injury. The availability of this defense depends, however, on the foreseeability of the alleged misuse or negligence and, on the nature of the alleged design defect.

In New Hampshire, the manufacturer is under a general "duty to design his product reasonably safely for the uses which he can foresee." This duty is necessarily limited " 'to foreseeing the probable results of the normal use of the product or a use that can reasonably be anticipated.' " Thus, before a defendant may successfully argue a third person's negligence or misuse as a superseding cause, he must prove that the negligence or misuse was not reasonably foreseeable.

However, by finding the machine defective in design, the jury has found that two-person use was foreseeable. It was the failure to guard against such foreseeable use that made the machine's design defective. This being so, that same use cannot be a superseding cause, even assuming that Davidson was negligent in not preventing that use. See generally Restatement (Second) of Torts §§ 442, 443 (1965)....

Remanded.

NOTES

1. **Defectiveness or superseding cause?** What is the most helpful way to think of the problem represented by *Reid*? (A) It is an issue whether the product is defective at all. (B) It is an issue whether there is legal cause or responsibility for a defective product. Are there other courts that treat misuse of a product as bearing on a different issue?

2. **Plaintiff's misuse as superseding cause.** We saw in Chapter 9, § 4, that some courts may regard a plaintiff's unforeseeable negligence as a superseding cause of harm, barring the plaintiff's recovery on proximate cause

grounds. In *Hood v. Ryobi America Corp.*, 181 F.3d 608 (4th Cir. 1999), the plaintiff was injured when a blade detached from a miter saw he was using. The plaintiff had removed the saw's guards in contravention of unambiguous warnings. In his suit against the manufacturer, *held*, summary judgment for defendant was proper. The plaintiff's act of alteration was the superseding cause of his harm. If the alternation had been foreseeable to the manufacturer, would the analysis and outcome change?

In *Jeld–Wen, Inc. v. Gamble*, 501 S.E.2d 393 (Va. 1998), parents sued a window and screen manufacturer for negligence and breach of warranty after their infant pushed on the screen and then fell two stories to the ground when it gave way. Could the child's own "misuse" constitute a complete defense? What do you see as the key arguments?

3. **Intended users.** Courts used to say that the product was not defective if it was reasonably safe for intended users. In *Phillips v. Cricket Lighters,* 841 A.2d 1000 (Pa. 2003), people died in a fire started by a two year old's use of a lighter that lacked available child-proofing. The lead opinion of a divided court held that the manufacturer would not be strictly liable because it intended the lighter to be used only by adults, even though child use was foreseeable. Other courts follow a test of foreseeability rather than intention. One of the claims arising from the September 11 crashes was for death and injury to persons on the ground. The plaintiffs claimed that the Boeing planes had defective cockpit doors that permitted terrorists to take control and ultimately to crash the planes. Boeing argued that "since the terrorists who hijacked the airplanes were not the intended users of the cockpit doors, one cannot say that the doors were unreasonably dangerous or unsafe in relation to the use that terrorists would be expected to make of the doors." *In re Sept. 11 Litig.,* 280 F. Supp. 2d 279 (S.D.N.Y. 2003). The court of course rejected that argument. For the most part, "intended user" is no longer the governing test, as shown in the next note.

4. **Foreseeability of misuse.** In many states, the manufacturer must ordinarily design a product reasonably in the light of known or foreseeable misuses, not merely for "intended" use. Thus the usual rule is that if a car will collapse when it is in a foreseeable collision, it may be defective, even though the manufacturer never intended it to be crashed. *Turner v. General Motors Corp.*, 584 S.W.2d 844 (Tex. 1979); *Slone v. General Motors Corp.*, 457 S.E.2d 51 (Va. 1995). Foreseeability has also become the test for bystander injury. When misuse is foreseeable and a reasonable alternative design would have prevented harm from the misuse, the manufacturer cannot avoid liability on the ground that the product was not defective or that the defect was not a proximate cause. *See, e.g., Perkins v. Wilkinson Sword, Inc.*, 700 N.E.2d 1247 (Ohio 1998) (rejecting argument by cigarette lighter manufacturer that it did not have to make its lighters childproof, since children are not the intended users). Bear in mind, however, that in some cases a plaintiff's "misuse" might be regarded as a form of contributory fault or assumed risk, with whatever defensive advantage those doctrines might produce.

5. **Foreseeability of excessive risk.** As always, it looks as if "foreseeability" is a kind of shorthand expression. Many harms can be foreseen but foreseeability probably refers only to those harms that are foreseeable and

also unreasonably risky under the circumstances. It is surely possible to foresee almost any harm from a product, but since some foreseeable risks are reasonable, the product is not necessarily defective merely because harm can be foreseen. So, once again, you cannot take the term literally: foreseeability is necessary but not sufficient to establish liability.

6. **Shifting responsibility.** Granted that the machine is defective in *Reid*, should a manufacturer nevertheless be permitted to shift responsibility to the employer, if the employer actually knows of the danger at the time of purchase? In *Robinson v. Reed–Prentice Division of Package Co.*, 403 N.E.2d 440 (N.Y. 1980), the defendant manufactured and sold a plastics molding machine to the employer, who wished to use it to mold plastic beads on a long string. The machine was equipped with a gate so that the operators' hands could not be in the molding area, but the employer cut a hole in it so that the operator could put his hands into the area and move the string or cord for continuous molding. This facilitated production, but it completely destroyed the safety feature. An operator's hands were seriously injured. Evidence showed that the manufacturer knew that the safety gate it had supplied made it impossible for the employer to mold beads on strings. The manufacturer also knew that other like machines had been modified and that in all probability this one would be modified as well. The court held that the manufacturer was not strictly liable. "Substantial modifications of a product from its original condition by a third party . . . are not the responsibility of the manufacturer. . . . Principles of foreseeability . . . are inapposite where a third party affirmatively abuses a product by consciously by-passing built-in safety features." Even so, "A manufacturer may be liable where plaintiffs adduce evidence to show that a product was purposefully manufactured to permit use without a safety feature." It is also possible that *Robinson* simply does not apply to consumer products, as distinct from industrial products. "*Robinson* and its progeny are not directly applicable to manufacturer liability for injuries caused by household consumer products." *Colon v. BIC USA, Inc.,* 199 F. Supp.2d 53 (S.D.N.Y. 2001). On what principle would you differentiate home users from injured industrial workers, who, after all, have no viable economic choice about facing product dangers? *Cf. Snyder v. LTG Lufttechnische GmbH,* 955 S.W.2d 252 (Tenn. 1997) (evidence that plaintiff's employer removed a safety device from its cotton press, resulting in plaintiff's injury, admissible to prove that product was not defective).

7. **Well-known dangers.** If a product's danger is well-known and generally understood, should the manufacturer be liable for foreseeable abuse? Manufacturers of alcohol can certainly foresee that users of that substance will on occasion, or even very often, become intoxicated and harm themselves or others. Is foreseeability of this misuse enough to make the manufacturer prima facie liable? In *Joseph E. Seagram & Sons, Inc. v. McGuire,* 814 S.W.2d 385 (Tex. 1991), the plaintiffs were alcoholics suing the manufacturers and distributors of the brands they drank. They claimed that the defendants depicted alcohol as safe when in fact it was not and that the defendants should have warned them of the danger and the addictive quality of alcohol. The court held that the danger of alcohol in causing alcoholism has been generally known and that no duty was owed the plaintiffs.

8. **Statutory solutions.** In some states, statutes resulting from "tort reform" initiatives by defense groups have addressed the issue just raised. A California statute provides:

> (a) In a product liability action, a manufacturer or seller shall not be liable if both of the following apply:
>
> (1) The product is inherently unsafe and the product is known to be unsafe by the ordinary consumer who consumes the product with the ordinary knowledge common to the community.
>
> (2) The product is a common consumer product intended for personal consumption, such as sugar, castor oil, alcohol, and butter, as identified in comment i to Section 402A of the Restatement (Second) of Torts.

CAL. CIV. CODE § 1714.45. Similar provisions have been enacted in other states as well. *E.g.*, N.J. STAT. ANN. § 2A:58C–3(a)(2).

VAUGHN v. NISSAN MOTOR CORP. IN U.S.A., INC., 77 F.3d 736 (4th Cir. 1996). The defendant manufactured a car called a Nissan Pulsar. Its voltage regulator failed, allegedly because of bad design and construction. This caused excessive current, which caused the battery fluid to boil. The plaintiff-driver claimed that fumes entered the car and caused her to suffer vocal chord dysfunction and reactive airway dysfunction, a severe asthma. The defendant argued that the plaintiff, who had been abused as a child, suffered from "somatization disorder," a psychological tendency to generate illnesses that have no apparent physiological cause and that there was no physical basis for her injury. Governing law adopted the older Restatement's consumer expectation test. On this basis, the trial judge instructed the jury that it could find a causal defect if the plaintiff inhaled the fumes, suffered asthma as a result, and was an ordinary consumer. The jury, so instructed, found for the defendant. *Held*, the instruction was error. The ordinary consumer is the test of a defect. But if a defect exists, the plaintiff need not be an ordinary consumer or suffer only damages that an ordinary consumer would suffer. This is borne out by the allergy cases. If a manufacturer should be aware that an appreciable number of consumers are unusually susceptible to injury from the product, it is under a duty to warn those with such unusual reactions.

STAHLECKER v. FORD MOTOR CO., 667 N.W.2d 244 (Neb. 2003). The plaintiffs alleged that their decedent was stranded alone after Firestone tires on her Ford tore apart. So stranded, she was murdered. In the claim against Ford and Firestone for negligence and strict products liability, *held*, the trial judge correctly dismissed the claim. The manufacturers may have been negligent and may have produced defective products, but they were under no duty to control a third person with whom they had no relationship, and there was no "causal relationship" between defect and murder.

C. MISUSE, DEFECTIVENESS, WARNINGS, AND DISCLAIM-
ERS

Warnings and misuse. Misuse is intimately related to questions about warnings, instructions, and obvious or generally known dangers. For instance, in *Hughes v. Magic Chef*, if Magic Chef had given no instructions or warnings about the number or location of pilot lights, it might be quite easy to say that the product was defective for lack of a warning or instructions and by the same token that the plaintiff's failure to light the third pilot was entirely foreseeable. Conversely, if the user is fully shielded by instructions and warnings, his violation of instructions or failure to heed warnings may quite easily count as an unforeseeable misuse. In *Halliday v. Sturm, Ruger & Co., Inc.*, 770 A.2d 1072 (Md. Ct. Spec. App. 2001) a father purchased a handgun and kept it under his mattress with shells located elsewhere. His three-year-old son allegedly found the gun there and managed to load the magazine. While playing with the gun he accidently shot himself. He died. The gun could have had a trigger lock to protect against such a discharge, but it did not. Still, the court held that the gun was not defective. One reasons was that the father was chargeable with unforeseeable misuse. Was it really unforeseeable? The plaintiff argued that the manufacturer was aware that parents left guns unlocked, but the court thought that the explicit warning that accompanied the gun made the father's action in storing the gun under the mattress unforeseeable as a matter of law.

Disclaimers. Granted that a manufacturer can exert a degree of control over the misuse issue by providing warnings or instructions about use, can the manufacturer or other supplier of a product simply disclaim liability altogether? Suppose the product were covered with embossed warnings in bright red letters saying "This product is dangerous. Use it at your own risk. The manufacturer is not liable for any injury that may result." Or suppose the manufacturer provided for a limited remedy by saying that it would be liable for any defects in the product, but only for the cost of repair or replacement.

(1) For tort law claims for personal injury, the usual answer is that the manufacturer cannot avoid liability by disclaimers. *See* RESTATEMENT OF PRODUCTS LIABILITY § 18 (1998).

(2) For warranty claims under the UCC, a warranty may be effectively disclaimed. UCC Art. 2–316. If it is effectively disclaimed, the plaintiff would have no warranty claim. If it is *not* effectively disclaimed, the seller can still limit remedies for consequential damages, except that, prima facie, it is unconscionable to limit damages for personal injury resulting from the breach of warranty. Unconscionable limitations are not enforceable in the courts. *Id.* UCC Art. 2–719.

Suppose the manufacturer or supplier sells an automobile that is dangerous if driven but perfectly harmless if used for scrap metal or old parts and tells the buyer, "this is for parts or scrap only, not to be driven." Suppose the buyer is a 16-year-old who actually drives the car and is injured when it cannot be controlled. Is the manufacturer's description and sale for a limited purpose a warning or a disclaimer? If it is a warning, is the buyer's misuse nevertheless foreseeable? And if it is foreseeable, is the risk great enough to justify imposing liability upon the seller?

REFERENCE: DOBBS ON TORTS § 370–71 (2000).

§ 10. COMPLIANCE WITH OVERRIDING STANDARDS—STATUTE, SPECIFICATIONS AND FEDERAL PREEMPTION

A. COMPLIANCE WITH STATUTE

DOYLE v. VOLKSWAGENWERK AKTIENGESELLSCHAFT

481 S.E.2d 518 (Ga. 1997)

HINES, JUSTICE.

This case is before the Court on a certified question from the United States Court of Appeals for the Eleventh Circuit. The question certified is:

> When an automobile manufacturer sells an automobile to a Georgia citizen and the automobile is in compliance with the National Automobile Safety Act, 15 U.S.C. 1381 et seq., does Georgia law preclude a personal injury product liability claim?

The answer to this question is no. Georgia common law permits a Georgia citizen to sue an automobile manufacturer despite the manufacturer's compliance with the standards established by the National Automobile Safety Act. . . .

[Victoria and Duffey Doyle sued Volkswagen for negligence, strict products liability and breach of the implied warranty of fitness after Victoria Doyle was seriously injured when her new 1989 Volkswagen Jetta was struck in the rear by another vehicle. An expert testified that her injuries were caused by the absence of a lap belt in the Jetta. Both the Jetta's driver's seat and front passenger seat were designed and equipped with automatic shoulder belts, but no lap belts. The Jetta's "passive restraint system" was authorized under Federal Motor Vehicle Safety Standard 208. Defendant moved for partial summary judgement, arguing "that because the Jetta seat belt system complied with federal motor vehicle safety standards, they were entitled to judgment as a matter of law because ... they had no duty under Georgia law to exceed federal standards." The trial court granted defendant's motion and plaintiffs appealed.]

The Eleventh Circuit agreed that the Jetta seat belt system complied with applicable federal standards governing automobile restraints. It was uncertain, however, whether the district court correctly interpreted Georgia law. . . .

[The notion that compliance with statute is a complete defense] is inconsistent with a risk-utility analysis. Under the risk-utility test, compliance with federal standards or regulations is a factor for the jury to consider in deciding the question of reasonableness, that is, whether the product design selected was a reasonable one from among the feasible choices of which the manufacturer was aware or should have been aware. It does not render a manufacturer's choice of design immune from liability. That is not to say that evidence of such compliance is not significant, for it is. But, instead of acting as an impenetrable shield from liability, compliance, more appropriately, is to be a piece of the evidentiary puzzle. . . . [O]ur state common law permits its citizens to pursue a personal injury product liability claim against an automobile manufacturer even if the automobile is in compliance with the Safety Act. This decision will not make the manufacturer an insurer of its product, for there is no duty to design an accident-proof vehicle. All we do today is affirm that proof of compliance with federal standards or regulations will not bar manufacturer liability for design defect as a matter of law.

Question answered.

NOTES

1. *Doyle* expresses the conventional view is that compliance with a statute does not conclusively demonstrate the absence of negligence. This is sometimes expressed by saying that the statute provides a minimum standard, a floor and not a ceiling on the defendant's duty. Compliance with a statute may be relevant, however, sometimes as one fact among many tending to indicate that the defendant was not negligent. For this reason, evidence of compliance with government regulations or statutes may be admitted, although compliance is not itself a defense. Statutes may make similar provisions. The Restatement Third is in accord, providing that compliance is to be considered but does not preclude a finding, as a matter of law, that the product was defective in particular cases. RESTATEMENT OF PRODUCTS LIABILITY § 4(b) (1998). What problems of justice or policy would you anticipate if compliance with statute were made a complete defense?

2. State statutes may go further and provide that a manufacturer's or seller's compliance with any federal or state statute or regulation raises a rebuttable presumption that the product is not defective with respect to design or information defects. *See, e.g.,* TENN. CODE ANN. § 29–28–104; TEX. CIV. PRAC. & REM. CODE § 82.008.

3. In rare cases courts may choose to adopt a regulatory standard as the standard of care in a products case. This occurred in *Ramirez v. Plough, Inc.,* 863 P.2d 167 (Cal. 1993), in which a young child developed Reye's Syndrome (a serious disease causing severe neurological damage) after his mother, not fluent in English, gave him aspirin manufactured by defendant. The aspirin package contained warnings about Reye's, but only in English. FDA regula-

tions required a warning about Reye's syndrome. But, except for Puerto Rico and areas where some other language predominates, the FDA only required a warning in English. California statutes were similar. The court held that the defendant was under no duty to provide a Spanish-language warning. "Given the existence of a statute expressly requiring that package warnings on nonprescription drugs be in English, we think it reasonable to infer that the Legislature has deliberately chosen not to require that manufacturers also include warnings in foreign languages. The same inference is warranted on the federal level. The FDA's regulations abundantly demonstrate its sensitivity to the issue of foreign-language labeling, and yet the FDA regulations do not require it. Presumably, the FDA has concluded that despite the obvious advantages of multilingual package warnings, the associated problems and costs are such that at present warnings should be mandated only in English." The task of specifying language of warnings, said the court, is best left to legislators and administrators.

B.   "PREEMPTION" OF LIABILITY RULES BY COMPLIANCE WITH OVERRIDING LAW

Federal preemption. Under the Supremacy Clause of the United States Constitution, U.S. Const. Art. 6, cl. 2, state law that conflicts with federal law is without effect. This means that Congress has the power to override state law, as long as it acts within the limits of its own constitutional powers. Congress can effectively forbid the enforcement of state law not only when the state law would conflict directly with federal statutes or regulation, but also when Congress wishes to impose a single scheme of regulation or control. Congress might thus "preempt" state law by (1) occupying the field with heavy regulation so that there is no room left for state law; (2) by passing laws that actually conflict with state laws; or (3) by providing for preemption in particular cases, either expressly or by implication. Even when Congress has expressly provided for preemption, courts must construe the statute to determine what was and what was not preempted. In general, the Supreme Court is reluctant to find preemption of state powers unless the Congress has clearly manifested its purpose. *See Medtronic, Inc. v. Lohr*, 518 U.S. 470 (1996). Congress has exhibited such a preemptive purpose with increasing frequency, however.

Effect in products cases. Preemption can be important in products liability cases. Suppose a federal statute sets a minimum standard for warnings that must be contained on labels of a dangerous product. A state law that required a better warning or additional information would not actually conflict with the federal statute and would therefore not be preempted under the actual conflict rule. Nevertheless, the federal labeling statute might either expressly or impliedly preempt state law. If it did, the result would be that the manufacturer who complied with the federal statute would not be liable for failing to comply with the state statute. Of course, where state laws are found to actually conflict with the federal statute, preemption is also found. *See, e.g., BIC Pen Corp. v. Carter*, 251 S.W.3d 500 (Tex. 2008) (Consumer Product Safety Commission regs preempt state law design-defect claim over disposable lighter);

Preemption is asserted by defendants under many of the important federal statutes and preemption not infrequently operates to bar the plaintiff's claim. Indeed, this is becoming more and more common in recent years. For example, in *Geier v. American Honda Motor Co.*, 529 U.S. 861 (2000), the plaintiff claimed that Honda was negligent in failing to equip its 1987 Accord with a driver's side airbag. The Court decided, 5–4, that plaintiff's state-law claim was impliedly preempted by federal regulations that had sought a "variety and mix of [restraint] devices" in cars in order to "help develop data on comparative effectiveness," to give "the industry time to overcome the safety problems and the high production costs associated with airbags," and to "facilitate the development of alternative, cheaper, and safer passive restraint systems." To allow the plaintiff to establish that Honda owed a duty under state law to install an airbag in its 1987 Accords would conflict with these federal goals; thus her claim was preempted. In *Riegel v. Medronic, Inc.*, ___ U.S. ___, 128 S.Ct. 999 (2008), the Court held that where the Food and Drug Administration has given premarket approval to a particular medical device, federal law preempts common-law claims challenging the safety or effectiveness of such a device. Federal railroad-crossing safety provisions and federal warning requirements on insecticide or herbicides are also commonly found to preempt state law and eliminate tort claims. although courts are not all in agreement about particular cases.

Preemption cases moved toward center stage in the 2008 term of the U.S. Supreme Court. After deciding *Riegel, supra,* the Court heard arguments in two other products/preemption cases. In both cases the courts below had determined that federal law did not preempt state law. In the first case, *Levine v. Wyeth*, 944 A.2d 179 (Vt. 2006), *cert. granted* (2008), a patient sued a drug manufacturer for failure to warn of the dangers of administrating a medication directly into the vein. The Vermont Supreme Court decided that such a claim is not preempted by FDA regulations on warnings, even where the manufacturer complied with such regulations. In the second case, *Good v. Altria Group, Inc.*, 501 F.3d 29 (1st Cir. 2007), *cert. granted sub nom., Altria Group, Inc. v. Good*, ___ U.S. ___, 128 S.Ct. 1119 (2008), the First Circuit held—contrary to some other courts—that the Federal Cigarette Labeling and Advertising Act did not preempt smokers' claims that tobacco companies misrepresented the safety of their "light" cigarettes in violation of the state unfair trade practices statute. The Supreme Court ultimately ruled 5–4 in *Altria*, ___ U.S. ___, 129 S.Ct. 538 (2008), that the FCLAA did not preempt "states' authority to prohibit deceptive statements in cigarette advertising," even if it would preempt state action that would require additional warnings on labels. The *Altria* case is the latest in a series of preemption cases on cigarettes that includes *Cipollone v. Liggett Group, Inc.*, 505 U.S. 504 (1992), in which a badly-divided Supreme Court plurality allowed the plaintiff to sue for negligent testing of tobacco, but found false advertising claims preempted by the FCLAA.

Federal statutes creating a federal tort right. The preemption discussed above may effectively destroy the plaintiff's claim. But some federal preemption works differently. Instead of effectively enacting a federal defense, some federal statutes enact a federal claim by granting the plaintiff a cause of action more favorable than he had under state law. The FELA (Federal Employers Liability Act) creates federal tort rights for interstate railroad workers and, when it was enacted, was substantially more favorable to the workers than was state tort law. The FELA claim is still more favorable in certain ways. Other federal statute may enact an alternative system of liability, with different claims, defenses, and procedures.

Federal preemptive statutes not creating a private right of action. Statutes creating a private federal right are rare, however. (Federal law making culture is oriented toward official regulation rather than toward private rights.) In most cases, then, the defendant's violation of a federal statute does not give the plaintiff a right of action for the violation, even if that violation harms the plaintiff. In such cases, the plaintiff's state tort claim may be barred by preemption and the plaintiff has no federal claim at all because the preempting statute created no private right of action.

C. COMPLIANCE WITH SPECIFICATION: GOVERNMENT CONTRACTORS AND OTHERS

BOYLE v. UNITED TECHNOLOGIES CORP., 487 U.S. 500 (1988). A U.S. Marine helicopter copilot was killed when his helicopter crashed during a training exercise. His father sued Sikorsky Division of United Technologies Corporation (Sikorsky), which built the helicopter under contract for the United States. Plaintiff alleged two state-law claims: (1) that Sikorsky had defectively repaired a device called the servo in the helicopter's automatic flight control system, which allegedly malfunctioned and caused the crash, and (2) that Sikorsky had defectively designed the copilot's emergency escape system. The jury found for plaintiff and awarded him $725,000. The Court of Appeals reversed and remanded with directions that judgment be entered for Sikorsky, partly because it was protected by what the court called the "military contractor defense." *Held*, "Liability for design defects in military equipment cannot be imposed, pursuant to state law, when (1) the United States approved reasonably precise specifications; (2) the equipment conformed to those specifications; and (3) the supplier warned the United States about the dangers in the use of the equipment that were known to the supplier but not to the United States." The governing principle underlying this defense is the FTCA's discretionary immunity clause, which retains immunity for the federal government itself for tort cases "based upon the exercise or performance or the failure to exercise or perform a discretionary function or duty on the part of a federal agency or an employee of the Government, whether or not the discretion involved be abused." The government's selection of the design of military equipment "is assuredly a discretionary function within the meaning of this provision. . . . It makes little sense to insulate the Government against financial liability for the judgment that a particular feature of military equipment is necessary when the Government produces the equipment itself, but not when it contracts for the production. In sum, we are of the view that state law which holds Government contractors liable for design defects in military equipment" must be displaced under the circumstances presented here.

NOTES

1. **Manufacturing defects.** What if the plaintiff is injured by a product made for the government and to government specification, but the injury results because of a manufacturing rather than a design defect? What if the plaintiff claims that the contractor could have supplied a warning to make the product safer? *See Densberger v. United Tech's. Corp.*, 297 F.3d 66 (2d Cir. 2002).

2. ***Boyle* as a compliance case.** *Boyle* turns on the defendant's compliance with overriding law affecting product design. If the plaintiff's injury results from the contractor's non-compliance rather than its compliance with specifications, the *Boyle* defense would not apply. The compliance required to trigger the *Boyle* defense, however, is not a compliance with a legislative enactment, but with specifications used by the government in making a private contract.

3. **The *Richardson* case.** In *Richardson v. McKnight*, 521 U.S. 399 (1997), the Court held that the qualified immunity accorded to government employees in § 1983 actions does not extend to prison guards who are employees of a private prison management firm. The Court stressed that the private firm had "limited direct supervision by the government." Is this consistent with *Boyle*?

4. **Is *Boyle* limited to military contractors or product manufacturers?** Up until *Boyle*, some of the courts of appeal had been much taken with the military aspects in government contractor cases and some had even referred to the "military contractor" defense. These cases emphasized the impropriety of judicial interference with military decisions and they grounded the defense partly in those concerns. Does the *Boyle* rationale make it clear that the defense is much broader than that?

5. ***Feres* and *Boyle*.** Under the *Feres* doctrine (see Chapter 15 § 2), military service members are barred from suing the federal government for injuries that are "incident to service." The *Boyle* court declined to rest its decision on *Feres*, but also avoided deciding whether *Feres* immunity could ever be applied derivatively to a federal military contractor. In *McMahon v. Presidential Airways, Inc.*, 502 F.3d 1331 (11th Cir. 2007), the issue was joined. Survivors of U.S. soldiers who were killed when the airplane in which they were being flown crashed in Afghanistan filed a negligence suit against the civilian contractors who provided air transportation and support services to the government. The defendant argued "that it is entitled to claim the whole of the government's *Feres* immunity under the doctrine of derivative sovereign immunity." The court held that derivative *Feres* immunity should not be recognized in the case because "it would single out soldiers" and would

not protect sensitive military judgments in suits brought by anyone else, including journalists or private contractor employees. The court said that "we do not mean to foreclose the possibility" of a government contractor immunity but that "any such immunity must, if it is to have any basis in reason, apply to civilians as well as soldiers: including the employees of private contractors, and other civilians." Does *McMahon* conflict with *Boyle*?

6. **State (not federal) contractors.** *Boyle* was distinguished in *Conner v. Quality Coach, Inc.*, 750 A.2d 823 (Pa. 2000). In that case, a private company had contracted with a state agency to provide modifications on the vehicles of disabled persons. The plaintiff alleged that the defendant contractor utilized a defective design for its brake/throttle control, resulting in an injury-causing accident. The defendant argued that it was immune under *Boyle,* but the state court disagreed. *Boyle* is limited to federal contractors. In Pennsylvania, the courts have abolished common law immunity, leaving only immunities established by the legislature, which has established none here. Contractors are protected when they reasonably rely upon specifications, but only because in that case they are not negligent at all. When they participate in the design decision, as here, they are liable for their negligence. Any general policy to lower government procurement costs by protecting government contractors is "lacking in empirical support," and is "ill-suited to serve as a counterweight to the policies favoring just compensation underlying our tort system."

7. **Private contractors providing products to private customers.** Suppose the local bus company orders a fleet of buses, specifying a gas tank in a dangerous location and in fact the gas tank blows up when the bus is rammed by a car. Would an injured bus passenger have a products liability claim against the manufacturer?

§ 11. STATUTES OF LIMITATION

1. *Choice of statute. (a) Negligence and strict liability.* Many states have special products statutes, setting up some rules about products liability and also a special statute of limitations that may be different from the ordinary negligence/personal injury statute. Suppose the products statute is two years, while the negligence statute is four. The plaintiff sues the manufacturer of a machine for injury resulting when the manufacturer installed it at the plaintiff's employer's business without assuring ventilation needed to make it safe. Suit was filed three years after the injury. Is the suit timely?

(b) Warranty. When the plaintiff sues on a warranty theory, or includes a warranty theory among others, the statute of limitations intended to govern "contract" or warranty claims may apply. The UCC in fact specifies in Art. 2–725(1):

> An action for breach of any contract for sale must be commenced within four years after the cause of action has accrued.

A number of courts have held that this provision governs a warranty claim, even where the damage claimed is for personal injury. This is important in a state—Alabama, for instance—in which strict tort liability is not accepted as such and in which most strict liability may be based on a warranty theory.

Other courts, however, seem more interested in determining whether the underlying claim is the kind tort law has sought to protect, and in these courts the fact that "warranty" is the theory might not be determinative if the underlying claim is a claim for physical harm to person or property of the same kind a products tort liability case might cover. The New York Court of Appeals said something like this in *Victorson v. Bock Laundry Machine Co.*, 335 N.E.2d 275 (N.Y. 1975). Quoting PROSSER ON TORTS, the court said that "The fundamental difference between tort and contract lies in the nature of the interests protected." Even if warranty is part of the verbiage used to state the claim, if physical harm is the damage claimed, the warranty statute of limitations is inappropriate, and whatever statute governs torts or personal injury claims would be chosen instead. This view is consistent with the distinction drawn in Section 3, supra, between economic harm, for which warranty is especially suited, and physical harm, for which tort doctrine seems to work better.

2. *Accrual of the claim.* (a) *Sales or later date.* If the claim is for personal injury and based solely on tort doctrine, the tort statute, however that may be phrased in a particular state, will govern. When will the statute begin to run? In tort law this ordinarily occurs when injury is inflicted, subject to the discovery rule. Certainly, it does *not* begin to run on the date of sale. If the claim is based on a warranty theory, however, and if the UCC statute is applied, it is quite possible that the statute begins to run from the time the product is sold by the defendant. This is, in fact, the express provision of UCC Art. 2–725(2): "A breach of warranty occurs when tender of delivery is made...." Although the UCC statute is for four years, and although this is longer than most tort statutes, it begins running before injury. In *Waldrop v. Peabody Galion Corp.*, 423 So.2d 145 (Ala. 1982), the defendants sold (or "tendered delivery" of) a garbage truck in 1974. The plaintiff, a city employee working on the truck was injured, allegedly by a defect, in 1976. At that time the statute had already been running two years. When his suit was actually brought in 1979 it was barred by the four-year statute. If he had been able to sue on a tort theory and a three-year tort statute had applied, his suit would have been timely.

(b) *Injury or later date.* Most states will not force an injured plaintiff to use warranty theory to pursue a products liability claim, but will permit or even require use of a tort theory instead. Under the general statutes of limitation applied to tort claims, the claim does not accrue until injury; and the statute cannot start running before injury. Under the discovery rule seen in Chapter 9, the statute does not begin to run until the harm is or should have been discovered.

3. *Statutes of repose.* (a) *The Problem.* The typical statute of limitations in tort cases has run from the time of injury or some later date.

After the initial explosive expansion of product liability, manufacturers and others in the commercial world exerted considerable effort to restrict liability. One special problem was the "long tail" of possible liabilities that could occur. A product sold in 1959 might not cause harm until 1999. If the victim sued immediately, he would not be barred by an ordinary statute of limitations, which does not begin to run until injury occurs, or later. But this would mean that a manufacturer would have to plan for potential liabilities 20, 30, 40 years into the future, or even more.

(b) *Statutory response.* With ideas like these in mind, many legislatures have passed statutes of "ultimate repose," under which products claims are barred if injury occurs more than, say, 12 years after the product was initially sold or delivered.

Similar statutes of repose have been passed in some states to protect architects, engineers, real estate developers and doctors. All these are structured like the products statute: the statutory period is a long one, but it begins to run from the time the product was sold, or the work or service completed.

(c) *Constitutionality.* Some of these statutes have been held unconstitutional under the provisions of state constitutions. New Hampshire also held its statute to be in violation of its State constitution partly because it denied equal protection to products plaintiffs and partly because it denied reasonable access to courts. The court commented:

> The unreasonableness inherent in a statute which eliminates a plaintiff's cause of action before the wrong may reasonably be discovered was noted by Judge Frank [who] condemned the Alice in Wonderland' effect of such a result:
>
>> 'Except in topsy-turvy land, you can't die before you are conceived, or be divorced before you marry, or harvest a crop never planted, or burn down a house never built, or miss a train running on a non-existent railroad. For substantially similar reasons, it has always heretofore been accepted, as a sort of logical "axiom," that a statute of limitations does not begin to run against a cause of action before that cause of action exists, i.e., before a judicial remedy is available to a plaintiff.'

Heath v. Sears, Roebuck & Co., 464 A.2d 288 (N.H. 1983).

The quotation from Judge Frank is a beautiful example of effective rhetoric. Is there, however, any rule of state constitutions that requires the legislature to accept logical axioms? Given the difficult problem, can you be sure that the solution of the legislature is not only unjust but a violation of the constitution? Local constitutional provisions are most important in these cases.

(d) *Continuing duty to warn.* Whatever the constitutionally of the statutes of repose in the ordinary case, can they apply at all to the case in which the defendant's liability is based, not upon defect at the time of sale, but upon failure to warn of the defect it discovers after sale? Five years after a car is marketed, the manufacturer discovers a steering defect and does nothing. Unwarned, the plaintiff has a horrible wreck six years after that. Should the statute of repose apply to such a case? *See, e.g., Watkins v. Ford Motor Co.*, 190 F.3d 1213 (11th Cir. 1999). What if liability is based on failure to warn of an unknown defect?

REFERENCE: DOBBS ON TORTS § 374 (2000).

SUBCHAPTER D. EXTENDING THE SCOPE OF PRODUCTS LIABILITY
§ 12. BEYOND THE MANUFACTURER OF NEW GOODS

In the earlier days of products liability expansion, there was uncertainty about a good many details. Did this liability extend to all goods, or only to foods or to intimate products? Did it extend to containers, or only the goods themselves? These questions have long since been answered favorably to the consumer, provided only that a defect is proven. This section considers whether strict liability is imposed upon persons besides manufacturers and whether it is imposed for defects besides those in "goods."

A. TANGIBLE GOODS AND PROPERTY

1. *Distributors and only distributors.* Persons who count as distributors and only such persons are subject to the products liability rules. *See, e.g., Burnett v. Covell*, 191 P.3d 985 (Alaska 2008) (law office owner who provided chair to visitor was not a distributor of the chair and thus not subject to strict products liability). All commercial providers of products are distributors. Noncommercial providers generally are not distributors. See RESTATEMENT OF PRODUCTS LIABILITY § 1, cmt. *c.* For instance, if you are not in the car business, you are not a distributor when you sell your car. The commercial-noncommercial distinction may not fully capture the idea, however. *Cf. New Texas Auto Auction Services, L.P. v. Gomez*, 249 S.W.3d 400 (Tex. 2008) (automobile auctioneer could not be held strictly liable for defect in car he sold because he did not actually place the product in the stream of commerce). Suppose a non-profit organization devoted to health has a massive continuing program for providing, free, a drug to help respiratory patients and the drug proves to be defective, causing injuries. Could its systematic provision of the drug make it a distributor?

What about a business that sells a product outside its usual line, in a "casual sale"? In *Griffin Industries, Inc. v. Jones*, 975 S.W.2d 100 (Ky. 1998), plaintiff brought a products liability case against defendant, which had manufactured and sold to plaintiff's employer a conveyor belt system that caused the injury. The defendant's main business was rendering animal waste. It manufactured the belts for its own use, did not market them, and sold the belts to plaintiff's employer in an isolated transaction. Held, defendant is an "occasional seller," thus not liable in a products suit. See RESTATEMENT OF PRODUCTS LIABILITY § 1, cmt. *c.* What about a "custom fabricator" who builds, for the first time, a particular kind of retractable floor to suit a customer's specific needs? In *Sprung v. MTR Ravensburg, Inc.*, 788 N.E.2d 620 (N.Y. 2003), the court held that the defendant was not merely a "casual seller" because "the product was built for market sale in the regular course of the manufacturer's business," even if it was a one-time, custom fabrication. The court said that custom fabricators "hold themselves out as having expertise in manufacturing their custom products, have the opportunity and incentive to ensure safety in the process of making those products, and are better able to shoulder the costs of injuries caused by defective products than injured consumers or users."

2. *Retailers, wholesalers, component manufacturers.* Distributors subject to the products rules include manufacturers, wholesalers, and retailers. Under some circumstances, even an endorser, or a franchisor/trademark licensor might be strictly liable for the product that bears the franchise name. *See Torres v. Goodyear Tire & Rubber Co., Inc.*, 786 P.2d 939 (Ariz. 1990). The Restatement of Products Liability provides in § 14 that one who "distributes as its own a product manufactured by another" is liable as if it were the manufacturer. A retailer or wholesaler who is held liable usually has an indemnity claim in its favor against the manufacturer.

3. *The former requirement of a sale; lessors.* At one time it was supposed that products liability could be triggered only when there was a "sale" of goods. It now seems well accepted that a technical sale is not required, and a plaintiff injured by the explosion of a defective soft drink bottle in the grocery store recovers whether the explosion occurred after he paid for it or before. And suppliers who do not sell are also liable for defects, provided they are in the business of supplying goods. This covers lessors of goods, for example. What if a retailer gives away chewing gum to shoppers as part of a promotion and the gum proves to be deleterious?

4. *Used goods.* An individual who sells her car is not in the business of selling cars and is thus not liable as a distributor. What about a dealer in used cars? The dealer in used goods may be held liable for negligence, misrepresentation, or breach of any express warranty. UCC Art. 2–316(a) permits exclusion of warranty when selling goods "as is" with all faults. For personal injury cases, strict tort liability represents the most interesting possibility. The cases are somewhat divided. What about letting the commercial seller of used goods use an "as is" disclaimer, even for strict products liability? Do you expect to have more difficulty in judging defectiveness of a used product? What about a used product sold for a limited purpose, as where an old car is sold for scrap metal?

5. *Builders and sellers of real property.* The common law rule was that a contractor who negligently built or repaired real property (including buildings) could not be liable for injuries caused by his negligence once the

property was turned over to the owner and accepted by him. This rule no longer holds, and contractors and builders are liable for their negligence.

The law of warranty developed in chattel cases did not historically apply to real property sales. The deed was thought to express the whole obligation of the parties. Since the deed did not express any warranty of safety, there could be no implied warranty at odds with the deed. However, in 1965 New Jersey applied an implied warranty of habitability to the sale of mass production homes by a builder whose failure to install a valve permitted scalding water to flow from a faucet and to burn a child. *Schipper v. Levitt & Sons, Inc.*, 207 A.2d 314 (N.J. 1965). Although the vendor might be liable without privity in such cases, it would seem that only vendors in the business of selling (and perhaps only those in the business of building) houses would be held. Strict liability has also been applied to home builders in some cases. *See, e.g., Hyman v. Gordon*, 111 Cal.Rptr. 262 (Ct. App. 1973) (builder-designer of a house could be strictly liable for a design defect because of the dangerous location of a heater). *Cf.* Restatement of Products Liability § 19, cmt. *e* (contractor who sells a building with appliances or other manufactured equipment in it is considered a product seller of that equipment, and builders of pre-fabricated buildings may be considered product sellers with respect to the building itself).

There are, however, decisions refusing to apply strict liability in real property cases, and the issue is not resolved yet in most jurisdictions. If you were suing or defending such an action in a state with no decisions on point, what arguments would you invoke for strict liability? Against it?

6. *Lessors of real property.* Landlords are traditionally not strictly liable for defects in premises; indeed, even their liability for negligence was traditionally limited along the lines seen in Chapter 12. A few states have imposed an implied warranty of habitability on lessors, but most of these cases involve only economic harm, that is, the lessened value of the leased premises because of the defects, or else cases in which the lessor had notice of a defect and did not correct it. If lessors are held strictly liable, should this include any lessor, or only lessors of multiple unit dwellings? Would it matter whether the premises were furnished or unfurnished? Whether the lease was a short-term, month-to-month, or long-term, for years, lease?

In *Becker v. IRM Corp.*, 698 P.2d 116 (Cal. 1985), the California Court imposed strict liability upon landlords for premises defects. Ten years later, however, it repudiated that decision in *Peterson v. Superior Court*, 899 P.2d 905 (Cal. 1995). The court reasoned that the landlord was not in a stream of commerce in the defective goods and not in a good position to urge the manufacturer of the defective item to make it safer. It said the landlord is more in the position of a seller of used goods and consumers cannot expect the same safety. The court also feared economic ruin for landlords. Thus it thought the law of negligence was quite adequate. It did not mention nondelegable duties.

Lead-based paint has poisoned children for many years. When the paint peels, small children pull the peelings off the wall and put them in their mouths. Should landlords be strictly liable for using or failing to remove such paint, or should the debilitated child hope that someone will sue his parents for the permanent injuries? *Compare Ankiewicz v. Kinder*, 563 N.E.2d 684 (Mass. 1990) *with Gore v. People's Savings Bank*, 665 A.2d 1341 (Conn. 1995).

7. *Animals and animal products.* Is there any reason to say that animals and animal bodily products are not "products" for the purpose of product liability law? *Compare Kaplan v. C Lazy U Ranch*, 615 F.Supp. 234 (D. Colo. 1985) (horse with bad behaviors tending to cause harm was not a product) *with Sease v. Taylor's Pets, Inc.*, 700 P.2d 1054 (Or. Ct. App. 1985) (rabid skunk sold by store as a pet was a product).

B. INTANGIBLES—SERVICES AND ENDORSEMENTS

NEWMARK v. GIMBEL'S INC.

258 A.2d 697 (N.J. 1969)

FRANCIS, J.

[The plaintiff, Mrs. Newmark, went to one of defendant's beauty shops where she had a standing appointment. Her regular operator, Valante, made a recommendation about a permanent and she accepted it. During the treatment she felt a "burning" on more than one occasion, and Valante took steps to diminish it. However her forehead later blistered and her hair fell out. A dermatologist concluded she had contact dermatitis resulting from the application of the permanent solution. The trial court dismissed Mrs. Newmark's claim in warranty on the ground that the defendant was rendering a service, not making a sale. The Appellate Division reversed this, holding that there might be an implied warranty as to the lotion applied.]

Valante identified the permanent wave solution as "Candle Glow," a product of Helene Curtis. He said the liquid was mild but could damage a scalp which had scratches on it or could cause a sting if the solution were rubbed into the scalp. He applied the solution as it came from the original package or container, and his experience had shown that a tingling or burning sensation, the degree varying with different persons, was fairly common. The label on the package contained a caveat for the beauty operator. It said:

> "Always wear rubber gloves when giving a wave. Make sure patrons hair and scalp are in condition to receive a cold wave. Never brush or rub the scalp vigorously either before or after shampooing. If the scalp is excessively tender or shows evidence of sores or abrasions, the wave should not be given. Ask the patron her previous experience with cold waves to be sure she does not have a sensitivity to waving lotion."

Mrs. Newmark did not see this label, and there is nothing in the record to indicate Valante asked her about any previous experience with cold waves. It does appear, however, that she had four permanent waves without ill effects after the incident involved here and before trial of this case. . . .

If the permanent wave lotion were sold to Mrs. Newmark by defendants for home consumption or application or to enable her to give herself the permanent wave, unquestionably an implied warranty of fitness for that purpose would have been an integral incident of the sale. Basically defendants argue that if, in addition to recommending the use of a lotion or other product and supplying it for use, they applied it, such fact (the application) would have the effect of lessening their liability to the patron by eliminating warranty and by limiting their responsibility to the issue of negligence. There is no just reason why it should. On the contrary by taking on the administration of the product in addition to recommending and supplying it, they might increase the scope of their liability, if the method of administration were improper (a result not suggested on this appeal because the jury found no negligence).

The transaction, in our judgment, is a hybrid partaking of incidents of a sale and a service. It is really partly the rendering of service, and partly the supplying of goods for a consideration. Accordingly, we agree with the Appellate division that an implied warranty of fitness of the products used in giving the permanent wave exists with no less force than it would have in the case of a simple sale. Obviously in permanent wave operations the product is taken into consideration in fixing the price of the service. The no-separate-charge argument puts excessive emphasis on form and downgrades the overall substance of the transaction. If the beauty parlor operator bought and applied the permanent wave solution to her own hair and suffered injury thereby, her action in warranty or strict liability in tort . . . against the manufacturer-seller of the product clearly would be maintainable because the basic transaction would have arisen from a conventional type of sale. It does not accord with logic to deny a similar right to a patron against the beauty parlor operator or the manufacturer when the purchase and sale were made in anticipation of and for the purpose of use of the product on the patron who would be charged for its use. Common sense demands that such patron be deemed a consumer as to both manufacturer and beauty parlor operator.

A beauty parlor operator in soliciting patronage assures the public that he or she possesses adequate knowledge and skill to do the things and to apply the solution necessary to produce the permanent wave in the hair of the customer. When a patron responds to the solicitation she does so confident that any product used in the shop has come from a reliable origin and can be trusted not to injure her. She places herself in the hands of the operator relying upon his or her expertise both in the selection of the products to be used on her and in the method of using them. The ministrations and the products employed on her are under the control and selection of the operator; the patron is a mere passive recipient. . . .

It seems to us that the policy reasons for imposing warranty liability in the case of ordinary sales are equally applicable to a commercial transaction such as that existing in this case between a beauty parlor operator and a patron.

Defendants claim that to hold them to strict liability would be contrary to Magrine v. Krasnica, 94 N.J. Super. 228, 227 A.2d 539 (Cty. Ct. 1967), aff'd sub nom. Magrine v. Spector, 100 N.J. Super. 223, 241 A.2d 637 (App. Div. 1968), aff'd 53 N.J. 259, 250 A.2d 129 (1969). We cannot agree. Magrine, a patient of the defendant-dentist, was injured when a hypodermic needle being used, concededly with due care, to administer a local anesthetic broke off in his gum or jaw. The parties agreed that the break resulted from a latent defect in the needle. It was held that the strict liability in tort doctrine was not applicable to the professional man, such as a dentist, because the essence of the relationship with his patient was the furnishing of professional skill and services. We accepted the view that a dentist's bill for services should be considered as representing pay for that alone. The use of instruments, or the administration of medicines or the providing of medicines for the patient's home consumption cannot give the ministrations the cast of a commercial transaction. Accordingly the liability of the dentist in cases involving the ordinary relationship of doctor and patient must be tested by principles of negligence, i.e., lack of due care and not by application of the doctrine of strict liability in tort.

Defendants suggest that there is no doctrinal basis for distinguishing the services rendered by a beauty parlor operator from those rendered by a dentist or a doctor, and that consequently the liability of all three should be tested by the same principles. On the contrary there is a vast difference in the relationships. The beautician is engaged in a commercial enterprise; the dentist and doctor in a profession. The former caters publicly not to a need but to a form of aesthetic convenience or luxury, involving the rendition of non-professional services and the application of products for which a charge is made. The dentist or doctor does not and cannot advertise for patients; the demand for his services stems from a felt necessity of the patient. In response to such a call the doctor, and to a somewhat lesser degree the dentist, exercises his best judgment in diagnosing the patient's ailment or disability, prescribing and sometimes furnishing medicines or other methods of treatment which he believes, and in some measure hopes, will relieve or cure the condition. His performance is not mechanical or routine because each patient requires individual study and formulation of an informed judgment as to the physical or mental disability or condition presented, and the course of treatment needed. Neither medicine nor dentistry is an exact science; there is no implied warranty of cure or relief. There is no representation of infallibility and such professional men should not be held to such a degree of perfection. There is no guaranty that the diagnosis is correct. Such men are not producers or sellers of property in any reasonably acceptable sense of the term. In a primary sense they furnish services in the form of an opinion of the patient's condition based upon their experienced analysis of the objective and subjective complaints, and in the form of recommended and, at times, personally administered medicines and treatment. . . .

Thus their paramount function—the essence of their function—ought to be regarded as the furnishing of opinions and services. Their unique status and the rendition of these *sui generis* services bear such a necessary and intimate relationship to public health and welfare that their obligation ought to be grounded and expressed in a duty to exercise reasonable competence and care toward their patients. In our judgment, the nature of the services, the utility of and the need for them, involving as they do, the health and even survival of many people, are so important to the general welfare as to outweigh in the policy scale any need for the imposition on dentists and doctors of the rules of strict liability in tort. . . .

Strict liability to the injured consumer does not leave the dealer without remedy. He has an action over against the manufacturer who should bear the primary responsibility for putting defective products in the stream of trade. . . .

The judgment of the Appellate Division is affirmed for the reasons stated, and the cause is remanded for a new trial.

NOTES

1. **Pure services.** Defendants are not strictly liable for delivering defective services. Thus a surgeon is not strictly liable when an operation goes horribly wrong, nor a lawyer when he loses an easy case. *See* RESTATEMENT OF PRODUCTS LIABILITY § 19 (b) ("Services, even when provided commercially, are not products.").

2. **Hybrid transactions.** Many transactions involve both the transfer of tangible items and also the delivery of a service. *Newmark* is the leading decision dealing with such transactions. Does *Newmark* mark a satisfactory line between cases of strict liability and cases that will require proof of negligence? What do you think of a rule that says the hybrid transaction will be treated as a service unless the sale of goods aspect is predominant?

3. **Hybrid medical transactions.** What if a doctor selects a medical prosthesis, then surgically implants it. The prosthesis proves to be defective and its manufacturer is bankrupt. Should the doctor be strictly liable as a seller or distributor? *Cafazzo v. Central Med. Health Servs., Inc.*, 668 A.2d 521 (Pa. 1995), held not, arguing that first and most simply there was no sale, but that in any event the policy basis of strict products liability had no application. Doctors could not get better safety for products approved by the Food and Drug Administration. The health care system should not bear and spread the costs of bad medical prostheses because that would "further endanger the already beleaguered health care system." *Accord, In re Breast Implant Prod. Liab. Litig.*, 503 S.E.2d 445 (S.C. 1998) (health care providers who implanted breast implants were not "sellers" of medical devices and thus could not be held strictly liable). What about a pharmacist who dispenses prescriptions? In

Madison v. Home Products Corp., 595 S.E.2d 493 (S.C. 2004), the plaintiff sued a pharmacy for properly filling a prescription for anti-depressants that allegedly caused her to attack her son and attempt suicide. The court held that strict products liability could not apply because the pharmacy was providing a service, not selling a product.

4. **Separate billing.** A repair shop makes repairs on your car, installing various needed parts. The bill reflects separate charges for labor and parts. When you drive off, the brakes fail due to a defective cylinder installed by the shop. Could the separate billing for parts and labor possibly determine whether there was a "sale" for which strict liability could be imposed? *See Bell v. Precision Airmotive Corp.,* 42 P.3d 1071 (Alaska 2002).

5. **Products must be tangible; dangerous media communications.** The Products Restatement asserts in section 19 that only tangible things can count as products that can be defective. A number of cases have involved violent or dangerous activities depicted in movies, television and video games. If it can be established that these depictions desensitize viewers and players and actually triggered violence against the plaintiff, would the plaintiff have a strict products liability claim? The cases have rejected strict liability, sometimes on the ground that First Amendment free speech principles protect such communicative behavior, and sometimes on the formal ground that the plaintiff is not complaining of a tangible product but about the intangible message. *See James v. Meow Media, Inc.,* 300 F.3d 683 (6th Cir. 2002) (teenager shooting classmates at high school allegedly induced by video games and web sites); *Wilson v. Midway Games, Inc.,* 198 F. Supp. 2d 167 (D. Conn. 2002) (boy killing friend in manner of interactive video killing he had become obsessed with); *Walt Disney Prods., Inc. v. Shannon,* 276 S.E.2d 580 (Ga. 1981) (dangerous acts shown on TV, emulated by small child).

6. **Should some providers be strictly liable for pure service defects?** If strict liability is right in principle, why exempt service providers? Suppose a plane from Houston to Atlanta crashes without anyone's fault due to a bizarre failure of radar. What passengers bought was a service—transport—not a product. Still, wouldn't it serve the purposes of strict liability to impose liability?

7. **Blood and other body products.** Statutes typically provide, directly or indirectly that suppliers of blood and related products such as body organs or tissues, are not strictly liable. Some statutes attempt to prohibit strict tort liability by providing that the provision of blood is the provision of a service, not the sale of a product. Others directly state that the supplier of blood is not to be held strictly liable. The Restatement Third imports the statutory rules, treating them as a common law rule by providing that human blood is not subject to the rules of the Restatement. RESTATEMENT OF PRODUCTS LIABILITY § 19(c).

REFERENCE: DOBBS ON TORTS §§ 375–76 (2000).

*

PART 5

PRACTICALITIES AND VALUES

■ ■ ■

CHAPTER 25

SETTLEMENT AND APPORTIONMENT

■ ■ ■

Settlement entails a prediction of what would happen if the case were tried. That in turn requires lawyers to know both the substantive tort doctrine and the rules of damages. It also requires lawyers to estimate whether the defendant has assets or insurance that would pay the award. And since most torts involve at least two potential defendants, intelligent settlement also requires lawyers on all sides to know how liability can be apportioned among defendants.

Although the next chapter expressly considers some criticisms of tort law, the practical concerns in this chapter also raise important questions about values and goals.

SUBCHAPTER A.   INSURANCE AND SETTLEMENT

§ 1.   AN INTRODUCTION TO THE INSTITUTION OF INSURANCE

A.   THE BASIC INSURANCE COVERAGES

1. *First party insurance—fire and collision.* Two common examples of "first party" insurance are fire insurance, in which one's property is insured against fire, and collision insurance, in which one's car is insured against damage in a collision. There are many variations and additional protections that can be obtained under these policies. These forms of insurance are "first party" insurance in the sense that the insured party is the first and only party besides the insurer. If there is a loss, the insured person reports it to his own insurer and makes a claim. The rights of the insured are governed by the insurance contract.

A second common feature of these policies is that the insured is entitled to recover upon proof of loss covered by the policy and it is not necessary to show fault on the part of anyone. Indeed, even the insured's own fault, short of intentional damage to his own property, is irrelevant. You recover on your contract, not in tort.

2. *Subrogation.* Subrogation is a key feature of much first party insurance. You insure your house against fire loss by obtaining a policy with the Kentuckasee Insurance Company. Durfee Construction Company negligently excavates, cutting a gas line and causing a fire that burns your house down. You could ignore the fire policy and sue Durfee in tort, but if the policy is adequate to protect your loss, you might simply make a claim with your insurer. Subrogation permits the insurer to "stand in the shoes" of its insured, and take over any claim the insured has against the tortfeasor. Having paid for your loss, Kentuckasee will thus pursue its subrogation right against Durfee Construction. If it proves Durfee's negligence toward you and the other elements of a tort claim you yourself could have made, it will be entitled to recover against Durfee. The same principle applies in the case of collision insurance on your car, although usually with a "deductible" amount that you must pay.

Subrogation does not apply in *all* first party insurance. It has no application, for example, in life insurance. The survivors of one who is negligently killed have *both* a claim against the life insurance company which insured his life *and* a claim against the tortfeasor.

3. *Liability insurance.* First party insurance is based on the idea of "indemnity"—that is, a recompense or paying back for a loss suffered. In the latter part of the 19th century, this idea was expanded to cover a new kind of loss, namely, loss through legal liability. If an industry's factory burned down, it would need first party fire insurance to protect against loss. If the industry negligently injured a worker and were required to pay a judgment in his favor, it would need liability insurance to protect against loss. Since liability could arise from many kinds of risks, this form of insurance expanded further, and it became quite common for owners of vehicles to purchase liability policies covering risks from their operation. Liability insurance has played an important part in providing indemnity for many other unintended torts as well.

The liability insurance policy as originally conceived had two important characteristics. The first was that it covered only the legal liability of the insured. If the insured caused harm, but was not legally liable for it, the insured would not be liable and neither would the insurer. The insurer, in other words, could take advantage of any fact and legal rule that favored the insured.

The other characteristic of the liability policy as originally conceived was that it could be invoked only by the insured himself, not by his victim. If the insured tortiously injured a plaintiff, and was legally liable to pay him, the injured plaintiff had no claim against the insurance funds. He would be obliged to collect directly against the insured tortfeasor or not at all. If he did collect, the tortfeasor could in turn obtain the indemnity promised by his insurer. But if the tortfeasor was insolvent or for any other reason avoided payment to the injured person, the tortfeasor's liability insurer had no responsibility. This was true even if the insured tortfeasor was legally liable, so long as he had not actually paid the victim.

As liability insurance became more common, the public began to regard it as a source of recompense for injury rather than as an indemnity for the tortfeasor's loss. As a result of these changing ideas, statutes or policies themselves now permit the injured person to reach the insurance funds (up to the limits of the policy) once legal liability is shown. It is no longer possible for an insurer to escape liability merely because its insured is insolvent. This reflects an increased "socialization" of insurance, in which liability insurance is seen in part as a tool for financing injury loss rather than simply as a tool for indemnity of the tortfeasor. However, this social use of liability insurance to spread the costs of injury loss is incomplete, since "legal liability" of the insured person is still the first prerequisite to recovery. In other words, the liability policy is still not an accident or health policy.

4. *Liability insurance as second party insurance.* The shift from the view of liability insurance as an indemnity arrangement between the insured and insurer to a more "social" view of insurance as a device for assisting the injured has consequences in practice. One consequence is that the insurer controls the investigation and defense of the claim. This means that the injured person who makes the claim must deal with the tortfeasor's insurer rather than his own. In this respect liability insurance is now quite distinct from the first party insurance coverage in, say, collision insurance. It also differs, of course, in that liability turns not on loss to the injured person, but on the legal liability of the insured.

5. *Other forms of insurance.* Since you might be injured by the fault of an uninsured driver, the protections afforded by liability insurance are incomplete. Many drivers now purchase additional insurance such as medical payments insurance, which covers certain limited medical expenses resulting from auto accidents without regard to fault, and uninsured motorist insurance. For more information on no-fault insurance plans, *see* Chapter 30, *infra*.

6. *The impact of liability insurance.* One important effect of liability insurance is that it provides a fund available to pay judgments, without which legal liability might be meaningless. But the existence of liability insurance could at times encourage excessive damages awards, and maybe even the expansion of tort liability itself. Whether that is true or not, does liability insurance protection undercut the whole idea of individual accountability?

B. THE LIABILITY INSURER'S DUTIES

The liability insurer's exact duties depend primarily on the contract between it and the insured, that is, upon the policy terms. Lawyers for both the insured defendant and for the plaintiff must be aware of the policy's terms and limits. For example, a term of the policy might exclude all coverage in a particular case. In cases of this sort, the insurer is said to have a "policy defense" or a "coverage defense," and if that defense is sound, the policy is not operative at all.

In most cases, the insurer's defense to a claim against its insured is not a policy defense but a defense on the merits. The insurer asserts that the insured defendant was not negligent, or that the injured plaintiff was guilty of contributory negligence, or that the insured's behavior was not a proximate cause, or that damages are insignificant. This kind of defense, unlike the policy defense, does not deprive the insured of coverage under the policy. If the defense is successful the insured will be protected, but if it is not, the insurer will still be obliged to pay the injured plaintiff up to its policy limits.

Most policies today provide that the insurer has two main obligations, if there is coverage at all. One is to pay any judgment against the insured based on risks covered by the policy and up to the limits of the policy. The other is to defend the insured. The obligation to defend the insured, like the obligation to pay, applies only if the policy is actually in force. The obligation to defend is not limited to cases in which the plaintiff sues the insured defendant in good faith, but extends to any case even if such suit is groundless, false or fraudulent.

The duty to defend carries with it the insurer's right to be involved in, if not to control, the investigation, negotiation and settlement of the case. It imposes upon the insurer the obligation to retain an attorney to defend the insured's interests. The result of all this is that to a very large extent the insurer is the *de facto* defendant, though in most states the named defendant in court is the insured, not the insurer. The lawyer, even if retained by the insurer, continues to owe his primary duty to the insured as the client, but must cooperate with the insurer except where the insurer and the insured's interests conflict.

The insurer's influence over the process of negotiation, settlement and trial affects lawyers on both sides. Suppose an insured defendant has, perhaps negligently, run over a spouse or best friend. If the defendant is fully covered by insurance, will he have an interest in defeating the plaintiff's claim or assisting it? What can the insurer do in such a case except to insist upon its policy right to the cooperation of its insured? If the insurer is vulnerable in such a case, what is its position when dealing with an injured person who has no lawyer? Does the fact that the adjusters are experienced and knowledgeable have any practical effects on the rights of the injured person? How exactly does the defendant's insurer deal with negotiation and settlement? Many of the nuances of this problem must be left to specialized courses in insurance and professional responsibility. But the predominant role of insurance is worth keeping in mind in considering the problems of settlement raised in the next section.

§ 2. SETTLEMENT AND NEGOTIATION

A. SETTLEMENT

Importance of settlement. The great majority of tort cases are settled by negotiation. The plaintiff accepts a sum of money and gives the defendant a document, usually a "release," the effect of which is to absolve the defendant of further liability. Settlement is economically important to the public and to the parties. If all cases had to be tried, the legal system could not bear the weight of the work and the parties probably could not bear the weight of the delay. The tort system works, then, partly because settlement is the usual method of dealing with claims.

Protecting the effort to settle. The process of settlement negotiation is important enough to deserve some protection. Suppose D offers to settle for $100,000 and P rejects the offer. Can P show in court that D made the offer and therefore that he must have been admitting negligence? The usual answer is no. If negotiation terms could be admitted in court, the parties might be afraid to negotiate—a counterproductive result, because settlements produced by negotiation are needed to keep the system running.

Statutes in about a dozen states contain a provision of great tactical significance in settlement negotiations. These statutes, with some variation, provide that a defendant may make a written offer to settle a claim for a certain amount (called an "offer of judgment"). If the plaintiff rejects this offer and then fails to obtain a more favorable judgment at trial, the plaintiff must pay all of the defendant's costs, including attorney fees, from the time of the offer. *See, e.g.,* N.Y. MCKINNEY'S CIV. PRAC. LAW § 3221; CAL. CODE CIV. PROC. § 998 (also applying, in a limited way, to plaintiffs' offers). What impact do such provisions have on settlement strategy? What goals are served by such laws?

The lawyers' obligations. Parties in personal injury litigation often negotiate a settlement without lawyers; the insurance adjuster pays the injured person an agreed sum and takes a release. Once the claim has reached lawyers on both sides, negotiation is still overwhelmingly likely and it usually produces settlement. The client has the ultimate authority to accept or reject settlement of a matter, and the lawyer is obligated to explain the ramifications of settlement offers with sufficient clarity to allow the client to reach such a decision. This is both an ethical and a legal obligation. RESTATEMENT OF THE LAW GOVERNING LAWYERS § 22 (2000); ABA MODEL RULES OF PROFESSIONAL CONDUCT 1.2(a) & 1.4.

Factors in settlement. Styles of negotiation differ a great deal, often embodying personal preferences of the lawyers, sometimes, too, embodying local traditions or practices. However, all negotiation in legitimate cases must proceed from the lawyers' estimates of what would happen if the case were tried. The lawyer can negotiate competently and effectively only when investigation is complete and when all legal points have been thoroughly researched and understood. For example, if the plaintiff's lawyer negotiates a settlement before the client has had a good medical examination, the client may wind up with a settlement that falls far short of compensating for real injuries that would have been revealed by the examination. The lawyer must estimate the evidence and its effect on the judge. (Is a directed verdict a distinct possibility?) It also requires the lawyer to estimate the effect of evidence on the jury. (Will the jury find for the defendant or bring in a low verdict even though the judge has refused to direct a verdict?) These estimates in turn can be made only when the lawyer has formed an opinion about the judge, the jury and the opposing counsel in the case.

None of these estimates can be made with certainty, and when they are finally made the lawyer may be able to say only that the case has a small probability of coming in at $1 million and a high probability of coming in at $100,000. Every variable in the case will have an impact on the final figure each side will be willing to settle for. If the plaintiff is an unattractive personality the case may settle for $90,000, whereas it would go for $100,000 if the plaintiff were an ordinary person. The same is true with counsel. If the plaintiff's counsel is a poor lawyer, or makes a bad impression on juries, or usually settles instead of trying a case, the defense lawyer will recommend a smaller settlement than if plaintiff's counsel is an excellent lawyer, effective with juries and quite willing to try cases that cannot be fairly settled. It is obviously impossible to detail every kind of fact that will go into deciding the value of a case, but it will not be an overemphasis to say that the lawyer's evaluation of both law and the rational import of the evidence are as critical as the lawyer's evaluation of personalities involved in the trial.

B. IMPROVIDENT SETTLEMENT

GLEASON v. GUZMAN

623 P.2d 378 (Colo. 1981)

QUINN, J.

On September 29, 1970, Darlene Benavidez, then a fourteen-year-old minor, was struck on the head by a vending machine that fell from a truck operated by Irwin Gleason in the course of his employment with Coin Fresh, Inc. (defendants). Darlene Benavidez has since married and is now known as Darlene Guzman (plaintiff). Immediately after the accident she was taken to Denver General Hospital for examination. She complained of headache, vomiting and some disorientation and, after two days of observation and testing, her injury was diagnosed as a left temporal lobe contusion and she was released as improved. On October 13, 1970, the plaintiff was readmitted to the hospital with complaints similar to those previously experienced. Further testing resulted in a diagnosis of left intratemporal lobe hematoma and the plaintiff was discharged as improved on October 20, 1970. Shortly thereafter plaintiff returned to high school and a normal routine. She and her parents, Mr. and Mrs. Benavidez, believed that plaintiff had fully recovered from the injury.

In November 1970 the plaintiff's parents retained an attorney in connection with their daughter's claim. Approximately two years later this attorney initiated settlement negotiations with the defendants' insurance carrier. It was mutually agreed that the case be settled for $6,114.35. The insurance carrier hired an attorney to prepare a petition for the probate court's approval of settlement and the appointment of the plaintiff's father, Mr. Benavidez, as guardian of his minor daughter's estate. The probate court approved the settlement and Mr. Benavidez, as duly appointed guardian, executed a general release of his daughter's claim against the defendant.

In May 1974, approximately forty-four months after the accident, the plaintiff experienced her first epileptic seizure during her senior year in high school. Other seizures followed. Having become emancipated through marriage, she retained her present attorneys and a complaint was filed in November 1975. The complaint sought money damages against the defendants for negligently causing personal injuries to the plaintiff in the accident of September 29, 1970. The defendants in their answer raised as an affirmative defense the release executed by the guardian and endorsed on their answer a demand for a jury trial. Thereafter, the defendants filed a motion for summary judgment on the basis of the guardian's release. The plaintiff countered with a motion to set aside the release on the ground that it was executed under a mistake as to the nature of the injury actually sustained. The court heard both motions in a consolidated hearing on November 14, 1977.

[The trial judge granted the defendant's motion for summary judgment and denied the plaintiff's motion to set aside the release. The court of appeals reversed the entry of summary judgment.]

The defendants urge two reasons why the court of appeals erred in reversing the trial court's entry of summary judgment. First, they argue that the mistake related to a future complication of a known injury, as distinct from a mistake about the nature of the injury actually suffered in the accident. Next, they contend that the release was a general release encompassing both known and unknown injuries and it thereby precluded rescission even for a mistake as to an unknown injury....

Cases addressing the problem of mistake in the settlement of personal injury claims reflect a tension stemming, on the one hand, from the general need for finality in the contractual settlements of actual or potential lawsuits and, on the other hand, from a recognized need to alleviate the distorting and unintended effects which human error can impose on a transaction. See, e.g., II G. Palmer, The Law of Restitution § 11.2,12.22 (1978); Dobbs, Conclusiveness of Personal Injury Settlements: Basic Problems, 41 N.C.L. Rev. 665 (1963). Although the approaches are not totally discrete, they do lean in different directions. One approach denies rescission even though the injuries were not known or suspected at the time of the settlement. Under this view the releasor assumes the risk that the nature and extent of known injuries might be more severe than was believed at settlement. Another approach allows rescission based on any mistake as to the condition of the injured claimant, whether the mistake relates to the nature of the injuries or to their further consequences. Midway between these approaches is the view that rescission is available for mistakes relating to the nature of known injuries but not for mistakes as to the future course and effects of those injuries. The assumption here is that rescission must be based on mistake, and mistake for legal purposes must relate to a past or present fact rather than an opinion or prophecy about the future.

This latter approach represents the rule in this jurisdiction. [In *McCarthy v. Eddings*] the plaintiff suffered a broken arm but, based on his doctor's representation, believed that the injury was temporary in duration and executed a release. Thereafter, he discovered that the broken bones in the arm had not united and the resulting disability was permanent. We affirmed the jury verdict for the plaintiff and held that a release obtained as the result of a mutual basic mistake could be set aside as ineffective.

The *McCarthy* rule was further refined in *Davis v. Flatiron Materials Co.*, 511 P.2d 28 (Colo. 1973), which upheld the validity of a release.... Noting that the injury was correctly diagnosed and that the plaintiff was fully informed about the nature of her condition, we held that to justify rescission the mistake "must relate to a present existing fact or a past fact," rather than as there present, a mistake concerning the future course of recovery from the known injury.

We again addressed this problem in *Scotton v. Landers*, 543 P.2d 64 (Colo. 1975), where the plaintiff, believing that he suffered a fractured rib and bruises in an automobile accident, executed a general release only to discover shortly thereafter that his spleen had been ruptured and had to be surgically removed. We concluded that the mistake was sufficient to avoid the release because it was grounded in the nature of injuries suffered in the accident.

As *McCarthy, Davis* and *Scotton* demonstrate, the distinction between unknown injuries and unknown consequences of known injuries is a useful analytic standard but it does not yield a litmus-type resolution to these problems. The words we use, "though they have a central core of meaning that is relatively fixed, are of doubtful application to a considerable number of marginal cases." Indeed, this is such a marginal case. With respect to post-traumatic epilepsy, the margin of difference between a mistake in diagnosis and a mistake in prognosis, or the difference between that condition as an injury and as a consequence, cannot easily be fitted into predetermined categories of exclusivity.

Judge Learned Hand pointed up the difficulty of conceptual differentiation in these matters:

"There is indeed no absolute line to be drawn between mistakes as to future, and as to present facts. To tell a layman who has been injured that he will be about again in a short time is to do more than prophesy about his recovery. No doubt it is a forecast, but it is ordinarily more than forecast; it is an assurance as to his present condition, and so understood."

Scheer v. Rockne Motors Corp., 68 F.2d 942 (2d Cir. 1934)....

Knowledge of the nature of an injury requires an awareness and some appreciation of its extent, severity and likely duration. Admittedly, line-drawing here is difficult and its direction may well vary with the thrust of evidence. These basic components of knowledge, however, relate primarily to a comprehension of the basic character of the injury as distinct from a prediction or opinion about the future course of recovery when its basic nature is otherwise known....

The record before us provides an adequate basis from which one may reasonably infer the existence of mistake in the execution of the release by the guardian. He had little formal education and was not adept or articulate in the English language. According to the deposition testimony of the attorney who originally represented the plaintiff, the most sophisticated concept used by the guardian in connection with the injury was "concussion."

As noted by the court of appeals, from the date of the accident through the settlement the plaintiff experienced only minor symptoms. It may reasonably be inferred that when the release was executed the guardian believed the injury was minor, that it posed no risk of complication, that it was temporary in duration, and that his daughter had fully recovered. There is no evidence that anyone, including physicians and the original attorney, disabused the guardian of these beliefs. In fact, the attorney's legal preparation and his settlement correspondence to the defendants' insurance carrier belie any awareness that the injury posed any risk of brain dysfunction, much less post-traumatic epilepsy. This attorney's belief that the plaintiff had fully recovered from her injury is clearly discernible in his representations to the probate judge at the settlement hearing....

When the record is examined in its entirety, it is apparent that there exists a genuine factual issue on whether the guardian was mistaken about the nature of his daughter's injury when he executed the release. Under these circumstances, summary judgment was inappropriate....

The defendants argue that the guardian's release constitutes a bar to the plaintiff's claim as a matter of law because its terms are all inclusive and encompass unknown injuries that may later develop or be discovered as well as their effects and consequences.

Although some jurisdictions give effect to the language of a release so as to preclude avoidance even as to unknown injuries, the tendency of the law is to the contrary. Most courts provide for avoidance in appropriate circumstances, such as mistake or lack of intent, despite the presence of language in the release broad enough to cover the claim in question....

Resolution of the intent issue necessarily means going behind the language of the release. If unknown injuries were not within the contemplation of the parties, the release will be set aside....

[Judgment of the Court of Appeals, reversing the trial court's judgment, is affirmed. Concurring and dissenting opinions are omitted.]

NOTES

1. Is it clear how you can apply the rule in *Gleason*? In *Nevue v. Close*, 867 P.2d 635 (Wash. 1994) the plaintiff thought she had a neck sprain and settled for $150, then discovered a back injury. The court said its rule was that "where there are known injuries, here the neck sprain, the release is binding as to those injuries and as to the unknown consequences of the known injury. However, as to an injury unknown to the plaintiff, and not within the contemplation of the parties to the release, the release should not be binding per se. The plaintiff should bear the burden of proving that the injury was reasonably unknown and not within the contemplation of the parties." This rule seems to be about the same as the rule in *Gleason*. Given that rule, how would the court decide the case?

2. In *Maglin v. Tschannerl*, 800 A.2d 486 (Vt. 2002), the court said: "[P]laintiff has to show, at the very least, that the mistake was mutual. But plaintiff showed only that *she* was mistaken as to her injuries. Without a mutual mistake of fact 'one of the parties can no more rescind the contract without the other's express or implied assent, than he alone could have made it.' " Does this mean releases could never be set aside? After all, the defendants' insurers intend to secure a release for both known and unknown injuries, and releases in fact usually so state. If the insurer knows that it doesn't know all the injuries and doesn't care, because it only wants to shed responsibility, how can you say it is mistaken? Conscious ignorance—an awareness that you do not know—may negate any idea that you are mistaken. *See* 2 DAN DOBBS, LAW OF REMEDIES § 11.2 (1993). On this analysis, perhaps no releases should be set aside for "mistake." Or do you think that the mistake rules used in ordinary commercial contract cases are inappropriate in injury release cases?

3. In *Bernstein v. Kapneck*, 430 A.2d 602 (Md. 1981), a child was injured in 1975 in a car crash. Doctors diagnosed her with a laceration on the forehead, fractured nasal bones, a broken shoulder and a "moderately severe traumatic neurosis." Her mother, on advice of counsel, accepted a settlement of $7,500 and signed a release that covered all claims for "bodily injuries, known and unknown, and which may have resulted or main the future develop." Much later the child developed epileptic symptoms diagnosed to have resulted from a brain injury sustained in the 1975 accident. The mother went to court to have the release set aside on the ground of mistake. The court said no. Where as here there was a "mutually intended release of unknown injuries then the nature and extent of the misfortune is beside the point."

4. If the release itself provides that the injured person assumes the risk of, or releases her claims for unknown injuries, should that prevent a recovery later if the plaintiff can show that she never had any intent to assume the risk? *See Smothers v. Richland Mem. Hosp.*, 493 S.E.2d 107 (S.C. 1997) (release bars claims for unknown injury); *Williams v. Glash*, 789 S.W.2d 261

(Tex. 1990) (intent governs but cannot be judged by the release language alone; the parties' knowledge and other factors would be considered); 2 DAN DOBBS, LAW OF REMEDIES § 11.9 (1993).

5. Consider what you would do as a lawyer to fulfill your special responsibility to ascertain the client's condition before advising a settlement.

6. Notice that if the release is set aside, the plaintiff must still prove her case. Suppose that the jury ultimately finds for the defendant. The defendant is out the money paid for the release and didn't get the peace that settlement was supposed to bring either. Would the alternative be to require the plaintiff to restore the consideration paid for the release as a prerequisite to a suit on the merits?

7. Fraud, coercion, and incapacity are also grounds for avoiding a release. Incapacity represents a serious problem if the injured person is approached for settlement in the hospital, or is under sedation. Some states have enacted statutes designed to provide safeguards. New York makes it unlawful to enter a hospital to negotiate a settlement or obtain a release in most instances. N.Y. JUD. LAW § 480 (McKinney 2005). Maryland provides that any personal injury release signed within five days of the injury is voidable for the next sixty days. MD. CODE ANN. CTS. & JUD. PROC. § 5–401.1.

ALFONE v. SARNO, 432 A.2d 857 (N.J. 1981). Concetta Alfone sued Dr. Sarno in 1968, alleging medical malpractice. She recovered a general verdict of $100,000. Thereafter she died and the present action was brought by her father as administrator of her estate, alleging that Sarno's malpractice had caused her death and seeking damages, including losses to Concetta's mother, himself and her daughter. The trial judge granted summary judgment for the defendant on the ground that the personal injury action barred any recovery. The intermediate court reversed. *Held*, the personal injury recovery does not necessarily bar a second recovery for death; remanded for further development of facts. In some respects death actions are derivative. Thus there can be no claim unless there was a tort to the decedent. However, once it is established that the defendant's act was tortious, the fact that there is some personal defense that would have barred the decedent's own claim is not necessarily a bar to the dependent's claims, which are partly independent. Here the prior judgment for Concetta would bar her, were she alive and suing, but it should not necessarily bar dependents who have losses from her death. However, certain issues may not be relitigated. If the defendant wins in the first action, no new action may be brought when death occurs. Likewise, determinations as to percentages of negligence will be binding. And plaintiff may not assert new theories. Where the first action is terminated by settlement, whether these issues can be litigated "may depend upon the terms of such settlement or release." In any event, it will be necessary in the death action to prove what elements of damages were recovered in the first suit or in the settlement to avoid duplication of damages, and to preclude all recoveries that could have been made in the first action.

NOTES

1. What exactly is the danger of duplicated damages? Recall the measures of damages awarded in death actions. Suppose Concetta had proved she was permanently injured and would never work again. Is there any way to know that the $100,000 awarded by the jury covered that item? If it did, would any substantial recovery in the wrongful death action duplicate the earlier award?

2. Suppose Concetta had not died, but had received an inadequate award or accepted an improvidently low settlement. If she could not attack the award or settlement, neither could her dependents. Why should they be better off when she has died? Or, alternatively, would you want to say that although the injured victim is bound by a release, her dependents are not?

3. In *Gershon v. Regency Diving Center, Inc.*, 845 A.2d 720 (N.J. Super. Ct. 2004), the decedent, before engaging in scuba training with the defendants, released them from all claims, including all claims by his "heirs" and family. The decedent died under water. In a wrongful death action, the court held that the release could not affect his family or heirs, who would instead be permitted to claim against the defendants in spite of the release. Doesn't a valid release in advance merely relieve the defendant of a duty or show that he has breached no duty? If so, how could the defendant be liable to anyone?

4. If you were an insurance attorney in New Jersey and you wanted to settle a routine injury case, what could you do to protect your client against a second suit? The problem might be the same even after trial of the injured person's claim. Is there anything you can do to bring this dispute to an end when the trial is over?

5. The traditional rule is that a settlement in the injured person's lifetime, or a judgment for either party, will bar the death action. *See Varelis v. Northwestern Mem. Hosp.*, 657 N.E.2d 997 (Ill. 1995). A few courts take the *Alfone* position, including the Supreme Court for one narrow band of admiralty cases based on judge-made law. *Sea–Land Serv. v. Gaudet*, 414 U.S. 573 (1974).

NOTE: CLIENTS' RIGHTS AGAINST THEIR OWN LAWYERS

1. *Scope of lawyer's authority.* The law and ethics rules pertaining to lawyers provides that it is the client's decision, not the lawyer's, whether and on what terms to settle a claim. *See* RESTATEMENT (THIRD) OF THE LAW GOVERNING LAWYERS § 22 (2000); ABA MODEL RULES OF PROFESSIONAL CONDUCT, Rule 1.2(a) (2008). The lawyer who fails fully to inform his client about acceptance of a settlement is subject to liability for malpractice. *Wood v. McGrath, North, Mullin & Kratz, P.C.*, 589 N.W.2d 103 (Neb. 1999).

2. *Negligently advising settlement.* If a lawyer advises a client to settle and the client executes a release and accepts (or gives up) money,

the court will likely not set aside the release even where the client later proves that the lawyer's advice was negligent. But if the client can prove that the lawyer's negligence caused a worse result than would have been obtained by competent counsel, many states allow a legal malpractice claim. The measure of damages in such a case is the dollar difference between what the negligent lawyer recommended and what a competent lawyer would have obtained. *See* PAUL T. HAYDEN, ETHICAL LAWYERING 73-75, 99 (2d Ed. 2007).

3. *Settling aggregate claims.* A special problem arises when a lawyer represents two or more clients in the same case. The rule here is that a lawyer cannot settle the claims aggregately without the informed written consent of each client. ABA MODEL RULE 1.8(g). Suppose a lawyer has ten clients with claims against various defendants but all the defendants are insured by the same liability insurance company. Try to imagine how a negotiation between the lawyer and the insurance company's lawyer might proceed and how a single client's interest might be hurt.

SUBCHAPTER B. SETTLEMENT AND TRIAL WITH MULTIPLE DEFENDANTS

§ 3. THE TRADITIONAL ALLOCATION OF RESPONSIBILITY AMONG MULTIPLE DEFENDANTS

NOTE: REVIEWING JOINT AND SEVERAL LIABILITY

We have already seen that several defendants might be held liable together, jointly and severally, so that the plaintiff might enforce a judgment entirely against any one of them. Recall that under the rule of joint and several liability, if one defendant pays more than his share, he could obtain contribution from the other tortfeasors. Recall also that the plaintiff could enforce her judgment in part against one and in part against another, but that in no event could she recover a total of more than the total amount of her judgment. Finally, recall that this system helps assure the plaintiff of compensation when one or more tortfeasors have insufficient funds to pay the judgment.

The rule of joint and several liability applies in four distinct situations.

(1) *Concerted action.* Joint and several liability applies to true joint torts, those in which A and B act in concert to commit an unlawful act. This includes intentional torts pursued jointly, as where A and B agree, tacitly or formally, to beat the plaintiff. It also includes intended law violations, as where A and B agree to race on the public highway and in the course of the race A collides with the plaintiff.

(2) *Indivisible injury.* The rule of joint and several liability applies in cases of concurrent torts where there is no concert or agreement, but where the acts of A and B produce a single indivisible injury. In one kind

of case in this category, A's act standing alone and B's act standing alone would have been sufficient to cause the same harm. In a distinct kind of case, A's act would not suffice to cause all of the harm done, but it is still impossible to determine how much of the harm was caused by A and how much by B.

(3) *A creates a risk of harm by B.* The rule of joint and several liability applies in part when A's negligence not only creates a harm to the plaintiff, but also creates a risk of further harm by reason of B's negligence. A negligently runs the plaintiff down and leaves him concussed and unconscious, but otherwise unharmed, in the street. B later negligently runs over and breaks the plaintiff's leg. Although B can only be held liable for the separate injury he caused, A is jointly and severally liable for the entire harm under the rules of "proximate cause, since he created a foreseeable risk of harm from B." Thus if B proved to be uninsured and insolvent, the plaintiff would be entitled to recover his entire damages from A. This is the import of the proximate cause rules. Similarly, if A does not directly harm the plaintiff but creates a risk that B will do so, joint and several liability is no doubt proper. For instance, in *Nallan v. Helmsley–Spear, Inc.*, 407 N.E.2d 451 (N.Y. 1980), a building owner failed to protect an invitee from a gunman. The building owner was held fully liable, not limited to its comparative share.

(4) *A defendant is vicariously liable.* An employer is liable for the torts of an employee committed in the scope of employment. The employee is also liable for his own torts. The result is that they are jointly and severally liable.

NOTE: REVIEWING CAUSAL APPORTIONMENT

Plaintiff drives to work and on her way is struck from behind by a car driven by A. Her neck is sore, but she goes on to work. On her way home in the evening she is struck by a car driven by B, aggravating her neck condition, which becomes serious. This looks very much like a case in which joint liability could be imposed upon A and B on the basis of the second rule, because a single indivisible injury has resulted. But none of the other grounds for joint liability appear sufficient. Now suppose that the plaintiff's neck is injured in the collision with A, but that the collision with B is not a rear end collision but a T-bone collision and that B's collision causes the plaintiff a broken arm without aggravating her neck condition at all. In this instance, the harms flow from two injuries, not one. Since the other grounds for joint liability are also lacking, A and B are severally liable for the injury each has produced, but not jointly liable at all.

Many cases of injury are not so clear. How can one be sure, for example, that the collision with B did not in fact aggravate the neck injury that occurred a few hours earlier? This kind of question presents serious problems of proof. Should the burden of proving that damages are divisible fall upon the party who seeks to avoid responsibility for the whole? *See* RESTATEMENT OF APPORTIONMENT § 26, cmt. *h.* (yes). In the case of the rear-end and the T-bone collision, what is the practical effect of this rule?

Recall that where causal apportionment is not feasible, comparative fault apportionment can be used instead, not only as between defendant A and defendant B but also as between a defendant and the plaintiff. *See Owens Corning Fiberglas Corp. v. Parrish,* 58 S.W.3d 467 (Ky. 2001).

NOTE: TRADITIONAL FORMS OF SETTLEMENT WITH ONE OF SEVERAL TORTFEASORS

And now for something completely different. Suppose that instead of getting a judgment against all tortfeasors, the plaintiff settles with one of them. Imagine that the plaintiff has damages of $200,000 and A offers to settle his share for $100,000. Can the plaintiff accept this settlement and then pursue B for the remainder?

1. *Plaintiff's claim is fully satisfied.* If the plaintiff sues A separately, and recovers a judgment that is then paid by A, he has no claim against B for the same indivisible injury, even if the written satisfaction stipulates that the claim against B is not released. *See Saichek v. Lupa,* 787 N.E.2d 827 (Ill. 2003). The reason lies in the rule that the plaintiff may recover full compensation only once. Her claim is said to be satisfied and extinguished because it is paid and she is compensated. The same kind of consideration governs settlements. If A has fully paid the plaintiff's claim in a settlement, the plaintiff has no just claim against B. But since a settlement may not always represent full payment, it is obviously more difficult for B to take advantage of this rule in such cases.

2. *Releases under common law rule.* A very different rule at common law was that release of one tortfeasor was a release of all those who were jointly and severally liable. This rule was independent of the rule about satisfaction of the claim. Thus if the plaintiff settled with A for $10,000, when his total damages were $100,000, he would not be barred by the satisfaction rule from a recovery against B. But if he gave a release to A upon payment of the settlement monies, he would then be barred from any recovery against B under the release rule. The idea was that a release extinguished the cause of action itself, so that there was no ground left on which to sue B.

3. *Covenants not to sue.* In the situation just described, settlement would be unlikely. The plaintiff would not give a release, since that would end his claim against B. A would not make a payment unless he could be assured by a release that he would not be held liable a second time. To effect a settlement in this situation, lawyers came up with a new kind of settlement document—a "covenant not to sue." This was not a release of the claim at all, but merely a contract or covenant by the plaintiff not to sue A and in fact to indemnify A if he were held liable. Thus if a plaintiff

wished to settle with one tortfeasor and still sue the other, this was the settlement paper he would use.

4. *Modern developments*. In some states, statutes or court decisions have changed all this. The UNIFORM CONTRIBUTION AMONG TORTFEASORS ACT (1955) § 4 provides expressly that a release of one tortfeasor "does not discharge any of the other tortfeasors from liability ... unless its terms so provide...." Lawyers effecting a settlement with one tortfeasor will obviously have to be alert to local law provisions, but in one way or another it is now practical to attain a settlement with fewer than all tortfeasors.

NOTE: CONTRIBUTION AND INDEMNITY

1. *Contribution. (a) General availability.* In Chapter 6 § 2, we saw that if one tortfeasor, A, paid more than his fair share of damages, he could recover contribution from the other tortfeasors to rectify their respective liabilities. The common law rule was opposed to contribution and contribution may still be denied among intentional tortfeasors. Otherwise, however, the states generally permit contribution when A pays more than his share of a judgment for the plaintiff.

(b) The common liability rule. The person claiming contribution must show that both tortfeasors were liable to the plaintiff. Thus if one defendant is immune from suit, for example, no contribution could be had from him. *See, e.g., Crotta v. Home Depot, Inc.*, 732 A.2d 767 (Conn. 1999) (intra-familial immunity); *Stencel Aero Engineering Corp. v. United States*, 431 U.S. 666 (1977) (governmental immunity).

(c) Payment in settlement. In some states A can obtain contribution from B only when A has paid a judgment for the plaintiff. That rule would deny contribution if A paid the plaintiff's claim in a settlement rather than by paying off a final judgment. Such an approach is now outdated. If A settles with P for full compensation, A is usually entitled to contribution from B.

(d) Traditional amount of contribution. The amount of the appropriate share to be paid in contribution may not be obvious. However, the traditional rule is quite clear: if there is a single indivisible injury caused by two tortfeasors, each should pay one-half. Thus if A pays the entire $200,000, B would be liable to make contribution to A of $100,000. This rule is known as the pro rata share rule. The leading article is Robert A. Leflar, *Contribution and Indemnity Between Tortfeasors*, 81 U. PA. L. REV. 130 (1932). *See generally* DOBBS ON TORTS § 386 (2000).

2. *Indemnity.* In a few situations, A may be technically liable to the plaintiff, but it may be that B is the only person really at fault. If A, because of a technical liability, pays the entire amount of the plaintiff's damages, A may recover, not merely a share from B, but the entire sum.

This is known, traditionally, as indemnity. Thus while contribution involves a sharing of liability between the tortfeasors, indemnity involves a shifting of that liability.

There are not many occasions for indemnity in this sense. The chief example involves the negligence of the employee for which the employer is vicariously liable. In such a case the employer has a right of indemnity against the negligent employee, though it is not a right often exercised in practice. There is also a right of indemnity in some products cases, as where the retailer is held strictly liable for a defective product supplied by the manufacturer: the retailer will be entitled to recover indemnity from the manufacturer.

§ 4. NEW FORMS OF APPORTIONMENT AMONG TORTFEASORS

AMERICAN MOTORCYCLE ASS'N v. SUPERIOR COURT, 578 P.2d 899 (Cal. 1978). Glen Gregos, a teen-aged boy, was seriously injured in a motorcycle race sponsored by American Motorcycle Association (AMA). He brings this action against AMA for negligence, and AMA seeks to bring in the parents on a claim that they were also negligent and should share in liability. AMA also argued that it should not be jointly and severally liable with the parents or any other tortfeasors, but should, after the adoption of comparative negligence, be held only for its own percentage share of negligence. *Held*: (1) Adoption of comparative negligence does not abolish joint and several liability. In some cases each defendant's act alone would be sufficient to cause the whole harm, and in others it is impossible to tell how much would have been caused by each defendant. It is no answer to limit such defendants' liability in proportion to their negligence when that negligence may have caused the entire harm. Joint and several liability continues to help guarantee adequate compensation in cases where individual tortfeasors may be unable to pay their share. (2) Although the state has a contribution statute limiting contribution to cases involving a joint judgment and in such cases providing for pro rata contribution, this is not intended to prevent judicial development of equitable sharing arrangements. In the past this has been done under the all-or-nothing concept of "indemnity" but that concept will now be adapted to permit tortfeasors to share liability in proportion to fault. Thus if a tortfeasor guilty of 10% of the fault is made to pay all of the plaintiff's damages, that tortfeasor will be entitled to "equitable indemnity" for the 90%.

Notes

1. **Effect of comparative negligence on joint and several liability.** In § 6 below, we'll consider how the facts in *American Motorcycle* might play out in a proportionate fault jurisdiction. For now, can we say that under the rule in *American Motorcycle,* the comparative negligence system does *not* do away with joint and several liability?

2. **Effect of comparative negligence on contribution.** Can we say that under the rule in *American Motorcycle,* the comparative negligence system *does* change the way contribution is calculated? Remember that before the adoption of comparative negligence, contribution among tortfeasors was usually based on equal ("pro rata") shares. If there were two tortfeasors each should pay one-half; if one paid the whole judgment for the plaintiff, that one would be entitled to recover one-half from the other. This did not apportion according to fault but according to the number of tortfeasors. Exactly how is that changed under the *American Motorcycle* rule?

3. **"Indemnity."** *American Motorcycle* speaks of "indemnity." The term indemnity does not track traditional usage because the claim looks like an ordinary contribution claim. Perhaps the courts used the indemnity terminology because contribution statute did not permit contribution based on settlement, as distinct from judgment.

4. **Fault apportionment.** With the advent of comparative fault, the all-or-nothing system was abandoned. Juries might apportion some responsibility to the plaintiff, some to A and some to B. If the plaintiff suffers an indivisible injury, then under *American Motorcycle* and the general rules of comparative fault, each party is ultimately responsible for a share of the losses proportioned to his fault.

SAFEWAY STORES, INC. v. NEST–KART

579 P.2d 441 (Cal. 1978)

TOBRINER, JUSTICE.

In January 1972, plaintiff Rita Elliot was injured in a Safeway supermarket when the shopping cart she was using broke and fell on her foot, causing serious injuries requiring surgery. Plaintiff brought suit against Safeway (the owner of the shopping cart who had made it available for customers' use), Nest–Kart, a division of Folding Carrier Corporation (the manufacturer of the cart), and Technibilt Corporation (a company that, on occasion, had repaired some of Safeway's shopping carts), alleging that the various defendants were liable for her injuries under both strict product liability and negligence principles; defendants, in response, claimed that the plaintiff's own negligence was a proximate cause of the accident. At trial, the jury absolved both plaintiff and Technibilt of any responsibility for the accident, and returned a verdict for plaintiff of $25,000 against both Safeway and Nest–Kart.

[The jury made "special findings," that Safeway was liable both on negligence and strict liability grounds and that Nest–Kart was liable solely on strict liability grounds. The jury found that the "comparative fault" was 80% for Safeway and 20% for Nest–Kart.]

Thereafter, the trial court entered a judgment of $25,000 in favor of plaintiff and against Safeway and Nest–Kart. After the judgment had initially been satisfied by Safeway and Nest–Kart on an 80 percent–20 percent basis, Safeway moved in the trial court for a judgment of contribution to require Nest–Kart to pay an additional 30 percent of the judgment to Safeway, so as to achieve an equal 50–50 apportionment between the two tortfeasors.... [T]he trial court granted Safeway's motion and ordered each defendant to bear 50 percent of the judgment. It is from this order that Nest–Kart appeals....

American Motorcycle has now explicitly held that, contrary to the trial court's conclusion, the existing contribution statutes do not in themselves necessarily prohibit apportionment of liability among multiple tortfeasors on a comparative fault basis.

The question remains, however, whether the comparative indemnity doctrine, recognized in *American Motorcycle* as a permissible basis for apportioning liability among multiple negligent tortfeasors, may also be applied to apportion liability when, as in the instant case, the liability of one or more defendants derives from principles of strict liability....

First, and most significantly, we believe that the basic equitable considerations that led our court to adopt a rule permitting comparative apportionment of liability among multiple tortfeasors apply equally in the instant setting....

Nothing in the rationale of strict product liability conflicts with a rule which apportions liability between a strictly liable defendant and other responsible tortfeasors. Although one of the principal social policies served by product liability doctrine is to assign liability to a party who possesses the ability to distribute losses over an appropriate segment of society (see Greenman v. Yuba Power Products, Inc....), this policy has never been viewed as so absolute as to require, or indeed as to permit negligent tortfeasors who have also contributed to the injury to escape all liability whatsoever....

It is sometimes suggested, however, that while apportionment between strictly liable and negligent defendants may be a desirable goal, we encounter a fundamental doctrinal obstacle to any such apportionment in that no logical basis can be found for comparing the relative "fault" of a negligent defendant with that of a defendant whose liability rests on the "no fault" concept of strict product liability.... As our recent decision in Daly v. General Motors Corp., supra, explains, however, the suggested difficulties are more theoretical than practical, and experience in other jurisdictions demonstrates that juries are fully competent to apply comparative fault principles between negligent and strictly liable defendants....

Finally, we note that a contrary conclusion, which confined the operation of the comparative indemnity doctrine to cases involving solely negligent defendants, would lead to bizarre, and indeed irrational, consequences. Thus, if we were to hold that the comparative indemnity doctrine could only be invoked by a negligent defendant but not a strictly liable defendant, a manufacturer who was actually negligent in producing a product could frequently be placed in a better position than a manufacturer who was free from negligence but who happened to produce a defective product, for the negligent manufacturer would be permitted to shift the bulk of liability to more negligent co-tortfeasors, while the strictly liable defendant would be denied the benefit of such apportionment. Because we can discern no policy considerations that demand or justify such a result, we hold that in a case such as the instant one, the comparative indemnity doctrine may be utilized to allocate liability between a negligent and a strictly liable defendant. . . .

[Concurring and dissenting opinions omitted.]

NOTES

1. **Apportioning contributory negligence and strict liability.** The principle that comparative fault can operate to reduce recovery from a person who is strictly liable is applied in *Safeway* on the contribution issue. If it is a valid principle there, then presumably it is equally valid to reduce the recovery of a faulty plaintiff under contributory negligence/comparative fault rules. *See Daly v. General Motors Corp.*, 575 P.2d 1162 (Cal. 1978).

2. **Apportioning tortfeasor fault and strict liability.** On its facts, *Safeway* operates to deny a negligent party any contribution from a non-negligent party who has paid its "comparative fault" share. But is this the legal significance of the case? Suppose Nest–Kart had paid the entire judgment in favor of the plaintiff and had sought contribution. Does the principle adopted in the case limit Nest–Kart's recovery from Safeway to 80%? If so, is this justified, given the fact that Nest–Kart is not shown to be guilty of any fault and Safeway is?

3. **Where one tortfeasor pays the full judgment.** The same problem may arise if Safeway had paid the entire sum and sought contribution (or "equitable indemnity"). Is it clear that the case would allow Safeway, though negligent, to recover 20% from Nest–Kart? This view was adopted in *Cartel Capital Corp. v. Fireco of New Jersey*, 410 A.2d 674 (N.J. 1980). Why not hold that as between a faulty and a non-faulty party, the burden should fall entirely upon the party guilty of fault?

4. **Apportionment methods.** Consider how apportionment of liability can be accomplished. We first saw a but-for cause kind of apportionment: where harm was divisible, each defendant was liable for the harm he caused, no more and no less. We have now seen the possibility of a fault-based apportionment (under comparative negligence rules), an equal shares apportionment (in contribution claims), and whatever kind of apportionment is accomplished in the *Safeway* case. What is it exactly that is being apportioned there? Is it possible to apportion something other than separable injuries or fault?

5. **Comparative causation.** A number of courts and some of the comparative fault statutes say that we must be apportioning responsibility by comparative causation. That is, we must be deciding the relative importance of two or more causes of the plaintiff's harm. *E.g., Duncan v. Cessna Aircraft Co.*, 665 S.W.2d 414 (Tex. 1984); Robert N. Strassfeld, *Causal Comparisons*, 60 FORDHAM L. REV. 913 (1992).

6. **Comparing causation by the leap of intuition.** Is it feasible to base apportionment on the relative importance of causation? One way to do this might be to make a rough or intuitive judgment. This sounds much like what the trier must do in deciding proximate cause issues. The trier might conclude, for example, that the defendant was negligent and also a but-for cause of harm, but that the defendant's causal connection was too insignificant to warrant liability. Could the trier go beyond that and decide that the causal significance of one cause should be rated at 20% and another at 80%? Remember that the trier should be excluding judgments about fault.

7. **Comparing causation by comparing causal potency.** Another way to rate the significance of two causes would be to estimate their respective capacities for harm. Suppose that the plaintiff suffers cancer as a result of exposure to two different products and that the two manufacturers are wholly without fault but are strictly liable. Valid epidemiological studies show that exposure to the first product increases the probability of cancer by .40 and that exposure to the second increases the probability of cancer by .80. Finally, suppose the combination of the two adds nothing to the risk. Could you apportion liability between the two manufacturers if the plaintiff's total recovery was $1,200,000? *See* Mario J. Rizzo & Frank S. Arnold, *Causal Apportionment in the Law of Torts: An Economic Theory*, 80 COLUM. L. REV. 1399 (1980). Notice that the apportionment formula suggested by this example is not based on "how much" harm was caused by each product in this particular case.

8. **Strassfeld's criticisms.** Professor Strassfeld criticizes all the approaches to comparative causation, including that suggested by the preceding paragraph. He thinks judgments about comparative causation are possible even though they are largely unquantifiable, but they can be "cumbersome, unpredictable and subjective." Consequently, he favors using causal apportionment only when comparing fault is not possible. See Strassfeld, *supra* Note 5. In the practical world of trials and settlements would it be better to use a rule of thumb, such as pro rata apportionment when comparative fault is impossible? Or go back to liability for fault with true comparative negligence apportionment?

9. **Restatement of Apportionment.** Recognizing that comparing negligence, intentional wrongdoing, and activities that warrant strict liability requires the trier to compare incommensurable qualities, the Restatement of Apportionment rejects the terms comparative negligence and comparative fault altogether in favor of comparative responsibility. *See* RESTATEMENT OF APPORTIONMENT § 8, cmt. *a*. Under this section, the trier considers various factors in assigning responsibility. "The nature of each person's risk-creating conduct includes such things as how unreasonable the conduct was under the circumstances, the extent to which the conduct failed to meet the applicable legal standard, the circumstances surrounding the conduct, each person's abilities and disabilities, and each person's awareness, intent, or indifference with respect to the risks." *Id.*, cmt. *c*.

Is this merely one way of saying the trier considers the *Carroll Towing* factors? If not, then does this approach invite the triers to exercise their biases? How can an appellate court review the sufficiency of evidence for any particular assignment of "responsibility?"

HYMOWITZ v. ELI LILLY & CO.

539 N.E.2d 1069 (N.Y. 1989)

WACHTLER, CHIEF JUDGE.

[In 1941, the Food and Drug Administration (FDA) approved marketing of a drug known generically as diethylstilbestrol or DES. Over the years the drug was marketed for use by pregnant women. One of its purposes was to prevent miscarriages. The drug was a generic drug, that is, not the patented property of any one company. New companies would market the drug, others would drop out. Some 300 companies in all sold the drug for varying lengths of time to varying numbers of consumers.

[Although the drug first appeared to be safe, it later appeared that female children of mothers who used the drug were at risk for vaginal cancers and terrible complications when they reached adult years. It was often impossible for mothers to know or recall the name of the manufacturer of a drug she had taken twenty years earlier. For this reason, a DES daughter might be unable to show which of the manufacturers produced the particular specimen ingested by her mother.

[The cases before the Court here are suits by DES daughters against one or more DES manufacturers. In the trial court, the defendants moved for summary judgment on the ground, among others, that the defendant which had produced the particular chemical ingested by the plaintiffs' mothers could not be identified. These motions were denied. The Appellate Division affirmed.]

The paradigm of alternative liability is found in the case of Summers v. Tice, (33 Cal.2d 80, 199 P.2d 1). In Summers, plaintiff and the two defendants were hunting, and defendants carried identical shotguns and ammunition. During the hunt, defendants shot simultaneously at the same bird, and plaintiff was struck by bird shot from one of the defendants' guns. The court held that where two defendants breach a duty to the plaintiff, but there is uncertainty regarding which one caused the injury, "the burden is upon each such actor to prove that he has not caused the harm" The central rationale for shifting the burden of proof in such a situation is that without this device both defendants will be silent, and plaintiff will not recover; with alternative liability, however, defendants will be forced to speak, and reveal the culpable party, or else be held jointly and severally liable themselves. Consequently, use of the alternative liability doctrine generally requires that the defendants have better access to information than does the plaintiff, and that all possible tortfeasors be before the court It is also recognized that alternative liability rests on the notion that where there is a small number of possible wrongdoers, all of whom breached a duty to the plaintiff, the likelihood that any one of them injured the plaintiff is relatively high, so that forcing them to exonerate themselves, or be held liable, is not unfair.

In DES cases, however, there is a great number of possible wrongdoers, who entered and left the market at different times, and some of whom no longer exist. Additionally, in DES cases many years elapse between the ingestion of the drug and injury. Consequently, DES defendants are not in any better position than are plaintiffs to identify the manufacturer of the DES ingested in any given case, nor is there any real prospect of having all the possible producers before the court. Finally, while it may be fair to employ alternative liability in cases involving only a small number of potential wrongdoers, that fairness disappears with the decreasing probability that any one of the defendants actually caused the injury. . . .

Nor does the theory of concerted action, in its pure form, supply a basis for recovery. This doctrine, seen in drag racing cases, provides for joint and several liability on the part of all defendants having an understanding, express or tacit, to participate in "a common plan or design to commit a tortious act" (Prosser and Keeton, Torts § 46, at 323 [5th ed.];) As . . . the present record reflects, drug companies were engaged in extensive parallel conduct in developing and marketing DES. There is nothing in the record, however, beyond this similar conduct to show any agreement, tacit or otherwise, to market DES for pregnancy use without taking proper steps to ensure the drug's safety. Parallel activity, without more, is insufficient to establish the agreement element necessary to maintain a concerted action claim. Thus this theory also fails in supporting an action by DES plaintiffs.

In short, extant common-law doctrines, unmodified, provide no relief for the DES plaintiff unable to identify the manufacturer of the drug that injured her. This is not a novel conclusion; in the last decade a number of courts in other jurisdictions also have concluded that present theories do not support a cause of action in DES cases. Some courts, upon reaching this conclusion, have declined to find any judicial remedy for the DES plaintiffs who cannot identify the particular manufacturer of the DES ingested by their mothers. Other courts, however, have found that some modification of existing doctrine is appropriate to allow for relief for those injured by DES of unknown manufacture.

We conclude that the present circumstances call for recognition of a realistic avenue of relief for plaintiffs injured by DES. . . .

Indeed, it would be inconsistent with the reasonable expectations of a modern society to say to these plaintiffs that because of the insidious nature of an injury that long remains dormant, and because so many manufacturers, each behind a curtain, contributed to the devastation, the cost of injury should be borne by the innocent and not the wrongdoers. This is particularly so where the Legislature consciously created these expectations by reviving hundreds of DES cases. Consequently, the ever-evolving dictates of justice and fairness, which are the heart of our common-law system, require formation of a remedy for injuries caused by DES.

We stress, however, that the DES situation is a singular case, with manufacturers acting in a parallel manner to produce an identical, generically marketed product, which causes injury many years later, and which has evoked a legislative response reviving previously barred actions. Given this unusual scenario, it is more appropriate that the loss be borne by those that produced the drug for use during pregnancy, rather than by those who were injured by the use, even where the precise manufacturer of the drug cannot be identified in a particular action. We turn then to the question of how to fairly and equitably apportion the loss occasioned by DES, in a case where the exact manufacturer of the drug that caused the injury is unknown. . . .

In Sindell v. Abbott Labs, [607 P.2d 924 (Cal. 1980)], the court synthesized the market share concept by modifying the Summers v. Tice alternative liability rationale in two ways. It first loosened the requirement that all possible wrongdoers be before the court, and instead made a "substantial share" sufficient. The court then held that each defendant who could not prove that it did not actually injure plaintiff would be liable according to that manufacturer's market share. The court's central justification for adopting this approach was its belief that limiting a defendant's liability to its market share will result, over the run of cases, in liability on the part of a defendant roughly equal to the injuries the defendant actually caused.

In the recent case of Brown v. Superior Ct., 44 Cal.3d 1049, 245 Cal.Rptr. 412, 751 P.2d 470, the California Supreme Court resolved some apparent ambiguity in Sindell v. Abbott Labs., and held that a manufacturer's liability is several only, and, in cases in which all manufacturers in the market are not joined for any reason, liability will still be limited to market share, resulting in a less than 100% recovery for a plaintiff. Finally, it is noteworthy that determining market shares under Sindell v. Abbott Labs. proved difficult and engendered years of litigation. After attempts at using smaller geographical units, it was eventually determined that the national market provided the most feasible and fair solution, and this national market information was compiled.

Four years after Sindell v. Abbott Labs., the Wisconsin Supreme Court followed with Collins v. Eli Lilly & Co., 116 Wis.2d 166, 342 N.W.2d 37. Deciding the identification issue without the benefit of the extensive California litigation over market shares, the Wisconsin court held that it was prevented from following Sindell due to "the practical difficulty of defining and proving market share" (id., at 189, 342 N.W.2d, at 48). Instead of focusing on tying liability closely to the odds of actual causation, as the Sindell court attempted, the Collins court took a broader perspective, and held that each defendant is liable in proportion to the amount of risk it created that the plaintiff would be injured by DES.

Under the Collins structure, the "risk" each defendant is liable for is a question of fact in each case, with market shares being relevant to this determination (id., at 191, 200, 342 N.W.2d 37). Defendants are allowed, however, to exculpate themselves by showing that their product could not have caused the injury to the particular plaintiff (id., at 198, 342 N.W.2d 37).

The Washington Supreme Court, writing soon after Collins v. Lilly & Co., took yet another approach (see Martin v. Abbott Labs., 102 Wash.2d 581, 689 P.2d 368). . . .

Under the Washington scheme, defendants are first allowed to exculpate themselves by proving by the preponderance of the evidence that they were not the manufacturer of the DES that injured plaintiff. Unexculpated defendants are presumed to have equal market shares, totaling 100%. Each defendant then has the opportunity to rebut this presumption by showing that its actual market share was less than presumed. If any defendants succeed in rebutting this presumption, the liability shares of the remaining defendants who could not prove their actual market share are inflated, so that the plaintiff received a 100% recovery (id., at 605–606, 689 P.2d 368).[7] The market shares of defendants is a question of fact in each case, and the relevant market can be a particular pharmacy, or county, or State, or even the country, depending upon the circumstances the case presents (George v. Parke–Davis, 107 Wash.2d 584, 733 P.2d 507).

[W]e are led to the conclusion that a market share theory, based upon a national market, provides the best solution. As California discovered, the reliable determination of any market smaller than the national one likely is not practicable. Moreover, even if it were possible, of the hundreds of cases in the New York courts, without a doubt there are many in which the DES that allegedly caused injury was ingested in another State. Among the thorny issues this could present, perhaps the most daunting is the spectre that the particular case could require the establishment of a separate market share matrix. We feel that this is an unfair, and perhaps impossible burden to routinely place upon the litigants in individual cases.

Nor do we believe that the Wisconsin approach of assessing the "risk" each defendant caused a particular plaintiff, to be litigated anew as a question of fact in each case, is the best solution for this State. Applied on a limited scale this theory may be feasible, and certainly is the most

---

7. The actual operation of this theory proved more mathematically complex when the court was presented with the question of what to do about unavailable defendants. Recognizing that the possibility of abuse existed when defendants implead unavailable defendants, who would then be assumed to have had an equal share of the market, the court placed the burden upon appearing defendants to prove the market share of the absent ones (George v. Parke–Davis, 107 Wash.2d 584, 733 P.2d 507). If this can be proved, the plaintiff simply cannot recover the amount attributable to the absent defendant, and thus recovery in the case is less than 100%. If the market share of the absent defendant cannot be shown, the remaining defendants who cannot prove their market shares have their shares inflated to provide plaintiff with full recovery. Finally, if all appearing defendants can prove their market shares, their shares are never inflated, regardless of whether the market share of a nonappearing defendant can be proved or not; thus, in this situation, the plaintiff again will not recover her full damages (id.).

refined approach by allowing a more thorough consideration of how each defendant's actions threatened the plaintiff. We are wary, however, of setting loose, for application in the hundreds of cases pending in this State, a theory which requires the fact finder's individualized and open-ended assessment of the relative liabilities of scores of defendants in every case. Instead, it is our perception that the injustices arising from delayed recoveries and inconsistent results which this theory may produce in this State outweigh arguments calling for its adoption.

Consequently, for essentially practical reasons, we adopt a market share theory using a national market. We are aware that the adoption of a national market will likely result in a disproportion between the liability of individual manufacturers and the actual injuries each manufacturer caused in this State. Thus our market share theory cannot be founded upon the belief that, over the run of cases, liability will approximate causation in this State. Nor does the use of a national market provide a reasonable link between liability and the risk created by a defendant to a particular plaintiff. Instead, we choose to apportion liability so as to correspond to the over-all culpability of each defendant, measured by the amount of risk of injury each defendant created to the public-at-large. Use of a national market is a fair method, we believe, of apportioning defendants' liabilities according to their total culpability in marketing DES for use during pregnancy. Under the circumstances, this is an equitable way to provide plaintiffs with the relief they deserve, while also rationally distributing the responsibility for plaintiffs' injuries among defendants.

To be sure, a defendant cannot be held liable if it did not participate in the marketing of DES for pregnancy use; if a DES producer satisfies its burden of proof of showing that it was not a member of the market of DES sold for pregnancy use, disallowing exculpation would be unfair and unjust. Nevertheless, because liability here is based on the over-all risk produced, and not causation in a single case, there should be no exculpation of a defendant who, although a member of the market producing DES for pregnancy use, appears not to have caused a particular plaintiff's injury. It is merely a windfall for a producer to escape liability solely because it manufactured a more identifiable pill, or sold only to certain drugstores. These fortuities in no way diminish the culpability of a defendant for marketing the product, which is the basis of liability here.

Finally, we hold that the liability of DES producers is several only, and should not be inflated when all participants in the market are not before the court in a particular case. We understand that, as a practical matter, this will prevent some plaintiffs from recovering 100% of their damages. However, we eschewed exculpation to prevent the fortuitous avoidance of liability, and thus, equitably, we decline to unleash the same forces to increase a defendant's liability beyond its fair share of responsibility.

[The court also upheld the constitutionality of the statutory renewal of causes of action theretofore barred by the statute of limitations.]

MOLLEN, JUDGE [concurring in part and dissenting in part].

. . . I respectfully disagree with the majority's conclusion that there should be no exculpation of those defendants who produced and marketed DES for pregnancy purposes, but who can prove, by a preponderance of the evidence, that they did not produce or market the particular pill ingested by the plaintiff's mother. Moreover, in order to ensure that these plaintiffs receive full recovery of their damages, as they are properly entitled to by any fair standard, I would retain the principle of imposing joint and several liability upon those defendants which cannot exculpate themselves. . . .

NOTES

1. **The *Sindell* adoption of market-share.** Market-share apportionment is one of those rules that has a specific beginning point. Building on the suggestion of a law review writer, Comment, *DES and a Proposed Theory of Enterprise Liability*, 46 FORDHAM L. REV. 963 (1978), the California Supreme Court initiated market-share liability in *Sindell v. Abbott Laboratories*, 607 P.2d 924 (Cal. 1980).

2. **Several, not joint liability.** The idea was so new that the California Court itself may initially have had some kind of idea that it involved joint and several liability. The California Court later made it clear that the market-share idea is not one of joint and several liability. It is several liability apportioned according to the defendant's relative share of the market in the drug that caused injury. Thus it is not (a) liability apportioned according to fault; (b) it is not liability apportioned on the basis of relative causation; and (c) it is not joint and several liability. *See Brown v. Superior Court*, 751 P.2d 470 (Cal. 1988).

3. **Market-share and probabilistic causation.** Is market-share similar to the idea we first saw in *Lord v. Lovett* in Chapter 7? That case and some others have seemingly approved a recovery for the lost *chance* of good health, even if that chance was not a very large one; and, correspondingly, such cases seem to contemplate that damages would be proportional to the chance, which would be only a fraction of the damage caused by the injury itself. Professor Farber has described "proportional" recovery as one that "spreads compensation over all possible victims, fully compensating no one but paying something even on the weakest claim." Daniel A. Farber, *Toxic Causation*, 71 MINN. L. REV. 1219 (1987). Notice, however, that the market-share solution addresses only the defendants' causal responsibility for *exposure* to the drug. The connection between exposure and subsequent injury remains an issue of fact.

4. **Acceptance of market-share theories.** Several courts have accepted the central thrust of the market-share idea but have modified some details. *See, e.g., Smith v. Cutter Biological, Inc.*, 823 P.2d 717 (Haw. 1991). *Cf. Thomas v. Mallett*, 701 N.W.2d 523 (Wis. 2005) (allowing "risk-contribution theory" against lead carbonate manufacturers, without deciding how damages might be apportioned among liable manufacturers). But several states have expressly rejected the market-share approach. Illinois, for instance, rejected market-share on the ground that the plaintiff's burden of proving causation

was a fundamental principle of tort law. *Smith v. Eli Lilly & Co.*, 560 N.E.2d 324 (Ill. 1990). Ohio took a similar line in *Sutowski v. Eli Lilly & Co.,* 696 N.E.2d 187 (Ohio 1998). Rhode Island rejected the whole thing in two conclusory sentences, without giving a single reason pro or con. *Gorman v. Abbott Labs.*, 599 A.2d 1364 (R.I. 1991). Missouri rejected the theory as applied to a lead-paint case in *City of St. Louis v. Benjamin Moore & Co.*, 226 S.W.3d 110 (Mo. 2007), saying even if the plaintiff could prove "that a particular defendant held a certain share of the lead paint market in the city at the relevant time or even if it could prove that because of defendant's market share there was a statistical probability that its paint was in a certain percentage of the properties at issue, that would not establish that the particular defendant actually caused the problem."

5. **Alternative causation.** Michigan rejected market share in favor of a *Summers v. Tice* approach; but then it hampered practical use of that approach by requiring the plaintiff to bring in all the actors and to prove negligence rather than strict liability. *Abel v. Eli Lilly & Co.*, 343 N.W.2d 164 (Mich. 1984).

6. **Concert of action, enterprise liability.** A theory often raised in these cases but almost never accepted is that all of the manufacturers should be held jointly and severally liable because they acted in concert. The conscious parallel actions in the way they produced or warned of the product might be interpreted as an implicit agreement, just as two drag racers who take off together from a stop light might be regarded as having agreed to race even if no one spoke a word. The concert of action theory appeals to the oldest form of joint and several liability, and it works in the drag racing case. But in the products liability cases it has not been accepted on the basis of parallel business practices alone. A variation on the idea of concerted action is sometimes called "enterprise liability." It is based on common adherence to an industry-wide standard, which only seems to be a different form of proof. Most decisions have refused to apply these theories to products liability cases.

Two unusual cases that found enough on the particular facts to justify potential liability on an "enterprise liability" or concerted action theory are *Hall v. E.I. DuPont de Nemours & Co.*, 345 F.Supp. 353 (E.D.N.Y. 1972) (six manufacturers produced all the dynamite caps, none labeled, followed practices of trade association) and *Nicolet, Inc. v. Nutt*, 525 A.2d 146 (Del. 1987) (actual conspiracy to fraudulently conceal dangers of asbestos alleged).

7. **Cases for excluding market-share liability?** Should market-share liability, if appropriate in DES cases, be used in any of the following: (a) The strict liability claim is not based on the claim of a design defect but only a manufacturing flaw. (b) The defendant's product is one of many using the dangerous substance, but the various products use the substance in different amounts. For example, shipyard workers were once exposed heavily to asbestos in working around insulating materials but they might also be exposed if they had used hair dryers in the same period of time. (c) Only a small number of people are exposed to the dangerous substance in quantities that create a risk of harm.

8. **Blood products.** People whose blood does not readily coagulate (hemophiliacs) sometimes need a blood protein called a "factor" in order to

control bleeding. The factor is derived from donated blood and can carry the AIDS virus or HIV. Plaintiff has tested positive for AIDS. The virus was apparently communicated through the Factor VIII administered to the plaintiff. It was produced by one of several manufacturers, but no one can say which one. The blood shield law provided against liability except that each entity "shall remain liable for . . . its own negligence or wilful misconduct." Does "its own negligence" mean that no entity supplying blood can be liable on market-share theories? In any event, notice that the blood factor provided is not uniform, because not all units will contain HIV. Should the producers nevertheless be held on a market share theory? *Smith v. Cutter Biological, Inc.*, 823 P.2d 717 (Haw. 1991).

9. **Useful drugs.** When a plaintiff attempted to apply market-share theories to an injury from a childhood vaccine (DPT), the New Jersey Court drew back. Although the court did not reject market-share generally, it did reject that theory as applied to the vaccine involved. Because the vaccine was "essential to public welfare," and because some manufacturers had withdrawn from the market due to threats of products liability, the court feared market-share liability would either diminish manufacture of the drug or diminish safety research. It might also prevent development of other important drugs, such as a vaccine against AIDS. In addition, the court was persuaded that the right of vaccine-injured plaintiffs to recover compensation under the National Childhood Vaccine Injury Act provided an adequate, non-tort remedy. *Shackil v. Lederle Labs.*, 561 A.2d 511 (N.J. 1989). The Vaccine Injury Act creates a fund for payment of specified vaccine injuries by levying a tax on the vaccines. The fund is then liable for individual injuries covered by the statute. Doesn't this work out to be a form of market-share liability?

10. **Questions for evaluation.** If market-share liability works in practice as its theory predicts, would it impose any liabilities greater than the liability that would be imposed if we knew all the facts about causation? If the concern is that liability may drive manufacturers from the market or from desirable research, is that concern limited to market-share claims, or does it apply to *any* liability? And why do we ordinarily argue that liability will encourage more safety research but think that it would prevent such research in the drug or vaccine case? These or similar ideas are discussed by Justice O'Hern in his dissent in *Shackil, supra* Note 9. Is it possible to think of the *Shackil* rule as an exemption from liability which amounts to a subsidy paid by the injured persons?

§ 5. MULTIPLE DEFENDANTS: SETTLEMENT AND SUIT IN A JOINT AND SEVERAL LIABILITY SYSTEM

PROBLEM

Perkins v. Alter and Bain

Alter and Bain, each driving a vehicle, collided when Alter made a left turn and Bain, who was attempting to pass, drove into the left front of the Alter car. This collision caused both drivers to lose control and the two cars went off the highway. One or both struck Perkins, who was seriously injured. You represent Bain, having been hired by her liability insurance company for this purpose. Perkins has brought an action against your client and Alter, claiming joint and several liability. Investigation and discovery are complete. You estimate that Perkins will recover against both Alter and Bain, though each defendant contends the other was guilty of the only causal negligence. You also estimate that Perkins will recover a sum between $100,000 and $150,000, but you believe it will be closer to the low end of that estimate. At the same time, you recognize there is some chance that the jury would return a very large verdict, in excess of $200,000. Perkins has made some settlement overtures and you believe you could reach a settlement with his attorney for about $100,000. Your company would be willing to pay $50,000 if Alter's is willing to pay the other half. Alter's attorney, however, has been adamant. She believes that Alter was not at fault and further believes that liability would not exceed about $50,000 in any event. The liability insurer for Alter, according to his attorney, would be willing to contribute no more than $10,000 to a settlement. Perkins' attorney has made it clear that there is no point in discussing any offers of less than $100,000.

Consider whether you want to recommend to Bain's insurer that it pay $100,000 in settlement. What issues will you need to research? What document would you use? Assume that a joint judgment is not required and that contribution is available to a tortfeasor who settles the plaintiff's claim in full and who has paid more than his share of common liability.

NOTE

"A settling defendant is barred from seeking contribution against another defendant unless the settling defendant has discharged the liability of that defendant." *Fetick v. American Cyanamid Co.,* 38 S.W.3d 415 (Mo. 2001).

PROBLEM

Parrott v. Amlyn and Bumgartner

Parrott was injured severely when Amlyn, driving a car rented to him by Bumgartner, ran over him in a crosswalk. Parrott alleged that Amlyn was intoxicated, driving at a high speed and not keeping a proper lookout. He alleged that Bumgartner knew or should have known of Amlyn's intoxication and should not have rented a car to him under those circumstances; and that, in addition, the brakes on the car supplied were wholly inadequate. Parrott joined both and claimed against them jointly and severally.

Parrott's injuries were quite serious and permanent. Bumgartner took the position that if Amlyn was intoxicated, his servants neither knew nor had reason to know it, and also disputed the evidence that the brakes were defective. In any event, Bumgartner has said in negotiations that it is unlikely that better brakes could have made anything different if Amlyn was as drunk as Parrott claimed. Bumgartner has refused to pay more than a modest sum in settlement, and Parrott has refused to accept this offer.

Amlyn, through his liability insurer and lawyer, has taken a different position. Amlyn believes damages may well exceed $500,000. Amlyn's liability insurance policy is for only $300,000. The insurer, following recommendations by the attorney it retained on Amlyn's behalf, has told Parrott they are interested in settling at the policy limit if it can be worked out. Parrott is willing to settle for this sum if he can pursue his claim against Bumgartner, since he believes Bumgartner will be found liable.

If you represent Amlyn at this stage, do you settle or not? What documents would you propose? What concerns must you deal with and reveal to your client and to the liability insurer? After you have made some preliminary notes about the problems you foresee, consult the materials that follow.

NOTES

1. As counsel for Amlyn, would you consider the possibility that Bumgartner might be held liable for a large sum of money, say, $900,000? If that happened, what would Bumgartner then consider doing?

2. Some states, once said to be a majority, have indicated that if A settles with the plaintiff, B may still have contribution from A if B later settles for a greater sum or is forced to pay a larger judgment. *See Skaja v. Andrews Hotel Co.*, 161 N.W.2d 657 (Minn. 1968).

3. If the Minnesota rule is followed in your jurisdiction, would you advise Amlyn to settle?

4. Both your client and the plaintiff want to settle, and the sum is agreed upon. The only difficulty is your client's potential liability for contribution to Bumgartner if Parrott recovers a large judgment against him. Your client, is unwilling to settle so long as that potential exists. Can you draft some form of settlement that will protect Amlyn from potential contribution claims by Bumgartner? Assume that your jurisdiction follows the common law pro rata rule of contribution and that you expect Parrott to get a judgment from Bumgartner of any amount up to $900,000. Your insurer will pay and Parrott will accept $300,000. What agreement can you devise to protect Amlyn from contribution if this scenario is played out?

5. If you can't devise an agreement that suits you, research will reveal helpful cases like *Pierringer v. Hoger*, 124 N.W.2d 106 (Wis. 1963), where the parties had similar problems. In that case plaintiff settled with A, accepting payment of settlement sums and giving an agreement that the plaintiff would reduce his claim against B to B's proportionate liability, whatever that turned out to be. In addition the plaintiff agreed to guarantee that if for any reason B was allowed contribution against A, the plaintiff would indemnify A to that extent.

6. Is it clear how this protects Amlyn? Suppose Amlyn pays $300,000 in settlement and Parrott proceeds with the claim against Bumgartner. In that action the jury finds the total damages were $900,000. If the plaintiff is not permitted to recover more than his total loss, his judgment against Bumgartner must be reduced to $600,000, since $300,000 has already been paid. But even so, this would leave Bumgartner paying twice as much as Amlyn, clearly

more than his pro rata share. He might be permitted, then, under the rule in states permitting contribution against a settling tortfeasor, contribution from Amlyn in the sum of $150,000. This would equalize the payments of the two tortfeasors at $450,000 each, but it would deprive Amlyn of the benefit of the settlement. However, under the *Pierringer* type agreement (Note 5, *supra*), Amlyn could then claim indemnity from Parrott and thus recoup the $150,000 and have the benefit of his settlement agreement. There is a simpler way to achieve all this, isn't there? The plaintiff simply reduces his judgment against Bumgartner to achieve this equalization. Bumgartner then has no claim for contribution because he will not have paid more than his share. And plaintiff will not be forced to pay indemnity since Amlyn will not have paid contribution. The same principle can be applied under a comparative fault apportionment rule.

CAL. CODE CIV. PROC. § 877

Where a release, dismissal with or without prejudice, or a covenant not to sue or not to enforce judgment is given in good faith before verdict or judgment to one or more of a number of tortfeasors claimed to be liable for the same tort . . . it shall have the following effect:

(a) It shall not discharge any other such party from liability unless its terms so provide, but it shall reduce the claims against the others in the amount stipulated by the release, the dismissal or the covenant, or in the amount of the consideration paid for it whichever is the greater.

(b) It shall discharge the party to whom it is given from all liability for any contribution to any other parties. . . .

CARDIO SYSTEMS, INC. v. SUPERIOR COURT, 176 Cal. Rptr. 254 (Ct. App. 1981). Manoocher Kafai died in the defendant Hospital while he was undergoing open heart surgery, apparently because a hospital employee connected a heart-lung machine incorrectly and caused air to reach his heart. The machine arguably should have been designed to prevent such a misconnection. It was manufactured by CINCO and distributed by Cardio. Kafai's survivors sued Hospital, Cardio and others. Plaintiff's trial counsel concluded that the presence of Cardio would only complicate a case of clear liability against the hospital, although he also believed he had a good tort claim against Cardio. As a matter of tactics he agreed to settle with Cardio in exchange for Cardio's waiver of any claim for costs. After this settlement, the plaintiffs accepted a settlement with Hospital for $1 million. Hospital now seeks contribution from Cardio. *Held*, the settlement with Cardio was in good faith and Cardio is thus protected under § 877, which applies to equitable indemnity claims under *American Motorcycle* as well as to contribution claims.

NOTES

1. **Good faith settlement.** *Cardio* and similar decisions on "good faith" were disapproved by name in *Tech–Bilt, Inc. v. Woodward–Clyde & Associate*, 698 P.2d 159 (Cal. 1985). The court held that the statutory good faith rule required a judicial review of the settlement to assure that appropriate settlements would be encouraged and that one defendant would not be held for an unfair share of the costs. The court appeared to think that a settlement like that in *Cardio* was, as a matter of law, not a good faith settlement. Yet, as some courts have recognized, it is hard to know what counts as good faith or bad faith under the statute, which does not define the term. *See Johnson v. United Airlines*, 784 N.E.2d 812 (Ill. 2003). What costs and benefits are added by a court hearing on the good faith issue?

2. **Applying the rule.** In *Baker v. ACandS*, 755 A.2d 664 (Pa. 2000), an asbestos cancer case, three defendants settled with the plaintiff, taking a release that specified a pro rata credit. The fourth defendant, the trust for bankrupt Manville, settled for a relatively small amount, $30,000, taking a release that specified a pro tanto credit. The fifth defendant went to trial. The judge as trier found that the defendants were jointly and severally liable and that each defendant's share of the $2,200,000 damages was $440,000. Under provisions similar to California's, what must the fifth defendant pay?

3. **Secret settlements.** At times a plaintiff might want to settle with one defendant while pursuing others in court, but keep the fact of settlement secret from the court and from the other defendants. In a so-called "Mary Carter agreement," the settling defendant actually agrees to continue as an active party in court while working to assist the plaintiff's case; in return, the settling defendant's maximum liability is diminished proportionately by increasing the liability of the non-settling defendants. Such agreements are disallowed flatly by some courts. *See, e.g., Dosdourian v. Carsten*, 624 So.2d 241 (Fla. 1993). Another kind of secret settlement is a "high-low agreement," in which the parties agree to a minimum and maximum amount of a settlement, depending on what verdict is obtained at trial. For example, a defendant might agree to pay $100,000 if the jury verdict is for $250,000 or less, and $1 million if the jury verdict is above $250,000. Do you see anything wrong with a high-low agreement? Should the judge be informed of it before the jury begins deliberations? *See Monti v. Wenkert*, 947 A.2d 261 (Conn. 2008).

CARTEL CAPITAL CORP. v. FIRECO OF NEW JERSEY

410 A.2d 674 (N.J. 1980)

SCHREIBER, J.

[Plaintiff, Country Burger, operated a place of business equipped with a fire extinguishing system manufactured by Ansul. Fireco distributed and serviced the equipment. A fire occurred, perhaps partly because of grease buildup and the stacking of paper plates near the grill. The fire equipment failed, and as a result the fire did considerable damage. Fireco was found to be negligent and Ansul's equipment was found to be defective. The "fault" was allocated by the jury as follows: Country Burger, 41%, Ansul, 29% and Fireco, 30%. The total damages were found to be $113,400. However, Ansul had settled with the plaintiff for $50,000. Plaintiff's claim against Ansul, and Fireco's cross claim for contribution or indemnity, were dismissed. Both plaintiff and Fireco appealed. The court first held that the plaintiff's conduct in creating risks of fire was not to be considered at all, since it did not constitute an unreasonable and voluntary exposure to a known risk. It then turned to Fireco's contribution claim against Ansul.]

We have previously held that the Contribution Law does not require that joint tortfeasors be liable on the same theory of recovery, so that a defendant whose responsibility arises out of strict liability and another defendant whose responsibility is due to negligence may be joint tortfeasors under that law. . . .

As indicated previously a joint tortfeasor's recovery is limited under the Contribution Law to any excess paid over "his pro rata share." N.J.S.A. 2A:53A–3. In this respect it is important to note the effect on the Joint Tortfeasors Contribution Law of the Comparative Negligence Act, N.J.S.A. 2A:15–5.1 et seq. Under the act the percentage of each party's fault must be found and "[a]ny party who is so compelled to pay more than such party's percentage share may seek contribution from the other joint tortfeasors." N.J.S.A. 2A:15–5.3.[7] Thus the Legislature has seen fit to redefine the "pro rata" allocation to be a party's "percentage share" in the contribution scheme between and among joint tortfeasors. . . .

Under the joint tortfeasors law we had held that a settlement with a joint tortfeasor, even though for less than a pro rata share of the total claim, reduced the plaintiff's total claim against the nonsettling codefendant or codefendants by the pro rata share and thus barred contribution from the settling tortfeasor. Theobald v. Angelos, 44 N.J. 228, 208 A.2d 129 (1965). Now the effect on the plaintiff of a joint tortfeasor's settlement will depend upon the percentage of fault found against him. When one defendant settles, the remaining codefendant or codefendants are chargeable with the total verdict less that attributable to the settling defendant's percentage share. . . .

Applying the foregoing principles, we find that the total relevant fault is that of Ansul and Fireco, there being no contributory negligence as a matter of law. Ansul's 29% and Fireco's 30%, or 59%, constitute the total fault in the case. In a sense, the 59% is 100%. Thus, Fireco's responsibility is 30/59ths or 50.8% and Ansul's is 29/59ths or 49.2%. It follows that Fireco's proportionate share of the entire damages of $113,400 is $57,661.01 and Ansul's proportionate share is $55,738.99. Ansul, however, had settled its obligation to the plaintiff for $50,000. Fireco remains liable for its share, namely $57,661.01.

---

7. We have previously held that the Comparative Negligence Act pertains to fault emanating from strict product liability. Suter v. San Angelo Foundry & Machine Co., 406 A.2d 140.

NOTES

1. **Solving the contribution problem.** Accord, that the judgment against a tortfeasor who goes to trial is reduced by the comparative fault share attributable to the settling tortfeasor, RESTATEMENT OF APPORTIONMENT § 16. Does this solution resolve all the problems? The non-settling tortfeasor would never need to seek contribution from the settling tortfeasor, since it would be liable only for its relative fault share.

2. **Solving the *Cardio*/good faith problem.** Are there any other advantages to New Jersey's solution? If California applied this rule, would the plaintiff have risked a settlement with *Cardio Systems* in that case? If not, is that a problem, since the plaintiff did not want to complicate the trial with the *Cardio Systems* defendants?

3. **Potential windfalls.** In *Duncan v. Cessna Aircraft Co.*, 665 S.W.2d 414 (Tex. 1984), a products liability case, the Texas Court had this to say against the pro tanto or "dollar credit" rule:

> A dollar credit reduces the liability of non-settling defendants, pro tanto, by the dollar amount of any settlement. The defendant's liability may thus fluctuate depending on the amount of a settlement to which he was not a party. This fluctuation cannot be reconciled with the policy of apportioning liability in relation to each party's responsibility, the conceptual basis of comparative causation. A dollar credit also encourages collusion by shielding plaintiffs from the effect of bad settlements while denying them the benefit of good settlements.

The court accordingly adopted what it called a "percent credit" under which the settlement with A reduces B's liability by A's percentage share of causal responsibility. If A's percentage share was only 10%, but A paid 50% of the plaintiff's damages, the plaintiff could still recover 90% of his damages from B. The plaintiff in such a case would obtain a 140% recovery, but the Texas Court thought the plaintiff was entitled to the advantage of a good settlement if he was going to be held to the disadvantages of a bad one.

4. **Windfalls and accountability.** Conceivably, the policy of accountability for fault would require use of a comparative fault or comparative causation rule of contribution. In *Dobson v. Camden*, 705 F.2d 759 (5th Cir. 1983) a restaurant asked police for assistance in dealing with a customer who was thought to be spending too much time in the restroom. The police beat him. The customer filed an action against the restaurant and the police officer under § 1983. The restaurant settled for $30,000 and the jury then brought in a verdict against the officer for $25,000. The pro tanto rule would relieve the officer of any direct liability to the plaintiff. Would this violate the policy thrust of § 1983?

5. **The problem of settlement with an underinsured tortfeasor.** What would be done under the New Jersey rule if the plaintiff had settled with Ansul for only $10,000 because that was the limit of Ansul's resources? Is there any way to combine the New Jersey rule with the joint liability rule of *American Motorcycle*? Or would a settlement like this mean that the plaintiff in the *Cartel Capital* would recover only the $10,000 of its Ansul

settlement plus the $57,000 from its award against Fireco, leaving plaintiff well short of a full recovery?

Alternatively, Fireco could be held jointly and severally liable for the entire damages, with a credit only for what Ansul had actually paid. This would impose liability beyond the relative fault of Fireco, but this might be justified, even in a relative fault jurisdiction, if the settling tortfeasor's resources were exhausted by the settlement. How should the rule be written?

6. **Trial: What should the jury know about previous settlements?** A problem of tactics, quite distinct from the calculation of contribution, arises for both lawyers in these cases. Put yourself in the shoes of counsel for one side or another. Plaintiff has settled with one tortfeasor and is ready to go to trial against defendant. Does either party want the jury to know about the settlement?

§ 6. MULTIPLE DEFENDANTS: SETTLEMENT AND SUIT (MOSTLY) IN A PROPORTIONATE SHARE SYSTEM

A. ABOLISHING OR LIMITING JOINT AND SEVERAL LIABILITY

CAL. CIV. CODE § 1431.2

(a) In any action for personal injury, property damage, or wrongful death, based upon principles of comparative fault, the liability of each defendant for non-economic damages shall be several only and shall not be joint. Each defendant shall be liable only for the amount of non-economic damages allocated to that defendant in direct proportion to that defendant's percentage of fault, and a separate judgment shall be rendered against that defendant for that amount.

(b)(1) For purposes of this section, the term "economic damages" means objectively verifiable monetary losses including medical expenses, loss of earnings, burial costs, loss of use of property, costs of repair or replacement, cost of obtaining substitute domestic services, loss of employment and loss of business or employment opportunities.

(2) For the purposes of this section, the term "non-economic damages" means subjective, non-monetary losses including, but not limited to, pain, suffering, inconvenience, mental suffering, emotional distress, loss of society and companionship, loss of consortium, injury to reputation and humiliation.

NOTES

1. **Scope.** Remember that with the adoption of a comparative fault system, no defendant was liable to a plaintiff for the *plaintiff's* comparative fault share. Statutes abolishing joint and several liability do not affect that rule. Rather, they change the rule that defendants could be treated as a group so that each was liable for the comparative fault share of all defendants.

Notice that the California statute applies only when an action is "based upon principles of comparative fault." Does this mean that the statute does not apply at all to a strict products liability case? The court in *Bostick v. Flex Equip. Co.*, 54 Cal.Rptr.3d 28 (Ct. App. 1997), so held.

2. **Effects.** The most obvious effect of abolishing joint and several liability is that the plaintiff, not the tortfeasor, will bear the risk of a second tortfeasor's inability to pay. If A's share is 60% and B's is 40% but B is insolvent, the plaintiff will recover only 60% of her loss from A and none from B, even though A is a proximate cause of the entire harm.

3. **Causal apportionment.** A, speeding furiously, strikes P a glancing blow as P crosses in the crosswalk. This breaks P's arm. A moment later, B, driving moderately but distracted by a sudden yell from a baby in the car, runs P down, causing serious breaks in pelvic bones. If the plaintiff sues A for the broken arm and B for the broken pelvic bones, would statutes abolishing joint and several liability have any effect?

4. **Adoption of several liability statutes.** By 1990 the tort reform lobbyists had obtained statutory change in the traditional joint and several liability rules in about half the states, relieving defendants of joint liability in a wide range of cases.

5. **Constitutionality.** So far, courts have generally upheld statutes of this kind. *E.g.,State Farm Ins. Cos. v. Premier Manufactured Systems, Inc.*, 172 P.3d 410 (Ariz. 2007); *Evangelatos v. Superior Court*, 753 P.2d 585 (Cal. 1988). However, other states have found them violative of violations of various state constitutional provisions. *Best v. Taylor Mach. Works,* 689 N.E.2d 1057 (Ill. 1997); *State v. Sheward*, 715 N.E.2d 1062 (Ohio 1999).

6. **Federal statutes.** Some federal statutes impose joint and several liability for matters within their scope. This is the rule under CERCLA, a statute imposing liabilities for hazardous substances. *See United States v. Stringfellow*, 661 F.Supp. 1053 (C.D. Cal. 1987). The Supreme Court has also retained joint and several liability in FELA cases. *Norfolk & Western Railway v. Ayers,* 538 U.S. 135 (2003).

7. **The economic/non-economic distinction.** The California statute is one of a group which *retains* joint and several liability for actual pecuniary ("economic") losses. New York is another such state. *See* N.Y. C.P.L.R. § 1601.

8. **The relative fault distinction.** Another kind of statute retains some joint and several liability when the plaintiff's fault is small or the defendant's is great. New York's statute, for example, limits a defendant's liability for non-economic damages to his comparative fault share but only when his liability is "fifty percent or less of the total liability assigned to all persons liable." N.Y. C.P.L.R. § 1601. Illinois offered similar protection to defendants whose fault is less than 25% of the total relevant fault. 735 ILCS 5/2–1117. Both statutes, like others, include qualifications and exceptions that are sometimes intricate. *See Unzicker v. Kraft Food Ingredients Corp.*, 783 N.E.2d 1024 (Ill. 2002); *Lubecki v. City of New York*, 758 N.Y.S.2d 610 (App. Div. 2003).

9. **Combination systems.** A number of statutes combine the non-economic loss distinction with the relative fault distinction in some way. For instance, Florida Statutes § 768.81(3), prescribes:

> In cases to which this section applies, the court shall enter judgment against each party liable on the basis of such party's percentage of fault and not on the basis of the doctrine of joint and several liability; provided that with respect to any party whose percentage of fault equals or exceeds that of a particular claimant, the court shall enter judgment with respect to economic damages against that party on the basis of the doctrine of joint and several liability.

10. **The more severe statutes.** Another group of statutes is more severe, abolishing joint and several liability as to all the plaintiff's damages, both pecuniary and non-pecuniary, and regardless of the plaintiff's lack of fault. *E.g.,* ARIZ. REV. STAT. § 12–2506. As with most other statutes, some of these exempt particular torts, such as those based on hazardous wastes or pollution.

11. **Judicial adoption of several liability.** Several state courts have rejected the traditional joint and several liability rule, setting up a judicially created several liability system, seemingly along the lines of the more severe statutes. *See, e.g., Volz v. Ledes,* 895 S.W.2d 677 (Tenn. 1995).

12. **The Uniform Apportionment Act.** In 2002, still another effort to resolve apportionment issues was put in play when the Commissioners on Uniform State Laws promulgated a new Uniform Apportionment of Tort Responsibility Act (hereafter, The Uniform Apportionment Act). Some of its provisions will be mentioned at appropriate points.

13. **Nonsettling tortfeasors in a several liability system.** Recall the three methods for reducing a nonsettling tortfeasor's liability to the plaintiff when the plaintiff had settled with another tortfeasor—a reduction pro rata, pro tanto, or a reduction by the settling tortfeasor's comparative fault share. What happens in a several liability system when one tortfeasor settles and the other loses at trial? *See Nilsson v. Bierman,* 839 A.2d 25 (N.H. 2003).

B.　COMPARATIVE FAULT EFFECTS AND ADJUSTMENTS

PRICE v. KITSAP TRANSIT, 886 P.2d 556 (Wash. 1994). The plaintiff, already suffering from a whiplash in an earlier bus accident, was riding the defendant's bus. A four-year-old boy, walking in the aisle and holding his father's hand, suddenly reached into the driver's area and engaged an emergency stop switch, bringing the bus to a sudden halt and causing serious injury to the plaintiff. The jury found that the boy was guilty of 80% of the negligence, his father 10% and the bus company 10%. Tort reform legislation required the jury to apportion fault among "every entity which caused the claimant's damages, including the claimant or person suffering personal injury or incurring property damage, defendants, third-party defendants, entities released by the claimant, entities immune from liability to the claimant and entities with any other individual defense against the claimant. . . ." *Held,* no fault can be apportioned to the boy.

Children under six years of age are incapable of negligence. Although fault of an immune entity is to be considered, the boy is not immune; rather, he is not at fault. "This interpretation agrees with the fundamental practice of not assigning fault to animals, inanimate objects, and forces of nature which are not considered 'entities' under the statute."

NOTES

1. **Effects of eliminating tortfeasors from the calculus.** As *Price* suggests, the effects of abolishing joint and several liability may be mitigated if the negligence of some persons is disregarded in calculating comparative fault. Notice that the result in *Price* does not quite mimic the result of a joint and several liability system. The bus company is not liable for 90% but presumably only 50%.

2. **Eliminating remote causes.** What other fault should be disregarded besides that of minors too young to be guilty of legal fault at all? Presumably courts should disregard any fault that is not a proximate cause of the plaintiffs harm. This could lead plaintiffs to argue that the fault of insolvent parties is too remote to count. This might, however, be an uncongenial argument for lawyers who regularly represent plaintiffs, because a narrow view of proximate cause in today's case might cut off liability of the only solvent party in tomorrow's case.

3. **Phantom tortfeasors.** Plaintiffs have sometimes argued that the fault of any person who is not joined as a party in the suit should be ignored, so that only the fault of the plaintiff and the actual defendants should be compared. The plaintiff would not join an insolvent tortfeasor and could not join an unknown tortfeasor like a hit and run driver. Some courts have held that the fault of everyone, joined or not joined, is to be considered. *E.g., Fabre v. Marin*, 623 So.2d 1182 (Fla. 1993). However, the Uniform Apportionment Act allocates responsibility among those who are actual parties to the litigation and disregards the fault of all nonparties except released persons. *See* UNIFORM APPORTIONMENT OF TORT RESPONSIBILITY ACT, Preface, Apportioning Tort Responsibility in this Act (2002).

4. **Immune tortfeasors.** Many courts have counted the negligence of immune tortfeasors when assessing fault of the others. The inevitable result is that the amount of fault attributable to the solvent and non-immune defendant is reduced, and his liability along with it. Sometimes statutes so provides. *See* LA. CIV. CODE § 2324 B. This is also the provision of the Uniform Apportionment Act. In *Unzicker v. Kraft Food Ingredients Corp.*, 783 N.E.2d 1024 (Ill. 2002), the plaintiff was not at fault at all. His employer was immune from tort liability to the plaintiff under the usual provision that liability for relatively small workers' compensation award precludes tort liability. His employer was guilty of 99% of the fault, while the other tortfeasor, the defendant, was guilty of only 1%. The statute abolished joint and several liability as to nonmedical expenses when the tortfeasor was guilty of less than 25% of the fault. The court refused to exclude the immune employer in counting up fault percentages. The result was that except for medical expense, the plaintiff could only recover 1% of his nonmedical damages.

5. **Settlement effects.** Suppose the plaintiff suffers $100,000 damages as a result of the combined negligence of A and B. A settles for $50,000. The plaintiff goes to trial against B and the jury finds her total damages to be $100,000 and B's negligence is 70%, while P's negligence is 10% of the total. If joint and several liability is abolished, isn't it clear that the plaintiff should recover $70,000 from B, even though that gives her a recovery in excess of the total damage? *See Wells v. Tallahassee Mem. Reg'l Med. Ctr., Inc.*, 659 So.2d 249 (Fla. 1995). The Uniform Apportionment Act considers the fault of and apportions responsibility to only those tortfeasors who are parties, *except* that it considers the fault of (a) immune persons and (b) persons who have settled with the plaintiff. Under this approach, if the plaintiff settles with A, then sues B, and the jury in the suit against B finds A's fault to be 75% and B's 25%, B owes only 25% of the damages. In contrast, Massachusetts has held that the fault of a settling tortfeasor is ignored in its joint and several liability system; the jury apportions 100% of the fault between the plaintiff and defendant. *Shantigar Found. v. Bear Mountain Builders*, 804 N.E.2d 324 (Mass. 2004).

D'AMARIO v. FORD MOTOR CO.

806 So.2d 424 (Fla. 2001)

PER CURIAM. . . .

Clifford Harris, a minor, was injured when the car in which he was riding as a passenger collided with a tree and then burst into flames. The car was driven by a friend of Harris who was allegedly intoxicated and speeding at the time of the accident. As described in the opinion below:

> A witness to the crash circled the car twice and noticed a fire in the engine area. Some minutes later, the fire spread and an explosion occurred, engulfing the car in flames. Harris was severely injured, losing three limbs and suffering burns to much of his body.

Harris, and his mother, Karen D'Amario, sued Ford alleging that a defective relay switch in the automobile caused Harris's injuries. The plaintiffs did not seek damages against Ford for the injuries to Harris caused by the initial collision with the tree. Rather, they sought damages for the injuries caused by the alleged defective relay switch only. Ford asserted as an affirmative defense that the injuries were proximately caused by the negligence of a third party, although in its answer to the complaint, Ford did not specifically identify the vehicle's driver as a non-party tortfeasor.

At trial, the two sides advanced conflicting theories as to the cause of the fire and Harris's injuries. The plaintiffs' "theory of liability was that a relay switch failed, thus preventing it from disrupting the flow of power to the fuel pump." Plaintiffs' experts "testified that gasoline continued to be pumped after the impact and caused the fire." On the other hand, Ford's experts countered that the relay switch and fuel pump properly worked and that the original crash caused an oil pan to burst, which resulted in an oil-based fire. . . .

[A]t trial, Ford moved to amend its affirmative defenses to include an allegation that Harris's injuries were caused by the fault of a third party, and proffered evidence of the driver's intoxication and excessive speed. The trial court granted Ford's request and held that an apportionment defense was available and evidence of the driver's actions in causing the initial accident could be admitted in support of such defense. In the face of such ruling, the parties stipulated to the jury that the negligent and excessive speed of the driver caused the initial accident and that at the time the driver had a blood alcohol level of .14 percent.

Following deliberations, the jury returned a verdict for the defense, finding that Ford was not a legal cause of the injuries to Harris. [The trial judge granted a new trial, but the intermediate appellate court reversed, upholding the defense verdict.]

... Outside of Florida, courts have wrestled with the comparative fault issue and have adopted conflicting views. Under what has been characterized by *Whitehead v. Toyota Motor Corp.*, 897 S.W.2d 684 (Tenn. 1995), as the "majority view," the fault of the plaintiff or a third party in causing the initial accident is recognized as a defense to a crashworthiness case against a product manufacturer. This line of cases reasons that the fault of the person causing the accident that created the circumstances in which the second accident occurred should be compared with the role of the automobile manufacturer's negligence in designing a defective product in assessing total responsibility for the claimant's injuries. [The court cited seven other cases supporting this view.

In contrast to the approach of the "majority" view, the "minority" view, rejecting the application of comparative fault principles, focuses on the underlying rationale for imposing liability against automobile manufacturers for secondary injuries caused by a design defect....

Jimenez pointed out that the rule of damages in crashworthiness cases also effectively acts to apportion fault and responsibility between the first and second collisions and their respective causes:

> ... *[T]he concept of "enhanced injury" effectively apportions fault and damages on a comparative basis; defendant is liable only for the increased injury caused by its own conduct, not for the injury resulting from the crash itself.* Further, the alleged negligence causing the collision is legally remote from, and thus not the legal cause of, the enhanced injury caused by a defective part that was supposed to be designed to protect in case of a collision.

Under this reasoning, concerns about fairness in apportioning responsibility for damages based upon fault in crashworthiness cases are satisfied by the limitation of liability of a manufacturer to only those damages caused by the defective product.

Hence, the primary reason offered by courts excluding evidence of the driver's fault in causing an accident is that the accident-causing fault is not relevant to whether an automobile manufacturer designed a defective product, and, further, that such evidence, if admitted, may be unduly prejudicial to the plaintiff. . . .

The automobile manufacturers urge us to adopt the "majority" view. . . . They cite section 768.81(3), Fla. Stat. (1997), which provides for the entry of "judgment against each party liable on the basis of such party's percentage of fault" and this Court's interpretation of the statute in *Fabre v. Marin,* 623 So.2d 1182 (Fla.1993).

In *Fabre* . . . [we] interpreted the term "party" to include all persons who contributed to the accident "regardless of whether they have been or could have been joined as defendants." However, it is not entirely clear that our holding in *Fabre* resolves the question presented today since *Fabre* involved a simple automobile accident involving joint and *concurrent* tortfeasors, and did not involve successive tortfeasors or enhanced or secondary injuries allegedly stemming from a manufacturing or design defect. . . .

We have searched for an appropriate analogy to help us resolve the issue. In the context of a medical neglect case, for example, courts in this state have concluded that (1) the cause of an initial injury which may require medical assistance is not ordinarily considered as a legal cause of injuries resulting from the subsequent negligence of the medical-care provider; and (2) an initial wrongdoer who causes an injury is not to be considered a joint tortfeasor with a subsequent medical provider whose negligence enhances or aggravates injuries caused by the initial wrong-doer. In other words, in cases involving medical malpractice, the cause of the underlying condition that brought the patient to the professional, whether a disease or an accident, is not to be compared to the cause of the independent enhanced injury allegedly resulting from medical neglect. . . .

In *Whitehead,* the plaintiff's decedent was brought to the defendant hospital after he attempted to commit suicide. While under the care of the treating doctor, Whitehead died. An expert testified that the care received by Whitehead deviated from the standard practice in the community and that but for the doctor's negligence, Whitehead would have survived. The jury was instructed that it could consider Whitehead's own conduct as a defense to the medical malpractice claim against the doctor and hospital and the jury returned a verdict for the defense.

On appeal, however, the First District reversed, holding that White-head's conduct was too remote and could not be considered the proximate legal cause of his injuries from the alleged professional malpractice. . . .

[C]rashworthiness cases involve separate and distinct injuries-those caused by the initial collision, and those subsequently caused by a second collision arising from a defective product. We agree that when viewed in this light, crashworthiness cases may be analogized to medical malpractice cases involving a successive negligent medical provider who is alleged to have either aggravated an existing injury or caused a separate and additional injury. Thus, just as the injury-causing fault of the patient in *Whitehead* was held not relevant in assessing the doctor's subsequent and separate negligence, the accident-causing fault of the driver would not be relevant in crashworthiness cases in assessing a manufacturer's neglect in designing an automobile or its parts. The initial accident merely furnished the occasion for the manufacturer's fault to be tested....

We are not unmindful of the concerns that a manufacturer not end up improperly being held liable for damages caused by the initial collision. Of course, we must remember that in crashworthiness cases the plaintiff not only has the burden of proving the existence of a defect and its causal relationship to her injuries, but she must also prove the existence of additional or enhanced injuries caused by the defect. In this regard, we are impressed with the reasoning of the federal district court in *Jimenez* that the proper application of the crashworthiness doctrine is also consistent with comparative fault principles. The major concern of those courts following the majority rule is in seeing that successive tortfeasors only be held liable for the damages they cause, and not be held liable for damages caused by the initial tortfeasor. We agree with this concern, but see no reason why it cannot be properly addressed, as in *Jimenez,* by a recognition of the crashworthiness doctrine's legal rationale limiting a manufacturer's liability only to those damages caused by the defect....

We also conclude that to inject the issue of the driver's fault in causing the initial accident into the trial of a crashworthiness case tends to unduly confuse the jury by focusing attention on the conduct giving rise to the accident instead of the issues of the existence of a defect and its role in causing the enhanced injuries....

[The decision of the District Court of Appeal upholding the verdict for Ford is quashed.]

NOTES

1. After *D'Amario,* a Florida Court of Appeals panel considered its scope in *Jackson v. York Hannover Nursing Centers,* 876 So.2d 8 (Fla. Dist. Ct. App. 2004). In that case, the Medical Center transferred a patient to the defendant nursing home. At time of transfer the patient suffered from pressure sores and was in a state of dehydration; but the Medical Center did not so advise the nursing home. The nursing breached its duty to assess the patient and to provide care for the dehydration and sores, and the patient died three weeks later. In a suit against the nursing home, the nursing home claimed that the Medical Center was negligent and that its negligence should be considered in apportioning fault, even though the Medical Center was not a party. The personal representative argued *D'Amario.* The court held that D'Amario had no application because there was no "distinct injury." Consequently, a jury verdict attributing 75% of the fault to the Medical Center and only 25% of the fault to the nursing home was upheld. Is *D'Amario* fundamentally about "distinct" injuries?

2. Do you think that *D'Amario* would control a case in which no one could show how much harm was caused by the second impact? In that case,

how should responsibility be apportioned where joint and several liability has been abolished? *See* Restatement of Products Liability § 16 (1998).

C. COMPARING NEGLIGENCE WITH INTENTIONAL AND STRICT LIABILITY WRONGS

BOARD OF COUNTY COMN'RS OF TETON COUNTY v. BASSETT

8 P.3d 1079 (Wyo. 2000)

Grant, District Judge. . . .

The Wyoming Highway Patrol pursued Ortega from Dubois at high speeds. [Ortega was wanted in two jurisdictions and considered to be armed and dangerous.] Ortega repeatedly swerved from his own lane toward oncoming traffic, and otherwise presented a menace to the traveling public in an apparent attempt to cause a crash which would divert the pursuing officers or involve them in a crash. These efforts failed, but the officers were unable to stop Ortega, making the roadblock necessary.

[Sheriff's deputies decided to establish the roadblock] beyond the intersection of U.S. Highway 89 and Antelope Flats Road. At that location, they placed improvised road spikes in the hope that Ortega would turn off of the highway onto the road and be stopped when the spikes disabled his vehicle. Ortega did not turn off of the highway, and continued on until he was stopped by the crash just on the Jackson side of the roadblock.

As these events were unfolding, appellees, Michael Coziah (Coziah) and Rayce Bassett (Bassett), were enroute home from fishing at Coulter Bay. As they approached Moran Junction, where they would turn south toward Jackson, they passed several officers who were at the right of the road. These were Sergeant Wilson of the Wyoming Highway Patrol and park police whom he was briefing. None of these officers made any effort to warn appellees of the hazardous situation developing on U.S. Highway 89 onto which appellees' vehicle turned.

As appellees approached the roadblock, surprised officers began frantically gesturing for them to go through as a deputy sheriff moved his car for their passage. Ortega, approaching at 100 miles per hour or more, went through the same opening, smashing into Coziah's car which was going approximately thirty miles per hour. Coziah and Bassett were injured, and Ortega was arrested.

. . . [Bassett and Coziah sued.] The jury allocated 0% fault to Coziah, 40% fault to the Wyoming Highway Patrol, 20% fault to the Sheriff's officers, and 40% fault to the National Park Service. . . .

Since it is dispositive, we turn first to the question of whether Ortega, whose conduct was willful and wanton or intentional, should have been included among the actors whose fault would be determined and compared with that of the other actors by the jury in apportioning fault among the actors as required by Wyo. Stat. Ann § 1–1–109. Appellees contend, and the district court held, that Ortega's willful and wanton or intentional conduct could not be compared with the conduct of appellants....

Unlike the version before the 1994 amendment to Wyo. Stat. Ann. 1-1-109, which used "negligence," its present iteration introduces the more inclusive term "fault" and defines it as including conduct that is "in any measure negligent" eliminating degrees or varieties of negligence consistent with one of the purposes of the statute, that is to ameliorate the harshness of the doctrine of contributory negligence. The comparative negligence statute remedied the injustice of the doctrine of contributory negligence by stating that a plaintiff's negligence prevents recovery only in proportion as it causes plaintiff's damages.

The use of the word "includes" is significant because "includes" generally signifies an intent to enlarge a statute's application, rather than limit it, and it implies the conclusion that there are other items includable, though not specifically enumerated.

Appellees insist this is not so because the words "reckless," "wanton," "culpable" or "intentional" were stricken from the definition of "fault" in Senate File No. 35 evincing clear intent that they were not included in the definition of "fault" as conduct "in any measure negligent." This argument reads more into the deletion than we think justified. It leaves unexplained the legislature's expansion of "negligence" to "fault" which includes conduct "in any measure negligent." It may be as reasonable to attribute the deletions to a belief that the deleted words are subsumed in the phrase "in any measure negligent" as it would be to attribute them to other motives....

Application of Wyo. Stat. Ann. § 1-1-109 in this case to include Ortega as an actor is also consistent with the other purpose of the statute, the elimination of joint and several liability. Subsection (e) provides that "[e]ach defendant is liable only to the extent of that defendant's proportion of the total fault * * *." To leave an actor such as Ortega out of the apportionment calculation exposes the remaining appellants to the possibility that they will be held to answer for his misconduct. Such a result does act as an incentive to those with a duty to protect against intentional harm, and "[a] number of courts therefore have concluded that persons who negligently fail to protect against the specific risk of an intentional tort should bear the risk that the intentional tortfeasor is insolvent." Restatement (Third) of Torts § 24 cmt. b at 164 (Proposed Final Draft (Revised) 3/22/99). The statutory elimination of joint and several liability, however, forecloses our consideration of the merits of such a policy....

The exclusion of Ortega from the verdict form frustrates the legislature's expressed intent, and the defendants were entitled to have the causation rule of DeWald given as an instruction to the jury. We reverse and remand for a new trial.

NOTES

1. **Comparing negligence with intentional wrongdoing.** Several courts agree with the proposition that negligence of one defendant can be compared with intentional or wilful wrongdoing of another. *Slack v. Farmers Ins. Exch.,* 5 P.3d 280 (Colo. 2000) (statute construed to require comparison of intentional wrong and negligence where defendant referred plaintiff to a chiropractor it should have known might sexually assault her); *see Barth v. Coleman,* 878 P.2d 319 (N.M. 1994) (bar owner negligently failed to oust or control a threatening attacker, he attacked plaintiff; fault must be apportioned between bar owner and attacker; held, bar owner liable only for his own percentage of fault); *Rodenburg v. Fargo–Moorhead Young Men's Christian Ass'n,* 632 N.W.2d 407 (N.D. 2001) ("A negligent tortfeasor's conduct is compared with an intentional tortfeasor's conduct"). For a different view, see the next case.

2. **Attributing less fault to an intentional tortfeasor.** Could a jury ever attribute less fault to an insolvent, intentional tortfeasor? In *Hutcherson v. City of Phoenix,* 961 P.2d 449 (Ariz. 1998), a woman made a 911 call reporting a credible threat that she would be killed in a few minutes. She was, and it could have been prevented if the dispatcher had categorized the call as a priority one call, which would have provided an immediate police response. The jury allocated 75% of the fault to the city based upon the dispatcher's negligence and only 25% to the killer. This was upheld.

3. **Plaintiff-defendant comparisons.** Distinguish: plaintiff, chargeable with contributory fault, sues an intentional tortfeasor. Ellen M. Bublick, *The End Game of Tort Reform: Comparative Apportionment and Intentional Torts,* 78 NOTRE DAME L. REV. 355 (2003), notes that courts rarely call for apportionment of responsibility as between a contributorily negligent plaintiff and an intentionally wrongdoing defendant. In *Landry v. Bellanger,* 851 So.2d 943 (La. 2003), the court, governed in part by a statute, held: (1) the plaintiff who negligently provokes an intentional tort will recover full damages against the intentional tortfeasor; (2) the plaintiff who is herself an intentional tortfeasor can recover against an intentional tortfeasor defendant with damages reduced for comparative fault; (3) the plaintiff can recover nothing against a defendant whose intentional attack is privileged, as in the case of self defense.

TURNER v. JORDAN, 957 S.W.2d 815 (Tenn. 1997). The plaintiff was a nurse and the defendant a psychiatrist at the same facility. One of the defendant's patients had a known history of violence, but the psychiatrist took no steps to protect those who might be attacked. He later said he did not know the patient's history of violence, but he himself had been attacked by the patient, and he had referred to that history in suggesting that the patient be encouraged to leave "against medical advice." The patient beat the plaintiff, causing a severe head injury. The jury attributed all the fault to the psychiatrist and awarded the plaintiff $1,186,000. The trial judge, however, thought the allocation of fault unjustified and ordered a new trial. *Held*, reversed and remanded for reinstatement of the jury verdict. The key issue is "whether the negligent act of a defendant should be compared with the intentional act of another in determining comparative fault.... [T]he concern in cases that compare the negligence of a defendant with the intentional act of a third party is not burdening the negligent tortfeasor with liability in excess of his or her fault; conversely, the primary concern in those cases that do not compare is that the plaintiff not be penalized by allowing the negligent party to use the intentional act it had a duty to prevent to reduce its liability. In our view, the conduct of a negligent defendant should not be compared with the intentional conduct of another in determining comparative fault where the intentional conduct is the foreseeable risk created by the negligent tortfeasor." Such a comparison presents practical difficulties in comparing acts that are different in both degree and kind and "reduces the negligent person's incentive to comply with the applicable duty of care." Further, a negligent defendant "should not be permitted to rely upon the foreseeable harm it had a duty to prevent so as to reduce its liability."

Notes

1. **Rejecting apportionment between intentional and negligent torts.** A number of cases or statutes side with *Turner* by holding or providing that apportionment between a negligent defendant and an intentional tortfeasor is not permitted, at least not in situations like the one reflected in *Bassett* and *Turner. See Bhinder v. Sun Co.,* 819 A.2d 822 (Conn. 2003); *Kansas State Bank & Trust Co. v. Specialized Transp. Servs., Inc.,* 819 P.2d 587 (Kan. 1991); *Veazey v. Elmwood Plantation Assocs., Ltd.,* 650 So.2d 712 (La. 1994). In *Brandon v. County of Richardson,* 624 N.W.2d 604 (Neb. 2001), the court construed its statutes to exclude comparison between negligence and intent, but also observed that "it would be irrational to allow a party who negligently fails to discharge a duty to protect to reduce its liability because there is an intervening intentional tort when the intervening intentional tort is exactly what the negligent party had a duty to protect against."

2. **Intent and negligence under the Apportionment Restatement.** The Restatement of Apportionment favors comparison of all forms of culpability, so that the trier assigns a percentage of responsibility both to the negligent and to the intentional actor. However, when a negligent defendant specifically risks an intentional tort to the plaintiff, there is no apportionment to reduce the plaintiff's damages—the negligent defendant remains jointly and severally liable to the plaintiff. Restatement of Apportionment § 14 (2000). And the intentional tortfeasor is always jointly and severally liable for the entire damage. *Id.* § 12; *cf. Woods v. Cole,* 693 N.E.2d 333 (Ill. 1998) (joint and several liability remains for concerted action).

3. **Intentional tortfeasor's indemnity obligation.** If a negligent tortfeasor is held liable for the entire amount of the plaintiff's damages, could

he obtain an indemnity judgment against the intentional tortfeasor? *See Degener v. Hall Contracting Corp.*, 27 S.W.3d 775 (Ky. 2000).

4. **Causal apportionment?** In *Welch v. Southland Corp.*, 952 P.2d 162 (Wash. 1998), the court held that apportionment of "fault" under the statute only includes some species of negligence, not intentional wrongdoing, so the defendant who negligently permits an intentional tortfeasor to harm the plaintiff is liable without apportionment. Yet in *Tegman v. Accident & Medical Investigations, Inc.*, 75 P.3d 497 (Wash. 2003), the same court said that while the negligent tortfeasor could not apportion "fault" to the intentional tortfeasor, the negligent tortfeasor would not be liable for damages caused by the intentional tortfeasor. Under standard concepts of causation, how could this work?

5. **Single, indivisible injury; either defendant's act is sufficient to cause harm.** Suppose two defendants negligently set separate fires. Each fire is blown by winds towards the plaintiff's farm. Either would suffice to burn the house down, but by happenstance of the winds, the two fires "combine" before they reach the plaintiff's farm. It is then burned down by the combined fire. Defendant A is fully insured but B has no insurance and no assets. Should A be liable for only one-half the damages? Notice that (a) his negligence is exactly the same as if B did not exist, and (b) the damage is exactly the same as if B did not exist.

6. **A's negligence creates B's opportunity for harm.** In one kind of traditional joint and several liability case, the first tortfeasor's negligence makes the second tortfeasor's fault possible. In *Hines v. Garrett*, 108 S.E. 690 (Va. 1921), the railroad was responsible for putting the plaintiff at risk of rape by unknown persons. She was in fact raped and the railroad was held liable. The railroad's fault is significant but obviously not in the category with that of the rapists. Does it really make any sense to apportion fault at all in this kind of case, and, if so, to limit the railroad's liability?

7. **A problem.** Suppose that Tenant leases premises from Landlord. The landlord's duty to the tenant is to warn of dangers of which the landlord actually knows and the tenant does not. The landlord knows the floor is flimsy and could collapse and he does warn the tenant. The tenant thereafter invites a social guest to the premises without warning the guest. The floor collapses with the guest, causing her injuries. What liabilities if any should be visited upon Landlord and Tenant in a state that has abolished joint and several liability? *Rittenour v. Gibson*, 656 N.W.2d 691 (N.D. 2003).

CHAPTER 26

DAMAGES

■ ■ ■

§ 1. COMPENSATORY DAMAGES GENERALLY

Factors affecting settlement are largely factors that affect the trial and ultimate award. As a plaintiff you don't accept an offer of $100 if you think the jury will award you $100,000. As a defendant you don't offer $100,000 if you think the jury will award nothing at all. Estimating probable jury awards is no easy matter. Lawyers must consider matters having little to do with legal rules—the probable evidence that the jury will hear and the jurors' probable reaction to that evidence, for example. However, lawyers must also know the legal rules that guide, counsel, and constrain jurors—rules that may be enforced by the judge's instructions, directed verdict, or reduction in awards for excessiveness. *Cf. Cole v. Esquibel*, 182 P.3d 709 (Idaho 2008) (reversing trial judge's refusal to order a new trial or to remit award of future medical expenses when evidence did not support jury's award).

A. PROVING AND COMPUTING BASIC DAMAGES

The topic of tort damages is a small part of two larger fields. One field might be called "trial practice," which concerns itself with strategy, tactics, and rules of procedure and evidence governing trials. This is not only a field in itself, but is one that can be best appreciated in the circumstances of particular cases in practice rather than through the medium of appellate opinions. Accordingly, the trial tactics side of damages appears here only incidentally. The other field is that of "remedies," which includes not only the damages remedy but also the remedies of injunction and restitution. All three remedies are available in many tort cases. The field of remedies, however, is a broad one, summarized in three volumes in DAN B. DOBBS, THE LAW OF REMEDIES (2d ed. 1993) (hereafter cited as DOBBS, REMEDIES). Consequently, coverage of all tort remedies and remedial rules is impractical in any torts course, including this one.

Constitutional torts. We have seen that the plaintiff might have a personal injury or property damage claim under § 1983 based on the defendant's violation of his constitutional rights. In such cases, courts apply the damages rules they apply in any personal injury or property damage case. Some constitutional violations, however, cause no obvious physical injury, either to person or property. For instance, suppose you are denied the right to vote, or your right to free speech is infringed in violation of the Constitution. In these cases the Supreme Court has so far insisted that you must prove actual damages, such as pecuniary loss or at least actual mental distress, in order to recover anything more than nominal ($1) damages. This problem is discussed in Jean C. Love, *Presumed General Compensatory Damages in Constitutional Tort Litigation: A Corrective Justice Perspective*, 49 WASH. & LEE L. REV. 67 (1992); 2 DOBBS, REMEDIES § 7.4.

Property torts. Quite a few torts involve physical injury to, or dispossession of, tangible property, real or personal. We have already seen that for total dispossession of personalty there is a conversion action, in which damages are measured by the full market value of the thing converted. When there is similar dispossession of real property, there is no analogous damages claim. Instead the plaintiff recovers the rental value of the property during the time of dispossession. When physical harm is done to tangible property, the measure of damages is very often the diminished value of the property. Thus if A trespasses on Blackacre and damages a house, the owner or possessor will be entitled to recover a sum equal to the difference between the value immediately before and the value immediately after the damage.

The same diminished value rule, based on the market value, is applied in cases of damage to chattels, such as automobiles. However, for a number of reasons, the cost of repair may be substituted as a measure of damages in certain cases, especially where the repair is not likely to enhance the damaged property and make it more valuable than before.

The injunctive remedy is also important in certain tort cases. If the defendant repeatedly trespasses on the plaintiff's land, or threatens to trespass in some way that will cause irreparable harm, as by cutting down old oak trees, the plaintiff may be entitled to an injunction prohibiting such a tort. Injunction is also important in many cases involving intangible property, such as a trademark, and in other business tort cases, such as those involving interference with contracts. *See generally,* 1 DOBBS, REMEDIES, Chapter 5.

Personal injury torts. Personal injuries may occur through intentional torts, through negligence or through strict liability torts. The damages, however, are the same for any given broken jaw, without regard to whether the jaw was broken through intent, negligence or wholly without fault. Punitive damages may be warranted in some cases, where the defendant's conduct is "malicious" or wanton. Those damages aside, the main elements of damages for personal injuries can be stated quite easily.

(1) Damages for reasonably incurred medical expenses resulting from the tort.

(2) Damages for lost earning capacity or wage loss resulting from the tort.

(3) Damages for pain and suffering resulting from the tort, including mental pain and suffering.

(4) In a limited number of cases, an award to pay for the cost of medical monitoring of the plaintiff's condition to intercept a prospective disease, such as cancer, that may develop in the future.

(5) Any other specifically identifiable harm that has resulted from the tort, such as special expenses necessary to travel for medical attention.

In each category, the plaintiff is entitled also to recover for future damages if they are reasonably certain to occur. How difficult is it to calculate these elements of damage?

MARTIN v. UNITED STATES

471 F.Supp. 6 (D. Ariz. 1979)

JAMES M. BURNS, DISTRICT JUDGE.

[Federal Tort Claims Act case tried to the judge. The plaintiffs, two school boys, riding a motorbike, struck a sagging power line negligently maintained by the government. Each "suffered tragically severe and permanent injuries" from the burns.]

As to the plaintiff Melvin Burrows II, the court first noted that he sustained severe burns to his face, head, back, buttocks, arms and legs. Before considering loss of earning capacity, the court found that medical expenses to Burrows to the time of trial came to $48,130.97, and that future medical expenses would come to about $49,000 additional. Finally, the court awarded $5,000 for psychological treatments.

Clarence Martin is principal of the Florence middle school, owner of a roofing business that employs Melvin Burrows' father, and uncle of the other plaintiff in this case. He testified upon the basis of his observation of Melvin during the seven years he has known him and the month and a half that Melvin had attended the middle school prior to the accident. He believed that Melvin was average or above average in intelligence and probably would have become a skilled worker, perhaps a mechanic or a carpenter. Dr. Glenn Wilt, an associate professor of finance at Arizona State University and an investment counselor stated:

[I]t can be reasonably presumed that, but for their injuries, both Melvin and Jeffrey would have gravitated into positions in one of the construction trades. Clearly, that is exactly what most of their uninjured classmates will do, and considering the general demand in this territory, due to the growth of population and need for attendant services in the construction field, a strong demand can be forecast for these jobs.

Dr. David Yandell, a clinical psychologist and vocational rehabilitation counselor called by the defendant, testified that the intelligence and aptitude tests administered by Dr. Donald Guinoud show that Melvin could not have pursued a career in the skilled crafts but instead probably would have become a laborer. Defendant's other witness, Dr. John Buehler, chairman of the department of economics at the University of Arizona, expressed his opinion that neither plaintiff probably would have become a worker in the skilled trades, but rather each would have earned average wages.

Based upon my evaluation of the testimony and the expertise and credibility of the witnesses, I conclude that Melvin Burrows probably would have become a skilled worker. Dr. Wilt stated that a carpenter would, at 1978 wage rates, earn about $9,450 per year during a four-year apprenticeship and during a subsequent 42-year career as a journeyman carpenter would earn about $18,900 annually in wages and $3,900 annually in fringe benefits. I accept these figures as reasonable approximations of Melvin's lifetime earnings had he not experienced this accident.

Dr. Guinourd testified that Melvin might be employable as a night watchman or night diesel mechanic not involved with the public interaction aspect of either business. Dr. Wilt concluded that, because of Melvin's disfigurement and intolerance to sunlight and perspiration, he would probably be unable to find a job suited to his handicap. Dr. Canter testified that Melvin would benefit psychologically from working even at a lowly position.

Based upon the testimony and my own observation of Melvin Burrows, I conclude that he probably will be able to work at an entry-level position for at least half of his normal working life. According to Dr. Wilt, such work would generate an annual income of $3,120 in 1978 dollars. Thus, Melvin is entitled to recover in 1978 dollars $6,330 per year for four years (apprenticeship period), then $19,680 per year for the following 42 years (journeyman period). . . .

I find that the award can presently be invested at very little risk and return 7.5% compounded annually. I find that 5.5% is a reasonable annual rate of wage inflation to be expected during Melvin's working lifetime.

I award an amount for the loss of Melvin's earning capacity sufficient when invested at a 7.5% annual rate of return to generate in 1978 dollars $6,330 per year for the four years 1983–1986 (hypothetical apprenticeship period) and $19,680 per year for the following 42 years 1987–2028 (hypothetical journeyman period). These amounts in 1978 dollars are to be converted to current dollars for each year by application of a 5.5% expected annual rate of wage inflation, then discounted at 7.5% per year back to 1979. By this method of calculation, the award for loss of Melvin's earning capacity amounts to $548,029.

The power line struck Melvin on the face, head and perhaps also on the back, causing severe and extensive burns on those areas and on "blowout holes" on his buttocks, legs, left arm and right hand, where the electric current left his body seeking the ground. More than 80% of his head and face was burned, 70% to the third degree or worse. He also suffered third degree burns on 40% of his back, on his entire left buttocks and on at least six blowout ulcers. Melvin regained consciousness soon after the accident and was found wandering in the desert near the scene.

Dr. Williams Clemans, a general practitioner in Florence, treated Melvin briefly in the back of a pickup truck outside the local hospital before having him sent to the burn treatment unit at the Maricopa County Hospital in Phoenix. Dr. Clemans testified that Melvin appeared to be in critical condition. He doubted whether Melvin would survive long enough to reach the burn unit.

At the Maricopa County Hospital where Melvin remained for four months, the surgeons removed the charred layers of skin and tissue from Melvin's face, head, buttocks and other areas of his body. They performed numerous skin grafts and attempted to fashion a functioning right eyelid, which Melvin still cannot close. Melvin lost his right ear entirely and the top third of his left ear. To graft skin onto his left temple, which had been burned down to the skull, the doctors ground the skull down to granulation tissue that would accept a graft. Restoring hair growth to this area would require an additional series of scalp rotation operations. The operations have left Melvin's face and scalp severely scarred, his mouth permanently contorted into a sneer. Because his facial nerves and muscles have been burned away, even additional surgery will never restore to him the ability to smile.

Of the expected eleven future operations, Melvin will undergo eight additional operations to his face. Skin grafts not infrequently dry out, crack, become infected and ulcerated and must be replaced by new grafts. Sunlight darkens grafted skin permanently, highlighting the injured area. Grafted areas are also more susceptible to skin cancer than normal tissue. Melvin testified that the grafted areas hurt and itch constantly. Dr. Sacks testified that additional plastic surgeries and skin grafts will not restore a normal appearance to Melvin.

Melvin has suffered psychologically as well as physically. At the burn unit Dr. Canter treated Melvin by hypnosis to relieve pain, prevent regurgitation of food and restore a will to live. Since emerging from the hospital Melvin has faced teasing and ridicule from his peers and startle reactions and revulsion from strangers.

For several months Melvin wore a mask to protect his healing face from further injury. His schoolmates labeled him "Maskatron." During a school outing children from another school saw him and ran away in horror. Strangers often ask, "What happened to you?" Clarence Martin testified that Melvin has become reclusive, reluctant to attend school. Dr. Canter stated that Melvin has become somewhat detached from life, blames himself for his father's heart trouble and may develop schizophrenic tendencies as a result of his injuries. Nor is it likely that Melvin will have a normal social or sexual life, given the severity of the injuries.

Based upon the testimony and my own observation of Melvin, I award $1,000,000 in compensation for pain and suffering.

[The Court here made a similar analysis of the claims by plaintiff Martin.]

I find that the plaintiffs are entitled to awards as follows:

	BURROWS	MARTIN
Past Medical	$48,130.97	$15,384.38
Future Medical	53,629.00	30,000.00
Loss of Earning Capacity	548,029.00	453,088.00
Pain and Suffering	1,000,000.00	750,000.00
Total	$1,649,788.97	$1,248,472.38

The foregoing shall constitute findings of fact and conclusions pursuant to Rule 52, Fed. R. Civ. P., together with earlier findings and conclusions set out in my oral opinion on February 14, 1979.

NOTES

1. **Proving causation.** The plaintiff must prove that damages claimed were caused in fact by the defendant's conduct. Suppose the plaintiff proves an impact and testifies to headaches, back pain, and sleeplessness but has no external injury such as cuts or bruises. Must the plaintiff provide expert medical evidence either to show that the pain was "real" or that the impact caused it? *See Choi v. Anvil,* 32 P.3d 1 (Alaska 2001). Suppose that the plaintiff also claims that her headaches and backaches will last the rest of her life?

2. **Inflation and reduction to present value.** Notice that the judge had to make an upward adjustment in the award for future loss in order to account for expected inflation. The judge also made a downward adjustment to account for the fact that although the loss will take place over many years in the future, all of the money to compensate the plaintiff will be paid now and can be invested. This reduction to present value requires the judge or the trier to determine the amount the plaintiff can earn in safe investments of the award. The reduction may also require expert testimony. *See* 1 DAN B. DOBBS, REMEDIES §§ 3.7 & 8.5. Still other adjustments are considered in *subsection b.* below.

3. **Periodic payments.** These adjustments would not be necessary if, instead of a lump sum award, future loss were compensated in periodic payments that could be varied as inflation occurred. Some states now authorize such payments in a limited class of cases. *See* Roger Henderson, *Designing a Responsible Periodic Payment System for Tort Awards,* 32 ARIZ. L. REV. 21 (1990).

4. **The scope of pain and suffering.** The pain and suffering recovery includes all forms of pain, including mental or emotional distress. As this implies, the recovery includes the negative emotional reactions to pain as well as the pain itself. For example, a disfiguring injury, no longer physically painful, may cause a plaintiff to become self-conscious or even to withdraw from social contact. If so, such reactions count as part of the pain for which damages may be assessed. See 2 DOBBS, REMEDIES § 8.1(4).

5. **Dollarizing pain.** Pain is notoriously difficult to measure or even to talk about meaningfully. In *District of Columbia v. Howell,* 607 A.2d 501 (D.C. 1992), a nine-year-old boy was badly burned in a chemical explosion in school.

"The chemicals burned at 5000 degrees Fahrenheit, and Dedrick was burned over 25% of his body including his hands, arms, chest, and face." The jury awarded $8 million in pain and suffering damages. If this award and Martin's had been made in the same year, could you say that one was wrong or even that one was closer to the mark than the other? In *Surette v. Islamic Republic of Iran,* 231 F. Supp. 2d 260 (D.C. 2002), a group encouraged by the Republic of Iran, tortured Buckley for a long period before he died of his mistreatment. In a suit for his death and for his pre-death pain and suffering, the court said: "Subject to adjustment for cases deviating from the more common experience of victims, this Court typically has awarded former hostages or their estates roughly $10,000 for each day of captivity."

6. **Considering comparable awards.** May the trier of fact consider awards in comparable cases to fix the amount of noneconomic damages? Many courts have disapproved of this kind of evidence at trial. *See, e.g., Richardson v. Chapman,* 676 N.E.2d 621 (Ill. 1997); *Ritter v. Stanton,* 745 N.E.2d 828 (Ind. Ct. App. 2001). Where the trial judge is the trier of fact, however, a number of appellate courts approve of, and perhaps even require, the consideration of such information, usually on the ground that the trial judge is required to explain the basis for her decision. *See, e.g., Arpin v. United States,* 521 F.3d 769 (7th Cir. 2008) (reversing trial judge's award of damages where he did not consider awards in similar cases). Of course, many appellate courts consider comparable cases when determining whether an award is excessive. *See, e.g., Bravo v. United States,* 532 F.3d 1154 (11th Cir. 2008); *Sloane v. Equifax Information Services,* LLC, 510 F.3d 495 (4th Cir. 2007); *Okraynets v. Metropolitan Transp. Authority,* 555 F.Supp.2d 420 (S.D.N.Y. 2008) (applying New York law that requires reviewing courts to "compare verdicts sustained by New York courts in similar cases"). Do you see any problems with allowing a jury to consider awards in prior cases? Do all of those problems disappear when a trial judge is making the determination?

7. **Argumentation.** Lawyers have developed some effective jury arguments, one of which is called the per diem or unit-of-time argument. It asks the jury to consider the value of pain by the minute or hour and then to multiply by the number of hours the plaintiff will continue to suffer pain over his lifetime. Evaluating the jury's conversion of proof and argument into dollar amounts is more difficult. Many commentators have expressed concern that our measurements are too crude and that results are not even-handed.

8. **Reinforcing pain.** Another and distinct problem with pain awards is that the award itself may conceivably reinforce some kinds of pain, that is, operate as a psychological factor that helps cause the pain to continue. *See* Ellen Smith Pryor, *Compensation and the Ineradicable Problems of Pain,* 59 GEO. WASH. L. REV. 239, 280 (1991).

9. **Pain and suffering pays attorney fees.** One important thing to bear in mind when you judge pain and suffering awards is the American Rule that each side pays its own attorney. See 1 DOBBS, REMEDIES § 3.10. That rule explains why the contingent percentage fee is so important in personal injury cases. Lawyers for injured people must recover their fee from the damages award, since hardly any individual would be able to pay a guaranteed hourly fee for the lawyer's services. If there were no substantial pain and suffering

award, lawyer's would often be unable to pursue the claim with the vigor it requires, simply because damages equal to the plaintiff's pecuniary loss would not bring enough money to justify the time invested.

McDOUGALD v. GARBER

536 N.E.2d 372 (N.Y. 1989)

WACHTLER, CHIEF JUDGE.

This appeal raises fundamental questions about the nature and role of nonpecuniary damages in personal injury litigation. By nonpecuniary damages, we mean those damages awarded to compensate an injured person for the physical and emotional consequences of the injury, such as pain and suffering and the loss of the ability to engage in certain activities. Pecuniary damages, on the other hand, compensate the victim for the economic consequences of the injury, such as medical expenses, lost earnings and the cost of custodial care. . . .

On September 7, 1978, plaintiff Emma McDougald, then 31 years old, underwent a Caesarean section and tubal ligation at New York Infirmary. Defendant Garber performed the surgery; defendants Armengol and Kulkarni provided anesthesia. During the surgery, Mrs. McDougald suffered oxygen deprivation which resulted in severe brain damage and left her in a permanent comatose condition. This action was brought by Mrs. McDougald and her husband, suing derivatively, alleging that the injuries were caused by the defendants' acts of malpractice.

[The trial court charged the jury that if Emma McDougald was so neurologically impaired that she was incapable of experiencing painful sensation or any emotional reaction to it, then there could be no recovery for pain and suffering. But the court went on to instruct the jury that the plaintiff could recover for loss of the pleasures and pursuits of life even if she was unaware of any loss.]

A jury found all defendants liable and awarded Emma McDougald a total of $9,650,102 in damages, including $1,000,000 for conscious pain and suffering and a separate award of $3,500,000 for loss of the pleasures and pursuits of life. The balance of the damages awarded to her were for pecuniary damages—lost earnings and the cost of custodial and nursing care. Her husband was awarded $1,500,000 on his derivative claim for the loss of his wife's services. On defendants' post-trial motions, the Trial Judge reduced the total award to Emma McDougald to $4,796,728 by striking the entire award for future nursing care ($2,353,374) and by reducing the separate awards for conscious pain and suffering and loss of the pleasures and pursuits of life to a single award of $2,000,000. Her husband's award was left intact. [The Appellate Division affirmed.] . . .

We conclude that the court erred, both in instructing the jury that Mrs. McDougald's awareness was irrelevant to their consideration of damages for loss of enjoyment of life and in directing the jury to consider that aspect of damages separately from pain and suffering.

We begin with the familiar proposition that an award of damages to a person injured by the negligence of another is to compensate the victim, not to punish the wrongdoer. The goal is to restore the injured party, to the extent possible, to the position that would have been occupied had the wrong not occurred. To be sure, placing the burden of compensation on the negligent party also serves as a deterrent, but purely punitive damages—that is, those which have no compensatory purpose—are prohibited unless the harmful conduct is intentional, malicious, outrageous, or otherwise aggravated beyond mere negligence.

Damages for nonpecuniary losses are, of course, among those that can be awarded as compensation to the victim. This aspect of damages, however, stands on less certain ground than does an award for pecuniary damages. An economic loss can be compensated in kind by an economic gain; but recovery for noneconomic losses such as pain and suffering and loss of enjoyment of life rests on "the legal fiction that money damages can compensate for a victim's injury." We accept this fiction, knowing that although money will neither ease the pain nor restore the victim's abilities, this device is as close as the law can come in its effort to right the wrong. We have no hope of evaluating what has been lost, but a monetary award may provide a measure of solace for the condition created.

Our willingness to indulge this fiction comes to an end, however, when it ceases to serve the compensatory goals of tort recovery. When that limit is met, further indulgence can only result in assessing damages that are punitive. The question posed by this case, then, is whether an award of damages for loss of enjoyment of life to a person whose injuries preclude any awareness of the loss serves a compensatory purpose. We conclude that it does not.

Simply put, an award of money damages in such circumstances has no meaning or utility to the injured person. An award for the loss of enjoyment of life "cannot provide (such a victim) with any consolation or ease any burden resting on him * * * He cannot spend it upon necessities or pleasures. He cannot experience the pleasure of giving it away."

We recognize that, as the trial court noted, requiring some cognitive awareness as a prerequisite to recovery for loss of enjoyment of life will result in some cases "in the paradoxical situation that the greater the degree of brain injury inflicted by a negligent defendant, the smaller the award the plaintiff can recover in general damages" (McDougald v. Garber, 132 Misc. 2d 457, 460, 504 N.Y.S.2d 383, supra). The force of this argument, however—the temptation to achieve a balance between injury and damages—has nothing to do with meaningful compensation for the victim. Instead, the temptation is rooted in a desire to punish the defendant in proportion to the harm inflicted. However relevant such retributive symmetry may be in the criminal law, it has no place in the law of civil damages, at least in the absence of culpability beyond mere negligence.

Accordingly, we conclude that cognitive awareness is a prerequisite to recovery for loss of enjoyment of life. We do not go so far, however, as to require the fact finder to sort out varying degrees of cognition and determine at what level a particular deprivation can be fully appreciated. With respect to pain and suffering, the trial court charged simply that there must be "some level of awareness" in order for plaintiff to recover. We think that this is an appropriate standard for all aspects of nonpecuniary loss. No doubt the standard ignores analytically relevant levels of cognition, but we resist the desire for analytical purity in favor of simplicity. . . .

We turn next to the question whether loss of enjoyment of life should be considered a category of damages separate from pain and suffering.

There is no dispute here that the fact finder may, in assessing nonpecuniary damages, consider the effect of the injuries on the plaintiff's capacity to lead a normal life. Traditionally, in this State and elsewhere, this aspect of suffering has not been treated as a separate category of damages; instead, the plaintiff's inability to enjoy life to its fullest has been considered one type of suffering to be factored into a general award for nonpecuniary damages, commonly known as pain and suffering.

Recently, however, there has been an attempt to segregate the suffering associated with physical pain from the mental anguish that stems from the inability to engage in certain activities, and to have juries provide a separate award for each.

Some courts have resisted the effort, primarily on the ground that duplicative and therefore excessive awards would result. Other courts have allowed separate awards, noting that the types of suffering involved are analytically distinguishable. . . .

We do not dispute that distinctions can be found or created between the concepts of pain and suffering and loss of enjoyment of life. If the term "suffering" is limited to the emotional response to the sensation of pain, then the emotional response caused by the limitation of life's activities may be considered qualitatively different. But suffering need not be so limited—it can easily encompass the frustration and anguish caused by the inability to participate in activities that once brought pleasure. Traditionally, by treating loss of enjoyment of life as a permissible factor in assessing pain and suffering, courts have given the term this broad meaning.

If we are to depart from this traditional approach and approve a separate award for loss of enjoyment of life, it must be on the basis that such an approach will yield a more accurate evaluation of the compensation due to the plaintiff. We have no doubt that, in general, the total award for nonpecuniary damages would increase if we adopted the rule. That separate awards are advocated by plaintiffs and resisted by defendants is sufficient evidence that larger awards are at stake here. But a larger award does not by itself indicate that the goal of compensation has been better served.

The advocates of separate awards contend that because pain and suffering and loss of enjoyment of life can be distinguished, they must be treated separately if the plaintiff is to be compensated fully for each distinct injury suffered. We disagree. Such an analytical approach may have its place when the subject is pecuniary damages, which can be calculated with some precision. But the estimation of nonpecuniary damages is not amenable to such analytical precision and may, in fact, suffer from its application. Translating human suffering into dollars and cents involves no mathematical formula; it rests, as we have said, on a legal fiction. The figure that emerges is unavoidably distorted by the translation. Application of this murky process to the component parts of nonpecuniary injuries (however analytically distinguishable they may be) cannot make it more accurate. If anything, the distortion will be amplified by repetition.

Thus, we are not persuaded that any salutary purpose would be served by having the jury make separate awards for pain and suffering and loss of enjoyment of life. We are confident, furthermore, that the trial advocate's art is a sufficient guarantee that none of the plaintiff's losses will be ignored by the jury.

The errors in the instructions given to the jury require a new trial on the issue of nonpecuniary damages . . . . .

TITONE, JUDGE (dissenting).

The majority's holding represents a compromise position that neither comports with the fundamental principles of tort compensation nor furnishes a satisfactory, logically consistent framework for compensating nonpecuniary loss. Because I conclude that loss of enjoyment of life is an objective damage item, conceptually distinct from conscious pain and suffering, I can find no fault with the trial court's instruction authorizing separate awards and permitting an award for "loss of enjoyment of life" even in the absence of any awareness of that loss on the part of the injured plaintiff. Accordingly, I dissent. . . .

The capacity to enjoy life—by watching one's children grow, participating in recreational activities, and drinking in the many other pleasures that life has to offer—is unquestionably an attribute of an ordinary healthy individual. . . .

As in the case of a lost limb, an essential characteristic of a healthy human life has been wrongfully taken, and, consequently, the injured party is entitled to a monetary award as a substitute, if, as the majority asserts, the goal of tort compensation is "to restore the injured party, to the extent possible, to the position that would have been occupied had the wrong not occurred." . . .

Significantly, this equation does not suggest a need to establish the injured's awareness of the loss. The victim's ability to comprehend the degree to which his or her life has been impaired is irrelevant, since, unlike "conscious pain and suffering," the impairment exists independent of the victim's ability to apprehend it. . . .

Moreover, the compensatory nature of a monetary award for loss of enjoyment of life is not altered or rendered punitive by the fact that the unaware injured plaintiff cannot experience the pleasure of having it. The fundamental distinction between punitive and compensatory damages is that the former exceed the amount necessary to replace what the plaintiff lost. . . .

NOTES

1. **Hedonic damages: the terminology.** In the 1980s, plaintiffs' lawyers and some judges began to use the term hedonic damages from the Greek word referring to pleasure or happiness. The term has acquired ambiguity because those who use it sometimes seem to suggest (a) a right of recovery for the plaintiff's awareness of lost pleasures, sometimes (b) a right of recovery for lost pleasures even when the plaintiff is not aware of the loss or in fact has died, and sometimes (c) a certain type of economic evidence. To avoid misunderstanding, the term is avoided here.

2. **Plaintiff aware of loss.** When the plaintiff has lost the ability to pursue life's pleasures and knows it, that knowledge or awareness is itself a source of unpleasant feelings, a sense of loss, and even anguish. Recovery is allowed in most courts nowadays without hesitation. *See Foradori v. Harris,* 523 F.3d 477 (5th Cir. 2008) (applying Mississippi law, affirming award of $10 million); *Leiker v. Gafford,* 778 P.2d 823 (Kan. 1989); *Kenton v. Hyatt Hotels Corp.,* 693 S.W.2d 83 (Mo. 1985) (emphasizing plaintiff's loss of ability to play tennis, ski, jog, and carry on other athletic activities). Should a jury be instructed that the plaintiff can recover both for pain and suffering and for loss of enjoyment of life? Some courts have approved this idea. *See, e.g., Kansas City S. Ry. Co. v. Johnson,* 798 So.2d 374 (Miss. 2001). Would it be less confusing to the jury to instruct broadly on pain and suffering and to make it clear that consciousness of lost enjoyment is a part of that pain and suffering? *See Gregory v. Carey,* 791 P.2d 1329 (Kan. 1990).

3. **Plaintiff unaware of loss.** When the plaintiff is unaware of her loss, as in *McDougald,* there is no tradition of awarding damages for that "loss," but when the issue has arisen more recently, cases have gone both ways. A number of cases, directly or indirectly, are aligned with *McDougald. E.g., Dillingham v. IBP, Inc.,* 219 F.3d 797 (8th Cir. 2000); *Bulala v. Boyd,* 389 S.E.2d 670 (Va. 1990). Several others have strongly argued for allowing the recovery for loss of enjoyment of which the plaintiff will never be aware. *See Flannery v. United States,* 297 S.E.2d 433 (W.Va. 1982). *Holston v. Sisters of Third Order of St. Francis,* 650 N.E.2d 985 (Ill. 1995), may have accomplished the same thing by permitting recovery for the "disability" of a comatose patient who died after a week.

4. **Proof.** How can a plaintiff prove hedonic damages to the jury? Could an expert testify about the value of the loss of enjoyment of life? *See Mercado v. Ahmed,* 974 F.2d 863 (7th Cir. 1992) (affirming trial judge's refusal to admit such testimony). *Montalvo v. Lapez,* 884 P.2d 345 (Haw. 1994), com-

mented that valuing the joy of life is "a uniquely human endeavor ... requiring the trier of fact to draw upon the virtually unlimited factors unique to us as human beings."

NOTE: THE SPECIAL CASE OF MEDICAL MONITORING DAMAGES

The plaintiffs—sometimes whole neighborhoods or an entire workforce—are exposed to a toxic substance which increases the likelihood of a disease, usually some form of cancer. However, the plaintiffs have no demonstrable physical injury at present. They might conceivably claim an increased present risk of cancer, a kind of lost chance claim, or emotional harm resulting from their fear of future disease. However, courts have typically denied both of those claims.

If the plaintiffs were suffering from any actual physical harm because of the toxic exposure, the defendant would be liable for that physical harm and also for medical monitoring damages, provided proof shows such monitoring is needed. That is, damages would include damages for the costs of periodic medical checks that could detect cancers in early stages so as to permit early intervention.

Some courts have gone further by allowing medical monitoring damages even when no physical harm has been done and no emotional harm claim is allowable. *Bower v. Westinghouse Elec. Co.*, 522 S.E.2d 424 (W.Va. 1999); *Burns v. Jaquays Min. Corp.*, 752 P.2d 28 (Ariz. Ct. App. 1987); *cf. Sutton v. St. Jude Medical S.C., Inc.*, 419 F.3d 568 (6th Cir. 2005) (increased risk serious enough to require medical monitoring qualifies as an injury-in-fact, conferring federal standing). But other courts have insisted that medical monitoring costs are not "actual harm" that supports a claim; instead, the plaintiff must prove actionable physical harm before medical monitoring costs can be recovered. *Sinclair v. Merck & Co.*, 948 A.2d 587 (N.J. 2008) (applying products liability statute); *Henry v. Dow Chemical Co.*, 701 N.W.2d 684 (Mich. 2005); *Wood v. Wyeth–Ayerst Labs.*, 82 S.W.3d 849 (Ky. 2002). Two commentators have suggested that any other rule would be judicial "madness." James A. Henderson, Jr. & Aaron D. Twerski, *Asbestos Litigation Gone Mad: Exposure-based Recovery for Increased Risk, Mental Distress, and Medical Monitoring*, 53 S.C. L. REV. 815 (2002). Do you agree?

B. CAPPING AND LIMITING DAMAGES

CAL. CIV. CODE § 3333.2

(a) In any action for injury against a health care provider based on professional negligence, the injured plaintiff shall be entitled to recover noneconomic losses to compensate for pain, suffering, inconvenience, physical impairment, disfigurement and other nonpecuniary damage.

(b) In no action shall the amount of damages for noneconomic losses exceed two hundred fifty thousand dollars ($250,000).

MD. CODE ANN., CT. & JUD. PROC. § 11–108

(a) In this section: (1) "noneconomic damages" means pain, suffering, inconvenience, physical impairment, disfigurement, loss of consortium, or other nonpecuniary injury; and (2) "Noneconomic damages" does not include punitive damages.

(b) In any action for damages for personal injury in which the cause of action arises on or after July 1, 1986, an award for noneconomic damages may not exceed $350,000. . . .

(c)(1) In a jury trial, the jury may not be informed of the limitation established under subsection (b) of this section. (2) If the jury awards an amount for noneconomic damages that exceeds the limitation established under subsection (b) of this section, the court shall reduce the amount to conform to the limitation.

Notes

1. **Caps on pain and suffering awards.** In theory, damages are compensatory. For this reason, tort damages have been limited only by the evidence, not by any arbitrary dollar amount or by any formula.

2. **Two statutory waves.** Two waves of statutes have been passed changing this common law tradition. The first resulted from the supposed medical malpractice insurance "crisis" of the 1970s. The second resulted from a supposed "crisis" in the 1980s. This second wave, however, was the product of long and persistent efforts by a much wider group of defendants and insurers who felt threatened by tort law. The statutory limits were based on a perception that there was a crisis in the affordability and availability of insurance, especially for target groups like health care providers and public entities, or sometimes simply on the claim that juries had gone wild. Whether this perception is justified is considered further in Chapter 24.

3. **Line-up of the states.** Some kind of cap or limit has been enacted in well over half of the states. As indicated below, however, some have been held unconstitutional, some are applied to only one particular kind of claim, and some are overridden by statutes such as California's Elder Abuse statute, which allows recovery for reckless neglect of the elderly without a cap. As to this last, *see Delaney v. Baker,* 971 P.2d 986 (Cal. 1999).

4. **Types of statute: which defendants covered.** *(a) All injury defendants vs. medical defendants.* Notice that the Maryland statute applies by its terms to "any action for damages for personal injury." The California statute, on the other hand, applies only to claims against health care providers and then only for professional negligence—in other words, to medical malpractice claims. Most of the statutes follow one of these two patterns, applying either generally or to some special group.

(b) Caps partially restoring lost immunities of favored defendants or limiting new statutory claims. In some states statutory caps for special defendants reflect traditional protective attitudes that the common law itself shared. For instance, the common law provided immunities to governmental

entities and charities. It is not surprising to see that, when liability is imposed on these defendants, legislative caps put a ceiling to that liability. *See, e.g.,* ME. REV. STAT. ANN. tit. 14 § 8105 ($300,000 cap on all claims against government entity or employees). The common law's protective attitude toward purveyors of alcohol, like the traditional attitude toward immunities, has been much modified, but again, it is no surprise to see legislative caps on dram shop recoveries. *E.g.,* UTAH CODE ANN. § 32A–14–101(5) ($100,000 cap). Similarly, some new statutory claims may be subjected to a dollar limit, as where parents are subjected to liability for the torts of their children. *E.g.,* W. VA. CODE § 55–74–2 ($5000). Finally caps may be indirectly imposed when a new compensation system is substituted for traditional tort law, as with the National Childhood Vaccine Injury Act, summarized in Chapter 29, *infra.*

5. **Types of statute: which damages covered.** Most of the statutes so far enacted cap nonpecuniary damages but do not cap the recovery for actual pecuniary loss. The cap on nonpecuniary damages, however, is serious to plaintiffs, since it is the nonpecuniary recovery that furnishes a basis for the attorney fee, without which attorneys often cannot afford to pursue complex and time-consuming claims. A few statutes go beyond the cap on nonpecuniary damages and place a cap that limits damages of any kind. *E.g.,* COLO. REV. STAT. § 13–64–302 (subject to a limited possibility that the plaintiff could recover pecuniary losses and punitive damages in excess of the cap).

6. **Capping plaintiffs vs. capping defendants.** Suppose the cap is $250,000 but the plaintiff has damages of $500,000. If two defendants are liable, could the plaintiff recover up to $250,000 from each? *General Elec. Co. v. Niemet,* 866 P.2d 1361 (Colo. 1994) (yes, as a matter of statutory construction, Colorado's cap applies to individual defendants, not to plaintiffs). A somewhat similar question arises when the spouse of an injured person claims lost consortium. Does the cap apply to both claims as a unit, or could each spouse recover a sum up to the cap's limit? *In re Certification of Questions in Knowles v. United States,* 544 N.W.2d 183 (S.D. 1996) (one action for liability purposes, but two actions with separate caps on damages).

7. **Caps and comparative fault.** Suppose the plaintiff has $300,000 in nonpecuniary damages as well as pecuniary loss that can be separately calculated. The state has a cap on nonpecuniary damages of $250,000 and a pure comparative fault statute. The jury finds the plaintiff to be chargeable with 20% of the negligence. What should the plaintiff recover? Consider:

(A) $300,000 reduced to the cap of $250,000, minus 20% of the $300,000 or $60,000 = a net of $190,000 for nonpecuniary damages.

(B) $300,000 reduced to the cap of $250,000, minus 20% of the damages as capped, or $50,000 = a net recovery of $200,000.

(C) $300,000 minus 20% = $240,000; since this falls below the cap, no further reduction is required.

See McAdory v. Rogers, 264 Cal.Rptr. 71 (Ct. App. 1989) ("There is no legitimate or logical reason for reducing that award to the $250,000 cap prescribed by section 3333.2 before reducing it further due to Ms. McAdory's 22 percent comparative fault.")

8. **Caps unconstitutional.** Several courts have found the capping statutes to be unconstitutional under various provisions of their respective state constitutions. *E.g., Ferdon v. Wisconsin Patients Compensation Fund*, 701 N.W.2d 440 (Wis. 2005); *State v. Sheward*, 715 N.E.2d 1062 (Ohio 1999); *Lakin v. Senco Prods., Inc.*, 987 P.2d 463 (Or. 1999); *Trujillo v. City of Albuquerque*, 965 P.2d 305 (N.M. 1998); *Best v. Taylor Mach. Works*, 689 N.E.2d 1057 (Ill. 1997); *cf. Clarke v. Oregon Health Sciences Univ.*, 175 P.3d 418 (Or. 2007) (tort claims act provision requiring substitution of public body as sole defendant, coupled with damages cap, unconstitutional as applied in malpractice action against public hospital employees).

9. **Constitutional themes.** The capping statutes, the state constitutional provisions, and the cases are varied. Some statutes have been condemned as special legislation or violation of right to trial by jury. Broad themes discussed, however, include some version of these ideas:

(a) the injured plaintiff cannot be made to bear the burden of reducing insurance costs for others or for society as a whole;

(b) it is arbitrary to select the particular group of defendants for special attention;

(c) no alternative redress or even assistance is provided for the injured plaintiff; the plaintiff shoulders the burden others are feeling without a quid pro quo;

(d) caps are in themselves arbitrary, especially when injuries may be quite different among those affected;

(e) no showing is made that the caps will actually resolve the supposed insurance crisis.

10. **Caps constitutional.** The California statute set out above was upheld in *Fein v. Permanente Medical Group*, 695 P.2d 665 (Cal. 1985). The Ohio Supreme Court, after striking down broad tort reform legislation that included caps in *State v. Sheward, supra* Note 8, later upheld a revised statute that caps noneconomic damages in some but not all cases and contains exceptions for "serious injuries." *Arbino v. Johnson & Johnson*, 880 N.E.2d 420 (Ohio 2007). A number of other recent decisions have upheld caps against claims that they violated jury trial rights, due process, equal protection, or various somewhat analogous state constitutional provisions, or that they contravened the Americans with Disability Act. *Garhart v. Columbia/Healthone, L.L.C.*, 95 P.3d 571 (Colo. 2004); *Gourley v. Nebraska Methodist Health Sys., Inc.*, 663 N.W.2d 43 (Neb. 2003); *Kirkland v. Blaine County Med. Ctr.*, 4 P.3d 1115 (Idaho 2000); *Patton v. TIC United Corp.*, 77 F.3d 1235 (10th Cir. 1996); *Murphy v. Edmonds*, 601 A.2d 102 (Md. 1992); *Adams v. Children's Mercy Hosp.*, 832 S.W.2d 898 (Mo. 1992).

11. **Attorney fees.** One function of the pain and suffering award is to provide a fund from which to pay the plaintiff's attorney the usual percentage fee. Without this fee, attorneys cannot afford to take difficult cases. Is there any way to cap damages without removing just claims from the judicial system?

12. **Reform as discrimination?** Certain kinds of cases produce non-economic (but real) harms. Some sexual abuse, for example, may be so

harmful that the victim is actually unable to work effectively, but very often the main component of damages is noneconomic. Not all sexual abuse victims are women, but most are. Does this mean that if tort reformers cap pain and suffering damages, they discriminating against women? *See* Thomas Koenig & Michael Rustad, *His and Her Tort Reform: Gender Injustice in Disguise*, 70 WASH. L. REV. 1 (1995).

13. **Side effects of caps.** Maybe caps will have some unintended side-effects. Would judges or juries be more inclined to resolve close questions of *liability* for the plaintiff where caps limit the *damages*? After the 9–11 terrorist attacks, Congress set up a victims' compensation scheme but permitted victims to opt for tort suits instead. If they opted for tort suits, however, damages were capped (except in suits against terrorist-associated defendants) at the total of the defendants' liability insurance. In *In re September 11 Litigation*, 280 F. Supp. 2d 279 (S.D.N.Y. 2003), one question was whether the airlines owed a duty of care to potential victims on the ground. The court held that they did. One factor: there would be no limitless liability because of the caps.

NOTE: ABOLISHING OR LIMITING
PAIN AND SUFFERING DAMAGES

Pain and suffering awards have long been questioned for various reasons, some of which are suggested below in connection with the difficulty of proving or measuring such damages. In recent years economic arguments have been advanced against pain and suffering awards. A simplified version of what is sometimes elaborate economic theory might go something like this: When pain and suffering damages are awarded, the defendant must add these liabilities to its cost of doing business and will normally pass along the costs to consumers in the form of higher prices. For example, a product manufacturer, held liable for an injury, will probably raise the costs of its goods. Consumers in the future will then be forced to pay an increased cost or premium for the goods—a premium that reflects costs of paying pain and suffering damages. Since the purchaser of goods or services cannot get them at a cheaper price by renouncing any intention of suing for pain and suffering damages, this amounts to a kind of compulsory insurance. If everyone wanted to purchase such insurance, that might be all right, but most consumers would be better off to take goods at a cheaper price than to enjoy the fruits of a large pain and suffering recovery if they are injured.

In addition, even if one wanted to be sure to recover for pain, recovery through liability insurance is, as will be seen in Chapter 30, an expensive way to do it. A direct purchase of pain and suffering insurance or ordinary accident insurance would be cheaper than a recovery through the elaborate mechanisms of the tort system.

Such arguments suggest that pain and suffering recoveries should be abolished or limited. Would abolition affect safety incentives of toxic tortfeasors or product producers?

REFERENCE: DOBBS ON TORTS §§ 377–379 (2000).

§ 2. ADJUSTMENTS IN DAMAGES

KEANS v. BOTTIARELLI

645 A.2d 1029 (Conn. App. Ct. 1994)

SCHALLER, JUDGE.

The defendant in this dental malpractice action appeals from the judgment of the trial court in favor of the plaintiff. The trial court awarded the plaintiff damages of $20,000, but reduced the award by $5034.46 after finding that the plaintiff had failed to mitigate her damages. . . .

The trial court could reasonably have found the following facts. On July 19, 1990, the plaintiff consulted the defendant, an oral surgeon, to have a tooth extracted. On the initial visit to the defendant, the plaintiff informed the defendant that she suffered from myelofibrosis, a rare blood disorder that inhibits production of red blood cells and platelets, thereby affecting the blood clotting ability of afflicted individuals. The plaintiff's condition requires her to receive frequent blood and platelet transfusions and to self-administer interferon injections. The plaintiff further informed the defendant that her platelet count was 39,000. The defendant performed the extraction without first consulting the plaintiff's hematologist, concluding that the plaintiff "looked good" and would not require a platelet transfusion. The plaintiff remained in the defendant's recovery room until the area around the extraction site stopped bleeding and was sent home with a prescription for penicillin and a pamphlet detailing postoperative instructions. After returning home, the extraction site began to bleed. The plaintiff's son called the defendant, who advised him that the plaintiff should bite down on a tea bag to release tannic acid to facilitate blood clotting. The plaintiff made no further effort to contact the defendant that day, despite worsening of her condition.

The next morning, the plaintiff contacted Richard Hellman, her hematologist, who admitted her to the hospital. The plaintiff, diagnosed with neutropenia, severe thrombocytopenia, severe anemia and myelofibrosis, was hospitalized for three days and was discharged on July 23, 1990, with no permanent injuries.

The trial court, finding the plaintiff's expert to be more credible than the defendant's experts, concluded that the plaintiff had sustained her burden of proof regarding her claim of malpractice. The plaintiff's expert testified that the defendant deviated from prudent and standard dental practice by failing to consult the plaintiff's hematologist prior to proceeding with the extraction.

In reliance on Preston v. Keith, 217 Conn. 12, 584 A.2d 439 (1991), the trial court concluded that the plaintiff's failure to follow the defendant's postoperative instructions led to the hospitalization, and determined that damages should be mitigated to the extent of the plaintiff's hospitalization expense. . . .

The trial court applied the doctrine of mitigation of damages and reduced the award by the amount of the plaintiff's hospitalization expense. Our Supreme Court has stated that "[w]e have long adhered to the rule that one who is injured by the negligence of another must use reasonable care to promote recovery and prevent any aggravation or increase of the injuries." "When there are facts in evidence that indicate that a plaintiff may have failed to promote his recovery and do what a reasonably prudent person would be expected to do under the same circumstances, the court, when requested to do so, is obliged to charge on the duty to mitigate damages."

The trial court concluded that the three requirements to establish a failure to mitigate damages. . . . The trial court found that the plaintiff's conduct exacerbated her initial injury. The trial court found that the plaintiff failed to take reasonable action to lessen the damages by neglecting to fill the prescription for penicillin and by not following the defendant's postoperative instructions. The trial court further found that this failure on the part of the plaintiff caused the need for her hospitalization. We conclude that the trial court's reduction of the damage award for this reason was not clearly erroneous. We, therefore, also reject the plaintiff's contention on cross appeal that the trial court improperly reduced her award. . . .

The judgment is affirmed.

NOTES

1. **Avoidable consequences.** The avoidable consequences or "mitigation" rule requires the plaintiff to exercise reasonable care to minimize damages and denies a recovery to the extent that damages should have been but were not reasonably minimized or avoided. *See generally* 1 DOBBS, REMEDIES §§ 3.9, 8.7. The common law rules of avoidable consequences worked quite differently from comparative fault rules. Comparative fault rules reduce damages in proportion to the plaintiff's fault. Avoidable consequences rules reduce damages for discrete identifiable items of loss caused by the plaintiff's fault. For example, if the plaintiff, after injury, unreasonably refuses to accept medical attention for a foot injury, and as a result ultimately suffers amputation of the foot which otherwise would have healed, then the avoidable consequences rule would deny recovery for loss of the foot, but would not affect any other damages. In other words, comparative negligence rules are fault apportionment rules while avoidable consequences rules are "causal" apportionment rules.

2. **Why the distinction is important.** Because avoidable consequences rules have never operated as a defense to the plaintiff's cause of action but only to eliminate identifiable items of damage, courts thought that any fault that would count as avoidable consequences should not count as comparative fault. *E.g., Cipollone v. Liggett Group, Inc.*, 893 F.2d 541 (3d Cir. 1990), *rev'd*

on other grounds, 505 U.S. 504 (1992). Such a view is important because if the plaintiff's fault in failing to avoid injury is counted as comparative fault in a modified comparative fault jurisdiction like New Jersey, it might add up to more than 50% and might bar the plaintiff. If it is not counted as comparative fault, then it would only bar damages that could be traced to that particular conduct. In addition, those states that still bar the plaintiff completely for contributory negligence, can allow a reduced recovery to the plaintiff by applying the avoidable consequences or mitigation rule instead of the rule of contributory fault. *Cf. Sawyer v. Comerci,* 563 S.E.2d 748 (Va. 2002) (patient was not chargeable with contributory negligence, but failure to follow doctor's instructions after discharge from emergency room justified an instruction that the patient's "estate may not recover for any portion of the harm which, by such care, could have been avoided" by reasonable care).

3. **Distinguishing comparative fault and avoidable consequences.** Courts and writers have often emphasized that avoidable consequences rules come into play after the plaintiff's injury or the defendant's act of negligence, while contributory or comparative fault comes into play before injury. But doesn't the real difference lie elsewhere, namely in the fact that one rule bases apportionment of responsibility on fault and one on "cause"? One of the advantages of fault apportionment is that fault can be estimated even when evidence cannot separate out items of damages. Fault apportionment works, for example, even when there is only one inseparable item of damage.

4. **Which applies, comparative fault or avoidable consequences?** As indicated in Chapter 9, the RESTATEMENT OF APPORTIONMENT § 3, cmt. *b*, uses a comparative responsibility approach to avoidable consequences cases. However, it is comparative fault only as to the separate injury caused by failure to minimize. Thus on the facts of *Keans* the Restatement's rule does not call for the *Keans* result; rather, the plaintiff's recovery in *Keans* for the hospital expenses would be reduced for the plaintiff's comparative fault. *See* ID. § 3, ill. 4. The Restatement view is that the doctor was alone in culpably causing the initial injury and is fully liable for that, but that he and the plaintiff together culpably cause the indivisible component of hospital expense. Since causal apportionment of the hospital expense is not possible—they both caused it—comparative fault apportionment for that item rather than causal apportionment is required.

NOTE: OTHER DAMAGES ADJUSTMENTS: THE COLLATERAL SOURCE RULE AND ITS COUSINS

1. *The collateral source rule.* Suppose the injured plaintiff, as a result of his injury, collects medical insurance, continues to receive full pay from his job while he is in the hospital, and is a recipient of a donation from sympathetic neighbors. The general rule is that in figuring the defendant's liability, all these "collateral benefits" to the plaintiff must be ignored. *See* 1 DOBBS, REMEDIES §§ 3.8, 8.6. The defendant pays the full medical expenses of the plaintiff even though they may have been paid already by the medical insurance. The defendant pays full lost earnings or

lost earning capacity even though the plaintiff collected full pay as a gift from his employer or as part of his job benefits.

2. *The windfall effect.* As perceived by many, the collateral source rule sometimes gives the plaintiff a kind of windfall; in effect she may collect twice for the medical expenses and the "lost" wages. In *Covington v. George,* 597 S.E.2d 142 (S.C. 2004), the plaintiff's hospital bills came to about $4,000, which were claimed as damages. The defendant offered evidence that the hospital actually accepted payments, apparently from Medicare, of about $700 in full payment. This evidence was excluded, even though it suggested that the reasonable value of the medical services was much less than the nominal value of $4,000. The court said: "While a defendant is permitted to attack the necessity and reasonableness of medical care and costs, he cannot do so using evidence of payments made by a collateral source."

3. *The subrogation protection effect.* At other times the collateral source rule merely preserves the subrogation right of the insurer who paid the plaintiff to recover back its loss from the tortfeasor. For instance, suppose that the plaintiff's car is damaged by defendant's negligence. The plaintiff's own collision insurer pays for repairs. In the ordinary case, the collision insurer is subrogated to the plaintiff's claim against the defendant to the extent that it has paid for the car damage. In such a case the plaintiff would be entitled to recover against the defendant for the plaintiff's personal injuries and also for the car damage, but the recovery for car damage goes, by way of subrogation, to the plaintiff's collision insurance company. This can be done only because the collateral source rule allows the plaintiff to recover in spite of the fact that he has been paid. If the plaintiff had no right to recover for car damages because his collision insurer had paid those damages, then the collision insurer could not recover by standing in the plaintiff's shoes. In this situation the collateral source rule does not give the plaintiff "double damages" for the car repair; it merely operates to say which insurer—the plaintiff's collision insurer or the defendant's liability insurer—will ultimately bear the loss.

4. *The direct source or direct benefits rule.* The collateral source rule does not apply to payments made by the defendant itself or by a source identified with the defendant, such as the defendant's insurer. For instance, suppose the defendant has "medical pay" insurance—a kind of accident insurance that protects occupants of the defendant's car even when the defendant is not at fault. If the medical payment insurance makes a payment to the injured occupant and that occupant later sues the defendant in tort, the defendant will be entitled to a credit for the payment. The difference between this situation and the collateral source situation is that here the payment comes from the defendant himself or from his insurer. What counts as a collateral and a direct source is sometimes an issue in the cases, but the principle that damages are reduced for benefits provided directly by the defendant or his behalf is generally accepted.

5. *Criticizing the collateral source rule.* (a) *Eliminating subrogation to eliminate transaction costs.* The collateral source rule has many critics. In the best case it protects an insurer's subrogation recovery. But even in this best case, it merely sets up a system where one insurer recovers from another. Since this shift of the loss entails costs, it might be better to abolish the collateral source rule. This would mean that the collision insurer would bear the loss instead of the liability insurer for the negligent defendant. In some sense this might be unfair, but perhaps in the next case the roles of the two insurers would be reversed, so that the losses might more or less average out. If so, the costs of shifting the loss could be avoided. Even if this were not the case, abolishing the collateral source rule might be a good idea because it would mean that the loss would be paid by collision insurers which operate more efficiently than liability insurers, and hence that the loss would be handled more cheaply.

(b) *Eliminating windfalls to eliminate windfall costs.* When the collateral source rule does not merely protect a subrogation right, it may be seen as a windfall to the plaintiff. This is not entirely so, because, in the case of insurance at least, the plaintiff has paid for the right to the insurance proceeds. Still, if the plaintiff is to recover twice for some elements of damages, the total cost is excessive. The excess is charged against insurers who must reflect it sooner or later in premiums. Eventually, all insurance purchasers would pay more for insurance or goods in order to give random claimants a windfall. Bear in mind the compulsory insurance arguments sketched above. Putting the compulsory insurance aspects of tort recoveries together with the collateral source rule, we find that citizens who would prefer lower premiums on their liability insurance must nevertheless pay the higher price entailed to provide the windfalls of double recovery.

The criticisms seem sound in theory. Whether elimination of the collateral source rule and the windfalls it may produce would actually reduce overall costs of liability insurance is not clear as a matter of fact.

6. *Abolishing the collateral source rule.* The tort reform movement of the 1980s sought to limit defendants' liabilities in a number of ways, one of them by abolishing or substantially altering the collateral source rule in selective cases, usually medical malpractice claims, or those against public entities. The collateral source rule has been abolished or limited in something like half the states or more. *E.g.*, ARIZ. REV. STAT. § 12–565; CAL. CIV. CODE § 3333.1; N.Y. C.P.L.R. § 4545 (c). Some of the limiting statutes have been upheld against constitutional attack, *see, e.g., Eastin v. Broomfield*, 570 P.2d 744 (Ariz. 1977), while others have been struck down, *see, e.g., Farley v. Engelken*, 740 P.2d 1058 (Kan. 1987).

7. *Crediting the defendant for the plaintiff's insurance under the tort reform rules.* Suppose the plaintiff proves that the defendant's tort caused her to suffer $100,000 in medical costs. Under the tort reform statutes, if she received $50,000 in medical benefits from her own insurance, the defendant may be credited with that sum as though he had paid it. That

would leave the defendant owing, not $100,000 in medical expenses, but only $50,000. However, there is one other adjustment to be made. Typically, the plaintiff has paid for the benefits she received by paying premiums. If the plaintiff paid $25,000 in premiums to get the $50,000 insurance benefits, the credit to the defendant must be reduced by the sum of $25,000 the plaintiff paid in premiums over the relevant time period. In *Woodger v. Christ Hospital,* 834 A.2d 1047 (N.J. Super. 2003), the defendant was given a credit for five years' of social security benefits the plaintiff received due to her injury, but that credit was then reduced by the contributions the plaintiff had made to the social security system for five years.

REFERENCE: DOBBS ON TORTS § 380 (2000).

§ 3. PUNITIVE DAMAGES

DAN B. DOBBS, THE LAW OF REMEDIES

Copyright © 1973, 1993 by West Publishing Co.
§ 3.11(1), pp. 453–455. 2d ed. 1993

A. GENERAL RULES

1. Punitive damages are awarded only for ... misconduct coupled with a bad state of mind involving malice or at least a reckless disregard for the rights of others.

2. The stated purposes of punitive damages almost always include (a) punishment or retribution and (b) deterrence. Sometimes the purpose also encompasses (c) the desire to assist in financing useful litigation by providing a source from which fees and costs can be paid. The purposes are somewhat conflicting in that they do not necessarily call for the same amount of punitive recovery.

3. If the judge decides that the facts warrant submission of the case to the jury on the punitive damages issue, the jury's discretion determines (a) whether to make the award at all and (b) the amount of the award, as limited by its purposes, subject only to review as other awards are reviewed.

4. Punitive damages are not per se unconstitutional under the double jeopardy, excessive fines, or due process provisions of the United States Constitution. However, extreme awards, given without appropriate guidance to the jury and without adequate review by judges, may violate due process.

5. Statutes in some states now limit the amount of punitive damages that can be awarded, or, alternatively, direct a portion of the award to some public entity. In addition, some double and treble damages statutes may have the effect of precluding ordinary punitive damages.

6. Punitive damages were traditionally proven by the ordinary civil standard of proof, a preponderance of the evidence. Some courts now demand clear and convincing evidence.

7. The jury is normally allowed to hear evidence about the defendant's wealth, income, or profits as a basis for determining an appropriate amount of punitive damages.

8. Under one rule, punitive awards may be levied against defendants who are only vicariously responsible. Under another rule, employers and others can be responsible for punitive damages for torts of agents or servants only if the employer participated in, encouraged, or ratified the tort.

9. Under one view, probably the majority, liability insurers whose policies do not eliminate coverage for punitive damages are liable for punitive damages judgments against the insured. Under another view, the "punishment" will not be effective if the wrongdoer can insure, so insurance coverage for such awards is against public policy.

10. A defendant whose wrongs have caused many harms to different people may be subjected to more than one punitive liability.

11. Courts sometimes say that punitive damages cannot be awarded unless the plaintiff suffers actual harm or recovers actual damages. Some courts now read this rule to mean only that the plaintiff cannot recover punitive damages unless she first establishes a cause of action.

12. Courts sometimes say that the amount of punitive damages must be in some reasonable proportion to actual damages, but normally this statement is no more than a rough guideline. It may conflict with some other rules.

NOTES

1. **State of mind.** Punitive or exemplary damages are given partly to punish. They thus share a criminal law purpose. What is the bad state of mind required to trigger punitive damages? It is usually said that the defendant must act with malice or at least wanton or reckless disregard of the rights of others. *See, e.g., Ross v. Louise Wise Services, Inc.*, 868 N.E.2d 189 (N.Y. 2007) (holding that punitive damages were unavailable where there was no evidence of malicious or vindictive intent, or a high degree of moral turpitude). Reckless disregard of the rights of others includes conscious indifference to the risk. Although the wantonness standard is less demanding than the malice standard, both require some kind of bad state of mind, not merely extremely negligent conduct. Notice too that it is not enough that the defendant "act intentionally" if there is no malice or bad state of mind. *Id.; Doe v. Isaacs*, 579 S.E.2d 174 (Va. 2003) (intentional violation of traffic law does not support punitive award, without more).

2. **Serious misconduct.** Punitive damages are typically awarded only when the defendant's conduct and state of mind both depart seriously from ordinary expectations in a civil society. However, part of what makes us regard conduct as particularly wrong is the bad actor's state of mind. For this reason, the Supreme Court has held that no separate test of egregious misconduct is required in a federal job discrimination suit under Title VII beyond the defendant's discrimination itself and his awareness that his

conduct may violate the federal law. *Kolstad v. American Dental Ass'n*, 527 U.S. 526 (1999).

3. **Punitive damages in negligence cases.** You might think that punitive damages are thus unavailable in a negligence case, but that is not always true. A plaintiff may bring a case founded on a negligence theory, but may be entitled to punitive damages where he can show further that the defendant exhibited a conscious indifference to the consequences of his acts, or knew that his conduct was substantially certain to violate the plaintiff's rights. *See McCoy v. Montgomery*, 259 S.W.3d 430 (Ark. 2007) (medical malpractice claim); *Hutchison v. Luddy*, 896 A.2d 1260 (Pa. 2006) (negligent hiring and supervision claim); *Strenke v. Hogner*, 694 N.W.2d 296 (Wis. 2005) (negligent driving claim).

4. **Comparative fault reductions?** What if a plaintiff is injured by a reckless driver who acts so callously as to support an award of punitive damages, but at trial the plaintiff is found to have been contributorily negligent in the crash? Should the jury be told to reduce not only the compensatory damages but also the punitive damages based on the percentage of plaintiff's fault? *See Clark v. Cantrell*, 529 S.E.2d 528 (S.C. 2000) (holding no, because to shift a portion of the punitive award back to the plaintiff would undermine its deterrent function).

5. **Some settings for punitive damages.** Courts often talk as if the punitive award was created to punish the bully who deliberately beats or sexually abuses the plaintiff, and there are indeed cases like that. *Cf. Mrozka v. Archdiocese of St. Paul & Minneapolis*, 482 N.W.2d 806 (Minn. Ct. App. 1992) (bishops and archbishop knew of priest's long continued sexual molestation of young boys, refused to do anything significant about it; punitive award justified in spite of First Amendment). But punitive damages in contemporary law have been applied to a wide variety of defendants and in a wide variety of circumstances. Very commonly today, punitive damages are imposed upon defendants who have reaped financial profit from tortious activity and are likely to continue to do so unless deterred by punitive awards.

6. **Exclusions.** Punitive damages are seldom granted for breach of contract unaccompanied by tortious acts. Punitive damages are almost always denied in suits against public entities as well, in the absence of a statute to the contract. There are also statutory causes of action which permit only compensatory damages. *See Barnes v. Gorman*, 536 U.S. 181 (2002) (Americans with Disabilities Act does not authorize punitive damages.)

––––––––

OWENS–CORNING FIBERGLAS CORP. v. BALLARD, 749 So.2d 483 (Fla. 1999). Ballard proved that he had developed mesothelioma, a cancer of the chest lining, due to thirty years of exposure to asbestos in the defendant's product, Kaylo. Evidence showed that "for more than thirty (30) years Owens–Corning concealed what it knew about the dangers of asbestos. In fact, Owens–Corning's conduct was even worse than concealment, it also included intentional and knowing misrepresentations concerning the danger of its asbestos-containing product, Kaylo. For instance, in 1956, Owens–Corning, after having been told by the Saranac Laboratory that Kaylo dust was "toxic," and that asbestos was a carcinogen, advertised Kaylo as being "non-toxic." In 1972, after Owens–Corning developed an asbestos-free version of the Kaylo product, Owens–Corning knowingly and intentionally contaminated the new product with asbestos containing debris from its old Kaylo, and then intentionally and knowingly claimed falsely that the new Kaylo product was "asbestos-free." The jury awarded compensatory damages of $1.8 million and punitive damages of $31 million. *Held,* affirmed.

NOTES

1. **Deterrence function.** This case represents the tort-for-profit punitive damage case in contrast to the bully or excess testosterone case. The defendant in such cases has a motive to continue its tortious activity unless the total expected damages liability will be greater than the profit. Although the courts always focus on the defendant's bad state of mind as a justification for awarding punitive damages, deterrence seems to be the major goal in many cases. In *Ex parte Thicklin,* 824 So.2d 723 (Ala. 2002), the court held that a contract in which the plaintiff purportedly gave up any right to assert punitive damages for product defects would be unconscionable and unenforceable.

2. **Illustration.** Suppose the defendant is making so much money from the sale of the product that compensatory damages awards will never induce the defendant to take it off the market. That might be because, although damages are high, some victims do not discover that the defendant caused their harm. A national products manufacturer which deliberately markets a dangerous product like the Dalkon Shield after its dangers are known may continue to do so (as the Robins company did) unless punitive damages are enough to deny it any profit. See the shocking behavior of the manufacturer as described in *Tetuan v. A.H. Robins Co.,* 738 P.2d 1210 (Kan. 1987). *See also Gonzales v. Surgidev Corp.,* 899 P.2d 576 (N.M. 1995); Dan B. Dobbs, *Ending Punishment in "Punitive" Damages: Deterrence–Measured Remedies,* 40 ALA. L. REV. 831 (1989); Thomas Galligan, *Augmented Awards: The Efficient Evolution of Punitive Damages,* 51 LA. L. REV. 3 (1990). Or perhaps the right amount of punitive damages would be to bring the manufacturer's total liability up to the level it would have paid in ordinary compensatory damages if all victims had appropriately recovered. *See* A. Mitchell Polinsky & Steven Shavell, *Punitive Damages: an Economic Analysis,* 111 HARV. L. REV. 869 (1998).

3. **Strict liability cases.** Defendants used to argue that punitive awards could not be made in strict liability claims, even if the underlying conduct involved the kind of knowing wrong seen in cases like *Owens–Corning Fiberglas Corp. v. Ballard.* This has now changed and punitive damages are understood to be warranted by conduct and state of mind, not by the name of the legal theory used. The classic article is David G. Owen, *Punitive Damages in Products Liability Litigation,* 74 MICH. L. REV. 1256 (1976).

4. **Litigation finance function.** As cases sometimes explicitly point out, punitive damages may serve goals besides pure deterrence—societal condemnation, an example to others as well as deterrent to the defendant, and a source for payment of proper attorney fees, for example. *See Haralson v. Fisher Surveying, Inc.,* 31 P.3d 114 (Ariz. 2001) (holding that punitive damages could be assessed against the estate of a deceased tortfeasor in light of these larger societal effects, even though the deceased himself could not be deterred); *A.C. v. Estate of Crabtree,* 809 N.E.2d 433 (Ind. Ct. App. 2004) (deterrence of others even though tortfeasor cannot be deterred). More particularly, punitive damages may encourage lawyers to invest the large amounts of time necessary to prevail in major cases that require extensive technical investigation and evidence. While the lawyer works on the plaintiff's case, she is not earning money in other cases. The lawyer will not pursue the difficult case unless there is reason to hope for a large award sufficient to pay her a reasonable fee. In some cases the lawyer's investment is so large that she must expect a punitive award to cover her fee and expenses, else give up the case. Can you think of any contemporary cases in which this might be a problem? If so, you can see why a punitive award is a part of the practical financing of litigation in a system where the loser does not pay the winner's attorney fees. In this view, punitive damages may not be a windfall at all.

B. MEASUREMENT OF PUNITIVE DAMAGES

NOTE: TRADITIONAL FACTORS IN MEASURING PUNITIVE DAMAGES

1. *Reprehensibility of the defendant's misconduct.* If punitive damages are warranted by the defendant's serious misconduct, courts must then identify an appropriate sum. You might think that the most important consideration would be to identify the amount necessary to ensure that the defendant does not repeat the wrong. However, courts have often said that the degree of reprehensibility of the defendant's conduct is the most important single consideration. *State Farm Mut. Auto. Ins. Co. v. Campbell,* 538 U.S. 408 (2003). At the same time, courts identify other factors, not necessarily consistent.

2. *Wealth.* Courts have traditionally admitted evidence of the defendant's wealth as bearing on punitive damages, on the theory that a person of great wealth might not be deterred by a small award. *See, e.g., Tarr v. Bob Ciasulli's Mack Auto Mall, Inc.,* 943 A.2d 866 (N.J. 2008). If the tort itself is profitable, profits from the wrongdoing would also be highly relevant. *Must* the plaintiff introduce wealth evidence to warrant punitive damages? The California Court said so in *Adams v. Murakami,* 813 P.2d 1348 (Cal. 1991). Judge Posner incisively criticized this view in *Kemezy v. Peters,* 79 F.3d 33 (7th Cir. 1996), on the ground that the introduction of wealth evidence risks prejudice to the wealthy defendant. Partially because of this problem, it is now common to bifurcate the trial so that the punitive damages evidence is excluded until the jury has already found fault.

3. *Ratio rules*. Courts have long said that punitive damages should bear some kind of reasonable comparison to the compensatory damages, or to actual or potential harm done. In its crudest form, this ratio rule suggests limits incompatible with the purposes of punitive damages in the first place. Suppose the defendant malevolently and repeatedly fires his rifle at the plaintiff, but has so far only chipped the plaintiff's $10 sunglasses. If the jury awards $10 compensatory damages, the ratio rule suggests that punitive awards should be some modest multiple of that sum. It is apparent that this cannot be right under either a punitive or deterrence rationale and it is even less right if the defendant's conduct is profitable even after he pays compensatory damages. The more sophisticated form of the rule does not compare punitive awards to compensatory awards. It compares punitive awards to the potential actual harm that could have resulted from the defendant's conduct. This form of the ratio rule is in fact merely a way of measuring the seriousness of the defendant's misconduct.

4. Some other factors are sketched in discussing the constitutional decisions in the next Note.

NOTE: LIMITING PUNITIVE AWARDS

1. *Moves to limit punitive awards*. There is a perception that punitive damages awards are common, but that perception is incorrect. Recent studies show that punitive damages are awarded in only two to five percent of all cases in which plaintiffs prevail. Remember that most cases do not even go to trial. "Thus, for every 1,000 tort claims filed, typically only 50 are resolved by trial, only 25 produce trial outcomes favorable to the plaintiff, and only 1.25 have a punitive damages award." Thomas A. Eaton, David B. Mustard & Susette M. Talarico, *The Effects of Seeking Punitive Damages on the Processing of Tort Claims*, 34 J. LEGAL STUD. 343 (2005). Another common misperception is that punitive damages awards are primarily a problem produced by "runaway juries." Studies prove that judges award such damages at about the same rate as juries. *See* Theodore Eisenberg, Neil LaFountain, Brian Ostrom, David Rottman & Martin T. Wells, *Juries, Judges, and Punitive Damages: An Empirical Study,* 87 CORNELL L. REV. 743 (2002). However, repeat defendants greatly fear punitive awards. Because punitive damages are not reliably measurable, the trier of fact is free to vent any bias or anger they may feel by inflicting an award that cannot be evaluated against any effective standard. As punitive damages have been sought more frequently, and as amounts have sometimes run into the millions of dollars, defendant-oriented lobbies have tried to find ways to limit those awards, both in statutes and by more restrictive judicial decisions.

2. *Two types of limitations*. Although several means have been used to limit punitive awards, they fall mainly into two large categories. Since the main problem with punitive damages is to find a suitable measure or standard for guiding the award and evaluating it afterward, some legal changes attempt to enhance the methods for measuring the awards. A

second and much broader way to limit total damages awarded is not to limit the amount of the award but to limit the number of cases in which punitive damages may be awarded. Some courts and statutes have attempted this approach, too.

3. *Increased proof standards.* One way to filter out potential punitive damages claims is to increase the plaintiff's burden of proof. A number of courts and legislatures have done this, usually requiring the plaintiff to prove grounds for punitive damages by clear and convincing evidence rather than by a mere preponderance.

4. *Single liability statute.* Georgia enacted a statute that immunized a product liability defendant from all punitive liability for a given product, once the defendant had been vaccinated by a single punitive award. So the first plaintiff to recover was the only one to do so.

5. *Specific malice requirement.* Another effort to cut punitive damages off at the pass requires the plaintiff to prove some specific malice or oppressive intent toward the plaintiff, eliminating wanton and reckless misconduct as a basis. *See* KY. REV. STAT. ANN. § 411.184.

6. *Redirection of awards and the problem of financing tort suits.* A fourth line of legislative attack that is intended to cut down the number of claims rather than the amount of the award is the statute that redirects a portion of any punitive award so that it does not go to the plaintiff (or the plaintiff's attorney) but to the state or some designated beneficiary. *E.g.,* IOWA CODE ANN. § 668A.1. These statutes can retain the full capacity for deterring the defendant once the award is made because they do not necessary reduce or cap the award. In *Kirk v. Denver Public Co.,* 818 P.2d 262 (Colo. 1991), the court held one such statute unconstitutional as a taking of property without just compensation. *Cheatham v. Pohle,* 789 N.E.2d 467 (Ind. 2003) disagreed, upholding the statute against an argument that it was a taking of property without just compensation.

7. *Assessing the filters.* What is your assessment of these efforts? One trouble with them is that they do nothing at all about the problem of measurement. Once a case gets past these filters, the problem of standardless punitive awards remains. Another problem is that the filters may be too fine. Is there a good chance, in your view, that the deterrence function or the litigation finance function of punitive awards will be needed in some of the cases filtered out by these rules?

8. *Statutory ratios, multiples or caps.* With the push for tort reform, some statutes have enacted ratio cap statutes. For instance, Colorado limited punitive awards to no more than actual damages, with the added possibility of punitive damages up to three times actual damages if the defendant's misconduct continued during the trial. WEST'S COLO. REV. STAT. ANN. § 13–21–102. Utah, by court decision, has produced a kind of sliding scale ratio rule that varies according to whether the compensatory damages awarded were low or high. *Crookston v. Fire Ins. Exch.,* 817 P.2d 789 (Utah 1991) (3–1 ratio for punitive awards under $100,000, much closer ratio for higher awards). Georgia enacted a flat cap limiting punitive

damages in some cases to $250,000. GA. CODE § 51–12–5.1. In *Rhyne v. K–Mart Corp.*, 594 S.E.2d 1 (N.C. 2004), the court held constitutional a statute providing for caps on punitive damages of three times compensatory damages or $250,000, whichever is greater. Compensatory damages for each of the two plaintiffs came to a rather paltry sum, so the statute had the effect of capping punitive damages at $250,000. But the court also held that the statute applied "per plaintiff." The result was that each of the two plaintiffs could recover $250,000 in punitive damages and the defendant's total liability would be $500,000.

STATE FARM MUT. AUTO. INS. CO. v. CAMPBELL

538 U.S. 408 (2003)

JUSTICE KENNEDY delivered the opinion of the Court. . . .

In 1981, Curtis Campbell (Campbell) was driving with his wife, Inez Preece Campbell, in Cache County, Utah. He decided to pass six vans traveling ahead of them on a two-lane highway. Todd Ospital was driving a small car approaching from the opposite direction. To avoid a head-on collision with Campbell, who by then was driving on the wrong side of the highway and toward oncoming traffic, Ospital swerved onto the shoulder, lost control of his automobile, and collided with a vehicle driven by Robert G. Slusher. Ospital was killed, and Slusher was rendered permanently disabled. The Campbells escaped unscathed.

In the ensuing wrongful death and tort action, Campbell insisted he was not at fault. Early investigations did support differing conclusions as to who caused the accident, but "a consensus was reached early on by the investigators and witnesses that Mr. Campbell's unsafe pass had indeed caused the crash." Campbell's insurance company, petitioner State Farm Mutual Automobile Insurance Company (State Farm), nonetheless decided to contest liability and declined offers by Slusher and Ospital's estate (Ospital) to settle the claims for the policy limit of $50,000 ($25,000 per claimant). State Farm also ignored the advice of one of its own investigators and took the case to trial, assuring the Campbells that "their assets were safe, that they had no liability for the accident, that [State Farm] would represent their interests, and that they did not need to procure separate counsel." To the contrary, a jury determined that Campbell was 100 percent at fault, and a judgment was returned for $185,849, far more than the amount offered in settlement.

At first State Farm refused to cover the $135,849 in excess liability. Its counsel made this clear to the Campbells: " 'You may want to put for sale signs on your property to get things moving.' " Nor was State Farm willing to post a supersedeas bond to allow Campbell to appeal the judgment against him. Campbell obtained his own counsel to appeal the verdict. During the pendency of the appeal, in late 1984, Slusher, Ospital, and the Campbells reached an agreement whereby Slusher and Ospital agreed not to seek satisfaction of their claims against the Campbells. In exchange the Campbells agreed to pursue a bad faith action against State

Farm and to be represented by Slusher's and Ospital's attorneys. The Campbells also agreed that Slusher and Ospital would have a right to play a part in all major decisions concerning the bad faith action. No settlement could be concluded without Slusher's and Ospital's approval, and Slusher and Ospital would receive 90 percent of any verdict against State Farm.

In 1989, the Utah Supreme Court denied Campbell's appeal in the wrongful death and tort actions. State Farm then paid the entire judgment, including the amounts in excess of the policy limits. The Campbells nonetheless filed a complaint against State Farm alleging bad faith, fraud, and intentional infliction of emotional distress. The trial court initially granted State Farm's motion for summary judgment because State Farm had paid the excess verdict, but that ruling was reversed on appeal. On remand State Farm moved *in limine* to exclude evidence of alleged conduct that occurred in unrelated cases outside of Utah, but the trial court denied the motion. At State Farm's request the trial court bifurcated the trial into two phases conducted before different juries. In the first phase the jury determined that State Farm's decision not to settle was unreasonable because there was a substantial likelihood of an excess verdict. . . .

[The Utah Court summarized evidence in phase II:] "State Farm argued during phase II that its decision to take the case to trial was an 'honest mistake' that did not warrant punitive damages. In contrast, the Campbells introduced evidence that State Farm's decision to take the case to trial was a result of a national scheme to meet corporate fiscal goals by capping payouts on claims company wide. This scheme was referred to as State Farm's 'Performance, Planning and Review,' or PP & R, policy. To prove the existence of this scheme, the trial court allowed the Campbells to introduce extensive expert testimony regarding fraudulent practices by State Farm in its nation-wide operations. Although State Farm moved prior to phase II of the trial for the exclusion of such evidence and continued to object to it at trial, the trial court ruled that such evidence was admissible to determine whether State Farm's conduct in the Campbell case was indeed intentional and sufficiently egregious to warrant punitive damages."

Evidence pertaining to the PP & R policy concerned State Farm's business practices for over 20 years in numerous States. Most of these practices bore no relation to third-party automobile insurance claims, the type of claim underlying the Campbells' complaint against the company. The jury awarded the Campbells $2.6 million in compensatory damages and $145 million in punitive damages, which the trial court reduced to $1 million and $25 million respectively. Both parties appealed.

The Utah Supreme Court sought to apply the three guideposts we identified in [*BMW of North America, Inc. v. Gore,* 517 U.S. 559 (1996)] and it reinstated the $145 million punitive damages award . . . . .

While States possess discretion over the imposition of punitive damages, it is well established that there are procedural and substantive constitutional limitations on these awards The Due Process Clause of the Fourteenth Amendment prohibits the imposition of grossly excessive or arbitrary punishments on a tortfeasor. The reason is that "[e]lementary notions of fairness enshrined in our constitutional jurisprudence dictate that a person receive fair notice not only of the conduct that will subject him to punishment, but also of the severity of the penalty that a State may impose."

Although these awards serve the same purposes as criminal penalties, defendants subjected to punitive damages in civil cases have not been accorded the protections applicable in a criminal proceeding. This increases our concerns over the imprecise manner in which punitive damages systems are administered. We have admonished that "[p]unitive damages pose an acute danger of arbitrary deprivation of property. Jury instructions typically leave the jury with wide discretion in choosing amounts, and the presentation of evidence of a defendant's net worth creates the potential that juries will use their verdicts to express biases against big businesses, particularly those without strong local presences." Our concerns are heightened when the decisionmaker is presented, as we shall discuss, with evidence that has little bearing as to the amount of punitive damages that should be awarded. Vague instructions, or those that merely inform the jury to avoid "passion or prejudice" do little to aid the decisionmaker in its task of assigning appropriate weight to evidence that is relevant and evidence that is tangential or only inflammatory.

In light of these concerns, in *Gore, supra,* we instructed courts reviewing punitive damages to consider three guideposts: (1) the degree of reprehensibility of the defendant's misconduct; (2) the disparity between the actual or potential harm suffered by the plaintiff and the punitive damages award; and (3) the difference between the punitive damages awarded by the jury and the civil penalties authorized or imposed in comparable cases. We reiterated the importance of these three guideposts in *Cooper Industries* and mandated appellate courts to conduct *de novo* review of a trial court's application of them to the jury's award. Exacting appellate review ensures that an award of punitive damages is based upon an " 'application of law, rather than a decisionmaker's caprice.' "

Under the principles outlined in *BMW of North America, Inc. v. Gore,* this case is neither close nor difficult. It was error to reinstate the jury's $145 million punitive damages award. We address each guidepost of *Gore* in some detail.

"[T]he most important indicium of the reasonableness of a punitive damages award is the degree of reprehensibility of the defendant's conduct." We have instructed courts to determine the reprehensibility of a defendant by considering whether: the harm caused was physical as opposed to economic; the tortious conduct evinced an indifference to or a reckless disregard of the health or safety of others; the target of the conduct had financial vulnerability; the conduct involved repeated actions or was an isolated incident; and the harm was the result of intentional malice, trickery, or deceit, or mere accident. The existence of any one of these factors weighing in favor of a plaintiff may not be sufficient to sustain a punitive damages award; and the absence of all of them renders any award suspect. It should be presumed a plaintiff has been made whole for his injuries by compensatory damages, so punitive damages should only be awarded if the defendant's culpability, after having paid compensatory damages, is so reprehensible as to warrant the imposition of further sanctions to achieve punishment or deterrence.

. . . While we do not suggest there was error in awarding punitive damages based upon State Farm's conduct toward the Campbells, a more modest punishment for this reprehensible conduct could have satisfied the State's legitimate objectives, and the Utah courts should have gone no further.

This case, instead, was used as a platform to expose, and punish, the perceived deficiencies of State Farm's operations throughout the country. The Utah Supreme Court's opinion makes explicit that State Farm was being condemned for its nationwide policies rather than for the conduct direct toward the Campbells. . . .

A State cannot punish a defendant for conduct that may have been lawful where it occurred. Nor, as a general rule, does a State have a legitimate concern in imposing punitive damages to punish a defendant for unlawful acts committed outside of the State's jurisdiction. Any proper adjudication of conduct that occurred outside Utah to other persons would require their inclusion, and, to those parties, the Utah courts, in the usual case, would need to apply the laws of their relevant jurisdiction.

Here, the Campbells do not dispute that much of the out-of-state conduct was lawful where it occurred. They argue, however, that such evidence was not the primary basis for the punitive damages award and was relevant to the extent it demonstrated, in a general sense, State Farm's motive against its insured. This argument misses the mark. Lawful out-of-state conduct may be probative when it demonstrates the deliberateness and culpability of the defendant's action in the State where it is tortious, but that conduct must have a nexus to the specific harm suffered by the plaintiff. A jury must be instructed, furthermore, that it may not use evidence of out-of-state conduct to punish a defendant for action that was lawful in the jurisdiction where it occurred. A basic principle of federalism is that each State may make its own reasoned judgment about what conduct is permitted or proscribed within its borders, and each State alone can determine what measure of punishment, if any, to impose on a defendant who acts within its jurisdiction.

For a more fundamental reason, however, the Utah courts erred in relying upon this and other evidence: The courts awarded punitive damages to punish and deter conduct that bore no relation to the Campbells' harm. A defendant's dissimilar acts, independent from the acts upon which liability was premised, may not serve as the basis for punitive damages. A defendant should be punished for the conduct that harmed the plaintiff, not for being an unsavory individual or business. Due process does not permit courts, in the calculation of punitive damages, to adjudicate the merits of other parties' hypothetical claims against a defendant under the guise of the reprehensibility analysis, but we have no doubt the Utah Supreme Court did that here. Punishment on these bases creates the possibility of multiple punitive damages awards for the same conduct; for in the usual case nonparties are not bound by the judgment some other plaintiff obtains.

The same reasons lead us to conclude the Utah Supreme Court's decision cannot be justified on the grounds that State Farm was a recidivist. Although "[o]ur holdings that a recidivist may be punished more severely than a first offender recognize that repeated misconduct is more reprehensible than an individual instance of malfeasance," in the context of civil actions courts must ensure the conduct in question replicates the prior transgressions.

The Campbells have identified scant evidence of repeated misconduct of the sort that injured them. Nor does our review of the Utah courts' decisions convince us that State Farm was only punished for its actions toward the Campbells. Although evidence of other acts need not be identical to have relevance in the calculation of punitive damages, the Utah court erred here because evidence pertaining to claims that had nothing to do with a third-party lawsuit was introduced at length. Other evidence concerning reprehensibility was even more tangential. For example, the Utah Supreme Court criticized State Farm's investigation into the personal life of one of its employees and, in a broader approach, the manner in which State Farm's policies corrupted its employees. The Campbells attempt to justify the courts' reliance upon this unrelated testimony on the theory that each dollar of profit made by underpaying a third-party claimant is the same as a dollar made by underpaying a first-party one. For the reasons already stated, this argument is unconvincing. The reprehensibility guidepost does not permit courts to expand the scope of the case so that a defendant may be punished for any malfeasance, which in this case extended for a 20-year period. In this case, because the Campbells have shown no conduct by State Farm similar to that which harmed them, the conduct that harmed them is the only conduct relevant to the reprehensibility analysis.

Turning to the second *Gore* guidepost, we have been reluctant to identify concrete constitutional limits on the ratio between harm, or potential harm, to the plaintiff and the punitive damages award. We decline again to impose a bright-line ratio which a punitive damages award cannot exceed. Our jurisprudence and the principles it has now established demonstrate, however, that, in practice, few awards exceeding a single-digit ratio between punitive and compensatory damages, to a significant degree, will satisfy due process. In *Haslip,* in upholding a punitive damages award, we concluded that an award of more than four times the amount of compensatory damages might be close to the line of constitutional impropriety. We cited that 4–to–1 ratio again in *Gore*. The Court further referenced a long legislative history, dating back over 700 years and going forward to today, providing for sanctions of double, treble, or quadruple damages to deter and punish. While these ratios are not binding, they are instructive. They demonstrate what should be obvious: Single-digit multipliers are more likely to comport with due process, while still achieving the State's goals of deterrence and retribution, than awards with ratios in range of 500 to 1, or, in this case, of 145 to 1.

Nonetheless, because there are no rigid benchmarks that a punitive damages award may not surpass, ratios greater than those we have previously upheld may comport with due process where a particularly egregious act has resulted in only a small amount of economic damages. The converse is also true, however. When compensatory damages are substantial, then a lesser ratio, perhaps only equal to compensatory damages, can reach the outermost limit of the due process guarantee. The precise award in any case, of course, must be based upon the facts and circumstances of the defendant's conduct and the harm to the plaintiff. . . .

The compensatory award in this case was substantial; the Campbells were awarded $1 million for a year and a half of emotional distress. This was complete compensation. The harm arose from a transaction in the economic realm, not from some physical assault or trauma; there were no physical injuries; and State Farm paid the excess verdict before the complaint was filed, so the Campbells suffered only minor economic injuries for the 18-month period in which State Farm refused to resolve the claim against them. The compensatory damages for the injury suffered here, moreover, likely were based on a component which was duplicated in the punitive award. Much of the distress was caused by the outrage and humiliation the Campbells suffered at the actions of their insurer; and it is a major role of punitive damages to condemn such conduct. Compensatory damages, however, already contain this punitive element.

The third guidepost in *Gore* is the disparity between the punitive damages award and the "civil penalties authorized or imposed in comparable cases." We note that, in the past, we have also looked to criminal penalties that could be imposed. The existence of a criminal penalty does have bearing on the seriousness with which a State views the wrongful action. When used to determine the dollar amount of the award, however, the criminal penalty has less utility. Great care must be taken to avoid use of the civil process to assess criminal penalties that can be imposed only after the heightened protections of a criminal trial have been observed, including, of course, its higher standards of proof. Punitive damages are not a substitute for the criminal process, and the remote possibility of a criminal sanction does not automatically sustain a punitive damages award.

Here, we need not dwell long on this guidepost. The most relevant civil sanction under Utah state law for the wrong done to the Campbells appears to be a $10,000 fine for an act of fraud an amount dwarfed by the $145 million punitive damages award. The Supreme Court of Utah speculated about the loss of State Farm's business license, the disgorgement of profits, and possible imprisonment, but here again its references were to the broad fraudulent scheme drawn from evidence of out-of-state and dissimilar conduct. This analysis was insufficient to justify the award.…

The punitive award of $145 million, therefore, was neither reasonable nor proportionate to the wrong committed, and it was an irrational and arbitrary deprivation of the property of the defendant. The proper calculation of punitive damages under the principles we have discussed should be resolved, in the first instance, by the Utah courts.

The judgment of the Utah Supreme Court is reversed, and the case is remanded for proceedings not inconsistent with this opinion.

It is so ordered.

[Justices Scalia and Thomas dissented, both essentially on the ground that there was no Constitutional, substantive due process constraint on punitive awards.]

JUSTICE GINSBURG, dissenting.…

The large size of the award upheld by the Utah Supreme Court in this case indicates why damage-capping legislation may be altogether fitting and proper. Neither the amount of the award nor the trial record, however, justifies this Court's substitution of its judgment for that of Utah's competent decisionmakers. In this regard, I count it significant that, on the key criterion "reprehensibility," there is a good deal more to the story than the Court's abbreviated account tells.…

"[T]he Campbells presented considerable evidence," the trial court noted, documenting "that the PP & R program … has functioned, and continues to function, as an unlawful scheme … to deny benefits owed consumers by paying out less than fair value in order to meet preset, arbitrary payout targets designed to enhance corporate profits." That policy, the trial court observed, was encompassing in scope; it "applied equally to the handling of both third-party and first-party claims."

Evidence the jury could credit demonstrated that the PP & R program regularly and adversely affected Utah residents. Ray Summers, "the adjuster who handled the Campbell case and who was a State Farm employee in Utah for almost twenty years," described several methods used by State Farm to deny claimants fair benefits, for example, "falsifying or withholding of evidence in claim files." A common tactic, Summers recounted, was to "unjustly attac[k] the character, reputation and credibility of a claimant and mak[e] notations to that effect in the claim file to create prejudice in the event the claim ever came before a jury." State Farm manager Bob Noxon, Summers testified, resorted to a tactic of this order in the Campbell case when he "instruct[ed] Summers to write in the file that Todd Ospital (who was killed in the accident) was speeding because he was on his way to see a pregnant girlfriend." In truth, "[t]here was no pregnant girlfriend." . . .

Regarding liability for verdicts in excess of policy limits, the trial court referred to a State Farm document titled the "Excess Liability Handbook"; written before the Campbell accident, the handbook instructed adjusters to pad files with "self-serving" documents, and to leave critical items out of files, for example, evaluations of the insured's exposure. Divisional superintendent Bill Brown used the handbook to train Utah employees. While overseeing the Campbell case, Brown ordered adjuster Summers to change the portions of his report indicating that Mr. Campbell was likely at fault and that the settlement cost was correspondingly high. . . .

The trial court further determined that the jury could find State Farm's policy "deliberately crafted" to prey on consumers who would be unlikely to defend themselves. In this regard, the trial court noted the testimony of several former State Farm employees affirming that they were trained to target "the weakest of the herd"—"the elderly, the poor, and other consumers who are least knowledgeable about their rights and thus most vulnerable to trickery or deceit, or who have little money and hence have no real alternative but to accept an inadequate offer to settle a claim at much less than fair value."

The Campbells themselves could be placed within the "weakest of the herd" category. At the time of State Farm's wrongful conduct, "Mr. Campbell had residuary effects from a stroke and Parkinson's disease."

To further insulate itself from liability, trial evidence indicated, State Farm made "systematic" efforts to destroy internal company documents that might reveal its scheme. . . .

State Farm's inability to produce the manuals, it appeared from the evidence, was not accidental. Documents retained by former State Farm employee Samantha Bird, as well as Bird's testimony, showed that while the Campbells' case was pending, Janet Cammack, "an in-house attorney sent by top State Farm management, conducted a meeting . . . in Utah during which she instructed Utah claims management to search their offices and destroy a wide range of material of the sort that had proved damaging in bad-faith litigation in the past—in particular, old claim-handling manuals, memos, claim school notes, procedure guides and other similar documents." . . .

"As a final, related tactic," the trial court stated, the jury could reasonably find that "in recent years State Farm has gone to extraordinary lengths to stop damaging documents from being created in the first place." . . .

The Court dismisses the evidence describing and documenting State Farm's PP & R policy and practices as essentially irrelevant, bearing "no relation to the Campbells' harm." It is hardly apparent why that should be so. What is infirm about the Campbells' theory that their experience with State Farm exemplifies and reflects an overarching underpayment scheme, one that caused "repeated misconduct of the sort that injured them"? The Court's silence on that score is revealing: Once one recognizes that the Campbells did show "conduct by State Farm similar to that which harmed them," it becomes impossible to shrink the reprehensibility analysis to this sole case, or to maintain, at odds with the determination of the trial court, that "the adverse effect on the State's general population was in fact minor."

Evidence of out-of-state conduct, the Court acknowledges, may be "probative [even if the conduct is lawful in the state where it occurred] when it demonstrates the deliberateness and culpability of the defendant's action in the State where it is tortious...." "Other acts" evidence concerning practices both in and out of State was introduced in this case to show just such "deliberateness" and "culpability." The evidence was admissible, the trial court ruled: (1) to document State Farm's "reprehensible" PP & R program; and (2) to "rebut [State Farm's] assertion that [its] actions toward the Campbells were inadvertent errors or mistakes in judgment." Viewed in this light, there surely was "a nexus" between much of the "other acts" evidence and "the specific harm suffered by [the Campbells]." ...

No longer content to accord state-court judgments "a strong presumption of validity," *TXO*, 509 U.S., at 457, 113 S.Ct. 2711, the Court announces that "few awards exceeding a single-digit ratio between punitive and compensatory damages, to a significant degree, will satisfy due process." ...

I remain of the view that this Court has no warrant to reform state law governing awards of punitive damages. Even if I were prepared to accept the flexible guides prescribed in *Gore,* I would not join the Court's swift conversion of those guides into instructions that begin to resemble marching orders.

NOTES

1. **The tort: Bad faith failure to settle within policy limits.** States generally hold that (a) an insurer has no obligation to pay more than its policy limit, but (b) when judgment against its insured is likely to be much higher than the limit and the insurer can settle for its policy limit or less, it must use good faith or maybe even reasonable care to do so to protect its insured. If it does not do so and an excess judgment is entered against its insured, the insurer may be liable for that judgment and for other damages its misconduct has inflicted upon the insured. Frequently, as in *Campbell,* the insured's right of action is in effect sold in whole or part to the injured persons in exchange for a release, so the injured, not the insured, will be the only or primary beneficiary of any recovery.

2. **Relevance of out-of-state conduct?** Granted that Utah cannot punish out-of-state conduct that has no effect in Utah, does that mean that

out-of-state conduct is irrelevant to every issue in the case? In *Campbell*, wouldn't State Farm's pattern of conduct elsewhere tend to rebut its argument that it just made an innocent mistake?

3. **Relevance of out-of-state conduct on the award itself?** Couldn't out of state patterns of conduct be relevant even to a punitive award and not just as evidence on some other issue? Suppose a state insurance commissioner has power to exclude insurers from selling insurance in the state if their conduct has demonstrated a substantial risk that consumers will be injured. Suppose the insurance commissioner is not merely a creature of the insurance industry and that the federal Congress has not seen fit to preempt his powers. Would the commissioner be acting unconstitutionally if she concluded that State Farm should be excluded from selling insurance in the state because of its pattern of evil practices elsewhere? During the run-up to World War II, would it have been wrong to prohibit immigration of Nazis because of their activities in Germany? After all, the Nazi party and its atrocities were legal in Germany.

4. **What is similar conduct?** The Court in *Campbell* seems to recognize that some outside activities are relevant, but insists that they must be similar to those that injured the insured. What is similar, though, depends on characterization and the level of generalization you are prepared to accept. If you characterize State Farm's misbehavior as lying and cheating its own customers, that covers both the *Campbell* conduct and the out-of-state conduct. Is that a fair description of the conduct?

5. **Ratio rule limitations.** Is there really any basis for saying that punitive awards should bear some more or less specific ratio to compensatory awards? After *Campbell* courts have struggled to draw a ratio-based constitutional line. *See, e.g., Goddard v. Farmers Ins. Co.*, 179 P.3d 645 (Or. 2008) (as a general rule, the constitution prohibits a punitive award more than four times the compensatory award, at least where the injuries to the plaintiff are economic rather than physical); *Flax v. DaimlerChrysler Corp.*, 2008 WL 2831225 (Tenn.) (upholding a punitive award 5.35 times greater than the compensatory award, in a products liability suit involving a child's death). In *Exxon Shipping Co. v. Baker*, ___ U.S. ___, 128 S.Ct. 2605 (2008), the court held that a 1:1 ratio of compensatory to punitive damages was the constitutional limit for admiralty cases. It is not clear how broadly the Baker holding might be extended, although the Court itself was careful to limit its holding to the facts and maritime law setting.

6. **Profit or attorney fee as a limit.** Courts sometimes seem to approach punitive damages as if the wrongdoer were simply guilty of disinterested malevolence, like the bully who picks a fight in a bar. But in fact the major modern cases involve the wrongdoer who engages in wrong in order to make a large profit. Shouldn't profit from the wrong be far more relevant than any ratio between compensatory and punitive awards? The point would be to retain full deterrence by eliminating the profits and to retain the capacity of the punitive award to provide appropriate incentives to sue. See Dan B. Dobbs, *Ending Punishment in "Punitive" Damages: Deterrence–Measured Remedies*, 40 ALA. L. REV.831 (1989).

PHILIP MORRIS USA v. WILLIAMS, 549 U.S. 346 (2007). The widow of a heavy cigarette smoker sued the cigarette manufacturer for negligence and deceit, seeking both compensatory and punitive damages after her husband died of lung cancer. The jury found in her favor and awarded $821,000 in compensatory damages and $79.5 million in punitives. The trial judge reduced the compensatory damages to $500,000 and the punitive award to $32 million After several interim rulings and decisions after remand, the case came to this Court. Defendant now argues that the trial judge should have instructed the jury that it could not punish the defendant for injury to persons not parties before the court. *Held*, a punitive damages award based in part on a jury's desire to punish a defendant for harming nonparties violates due process. A state may properly impose punitive damages, but it must do so in a way to cabin the jury's discretionary authority, and give the defendant "fair notice ... of the severity of the penalty." Penalizing a defendant for misconduct towards nonparties who are "strangers to the litigation" adds a nearly standardless dimension to the punitive damages equation, and magnifies this Court's due process concerns in these cases: arbitrariness, uncertainty, and lack of notice. There is no authority at all for using punitive damages awards to punish a defendant for harming persons not before the court. While evidence of harm to nonparties may show that a defendant's conduct was particularly reprehensible, a jury may not go further and use a punitive damages award to punish a defendant directly for harms to such nonparties. States must develop procedures to insure that harm to nonparties is considered only on the reprehensibility issue and does not form the basis of the amount of the punitive award itself.

NOTES

1. The Court did not reach the issue of whether the amount of punitive damages was excessive, instead remanding for further proceedings. On remand, the Oregon Supreme Court held that the trial court did not err in refusing to give the particular jury instruction the defendant had requested, and remanded for further proceedings. *Williams v. Philip Morris Inc.*, 176 P.3d 1255 (Or. 2008).

2. In *White v. Ford Motor Co.*, 500 F.3d 963 (9th Cir. 2007), the jury in a products liability action involving a child's death awarded $52 million in punitive damages against Ford. The Ninth Circuit reversed on the basis of *Williams*, holding that the trial judge was required by due process to instruct the jury that while it could consider evidence of actual harm to nonparties as part of its reprehensibility determination, it may not use its punitive damages verdict to punish the defendant directly. Can a trial court make that distinction understandable to a jury?

3. Four justices (Stevens, Thomas, Scalia and Ginsburg) dissented in the U.S. Supreme Court's *Williams* decision. Justice Stevens commented on the majority's distinction between using harm to nonparties as evidence of reprehensibility but not to punish the defendant, "This nuance eludes me." He added, "A murderer who kills his victim by throwing a bomb that injures

dozens of bystanders should be punished more severely than one who harms no one other than his intended victim." Thus, in his view, the jury should be free not only to take conduct towards nonparties into account on the reprehensibility issue, but also to punish the defendant on that very basis. Do you agree?

PROBLEM

O'Brien v. Spring Department Store, Inc.

James O'Brien was 16 years of age. He was an African–American employed at the Spring Department Store. The store's "security" agents accused him of theft. They imprisoned him for hours in a small windowless room and refused to let him leave or call his parents. During this period, they coerced a confession. They now concede that the confession was false and a product of coercion.

After the security agents obtained a confession, they permitted O'Brien to leave. He discussed the events with his parents, who then took him back to the store to discuss these events with the manager. The manager, Bob Hurley, said in this discussion: "You people—you nigger boys make me sick, but you're going to burn for this, you sucker."

James was charged criminally for the supposed theft. However, there was no evidence that he stole anything or indeed that anything at all had been stolen. He then sued for false imprisonment and some other torts. The jury found in his favor in the first trial and besides compensatory damages awarded $350,000 in punitive damages. The highest state court reversed because some of the tort theories pursued at trial were invalid and the punitive award might have been generated in part because of multiple tort claims.

On a second trial, the jury awarded compensatory damages and $9 million in punitive awards. The defendant argued that this was excessive and should be reduced as a matter of law. You are the trial judge. Do you reduce the award? If so, what sum of punitive damages would you permit? Because substantial sums are involved no matter what you decide, your decision on this point is likely to be reviewed by the state's highest court. Consequently, you want to give persuasive reasons for your decision.

REFERENCE: DOBBS ON TORTS §§ 381–384 (2000).

CHAPTER 27

EVALUATING TORT LAW

■ ■ ■

There are at least two distinct tort systems—one based on "fault" and the other on strict liability. How good are these systems at coping with the problem of injury in modern American life? Any system used to deal with the injury problem will be severely strained. According to the National Safety Council, Americans suffer

- about 20.4 million disabling injuries per year, of which more than 2 million are from motor vehicle accidents.

- 120,000 accidental deaths a year as of 2006; about 44,000 from motor vehicle accidents alone.

- almost 4 million disabling work-related injuries.

- economic impact of unintended injury of $652.1 billion in 2006. This is equivalent to about $2,200 per capita, or about $5,700 per household.

§ 1. RULES, PRACTICES AND THEORIES OF TORT LAW

Looking back over the rules of torts, would you have any major criticisms? The rule of contributory negligence and the rules of assumed risk and fellow-servant were often the butt of serious criticisms until the recent past. These rules no longer automatically bar recovery. Do new rules of comparative fault and apportionment resolve all problems? What, in the fault system today would you find that warrants substantial change?

The strict liability system has been confined to a fairly narrow set of cases in recent years. Should it be applied more broadly? Does a more restricted strict liability system mean that tort recoveries will contract? An astute and careful observer argued that the expansion of tort liability that occurred in the latter half of the 20th century was accomplished largely through negligence law, not strict liability, and that tort law had become stabilized by the late 1980s. Gary T. Schwartz, *The Beginning and the Possible End of the Rise of Modern American Tort Law*, 26 GA. L. REV. 601 (1992).

The practical application of tort law seen in Chapters 25 and 26 may give some ground for concern. Are there practices that cause serious problems?

What about theoretical problems in tort law? Is there any need to move from a theory based predominantly on fault to a theory based on, say, general deterrence? On compensation? Would changes in tort theory, if they occurred, resolve the practical problems of administering tort law on a massive scale? Might some sort of compensation fund or other injury-response program fare better?

§ 2. TORT WARS

The New Tort Reform

Major Criticisms Advanced by the Tort Reformers

According to a common complaint of critics, a litigation explosion occurred in the 1980s; suddenly, everyone was suing everyone else. Critics say the tort system is running amok; liability is everywhere; the American public wants to sue whenever anything goes wrong; and lawyers' greed has brought the country to the brink of disaster. Some of these charges lead to long battles about whether litigation really has increased.

More soberly, tort reformers say that the tort system as presently administered has caused specific problems because of the costs it imposes on defendants and insurers:

> (1) liability insurance costs too much, especially for certain defendants like malpractice defendants (the affordability crisis);

> (2) insurance has or may become unavailable for some defendants (the availability crisis);

> (3) some goods or services of vast importance may become unavailable because the threat of tort liability is driving some producers out of the market, as perhaps the diminished availability of certain vaccines suggests.

Evaluating the Criticisms

The data suggest that injured people actually should be claiming redress more often than they do and that juries, far from running amok, award recoveries less often than judges do. Here are some major items of information.

- Most suits filed, around 80 million a year, deal with crimes, divorce, juvenile proceedings, debt claims, and traffic and parking infractions. Although the total number of cases filed has increased somewhat in recent years, the number of tort claims filed has actually decreased. A full 60% of the tort cases that are filed stem from automobile accidents. *See* N{{ATIONAL}} C{{ENTER}} FOR S{{TATE}} C{{OURTS}}, B{{RIAN}} O{{STROM}}, N{{EAL}} K{{AUDER}}, N{{EIL}} L{{A}}F{{OUNTAIN}}, E{{XAMINING}} THE W{{ORK}} OF S{{TATE}} C{{OURTS}} 2002, 24 (2003), available at www.ncsconline.org.

See also Deborah Jones Merritt & Kathryn Ann Barry, *Is the Tort System in Crisis? New Empirical Evidence,* 60 OHIO ST. L.J. 315 (1999); Michael J. Saks, *Do We Really Know Anything About the Behavior of the Tort Litigation System—And Why Not?,* 140 U. PA. L. REV. 1147 (1992); Joseph Sanders and Craig Joyce, *"Off to the Races": The 1980s Tort Crisis and the Law Reform Process,* 27 HOUS. L. REV. 207 (1990).

- Only about 10% of injured people make any claim at all; probably many more could justly assert claims. *See* Marc Galanter, *Real World Torts: An Antidote to Anecdote,* 55 MD. L. REV. 1093 (1996).

- Settlements, which constitute the great majority of tort dispositions, on the average probably undercompensate. See Deborah L. Rhode, *Frivolous Litigation and Civil Justice Reform: Miscasting the Problem, Recasting the Solution,* 54 DUKE L. J., 447, 460 (2004) (contending that "although excessive litigation is the pathology dominating public discussion and policy agendas, systematic research reveals that the more serious problems are undercompensation of victims").

- A Bureau of Justice Statistics study showed that the median total award in a sample of tort cases was only $24,000, although the National Safety Council estimates that the average economic cost (apart from human cost) of incapacitating injury in automobile cases is much greater—about $52,000. *See* BUREAU OF JUSTICE STATISTICS, CIVIL BENCH AND JURY TRIALS IN STATE COURTS, 2005 (October 2008); and NATIONAL SAFETY COUNCIL, INJURY FACTS 91 (2003).

- Juries have not run amok; in a Bureau of Justice Statistics sample, juries found for the plaintiff in only 52% of the cases. Judges found for the plaintiff only a little more often. When judges act as triers of fact, their awards resemble those of juries, even with punitive damages. *See* Theodore Eisenberg, Neil LaFountain, Brian Ostrom, David Rottman & Martin T. Wells, *Juries, Judges, and Punitive Damages: an Empirical Study,* 87 CORNELL L. REV. 743 (2002).

- Some torts, with disastrous consequences to human beings, really are being committed. Litigation should be perceived as a problem only if litigation outruns actionable injury. Striking studies show that in fact many more tortious injuries are caused than are sued for. *See* Michael J. Saks, *Do We Really Know Anything About the Behavior of the Tort Litigation System—And Why Not?,* 140 U. PA. L. REV. 1147 (1992); Localio, et al., *Relation between Malpractice Claims and Adverse Events Due to Negligence,* 325 N. ENG. J. MED. 245 (July 25, 1991). The question perhaps should be, not whether the amount of litigation has increased in any given time period, but whether it is too extensive or not enough and whether there are better alternatives. *See* Dan B. Dobbs, *Can You Care for People and Still Count the Costs?,* 46 MD. L. REV. 49 (1986) (commenting on

Marc Galanter, *The Day After the Litigation Explosion*, 46 Md. L. Rev. 3 (1986)).

In the light of the data, why have some people claimed that the courts are giving money away in ridiculous cases?

In part, this may reflect bias against courts—which, after all, are independent and on the whole not subject to political pressure or legislative control.

In other cases, opinion has been molded by anecdotes that shamefully distort the cases they purport to report. For example: (1) The story was that a burglar recovered when he fell through a skylight of a building he was trying to burglarize; the fact was that it was a student who fell when he was on the roof of a school to fix a floodlight. (2) The story was that a man who was struck by a car while he was in a telephone booth recovered from the phone company; the fact was that he tried desperately to get out of the booth when he saw the car coming, but the door jammed and he was trapped. Even if anecdotes were correct, they would tell us little about the system as a whole. When they are so terribly misleading, they generate conflict but not information. On the anecdotes, see Joseph Page, *Deforming Tort Reform*, Book Review of PETER W. HUBER, LIABILITY: THE LEGAL REVOLUTION AND ITS CONSEQUENCES (1988), 78 GEO. L. J. 649 (1990); Saks, *supra*. To read about the campaigns to shape public opinion in a misleading way, see Elizabeth G. Thornburg, *Judicial Hellholes, Lawsuit Climates and Bad Social Science: Lessons from West Virginia*, 110 W. VA. L. REV. 1097 (2008). For a thorough review of many empirical studies, see John T. Nockelby, *How to Manufacture a Crisis: Empirical Claims Behind "Tort Reform,"* 86 OR. L. REV. 533 (2007).

§ 3.　THE IMPACT OF TORT LAW ON THE INJURY PROBLEM

The Old Tort Reform

The tort reform movement discussed above was and is fueled mainly by industries, insurers and others who wish to see greater protection for defendants. The first tort reformers approached tort law with different questions and a different orientation. They were not focused on liability reduction, but asked in part: How well does the tort system work in the real world? Does it cope adequately with the problem of massive injury? Does it adequately deter wrongdoing? Compensate the injured? Encourage rehabilitation and otherwise minimize economic loss?

People can bring many viewpoints to the problem of injury. Here are two that may account in part for some of the criticisms we see of injury systems:

(1) Insurance funds, created by premiums to which many of us contribute, might be regarded as community funds, to be used in the interest of those whose contributions make them up. They are, in a sense,

a bit like public funds created by tax contributions. The taxpayer or premium payer should have something to say about how they are used. In other words, the premium payer might like to "buy" more or less liability insurance, but what in fact is bought must depend largely on what the law says about the extent of liability. The premium payer might want the law to contract or expand liability so that the insurance funds are distributed differently. Not only might the premium payer be interested in how the insurance pie is cut, one might also be interested in how efficiently it is cut. The premium payer might want to find ways to reduce overhead costs and hence to minimize the premium paid. Since liability insurance is the fuel of the torts system, these concerns, however, cannot be dealt with directly by the insurance market, because the market must reflect the legal liability. If anyone is interested in changing the distribution or efficiency of liability insurance, then, that person must first change the law of torts.

(2) Injury on the massive scale we know it in contemporary American society is a social problem. Injury that causes economic loss, at least, has radiating effects that impose losses on others—family members, employers, and society as a whole. The effects are not necessarily only economic in nature, and society also has an interest in seeing to it that uncompensated economic harm to a worker, for example, does not lead to a spiraling disintegration of the family structure itself. This view might result in the feeling that some minimal compensation would be more important than a careful determination of fault.

Nine points involving some of these criticisms are set out below for discussion. To what extent are these points predicated upon one or both of the viewpoints stated above?

Problems with the Tort System?

1. *Undercompensation.* Studies have repeatedly shown that many claimants are not fully compensated. This point has three parts: (a) undercompensation is itself a failure of the tort system to achieve its own goals; (b) undercompensation has social consequences—the hardships on the injured and their families may be translated into welfare claims on society, or into crime and juvenile delinquency; (c) undercompensation of some groups of claimants is part of a larger picture in which some other groups are—according to many thinkers—overcompensated, with the result that the system not only fails its goals, but also provides a "maldistribution" of the insurance pie and fails to treat people equally.

How does undercompensation come about under the tort systems? Consider these possibilities: (1) The cost of going to court is such that settlement is imperative; in many ranges of injury, lawyers will encourage settlement and, with or without encouragement, plaintiffs will be compelled to accept a fraction of their actual losses. (2) Delay in trial may force the claimant to accept a settlement now. (3) Other factors would encourage a settlement for less-than-loss. These include estimates of liability, and estimates about problems in proof, effectiveness of witnesses and the bias of juries. (4) In spite of compulsory insurance laws, one in five or six drivers is uninsured and often insolvent, so that their victims have little chance of collecting any compensation, much less adequate compensation. This is a very serious problem the states have not dealt with adequately. A recent California statute provides that a vehicle owner cannot recover pain and suffering damages for injuries he sustains in an accident with his vehicle if that vehicle is uninsured. CAL. CIV. CODE § 3333.4. Do you think this would adequately address the problem of the underinsured motorist?

One of the earliest studies was CONARD, MORGAN, PRATT, VOLZ & BOMBAUGH, AUTOMOBILE ACCIDENT COSTS AND PAYMENTS (1964), hereafter cited as CONARD. Of 86,000 persons who suffered economic loss, some 20,000 received no compensation from any source. Of those who were compensated, the majority received compensation from their own insurance, workers' compensation or the like—not from the tort system. More recent figures suggest that more than two-thirds of those injured in vehicle accidents receive at least some compensation, although because of the problem of uninsured motorists, that compensation may be from their own uninsured motorist coverage. *See* Gary T. Schwartz, *Auto No-fault and First-party Insurance: Advantages and Problems,* 73 S. CAL. L. REV. 611, 624 (2000).

Are the individual and social consequences of these facts significant enough to warrant changing the tort system if this is the only objection?

2. *Overcompensation.* Students of accident compensation have repeatedly found that some claimants are grossly overcompensated. Although one expects that many claimants will recover more than their financial losses—because of pain and suffering recoveries—this does not seem to explain the enormous overcompensation at the lower end of the scale. The Department of Transportation completed an extensive study of the auto accident problem in the early 1970s. This showed, in line with some other studies, that where the economic loss was low, the average recovery might more than double the loss. For instance, if the average economic loss was $330, the average recovery was $829. WESTAT RESEARCH CORP., ECONOMIC CONSEQUENCES OF AUTOMOBILE ACCIDENT INJURIES 38 (Department of Transportation Automobile Ins. and Compensation Study, 1970) (hereafter cited as ECONOMIC CONSEQUENCES). At the upper end of the scale, where pain and suffering would be likely to be more, the reverse was true, and undercompensation was common.

Knowing what you do about the tort system and how it works, what is your best guess as to the reason for this overcompensation feature?

What impact does this overcompensation have? Is it, standing alone, sufficient to warrant changing the tort system?

3. *Misuse of limited resources.* The DOT study concluded that the personal economic losses from auto accidents in the year 1967 were between $5 and $9 billion. *See* ECONOMIC CONSEQUENCES at 40. Whatever the figure, it will continue to be extremely large, year in and year out. And

the figure does not include either pain and suffering or social losses, such as lost production. The same study concluded that the tort-insurance system paid net compensation of about .8 billion dollars or less than 20% of the actual economic losses. *See id.* at 146.

Do figures like these reflect any misuse of resources? Some of the division of the "insurance pie" goes for pain and suffering claims. Every dollar paid for pain and suffering is a dollar that cannot be used to pay basic economic loss. The result is that while some claimants recover for pain, other claimants don't even get their medical bills or lost wages paid. There simply is not enough in the premium fund to go around.

Is this, as some critics argue, a misuse of the limited resources available? If it is, would this be ground, standing alone, for changing the tort system in any substantial way? Would you, instead, favor multiplying liability insurance premiums several fold in order to cover all economic losses?

Notice that the misuse of resources argument as it is cast here could be resolved in part by eliminating the pain and suffering recovery in tort. Would that be desirable, neutral, or undesirable?

4. *Inefficiency of the tort-liability insurance system.* Without liability insurance there would be no tort system as we know it in auto accident cases. The liability insurance system is, however, a three-party system, in which you buy insurance from the company, who will pay a third person— the plaintiff. This builds in certain costs and the tort system itself builds in more. The insurer must investigate fault, cause, damage, and, sometimes, complex legal issues as well. Given fault as a trigger of liability, much of the premium dollar must be devoted to administration costs.

In addition to the costs of the parties and the insurer, the tort system imposes costs on the public because it entails the cost of judges, courthouses, juries, clerks and other apparatus of the judicial system. Special problems appear in class actions, that literally involve hundreds of thousands of claims.

A rather different inefficiency comes from the fact that in mixing a liability insurance system with other kinds of insurance, there will be double coverage on some items. Double coverage means more premium charges. If you and your brother each drove a car and each had hospital insurance, you might agree between yourselves that if one of you negligently injured the other, the injured person would not hold the other liable for hospital costs, and the injured person would collect from the hospital insurance instead. (This would utilize the more efficient premium dollar.) The two of you might then approach your insurance agent and ask to have your liability policy amended accordingly and your premium reduced. "I'll never be liable to pay for the hospital costs," you might say, "because my brother will guarantee to rely on his own hospital insurance. So reduce my premium." If you could agree with all persons who might be hurt by your driving to rely on their hospital insurance, this plan might work and the liability insurer might indeed reduce the premium because it would have reduced its risks of liability. But you cannot agree with the whole world, so the scheme won't work. The result is that for practical purposes the law forces you to purchase the same insurance twice.

Would the inefficiencies suggested in these paragraphs be enough, standing alone, to warrant any attempt to find substitutes for the tort system in auto accident cases?

5. *Delay in payment under the tort system.* If a claimant is entitled to recover but cannot be paid for months or even years, a number of harmful consequences come about. This is not a problem peculiar to torts. All law attempts to make a careful investigation into the facts and to give full opportunity to debate the legal issues. These good points of law, however, carry a heavy price in forcing delay. In tort cases, the substantive rules requiring proof of fault, cause and damage, along with the ambiguities of many rules, require especially intensive investigation and especially intensive trials. Delay seems unavoidable.

Delay is also due to the fact that the claimant must assert all claims for the future in one legal action. This may require a period of waiting to better estimate future losses and it certainly requires extensive proof about the future.

Delay may also be used strategically by defendants. The procedural system, aimed at supporting the law's aim of full investigation and complete opportunity to be heard, is readily manipulated to delay trial. Defendants can, within the ethics of the system, often delay trial and hence delay settlement or payment. This is useful from the defendant's point of view, since the plaintiff, deprived of wages, will feel more and more pressure to accept smaller and smaller settlements as time goes by.

Would these problems of delay warrant making a substantial change in the tort system if they stood alone? Could you eliminate some of the problems of delay without eliminating the tort system?

6. *The failure to deter or compensate.* The tort system begins with a determination to fix fault. It assumes that fault can be determined in a rational way, and that when it is determined, the imposition of liability in accord with fault will accomplish two purposes: (a) it will administer justice by imposing liability upon faulty persons, and (b) it will deter similar faulty conduct in others. To some, the justice argument itself fails. We have all been faulty in driving at one time or another, quite probably very often by today's standards of negligence in auto cases. Since we are all at fault, according to this view, it is largely a matter of fortuity that some of us get involved in an accident because of fault and some escape an accident. It is even more a matter of fortuity that some of us may cause large damages and some may cause quite small damages. *Cf.* Marc Franklin, *Replacing the Negligence Lottery*, 53 VA. L. REV. 774 (1967). Under these circumstances, it is less than clear that imposing liability in accord with fault is truly "just."

Whatever may be said about the justice side of the argument, the deterrent effect of tort liability is undercut by the presence of liability insurance. When a defendant is held liable, that defendant does not ordinarily make payments to the injured plaintiff in the tort system. The liability insurer does so. In many states, punitive as well as compensatory damages are covered by insurance, so that insurance may protect even a reckless defendant from any personal accountability in money. In addition, the court's desire to compensate the plaintiff has led to many cases in which "fault" is found in a defendant who has behaved in a way that, but for insurance, most people would not find faulty at all. In this view, then, the tort system fails to accomplish one of its main purposes—deterrence.

Is it true that the tort system does not accomplish any of its main goals—justice, deterrence, compensation? If it is true, would this criticism standing alone lead you to seek a substitute system?

7. *Participation in the insurance fund—lack of reciprocity.* Although the tort system is fueled on liability insurance, not everyone purchases such insurance. Among those who do purchase it, many have procured only low-limit policies, inadequate to protect a seriously injured plaintiff. A person who purchases only minimal insurance protection or none at all may nevertheless be the beneficiary of a high-limits policy purchased by someone else. Suppose X buys no insurance, but, while driving recklessly, causes serious harm to C. Unless X has extraordinary personal resources, the result will be that C will recover little or nothing from X and will rely instead on public resources or on his own private resources. But X, having failed to provide even minimal compensation for his own negligence, is in no way limited in his own recovery. If X is injured by D's negligence, and D has provided himself with adequate insurance, X will receive full compensation. He can, in short, draw on the insurance others have provided, without providing his share of the protection for others. This is only one of several peculiarities of using liability insurance in which the protection of one rests in the hands of others. Is this justified on the ground that, after all, X may be relatively poor and may find it possible to drive only because he does not purchase liability insurance?

A second problem of reciprocity in the participation in insurance funds can be seen if one imagines that poor people as a class will draw less of the insurance pie than others because for any given injury they will have less wage loss. Yet they will pay the same premiums paid by wealthier persons. Again, this is a result of the fact that injury is compensated through the insurance of others, not through one's own insurance.

Do these observations amount to a criticism of the tort system? If so, would this criticism standing alone warrant an effort to change the tort system?

8. *Is the tort system a lottery?* Some lawyers think so. There are at least three senses in which this may be so.

(a) There is a large element of fortuity from the injured person's point of view. If a woman is injured in an ordinary car collision, she will have to prove negligence to recover. If the collision occurs while she is in the course of employment, she will not be required to prove negligence, though her workers' compensation recovery will be limited to economic losses. If the collision occurs because of a defective steering apparatus, she will be entitled to recover from the manufacturer without proving negligence and she will not be limited to economic losses. From her point of view, her legal rights depend almost wholly on the luck of the case— whether she was working or not, whether her injury was caused by the manufacturer or by another driver. There are a number of these fortuitous elements in the negligence case. Consider: The defendant is negligent, but by luck he causes no harm at all; or the defendant is negligent, but by luck the plaintiff was also guilty of substantial negligence, though the defendant would have caused the same harm to a non-negligent plaintiff. See Franklin, supra.

(b) The torts system may be viewed as a lottery for more quotidian reasons. Consider: the plaintiff is injured, but as luck would have it, the plaintiff herself is not very attractive and does not capture the jury's sympathy; or the only witness is quite truthful, but has an abrasive personality and makes a bad impression; or there is no witness at all; or defendant's witnesses have been packaged and stage managed to create the best impression; or the defendant is a sympathetic local person and the plaintiff is an outsider. Similarly, lawyers' abilities to deal with complex issues vary greatly; some plaintiffs lose because their lawyers were not up to the demands of the particular case, not because the case itself was unworthy.

(c) A final sense in which the tort system may be considered a lottery is rather different. Tort damages range from quite trivial sums to many millions. Suppose a defense attorney, defending a case in which the plaintiff is seriously injured but the defendant does not appear to be at fault, makes a small offer of settlement. The plaintiff's attorney might believe that the plaintiff will in fact lose the case on a directed verdict and that, therefore, a small offer should be accepted. But the lawyer might also believe that there is one chance in a thousand that the trial judge will let the case go to the jury and that there is one chance in ten that the jury, if it gets the case, will bring in a very large judgment indeed. If so, the lawyer may press on to trial. The result is that many weak cases that probably should not win may yet go to trial, and at times they might pay off.

Are any of these "lottery" reasons ground for reconsidering the tort system?

9. *Are the lump-sum award and pain and suffering compensation justifiable?* The instinctive answer of almost everyone is that something should be paid for pain and suffering, at least when that pain is caused by wrongdoing of others. Yet the pain and suffering award does not compen-

sate in the ordinary sense. If wages are lost, money can repay that loss. If one is in pain, the money award cannot relieve the pain. (Pain relievers are covered under medical expense awards.) To the extent these awards are used to pay lawyers' fees, they are explicable in practical terms; but lawyers are needed in the first place chiefly because the tort system requires detailed analysis of fault, cause and damage. If the system were changed, the role of lawyers would be very different, as it is in workers' compensation systems. Perhaps pain awards are symbolically important and important in deterrence. What do you think?

If you think there is something wrong with pain awards, do you also think that is ground standing alone to reconsider the whole tort system?

New Directions

If either the old or the new tort reformers are right or partly right in their central perceptions, would it be a good idea to find alternatives to some or all parts of the tort system?

Many of the criticisms summarized above are reviewed by Professor Sugarman, who insists that tort law fails in the goal of inducing safety, providing compensation, or doing justice if you look at the system as a whole and consider alternatives. STEPHEN SUGARMAN, DOING AWAY WITH PERSONAL INJURY LAW (1989). Sugarman proposes a comprehensive welfare program that would take care of injuries as well as any other misfortune. Employers would cover short term needs, government the rest. Safety incentives would be provided by regulation, not by threat of liability. But regulation does not always work or work efficiently and we do not know a great deal about how to make it effective as a substitute for liability. *See* JERRY MASHAW & DAVID HARFST, THE STRUGGLE FOR AUTO SAFETY (1990); Michael J. Trebilcock, *Requiem for Regulators: The Passing of a Counter-Culture?*, 8 YALE J. REG. 497 (1991).

Others among the newer critics have suggested that society should allocate certain kinds of injury problems to some institutions other than tort law, but that tort law should be retained for at least some kinds of cases. *E.g.*, Richard B. Stewart, *Crisis in Tort Law? The Institutional Perspective*, 54 U. CHI. L. REV. 184 (1987); W. Kip Viscusi, *Toward a Diminished Role for Tort Liability: Social Insurance, Government Regulation, and Contemporary Risks to Health and Safety*, 6 YALE J. REG. 65 (1989). See also the good short discussion as to toxic torts in Robert Rabin, *Book Review*, 98 YALE L. J. 813 (1989) (reviewing PETER SCHUCK, TORT SYSTEM ON TRIAL: THE BURDEN OF MASS TOXICS LITIGATION (1987)).

One alternative "institution" for dealing with injury might be specific regulation, such as regulation requiring air bags or seat belts. Another institution might be the free market, leaving people to contractual arrangements. Finally, some form of social or private insurance might provide the best institution for dealing with certain injuries not suited to the tort system. In evaluating the tort reform movement, and tort law itself, some of these alternatives must be considered. Some of the major ones other than regulation or contract are considered next.

*

PART 6

ALTERNATIVES TO TORT LAW

■ ■ ■

For many, including many legislatures, the disadvantages of the tort system have outweighed the advantages, at least in particular settings. In consequence, legal thinkers and state and federal legislatures have provided several non-tort alternatives to the tort system. All of these, however, have limited application, for example, to employment injuries or automobile injuries.

This subpart introduces some of those alternatives. In many ways they are enormously different from tort systems. But this should not obscure the similarities. In considering these alternatives, consider whether the same issues must be resolved and whether, in new language, similar problems arise for the judiciary. More importantly, consider whether any of these alternative systems is better than the tort system. If they are not to wholly supplant the tort system, can they be satisfactorily meshed with tort law?

CHAPTER 28

WORKERS' COMPENSATION

■ ■ ■

§ 1. INTRODUCTION

A. THE EMPLOYER'S TORT LIABILITY AT COMMON LAW

In the pre-industrial period in England, servants injured in the service of a master were often living in the household as apprentices or indentured servants. At least at some times and places, the practice and legal obligation of masters was to take care of the injured servant by furnishing him room and board during the period of the indenture or contract. A similar practice developed in the maritime law, and seamen injured in the service of the ship were entitled to "maintenance and cure"—basic support and medical attention. The assistance received by the servant or seaman in such cases was no doubt minimal compared to a tort remedy, but was available without respect to the employer's fault. In addition, the seaman injured by an "unseaworthy" condition of a ship had a strict liability claim against the owner. *See* THOMAS SCHOENBAUM, ADMIRALTY AND MARITIME LAW § 4–28–4–35 (1994); 5 U.S.C.A. § 8102.

With the development of industrial plants, the picture was very different. The force of machinery was multiplied through levers, pulleys and gears, then through water and steam power. The injuries caused by massive forces in the factory or on the rails were both numerous and horrible. At the very time injury was becoming the formidable problem it remains today, the system of apprentices and indentured servants was becoming obsolete. An injured plant worker could not expect that the employer would provide for him when injury made work impossible.

The common law tort system might have provided a very handsome remedy for the injured worker had it retained or developed the notion that an actor was liable for *trespassory* torts to the person, even without intent or negligence. But as we saw in Chapter 23, that notion largely went underground with the decision in *Brown v. Kendall*. The result was that the injured employee was required to prove employer negligence in all injury cases.

This might not have been an intolerable burden in many instances, but the defenses erected against the employee were effective barriers to many claims. The absolute common law defenses of contributory negligence, assumed risk and fellow servant barred a great many claims. The fellow servant rule in particular was often a hardship. That rule, supposedly grounded in assumed risk, held that the worker could not recover against the employer for negligence of the worker's fellow servant. Even though the master would be liable for the torts of a servant, he would not be liable for the torts of one servant to another.

Injured industrial workers in the 19th century were in difficult straits. They were without insurance or health benefits, without modern social services, and very often without a tort remedy. Piecemeal efforts were made in legislatures to ameliorate this situation. Factory acts sometimes attempted to provide safer working conditions. One example of safety legislation was the Federal Safety Appliance Act, 45 U.S.C.A. § 1 et seq., enacted in 1893 and requiring railroads to use such safety devices as automatic couplers and brakes operable by the engineer. In 1908, the Federal Employers' Liability Act, (FELA) 45 U.S.C.A. § 51 et seq. was passed. This attacked some major sources of the problem by abolishing the defenses of fellow servant and assumed risk and by adopting a comparative negligence scheme. The statute applied to railroad workers in interstate commerce, and as it stands today, it applies to virtually all railroad workers.

The FELA did not address the problems of factory or other workers. Nor did it address the fundamental problem of delay. The worker who was injured by an employer's negligence could indeed recover once the defenses were abolished. But recovery might take years if litigated in the court system. Since urban workers had little if any support if they were unable to work, even a good tort remedy might in practice be illusory.

This was the situation when workers' compensation provisions were first considered.

B. THE ADOPTION OF WORKERS' COMPENSATION

The first workers' compensation scheme was adopted in Germany in 1884. Although German philosophers had laid down the foundations of the idea in their conception of the state as a protector of the citizens, there were more immediate reasons for the adoption of the scheme, the foundation of which is compulsory insurance. One reason may have been that the German state, united under Prussian leadership in 1870, was a convenient means through which to organize the capital necessary to manage a widespread insurance scheme. An even more immediate reason was Bismarck's fear that, without some such plan, radical Marxist movements would be successful. With Bismarck's support, workers' compensation was adopted to provide a sufficient level of support to undermine Marxism. *See generally* Arthur Larson, Workers' Compensation (1992).

American states began enacting workers' compensation statutes, some quite limited, just after the turn of the century. The first comprehensive act was the 1910 New York statute. It was quickly declared unconstitutional in *Ives v. South Buffalo Railway Co.*, 94 N.E. 431 (N.Y. 1911) on the ground that in imposing liability without fault of the employer, the statute was a taking of property without due process of law. "When our Constitutions were adopted, it was the law of the land that no man who was without fault or negligence could be held liable in damages for injuries sustained by another." The liability of the employer to pay workers' compensation under a compulsory insurance scheme "is a liability unknown to the common law, and we think it plainly constitutes a deprivation of liberty and property...."

New York amended its constitution, however, and a new statute was passed in 1913. Other states began enacting workers' compensation statutes, sometimes avoiding constitutional challenge by making the provisions elective. Most states had enacted a statute by 1920, and all states eventually did so. There is a separate federal statute for federal employees and another for longshoremen and harbor workers.

C. CHARACTERISTICS OF THE STATUTES

Although the statutes are varied in detail, they are alike in these characteristic provisions:

1. *Strict liability.* Employers are made strictly liable for on-the-job injury of employees. Thus a worker injured on the job is entitled to compensation even if the employer is not negligent.

2. *Defenses are abolished.* Contributory negligence, assumed risk and fellow servant defenses are abolished completely. This is not a rule of comparative negligence. Even the employee who is guilty of contributory negligence recovers full compensation.

3. *Limited liability.* The employer's liability is limited. The compensation provided is not common law damages, but relatively fixed amounts, expressed as specific sums for certain injuries like the loss of a thumb, or as a percentage of average wages where there is total disability. Liability includes compensation for medical needs and wage loss, but nothing for pain and suffering. This limited liability is a trade-off for strict liability and sometimes is emphasized as a constitutional justification for the strict liability.

4. *Immediate and periodic payment.* An injured worker is entitled, after a short waiting period, to immediate periodic payments. This is in contrast to the common law lump-sum method. Payments continue as long as the disability exists, subject to any statutory maximum amounts.

5. *Enforcement and administration.* Where there is no dispute, the employer (or its insurer) pays directly to the worker on a periodic basis. If there is a dispute, the worker reports the claim to an administrative agency, called the Industrial Commission, Workers' Compensation Commission or something similar. The agency usually sends a hearing officer or referee to the locality to hold an informal hearing and settle the dispute. The statutes contemplated that there would be no need for lawyers, but today lawyers do in fact appear in many of these hearings. However, the procedure is relaxed and informal, and there are no rules of

evidence, so it remains true at least in theory that lawyers are not required.

6. *Financing.* The scheme is essentially a compulsory insurance scheme, though in some states the "insurance" fund is managed by the state rather than by private insurers. The employer is required by statute to purchase insurance. The insurance must provide coverage as outlined by the statute.

7. *Courts.* Courts have a most limited role in workers' compensation. They do, however, decide the meaning of the statute and whether evidence is sufficient to warrant the decisions of the administrators who decide disputes under the statute. In other words, one may appeal from an award of the compensation tribunal, but the courts will not overturn the award if there is evidence to support it and it is based on a correct interpretation of the law. There is no jury trial in either the initial hearing or in the appeal to the courts.

8. *Exclusive remedy and third-party claims.* Most statutes provide that the injured employee's remedy against the employer is workers' compensation, and that this remedy is exclusive of any other remedy. In other words, with few exceptions, there is no tort action against the employer. The exclusive remedy provision, however, is aimed only at preventing suits against the employer. The employee injured by a third person, such as a manufacturer of a machine used on the job, still has a tort suit against that third person.

D. COVERAGE

No state has enacted workers' compensation benefits for every single worker within the state. Several devices in the statutes operate to limit coverage of workers.

1. *Election of coverage.* At one time, many of the statutes provided that workers' compensation coverage was not compulsory, but was elective only. The employer could elect not to be covered, but if this happened, the employer would be liable in tort and would be deprived of the common law defenses. The employer was thus encouraged to elect workers' compensation. The employee also had an election, but was presumed to elect in favor of compensation in the absence of some active rejection of it. This system has met with much disapproval, and many states now use a fully compulsory system. In states where an election is possible, an election by either employer or employee may eliminate workers' compensation coverage in particular cases.

2. *Definition of employer.* Several of the critical determinants of compensation are hidden in definitional sections of the statutes. The statute may define "employer" or "employee" or both, and the statutory definitions will necessarily exclude certain persons from coverage. Many statutes exclude from coverage the following groups of workers, usually by definition of terms like "employee":

(A) *"Casual workers."* Example: someone who trims your hedge for you on one occasion. Obviously this category can present line-drawing problems, but it is not a major problem.

(B) *Domestic workers.* Example: a home cleaning person. Notice this is not the same as "janitorial."

(C) *Agricultural workers.*

(D) *Non-business employees.* This seems broader in some ways than "domestic workers."

(E) *Small employers.* Several states exempt employers whose employees are not numerous. The cut-off varies from two to six employees.

Since the definition of employee may take several pages of statutory print, there are a good many details to be assessed under particular statutes. Although many states do not cover agricultural employees, public employees and corporate executives are often covered. Even prisoners may be covered. Obviously the governing statute must be consulted.

3. *Expanding coverage.* In some situations an enterprise that would not normally be considered an employer will be defined as an employer under the compensation statute. Material on "statutory employers" and "loaned employees" is considered in § 3.

E. BENEFITS

If an entire section could be devoted to a study of the benefits payable under workers' compensation, quite a few major issues would emerge. Some of the decisions and some of the statutes would be subject to various criticisms. In some cases, benefits are woefully inadequate. In others, courts seem to have moved to a more tort-like assessment of liability. However, the mainstream cases and the principles of workers' compensation benefits are fairly straightforward. In general they look something like this:

1. *Death benefits.* If the worker dies from an on-the-job injury, death benefits based on his or her earnings are paid to certain survivors. Often, these are dependents rather than heirs. In this respect, some workers' compensation statutes differ from many of the wrongful death statutes governing tort liability.

2. *Medical benefits.* Statutes now provide more or less unlimited medical benefits, including all forms of needed care, prosthetic devices, and the like. For the most part, issues over medical care have been extremely narrow and minor.

3. *Disability benefits.* In principle, workers' compensation statutes sought to replace or avoid economic loss suffered from injury. There was no award for pain and suffering. The award was intended instead to replace wages lost due to disability. Thus if a worker was injured and disabled for six months, during which time he or she could earn no wages, the ideal benefit would be equal to six months' wages. And if the worker

regains part of her earning capacity, benefits would be reduced accordingly. *See Metropolitan Stevedore Co. v. Rambo,* 515 U.S. 291 (1995).

Limits on benefits. No statute affords 100% wage replacement in providing disability benefits. If a worker collected 100% of wages during disability, there would be an incentive to feign injury or disability. Even if that did not happen, there might be an unconscious tendency to prolong disability. In addition, federal law makes payments for personal injury tax-exempt. Workers' compensation benefits, since they are not taxable, are "worth more" than the wages themselves. For these and similar reasons, compensation is limited to a percentage of average wages. This percentage is often fixed at two-thirds of the average wage, and it is, ordinarily, paid on a weekly or monthly schedule. There are, in some instances, also limits on the total amount in any given week. This might be expressed in terms of a dollar amount, such as $200 per week. Or it might be expressed as a percentage of the average wage for the entire state. In either event, very high-earning employees might be entitled to considerably less than their actual wage loss. Finally, there may be limits on the total number of weeks for which compensation is payable.

Classifications of disability. Disability is typically classified as temporary or permanent on the one hand, and as either partial or total on the other. Most industrial injuries cause some temporary total disability, as where an employee is injured and cannot work at all for two months. Such an employee would ordinarily be entitled to two months' compensation. If the disability is permanent, compensation may run for life, but in some states it may be limited to a specified period, such as 500 weeks or 600 weeks. In the case of partial disability there may be compensation due, but at a reduced level.

Scheduled injuries. Injuries that were painful but caused no wage loss were not originally compensable at all, since there was no claim for pain and suffering. A worker who lost testicles or was sexually disfigured might, therefore, recover medical benefits and wage loss during any healing period, but since these injuries would not prevent work, there would be no compensation after the healing period. Some statutes have now added a small compensatory sum in the case of "disfigurement." More importantly, virtually all states have a "schedule" of benefits for certain injuries. For example, if a worker loses the sight in one eye in an industrial injury, the schedule specifies a fixed amount of compensation. Such a worker might receive 66 2/3% of the average monthly wage for 30 months. This would be awarded even if there was no demonstrable "disability," as reflected in wage loss. An unscheduled injury, in comparison, would be compensable only if it resulted in a disability.

Functional or industrial disability. The principle of computing benefits by schedule and the principle of computing by actual wage loss are obviously at odds. The original idea was to replace wages, or at least a reasonable percentage of wages. Over the years, the principle behind the schedules has moved courts and legislatures toward a "functional" assessment of disability and away from the wage-loss or "industrial" assessment of disability. This may permit courts to say that, though the claimant has not lost work time except for a healing period, nevertheless the body as a whole is impaired in function, and a disability should be found accordingly. Different statutes and different courts may thus get quite different results when a worker is injured in a way that impairs bodily function but does not seriously affect earning capacity. This particular problem is treated by Professor Larson in a section entitled "Disability: Wage Loss Versus Medical Incapacity." This section and the next, which deals with scheduled benefits, runs over 300 pages. ARTHUR LARSON, WORKMEN'S COMPENSATION §§ 57–58.

These notes suggest that problems arise in computing benefits. In addition, benefits may tend to under-compensate, as where there is a 500–week limit on compensation for total and permanent disability. And benefits may over-compensate where the principle of the schedule is carried out. All of these problems and others, that could be identified in computing benefits, are problems worthy of attention by those who could improve the law. But, especially for the purpose of comparisons to tort law, the central features of benefits payable under workers' compensation statutes are quite simple. In the great majority of cases, benefits will be paid regularly and without dispute as long as disability continues, but in most cases, benefits will reflect something less than actual wage loss.

On the theoretical side, workers' compensation was justified on grounds much like those that were advanced later for vicarious liability and strict products liability. The idea was that enterprise ought to bear responsibility for the costs it typically or recurrently imposed and pass those costs along to consumers. As workers were routinely injured, the costs of their injuries should be treated as a cost of doing business and internalized by the business. *See* George L. Priest, *The Invention of Enterprise Liability: A Critical History of the Intellectual Foundations of Modern Tort Law,* 14 J. LEGAL STUD. 461, 465–67 (1985).

Pragmatic justifications were different. Workers' compensation statutes attempted to provide for some minimum well-being for injured workers. But they also attempted to provide a quick, efficient remedy, one that would not bog down in litigation, and that would provide payments quickly and with relative certainty. They thus attempted to provide a system that allowed only a minimum range of dispute. Benefits, for example, were relatively fixed and certain; there were no long trials devoted to proving extensive pain and suffering. Likewise, by eliminating investigations into fault, grounds for dispute were minimized.

With fault out of the picture and little ground for litigating over benefit levels, did they provide for that Utopia, long sought by citizens the world over, a system that worked without lawyers? That was, quite clearly, the drafters' goal. To achieve it, they would have to provide what is missing in some of the torts cases—an efficient trigger for liability. In the workers' compensation statutes, the trigger for liability is only job relatedness; that is, the injury must be one "arising out of and in the course of employment." The next section explores how efficient this trigger is.

§ 2. JOB–RELATED INJURY

A. ARISING OUT OF AND IN THE COURSE OF EMPLOY-MENT

WAIT v. TRAVELERS INDEMNITY CO. OF ILLINOIS

240 S.W.3d 220 (Tenn. 2007)

William M. Barker, C.J.

[Plaintiff Kristina Wait worked as an executive with the American Cancer Society ("ACS"). Due to a lack of office space in its Nashville facility, ACS allowed Wait to work from her East Nashville home. She converted a spare bedroom into an office, and ACS furnished office equipment and a budget to purchase office supplies. She performed all her daily work for ACS at her home office, and her supervisor and co-workers attended meetings at her home office. Her work did not require her to open her house to the public. One day as plaintiff was preparing her lunch she opened her door to a neighbor, Nathaniel Sawyers, who brutally beat her for no apparent reason. Plaintiff sought workers' compensation bene-fits from Travelers Indemnity, the insurer of ACS. The chancery court granted summary judgment for defendant on the grounds that the injuries did not arise out of or occur in the course of her employment.]

... The Workers' Compensation Act ("Act"), codified at Tennessee Code Annotated sections 50–6–101 to–801 (2005), is a legislatively created quid pro quo system where an injured worker forfeits any potential common law rights for recovery against his or her employer in return for a system that provides compensation completely independent of any fault on the part of the employer. The Act should be liberally construed in favor of compensation and any doubts should be resolved in the employee's fa-vor. . . .

This case requires us to apply the Act to a new and growing trend in the labor and employment market: telecommuting. An employee telecom-mutes when he or she takes advantage of electronic mail, internet, facsimile machines and other technological advancements to work from home or a place other than the traditional work site. In 2006, approxi-mately thirty-four million American workers telecommuted to some de-gree. . . . [T]his innovative working arrangement has resulted in an issue of first impression: whether the injuries a telecommuter sustains as a result of an assault at her home arise out of and occur in the course of her employment.

It is well settled in Tennessee, and in many other jurisdictions, that for an injury to be compensable under the Act, it must both "arise out of" and occur "in the course of" employment. Tenn. Code Ann. § 50–6–103(a) (2005). Although both of these statutory requirements seek to ensure a connection between the employment and the injuries for which benefits are being sought, they are not synonymous. As such, the "arising out of" requirement refers to cause or origin; whereas, "in the course of" denotes the time, place, and circumstances of the injury. Furthermore, we have consistently abstained from adopting any particular judicial test, doctrine, formula, or label that purports to clearly define the line between accidents and injuries which arise out of and in the course of employment and those which do not.

In this case, we will consider the second requirement first. An injury occurs in the course of employment "when it takes place within the period of the employment, at a place where the employee reasonably may be, and while the employee is fulfilling work duties or engaged in doing something incidental thereto." *Blankenship,* 164 S.W.3d at 354 (quoting 1 Arthur Larson, *Workers' Compensation Law* § 12 (2004)).

Generally, injuries sustained during personal breaks are compensable. *Holder v. Wilson Sporting Goods Co.,* 723 S.W.2d 104, 107 (Tenn.1987). In *Holder,* we affirmed an award of workers' compensation benefits for an employee who slipped and fell in his employer's parking lot while he was putting his lunch box into his vehicle after finishing his meal. We noted that "[t]he remedial policies of the Worker's Compensation Act would be undermined if too severe a line were drawn controlling the compensability of injuries that occur during the normal course of the work day after employees have arrived for work, have started working, and before they have left for the day."

Much like the defendant in *Holder,* the defendant here argues that the plaintiff's injuries are not compensable because the plaintiff was not "fulfilling a work duty" in admitting Sawyers into her kitchen. It is true that the plaintiff suffered her injuries while preparing her lunch in the kitchen of her home; however, the plaintiff's work site was located within her home. Under these circumstances, the plaintiff's kitchen was comparable to the kitchens and break rooms that employers routinely provide at traditional work sites.... It is reasonable to conclude that the ACS realized that the plaintiff would take personal breaks during the course of her working day including "such incidental acts as eating, drinking, smoking, seeking toilet facilities, and seeking fresh air, coolness or warmth." *Carter v. Volunteer Apparel, Inc.,* 833 S.W.2d 492, 495 (Tenn. 1992) (citing 1A Arthur Larson, *Workmen's Compensation Law* §§ 21.10– 21.50 (1990)).

Thus, after careful review, we conclude that the injuries the plaintiff sustained while on her lunch break, like the injuries at issue in *Holder,* occurred during the course of the plaintiff's employment.... Unless instructed otherwise by the employer, an employee working from a home office who answers a knock at her door and briefly admits an acquaintance into her home does not necessarily depart so far from her work duties so as to remove her from the course of her employment. This is not to say, however, that situations may never arise where more prolonged or planned social visits might well remove the employee from the course of the employment. . . .

In arguing that the plaintiff's injury did not occur "in the course of" her employment, the defendant maintains that the plaintiff's decision to admit Sawyers into her home was not a work duty. However, this argument misses the mark on this requirement because the Act does not explicitly state that the employee's actions must benefit the employer; it only requires that the injuries occur in "the course of" the employment. . . . The question is not whether the plaintiff's injuries occurred while she was performing a duty owed to the ACS, but rather whether the time, place, and circumstances demonstrate that the injuries occurred while the plaintiff was engaged in an activity incidental to her employment. . . .

Even though the plaintiff's injuries occurred "in the course of" her employment, we nevertheless hold that they did not "arise out of" her job duties with the ACS. The phrase "arising out of" requires that a causal connection exist between the employment conditions and the resulting injury. With respect to whether an assault arises out of employment, we have previously delineated assaults into three general classifications:

> (1) assaults with an "inherent connection" to employment such as disputes over performance, pay or termination; (2) assaults stemming from "inherently private" disputes imported into the employment setting from the claimant's domestic or private life and not exacerbated by the employment; and (3) assaults resulting from a "neutral force" such as random assaults on employees by individuals outside the employment relationship.

Woods v. Harry B. Woods Plumbing Co., 967 S.W.2d 768, 771 (Tenn.1998).

When an assault has an "inherent connection" to the employment it is compensable. On the other hand, assaults originating from "inherently private" disputes and imported into the work place are not compensable. However, whether "neutral assaults" are compensable turns on the "facts and circumstances of the employment."

The assault in this case is best described as a "neutral assault." . . . A "neutral force" assault is one that is "neither personal to the claimant nor distinctly associated with the employment." 1 Arthur Larson, *Workers' Compensation Law* § 3.05 (2007). The *Woods* categories focus on what catalyst spurred the assault, i.e., was it a dispute arising from a work-related duty, was it a dispute arising from a personal matter, or was it unexplained or irrational? An assault that is spurred by neither a catalyst inherently connected to the employment nor stemming from an inherently private dispute is most aptly labeled as a "neutral force" assault. Here, the undisputed facts clearly show that the assault had neither an inherent connection with the employment, nor did it stem from a personal dispute between Sawyers and the plaintiff. Therefore, we must focus our attention on the facts and circumstances of the plaintiff's employment and its relationship to the injuries sustained by the plaintiff.

Generally, for an injury to "arise out of" employment, it must emanate from a peculiar danger or risk inherent to the nature of the employment. Thus, "an injury purely coincidental, or contemporaneous, or collateral, with the employment ... will not cause the injury ... to be considered as arising out of the employment." *Jackson v. Clark & Fay, Inc.*, 197 Tenn. 135, 270 S.W.2d 389, 390 (1954). However, in limited circumstances, where the employment involves "indiscriminate exposure to the general public," the "street risk" doctrine may supply the required causal connection between the employment and the injury. [We have held that] the "street risk" doctrine applies where an employee's "indiscriminate exposure to the general public is one of the conditions under which her work [is] required to be performed, and the actions of those persons on the premises are reasonably considered hazards of the employment." . . .

The plaintiff argues that had it not been for her employment arrangement, she would not have been at home to suffer these attacks. However, we have never held that any and every assault which occurs at the work site arises out of employment.... The "street risk" doctrine is not a limitless means of allowing recovery for every situation. As such, this case presents us with an opportunity to outline the boundaries of the doctrine. When an employee suffers a "neutral assault" within the confines of her employer's premises—whether the premises be a home office or a corporate office—the "street risk" doctrine will not provide the required causal connection between the injury and the employment unless the proof fairly suggests either that the attacker singled out the employee because of his or her association with the employer or that the employment indiscriminately exposed the employee to dangers from the public. The facts of this case clearly illustrate that the "street risk" doctrine does not apply. There is nothing in the record to fairly suggest or provide any weight to the assertion that the plaintiff's injuries were causally connected with the nature of her employment. Therefore, the chancery court's holding that the plaintiff's injuries did not arise out of her employment is affirmed.

In sum, the plaintiff's injuries were suffered during the course of her employment; however, they did not arise out of her employment.... We therefore affirm the judgment of the chancery court dismissing the complaint.

NOTES

1. **Increased risk.** Courts no longer insist that the employment risk be "peculiar" to the employment in the sense that it is different in its nature from risks faced by people in general. They very commonly do, however, insist that employment must somehow increase these risks. Thus if employment requires a worker to drive a van delivering flowers, injury in a collision on the street will be one arising out of employment, even though everyone is

subjected to "street risks." The worker in such a case has increased exposure, though the nature of the risk is the same. *See, e.g, Jivan v. Economy Inn & Suites*, 260 S.W.3d 281 (Ark. 2007) (hotel assistant manager required by employer to live in hotel was put at greater risk of injury by hotel fire than someone who did not live there). Some courts would impose liability for compensation in such a case even if the employment only occasionally puts the employee on the streets, so long as it in fact does so. *See* ARTHUR LARSON, WORKMEN'S COMPENSATION § 9.00 *et seq.* Does the *Wait* court's formulation of the "street risk" doctrine as it applies to attacks at the workplace provide a workable test for future cases?

2. **Positional risks.** The increased risk test is commonly used, but some courts have adopted and used a "positional risk" test for risks that are not purely personal. This is basically a rule that liability for compensation is triggered if the employment is a but-for cause of injury. A well-known decision is *Industrial Indemnity Co. v. Industrial Accident Commission*, 214 P.2d 41 (Cal. App. 1950). In that case, an angry wife entered a bar and fired a shot at her husband. The shot ricocheted off the bar and struck a waitress, who had nothing to do with the quarrel but who died as a result. Conceivably, one could say that risk of injury of bar employees as a result of angry customers (or spouses) is somewhat increased by their employment. The court took a much broader line, however, emphasizing that "her employment required her to be in what turned out to be a place of danger." It would be sufficient for liability, the court said, that "injury results from a danger to which [the employee] was exposed as an employee." *See also Kolson v. District of Columbia Dept. of Employment Services*, 699 A.2d 357 (D.C. 1997) (bus driver attacked on the street while walking to a hotel after completing his shift at 4:30 a.m.; injury "grew out of his employment because it resulted from a risk created by his employment—his arrival at odd hours in places away from his home and the necessity of using the public streets to seek lodging"). What about a case in which a supervisor orders an employee to come out to see someone at the place of business, and that person shoots the employee in connection with a personal dispute? *See Kerr–McGee Corp. v. Hutto*, 401 So.2d 1277 (Miss. 1981) (held, "the employee's death was so strongly connected to the directive of his superior that it cannot be completely disassociated from his employment").

3. **"In the course of" employment and the going and coming rule.** Compensation for an injury requires that it occur "in the course of" employment, which emphasizes time and place—injury must occur "at work" and during working hours. This means that an injury that occurs while an employee is going to or coming from work is not compensable. *See, e.g., Harris v. Westin Management Co. East*, 230 S.W.3d 1 (Mo. 2007); *MGM Mirage v. Cotton*, 116 P.3d 56 (Nev. 2005); *Jaeger Baking Co. v. Kretschmann,* 292 N.W.2d 622 (Wis. 1980). There are exceptions, however, including where a commuting employee is running a "special errand" for the employer, *see Bob Allyn Masonry v. Murphy*, 183 P.3d 126 (Nev. 2008), or where the employer receives some "incidental benefit" from the employee's commute that were not common to ordinary commutes, *see Salt Lake City Corp. v. Labor Com'n*, 153 P.3d 179 (Utah 2007). What if an employee's commute is made more

hazardous by the employer's "extraordinary demands" for overtime work? *See Snowbarger v. Tri–County Elec. Coop.*, 793 S.W.2d 348 (Mo. 1990).

4. **Traveling employees.** Employees who routinely work away from home are known as "traveling employees." Under the traveling employee doctrine, also known as the "commercial traveler rule," or the "continuous coverage rule," such employees are considered to be "in the course of employment continuously during the entire trip, except during a distinct departure on a personal errand." *Ball–Foster Glass Container Co. v. Giovanelli*, 177 P.3d 692 (Wash. 2008). A number of cases hold that traveling employees are "in the course of" employment even when they are injured during recreational or social activities. *See, e.g., McCann v. Hatchett*, 19 S.W.3d 218 (Tenn. 2000) (employee drowned in hotel pool at 10 p.m.); *Giovanelli, supra* (employee was walking to a park near his hotel to listen to music). The traveling employee doctrine may also be seen as an exception to the going and coming rule. *See Labadie v. Norwalk Rehabilitation Services, Inc.*, 875 A.2d 485 (Conn. 2005) (home health care worker injured going to her first assignment of the day). Should the traveling employee rules apply to telecommuters?

5. **Incidental departures from working.** The *Wait* court holds, as most courts do, that an employee who is on a momentary break, or having lunch at the workplace, remains "in the course of" employment. Such "personal comfort missions" are not considered outside the course of employment. *See, e.g., K–Mart Corp. v. Herring*, 188 P.3d 140 (Okla. 2008) (night watchman who was shot during a trip to a fast-food restaurant during a 7–hour shift with no scheduled breaks was still acting in the course of employment); *Gooden v. Coors Technical Ceramic Co.*, 236 S.W.3d 151 (Tenn. 2007) (employee's heart attack while playing basketball on company premises during work break was in the course of employment). A substantial departure will take the employee out of the course of employment, although "reentry" may occur at some point. This is true even with traveling employees. *See, e.g., Ray Bell Const. Co. v. King*, 642 S.E.2d 841 (Ga. 2007). Does this remind you of a rule we saw in Chapter 22 on vicarious liability of an employer for the torts of an employee?

CARVALHO v. DECORATIVE FABRICS CO.

366 A.2d 157 (R.I. 1976)

BEVILACQUA, CHIEF JUSTICE.

[The employee worked in a factory handling yarn. At the end of the shift fellow employees customarily assisted removing lint from each other's clothes by using an air hose. On this occasion a fellow worker placed the air hose "in the vicinity of petitioner's rectum," and the petitioner felt his stomach blow up. He was unable to work the next day and later went to the emergency room in pain. He was found to have a perforated rectum. The commission denied compensation on the ground that this involved horseplay and assault and was therefore not arising out of employment.]

In the early workmen's compensation cases involving "horseplay" (sometimes referred to as "sportive assault," "larking" or "skylarking") courts were reluctant to award compensation, even to the innocent, non-participating victim. Reasoning that employees were hired to work and not to play, courts concluded that injuries resulting from "horseplay" did not arise out of and in the course of employment. In addition, courts denied compensation sustaining the defense that the claimant was a "participant" in or "instigator" of "horseplay." However, these decisions are contrary to the scope and intent of the Workmen's Compensation Acts. These Acts were designed to provide compensation to victims of work-connected injuries and to eliminate the tort defenses of negligence and fault. In effect, these early decisions judicially reinstituted common law defenses which had been abolished by statute.

Later courts recognized that the primary purpose of workmen's compensation is to provide economic assistance to an employee who is injured and thereby suffers a loss of earnings; such legislation "... was intended to impose upon the employer the burden of taking care of the casualties occurring in his employment, thus preventing the injured employee from becoming a public charge." Moreover, the worker need no longer be free from fault to receive compensation....

In the case of the victim who does not participate in the "horseplay" and is innocent of any wrongful conduct, we need no extended justification to hold that the injuries received are compensable. In *In re Leonbruno v. Champlain Silk Mills*, supra, the late Mr. Justice Cardozo stated:

> "The claimant was injured, not merely while he was in a factory, but because he was in a factory, in touch with associations and conditions inseparable from factory life. The risks of such associations and conditions were risks of the employment." Id. at 472, 128 N.E. at 711.

When people are placed together and are in close association with one another in performing their work there is a natural instinct to fool around and play pranks on one another. Such activity is part of the work environment, an incident of the employment. The claimant need only establish that the injury arose out of and in the course of employment: a nexus or causal connection between the injury and the employment must be shown....

The injured claimant should not be denied compensation merely because of his participation in "horseplay." As the court in *Maltais v. Equitable Life Assur. Soc'y of United States*, 40 A.2d 837 (N.H. 1944) stated:

> "... to hold that an injury arises out of the employment if it is inflicted on a workman attentive to duty by the sportive conduct of a fellow-employee, but that it does not so arise if the injured workman participates, however slightly, in the sport is to draw a distinction based on the injured workman's fault, when the only faults specifically named in the statute as precluding recovery are intoxication, violation of law, and serious or wilful misconduct."[1]

---

1. In *Maltais,* two workers, while cleaning each others' clothes off with an air hose, began fooling around with it, causing claimant's death. Although claimant participated in the "horseplay," compensation was awarded.

Clearly, where horseplay has become customary, a participant can recover since his act is an incident of the work environment. However, where there is no evidence that "horseplay" is customary, the issue is whether the "horseplay" constituted a substantial deviation from the employment. The substantiality of the deviation should be determined not by the seriousness of the resulting injuries but solely by the extent to which the "horseplay" constitutes a departure from the course of the employment. 1 ARTHUR LARSON, WORKMEN'S COMPENSATION LAW, § 23.63 (1972).

Where the use of an air hose to clean off clothes is a daily practice, play with the hose is a risk of the employment and part and parcel of the working environment. Such activity should be regarded as part of the course of employment, particularly where, as in the instant case, the employer places in the hands of the employee the instrumentality which was used in the "horseplay" and caused the injury. . . .

NOTES

1. **Workers' comp versus tort claim.** If an injury is not compensable under workers' compensation, then the injured worker might well be able to bring a tort claim against a co-worker for an injury resulting from "horseplay." *Grabowski v. Mangler*, 938 A.2d 637 (Del. 2007). Larsen's treatise, in § 23.01, points to four important factors in making a coverage determination: "(1) the extent and seriousness of the deviation from work; (2) the completeness of the deviation (i.e., whether it was co-mingled with the performance of duty or involved an abandonment of duty); (3) the extent to which the practice of horseplay had become an accepted part of the employment; and (4) the extent to which the nature of the employment may be expected to include some horseplay." What about a case in which a an emergency medical technician with a reputation as a "kid in an adult's body" suddenly picks up a cardiac defibrillator while riding in an ambulance and shocks a co-worker, resulting in her death? What additional facts would you want to know? *See Hilton v. Martin*, 654 S.E.2d 572 (Va. 2008).

2. **Instigators.** Even the instigator of horseplay may claim compensation for horseplay injury, provided that the horseplay is not a substantial deviation from the job. *See Prows v. Industrial Comm'n of Utah*, 610 P.2d 1362 (Utah 1980).

3. **Intended battery.** Even an intended battery by a co-worker, distinct from a playful injury, could be considered to be within the scope of employment if it arises from a job-related dispute. *See, e.g., Ford Motor Co. v. Industrial Commission*, 399 N.E.2d 1280 (Ill. 1980); *PF Chang's v. Industrial Com'n of Arizona*, 166 P.3d 135 (Ariz. Ct. App. 2007).

4. **Company-sponsored recreation.** Sometimes unintended injuries occur during company social or recreational events. Courts often scrutinize the facts of these cases very carefully. If the employer actually sponsors the event, expects employee attendance, and pays the costs, injury during the event is likely to be one that arises from employment. If any of these elements

is missing, courts may hold that injury is unrelated to employment. *See, e.g., Frost v. Salter Path Fire & Rescue*, 639 S.E.2d 429 (N.C. 2007).

UNION COLLIERY CO. v. INDUSTRIAL COM'N, 132 N.E. 200 (Ill. 1921). This is a claim for compensation by a widow and children of a deceased worker. The deceased was employed in the employer's coal mine, working at the top of the "cage" or elevator on which coal was hoisted. He was to dump the coal when the cage arrived at the top, but he also had underground duties. On the night of his death, he rode up on the cage with a load of coal. Circumstantial evidence suggested he was crushed between the cage and a beam. To ride up in a loaded cage or hoist was a violation of the state statutes on mining safety. The Industrial Commission made an award of compensation, but the trial court, reviewing this, set it aside. *Held*, compensation should be awarded. The employer argues that violation of the statute, like violation of an employer's instruction, would show that the injury and death "did not arise out of and in the course of employment." However, violation of the statute would at most show negligence. Nor does violation of an employer's rules automatically place the employee outside the sphere of his employment. In this case, injury arose out of employment.

NOTES

1. Conceivably, some violations of statute or employer rules would show more than negligence. What would have to be shown?

2. Early cases sometimes took a narrow view about what injuries arose in employment. On facts similar to those in *Union Colliery*, the Pennsylvania Court barred recovery in *Pokis v. Buck Run Coal Co.*, 132 A. 795 (Pa. 1926). In so doing it relied in part on an earlier decision in which a worker entered a portion of the mine known to contain gas. This was prohibited by law. The court said that "as to this danger zone, he had no employment," and that the injury was not therefore one arising out of employment. *Walcofski v. Lehigh Valley Coal Co.*, 122 A. 238 (Pa. 1923).

3. Narrow decisions of this kind no longer represent the courts' approach to the issue of "arising out of employment," although an employee's willful misconduct may in some instances be a defense. *See, e.g., Brackett v. Focus Hope, Inc.*, 753 N.W.2d 207 (Mich. 2008) (state statute bars compensation where employee has engaged in "intentional and willful misconduct"). The modern approach is and long has been to give a very liberal interpretation to coverage under workers' compensation statutes and to resolve doubts in favor of the employee's coverage.

B. ACCIDENT, INJURY AND DISEASE

NOTE: "ACCIDENT" AND "ACCIDENTAL INJURY"

1. *Injury by accident; accidental injury.* Workers are initially covered for compensation only when injury arises out of and in the course of

employment and when, in addition, they are injured by "accident" or suffer "accidental injury." These requirements remain today except that workers may recover for disability resulting from certain occupational diseases.

2. *Meaning of accident/accidental terminology.* The statutory phrase, "injury by accident," or the more liberal "accidental injury," has been made to bear the weight of a multitude of legal issues. The requirement of accident might mean: (a) the injury must not have been intentional on the part of the worker; or (b) the injury must have occurred on some definite occasion, or "event;" or (c) the injury must have proceeded from external causes, as distinct from a degenerative breakdown within the body, or some combination of these three ideas. Actually, analysis reveals even further ambiguities. If the word "accident" refers to something that is not expected, is it the cause, or is it the result? If it refers to a definite occasion or event, is it the cause or the result?

3. *Accident/accidental: Suicide.* Statutes frequently exclude from coverage the self-inflicted injury, including suicide and injuries resulting from intoxication. The requirement of "accident" would perhaps have sufficiently covered the self-inflicted injury. When the self-inflicted injury is suicide, complications occur. If injury on the job causes insanity, which in turn leads to suicide, the resulting death may still be considered part of the "accident," and, on reasoning like that used in the tort cases, not the product of a "moral being." The death in such cases is compensable. Thus the legal cause reasoning is imported into the workers' compensation area. *See, e.g, Vredenburg v. Sedgwick CMS*, 188 P.3d 1084 (Nev. 2008). The exact kind of insanity—or "depression"—sufficient to permit this causal analysis in favor of the workers' dependents had been subject to debate and vacillation. It is perhaps fair to say that nothing like "insanity" is really required in many of the cases, and that pain and depression will be sufficient instead. *See* ARTHUR LARSON, WORKMEN'S COMPENSATION § 36.

4. *Accident/accidental: Self-inflicted injury.* The term "accident" may exclude cases that "self-inflicted injury" would not exclude. A worker has an unsatisfactory conversation with his superior and kills himself. Is this an accident? *Zach v. Nebraska State Patrol*, 727 N.W.2d 206 (Neb. 2007).

5. *Accident/accidental: The definite occasion aspect.* In an old case from Minnesota, the statute actually defined "accident" to mean a sudden, unforeseen event. A worker worked for years at a machine which vibrated. Her nerves were gradually killed and the muscles atrophied, so that use of the arms was no longer possible. This was held to be no "accident," since there was no sudden event. *Young v. Melrose Granite Co.*, 189 N.W. 426 (Minn. 1922).

HARRIS v. BOARD OF EDUCATION
OF HOWARD COUNTY

825 A.2d 365 (Md. 2003)

ELDRIDGE, JUDGE. . . .

In January 1999, the petitioner, Vernell Harris, was fifty-eight years old and had been employed by the respondent, the Howard County Board of Education, for twelve years at Wilde Lake High School, as a "Food and Nutritional Service Assistant I." Ms. Harris's duties included preparing lunches for the students, tending to the cash register, cleaning the kitchen area, and laundering all linens used throughout the day. It is undisputed that Ms. Harris's regular work involved lifting boxes of frozen food weighing approximately thirty-five pounds from the freezer and carrying them to the appropriate food preparation area.

On the day that she incurred her injury, January 25, 1999, Ms. Harris was doing laundry with a co-worker, as she typically did at the end of her workday. [Ms. Harris had to drag a heavy box of laundry detergent, then lift the inner bag of powder.] After bending down to scoop some soap detergent into a cup, Ms. Harris bent down a second time to tie up the bag of soap powder. At that point, her back "cracked" and she screamed. Ms. Harris was unable to stand upright, and, when a co-worker brought her a chair, she was unable to sit. She appeared to be in excruciating pain. With the aid of another co-worker, Ms. Harris walked to the cafeteria manager's office who gave her an incident form authorizing her to see a doctor at a nearby medical office.

Ms. Harris was seen by Dr. Prudence Jackson at the Concentra Medical Center later that afternoon. Dr. Jackson testified that it was her expert medical opinion, within a reasonable degree of medical certainty, that dragging the heavy box of laundry soap outside caused Ms. Harris's back injury.

[Ms. Harris' claim was allowed by the Workers' Compensation Commission, but on judicial review in the Circuit court, the judge left to the jury the question whether the injury arose out of "unusual activity." The jury returned a verdict in favor of the employer. The intermediate appellate court affirmed and the case is now before Maryland's highest court.]

The current Maryland Workers' Compensation Act, in § 9–101(b) of the Labor and Employment Article, defines "accidental personal injury" as follows:

§ 9–101. DEFINITIONS.

(a) *In general.*—In this title the following words have the meanings indicated.

(b) *Accidental personal injury.*—"Accidental personal injury" means:

(1) an accidental injury that arises out of and in the course of employment. . . .

The above-quoted language contains no mention of "unusual activity." Under the plain language of the statute, what must be "accidental" is the *injury* and not the activity giving rise to the injury. The activity giving rise to the injury need only "arise[ ] out of and in the course of employment," and not be otherwise excluded by the Act....

The line of cases in this Court requiring that an accidental personal injury arise out of "unusual activity" for there to be coverage obviously adds a requirement not contained in the statutory language. That line of cases requires both (1) that the accidental injury arise out of and in the course of employment and (2) that the accidental injury arise out of "unusual activity." Such cases cannot be reconciled with the often-repeated principle that this Court will "neither add nor delete words in order to give the statute a meaning not otherwise communicated by the language used." ...

The Court in *Victory Sparkler* concluded as follows (147 Md. at 382, 128 A. at 640):

> "The Maryland act is remedial and should receive a liberal construction so as to give to it the most beneficial operation; and when it contains positive direction that should 'be so interpreted and construed to effectuate its general purpose,' the Court must act under the compulsion of this mandate, and not disappoint an explicit provision, plainly expressed...."

The requirement that an accidental injury, arising out of and in the course of employment, must also arise out of unusual activity for there to be coverage, directly conflicts with this "mandate" set forth in *Victory Sparkler*. Instead of a "liberal construction so as to give to it the most beneficial operation," the respondent's position makes the Maryland Act the most restrictive in the nation....

If the decisions of this Court had uniformly required that an injury, arising out of and in the course of employment, must also result from unusual activity in order to be covered by the Workers' Compensation Act, a not unreasonable argument could be made that our erroneous insertion of language into the statute had become too ingrained to be corrected by judicial decision and that any correction should be made by the Legislature. Our decisions, however, have not been uniform or consistent. We have on numerous occasions held that accidental injuries were compensable even though they did not result from unusual activities....

Under *Schwind*, an injury is an "accidental injury" if it is the result of an "untoward event which [the employee] neither expected nor intended." Applying this principle to the present case clearly mandates coverage....

There is another line of Maryland cases which hold that the "unusual activity" requirement is pertinent only when there is no apparent causal connection between the accidental injury and the employment. In other words, under the opinions, the presence or absence of "unusual activity" is an aspect in the "arising out of the course of employment" analysis. Judge Markell for the Court in the often-cited opinion, *Perdue v. Brittingham,* thus explained (emphasis added):

> "It must always be shown that the injury arose not only 'in the course of [the] employment' but also 'out of the employment.' ... There must be a 'causal connection between the conditions under which the work is required to be performed and the resulting injury.' ... The causal connection may relate either (a) to the act or event, *e.g.,* a fall, which produces the injury or (b) to the consequences of the particular act or event. If there is other evidence that the work causes the act or event, *then it is immaterial how usual or trivial the act or event is,* or how unusual or abnormal the consequence.... If, however, there is no apparent causal connection between the work and the event, *e.g.,* a cerebral hemorrhage or an epileptic fit, then *unusual or extraordinary conditions* of the employment, constituting a risk peculiar to the work, *may establish the causal connection* between the work and the injury." ...

In still other cases, purporting to require that an injury arise out of unusual activity, this Court and the Court of Special Appeals have strained to label as "unusual" activities which appear to be entirely normal in the particular employments, and thus have upheld coverage....

In other areas of the law, where a judicially created standard has not been uniformly followed, has been inconsistently applied, and has treated differently persons who were similarly situated, this Court has not hesitated to change or abandon the standard....

Only a small minority of other jurisdictions have adopted the "unusual activity" requirement with regard to continuing conditions in the workplace.... With regard to of the type involved in the present case, namely injuries arising out of and in the course of employment and based on specific, sudden, unexpected and unintended events, the line of Maryland cases following *Atlantic Coast Shipping Co. v. Stasiak,* requiring "unusual activity," seems to constitute a minority of one. A review of decisions under the workers' compensation statutes of the other states, as well as the federal workers' compensation acts, indicates that no other jurisdictions presently require that an accidental injury of the type here involved arise out of "unusual activity" for there to be coverage....

[W]e reverse the judgments of both courts below and direct that the decision of the Workers' Compensation Commission be affirmed. In addition, we overrule the holdings in *Slacum v. Jolley, supra,* 153 Md. 343, 138 A. 244; *Miskowiak v. Bethlehem Steel Co., supra,* 156 Md. 690, 145 A. 199; *Atlantic Coast Shipping Co. v. Stasiak, supra,* 158 Md. 349, 148 A. 452, and similar holdings.

NOTES

1. **Scope and meaning of *Harris*.** A worker, doing nothing unusual at her job, suffers a heart attack and can never work again. Does *Harris* mean that the worker is entitled to compensation? Many courts have said that in such cases, unusual exertion or some kind of sudden or external event is required for various "internal" injuries such as heart attacks, strokes, hernias, and general backache, and statutes sometimes address the problem.

2. **Alternative tests.** Some heart attacks or strokes are merely part of the worker's genetic heritage or aging rather than a result of the work. The unusual exertion test might exclude some of those. Consider whether there might be alternative tests. In *Farrington v. Total Petroleum, Inc.*, 501 N.W.2d 76 (Mich. 1993), the court, applying a statutory rule, said: "The heart injury must be significantly caused or aggravated by employment considering the totality of all the occupational factors and the claimant's health circumstances and nonoccupational factors." It went on to say that ordinary everyday work, without unusual exertion, might contribute to a heart attack, but to determine whether work was a significant cause, the "factfinder must also consider the causal effect of every-day work activities in relation to the claimant's other, nonoccupational factors. These factors would include, for example, age, weight, diet, previous cardiac ailments or injuries, genetic predispositions, and the claimant's consumption of alcohol and use of tobacco or other drugs." What would the claimant need to prove if a preexisting neck injury was aggravated while she was working? *Rakestraw v. General Dynamics Land Sys., Inc.*, 666 N.W.2d 199 (Mich. 2003).

3. **Statutes.** Although courts may reject the unusual exertion test in many instances, see ARTHUR LARSON, WORKMEN'S COMPENSATION § 38.20, the job must still cause the harm if it is to be compensable. Statutes may add specific proof requirements in heart attack and similar cases. For instance, a statute may enact the unusual exertion requirement. *E.g.*, KAN. STAT. ANN. § 44–501(e). Or it may go further, requiring not only that the job be a direct cause of the heart condition, but that the "acute symptoms of the cardiac condition are clearly manifested not later than four (4) hours after the alleged causative exertion." WYO. STAT. § 27–14–603 (b).

4. **Pre-existing conditions and amount or award.** In tort cases, it is at least theoretically possible that, though the defendant takes the plaintiff as he finds him, the plaintiff's damages will be calculated with the fact in mind that his pre-existing conditions would sooner or later have caused the same kind of harm. *Cf. Dillon v. Twin States Elec. Co.*, *supra* Ch. 7, § 2(c). Is there room in the workers' compensation statutes for any adjustment of the award to accomplish the same end if the job triggers a heart attack, but the plaintiff would have suffered such an attack sooner or later even without working?

SHEALY v. AIKEN COUNTY, 535 S.E.2d 438 (S.C. 2000). Claimant was an undercover officer of the Sheriff's department working deep cover without police backup or identification. As such, he was subjected to continual stress. He eventually became unable to work and claimed compensation. "Mental or nervous disorders are compensable accidental injuries under the statute when 'the emotional stimuli or stressors are incident to or arise from unusual or extraordinary conditions of employment.' [C]ourts should use the 'heart attack standard' to determine when a mental-mental injury is compensable. A heart attack suffered by an employee constitutes a compensable accident if it is induced by unexpected strain or overexertion in the performance of his duties of employment, or by unusual and extraordinary conditions in employment." That standard is met here. "Over several months in 1992, Shealy experienced death threats, gun incidents with violent drug dealers, high tension confrontations, fear of losing his cover, loss of security as a police officer, and loss of his insurance. Knowing that a specific plot has been developed for one's murder by people who are willing and able to commit such a crime is certainly extraordinary. Furthermore, to have knowledge of an imminent death threat and then be stripped of the protection of the Sheriff's Department constitutes an extraordinary condition of employment." Even so, the claimant cannot recover. "Shealy was suffering from financial problems that led to bankruptcy; marital problems, including a divorce and a custody battle over his son; memories of a gun fight and shooting a man during a previous employment; and the constant stress of fighting alcoholism. Based on these non-job stressors," the trier properly found that the job was not a cause of his disability.

NOTES

1. **Mental or emotional disorders: Sudden event in the fright-shock pattern.** When the worker is physically injured on the job and suffers emotional or mental disability as a result, courts can easily feel that the statutory requirement of accidental injury arising out of and in the course of employment has been met. In the "mental-mental" case—when the employee is subjected to some kind of mental or emotional stress causing mental or emotional injury without physical injury—courts may feel less certain. Overall, the stronger case for compensation with mental injuries resulting from mental stimuli is probably one in which a sudden on-the-job event causes or triggers the emotional reaction, and some states require that. *See, e.g., McGrath v. State Dept. of Public Safety*, 159 P.3d 239 (Nev. 2007). Such a case would be similar to the old fright-shock pattern of tort claims for negligent infliction of emotional distress. An example is *Ivey v. Trans Global Gas & Oil*, 3 S.W.3d 441 (Tenn. 1999), where a robber pointed a gun at the face of an employee of a convenience store and compensation was permitted. What would the same court do if the worker suddenly came in contact with blood of a fellow worker and was disabled by fear of AIDS? *Guess v. Sharp Mfg. Co. of America*, 114 S.W.3d 480 (Tenn. 2003).

2. **Mental or emotional disorders: Cumulative stress.** Cumulative job stress—meeting deadlines, arguing with co-workers and superiors, for example—is probably overall less likely to yield a compensable mental-mental

claim. *See, e.g., Martin v. Rhode Island Public Transit Auth.*, 506 A.2d 1365 (R.I. 1986). Such claims may present serious causation issues. *See, e.g., Verga v. Workers' Comp. Appeals Bd.*, 70 Cal.Rptr.3d 871 (Ct. App. 2008). Still, individual facts count, as does the exact statutory language. If the events triggering disability from emotional distress amount to discrimination of a kind outlawed by statute, courts may feel that the discrimination statutes, rather than workers' compensation statutes, should control.

3. **Occupational disease.** Is there either injury or accident if the worker develops cancer or arthritis while employed as a high school teacher? What if a hospital worker with access to drugs becomes a drug addict? Statutes now provide for some degree of coverage for occupational diseases. Coverage is usually more restrictive than for "injury by accident." First, the disability must count as a "disease." See *Stenrich Group v. Jemmott*, 467 S.E.2d 795 (Va. 1996) (repetitive stress injuries neither a "disease" nor an "injury by accident"). Second, courts may insist that a disease is not compensable unless it is somehow especially related to the job. What about someone who suffers serious respiratory disability from second hand smoke on the job? Since one might be subjected to smoke in many places, does that mean the disability is not compensable as a disease? See *Palmer v. Del Webb's High Sierra*, 838 P.2d 435 (Nev. 1992) (environmental smoke in casino where claimant worked was not uniquely incident to employment, bronchitis not compensable). However, in *Johannesen v. New York City Dep't of Housing Etc.*, 638 N.E.2d 981 (N.Y. 1994), the court held that injury from second hand smoke is compensable as accidental injury rather than as an occupational disease. What about post traumatic stress disorder resulting from cumulative stress? That would definitely not sound like an "accident," but could it be an occupational disease in stressful occupations—like police work? See *Brunell v. Wildwood Crest Police Dept.*, 822 A.2d 576 (N.J. 2003).

C. MULTIPLE EXPOSURE OR INJURY

UNION CARBIDE CORP. v. INDUSTRIAL COM'N, 581 P.2d 734 (Colo. 1978). Benally worked as a uranium miner from 1955 to 1970 and died of lung cancer. He worked for Climax Uranium for four years before he was hired on April 28, 1970 by Union Carbide. The Union Carbide hiring was based upon a proviso that he pass a physical examination, but he began work before the test results were in. He worked eight days for Union Carbide before the tests came back and showed lung cancer. He was dismissed under the original proviso of his hiring. He was exposed to radiation during his short tenure at Union Carbide as well as at his earlier employment. *Held*, Union Carbide is liable for the worker's compensation death benefits since Benally's last injurious exposure was there. "[T]his rule makes good sense.... If the employee has worked for many different employers, it may well be that no single exposure with any employer was in fact sufficient, in itself, to cause the disease.... [A] test for liability based upon the employee's actual length of exposure with each employer could well deny the employee any recovery for the disease. In contrast, the 'last injurious exposure' rule looks at the concentration of radiation received during the last employment to determine whether the employee was exposed to a harmful quantity.... If the rule were otherwise, the employee would be burdened with the almost impossible task of apportioning liability among his several employers."

BRACKE v. BAZA'R, INC., 646 P.2d 1330 (Or. 1982). Bracke worked as a meat wrapper from 1974 until early 1977 for Baza'r. In early 1977, she also worked part time for Albertson's and Thriftway food markets. Her last employment with Baza'r ended March 30, with Albertson's on May 9, and with Thriftway on May 13. Claiming "meat wrapper's asthma," she applied for compensation with all three, and all denied her claim. She did not seek a hearing as to Thriftway's denial within the required 60–day limit. The Worker's Compensation Board found she suffered an occupational disease and that Thriftway would have been responsible because of the last injurious exposure rule, except that no hearing had been requested. Since Thriftway was the last injurious exposure, neither other employer was responsible. The Court of Appeals reversed this order of the board. In the Supreme Court of Oregon, *held*, the Court of Appeals judgment is affirmed. Testimony showed that with this disease there is no problem until one becomes sensitized by exposure to the fumes involved in cutting plastic wrap with a hot wire and dealing with price labels. But once one is sensitized, there will always be an allergic reaction thereafter. Sensitization occurred while the plaintiff was working for Baza'r, and later work does not make this "sensitization" any worse. Justification for the several variants of the last injurious exposure rules may be found "not in their achievement of individualized justice, but rather in their utility in spreading liability fairly among employers by the law of averages and in reducing litigation.... It is fair to employers only if it is applied consistently so that liability is spread proportionately among employers by operation of the law of averages." Hence the employer may assert the rule as a defense, as Baza'r does here, since this will "assure that they are not assigned disproportionate share of liability relative to other employers...." But in this case Baza'r was properly held liable, because subsequent employment "did not cause or aggravate the underlying disease. Had that occurred, a later employer would be liable.... Rather, claimant's subsequent employment only activated the symptoms of a preexisting disease."

NOTES

1. **Where the last injurious exposure rule does not apply.** Several problems must be distinguished. One problem is whether any employer is responsible for injury or disease. In the case of a disease, it must not be merely a disease to which everyone is more or less equally at risk. What is the test of liability for compensation where both work and non-work exposures contribute to the disease? *See Deschenes v. Transco*, 953 A.2d 13 (Conn. 2008) (considering several alternatives, and deciding that a proportional reduction of benefits is appropriate when an employer proves that a disability is caused in part by work-related disease processes and in part by non-work-related processes). Is there any comparable problem in cases of injury by accident?

2. **Where the last injurious exposure rule does apply.** A separate problem is to allocate responsibility among employers where several have, or may have, contributed to disease or injury. The last injurious exposure rule deals with this problem. What is the test of liability under that rule?

3. **Second injury funds.** In addition to the two problems just identified, there are two other broad problem areas. The first involves the worker who comes to the job with an existing injury or disability. If he is injured on the job, his pre-existing condition may mean that the job injury will be much more serious than otherwise it would have been. For example, if he comes to the job with one eye, an injury to his good eye may mean total blindness, not merely the partial loss of vision. Total blindness in turn might mean that the employer would be liable for a great deal more compensation than if a worker merely lost one of two good eyes. Given this situation, an employer might discriminate heavily against workers with an existing disability. To avoid this employer discrimination, most states created a second-injury fund which would pay any added compensation needed in such situations. The result is that the employer in the example given pays for the loss of one eye, not for total blindness; the additional compensation is paid from the fund. The fund itself is created in various ways, sometimes by what amounts to a special tax levied against compensation insurance carriers.

4. **Compensable injury causing further injury.** The employer may be held liable for compensation not only for the original injury, but for medical aggravation.

§ 3. WORKERS' COMPENSATION AS THE EXCLUSIVE REMEDY

The liability of an employer under this act shall be exclusive and in place of any and all other liability to such employees, their legal representative, husband or wife, parents, dependents, next of kin or anyone otherwise entitled to damages in any action at law or otherwise on account of any injury or death or occupational disease as defined in this Act.

———

In one form or another, workers' compensation statutes contain such an exclusive remedy provision, in effect forbidding the employee's tort recovery against the employer. Seamen, interstate railroad workers, and job discrimination victims all have tort claims under federal statutes. These are not barred by the workers' compensation claim. Otherwise, the exclusive remedy provision had broad impact to immunize both employers and co-workers from liability to victims of on-the-job injury. Co-workers share the employer's immunity on the ground that the statute intended to put the burden on the enterprise as a whole, and most definitely not upon individual workers. Employers enjoy the tort immunity on the ground that it represents the price workers paid to get workers' compensation rights.

SNYDER v. MICHAEL'S STORES, INC., 945 P.2d 781 (Cal. 1997). The plaintiff, Mikayla Snyder, sued her mother's employer in tort, claiming that she had been exposed in utero to a gas at her mother's workplace and suffered injury as a result. The trial court sustained the employer's demurrer on the ground that the claim was derived from her mother's exposure and that it was barred because her mother's tort claim would be barred by the exclusive remedy provision. The court of appeals reversed. *Held,* the court of appeals is affirmed. Mikayla's action is for her own injuries, not her mother's. The trial court therefore should have overruled Michael's Stores' demurrer.

HESSE v. ASHLAND OIL, INC., 642 N.W.2d 330 (Mich. 2002). Parents of a 16-year-old "witnessed" his on-the-job death. *Held,* an exclusive remedy provision that bars the claims of "any other person to whom a claim accrues by reason of the [employee's death]" bars the parents' claim for negligent infliction of emotional distress resulting in the death of their son. Marilyn J. Kelly, J., dissenting: "Plaintiffs allege an injury to themselves, not to their son. [T]heir claim falls outside the scope of the act" and is actionable.

MARTIN v. LANCASTER BATTERY CO.

606 A.2d 444 (Pa. 1992)

LARSEN, JUSTICE. . . .

[A]ppellant Stuart C. Manix (Mr. Manix) was a part owner and manager of the Lancaster Battery Company, Inc. Appellant Lancaster Battery Company, Inc. (LBC) manufactured automotive/truck wet storage batteries. The manufacturing process involved extensive employee exposure to lead dust and fumes. Federal safety regulations require that employees in such working environments be tested on a regular basis for lead content in their blood. Appellee Joseph H. Martin, Sr. (Mr. Martin) was employed by LBC, and his blood was tested along with the other employees of LBC who were exposed to lead. Mr. Manix, who oversaw and administered the blood testing at LBC, willfully and intentionally withheld from Mr. Martin the results of Mr. Martin's blood tests between January 1, 1982, and July, 1985. In addition, Mr. Manix intentionally altered blood test results before forwarding the results to Mr. Martin. Subsequently, Mr. Martin was diagnosed with chronic lead toxicity, lead neuropathy, hypertension, gout, and renal insufficiency. The severity of his condition would have been substantially reduced if his employer had not perpetrated a delay by failing to accurately report the elevated levels of lead in Mr. Martin's blood.

[Martin and his wife sued LBC and Manix in tort, alleging intentional and willful misconduct by Manix. The trial court sustained the defendant's objections in the nature of a demurrer. The appellate court reversed, holding that the tort claim could proceed in spite of the exclusive remedy provision.]

We agree with the Superior Court that the cases cited by the trial court regarding the exclusivity issue are not applicable to the instant action. In sustaining LBC's preliminary objections, the trial court cited this Court's decision in Poyser v. Newman & Co., 514 Pa. 32, 522 A.2d 548 (1987). In that case, we held that the exclusivity provision of the Workmen's Compensation Act precluded an employee from bringing an action against his or her employer for a work-related injury caused by the employer's willful and wanton disregard for employee safety as manifested by the employer's fraudulent misrepresentation of factory safety conditions to federal safety inspectors. Poyser is distinguishable from the case presently before the Court in that the fraudulent misrepresentation in Poyser was made to a third party and was not made to the injured employee. In the case sub judice, it has been alleged that the fraudulent misrepresentation was made directly to the employee. Moreover, Poyser did not involve a claim for the aggravation of a work-related injury as is the case herein. . . .

Courts in [some] other jurisdictions have considered the exclusivity issue presently before this Court and some have determined that the applicable workmen's compensation statute is not the exclusive remedy for the aggravation of an employee's work-related injury where the employer's fraudulent misrepresentation has been alleged. The reasons advanced to support recovery for such injuries in a common law action include the following: 1) "[a] hazard of employment does not include the risk that the employer will deprive an employee of his workers' compensation rights to medical treatment and compensation," 2) there is a strong state interest in deterring an employer from deliberately concealing the nature and extent of the danger following an initial injury, and 3) "[a]n employer's fraudulent concealment of diseases already developed is not one of the risks an employee should have to assume. Such intentionally-deceitful action goes beyond the bargain struck by the Compensation Act."

In [still other] jurisdictions, the courts have determined that such injuries are exclusively compensable under the applicable workmen's compensation statute. The courts refusing to permit common law actions where employees allege fraudulent misrepresentation are generally concerned with employees receiving duplicate monetary awards for single injuries.

We do not find the reasoning of the courts refusing to permit common law actions under these circumstances to be persuasive. The employee herein has alleged fraudulent misrepresentation on the part of his employer as causing the delay which aggravated a work-related injury. He is not seeking compensation for the work-related injury itself in this action. Clearly, when the Legislature enacted the Workmen's Compensation Act in this Commonwealth, it could not have intended to insulate employers from liability for the type of flagrant misconduct at issue herein by limiting liability to the coverage provided by the Workmen's Compensation Act. There is a difference between employers who tolerate workplace conditions that will result in a certain number of injuries or illnesses and those who actively mislead employees already suffering as the victims of workplace hazards, thereby precluding such employees from limiting their contact with the hazard and from receiving prompt medical attention and care. The aggravation of the injury arises from and is related to the fraudulent misrepresentation of the employer. Thus, the appellees are not limited to their remedies under the Workmen's Compensation Act and are not precluded from bringing a common law action against LBC....

With these standards in mind, and reviewing appellees' complaint in light of all reasonable inferences deducible therefrom, we find that the appellees have pleaded facts sufficient to support a cause of action for fraudulent misrepresentation. A cause of action for fraudulent misrepresentation is comprised of the following elements: "(1) a misrepresentation, (2) a fraudulent utterance thereof, (3) an intention by the maker that the recipient will thereby be induced to act, (4) justifiable reliance by the recipient upon the misrepresentation, and (5) damage to the recipient as the proximate result."

Nᴏᴛᴇs

1. **General rule.** When the employee suffers physical injury, the workers' compensation statute routinely applies and limits recovery to that provided in the statute. This will ordinarily include not only the original injury but subsequent aggravations.

2. **Negligence of employer.** Suppose the employer negligently constructs a catwalk workers must use and it gives way with a worker, who falls many feet and suffers a disastrous injury. Is the employer liable in tort? Now suppose that after the employer's negligence, it sells the plant to a third person, who becomes the worker's employer and the fall occurs after that. Is the original employer liable for its negligence or does it have the exclusive remedy immunity? *See Weaver v. Kimberly Clark Corp.,* 871 So.2d 827 (Ala. 2003); *Burns v. Smith,* 214 S.W.3d 335 (Mo. 2007). If you cannot resolve this on principle or logic, what specific research would you do if you represented one of the parties?

3. **Intentional torts of the employer.** One way to deal with intentional torts of the employer is to permit recovery in tort where the employer is guilty of a "deliberate intention" to injure or kill the employee. *See, e.g., Ryan v. Clonch Industries, Inc.,* 639 S.E.2d 756 (W.Va. 2006). Another is to retain the exclusive remedy provision but to raise the workers' compensation benefits substantially. Some states permit both compensation and tort recovery. California merely increases compensation for ordinary intentional torts, but when the intentional tortious conduct takes the case "beyond the boundaries of the compensation bargain," the tort recovery is permitted. This occurs if the conduct goes beyond the normal risk of employment. See the summary of California's system in *Vuillemainroy v. American Rock & Asphalt, Inc.,* 83 Cal.Rptr.2d 269 (Ct. App. 1999). What if the employer knowingly fails to maintain brakes on a heavily loaded truck and the employee is killed when brakes fail on a steep hill?

4. **Intentional torts of coworker.** As we've seen, coworkers are ordinarily immunized by the exclusive remedy provision. What if, in the course and scope of employment, the coworker intentionally shoots the plaintiff? *See, e.g., Mayberry v. Dukes,* 742 A.2d 448 (D.C. 1999) (coworker liable in tort).

5. **Intentional torts of insurance carrier.** What if the employee's harm is also caused by the workers' compensation insurer's intentional conduct in delaying the claim? In *Aguilera v. Inservices, Inc.,* 905 So.2d 84 (Fla. 2005), the employee was allowed to sue the carrier in tort for intentional infliction of emotional distress.

BERCAW v. DOMINO'S PIZZA, INC., 630 N.E.2d 166 (Ill. App. Ct. 1994). A pizza delivery driver was attacked and killed while making a delivery to a suspicious address in response to a pay-phone order. Survivors sued the pizza business, claiming negligence in the business' training about dangers and in its acceptance of suspicious orders to be delivered in dangerous circumstances. *Held,* the exclusive remedy provision is a bar to the suit. "Plaintiffs argue that Bercaw's death was 'not accidental' in that Shipman knew with substantial certainty that sending the untrained Bercaw out to deliver an order placed on a pay phone would result in an assault on Bercaw. Shipman claims that Bercaw's death was accidental because Shipman did not specifically intend to injure Bercaw.... We believe ... that use of the substantial certainty standard would be unduly difficult to employ in distinguishing between accidental and nonaccidental injuries and that adoption of the substantial certainty test would upset the Act's balance of interests.... Specifically, use of the substantial certainty test could well lead to a proliferation of suits against employers whose employees' jobs entail a high risk of injury. It would be open to argument and speculation at what point an employer's knowledge that a certain task presented a risk of employee injury became knowledge on the part of the employer that injury was substantially certain to occur. Here ... plaintiffs have not alleged a specific intent by Shipman to harm Bercaw, and we believe they could not credibly do so on the facts alleged. While an employer that requires employees to work day after day in an asbestos-contaminated workplace easily could be said to have intended to harm its employees, the same conclusion does not follow from an employer's sending a pizza deliveryman out to deliver an order made from a pay phone."

NOTES

1. Some courts have invoked what they said was the substantial certainty test of intent, and, finding intent on that ground, concluded that the exclusive remedy provision was no bar. *See, e.g., Bakerman v. The Bombay Co.,* 961 So.2d 259 (Fla. 2007). But some of the cases seem to apply "substantial certainty" for what is no more than a substantial *risk* of harm. In *Padney*

v. MetroHealth Medical Center, 764 N.E.2d 492 (Ohio Ct. App. 2001), the court held that a jury could find substantial certainty intent to harm when an employer ran a risk that may have been a little more than 35%. The court also thought that the seriousness of harm that might occur would also tend to show substantial certainty of harm. Is it clear that "substantial certainty" as so conceived is not about certainty at all?

2. Instead of rejecting the substantial certainty definition of intent as in *Bercaw,* some courts have simply applied the substantial certainty test in a straightforward manner, insisting that certainty means virtual certainty and that risk, even intended risk, is not enough to show intent. Thus in *Tomeo v. Thomas Whitesell Construction Co.,* 823 A.2d 769 (N.J. 2003) an employer intentionally created a risk to employees by circumventing a safety device, but the court held that this was only an intended risk of harm, not an intended infliction of harm. That's pretty much the orthodox understanding of substantial certainty, isn't it?

KERANS v. PORTER PAINT CO., 575 N.E.2d 428 (Ohio 1991). Sally Kerans worked as a decorator for Porter Paint. Kerans claimed that she was sexually molested on five occasions by her store manager, Al Levine. Kerans and her husband sued Levine and Porter Paint. Plaintiffs settled with Levine but pursued their claim against Porter Paint for, *inter alia,* intentionally or negligently maintaining a policy of encouraging, permitting, or condoning sexual harassment by Levine, inflicting emotional distress, and negligently hiring and/or retaining Levine. The trial court granted summary judgment for defendant on the basis of the exclusive remedy provisions of the workers' compensation statute. *Held,* reversed. First, this is not an "injury" as defined in the statute; rather, it is a "nonphysical injury with purely psychological consequences . . . If the workers' compensation scheme were adjudged to be the exclusive remedy for claims based upon sexual harassment in the workplace, as appellee urges, victims of sexual harassment would often be left without a remedy." Workers' compensation laws and sexual harassment laws are aimed at vastly different concerns. "Workers' compensation addresses purely economic injury; sexual harassment laws are concerned with a much more intangible injury to personal rights."

Further, there is a material issue of fact concerning whether Levine was acting within the scope of his employment. Even if he was not, "both state and federal courts have held that an employer may be liable for failing to take appropriate action where that employer knows or has reason to know that one of its employees poses an unreasonable risk of harm to other employees. . . . [W]here a plaintiff brings a claim against an employer predicated upon allegations of workplace sexual harassment by a company employee, and where there is evidence in the record suggesting that the employee has a past history of sexually harassing behavior about which the employer knew or should have known, summary judgment may not be granted in favor of the employer, even where the employee's actions in no way further or promote the employer's business. An employ-er has a duty to provide its employees with a safe work environment and, thus, may be independently liable for failing to take corrective action against an employee who poses a threat of harm to fellow employees, even where the employee's actions do not serve or advance the employer's business goals."

NOTES

1. How much of a difference did it make in *Kerans* that the workers' compensation statute did not at the time define "injury" to include emotional distress? In *Driscoll v. General Nutrition Corp.*, 752 A.2d 1069 (Conn. 2000), the plaintiff, a sales clerk for the defendant, was at work when Gregory Popielarczyk entered, forced her into a back room, and forced her to perform fellatio. The plaintiff sued her employer for emotional distress. The court found it was barred by the exclusive remedy provision, reasoning that the legislature defined personal injury to exclude emotional harm when that harm does not arise from personal injury, but in this case the emotional harm was a direct result of physical injury—the sexual assault perpetrated by Popielarc-zyk. Hence the harm is a personal injury covered by workers' compensation statute and the exclusive remedy provision applies to bar this tort suit.

2. In *Horodyskyj v. Karanian*, 32 P.3d 470 (Colo. 2001) the plaintiff alleged sexual harassment by a fellow employee and sued the company for battery and other torts. The court first classified "assaults:" (a) those inher-ently employment related, as where they arise out of arguments over work equipment; (b) those inherently private, as where they arise from private relationships unrelated to the job; and (c) those that are neutral. It thought that since private matters are not within the statute's coverage, the exclusive remedy would be no bar to tort claims for such injuries.

3. Suppose the employee, working at her job, is sexually assaulted by a co-worker. The attack did not grow out of job conditions, only the personal psychology of the attacker. If the employer knew that the attacker was dangerous to other employees but did nothing, could the victim sue in tort (a) under *Kerans?* (b) under *Horodyskyj*, Note 2, *supra?*

4. In *Byrd v. Richardson–Greenshields Securities, Inc.*, 552 So.2d 1099 (Fla. 1989), the Florida court suggested still another rationale for allowing the tort claim that might be independent of the *Kerans'* rationale: the exclusive remedy provision should not be applied to bar sexual harassment claims if that would conflict with policies expressed in anti-discrimination and anti-harassment statutes.

5. Distinguish two questions: (a) Did the employer commit a tort, either vicariously or directly?, and (b) Is there ground for holding a tortious employer liable in spite of the exclusive remedy clause?

6. *Case A*: The plaintiff is sexually harassed but suffers no physical harm and incurs neither medical bills nor wage loss. *Case B*: The plaintiff is physically harmed by a sexual assault, incurs medical bills and suffers wage loss during a period of healing. If the employer is not guilty of any negligent or intentional wrongdoing, no tort action would lie even if the exclusive

remedy clause were repealed. Should there be a workers' compensation claim in either case? Could you possibly write a statute to give the plaintiff a workers' compensation claim where it is needed and still permit a tort claim where the employer was at fault? See the excellent discussion in Jean C. Love, *Actions for Nonphysical Harm: Relationship Between the Tort System and No–Fault Compensation (With an Emphasis on Workers' Compensation)*, 73 CAL. L. REV. 857 (1985).

7. Several federal statutes provides rights to workers that can potentially overlap or conflict with workers' compensation rights. These include:

(1) *Title VII*. Title VII forbids discrimination against workers on the basis of gender or race, for example, and under some circumstances permits a federal suit if the employer violates the statute. 42 U.S.C.A. § 2000e.

(2) *ADA*. The Americans with Disabilities Act (ADA) and some similar federal legislation forbids employer discrimination against employees with disabilities and provides that employers must make reasonable accommodations to permit the employee to work. This may require adjustments in work schedules, temporary leave, or addition of special features to the worksite. This statute, too, permits a suit by an employee whose rights under the statute are violated.

(3) *FMLA*. The Family and Medical Leave Act requires employers to grant up to twelve weeks unpaid leave to an employee who becomes a parent, adopts a child or becomes a foster parent, or when the employee suffers "a serious health condition that makes the employee unable to perform the functions of the position of such employee." 29 U.S.C. § 2612.

(4) *Social Security Disability*. The disability provisions of the social security statutes permit totally disabled persons to receive monthly benefits equivalent to early retirement. If the disability results from injury compensable under workers' compensation, adjustment is made, either in the compensation benefits or in the social security benefits. Social security disability is considered in the next chapter.

Many problems arise when two or more of these statutes could apply in the same case. The interaction of these statutes must be left to courses in employment law. However, it is important to notice here that since state law cannot control federal rights, the exclusive remedy provision of the states' workers' compensation statutes does not prevent a worker from claiming her rights under any of these federal statutes

8. State statutes may also give the plaintiff rights against an employer who engages in forbidden discrimination. As a matter of construing the statutes, the court may conclude that the exclusive remedy provision does not bar either the discrimination claim or a claim for emotional harm that grows out of the discrimination. *See Murray v. Oceanside Unified Sch. Dist.,* 95 Cal.Rptr.2d 28 (Ct. App. 2000).

§ 4. TORT CLAIMS AGAINST THIRD PARTIES

Virtually all states permit the injured worker to sue a third party or outsider who tortiously causes an on-the-job injury. In such a case, the worker may have both a tort claim against the outsider and a compensation claim against the employer, subject only to certain adjustments to prevent "double recovery." This raises a number of questions of practice, procedure and principle.

A. WHO IS A "THIRD PARTY?"

1. *Co-employees in the scope of employment.* In most states a co-employee who negligently causes injury to the worker is not regarded as a third party who can be sued in tort. Instead, the co-employee shares the employer's immunity under the exclusive remedy rule. *See, e.g., Progressive Halcyon Ins. Co. v. Philippi*, 754 N.W.2d 646 (S.D. 2008). The chief reason for this is that the compensation scheme is intended to put the burden of industrial injuries upon the enterprise and to shift them away from the employees. The enterprise itself is thought to be the source of injury, and the products should, in this view, reflect the costs that are inevitable parts of that enterprise.

2. *Co-employees* not *in the scope of employment.* If the injuring co-employee deviates sufficiently from employment, engaging in a personally motivated, intentional tort, he loses the immunity. *Cf. Stringer v. Minnesota Vikings Football Club, LLC*, 705 N.W.2d 746 (Minn. 2005) (but holding that team medical services coordinator and trainer did not so act). Likewise when the co-employee responsible for injury acts in another capacity, then he may be liable for injuries arising from that other capacity, as where the landlord/co-employee maintains a defective stair. *Sauve v. Winfree*, 907 P.2d 7 (Alaska 1995).

3. *Workers' compensation insurance carriers.* The insurance carrier may provide safety inspections of the insured working situation, and may offer more attractive rates if its safety demands are met. Suppose such an insurer makes a negligent inspection, failing to recommend a safety device that clearly is needed. Again distinguish the two questions: (a) Did the insurer commit a tort? and (b) Is the insurer a third party or is it merely acting in the stead of the employer? In *Pratt v. Liberty Mutual Insurance Co.*, 952 F.2d 667 (2d Cir. 1992), the employer's insurance carrier had advertised extensively about its loss prevention program to make the insureds' operations safe. It had in fact inspected the employer's workplace and had concluded that the work done by the plaintiff needed to be safer, but it had failed to recommend appropriate changes. As a result, the plaintiff was injured. The court held that the advertising materials should have been admitted in evidence, even though the plaintiff did not show she relied upon them. To what issue would the advertising be relevant?

B. THE STATUTORY EMPLOYER AND BORROWED SERVANTS

1. *Statutory employers.* Workers' compensation statutes usually provide that when an employer hires independent contractors to carry out the employer's regular work or business, the employer is to be treated as the "statutory employer" of the independent contractor's employees. A, a general contractor, hires B to do the framing on a building A is building. B hires five workers, one of whom is injured on the job. The statutory employer provision permits B's injured worker to claim worker's compensation benefits from A. This will normally be a significant advantage only if B has not secured his own workers' compensation insurance. So A will usually protect himself by requiring his contractors to have workers' compensation insurance coverage.

2. *Statutory employer's immunity from tort suits.* Can the injured worker sue A in tort? The theory would be that the worker is employed by B, not A, so that A is a third person and does not enjoy the employer's immunity. However, if A is a statutory employer, he presumably gets the protection that all employers obtain when they are liable for workers' compensation—complete immunity from tort suits.

3. *Borrowed servants.* A supplies temporary employees to B, who controls the details of their work in B's business. Suppose such an employee is injured by B's negligence. Does the exclusive remedy provision bar a tort claim against B? *Kaiser v. Millard Lumber, Inc.,* 587 N.W.2d 875 (Neb. 1999) (when labor broker who employs worker then provides worker to business that controls his work, the worker is the employee of both and workers' compensation is his only remedy).

C. ADJUSTMENTS AMONG THE PARTIES

1. *The employer's lien rights against tortfeasors who injured the employee.* The employer who pays workers' compensation benefits to an injured employee has a lien on the employee's tort claim against third persons to the extent of the employer past or future benefits payments. *See, e.g., Sourbier v. State,* 498 N.W.2d 720 (Iowa 1993). If the tort suit is successful, the payments made by the tortfeasor will go in part to the employer (or its workers' compensation insurer).

2. *The employer's subrogation rights against tortfeasors who injured the employee.* If the injured employee does not bring a tort suit against the third person tortfeasor within a time specified in the statute, the employer is subrogated to the employee's rights against the tortfeasor, to the extent the employer has paid benefits. The employer may thus sue the tortfeasor, recover the damages due to the injured person, repay himself for the workers' compensation benefits, and turn over the balance to the employee.

3. *The third person tortfeasor's claim against the negligent employer in a joint and several liability system.* Frequently both the employer and a third person negligently cause injury to the employee. Because the em-

ployee cannot recover in tort against the employer, his tort suit will run against the third person. Traditionally, the third person tortfeasor would be liable for all the employee's damages and would not be entitled to contribution against the immune employer. Thus the third person would bear all the loss and the negligent employer none. A few courts have slightly mitigated this extreme result by permitting limited contribution against the employer up to the amount of it workers' compensation benefits, but most courts have not.

4. *The third person tortfeasor's claim against the negligent employer where joint and several liability is abolished.* Where joint and several liability has been abolished, the employer would still be immune and the third person tortfeasor would pay only his comparative fault share. That would leave the employee with only a percentage of his tort damages even if the employee herself was not at fault and the employer was.

CHAPTER 29

PUBLIC COMPENSATION SYSTEMS, INCLUDING SOCIAL SECURITY

■ ■ ■

§ 1. PROTECTING INDUSTRIES THROUGH COMPENSATION SCHEMES THAT REPLACE TORT LIABILITY

A. TAXING INDUSTRY AND ELIMINATING ITS TORT LIABILITY

Is some kind of public system for compensating injury a good idea, either to supplement or to replace the tort and workers' compensation systems? One approach might be to add a tax upon industries that cause harm and use the fund so created to pay for the harms done.

Something like this has been done in the National Childhood Vaccine Injury Act, 42 U.S.C.A. § 300aa–1. Compulsory vaccination is an overall health benefit, but vaccines cause devastating side effects with permanent brain damage to particular infants. A child who is entirely normal at birth may be so damaged by a vaccine that he cannot move, talk, or feed himself. Such a child will require a lifetime of care and may suffer other medical problem such as repeated seizures. The Vaccine Act addresses this problem and is an important experiment in alternatives to tort law. Judge Breyer (now Justice Breyer) summarized the vaccine act this way in *Schafer v. American Cyanamid Co.*, 20 F.3d 1 (1st Cir. 1994):

"The National Childhood Vaccine Injury Act provides a special procedure to compensate those who are injured by certain vaccines. The Act bars those who accept an award under that procedure from later bringing a tort suit to obtain additional compensation. The question before us in this appeal ... is whether the Act also bars the family of such a person from bringing a tort suit to obtain compensation for their own, related, injuries, in particular, for loss of companionship or consortium....

"The National Childhood Vaccine Injury Act represents an effort to provide compensation to those harmed by childhood vaccines outside the framework of traditional tort law. Congress passed the law after hearing testimony 1) describing the critical need for vaccines to protect children from disease, 2) pointing out that vaccines inevitably harm a very small number of the many millions of people who are vaccinated, and 3) expressing dissatisfaction with traditional tort law as a way of compensating those few victims. Injured persons (potential tort plaintiffs) complained about the tort law system's uncertain recoveries, the high cost of litigation, and delays in obtaining compensation. They argued that government had, for all practical purposes, made vaccination obligatory, and thus it had a responsibility to ensure that those injured by vaccines were compensated. Vaccine manufacturers (potential tort defendants) complained about litigation expenses and occasional large recoveries, which caused insurance premiums and vaccine prices to rise, and which ultimately threatened the stability of the vaccine supply. . . .

"The Vaccine Act responds to these complaints by creating a remedial system that tries more quickly to deliver compensation to victims, while also reducing insurance and litigation costs for manufacturers. The Act establishes a special claims procedure involving the Court of Federal Claims and special masters (a system that we shall call the "Vaccine Court"). 42 U.S.C. § 300aa–12. A person injured by a vaccine may file a petition with the Vaccine Court to obtain compensation (from a fund financed by a tax on vaccines). He need not prove fault. Nor, to prove causation, need he show more than that he received the vaccine and then suffered certain symptoms within a defined period of time. The Act specifies amounts of compensation for certain kinds of harm (e.g., $250,000 for death, up to $250,000 for pain and suffering). And, it specifies other types of harm for which compensation may be awarded (e.g., medical expenses, loss of earnings).

"At the same time, the Act modifies, but does not eliminate, the traditional tort system, which Congress understood to provide important incentives for the safe manufacture and distribution of vaccines. The Act requires that a person injured directly by a vaccine first bring a Vaccine Court proceeding. Then, it gives that person the choice either to accept the Court's award and abandon his tort rights (which the Act transfers to the federal government) or to reject the judgment and retain his tort rights. (He can also keep his tort rights by withdrawing his Vaccine Court petition if the Court moves too slowly.)

"The Act additionally helps manufacturers by providing certain federal modifications of state tort law. For example, it forbids the award of compensation for injuries that flow from 'unavoidable side effects'; it frees the manufacturer from liability for not providing direct warnings to an injured person (or his representative); it imposes a presumption that compliance with Food and Drug Administration requirements means the manufacturer provided proper directions and warnings; it limits punitive damage awards; and it requires that the trial of any tort suit take place in three phases (liability; general damages; punitive damages)."

Data from the Department of Health and Human Services show that between 1988 and 2008, over 8500 claims had been filed by claimants alleging injuries from vaccines administered after Oct. 1988, the effective date of the Act. Almost two-thirds of those claims allege that vaccines caused autism. In the same period, just over 1000 claims had been granted, with awards and costs totaling about $1 billion, and 1500 claims have been dismissed. According to the HHS, claims take between two and three years to adjudicate, so many claims remain to be adjudicated . . Critics of the Act's actual operation have pointed out that causation in fact is still an issue. See Katherine E. Strong, *Note, Proving Causation Under the Vaccine Injury Act: A New Approach for A New Day*, 75 GEO. WASH. L.REV. 426 (2007). Most of those who find no compensation under the Vaccine Act find none in the tort system either. *See* Elizabeth A. Breen, *A One Shot Deal: the National Childhood Vaccine Injury Act*, 41 WM. & MARY L. REV. 309 (1999). The claims are handled by a handful of special masters who have wide decision-making authority. Claimants have a markedly better chance with some special masters than others. *See* Derry Ridgway, *No-fault Vaccine Insurance: Lessons from the National Vaccine Injury Compensation Program*, 24 J. HEALTH POL. POL'Y & L. 59 (1999).

If the problems raised by critics are fixable, the statute still raises many issues of policy and justice. It uses public powers for the direct benefit of one class of manufacturers. Among the many questions you might consider are these: (1) What happens to safety incentives under the statute and how would you compare it on that point with workers' compensation? (2) Do you think it is harmful to the interests of vaccine-injured plaintiffs as a whole? (3) How do you rate the Act as a solution to the problem of compensation for injury—is it a good model for developing broader solutions?

B. TAXING THE PUBLIC TO PROTECT INDUSTRIES AND PROVIDE COMPENSATION TO VICTIMS—THE 9–11 COMPENSATION SYSTEM

A federal statute, known as the Air Transportation Safety and System Stabilization Act (ATSSSA), 49 U.S.C.A. § 40101, creates a unique system for dealing with the injuries and fears arising from events of September 11, 2001. First, the bail-out provisions use public money as direct compensation and as loans for airlines to cover losses incurred from the terrorist attacks. Second, the statute sets up an optional administrative compensation scheme. If claimants choose this option, they cannot sue the airlines in tort. And when they are paid, they are paid from public funds, not the funds of the airlines or their insurers.

The compensation system from public monies is administered by a federal administrator called a Special Master. Only those present at the 9–11 sites and their families qualify to assert claims for losses. Although the act aims to provide complete recovery of economic losses and limited recovery of non-economic losses, the Special Master promulgated regulations governing amounts of compensation for some losses and guidelines for others. To manage the large numbers of claims expeditiously, he provided calculations on work-life expectancy, on probable wage increases, taxes, and other matters, then promulgated a table of presumed awards for each age/earnings group. There is also a floor in death cases—$500,000 for a victim with a spouse or dependent, for example. Besides calculation of economic losses by way of the table, there is a flat $250,000 for non-economic loss. Collateral source payments are deducted, including some not normally deducted under the state tort reform statutes, such as life insurance. These regulations leave room for some individualization of awards. In particular, the Master will, to some extent, take into account the financial needs of the claimant. 28 C.F.R. § 104.41. The point seems to be to flatten the awards to high earners to minimize the difference between awards for death of low-earning victims and death of those whose earnings are quite modest.

If a claimant pursues the compensation alternative, she cannot sue in tort. But she can choose to sue in tort instead of claiming compensation. However, she must sue in a federal court in New York and total liability of the airlines is limited by the amount of their insurance coverage. There is, of course, no guarantee that the tort claimants would win, but it has been held that the airlines at least owe a duty of care to victims on the ground. *In re Sept. 11 Litig.*, 280 F. Supp. 2d 279 (S.D.N.Y. 2003).

NOTES

1. Compare the financing features of the Vaccine Act with ATSSSA. Could you mount an argument that one financing system is better than the other?

2. Notice that both the Vaccine Act and ATSSSA give the plaintiff the option of seeking a kind of strict-liability-and-limited-compensation or suing in tort, although the tort option may be burdened with new disadvantages. Compare the workers' compensation system, which, under the exclusive remedy clause, denies the worker any option to sue in tort.

3. Is this public compensation a good model for other injury cases? If so, why wasn't it applied to, say, the victims of Timothy McVeigh's bombing of the federal building in Oklahoma City? Or for that matter, to any victims of injury? *See* John G. Culhane, *Tort, Compensation, and Two Kinds of Justice*, 55 RUTGERS L. REV. 1027 (2003); Betsy J. Grey, *Homeland Security and Federal Relief: A Proposal for a Permanent Compensation System for Domestic Terrorist Victims*, 9 N.Y.U. J. LEGIS. & PUB. POL'Y 663 (2006).

4. There are a number of federal compensation schemes, and/or liability caps for industries. Compensation systems include, for example, no-fault benefits for miners suffering from Black Lung and victims of swine flu vaccines. Liability caps are imposed for the protection of involved industries in certain environmental contamination and the nuclear energy industry.

§ 2. SOCIAL SECURITY DISABILITY BENEFITS

The Social Security Act of 1935 is aimed at increasing economic security by providing, among other things, unemployment compensation, retirement benefits, and survivor's benefits. Later amendments included Medicare and Medicaid provisions. This chapter introduces another feature—benefits paid for serious disabilities that prevent work.

The program has enormous public importance. Although the figures vary from month to month, over 10 million disabled workers are receiving benefits. In fiscal year 2004 there were 4.5 million new disability claims. *See* Frank S. Bloch, *Medical Proof, Social Policy, and Social Security's Medically Centered Definition of Disability,* 92 CORNELL L. REV. 189 (2007). The annual payout in benefits to the disabled and their families exceeds $20 billion.

At the most immediate professional level, lawyers must be aware that an injured client may be entitled to social security benefits. In some cases, the existence of those benefits will figure in a large way in pursuit or defense of a tort claim. Social security benefits may keep the plaintiff going while the tort claim is developed. Or lawyers may find they can reach a settlement only because the total package of benefits, including those under social security legislation, is high enough to provide adequate care. Tort settlements must also be structured with trusts or otherwise to protect the client's rights to public assistance programs such as Medicaid. More broadly, does the disability benefit system suggest an alternative to, or improvement in, tort law?

42 U.S.C.A. § 423

As amended 2004

(a) Disability insurance benefits

(1) Every individual who—

(A) is insured for disability insurance benefits (as determined under subsection (c)(1) of this section),

(B) has not attained retirement age . . . ,

(C) [meets certain requirements of non-citizens or non-U.S. nationals,]

(D) has filed application for disability insurance benefits, and

(E) is under a disability (as defined in subsection (d) of this section), shall be entitled to a disability insurance benefit . . .

(d) "Disability" defined

(1) The term "disability" means—

(A) inability to engage in any substantial gainful activity by reason of any medically determinable physical or mental impairment which can be expected to result in death or which has lasted or can be expected to last for a continuous period of not less than 12 months; or

(B) in the case of an individual who has attained the age of 55 and is blind ... inability by reason of such blindness to engage in substantial gainful activity requiring skills or abilities comparable to those of any gainful activity in which he has previously engaged with some regularity and over a substantial period of time.

(2) For purposes of paragraph (1)(A)—

(A) An individual shall be determined to be under a disability only if his physical or mental impairment or impairments are of such severity that he is not only unable to do his previous work but cannot, considering his age, education, and work experience, engage in any other kind of substantial gainful work which exists in the national economy, regardless of whether such work exists in the immediate area in which he lives, or whether a specific job vacancy exists for him, or whether he would be hired if he applied for work. For purposes of the preceding sentence (with respect to any individual), "work which exists in the national economy" means work which exists in significant numbers either in the region where such individual lives or in several regions of the country.

(B) In determining whether an individual's physical or mental impairment or impairments are of a sufficient medical severity that such impairment or impairments could be the basis of eligibility under this section, the Commissioner of Social Security shall consider the combined effect of all of the individual's impairments without regard to whether any such impairment, if considered separately, would be of such severity. If the Commissioner of Social Security does find a medically severe combination of impairments, the combined impact of the impairments shall be considered throughout the disability determination process.

(C) An individual shall not be considered to be disabled for purposes of this subchapter if alcoholism or drug addiction would (but for this subparagraph) be a contributing factor material to the Commissioner's determination that the individual is disabled.

(3) For purposes of this subsection, a "physical or mental impairment" is an impairment that results from anatomical, physiological, or psychological abnormalities which are demonstrable by medically acceptable clinical and laboratory diagnostic techniques. . . .

(5)(A) An individual shall not be considered to be under a disability unless he furnishes such medical and other evidence of the existence thereof as the Commissioner of Social Security may require. An individual's statement as to pain or other symptoms shall not alone be conclusive evidence of disability as defined in this section; there must be medical signs and findings, established by medically acceptable clinical or laboratory diagnostic techniques, which show the existence of a medical impairment that results from anatomical, physiological, or psychological abnormalities which could reasonably be expected to produce the pain or other symptoms alleged and which, when considered with all evidence required to be furnished under this paragraph (including statements of the individual or his physician as to the intensity and persistence of such pain or other symptoms which may reasonably be accepted as consistent with the medical signs and findings), would lead to a conclusion that the individual is under a disability. Objective medical evidence of pain or other symptoms established by medically acceptable clinical or laboratory techniques (for example, deteriorating nerve or muscle tissue) must be considered in reaching a conclusion as to whether the individual is under a disability. . . .

NOTES

1. **Procedures for claim.** A disability claim is initially administrative, not judicial. The claimant files a claim in the social security office, but it is initially determined by a state agency. The claimant may appeal to a federal Administrative Law Judge (ALJ), who holds a hearing. *See* 1 HARVEY L. MCCORMICK, SOCIAL SECURITY CLAIMS AND PROCEDURES § 1:8 (5th Ed. 2008). After administrative appeals from his decision have been exhausted, the claimant can seek review in the United States District Court. The District Judge must affirm the ALJ's factual findings if they are supported by substantial evidence, but may reverse or remand for errors in law and may reject factual findings not supported by substantial evidence. 42 U.S.C.A. § 405(g).

2. **Insured status.** The claimant under § 423 must meet the requirements listed in subsection (a)(1), including insured status. The claimant recovers benefits only because she has worked and paid "premiums" in the form of payroll tax deductions. However, a welfare component of the social security laws provides similar benefits for similar disabilities to persons who have made no contributions or insufficient contributions to the system. This is known as Supplemental Security Income or SSI. The SSI claimant must meet a "needs" test and cannot recover benefits if he or she has assets or income beyond certain levels.

3. **Benefits.** Disability may be viewed as a form of involuntary early retirement, and indeed the benefits provided are calculated as if the claimant were 62 when disability struck. The actual computation is complex, because it takes into account the claimant's monthly wages over a lifetime of employment and also "indexes" the wages so that inflation can be factored out and all wages can be on the same scale. In general you can say that benefits are not generous but that they matter greatly to anyone unable to work and lacking independent income.

4. **Disability.** Subsection (d) defines disability, and it has two main components, one medical and one work-related. There must be a medical "impairment," and that medical condition must render the claimant unable to engage in any substantial gainful employment in the national economy for a

period of at least 12 months, given the claimant's age, education and work experience.

———

McLAIN v. SCHWEIKER, 715 F.2d 866 (4th Cir. 1983). McLain is 49 years old, has completed high school and two years of college. He has in the past been employed as a traveling sales representative for a cheese-cake company and later as a security guard. His testimony is that he can no longer work in these stressful environments, as he cannot tolerate noise, including telephones, and typewriters. Doctors and psychiatrists report a 20 year history of nervous disorders and "inadequate personali-ty." Dr. Katherine Kemp, a psychiatrist, reported a paranoid-like trend in his thoughts and stated he could not "interrelate" with others and would be unable to withstand the pressures of the employment world. The ALJ found an impairment, but concluded that McLain would be able to perform his previous work in "nonstressful environments," noting that this might include telephone sales work and sedentary security guard positions. He therefore denied benefits. The Secretary then denied bene-fits and the district court affirmed. McLain appeals. *Held*, vacated and remanded. McLain "presented a prima facie case of disability by showing that he was unable to perform his previous work.... [T]he medical findings and opinions unanimously support the conclusion that McLain has a serious psychiatric disorder. It is clear that McLain's impairment prevents him from performing the demands of his previous jobs as a salesman and security guard." Once he made that case, the Secretary could prevail only by showing that "could perform an alternative job existing in significant numbers in the national economy."

NOTES

1. **Applying the statute.** (a) Suppose the claimant could do limited work sorting potatoes into bins. The only place where such employment is possible is 1,000 miles from the claimant's life-long residence. Is the claimant disabled? What does the statute say?

(b) What if the claimant could do limited work sorting potatoes into bins, and such employment actually exists, but there is no job open and long lines of people are on the waiting list? What does the statute say?

2. **The five-step analysis.** The regulations provide for a five-step process or decision tree that goes something like this: (1) Is the claimant currently engaged in substantial gainful activity? If yes, the claimant is not disabled. If no, then (2) does the claimant have a severe impairment that limits her ability to work? If no, she is not disabled, but if yes, then (3) is the impairment in the listings (Note 4, below)? If yes, disability is proved and benefits computed. If no, then (4) in spite of impairment, can the claimant perform her past work? If yes, she is not disabled. If not, (5) she is presump-tively disabled and the burden falls upon the Commissioner to show that there is a job in the national economy that she would be able to perform.

3. **Burden-shifting and older workers.** Although disability is determined by the claimant's ability to perform jobs rather than on her ability to obtain them, the burden-shifting in the five-step analysis can greatly assist the claimant. In addition, claimants over 60 get a break. If they suffer a severe impairment, the burden not only shifts to the Commissioner under the five-step analysis, but the burden becomes qualitatively more difficult. The Commissioner must show not only that the over–60 claimant has transferrable skills but also that they are "highly marketable." *See, e.g., Kerns v. Apfel*, 160 F.3d 464 (8th Cir. 1998).

4. **The Listings.** At one time each case was decided on the proof adduced in the hearing before the ALJ. This often led to vocational testimony about kinds of jobs the claimant might or might not do. This could be repetitious and wasteful. In some instances, disability was a very likely finding, as in the case of blindness or severe visual impairment. Although some individuals might be able to work with such impairments, most would not. What would you propose? How about a schedule of impairments that would automatically qualify as "disability?" This is what the Secretary provided in the governing administrative regulations, which, like other federal regulations, are codified in the Code of Federal Regulations or CFR. In this case the regulations are known as the "listings" and are found in 20 CFR part 404, Subpart P, Appendix I. Although the listings can be used to provide automatic awards, they cannot be used the other way around, to foreclose awards for disabilities that are not listed. Each claimant is entitled to proceed on the evidence if he fails to succeed under the listings. *See Sullivan v. Zebley*, 493 U.S. 521 (1990).

NOTE: THE MEDICAL–VOCATIONAL GUIDELINES (THE GRIDS)

Federal regulations referred to as "the grids" come into play when there is no automatic disability found in the Listings of Appendix I. The grids provide a disability profile of the claimant by setting up a table of several factors: (1) Degree of medical impairment or Residual Functional Capacity; (2) Age; (3) Education; (4) Previous work experience. These four factors are in turn broken down into subcategories. One might have an RFC that permits only sedentary work, or an RFC that permits "limited to light work", or "limited to medium work." Age might be "advanced," "approaching advanced," "younger," and so on. Similarly, education and work experience are categorized.

The Code of Federal Regulations reduces these factors to a set of tables or grids. The ALJ may simply determine the RFC, age, education and experience and then automatically come up with a decision. It is, in short, a simple mechanical version of what a computer might do. Reading the combination of factors on the appropriate grid leads the ALJ to a definite conclusion—disability or no disability.

Here is a sample of one of the grids based upon the Code of Federal Regulations, the compiled regulations of federal administrative agencies, 20 C.F.R. Pt. 404, Subpt. P, App. 2. Note that the title of the table sets one of the conditions that determines the outcome, with the column at the far right indicating the outcome of the claim based on the presence of the variables in the preceding columns.

Table No. 1--Residual Functional Capacity: Maximum Sustained Work Capability Limited to Sedentary Work as a Result of Severe Medically Determinable Impairment(s)

Rule	Age	Education	Previous work experience	Decision
201.01	Advanced	Limited or less	Unskilled or none	Disabled.
201.02	same	same	Skilled or semiskilled-skills not transferable	Disabled.
201.03	same	same	Skilled or semiskilled-skills transferable	Not disabled.

The grids channel decision-making in a very firm way and probably provide a uniformity and simplicity of decision-making that would not otherwise exist. Are they nevertheless unfair?

HECKLER v. CAMPBELL

461 U.S. 458 (1983)

JUSTICE POWELL delivered the opinion of the Court.

The issue is whether the Secretary of Health and Human Services may rely on published medical-vocational guidelines to determine a claimant's right to Social Security disability benefits.

The Social Security Act defines "disability" in terms of the effect a physical or mental impairment has on a person's ability to function in the work place. It provides disability benefits only to persons who are unable "to engage in any substantial gainful activity by reason of any medically determinable physical or mental impairment." And it specifies that a person must "not only [be] unable to do his previous work but [must be unable], considering his age, education, and work experience, [to] engage in any other kind of substantial gainful work which exists in the national economy, regardless of whether such work exists in the immediate area in which he lives, or whether a specific job vacancy exists for him, or whether he would be hired if he applied for work."

Prior to 1978, the Secretary relied on vocational experts to establish the existence of suitable jobs in the national economy. After a claimant's limitations and abilities had been determined at a hearing, a vocational expert ordinarily would testify whether work existed that the claimant could perform. Although this testimony often was based on standardized guides, vocational experts frequently were criticized for their inconsistent treatment of similarly situated claimants.

To improve both the uniformity and efficiency of this determination, the Secretary promulgated medical-vocational guidelines as part of the 1978 regulations. See 20 CFR pt. 404, subpt. P, app. 2 (1982).

These guidelines relieve the Secretary of the need to rely on vocational experts by establishing through rulemaking the types and numbers of jobs that exist in the national economy. They consist of a matrix of the four factors identified by Congress—physical ability, age, education, and work experience—set forth rules that identify whether jobs requiring specific combinations of these factors exist in significant numbers in the national economy. Where a claimant's qualifications correspond to the job requirements identified by a rule, the guidelines direct a conclusion as to whether work exists that the claimant could perform. If such work exists, the claimant is not considered disabled.

In 1979, Carmen Campbell applied for disability benefits because a back condition and hypertension prevented her from continuing her work as a hotel maid. After her application was denied, she requested a hearing *de novo* before an Administrative Law Judge. He determined that her back problem was not severe enough to find her disabled without further inquiry, and accordingly considered whether she retained the ability to perform either her past work or some less strenuous job.

He concluded that even though Campbell's back condition prevented her from returning to her work as a maid, she retained the physical capacity to do light work.... Relying on the medical-vocational guidelines, the Administrative Law Judge found that a significant number of jobs existed that a person of Campbell's qualifications could perform. Accordingly, he concluded that she was not disabled....

The Court of Appeals held that "[i]n failing to show suitable available alternative jobs for Ms. Campbell, the Secretary's findings of 'not disabled' is not supported by substantial evidence." It thus rejected the proposition that "the guidelines provide adequate evidence of a claimant's ability to perform a specific alternative occupation," and remanded for the Secretary to put into evidence "particular types of jobs suitable to the capabilities of Ms. Campbell." The court's requirement that additional evidence be introduced on this issue prevents the Secretary from putting the guidelines to their intended use and implicitly calls their validity into question. Accordingly, we think the decision below requires us to consider whether the Secretary may rely on medical-vocational guidelines in appropriate cases.

The Social Security Act directs the Secretary to "adopt reasonable and proper rules and regulations to regulate and provide for the nature and extent of the proofs and evidence and the method of taking and furnishing the same" in disability cases.

We do not think that the Secretary's reliance on medical-vocational guidelines is inconsistent with the Social Security Act. It is true that the statutory scheme contemplates that disability hearings will be individualized determinations based on evidence adduced at a hearing. But this does not bar the Secretary from relying on rulemaking to resolve certain classes of issues. The Court has recognized that even where an agency's enabling statute expressly requires it to hold a hearing, the agency may rely on its rulemaking authority to determine issues that do not require case-by-case consideration. A contrary holding would require the agency continually to relitigate issues that may be established fairly and efficiently in a single rulemaking proceeding.

. . . As noted above, in determining whether a claimant can perform less strenuous work, the Secretary must make two determinations. She must assess each claimant's individual abilities and then determine whether jobs exist that a person having the claimant's qualifications could perform. The first inquiry involves a determination of historic facts, and the regulations properly require the Secretary to make these findings on the basis of evidence adduced at a hearing. We note that the regulations afford claimants ample opportunity both to present evidence relating to their own abilities and to offer evidence that the guidelines do not apply to them. The second inquiry requires the Secretary to determine an issue that is not unique to each claimant—the types and numbers of jobs that exist in the national economy. This type of general factual issue may be resolved as fairly through rulemaking as by introducing the testimony of vocational experts at each disability hearing.

As the Secretary has argued, the use of published guidelines brings with it a uniformity that previously had been perceived as lacking. To require the Secretary to relitigate the existence of jobs in the national economy at each hearing would hinder needlessly an already overburdened agency. We conclude that the Secretary's use of medical-vocational guidelines does not conflict with the statute, nor can we say on the record before us that they are arbitrary and capricious.

We now consider Campbell's argument that the Court of Appeals properly required the Secretary to specify alternative available jobs. . . . Rather the court's reference to notice and an opportunity to respond appears to be based on a principle of administrative law—that when an agency takes official or administrative notice of facts, a litigant must be given an adequate opportunity to respond.

This principle is inapplicable, however, when the agency has promulgated valid regulations. Its purpose is to provide a procedural safe-guard: to ensure the accuracy of the facts of which an agency takes notice. But when the accuracy of those facts already has been tested fairly during rulemaking, the rulemaking proceeding itself provides sufficient procedural protection.

The Court of Appeals' decision would require the Secretary to introduce evidence of specific available jobs that respondent could perform. It would limit severely her ability to rely on the medical-vocational guidelines. We think the Secretary reasonably could choose to rely on these guidelines in appropriate cases rather than on the testimony of a vocational expert in each case. Accordingly, the judgment of the Court of Appeals is

Reversed.

[Concurring and dissenting opinions omitted.]

NOTES

1. **Beating the grids.** Is Campbell's position a reasonable one? Suppose Campbell has diligently searched for work that fits her skills, education and capacity. She or her attorney consults the grids and determines that they will require the ALJ to deny disability. Can she prove there is really *not* a job she can do? Can she effectively dispute the "hidden" premises of the grids—that somewhere there is some undefined job she can somehow find? Just how can the Secretary determine, once and for all, what jobs are available for persons of given impairments?

2. **Nonexertional limitations.** The grid system does not apply to nonexertional limitations. *E.g., Reddick v. Chater,* 157 F.3d 715 (9th Cir. 1998). For example, limited intellectual capacity is a nonexertional impairment, meaning one that does not vary with exertion. Hence a claimant who is found to have a significant mental impairment must be given benefits unless the ALJ hears a vocational expert who establishes that there are jobs the claimant can perform. *Foreman v. Callahan,* 122 F.3d 24 (8th Cir. 1997).

3. **Pain.** Both pain and psychological impairments can count as, or cause, disability. What if the claimant merely testifies to pain, but neither he nor anyone else can find a medical source of the pain? See § 423 (d)(5). What if the claimant testifies to his severe pain, and doctors provide objective medical evidence of the underlying impairment that could reasonably be expected to cause pain, but the doctors cannot opine about the severity of that pain? *See Lingenfelter v. Astrue,* 504 F.3d 1028 (9th Cir. 2007) (error for ALJ to rule against claimant on such facts, at least without specific findings about why the claimant was not credible).

4. **Sparta vs. Athens.** When disability results from injury would it be better from a public point of view if the loss were borne by the activity that caused the harm rather than from public revenues? Reconsider Calabresi's Sparta and Athens example, *supra,* Ch. 24.

5. **Expanding welfare programs to eliminate tort law?** Professor Sugarman proposes a system of comprehensive coverage for people in need, without regard to whether their need derives from injury or something else. His program would substantially expand the social program we have just glanced at and do away with tort law altogether. The welfare program would provide compensation, and safety and deterrence would be achieved through regulation. *See* STEPHEN SUGARMAN, DOING AWAY WITH PERSONAL INJURY LAW (1989). This program would significantly reduce costs now borne by the tort system, he thinks, and could be financed in part by that reduction. What do you think?

CHAPTER 30

PRIVATE INSURANCE SOLUTIONS

■ ■ ■

Can private insurance solve the injury problem? If it is to improve on the tort system, workers' compensation and social security benefits, it would have to provide at least a large portion of the following:

(1) Basic coverage for most injuries causing medical loss or work-disability; (2) efficient return on premiums; (3) coverage for most if not all persons who may be injured; (4) a limit on any public subsidy; (5) a system of safety incentives. Is it possible that this could be done by private insurance?

NOTE: INSURANCE INSIDE AND OUTSIDE THE TORT SYSTEM

Within the tort system. The principal insurance schemes that work strictly within the confines of the tort system have been directed at one narrow but severe problem of those systems—the negligent driver who has insufficient liability insurance or none at all. Legislatures have enacted financial responsibility laws, under which, after an auto accident, the driver is required to show that he has insurance or the ability to pay damages; but these laws did not require the driver to purchase insurance before an accident occurred and they seldom worked to assure compensation. A few states added a provision for unsatisfied judgment funds, created by assessing an extra fee in licensing. These funds were used to help satisfy claims of injured victims when the defendant could not do so. This might secure a degree of compensation, not by putting responsibility upon negligent drivers but upon drivers as a class, "distributing" the costs of driving in much the way that products liability rules might "distribute" the cost of products to users. A third system simply permits drivers to buy their own insurance against the possibility of injury by uninsured, or underinsured, motorists.

In the last generation, most states have dealt with the uninsured motorist problem by mandating liability insurance for all vehicles. That has proved to be surprisingly ineffective because some drivers leave cars unregistered to avoid insurance, or purchase insurance to register, then cancel it. If you are injured by a negligent driver, chances are about one in five that he won't be insured even under compulsory insurance laws.

Outside the tort system. Uninsured motorists are not the only problem with the tort way of handling vehicle accidents. The time and expense of shifting loss through adjudication and the consequent premium cost for insurance also represent serious problems. Several kinds of insurance that do not require adjudication of fault are available to help protect against losses from injury. You can buy for yourself collision insurance (to pay for damages to your own car), accident insurance (to pay predetermined sums for specified injuries to yourself), or medical payment insurance (to pay limited sums for medical costs resulting to you or occupants of your car in a collision). These methods of covering costs of injury are limited, but they have some advantages. For instance, you yourself decide whether collision insurance is worth buying, how much coverage to buy, and what deductible to use. If you do buy such insurance, you can be assured that your car will be repaired whether or not you can prove that someone else was at fault, and you can handle the matter more or less expeditiously, without going to court. Could these advantages be generalized to supplant tort law for all cases of relatively small injuries, and thus to guarantee compensation without resort to the courts?

NOTE: NO–FAULT AUTO INSURANCE

No-fault auto insurance plans were first proposed by Robert Keeton and Jeffrey O'Connell in a now-classic book, BASIC PROTECTION FOR THE TRAFFIC VICTIM (1965). Their proposal contains several specific new ideas for reform. It envisions a two-tier system of injury law. Tort law is retained for larger claims, but smaller claims would be handled by insurance similar to medical and disability insurance. The insurer's liability is not based on fault, but on the fact of an auto injury. Yet it is not strict liability in the ordinary sense, because the injured victim merely claims against her own insurer for benefits ... Benefits include only a percentage of wage loss and all medical expenses (with a cap) with nothing for pain and suffering. If injury is more serious, the victim may then move to the second tier and "re-enter" the tort system.

Principal features of the Keeton–O'Connell plan are as follows:

1. *Insurance is compulsory.* The no-fault insurance is compulsory. The person registering a car must show proof that such insurance covers the car for injury arising from ownership, maintenance or use.

2. *Insurance is "first-party."* The no-fault insurance covering the car provides, by the insurance contract, benefits for auto injury to driver and all occupants, and in addition, to any injured pedestrian. This contemplates that the injured person claims against her own insurer, not against another's insurer. Even the pedestrian is a kind of third party beneficiary of the insurance purchased by the owner of the car. In other words, the claim is like a claim for medical or disability insurance, not a liability insurance claim.

3. *Tort claims abolished.* In all small claims covered by no-fault, an injured person is deprived of the tort claim altogether and must rely

exclusively on no-fault insurance (and any other added insurance that may cover the victim). Correlatively, even a negligent defendant is protected from liability as to these small claims.

4. *Re-entering the tort system.* If injury is severe, the victim will be permitted to sue in tort for injury not compensated by no-fault insurance. One could sue in tort if pain and suffering would exceed $5,000 or economic loss would exceed $10,000 (in 1965 dollars, remember). In such a case, the victim would first collect no-fault benefits and then sue in tort. If the damages exceeded these sums, the defendant would be liable, but liability would be reduced by $5,000 for pain and suffering and $10,000 for other damages. In other words, no-fault insurance superseded tort liability as to the first $10,000 of economic loss and the first $5,000 of pain and suffering.

Since there is potential tort liability for larger injuries, liability insurance is a part of the no-fault insurance package. But since that portion of the insurance is not responsible for the smaller injuries, the premium would be less in no-fault states.

5. *Benefits.* As with all no-fault laws, the Keeton–O'Connell benefits excluded all recoveries for pain and suffering. However, one could purchase added protection for greater benefits (at a higher premium). Added benefits could include coverage for pain and suffering. The limits on benefits might vary from state to state; the plan itself called for a maximum limit of $10,000 and also imposed a $100 work-loss deductible. Wage losses were also subject to a monthly maximum. Property damage was not covered at all.

The plan also adopted a coordination of benefits approach in many respects, in effect rejecting the collateral source rule. This was done by providing that all benefits received or receivable because of injury, from sources other than basic or added no-fault insurance, would be "subtractable." No subtraction would be made, however, for benefits from family members, life insurance, or inheritance.

All the existing no-fault plans follow the Keeton–O'Connell Plan by providing for periodic payments of benefits as the losses accrue. It is interesting to notice that periodic payment—rather than a lump sum payment—is characteristic also of workers' compensation, social security benefits and "structured settlements" of tort claims.

NEW YORK INSURANCE LAW

§ 5103. Entitlement to first party benefits; additional financial security required

(a) Every owner's policy of liability insurance [for automobiles and any other device intended to comply with the compulsory insurance requirements] shall also provide for ... the payment of first party benefits to:

(1) Persons, other than occupants of another motor vehicle or a motorcycle, for loss arising out of the use or operation in this state of such motor vehicle....

(2) The named insured and members of his household, other than occupants of a motorcycle, for loss arising out of the use or operation of (i) an uninsured motor vehicle or motorcycle, within the United States, its territories or possessions, or Canada; and (ii) an insured motor vehicle or motorcycle outside of this state and within the United States, its territories or possessions, or Canada....

(4) The estate of any covered person, other than an occupant of another motor vehicle or a motorcycle, a death benefit in the amount of two thousand dollars for the death of such person arising out of the use or operation of such motor vehicle which is in addition to any first party benefits for basic economic loss.

(b) An insurer may exclude from coverage required by subsection (a) hereof a person who:

(1) Intentionally causes his own injury.

(2) Is injured as a result of operating a motor vehicle while in an intoxicated condition or while his ability to operate such vehicle is impaired by the use of a drug within the meaning of section eleven hundred ninety-two of the vehicle and traffic law.

(3) Is injured while he is: (i) committing an act which would constitute a felony, or seeking to avoid lawful apprehension or arrest by a law enforcement officer, or (ii) operating a motor vehicle in a race or speed test [or carrying out certain other acts].

NOTES

1. "First party benefits" required by § 5103 "means payments to reimburse a person for basic economic loss on account of personal injury arising out of the use or operation of a motor vehicle, less: (1) Twenty percent of lost earnings.... (2) Amounts recovered or recoverable on account of such injury under state or federal laws providing social security disability benefits, or workers' compensation benefits, [and certain other benefits]." § 5102(b).

2. "Basic economic loss" for which the first party benefits are to compensate is capped at $50,000, but, subject to that cap, covers all necessary medical or "remedial" expenses, loss of earnings from work that the injured person otherwise would have performed, substitute services expense, and "all other reasonable and necessary expenses incurred, up to twenty-five dollars per day for not more than one year from the date of the accident causing the injury." § 5102(a).

NEW YORK INSURANCE LAW

§ 5104. Causes of action for personal injury

(a) Notwithstanding any other law, in any action by or on behalf of a covered person against another covered person for personal injuries arising out of negligence in the use or operation of a motor vehicle in this state, there shall be no right of recovery for non-economic loss, except in the case of a serious injury, or for basic economic loss. . . .

(b) In any action by or on behalf of a covered person, against a non-covered person, where damages for personal injuries arising out of the use or operation of a motor vehicle or a motorcycle may be recovered, an insurer which paid or is liable for first party benefits on account of such injuries has a lien against any recovery to the extent of benefits paid or payable by it to the covered person. . . .

NOTES

1. **Economic losses.** This section creates the tort exemption and sets the threshold for reentry into the tort system. There is no right of recovery for "non-economic loss" unless it is "serious," and no right of recovery for economic losses except so far as they exceed "basic economic loss." Thus the first $50,000 of economic loss must come from the no-fault or PIP benefits, not from the tort claim.

2. **Non-economic losses.** Non-economic loss such as pain and suffering is limited to cases involving "serious injury." Serious injury is defined in § 5102 (d) to mean "a personal injury which results in death; dismemberment; significant disfigurement; a fracture; loss of a fetus; permanent loss of use of a body organ, member, function or system; permanent consequential limitation of use of a body organ or member; significant limitation of use of a body function or system; or a medically determined injury or impairment of a non-permanent nature which prevents the injured person from performing substantially all of the material acts which constitute such person's usual and customary daily activities for not less than ninety days during the one hundred eighty days immediately following the occurrence of the injury or impairment."

Is this a better "threshold" than the dollar amount envisioned in the original Keeton–O'Connell proposal?

Statutes, of course, differ in many such details. It will be helpful, however, to apply the statute to a concrete case:

PROBLEM

In re Claims of Picklesimer, et al.

Since obtaining the basic facts, Mr. Picklesimer has furnished us the following information about damages to date:

Dr. Doubs $1,250.00

Murphey Med. Center 3,500.00

Dr. Doubs' bill does not include any charge for treatment following the complications. Mr. Picklesimer says that his medical insurance paid $2,800 of the hospital and doctor's bill. Dr. Doubs and our own consulting physician,

Dr. Newton, say that there will be further treatments over Picklesimer's lifetime, probably calling for $7,500 in future medical expenses (for drugs, perhaps prosthetics, and for examination and treatment). They also say that he will have limited motion the rest of his life, though he is mobile.

Please give me a brief memo on the following problems:

(1) Under the no-fault law, do we have any tort suit at all?

(2) Are our no-fault claims likely to be prejudiced by claims of Patrick or Plangent? Specifically, might their claims use up the no-fault coverage?

NOTES

1. Should Picklesimer be permitted to sue the landowner, car manufacturer, medical defendants, and the state responsible for the road design, even if his damages do not reach the tort threshold? Suppose, for example, his pain and suffering is less than $5,000 and his total economic damages are less than $10,000.

2. Could Dalzell claim against Picklesimer's policy for damage to his land if any was done?

3. If Picklesimer's injuries result partly from injury on Dalzell's land after the car came to a stop, and partly from medical negligence, are these injuries covered at all by no-fault? What phrase in the New York statute would be most relevant to resolution of this question? Is there any similar problem in tort law?

4. Suppose Picklesimer recovers several thousand dollars in PIP benefits under his no-fault policy and then recovers in tort from Dalzell, the state agency responsible for road design, the doctor, or the car manufacturer. Should he be compelled to share the tort recovery with his insurer, much as the injured worker must share the tort recovery with the workers' compensation insurer? Does § 5103 cover this situation?

5. Legislatures have had difficulty in defining the cut-off point or the "threshold" for reentering the tort system. Keeton and O'Connell used pain and suffering as one of the doorways back into tort, and relatively high economic loss as the other. The New York statute does not use pain and suffering as such, but rather lists a number of injury qualities that might suggest pain. See the Note following § 5104 above. Economic loss in excess of $50,000 is also a threshold. How serious a problem is this matter of defining the threshold?

LICARI v. ELLIOTT

441 N.E.2d 1088 (N.Y. 1982)

JASEN, JUDGE.

The issue raised on this appeal is whether the plaintiff in this negligence action brought to recover damages for personal injuries has established a prima facie case that he sustained a "serious injury" within the meaning of ... the "No–Fault" Law.

On February 13, 1979, plaintiff was injured in a motor vehicle accident. After being examined at the hospital, plaintiff was diagnosed as having a concussion, acute cervical sprain, acute dorsal lumbar sprain and a contusion of the chest. He was released two hours later and went home. Later that day, plaintiff consulted his family physician and, after relating the events of the day, was told to rest in bed. On February 15, 1979, plaintiff again consulted his physician and complained that he was coughing up reddish phlegm. Concerned about possible rib damage, his physician had plaintiff admitted to the hospital for tests. The test results showed no rib damage and that plaintiff's lungs were clear. The hospital physician examined plaintiff upon his admission and testified at trial that plaintiff's lungs were clear, reflexes normal, and that he suffered only a "very mild limitation" of movement in the back and neck areas. No further medical testimony was elicited with respect to the extent of plaintiff's limitation of movement. On February 17, 1979, plaintiff stated that he felt better and requested his release from the hospital. He was discharged and returned home. On March 9, 1979, 24 days after the accident, plaintiff returned to his job as a taxi driver. Immediately upon returning to work, plaintiff resumed driving a taxicab 12 hours per day, 6 days a week, as he had prior to the accident. The only proof of limitation with respect to his work performance was plaintiff's own testimony that he was unable to help some of his fares with their luggage "if they happened to have luggage." Plaintiff also testified that he could not help his wife with various household chores as much as he had before the accident. Finally, plaintiff stated he had occasional transitory headaches and dizzy spells which were relieved by aspirin.

After the close of evidence, defendant moved to dismiss the complaint on the ground that plaintiff failed to establish that his injury met any of the threshold requirements of a serious injury.... The court reserved decision on the motion and submitted the case to the jury on the theories that, in order to recover, plaintiff had to establish, by a preponderance of the evidence, that he had suffered either a medically determined injury of a nonpermanent nature which prevented him from performing substantially all his daily activities for not less than 90 days during the 180 days immediately following the accident or that as a result of the accident he sustained a significant limitation of use of a body function or system....

[The jury found for plaintiff on both grounds. The Appellate Division reversed, finding that plaintiff failed as a matter of law to prove "serious injury" under either definition.]

In construing the statutory definition of serious injury, it is necessary to examine the policies and purposes underlying this State's no-fault legislation. The so-called No–Fault Law was adopted by the Legislature to correct certain infirmities recognized to exist under the common-law tort system of compensating automobile accident claimants.

The Legislature provided that "there shall be no right of recovery for non-economic loss [i.e., pain and suffering] except in the case of a serious injury, or for basic economic loss." ... Although the statute sets forth eight specific categories which constitute serious injury, we are only concerned on this appeal with construing two of them, to wit: whether the plaintiff suffered a serious injury which resulted in either (1) a "significant limitation of use of a body function or system"; or (2) "a medically determined injury or impairment of a nonpermanent nature" which endured for 90 days or more and substantially limited the performance of his daily activities....

There can be little doubt that the purpose of enacting an objective verbal definition of serious injury was to "significantly reduce the number of automobile personal injury accident cases litigated in the courts, and thereby help contain the no-fault premium." "The verbal definition provided in the [legislation placed] a reasonable restriction and further limitation on the right to sue, in order to preserve the valuable benefits of no-fault, at an affordable cost." The Governor voiced his support of these policies when he signed the legislation into law. While it is clear that the Legislature intended to allow plaintiffs to recover for noneconomic injuries in appropriate cases, it had also intended that the court first determine whether or not a prima facie case of serious injury has been established which would permit a plaintiff to maintain a common-law cause of action in tort.

In light of this mandate, plaintiff's argument that the question of whether he suffered a serious injury is always a fact question for the jury is without merit. It is incumbent upon the court to decide in the first instance whether plaintiff has a cause of action to assert within the meaning of the statute. By enacting the No–Fault Law, the Legislature modified the common-law rights of persons injured in automobile accidents, to the extent that plaintiffs in automobile accident cases no longer have an unfettered right to sue for injuries sustained. Thus, to the extent that the Legislature has abrogated a cause of action, the issue is one for the court, in the first instance where it is properly raised, to determine whether the plaintiff has established a prima facie case of sustaining serious injury. Since the purpose of the No–Fault Law is to assure prompt and full compensation for economic loss by curtailing costly and time-consuming court trials requiring that every case, regardless of the extent of the injuries, be decided by a jury would subvert the intent of the Legislature and destroy the effectiveness of the statute. The result of requiring a jury trial where the injury is clearly a minor one would perpetuate a system of unnecessary litigation.... Thus, we believe the Legislature intended that the court should decide the threshold question of whether the evidence would warrant a jury finding that the injury falls within the class of injuries that, under no-fault, should be excluded from judicial remedy. If it can be said, as a matter of law, that plaintiff suffered no serious injury within the meaning of ... the Insurance Law, then plaintiff has no claim to assert and there is nothing for the jury to decide.

... Since plaintiff was able to maintain his daily routine for most of each day after returning to work, it should be abundantly clear that plaintiff was not prevented from performing substantially all of his daily activities during anything close to 90 days following the occurrence of the injury. Thus, the Appellate Division correctly held, as a matter of law, that plaintiff did not meet the statutory standard of serious injury. . . .

It requires little discussion that plaintiff's subjective complaints of occasional, transitory headaches hardly fulfill the definition of serious injury. Plaintiff offered no proof that his headaches in any way incapacitated him or interfered with his ability to work or engage in activities at home. In fact, plaintiff testified that such headaches occurred only once every two or three weeks and were relieved by aspirin. . . .

To hold that this type of ailment constitutes a serious injury would render the statute meaningless and frustrate the legislative intent in enacting no-fault legislation.

As to plaintiff's contention that he suffered a "significant limitation of use of a body function or system," taken in its most favorable light, the evidence at trial established only that plaintiff suffered a painful sprain which limited the movement of his neck and back. Plaintiff offered no evidence as to the extent of the limitation of movement. . . .

Accordingly, the order of the Appellate Division should be affirmed, with costs.

NOTES

1. **Proof.** What kind of proof is required to prove "serious injury" under the New York statute? In *Toure v. Avis Rent A Car Systems, Inc.*, 774 N.E.2d 1197 (N.Y. 2002), the court held that there must be "objective proof" by an expert—usually a medical expert, of course—and that "subjective complaints alone are not sufficient. Applying that rule to three consolidated cases, the court found that in two of them, the plaintiff had adduced sufficient proof, through doctors who testified to having performed various tests, including MRI's, to meet the "serious injury" threshold. In the third, however, where the plaintiff relied solely on her own testimony and that of her chiropractor, who did not indicate "what test, if any" he performed to ascertain the nature of her injuries, her proof was insufficient as a matter of law.

2. **Adoption of no-fault.** Existing no-fault plans in the United States are varied in detail. *See* Roger C. Henderson, *No–Fault Insurance for Automobile Accidents: Status and Effect in the United States*, 56 OR. L. REV. 287 (1977). About 15 states have enacted a no-fault system. Another ten permit the driver to buy extra no-fault insurance but these are added-cost systems. All of the statutes are so-called modified or "hybrid" rather than pure statutes—meaning that they envision no-fault only for one tier of accidents, not as a complete replacement of the tort system. A pure system would guarantee very high or unlimited payments for actual economic losses, and no access to the tort system at any time. In a few of those states, notably New York and Michigan, the caps on benefits are fairly high. No-fault in those states comes closer to a pure no-fault system.

3. **Outside the vehicle accident setting.** The no-fault idea has generated a second-generation of smaller no-fault plans with different mechanisms for other kinds of injury. We have seen one form in the Childhood Vaccine Injury Act, 42 U.S.C.A. §§ 300aa–1, providing limited but certain compensation in lieu of tort liability for injuries resulting from childhood immunization programs. For a comparison of several no-fault systems, *see* Robert L. Rabin, *The Renaissance of Accident Law Plans Revisited*, 64 MD. L. REV. 699 (2005).

4. **No-fault and deterrence.** Does a no-fault system deter bad behavior? Professor Gary Schwartz argued in *Auto No-fault and First-party Insurance: Advantages and Problems*, 73 S. CAL. L. REV. 611 (2000), that it has about the same deterrent effect as tort law, because if no-fault insurance premiums are left to the market, insurers will tend to raise premiums for bad no-fault drivers, and also for good drivers who are members of a dangerous group like teenagers. Uninsured drivers may have no assets to protect and may not be deterred under either system. J. David Cummins, Richard D. Phillips & Mary A. Weiss, *The Incentive Effects of No-fault Automobile Insurance*, 44 J.L. & ECON. 427 (2001), presents an empirical study and concludes that no-fault weakens safety by weakening deterrence effects of tort law, but that, as Schwartz suggested, rating systems that increase insurance costs of bad drivers would restore some of the deterrence effect.

5. **Pure vs. hybrid no-fault.** Professor Schwartz also concluded that hybrid no-fault systems, though not losers, are definitely not winners. On the other hand, a pure no-fault systems—one that excludes tort law altogether—is a clear winner. Recall that this would eliminate all pain and suffering damages. On the other hand, it would take care of the most serious injuries as well as minor ones. And it would entail much more efficient use of premium dollars, returning as much as 93% of the premium dollar in compensation to the injured. What do you think? Would you favor pure over hybrid no-fault? Over the tort system?

6. **Pain.** If you think pain and suffering represents real loss for which, in justice, the defendant should compensate the plaintiff, it will be hard for you to approve a pure no-fault system. But there is evidence suggesting that awards may actually reinforce some kinds of pain. *See* Ellen Smith Pryor, *Compensation and the Ineradicable Problems of Pain*, 59 GEO. WASH. L. REV. 239 (1991). If it is true that awards not only don't help get over pain but actually encourage it, are you willing to eliminate all claims for pain?

CHAPTER 31

EVALUATING INJURY SYSTEMS:
A DISCUSSION AGENDA

■ ■ ■

This book has explored many facets of tort law. In the last three chapters it has also looked at some prominent alternative systems for dealing with torts that cause physical harm. This chapter poses a few of the many questions that can promote evaluation of the different ways we as a society could deal with accidental injuries.

1. *Judicial Process*

You might notice that some critics of tort law distrust of the judicial system—judges, juries, and lawyers. Some of them, for example, believe that many fraudulent claims succeed in the "tort system"—meaning in courtrooms where judges and juries actually see and hear each claimant and defendant. What is your guess—that critics know that persons they've never seen are fraudulent while judges and juries somehow systematically miss this fact?

The question is important not because it deals with fraud but because it deals with the judicial process. One salient characteristic of tort law and the judicial process generally is that each claim is judged on its own merits. Judges decide nothing about whether humans are generally fraudulent or whether plaintiffs lie more than defendants. Instead judges and juries look at the particular plaintiff and the particular defendant asserting claims and defenses about their individual facts. Neither is a token in a board game or an icon who stands for a group. To the extent that rules of law eliminate individual characteristics and particular facts from consideration this essential idea of justice is lost.

How do you think alternative systems stack up in this regard? Are any important individual facts—fault or extent of injury, for example—discarded under workers' compensation, social security disability, or no-fault? If so is that good or bad?

2. *Personal accountability and social responsibility—fairness or justice*

If personal responsibility for wrongs done is an ideal, does tort law actually enforce that accountability? If so, is something lost in moving to workers' compensation, social security, or no-fault? If not, should we rate the systems as equal on this score?

3. *Safety and deterrence*

(a) Some risks are desirable, otherwise nothing is accomplished; but too many risks are not. Does tort law promote optimal risk-taking? Does it appropriately deter undesirable risks? Indeed, does it deter any conduct at all? If your answer is that tort law (perhaps along with cultural constraints) does provide some deterrence, would that be lost in any of the other systems considered here?

(b) Even if, by and large, tort theories do not encourage safety in most instances, might some other injury systems have an adverse effect on safety? In a no-fault system, could that depend in part on whether the driver's no-fault insurance premiums are raised when he shows a propensity for numerous accidents?

(c) Before making a final decision, consider whether non-tort systems might have some non-obvious deterrence or safety effects. Maybe workers' compensation insurers inspect factories and encourage safer practices. Maybe no-fault insurers would reduce premiums for insureds who have airbags or other safety devices. Could such devices actually create better conditions for safety? If so, would that judgment apply only to vehicle accidents or would it apply equally to, say, toxic tort cases or medical malpractice cases?

4. *Costs*

Pure (not hybrid) no-fault might lead to a highly efficient use of the premium dollar—returning 90% or more in benefits, compared to something around 50% return of the liability insurance dollar. What is the trade-off for this great efficiency? Is it worth it? What do you think about the probable cost comparisons of a welfare system for injury modeled on social security disability or workers' compensation? Should we as a society seek to get highly reliable data?

5. *Delay in payment*

One criticism of the courts is that they can take a very long time to produce a decision. Due process is expensive and perhaps not every dispute should be subjected to its rigors. An early study indicated that under Massachusetts' no-fault system, medical expenses were paid in about seven days from the time the insurer received the necessary documentation. Will concerns about medical expenses lessen if more people are covered?

6. *The most important question*

Questions about fairness, efficiency and deterrence are endless. The editors of this book believe that the most important questions readers should consider are those that trouble them most. What do you see as the most important issue about injury law?

*

PART 7

ECONOMIC AND DIGNITARY TORTS

■ ■ ■

CHAPTER 32

COMMUNICATION OF PERSONALLY HARMFUL IMPRESSIONS TO OTHERS

▪ ▪ ▪

§ 1.   DEFAMATION—LIBEL AND SLANDER

A.   THE COMMON LAW RULES

CASSIDY v. DAILY MIRROR NEWSPAPERS, LTD., [1929] 2 K.B. 331, 69 A.L.R. 720. "Scrutton, L.J. The facts in this case are simple. A man named Cassidy, who for some reason also called himself Corrigan and described himself as a General in the Mexican Army, was married to a lady who also called herself Mrs. Cassidy or Mrs. Corrigan. Her husband occasionally came and stayed with her at her flat, and her acquaintances met him. Cassidy achieved some notoriety in racing circles and in indiscriminate relations with women, and at a race meeting he posed, in company with a lady, to a racing photographer, to whom he said he was engaged to marry the lady and the photographer might announce it. The photographer, without any further inquiry, sent the photograph to the Daily Mirror with an inscription: 'Mr. Corrigan, the race horse owner, and Miss X.'—I omit the name—'whose engagement has been announced,' and the Daily Mirror published the photograph and inscription. This paper was read by the female acquaintances of Mrs. Cassidy or Mrs. Corrigan, who gave evidence that they understood from it that the lady was not married to Mr. M. Corrigan and had no legal right to take his name, and that they formed a bad opinion of her in consequence. Mrs. Cassidy accordingly brought an action for libel against the newspaper setting out these words with an innuendo, meaning thereby that the plaintiff was an immoral woman who had cohabited with Corrigan without being married to him." *Held*: the plaintiff has an action for damages. The words were capable of defamatory meaning by suggesting that Mrs. Cassidy was not married to the man who stayed at her flat. And the fact that the newspaper did not know the facts that would permit some persons to draw the defamatory conclusion is no defense. The publisher must take the consequences even if it has no intent to speak about the plaintiff at all.

890

NOTE

Strict liability at common law. *Cassidy* shows the essential strict liability of traditional common law libel. The plaintiff had to prove only that (a) the defendant published (b) defamatory material (c) "of and concerning" the plaintiff. That proved, the plaintiff could recover damages, sometimes awarded in large sums. The plaintiff was not required to prove falsehood, dishonesty, or even damages. The fact that the defendant honestly believed what it published or even investigated carefully was no defense. Some, but not all, of these rules have changed today.

———————

STANTON v. METRO CORP., 438 F.3d 119 (1st Cir. 2006). The teenaged plaintiff's photograph appeared in *Boston* magazine, a monthly general-interest publication, accompanying an article about teenage sexual promiscuity in Massachusetts. The cover refers to the article with the phrase, "Fast Times at Silver Lake High: Teen Sex in the Suburbs." Inside, the plaintiff is one of five teenagers pictured. The photo was taken at a high school dance. Three of the students are smoking cigarettes, but plaintiff is simply looking at the camera, smiling slightly. A "superhead" reads, "They hook up on line. They hook up in real life. . . ." The article describes the frequent, casual and drunken sexual encounters of several teenagers, quoting many by their first names. Small type at the bottom of the first page says that the photographs in the article were taken as part of a "five-year project on teen sexuality," and that "the individuals pictured are unrelated to people or events described in this story." Plaintiff, who lives in New Hampshire, sued the magazine's publisher for defamation. The trial court dismissed the complaint. *Held*, reversed. A reasonable jury could find the publication defamatory, meaning that it had a reasonable tendency to injure her reputation, and could also find that she was one of the teenagers described in the story. There need not be any express connection between the article and the photo to make the communication defamatory. Nor is the disclaimer determinative, because it could be ignored or missed by a reasonable reader. Her complaint also sufficiently alleges that the defendant published the article with negligent disregard for the truth.

NOTES

1. **Common law evolution.** The common law rarely remains static, and the rules on defamation are no exception. The Massachusetts defamation rules applied in *Stanton* require proof that (a) the defendant negligently published (b) a false and defamatory statement (c) of and concerning the plaintiff. A plaintiff must prove economic loss in some cases, but not in others. How does this differ from what was required in *Cassidy* to state a claim?

2. **Publication.** "Publication" is a term of art, and does not necessarily mean a media publication. Any communication to a third person is sufficient.

Defendant tells his neighbor that the minister at the church is having an affair with the choir mistress. This is a publication of the kind called slander, since it is oral. Or defendant writes his cousin that a city councilwoman has taken a bribe. This is also a publication, and since it is in writing it is called libel. The traditional common law rule we saw in *Cassidy* required that publication be made intentionally or negligently to support a defamation claim, but did not require any fault on the part of the defendant. Many courts have now said that negligence in making a false or defamatory statement is required, apparently rejecting the tradition reflected in *Cassidy*.

3. **Repeaters as publishers.** A newspaper publishes a libel about the plaintiff. Readers and other newspapers report what the newspaper said, correctly attributing the defamation to the first newspaper. Under the rule that repeaters are publishers, they are also subject to liability unless they have a privilege.

4. **Reference to the plaintiff.** The defendant's publication is not actionable for defamation of the plaintiff unless people can reasonably take it as referring to the plaintiff. As *Cassidy* and *Stanton* indicate, this rule did not and does not require reference to the plaintiff by name, if in fact some readers would reasonably understand that the plaintiff was referred to. The readers' reasonable understanding, not necessarily intent of the author, controls. Thus, reasonable inferences from the published material, or even from outside facts, might lead a reader to believe the defamatory material refers to the plaintiff. If a fictional movie depicted a man who founded a Little League for poor children in Chicago and contained defamatory implications about him, could a real person who founded such a league recover for defamation? *See Muzikowski v. Paramount Pictures Corp.*, 322 F.3d 918 (7th Cir. 2003).

5. **Defamatory meaning.** Publications are actionable as defamation only if they carry some negative implication, something that makes the publication "defamatory." A publication that engenders "hatred, ridicule or contempt" for the plaintiff would qualify, but so would publications that merely lower esteem for the plaintiff among some substantial segment of the community. This hypothetical segment of the public is hypothetically allowed, as in *Cassidy* and *Stanton*, to draw a string of quite uncharitable inferences. And defamatory content may be found not only in factual statements, but also in certain opinions, witticisms and satirical jabs. "In my opinion, his best friends are all members of the Mob," probably easily qualifies as defamatory. On the other hand, mere name calling is not enough. "He's a jerk" with nothing more is not actionable. The defamatory quality of a publication is a core issue in many cases. *See, e.g., Damon v. Moore*, 520 F.3d 98 (1st Cir. 2008) (army reservist's non-consensual placement in Michael Moore's anti-war documentary Farenheit 9–11 could not reasonably be viewed as "discrediting the reservist in the minds of any considerable an respectable class of the community to which the statement was addressed").

6. **Judge and jury.** Defamatory meaning is generally a jury question, but where reasonable people could not interpret a publication as defamatory, the judge will properly find against the plaintiff. *See, e.g., Knievel v. ESPN*, 393 F.3d 1068 (9th Cir. 2005) (caption under photo of sports celebrity and his wife on defendant's website that said, "Evel Knievel proves that you're never

too old to be a pimp," could not be construed by a reasonable person to mean that Knievel was a pimp and that his wife was a prostitute, given that the tone of the entire website was "lighthearted and jocular."

7. **Damages.** In many cases, including all cases of libel, the traditional common law presumed that the plaintiff suffered damages. This meant that in most cases the plaintiff could recover without proving any actual losses at all. Recovery might be augmented by proof of pecuniary loss, as where the plaintiff lost a job because of the libel. But the derogatory words would be sufficient to warrant a recovery. The damages thus recovered were not merely nominal but were quite substantial. Many states have changed this rule today, but damages may still be presumed in certain kinds of defamation cases. Indeed, libel verdicts in the millions are sometimes recovered. *See* David A. Logan, *Libel Law in the Trenches: Reflections on Current Data on Libel Litigation,* 87 VA. L. REV. 503 (2001).

8. **Libel and slander.** The traditional common law carefully distinguished libel from slander and made different rules of damages for the two forms of defamation. Libel was originally thought of as written material; slander as oral. Radio, television, movies, and electronic publication have put the libel/slander categories in doubt. However, it is a good guess that that media publications will all be treated as libel if the distinction continues to matter, though there may be close cases, such as the use of a loudspeaker system without broadcast or recording.

9. **Slander per se.** The common law traditionally treated virtually all libel as libel per se, meaning that damages would be presumed. Slander, however, required that the plaintiff prove pecuniary loss, meaning the loss of money or money's worth. This might happen, for example, if the plaintiff were to lose her job because of slanderous statements. Three or four kinds of slander, however, were regarded as being especially serious and to warrant a presumption of damages. In such cases it was said that the slander was per se and it was not necessary for the plaintiff to prove pecuniary loss to sustain a claim. Damages were presumed if the publication imputed that the plaintiff (1) had committed a serious crime; (2) had a loathsome disease, historically leprosy and venereal diseases; (3) had traits or had engaged in conduct incompatible with plaintiff's business, trade or profession, such as saying of a minister that she is drunk while off-duty; and (4) had engaged in serious sexual misconduct.

10. **Truth defeating the claim.** If defamatory content was shown, the traditional common law approach was to presume that the statement was untrue. This left the defendant with the entire burden of proving the truth of the statements made. The rule made the defendant liable for the sting of his statement, even where it was literally true. In many situations in many states, the burden of proof on "truth" now rests with the plaintiff, as we will see in subpart b below. Still, however, courts do not focus exclusively on the literal truth or falsity of a statement, but rather on its gist. An inaccurate statement may be substantially true. For example, what if the defendant says the plaintiff is serving prison time for fraud when in fact she has been convicted but is awaiting sentence which could include prison time? Notice also that just because you truthfully quote a defamer you may not escape liability; instead

the "repeater's rule" governs. *See Flowers v. Carville,* 310 F.3d 1118 (9th Cir. 2002).

NOTE: COMMON-LAW PRIVILEGES

1. *Judge-made privileges.* Under the traditional common law rules a publisher might be held in damages not only in cases in which he was not at fault but also in cases in which what he published was strictly accurate. To mitigate this, courts developed a series of privileges—affirmative defenses that could in special cases provide protection, provided the defendant was able to shoulder the burden of proving them. Most of these privileges remain in place today, at least where not displaced by constitutional rules described in subpart b. The chief privileges include:

A. *Official privileges. (1) The litigation privilege.* Judges, lawyers, and witnesses enjoy an absolute privilege to defame when they communicate in the course of and in relation to the subject matter of litigation. *See, e.g., Mahoney & Hagberg v. Newgard,* 729 N.W.2d 302 (Minn. 2007). This privilege has been expanded to encompass adversary work before administrative agencies and other quasi-judicial adjudicative bodies. *See, e.g., Rosenberg v. MetLife, Inc.,* 866 N.E.2d 439 (N.Y. 2007) (privilege applied to termination notice filed with national stock exchange). Whether this absolute privilege is really necessary to assure vigorous and unfettered advocacy is debatable. *See* Paul T. Hayden, *Reconsidering the Litigator's Absolute Privilege to Defame,* 54 Ohio St. L. J. 985 (1993). *(2) Legislative privilege.* Federal legislators are given an absolute privilege to utter defamatory statements in the course of their official duties by the U.S. Constitution, Art. I, § 6. State and local legislators usually enjoy a similar privilege. *(3) Executive privilege.* Executive officers have mostly enjoyed only a qualified privilege, one destroyed if there is actual malice, although there are still some cases in which federal executives still enjoy an absolute privilege as to utterances in the scope of their duties.

B. *The privilege to communicate in one's own interest, the interest of third persons, or in common interest of publisher and recipient.* These vaguely worded privileges permit defendants in some cases to indulge in self-defense ("I didn't do it, he did"), protection of loved ones ("Don't trust him, daughter, he's no good") and sharing of important information within a group ("Our minister is having an affair with the Church Secretary"). This privilege often applies to protect an employer who sends a negative reference letter to an employee's prospective new employer. *See, e.g, Miron v. University of New Haven Police Dept.,* 931 A.2d 847 (Conn. 2007). The privilege is destroyed if abused, as where the speaker has an improper purpose or malice, or publishes excessively.

C. *The privilege to report information pertaining to crime or the like to appropriate officers.* Again, the privilege may be lost if there is malice and perhaps if there is negligence. *See, e.g., Gallo v. Barile,* 935 A.2d 103 (Conn. 2007) (witnesses who made false statements to police lost qualified privilege).

D. *The privilege to report a public document, meeting or activity*. Example: a report of a trial. This privilege is lost only if the report is biased or inaccurate.

E. *Fair comment*. A person is privileged to comment about accurately stated facts concerning some matter of public concern, including political, social, and artistic matters. This is limited to comment about facts that are accurately stated. Comment without statement of facts (and an accurate statement at that) is not protected.

2. *Statutory privileges or immunities*. Statutes may create additional privileges. The advent of the internet has made it possible for almost anyone to post defamatory material on web bulletin boards, in chat rooms, or other sites controlled by a provider. Is the internet provider liable for defamation for failing to remove or prohibit a defamatory message posted by others? A federal statute, the Communications Decency Act, 47 U.S.C.A. § 230(c)(1), gives internet providers or message board operators immunity from liability for allegedly defamatory postings made by third party subscribers. *See, e.g., Universal Communication Systems, Inc. v. Lycos, Inc.*, 478 F.3d 413 (1st Cir. 2007); *Zeran v. America Online, Inc.*, 129 F.3d 327, 333 (4th Cir. 1997).

REFERENCES: DOBBS ON TORTS §§ 400–16 (2000); DAN B. DOBBS & ELLEN M. BUBLICK, ADVANCED TORTS: ECONOMIC AND DIGNITARY TORTS Ch. 1 & 2 (2006).

B. THE CONSTITUTIONAL CONSTRAINTS OF FREE SPEECH

NEW YORK TIMES CO. v. SULLIVAN

376 U.S. 254 (1964)

[The New York Times published an advertisement signed by a committee of distinguished persons and asking for donations to help defend Dr. Martin Luther King, Jr. in a perjury indictment against him and for other civil purposes. It said that efforts to enforce civil rights had been met with a "wave of terror," and that "Southern violators" had "bombed his home," and had "arrested him seven times" on various charges. The advertisement referred to the police "ringing" the campus at Alabama State College, and said that "authorities" had padlocked the campus dining hall in an effort to starve the student body into submission.]

[The plaintiff in this case is L.B. Sullivan, elected Commissioner of the City of Montgomery, Alabama. In that capacity he is in charge of the Police Department. He was not named in the advertisement, but he contends that references to the police must be read as implicating him; and similarly that references to "arrests" must be read as accusing him of intimidation and violence. The trial judge charged the jury that the statements were libelous per se, that falsity, malice and damages were presumed. The jury awarded $500,000 and the Supreme Court of Alabama affirmed.]

[BRENNAN, J. delivered the opinion of the Court.]

We reverse the judgment. We hold that the rule of law applied by the Alabama courts is constitutionally deficient for failure to provide the safeguards for freedom of speech and of the press that are required by the First and Fourteenth Amendments in a libel action brought by a public official against critics of his official conduct. We further hold that under the proper safeguards the evidence presented in this case is constitutionally insufficient to support the judgment for respondent. . . .

Under Alabama law as applied in this case, a publication is "libelous per se" if the words "tend to injure a person in his reputation" or to "bring [him] into public contempt"; the trial court stated that the standard was met if the words are such as to "injure him in his public office, or impute misconduct to him in his office, or want of official integrity, or want of fidelity to a public trust." The jury must find that the words were published "of and concerning" the plaintiff, but where the plaintiff is a public official his place in the governmental hierarchy is sufficient evidence to support a finding that his reputation has been affected by statements that reflect upon the agency of which he is in charge. Once "libel per se" has been established, the defendant has no defense as to stated facts unless he can persuade the jury that they were true in all their particulars.

His privilege of "fair comment" for expressions of opinion depends on the truth of the facts upon which the comment is based. Unless he can discharge the burden of proving truth, general damages are presumed, and may be awarded without proof of pecuniary injury. . . .

The general proposition that freedom of expression upon public questions is secured by the First Amendment has long been settled by our decisions. The constitutional safeguard, we have said, "was fashioned to assure unfettered interchange of ideas for the bringing about of political and social changes desired by the people."

> "The maintenance of the opportunity for free political discussion to the end that government may be responsive to the will of the people and that changes may be obtained by lawful means, an opportunity essential to the security of the Republic, is a fundamental principle of our constitutional system." "[I]t is a prized American privilege to speak one's mind, although not always with perfect good taste, on all public institutions," and this opportunity is to be afforded for "vigorous advocacy" no less than "abstract discussion."

The First Amendment, said Judge Learned Hand, "presupposes that right conclusions are more likely to be gathered out of a multitude of tongues, than through any kind of authoritative selection. To many this is, and always will be, folly; but we have staked upon it our all."

Mr. Justice Brandeis, in his concurring opinion in Whitney v. California, 274 U.S. 357, 375–376, 47 S.Ct. 641, 648, 71 L.Ed. 1095, gave the principle its classic formulation:

"Those who won our independence believed ... that public discussion is a political duty; and that this should be a fundamental principle of the American government. They recognized the risks to which all human institutions are subject. But they knew that order cannot be secured merely through fear of punishment for its infraction; that it is hazardous to discourage thought, hope and imagination; that fear breeds repression; that repression breeds hate; that hate menaces stable government; that the path of safety lies in the opportunity to discuss freely supposed grievances and proposed remedies; and that the fitting remedy for evil counsels is good ones. Believing in the power of reason as applied through public discussion, they eschewed silence coerced by law—the argument of force in its worst form. Recognizing the occasional tyrannies of governing majorities, they amended the Constitution so that free speech and assembly should be guaranteed."

Thus we consider this case against the background of a profound national commitment to the principle that debate on public issues should be uninhibited, robust, and wide-open, and that it may well include vehement, caustic, and sometimes unpleasantly sharp attacks on government and public officials.

The present advertisement, as an expression of grievance and protest on one of the major public issues of our time, would seem clearly to qualify for the constitutional protection. The question is whether it forfeits that protection by the falsity of some of its factual statements and by its alleged defamation of respondent.

Authoritative interpretations of the First Amendment guarantees have consistently refused to recognize an exception for any test of truth—whether administered by judges, juries, or administrative officials—and especially one that puts the burden of proving truth on the speaker.... That erroneous statement is inevitable in free debate, and that it must be protected if the freedoms of expression are to have the "breathing space" that they "need ... to survive," was also recognized by the Court of Appeals for the District of Columbia Circuit in Sweeney v. Patterson....

If neither factual error nor defamatory content suffices to remove the constitutional shield from criticism of official conduct, the combination of the two elements is no less inadequate. This is the lesson to be drawn from the great controversy over the Sedition Act of 1798....

[The Court here discussed the Sedition Act, which made it a crime to publish "false, scandalous and malicious writing" against the government or its main officers. The act was attacked by many of the Founders and eventually repealed on a consensus that it was inconsistent with the First Amendment.]

What a State may not constitutionally bring about by means of a criminal statute is likewise beyond the reach of its civil law of libel. The fear of damage awards under a rule such as that invoked by the Alabama courts here may be markedly more inhibiting than the fear of prosecution under a criminal statute....

The state rule of law is not saved by its allowance of the defense of truth. A defense for erroneous statements honestly made is no less essential here than was the requirement of proof of guilty knowledge which, in Smith v. California, 361 U.S. 147, 80 S.Ct. 215, 4 L.Ed.2d 205, we held indispensable to a valid conviction of a bookseller for possessing obscene writings for sale.... A rule compelling the critic of official conduct to guarantee the truth of all his factual assertions—and to do so on pain of libel judgments virtually unlimited in amount—leads to a comparable "self-censorship." Allowance of the defense of truth, with the burden of proving it on the defendant, does not mean that only false speech will be deterred.... Under such a rule, would-be critics of official conduct may be deterred from voicing their criticism, even though it is believed to be true and even though it is in fact true, because of doubt whether it can be proved in court or fear of the expense of having to do so. They tend to make only statements which "steer far wider of the unlawful zone." The rule thus dampens the vigor and limits the variety of public debate. It is inconsistent with the First and Fourteenth Amendments. The constitutional guarantees require, we think, a federal rule that prohibits a public official from recovering damages for a defamatory falsehood relating to his official conduct unless he proves that the statement was made with "actual malice"—that is, with knowledge that it was false or with reckless disregard of whether it was false or not.... Since respondent may seek a new trial, we deem that considerations of effective judicial administration require us to review the evidence in the present record to determine whether it could constitutionally support a judgment for respondent. This Court's duty is not limited to the elaboration of constitutional principles; we must also in proper cases review the evidence to make certain that those principles have been constitutionally applied....

[W]e consider that the proof presented to show actual malice lacks the convincing clarity which the constitutional standard demands, and hence that it would not constitutionally sustain the judgment for respondent under the proper rule of law....

[The Court rejected the argument that "actual malice" could be found because the Times did not retract and because it did not check the accuracy against news stories in its own files. The imputed knowledge from its own files was not sufficient to show an actual state of mind necessary to support a finding of knowing or reckless falsehood. The Court also thought the evidence was constitutionally deficient because criticisms did not clearly refer to the plaintiff. This was thought too much like permitting an action for criticism of government itself.]

[JUSTICES BLACK and DOUGLAS and GOLDBERG, in two concurring opinions, argued for an absolute right to speak, with no liability even for knowing falsehoods.]

NOTES

1. **Public officials and public figures.** The rules in *Times–Sullivan* originally applied only to public officials, either appointed or elected. In 1967, a much-divided Court extended the same rules to cover "public figures," who were neither candidates for office nor actual public employees. *Curtis Publ'g Co. v. Butts*, 388 U.S. 130 (1967). One rationale for this extension was that many private citizens have an key role in influencing social policy and in "ordering society."

2. **Actual malice.** In protecting publications about public officials (and later public figures), the *Times–Sullivan* Court drew on familiar words in holding that "actual malice" was required as a condition of liability, but the words proved confusing in the end because the court was not referring to spite or ill-will. Instead, the plaintiff must prove that the defendant knew the publication was false or, just short of this,that the defendant published "recklessly." It is now established that recklessness in this sense requires a "high degree of awareness of probable falsity," or that the publisher "in fact entertained serious doubts as to the truth of his publication." *St. Amant v. Thompson*, 390 U.S. 727 (1968). A deliberate intent to avoid the truth coupled with knowledge of an allegation's probable inaccuracy may establish actual malice. *Murphy v. Boston Herald, Inc.*, 865 N.E.2d 746 (Mass. 2007). Mere negligence, as in a failure to investigate, is clearly insufficient.

3. **Fair comment.** Would the common law fair comment privilege ever protect a publication that would not be protected under *Times–Sullivan*?

4. **Truth.** In the early years after *Times–Sullivan*, libel lawyers continued to think in common law terms and often spoke of the case as erecting a "Constitutional privilege." But common law privileges were affirmative defenses, and it gradually became clear that *Times–Sullivan* rewrote the elements of the plaintiff's prima facie case in all claims brought by public officials (and later extended to public figures). Thus the plaintiff in such a case must prove that the published statements are false; the burden is no longer on the defendant to prove truth.

GERTZ v. ROBERT WELCH, INC.

418 U.S. 323 (1974)

[The plaintiff, Elmer Gertz, is a lawyer. A police officer named Nuccio shot and killed a youth named Nelson and was convicted of second degree murder. Gertz represented the Nelson family in civil claims against Nuccio. The defendant publishes an organ known as American Opinion, representing the views of the John Birch Society. This organ, arguing that the prosecution of Nuccio was a part of the Communist campaign against police, portrayed Gertz as an architect of the "frame-up" of Nuccio, and went on to identify him as a Leninist and Communist-fronter. In fact Gertz had nothing to do with the criminal prosecution and there was no basis for claiming him to be a Leninist or Communist fronter. Gertz sued. The trial court concluded that Gertz was not a public official or a public figure, but that the *Times–Sullivan* rules applied anyway. Accordingly, it entered a judgment for the defendant. The Court of Appeals concluded that there was no clear and convincing evidence of "actual malice," and it affirmed.]

[JUSTICE POWELL delivered the Court's opinion.]

The principal issue in this case is whether a newspaper or broadcaster that publishes defamatory falsehoods about an individual who is neither a public official nor a public figure may claim a constitutional privilege against liability for the injury inflicted by those statements. The Court considered this question on the rather different set of facts presented in *Rosenbloom v. Metromedia, Inc.*, 403 U.S. 29, 91 S. Ct. 1811, 29 L. Ed.2d 296 (1971). Rosenbloom, a distributor of nudist magazines, was arrested for selling allegedly obscene material while making a delivery to a retail dealer. The police obtained a warrant and seized his entire inventory of 3,000 books and magazines. He sought and obtained an injunction prohibiting further police interference with his business. He then sued a local radio station for failing to note in two of its newscasts that the 3,000 items seized were only "reportedly" or "allegedly" obscene and for broadcasting references to "the smut literature racket" and to "girlie-book peddlers" in its coverage of the court proceeding for injunctive relief. He obtained a judgment against the radio station, but the Court of Appeals for the Third Circuit held the New York Times privilege applicable to the broadcast and reversed. 415 F.2d 892 (1969).

This Court affirmed the decision below, but no majority could agree on a controlling rationale. The eight Justices who participated in Rosenbloom announced their views in five separate opinions, none of which commanded more than three votes.... We begin with the common ground. Under the First Amendment there is no such thing as a false idea. However pernicious an opinion may seem, we depend for its correction not on the conscience of judges and juries but on the competition of other ideas. But there is no constitutional value in false statements of fact. Neither the intentional lie nor the careless error materially advances society's interest in "uninhibited, robust, and wide-open" debate on public issues....

Although the erroneous statement of fact is not worthy of constitutional protection, it is nevertheless inevitable in free debate.... The First Amendment requires that we protect some falsehood in order to protect speech that matters.

The need to avoid self-censorship by the news media is, however, not the only societal value at issue. If it were, this Court would have embraced long ago the view that publishers and broadcasters enjoy an unconditional and indefeasible immunity from liability for defamation....

The legitimate state interest underlying the law of libel is the compensation of individuals for the harm inflicted on them by defamatory falsehood....

The *New York Times* standard defines the level of constitutional protection appropriate to the context of defamation of a public person. Those who, by reason of the notoriety of their achievements or the vigor and success with which they seek the public's attention, are properly classed as public figures and those who hold governmental office may recover for injury to reputation only on clear and convincing proof that the defamatory falsehood was made with knowledge of its falsity or with reckless disregard for the truth.... We think that these decisions are correct, but we do not find their holdings justified solely by reference to the interest of the press and broadcast media in immunity from liability. Rather, we believe that the *New York Times* rule states an accommodation between this concern and the limited state interest present in the context of libel actions brought by public persons.... Because an *ad hoc* resolution of the competing interests at stake in each particular case is not feasible, we must lay down broad rules of general application. Such rules necessarily treat alike various cases involving differences as well as similarities. Thus it is often true that not all of the considerations which justify adoption of a given rule will obtain in each particular case decided under its authority.

With that caveat we have no difficulty in distinguishing among defamation plaintiffs. The first remedy of any victim of defamation is self-help—using available opportunities to contradict the lie or correct the error and thereby to minimize its adverse impact on reputation. Public officials and public figures usually enjoy significantly greater access to the channels of effective communication and hence have a more realistic opportunity to counteract false statements than private individuals normally enjoy. Private individuals are therefore more vulnerable to injury, and the state interest in protecting them is correspondingly greater.

More important than the likelihood that private individuals will lack effective opportunities for rebuttal, there is a compelling normative consideration underlying the distinction between public and private defamation plaintiffs. An individual who decides to seek governmental office must accept certain necessary consequences of that involvement in public affairs. He runs the risk of closer public scrutiny than might otherwise be the case. And society's interest in the officers of government is not strictly limited to the formal discharge of official duties. As the Court pointed out in Garrison v. Louisiana, 379 U.S. at 77, 85 S.Ct., at 217, the public's interest extends to "anything which might touch on an official's fitness for office.... Few personal attributes are more germane to fitness for office than dishonesty, malfeasance, or improper motivation, even though these characteristics may also affect the official's private character."

Those classed as public figures stand in a similar position. Hypothetically, it may be possible for someone to become a public figure through no purposeful action of his own, but the instances of truly involuntary public figures must be exceedingly rare. For the most part those who attain this status have assumed roles of especial prominence in the affairs of society. Some occupy positions of such persuasive power and influence that they are deemed public figures for all purposes. More commonly, those classed as public figures have thrust themselves to the forefront of particular public controversies in order to influence the resolution of the issues involved. In either event, they invite attention and comment.

Even if the foregoing generalities do not obtain in every instance, the communications media are entitled to act on the assumption that public officials and public figures have voluntarily exposed themselves to increased risk of injury from defamatory falsehood concerning them. No such assumption is justified with respect to a private individual. He has not accepted public office or assumed an "influential role in ordering society." ...

Thus, private individuals are not only more vulnerable to injury than public officials and public figures; they are also more deserving of recovery....

We hold that, so long as they do not impose liability without fault, the States may define for themselves the appropriate standard of liability for a publisher or broadcaster of defamatory falsehood injurious to a private individual. This approach provides a more equitable boundary between the competing concerns involved here. It recognizes the strength of the legitimate state interest in compensating private individuals for wrongful injury to reputation, yet shields the press and broadcast media from the rigors of liability for defamation. At least this conclusion obtains where, as here, the substance of the defamatory statement "makes substantial danger to reputation apparent." This phrase places in perspective the conclusion we announce today. Our inquiry would involve consideration somewhat different from those discussed above if a State purported to condition civil liability on a factual misstatement whose content did not warn a reasonably prudent editor or broadcaster of its defamatory potential....

Our accommodation of the competing values at stake in defamation suits by private individuals allows the States to impose liability on the publisher or broadcaster of defamatory falsehood on a less demanding showing than that required by *New York Times* .... But this countervailing state interest extends no further than compensation for injury. For the reasons stated below, we hold that the States may not permit recovery of presumed or punitive damages, at least when liability is not based on a showing of knowledge of falsity or reckless disregard for the truth.

... Under the traditional rules pertaining to actions for libel, the existence of injury is presumed from the fact of publication. Juries may award substantial sums as compensation for supposed damage to reputation without any proof that such harm actually occurred. The largely uncontrolled discretion of juries to award damages where there is no loss unnecessarily compounds the potential of any system of liability for defamatory falsehood to inhibit the vigorous exercise of First Amendment freedoms. Additionally, the doctrine of presumed damages invites juries to punish unpopular opinion rather than to compensate individuals for injury sustained by the publication of a false fact. More to the point, the States have no substantial interest in securing for plaintiffs such as this petitioner gratuitous awards of money damages far in excess of any actual injury. . . .

We also find no justification for allowing awards of punitive damages against publishers and broadcasters held liable under state-defined standards of liability for defamation. . . . Notwithstanding our refusal to extend the *New York Times* privilege to defamation of private individuals, respondent contends that we should affirm the judgment below on the ground that petitioner is either a public official or a public figure. . . .

Respondent's characterization of petitioner as a public figure raises a different question. That designation may rest on either of two alternative bases. In some instances an individual may achieve such pervasive fame or notoriety that he becomes a public figure for all purposes, and in all contexts. More commonly, an individual voluntarily injects himself or is drawn into a particular public controversy and thereby becomes a public figure for a limited range of issues. In either case such persons assume special prominence in the resolution of public questions.

Petitioner has long been active in community and professional affairs. He has served as an officer of local civic groups and of various professional organizations, and he has published several books and articles on legal subjects. Although petitioner was consequently well known in some circles, he had achieved no general fame or notoriety in the community. None of the prospective jurors called at the trial had ever heard of petitioner prior to this litigation, and respondent offered no proof that this response was atypical of the local population. We would not lightly assume that a citizen's participation in community and professional affairs rendered him a public figure for all purposes. Absent clear evidence of general fame or notoriety in the community, and pervasive involvement in the affairs of society, an individual should not be deemed a public personality for all aspects of his life. It is preferable to reduce the public-figure question to a more meaningful context by looking to the nature and extent of an individual's participation in the particular controversy giving rise to the defamation.

In this context it is plain that petitioner was a not a public figure. . . .

[Remanded for further proceedings. Concurring and dissenting opinions are omitted.]

NOTES

1. **The *Gertz* fault standard.** For public officials and public figures, the *Times–Sullivan* standard remains applicable after *Gertz*. For plaintiffs who are private persons, the *Gertz* Court held that there was no need to prove knowing or reckless falsehood. The Court did, however, put a Constitutional surcharge on the common law rules for private persons in *Gertz*-like cases: they can only recover if they prove (a) some kind of fault, to be specified by the states under state tort law, and (b) actual damages.

2. **The states' fault standard.** Most states, accepting *Gertz'* invitation to apply any fault standard they chose, fell back on the most familiar word—negligence. Thus liability would be imposed in most states on *Gertz*-type claims if the jury found defendant published "negligently." A few states have decided on a tougher standard and have kept the *Times–Sullivan* standard even for private person cases, or have adopted some other variation, such as "grossly irresponsible," or the professional standards of journalists.

3. **Types of fault.** Is it really possible to carry over the negligence standard to these cases? What kind of conduct and what kind of risks are entailed in the fault required here? The *Gertz* Court almost certainly had in mind fault as to the truth or falsity of the defamatory statements, as for example, fault in failure to investigate unsubstantiated charges. Would a negligence analysis work just as well when the fault, if any, lies in a reporter's perception of fast-moving events? Suppose a reporter writes that the plaintiff was leading demonstrating trespassers at a nuclear power plant, but plaintiff says he was merely out in front watching? What about fault that does not bear on the truth or falsity at all, for example, spite or ill-will? What about fault in writing an ambiguous sentence, in which one meaning is defamatory but the meaning intended is not?

4. **Actual damages.** Suppose the private-person plaintiff proves the defendant was guilty of a knowing or reckless falsehood, so that the test laid down in *Times–Sullivan* is met. Would both presumed and punitive damages then be available?

5. **Public figures under *Gertz*.** After the decisions in *Times–Sullivan* and *Gertz*, one of the central issues has been whether the plaintiff in a libel action is a public figure or whether he is a private person, since this determines the kind of proof required. The common law notion of public figures was rather broad, although not necessarily well defined. *Gertz* limited the concept of public figures quite stringently. Justice Powell seemed to concede that a plaintiff might be "drawn into a particular public controversy and thereby [become] a public figure." But his main emphasis seems to be on the case in which the plaintiff "voluntarily injects himself" into a public issue or has "thrust" himself "to the forefront of particular public controversies." Later cases have emphasized this "thrusting" and also the idea that true public figures have a greater access "to the channels of effective communication." *See, e.g., Hatfill v. New York Times Co.*, 532 F.3d 312 (4th Cir. 2008) (research scientist held to be a public figure); *American Future Systems, Inc. v. Better Business Bureau of Eastern Pennsylvania*, 923 A.2d 389 (Pa. 2007) (telemarketer held to be a public figure); *Cf. O'Connor v. Burningham*, 165 P.3d 1214 (Utah 2007) (public high school basketball coach not a public figure because she lacked authority to make policy about public issues such as life, liberty and property).

6. **Development of public figures.** Some Supreme Court cases have taken these stringent tests of public figurehood to extremes. The Court has held a party to a lawsuit, at least if it is a divorce, is not a public figure for that reason alone, with the result that a publisher who inaccurately states the court's opinion may be denied the *Times–Sullivan* protections. *Time, Inc. v. Firestone*, 424 U.S. 448 (1976). In *Wolston v. Reader's Digest Ass'n, Inc.*, 443

U.S. 157 (1979), the Court held that a person who is charged with and convicted of crime is not a public figure merely for that reason because he did not "voluntarily thrust" himself into a public controversy.

7. **Public officials.** The decision that some public employees are not public figures puts renewed emphasis on the idea of a public official. The Court has long recognized that not every public employee is a public official for *Times–Sullivan* purposes. It has so far not clearly delineated its ideas on this subject, but it has said that an employee is not a public official unless "[t]he employee's position [is] one which would invite public scrutiny and discussion of the person holding it, entirely apart from the scrutiny and discussion occasioned by the particular charges in controversy." *Rosenblatt v. Baer*, 383 U.S. 75 (1966). What if there is evidence that a janitor at the local high school is selling heavy drugs to students? Presumably he would not be an "official" under the *Rosenblatt* test. Presumably also he did not thrust himself into a controversy. Might the Court might find he is a public figure because he is "drawn into" a public controversy?

8. **Publishers and broadcasters.** The common law of defamation used the term "publication" and "publisher" to refer to any communication to someone other than the plaintiff. Justice Powell in *Gertz* repeatedly refers, however, to "publishers and broadcasters," and even to "news media." Does he mean to limit *Gertz* to cases in which a private citizen sues a media publisher? Suppose an employer or the dean of a college writes a letter about an employee or a college student. If there is reason to require both fault and actual damages in media cases, does it apply equally to private publications as well? There are a few cases saying that it does not and that the common law rules apply in full force to the private letter writer.

9. **Truth (redux).** We saw above that *Times–Sullivan* changed the role of truth from an affirmative defense to an element of the plaintiff's prima facie case if the plaintiff is a public figure. In *Philadelphia Newspapers, Inc. v. Hepps*, 475 U.S. 767 (1986), the court held that a *Gertz*-type plaintiff must similarly prove falsity as part of the prima facie case. The Court has not yet decided, however, whether the states could constitutionally presume falsity when the plaintiff is a private person and the subject matter of the publication is of no public concern.

10. **Constitutional protection for "opinion" statements.** "[T]here is no such thing as a false idea." This statement in *Gertz* seemed to create a new limitation on recovery for defamation. The common law denied recovery for mere name-calling, but at least on occasion could impose liability for statements of opinion and even for unkind satire. *Gertz* seemed to commit the Court to the proposition that the defamation must involve a factual misstatement and that it must be reasonably understood as such. Later, in *Hustler Magazine v. Falwell*, 485 U.S. 46 (1988), the defendant published a nasty parody of an ad that used "first time" as its theme. The parody presented Falwell, a famous evangelist, as having his "first time" with his own mother. No one believed that the publisher intended this parody to be taken as a fact and no one did take it as a fact. The Court held that the defendant could not be liable because the plaintiff could not prove that the defendant knowingly or recklessly published a "fact." Two years later, the Court said there was no

separate constitutional protection for "opinion," but reiterated its holdings that liability depended upon statements or at least implications of something "provably false." *Milkovich v. Lorain Journal*, 497 U.S. 1 (1990). What if protestors at an abortion clinic carry signs saying "This clinic murders babies"? *Cf. Horsley v. Rivera*, 292 F.3d 695 (11th Cir. 2002) ("You are an accomplice to homicide" said of anti-abortion activist who maintained a website listing names of abortion doctors, graying out those who had been wounded and x-ing out those who had been killed).

DUN & BRADSTREET, INC. v. GREENMOSS BUILDERS, INC., 472 U.S. 749 (1985). The defendant, Dun & Bradstreet, supplied a confidential credit rating report about the plaintiff to five subscribers. The report was negligently compiled by a reporter who misinterpreted or mistranscribed some court documents. It erroneously stated that plaintiff, which was a business operation, had filed a petition for bankruptcy. The plaintiff feared the report would seriously affect credit or other business affairs. He asked for correction and for the names of the subscribers who had received the report. The defendant gave a correction, but the plaintiff regarded it as inadequate. The defendant refused altogether to give him the names of subscribers. In the trial court, the plaintiff recovered $50,000 presumed compensatory and $300,000 punitive damages, which the Vermont Supreme Court upheld, saying that *Times–Sullivan* had no application to non-media defendants. In the Supreme Court of the United States, *held*, presumed and punitive damages are recoverable in this case without proof of *Times–Sullivan* malice. *Gertz* held that a private individual could obtain only restricted damages from a publisher of a libel that involved a matter of public concern, but did not address the case of a private person libeled on a matter of private concern. In the private-figure/private-concern case, the state's interest in compensation is just as strong as elsewhere, but the First Amendment interest is weak. The speech here is not on a matter of public concern, as determined by "content, form, and context." The interest is of the individual speaker and its specific business audience; no free flow of information is involved, since Dun & Bradstreet prohibited subscribers from passing the information on. The speech is also hardy and unlikely to be deterred by "incidental state regulation," because profit motive is involved.

NOTES

1. *Gertz* seemed to focus on the character of the plaintiff rather than the nature of the issue under discussion as the basis for invoking *Times–Sullivan* or avoiding it. For this reason, *Dun & Bradstreet* was a surprise to many observers.

2. After *Dun & Bradstreet*, the rules to be applied with respect to proof and damages for defamation appear to be a function of at least two variables: First, is the plaintiff a public figure? And second, was the issue under

discussion or the communication involved a matter of public interest? *Dun & Bradstreet* addressed the case in which the answer to both questions was "no," and in that case allowed the plaintiff to recover presumed damages without proof of the knowing or reckless falsehood required by *Times–Sullivan*.

3. *Dun & Bradstreet* involved only the question whether the plaintiff could recover common law "presumed" damages. This means that one of the two main rules in *Gertz* has no application in cases of private person plaintiffs and private concern issues. What is your prediction about the other rule in *Gertz*?

4. The Supreme Court's decisions on defamation are constitutional rules which govern the states. But they only prescribe minimum protections for free speech, meaning that states may provide more protection for speakers and less for victims of defamation. *See Wilkow v. Forbes, Inc.*, 241 F.3d 552 (7th Cir. 2001) (subjective opinion statements protected under Illinois law); *Newberry v. Allied Stores, Inc.*, 773 P.2d 1231 (N.M.1989) (rejecting the new liabilities permitted by *Dun & Bradstreet*).

REFERENCES: DOBBS ON TORTS §§ 417–23 (2000); DAN B. DOBBS & ELLEN M. BUBLICK, ADVANCED TORTS: ECONOMIC AND DIGNITARY TORTS Ch. 3 & 4 (2006).

§ 2.   MALICIOUS PROSECUTION AND OTHER ABUSES OF THE LEGAL SYSTEM

A.   MALICIOUS PROSECUTION

Illustration 1

Max Parrillo owned a socket wrench purchased from Lambert's Hardware. He wished to replace a socket used on the wrench, so he took the wrench and socket to Lambert's store. He went directly to the wrench display where he took his own wrench out of his pocket and made some comparisons. Not finding the right size, he put his wrench in his pocket and walked out of the store. Right outside the store, a store detective employed by Lambert's stopped him and accused him of stealing the wrench. The detective called the police and told the officer that Parrillo had stolen the wrench. Up until this time, the detective had refused to listen to Parrillo's side of the story. The detective told the officer that he had watched Parrillo the whole time and that he had stolen the wrench. Parrillo was prosecuted on the basis of this information, but was found not guilty. He then sued Lambert's Hardware. These facts will justify a recovery of any special damages, such as cost of defending the criminal trial, plus "general" damages and punitive damages.

Illustration 2

Penny Pfennig saw an officer in the act of arresting a friend of Pfennig's, Shirley Schilling. Schilling, it appeared, had been driving while intoxicated. Pfennig stopped her car and walked back to the scene of the arrest. She said: "I don't want to interfere, but this is a friend of mine. Can I help her in any way?" At this point another officer, Rex Stebbins, pulled up and strode aggressively over to the scene. Apparently he assumed that Pfennig was also under arrest; he pushed her back and told her to get on the sidewalk. Pfennig's husband, Thaler, then arrived and protested Stebbins' actions, whereupon Stebbins arrested Pfennig and Thaler for obstructing justice and interfering with an arrest. After they were found not guilty, they sued Stebbins and the city for (a) false arrest and (b) malicious prosecution. They are entitled to recover for false arrest for damages from the time of detention until formal prosecution was begun, and for malicious prosecution for damages arising after prosecution was begun.

The malicious prosecution claim is often compared to a *false imprisonment*, and there is much resemblance. But false imprisonment is a trespassory tort, involving direct physical detention of the person. Prosecution is indirect interference. In the case of false imprisonment, the plaintiff makes a prima facie case by showing an intended detention of which the plaintiff was aware. Any privilege based on the existence of a warrant or probable cause for arrest must be shown affirmatively by the defendant. In the malicious prosecution case, on the other hand, the plaintiff cannot recover unless he affirmatively shows that the accuser lacked probable cause and was also motivated by malice. Damages in the two torts are different, too. The false arrest or imprisonment damages include any damages from the time of detention to the time of prosecution, but no more. Damages for malicious prosecution include any damages occurring after prosecution has begun. Thus in many cases the plaintiff may have both claims, and may need to assert both to collect full damages.

Defamation and malicious prosecution. In some ways, malicious prosecution more closely resembles a defamation claim. All malicious prosecution claims necessarily involve a defamatory communication—an accusation of crime. Under the law of defamation, there is a privilege to report a crime and other facts to responsible officials, so that under the ordinary law of libel there could be no recovery for a good faith report which resulted in prosecution. The law of malicious prosecution is, in a sense, a special case of defamation with special rules. What the common law sought in these rules was a system that would redress genuine grievances of the wrongly-prosecuted plaintiff without discouraging defendants from reporting crimes or suspected crimes. In a very real way, this parallels the *Times–Sullivan* concern to redress injury while avoiding self-censorship.

The common law rule. The common law solution, like that of *Times–Sullivan*, is something of a compromise, and one intended to protect similar values. But the common law solution is structured quite differently from that in *Times–Sullivan*. The common law rule denies the plaintiff any claim unless:

(1) *There is a prosecution.* This is a requirement that the only kind of damage recognized is prosecution itself, and mere report of a crime to an officer is not itself sufficient.

(2) *The defendant in the malicious prosecution suit instigated the prosecution.* Either a private citizen or an officer might instigate the prosecution; indeed, there may be several instigators. The idea is to locate one or more persons who played a significant role in causing prosecution. An honest factual report to an officer, not accompanied by any pressure to prosecute, will ordinarily not be sufficient. On the other hand, it is clear that the store detective in Illustration 1 and the officer in Illustration 2 both are instigators.

(3) *The defendant acted maliciously.* Malice is a specialized term in tort law. It may at times mean spite or ill-will, but is seldom limited to that meaning. Many of the results of cases suggest that any improper purpose will do, and so will abuse of position or authority or denial of ordinary decencies to the accused. Thus in both Illustrations, the defendants refused to hear the plaintiff's side of the story, and considering they acted from positions of power or authority, this may have justified a finding of malice.

(4) *The defendant acted without probable cause.* The false report of a crime is not by itself enough, even if the defendant acts maliciously. The defendant must also have acted without probable cause, that is, without reasonable cause for believing that the plaintiff has committed the crime charged. *See, e.g., Papa John's Intern., Inc. v. McCoy*, 244 S.W.3d 44 (Ky. 2008). Where facts are capable of dispute, the accuser may be under some obligation to check the facts where this is reasonably possible. This is one of the grounds on which the store detective could be found to lack probable cause in Illustration 1.

(5) *The criminal action is terminated in favor of the present plaintiff.* The plaintiff cannot recover for malicious prosecution unless the criminal action against him has terminated and terminated in his favor. Thus he cannot sue for the tort while the criminal action is pending. And he cannot sue after it has terminated if he was convicted. In a third group of cases, the criminal action is terminated by compromise or some other procedure that does not determine guilt or innocence. In many courts this is not considered a termination favorable to the accused.

Defenses. The litigation immunities sketched in connection with defamation claims also apply to malicious prosecution and other torts. Thus the judge and the prosecutor are absolutely immune from malicious prosecution claims, so long as they are acting in their judicial and prosecutorial capacities respectively. The prosecutor who takes on police work, however, risks a loss of the absolute immunity. A second defense is "guilt-in-fact." Even if the accuser lacked probable cause for the accusation and acted with malice, and even if the accused is found not guilty in the criminal trial, the accuser may offer it as a defense in the malicious prosecution action that the plaintiff was in fact guilty. This is analogous to the truth "defense" in libel cases.

Malicious prosecution after Times–Sullivan. Since malicious prosecution involves communication, and invariably reputation as well, it may be regarded as merely a special case of defamation. Would *Times–Sullivan* and *Gertz* apply, then, to restrict liability in these cases? Look back at the common law rule. Does it effectively provide the same protections provided by *Times–Sullivan* and *Gertz*? One element that may give trouble is the "presumed" damages in malicious prosecution cases. These were forbidden under the *Gertz* test.

B. IMPROPER CIVIL LITIGATION

The defendant in malicious prosecution cases has accused the plaintiff of a crime and instigated criminal prosecution. But in "malicious civil prosecution" the defendant has brought a civil action against the person who is now the plaintiff. If it was brought without probable cause, was malicious, and was terminated in favor of the person who is now plaintiff, there may be a cause of action for malicious civil prosecution under that name or under some other descriptive term. The rules in the two actions are much the same. Still, access to courts is a valuable individual right and civil suits often serve social purposes as well by breaking new ground. Consequently, one who complains that he was civilly sued must make a strong showing that the suit was unjustified. In one or two respects some courts have fashioned special limitations on the claim for improper civil litigation.

———

FRIEDMAN v. DOZORC, 312 N.W.2d 585 (Mich. 1981). Attorneys Dozorc and Golden sued Dr. Friedman for medical malpractice on behalf of a client. After the trial judge directed a verdict in the malpractice case for Dr. Friedman, Dr. Friedman sued the attorneys for negligence and malicious civil prosecution The trial judge granted the attorneys' motion for summary judgment, and the appeals court affirmed in part, reversed in part. *Held,* the trial court was correct in granting judgment on all claims. On the negligence claim, lawyers owe a duty of care to their clients, not to the adversaries in litigation. To hold otherwise would be "inconsistent with basic precepts of the adversary system" and create an "unacceptable conflict of interest." On the malicious civil prosecution claim, many American courts follow the rule that "in the absence of an arrest, seizure, or special damage, the successful civil defendant has no remedy, despite the fact that his antagonist proceeded against him maliciously and without probable cause." Even more courts follow the rule permitting such claims without a showing of "special injury." But Michigan follows the "special injury" requirement, and plaintiff here does not allege special injury. "Most commentators appear to favor abrogation of the special injury requirement to make the action more available and less difficult to maintain. Their counsel should, however, be evaluated skeptically. The lawyer's remedy for a grievance is a lawsuit, and a law student or tort professor may be particularly predisposed by experience and training to see the preferred remedy for a wrongful tort action as another tort action. In seeking a remedy for the excessive litigiousness of our society, we would do well to cast off the limitations of a perspective which ascribes curative power only to lawsuits.'' A lawyer who brings a claim to aid his client, even with knowledge that a claim is untenable, "should not be subject to liability on the thesis that an inference of an improper purpose may be drawn" therefrom.

NOTES

1. **The special injury rule.** As the court notes, there is a split in authority on whether proof of special injury is required in an improper civil litigation claim. In states that require it, the plaintiff must show that there was a seizure of property, as where property is attached or subjected to an injunction; or seizure of the person, as where one is civilly committed; or, in some cases, where there was repeated re-litigation of the same claim. The injury that may arise to a doctor's reputation from a malpractice claim is not sufficient.

2. **Physician countersuits.** The *Friedman* case represents a topic of considerable debate. One way to resolve it against the physician is to rely on the special injury rule. See, e.g., *O'Toole v. Franklin*, 569 P.2d 561 (Or. 1977) (retaining the rule in part to avoid chilling access to courts). Most courts, even where the special injury rule has been rejected, have found ways of excluding liability in the suits against lawyers like those in *Friedman* and *O'Toole*.

3. **Rules of ethics and procedure.** Rules of professional responsibility for lawyers provide that it is a disciplinary infraction for a lawyer to bring frivolous claims or make frivolous contentions in litigation. *See* ABA MODEL RULE OF PROFESSIONAL CONDUCT 3.1 (2008). Discipline may be severe. *See, e.g., In re Hawkley*, 92 P.3d 1069 (Idaho 2002) (3-year suspension for filing two frivolous lawsuits). A federal court may sanction a lawyer under Federal Rule of Civil Procedure 11 for filing a paper that is either frivolous or presented for an "improper purpose." *See, e.g., Whitehead v. Food Max of Mississippi, Inc.*, 332 F.3d 796 (5th Cir. 2003). A number of other state and federal statutes and rules provide for similar sanctions. Does the existence of these sanctions lessen the need for a civil cause of action?

C. ABUSE OF PROCESS

Illustration 1

Purtle broke into Dominic's house with felonious intent. Dominic caught him and turned him over to the police, having probable cause to believe he was guilty, which in fact he was. While Purtle was in jail, Dominic visited him. Dominic said "I will drop charges if you will work for one year in my guano factory at minimum wage." Dominic is guilty of an abuse of process.

Illustration 2

Cline, a patient of Dr. Tellman, suffered injury in the course of surgery. Cline consulted a lawyer, Dalmar, who brought suit against Tellman. Dalmar concluded that Dr. Puccinni had nothing to do with the injury suffered by Cline, but that, if sued, Puccinni would testify against Tellman in order to protect himself. For this reason, Dalmar made Puccinni a defendant as well. The jury in the malpractice case brought in a verdict for Puccinni. Dalmar is not guilty of an abuse of process.

Elements of abuse of process. Abuse of process involves misuse of legal process for an ulterior or improper purpose. The defendant may be held liable even if he rightly invoked the process and even if the person against whom it is invoked is in fact guilty of the crime or civilly liable. The reason for this is that the gist of the tort is misuse of the legal system for some personal end. Thus Illustration 1 reflects a typical case in which legal process is properly issued, but the instigator attempts to use it for extortionate purposes. The instigator is thus liable for abuse of process. However, courts have often said that some act, threat or demand must be made *after* process has issued in order to support recovery. Thus the tort is not made out in Illustration 2, since the lawyer there made no demand for favorable testimony from Dr. Puccinni after process was issued. Perhaps not all courts would require this, but a number have done so.

Settlement. Does the abuse of process claim chill the prospects of settling a lawsuit? In the criminal case it is arguable that no one should make any kind of bargain whatever with a person charged with crime. But consider civil cases. A brings an action against B, attaching B's car. While the car is attached, so that B has no means of transport, A offers to settle all claims between the parties, including some that have no bearing on the attached car. He offers to release the car if settlement is accepted. Does this offer run a risk that B will sue for abuse of process?

SLAPP suits. In recent years some environmentally concerned citizens have argued that some developers, whose projects might be opposed by environmentalists and others, have used lawsuits to discourage their opponents, for example, by suing critics for defamation, malicious prosecution, or abuse of process. These suits against critics are said to be Strategic Lawsuits Against Public Participation (SLAPP suits), and some states have enacted laws (anti-SLAPP statutes) to deter them. They have since been applied to a number of situations beyond the developer context. *See, e.g., Taus v. Loftus*, 151 P.3d 1185 (Cal. 2007) (suit brought against author of scholarly articles). These statutes may require the plaintiff to prove before trial or discovery that he will probably win. *See* CAL. CODE CIV. PROC. § 425.16. In effect, it represents a kind of defensive use of the abuse of process idea. Perhaps there is room for caution. The Massachusetts court observed in *Baker v. Parsons,* 750 N.E.2d 953 (Mass. 2001), that in dismissing the plaintiff's complaint before factual development, the statute protects "one party's exercise of its right of petition [but] impinges on the adverse party's exercise of its right to petition." In *Opinion of the Justices (SLAPP Suit Procedure)*, 641 A.2d 1012 (N.H. 1994), the court ruled that a proposed statute unconstitutionally infringed on the right to jury trial.

§ 3. PRIVACY

For many years, courts recognized certain rights that might today be labeled rights of privacy but which were originally protected under some other name. And there are still cases today in which interests in privacy are protected under other theories. For instance, if someone enters your apartment without permission, the law will protect your rights of privacy by imposing liability under a trespass theory. If someone publishes your private papers, the law may offer redress under a theory of copyright or conversion. Recognizing this, "two young Boston lawyers" argued that the law court recognizes a separate tort for any invasion of privacy. In part they were offended by gossip columnists. But they also saw law as a source of protection for the core of human dignity and they wanted a law of privacy to support the individual's self-development and self-conception by guaranteeing privacy. Long before the term "self-image" came into popular use, they wanted to protect the individual's "estimate of himself." Samuel Warren & Louis Brandeis, *The Right to Privacy*, 4 Harv. L. Rev. 193 (1890). Gradually the courts accepted the idea and today privacy claims are recognized in some form everywhere.

A wide variety of claims have been brought as privacy claims, although some of them involve privacy only in the most attenuated sense. For instance, non-physical sexual harassment, obnoxious and harassing debt collection methods, even stalking and threats have been characterized as privacy claims. *E.g., Rumbauskas v. Cantor*, 649 A.2d 853 (N.J. 1994). Prosser, attempting to make sense out of the mass of cases, came up with the proposition that modern cases really involved four distinct torts, all using the name "privacy." William Prosser, *Privacy*, 48 Cal. L. Rev. 383 (1960). Perhaps not all "privacy" cases fit comfortably within these categories, but they remain the chief modes of privacy analysis. They are:

1. *Intrusive invasions.* Short of trespass, one might still intrude in unpermitted ways on solitude, as by using electronic listening devices. What about harassing telephone calls made by one person? Made by telemarketers as a group?

2. *Commercial appropriation.* One might publish the plaintiff's name, face or figure in a commercial advertisement without the plaintiff's permission. This might not libel the plaintiff, but the plaintiff should still control how her face or name is used for commercial purposes.

3. *False light.* The plaintiff might be presented in a false light, again without libel. For example, it might be reported that the plaintiff had emotions which were perfectly commendable, but which the plaintiff did not feel or did not wish revealed; or associated with a political cause that was perfectly uplifting but which the plaintiff did not support.

4. *Public revelation of private facts.* The defendant might publish true statements about the plaintiff on matters utterly private. This would not be libelous even if the facts were derogatory since truth could be shown; but it might still be an invasion of privacy.

This chapter deals solely with false light and private facts cases, both of which involve publication and hence potential free speech issues.

SOLANO v. PLAYGIRL, INC.

292 F.3d 1078 (9th Cir. 2002)

FISHER, CIRCUIT JUDGE.

The January 1999 issue of Playgirl magazine featured a cover photograph of actor Jose Solano, Jr., best known for his role as "Manny Gutierrez" on the syndicated television program "Baywatch" from 1996 to 1999. Solano was shown shirtless and wearing his red lifeguard trunks, the uniform of his "Baywatch" character, under a heading reading: "TV Guys. PRIMETIME'S SEXY YOUNG STARS EXPOSED." Playgirl, ostensibly focused on a female readership, typically contains nude photographs of men in various poses emphasizing their genitalia, including some showing them engaged in simulated sex acts. The magazine also contains written editorial features. Although Solano—who did not pose for or give an interview to Playgirl—did not in fact appear nude in the magazine, he sued Playgirl alleging it deliberately created the false impression that he did so, making it appear he was willing to degrade himself and endorse such a magazine....

As indicated above, Solano appeared bare-chested wearing his red trunks, dominating the cover. In the upper left corner was a red circle containing the words, "TV Guys," followed by the headline, "Primetime's Sexy Young Stars Exposed," which ran across the top of Solano's head. Immediately to the left of Solano's picture, the magazine proclaimed, "12 Sizzling Centerfolds Ready to Score With You." The "s" in "Centerfolds" was superimposed on Solano's right shoulder. Also placed to the left of Solano, running down the left margin, the cover touted "Countdown to Climax: Naughty Ways to Ring in the New Year," "Toyz in the Hood: The Best in Erotic Home Shopping" and "Bottoms Up!: Hot Celebrity Buns." In the cover's lower right hand corner was the headline, "Baywatch's Best Body, Jose Solano."

Solano's sole appearance inside the magazine was on page 21, in a quarter-page, head-and-shoulders photograph—showing him fully dressed in a tee shirt and sweater—alongside a brief, quarter-page profile of the actor.... Significantly, Playgirl issues are displayed on newsstands packaged in plastic wrap to prevent potential customers from flipping through the pages to view the magazine's contents.

[The district court granted summary judgment for Playgirl, and Solano appeals.]

To prevail on this false light claim, Solano must show that: (1) Playgirl disclosed to one or more persons information about or concerning Solano that was presented as factual but that was actually false or created a false impression about him; (2) the information was understood by one or more persons to whom it was disclosed as stating or implying something highly offensive that would have a tendency to injure Solano's reputation; (3) by clear and convincing evidence, Playgirl acted with constitutional malice; and (4) Solano was damaged by the disclosure....

[A] jury reasonably could conclude that the Playgirl cover conveyed the message that Solano was not the wholesome person he claimed to be, that he was willing to—or was "washed up" and had to—sell himself naked to a women's sex magazine.

Although Solano has established a genuine issue as to whether the cover created a false impression, to survive summary judgment he must, as a public figure, also establish by clear and convincing evidence that Playgirl's editors knowingly or recklessly created this false impression.... [Evidence that some editors had been worried about the possible false impression was sufficient to satisfy that requirement. Damages are required but they are sufficiently shown by Solano's testimony that he was embarrassed.]

NOTES

1. **Libel vs. false light privacy invasion.** From *Solano,* can you detect any difference between libel and and false light invasion of privacy?

2. **Restatement § 652E.** Under RESTATEMENT (SECOND) OF TORTS § 652E, the plaintiff has a false light claim when "publicity" places her in a false light that would be "highly offensive" to a reasonable person. Publicity means communication to the public at large, not merely to a few people. The "highly offensive" element is not the same as "defamatory," is it? The Restatement would allow recovery for publicity by way of a fictional presentation of the plaintiff's life, picturing her as having a perfectly legitimate romance she did not have. See *Id.* cmt. *b,* Ill. 5.

3. **Rejecting the false light tort.** Several courts have rejected the false light claim, arguing that it largely or wholly duplicates defamation claims or needlessly raises free speech problems, or both. *See Jews for Jesus, Inc. v. Rapp,* 2008 WL 4659374 (Fla.); *Denver Pub. Co. v. Bueno,* 54 P.3d 893 (Colo. 2002); *Lake v. Wal–Mart Stores, Inc.,* 582 N.W.2d 231 (Minn. 1998). This is also the more or less accidental result in states that only recognize the commercial appropriation version of the tort. On the other hand, *Godbehere v. Phoenix Newspapers, Inc.,* 783 P.2d 781 (Ariz. 1989) defended the tort as filling a gap not covered by defamation law.

4. **Constitutional limits.** *Solano* reflects constitutional limitations on the tort—a requirement of knowing or reckless falsehood in the case of public officials and public figures. In *Time v. Hill*, 385 U.S. 374 (1967), the Supreme Court applied the knowing or reckless falsehood test even to a *private person plaintiff* suing for false light, but that was before it had decided *Gertz* and presumably the "some fault" standard would now apply. Would you expect "opinion" statement to receive the same constitutional protection as in libel cases? See *Veilleux v. National Broadcasting Co.*, 206 F.3d 92 (1st Cir. 2000).

THE FLORIDA STAR v. B.J.F., 491 U.S. 524 (1989). The plaintiff was a rape victim. A Florida statute makes it unlawful to publish the name of any victim of a sexual offense. A reporter-trainee for the defendant was sent to the police press room to compile material for the paper's "Police Reports" section. He copied the rape report verbatim. The resulting "Police Reports" notation under the heading of "Robberies" reported the rape, the plaintiff's name, and the location. This violated internal policy of the paper as well as Florida law. The plaintiff suffered emotional distress not only from hearing about it from fellow workers but in receiving threatening phone calls. *Held*, to impose liability would violate the First Amendment. In *Cox Broadcasting Corp. v. Cohn*, 420 U.S. 469 (1975), the publisher took the victim's name from court records open to the public. "Significantly, one of the reasons we gave in *Cox Broadcasting* for invalidating the challenged damages award was the important role the press plays in subjecting trials to public scrutiny and thereby helping guarantee their fairness. That role is not directly compromised where, as here, the information in question comes from a police report prepared and disseminated at a time at which not only had no adversarial criminal proceedings begun, but no suspect had been identified. Nor need we accept appellant's invitation to hold broadly that truthful publication may never be punished consistent with the First Amendment." However, where the publisher "lawfully obtains truthful information about a matter of public significance then state officials may not constitutionally punish publication of the information, absent a need to further a state interest of the highest order." That need has not been demonstrated here given the government's power to prevent access to the information in the first place and its failure to prohibit dissemination of the information except by mass media.

R_EFERENCE: D_OBBS ON T_ORTS §§ 424–28 (2000).

§ 4. INTERFERENCE WITH FAMILY RELATIONSHIPS

In an early period of the common law, a master could have a real interest in his servant's health. If the servant were injured, the master might be obliged to continue support of the servant, but without getting the work he expected in return. It is not surprising, then, that the common law gave the master a tort action against anyone who beat and injured the servant. It later came to be thought that the husband stood in a similar relationship to his wife. Consequently, anyone who tortiously injured a wife was subject to tort liability to her husband, and it is true even today that either spouse may have a consortium claim for the injury to the other.

These earlier lines of cases were expanded to permit three other recoveries by the husband, and then later by the wife:

1. *Abduction.* Defendant carried one spouse away from the other, or "harbored" a spouse who wished to escape the marital bonds. Abduction of children, especially by former spouses, is a major problem, but is outside the scope of this chapter on communicative torts.

2. *Criminal conversation.* Defendant had sexual relations ("conversation") with the plaintiff's spouse. Even if this did not disrupt the marriage or cause other harm, it was regarded as a dishonor to the non-participating spouse. Consent of the participating spouse was no defense.

3. *Alienation of affections.* The defendant secured the affection of the plaintiff's spouse, or at least alienated those affections from the plaintiff. This might or might not be accompanied by sexual attentions; sometimes friends or relations simply persuaded one spouse to leave the other.

These torts required affirmative action by the defendant, and that the act caused harm, though not necessarily financial harm. The only fault required was an intent to interfere in the prohibited way. For example, if a defendant intended to persuade the wife to leave her husband, the defendant would be liable for alienation if he succeeded, unless he could affirmatively prove a privilege. The main privilege was a good faith effort by a relative or disinterested party to persuade the wife to leave her husband for her own good, which in some cases also protected religious advisors. Love and affection were not entitled to any similar protection, however, and the woman who persuaded a man to leave his wife, or the man who induced a woman to leave her husband, would be liable for alienation or criminal conversation, or both.

If parents sued for interference with their relationships with their children, the rights were substantially constricted. One would be liable for enticement of a child, or abduction, or seduction of a minor, but there is scant authority for permitting a claim for alienating the child's affections. A few states allow a cause of action for tortious interference with a parental or custodial relationship, *see Kessel v. Leavitt*, 511 S.E.2d 720 (W.Va. 1998), or interference with child custody and visitation rights, *see Khalifa v. Shannon*, 945 A.2d 1244 (Md. 2008). Children have been given almost no rights when an outsider interferes with parental relationships. If one parent is induced to leave the home and run off with a "home-wrecker," the children may have claims in only a couple of states.

Since the 1930s, about half the states have abolished or severely limited the action for alienation of affections, or for criminal conversation, or both. Sometimes this is accompanied by abolishing the action for breach of a promise to marry as well. Abolition has been accompanied in many instances through legislation, but in some cases courts themselves have abolished the action, and some jurisdictions have never recognized it. Some of the reasons have been that the action leads to blackmail, that interference without violence or other tortious activity probably has little effect on a healthy family relationship, and that recovery in these actions does not accomplish any real good. In addition, it has been suggested that the criminal conversation and alienation of affections actions imply that one spouse has ownership rights in another, and that they interfere with personal autonomy. See Dan B. Dobbs, *Tortious Interference with Contractual Relationships,* 34 ARK. L. REV. 335, 358–59 (1980).

However, in a few states, the alienation of affection action or the criminal conversation action or both are alive and kicking. *See, e.g., Nunn v. Allen,* 574 S.E.2d 35 (N.C. Ct. App. 2002); *see also* William R. Corbett, *A Somewhat Modest Proposal to Prevent Adultery and Save Families: Two Old Torts Looking for a New Career,* 33 ARIZ. ST. L.J. 985 (2001) (supporting a kind of criminal conversation liability to "prevent adultery and save families").

Are there free speech (or privacy) arguments for abolishing liability based on love or sex between two consenting and competent parties? Suppose defendant says, "I love you; leave your wife and come live with me." Given *Times–Sullivan* and *Gertz,* are the states free to make this a tort? For that matter, isn't it invasion of privacy by the state?

Even after abolition of the alienation of affections tort, some kind of tort claims may still be viable in extreme cases, as where the marriage counselor takes advantage of the therapeutic relationship to alienate the affections of one spouse.

REFERENCE: DOBBS ON TORTS §§ 441–44 (2000).

CHAPTER 33

COMMUNICATION OF COMMERCIALLY HARMFUL IMPRESSIONS TO OTHERS

■ ■ ■

In Chapter 32, all of the torts involved communication of facts or impressions about the plaintiff to some other person or persons. In each of these cases, the harm caused might have been partly economic. One who is libeled or maliciously prosecuted, for example, might lose a job. However, the torts involved in that chapter have also involved intensely personal elements, mainly reputation and privacy. No matter how much economic harm is done in those cases, the tort cannot fail to reach a highly personal level. They are, preeminently, dignitary torts.

In the present chapter the torts involved also turn on communication to third persons, but in contrast they are preeminently commercial. Some of them at times touch highly personal or dignitary interests as well; but by and large they are important as means of gaining or preserving some commercial value. They also at times raise questions about political and social values. Since they are communicative torts, there is at least the possibility that First Amendment values will be implicated.

§ 1. INJURIOUS FALSEHOOD

BRUNSON COMMUNICATIONS, INC. v. ARBITRON, INC.

266 F. Supp. 2d 377 (E.D. Pa. 2003)

BAYLSON, JUDGE. . . .

[The plaintiff alleged: The plaintiff owned a small independent television station. Defendant purported to measure the number of viewers watching each television station in the market area at any given time and purported to measure the entire market, but in fact did not measure the viewers watching the plaintiff's station. This led to biased or erroneous information. Defendant published this erroneous information about the number of viewers to "advertising agencies, advertisers, television stations and other media sources, representing that the data were complete and accurate." Defendant moved to dismiss. That motion is before the court.]

919

In its commercial disparagement count, Plaintiff asserts that Defendant's false statements as to the accuracy and completeness of its test surveys caused substantial pecuniary loss to Plaintiff, in that prospective advertisers would conclude from the data that WGTW's viewership was "so insignificant as not to warrant either inclusion in the survey or recognition of the exclusion, as was foreseen by the defendant."....

The Court of Appeals for the Third Circuit has recently predicted that the Pennsylvania Supreme Court would adopt a Restatement of Torts section regarding commercial disparagement. That Restatement section, § 623A, provides that:

> One who *publishes a false statement harmful to the interests of another* is subject to liability for *pecuniary loss* resulting to the other if

> (a) he *intends* for publication of the statement to result in harm to interests of the other having a pecuniary value, *or* either recognizes or should *recognize that it is likely* to do so, *and*

> (b) he *knows* that the statement is *false* or acts in *reckless disregard* of its truth or falsity.

Restatement (Second) of Torts § 623(A) (1977) (emphasis added)....

Thus, to sustain its cause of action for commercial disparagement, Plaintiff must allege, 1.) that Defendant made a false statement, which caused pecuniary loss to Plaintiff, 2.) that Defendant intended for publication of the statement to result in harm to Plaintiff's pecuniary interests, or either recognized or should have recognized that it was likely to do so, and 3.) that Defendant knew that the statement was false or acted in reckless disregard of its truth or falsity....

Under notice pleading, these allegations fulfill the requirement of a "false statement," the requirement that Defendant should have recognized the potential harm the statement could cause, and the requirement that Defendant knew the statement was false or acted in reckless disregard of its truth or falsity. Although Plaintiff does not allege that Defendant made any statements *directly referring to WGTW,* this Court concludes that Plaintiff has made out a disparagement case strong enough to withstand the present motion to dismiss. While Defendant may not have expressly mentioned WGTW in any of its statements, Plaintiff may, nevertheless, be able to prove that the total effect of Defendant's various statements and actions was to disparage Plaintiff's business—and to reduce WGTW's standing in the eyes of the persons and companies it must solicit to buy the station's product.

However, as noted above, Plaintiff has not specifically identified a pecuniary loss resulting from the allegedly false statements. Rule 9(g) provides that "[w]hen items of special damage are claimed, they shall be specifically stated." This Court has previously held that, to successfully plead a cause of action for disparagement, a plaintiff must allege facts showing an established business, the amount of sales for a substantial period preceding publication, and amount of sales subsequent to the publication, facts showing that such loss in sale were the natural and probable result of such publication, and the facts showing the plaintiff could not allege the name of particular customers who withdrew or withheld their custom....

In the case at bar, Plaintiff does not allege a general decline in business, much less a specific type of pecuniary loss. However, because the allegedly disparaging statements were made approximately one year ago, Plaintiff should now be able to readily determine and specifically allege the type and extent of its economic damages. *See* Plaintiff's Motion for Leave to Amend at ¶ 4 (suggesting that "now that a year has passed," Plaintiff may be able to "quantitatively assess the actual damage"). Therefore, this Court will dismiss Plaintiff's commercial disparagement claim without prejudice to Plaintiff's right to file a Third Amended Complaint within twenty days, alleging facts showing specific types and amounts of damages, such as alleging the amount of sales for a substantial period preceding Defendant's statements, and the amount of sales subsequent to Defendant's statements, and also alleging specific facts showing that such losses in sales were the natural and probable result of Defendant's statements....

[As to the plaintiff's claim of negligence:] This Court cannot conclude that Defendant owed a legal duty of care to Plaintiff under the circumstances set forth in the Second Amended Complaint. While Plaintiff has cited numerous Pennsylvania negligence cases in its brief, not one of the cases cited establishes the formation of a duty based upon the type of business activity involved in this case.

NOTES

1. **Injurious falsehood defined.** Commercial disparagement is a form of the tort the Restatement (Second) of Torts calls injurious falsehood. Another tort within the "injurious falsehood" umbrella is slander of title, in which the defendant falsely casts aspersions on plaintiff's ownership of real or personal property. Slander of title requires plaintiff to prove (1) some interest in the property, (2) that the words published were false, (3) that the words were published with malice, and (4) that the plaintiff suffered pecuniary loss or injury as a result of the false statement. *See, e.g., Jeffrey v. Cathers*, 104 S.W.3d 424 (Mo. Ct. App. 2003).

2. **Connection to defamation.** The torts in the injurious falsehood family involve assertions that disparage the plaintiff's title or ownership rights (in the case of slander of title) or the plaintiff's product, (in the case of commercial disparagement) but do not qualify as ordinary libel or slander. Some courts allow a defamation case based on statements that disparage a plaintiff's business, *see, e.g., Senna v. Florimont*, 958 A.2d 427 (N.J. 2008), but it is not personally libelous to print that the plaintiff does not own Blackacre or that his product is not so good. Notice that the rules for the

injurious falsehood tort demand proof that is far more demanding than required by common law libel rules. In fact, don't the rules come close to requiring the same proof that would be required in a libel suit by a public figure?

3. **Statutory actions.** The common law tort of injurious falsehood is generally if not universally recognized by the courts, but injurious falsehood or commercial disparagement may also count as a statutory tort under state unfair competition or deceptive trade practices acts. In addition, the plaintiff in such cases may have a cause of action under the now expanded version of the federal trademark legislation, § 43(a) of the Lanham Act, 15 U.S.C. § 1125(a). The statutory actions might carry certain advantages or disadvantages—federal jurisdiction in some cases, perhaps a right to recover attorney fees if the plaintiff prevails.

§ 2. INTENTIONAL INTERFERENCE WITH CONTRACT AND OTHER ECONOMIC VALUES

A. PRIMA FACIE LIABILITY FOR INTERFERENCE

LUMLEY v. GYE, 2 El. & Bl. 216, 118 Eng. Rep. 749 (1853). The plaintiff operated an opera theater. He had retained a singer, Wagner, to perform exclusively at his theater. Before the term of her contract was up, the defendant, knowing of the contract, "enticed" or induced Wagner to cease further performance for the plaintiff and to perform at the defendant's theater instead, to the plaintiff's damage. The plaintiff sued the defendant claiming that inducing a breach of contract was a tort. *Held*, for the plaintiff. Erle, J.: "[P]rocurement of the violation of the right is a cause of action...."

NOTES

1. **The basis of liability.** *Lumley* made inducing breach of contract, by itself, a tort. The defendant is liable if he intends to interfere with a known contract, even if he uses no wrongful means. The defendant might be able to justify his actions, but that would come in as a defense if it comes in at all, and the burden would be on the defendant to persuade judges and juries that his conduct was truly justified.

2. **Inducing and other forms of interference.** *Lumley* involved only inducing breach, but today other forms of intentional interference with contract are also actionable. This can occur in many ways. One example: Employees of the Pershing Company validly contract to continue work for Pershing for one year and not to work for a competitor during that year. Eloise Empson leaves Pershing after one month and goes to work for the Damich Company. Two weeks later, Damich learns that Empson is breaching her non-competition covenant but Damich continues to employ her. Damich has not induced a breach but nevertheless has intentionally interfered with the contract and is liable to Pershing. *Fowler v. Printers II, Inc.*, 598 A.2d 794 (Md. Ct. Spec. App.1991).

3. **Negligent interference with contract.** Intentional interference is normally required to state a claim for interference with contract; negligence is not enough. *See, e.g., Telemundo Network Group, LLC v. Azteca Int'l Corp.*, 957 So.2d 705 (Fla. Dist. Ct. App. 2007). However, there are certain cases in which negligence will suffice. For example, suppose that A contracts with B to keep B's private road in good repair. D negligently crashes an oil truck into a tree nearby, there is an explosion and the road is heavily damaged. As a result, A must spend additional money in keeping her contract to repair. A has a claim against D. This pattern of cases is equivalent to the subrogation pattern in which A insures B's car. When D negligently damages B's car, A pays and is then "subrogated" to B's rights against D. The damages claimed are the same damages that could have been claimed by someone even if there was no contract at all. In these cases, then, to permit A's claim is merely to say that A, rather than B, is the plaintiff. Hence if negligence would warrant a claim by B, it would equally warrant substituting A as the plaintiff. Several cases, however, have gone beyond this pattern and have ostensibly allowed recovery for negligent interference with contract. *J'Aire Corp. v. Gregory*, 598 P.2d 60 (Cal. 1979) is such a case, although it might have been explained on a contract theory with the plaintiff a third party beneficiary. The plaintiff in *J'Aire* operated a restaurant in an airport. Defendant contracted with the airport for a reasonably expeditious improvement. Operation of the restaurant was impossible while the work was being done and the defendant negligently delayed completing the work, to the restaurant's loss. This was held actionable. A few other cases involving close relationships among landowners, construction contracts, and architects or engineers also allow recovery for negligent interference with contract.

4. **Independent torts causing interference; distinguishing the fact of interference from the tort of interference.** The striking characteristic about interference with contract is that the defendant may be liable without doing anything wrong besides making a business deal. But some interference with contract occurs through the commission of particular torts. For example, if A contracts to sell a supply of vaccine to B for distribution, the defendant might steal the vaccines so that A could not perform his contract with B. Or the defendant might libel B, representing that he represents a terrorist group or foreign power which will misuse the vaccines. When the defendant interferes with contract by converting the goods involved or libeling the promisee, we describe the facts by saying he interfered with the contract. Yet we usually think that the tort involved is conversion or libel, not *the tort* of interference with contract. In those cases, we ordinarily expect that the rules applied are the rules of conversion or libel, although damages may include the loss of the contract.

5. **Interference by disparagement.** But wait. If the defendant in *Lumley* merely offered the singer a better contract, the defendant is liable, period. The plaintiff need not prove fraud, or libel, or any other wrongdoing. Suppose, however, that the defendant in *Lumley* induced Miss Wagner to breach her contract with plaintiff by telling her that the plaintiff's opera house was losing money and might cease to exist, or that its productions were generally of low quality. That sounds like disparagement. We know that for injurious falsehoods the plaintiff must prove knowing or reckless falsity and

pecuniary damages. Would these disparagement rules apply in such a case, or could the plaintiff simply ignore disparagement and claim the interference with contract tort? If the answer is that we can ignore the stringent rules of disparagement, then isn't that tort obsolete? If the answer is that the plaintiff must prove knowing falsity, isn't it strange or even irrational to say that if the defendant merely persuades a contracting party to breach he is automatically liable but that if he does so by disparagement he can shield himself with the rules requiring knowing or reckless falsity? Is it possible that it was a mistake to recognize interference with contract as a tort?

ALYESKA PIPELINE SERVICE
v. AURORA AIR SERVICE

604 P.2d 1090 (Alaska 1979)

CONNOR, JUSTICE.

[Alyeska, involved in the Alaska oil pipeline, contracted with RCA to provide a communications system along the line. RCA was required to use an aircraft as part of its bargain. RCA contracted with Aurora to provide a plane, pilot, parts and services along part of the pipeline, and provided that this could be terminated at RCA's option. RCA's contract with Alyeska could, in turn, also be terminated at Alyeska's option. Services began under the RCA–Alyeska contract and Aurora began providing flight services as prescribed under the RCA–Aurora contract. However, Alyeska and Aurora had a dispute about payment under an earlier arrangement, and Alyeska then exercised its option under the RCA contract to take over the flight services itself. This resulted in RCA's termination of Aurora under the RCA–Aurora contract. Aurora then brought this action against Alyeska, alleging that Alyeska induced breach of contract by terminating RCA. The trial court denied Alyeska's motion for summary judgment, holding that although Alyeska was entitled under its contract with RCA to terminate RCA (and hence, indirectly to terminate Aurora), it would be liable if it did so in bad faith. It submitted this question to the jury which found for Aurora in the sum of $362,901.]

The unilateral right to modify the Alyeska–RCA contract, accepting the superior court's ruling that there was no ambiguity in regard to the interpretation of "work," was vested in Alyeska, but it had to be exercised in good faith. We reject Alyeska's contention that a privilege arising from a contractual right is absolute and may be exercised regardless of motive. It is a recognized principle that a party to a contract has a cause of action against a third party who intentionally procured the breach of that contract by the other party without justification or privilege. The weight of recent authority holds that even though a contract is terminable at will, a claim of unjustifiable interference can still be made, for "[t]he wrong for which the courts may give redress includes also the procurement of the termination of a contract which otherwise would have [been] continued in effect." . . .

Alternatively, Alyeska asserts that its overriding economic and safety interests constituted a sufficient privilege to require dismissal of Aurora's action as a matter of law. One is privileged to invade the contractual interest of himself, others, or the public, if the interest advanced by him is superior in social importance to the interest invaded. However, if one does not act in a good faith attempt to protect his own interest or that of another but, rather, is motivated by a desire to injure the contract party, he forfeits the immunity afforded by the privilege.

The question of justification for invading the contractual interest of another is normally one for the trier of fact, particularly when the evidence is in conflict.

In the case at bar, the central factual issue, as to which there was evidentiary conflict, was whether Alyeska was genuinely furthering its own economic and safety interests or was using them as a facade for inflicting injury upon Aurora. There was sufficient evidence upon which the jury could properly find that Alyeska was acting out of ill will towards Aurora, rather than to protect a legitimate business interest.[5] The trial judge correctly denied Alyeska's motion for summary judgment and submitted this issue to the jury....

Alyeska next claims that it was error not to give its proposed Instruction No. 10, which stated:

> "[P]laintiff has the burden of proving by a preponderance of the evidence that defendants actions were malicious and committed with the sole intent of injuring plaintiff."

Alyeska argues that Aurora's evidence of the termination of its contract, intentionally procured, made out a prima facie case, that the burden of proof shifted to Alyeska to show justification, and that Alyeska satisfied that requirement by producing evidence of its contract with RCA and its primary interest in the performance of the RCA contract. It is urged that if, in spite of such evidence, the good faith of Alyeska was still a valid issue, the burden of proving Alyeska's lack of good faith should have shifted back to Aurora.

Alyeska supports this argument by reference to the commentary accompanying a recent redraft of the Restatement of Torts (Second) § 767 Comment k at 37–38, in which the drafters note that the rule on allocating the burden of proof is in an unsettled state. The drafters of the commentary leave that question open. However, in *Long v. Newby*, 488 P.2d 719, 722 (Alaska 1971), we laid down the general rule that when a prima facie case is made out by showing that a breach was intentionally procured, it is incumbent upon the defendant to show justification.

Alyeska argues that the case at bar presents a special fact pattern, that Alyeska had the right to change the Alyeska–RCA contract, and that

---

5. Alyeska maintains that its primary consideration in taking over the air transportation was safety. Aurora presented evidence that its safety record was far better than that of the Alyeska contracted aircraft that replaced it.

the burden of showing further that Alyeska acted in bad faith or with malice should be part of plaintiff's case. We are not persuaded. The issue presented here was whether Alyeska really did exercise its rights in good faith or whether it acted from an ulterior motive. We think that such proof goes to the question of justification, and that it was not part of Aurora's prima facie case, which only requires a showing that a breach was intentionally procured. Nor do we think that Alyeska has submitted sufficient proof of justification to trigger another shifting of the burden of proof and to require Aurora to rebut such evidence. There may be exceptional situations in which such a treble shifting of burdens should occur, but we do not view this case as one of them. On this point there was no error.

[The court found an error in computing damages and reversed as to permit a correction. Otherwise the lower court opinion was affirmed.]

NOTES

1. **Expansion to permit recovery for interference with economic opportunities, business relationships or prospective advantage.** *Alyeska* reflects the generally accepted expansion of liability to cover not only interference with enforceable contract but other reasonably strong economic expectations. Although the defendant who interferes with economic opportunities may have a broader range of privileges—he is free to compete for business, for example, and to offer better prices in doing so—the tort is still a prima facie tort. *See, e.g., Siegel v. Ridgewells, Inc.*, 511 F.Supp.2d 188 (D.D.C. 2007). Once an intentional interference with prospective business opportunity is shown, the defendant is prima facie liable and the burden under traditional rules is on the defendant to justify his interference.

2. **Conduct vs. motive.** Notice that Alyeska's conduct as distinct from motives you might attribute to its corporate mind, was perfectly legal and appropriate; if safety was a reasonable concern, Alyeska's action was also socially desirable. *See* Harvey Perlman, *Interference with Contract and Other Economic Expectancies: A Clash of Tort and Contract Doctrine*, 49 U. CHI. L. REV. 61 (1982); Dan B. Dobbs, *Tortious Interference with Contractual Relationships*, 34 ARK. L. REV. 335 (1980).

3. **Damages in contract and tort.** Aurora could not have recovered against RCA at all, since RCA, having a privilege to terminate, was not in breach. In most interference cases, the contract promisor, however, has itself breached the contract. The plaintiff may recover either on contract against his promisor or in tort. Should the damages be the same? There are cases permitting recovery in the tort claim that would not be permitted in the contract claim-punitive damages and mental distress damages, for example. *See, e.g., Mooney v. Johnson Cattle Co., Inc.*, 634 P.2d 1333 (Or. 1981).

B. TRADITIONAL PRIVILEGES AND CHANGING RULES

1. *Two identifiable privileges.* Under the traditional rules, defendant would be liable both for intentional interference with contract and intentional interference with economic prospects, but in either case might

defeat liability by showing a privilege or justification for the interference. Two privileges are fairly well-defined. These are (1) the privilege to interfere with a promise to marry and (2) the privilege to interfere with economic expectancies (but not actual contracts) by competing for business. On the latter, suppose that another air service company, competing with Aurora, had approached RCA and persuaded RCA to exercise its contractual option to terminate Aurora in the hope of getting RCA's business for itself. Since the competitor was only using words and was not communicating falsehoods, wouldn't he enjoy protection of the common law privilege and maybe the First Amendment as well?

2. *Good motive and other uncertain privileges.* Otherwise the domain of privilege was an uncharted sea, or maybe just an uncharted bond. RESTATEMENT (SECOND) OF TORTS § 767 (1979) advises courts to consider the defendant's conduct and motive, the interests of the parties, and the social interests in protecting the defendant's actions. The implication is that a consumer advocate who interferes with a consumer's contract to purchase a refrigerator for an outrageous price, if he acts with a disinterested motive, might not be liable to the seller who is deprived of his unfair sale, and that other "good" but undescribed motives might similarly be protected.

3. *Mixed motive.* Motive has been particularly important when the defendant interferes with prospects rather than contracts, as in *Alyeska*. The interference torts are among the very few that turn on motive for an intentional act rather than upon an intent to act in a described way. Is this desirable? What is to be done about mixed motives, one good and one the court thinks is "bad"? Specifically, consider what the jury should be told to do in *Alyeska*, if Alyeska had a genuine motive to provide more safety and also a motive to retaliate against Aurora? If Alyeska had both motives, and the safety motive was strong enough standing alone to induce its termination, should it be liable merely because it was even more motivated by malice? *See Mt. Healthy City Sch. Dist. Bd. of Educ. v. Doyle*, 429 U.S. 274 (1977).

4. *Putting the burden on the plaintiff.* What about requiring the plaintiff to establish wrongdoing in the first place instead of putting the burden on the defendant to justify his conduct? If you would go that far, would you also require the plaintiff to establish wrongful means of interference, or would you be content to allow recovery solely because of the defendant's "bad" motive?

———————

WAL–MART STORES, INC. v. STURGES, 52 S.W.3d 711 (Tex. 2001). Wal–Mart owned a store on parcel 1 and had the right to reject any modification of a site plan on the adjoining land, parcel 2. That plan limited the size of any building to 36,000 square feet. Hearing that Fleming Foods wanted a store in the area, the plaintiff obtained an option to purchase parcel 2, then a tentative commitment from Fleming to lease it. But Fleming wanted 51,000 square feet. Wal–Mart, wishing to expand its store, refused to consent to the change in the site plan and told Fleming that if Wal–Mart could not expand into parcel 2, Wal–Mart would move. That was indeed Wal–Mart's policy—expand by preference but move to a larger store if necessary. Fleming, needing Wal–Mart, had no interest in moving to that location if Wal–Mart moved. Fleming therefore cancelled its tentative agreement with the plaintiff. The plaintiff sued Wal–Mart for interference with prospects. *Held,* (1) Interference with prospects is a radically different tort from interference with contract. (2) "[L]awful conduct is not made tortious by the actor's ill will towards another, nor does an actor's lack of ill will make his tortious conduct any less so." (3) "The concepts of malice, justification, and privilege have not only proved to be overlapping and confusing, they provide no meaningful description of culpable conduct" required. (4) Hence, the interference with prospects claim cannot be maintained unless the plaintiff proves that the defendant was guilty of independently tortious conduct such as fraud or defamation addressed to a third person that leads the third person to cease doing business with the plaintiff. Such conduct need not necessarily be actionable by the third person; for example, the third person might not rely upon the fraud. However, the independently tortious conduct is not ground for an interference with prospects claim if that conduct was privileged.

Notes

1. **Wrongfulness.** Several recent cases require the plaintiff to prove that the defendant's interference was wrongful in some sense, although they do not necessarily require an independent tort. *See, e.g., Mason v. Wal–Mart Stores, Inc.,* 969 S.W.2d 160 (Ark. 1998); *Della Penna v. Toyota Motor Sales, U.S.A., Inc.,* 902 P.2d 740 (Cal. 1995).

2. **Boycotts.** One form of interference with contract or prospective advantages is the boycott, which is a refusal to deal. Apart from statutes, such as anti-discrimination statutes, any one individual may refuse to deal with any other for any reason whatever. When the individual organizes others or calls upon them to join in this refusal, it is a boycott and analysis becomes more complicated. For example, some boycotting activity, in which people may make speeches and picket in order to make others aware of their grievances, is constitutionally protected. See *NAACP v. Claiborne Hardware Co.,* 458 U.S. 886 (1982) (business boycotts by NAACP).

3. **Anti-competitive boycotts.** Some boycotts are illegal because of serious anti-competitive elements in them. Suppose T, who controls the entire supply of a rock star's new recording, agrees with retailers A, B, and C that the recording will not be sold to retailer D. D, unable to obtain this popular recording, may be unable to compete, not only in this item, but on others. This kind of boycott, which usually involves a combination of several actors, will very likely be found to violate federal and state antitrust laws. Frequently a complaint in cases of this kind may contain both a claim for antitrust violations and also a common law claim for interference with contract.

4. **Secondary boycotts.** Suppose T has a dispute with B. T, seeking to induce B to discharge certain employees of B, tells B "I won't buy your products until you fire those people." If B agrees, the discharged employees might have a claim for interference with contract on prospects. Suppose, however, T goes further and tells A: "You must also pressure B to discharge the employees, and if you do not do so, I will also quit buying *your* product." This is called secondary boycott. It draws A into a dispute in which he has no part and holds him hostage for B's good behavior. These boycotts are almost always condemned for this reason. If B loses business because of this kind of boycott, B would have a claim. Conceivably A might also have a claim.

5. **Labor boycotts.** Strikes by labor organizations were once considered illegal because they were interferences with contract or with business relations. The union calling a strike was inducing employees not to continue work and it was liable in tort. Over a very long period of time this has been changed by federal statute. Although certain strikes involving secondary boycotts are impermissible under federal law, most others are entirely legal. And to a very large extent federal law has preempted the field of labor organizations. This topic is thus a part of advanced courses in labor law.

6. **Free speech and interference with business claims.** If the defendant's only "wrong" is to offer the singer a better contract, shouldn't the defendant be protected by First Amendment free speech rights? *See* David A. Anderson, *Torts, Speech, and Contracts*, 75 TEX. L. REV. 1499 (1997); Dan B. Dobbs, *Tortious Interference with Contractual Relationships*, 34 ARK. L. REV. 335 (1980). Should First Amendment protection be afforded for all interferences based on words used rather than conduct that is tortious by some independent standard?

REFERENCE: DOBBS ON TORTS §§ 445–55 (2000).

§ 3. INTELLECTUAL PROPERTY AND UNFAIR COMPETITION—TRADEMARK INFRINGEMENT

NOTE: INTELLECTUAL PROPERTY AND UNFAIR COMPETITION

1. *What is intellectual property?* Intellectual property includes rights in intangibles such as (a) patents, (b) copyrights, (c) marks (such as trademarks) that identify a business or goods it sells, and (d) trade secrets. Personality of "identity" of performers might be included, but we deal with that in the next section. The term "unfair competition," long identified especially with one person's misuse of another's trademark or misappropriation of some intangible commercial value, is now often used to refer to almost any form of competitive misconduct. Each of the fields of intellectual property is large in itself and supports large books and many lawyer specialists. We sketch a few high points, mainly about trademarks and unfair competition.

2. *Patents.* This chapter concerns commercial communications, but we mention patents briefly as one kind of intellectual property. Only the federal government can grant a patent, which is a monopoly for a limited

period of time, meant to encourage inventions. You can have a valid patent for inventing a machine (or even a part or a process) that is novel and inventive and not an extension of prior "art," but only if the knowledge is not already in the public domain. Besides all this, you have to reveal quite precisely all the knowledge necessary to make the machine, which goes on file open to the public at the Patent and Trademark Office (a federal agency). The point is to encourage invention by giving the inventor a monopoly, but only for the ultimate purpose of getting the knowledge into the public domain. So your patent will expire in 17 years and after that anyone can use the knowledge to make the machine and even go into competition against you. States cannot offer more protection by making it a tort to copy the useful features of an unpatented article or one in which the patent has expired. All this is explored in *Bonito Boats, Inc. v. Thunder Craft Boats, Inc.,* 489 U.S. 141 (1989). Although the mechanical invention is the prototype or fundamental model for patent, today's patent law now affords the patent monopoly to some surprising other items, such as genes and gene sequences that are by no means invented but have been discovered by scientists.

3. *Copyrights.* Copyright protection is also exclusively federal. If you are the "author" of any original work of tangible expression you are entitled to copyright protection. "Author," includes any creator, such as composers, painters, and photographers. Filing copies with the Library of Congress and filling out a form will enhance your protection but is not necessarily required. The copyright monopoly is now for a very long period—life of the author plus 70 years. You can have a copyright even if your work is not creative; it must be original in the sense that it originated with you and in the sense that it is something more than a mere alphabetical list like a telephone book. Since copyright law gives a monopoly over expression, doesn't that impair free speech rights? There are two free speech protections for free speech. First, only the specific expression you created is copyrighted; anyone can use the ideas and the facts, just not your expression or a close imitation of it. Second, the statute itself permits "fair use" of copyrighted material. What counts as fair use, though, may not be easy to determine in advance and that fact may dampen free speech. The factors to be considered in determining fair use are vaguely expressed in the statute: "(1) the purpose and character of the use, including whether such use is of a commercial nature or is for nonprofit educational purposes; (2) the nature of the copyrighted work; (3) the amount and substantiality of the portion used in relation to the copyrighted work as a whole; and (4) the effect of the use upon the potential market for or value of the copyrighted work." What if an evangelist copies a page of copyrighted material from Hustler Magazine and mails it to many supporters, presumably to show the nature of the enemy. He requests donations and reaps $700,000. Does the copyright owner have a claim or is this fair use? *Hustler Magazine Inc. v. Moral Majority Inc.,* 796 F.2d 1148 (9th Cir. 1986).

4. *Trade secrets.* Any information that can be used to economic advantage in the operation of an enterprise can qualify as a trade secret. *See* RESTATEMENT (THIRD) OF UNFAIR COMPETITION § 39 (1993). Examples: chemical formulas, production techniques. The secret must have economic value in part because it is not generally known and in fact is kept secret. Once trade secrets are generally known, they no longer get legal protection. Typical trade secret cases involve employees or former employees who reveal a business' secret to competitors for a price, or else use the secret to go into business competing with the former employer. The tort is almost always committed by violating the plaintiff's rights of confidentiality. If a stranger simply buys the plaintiff's product on the market, and figures out the secret for himself, he has committed no tort. He can then go into competition with the erstwhile owner of the secret, manufacturing and selling the same product based on the same secret. Would a business ever prefer to use trade secret protections for an important formula rather than patent law?

5. *Trademarks and unfair competition.* The common law of trademarks began with the tort often called "passing off." The customer asks for a brand name item, Mopsy; the seller secretly substitutes his own brand, Flopsy, instead. If you want to protect consumers in their right to choose what they buy, you let the manufacturer of Mopsy sue and recover an injunction or damages (he lost a customer). This is the rudimentary point of traditional unfair competition or "trademark" law.

QUALITEX CO. v. JACOBSON PRODUCTS CO.

514 U.S. 159 (1995)

JUSTICE BREYER delivered the opinion of the Court. . . .

[The plaintiff sells pads to dry cleaners for use of their pressing machines. The pads are a distinctive green-gold color. The defendant, Jacobson, a competitor, started selling pads of the same color. The plaintiff registered its pad color with the Patent and Trademark Office and sued Jacobson under the Federal Lanham Act.]

The Lanham Act gives a seller or producer the exclusive right to "register" a trademark, and to prevent his or her competitors from using that trademark. Both the language of the Act and the basic underlying principles of trademark law would seem to include color within the universe of things that can qualify as a trademark. The language of the Lanham Act describes that universe in the broadest of terms. It says that trademarks "includ[e] any word, name, symbol, or device, or any combination thereof." Since human beings might use as a "symbol" or "device" almost anything at all that is capable of carrying meaning, this language, read literally, is not restrictive. The courts and the Patent and Trademark Office have authorized for use as a mark a particular shape (of a Coca–Cola bottle), a particular sound (of NBC's three chimes), and even a particular scent (of plumeria blossoms on sewing thread). If a shape, a sound, and a fragrance can act as symbols why, one might ask, can a color not do the same?

A color is also capable of satisfying the more important part of the statutory definition of a trademark, which requires that a person "us[e]" or "inten[d] to use" the mark "to identify and distinguish his or her goods, including a unique product, from those manufactured or sold by others and to indicate the source of the goods, even if that source is unknown." True, a product's color is unlike "fanciful," "arbitrary," or "suggestive" words or designs, which almost automatically tell a customer that they refer to a brand. The imaginary word "Suntost," or the words "Suntost Marmalade," on a jar of orange jam immediately would signal a brand or a product "source"; the jam's orange color does not do so. But, over time, customers may come to treat a particular color on a product or its packaging (say, a color that in context seems unusual, such as pink on a firm's insulating material or red on the head of a large industrial bolt) as signifying a brand. And, if so, that color would have come to identify and distinguish the goods—i.e. "to "indicate" their "source"—much in the way that descriptive words on a product (say, "Trim" on nail clippers or "Car–Freshner" on deodorizer) can come to indicate a product's origin. In this circumstance, trademark law says that the word (e.g., "Trim"), although not inherently distinctive, has developed "secondary meaning."
. . .

In principle, trademark law, by preventing others from copying a source-identifying mark, "reduce[s] the customer's costs of shopping and making purchasing decisions," 1 J. McCarthy, McCarthy on Trademarks and Unfair Competition § 2.01[2], p. 2–3 (3d ed. 1994) (hereinafter McCarthy), for it quickly and easily assures a potential customer that this item—the item with this mark—is made by the same producer as other similarly marked items that he or she liked (or disliked) in the past. At the same time, the law helps assure a producer that it (and not an imitating competitor) will reap the financial, reputation-related rewards associated with a desirable product. The law thereby "encourage[s] the production of quality products," and simultaneously discourages those who hope to sell inferior products by capitalizing on a consumer's inability quickly to evaluate the quality of an item offered for sale. It is the source-distin-guishing ability of a mark-not its ontological status as color, shape, fragrance, word, or sign-that permits it to serve these basic purposes. . . .

Neither can we find a principled objection to the use of color as a mark in the important "functionality" doctrine of trademark law. The functionality doctrine prevents trademark law, which seeks to promote competition by protecting a firm's reputation, from instead inhibiting legitimate competition by allowing a producer to control a useful product feature. It is the province of patent law, not trademark law, to encourage invention by granting inventors a monopoly over new product designs or functions. . . . If a product's functional features could be used as trade-marks, however, a monopoly over such features could be obtained without regard to whether they qualify as patents and could be extended forever (because trademarks may be renewed in perpetuity). Functionality doctrine therefore would require, to take an imaginary example, that even if customers have come to identify the special illumination-enhancing shape of a new patented light bulb with a particular manufacturer, the manufacturer may not use that shape as a trademark, for doing so, after the patent had expired, would impede competition—not by protecting the reputation of the original bulb maker, but by frustrating competitors' legitimate efforts to produce an equivalent illumination-enhancing bulb. This Court consequently has explained that, "[i]n general terms, a product feature is functional," and cannot serve as a trademark, "if it is essential to the use or purpose of the article or if it affects the cost or quality of the article," that is, if exclusive use of the feature would put competitors at a significant non-reputation-related disadvantage. Although sometimes color plays an important role (unrelated to source identification) in making a product more desirable, sometimes it does not. And, this latter fact—the fact that sometimes color is not essential to a product's use or purpose and does not affect cost or quality—indicates that the doctrine of "functionality" does not create an absolute bar to the use of color alone as a mark. . . .

Third, Jacobson points to many older cases—including Supreme Court cases—in support of its position. . . .

These Supreme Court cases, however, interpreted trademark law as it existed before 1946, when Congress enacted the Lanham Act. The Lanham Act significantly changed and liberalized the common law to "dispense with mere technical prohibitions," most notably, by permitting trademark registration of descriptive words (say, "U–Build–It" model airplanes) where they had acquired "secondary meaning." The Lanham Act extended protection to descriptive marks by making clear that (with certain explicit exceptions not relevant here), "nothing . . . shall prevent the registration of a mark used by the applicant which has become distinctive of the applicant's goods in commerce." This language permits an ordinary word, normally used for a nontrademark purpose (e.g., description), to act as a trademark where it has gained "secondary meaning." . . .

[W]e conclude that the Ninth Circuit erred in barring Qualitex's use of color as a trademark. For these reasons, the judgment of the Ninth Circuit is

Reversed.

Notes

1. **Infringement.** How do you infringe a trademark? You use a symbol or device with enough similarity to create confusion or likelihood of confusion among potential consumers. *See, e.g., North American Medical Corp. v. Axiom Worldwide, Inc.*, 522 F.3d 1211 (11th Cir. 2008) (infringement by using competitor's trademarks within defendant's "meta tags" on its website).

Suppose you start manufacturing canned soup sold with red and white labels and call it "Camp's Soup." Some customers would unthinkingly pick up your soup when they meant to pick up Campbell's. Expect to hear from Campbell's.

2. **Dilution.** Notice that traditional trademark law protected the consumer (albeit by giving a cause of action to the trademark holder). State legislatures, followed by the federal, then went beyond that protection and created a cause of action for the trademark owner based on dilution of the trademark value. Suppose you manufacture and market "TIFFANY'S CAT CHOW" or "TIFFANY'S PLASTIC STAINED GLASS." Nobody who buys cat chow is likely to think he is getting an exquisite Fifth Avenue creation, so the requisite consumer confusion is lacking. However, you can see why a jeweler might not want to be identified with cat chow, however much you might love cats. This is an example of dilution by "tarnishment." It would also be possible to dilute by "blurring." Judge Posner gave an illustration in *Ty Inc. v. Perryman*, 306 F.3d 509 (7th Cir. 2002). He imagined an upscale restaurant calling itself Tiffany. No one is likely to think the jeweler has opened a restaurant, so there is no confusion. But the association of the two *Tiffany's* tends to blur the unique standing of the *Tiffany's* mark. The state and federal statutes now authorize trademark owners to sue for dilution. The federal statute limits this antidilution protection to owners of "famous" marks.

3. **Free speech: trademark cases.** We saw that copyright law withdrew some of its protection for authors in the interest of free speech. Is there anything similar with trademarks? Suppose a group of nutritionists tries to persuade members of Congress that the cold cereal industry should be regulated by federal law. To do this, the group publishes: (1) a booklet reproducing cereal ads in an effort to show that these ads are misleading consumers about the nutritional content of cereals, and (2) posters on which pictures of actual cereal boxes are reproduced, with a stamp across them saying "Dangerous to Your Health." Suppose in each case the reproductions include reproductions of trademarks or trade names. Is there a free speech issue?

REFERENCES: RESTATEMENT (THIRD) OF TORTS, UNFAIR COMPETITION, §§ 9–17 (1995); J. THOMAS MCCARTHY, TRADEMARKS AND UNFAIR COMPETITION (4th Ed. 1998); DOBBS ON TORTS §§ 457–58 (2000).

§ 4. MISAPPROPRIATION OF COMMERCIAL VALUE

A. APPROPRIATION OF PERSONALITY OR "IDENTITY"

CARSON v. HERE'S JOHNNY PORTABLE TOILETS, INC., 698 F.2d 831 (6th Cir. 1983). Plaintiff John W. Carson is a famous entertainer, whose "Tonight Show" on television is introduced with the phrase "Here's Johnny." The phrase is generally associated with Carson and the show by a substantial segment of the television viewing public. Carson has authorized use of the phrase by others, who have used it to identify restaurants, men's clothing and men's toiletries. The defendant is a corporation which rents and sells portable toilets under the name "Here's

Johnny." The founder was aware of the television significance of the phrase when he adopted it for the toilets. Carson sued. The trial court dismissed the claim. Held, vacated and remanded for further proceedings. (1) The "Here's Johnny" mark is a relatively "weak" mark, so that its use on other goods should not be entirely foreclosed, and there is insufficient evidence to establish a likelihood of confusion. Consequently the trademark claim fails. (2) Prosser delineated four types of the right of privacy, including intrusion upon solitude, public disclosure of embarrassing private facts, publicity that places one in a false light, and commercial appropriation of one's name for the defendant's advantage. The first three involve the right to be let alone, but the fourth is best referred to, not as a privacy claim, but as a right of publicity. In this case there is no violation of any real right to privacy, even though Carson may be embarrassed to be associated with the defendant's product. However, there is an invasion of the right of publicity, since the plaintiff's identity is valuable in the promotion of products and he has an interest in preventing unauthorized commercial exploitation of that identity.

Notes

1.   **Privacy/right of publicity.** Prosser's insights in identifying the four kinds of "privacy" have been generally recognized, but, as in *Carson*, courts and writers now believe that it would be more accurate in this "commercial appropriation" version of privacy to label the right as one of "publicity." "[T]he right of publicity protects the right to control the commercial value of one's identity." *Montgomery v. Montgomery*, 60 S.W.3d 524 (Ky. 2001). Commercial advertising includes ads using the plaintiff's unique vocal sounds, *Midler v. Ford Motor Co.*, 849 F.2d 460 (9th Cir. 1988), or the plaintiff's style of dress as seen on a television game show, *White v. Samsung Elec. Am., Inc.*, 971 F.2d 1395 (9th Cir. 1992) (Vanna White). Products embodying the plaintiff's likeness have been treated the same way. *See Comedy III Productions, Inc. v. Gary Saderup, Inc.*, 21 P.3d 797 (Cal. 2001) (sweatshirts bearing the likeness of the Three Stooges as sketched and lithographed by the defendant); *Martin Luther King, Jr., Center for Social Change, Inc. v. American Heritage Prod's., Inc.*, 296 S.E.2d 697 (Ga. 1982) (busts of Martin Luther King).

2.   **Duration.** Should your rights not to have your personality exploited commercially be passed down to your heirs and their heirs in perpetuity? Should descendants of Thomas Jefferson get royalties for the use of his picture? Some states treat the right as "descendible." In that case should we follow the guide of copyright and patent law and put a time limit on the right? Or should we follow the trademark practice and permit the right to run in perpetuity?

3.   **Commercial use.** Commercial use is primarily use associated with sales. An advertisement is a commercial use, but feature stories, biographies, news, and creative works like movies are not considered commercial. Use of the plaintiff's identity in noncommercial works is thus fully permissible, both because the right of publicity does not extend to such uses and because

constitutional free speech rights protect against liability. In *Hoffman v. Capital Cities/ABC, Inc.,* 255 F.3d 1180 (9th Cir. 2001), a feature story on fashion, using a computer to graft new fashion designs on famous Hollywood figures, including the actor Dustin Hoffman, was not deemed commercial; in addition, the court thought that *Times–Sullivan* rules would apply to require a knowing or reckless falsehood. The court entered judgment for the publisher.

4. **Private individuals.** Some cases have involved celebrities who, if given the protection invoked in *Carson*, would be able to sell their names, faces, or endorsements for a price. But private individuals, whose face or endorsement would sell for little or nothing, also have a protectible interest. The fact that a citizen is unknown does not permit an advertiser to use her picture to accompany its advertising. If the picture or name is used to advertise a product the plaintiff finds offensive or demeaning, there is undoubtedly a very personal interest involved and not merely a commercial one. Is there also such an interest in *Carson?* Should the court have recognized a privacy right and not a publicity right? Would there be a First Amendment difference?

B. MISAPPROPRIATION OF COMMERCIAL VALUES

INTERNATIONAL NEWS SERVICE v. ASSOCIATED PRESS, 248 U.S. 215 (1918). Associated Press (the AP) and INS were competitors, each collecting news at its source and supplying accounts to subscriber or member newspapers, who then published the news in their columns. During World War I, AP was able to get news from Europe, but INS was prohibited by foreign governments from doing so. It is alleged that INS provided the news to its subscribers by copying the AP news bulletins on public view in eastern newspaper offices, or copying the AP news as printed in eastern papers. This was then sent to INS' western subscribers, where it was still fresh news because of the time difference between the east and west coasts. AP brought this suit to enjoin the copying and republication, although the material enjoyed no copyright protection. *Held*: the injunction should be granted. The news is not copyrighted and the Copyright Act does not confer upon anyone the exclusive right to report a historic event, and news of current events may be regarded as common property. But although AP has no property interest in the news as against the general public, it has certain interests as against competitors. It has utilized its enterprise, organization, skill, labor and money to get the news and as against competitors, this gives AP a "quasi property" in it. The defendant INS, "in appropriating it and selling it as its own is endeavoring to reap where it has not sown...."

SEARS, ROEBUCK & CO. v. STIFFEL CO.

376 U.S. 225 (1964)

MR. JUSTICE BLACK delivered the Opinion of the Court.

The question in this case is whether a State's unfair competition law can, consistently with the federal patent laws, impose liability for or prohibit the copying of an article which is protected by neither a federal patent nor a copyright. The respondent, Stiffel Company, secured design and mechanical patents on a "pole lamp"—a vertical tube having lamp fixtures along the outside, the tube being made so that it will stand upright between the floor and ceiling of a room. Pole lamps proved a decided commercial success, and soon after Stiffel brought them on the market Sears, Roebuck & Company put on the market a substantially identical lamp, which it sold more cheaply, Sears' retail price being about the same as Stiffel's wholesale price. Stiffel then brought this action against Sears in the United States District Court for the Northern District of Illinois, claiming in its first count that by copying its design Sears had infringed Stiffel's patents and in its second count that by selling copies of Stiffel's lamp Sears had caused confusion in the trade as to the source of the lamps and had thereby engaged in unfair competition under Illinois law. There was evidence that identifying tags were not attached to the Sears lamps although labels appeared on the cartons in which they were delivered to customers, that customers had asked Stiffel whether its lamps differed from Sears', and that in two cases customers who had bought Stiffel lamps had complained to Stiffel on learning that Sears was selling substantially identical lamps at a much lower price.

The District Court, after holding the patents invalid for want of invention, went on to find as a fact that Sears' lamp was "a substantially exact copy" of Stiffel's and that the two lamps were so much alike, both in appearance and in functional details, "that confusion between them is likely, and some confusion has already occurred." On these findings the court held Sears guilty of unfair competition, enjoined Sears "from unfairly competing with [Stiffel] by selling or attempting to sell pole lamps identical to or confusingly similar to" Stiffel's lamp, and ordered an accounting to fix profits and damages resulting from Sears "unfair competition."

The Court of Appeals affirmed. 313 F.2d 115. That court held that, to make out a case of unfair competition under Illinois law, there was no need to show that Sears had been "palming off" its lamps as Stiffel lamps; Stiffel had only to prove that there was a "likelihood of confusion as to the source of products"—that the two articles were sufficiently identical that customers could not tell who had made a particular one. Impressed by the "remarkable sameness of appearance" of the lamps, the Court of Appeals upheld the trial court's findings of likelihood of confusion and some actual confusion, findings which the appellate court construed to mean confusion "as to the source of the lamps." The Court of Appeals thought this enough under Illinois law to sustain the trial court's holding of unfair competition, and thus held Sears liable under Illinois law for doing no more than copying and marketing an unpatented article. We granted certiorari to consider whether this use of a State's law of unfair competition is compatible with the federal patent law. . . .

The grant of a patent is the grant of a statutory monopoly; . . . Patents . . . are meant to encourage invention by rewarding the inventor with the right, limited to a term of years fixed by the patent, to exclude others from the use of his invention. During that period of time no one may make, use, or sell the patented product without the patentee's authority. 35 U.S.C. § 271. But in rewarding useful invention, the "rights and welfare of the community must be fairly dealt with and effectually guarded." To that end the prerequisites to obtaining a patent are strictly observed, and when the patent has issued the limitations on its exercise are equally strictly enforced. To begin with, a genuine "invention" or "discovery" must be demonstrated "lest in the constant demand for new appliances the heavy hand of tribute be laid on each slight technological advance in an art." Once the patent issues, it is strictly construed. . . . Finally, and especially relevant here, when the patent expires the monopoly created by it expires, too, and the right to make the article—including the right to make it in precisely the shape it carried when patented—passes to the public.

Thus the patent system is one in which uniform federal standards are carefully used to promote invention while at the same time preserving free competition. Obviously a State could not, consistently with the Supremacy Clause of the Constitution, extend the life of a patent beyond its expiration date or give a patent on an article which lacked the level of invention required for federal patents. To do either would run counter to the policy of Congress of granting patents only to true inventions, and then only for a limited time. Just as a State cannot encroach upon the federal patent laws directly, it cannot, under some other law, such as that forbidding unfair competition, give protection of a kind that clashes with the objectives of the federal patent laws.

In the present case the "pole lamp" sold by Stiffel has been held not to be entitled to the protection of either a mechanical or a design patent. An unpatentable article, like an article on which the patent has expired, is in the public domain and may be made and sold by whoever chooses to do so. What Sears did was to copy Stiffel's design and sell lamps almost identical to those sold by Stiffel. This it had every right to do under the federal patent laws. That Stiffel originated the pole lamp and made it popular is immaterial. "Sharing in the goodwill of an article unprotected by patent or trade-mark is the exercise of a right possessed by all—and in the free exercise of which the consuming public is deeply interested." To allow a State by use of its law of unfair competition to prevent the copying of an article which represents too slight an advance to be patented would be to permit the State to block off from the public something which federal law has said belongs to the public. The result would be that while federal law grants only 14 or 17 years' protection to genuine inventions, see 35 U.S.C. §§ 154, 173, States could allow perpetual protection to articles too lacking in novelty to merit any patent at all under federal constitutional standards. This would be too great an encroachment on the federal patent system to be tolerated.

Sears has been held liable here for unfair competition because of a finding of likelihood of confusion based only on the fact that Sears' lamp was copied from Stiffel's unpatented lamp and that consequently the two looked exactly alike. Of course there could be "confusion" as to who had manufactured these nearly identical articles. But mere inability of the public to tell two identical articles apart is not enough to support an injunction against copying or an award of damages for copying that which the federal patent laws permit to be copied. Doubtless a State may, in appropriate circumstances, require that goods, whether patented or unpatented, be labeled or that other precautionary steps be taken to prevent customers from being misled as to the source, just as it may protect businesses in the use of their trademarks, labels, or distinctive dress in the packaging of goods so as to prevent others, by imitating such markings, from misleading purchasers as to the source of the goods. But because of the federal patent laws a State may not, when the article is unpatented and uncopyrighted, prohibit the copying of the article itself or award damages for such copying. The judgment below did both and in so doing gave Stiffel the equivalent of a patent monopoly on its unpatented lamp. That was error, and Sears is entitled to a judgment in its favor.

Reversed.

NOTES

1. ***Bonito Boats.*** Bonito developed a new kind of boat hull. Fiberglass allegedly copied the hull exactly, perhaps by making a direct mold. A state statute prohibited direct molding and selling of the copied hulls. In *Bonito Boats, Inc. v. Thunder Craft Boats, Inc.*, 489 U.S. 141 (1989), the Court held that the statute was preempted by patent law. Justice O'Connor emphasized that the "bargain" set up by patent laws must be attractive to inventors, so that states must not be free to offer a better protection. Put differently, competitors must be free to compete freely with all unpatented ideas. At the same time the Court made it clear that states would be free to give trademark-like protection to "trade dress." If a product's packaging or design itself works like a trademark, identifying the maker of the product by a design that is not "functional," the design could be protected like any other trademark.

2. **The status of *INS*.** What is the status of *International News Service v. Associated Press*? The *INS* case was actually a diversity case, decided before *Erie*. In other words it was decided under a belief that there was some general federal law. That being so, it has never been overtly overruled and seems to twist and turn in an uncertain limbo. Perhaps the question should be: Can a state be permitted under *Sears* and *Bonito* to follow the rule announced in *INS*?

ZACCHINI v. SCRIPPS–HOWARD BROADCASTING CO., 433 U.S. 562 (1977). Zacchini performed an act as a human cannonball. He was one of the acts shown in the Geauga County Fair in Ohio. The act consists of being shot from a cannon into a net 200 feet away. It takes 15 seconds for the entire performance. This took place in an area open to all those who had properly entered the fair grounds. There was no separate charge. Defendant filmed the entire act, against Zacchini's express wishes. The film was shown on the defendant's television news. The "entire act" was shown. Television commentary was favorable and recommended seeing the act in person. Zacchini sued. The Ohio Court concluded that, under Ohio law, the defendant was guilty of the kind of privacy invasion Prosser had identified as commercial appropriation and which is sometimes called a right of publicity. It thought, however, that recovery was barred by the First Amendment and that the publisher was "privileged" to provide an accurate report. In the Supreme Court of the United States, *held*, reversed. Ohio may apply any state law privilege, but the Constitution does not provide one here. Ohio's preference for enforcing property interest in this act does not offend the decisions in *Times–Sullivan* and *Gertz*. Those decisions did not deal with the appropriation of an entire act. "The Constitution no more prevents a State from requiring [a defendant] to compensate [a plaintiff] for broadcasting his act on television than it would privilege [a defendant] to film and broadcast a copyrighted dramatic work. . . ." The policy of recognizing a property interest here is partly to compensate for efforts already made, but more significantly to provide economic incentive to do further work of interest to the public. These are indeed the policies behind the copyright and patent statutes. Thus Ohio is free to impose liability if it so chooses, and the federal Constitution does not require otherwise.

NOTE

When would the First Amendment bar a commercial appropriation claim? In *C.B.C. Distribution and Marketing, Inc. v. Major League Baseball Advanced Media, L.P.*, 505 F.3d 818 (8th Cir. 2007), a producer of fantasy major league baseball games sought a declaratory judgment that it had the right to use the names and statistics of actual players in its games without obtaining a license to do so. The licensee counterclaimed and the players' association intervened. A federal magistrate hearing the case granted summary judgment for the producer. The appeals court affirmed, holding that while the players "offered sufficient evidence to make out a cause of action for violation of their rights of publicity under Missouri law," under *Zacchini* the right of publicity must give way to First Amendment considerations. The court gave three reasons: (1) "the information used in CBC's fantasy baseball games is all readily available in the public domain, and it would be strange law that a person would not have a first amendment right to use information that is available to everyone." (2) "Courts have also recognized the public value of information about the game of baseball and its players," and discussions of baseball statistics "command a substantial public interest," making it "a form of expression due substantial constitutional perspective." (3) The facts in this case "barely, if at all, implicate the interests that states typically intend to vindicate by providing rights of publicity to individuals." Those interests include encouraging a person's productive activities, protecting consumers from misleading advertising, protecting natural rights, rewarding celebrity labors, and avoiding emotional harm. "We do not see that any of these interest are especially relevant here...."

REFERENCES: RESTATEMENT THIRD OF TORTS, UNFAIR COMPETITION § 38 (1995); J. THOMAS MCCARTHY, THE RIGHTS OF PUBLICITY AND PRIVACY (2d Ed. 2000); DOBBS ON TORTS § 460 (2000); DAN B. DOBBS & ELLEN M. BUBLICK, ADVANCED TORTS: ECONOMIC AND DIGNITARY TORTS Ch. 10–11, 13 § 3–5 (2006).

CHAPTER 34

MISREPRESENTATION
AND OTHER MISDEALINGS

■ ■ ■

§ 1. THEORIES OF LIABILITY
AND THEIR CONSEQUENCES

Illustration 1

DuBois was negotiating to sell his house to Pace. DuBois told Pace that the roof was in good condition and never gave any problems. In fact, as DuBois knew, a tree had fallen on the roof and caused serious damage. This had happened over a year ago and deterioration was now substantial. Pace, relying upon DuBois' statement, purchased the house for $100,000. This would have been its value if the roof had been in good condition, but because of the condition of the roof, the house was worth no more than $90,000. When Pace discovered this, she sued DuBois for fraud. Pace is entitled to recover $10,000.

This illustration typifies many fraud or misrepresentation claims for money damages at common law. The case differs from the kinds of cases involved in the two preceding chapters in that while there is a communication by the defendant, it is made directly to the plaintiff, not to third persons. The fraud claim usually arises in a bargaining situation. The claim is frequently asserted against the seller, or someone representing the seller. Finally, the claim is very often found in real property cases or the sale of securities, such as corporate stocks or bonds. The reason for this is that the law of warranty, with its strict liability, is likely to govern the liability of chattel sellers, so it is only in other cases that the plaintiff will fall back on the law of tort, attempting to prove "fraud."

Misrepresentation is a factual element in many kinds of tort claims. You might intentionally or recklessly inflict emotional distress by a misrepresentation, or you might risk physical harm to a person by misrepresenting the safety of a scaffold. Although a misrepresentation is important in such cases, they are not cases we think of when we speak of fraud or deceit. The traditional fraud or deceit claims—or today, the negligent misrepresentation claim—is about economic loss in a bargaining transaction.

DERRY v. PEEK, 14 App. Cas. 337 (H.L. 1889). Defendants, selling shares of stock in a Tramways company, represented that they had the right under an act of Parliament, to use steam or mechanical power as well as horses. In fact, they could use steam power only if the Board of Trade consented, though defendants believed that such consent would be given as a matter of course. They were wrong; the consent was never given, and the corporation failed. In the meantime, relying on the statement that the company was authorized to use steam power, the plaintiff had purchased shares of stock. When the corporation failed, he lost his investment and he sued for fraud. The Court of Appeals held that defendants honestly believed their statements to be true, but that they were nonetheless liable to the plaintiff. In the House of Lords, *held*, reversed. (a) A rescission of the contract may be had where there is an innocent misrepresentation, but (b) damages for fraud may not be recovered unless the defendant made a false representation "(1) knowingly or (2) without belief in its truth, or (3) recklessly, careless whether it be true or false."

NOTES

1. **Scienter.** The requirement of an intent to deceive—a knowing or reckless falsehood—was called scienter and taken as the common law rule until recent years. It still remains the favored ground for recovery. Does the language sound familiar?

2. **Negligence.** It is now generally accepted that negligence can also form a basis of liability for misrepresentations. However, the conditions for imposing liability are more stringent, and the scope and amount of liability are also limited.

The rule of the RESTATEMENT (SECOND) OF TORTS § 552 (1965) would impose liability for negligent misrepresentation only when the defendant makes a representation in the course of business or employment, or in a case in which he has a pecuniary interest. In *Onita Pacific Corp. v. Bronson Trustees*, 843 P.2d 890 (Or. 1992), the court held that a negligent misrepresentation would be actionable only if the defendant was in the business of supplying information and would not be actionable as against an adversarial bargainer. As in other cases, the plaintiff must justifiably rely on the representation in order to have a claim. In *Westby v. Gorsuch,* 50 P.3d 284 (Wash. Ct. App. 2002), the plaintiff had a "ticket" from the Titanic. Needing money immediately, he took it to the defendant, a dealer in antiques. The dealer indicated that it had little value, but eventually paid the plaintiff $1,000 for the ticket. It turned out to be quite valuable. Would the dealer be under a duty of reasonable care so that, even if he did not act fraudulently, he would be liable for negligence?

3. **Representations creating physical risks.** The limitations of the Restatement do not apply to communications that create a physical risk. D tells P that his brakes are safe when D should have known better. In reliance, P drives the car and is injured when the brakes don't work. P has a good claim. What if an employer writes a positive letter of recommendation that fails to disclose that the employee had been subject to complaints about sexual improprieties with students. The employee accepts the new job, working with middle-school students, one of whom he allegedly molests. Would the former employer be liable for those physical harms? *See Randi W. v. Muroc Joint Unified Sch. Dist.*, 929 P.2d 582 (Cal. 1997). What if the publisher of a telephone directory creates and publishes a Yellow Pages advertisement that intentionally misrepresents a doctor's qualifications. A patient who relies on the advertisement suffers physical harm from the liposuction surgery performed on him by the doctor. Is the publisher liable for those physical harms? See *Knepper v. Brown*, 195 P.3d 383 (Or. 2008).

4. **Emotional harm recovery.** What if a prospective employer makes misrepresentations in a job interview with the plaintiff about the company's growth prospects. The plaintiff suffers no physical harm, but does allege emotional harm. Liability? *Brogan v. Mitchell Int'l, Inc.*, 692 N.E.2d 276 (Ill. 1998) (no recovery). What about a misrepresentation by an employer that plaintiff was covered by health insurance when he was not, which causes only emotional and not physical harm. *See Southern Alaska Carpenters Health & Sec. Trust Fund v. Jones*, 177 P.3d 844 (Alaska 2008) (allowing recovery). Are the two cases distinguishable?

5. **Representations by non-parties.** Most representations are made by parties to a negotiation which is followed by a contract or sale. However, outsiders could also be held liable for misrepresentations if they were fraudulent. If, in Illustration 1, DuBois' representation is repeated to the plaintiff by a neighbor, who also knows its falsity, the neighbor would also be liable. This rule applies only to fraud; warranty claims require privity.

Suppose in Illustration 1 that DuBois had represented to A that his roof was sound and that A repeated it later to B, who then bought the house for $100,000 from DuBois. Should B, to whom no representation was made, have a fraud action? Some older cases took a tough line about this, denying liability to plaintiffs who were merely foreseeable. But according to the Restatement Second § 533, the defendant is liable not only to the person to whom the representation is made, but also to third persons if he "intends or has reason to expect that its terms will be repeated. . . ." This raises the problem seen in the next case.

ULTRAMARES CORP. v. TOUCHE, NIVEN & CO.
174 N.E. 441 (N.Y. 1931)

CARDOZO, C.J.

[Defendants were public accountants. Pursuant to a contract with Stern they undertook to prepare an independent audit of the business, showing its net worth. As defendants knew, this was to be used by potential lenders, who, relying upon defendants' independent assessment of Sterns' financial situation, would lend money to Stern. The audit showed a net worth of over a million dollars, and defendants certified this as accurate and prepared 32 originals for Stern to show potential lenders. In fact, relying on the audit and balance sheet furnished by defendants, the plaintiff loaned $165,000 to Stern. When Stern collapsed, the plaintiff was unable to obtain repayment of the loan. The plaintiff brought this action against the defendants for the damages thus suffered, claiming both scienter fraud and negligent misrepresentation. There was evidence that the defendants did not examine Stern's books with appropriate care, and that had they done so, discrepancies would have been revealed which would have led to a more accurate audit. The trial judge set aside jury's verdict for the plaintiff. The Appellate Division thought that the fraud action should be dismissed, but not the negligence claim.]

We are brought to the question of duty, its origin and measure.

The defendants owed to their employer a duty imposed by law to make their certificate without fraud, and a duty growing out of contract to make it with the care and caution proper to their calling. Fraud includes the pretense of knowledge when there is none. To creditors and investors to whom the employer exhibited the certificate, the defendants owed a like duty to make it without fraud, since there was notice in the circumstances of its making that the employer did not intend to keep it to himself. A different question develops when we ask whether they owed a duty to these to make it without negligence. If liability for negligence exists, a thoughtless slip or blunder, the failure to detect a theft or forgery beneath the cover of deceptive entries, may expose accountants to a liability in an indeterminate amount for an indeterminate time to an indeterminate class. The hazards of a business conducted on these terms are so extreme as to enkindle doubt whether a flaw may not exist in the implications of a duty that exposes to these consequences. We put aside for the moment any statement in the certificate which involves the representation of a fact as true to the knowledge of the auditors. If such a statement was made, whether believed to be true or not, the defendants are liable for deceit in the event that it was false. The plaintiff does not need the invention of novel doctrine to help it out in such conditions. . . .

The assault upon the citadel of privity is proceeding in these days apace. How far the inroads shall extend is now a favorite subject of juridical discussion. In the field of the law of contract there has been a gradual widening of the doctrine of Lawrence v. Fox, 20 N. Y. 268, until today the beneficiary of a promise, clearly designated as such, is seldom left without a remedy. Even in that field, however, the remedy is narrower where the beneficiaries of the promise are indeterminate or general. Something more must then appear than an intention that the promise shall redound to the benefit of the public or to that of a class of indefinite extension. The promise must be such as to "bespeak the assumption of a duty to make reparation directly to the individual members of the public if the benefit is lost." *Moch Co. v. Rensselaer Water Co.*, 247 N.Y. 160, 164; Restatement of the Law of Contracts, § 145. In the field of the law of torts a manufacturer who is negligent in the manufacture of a chattel in circumstances pointing to an unreasonable risk of serious bodily harm to those using it thereafter may be liable for negligence though privity is lacking between manufacturer and user. *MacPherson v. Buick Motor Co.,* 217 N.Y. 382; Restatement of the Law of Torts, § 262. . . .

Liability for negligence if adjudged in this case will extend to many callings other than an auditor's. Lawyers who certify their opinions as to the validity of municipal or corporate bonds, with knowledge that the opinion will be brought to the notice of the public, will become liable to the investors, if they have overlooked a statute or a decision, to the same extent as if the controversy were one between client and adviser. Title companies insuring titles to a tract of land, with knowledge that at an approaching auction the fact that they have insured will be stated to the bidders, will become liable to purchasers who may wish the benefit of a policy without payment of a premium. These illustrations may seem to be extreme, but they go little, if any, farther than we are invited to go now. Negligence, moreover, will have one standard when viewed in relation to the employer, and another and at times a stricter standard when viewed in relation to the public. Explanations that might seem plausible, omissions that might be reasonable, if the duty is confined to the employer, conducting a business that presumably at least is not a fraud upon his creditors, might wear another aspect if an independent duty to be suspicious even of one's principal is owing to investors. "Every one making a promise having the quality of a contract will be under a duty to the promisee by virtue of the promise, but under another duty, apart from contract, to an indefinite number of potential beneficiaries when performance has begun. The assumption of one relation will mean the involuntary assumption of a series of new relations, inescapably hooked together." Moch Co. v. Rensselaer Water Co., *supra,* at page 168. "The law does not spread its protection so far." Robins Dry Dock & Repair Co. v. Flint, *supra,* at page 309 of 275 U.S.

Our holding does not emancipate accountants from the consequences of fraud. It does not relieve them if their audit has been so negligent as to justify a finding that they had no genuine belief in its adequacy, for this again is fraud. It does no more than say that, if less than this is proved, if there has been neither reckless misstatement nor insincere profession of an opinion, but only honest blunder, the ensuing liability for negligence is one that is bounded by the contract, and is to be enforced between the parties by whom the contract has been made. We doubt whether the average business man receiving a certificate without paying for it, and receiving it merely as one among a multitude of possible investors, would look for anything more. . . .

[Remanded for trial as to the fraud claim and dismissed as to the negligence claim.]

NOTES

1. Suppose Stern had told the accountants to send one copy directly to the plaintiff as quickly as possible, because the plaintiff might make a loan. Would the defendant then be liable for negligence?

2. Suppose the defendant, a jeweler, certifies that a diamond owned by S is genuine. Defendant knows that S will distribute numerous copies of this certificate in an attempt to sell the diamond. S does so and one reader of the certificate buys the diamond in reliance. If the defendant was merely negligent, does *Ultramares* bar recovery against the defendant?

3. Does *Ultramares* make sense to you? Consider another Cardozo decision, *Moch v. Rensselaer Water Co.* Presumably the water sold there was priced by the unit of water, not according to the value of houses served by the fire hydrants. Presumably the services of the accountant are priced by the hour or unit of work, not according to the amount of loans that might be made in reliance on the statement. The implication of the price seems to be that indeterminate liabilities to third persons are not part of the bargain. Would it even be possible for a prudent insurer to calculate a premium to insure for accountant's liabilities? After all, we do not know whether any sum will be loaned or how much it will be.

4. Whatever sense *Ultramares* might have made, the Restatement's § 552 took a more liberal position, extending liability to all those in a "limited group of persons for whose benefit and guidance" the information is supplied, if the transaction is similar to the one he expected to influence. *See Audler v. CBC Innovis Inc.*, 519 F.3d 239 (5th Cir. 2008) (Louisiana law). California has adopted a rule similar to the Restatement's rule, allowing a recovery only by specifically identifiable plaintiffs. *Bily v. Arthur Young & Co.*, 834 P.2d 745 (Cal. 1992). New York extends liability to third persons only when the defendant has a close "bond" with the plaintiff, as by some direct contact or representation. *See Credit Alliance Corp. v. Arthur Andersen & Co.*, 483 N.E.2d 110 (N.Y.1985). One or two states go further in negligent misstatement cases, imposing liability for all proximately caused economic harms. *Touche Ross v. Commercial Union Ins.*, 514 So.2d 315 (Miss. 1987); *Citizens State Bank v. Timm, Schmidt & Co.*, 335 N.W.2d 361 (Wis. 1983). In the latter case the court added, however, that public policy might preclude liability on the facts of particular cases, emphasizing factors such as highly extraordinary harm, remoteness, and disproportion between negligence and harm.

5. Suppose the plaintiff is foreseeable, and even within a limited class for whose guidance the information is purchased, but the plaintiff relies on the information in a wholly unsuspected way: instead of lending money to the business that has been audited, the plaintiff buys its stock. What kind of issue does this raise?

Illustration 2

Durham sells a bull to Bynum, who purchases in reliance on a knowingly false representation by Durham that the bull is a pedigreed

Guernsey. If this had been true the bull would have been worth $90,000. It was not true and the bull was worth only $5,000. Bynum paid $80,000 for the bull. He is entitled to recover a sum sufficient to give him the benefit of his bargain. Since, if the bull had been as represented, he would have made a gain of $10,000, he is entitled to recover a sum sufficient to put him in that position. This will require $85,000 in damage. This, added to the value of the bull which he has, will give him $90,000—the benefit of his bargain, for which he paid $80,000.

Illustration 3

Danton, an art dealer, negligently inspected a painting and concluded it was a genuine Giaccomo Jones. He represented this to be the case and relying on this representation Pierre bought it for $200,000, expecting to resell it for $250,000. He would have been able to do so if it had been a genuine Jones, but it was not. It was worth only $175,000. Pierre's loss of bargain is $50,000, but he can only recover his "out-of-pocket," $25,000.

Illustration 4

The facts are the same as in Illustration 3, except that Pierre incurred $10,000 in brokerage fees to sell the painting, and would have incurred no brokerage fee to sell it if it had been a Jones. He is entitled to recover his out-of-pocket damages of $25,000 plus his consequential or special damages of $10,000.

NOTES

1. **Scienter fraud: Benefit of the bargain measure.** If the defendant is guilty of a scienter fraud, the plaintiff may recover the benefit of his bargain in most jurisdictions. This is a sum sufficient to give him the gain in asset value he would have made had the representation been true. *See* RESTATEMENT (SECOND) OF TORTS § 549 (1977); 2 DAN B. DOBBS, THE LAW OF REMEDIES § 9.2 (1) (2d ed. 1993). Even in the case of scienter fraud, New York limits recovery to the out-of-pocket measure described below and does not permit the usual loss of bargain damages.

2. **Scienter fraud: Optional out-of-pocket measure.** The plaintiff who proves scienter fraud also has an option to claim a different measure, the out-of-pocket damages, plus any consequential damages. The out-of-pocket measure can be seen in Illustration 3. This represents the difference between what the plaintiff paid and what he got. In Illustration 3 it is obviously less than the loss of bargain measure, which would have given the plaintiff a recovery of $75,000 (to give him his $50,000 expectancy). The out-of-pocket measure simply puts the plaintiff in the financial position he would have been in had there been no transaction at all. Why would a plaintiff ever choose this measure of damages if he could claim the loss of bargain?

3. **Consequential damages.** If the plaintiff recovers the out-of-pocket measure, he can also recover appropriate consequential or special damages. This would include any special expenses he incurred because of the fraud. *See*

Illustration 4. These might be denied in New York in order to make its out-of-pocket rule effective.

4. **Negligent misrepresentation.** When the defendant is guilty of negligence, but not scienter fraud, the damages are limited to the out-of-pocket plus the consequential damages. *BDO Seidman, LLP v. Mindis Acquisition Corp.,* 578 S.E.2d 400 (Ga. 2003); RESTATEMENT (SECOND) OF TORTS § 552B (1977). Thus in Illustration 3 above, the plaintiff cannot recover the $50,000 loss of bargain.

GAUERKE v. ROZGA

332 N.W.2d 804 (Wis. 1983)

CECI, JUSTICE.

[The Rozgas owned a hotel property, which they listed for sale with the Gudim Realty. They told Gudim that, according to former owners, the property was five and one-half acres. Gudim seems to have put this information in a specification sheet. In the meantime, the Gauerkes were looking for hotel property and asked Robert Frost Realty, Inc. to act for them. A Frost agent contacted Gudim, obtained the specification sheet, put a Frost card at the top, and submitted it to the Gauerkes. The Gauerkes eventually purchased the property, but two years later they discovered that the property contained less than three acres. They brought this action against the Rozgas, Robert Frost Realty, and Gudim. Gudim settled and the case was submitted to a jury against Robert Frost and its agent. A jury found for the plaintiff and Frost was held liable on a "theory of strict responsibility for the misrepresentations."]

Frost argues that the theory of strict responsibility should not have been submitted to the jury, because that theory is only applicable where the defendant could normally be expected to know the facts represented to be true without investigation.... The court of appeals reasoned that "in strict liability the loss is to fall on the innocent defendant rather than the innocent plaintiff...."

[Wisconsin requires] (1) a representation made as of defendant's own knowledge, concerning a matter about which he purports to have knowledge, so that he may be taken to have assumed responsibility as in the case of warranty, and (2) a defendant with an economic interest in the transaction into which the plaintiff enters so that defendant expects to gain some economic benefit. In other words, strict responsibility applies in those circumstances which 'indicate that the speaker either had particular means of ascertaining the pertinent facts, or his position made possible complete knowledge and the statements fairly implied that he had it.' Therefore, the speaker ought to have known or else ought not to have spoken.

We agree with the court of appeals that the applicability of the doctrine of strict responsibility does not depend upon the actual source of the speaker's knowledge' rather, this element is satisfied if the speaker professes or implies personal knowledge. The other key element is the buyer's justifiable reliance on the statement. If the fact represented is something that one would not expect the speaker to know without an investigation, this might be a factor in determining there was justifiable reliance on the part of the buyer.... [Money award to the plaintiff affirmed.]

NOTES

1. **Strict liability for physical harm.** When should there be strict liability for misrepresentations?

— A seller of staples honestly and reasonably represents them as safe for use in the buyer's staple gun. In fact they are not safe; a small piece breaks off and puts out the plaintiff's eye. Is there any doubt about strict liability? *See* RESTATEMENT OF PRODUCTS LIABILITY § 9 (1998).

— A homeowner has her roof repaired in May. In June she tells a would-be buyer, "The roof is in excellent shape." She is honest and reasonable, but in fact the roofer has done a poor job and the roof is already developing hidden cracks. Is there to be strict liability?

2. **Strict liability and consciously ignorant representations.** In some instances a speaker may be guilty of a scienter fraud if he states facts as if he had knowledge of them when in truth he knows that he does not know the facts. Seller says: "The well on this farm will pump enough to water 500 head of cattle." The seller has never tried to pump that much, though he honestly and reasonably believes it is so based on pump specifications. However, it is not in fact the case. If he is consciously aware of his own ignorance is he not guilty of a scienter fraud?

3. **Warranty strict liability.** One basis for strict liability is that the buyer may reasonably believe the seller is warranting the statement to be true. But if the theory is warranty or an analogy to warranty, should the claim then be defeated if there is a disclaimer or a merger clause in the deed? The disclaimer or merger clause would often not suffice to defeat an actual scienter fraud claim.

Other Bases for Strict Liability

4. **Rescission.** Under contract a mutual mistake of basic fact may be sufficient to avoid a contract and justify rescission, sometimes on the theory that, given such a mistake, there was no contract at all. The case of an honest misstatement by one party and belief by the other is obviously a special instance of mutual mistake and just as good a ground for rescission. Thus, as recognized in *Derry v. Peek*, neither negligence nor scienter is required when the plaintiff seeks rescission. Should rescission be granted also for misrepresentation of any material fact? Rescission would be granted for misrepresentation that "this is a Guernsey," when in fact it was a polled Hereford. Should rescission also be granted for a misrepresentation that "this cow won first prize at the fair" when in fact it won second?

5. **Fiduciaries.** Fiduciaries, such as trustees in relationship to the beneficiaries of their trusts and lawyers in relationship to their clients, are obliged to exercise the utmost good faith, and to act in each transaction for the best interest of the beneficiary. For failure to do this they may be held for constructive fraud. The effect is strict liability. A similar idea may extend to persons who are not classic fiduciaries, but who have led the plaintiff to place special trust and confidence in them.

6. **Statutory strict liability.** Federal and state statutes sometimes provide for strict liability for particular misstatements, although the situations in which this is true are limited. More frequently statutes, particularly in the areas of securities and mass sales of real property, require scienter. *See, e.g.,* 15 U.S.C.A. §§ 77a et seq. (securities); §§ 1701 et seq. (land).

Scope of Strict Liability and Damages

7. **The *Ultramares* problem.** Reconsider the *Ultramares* problem. To what group of potential plaintiffs should strict liability extend? Only to the very person to whom the representation was made? This is the provision of the RESTATEMENT (SECOND) OF TORTS § 552C, cmt. *d* (1977).

8. **The damages problem.** What damages should be available when strict liability is imposed? The Restatement (Second) would limit damages to out-of-pocket measure. This eliminates recovery of the benefit of the bargain damages and also consequential damages. See § 552C(2) & cmt. *f*.

§ 2. RELIANCE
AND RELATED DOCTRINES

1. *Reliance in fact.* If the plaintiff pays no attention to the defendant's misrepresentation, or does not care, or relies on his own investigation instead, then the defendant's representations have in fact caused no harm. That is, the normal requirement of actual cause is met in this context by the rule that the plaintiff must have relied in fact on the false statement (or a false implication of silence). *See, e.g., Smalley v. Dreyfus Corp.*, 882 N.E.2d 882 (N.Y. 2008). If not, then the plaintiff cannot recover under any of the misrepresentation theories.

In rare cases, the plaintiff may be permitted to show that she relied indirectly upon the defendant's representation by relying upon market values that were themselves influenced by the misrepresentation. This is the "fraud on the market" theory, presently available only under federal securities laws. *See Mirkin v. Wasserman*, 858 P.2d 568 (Cal. 1993) (rejecting the fraud on the market theory for state-law claims); *Kaufman v. i-Stat Corp.*, 754 A.2d 1188 (N.J. 2000) (same).

2. *Contributory negligence/comparative fault.* At a time when all actionable misrepresentations were scienter frauds under *Derry v. Peek*, the tort was necessarily an intentional one. As a result, contributory negligence could not furnish any defense. This remains the rule today as to scienter frauds. As to negligent misrepresentations, however, contributory negligence is usually taken into account either to bar the claim or,

under comparative fault rules, to reduce a plaintiff's damages. *See, e.g., Williams Ford, Inc. v. Hartford Courant Co.*, 657 A.2d 212 (Conn. 1995); RESTATEMENT (SECOND) OF TORTS § 552A (1977).

3. *Justified reliance.* Somewhat strangely, the law has required that the plaintiff not only rely, but that the reliance must be "justified." This rule applies not only to negligent misrepresentations, but also to actual fraud. *See, e.g., Doe v. Dilling*, 888 N.E.2d 24 (Ill. 2008). Is the rule distinguishable from a rule of contributory negligence? The Restatement suggests that justified reliance is more subjective and personal to the particular plaintiff and does not impose a community standard of care. *See* RESTATEMENT (SECOND) OF TORTS § 545A, cmt. *b*. Thus perfect fools have been allowed to recover for representations that would not take in the ordinary prudent person. Courts have held that a plaintiff "justifiably relied" on a misrepresentation, but was negligent in doing so, resulting in a reduction of damages rather than none at all. *See, e.g., ESCA Corp. v. KPMG Peat Marwick*, 959 P.2d 651 (Wash 1998). On the other hand, the law has developed out of the "justified reliance" requirement a series of rather formalized rules about cases that do not ordinarily justify reliance. These include representations that are not material and representations that are not factual. The latter includes most representations of opinion, representations about law, and representations about the future. Perhaps the justified reliance requirement is an indirect way to determine whether the plaintiff actually relied, and whether the defendant really made the representation and intended to induce reliance.

4. *Legal cause.* The RESTATEMENT (SECOND) OF TORTS § 548A provides that a fraudulent misrepresentation is a legal cause of loss only if the loss might reasonably be expected to result from reliance on that representation. Is this congruent with the scope of risk rules that we saw in Chapter 8? In *Richey v. Philipp*, 259 S.W.3d 1 (Mo. App. 2008), the plaintiff was seriously injured when he fell from his sister's roof while trying to remove a tree limb. He sued his sister's insurance company for misrepresentation (both fraudulent and negligent), pointing to an insurance agent's false representation that the sister did not have homeowner's insurance coverage for removal of the tree limb. How would you frame the question on causation? Might his claim succeed?

5. *Materiality.* The representation must be material and reliance on an immaterial statement is not justified. Example: Defendant, attempting to sell a car, says to the plaintiff, "Oh, are you a member of the Elks Club? Me, too." Defendant is not a member and has no reason to think that the plaintiff's decision would hinge on the representation, though he does expect to win the plaintiff's good will by this lie.

PINNACLE PEAK DEVELOPERS v. TRW INVESTMENT CORP.,

631 P.2d 540 (Ariz. Ct. App. 1980). TRW purchased 40 acres from Pinnacle Peak for a residential subdivision. The purchase agreement

required TRW to make certain off-site improvements, such as roads, and electrical, telephone, and water distribution systems. TRW had a written option to purchase additional acreage, but only if a certain portion of the off-site improvements had not been completed by the option deadline. When the option deadline was reached, the improvements had not been made and the seller took the position that the option had therefore expired. TRW took the position that the seller had fraudulently induced TRW to forego the improvements and that for this reason the option should be treated as extant. TRW argues that it was induced to enter into the purchase and option agreement by reliance on Pinnacle Peak's representation that the off-site improvements would be no obstacle to the exercise of the option so long as there was reasonable progress on those improvements, and that this representation was false when made. The trial court granted summary judgment for the seller. *Held,* affirmed. "A promise, when made with a present intention not to perform it, is a misrepresentation which can give rise to an action of fraud.... Representations which give rise to an action of fraud must, of course, be of matters of fact which exist in the present, and not merely an agreement or promise to do something in the future, or an expression of opinion or judgment as to something which has happened or is expected to happen. To this there is one exception, that when a promise to perform a future act is made with the present intention on the part of the promisor that he will not perform it, it is such a representation as will give rise to an action of fraud."

However, the trial court properly held that the parol evidence rule bars the introduction of evidence of the allegedly fraudulent representation here, which was made prior to execution of the written option agreement. The parol evidence rule "renders inadmissible any evidence of prior or contemporaneous oral understandings and of prior written understandings, which would contradict, vary or add to a written contract which was intended as the final and complete statement or integration of the parties' agreement." The states are split on "whether to permit parol evidence which contradicts a writing when fraud in the inducement is alleged." Many courts have applied the parol evidence rule even to allegedly fraudulent misrepresentations where the parties have "expertise and business sophistication" and have freely negotiated a formal written contract. Here, the parties were sophisticated and represented by counsel during their negotiations, justifying the trial judge's ruling.

NOTES

1. **Rule.** It is generally agreed that one's present intention to do some future act is a fact about one's state of mind, and that a misrepresentation about that state of mind is actionable as fraud.

2. **Proof.** What proof would suffice to show that the speaker did not have the intention at the time the statement was made? Since nonperformance of the stated intention might simply result from a change of heart, the plaintiff's proof can be difficult; mere proof that the statement was made and

not performed would not suffice. *See Milwaukee Auction Galleries Ltd. v. Chalk*, 13 F.3d 1107 (7th Cir. 1994). What if a defendant represents an intention to build a swimming pool for the benefit of those who buy a condominium, but he does not have the money to do so and no prospects of getting any?

3. **Contract doctrines.** The statute of frauds, the parol evidence rule, and disclaimers or merger clauses in deeds might each prevent a recovery in the case of oral representation. The view of most courts has been that the statute of frauds does not prevent a recovery for a fraudulent misrepresentation, though it would bar enforcement of a promise. As to the parol evidence rule, it is more likely to prevent recovery the greater the sophistication of the parties; courts also look at the extent of the contradiction between precontract representations and the final contract. Disclaimers may appear in several forms. One is the merger clause, which provides that all promises and agreements are contained in the written documents. This is a contractual form of the parol evidence rule. Disclaimers may also state that the vendor has made no representations, or that the buyer does not rely on representations. If the plaintiff is induced to enter the contract, including the disclaimer, by fraud, then the disclaimer may not protect the defendant from liability. But a statement in the written documents that no representations have been made, or that the buyer does not rely upon them, will at least raise the question whether the buyer's reliance was reasonable in the light of the notice these documents gave that reliance was not expected. *See Wittenberg v. Robinov*, 173 N.E.2d 868 (N.Y. 1961).

4. **Economic loss rule.** Problems once dealt with by considering disclaimers, merger clauses, or the parol evidence rule may now be addressed through the economic loss rule. Recall that in *Moorman Manufacturing Co. v. National Tank Co.*, 435 N.E.2d 443 (Ill. 1982) (Chapter 24, § 3), the court held that a product purchaser who claimed stand-alone economic loss rather than physical harm to person or property must sue under contract or warranty and could not sue in tort for strict liability or negligence. The idea of this economic loss rule is to honor the contract and to emphasize the potential role of contracts in resolving disputes between contracting parties. Courts are not always consistent in applying the economic loss rule to misrepresentation cases. *See* Dan B. Dobbs, *An Introduction to Non–Statutory Economic Loss Claims*, 48 ARIZ. L. REV. 713, 728–33 (2006). A number of courts have barred negligent or innocent misrepresentation claims on this ground. *See, e.g., Stieneke v. Russi*, 190 P.3d 60 (Wash Ct. App. 2008) (barring negligent misrepresentation claim by purchaser of home). Some courts are now applying a modified version of the economic loss rule to bar fraud claims. *See, e.g., Below v. Norton*, 751 N.W.2d 351 (Wis. 2008) (economic loss rule bars all intentional misrepresentation claims in connection with residential real estate transactions). In *Digicorp, Inc. v. Ameritech Corp.*, 662 N.W.2d 652 (Wis. 2003), a fragmented court held that a claim of fraud would be barred unless the fraud was "extraneous" to the contract. It actually barred the fraud claim even though the alleged fraud did not actually contradict the contract provisions. Would that be more justified in the case of negligent misrepresentations?

§ 3. DUTY TO DISCLOSE

OLLERMAN v. O'ROURKE CO.

288 N.W.2d 95 (Wis. 1980)

ABRAHAMSON, JUSTICE.

[Ollerman purchased a lot from O'Rourke Co. When he excavated to build a house, an underground well was uncovered and uncapped, and water was released. Ollerman alleged he had spent over $2700 to cap the well and that building changes costing over $10,500 were necessitated by its presence. He alleged that O'Rourke Co. knew of the underground well but did not disclose it. The trial court overruled the defendant's motion to dismiss.]

[The court first held that silence where there is a duty to disclose is equivalent to a misrepresentation of fact and that a seller obliged to disclose could be held liable for an "intentional" representation.]

We recognize that the traditional rule in Wisconsin is that in an action for intentional misrepresentation the seller of real estate, dealing at arm's length with the buyer, has no duty to disclose information to the buyer and therefore has no liability in an action for intentional misrepresentation for failure to disclose. . . .

Under the doctrine of caveat emptor no person was required to tell all that he or she knew in a business transaction, for in a free market the diligent should not be deprived of the fruits of superior skill and knowledge lawfully acquired. The business world, and the law reflecting business mores and morals, required the parties to a transaction to use their faculties and exercise ordinary business sense, and not to call on the law to stand *in loco parentis* to protect them in their ordinary dealings with other business people.

Over the years society's attitudes toward good faith and fair dealing in business transactions have undergone significant change, and this change has been reflected in the law. Courts have departed from or relaxed the "no duty to disclose" rule by carving out exceptions to the rule and by refusing to adhere to the rule when it works an injustice. Thus courts have held that the rule does not apply where the seller actively conceals a defect or where he prevents investigation; where the seller has told a half-truth or has made an ambiguous statement if the seller's intent is to create a false impression and he does so; where there is a fiduciary relationship between the parties; or where the facts are peculiarly and exclusively within the knowledge of one party to the transaction and the other party is not in a position to discover the facts for himself.

On the basis of the complaint, the case at bar does not appear to fall into one of these well-recognized exceptions to the "no duty to disclose" rule. However, Dean Prosser has found a "rather amorphous tendency on the part of most courts toward finding a duty of disclosure in cases where the defendant has special knowledge or means of knowledge not open to the plaintiff and is aware that the plaintiff is acting under a misapprehension as to facts which could be of importance to him, and would probably affect his decision."

Dean Keeton described these cases abandoning the "no duty to disclose" rule as follows:

> "In the present stage of the law, the decisions show a drawing away from this idea [that nondisclosure is not actionable], and there can be seen an attempt by many courts to reach a just result in so far as possible, but yet maintaining the degree of certainty which the law must have. The statement may often be found that if either party to a contract of sale conceals or suppresses a material fact which he is in good faith bound to disclose then his silence is fraudulent.
>
> "The attitude of the courts toward nondisclosure is undergoing a change and ... it would seem that the object of the law in these cases should be to impose on parties to the transaction a duty to speak whenever justice, equity, and fair dealing demand it. This statement is made only with reference to instances where the party to be charged is an actor in the transaction. This duty to speak does not result from an implied representation by silence, but exists because a refusal to speak constitutes unfair conduct." *Fraud—Concealment and Nondisclosure*, 15 Tex. L. Rev. 1, 31 (1936).

The test Dean Keeton derives from the cases to determine when the rule of nondisclosure should be abandoned—"whenever justice, equity and fair dealing demand it"—present, as one writer states, "a somewhat nebulous standard, praiseworthy as looking toward more stringent business ethics, but possibly difficult of practical application." Case Note, *Silence as Fraudulent Concealment—Vendor & Purchaser—Duty to Disclose*, 36 Wash. L. Rev. 202, 204 (1961)....

The draftsmen of the most recent Restatement of Torts (Second) (1977) have attempted to formulate a rule embodying this trend in the cases toward a more frequent recognition of a duty to disclose. Sec. 551(1) of the Restatement sets forth the traditional rule that one who fails to disclose a fact that he knows may induce reliance in a business transaction is subject to the same liability as if he had represented the nonexistence of the matter that he failed to disclose if, and only if, he is under a duty to exercise reasonable care to disclose the matter in question.... Sec. 551(2) (e) is the "catch-all" provision setting forth conditions under which a duty to disclose exists; it states that a party to a transaction is under a duty to exercise reasonable care to disclose to the other "facts basic to the transaction, if he knows that the other is about to enter into it under a mistake as to them, and that the other, because of the relationship between them, the customs of the trade or other objective circumstances, would reasonably expect a disclosure of those facts." ...

Section 551(2) (e) of the Restatement (Second) of Torts limits the duty to disclose to disclosure of those "facts basic" to the transaction.

Comment *j* to sec. 551 differentiates between basic facts and material facts as follows:

> "A basic fact is a fact that is assumed by the parties as a basis for the transaction itself. It is a fact that goes to the basis, or essence, of the transaction, and is an important part of the substance of what is bargained for or dealt with. Other facts may serve as important and persuasive inducements to enter into the transaction, but not go to its essence. These facts may be material, but they are not basic."

However, the draftsmen of the Restatement recognized that the law was developing to expand the duty to disclosure beyond the duty described in sec. 551. . . . The seller contends, in its brief, that if this court affirms the circuit court's order overruling the motion to dismiss and allows the buyer to proceed to trial, the court is adopting "what really amounts to a strict policy of 'let the seller beware.' " The seller goes on to state, "Woe indeed to anyone who sells a home, a vacant lot or other piece of real estate and fails to itemize with particularity or give written notice to each prospective buyer of every conceivable condition in and around the property, regardless of whether such a condition is dangerous, defective or could become so by the negligence or recklessness of others. A seller of real estate is not and should not be made an insurer or guarantor of the competence of those with whom the purchaser may later contract." . . .

The seller's arguments are not persuasive in light of the facts alleged in the complaint and our narrow holding in this case.

Where the vendor is in the real estate business and is skilled and knowledgeable and the purchaser is not, the purchaser is in a poor position to discover a condition which is not readily discernible, and the purchaser may justifiably rely on the knowledge and skill of the vendor. Thus, in this instant case a strong argument for imposing a duty on the seller to disclose material facts is this "reliance factor." The buyer portrayed in this complaint had a reasonable expectation of honesty in the marketplace, that is, that the vendor would disclose material facts which it knew and which were not readily discernible. Under these circumstances the law should impose a duty of honesty on the seller.

. . . [W]e hold that a subdivider-vendor of a residential lot has a duty to a "non-commercial" purchaser to disclose facts which are known to the vendor, which are material to the transaction, and which are not readily discernible to the purchaser. A fact is known to the vendor if the vendor has actual knowledge of the fact or if the vendor acted in reckless disregard as to the existence of the fact. This usage of the word "know" is the same as in an action for intentional misrepresentation based on a false statement. A fact is material if a reasonable purchaser would attach importance to its existence or nonexistence in determining the choice of action in the transaction in question; or if the vendor knows or has reason to know that the purchaser regards or is likely to regard the matter as important in determining the choice of action, although a reasonable purchaser would not so regard it.

NOTES

1. In *Van Dinter v. Orr*, 138 P.3d 608 (Wash. 2006), a seller did not disclose to a purchaser of unimproved property that a capital facilities rate for sewer construction would be imposed once the land was developed. The buyer sued for negligent misrepresentation, but the court held there was no duty to disclose. In *Nei v. Burley*, 446 N.E.2d 674 (Mass. 1983), a seller knew that the water table on his property was high and that there was a seasonal stream which was not apparent in dry season. He revealed neither. The buyer was required to spend more to install a septic tank because of these unrevealed features of the land. The court followed the traditional rule that there was no duty to disclose. Would the Wisconsin Court, on the basis of *Ollerman*, get a different result in *Van Dinter* or *Nei*? Notice that the limitation of the duty is to "basic" facts. In *Maybee v. Jacobs Motor Co.*, 519 N.W.2d 341 (S.D. 1994), the seller of a used vehicle did not tell the buyer that the engine had been rebuilt and that it used a gas not now generally available. The court held that if these were basic facts, the seller was under a duty to disclose and that it was up to the jury to determine whether the facts were basic.

2. V, attempting to sell a vacant lot, tells P: "I want to warn you—there is an easement across the edge of this property." P finds this acceptable and purchases the property. She then discovers that there is another easement in the middle and she cannot use the property for her purposes. The cases are agreed that P can recover. What is the principle? What if V honestly and reasonably believes there is only the one easement but later, before any contract for sale is signed, discovers the second one?

3. S, attempting to sell a car, moves its odometer back from 65,000 miles to 30,000 miles. He says nothing whatever about the mileage and P does not ask. If P buys in reliance on the odometer, has he a claim? On the basis of what rule?

4. L, a lawyer who represents C, offers to sell C shares of stock in a corporation. He says nothing about the fact that the corporation has manufactured, among other things, asbestos, and may be subject to catastrophic liabilities for injuries. C purchases, then the corporation goes bankrupt over asbestos liabilities. Has C a claim against her lawyer? On the basis of what rule?

5. The securities laws, the Interstate Land Sales Act, and other statutes, including some state statutes, frequently impose affirmative duties to disclose material. In some states, consumer protection acts have been passed which may also require disclosure. A claim for nondisclosure therefore requires a careful study of the statutes.N

REFERENCES: DOBBS ON TORTS §§ 469–483 (2000); Fleming James, Jr. and Oscar S. Gray, *Misrepresentation*, 37 MD. L. REV. 286, 488 (Parts I & II, 1978); 2 HARPER, JAMES & GRAY, THE LAW OF TORTS, Chapter 7 (3d ed. 2006); DAN DOBBS, THE LAW OF REMEDIES § 9.2 (6) (2d ed. 1993).

AN END NOTE

∎ ∎ ∎

———————

Daunting as it may seem, plenty of tort claims not covered in this book dot the legal landscape. Although this book has touched upon some important economic and dignitary torts, many torts and issues remain for exploration in advanced tort courses. This book has also touched upon some civil rights torts claims for physical injury. Yet many other claims for economic harm or discrimination without physical injury caused by civil rights violations must be left for more specialized advanced courses. Such claims might include cases in which government officers libel the plaintiff or invade her privacy, but perhaps more commonly involve claims of employment discrimination under a number of different statutes.

So you can find many more tort issues in upper level courses with many names—courses called Economic and Dignitary Torts or Advanced Torts, and courses in employment law, civil rights, and intellectual property, including copyright, patents, or unfair competition and others.

In that light, this page brings us, not to the end of tort law, but only to the end of the beginning.

*

INDEX

Using the Index

This index refers to key words, legal rules or ideas, legal issues, key parties, and important factual settings. It is not a concordance or a computer generated word list. Hence not every instance of a word is listed. Equally, the referenced page may discuss or exemplify the legal idea indexed without using the indexing word. References are to pages. When indexed material appears in a main case, only the first page of the case is given, unless inclusive references are more practical. When indexed material appears in notes, the first page of an inclusive reference is the page on which the note begins.

---

†